MW01503352

ARCHIVES BRANCH 1905.

The Honourable S. A. Fisher, M.P., Minister of Agriculture.

George F. O'Halloran, B.C.L., Deputy Minister.

CLERKS.

Miss M. Casey, Miss M. Greaves, Miss F. McDonald, Miss M. Robertson.

A. Archambault, F. J. Audet, B. Boutet, A. G. Doughty, A. Duff, H. R. Holmden, R. Laidlaw, Dr. L. M. Pelletier.

GENEALOGIST.

Placide Gaudet.

Facsimile Reprint Published 1994 By

HERITAGE BOOKS, INC.

1540-E Pointer Ridge Place, Bowie, Md., 20716
(301) 390-7709

ISBN 0-7884-0031-2

REPORT

CONCERNING

CANADIAN ARCHIVES

FOR THE YEAR 1905

IN THREE VOLUMES

CONTENTS OF VOLUME II.

The Contents of the other Volumes forming the report on the Archives for 1905, are as follows :—

CONTENTS OF VOLUME I.

CONTENTS OF VOLUME III.

LIST OF MAPS AT THE RECORD OFFICE.

America—Map of the British Empire in, with the French and Spanish settlements adjacent thereto, by Henry Popple—1733 .... Case 35.   No. 4.

North America—New map of the English Empire in, Morden (early) 7.19

N. America, chart of the sea coasts—mount and page—1716 ....   34.6

N. America—General map of—Sanson & Berry—1718 .... Library 18.5

M.S. North America—Old map of part of, about 1720. Very curious 7.18

North America, chart of the North Seas with Davids' and Hudson's Straits—Mortier.... Library 29.19 2

Amerique Septentrionale, map of—D'Anville, 1746 ....   7.6

"   "   "   in two sheets 27.17.18

"   "   "   " 24.38.39

North America, map of, Vaugondy 1750.26.97

"   ....Case 36.   No. 13

"   1752—D'Anville & Bolton. Translated from the French................   7.11

"   map of the British Colonies in North America—First Edition—John Mitchell—1755 ....Case 36.   No. 15

"   "   "   "   2nd edition.............. "   35.   "   6

"   "   "   "   "   in 8 sheets... "   36.   "   16

"   another copy .... "   36.   "   17

North America—Map of the British Colonies in North America—John Mitchell, 1755—Another copy with many MS. additions in red ink .... "   36.   "   18

North America—Map of the British Colonies in North America—John Mitchell, 1755—with MSS. corrections and additions, in the locality of the Rivers St. Croix and St. John's.. "   36.   "   19

America, North—Accurate map of, describing and distinguishing the British, Spanish and French Dominions, according to the Treaty of Paris, 1763—Bowen and Gibson.. "   36.   "   20

Another copy, coloured.... .... "   36.   "   21

North America—Map of—according to the Treaty of Paris, 1763—Bowen & Gibson. ...   7.1

North America—Map of the Southern Indian District of North America, compiled under the direction of John Stuart, Esq., Superintendent of Indian Affairs, by Joseph Purcell, 1775 (?) ....Case 36.   No. 11

North America—Map of the Southern Indian District of North America, compiled under the direction of John Stuart, Esq., Superintendent of Indian Affairs, by Joseph Purcell, 1781, most elaborate and beautifully executed............................ "   36.   "   12

Annapolis Royal—Geo. Seely, 1716..... ....   9.73

"   Plan of settlements, &c. Transmitted in Govr. Shirley's letter, 27th April, 1749 ....   9.40

"   Chart of—Des Barres, 1776 ....   1.14

"   Plan of surveys and lands granted to loyal emigrants, disbanded corps and others in the Township of Clements and County of Annapolis —C. Morris, 1785 ....Case 36.   No. 26
      (Received 9th July, 1786, by Mr. Gibbons.)

Bay of Bulls and Harbour Grace (Newfoundland). Early chart of.... .. ..   28. 2

Beau Basin (Nova Scotia). Sketch of 9.41

Beaver Harbour. Chart of. Des Barres, 1776.......... ....   1.4¹

"   "   "   " 2.43

Belle Isle. Chart of the Straits of, with part of the coasts of Newfoundland and Labradore, from actual surveys. Sayer & Bennett, 1770....................... ..... Case 37.   No. 3

Bonaventure. Survey and plan of—in the Bay of Chaleurs, with situation of allotments, etc. John Collins, 1765.... .... "   37.   "   20

5-6 EDWARD VII., A. 1906

SESSIONAL PAPER No. 18

APPENDIX A

PART I

TOUR OF INSPECTION MADE BY THE SIEUR DE LA ROQUE.

CENSUS.

1752.

The journal and census of the Sieur de la Roque, from the Archives in Paris, were prepared under the direction of M. le comte de Raymond, in the year 1752. La Roque commenced his work in the midst of winter and had to encounter many hardships in the performance of his task.   The census appears to have been carefully made and furnishes many details of interest to-day. As an introduction to the work of the Sieur de la Roque we quote a letter of M. le comte de Raymond to the Minister, dated the 5th of December, 1752, as it contains the instructions given to the surveyor, particulars concerning his qualifications, and the progress made with the census up to the end of the year.

LETTER OF THE COMTE DE RAYMOND TO THE MINISTER.

LOUISBOURG, 5th December, 1752.

MY LORD,

The ship which is to carry the despatches is not yet ready to sail, and is not likely to leave for eight or ten days.

I do not know whether the Sieur de la Roque, one of the land surveyors of the colony, has as yet arrived in Paris, where he is going after he has entered into possession of an inheritance at Toulouse.

I would be sorry, My Lord, if you were not apprised before his arrival there, of his qualifications. He is a very good man, full of zeal and talent. He is the son of one of the King's Musketeers, of good family, and has rendered excellent service during the last war.

He has done wonderful things here for me. It is he, who last year made a tour of Ile Royale to inspect, according to my instructions, all the ports and harbours, search for a new route to Ile au Justaucorps, which is feasible and would shorten the sea voyage between this island and Ile Royale more than fifty leagues.

I had also intrusted him with the making of a general census of the settlers on the island, name by name, men as well as women and children, their respective ages and professions, the numbers of arpents each has of improved land, the number of their cattle, their species, fowl, &c., &c., distinguishing the good workmen from those who are not, and the character of each individual. He was instructed also to examine, and inspect the most percipitous places in the island; those where troops could be most easily landed ; how many ships each harbour could accommodate, and their tonnage ; the difficulties of making each harbour, the rocks and breakers at their entrances ; what disputes exist concerning concessions, and lastly a general survey of everything.

18—1½

5-6 EDWARD VII., A. 1906

I instructed him to do the same during the summer at the Ile St. Jean. He acted as my forerunner there, and I have seen with pleasure, My Lord, during the general tour which I have made, that when I have personally reviewed the reports which he has made to me, they have all been proved correct.

This man being of good family is desirous of rising above the average and asks a brevet as sub-engineer, which I pray you to be pleased to grant. Monsieur Franquet has already taught him much, and he intends to perfect himself during his stay in France, but at the same time, I have arranged with him that at present he shall not cease to be a surveyor. He will be of the very greatest assistance in the general survey, which I intend to make of this colony, as well as of Ile St. Jean, in order to come to some definite settlement of the concessions. He will take with him two other surveyors, and with his knowledge of the country, and of each concession, he will be well fitted to satisfactorily carry out the work.

I pray you, My Lord, to not only grant him the favour he greatly desires, but also to show him more kindness and allow him to return by the first boat coming here.

If you intend to send us a fourth surveyor who has some knowledge of engineering and who has the instruments necessary for the survey of this country, it would be very fitting to expedite this most interesting work.

Two surveyors could go one way and two the other. I know that to maintain four surveyors here will be putting the King to much expense, but I also know that at the present time they are very necessary, and will be so until the land granting business is cleared up, and all the concessions have been put in order and the boundaries determined ; a work which cannot be begun too soon. It would not be necessary to keep more than two afterwards, one in this colony, and the other at Ile St. Jean. The two others could be utilised on other work, or returned to France.

Les Sieurs Chatton and Roche who are the other two surveyors, and of whom nothing but good can be said, have not yet received payment of the three hundred livres which you had the goodness to grant to each of them towards the cost of their passage to this country. I beg you, My Lord, to be pleased to send orders that they be paid, for I assure you they have great need of this small sum, as they cannot live here within the limits of their eight hundred livres of pay.

I have the honour, etc.,

Le Comte de RAYMOND.

TOUR OF INSPECTION UNDERTAKEN BY LE SIEUR DE LA ROQUE.

Tour of inspection undertaken by le Sieur de la Roque, King's Surveyor, by order of M. le Comte de Raymond, Chevalier, Seigneur d'Oye, la Cour and other places ; Brigadier General ; His Majesty's Lieutenant of the Towns and Castles of Angoulême ; Governor and Commandant of Isles Royale, St. Jean and others and their dependencies.

This tour through all the ports, harbours, creeks, rivers and to all places in Isle Royale, generally, where there are settlers, was commenced on the fifth of February, 1752.

This said 5th day of February, 1752, we, Joseph de la Roque, in consequence of orders and instructions given to us by M. le Comte de Raymond, left the town of Louisbourg, the capital of Isle Royale, at one o'clock in the afternoon, in rainy weather, and at four o'clock in the evening of the same day arrived at the dwelling of the Sr. Pierre Boisseau, situate on the road to Miré, two leagues from Louisbourg.

We found in the said house an old soldier of the garrison of Louisbourg, Pierre Bonne, aged 61. He is a native of St. Pierre de Roumoulon, diocese of Xaintes, has neither trade nor profession, and is in the service of the said Pierre Boisseau.

On being asked the extent of the concession, by whom granted and when ; the quantity of cleared and meadow land and of fallow land ; and what use could be made of the land ; he answered us that he knew nothing about the extent or boundaries of the concession ; in regard to the cleared land, that was in grass, and from it they had harvested from 130 to 140 quintals of hay, the nature of the soil being most favourable for growing hay.

The said Sieur Boisseau had no live stock.

Except a lake lying to the left of the road we observed nothing worthy of note throughout the whole distance of two leagues. This lake discharges its water into the stream of Pointe Plate, by which stream they are carried to the sea at the harbour of Gabarus. The land is clothed with fir of all descriptions.

Between six and seven o'clock in the morning, in bright sunshine, we set out from the said dwelling for Gabarus. We continued to follow the highway for half a league, and then took a blazed road, which led us to the further end of the gorge of the Montagne du Diable, on the sea shore at the harbour of Gabarus. The length of this road is placed at three leagues.

All the woods are of beech and the surface of the ground is extremely rough.

THE BAY OF GABARUS.

This bay is formed by the Pointe du Dehors and the Pointe Blanche. These points lie about north-east and south-west, at a distance from each other of some three leagues, giving the bay a circuit of six leagues inland on the north-west of the island.

Between Pointe Blanche and Cormorandière, a good half league distant from Louisbourg, lies Pointe Plate, the exact place on which the English made a descent and landed the army in the year 1745. The land between the town of Louisbourg and this point is very rough and marshy, with ten to twelye feet of peat, which neither dries up, nor condenses owing to the great quantity of water with which every part is usually covered.

Nor would it be easy to make practical drainage for the reason that nearly all the marshes are pierced by ridges which partake of the nature of rocks. The bottom beneath the ten or twelve feet of peat is a mixture of rich soil full of and traversed by rocks, the whole producing a petrified mass and extremely difficult to remove.

All these considerations lead to the conclusion that should the enemy attempt to make a descent at this part of the bay, they would find it very difficult if not impracticable to transport artillery across such rough country.

The distance from Cormorandière to Pointe aux Basques, or to Point du Dehors is estimated at four leagues. Within this distance we find :—

1. Between la Cormorandière and the gorge of the above mentioned Montagne du Diable there lie several creeks practicable for landing from boats. These creeks are, respectively, half a league, a league, and a league and a half distant from the site of one of the projected redoubts on the said Cormorandière, on which a landing could be made without running any risk of danger. The distance between the gorge of the said mountain to the Pointe du Dehors is about two leagues, and (between them) there rises a bank of sand half a league in length, and from 40 to 50 toises in width, extending from the foot of the said mountain to a stream which forms the boundary of the homesteads of the Sieur Duchambon, and the heirs of Pierre Rondeau.

On this bank it would be possible to effect a landing at all times and tides except during a heavy gale, and the redoubts to be thrown out on Pointe Plate and on the Cormorandière would offer no opposition on account of their distance.

But it is probable that these two projected redoubts will be very useful in preventing the enemy from effecting a landing as near the place as they did during the last war, and should a landing on the said sand bank be effected, even then the impracticable roads they must follow in order to attack the said redoubts, and gain the road to Miré, are the true guarantees for their security, seeing that it is morally impossible to tranport any kind of artillery across the lands in this locality or by way of the perpendicular banks of the streams which intersect them.

It is estimated that the distance between the said sand bank and the Pointe du Dehors is two leagues, and at a quarter of a league to the south east lies a creek where

5-6 EDWARD VII., A. 1906

vessels anchor in four or five fathons of water, and sheltered generally from all winds except from the north which blows off land.

This bay, where a very promising commencement for the settlement of a colony has been made is suitable for the cod fishery; there is also an abundance of pasturage for raising a great quantity of live-stock and the land is also good for cultivation.

CENSUS.

The homesteads that have been granted on the said Bay of Gabarus, and the inhabitants who have settled there, men as well as women, boys, girls, domestics, thirty-six months men, live stock, schooners, bateaux, skiffs, boats, &c.

M. Degouttin, a lot situated on the Pointe du Dehors, unimproved.

T M. Daillebou, a piece of land situated along the coast. Not cultivated.

M. Thiery, a piece of ground situated on the coast, (adjoining the above). Uncultivated.

M. de St. Ovide, and now occupied by M. St. de Chambon. There are at present two settlers on it.

M. Rondeau, a piece of ground situated in the middle of the said bay. There is one settler at work thereon. Sixton Huiker, ploughman, native of Switzerland, aged 42 years, married to Marie Jeanne Esteruine, native of Dailledan, Switzerland, aged 35 years, and their children as follows :—

Joseph Huiker, aged 16 years.

Angelique Huiker, aged 9 years.

Both natives of Louisbourg. The man occupies about two arpents of cleared land to make a garden in which he will sow all kinds of grain as an experiment to discover which will do best. He has a skiff.

The land on which he is settled belongs to M. du Chambon.

Jeanne Baudry, widow, of François Clermont, native of Plaisance, aged 45 years. She has three children, who are :—

François Clermont, aged 33 years of age ;

Pierre Clermont, aged 27 years ;

Jeanne Clermont, aged 15 years.

Three hired fishermen, who are :

Etienne Daguerre, native of Louisbourg, aged 33 years ;

Pierre Tuillier, native of Dieppe, aged 27 years ;

François Durand, native of Dinant, aged 27 years.

Three boats, one sow and five young pigs.

The land on which she is settled is situated on the creek au Major, a part of the homestead of M. du Chambon.

Pierre Duport, ploughman, settler in the Colony for one year, having received rations for that time for himself and his family, native of the parish of Sonneville, in Abbeville, diocese of La Rochelle, aged 32 years ; Jeanne Metayer, his wife, native of the same parish, aged 24 years. They have three children, two sons and one daughter, who are :—

Pierre Duport, aged 6 years ;

Jean Duport, aged 4 years ;

The daughter is not yet baptised.

They have with them,

Jeanne Rousseau, widow of Jean Metayer, their mother, aged 45 years ;

Elizabeth Metayer, their sister, aged 18 years.

The land on which they are settled belongs to and forms part of the homestead of Sr. Rondeau.

On the 8th at 7 o'clock in the morning we took our departure from the said Gabarus to proceed to the harbour of Fourché, which we reached about 3 o'clock in the afternoon of the same day.

The harbour of Fourché lies on the south-west coast of the island about three leagues distant from Gabarus. In leaving the said harbour of Gabarus, we crossed the lake on the land of Madame Rondeau, which lies behind the sand bank already referred to. In keeping to the west for a quarter of league the lands are covered with hard wood fit for fuel. Making west-south-west, during the second stage we reached a portage of about 80 toises, which brought us to a second lake with no outlet for its waters save that of filtration. This is a very extensive sheet of water. Keeping the same course we followed this lake for 200 toises, and entering a wood went south-west for a quarter of a league, which brought us out on the Grand lac du Gabarus. This lake has three arms, running well inland to the north, north-east, and south-west. The river Barachois de Bellefeuille rises here, lying in the north arm and is the only outlet from the said lake of Gabarus.

On leaving the wood for the first stage we followed the river in a south-westerly direction for about 400 toises, and then west quarter north-west for a quarter of a league, all the woods being composed of fir. At the end of this distance we reached a small portage of about 70 or 80 toises through hard wood, which brought us to a fourth unnamed lake. In continuing our journey we followed this lake its entire length, which is not very great. The timber in this locality is fir, and further on we re-entered the wood going south-west for some 400 toises. This brought us immediately to the further end of the Barachois de Bellefeuille. Towards the end of the way we found all kinds of hard wood.

THE BARACHOIS DE BELLEFEUILLE.

The Barachois de Bellefeuille is very extensive. It forms several arms, which run deep inland on the north-east, the north and the north-west. We crossed, at first holding south-west for about five toises, and then going west, a quarter north-west for a good quarter of a league. The banks as well as the lands in the interior are wooded with inferior fir. The entrance to the said Barachois de Bellefeuille lies north and south. At high tide an empty boat might succeed in making the passage, which is hardly two toises in width. The land is mostly peaty and marshy, being only good for pasturage. In front of the said barachois a sand bank extends a quarter of a league in length by 30 to 40 toises in width. It runs north-east and south-west. Besides the sand bank lying outside the entrance, the water is full of shoals and reefs; vessels would be unable anywhere to find shelter from the winds, or to ride in safety in case of a light wind springing up. Further, as everyone knows, the weather on this coast is so changeable that an enemy would never be so imprudent as to land without making sure of being able to reembark in case of a repulse or if the state of the weather should render such a course necessary.

But even with a favourable wind what advantage would a landing offer ? If they should proceed inland to reach Gabarus Bay how could they pass through a country so marshy as that described above ?

Leaving this Barachois going west-south-west, we passed an alder plot of some 400 toises in extent, which brought us to the Barachois Marcoche.

The Barachois de Marcoche is very extensive, being a league across. We followed it, making many points of the compass, which we reduced to the south-west. The Barachois has a number of arms running inland for a league, and one running to the north-west a good league and a half. There are several islets and peninsulas on it, whilst the banks are covered with fir trees. The entrance, which is perhaps fifteen toises across, lies north and south. Loaded boats pass at high tide. There is a rock on the starboard side as one enters, and a sand bank on the larboard, leaving room for only one boat to pass. A sand bank very similar to that in front of the Barachois de Bellefeuille lies before the entrance. About a league outside the two Barachois there are a number of reefs, visible only at low tide. From the said lake we skirted the coast which is full of reefs and shoals as far as the mouth of the Harbour de Fourchè, a distance of a quarter of a league.

THE HARBOUR OF FOURCHÉ.

The harbour of Fourché is one of the best harbours for the cod-fishery on the coast. The only thing against it is the difficulty of the entrance on account of shoals near it.

5-6 EDWARD VII., A. 1906

It is divided into two arms, the one running to the west, north-west, and the other to the west. The latter was well settled before the war, there being twelve or fifteen families all doing well.

The English burned the whole place with the exception or a storehouse, 100 feet long, on the homestead of the late M. Daccarette, still in existence to-day and used for the raising of cattle.

Leaving Fourché on Wednesday the ninth instant, holding north-west for a quarter of a league, past spruce woods rendered impracticable owing to their heavy growth, the route brought us to Lake Ablin, which may be a quarter of a league in length by 200 toises in breadth. It divides at the further end into two branches, and runs about north-east and south-west. The shores are entirely covered with fir. The lake discharges itself into the Barachois de la Grande Framboise by means of a stream, which we followed until we came to an arm of the said Barachois de la Framboise. The distance between the two points is possibly an eighth of a league.

THE BARACHOIS DE LA GRANDE FRAMBOISE.

The Barachois de la Grande Framboise is situated half a league from the Harbour Fourché. The entrance lies north-north-west, and south-south-east ; its width may be placed at 450 toises.

There are two reefs opposite the entrance. A boat of the capacity of five or six cords of wood can pass, while outside there is anchorage. It is estimated that it runs inland for a league and a half, throwing out several arms that extend, some deeper than others into the land in a north-north-westerly direction forming many islands and points, in its middle; its width may be considered to be a good half league. The banks are covered with poor fir. The chief product of these Barachois, creeks and lakes consists of hay, seeing that the country is very marshy. Leaving the Barachois we took a westerly course past an alder plot of about 200 toises in extent, which brought us to the Barachois de la Petite Framboise.

THE BARACHOIS DE LA PETITE FRAMBOISE.

The Barachois de la Petite Frambois lies two leagues from the Harbour Fourché and four from that St. Esprit. Its entrance is not suited for anything more than a canoe. The Barachois is a league in width north-east and south-west, and has several arms which run inland for a distance of about two leagues, forming islands and points, and it is stated that the arm to the north-north-east discharges its waters through a river into the lake of the river Miré. All the shores as well as the lands of the interior grow poor fir. From the Barachois we continued to skirt the coast as far as St. Esprit. In this distance of four leagues we found only two creeks where boats could shelter in bad weather from winds blowing from west-quarter-north-west to north-north-east. There was much greater shelter in the creek that has been named the Creek du Caplan. With these two exceptions the rest of the coast consists of high lands and rocks which are impracticable owing to their extreme abruptness.

ST. ESPRIT.

St. Esprit is well settled. It is adapted to the cod fishery, the raising of cattle, and for gardening, the soil being sandy in character.

The harbour of St. Esprit is in truth an open roadstead. Its mouth lies east-north-east and west-south-west. Vessels of sixty to seventy tons can enter and anchor in the middle of the roadway with from ten to twelve fathoms of water at high tide. There are two reefs which one leaves, the one on the starboard and the other on the larboard. Behind the roadstead is a Barachois which runs inland in a north-westerly direction for about a league. The settlers cut what hay they require on the banks of this Barachois. Its mouth lies north-east and south-west.

There is sufficient water at high tide to allow of the passage of a boat laden with five or six cords of wood. All the lands in the neighbourhood of St. Esprit are covered with fir wood only.

CENSUS.

Census of the settlers, bachelors, hired fishermen, thirty-six months men, live stock, schooners, bateaux, and boats of St. Esprit.

Le Sieur Perriez, conducting a fishery, native of Plaisance, aged 42 years, married to Marguerite Dion, native of La Cadie, aged 48 years. They have three hired fishermen, two boats, three cows, three geese, two turkey-hens and nine fowls.

The land that he occupies was granted him, verbally by M. de St. Ovide, and M. Lenormant de Mézy.

It includes a beach and scaffolding for the drying of the fish of two boats, and a large garden where they grow all kinds of vegetable produce.

François Picard, fisherman, native of Pléhérel, diocese of St. Brieux, aged 39 years, of which he has passed 24 years in the colony ; married to Anne Barbudeau, native of the place, aged 28 years. They have been granted rations for two years.

They have four children :—

Jullien, aged 8 years.

Suzanne, aged 5 years.

Angélique, aged 2 years.

Françoise, aged 1 year.

Five hired fishermen, namely :—

Jean Gauthier, aged 36 years, native of Mandes, diocese of St. Malo.

Julien Thomas, native of Couet, diocese of St. Malo, aged 30 years.

Jean Colinet, aged 22 years, native of Trebedeau, diocese of St. Malo.

Pierre Briand, native of St. Carlé, diocese of St. Malo.

Toussaint Picard, native of Pléhérel, diocese of St. Brieux, aged 17 years.

Three other hired men who are at Louisbourg.

Two boats, a half boat, one cow and six fowls.

Le Sieur François Picard has no dwelling.

Jean Granne, fisherman, native of Tadé, diocese of St. Malo ; and 35 years : of which he has passed 17 in this colony ; married to Marie Papou, native of St. Pierre, aged 30 years.

They have one son and three daughters :—

Augustin, aged 3 years.

Isabelle, aged 7 years.

Agathe, aged 5 years.

Geneviève, aged 14 months.

Nine hired fishermen of whom six are working for their board :—

Jean Fougère, native of Chateauneuf, diocese of St. Malo, aged 39 years.

André Groey, aged 24 years, native of Caronne, diocese of Avranches.

Toussaint Tramond, aged 15 years, native of Hebedau, diocese of St. Malo.

Julien Papou, aged 24 years, native of St. Esprit.

Pierre Jourgouche, native of Bayonne, aged 22 years.

Gabriel Touria, aged 30 years, native of Bayonne.

Two boats, two cows, one calf and six fowls.

The dwelling that he occupies was sold to him by the widow Seau. In the deed of sale the number of toises the land contains, either frontage or surface measurement, is not mentioned.

Georges Barbudeau, master-surgeon of St. Esprit, native of the island of Oléron, diocese of Saintes. He has been 36 years in the colony ; married to Françoise Vrigneau, aged 52 native of Plaisance. They have with them their nephew Simon Halbert, native of the island of Oléron, aged 16 years. He is to remain in the country in the capacity of a surgeon.

They have no grant of the land they occupy. They have a garden but no live stock or poultry.

Herbe Desroches, fisherman, native of Coral, diocese of Avranche, has been in the colony 22 years ; aged 35 years ; married to Marie Barbudeau, native of this place, aged 30 years.

5-6 EDWARD VII., A. 1906

They have three sons and one daughter.

François, aged 8 years.

Jean, aged 3 years.

Pierre, aged 3 months.

Margueritte, aged 10 years.

Louise Duneau, aged 14, native of Louisbourg, in the capacity of servant.

Three hired fishermen :—

Yves Galles, aged 30 years, native of the parish of Guillé, diocese of St. Malo.

Alexis Renard, aged 30 years, native of Ste. Broulade de Hol.

Louis Mange, aged 23 years, native of Carmel, archdiocese of Paris.

One boat, one half boat, one cow and eight fowls.

The dwelling that he occupies was given, verbally, by M. Bigot and contains platforms and scaffoldings for drying the fish of two boats.

Isabelle Longue Epée, widow of the late Jean Papou, native of the coast of Plaisance ; aged 52 years.

She has four sons :—

Charles, aged 29 years ;

Julien, aged 25 years ;

Jean, aged 22 years ;

François, aged 18 years, all natives of St. Esprit.

The land they occupy was given them verbally by the authorities. They have a garden.

Jean Clément, fisherman, native of the parish of Jeffrets, diocese of Coutances, aged 45 years, of which he has passed 30 in the colony. Married to Marie Brus, aged 40 years, native of la Cadie.

They have five sons and one daughter :—

Jean, aged 20 years ;

Pierre, aged 18 years ;

Jean, aged 11 years ;

Pierre, aged 9 years ;

Chapin, aged 10 months ;

Louise, aged 4 years, all natives of St- Esprit.

One boat, one cow, one calf, and six fowls.

George Bonin, fisherman, native of the place, aged 28 years, married to Marie Diers, native of Niganiche, aged 19 years.

They have one daughter not yet named, aged 21 days, and Madeleine Diers, her sister aged 9 years.

One mare, three fowl, two geese, and two turkey hens.

The land they occupy was granted to them by Messrs. de St. Ovide and Le Normand, but they lost the title deed in the war.

Jacques Lirard, fisherman, native of the parish of Plerin, diocese of St. Brieux, aged 40 years of which he has passed 26 in the colony. Married to Catherine Clément, aged 22 years, native of Port Toulouse.

They have one daughter Marie, aged 14 months.

Two hired fishermen.

Nicolas Joasse, aged 18 years, native of Quarolle, diocese of Avranche.

Joannes Dharouenaut, aged 24 years, native of Charau, diocese of Bayonne.

Five fowls. They have no dwelling place.

Francois Le Hardy, fisherman, native of St. Modé, diocese of St. Malo, married to Marguerite Clément, aged 15 years, native of the place.

Their whole wealth consists of seven fowls, they have no dwelling place.

Madeleine Robert, widow of the late Jean Bradon, native of la Cadie, aged 52 years.

She has three children, two sons and one daughter.

Jean Bradon, aged 24 years ;

Pierre Bradon, aged 32 years ;

Marguerite Bradon, aged 18 years,

Etienne Porier, her nephew, aged 7 years.

All natives of Ile Royal.

One heifer, and five fowls. She has no dwelling place.

Jean Beaulieu, fisherman, native of Bourneuf, diocese of Nantes, aged 48 years of which he has passed 30 in the colony. Married to Marie Hulin, native of Grandville, diocese of Coutances, aged 48 years.

They have two sons:

Pierre, aged 6 years;

Jean, aged 2 years;

Four fowls, and they have no dwelling place.

Francois Bonnieu, fisherman, native of the place, aged 24 years. Married to Marguerite Lavaudiere native of Port Toulouse.

They have one son and one daughter.

Jean aged 5 months.

Barbe, aged 3 years.

And one mare for the whole of their live stock.

Anselme Blanchard, farmer for M. Dola Barras, Captain of the port, native of Cobeguy, aged 33 years. Married to Marguerite Diron, native of la Cadie aged 32 years.

They have 6 children.

Joseph, aged 10 years;

Marie Marthe, aged 15 years;

Isabelle, aged 7 years;

Margueritte, aged 4 years;

Jeanne, aged 3 years.

Cloty, aged 2 years.

A cow with her calf.

They have not yet cleared any land.

NOTE.—As regards St. Esprit there was a greater number of boats before the war than to-day.

Left St. Esprit on the 11th of February and arrived at l'Ardoise about 6 o'clock in the afternoon of the same day. The distance between the two points is estimated at six leagues. We noticed, first, that a bank of sand on which there is a great deal of grass, extends from St. Esprit to the Creek de la Choui, and, further, that this Creek de la Choui affords excellent anchorage from the south-west; north-west, and north-quarter-north-east winds, but it is open to the full force of winds from other points. It has an area of three quarters of a league, and in the centre seven or eight fathoms of water. There are two submerged reefs outside the said creek that are left to starboard on entering. The Grande Rivière runs into the said creek. The narrow entrance of the creek lies north and south. It runs inland about three leagues and after dividing into three arms penetrates inland to the west, north-west and north. Vessels of seventy tons, if they could only effect an entrance, might pass up the creek for two leagues, but the passage is only practicable for vessels drawing six or seven feet of water, and that only at high tide. It's shores are covered with all kinds of hard wood, with quantities of pine or, spruce on the high ground, and on the banks of the three arms. During the remainder of the distance, which is estimated at four leagues, we did not find any place suitable as a place of refuge for boats. It is all composed of abrupt declivities and chains of rocks impracticable for vehicles. All the land in the vicinity of the sea is covered with fir and poor spruce.

The bay de l'Ardroise is adapted to the cod-fishery. The family of the Sieur Coste, who took refuge here at the time of the last war with the English, makes good catches of codfish of very merchantable quality. The bay is divided into two parts; the one that is settled being very small and exposed to the winds blowing in from the open sea, but it was preferred to the larger arm seeing that that does not run so far inland, and is therefore more exposed to the full force of the wind. In the larger branch vessels find shelter from winds from every point generally, and when they are to lie there for some time, without proceeding on their way, they can by using precaution

5-6 EDWARD VII., A. 1906

find anchorage. It runs inland for a good half league, but the water is only deep enough for boats. The banks are covered with hardwood. The soil is known to be largely sandy in its composition and suited only for the cultivation of hay, and garden stuff.

CENSUS OF THE FAMILY OF SR. FRANÇOIS COSTE.

François Coste, native of the parish of Martegue, diocese of Marseille, aged 90 years ; has been in the colony 30 years. Married to Madeleine Martin, native of Port Royal, aged 89 years.

They have with them :

Joseph Dugas, aged 21 years ;

Madeleine Dugas, aged 12 years ; their grand son ;

Louis Mercier, aged 17 years, native of Canada, engaged for one year in the capacity of servant.

Five cows, two mares, one sow, six fowls, and a garden.

Pierre Boy, fisherman, native of St. Jean des Camps, disocese of Coutances, aged 70 years of which he has spent 40 in the colony. Married to Marie Coste, aged 56 years, native of Port Royal.

They have two sons, and five daughters.

Joseph, aged 19 years ;

Francois, aged 17 years ;

Judith, aged 27 years ;

Cecile, aged 21 years ;

Madeleine, aged 17 years ;

Charlotte, aged 14 years ;

Geneviève, aged 11 years.

One ox, two cows, three calves, one bull, two pigs, seven fowls, one boat and a large garden.

Madeleine Coste, widow of the late Barthelemy Petitpas, native of Port Royal, aged 54 years.

She has five sons and one daughter :

Jean Petitpas, aged 24 years ;

Pierre Petitpas, aged 21 years ;

Claude Petitpas, aged 18 years ;

Guillaume Petitpas, aged 17 years ;

Paul Petitpas, aged 12 years ;

Pelajie Petitpas, aged 14 years. All natives of Port Toulouse.

One ox, four cows, one calf, two pigs, five fowls, one boat, and a large garden.

Gervais Brisset, fisherman, native of Condé, diocese of Bayou, aged 50 years, of which he has passed 30 in this colony. Married to Marie Joseph Le Roy, native of Port Toulouse, aged 36 years.

They have five daughters :

Marie Josephe, aged 16 years ;

Catherine, aged 12 years ;

Brigide, aged 8 years ;

Suzanne, aged 6 years ;

Gervaise, aged 3 years.

One ox, one cow, two pigs, six fowls, one schooner of the capacity of 15 cords of wood, and a garden like the others.

Charles Lavigne, coaster, native of Port Royal, aged 34 years. Married to Madeleine Petitpas, aged 34 years, native of Port Toulouse.

They have two sons and three daughters :

Benoist, aged 3 years ;

Joseph, aged 5 months ;

Anne, aged 9 years ;

Charles, aged 6 years ;

Cecile, aged 5 years.

Gilles Poirier, aged 13 years, native of St. Esprit, in the capacity of a domestic.

One ox, four cows, one calf, two pigs, seven fowls, one boat of the capacity of ten cords of wood and a garden.

Joseph Petitpas, fisherman, native of the Port de Toulouse, aged 29 years. Married to Anne Lafargue, aged 25 years, native of Petit Degras.

They have one son aged 15 months.

One cow, five fowls and a garden.

Jean Coste, coaster, native of Port Royal, aged 38 years. Married to Madeleine Lafargue, native of Petit Degra, aged 29 years.

They have four sons and one daughter :

François, aged 11 years ;

Pierre, aged 9 years ;

Jean, aged 6 years ;

Etienne, aged 6 months ;

Geneviève, aged 3 years ;

Madeleine, aged 16 years.

Ambroise Lebandon, aged 24 years, native of Port Toulouse, in the capacity of domestic.

Six head of cattle, one mare, two pigs, seven fowls, one boat of the capacity of 15 cords of wood and a garden.

Pierre Brisson, fisherman, native of Nantes, aged 52. Married to Anne Boy, native of Port Toulouse, aged 33 years.

They have two sons and one daughter :

Jean, aged 5 years ;

Pierre, aged 18 months :

Marie, aged 11 years.

Louis Minereau, native of Rochfort, aged 20 years, as a domestic.

Five head of cattle, one mare, two pigs, five fowls, one boat and a garden.

Noel Amiot, fisherman, native of Quiberon, diocese of St. Malo, aged 40 years, and in the Colony since 1728. Married to Marguerite Boy, native of Port Toulouse, aged 30 years.

They have two sons and two daughters.

Jean, aged 4 years, and the other is not yet named ;

Margueritte, aged 8 years ;

Madeleine, aged 2 years.

Seven head of cattle, one pig, five fowls, one boat, and a garden.

The land on which the family of François Coste is settled was granted to Sieur Coste by Messrs. de Saint Ovide and de Soubras. It extends half a league on the sea shore. The small quantity of meadow land is situated on the banks of the Grande Baye. They would not know where to obtain sufficient hay for their live stock, unless they carried it from the lands of Canceau. The beach is naturally enclosed and there are scaffoldings for drying the fish.

NOTE.—That all those settlers as well as those at Saint Esprit and at Gabarus have received rations for two years.

Left l'Ardoise on the 13th and arrived at Port Toulouse on the same day, the distance between the two points being estimated at two leagues.

About two hundred toises from the bay de l'Ardoise, settled by le Sieur François Coste, we found a second very extensive bay. The entrance to it lies south-east and north-west with a depth of four fathoms of water ; and vessels, once inside find anchorage in 15 to 16 feet of water, and shelter from winds from the south-quarter-south-west; west, north-west ; north; and north-quarter; north-east. In truth they are not secure in case of heavy weather, for the bottom is composed of moving sands, and vessels are liable to drag their cables, and drive on to the rocks of the Cap de l'Ardoise, or run aground on a sand bank that extends to the further end of the bay. It is little frequented by the sailors during the autumn, which is the season for gales, and vessels only go there to load with cord wood. A quarter of a league outside the bay to the south, quarter south-west, lies an island of the same name, which may be half a league

5-6 EDWARD VII., A. 1906

in extent. It is close to the lands Grand Isle, near the cape at the south-west of the said bay. All the shore as well as the interior is covered with hard timber. Leaving the bay we pass through an alder plot about an eighth of a league in extent, which leads to a species of barachois, afterwards following the shore for half a league before striking the Barachois des Sept Islots. This barachois is not of much importance.

It has little water and it seems probable that at some remote date it was meadowland, which has been submerged with the waters left by the incursions of the sea into the island. One sees where in reality there is the grass still at the bottom, and at low tide there is at the most only a foot of water over it. The bottom is very muddy. Outside there are seven small islands which give to this place the name Sept Islots.

Finally a blazed road is taken which leads to the further end of the barachois to the east of Port Toulouse. All this part of the country is covered with mixed timber, but fir is the predominant wood.

PORT TOULOUSE.

Port Toulouse is situated to the right as you enter the little channel. The mouth is formed by the Pointe à Coste, on the lands of Isle Royale, and the Cap de la Ronde, on the isles Madame. The port extends three leagues running east and west. The breadth varies at divers points but is estimated to average from 150 to 200 toises. Vessels of 150 tons could not pass on account of two shoals that are in the centre of the said channel and it would take good seamanship to work small vessels through.

Port Toulouse is formed by the Pointe à Coste and the Pointe de la Briquerie, which are reckoned to lie north-west and south-east, and to be three quarters of a league apart. There is one channel which the King's vessels of 30 to 36 pieces of cannon could enter, but it is winding, and it is necessary to buoy the course on port and starboard in order that vessels may pass up the middle of the channel without fear of coming to grief. It is a pity that this port is not practicable to vessels of all kinds; it presents a charming perspective and could be easily fortified, but it would be impossible to prevent an enemy effecting the landing of troops without the construction of several forts at the various points suitable for that purpose, between the Pointe de l'ancienne Intendance and the rivière à Tillard. On this rivière Tillard, in the creek of la Briquerie défence is everywhere quite easy, and without being visible from the present settlement. When near the land one estimates that la Briquerie is a good league from the settlement, and the rivière à Tillard three-quarters of a league. Vessels of 100 tons can enter and find shelter in this river, secure from winds from all points generally. The basin is not very large but is well adapted for sheltering ships. The settlers of Port Toulouse beach their boats and schooners here for the winter. It is the only spot that is concealed from observation from the King's Post. From Pointe à Coste to the King's Post there lies a sand bank which leaves a small space between it and the land on the north side where the Post stands and between this sandbank and the land on the north side, there is an arm running inland to the east for about a good half league. It is just as easy to effect a landing in this spot as in the preceeding. The land of l'ancienne Briquerie is found to be stony and not capable of producing marketable stuff. Half a league east-south-east from Port Toulouse lies the Grande Grave. It is bordered by Pointe Pinet on the east and by Pointe à Coste on the west. The entrance lies north-east by south-west. Vessels can find anchorage here and shelter from winds from almost every point, only those blowing off shore being dangerous. They anchor in five to six fathoms of water. Two reefs lie opposite to pointe à Coste. They are visible at low water and left on the starboard beam as one enters. At the far end of the creek there is a barachois running a good quarter of a league inland in a north-westerly direction. All this section is covered, with a mixed timber.

CENSUS OF THE SETTLERS OF PORT TOULOUSE.

Jean Baptiste Martel, coaster, native of Quebec, aged 42 years. Married to Marie Poujet, native of Port Royal, aged 48 years.

They have three sons and two daughters :—

Charles, 18 years ;

Joseph, aged 16 years ;

Baptiste, aged 13 years ;

Madeleine, aged 11 years ;

Epotille, aged 8 years ;

Four oxen, eight cows, one horse, eleven fowls, three ducks, six geese, and a gander. The land for his dwelling place was sold him by Jean Clement. He did not know the extent, nor that of a meadow from which he carries hay for wintering his live stock.

Jean Boy, coaster, native of the neighbourhood, aged 22 years. Married to Judict Coujet, native of Port Toulouse, aged 23 years.

They have one cow with a calf, four turkey hens, five geese, three fowls, and one schooner.

The land they occupy was sold to them by le Sieur Boudrot. They have partly cleared a piece of ground for a garden. They, as well as the preceeding family, have been granted rations for two years.

Nicolas Beriot, coaster, native of la Cadie, aged 49 years. Married to Ursul le Gotre, native of des Mines, diocese of Quebec, aged 34 years. They have taken refuge in the island for two years.

They have three sons and three daughters :—

Olive, aged 12 years ;

Pierre, aged 10 years ;

Joseph, aged 7 years ;

Marie, aged 16 years ;

Joseph, aged 14 years ;

Madeleine, aged 4 years.

One cow, three geese, and five fowls.

The land they occupy was granted them in 1749 by M. Duhaget, then Commandant at Port Toulouse. They have made a small clearing for a garden, and uncultivated land for a meadow. They have been granted rations for two years.

Pierre Degrê, carpenter, native of la Cadie, aged 56 years. Married to Marie Testard, widow of the late Charles Pinet Jr., native of Port Royal, aged 41 years.

She has five children by her first marriage, three sons, and two daughters :—

Joseph Pinet, aged 24 years ;

Pierre Pinet, aged 22 years ;

Pierre Pinet, aged 12 years ;

Marie Joseph, aged 23 years ;

Madeleine Pinet, aged 15 years ;

All natives of Port Toulouse.

The land they occupy was given them by M. de Rouville, then Commandant at Port Toulouse.

The only clearings they have made are one for a garden, and one for pasturage, where they cut about thirty quintals of hay. They receive rations according to the King's regulations.

Three cows and nine fowls.

Michel Samson, coaster, native of la Cadie, aged 40 years, of which he has spent 25 years in the colony. Married to Jeanne Testard, native of Port Royale, aged 35 years. They have been granted two years rations.

They have four sons and four daughters :—

Jean, aged 17 years ;

Michel, aged 13 years ;

Sebastien, aged 11 years ;

Fabien, aged 11 years ;

Jeanne, aged 22 years ;

Jeanette, aged 15 years ;

Judic, aged 8 years ;

Joseph, aged 3 years.

5-6 EDWARD VII., A. 1906

The land they occupy was granted verbally by Messieurs de Saint Ovide and Le Normand. They have two oxen, eight cows and six fowls.

They have cleared two or three arpents of land, which they have turned into meadows, where hay comes up best, and a garden where vegetables thrive best.

Charles Pinet, coaster, of Port Toulouse, native of that place, aged 27 years ; married to Jeanne Samson, native of Port Royale, aged 32 years.

They have one son who is not named.

The land on which they dwell belongs to Sr. Samson, their father-in-law, and he has given them land for building and to make a small garden where garden products do best. They have two cows and six fowls. They have been granted two years rations.

Mathieu Samson, coaster, native of Port Royal, aged 42. Married to Marguerite Lapierre, native of la Cadie, aged 42 years.

They have four sons and three daughters :—

Pierre Samson, aged 17 years ;
Jean Samson, aged 16 years ;
François Samson, aged 14 years ;
Bruneau Samson, aged 7 years ;
Isabelle Samson, aged 13 years ;
Charlotte Samson, aged 8 years ;
Jeanne Samson, aged 3 years.

They have been granted two years rations, and have beeen in the colony since 1730. They have three oxen, two cows, and seven fowls.

The land they occupy was granted to them verbally by Messieurs de St. Ovide and Le Normand. They have made a clearing for a garden and a piece of ground four arpents in extent for a meadow.

Habraham Du Gas, coaster, native of Mount Royal, aged 36 years ; married to Marguerite Fougère, native of La Cadie, aged 28 years.

They have five children :—

Jean Dugas, aged 13 years ;
Marguerite, aged 16 years ;
Marie Dugas, aged 11 years ;
Geneviève, aged 9 years ;
Joseph, aged 18 months.

They have been in the colony since 1719, they have been granted rations conformably to the King's ordinance.

The land on which he is settled was granted to him, verbally, by Messieurs de St. Ovide, and Le Normand. They have made a clearing for a garden, and the rest is in pasture, with a second meadow above the dike of the Isles Madame.

Their live stock consists of two oxen ; three cows ; one sow ; seven fowls ; and one batteau.

Marie Marchand, widow of the late Charles Pinet, native of la Cadie ; aged 43 years.

She has three sons and two daughters :—

Jean Pinet, aged 21 years ;
Jean Baptiste, aged 13 years ;
Jeanne Pinet, aged 18 years ;
Angelique, aged 12 years.

The land she occupies was granted in form to Sr. Louis Marchand by Messieurs de St. Ovide, and le Normand, but they lost their title deed during the late war. She has no clearing except for a small garden.

Charles Pinet, Jr., coaster, native of the place, aged 25 years. Married to Helène Guedry, native of la Cadie, aged 22 years.

They have neither live stock nor dwelling place.

Pierre Sauvage, coaster, native of la Cadie, aged 27 years. Married to Jeanne Pinet, native of Port Toulouse, aged 22 years.

They have Josette Sauvage, their daughter, aged 17 months.

They have neither live stock nor dwelling place.

Louis Dantin, native of Paris, aged 50 years.   Married to Marguerite La Soude, a tive of Saint Pierre, aged 36 years.

They have four sons and one daughter :
Gabriel Dantin, aged 10 years ;
Louis Dantin, aged 7 years ;
Barthélémy, aged 4 years ;
Joseph Dantin, aged 2 years ;
Jeanne Dantin, aged 9 years.

One ox, one cow and one hen.

Their house is situated on the land of Marc la Soude, their father.

Judicth Petitpas, aged 60 years, native of Port Royal, widow of the late Marc la Soude.

She has two sons :—
Jean Baptiste La Soude, aged 24 years ;
Joseph La Soude, aged 21 years.

They had a grant in form of the land they occupied from Messieurs de Saint-Ovide and Le Normand, but they lost the deed in the late war.

One ox, three cows, two calves and four fowls.

They make their hay on the banks of the rivière à Tillard, where their meadows lie.   They were granted to them in the same deed as their homesteads.

Honoré Boucher, native of la Cadie, aged 36 years, of which he has passed 30 in the colony.   Married to Marie Anne La Soude, native of Port Toulouse, aged 24 years.

They have two sons and one daughter :—
Bellony Boucher, aged 8 years.
Jean Boucher, aged 2 years ;
Marie Joseph, aged 4 years ;

They have two oxen, two cows, and four fowls.   Their house is on their mother's homestead.

Michel Boudreau, coaster, native of la Cadie, aged 35 years.   Married to Jeanne Fougère, native of Port Toulouse, age 27 years.

They have one son and one daughter :—
Joseph Boudrot, aged 2 months ;
Jeanne Boudrot, aged 2 years.

One ox, one sow ; six fowls and one schooner.

The land they occupy was granted to them by Messieurs Saint Ovide and Le Normand.   They have made a small clearing for a garden.

Jacques Coste, builder, native of Port Royal, aged 47 years.   Married to Françoise Petitpas, native of la Cadie, aged 45 years.

They have Claude Coste, their son aged 22 years.

They hold in live stock, two oxen, three cows ; two pigs, one horse ten fowls ; one bateau and a skiff.

The land on which they are settled was given them verbally by Messieurs de Saint Ovide, and Le Normand.   They know nothing as to its extent, and have cleared ground for a garden only.

Joseph Dugas, coaster, native of la Cadie, aged 38 years, widower of the late Margueritte Le Blanc.

He has one son and four daughters :—
Joseph, aged 5 years ;
Margueritte, aged 10 years ;
Anne, aged 8 years ;
Françoise, aged 3 years :
Marie, aged 5 years, Marie Braud, his niece, native of la Cadie, aged 22 years.

One ox, two cows, two pigs, and 12 fowls.

The land on which he is settled was granted to his late father, by Messieurs de Saint-Ovide and Le Normand, but they lost the deed in the last war.   They have cleared about two arpents of land where they have several times sown turnips, but they have never come up well.

5-6 EDWARD VII., A. 1906

Pierre Boy, coaster, native of the place, aged 19 years. Married to Jeanne Dugas, native of Louisbourg, aged 22 years.

They are on the land of Joseph Dugas, their father. They have two cows and one hen.

Claude Clerget, coaster, native of the parish of Acre, diocese of Langres, aged 60 years, of which he has passed 25 in the country. Married to Françoise Lavergne, native of Port Royal, aged 50 years.

Three have three sons and three daughters :—

Joseph Petitpas, aged 21 years ;

Abraham La Vaudière, aged 17 years ;

Gabriel Clerget, aged 14 years, natives of the place ;

Felicité Clerget, aged 12 years ;

Françoise Clerget, aged 11 years ;

Anne Clerget, aged 10 years.

They have live stock consisting of two oxen, two cows, two heifers and three fowls.

The land they occupy is situated at the further end of Bras d'Or. It was granted to them by Messieurs de St. Ovide and le Normand. They have cleared about two arpents of ground, where they raise all sorts of garden stuff.

Jacques Petitpas, of Port Toulouse, is a coaster, and native of Canceau, aged 28 years. Married to Françoise Breaud, native of la Cadie, aged 28 years.

They have Marie Petitpas, their daughter, nine days old.

One ox, one sow, four fowls and a bateau. The land they occupy was given them by their mother, out of her homestead.

Anne Baudreau, widow of Jean Braud, native of la Cadie, aged 54 years.

She has two sons and four daughters :—

Joseph, aged 26 years ;

Ernant, aged 20 years ;

Marie, aged 22 years ;

Anne, aged 18 years ;

Margueritte, aged 15 years ;

Magdeleine, aged 14 years.

She has no dwelling place, and has been granted a year's rations. Her children follow the coasting trade.

Jean Petitpas, coaster, native of la Cadie, aged 30 years ; married to Françoise Monthory, native of la Cadie, aged 27 years. They have been settled in the Colony ten years.

They have Jean, their son, 5 months old and are settled in the dwelling place of her mother.

The character of the land in the further end of Bras d'Or is very well suited to the cultivation of much garden stuff, such as peas and other vegetables. Notwithstanding that the fogs are as prevalent as at Louisbourg in the spring, the Sr. Petitpas told me that one year his father sowed wheat and that it came up in fine condition and well nourished.

Joseph Vigneau, coaster, native of la Cadie, aged 37 years ; married to Catherine Arceneau, native of Port Royal aged 33 years. They have been settled in the Colony 14 years.

They have five sons and two daughters :

Joseph, aged 13 years ;

Nicolas, aged 11 years ;

Jean, aged 10 years ;

Pierre, aged 6 years ;

Hippolite, aged 3 years ;

Rose, aged 15 years ;

Marguerite, aged 7 years.

And in live stock, two oxen, two cows, four pigs, ten fowls, and one bateau. They have Baptiste Bareu in the capacity of a domestic. He is to settle in the colony.

They have verbal permission from Messrs. Desherbiers and Prévost to settle on the land they occupy, and they have turned the whole into pasture.

SESSIONAL PAPER No. 18

Madeleine Soret, widow of the late Pierre du Mas, native of Quebec, aged 46 years.

She has two sons and one daughter :

Dominique Coulon, aged 20 years, by her first marriage.

Pierre Dumas, aged 12 by her second marriage.

Margaret Coulon, aged 18 years.

She has been in the colony 29 years.

Her land was granted to her by Messieurs. de St. Ovide and Le Normand, but she lost the deed in the war. She has turned all the forepart of her homestead into meadow land from which she saves from 130 to 140 quintals of hay. She has no live stock.

Joseph Fougère, coaster, native of Port Royal, aged 36 years ; married to Marguerite Coste, native of Port Toulouse, aged 32 years. They are in the colony 28 years.

They have Modeste Fougère, aged 4 years.

Marie Madeleine, aged 12 years, native of la Cadie, as a domestic.

In live stock, they have one ox, one cow, one heifer, two geese, four fowls, and a share in a vessel.

The dwelling in which he is settled, was sold to him by Claude Dugas.

Claude Dugas, coaster, native of this place, aged 26 years, married to Madeleine Béliveau, native of Port Royal, aged 34 years, widow of the late Jean Fougère.

They have four sons and two daughters :

Louison Fougère, aged 18 years ;

Jean Fougère, aged 10 years ;

Michel Fougère, aged 9 years ;

Joseph Dugas, aged 2 months ;

Isabeau Fougère, aged 17 years ;

Barbe Fougère, aged 16 years.

In live stock they have two oxen, two cows ; one mare ; one goose, one pig, and five fowls. They have cleared a garden, and the remainder of the homestead is in meadow land from which they draw 20 to 30 quintals of hay.

The land they occupy was sold to them by the late Jean Robert Henry. The extent of the said land was not specified in the deed of sale.

Nicolas Préjean, coaster of Port Toulouse, native of Port Royal, aged 42 years.

He has two sons and four daughters :—

Louison, aged 18 years ;

Gabriel, aged 1 year ;

Marie, aged 16 years ;

Jeanne, aged 9 years ;

Rose, aged 8 years :

Cecille, aged 4 years.

Two cows, two fowls, and a bateau.

The dwelling he occupies was sold to him, by the late Jean Robert Henry. There is a garden and the rest of the land is pasture.

Nicolas Lavigne, coaster, native of St. Denis, aged 68 years, of which he has spent 25 in the colony, married to Marie Anne Demanceau, aged 43 years.

They have one son and five daughters :—

Nicolas, aged 14 years ;

Anne, aged 19 years ;

Marguerite, aged 15 years ;

Madeleine, aged 11 years ;

Barbe, aged 7 years ;

Geneviève, aged 2 years.

Of live stock they have two oxen, two cows, two bulls, four geese, and seven fowls.

The homestead on which they are was merely granted to them verbally by Messieurs de Saint-Ovide, and Le Normand. They have made a clearing for a garden and the rest of the land is in pasture.

5-6 EDWARD VII., A. 1906

Orré Marchand, widow of the late Breau, native of the said place, aged 36 years. She has five sons and two daughters :—

Joseph, aged 15 years ;
Pierre, aged 14 years ;
François, aged 11 years ;
Jean, aged 7 years ;
Georges, aged 4 years ;
Jeanne, aged 20 years ;
Célestine, aged 9 years.

In live stock she has two cows, and one sow.

The land she occupies was granted to her by Messieurs de Saint Ovide, and Le Normand. In the grant the extent of frontage of the said land is not stated, but it is clearly specified that its depth extends from the settlement to the further end of Bras d'Or.

Jean Marchand, coaster, native of Port Royal, aged 40 years ; married to Geneviève Pouget, aged 35 years, native of Port Royal.

They have two sons :—

Eustache, aged 2 years,
Louis, aged 1 year.

In live stock they have four oxen, two cows, eight geese, five turkey hens, eight fowls, and one skiff.

Their meadows are situated on the Grand Passage, from la Platriere to the Isle de l'Ours, the distance between these boundaries being one league, where they gather 60 to 70 quintals of hay.

They have two other dwellings, one granted verbally by M. de la Valière, subject to the good pleasure of Messieurs de St. Ovide and de Mézy. The other was sold to them by the widow Boudreau.

Note, that all the settlers enumerated above, were given two years rations, with the exception of several who complained of not having received their supplies from the store house, because the storekeeper had taken their orders from them, and gave them a supply on account, telling them to return another time, and when they went back for the balance le Sr. Lartigue did not remember the occurrence, and they never received the balance due to them.

Census of new settlers, refugee Acadians, throughout the command of Port Toulouse.

Jean Boudrot, native of Port Royal, aged 29 years, married to Francoise Harsenot, native of la Cadie, aged 23 years. They have been in the colony two years and have received rations during that period.

They have two sons and one daughter.
Joseph, aged 3 years, native of la Cadie.
Jean, aged 2 years, native of the same place.
Angélique, aged three months.
Nicolas La Treille, native of la Cadie, aged 10 years, a relative.

They have neither live stock nor dwelling. They have ten fowls, and a bateau they are building to carry wood to Louisburg.

Baptiste Vigneau, native of Port Royal, aged 25 years, married to Anne Poirier, native of la Cadie, aged 28 years. They have been in the colony half a year, and have been granted rations for two years.

They have two sons and four daughters :—

Jean Baptiste, aged 10 years ;
Amant, aged 6 years ;
Marie, aged 12 years ;
Téotiste, aged 8 years ;
Marguerite, aged 4 years ;
Nastazie, aged 1 year.

In animals, one cow, one calf, one sow, eleven fowls, and a bateau. They have no dwelling place.

The land on which they are settled was marked out for them by M. de Villejoint. They have made no clearing.

Joseph Poirier, native of la Cadie, aged 47 years. Married to Jeanne Godet, native of Port Royal, aged 35 years. They have been in the colony two years, and have been granted rations for that time.

They have a son and three daughters :—

Joseph, aged 15 years ;
Anne, aged 18 years ;
Marie, aged 10 years ;
Modeste, aged 4 years ;

In animals, one ox, one cow, one calf, four pigs, eleven fowls, and one bateau.

The land on which they are settled was given them by M. de. Villejoint. It was long ago cleared by fire. They have done no clearing.

Vincent Arceneau, native of la Cadie, aged 32 years. Married to Marguerite Poirier, native of Port Royal, aged 21 years. They have been in the colony two years, and have been granted rations for that period.

They have only one cow.

The land they have was granted to them by M. de Villejoint. They have done no clearing.

Jean Maurice, coaster, native of la Cadie, aged 48 years. Married to Isabelle Arceneau, native of des Mines, aged 37 years. They have been for two years in the colony and have been given rations during that time.

They have three daughters and two orphans :—

Marguerite, aged 18 years ;
Anne, aged 15 years ;
Marie, aged 9 years ;
Charles Bourd, aged 14 years ;
Simon Poirier, aged 8 years.

In live stock they own two oxen, one cow, two pigs, three geese, six fowls, and a bateau.

The land on which they are settled was marked out for them by M. de Villejoint. They have made a clearing for a garden.

Jean Bte. Bouteau, of Port Toulouse, native of la Cadie, aged 27 years. Married to Jeanne Quéry, native of Port Royal, aged 23. They have been in the country for 18 months and have been granted rations for two years.

They have Margueritte, their daughter, aged 8 months, and Anne Clémenceau, aged 7 years.

One ox forms their whole stock.

The land which they have improved was given them by M. de Villejoint.

They have cleared about two arpents to make a meadow and a garden ; for as regards grain not only is the nature of the soil unsuitable for its growth but the fogs that prevail in the spring prevent it from being productive.

André Temple, native of the parish of Menibec (?) bishopric of Avranches, aged 24 years. Married to Marie Devot, native of la Cadie, aged 22 years. They have been three years in the colony, and have received rations during that period.

They have Margueritte, their daughter, aged three months.

The land they occupy was marked out for them by M. de Villejoint. They have made a clearing for a garden, and another of about four arpents in extent for a meadow.

Marie Quéry, native of la Cadie, aged 55 years, widow of Pierre Devot.

She has Pierre, her son, aged 18 years, and Anne, aged 13 years.

In live stock, one ox, one cow and calf, one sow, ten fowls, three geese.

She is in the country since the month of August last, and she lives in the house of André Temple, her son-in-law.

5-6 EDWARD VII., A. 1906

Charles Poirier, native of la Cadie, aged 30. Married to Margueritte Vigneau, native of Port Toulouse, aged 25 years. They have been in the country 18 months, and have been granted rations for three years.

They have Charles, their son, aged 18 months.

In live stock they have one sow and ten fowls.

The homestead on which they are settled is owned by a man named Langlois, a settler in the Isles Madame. When they came there he promised to give them the freehold, but on seeing that they had improved the property and built a house on it, he declined to fulfil his promise and demanded the sum of 100 écus in settlement.

Joseph Le Blanc, native of la Cadie, aged 55 years. Married to Anne Bourg, native of Des Mines, aged 53 years. They have been in the colony three years, and have received rations during that time.

They have two sons and one daughter :—

Alexandre, aged 20 years ;

Paul, aged 17 years ;

Anne, aged 10 years ;

Joseph Le Blanc, aged 6 years, their nephew.

Anne Alain, aged 18 years, native of la Cadie.

Marie Joseph Alain, aged 15 years, their nieces.

Alexandre Bourg, her father, a native of la Cadie, aged 84 years, lives with them.

In live stock they have twenty-five cattle, ten fowls, and one skiff.

The dwelling in which they are belongs to Joseph Dugas, their son-in-law. He allows them to occupy it until such time as they are given land.

OLD SETTLERS IN LA BRIQUERIE.

Honoré Préjean, coaster, native of la Cadie, aged 40 years. Married to Marie Brossard, native of Port Royal, aged 30 years.

They have five sons and three daughters :—

Fœlix, aged 11 years ;

Ciprien, aged 5 years ;

Julien, aged 2 years ;

Two sons, each aged two and a half months, not yet named ;

Marie Anne, aged 9 years ;

Felicité, aged 7 years ;

Madeleine, aged 2 years.

Thomas Nolen, aged 27 years, native of Ireland, in the capacity of a domestic.

In live stock, one ox, three fowls, one bateau. He is in the colony since 1732.

The land on which Sr. Honoré Préjean has built was sold to him by Charles Béoudrot. He has done no clearing.

Margueritte Dugas, widow of the late Joseph Boudrot, native of Port Royal, aged 46 years.

She has two sons and one daughter :—

Louison, aged 19 years ;

Charles Boudrot, aged 14 years ;

Margueritte, aged 16 years ;

Joseph Boudrot, coaster, her son, native of Port Toulouse, aged 30 years. Married to Judict Fougère, native of said place, aged 19 years.

They have Jeanne, their daughter, aged 4 months.

Pierre Boudrot, coaster, native of the said place, aged 25 years. Married to Josette Dugas, native of petit Saint Pierre, aged 19 years.

They have two cows, two calves, and eight fowls.

The land on which they are located was given them verbally by Messrs. de Saint-Ovide, and Le Normand, and is situate on the coast of Saint Pierre. They have made a clearing for a garden, and the rest of the place is pasture land. Their meadows are on the Barachois à Descouts on the lands of the Isles Madame.

They could cut one hundred quintals of hay, if only it could be well saved, but they only grow, and cut grass sufficient for the live stock they have.

The lands were granted to them by the late Monsieur La Vallière, Commandant at Port Toulouse.

We left Port Toulouse on the twentieth of February and arrived at the rivière à Bourgeois at six o'clock in the evening of the same day.

The rivière à Bourgeois empties its waters in the little channel a league and a half from Port Toulouse. It takes its source in a large basin situated a quarter of a league from its mouth in the northern part of Isle Royale. It lies east and west, and is estimated as being a half league in length. The breadth of the river is unequal but its average width is estimated at 150 toises. Its entrance lies north and south. At high tide there are 15 to 16 feet of water in the river throughout its whole course of a quarter of a league in extent, whilst over the whole area of the basin already mentioned the depth varies from three to five feet. Vessels of 100 tons burden can enter and load with the cordwood and dimension timber, which is cut by the settlers of Port Toulouse during the winter. All the shores of the basin as well as the lands in the interior are covered with hard wood.

On February the 21st we left rivière à Bourgeois, and reached the creek à Descoust, situated in the lands of the Isles Madame the same day.

On leaving the basin of the rivière à Bourgeois one has to make a portage of about a quarter of a league. It is covered with fir and leads to the large creek.

This large creek would form part of the little channel, if there were not two islands, close to one another, lying in a line with the lands north of the said channel, and causing a break in the connection. The two entrances to the said creek lie at the two extremities of these islands. The eastern entrance is the most used ; it lies north and south. Vessels of 100 tons burden can make the passage, and find anchorage in from three to nine fathoms of water in any part of the creek.

The entrance to the west can only be used by vessels drawing six or seven feet of water, and at high tide. It lies north-east and south-west. The length of this creek is estimated at three quarters of a league. It runs east and west, with a breadth of a quarter of a league, towards the northern lands. All the banks are wooded with fir, but to compensate for this, a quarter of a league inland from the creek there is nothing but hard timber. We next traversed the little channel above the Isle Brulée, at which place there may be 150 toises of land.

THE ISLES MADAME AND THEIR SMALL CHANNEL.

Isles Madame lie to the south-south-west of Port Toulouse, and are separated from the lands of Ile Royale by the little channel. Isle Madame is estimated to be three leagues in length, by one league in breadth. Lengthwise it lies east and west, as does the channel, whilst its breadth lies north and south. The nature of the soil is not suitable for cultivation, as in addition to the fact that fogs are constantly prevalent during the whole of spring, the quality of the soil can only be described as a mixture of earth largely composed of clay, and an infinite number of rough stones heaped one upon the top of another. The land in the interior is wooded in places with beech-wood and the wild cherry tree, the remainder being covered with spruce and fir. The settlers on this island follow various callings, in order to secure a livelihood.

Those who are not engaged in the cod fisheries, are employed in navigation during the summer, whilst in the winter they make cord wood, which they sell at 9 livres a cord, delivered at the coast, whilst as a general rule all the settlers endeavour to add to their earnings by finding keep for a few head of cattle. The whole coast is practicable for small vessels, and a landing can be very easily effected at almost any point.

CENSUS OF OLD SETTLERS.

Census of the old settlers who are located on the north coast of the Isles Madame only.

Pierre Bernard, coaster, native of St. Malo, aged 66 ; married to Cecille Longue-Epée, native of la Cadie, aged 50 years. They have spent 30 years in this island.

5-6 EDWARD VII., A. 1906

They have eight children, four sons and four daughters :—
François, aged 22 years.
Nicolas, aged 18 years ;
Charles, aged 8 years ;
Isaac, aged 4 years ;
Anne, aged 24 years ;
Geneviève, aged 17 years ;
Françoise, aged 15 years ;
Froisille, aged 10 years.

In live stock they own one ox, two cows, two pigs and four fowls.

The land on which he has been located since 1720 was granted to him verbally by Messieurs de St. Ovide and Le Normand.

He has done a large amount of clearing and there is a fair amount of improved land. Sr. Pierre Bernard has made several attempts to grow wheat, but though it has always come up well, it has not ripened.

Jean Bernard, coaster, native of this place, aged 30 years; married to Catherine Langlois, native of Isles Madame, aged 28 years.

They have Madeleine Bernard, their daughter, aged 16 months, and a man named Pancros, aged 20 years, a native of Dieppe, who follows the fishery at Petit Degra, during the summer.

They own one ox, one cow and six fowls.

François Langlois, a settler in the colony for 30 years, native of Paris, aged 42 years. Married to Madeleine Coumeau, native of Port Royal, aged 65 years.

They have one son, Joseph, born in this place, aged 18 years.

They own a skiff, two cows, three calves, and two fowls.

The land on which he is settled was given to him verbally by Messrs. Saint Ovide and Le Normand. All the clearing he has made is contained in two gardens, but he also has a large piece of cleared ground which serves as a meadow.

Pierre Poujet, coaster, native of Port Royal, aged 40 years; Married to Madeleine Langlois, native of la Cadie, aged 30 years.

They have three sons and two daughters :—

Pierre, aged 9 years.
Jean, aged 7 years ;
François, aged 2 years ;
Madeleine, aged 14 years.
The youngest is not yet named. She is three weeks old.

They are settled on land owned by Langlois, père. They have made a clearing of about a quarter of an arpent in extent for a garden.

In live stock they own, four cows, three calves, one ox, one pig, and three fowls.

François Josse, coaster, native of St. Glam, bishopric of Dolle, aged 56 years. Married to Marie Langlois, aged 48 years, native of Port Royal.

They have five sons and two daughters:—

Pierre, aged 23 years.
Mathieu, aged 17 years ;
Guillaume, aged 13 years ;
Gabriel, aged 11 years ;
Jean, aged 6 years ;
Joseph, aged 22 years ;
Aimable, aged 8 years.
In live stock they own, three cows, one calf, and three fowls.

The land on which he is settled was given him verbally by the authorities. The quality of the soil renders it unsuitable for cultivation, and the most they can do is, by using a large amount of manure, to raise a little garden produce.

Mathurin Joseph, fisherman, native of Plangrenoy, bishopric of St. Brieux, aged 45 years, of which he has spent 23 in the colony. Married to Marie Gourde, native of Louisbourg, aged 31 years.

They have three daughters :—

Louise, aged 11 years;
Elenne, aged 10 years;
Cecille, aged 2 years.
All natives of the Isles Madame.
He has no land and is obliged to rent.

François Josse, coaster, native of Port Toulouse, aged 26 years, Married to Marie Margueritte Tardif, native of Louisbourg, aged 22 years.

They have one daughter, Jeanne, aged one year.

They own a cow, and a bateau.

The land he occupies was given to him verbally by the authorities. He has cleared about an arpent of land to make a garden.

François Langlois, fisherman, native of Port Royale, aged 44 years. Married to Henriette Bernard, native of the place, aged 33 years.

They have one daughter, Henriette, aged 14 months.

They own two cows, a calf, and three fowls.

Their house is built on land owned by Langlois' father. They have cleared land to make a garden.

Nicolas Langlois, fisherman, native of Port Toulouse, aged 29 years. Married to Isabelle Pouchet, native of Port Royal, age 27 years.

They have one son Nicolas, aged 2 years.

They own two cows ; three calves, an ox, a pig, and four fowls.

Their house is built on land owned by Langlois' father.

Jean Bouget, ploughman, native of la Cadie, aged 28 years. Married to Margueritte Langlois, native of Port Royal, aged 31 years.

They have one son, François aged one year.

In stock they own, four cows, three calves, two pigs, and four fowls.

Their land is the same as that of their father Langlois. Monsieur de Villejoint has given them a meadow situated on the river à Dumolin at the little channel. It is very extensive and they carry sufficient hay from it to keep 24 head of cattle.

All the above named settlers have been a long time in the colony, and have had rations granted them for two years only.

CENSUS OF NEW SETTLERS.

Census of the new settlers, refugees from la Cadie, on the Isles Madame.

Namely :—

Herne Lambert, ploughman, native of la Cadie, aged 65 years, married to Marie Longue Epée, aged 54 years, native of Cobeyt. They have been three years in the colony, and have been granted rations for that time.

They have two sons and two daughters :—

François, aged 21 years ;
Ambroise, aged 19 years ;
Jeanne, aged 15 years ;
Isabelle, aged 14 years.

And Olivier Lambert, ploughman, native of la Cadie, married to Marie Anne Pichot, native of Petit Degra, aged 17 years.

The land they occupy was located for them by Monsieur de Villejoint.

They have made a clearing, by cutting as much cord-wood as they possibly could along the shore, choosing to work on that part of the land, where they could make a living by cutting cordwood, as the nature of the soil makes no return for cultivation.

Claude Giroir, ploughman, native of la Cadie, aged 55 years, married to Madeleine Vincent, native of Port Royal, aged 44 years.

They have five sons and three daughters :

Joseph, aged 23 years ;
Silvain, aged 14 years ;

5-6 EDWARD VII., A. 1906

Bazille, aged 11 years ;
Antoine, aged 8 years ;
Margueritte, aged 21 years ;
Marie Joseph, aged 16 years ;
Procède, aged 5 years.

They have been in the colony three years, and have been granted rations for that period.

In live stock they own, three oxen, two cows, one calf, one pig, and five fowls.

They are settled on land that was chosen for them by Monsieur de Villejoint, but have found that the nature of the soil would not repay cultivation.

They cleared ground, and made a garden, sowing cabbage and turnip seed, but though they used a prodigious quantity of manure, the seed did not come up very well.

Jean Daniqua. fisherman, native of Grave, bishopric of Coutances, aged 40 years. Married to Marie Sire, native of la Cadie, aged 26 years.

They have two daughters.

Marie, aged 2 years ;
Roze, aged 14 months.

He has no homestead, and no house built except in the bush. He has been in the colony since the month of August last. He has been granted rations for one year.

Jean Coumeau, ploughman, native of la Cadie, aged 37 years. He is a widower. He has five children, three sons and two daughters :—

Jean, aged 16 years ;
David, aged 7 years ;
Charles, aged 4 years ;
Margueritte, aged 14 years ;
Isabelle, aged 11 years ;

He has two cows.

He has been three years in the colony and has been granted rations for that period. He is settled on land located for him by Monsieur de Villejoint. He only took possession last autumn and made neither clearing nor improvement.

Pierre Gedry (Guedry) ploughman, native of la Cadie, aged 28 years ; married to Haniez Hiel (Friel), native of la Cadie, aged 27 years.

They have children :—

Simon, aged 5 years ;
Charles, aged 7 months ;
Marie, aged 7 years ;
Marguerite, aged 3 years ;
Philippe Turpin, their niece, aged 10 years.

They are in the colony since the month of August last, and have been granted rations for one year.

Pierre Friel, native of la Cadie, aged 74 years, married to Catherine Bourg, native of la Cadie, aged 68 years.

They live with Guedry their son-in-law.

They have one ox and two cows.

The land they occupy is situated on the Isle à Descoust. It was chosen for them by Monsieur de Villejoint. They have done no clearing.

Etienne Hamet, ploughman, native of Saint-Jean, bishopric of Coutances, aged 66 years. Married to Margueritte Benoist, native of la Cadie, aged 56 years. They have been in the colony two years and have been granted rations for a term of three years.

He has a cow and calf and three fowls.

The land he occupies is situated on the little creek. He is there by permission of Monsieur de Villejoint and has done a little clearing, sufficient for a garden.

Jean Baptiste Forin, ploughman, native of Des Mines, aged 30 years. Married to Marie Madeleine Le Blanc, native of la Cadie, aged 26 years.

They have two sons and one daughter :—

Olivier Le Blanc Forin, aged 6 years ;
Etienne, aged 1 year ;
Margueritte Théodose, aged 5 years.
They have been in the country two years, and have been granted rations for three.
His land is situated on the little creek. He has cleared ground for a garden.

Jacques Barican, ploughman, native of la Cadie, aged 47 years. Married to Marie
Turpin, native of Des Mines, aged 43 years.

They have three sons and six daughters :—

Jean, aged 20 years ;
Pierre, aged 18 years ;
Sifroy, aged 16 years ;
Marie Joseph, aged 22 years ;
Margueritte, aged 14 years ;
Marie, aged 12 years ;
Précède, aged 7 years ;
Ursulle, aged 4 years ;
Rosalie, aged 2 years ;
Margueritte Turpin, aged 7 years, her niece.

They are in the colony since the 16th of last July, and have been granted rations
for one year.

Monsieur de Villejoint settled them on land at the Pointe à Jacob. Since that
time they have built, and have cleared an arpent of land for a garden.

They have a horse and four fowls.

Charles Doiron, ploughman, native of la Cadie, aged 33 years. Married to Marie
Madeleine Tibouday, native of Port Royal, aged 35 years.

They have four sons and three daughters :—

Baptiste, aged 10 years ;
Zacharie Aimable, aged 8 years :
Joseph Marry, aged 6 years ;
Charles, aged 6 years ;
Marie, aged 12 years ;
Madeleine, aged 4 years ;
Marie Anne, aged 6 months.

He has been in the colony three years with all his family, and he has only a house
built in the wood and two fowls.

Eustache Le Jeune, coaster, native of la Cadie, aged 37 years. Married to Marie
Anne Beriaude, native of Port Royal, aged 25 years.

The children they have are :—

Agatte, aged 4 years ;
Marie Joseph, aged 17 months.

They have six fowls.

They have been three years in the colony, and have received rations for that time.

The land on which he is settled was located for him by Monsieur de Villejoint. It
is situated on the Point à Jacob. He has made a small clearing for a garden.

Throughout this account it is made very clear that if the settlers are obliged to
clear the land and are prohibited from fishing or embarking on vessels engaged in the
coasting trade, it is certain that they will not be able to make a living.

We left the creek à Descoust on the 23rd of February, and, following the shore,
arrived at Petit Degrat the same day.

The distance from the creek à Descoust, lying on the open coast directly opposite to
Port Toulouse, to the Cap à la Ronde, is estimated at a quarter of a league. Through
this distance the coast rises so abruptly from the open sea, and reefs and shoals are
so numerous that it is difficult to tell how to land. The Cap à la Ronde and the
Cap au Gros Né form the entrance to the Great Creek du Petit Degrat. They lie about
a league apart * * The entrance to this creek * * and it runs a league inland.

It makes a wide bend at the further end, where 200 toises from land, vessels can
anchor in five to six fathoms of water, and is sheltered from all winds, except those from

5-6 EDWARD VII., A. 1906

between the east north-east and south-east. With regard to other winds, they blow off shore and in the heavy autumnal gales that prevail here vessels would certainly not be safe. So commodious is this creek that the English, when they were in possession of the country, took vessels of three hundred tons burden there to load with cord wood.

In the centre are three islands lying together, and visible at any state of the tide. Small vessels can shelter here from the east, north-east and south-east winds. A shoal lies between these islands and the land. There is a channel between this shoal and the islands, and another between the shoal and the land, one on either side of the reef. At the entrance at an estimated distance of a quarter of a league from Cap à la Ronde, there lies a shoal which can be left either to starboard or larboard on entering, a channel lies between this shoal and the Cap à la Ronde. Throughout the whole of the district, to the west-north-west, to the north, and to the north-east there is nothing but hard timber, and throughout the remainder is poor fir.

The said creek lies only a quarter of a league distant from the Petit Degrat. Before the war the waters of these two places met by means of a channel which has been filled, but at the entrance only, by a surge of the sea. Vessels carrying five or six cords of wood, or other cargo formerly passed there loaded.

The local fishermen found this channel a great convenience, in taking their boats laden with supplies to Louisbourg. Once out of the great creek they found themselves crossing the Barachois de l'Ardoise, instead of being obliged, as they are to-day, to leave by the entrance to the harbour of Petit Degrat, to double the Cap Gros Né which projects far into the sea, and then go four or five leagues outside to make l'Ardoise.

The passage to the point of crossing the harbour of l'Ardoise; by way of the channel referred to, could be made in an hour, whilst in doubling the Cap du Gros Né, the fishermen are not sure of doing it in 24 hours and if they meet contrary winds they have to be driven ashore rather than run the risk of being driven ten or fifteen leagues out to sea.

It would be a convenience to the fishermen if they were able to take their boats in and out of the harbour of Petit Degrat, no matter what wind was blowing at the time.

It is estimated that the channel could be made as practicable for navigation as it was before for an outlay of not more than 300 livres, a small amount in comparison with the benefit to be derived. One is also led to believe that this creek could be used by fishing vessels. This would be a great benefit because fishing is not carried on in the autumn, which is the season of the gales.

Some superb beaches for drying cod-fish lie at the further end of this creek on the edge of the plain.

PETIT DEGRAT.

Petit Degrat is suitable only for the cod-fishery. None of the people who are settled there have any other occupation. Fish are very abundant and none finer are found at Ile Royale. This place lies on the south-east coast of the Isles Madame, opposite to the port of Canceau.

It is calculated that it lies about south-south-west and north-north-east, and that the distance between the two harbours is three leagues.

Petit Degrat harbour is formed by the Pointe à la Rivière, lying to the north-west of the harbour, and by the Cap de Fer lying to the south east. It is calculated that the entrance is an eighth of a league in breadth, that it lies north-east and south west, and that the harbour runs half a league inland to the south east, preserving the same breadth, or thereabouts.

A shallow at the entrance lies about a hundred toises from, and opposite to Cap de Fer. It is left to starboard on entering, and after entering, the land is coasted in taking the channel that passes this reef. The channel to larboard is very difficult to navigate even at low tide. The bottom is composed of nothing but impracticable rocks.

The harbour is practicable only to vessels of less than 150 tons burden. Vessels of heavier tonnage would experience difficulty in entering. There are only thirteen feet of water in the channel at high tide, but when one has gained the harbour, he can anchor his ships in the creek aux Navires, in four to five fathoms of water. This creek runs inland for a short distance.

The lands in the neighbourhood of the Petit Degrat are of a nature unsuitable for cultivation. They are composed of rocky bluffs, with spongy soil covered with a foot and a half of peat on the surface.

GENERAL CENSUS.

General census of men, women, boys, girls, live stock, schooners, bateaux, and boats of the Petit Degrat.

Namely :—

Nicolas Ecard, fisherman, native of the parish of Serance, bishopric of Coutances, aged 52, married to Marie Anne Pichaud, widow of the late Jean Embourg, native of Plaisance, aged 46 years.

She has by her first marriage, six sons and one daughter :—

Foelix d'Embourg, aged 19 years ;
Jean, aged 17 years ;
Jean Pierre, aged 16 years ;
François, aged 14 years ;
Martin, aged 12 years ;
Gerome, aged 8 years ;
Isabelle, aged 4 years.

Le Sr. Nicolas Ecard has four men engaged for the next fishery season.

Jean Daribot, native of Bayonne, aged 42 years.
Martin Detcheverry, aged 40 years, native of St. Jean de Luz.
Joannis Dorebida, native of St. Jean de Luz, aged 25 years.
Bernard Le Basque, native of Bayonne, aged 36 years.

Le Sieur Ecard owns the following live stock : two oxen, two cows, three heifers, one pig, six hens, with their rooster, and two boats.

The homestead on which he is settled was granted to the late Jean Embourg in 1722 by Monsieur de Rouville then commandant at Port Toulouse, without however, the quantity of land he could enter upon, being determined.

Margaret Rambourg, widow of the late Emanuel, native of the place, aged 29 years. She has one daughter, Marie Joseph, aged 14 years.

Her land lies at the further end of the great creek, and she has ground for two gardens cleared, but she does not cultivate them, as she has become dumb and is in her second childhood. She and her child live with her mother.

Nicolas Le Borgne, fisherman, native of Dieppe, aged 36 years, married to Marie Darembourg, native of Petit Degra.

They have two children :—

Michel Le Borgne, aged 3 years ;
Marie Anne, aged 14 months ;
Gérome Darembourg, aged 10 years ;
Françoise Emanuel, his niece, aged 8 years.

Three men for the fishery :—

Joannis Detcheverry, native of Dagitery, bishopric of Bayonne, aged 19 years.
Dominique La Reide, native of Bearix, bishopric of Bayonne, aged 36 years.
Joannis Detcheverry, native of Aquitary, bishopric of Bayonne, aged 58 years.

In live stock, they own one bull, three cows, seven fowls and one boat.

The land on which they are settled was given to them verbally by Messieurs Desherbiers and Prévost in 1749. Upon it are platforms, beach and scaffoldings for drying the fish from two boats.

Jean La Fargue, the elder, fisherman, native of St. Jean de Luz, aged 70 years. Married to Marie Anne Osselette, native of Plaisance, aged 58 years. They have one son and three daughters :—

Jean, aged 22 years ;

Cecile, aged 20 years ;
Charlotte, aged 16 years ;
Jeanne, aged 14 years.
Live stock ; three cows, nine fowls, and two boats.

His land, which he has improved, was only granted to him verbally by Messieurs Desberbiers and Prévost. He has on it a platform, beach and scaffolding for drying the fish from the two boats.

Marc Vilalong, fisherman, native of Trebeda, bishopric of Dol, aged 47 years ; married to Marie Jeanne Osselette, native of Plaisance, aged 38 years.

They have six daughters :—

Marie Jeanne, aged 20 years ;
Cecile, aged 18 years ;
Marie Anne, aged 16 years ;
Marie, aged 14 years ;
Margueritte, aged 10 years ;
Madeleine, aged 3 years.

They have three fowls and a boat.

The land they occupy was given to them verbally by Messieurs de St. Ovide and Le Normand in 1732. They have on it platforms, scaffoldings and beach for drying fish from two boats.

Mathurin Picard, fisherman, native of Pléhéret, bishopric of St. Brieux, aged 35 years ; married to Angélique Romain, native of St. Esprit, aged 21 years.

They have four men hired for the next fishing season.

Jean Desroches, native of Caret, bishopric of Avranches, aged 34 years.
Jean Dupont, native of Vins, bishopric of Avranches, aged 31 years.
Pierre Nourry, aged 21 years, native of Vins.
Etienne Barbudeau, native of Saint Esprit, aged 16 years.
One boat, three fowls.

The place he occupies was sold to him and another man named Jean Valois, by Pierre Brisson for the sum of 150 livres. There are upon it platforms, beach and scaffolding for drying the fish of two boats, whilst the extent of the concession granted to them is for four.

Jean Baloy, fisherman, native of Mourviron, bishopric of Avranches, aged 50 years. Married to Margueritte Beaument, native of Grandeville, aged 26 years.

They have one daughter, Margueritte Baloy, aged 16 months.
Robert Guitton, native of Rennes, aged 17 years.
Allain Reou, native of Quimper Bossever, bishopric of Trégnier, aged 2 (?) years.
He has two boats, and three fowls.

His dwelling is adjoining that of Mathurin Picard.

Census

Census of the fishermen of Petit Degrat, who have no house built at the fishery. Namely :—

Antoine Vilalong, fisherman, native of this place, aged 20 years. Married to Geneviève Darambourg, native of Petit Degra, aged 22 years. They have no dwelling here, but only a house built in the woods.

Etienne Saux, fisherman, native of Plaisance, aged 41 years. Married to Marie Anne La Fargue, aged 33 years, native of the place.

They have one son and four daughters ;

Jean Baptiste, aged 14 months,
Angélique, aged 12 years ;
Marie, aged 11 years ;
Margueritte, aged 8 years ;
Charlotte, aged 3 years ;

He has been in the colony for 30 years.
He has four fowls.

Louis Saux, fisherman, native of Saint Esprit, aged 24 years. Married to Marie Jeanne Lafargue, aged 27 years, native of the place.

They have one son, Etienne Saux, aged 18 months.

Jean Maréchal, fisherman, native of Carot, bishopric of Avranches. Married to Margueritte Doiron, native of la Cadie, aged 23 years.

They have no dwelling at the fishery. He has been in the country twenty years. He has a schooner which he uses to follow his calling.

François Cardet, fisherman, native of Rui, bishopric of Vannes, aged 55 years. Married to Marie Pitre, native of la Cadie, aged 40 years.

They have Pierre Cardet aged 4 years, and Marie Anne Cardet, aged 2 years, their children.

He has been 35 years in the colony.

Jean Daguerre, fisherman, native of St. Jean de Luz, bishopric of Bayonne, aged 24 years. Married to Marie Decheverry, native of Port Toulouse, aged 22 years.

They have one son Jean Daguerre, aged 4 months.

Jean Majet, fisherman, native of Plaisance, aged 35 years. Married to Claire Langlois, native of the Isles Madame, aged 47 years.

They have four sons and one daughter :—

Jean Marie, aged 12 years ;

Jean Pierre, aged 8 years ;

François, aged 6 years ;

The fourth is not yet named.

Marie, aged 3 years.

They own one ox, one cow, and four fowls.

They have built a house on the Barachois à Villedieu.

Pierre Giroir, fisherman, native of la Cadie, aged 24 years. Married to Cecille Detcheverry, native of the Isles Madame, aged 20 years.

They have one child, which is not yet named, and Madeleine Detcheverry, her sister, native of Port Toulouse, aged 17 years.

They have built their house in the woods.

They own two fowls.

NOTE. There is more than sufficient land around the harbour of Petit Degrat for the accommodation of all these settlers, who have no houses on the fishery, if once the boundary lines of the lands of those who have dwellings are defined in conformity to their letters of concession, and le Sieur Hiriart is once forced to make restitution of all those concessions, which he has appropriated on his own private authority. It can be most truthfully affirmed that le Sieur Hiriart, solely and also in common with his partner, holds possession of one half of the harbour, and of two thirds of the remaining half, and it is anticipated, unless the authorities take the matter in hand, that these two men will expel all the settlers one after the other, or contrive to enslave them, as will be shown in the proper place, when the truth of what is here stated will be duly manifested.

Julien Rabageois, fisherman, native of Vignac, bishopric of St. Malo, aged 24 years. Married to Marie Lambert, native of la Cadie, aged 22 years.

They have neither dwelling house nor live stock.

Isabelle Toulon, native of Plaisance, aged 36 years, widow of Herne Pichot.

She has François Pichot, her son, aged 14 years.

She owns, jointly with Madame Gerard, a dwelling situate on the line dividing their lands. Le Sieur Herne Pichot obtained a grant in form from M. de St. Ovide, and from M. de Soubras, of a parcel of land having a frontage on the sea-shore of forty toises, and a depth of sixty toises.

She has only three fowls.

NON-RESIDENT FISHERMEN.

Census of the fishermen engaged in the cod-fishery at Petit Degra, but who are not domiciled there.

Namely :—

5-6 EDWARD VII., A. 1906

Le Sr. Pierre D'Aroupet, partner of the Sr. Jean Hiriart, native of St. Jean de Luz, aged 50 years.

He has in his employ 37 fishermen :—

Martin Bourbide, native of St. Jean de Luz, aged 23 years ;
Pierre Davidard, native of St. Jean de Luz, aged 33 years ;
Pierre Lariard, native of St. Jean de Luz, aged 28 years ;
Joannis Courticou, native of St. Jean de Luz, aged 35 years ;
Behy Darenesguy, native of the same place, aged 24 years ;
Barcin Decelot, native of the same place, aged 23 years ;
Adam de Seilaonna, native of the same place, aged 23 years ;
Christonalle Detourbide, native of the same place, aged 21 years ;
Jean Detourbide, native of the same place, aged 18 years ;
Sabat Decheverry, native of the same place, aged 26 years ;
François Tertel, native of the same place, aged 40 years ;
Jean Dominique, native of the same place, aged 40 years ;
Christory Finade, native of the same place, aged 20 years ;
Pierre La Serre, native of the same place, aged 22years ;
Joannis Labonne, native of the same place, aged 25 years ;
Martin Daroste, native of the same, aged 24 years ;
Joannis Degoyet, native of the same place, aged 20 years ;
Martin Detouriac, native of the same place, aged 26 years ;
Martin Yvarin, native of the same place, aged 25 years ;
Maugon Designac, native of St. Jean de Luz, aged 56 years ;
Jean Darot, native of the dependency of St Jean de Luz, aged 50 years ;
Christophe Dafavora, native of the same place, aged 32 years ;
Pierre Capendia, native of the same place, aged 50 years ;
Pierre Detchevery, native of the same place, aged 31 years ;
Raimond Dalancet, native of the same place, aged 33 years ;
Pierre Laray, native of the same place, aged 28 years ;
Jean Hivery, native of the same place, aged 22 years ;
Bertrand Douzinague, native of Ridard, aged 27 years ;
Joannis Sindide, native of St. Jean de Luz, aged 25 years ;
Martin Mouleret, native of the dependency of St. Jean de Luz, aged 24 years ;
Thomas Lignognier, native of the same place, aged 28 years ;
Michel Degoiry, native of the same place, aged 28 years ;
Jean Decheverry, native of the same place, aged 20 years ;
Bernard Dechevery, native of the same place, aged 20 years ;
Baptiste Decheverry, native of St. Jean de Luz, aged 23 years ;
Sebastien de Sens, native of the dependency of St. Jean de Luz, aged 18 years ;
Joannis Decort, native of the same place, aged 15 years.

SIX THIRTY-SIX MONTHS MEN.

Namely :—

Martin Clavière, native of Bayonne, aged 33 years ;
Bernard Casteck, native of Agens, aged 18 years ;
Ballerie La Guerre, native of St. Jean de Luz, aged 30 years ;
David de Choun, native of the same place, aged 22 years ;
Etienne Darouspet, native of the same place, aged 18 years ;
Joannis Darouspet, native of the same place, aged 13 years ;
Ten boats and one schooner.

With Sr. Larcher, Merchant, in this colony, there are 39 men ;
Joannis Daguerre, native of the dependency of St. Jean de Luz, aged 52 years ;
Jean de Castillan, native of the dependency of St. Jean Luz, aged 52 years ;
Jean Yvarin, native of the same place, aged 49 years ;
Bernard Subiet, native of the same place, aged 38 years ;
Pierre de Chapara, native of the same place, aged 40 years ;

Etienne de Vivaren, native of the same place, aged 30 years ;
Joannis Larscabat, native of the same place, aged 40 years ;
Jean Pentieu, native of the same place, aged 30 years ;
Pierre La Serre, native of the same place, aged 30 years ;
Martin Decheverry, native of the same place, aged 28 years ;
Erimont Cascamond, native of the same place, aged 38 years ;
Lorent Baschez, native of the same place, aged 20 years ;
Michel Dechard, native of the same place, aged 28 years ;
Joannis Delamart, native of the same place, aged 21 years ;
Joannis Dharoscenca, native of the same place, aged 43 years ;
Baptiste Dechecé, native of the same place, aged 30 years ;
Martin Lefargue, native of the dependency of St. Jean de Luz, aged 19 years ;
Laurent de Sabat, native of the same place, aged 20 years ;
Joannis Dechouactis, native of the same place, aged 20 years ;
Martin de Bardhot, native of the same place, aged 47 years ;
Bernard Cassabon, native of the same place, aged 32 years ;
Nicolas Chabas, native of the same place, aged 30 years ;
Joannis Dolainde, native of the same place, aged 22 years ;
Joannis Dexonhonine, native of the same place, aged 22 years ;
Joannis Doucanard, native of the same place, aged 36 years ;
Dominique Apostien, native of the same place, aged 22 years ;
Jacques Maupeau, native of the same place, aged 20 years ;
Martin de Jean Sena, native of the same place, aged 16 years ;
Joannis de Bordox, native of the same place, aged 21 years ;
David de Fronseda, native of the same place, aged 38 years ;
Pierre Decheverry, native of the same place, aged 23 years ;
Joannis Faondo, native of the dependency of St. Jean de Luz, aged 31 years ;
Martin de Sibour, native of the same place, aged 21 years ;
Etienne Pevertin, native of the same place, aged 25 years ;
Pierre Cascos, native of the same place, aged 29 years ;
Jean Laleine, native of the same place, aged 28 years ;
Pierre Fagonde, native of the same place, aged 18 years ;
Bernard Doularoy, native of the same place, aged 19 years ;
Eight boats, one scow, one schooner and one bateau.

The Sieurs Hiriart and D'Aroupet are partners in their cod-fishery business. They have taken possession on their own authority solely, of four fishing lots to which there are heirs living.

To wit :—

First, that of the late Beauregard on which he can dry the fish of ten boats, and on which there were, when he took possession, sheds, together with cabins and beaches for the work.

That of the late Jacques Roland, dit la Rivière. The late owner had put his land in order throughout the whole extent of the concession. There is ground sufficient to dry the fish of twelve boats.

That of the late Duclos, and afterwards of the late des Cousces. Le Sr. Larcher, put this concession into working order, but ever since he did so the Sieurs Hiriart and D'Aroupet have sought to quarrel with him, and in order to effect a settlement le Sieur Larcher has paid them 40 quintals of merchantable cod fish, and for the second 50 (remains to be paid.) The concession is for four boats.

Also that of the late Jean Osselet, who for two years engaged in the fishery on this concession with two boats. The grant is for ground sufficient for drying the fish of four boats.

In addition to these, le Sieur Hiriart owns two other concessions, which are very extensive, and of which he has the title deeds.

The only source from which the settlers can obtain hay for the subsistence of their cattle is from Isle Verte, lying a quarter of a league out on the open sea, opposite Cap au Gros Nez. They have no other meadowlands whence they can

5-6 EDWARD VII., A. 1906

carry hay. Le Sieur Daroupet, however, some time ago became the principal proprietor of Isle Verte, and claims that no one can go there to make hay without previously obtaining his permission.

We left on the 26th of February and arrived at the harbour of Grand Nerichac the same day.

In order to travel from the harbour of Petit Degrat to the great harbour of Nerichac one enters the bush, the road is estimated as being half a league in length. The lands are covered with timber of all kinds.

The harbour of Grand Nerichac makes one of the finest ports that there is in the country. A survey shows that it is well fitted for those carrying on the cod-fishery by means of vessels.

It is enclosed by the lands of Isles Madame, and an island called Isle de Punot (Pichot), lying in the open sea. The harbour has two entrances, that to the east being the better. This entrance lies north-east and south-west, and is estimated to be barely a quarter of a league in breadth. At this entrance to the harbour, opposite the island are three reefs which are left to larboard by boats going in. In order to pass clear of these reefs, which lie almost in the middle of the entrance, boats have to sail close to the land. The second entrance, to the westward lies west-north-west and east-south-east, and is about half a league in breadth. Only vessels from 40 to 50 tons burden can use this entrance. The harbour is of great extent, running inland to the north west for a good league. The lands are covered with hard wood.

The harbour of Petit Nerichac is entered as one leaves that of Grand Neri-chac. Only small vessels can make the entrance. Its great area is composed of a vast number of creeks and barachois, stretching inland, and covered with hard wood. Then we hugged the shore as far as Cap Rouge, whence we passed through the little channel in order to reach the rivière des Habitants. From the harbour of Petit Nerichac to Cap Rouge the distance is estimated at a quarter of a league, and from Cap Rouge to rivière aux Habitants is counted as five leagues. From the time we left the channel we followed the right bank of the channel until we arrived at the great basin of the rivière aux Habitants. This river empts itself into the little channel of Froncak. The entrance to the basin lies east and west, and has seven fathoms of water at low tide. There is not the same depth of water in every part of the basin. The area of the basin is one league in length, running east-north-east, by a quarter of a league in breadth, and the depth of the water, which is more in some places than in others, is estimated as varying from nine to four fathoms.

There are three reefs in the said basin, lying a quarter of a league to starboard outside the rivière aux Habitants, but those entering the river by tacking, do not con-sider them at all dangerous.

The settlers on this river make most of their hay on the shores of this basin.

The rivière aux Habitants runs about six leagues inland in a direction which is about north-north-east by south-south-west, but making a zig-zag course. It is estimated that Isle Brulée, which lies in the centre of the basin that forms the rivière aux Habitants, is situated half a league from the mouth of the river.

This island is the highest point reached by vessels of sixty to seventy tons burden. It cannot be said that they can ascend no higher up the river, but they would not know how to navigate the river above the house of one Guillaume Benoist, and so winding and narrow is the channel that one requires to be an experienced pilot to succeed in taking a vessel so far up.

Although throughout the channel there is water to the depth of three or four fathoms, yet, on account of the rapids which are estimated to be about a league and a quarter above the mouth of the river, sailors would not even know how to take a boat higher up the stream than this island.

On this island le Sr. Guillaume Benoist has constructed an ordinary saw mill. The banks on the rest of the river are merely plateaux, where the settlers make hay, and which might be turned into fine meadow land, if only the residents would take the trouble. The country is covered with all kinds of hardwood and fine fir trees, out of which the people make lumber for carpentry purposes, and boards two inches thick, and 12 to 14 inches wide. The government has no idea of making any outlay, or of inducing the settlers to do so, in clearing the land, so that the residents could grow wheat, or rye, or above all buck-wheat, oats or peas but they should be directed to lay out meadow lands on the banks of the river, so that they could feed live stock.

GENERAL CENSUS.

General census of the settlers on the rivière aux Habitants.

Joseph Landry, carpenter, native of la Cadie, aged 36 years, married to Marie Brau, native of des Mines, aged 35 years.

They have three daughters:—

Anne, aged 11 years;

Margueritte, aged 9 years;

The third aged three years is not named.

Alexis le Jeune, aged 18 years his nephew, lives with them.

In live stock they own, two oxen, four cows; two heifers, a pig, and five fowls.

He has no dwelling place and for that reason has made no clearing.

They are in the colony since the 15th of last August, and are granted rations for one year.

Jean Bte. Landry, ploughman, native of la Cadie, aged 60 years, married to Marie Bouherut (Gautrot), native of Pepeguit, aged 59 years.

They have Jean Daigle, their nephew, aged 20 years, and Margueritte Landry their niece, aged 18 years, natives of la Cadie, living with them.

In live stock they own two oxen, two cows, one bull, one pig, and three fowls.

They have been in the colony since —————, and have been granted rations, as has Joseph Landry their son.

Alexis Landry, ploughman, native of la Cadie, aged 29 years. Married to Margueritte Aucoin, native of la Cadie, aged 29 years.

They have two sons:—

Jean Baptiste, aged 3 years;

Joseph, aged 2 years;

They have in live stock four oxen, five cows, one calf, two pigs and three fowls.

They are 18 months in the colony, and have been given rations for one year.

Jean Bte. Landry, ploughman, native of la Cadie, aged 39 years. Married to Marie Joseph Le Blanc, native of the same place, aged 32 years.

They have four sons and two daughters:—

Jean, aged 13 years;

Joseph, aged 11 years;

Charles, aged 9 years;

Pierre, aged 4 years;

Marie, aged 7 years;

Margueritte, aged 2 years;

All natives of la Cadie.

Their live stock consists of three oxen, two cows two pigs and five fowls.

They have been in the colony eight months, and have been granted rations for one year.

Guillaume Benoist, builder, and owner of a saw-mill, native of la Cadie, aged 46 years. Married to Joseph Benoist, native of the same place, aged 50 years.

They have four sons and two daughters:—

Pierre, aged 22 years;

Michel, aged 20 years;

Boniface, aged 15 years;

Simon, aged 13 years;

Judict, aged 15 years;

Geneviève, aged 9 years;

All natives of la Cadie.

18—3½

5-6 EDWARD VII., A. 1906

They have been in the colony three years, and have received rations for that period.

They have one ox, three cows, five heifers, one bull, three pigs, and five fowls in live stock.

This land which they have improved is situated on the right bank of the rivière aux Habitants, but they will not continue to cultivate it for any length of time on account of the serious and frequent inundations of the river, caused by the melting of the snows in the springtime. At these times, not only are they prevented from working on the land, but they find it almost impossible to prevent the mouth of the river from being closed by silt.

We left the rivière aux Habitants on the 29th of February and returned to Port Toulouse that same day.

On the 10th of March we left Port Toulouse taking the road for the Isle de la Sainte Famille, at which point we arrived on the same day.

The Isle de la Sainte Famille lies on lake Bras d'Or, at an estimated distance of two leagues from Port Toulouse, and in 45 degrees north latitude. The island lies north and south as regards its length and east and west as regards its breadth, which latter, varying in different parts, has been reduced to an average of 300 toises. Whilst the quality of the soil does not appear wholly bad, there is no evidence supplied as yet, which could justify certain assurance that any crops which might be grown would come to maturity. The island is covered with all sorts of timber, but chiefly beech and wild cherry. There has been a settlement on the island, since the date when M. l'Abbé Maillard moved his mission to the Indians.

The Indians do not live on this Isle de la Sainte Famille, but they have their village on the lands of Grand Isle, opposite the Isle de la Sainte Famille, (the reason of this being that the wild dogs devoured all their domestic animals). The arm of the sea that separates these two islands is only a hundred toises wide. The Indians only live here during the summer, for there being no means of subsistence for them on the island in the winter, they are forced to disperse to fish and hunt in the various rivers existing in the district to the west of Bras d'Or and the district in the north of the island. They only return to the Isle of Sainte Famille in time for Easter and Whitsuntide when they make their religious duty.

Louis Petitpas, interpreter for the Indians, aged 26 years, lives on this island. He is married to Madeline Poujet, native of the said place, aged 23 years.

Baptiste Roma, native of Trois Rivières de l'Ile St. Jean, aged 19 years.

Live stock : one ox, two cows, one horse, two pigs, six ewes and six fowls.

They have made a clearing of about 36 toises square for a garden where cabbage and turnips have come up well, and they have grown several ears of wheat of a quality above the ordinary, and well filled, but it is considered that while these ears of wheat and the cabbage and turnips have done well on the cleared land where the manure of the live stock rotted in during the year, which had produced a hot-bed six inches deep, they have no assurance that unless the same quantity of manure is placed on all land where crops are sown they would come up with the same beauty, the same quantity and so perfectly matured.

We left the Isle de la Sainte Famille on the 11th of March and set out for the west end of Bras d'Or. We camped in the woods in the evening for the night of the 11th and 12th, arriving at the further end of Bras d'Or on the 12th. Here we camped for the night. The distance from Sainte Famille to the further end of Bras d'Or is counted to be six leagues. We walked nearly all the way on the ice, but in places on the Bras d'Or where the ice had thawed we were obliged to take to the bush, and put on our snowshoes in order to get over the snow. All this region of the Bras d'Or is covered with hard timber, mixed with a good deal of fir.

We took the road on the 15th day of the month of March, travelling north-north west. Whilst traversing the bush we came across a patch of spruce wood half a league in extent. The soil did not appear to be of a marshy character.

Next we came to a growth of beech, but only one of small importance, and in the third place to a second patch of spruce wood. As a matter of fact all sorts of wood are plentiful here, but fir is the most plentiful, in the three-quarters of a league, which we traversed before reaching the spur of the slope of the first mountain, where there is a stream of some three or four toises in width. We climbed the mountain to its highest point so as to make sure of our way. Its sides though somewhat precipitous are not sufficiently so to prevent the construction of a practicable road, by which loaded vehicles could ascend and descend by making a winding course. The slope is very even and covered with hard timber through which a horse could gallop. It is estimated to be 400 toises in length at most, and then it rises for half a league forming a declivity so gentle as to be just sufficient to determine the direction in which the water will flow. It is covered with all sorts of timber.

4th. In the third piece of sprucewood, half a league in extent, the soil appeared to be of a very moist character, nevertheless one could not be sure seeing that it was on the highest part of the mountain. Imperceptibly descending it led us to a section of the mountain which is in all respects impracticable, but turning aside from this point and passing half a league to the west we found a pass through which by making three zig-zags a road could be constructed, which could be made more practicable than those false roads over which 24 pounders have been taken. The land is covered with mixed timber. Having descended the mountain we camped at its foot. The whole descent may have been an eighth of a league in all. We estimated that we had travelled two leagues and two thirds on the road which we had taken and in that distance we took note of four small streams.

We resumed our journey on the 14th, in a direction north-west a quarter west. In the first two leagues we ascended and descended several mountains which require no special mention. The timber is mixed wood. Next for a good half league we descended an almost imperceptible slope until we came to the river aux Habitants. In order to cross this stream we had to cut down a fir tree and use it as a bridge over the narrowest part of the river, which we estimated at 30 feet at most, the depth of the stream is barely 6 or 8 feet

Its bed, like that of all the other streams we passed, is of a nature to lead us to conclude that the land in this section of the country is not swampy, even in the least. The bed is composed of red sand and pebbles, the water being extremely clear. The lands are known to be sandy. We followed one of the arms of the river for a quarter of a league, which brought us to the foot of the Grande Montagne.

We ascended this mountain as it lay in our road. The ascent is about a quarter of a league, through woods composed of beech. Owing to the height of this mountain it appears at first impracticable to build a carriage road across it, but by following a circuitous route and taking advantage of the passes between the small hillocks a road could certainly be constructed by which all, even loaded conveyances might ascend and descend. It must be remembered that such a work would entail a great deal of labour. We camped on the summit of this mountain.

On the 15th we resumed our journey travelling northward for a league, after which we left the river Judac on our left. Leaving the river we continued on our way always following the crest of the mountain, till it dies away gradually as one nears the harbour of the Isle aux Justeaucorps. The lands are covered with hardwood. That day we kept to the crest of the mountain for one league, being delayed by bad weather, and on the 16th we resumed our road, keeping north-north-west, and continued keeping to the top of the mountain till it sloped down to the harbour of the Isles aux Justeaucorps. We calculated that we made a league and a half that day. The lands in this section of the country are mostly covered with poor spruce.

On the two isles lying outside the harbour there are some freestone quarries from which the stone used in building the subterranean vaults, as well as the gates of the King's bastion, was taken. The stone was also used for the gates of the King's hospital, but the builder must have known how inferior its quality was, since part of the stone used in these buildings was brought from France. There is another kind of stone found in these islands which is suitable for grinding tools.

These two islands, situate in the open sea off the mainland, and one of which is touching the land, make the harbour a safe one, whilst it is said that a coal mine exists on the mainland.

5-6 EDWARD VII., A. 1906

After le Sr. LaRoque had completed his work at the harbour and on the coast, we re-entered the wood to "tander." "Tander" is to make a hole in the snow in which to sleep.

The 17th ; 18th ; 19th ; and 20th days of March were spent in returning, and we reached Port Toulouse on March 21st., having retraced our road.

We remained at Port Toulouse during the 22nd., 23rd and 24th., leaving on the 25th day of March to proceed to the Pointe la Jeunesse. We slept the night of the 25th and 26th at the Isle de la Sainte Famille, and reached Pointe la Jeunesse in the in the evening of the 26th. The distance between the Isle de la Sainte Famille and the Point la Jeunnesse is estimated at seven leagues ; and this is travelled in the winter on the ice, and in the summer by boat.

The Pointe à la Jeunesse is situate on the narrows of the great lake of Bras d'Or. The lands lie exceedingly high and are covered with all kinds of mixed wood.

The settlers are unanimous in reporting the ground as unsuitable for cultivation. It is freely traversed with rocks, which prevent its being worked.

GENERAL CENSUS OF THE SETTLERS AT THE POINTE A LA JEUNESSE.

Jean Benoist, ploughman, native of Port Royal, aged 69 years. Married to Marie Meran, native of cap de Sable, aged 67 years.

They are in the colony eight months and have been granted rations for eighteen months.

Jean Bourg, ploughman, native of la Cadie, aged 36 years. Married to Françoise Benoist, aged 31 years, native of Port Royal.

They have six children, three sons and three daughters :—

Martin, aged 11 years ;
Joseph, aged 2 years ;
The last, aged 4 months, is not yet named ;
Luce Perpétue, aged 8 years ;
Gertrude, aged 5 years ;
Anne Marie, aged 2 years.

They have in live stock, one ox, two cows and three pigs.

François le Blanc, ploughman, native of la Cadie, aged 38 years. Married to Isabelle Dugas, native of la Cadie, aged 31 years.

They have five children, two sons and three daughters :—

Joseph, aged 11 years ;
François, aged 2 years ;
Marie, aged 6 years ;
Isabelle, aged 4 years ;
The last, 18 days old, is not yet named.

They have one ox.

Charles Hebert, ploughman, native of la Cadie, aged 45 years. Married to Margueritte Dugas, native la Cadie, aged 49 years.

They have seven children, three sons and four daughters :—

Ambroise, aged 22 years ;
François, aged 17 years ;
Olivier, aged 7 years ;
Anne, aged 19 years ;
Isabelle, aged 15 years ;
Luce, aged 10 years ;
Sixte, aged 5 years ;
In animals : one cow ;

Ignace Caret, ploughman, native of la Cadie, aged 75 years. Married to Cécille Henry, native of Port Royal, aged 52 years.

They have eight children, six sons and two daughters :

Charles, aged 28 years ;
Joseph, aged 25 years ;

Honoré, aged 23 years ;

François, aged 18 years ;

Zenou, aged 16 years :

Ignace, aged 8 years ;

Marie, aged 20 years ;

Anne, aged 12 years ;

In live stock, two oxen, two cows, ten sheep three pigs, four fowls.

Pierre Bourg, ploughman, native of la Cadie, aged 25 years, Married to Madeleine Hebert, native of la Cadie, aged 24 years.

They have one child which is not yet named.

They own two oxen and one cow.

Anne Bourg, widow of the late Jean Hebert, native of la Cadie, aged 28 years.

She has two sons and one daughter :—

Bazille, aged 5 years ;

Jean Bte. Hebert, aged 2 years ;

Sarville Hebert, aged 7 years.

She owns one cow.

Antoine Henry, ploughman, native of la Cadie, aged 48 years. Married to Claire Hebert, native of la Cadie, aged 48 years.

They have seven children, four sons and three daughters :—

Joseph, aged 22 years ;

Eustache, aged 20 years ;

Aimable, aged 10 years ;

Paul, aged 8 years ;

Isabelle, aged 26 years ;

Claire, aged 24 years ;

Madeleine, aged 18 years.

Joseph Ebert, ploughman, native of la Cadie, aged 42 years. Married to Cecile, Nanson, aged 48 years.

They have 7 children, three sons and four daughters :—

Joseph Ebert, aged 17 years ;

Xavier, aged 13 years ;

Baptiste, aged 7 years ;

Anne Joseph, aged 17 years ;

Françoise, aged 13 years ;

Marie, aged 12 years ;

Isabelle, aged 8 years.

In live stock they own, one ox, one cow and two pigs.

Pierre Brau, ploughman, native of la Cadie, aged 26 years. Married to Margueritte Guedry, native of la Cadie, aged 24 years.

They have one daughter, 21 days old, not yet named, and Marie Joseph Brau, his sister, native of la Cadie, aged 18 years living with them.

They own one pig and four fowls.

Antoine Brau, ploughman, native of la Cadie, aged 33 years. Married to Cécile Bourg, aged 29 years.

They have four children, one son and three daughters :—

Blaise, aged 4 years ;

Angelique, aged 8 years ;

Cecile, aged 6 years ;

Suzanne, aged 1 year ;

And in live stock, one ox, two cows, two calves, four pigs and six fowls.

Jean Bte. Guérin, ploughman, native of la Cadie, aged 33 years. Married to Marie Madeleine Bourg native of Beaubassin, aged 32 years.

They have two sons :—

Jean Pierre, aged 2 years ;

The last, aged 2 months, is not named.

5-6 EDWARD VII., A. 1906

In live stock, they own one cow and two pigs.

Dominique Guérin, ploughman, native of la Cadie, aged 31 years. Married to Anne Le Blanc, native of la Cadie, aged 25 years.

They have three daughters :—
Anne Joseph, aged 5 years,
Nastay, aged 3 years.
Margueritte, aged 1 year ;
They have two pigs.

Olive Benoit, ploughman, native of la Cadie, aged 35 years. Married to Anne Part, native of Louisburg, aged 34 years.

They have four children, three sons and one daughter :—
Olive, aged 7 years ;
Clement, aged 4 years ;
Jean, aged 18 months ;
Marie Ange, aged 9 years ;
One pig is all the live stock.

Charles Ebert, ploughman, native of la Cadie, aged 27 years. Married to Margueritte Joseph Bourg, native of Beaubassin, aged 23 years.

They have two sons :—
Charles, aged 2 years ;
The last, aged 5 months, is not yet named.
In live stock they own one ox, one cow and one pig.

François Ebert, ploughman, native of la Cadie, aged 38 years. Married to Isabelle Bourg, native of la Cadie, aged 32 years.

They have eight children, four sons and four daughters :—
Olive Ebert, aged 13 years ;
Joseph, aged 8 years ;
François, aged 6 years ;
Marie, aged 3 years.
Françoise, aged 11 years ;
Ursulle, aged 10 years ;
Trazille, aged 5 years ;
The last is not named ; she is two months old.
They own in live stock, two oxen and three pigs.

Charles Guedry, ploughman, native of la Cadie, aged 26 years. Married to Madeleine Ebert, native of la Cadie aged 25 years.

They have two daughters :—
Marie Madeleine, aged 6 years ;
The last is not named ; she is 8 days old.
In live stock they have one ox and one pig.
There are with him four of his brothers, who are :—
Joseph Guedry, aged 20 years ;
Jean Femilien, aged 17 years.
Augustin, aged 12 years.
Aniez, aged 10 years ;

Benjamin Mieux, ploughman, native of la Cadie, aged 24 years. Married to Josephe Guedry, native of la Cadie, aged 30 years.

They have two daughters :—
Marie Joseph, aged 2 years ;
Nastay, aged 1 year ;
Margueritte Pelagie Brau, aged 6 years ;
And one ox.

Charles Benoist, ploughman, native of la Cadie, aged 26 years. Married to Marie Joseph Estebondon, native of Port Royal, aged 24 years.

They have one son and two daughters :—
François, aged 2 years ;
Marie Madeleine, aged 5 years ;

Margueritte, aged 16 months ;

And in live stock they own one ox, one cow and two pigs.

Martin Henry, ploughman, native of la Cadie, aged 35 years. Married to Marie Joseph Benoist, native of la Cadie, aged 29 years.

They have five children, four sons and one daughter :—

Bazile, aged 8 years ;

Jean Charles, aged 6 years ;

Simon, aged 4 years ,

The last is not named and is 15 days old ;

Anne, aged 2 years.

One pig is all their live stock.

Ambroise Hebert, native of la Cadie, aged 40 years. Married to Marie Madeleine Bourg, native of la Cadie, aged 36 years.

They have six children, four sons and two daughters :—

Bazile, aged 12 years ;

Ambroise, aged 7 years ;

Jean Pierre, aged 5 years ;

Isaac, aged 2 years ;

Marie Madeleine, aged 16 years ;

Françoise, aged 9 years ;

And in live stock they own one ox and three pigs.

Jacques Arete, ploughman, native of Port Toulouse, aged 30 years. Married to Roze Alitra, native of la Cadie, aged 28 years.

They have two daughters :—

Marie Roze, aged 2 years ;

The last is not yet named.

The only description of live stock they have consists of five fowls.

When all the settlers landed on their arrival from la Cadie in August last, they owned between them the number of 188 oxen or cows, 42 calves, 173 sheep or ewes, 181 pigs and 17 horses. A comparison with the recapitulation will easily show how many of these have perished from want of hay on which to feed. The settlers had not even water to give them within reach, and now all ask to leave so fully do they realize that they cannot live here.

The Sr. de la Roque left the Pointe à la Jeunesse on the morning of the 28th, and arrived at Port Dauphin the same day.

On leaving the Pointe à la Jeunesse one takes the ice in order to cross the little lake of Bras d'Or, and then going north-quarter-north-east for three leagues, reaches the Isle Rouge, lying in front of the harbour of la Cadie, and then holding north-east for a league, proceeds directly forward on the Rouillé road.

The Rouillé road runs nearly north-east quarter north, and south-west quarter south. It is reported to be two leagues and a half in length by ten feet in width. It is very winding in its course, the bridges are not built, neither are the bad places mended, nor the steep places cut down. The bluffs at the two extremities of the road are exceedingly steep, particularly the one lying at the further end of the bay of Port Dauphin, which is estimated to rise perpendicularly to a height of at least thirty feet.

The lands in the vicinity of Port Dauphin are extremely high and precipitous, and are traversed with masses of stone heaped one on top of another and crumbling away through the action of the wind and weather.

The land is mostly covered with hard wood. The nature of the soil as well as the position of the land is not favourable to cultivation. Any settlers who might be placed here for the purpose of improving the land might be given full liberty to make their living as best they could, they might subsist on the large herds of cattle they could raise, the country having an abundance of pasturage.

The roadstead of Port Dauphin is formed by the Cap Dauphin, situated on the lands to the north, and the Pointe Basse on those to the south. The Isles de Libore lie three quarters of a league out to sea to the east-south-east of the entrance. The island is estimated to be two leagues in depth, whilst the breadth between Cap Dauphin and the Pointe Basse is estimated as being more, though at the further end it is only half a league.

The harbour is formed by two banks of sand; the one lying to the north and the other to the south. The distance between these two banks is only 70 to 80 toises and forms the entrance to Port Dauphin.

The entrance lies north-east and south-west. The depth of water in the channel is twelve fathoms, whilst throughout the whole extent of the harbour there is fifteen to twenty fathoms of water.

CENSUS.

Census of the settlers of Port Dauphin.

Le Sr. Courtian, sub-delegate of the Admiralty authorities of the town of Louisbourg, native of Bayonne, aged 50 years. Married to Geneviéve La Forest, native of Rochefort, aged 43 years.

They have Catherine La Forest their niece, aged 17 years, native of Louisbourg living with them.

He owns two dwellings in Port Dauphin by grant of Messieurs de Costebelle and De Soubras. The first is situate on the borders of the roadstead and contains 150 toises front on the sea-shore; with regard to its depth, it is not determined. The second is above the pool, and has only 20 toises frontage.

He occupies two meadows to which he has not yet the titles. They are situated on the Rivière de Rouville, and contain about seven arpents.

In live stock, one cow, one heifer, three ducks and nine fowls.

Antoine Massé, being in the service of le Sr. Courtian in the capacity of a 36-months man.

Julien Gomeriets, native of Combourg, bishopric of St. Malo, engaged for one year in the service of Sr. Courtian.

Maurice Leveque, native of Boulan, bishopric of Avranches, aged 43 years, of which he has spent 35 years in the Colony. Married to Marie Anne Bernard, native of the place, aged 35 years.

They have three children :
Jean Baptiste, aged 3 years.
Marie, aged 11 years.
Joseph, aged 8 years.

Mathurin Doulet, fishing partner, native of St. Malo, aged 59 years.
One boat and nine fowls.

The land on which they are settled was granted to their late father, Bernard, by Messieurs de Costebelle and Soubras. They lost the title deed in the last war. They have made a clearing for a garden in which they have grown all sorts of garden produce, and in which they have six apple trees bearing fruit. The fruit does not ripen well.

Philippe Desmarets, ploughman, native of Amiens, aged 55 years, and who is three years in the colony. Married to Marie Anne Rondeau, native of Quebec, aged 58 years.

They have five fowls.

The land on which they are settled was given them verbally only by Messieurs Desherbiers and Prevost.

Julien Fouré, fisherman, native of Carbé, bishopric of St. Malo, aged 33 years. Married to Marie Anne Du Charme, native of Quebec, aged 21 years.

They have Julien Fourré, native of the Rivière de Miré, aged 2 years.
They have no dwelling house in the country.

Left Port Dauphin the 31st March and arrived the same day at Little Bras d'Or.

In leaving the King's Post we ascended the mountain to the south. It is covered with all sorts of wood, but chiefly fir trees. We descended on the Great Bras d'Or. It is estimated that there is one league of portage. We passed the Great Bras d'Or on the ice at the imminent risk of our lives, so rotten had the ice become owing to the effect of five or six days incessive thaws.

The great Bras d'Or lies between the lands of Port Dauphin and those of the Isle de Verderonne. The distance between the month of the great Bras d'Or and the little lake of Bras d'Or is estimated at seven leagues, which constitutes the length of the Isle de Verderonne, whilst its breadth is a good quarter of a league, though its entrance is at most 400 to 450 toises in width.

There is a reef lying off the lands of Port Dauphin which necessitates hugging the coast of the Isle of Verderonne, and one makes the passage in 15 to 20 fathoms of water.

Little Bras d'Or is settled by M. de la Boularderie. It is suited for Cod fishery, for agriculture and for the raising of quantities of live stock. The quality of the soil does not appear absolutely poor.

CENSUS OF THE SETTLERS OF THE PETITE BRAS D'OR.

Georges Diliart, fisherman, native of Chapeau Rouge, on the coast of Plaisance. Married to Marie Coupeau, native of St. Pierre, aged 47 years.

They have eight children, three sons and five daughters :

Alexandre, aged 26 years ;

Louis, aged 17 years ;

Georges, aged 10 years ;

Marie, aged 18 years ;

Jeanne, aged 17 years ;

Margueritte, aged 12 years ;

Madeleine, aged 11 years ;

Victoire, aged 6 years.   All natives of Bras d'Or.

They have two fishermen, Joseph Doex, aged 20 years, native of the bishopric of Bayonne.

Nicolas Richard, native of Grandville, aged 38 years.

Two boats and eight fowls.

The land he occupies was granted by the late M. de la Boularderie. He has built on it a beach and staging for drying the fish of two boats, and has made a clearing of about two arpents in extent.

Julien Durand, fisherman, native of Plaisance, aged 42 years. Married to Madeleine Vincent, native of Niganiche, aged 22 years.

They have Bernardine Vincent, native of Niganiche, aged 15 years.

Ten fishermen :

Jean Trouvé, aged 42 years ;

Vincent des Roches, aged 40 years ;

François Toré, aged 30 years ;

François Trogue, aged 27 years ;

Jacquês Le Troqué, aged 28 years ;

Jean Chesne, aged 30 years ;

Jean le Moine, aged 26 years ;

Jacob, aged 18 years ;

Jean Catelier, aged 22 years ;

Jean Pierre, native of St. Malo, aged 19 years.

All the others are natives of Grandville, bishopric of Coutances.

He has two boats, one-half boat and one small boat for the fishery.

The land he occupies was granted to him by M. de la Boularderie. It contains 45 toises fronting on the sea shore ; but with regard to the depth the extent is not determined. There are on it platform, beach and scaffolding for drying the fish of three boats and he has made a clearing of two arpents in extent.

François Gouet, fisherman, native of Plairier, bishopric of Dol, aged 55 years. Married to Marie Montagne, native of Plaisance, aged 45 years.

They have ten children, six sons and four daughters :

Jean Gouet, aged 25 years ;

Barthelemy, aged 23 years ;

François, aged 21 years ;

Jean François, aged 15 years ;

Pierre, aged 14 years ;

La Chesne, aged 16 years ;

Marie, aged 12 years ;

Georges, aged 10 years ;

Fauchon, aged 4 years ;

Jeanne Ouelle, her daughter, aged 18 years, widow of Guillaume Messer. She has a son aged 4 years.

Three hired fishermen,

Pierre Michel, native of St. Brieux, aged 30 years.

Jacques Poussard, native of Plaisance, aged 23 years.

Jacques Gresse de Grandville, aged 45 years.

The land he occupies was granted to him by M. de la Boularderie. It has about 100 toises frontage on the sea shore. There are on it platforms, beach and scaffolding for drying the fish of two boats. There is a great deal of land cleared, and still more uncultivated.

He owns in live stock, one cow, one bull, three goats and twelve fowls.

Jean Pichot, fisherman, native of Nerichac, aged 32 years. He is not married.

He has with him three men : Jean Rambourg, native of Grandville, aged 27 years ; and two others who live with De Broise, master Smith.

He has also two other little boys to look after the kitchen and superintend the platforms for drying the fish.

François Pagnon, native of Grandville, aged 40 years.

All these people are at Louisbourg. He does not know their age. He has two boats and fears that, for want of hands, he will only be able to send one to the fishery. He came here one year ago from Gaspé, where he was settled.

The homestead he occupies was given him by de la Boularderie. It contains about 80 toises fronting on the sea shore. There are on it platforms, beaches and scaffoldings for drying the fish of two boats. He has made a clearing sufficient for the sowing of a peck of wheat and for a very good garden. He has had rations given him for six months.

Three fowls,

Bazile Borny, fisherman, native of the coast of Plaisance, aged 50 years. Married to Jeanne Pichot, native of Nerichac, aged 33 years.

They have Jean Bazile, their son, aged 12 years, and two hired fishermen.

Joseph Pinçon, native of Britanny, aged 55 years.

Gilles Tosse, native of Combourg, bishopric of St. Malo, aged 22 years.

He owns one boat, one schooner and eight fowls.

They are in refuge at Labrador from Cap de Rés for a year, and have been given rations for six months.

The land he occupies was granted him by M. de la Boularderie. It has 100 toises front on the sea shore. There are on it platforms, beach and scaffoldings for the drying of the fish of two boats and enough land cleared to sow a barrel of wheat.

The land which M. de la Boularderie has had cleared on the little Brasdor is about 100 to 150 arpents with at least as much uncultivated land. There are two gardens which are very large and which contain all sorts of fruit trees particularly apple trees.

Antoine Berteau, dit Lyonnais, settler for one year past at Bras d'Or, native of Port aux Basques, where he managed the affairs of the English, aged 50 years. Married in that country first and having for issue two children :

Antoine, aged 24 years ;

Pierre, aged 19 years, who is still at Boston with the English.

Married a second time to Joseph Lemare, native of Niganiche, aged 27 years.

They have five children ; two sons and three daughters :

Jean Baptiste, aged 4 years ;

The last is not named. He is two years of age ;

Joseph, aged 11 years ;

Françoise, aged 7 years ;

The last, aged 9 months, not yet named.

In addition he has two boys for cooking hired at Niganiche, whose names and age he does not know.

He has his aunt Marie Linier, native of Plaisance, aged 90 years, living with him.

He has no live stock, but owns two boats and is building a third.

The place he occupies was given him by M. de la Boularderie. It consists only of a bank of sand on the sea shore, sufficient for drying the fish of three to four boats. There are on it platforms, beach and scaffolding for drying the fish of the said boats. The only clearing is for a garden.

THE BAYE DES ESPAGNOLS.

The baye des Espagnols is situated at two leagues distance from the narrows of the little Bras d'Or. It is formed by the Pointe aux Pommes, situate on the lands to the north and the Point Basse on the lands to the south. They lie north and south at an estimated distance of a half league, and are situate a league and a half from the entrance, which is formed by the sand bank de Brouillant, situated to the north of the said entrance, and of that of Berrichon to the south. The presence of these two banks leaves but a narrow space for vessels to enter, but large enough to leave nothing to fear. Boats can pass with a depth of water of eight fathoms. Inside the entrance the bay divides into two arms ; one runs inland to the south for a distance of about three leagues, the breadth in sight of the mouth being a small league which gradually diminishes toward the further end, where it is about 150 to 160 toises. It contains several small creeks, isles and points. The timber on the banks is mixed, hard wood, however, predominating. This hard wood is mostly suitable only for fuel, but a small proportion of it might be used in the construction of schooners, bateaux and boats. The settlers are unanimously of the assured opinion that the nature of the soil is suited to the production of all kinds of grain, vegetables and roots.

The second arm of the bay, as well as the narrow channel at its entrance runs west, south-west. It runs inland for about two leagues. The nature of the soil on this arm is even better than of that on the other arm, and above all of that which is found between the two arms, and which forms a sort of peninsula jutting out from the mainland, and having a breath of half a league.

From the beginning of this point, separating the two arms, up to the land at the north end this second arm of the bay preserves an equal breadth. At the further end there is a river navigable by boat for upwards of a league.

This stream rises in a large lake, which may be two and a half leagues in circumference, and which lies in the lands to the west. Around the lake is a belt of hardwood mixed with a little fir. A league and a half southward from the mouth of the lake there is a limestone quarry. Vessels can enter the bay with eight fathoms depth of water, and once inside can anchor in eight to twelve fathoms. Throughout the bay there is most secure anchorage.

The bottom is composed of strong tenacious mud, and the anchor can only be weighed with a good deal of difficulty.

Frequently the anchor comes up with 200 pounds of bottom clay attached to it, thus showing that vessels are not likely to drag their anchors here as they do in the port of Louisbourg. Winds no matter from what point they blow can hardly imperil vessels anchored in this bay, because even when winds from the east north-east blow in at the mouth of the western arm and there is a good deal of sea on, vessels have only to take refuge in the southern arm which is generally safe from any wind. No reefs or shoals exist in any part of the entrance.

CENSUS OF THE SETTLERS IN THE BAYE DES ESPAGNOLS.

Jean Cousin, navigator, native of St. Malo, aged 35 years, married to Jude Kedry, native of Boston, aged 30 years. They have been settled in the colony for two years and have been given rations for that time.

5-6 EDWARD VII., A. 1906

They have four children, two sons and two daughters :—

Bénomy, aged 9 years ;

Jean Baptiste, aged 5 years ;

Marie la Blanche, aged 7 years ;

Marie Madeleine. aged 2 years ;

One ox, two cows, two pigs and six fowls ; one boat.

The dwelling they occupy was granted only verbally by Messieurs Desherbiers and Prevost. They have made a small clearing on it where they have grown a large quantity of beans and turnips and have besides a large piece of fallow land, about five or six arpents in extent. They have no meadow land.

Germain Le Jeune, ploughman, native of la Cadie, aged 50 years. Married to Marie Guédry, native of la Cadie, aged 40 years. They have been in the country for 18 months and have been given rations.

They have four sons and one daughter :—

Joseph, aged 22 years ;

Chrisostome, aged 12 years ;

Germain, aged 11 years ;

Paul, aged 5 years ;

Margueritte, aged 16 years.

One cow and one pig.

The dwelling which they have improved, was given them only verbally by Messieurs Desherbiers and Prevost. They have made a clearing where half a barrel of wheat could be sown, they have sown cabbage, turnips, beans and pumpkins, all of which came up in great abundance. In addition they have made a large piece of uncultivated land of about 6 or 7 arpents in extent.

Paul Guedry, ploughman, native of la Cadie, aged 45 years. Married to Anne Mus, native of la Cadie, aged 43 years. They will have been in the Baye des Espagnols two years at the commencement of August, and have been given rations for that time.

They have five sons and one daughter :—

Jean, aged 22 years ;

Thomas, aged 19 years ;

Paul, aged 10 years ;

Petitjan, aged 9 years ;

François, aged 2 years ;

Margueritte, aged 20 years ;

They own two cows and seven pigs.

The dwelling in which they are settled was given them by Messieurs Desherbiers and Prevost. They have cleared land of about two arpents in extent, where they have grown cabbage, turnips and beans in abundance. In addition they have a good deal of fallow land where they will sow seed this year.

Jean Olivet, ploughman, native of Pepiguit, aged 35 years. Married to Josette Hebert, native of la Cadie, aged 25 years. They will soon have been in the colony two years, and have been given rations for that time.

They have four children, one son and three daughters :—

Jean Fournier, aged 2 months :

Anne Angelique, aged 2 years ;

Marie, aged 6 years ;

Anne Josette, aged 6 years ;

Anne Josette La Jeune, native of Port Royale, aged 110 years, her mother.

The only live stock they own is one pig.

The homestead on which they are settled was given to them verbally by Messieurs Desherbiers and Prevost. They have cleared land on it, of about two arpents and a half, where they have sown all sorts of roots which have come up well, and they have fallow land of about the same extent.

Joseph Guedry, ploughman, native of la Cadie, aged 38 years. Married to Josette Benoist, native of la Cadie, aged 24 years. They are in the country two years and have had food from the King for the said time.

47

They have three children, one son and two daughters.

Servant, aged 10 days.

Perrine, aged 13 years.

Jeanne, aged 3 years.

Their live stock consists of one pig.

The dwelling or the land in which they are settled, has been given to them verbally by Messieurs Desherbiers and Prevost. They have made a clearing of about twelve arpents from which they have gathered a large quantity of very fine turnips, cabbage and beans.

Antoine Boulin, ploughman, native of la Cadie, aged 40 years. Marrrid to Agathe Bigé, native of Cap de Sable, aged 40 years.

They have seven children, four sons and three daughters.

Jean Baptiste, aged 17 years.

Qualier, aged 12 years.

Joseph, aged 7 years.

Francois, aged 5 years.

Ruffine, aged 15 years.

Angelique, aged 9 years.

Agathe, aged 18 months.

In the month of September they will have been three years in the colony. They have been given rations for 33 months.

The land in which they are settled was given them by Messieurs Desherbiers and Prevost. They have made a clearing on it to sow half a peck of oats and half a bushel of peas.

Jean Boutin, père, native of la Cadie, aged 76 years. He is alone in a small house that his children have helped him to build. He makes hand barrows and other like things for his own amusement.

Paul Boutin, ploughman, native of la Cadie, aged 25 years. Married to Eustache Guedry, native of la Cadie, aged 21 years.

They have Pierre Guedry their brother, aged 11 years.

They have two sheep and one hen.

The land on which they are was given to them verbally by Messieurs Desherbiers and Prevost. They have made a clearing in which to sow a peck of oats and a bushel of peas.

Charles Boutin, ploughman, native of la Cadie, aged 29 years. Married to Joseph Guedry, native of la Cadie, aged 28 years.

They have three children, two sons and one daughter.

Jean Charles, aged 5 years.

Olive, aged 3 years ;

Marie Françoise, aged 3 months ;

Eleine Guédry, her sister, native of l'Acadie, aged 29 years.

Joseph Boutin, ploughman, native of la Cadie, aged 42 years. Married to Françoise Pitre, native of la Cadie, aged 42 years.

They have eight children, five sons and three daughters :—

Joseph, aged 20 years ;

Ambroise, aged 15 years ;

Bernard, aged 13 years ;

Paul, aged 9 years ;

Michel, aged one year ;

Ufrosine, aged 18 years ;

Marie, aged 6 years ;

Anne, aged 4 years.

Three sheep and three pigs.

The land on which they are settled was given to them by Messieurs Desherbiers and Prevost. They have made a clearing of two arpents, in which last year they sowed a quarter of a bushel of oats from which they gathered twelve bushels, making 48 pecks, each grain thus producing 47 and one more.

5-6 EDWARD VII., A. 1906

The family of the said Joseph Boutin have been thirty months in the colony, and they have been granted rations for 33 months,

Jean Bte. Le Jeune, ploughman, native of the East coast, aged 26 years. Married to Judith Vigne, native of Cap du Sable.

They have one son and one daughter :—

Claude Le Jeune, aged 3 years ;

Geneviève, aged 5 months.

Two sheep, one pig and two fowls.

The land on which they are settled was given to them by Messieurs Desherbiers and Prevost. They have made a clearing of one arpent in extent on it. They have been in the colony for two years, and have been given rations for that time.

Augustin Benoist, native of la Cadie, ploughman, aged 24 years. Married to Margueritte Le Jeune, native of la Cadie, aged 22 years.

They have Margueritte, their daughter, aged 16 months.

And in live stock, one pig and three fowls.

The land on which they are settled was given to them verbally by Messrs. Desherbiers and Prevost. They have made a clearing on which to sow a peck of oats.

Jean Le Jeune, ploughman, native of la Cadie, aged 52 years. Married to Françoise Guedry, native of la Cadie, aged 48 years.

They have eight children, five sons and three daughters :—

Eustache, aged 20 years ;

Gerôme, aged 17 years ;

Grégoire, aged 15 years ;

Barnabé, aged 11 years ;

Jean Charles, aged 3 years ;

Felicité, aged 13 years ;

Eleine, aged 9 years ;

Anne, aged 7 years ;

They have been in the colony 18 months, and have been granted rations for two years.

In animal stock they own two oxen, one sow and two sheep.

The land on which they are settled was given them by Messieurs Desherbiers and Prevost. They have made a clearing on it of two arpents. They have no other pasturage than they can find in the wood.

Olivier Trahan, ploughman, native of la Cadie, aged 35 years. Married to Isabelle Le Jeune, aged 26 years.

They live with their father, Jean Le Jeune.

Charles Trahan, ploughman, native of la Cadie, aged 31 years. Married to Margueritte Boudrot, native of the same place, aged 34 years.

They are in the colony for three years, and have been given rations for that time.

They have Cécile Boudrot, their daughter, aged 3 years.

Jean Baptiste Boudrot, their brother, native of la Cadie, aged 25 years.

In animal stock they own four oxen, four cows, three calves and one pig.

The land on which they are settled has been given to them verbally by Messieurs Desherbiers and Prevost. They have made a clearing on it of about two arpents. They do not know how to praise the beauty of the land sufficiently. Such an abundance of vegetables of very fine quality has been returned to them for the seed they have sown.

Jean Trahan, ploughman, native of la Cadie, aged 66 years. Married to Marie Giroir, native of the same place, aged 60 years.

They have been in the colony for three years and have been given rations for that time.

They have four children, one son and three daughters :

Paul Trahan, aged 19 years.

Lucie, aged 18 years.

Agathe, aged 15 years.

Margueritte, aged 9 years.

Allein Gredenguy, native of Brest, aged 19 years.

In live stock, one ox, two cows, two heifers, one pig and five fowls.

François Marteau, ploughman, native of Paris, aged 40 years. Married to Françoise Trahan, native of la Cadie, aged 25 years.

They have been in the colony three years, and were given rations for that time.

They have Joseph Marteau, their son, aged 8 months.

Honoré Trahan, ploughman, native of la Cadie, aged 26 years. Married to Marie Corperon, native of the same place, aged 33 years.

They have been in the colony three years, and have been given rations for that time.

They have one son and two daughters :

Pierre, aged 2 years.

Marie, aged 5 years.

Margueritte, aged 3 weeks.

In live stock they own two oxen, two cows, two calves, two pigs and one hen.

The land in which they are settled was given to them verbally by Messieurs Desherbiers and Prévost. They have made a clearing of four arpents.

Thomas Commere, dit La Chapelle, fisherman, native of Plaisance, aged 85 years. Married to Charlotte Vincent, native of the same place, aged 68 years. They have been given rations conformably to the King's order.

They have with them Louis Commere, native of Scatary, aged 30 years. Married to Margueritte Grossin, native of the harbour de Fourché, aged 24 years.

They have one son and one daughter :

Thomas, aged 18 months ;

Charlotte, aged 4 days.

Four goats are all their live stock.

Their dwelling place on the fishery is at Scatary. It was given to him in form by Messieurs de Costebelle and Soubras. It contains 24 toises fronting the sea shore, the depth not being determined.

Servant Commere, fisherman, native of Scatary, aged 29 years. Married to Anne La Forest, native of Louisbourg, aged 29 years.

They have four children, two sons and two daughters :

Jean, aged 9 years ;

Louis, aged 4 years ;

Marie, aged 3 years ;

Jeanne, aged 11 months.

They have four domestics including a 36 months man.

Yvon Brunet, native of St. Malo, aged 28 years. Married to Marie Touze, native of St. Jean, bishopric of St. Malo, aged 30 years.

Yves Carovent, native of Brest, aged 23 years. Married to Margueritte Le Jeune, native of la Cadie, aged 21 years.

Nicolas Tenguy, native of the parish of Ecovignas, bishopric of St. Malo, aged 22 years.

Simon Godet, in the capacity of a 36-months man, native of Plaisance, aged 17 years, who has two years more to complete his term and have his liberty. They own one boat.

Pierre Benoist, ploughman, native of la Cadie, aged 48 years. Married to Anne Marie Godet, native of the same place, aged 63 years.

They have Catherine Benoist, aged 20 years.

They have been three years in the colony and have had rations for that time.

The land in which they are settled was given to them verbally by Messieurs Desherbiers and Prévost. They have one arpent cleared.

Jean Benoist, ploughman, native of la Cadie, aged 25 years. Married to Anne Trahan, native of the place, aged 21 years.

They have been two years in the colony and have been given rations for the said time.

18—4

5-6 EDWARD VII., A. 1906

The land they occupy was given to them verbally by Messieurs Desherbiers and Prévost. They have made a clearing on it of an arpent square and has two arpents of fallow land.

Charles Roy, ploughman, native of Port Royal, aged 34 years. Married to Margueritte Le Jenne, native of the same place, aged 30 years.

They have been in the colony for one year, and have been given rations for the said time.

The land that they occupy was given to them by Messieurs Desherbiers and Prévost. They have made a clearing where they can sow half a peck in oats and peas.

Etienne Trahan, ploughman, native of la Cadie, aged 64 years. Married to Françoise Roy, native of Port Royal, aged 46 years.

They have two sons :

Charles, aged 18 years.

Francois, aged 16 years.

Ossite Corporan, their cousin, native of Port Royal, aged 17 years.

They have been three years in the colony and have been given rations for the said time.

In live stock, they have one cow, one sow, three fowls.

The land they occupy has been given to them by Messieurs Desherbiers and Prévost. They have made a clearing on it of half an arpent square.

Jean Bte. Le Jeune, ploughman, native of la Cadie, aged 24 years. Married to Margueritte Trahan, native of same place, aged 24 years.

They have three children, two sons and one daughter :

Jean, aged 3 years.

Blaise, aged 2 years.

Margueritte, aged 2 months.

Two pigs are all their live stock.

They are in the colony two years and a half, and have been granted rations for 33 months.

The land they occupy has been given them by Messieurs Desherbiers and Prévost. They have made a clearing on it half an arpent square.

Paul le Jeune, ploughman, native of la Cadie, aged 50 years. Married to Marie Benoist, native of la Cadie, aged 47 years.

They have nine children, three sons and six daughters :

Paul, aged 17 years ;

Pierre, aged 16 years :

Joseph, aged 7 years ;

Josephe, aged 20 years ;

Nastasie, aged 18 years ;

Reine, aged 14 years :

Anne, aged 10 years ;

Marie Roze, aged 5 years ;

Eleine, aged 4 months.

François Roy, native of the parish of Plumeau, bishopric of Brest, aged 50 years, his partner in a skiff that they have.

The land on which they are settled, was given to them verbally by Messieurs Desherbiers and Prévost. They have made a clearing on it to be able to sow a peck of wheat and a half peck of oats. They have a large piece of fallow land.

Pierre Le Roy, ploughman, native of la Cadie, aged 28 years. Married to Marie Le Jeune, native of the same place, aged 24 years.

They have three daughters :—

Henriette, aged 3 years ;

Roze, aged 2 years :

Suzane, aged one month.

They are in the country 30 months, and have been granted food from the King for 33 months.

In animal stock they own one cow and one pig.

The land they occupy was given them verbally by Messieurs Desherbiers and Prévost.

Charles Le Roy, ploughman, native of Paris, aged 52 years. Married to Marie Charlotte Chauvet, native of la Cadie, aged 52 years.

They have seven children, three sons and four daughters :—

Alexandre, aged 22 years ;

Charles, aged 18 years ;

Alexis, aged 16 years ;

Margueritte, aged 24 years ;

Anne, aged 16 years ;

Martine, aged 14 years ;

Ossite, aged 7 years ;

Jean Fournier, his son-in-law, fisherman, native of Quebec, aged 33 years. Married to Geneviève Le Roy, native of la Cadie, aged 26 years.

Charles Le Jeune, his son-in-law, ploughman, native of la Cadie, aged 23 years. Married to Marie Le Roy, native of the same place, aged 20 years.

They have in live stock three oxen, six cows, four pigs and sixteen fowls.

They will have been two years in the colony on the 22nd July, and have been given rations for the said time.

The land they occupy was given to them by Messieurs Desherbiers and Prévost. He has made a clearing on it for a garden of about half an arpent in extent, and has a large piece of fallow land. He has found pasturage situated at the distance of a league to the east-south-east from their dwelling place for feeding three or four head of cattle.

Joseph Le Jeune, ploughman, native of the colony, aged 48 years. Married to Cecille Pitre, aged 45 years.

They have seven children, six sons and one daughter :—

Joseph, aged 19 years, unfit for the militia ;

Bazile, aged 17 years ;

Chrisostome, aged 15 years ;

Olivier, aged 7 years ;

Athanaze, aged 5 years ;

Jacques, aged 2 years ;

Perpétue, aged 13 years.

They own in live stock two oxen, two cows, one calf, one pig and two fowls.

They are in the colony two years, and have been granted rations for 33 months.

The land they occupy was given to them verbally by Messrs. Desherbiers and Prévost. They have made a clearing of about one arpent in extent, and have a large piece of fallow land.

Paul Benjamin, ploughman, native of la Cadie, aged 27 years. Married to Cécile le Jeune, native of la Cadie, aged 21 years.

They have Jean Baptiste, their son, aged four months.

And in animals, two oxen, one cow, one calf and a pig.

They are in the colony two years and have been granted rations for 33 months.

The land on which they are settled was located for them by Messieurs Desherbiers and Prévost. They have made a clearing on it of about one arpent in extent and have a large piece of fallow land.

Marcel Trahan, widow of the late Pierre Boutin, native of la Cadie, aged 27 years.

She has been in the colony for two years and a half and has been given rations for the said time.

She has a son and two daughters :

Alexis, aged 3 years ;

Marie Joseph, aged 6 years ;

Anne, aged 5 years.

Alexis le Jeune, ploughman, native of la Cadie, aged 27 years. Married to Madeleine le Jeune, native of the same place, aged 23 years.

18—4½

5-6 EDWARD VII., A. 1906

They have two daughters :
Marie Joseph, aged 3 years ;
Madeleine, aged 18 months.

In the month of September they will have been three years in the colony and they have received rations for 33 months.

They have two pigs, two sheep and nine fowls.

The land on which they are settlers has been given them by Messieurs Desherbiers and Prévost. They have made a small clearing on it for gardening and have also a large piece of fallow land.

We left the Baye des Espagnols on the 5th April and arrived at four o'clock in the afternoon at the Bay de l'Indienne.

The distance between the bank of the Berichon to Pointe Basse is estimated at a league and a half. The coast lies about east-north-east by west south-west. Through-out this distance, so high are the shoals, that it is evident that an enemy would not be able to effect a landing. At low tide the shoals stand above water for a distance of more than a hundred toises from the foot of the cliff. In addition, about a quarter of a league out to sea, there lies a reef which is said to be half a league from Pointe Basse, and a league from the bank of the Berichon. The distance between the Pointe Basse and the Cap Charbon, lying at the entrance to the Baye de l'Indienne, is also estimated at a league and a half. Pointe Basse and Cap Charbon lie east-south-east and west-north-west. After having doubled Pointe Basse, and gone a quarter of a league, one reaches a creek of no great size, but in which, nevertheless the fishing boats take refuge when they cannot make the harbour. This proves that the creek is on the open coast, and it is only when the wind blows overland from the Isle that the boats can go out fishing.

Then, at a quarter of a league from this creek, there is a barachois, which runs inland, in a south-westerly direction, for a good quarter of a league, and which is about 40 toises in breadth. In this barachois vessels can lie sheltered from north-north-west ; west and south-south-east winds. Finally between this barrachois and the Cap au Charbon there is no place fitted as a place of refuge for boats.

THE BAYE DE L'INDIENNE.

The Baye de l'Indienne is only fitted for the cod-fishery and for the raising of plenty of live stock. The entrance to the bay is formed by the Cap au Charbon, lying on the lands at the north end of the harbour, and by the Cap de Table lying on the land to the south-west. The entrance lies north-west by south-east. It is estimated that the distance between these two points, Cap au Charbon and Cap de Table, is one league, and that there are from fifteen to sixteen fathoms of water on the line between them but then the bottom of the bay gradually shelves upwards towards the narrows, until there are but eleven feet of water at spring tide. The bay is restricted (in its accommodation) by a bank of sand, which crosses it from the south-west shore, leaving between it and the land on the north-east a space of from twenty to twenty-five toises only in breadth, in which space vessels repairing to the harbour for coal on the King's account are loaded. It is the only place to which vessels can go to take in cargo, and it is much to be deplored, because in lading coal falls into the water, and in course of time will fill the channel and thus render it impracticable.

Behind the bank of sand is a great barachois which runs very far inland in a westerly direction. It is estimated that its average breadth is three-quarters of a league with a length of one league.

Its banks are covered with grass, and the crop would be vastly increased if the settlers would go to the trouble of burning and cutting, or pulling out the roots of the fir brush. The lands around the barachois are covered generally with fir trees. Three small rivers flowing from the west, north-west, and north-north-west empty themselves into this barachois.

SESSIONAL PAPER No. 18

GENERAL CENSUS OF THE BAYE DE L'INDIENNE.

Census of men, women, boys, girls, fishermen, domestics, animals and vessels.

Baptiste La Guerre, ploughman, native of Bilbau in Spain, aged 50 years ; married to Brigide Trahan, native of la Cadie, aged 35 years.

They have eight children :—

Jean Baptiste, aged 13 years ;

Antoine, aged 8 years ;

Charles, aged 3 years ;

Pierre, aged 1 year ;

Madeleine, aged 14 years ;

Marie Roze, aged 12 years ;

Marie, aged 6 years ;

Isabelle, aged 4 months ;

In live stock, they own eight oxen, fourteen cows, three ducks and eight fowls.

In the month of August they will have been three years in the colony. They have been granted rations for 33 months.

The land on which they are settled was given to them verbally by Messieurs Desherbiers and Prévost. They have made a clearing of about ten arpents in extent.

Pierre Le Gros, carpenter, native of Paris, aged 34 years. Married to Servane Laman, native of Little Bras d'Or, aged 22 years.

They have Margueritte, their daughter, aged two years.

They have been given rations for two years.

They have no live stock of any kind.

The land on which he has settled has not been given to him ; he has placed himself there waiting for one which has not been imgroved, to be given him.

François Le Breton, fisherman, native of the parish of St. Léger, bishopric of Coutances, aged 48 years. Married to Marie Mordan, aged 32 years, native of Little Bras d'Or.

They have two sons and one daughter :—

François, aged 12 years ;

Charles, aged 7 years ;

Isabelle, aged 2 years ;

He has three fishing partners :—

Nicholas Le Breton, native of the parish of St. Léger, aged 24 years :

Pierre Tosse, native of the parish of Bruvilly, bishopric of St. Malo, aged 41 years.

Julien Tournier, native of the parish of Hedia, bishoprick of St. Malo, aged 22 years.

All these fishing partners have it in view to settle in this colony.

For 29 years the Sr. François Le Breton has been in this colony. He has been given rations for two years.

The dwelling in which he is settled belongs to his ather-in-law. He is settled on it, waiting to be given a location outside the narrows for where he now is he cannot put up platforms for drying fish, on account of the vessels loading there with coal for the King.

Catherine Le Bon, widow of the late Gabriel Borny, native of Coutances, aged 38 years.

She has four sons :—

Jean Borny, aged 20 years ;

Gabriel, aged 15 years ;

Jacques, aged 12 years ;

André, aged 3 years ;

Three fishing partners :—

Jean Maslarex, aged 36 years ;

Bertrand Anglade, aged 27 years ;

Mathieu Mourgue, aged 30 years, all of the department of Bayonne.

5-6 EDWARD VII., A. 1906

She owns two boats and four fowls.

She has been given rations for two years.

The concession she occupies on the property was given to her verbally by Messieurs. de St. Ovide and Le Normand without determining the extent. She has made a beach with scaffolding and platforms for drying the fish of two boats, and has made a garden.

François Dauphin, fisherman, native of the parish of St. Père, bishopric of Coutances, aged 45 years. Married to Perrine Mordan, native of Little Bras d'Or, aged 23 years.

They have two sons :

François, aged 12 years.

Claude Pierre, aged 18 months.

Three fishermen:

Claude Lamort, native of St. Planché, bishopric of Coutances, aged 43 years.

Pierre Colin, native of Dinan, bishopric of St. Malo, aged 30 years.

Jean Moreau, native of Limoges, aged 19 years.

He owns one boat and eleven fowls. He has been given rations for two years.

The dwelling on the fishery on which he is settled was granted to the late Jean Villedieu, his father-in-law by Messieurs de St. Ovide and de Mézy without delivering any title to him, or limiting the extent of the land. He has on it beach scaffolding and and platforms for drying the fish of two boats.

Nicolas, his fishery partner, native of Montanes, bishopric of Coutances, aged 45 years. Married to Marie Ebert, native of la Cadie, aged 50 years, He has been in the country 27 years.

They have no grant of the land they occupy, and no clearing except one for a small garden.

Note, that the beaches for drying the fish in the harbour, as well as those of Little Bras d'Or, are not made with stones as are those of Louisbourg, but with branches of birch and wild cherry. The reason is that the beaches made with pebbles do not allow of sufficient ventilation, and the cod becomes overheated by the great heat of the month of July.

We left Baye de l'Indienne on the 7th day of April, taking the road for the bay de Mordienne, and reached that place the same day.

After passing the Cap de Table we reached the coal mine from which the coal for the troops of the garrison is drawn. The English constructed a sort of entrenchment with palisades at this point, in order to protect themselves from attack by the Indians. The fortification is a square with a bastion, constructed of palisades at each angle. In the centre of the entrenchment is a block-house, built of logs, placed one on top of the other, the upper floor of which being intended for the placing of four pound cannon. Outside the entrenchments are two main buildings built of stakes, the one being sixty feet long by fifteen wide, and the other being twenty-five feet long by the same width as the first.

Vessels awaiting cargoes of coal cannot be loaded in every sort of weather, but only when there is no wind, or when it blows lightly off land from over the island. At other times vessels would find it impossible to lay alongside, so that when the sea is still, the soldiers, or other persons, superintending the drawing of the coal, hoist a pennon on a flagstaff, within sight of the vessels lying in the Baye de l'Indienne, as a signal to them to come in and load. It is stated that this coal mine extends along the whole coast to Little Bras d'Or. A quarter of a league along the road from the coal mine is the Cap de Table, which with the Cap Percé forms Glace Bay, situate half way between these two bays.

Cape de Table is so high and so precipitous that no vessel would be able to approach without running the risk of losing crew and cargo, but vessels can go down to Glace Bay with ease and safety. The bay is a league and half in breadth and runs inland about the same distance. Vessels anchor in the bay in six fathoms of water at the entrance, and find shelter from south and west winds, in absolute security. There is also shelter from north-west and south-east winds, but when these blow fiercely they are not secure. Over all the remainder of the bay there are two to three fathoms of water. At the further end of the bay is a bank of sand 200 toises in extent, that separates the bay from its barachois. There are four feet of water at the foot of this bank at hightide. No reefs or shoals are known to exist either in the bay or outside save one only, which lies a musket-shot outside Cap Percé, and which is not worth taking into account. The barachois of Glace Bay is very extensive. It extends inland to the west for at least a league, and has a breadth of half a league. The lands are covered with mixed wood, fir being the chief. The rest of the coast is not at all practicable.

THE BAYE DE MORDIENNE.

The Baye de Mordienne is good only for raising cattle, and for the cod-fishery though so far no fishing has been done. The bay is formed by a spur of Cap Percé and by Cap Mordienne, which are estimated as being a league apart. These points lie north by south and the entrance to the bay lies east and west. Vessels making the entrance tack in twelve fathoms of water, for a good quarter of a league, in nine, half a league, in four, and for one league, which is opposite to the present settlement in two and a half fathoms. There is no channel throughout the whole distance the bottom being so level. At a quarter of a league from the point opposite the present settlement there lies a sand bank that extends all across the bay, leaving only a narrow passage at each end, one to the south and the other the north, by which access can be had to the barachois. On the barachois there is only a foot to a foot and a half of water at low tide, and from five to from five and a half feet at high tide. The entrance to the south, which contains ten feet of water is the more accessible, and after passing that one comes to the channel leading to Fausse Baye. One takes a boat to cross the barachois which is a good half league long by a quarter of a league broad. All the lands in this district are covered with fir, with the exception of those to the north of the Baye de Mordienne which are common lands. The settlers make nearly all their hay here and in Glace bay.

GENERAL CENSUS.

GENERAL CENSUS of the settlers in the Baye de Mordienne.

Namely :—

Claude Teriau, ploughman, native of la Cadie, aged 56 years. Married to Marie Guérin, native of the same place, aged 53 years.

They have nine children, three sons and six daughters :—

Mathieu, aged 22 years ;
Romain, aged 12 years ;
Ignace, aged 6 years ;
Madeleine, aged 25 years ;
Téotite, aged 23 years ;
Margueritte, aged 20 years ;
Françoise, aged 18 years ;
Anne, aged 14 years ;
Eleine, aged 9 years.

They own in live stock : one ox, five cows, two pigs, one horse and twelve fowls.

On Michaelmas day next they will have been two years in the colony, and they have been given rations for that time.

The land on which they are settled is on the west point of the Lake de Mordienne on the lands lying south of the bay. The quality of the land does not seem to be at all suitable for the cultivation of wheat. It is reddish, sandy and very light. There is not more than a foot of soil to work, and under that is found a bed of rock. They have cleared sufficient ground to sow three bushels of oats between three settlers, who are there by permission of Messieurs Desherbiers and Prévost.

Pierre Teriau, ploughman, native of la Cadie, aged 58 years. Married to Margueritte Guérin, native of the same place, aged 45 years.

They have nine children, four sons and five daughters :—

Jean Baptiste, aged 24 years ;
Ancelme, aged 14 years ;

5-6 EDWARD VII., A. 1906

Fabien, aged 10 years ;
Brisset, aged 8 years ;
Margueritte, aged 20 years ;
Marie Madeleine, aged 19 years ;
Anne, aged 17 years ;
Françoise, aged 12 years ;
Geneviève, aged 4 years ; all natives of la Cadie.

In live stock, they own : two oxen, four cows, one horse and six fowls.

Joseph Teriau, ploughman, native of la Cadie, aged 23 years. Married to Marie Godet, native of the same place, aged 24 years. They have a cow with calf and two fowls.

Germain Teriau, ploughman, native of la Cadie, aged 47 years. Married to Catherine Joseph Benoist, native of the same place, aged 40 years.

They have ten children, four sons and six daughters :—
Chrisostôme, aged 16 years ;
Hilaire, aged 11 years ;
Ambroise, aged 9 years ;
Luc, aged 5 years ;
Marie Joseph, aged 19 years ;
Anne, aged 17 years ;
Marie Théodose, aged 14 years ;
Victoire, aged 9 years ;
Isabelle, aged 7 years ;
Françoise, aged 3 years ; all natives of la Cadie.

They own the following live stock : three oxen, two cows, one calf, five pigs, two horses and a cock.

On Michaelmas next they will have been two years in the colony, and have received rations for that time.

The land on which they are settled was given them verbally by Messieurs Desherbiers and Prévost. It is situated at Fausse baye but they have done scarcely any clearing.

Pierre Guérin, ploughman, native of la Cadie, aged 40 years. Married to Marie Joseph Bourg, native of the same place, aged 39 years.

They have seven children, three sons and four daughters :—
Pierre, aged 17 years ;
Isidor, aged 13 years ;
Louis, aged 10 years ;
Pelagie, aged 15 years ;
Luce, aged 8 years ;
Gertrude, aged 6 years ;
Marie Joseph, aged 3 years ;

They have been in the colony 18 months and have been granted rations for 21 months. They own in live stock : two cows, two pigs, six sheep, and three fowls.

Marie Joseph Teriau, widow of the late Jean Benoist, native of la Cadie, aged 45 years.

She has seven children, four sons and three daughters :
Joseph Benoist, aged 21 years ;
Baptiste, aged 13 years ;
Jean Louis, aged 11 years ;
Paul, aged 9 years ;
Anne, aged 23 years ;
Isabelle, aged 19 years ;
Ossitte, aged 19 years.

She has been in the country and received rations like others above mentioned. One sow and two fowls are all her live stock.

François Teriau, ploughman, native of la Cadie, aged 49 years. Married to Françoise Guérin, native of the same place, aged 42 years.

They have eleven children, four sons and seven daughters:—-
Pierre, aged 18 years ;
Theodose, aged 10 years ;
Cirille, aged 8 years ;
Joseph, aged 2 years ;
Marie, aged 22 years ;
Margueritte, aged 20 years ;
Madeleine, aged 16 years ;
Isabelle, aged 14 years ;
Perpétue, aged 12 years ;
Gertrude, aged 6 years ;
Anne, aged 4 years.

They will have been in the colony one year at the beginning of August next, and have been given rations for nine months.

Live stock : seven oxen, nine cows, eleven sheep, one mare, three pigs and four fowls.

They have not made an inch of clearing where they are, not having had time through change from one place to another. They are at Fausse Baye since the end of the month of September. They cut the hay for feeding their animals on the banks of the Barachois de Mordienne and of Fausse Bay. The quality of the land is similar to that at the Baye de Mordienne.

The settlers will not be able to live unless given entire liberty to do what suits them best to preserve their subsistence.

We left Fausse Baye on the 19th of the month of April and arrived the same day at the mouth of the river de Miré.

From Fausse Baye to the Bay of de Miré there is a bank of sand of about thirty to thirty-five toises in width to be crossed.

THE BAYE DE MIRÉ.

The true baye de Miré is formed by the Pointe Plate, lying to the north and by the Pointe de Catalogne to the south. It is estimated that these points lie north-north-west by south-south-east, and that the distance from one to the other is half a league, whilst from the said Pointe Plate to the river de Miré is three quarters of a league. In this distance several small creeks are found, which are very suitable for debarcation of troops, without any risk of the movement being perceived from the site of the projected redoubt, which it is proposed to build on one of the points of the river de Miré. A league from the river one strikes Pointe à Catalogne, at a point exactly opposite to the house of the Fathers of Charité.

In all this part there is only a bank of sand lying along the front of the said house of the Fathers of Charity, upon which it would be possible for an enemy to effect a landing, and it must be taken into consideration that any such attempt would be discovered from the projected redoubt, which is not only very near this place but stands on much higher ground.

The Bay de Miré is half a league in depth, with a good depth of water in almost every part. Large vessels can anchor in twelve fathoms of water at only a short distance from land, whilst boats and schooners can find three and four fathoms only a hundred toises off the shore, and from a bar that lies before the mouth of the river. Vessels can find shelter here from southerly to easterly winds, by lying under the land on the west and north sides, whilst as a rule there is good anchorage throughout the bay.

As above stated the Riviere de Miré lies between the points Plate and Catalogne. It takes its rise eight or nine leagues inland, and runs east and west. Vessels of the capacity of 15 or 16 cords of wood, can ascend loaded with the produce of the country, which consists up to the present only of wood, almost to the far end.

The name of Baye of Miré is applied indifferently to the whole coast lying between the Cap de Mordienne on the north side and the Cap de Menadon on the south. These

5-6 EDWARD VII., **A. 1906**

two points lie north-north west and south-south-east, at an estimated distance of two and a half leagues, and giving a circuit of five leagues. Fausse Bay is comprised in the stretch between the two capes; and is only a league distant from the Cap de Mordienne. So high and precipitous is the coast at the Cap de Mordienne that it is morally impossible for ships to approach it without incurring great danger of being cast away both crew and cargo ; but as if to compensate for this, it is possible to make a very easy attack by way of the bank of sand at Fausse bay, which is at the dividing line of the two bays. Fausse bay is so called because it is in sight both of the Bay de Miré and the bank of sand. It lies at a distance of a league and a half from Pointe Plate, and whilst the coast on this side is not nearly so high as on the other, it is almost as inaccessible owing to a chain of rocks extending along the front.

The true Baye de Miré is the barachois de Catalogne, which runs inland to the west for a league, and has an estimated breadth of 200 to 250 toises. It preserves the same width for half a league gradually widening towards the further end where it forms small isles and peninsulas. At this end the Rivière à Durand flows in from the north-west. Finally it is estimated that the distance from this barachois to Cap de Menadon is three quarters of a league. Several places were found where troops could be landed at any time and without risk.

General Census.

General Census of the Settlers at the Rivière de Miré.

Namely :—

Jean Bte. Villedieu, carpenter, native of Grandville, aged 58 years. Married to Catharine Grosset, native of St. Malo, aged 45 years.

They have five sons :

Nicolas, aged 17 years ;

Jacques Cruchon, aged 17 years ;

Laurent, aged 8 years ;

François, aged 7 years ;

Louis, aged 2 years :

All natives of Louisbourg.

Pierre Martin Villedieu, coaster, native of Petit Degra, aged 26 years. Married to Marie Perine Cruchon, native of St. Malo, aged 20 years.

They have been granted rations for 18 months.

They have in live stock one horse, three goats, and nine fowls.

The land on which they are settled was given them verbally by Messieurs Desherbiers and Prévost. They have made a small clearing on it and would have made a larger if they had not been disturbed by a settler who had previously obtained it to mine coal.

Pierre Varenne, ploughman, farmer for the Fathers Charity, native of Léon, aged 40 years. Married to Madeleine La Bauve, native of la Cadie, aged 26 years.

They have three daughters :

Angélique, aged 6 years ;

Marie, aged 4 years ;

Joseph, aged 2 years.

In live stock they own two oxen, ten cows, three calves, nine sheep, three pigs, three ducks and twenty-one fowls.

The farm of the Fathers Charity was originally one league in extent, but they obtained from Messieurs de St. Ovide and de Mézy an addition of three leagues which makes a homestead of four leagues square and they have had their farmers make a clearing of about sufficient extent to allow of the sowing of three barrels of oats and a bushel of wheat. They have their hay cut on the banks of the river.

Jean Guillaume, ploughman, native of Laitoure, bishopric of Auch, aged 32 years. Married to Marie Boila, native of Busset, bishopric of Lerou, aged 31 years.

They have Catherine, aged 6 years, and André Durocher, their partner, native of Condon, bishopric of Auch, aged 45 years.

They have been in the colony since the surrender of the place by the English, and have been given rations for three years.

In live stock, they own one cow, twelve fowls and three ducks.

The land on which they are settled was given to them verbally by Messieurs Desherbiers and Prévost.

It is situated on the creek à Dion. They have cleared land for sowing one barrel of oats. Their pasturage is on the Pointe à Dion.

Laurent Lhermitte, ploughman, native of Coutances, aged 37 years. Married to Marie Renée Bertrand, native of la Baleine, aged 28 years.

They have two sons :—

François, aged 7 years.

Pierre, aged 15 months.

He has been in the colony 22 years, and has been given rations for two years.

The land they occupy was given to them verbally by Messieurs Desherbiers and Prévost in 1750, and is situated on the Pointe au Razoir, where he has been promised twelve arpents fronting the river in consideration of land he had at Porte Dauphine which has been taken by the king. He has not yet done any clearing.

Marie Le Borgne, widow of the late Jean Bertrand. Hoping to settle on the river de Miré, she is wintering here with all her family.

Laurent Soly, ploughman, native of Spain, aged 33 years. Married to Jeanne Lécuyer, native of Louisbourg, aged 22 years.

They have two sons :—

Antoine Thomas, aged 2 years ;

Laurent Soly, aged 4 months ;

They have been granted rations for three years which is about the time they have been in the colony.

The land they occupy was given them verbally by M. le Comte de Raymond at the time of his visit to Miré. They have made no clearing, not having had time to work at it before the snow fell. They have been granted rations for three years.

Jean Tesse, coaster, native of Cap Freel, bishopric of St. Brieux, aged 53 years. Married to Marie Bodard, native of La Cadie, 40 years.

They have six children, five sons and one daughter :—

Pierre, aged 23 years ;

Jean, aged 15 years ;

Baptiste, aged 14 years ;

Etienne, aged 13 years ;

Servant, aged 4 years ;

Marie, aged 8 years.

They own the following live stock : one cow with calf, four fowls, and one bateau.

They have been given two years' rations.

The land on which they are settled was given to him verbally by Messieurs Desherbiers and Prevost. It is situated near the Isle de la Conférance. He has made a piece of fallow land of six or seven arpents in extent, and a small clearing for a garden.

Jean Mariadé, ploughman, native of La Chapelle, aged 52 years. Married to Madeleine Benoist, native of la Cadie, aged 44 years.

They have eleven children, six sons and five daughters.

Jean, aged 23 years ;

Pierre, aged 17 years ;

François, aged 13 years ;

Michel, aged 11 years ;

Jean Lucas, aged 9 years ;

Joseph, aged 6 years ;

Marie, aged 24 years ;

Marie Madeleine, aged 10 years ;

Anne la Blanche, aged 8 years ;

Judic, aged 4 years ;

Modeste, aged one year, all natives of la Cadie, with the exception of the last, who was born at St. Pierre.

They have been given rations for two years. They have no dwelling and no live stock. They are wintering in the house of one Tessé.

Mathurin Le Faucheux, ploughman, native of the parish of Jenelay, bishopric of Angers, aged 50 years. Married to Geneviève Meran, aged 54 years, native of la Chevrotière, bishopric of Quebec.

We have one son and one daughter :—

Guillaume, aged 16 years ;

Marie Louise Angélique, aged 12 years ;

Guillaume Fromant, their nephew, native of La Flèche, bishopric of Angers, aged 14 years.

Mathurin Charboneau, engaged for one year as a domestic, native of Trémontier, bishopric of Poitiers, aged 21 years. He intends settling in the colony.

They own the following live stock : four cows, three calves, two sheep, four lambs, three ducks, seven fowls, and one skiff.

He has been given two years rations.

The land he occupies was given to him by a deed of grant by Messieurs de St Ovide and Le Normand in 1734. The extent of the land is defined as being from the Isle de la Conférance to the creek of Charroy. The land between these two places, north and south belong to him for half a league in depth. He had made a very large piece of fallow land and a clearing where he might sow at least eight barrels of seed corn if he had men and oxen to work with. Before the war he always sowed a barrel of oats, which returned him a yearly average of twelve for one ; a peck of buckwheat which returned him fifteen to one, a plot of peas which always yielded ten to one, a peck of beans which usually gave fifteen for one, but with wheat he has never succeeded well. He has a meadow which was granted him at the same time as his homestead, the title deed of which he lost in the last war. It is situated to the north, quarter north-west of his land, and on it he can cut enough hay to feed eight head of cattle.

Jean Pierre St. Gla, ploughman, native of St. Fristre, bishopric of Castres, aged 30 years. Married to Jeanne de la Bonne, native of Begnac, aged 30 years.

They have Catherine their daughter, aged 11 months.

The land on which they are settled was given them by M. le comte de Raymond at the time of his journey to Miré. They made a large piece of fallow land during the winter, where they will sow oats. It is situated on a point that juts far into the river forming a peninsula.

Joseph Gracia, ploughman, native of Lerocgue, bishopric of Bucaye, aged 34 years. Married to Marie Depontigue, native of Dourescan, bishopric of Bayonne, aged 32 years.

The land on which they are settled was given verbally to them by M. le comte de Raymond. He has worked on it pretty well since he is on it. They have been given rations for two years, which is the time they have been in the colony.

Luc Le Chené, ploughman, native of Bordeaux, aged 34 years. Married to Laurens Seigneux, native of Dinan, aged 36 years.

He has been in the country two years and been given rations for eight months.

The land on which he is to build is situate on the Grande Pointe. He has not wintered there to do any clearing.

Thérèse Gruneau, widow of the late Guillaume Brebel, native of Plandieu, bishopric of Dol, aged 32 years.

The land she occupies was given to her verbally by Messieurs Desherbiers and Prévost. Her late husband made a small clearing on it.

She has one hen and two ducks.

Ignace Tallement, ploughman, native of Pragues, aged 26 years. Married to Esperchy, native of Bordeaux, aged 22 years.

They have two daughters :—

Marie, aged 3 years ;

Marie Catherine, aged 1 year.

He has been two years in the country and has been given rations for that time.

The land on which he is settled was given him verbally by Monsieur le comte de Raymond. He has made a small clearing where he can sow small quantities of oats and turnips.

Julien Bourneuf, ploughman, native of Médrillac, bishopric of St. Malo, aged 36 years. Married to Jeanne Guedry, native of la Cadie, aged 27 years.

They have four daughters :—

Anne, aged 12 years ;

Jeanne, aged 9 years ;

Julienne, aged 7 years ;

Sophie, aged 5 years.

Joseph Guedry, his brother-in-law, native of la Cadie, aged 17 years. Renée Guillaume, his sister, native of the parish of Argence, aged 20 years.

He owns in live stock : one pig and three fowls. He is in the colony three years, and has been given rations for that time.

The land on which he is settled is situated to the east of the dwelling place of Monsieur de la Borde, treasurer to the colony ; it was given to him verbally by Messieurs Desherbiers and Prévost. He has made a good clearing in which he can sow two pecks of oats.

Pierrre Courtiau, ploughman, native of the parish of Monmorency, bishopric of Dax, aged 31 years. Married to Marie Cortien, native of La Rochelle, aged 38 years.

They have a son of two months who has not been named.

Pierre la Cane, native of Bordeaux, aged 22 years, engaged for one year in their service, who intends settling in the colony.

They own in live stock one cow, one bull, one pig and six fowls.

The land in which he is settled belongs to Monsieur de la Borde. He has only been there since last autumn, and has made a small piece of fallow land and a clearing for a garden. He is in the colony two years, and has been given rations for the said two years.

François Gouret, ploughman, farmer for Monsieur de la Borde, native of the Parish of Provezien, bishopric of Grenoble, aged 22 years. He is not fit to enter the militia. Married to Toinette Eviard, of the same parish, aged 23 years.

They have Thérèse, their daughter, aged 18 months.

Jean Eu, engaged in the capacity of a domestic until the end of the month, native of St. Malo, aged 50 years. He is a fisherman by calling.

They will have been in the colony two years at the end of August next, and have been given rations for the said time. He has in all made a piece of fallow land and a clearing where he can sow a peck of oats.

François Chalot, ploughman, farmer for Monsieur de la Borde, native of Caen, bishopric of Bayeux, aged 49 years. Married to Marie Tanère, native of Grandville, bishopric of Coutances, aged 42 years.

They have Jean, their son, aged 22 years.

Pierre Comere, native of Bayeux, aged 27 years, engaged for one year, and intends settling in the colony.

He has made a large piece of fallow land and a clearing of three arpents in extent, where he intends to sow all sorts of grains experimentally to see which answer best. He is in this country three years and has been given rations for that time.

Jacques Guilant, ploughman, farmer for Monsieur de la Borde, native of the parish of Basse Mer, bishopric of Nantes, aged 52 years.

He is a partner with one named Sébastien Bourneuf, native of Combourg, aged 39 years.

They have four cows, one bull, three calves of this year.

They have made a large piece of fallow land and a clearing to sow a barrel of wheat.

From three bushels of wheat they sowed last year they have harvested one barrel and a half, with 24 bushels to the barrel ; bringing a profit of eleven for one. From

5-6 EDWARD VII., A. 1906

two bushels of oats they have gathered a barrel and a half, a return of seventeen to one.

Mathurin Donin, ploughman, native of Nantes, parish of St. Nicolas, aged 47 years. Married to Marie Catherine Courte, native of Daste, in Italy, aged 37 years.

They have two sons and one daughter :

Mathieu, aged 5 years.

Louis Mathurin, aged 4 months.

Christine, aged 2 years.

They are in the colony two years, and have been given rations for that time.

The land on which they are has been sold to them by widow Mathurin Germain. They have made fallow land and a clearing of no great extent for a garden.

Jean Chapin, ploughman, native of Amboise, bishopric of Tours, aged 32 years. Married to Catherine Robert, widow of the late Jean Gerat, native of la Cadie, aged 57 years.

They have two daughters :

Jeanne Gerat, aged 16 years.

Catherine, aged 14 years.

In live stock they own, three cows, one horse, two pigs and six fowls.

In the month of August next, they will have been in the colony three years, and have received rations for two years.

The land on which they are settled was given to them by Messieurs Desherbiers and Prévost by a deed which has been lost. They have made a clearing to sow cabbage and turnips.

Jacques Chemin, ploughman, native of the parish of Dumeny Brion, bishopric of Sez, aged 37 years. Married to Françoise Ange, native of St. Pierre d'Oléron, aged 27 years.

They have one daughter, Jeanne Chemin, aged six months.

The said Jacques Chemin intends settling on the river if the King will give him three years rations. He has received his pardon as a deserter from the troops.

We left the farther end of the Baye de Miré on the 9th April for Isle de Scatary, arriving there the same day.

The channel de Menadon is formed by the west point of the Isle de Scatary, and by the Cap de Menadon. It is navigated by several routes, the channel being the one where the traveller has to decide which is to be taken. Coasters of the country on leaving Louisburg take the corrected course east-south-east until they have cleared the Cap de Portanove, which lies to the east quarter south-east of the entrance of the Port of Louisbourg.

Navigators familiar with these waters know that from the time they sight the channel of Ménadon, they steer for the Cap au Nord until the Pointe aux Chats is west. This point lies in the harbour of Menadon, and is visible at a considerable distance as it stands boldly out into the bay. When sailors sight this point they make a north-west course in order to make the channel of Menadon, and hold the same course until they double the two islets lying in the channel, and coasting that lying to the starboard, leaving the cape to the north-west. This is the best channel. That to larboard must not be taken as is surrounded with shoals. After having doubled the two islets, one must take a westerly course in order to enter the Bay de Miré, and a north-easterly one to double Cap de Mordienne.

On the 12th day of the month of October in the year 1750, a vessel, named the Grand Saint Esprit, owned by the Sr. Rodrigue, shipowner of La Rochelle, commanded by the Sr. Coinrdet, and chartered by the King, being unable to make the port of Louisbourg owing to contrary winds, was obliged to seek refuge in the bay of Miré. On the 13th day of the month, the wind having veered to the north-east, anchors were weighed and and top-sails set. It was a question whether she could make the passage by the channel of Ménadon. Not an officer on board was familiar with the coast.

The captain asked M. Dolabarras if he believed very great danger would be incurred in attempting the passage ; and was told in reply that that gentleman had made the passage with vessels quite as large as the Grand Saint Esprit. Upon this le Sr. Coinrdet prepared to make the attempt. He kept two men constantly heaving the lead, the one in the port and the other on the staboard, and had the lines thrown alternately so that there would always be one in the water. At first he held to the east for a quarter of a league, finding twelve fathons of water, and then they made to the south-east, but did so too soon to make the passage de Menadon. This obliged them to hug the islet lying off the shore of Isle Royale too closely, but the vessel, drawing 13 to 14 feet of water, passed in three fathons ; instead of having as she might have in other places from seven to nine fathoms. Those familiar with the locality know their whereabouts as soon as Cap de Mordienne lies to the north north-east, and it is then that they change their course to south-east certain of being in safe water.

ISLE OF SCATARY.

The Isle of Scatary is suitable only for cod fishery. The situation is one of the best for trade, but, unfortunately, the ports and harbours are not safe. It lies in the sea opposite to Menadon. It is estimated to be two leagues in length, lying east and west with a breadth, north and south of half a league. Generally speaking the island is a mere rock. The nature of the ground varies, two kinds of soil being found. The one is wet and tenacious, and the other partakes of the character of marl. It is not by any means wooded, and there is no hard wood on it, neither is there fir or any description of pine suitable for the building of the platforms and scaffoldings, that are used on the island. The settlers have to bring their wood from the lands on the river Miré, or from those of the barachois de Catalogne which are near them.

THE GREAT AND THE LITTLE HARBOURS OF SCATARY.

The great and little harbours of Scatary are but one, all the difference being that vessels anchor in the great harbour, whilst in the little not even a skiff could enter at low tide without risk of being cast away on the reefs and shoals which are strewn over the whole bottom of the harbour. They are both formed by headlands to the north-east or by the islets of Scatary and the headlands of the south-west which front each other. The harbours lie north-east by south-west. It is estimated that the headlands are a good league distant from each other, and that the harbour is a quarter of a league in depth. In this area and in the same point of the compass at a distance of a quarter of a league from the easterly headland lies a small islet, some 500 or 550 toises in length called the Isle de la Tremblade or Isle aux Coucous. This islet is 100 to 150 toises in width, and on it, long before the late war a number of people engaged in cod fishing. They have now wholly abandoned it, and there are no other people offering to go there to settle. It seems more suitable for fishing with vessels than with boats.

The portion which is called the great harbour is formed by the headlands to the north-east and the islets of Scatary ; by the headland to the north-east of the Isle de la Tremblade, and by a third point formed by a huge bank of sand, lying to the north-west of the entrance 200 toises from the Isle de la Tremblade.

The entrance lies east and west, and has from 15 to 16 feet of water at high tide. One is obliged to coast the point or islets on the north-east, in order to avoid running ashore on the coast of the islet which runs far out into the entrance. Vessels having once passed the entrance run no risk, but can anchor in the harbour in four to five fathoms of water and sheltered from all winds. In addition the anchorage is good.

The little harbour is formed by the headland on the south-west of the Isle de la Tremblade, by the point on the south-west of the harbour and by that on the north-west of the entrance of the great harbour on an alignment drawn from the headland on the south-west of the Isle de la Tremblade to that on the south-west of the said harbour. About equi-distant between these two points lies an islet visible at all states of the tide which may be about 20 to 25 toises in extent. It is surrounded by a large number of reefs and shoals, so that in bad weather and even at high water, vessels dare not risk passing it. They prefer to go around the isle, and take the main channel.

5-6 EDWARD VII., A. 1906

Before the last war ten homesteads had been granted in the neighbourhood of this harbour, part being granted by patent and part verbally. These ten concessionaires have appropriated to their own use all the land around the harbour, under the pretext that their concessions were not delimited, and that their deeds prescribed no limits to their lands. Meantime it is certain that when these concessions are delimited there will be sufficient land on which to locate ten other settlers with ground for the erection of sheds for drying the fish from five boats apiece.

GENERAL CENSUS OF THE SETTLERS ON THE GREAT HARBOUR OF THE ISLE DE SCATARY.

Pierre Cezard Alexandre Le Grand, fisherman, native of the coast of Plaisance, aged 70 years. Married to Madeleine Diars, native of Newfoundland, aged 58 years.

They have been in the colony since 1715, and have been given rations for two years.

They have three sons and two daughters :—

Georges Le Grand, aged 26 years ;

Guy Alexandre, aged 21 years ;

Louis, aged 19 years ;

Marie, aged 22 years ;

Louise, aged 17 years ;

Mathurin Guillot, in the capacity of a domestic, native of Madrignac, bishopric of St. Brieux, aged 17 years.

He owns two boats and eight fowls.

The concession of this fishery was given him by Messieurs de Costebelle and de Soubras in 1715, and includes ground on which to make drying sheds for the fish of six boats.

Julien Jourdan, fisherman, native of Jean Servan (?) bishopric of Avranches, aged 35 years. He is in the colony 16 years, and is married to Marie Phelipeau, native of the country, aged 25 years.

They have two sons and one daughter :—

Jean, aged 5 years ;

Julien, aged 1 year ;

Marie, aged 3 years ;

Guillaume Rubé, fisherman, native of St. Martin des Champs, bishopric of Avranches, aged 35 years.

He owns two boats, two cows, and seven fowls.

The land on which he is settled is situated at the farther end of the great harbour, between the grounds of Pierre Le Grand and one Philipot. It was granted before the war to the late Jean Durand, whose heirs have never yet presented themselves to take possession of the land.

Monsieur Prévost has given it to him on condition that if the heirs of the deceased present themselves he will give them possession.

Jean Philipot, fisherman, native of Laide, bishopric of Coutances, aged 50 years. Married to Julienne Bassin, native of St. Michel des Loups, bishopric of Avranches, aged 35 years. He is in the colony 36 years.

They have seven children :—

Bazile, aged 24 years ;

Jean, aged 22 years ;

Guillaume Jean, aged 20 years ;

Guy Adrien, aged 20 years ;

Gabriel, aged 18 years ;

The other two are in France with their mother.

He owns one skiff, one boat, and five fowls.

ANCE DARANBOURG.

Ance Daranbourg lies on the north coast of the Isle of Scatary. It is formed by the Pointe Darambourg, on the east side, and by the Pointe des deux Cheminées on the west. It is scarcely suitable for cod fishing, above all in vessels, which are not sheltered from any winds except from those that come over the land from the isle. It is only large enough for two settlers.

GENERAL CENSUS OF THE SETTLERS OF ANCE DARANBOURG.

Le Sr. Silvain Jean Semidon Gation, surgeon, native of St. Servan, bishopric of St. Malo, aged 26 years. Married to Françoise Faye, native of Bordeaux, of the parish of St. Loy, aged 32 years.

They have three fowls.

The land on which they are settled is situated on the said Pointe Daranbourg. They have made a small clearing on it.

Marie Borgne, widow of the late Jean Nauguety, native of the coast of Plaisance, aged 54 years.

She has two sons and one daughter :

Thomas Nauguety, aged 17 years ;

Gabriel, aged 16 years ;

Marie, aged 14 years.

She owns one boat and six fowls.

Thomas Poirée, fisherman, native of Messy de Roy, bishopric of Coutances, aged 33 years. Married to Marie Vincent, native of Scatary, aged 25 years.

They have Marie Poirée, their daughter, aged 19 months.

They employ four thirty-six months men.

Jean Rabié, native of Ray, aged 20 years ;

Etienne Tutier, native of Dompierre, en Annis, aged 19 years.

Bousseau, aged 18 years, who does not know where he is from.

Jean Michel, native of Rochefort, aged 21 years.

These men complete their time in the month of June next and are thinking of remaining in the country.

He owns three boats and four fowls.

Charles Philbert, fisherman, native of la Bellière, bishopric of Coutances, aged 33 years. Married to Michel Borny, native of Scatary, aged 26 years.

They have three sons and one daughter :

Jean, aged 6 years.

Pierre, aged 4 years.

And the third, aged 3 months, is not named.

Marie, aged 2 years.

Living with him are three of his brothers and one sister :

Joseph Borny, aged 30 years.

Colas Borny, aged 19 years.

Thomas, aged 18 years.

Anne, aged 25 years.

He has two fishery partners :

Pierre Perron, native of la Bellière, aged 22 years.

Jean Le Gras, native of Laval, bishopric of St. Brieux, aged 25 years.

He employs two thirty-six months men :

Guillaume Beurrier, native of the bourg of Villedieu, bishopric of Coutances, aged 17 years.

François Beurrier, his brother, aged 15 years.

These men are to remain in the colony.

He owns four boats, one yawl, two sheep and eight fowls.

Pierre Le Berteau, fisherman, native of Plaisance, aged 48 years. Married to Jean Borny, native of the same place, aged 57 years. They are seven years in the colony.

They have four sons and one daughter :—

Charles Sabot, aged 35 years ;

Barthelemy Sabot, aged 25 years ;

Alexis Sabot, aged 20 years ;

Pierre Le Berteau, aged 12 years ;

Anne Sabot, aged 16 years.

18—5

Living with them are Reneé Camer, their mother, aged 102 years. Michel Chaineau, native of Angouléme, aged 20 years, engaged in the capacity of a domestic. He counts on remaining in the colony 3 to 4 years.

He owns one skiff of the capacity of ten cords of wood, one cow with calf, one sheep and thirteen fowls.

Antoine Sabot, fisherman, native of Cap de Rey, aged 29 years. Married to Jeanne Le Grand, native of Scatary, aged 23 years.

They have Jeanne, their daughter, aged 3 months.

He owns two boats and five fowls.

Guillaume Le Maréchal, fisherman, native of Carolle, bishopric of Avranches, aged 40 years. Married to Jeanne Sabot, native of Cap Breton, aged 30 years.

They have six children, two sons and four daughters.

Guillaume, aged 7 years ;
Jean Marc, aged 3 years ;
Jeanne, aged 12 years ;
Anne, aged 10 years ;
Madeleine, aged 8 years ;
Marie, aged one year.

He owns one boat.

Jean Dubarbier, fisherman, native of Bayonne, aged 34 years. Married to Marie Sabot, aged 24 years.

They have one son and one daughter :
Jean, aged 6 months ;
Marie Jeanne, aged 3 years.

He has one yawl to sell, and three fowls.

Sebastia Fond, fisherman, native of St. Vincent de Piros, bishopric of D'Ax, aged 40 years, in the colony 20 years. Married to Guillemette Sabot, native of Cap de Ré, aged 27 years.

They have two sons and one daughter :—
Sebastia La Fond, aged 10 years ;
Antoine, aged 3 years ;
Guillemette, aged one year.

He has six fowls.

Louis Grándville, fisherman, native of Calais, aged 35 years, in the colony 25 years. Married to Michelle Sabot, native of Cap de Ré, aged 24 years.

They have three sons :—
Louison, aged 4 years ;
Barthelemy, aged 3 years ;
Jean, aged one year.

Pierre Trely, native of the parish of la Bellière, bishopric of Coutances, aged 22 years, lives with them in the capacity of a domestic. He thinks of settling in the country.

They have one boat, one yawl, three sheep and four fowls.

All these settlers are without dwelling places at the fishery with the exception of Poirée and Philbert who are settled on the Pointe Darambourg by verbal permission of Messieurs Desherbiers and Prevost. The others hope to establish themselves on the harbour of Chetecamps ; at present they make their home in the woods. The settlers of the Isle de Scatary in general have had rations for two years.

ANCE DE BELLEFEUILLE.

The Ance de Bellefeuille is situated on the same coast of the Isle de Scatary as the preceding. It is much more exposed to gales than that of Darambourg.

There are settled :

Jean Nicolas de Malvillen, native of St. Malo, aged 48 years. Married to Madeleine Durand, native of Scatary, aged 37 years.

They have eleven children—seven sons and four daughters :

Jean, aged 18 years ;
Servant, aged 15 years ;
Charles, aged 11 years ;
Bazile, aged 10 years ;
Barthélemy, aged 8 years ;
Adrien, aged 5 years ;
The seventh is not named ;
Elizabeth, aged 19 years ;
Jeanne, aged 12 years ;
Jeanette, aged 4 years ;
Madeleine, aged 2 years.

Living with him is Pierre Brontin, native of Prouvale, bishopric of St. Malo, aged 22 years, engaged for 36 months and who has still two years to complete his time. He thinks of settling in the colony.

He has three fishery partners who neither know their names or where they are from.

He owns three boats and five fowls.

MENADON.

The harbour of Menadon is suitable for the cod fishery and the lands are fertile in pasture. It is formed of the point by the north-east of Menadon and by the Pointe au Chats. They lie north-west and south-east, and are estimated to be half a league distant from each other, the depth of the harbour running west-south-west and east-north-east being another half league. In the farthest recess of the harbour are several creeks. From the said Pointe aux Chats running to the east-south-east extends a bar a good quarter of a league in length with a breadth of 100 to 150 toises. Mariners distrust it much because it is so steep and there is little water in it. The best anchorage in the harbour is between an islet and the bar aux Chats. This islet is situated nearly in the middle of harbour and is seen at all states of the tide. Vessels anchor off it in four and five fathoms of water and are sheltered from the winds generally ; that most to be feared being from the north-east, and even this is broken by the north-east point of harbour.

Census.

Census of the settlers of the bay of Menadon :

Remy Bussac, ploughman, native of Angoulême, aged 39 years.

He has one ox, one cow with calf, and eight fowls.

He lives on land belonging to Madame Carrerot.

We left the harbour of Menadon on the 13th of April, and reached the harbour de la Baleine the same day.

On leaving the harbour of Menadon, and after doubling la pointe aux Chats, the creek of that name is reached. This creek, as well as the creek aux Cannes which adjoins it, but runs further into the interior of l'Ile Royale, is formed by the Pointe aux Chats and the Cap de Portanovo, These points lie north and south at an estimated distance from each other of two leagues. It is found that the ance aux Chats is impracticable by sea, owing to the chains of rocks existing there, but on the other hand, the ance aux Cannes is well suited for effecting a landing, and for the anchorage of vessels. These vessels lie under the lea of the Isle aux Cannes, sheltered from easterly and south-south-easterly winds. The Isle aux Cannes lies in the middle of the creek of that name, and is estimated to be 200 to 300 toises in length and 150 to 200 in breadth. The clear channel is on that on the north of this isle, that on the south side being impassable even for boats. A large bank of sand, well adapted to the drying of codfish, lies across the further end of this harbour. The creek is so situated as to be better suited to cod-fishing by means of vessels than by boats, though on the beach at the further end of the harbour of la Baleine, there is a road of an estimated length of about a quarter of a league, not altogether impracticable to foot passengers, but good for all

5-6 EDWARD VII., A. 1906

kinds of beasts of burden. The reason of this is that over the whole of this part of the country there is a layer of peat, in some places ten to fifteen feet in thickness, and in others so thick that it cannot be measured.

The distance between the Cap de Portanove, and the pointe à deux Doights, lying at the entrance to the harbour de la Baleine is placed at one league. The Cape and pointe lie south-east by north-west.

Between these points we found no creek, nor any place suitable for putting men ashore. The coast is strewn with shoals and reefs. A channel runs between Cap de Portanove and the land, but though it is a quarter of a league in length it is not considered safe even for a boat to navigate.

The Harbour of la Baleine.

The harbour of la Baleine is only suitable for the cod-fishing industry. It is formed by the pointe à Deux Doights lying to the north, and the pointe à Marcoche lying to the south. They lie west-north-west and east-south-east at an estimated distance of 400 toises, one from the other.

Two large rocks, which when seen from a distance resemble whales and were so named, lie immediately in the centre of the entrance. These two whales are left to the larboard in entering, but they can be safely passed quite closely owing to their precipitous character, whilst between lies a safe channel for a boat. Between the two whales and the pointe à Marcoche there is a channel good only for a boat, and in fine weather. Only merchantmen of not more than 200 tons burden can enter the harbour de la Baleine. The channel by which one enters turns to many points of the compass. Vessels that enter have three feet of water in which to anchor, and can have the same depth even in the further end of the bay, and are sheltered from nearly every wind. The harbour runs north-east by south-west for a distance of some 800 toises inland.

General Census.

General Census of the settlers of la Baleine.

Louis Gascot, fisherman, native of Vins, bishopric of Avranches, aged 50 years. Married to Jeanne Desroches, native of St. Qua, bishopric of St. Brieux, aged 30 years.

They have Marie their daughter aged 9 months.

They employ nine men for the fishing, and have five boats, one barque, three sheep with their lambs and ten fowls.

The fishery concession that he occupies was sold him by the heirs of the late Georges Tasson for the sum of one hundred quintals of cod, and includes ninety toises fronting the shore of the harbour ; the depth is not defined.

Marie Ostando, widow of the late Thomas Tompigue, aged 60 years.

She has with her four sons and two orphans :—

André Tompigue, native of the place, aged 32 years, widower of the late Cécile his wife, by whom he had :—

Etienne André, their son, aged 9 months ;

Etienne Tompigue, native of the country, aged 30 years, married to Marguerite Jean Tesse, native of St. Pierre, aged 21 years.

Thomas Pierre Tompigue, aged 24 years ;

Pierre François Tompigue, aged 22 years ;

Pierre Bertrand, aged 19 years, unfit to bear arms ;

Catherine Bertrand, aged 10 years ; all natives of la Baleine.

He owns a schooner of the capacity of eight cords of wood, and four fowls.

The land occupied by them was granted to them by patent of the court, dated the 24th June, 1718. It contains 60 toises front by 25 in depth. There are on it beaches and scaffolding for drying the fish of three boats.

André Paris fisherman, native of the parish of Brouillant, bishopric of Auch, aged 40. Married to Perrine Dupont, native of Baleine, aged 33 years.

They have five children ; four sons and one daughter :—

André Paris, aged 9 years ;

Jean Baptiste, aged 4 years ;

François, aged 3 years ;

François, aged 6 months ;

Marie, aged 14 years, all natives of la Baleine.

They employ one thirty six months man who finishes his time during the present month of April, Claude Rousset, native of Bourges, aged 24 years.

Monsieur Imbert, works his fishery with four boats of his own. He must ascertain the names and number of his fishermen.

The land of their fishery concession, situated on a beach which lies in the harbour, is for the fish of six boats and was granted to them by Messieurs de St. Ovide and de Soubras in 1715. It contains 100 toises fronting the sea shore with a depth of thirteen toises. There are on it two platforms, a beach and scaffolding for drying the fish of six boats. He has but one yawl with which he followed the fishing last year.

They own : one cow, one ewe, one boat and fourteen fowls.

He seeks a grant of an aditional 50 toises frontage, which have never been granted to anyone and which he has improved.

Catherine Gosselin, widow of the late Jean des Roches, native of la Baleine, aged 30 years.

She has left no children and lives with le Sr. Paris, her brother-in-law.

Jacques Le Tourneur, fisherman, native of the parish of St. Jean des Champs, bishopric of Coutances, aged 70 years. Married to Catherine Roger, native of Sirance, bishopric of Coutances, aged 75 years. They are settled in the colony since 1720.

They have Jean Philippe Guigoit, aged 9 years, their little grandson.

They employ nine fisherman :—

—————————————, native of the parish of Getary, bishopric of Bayonne, aged 66 years.

Julian Le Perchoix, native of the parish of Roulont, bishopric of Avranches, aged 56 years.

Pierre Le Maréchal, native of the parish of Chateauneuf, bishopric of St. Malo, aged 26 years.

Antoine Paris, native of the parish of Neudenenry, bishopric of Coutances, aged 38 years.

François Auger, native of the parish of St. Pierre de Lanzy, bishopric of Avranches, aged 25 years.

Mathieu Arieux, native of the parish of Gatary, aged 54 years.

Martin Martigon, native of the parish of St. Père, aged 22 years.

Martin Chaud, native of the parish of Gatary, bishopric of Bayonne, aged 21 years.

Pierre Desmalet, native of the parish of St. Père, aged 22 years.

He owns two boats and four fowls.

The land in their homestead is situated on a creek at the farther end of their homestead. It was granted to them by Messieurs de St. Ovide and Le Normand in 1733. There are on it platforms, beaches and scaffoldings for drying the fish of four boats.

Le Sr. Pierre Le Cerf, native of Dinan, bishopric of St. Malo, aged 37 years, Master Surgeon. Married to Therese Grandin, native of L'Indienne, aged 30 years. He has been in the colony since 1730.

They have four children, two sons and two daughters :—

Pierre, aged 10 years ;

Clement, aged 4 years ;

Anne, aged 12 years ;

Marie Jeanne, aged 18 months.

One domestic, named Julien Poulien, native of the parish of St. Targot de Sena, bishopric of Avranches, aged 22 years. He is going to follow the fishery this year at Madame Dupont's, of Laurenbec. He owns five fowls.

The land on which they are settled has never been granted to anyone. It is situated at the farther end of the harbour behind the dwelling places. They received

5-6 EDWARD VII., A. 1906

verbal permission from Messieurs Desherbiers and Prevost. He has built a house there and cleared a piece of ground for a small garden as well as a swamp in front for a meadow.

Le Sr. Daguaret carries on the fishery here with six boats and thirty fishermen.

We left the Harbour de la Baleine on the 15th of the month of April, taking road for the harbour of Laurenbec and arrived there the same day.

The distance between the pointe à Marcoche lying to the south and point Bordieu lying to the south-east of the harbour of Laurenbec is placed at a quarter of a league, wherein there is only one large creek which can be ascended by boats and barges. This creek is strewn with reefs and shoals visible at all tides, whilst the remainder of the coast is impracticable in every respect.

THE HARBOUR OF LITTLE LAURENBEC.

This harbour is scarcely suitable for the cod fishery. In runs inland a quarter of a league in a north-north-westerly direction. The harbour is in the form of a river. The breadth is irregular but is averaged at 60 toises. It is formed by a point to the south-east of the harbour, and by that of Michel Vallet lying to the west north-west. The distance between these points is placed at not more than 100 toises at most.

A large rock visible at all states of the tide lies almost in the middle of the channel. It is left to starboard in entering, and vessels hug the shore of the pointe de Michel Vallet. The entrance lies north and south, and the heaviest vessels that can enter the harbour are merchantmen of a capacity of 200 tons at most.

CENSUS OF THE SETTLERS AT LAURENBEC.

Pierre Le Tourneur, fisherman, native of the parish of St. Aubin des Préaux, bishopric of Coutances, settled in this country for twenty years, aged 41 years. Married to Marie Prieur, native of St. Malo, aged 31 years.

They have six daughters :—

Guillmette Vallet, aged 16 years ;
Marie Vallet, aged 14 years ;
Perrine, aged 10 years ;
Geneviève Le Tourneur, aged 8 years ;
Jeanne, aged 6 years ;
Perrine, aged 18 months.

He owns two outfits for the fishery. Living with him are Julien Gasseau, native of Vins, bishopric of Avranches, aged 40 years.

Louis Panear, native of St. Brieux, aged 35 years.
Servant Le Prieur, native of l'Isle Royale, aged 24 years.
Jean Le Noir, native of Charvé, bishopric of Dol, aged 25 years.
Jean Lapinet, native of Avranches, aged 45 years.
René Le Loquet, native of St. Aubin, bishopric of Coutances, aged 22 years.
François Gourdon, native of Limoges, aged 50 years.

None of these men have a fixed residence with the exception of Servant Le Prieur. He also hires Jean Baptiste D'Arnault, native of St. Pierre de la Martinique.

Barthélemy Chapereau, native of Brive, bishopric of Saintes, in the capacity of thirty-six months man.

Louis Gaultier, native of Dole, aged 20 years.
François Collet, native of Hénaut, bishopric of St. Brieux, also a 36 months man

These men have two years and a half to finish their time, and are thinking of settling in the country.

He owns three boats and a half boat ; eight fowls and two sheep.

His dwelling place was granted to him by a grant in form by Messieurs de Saint-Ovide and Le Normand de Mézy, dated May 15, 1736. It contains 72 toises fronting on the harbour by 90 toises in depth. On it are platforms, beaches and scaffoldings for drying the fish of three boats.

Perrine Desroches, widow of François Dupont, fisherman, native of the coast of Plaisance, aged 40 years.

She has two sons and two daughters :

François Dupont, aged 22 years ;

Pierre, aged 16 years ;

Françoise, aged 23 years ;

Perrine, aged 19 years, all natives of Laurenbec.

In her service are three, thirty-six months men, who finish their time at the end of this month.

Pierre Louis Viellard, native of Vailly, bishopric of Soissons, aged 30 years.

Jean Sonier, native of Tremuzon, bishopric of St. Brieux, aged 21 years.

Mathieu Deniseau, native of Lion, bishopric of St. Malo, aged 19 years.

They are undetermined whether they will remain in the colony or not.

He owns two boats and ten fowls.

The dwelling they occupy was granted in the name of François Dupont in 1733 by Messieurs de St. Ovide and Le Normand. It carries 70 toises of front on the harbour, With regard to the depth it is defined by two lines of separation. There are upon it one platform one beach and scaffoldings for the drying of the fish of four boats.

Simon Gaultier, fisherman, native of the parish of Vins, bishopric of Avranches, aged 46 years. Married to Catherine Doight, native of Lancieux, bishopric of St. Malo, aged 32 years. They are settled in the colony since 1722.

They have six fishermen, three of whom are at Louisbourg. Those who are with him at present are :

François Le Bessot, native of Vins, bishopric of Avranches, aged 40 years.

Louis Le Bessot, aged 33 years.

René Le Sellier, native of the same parish.

There are also two thirty-six months men, who have thirty months to finish their time.

Jacques Dupont, aged 22 years ;

Etienne Dupont, aged 22 years, both natives of Vins.

He has two boats and three head of poultry.

The land he occupies was sold to him under a deed in the year 1738 by the late Jean Durand, fisherman, for the sum of 465 livres. It contains 14 toises 4 feet facing the harbour and 66 toises 3 feet in depth. There are upon it a platform, beach and scaffolding for the drying of the fish of two boats and a small garden.

Antoine Deroches, fisherman, native of the place, aged 32 near. Married to Jeanne Boucher, native of Petit Degra.

They have four children and one lad who is under age.

Antoine, aged 4 years ;

Jeanne, aged 8 years ;

Toinette, aged 6 years ;

Perrine, aged one month.

Jean des Roches, aged 14 years.

He has three partners in the fishery, one workman who dries the cod on the beach and one thirty-six-months man.

Jean Lallemand, native of Lourendecus, bishopric of Coutances, aged 24 years.

Jean Poulard de Rennes, aged 22 years.

Jean Galles, native of Gennes, bishopric of Genois, aged 21 years.

They are thinking of remaining in the country.

The fishermen are :—

Joseph Dechery, native of Sibour, bishopric of St. Jean de Luz, aged 45 years ;

Bernard Claverie, native of Sard, bishopric of Bayonne, aged 30 years ;

Bertrand Le Gue, native of St. Pierre de Vins, bishopric of Avranches, aged 50 years. They are married in France.

He has two boats.

The dwelling place which they have improved was sold to them by Pierre Noblet for the sum of 450 livres and a ————— of Messieurs Desherbiers and Prevost. It

5-6 EDWARD VII., A. 1906

has 30 toises of front on the harbour, and 9 to 10 of depth. There are on it platforms, beach and scaffolding for the drying of the fish of two boats.

Charles Yvon, fisherman, native of the parish of St. Jean des Champs, bishopric of Coutances, aged 55 years. He is in the colony since 1726. Married a second time, namely, to Mathurine Dohiels, native of the parish of Lancieux, bishopric of St. Malo, aged 36 years.

They have six children, five sons and one daughter :—
Etienne Yvon, aged 17 years ;
Guillaume, aged 15 years ;
François, aged 13 years ;
Louis, aged 11 years ;
Pierre, aged 3 years ;
Jeanne, aged 5 months.

They employ one fisherman :—

Jean Henry, native of Vignac, bishopric of St. Malo, aged 46 years; and two thirty-six months men. One finishes his time in the commencement of the month of May, and the other his in the month of September.

François Colant, native of Canté, bishopric of St. Malo.

Jean Pras, native of Quesencé, bishopric of Treguier, aged 20 years.

He has three boats of which he lets two, following the fiishery with the third ; and three fowls.

His dwelling place was granted to him by Messieurs de St. Ovide and Le Normand, in 1733. It contains 23 toises front on the sea in the harbour and 90 in depth. There are a platform, beach and scaffold for the drying of fish of four boats.

Monsieur Didion is engaged in the fishery here with two boats. He will give the name of his fishermen to Pierre Lorent ; he stays at Louisbourg.

Margueritie Desroches, widow of Julien Banet, native of St. Pierre, on the coast of Plaisance, aged 38 years.

She has three children, two sons and one daughter :—
Pierre Banet, aged 14 years ;
Jean Pierre, aged 12 years ;
Marie, aged 17 years ;
She is working for her.

Jean Nicolas Camus, native of the parish of Dinan, aged 20 years. He is a thirty six months man. He finishes his time at the end of the month of May, and is thinking of remaining in the country.

The dwelling place was granted to them by Messieurs de St. Ovide and Le Normand by a concession in form of the date of 25th May, 1733. It contains 35 toises fronting the sea shore in the harbour by 90 in depth. It has on it a platform, three cabins, beach and scaffolding for drying the fish for four boats belonging to Monsieur Delort le Jeune. She has let her dwelling to him, as she is not capable of improving it by herself or to find fishermen by other means.

She has seven fowls.

Jacques Couzin, fisher, native of St. Martin de Condé, bishopric of Bayeux, aged 26 years. Married to Marie Grossin, widow of the late Algrain, native of St. Servan, aged 29 years.

They have three children, two sons and one daughter :—
Pierre, aged 2 years ;
Julien, aged 4 months ;
Marie Houze, aged 5 years.

Working for him is Mathurin Briaud, native of St. May, bishopric of St. Malo, a thirty-six months man, who finishes his time on the 27th May next.

They have three fowls.

The land on which he is settled was given to him verbally by Messieurs Desherbiers and Prevost. He has made a clearing on it of about one arpent in extent, and built a beach and scaffolding for the drying of the fish of two boats. He has no boat but hopes to hire one.

Françoiç Desroches, widow of Jean Dubordien, native of Plaisance, aged 48 years.
She has four children, three sons and one daughter :—
Felix Dubordien, aged 24 years ;
François, aged 22 years ;
Simon, aged 20 years ;
Marie, aged 17 years.
Josette des Roches, her niece, aged 11 years.

She has working for her four thirty-six months men who finish their time in the month of July.

Yvon de Kemaire, native of Treverant, bishopric of Tréguier, aged 28 years.
François Henry, native of Boco, bishopric of Tréguier, aged 22 years
Pierre Bellet, native of Painvenant, bishopric of Tréguier, aged 26 years.
Jacques Le Neveu, native of Morlais, aged 19 years.

They are to remain in the country for some time.

The concession which they have improved was previously in the possession of a man named Le Corps. It was granted her by Messieurs Desherbiers and Prevost, on the condition that in case the heirs, or anyone on behalf of the heirs, should appear to improve the concession her claim would cease ; but the time having passed without any claimant appearing the said widow prays Messieurs le Comte and Prevost to deliver her a grant in form that she may be guaranteed the work she and her children have done. There are on the concession a platform, beach, scaffolding and cabins for the drying of the fish of two boats. She has one boat and one half-boat for the fishery.

She has twelve fowls.

Joseph Mirande, fisherman, native of L'Indienne, aged 32 years. Married to Marie Barbe Elie Le Grand, native of Labrasdor, aged 24 years.

They have one son and one daughter :—
Jean Baptiste, aged 3 years ;
Josette, aged 8 months.

The land on which they are settled was given to the late Joseph Mirande their father, they could not tell me by whom, nor its extent.

They have three fowls.

Georges Chauvin, fisherman, native of the parish of Bassily, diocese of Avranches, aged 52 years. Married to Marie Mirande, native of L'Indienne, aged 39 years. He is in the colony since 1719.

They have two sons :—
Joseph, aged 20 years ;
Pierre, aged 12 years ;

He employs three fishermen :—
Pierre Poussin, native of Dinan, bishopric of St. Malo, aged 48 years ;
François Norber, native of La Rochelle, aged 23 years ;
Gabriel Lemarié, native of Vins, bishopric of Avranches, aged 23 years.

They have no settled residence in the colony.

Guillaume Bresset, native of Saint Brieux, aged 18 years, domestic.

He owns one boat and eight fowls.

The land of the concession was granted in 1733 by Messieurs de St. Ovide and Le Normand to one named Pierre Allain and his wife, and sold to said Georges Chauvin for 70 quintals of merchantable codfish, in 1738. It contains 38 toises frontage on the harbour, the depth not being defined.

There are upon it a platform, beach and scaffolding for the drying the fish of his boat.

Le Sr. Duplessis, master surgeon, native of Grandville, aged 43 years. Married to Marie Ferté, widow of the late Bealieu Collet, native of St. Malo, aged 38 years.

They have five daughters and one son :—
Thomas, aged 12 years ;
Françoise, aged 18 years ;
Gillette, aged 16 years ;
Jeanne, aged 9 years ;

5-6 EDWARD VII., A. 1906

Charlotte, aged 7 years ;

Also Anne Beaulieu, aged 18 years, living with them as well as Josseline de Rioguain, native of St. Malo, aged 60 years, their mother.

Louis Arnault, native of Orleans, aged 20 years, as assistant surgeon. He is not thinking of remaining in the colony.

The land on which they are settled is situated to the west of the dwelling of Monsieur Boucher, Engineer to the King.

They have no grant in form, only a verbal permission from M. le Comte de Raymond and M. Prevost. They have one house on it and are building another.

They have a garden and fifteen fowls.

Jacques Perrain, native of the parish of Plené, bishopric of St. Brieux, aged 30 years. Married to Marie Jeanne Dupont, native of the same parish aged 28 years.

They have one son and one daughter :—

Julien François, aged 12 years;

Marie Anne, aged 8 years.

He has six fowls.

Their homestead has been sold to them by M. Boucher for the sum of———————
On it they grow hay and garden produce.

François Malle, fisherman, native of Bouillon, bishopric of Avranches, aged 45 years. He is in the colony since 1728. Married to Anne Marie Le Large, native of Grandville, aged 45 years.

They have three sons :—

Francois, aged 11 years ;

Pierre, aged 6 years ;

Louis, aged 3 years.

He employs six fishermen, who are :

François Le Moine, native of Saint-Jean des Champs, bishopric of Coutances, aged 35 years ;

Jean Richard, native of Kintenay, bishopric of St. Brieux, aged 17 years.

Louis Chauvin, native of Bassile, bishopric of Avranches, aged 23 years.

François Bretet, native of Berepied, bishopric of Avranches, aged 20 years.

Justin Megray, native of Gipé, bishopric of Rennes, aged 31 years.

They are all without any fixed residence.

He owns two boats.

The land they occupy was sold to them by the Sr. Perrain for the sum of 300 livres and so small was the amount of land that le Sr. Perrain would tell them that they would not know where to dry the fish from two boats. The contract is not legally completed, but they have placed the purchase money in the hands of M. Fizel as guarantee to le Sr. Perrain. They hoped their land would extend from one stream to another according to the first agreement, but when the Sr. Perrain saw that the Sr. François Mallé could not withdraw because the season was so far advanced he would only let them have half the piece of ground between the said two streams.

They have made a platform beach and scaffolding for drying the fish of two boats.

Jean La Chou, fisherman, native of Prouvallain, bishopric of St. Malo, aged 55 years. Married to Marie Anne Borisse, native of Louisburg, aged 31 years.

They have Marie Joseph, their daughter, aged 4 years.

He employs four unmarried fishermen :—

Jean Albane, native of St. Jean de Luz, aged 20 years.

Pierre Amelin, native of Montiville, aged 50 years. Married in France.

Jacques Canivet, native of Normandy, aged 28 years.

Julien Chapelle, native of Normandy.

They are going to their homes at the close of the next fishing season.

Also Francois Danosa, native of Preiscalet, bishopric of Quimper, aged 26 years, who is a thirty six months man and will finish his time in two years. He will remain in the colony. M. La Chou owns one boat and three fowls.

The dwelling in which they are settled was granted to them by Messrs. Desherbiers and Prevost. It belonged previously to one named Jean Le Bessot. He died in

SESSIONAL PAPER No. 18

the English prison. The heirs have not presented themselves to claim their inheritance, there being a good many debts against the property ; neither have the creditors. A house has been built on the property and a beach and scaffolding for the drying of the fish of one boat built.

Jean Le Chau, fisherman, native of Lasserne, bishopric of Avranches, aged 42 years. Married to Marie Madeleine Corporon, native of Louisbourg, aged 36 years.

They have Jean Le Chau, their son, aged two years.

He employs fifteen fishermen, of whom eight have been boarded by him all the winter, the remaining seven wintering with other private persons :—

Louis Pepin, native of Sartilly, bishopric of Avranches, aged 22 years ;
Louis Noblé, native of Sartilly, bishopric of Avranches, aged 32 years ;
Jean Charles Corporon, native of Ile Royale, aged 30 years ;
Jean Baudry, native of Marenne, bishopric of La Rochelle, aged 33 years ;
Michel Le Roy, native of Nantes, aged 20 years ;
François Riché, native of l'Ile Royale, aged 14 years ;
Jean Baudry, native of Marenne, bishopric of La Rochelle, aged 11 y ars.

All these fishermen are to remain in the country.

Thomas Cousin, native Gené, bishopric of Avranches, aged 17 years ;
Jean Benoist, native of the parish of La Rochelle, bishopric of Avranches, aged 42 years ;
Herné Brindechamp, native of Cau, bishopric of of St. Malo, aged 25 years ;
Guy Hernand, native of Laucalu, bishopric of Dol, aged 25 years ;
Jacques Cacu, native of Plau, bishopric of Avranches, aged 60 years ;
Charles Cacu, aged 22 years ;
René Hernard, native of Dinan, aged 44 years ;
Mathurin Renouve, native of Dinan, bishopric of St. Malo, aged 28 years.

The land they occupy was granted to them by Messieurs de St. Ovide and Le Normand in 1733. It contains frontage on the shore of the harbour of,——————— by —of depth. There are on it two platforms, a beach and scaffolding for the drying of fish from three boats and a smack, which he actually owns.

Jude Rode, smith, native of the parish of Lolif Rode, bishopric of Avranches, aged 60 years. Married to Angelique Aller, native of the parish of St. Servant, bishopric of St. Malo.

He has Louis, his son, fisherman, aged 33 years.

They have been in the colony since 1720. They have Louis Joseph, their son, aged 10 months. They have no hired fishermen yet. They are awaiting the arrival of two crews from France.

He owns two boats and two half boats ; one ewe with her young and five fowls.

He has working for him three thirty-six months men :—

Jean Heu, native of the parish of St. Helen, bishopric of Dol, aged 45 years ;
Joseph Malivet, native of the parish of Derignac, bishopric of Saint Malo, aged 22 years ;
Julien Le Moine, native of Plené, bishopric of St. Malo, aged 20 years.

The first finishes his time next month, and the two others, in a year.

Living with them are Margueritte Baudry, native of Marenne, bishopric of La Rochelle, aged 10 years, their god-daughter.

The land on which they are was granted to them by Messieurs de St. Ovide and Le Normand in 1733. It extends from the place of the heirs of the late Rene to that of Desroches. There are on it a platform, beach and scaffolding for the drying of fish of three boats.

Adam Perré, fisherman, native of the coast of Plaisance, aged 36 years. Married to Jacinthe Grandien, native of l'Indienne, age 25 years.

They have two sons :—

Thomas, aged 18 months ;
Pierre Perré, aged one month ;
Two hired fishermen :—
Jean Nalet, native of Canada, aged 31 years ;

5-6 EDWARD VII., A. 1906

Martin Maurice, native of the parish of Tenac, bishopric of Saint Malo, aged 36 years.

Also two domestics engaged until St. Michel's Day ;

Jacques Amelin, native of Saint Jean des Champs, bishopric of Coutances, aged 19 years;

Guillaume Berry, native of the parish of Vignac, bishopric of Saint Malo, aged 55 years.

He owns two fishing boats and six fowls.

Their land was granted to them by Messieurs de Saint Ovide and Le Normand in 1733. It contains 45 toises fronting on the sea in the harbour, by 90 in depth. There are on it platforms, beach and scaffolding for drying the fish of two boats.

Gabriel Le Manquet, widow of the late Etienne Desroches, native of the coast of Plaisance, aged 70 years.

She has Guillaume Desroches, her son, native of Lorenbec, aged 27 years.

Two thirty-six months men ;

Herne Herbert, native of Carfanitin bishopric of Dol, aged 19 years :

Guillaume Guiton, native of the parish of Montigu, bishopric of Avranches, aged 18 years.

He has eleven men hired for the fishery and three boats. He has made use of the homestead of one named Adam Perré having no dwelling place of his own, that on which he built his house belonging to several brothers and sisters who refused to assist him to improve it, telling him that he could work on it himself if he chose. He very humbly supplicated the authorities to give him a written permit to work on said homestead so that if, after he had improved the property, the heirs desired to enter upon it they should be obliged to make good to him what expense he had been at for the improvements. They lost the title deed during the war ; a copy is with the clerk of the Conseil Superieur.

In his employ are :

Jean Gause, of the parish of Roulan, bishopric of Coutances, aged 28 years ;

Pierre Bourg, native of the parish of Pleumondat, bishopric o St. Malo, aged 58 years ;

François Loiselle, of the parish of St. Servant, aged 50 years.

François Boulier, of the parish of Vignac, bishopric of St. Malo, aged 47 years ;

Jean Valleé, native of the parish of St. Servant, bishopric of St. Malo, aged 50 years ;

Jean Le Pejoux, of the parish of Brou, bishopric of St. Malo, aged 48 years ;

Pierre Goulier, of the parish of Modet, bishopric of St. Malo, aged 27 years ;

Nicolas Le Chenechal, native of the parish of Vezant, bishopric of Avranches, aged 24 years ;

Raymond de Chegarey, of the parish of Bidart, bishopric of Bayonne, aged 32 years ;

Betrie Choubecte, of the parish of Sarre, bishopric of Bayonne, aged 36 years ;

Joseph Darostegay, of the parish of Durogne, bishopric of Bayonne, aged 36 years.

THE CREEK OF PORT LA JOYE.

The creek of Port La Joye, known also under the name of the Ance à la Pointe Prime, is formed by the point of that name lying to the south-south-east of the entrance to Port La Joye, and by the headland to the north-west of the lands on the north-west quarter north of the entrance of Port La Joye. These points lie south-east and north-west, at a distance from each other estimated at two leagues and a half in a direct line, by seven leagues around the bay, and two in depth.

The channel lies north a quarter north-east by south a quarter south-west to Port La Joye. It is a quarter of a league in breadth and has an average depth of five, six, seven, eight and nine fathoms of water at low tide. The most experienced sailors in the country hold that when in five fathoms of water they are not in the best channel, and no matter which way they are going, must luff up till they find it.

The Isle du Gouverneur is left to the starboard on entiring, in order to avoid the shoals which stretch out to sea and are composed of rocks.

The island is of a round shape being a league and a half in circumference and half a league across. It lies low and is wooded with all kinds of timber.

The Isle du Comte Saint-Pierre lies to the larboard on entering. One can sail much closer to this island than to the other owing to the fact that the shoals are more perpendicular. The island is a good quarter of a league long by four hundred and fifty toises in width, and wooded with pine, white spruce, fir and hemlock with but little of the last. At low tide one may walk dry shod from the head land on the north-west to the Isle du Comte Sainte Pierre. There is a bar that is uncovered at low tide.

PORT LA JOYE.

Port La Joye is situated at the farther end of the creek of that name, five leagues from Pointe Prime, making the circuit from headland to headland and two leagues from the north-east headland. It is formed by Pointe à la Framboise lying to the east, and by that of la Flame lying to the west. It is estimated that these points lie east quarter north-east by west quarter south-west; that the distance between them is about five hundred toises; that the channel lies equi-distant from both points, and that for a bare three hundred toises there are at low tide but eight fathons of water in the channel. The roadstead is a quarter of a league from the entrance. It lies between the points à Pierrot and à Margueritte. The distance between these points is seven hundred toises. In the harbour there is good anchorage in a muddy bottom, where three rivers, one from the west, the second from the north and the third from the north-east, discharge their waters.

The mouth of the river du Ouest is formed by Pointe à Pierrot, lying on the larboard going up the river, and the headland to the north of the river. The distance between these two points is placed at a quarter of a league, and they lie north by south. The river runs west for four leagues preserving an almost uniform breadth. In this stretch there are sixteen settlers cultivating the lands on its banks. The river then runs north, north-west for three leagues to where it takes its rise in fresh water. Its banks are covered with all kinds of timber, but hard wood is the chief. The land is clayey in its nature and affords fairly abundant pasturage.

The mouth of the river du Nord is formed by the point to the north of the Rivière du Ouest, and by the point on the east of the rivre du Nord. The distance between these points is seven (hundred) toises. They lie east and west. The river runs four leagues inland to the northward. Seven families are settled on its banks, and engaged in agriculture.

The lands on its banks are equal in quality to those of the river du Ouest, and the woods are also similar.

The mouth of the river du Nord-Est is formed by Pointe à Margueritte lying to the starboard and by Pointe à la————lying to the larboard. It is estimated that these points are eight hundred toises apart. The river runs nine leagues inland; in a north-easterly direction for three leagues; to the east north-east for two leagues, to the north north-east for one league, and to the east for half a league, being navigable to this point by vessels of 50 tons burden, it then runs north-east for a league and a half where it is navigable for boats carrying ten cords of wood. At this point the place called la Grande Source is reached.

GENERAL CENSUS

General Census of the settlers of Port La Joye, of men, women, boys, &c.

Jean Henry dit Maillardé, master tailor and ploughman, native of the parish of Orbin, Switzerland, aged 26 years, of which he has been in the country two months, having deserted Chibouctou. Married to Anne Barbe, native of the town of Bienne, Switzerland, aged 32 years.

They have Henry, their son, aged 17 days.

5-6 EDWARD VII., A. 1906

Living with them is Abraham Louis, bachelor, workman in cotton print, native of Lideau, in Switzerland, aged 20 years. He has been six weeks in the country.

The land on which they are settled is situated on the road from the wood, and was given to them verbally by Monsieur de Bonaventure.

Jasques Nicolas, master sugar refiner, native of the dependency of the bishopric of Beauvais in Picardy, aged 37 years ; has been one month in the country. Married to Marie Quilien, native of the town of Neis, in Ireland, aged 19 years. The land on which they are settled is situated on the road by which they go from Port La Joye to the wood, and was given to them verbally by M. de Bonaventure.

Margueritte Mieux, widow of the late Michel Hebert, native of the Cap de Sable, aged 36 years ; she has been two years in the country.

She has seven children, five sons and two daughters.

Cyprien Hebert, aged 15 years.
Joseph Nicodême, aged 13 years,
Ferdinand, aged 11 years.
Grégoire, aged 7 years.
Magloire, aged 5 years.
Magdelaine Barbe Hebert, aged 9 years.
Geneviève Hebert, aged 7 years.

In live stock she owns one sow and ten fowls.

The land on which she is settled was granted to her by Messieurs Bonaventure and Degoutin, and she has made a clearing for a garden.

Germain Henry, native of l'Acadie, aged 66 years ; he has been two years in the country. Married to Cecille Desveaux, native of l'Acadie. They have four sons and two daughters.

Jean Baptiste, aged 25 years.
Pierre, aged 18 years.
Joseph, aged 11 years.
Amand, aged 7 years.
Rozalie, aged 14 years.
Magdeleine, aged 9 years.

Jean Cayssy, orphan, native of l'Acadie, aged 27 years.

They have in live stock, one bull, one mare, three sows, four pigs, five geese and eight fowls.

They own no land.

François Siriés, ploughman, native of the parish of D'Albourg, bishopric of Cahors, aged 38 years. It is 22 months since he arrived from l'Acadie. Married to Anne Edon, native of the parish of la Franche, bishopric of Grenoble, aged 37 years.

They have Roze, their daughter, aged ten months.

They have in live stock, one ewe, one lamb, one pig, two geese and thirty fowls and chickens.

The land on whice they are settled was given them under rental from the minors of Jean Baptiste Mazierre. They have made a large clearing on it for a graden.

Joseph Benet, ploughman, native of Albiac, bishopric of Cahors, aged 30 years, in the country 22 months.

Married to Jennie Doillet, native of Cognac, bishopric of Cahors, aged 35 years. They have one son and one daughter.

Paul, aged 5 years and 6 months.
Rose, aged 5 months.

They have one pig and eight fowls.

The land on which they are settled was given them as above and on it they have made a clearing for a large garden.

Le Sr. Louis Jonisseaux, merchant, native of the parish of Balergant, bishopric of Quebec. Aged 30 years, he has been in the country 35 months. Married to Marie Therese Dauphin, native of the town of Quebec, aged 37 years.

They have Louis Marie Jonisseau, aged 2 years.

They have in live stock one horse, one cow, one heifer, one pig and thirty fowls.

They hold the land by virtue of the following purchases, namely : One of two arpents front and forty in depth, from Charles Haché Galland and Geneviève Lavergne his wife, and another of two arpents five perches front with a depth extending to the bank of the Barachois or Ance aux Sauvages from Louis la Bauve and Marie Landry his wife.

Jean Baptiste Perial, corporal of the company formerly of Bonaventure, native of Franche Comté, aged 25 years, and has been in the country three years. Married to Rosalie Commeau, native of l'Acadie, aged 32 years.

She has Joseph Caissy, her son by a previous marriage, aged 8 years.

Anne Caissy, orphan, native of l'Acadie, aged 15 years.

They have in live stock one sow, one pig and twenty fowls.

They hold their land under rental from the children of the deceased Jean Baptiste Mazierre. The said land has three arpents of front with a depth of forty.

Jean Roussin, navigator, native of the parish of St. Thomas de la Pointe à la Caille, bishopric of Quebec, aged 38 years, for four months a settler in the country. Married to Françoise Boudrot, native of l'Acadie, aged 21 years.

They have one cow.

They have no children and no land.

CENSUS OF RIVIÈRE DU OUEST.

Census of the settlers of Rivière du Ouest, of men, women, children, &c.:

Jean Bourg, ploughman, native of l'Acadie, aged 69 years. He has been fifteen months in the country. Married to Françoise Aucoin, native of l'Acadie, aged 64 years.

They have four children—one son and three daughters :

François Bourg, aged 20 years ;

Françoise, aged 28 years ;

Anne, aged 26 years ;

Marie, aged 23 years.

They have in live stock four cows, one calf, one sow, four pigs and eight fowls or chickens.

The land on which they are settled is situated on the south side of the said Rivière du Ouest and was given to them verbally by Monsieur de Bonnaventure. They have made a clearing on which they have sown three bushels of grain.

Charles Bourg, ploughman, native of l'Acadie, aged 32 years, has been fourteen months in the country. Married to Magdelaine Blanchard, native of l'Acadie, aged 26 years.

They have one son and two daughters :

Joseph, aged 5 years ;

Ludivinne, aged 3 years.

Margueritte Joseph, one year.

They have in live stock one cow, one calf, one mare, one sheep, two sows and two pigs.

The tenure of their land and its location are as in the preceding case. They have made a clearing for the sowing of two bushels of wheat.

Joseph Braud, ploughman, a native of l'Acadie, aged 40 years. He has been in the country two years. Married to Ursulle Bourg, native of l'Acadie, aged 38 years.

They have ten daughters, Margueritte Joseph, aged 16 years.

Marie Joseph, aged 15 years.

Ursulle, aged 12 years.

Perptue, aged 10 years.

Elisabeth Françoise, aged 8 years.

Luce, aged 6 years.

Anne Joseph, aged 5 years.

Angelique, aged 4 years.

Marie Jeanne, aged 3 years.

5-6 EDWARD VII., A. 1906

Rosalie, aged one year.

Living with them is Charles Braud, native of l'Acadie, age 26 years, unmarried.

In live stock they have two oxen, one cow, two heifers, one bull, one ewe, two sows and two pigs.

The land on which they are settled is situated on the north side of the said river du Ouest and was given to them verbally by Monsieur de Bonnaventure. They have made a clearing on it for the sowing of about four bushels of wheat.

Louis Henry, ploughman, native of l'Acadie, aged 30 years, has been in the country two years. Married to Magdelaine Pitre, native of l'Acadie, aged 25 years.

They have two daughters :—

Margueritte Joseph, aged 2 years.

Helenne two months.

In live stock they have two oxen, one cow, two heifers, three ewes, one sow and two pigs.

The land on which they are settled is situated as the preceding case, and was given to them, under similar conditions, and on it they have made a clearing where they can sow four bushels of grain.

Joseph Pitre, ploughman, native of l'Acadie, aged 53 years, and has been in the country fourteen months. Married to Elisabeth Boudrot, native of l'Acadie, aged 51 years.

They have four sons :—

Pierre, aged 27 years.

Joseph, aged 18 years.

Paul, aged 16 years.

Jean Baptiste, aged 14 years.

Marie Roze, orphan, native of l'Acadie, aged 8 years, lives with them.

They have in live stock three oxen, one cow, one calf, one ewe, two sows and four pigs.

The land on which they are settled is situated on the north side of the [said river du Ouest, and was given to them verbally by Monsieur de Bonnaventure, on it they have made a clearing for sowing about four bushels of wheat.

Jean Henry dit Le Neveu, native of l'Acadie, aged 48 years, has been in the country two years. Married to Magdelainne Terriot, native of l'Acadie, aged 48 years.

They have five children, four sons and one daughter :—

Pierre Henry, aged 18 years ;

Charles, aged 16 years ;

Laurent, aged 11 years ;

François, aged 6 years ;

Marie, aged 22 years.

In live stock they have three oxen, one calf, two sheep, two sows and one pig.

The land on which they are settled is situated as in the preceding case, and was given to them under similar conditions. They have made a clearing for the sowing of about twelve bushels of wheat.

François Pitre, ploughman, native of l'Acadie, aged 25 years, has been two years in the country. Married to Rozalie Henry, native of l'Acadie, aged 23 years.

They have one daughter :—

Victoire Pitre, aged 18 months.

In live stock they have two oxen, one cow, one calf, one wether, one ewe and four sows.

The land on which they are settled is situated on the north side of the river du Ouest, and was given to them verbally by Monsieur de Bonnaventure. On it they have made a clearing for the sowing of about four bushels of wheat.

Charles Guerin, ploughman, native of l'Acadie, aged 27 years, has been two years in the country. Married to Margueritte Henry, native of l'Acadie, aged 27 years.

They have one son and one daughter :—

Marin, aged 2 years ;

Terille, aged 5 years.

Elizabeth Aucoin, mother of the said Charles Guerin, native of l'Acadie, aged 74 years.

In live stock they have two oxen, one wether, one ewe, two sows, one pig and fourteen fowls or chickens.

The land on which they are settled is situated as in the preceding case, and was given to them under similar conditions. They have made a clearing for the sowing of about four bushels of wheat.

Jean Henry dit Le Neveu, junior, native of l'Acadie, aged 21 years, has been in the country two years. Married to Marie Pitre, native of l'Acadie, aged 21 years.

They have no children ; being married in the month of January only.

Live stock : Two pigs.

The land on which they are settled is situated as in the preceding case, and was given to them under similar conditions, and they have made a clearing for the sowing of about four bushels of seed.

Charles Pitre, ploughman, native of l'Acadie, aged 23 years, has been in the country fifteen months. Married to Anne Henry, native of l'Acadie, aged 21 years.

They have no children ; being married in the month of February only.

In live stock they have one cow, two pigs and one sheep.

The land on which they are settled is situated as in the preceding case, and was given to them under similar conditions. They have made a clearing for the sowing of four bushels of wheat.

Charles Thibodeau dit Charlie, ploughman, native of l'Acadie, aged 29 years, has been in the country two years. Married to Magdeliene Henry, native of l'Acadie, aged 26 years.

They have one daughter :—

Helenne, aged 7 months.

In live stock they have one cow, one calf, one horse, one ewe, one sow and one pig.

The land on which they are settled is situated on the north side of the Rivière du Ouest, and was given to them verbally by Monsieur de Bonnaventure. They have made a clearing for the sowing of about two bushels of wheat.

Jean Henry dit le Vieux, ploughman, native of l'Acadie, aged 68 years, has been in the country two years. Married to Marie Hebert, native of l'Acadie, aged 55 years.

They have five children, two sons and two daughters :—

Simon, aged 23 years ;

Charles, aged 15 years ;

François, aged 12 years ;

Marie Joseph, aged 29 years ;

Françoise, aged 19 years ;

In live stock they have five oxen, two cows, one calf, three sheep, three sows and three pigs.

The land on which they are settled is situated as in the preceding case, and has been given to them under similar conditions. They have made a clearing for the sowing of about ten bushels of wheat.

Joseph Terriaud, ploughman, native of l'Acadie, aged 53 years, has been in the country two years. Married to Françoise Melançon, native of l'Acadie, aged 44 years.

They have seven children, five sons and two daughters :—

Estienne Terriaud, aged 21 years ;

Jasques, aged 15 years ;

Thomas, aged 9 years ;

Ambroise, aged 4 years ;

Paul, aged one year ;

Margueritte Suzanne, aged 12 years ;

Marie Magdeleine, aged 7 years.

They have in live stock two oxen, two cows, one heifer, one calf, two sows and one pig.

18—6

5-6 EDWARD VII., A. 1906

The land on which they are settled is situated as in the preceding case, and was given to them under similar conditions.   They would be able next spring to sow about four bushels of wheat, but he leaves this locality to go to Bedecq to live, and Charles Henry, his son-in-law is coming to live on this lot.

Alexis Henry, ploughman, native of l'Acadie, aged 30 years and six months, has been in the country nine months.   Married to Margueritte Hebert, native of l'Acadie, aged 23 years.

They have one daughter :—

Victoire Henry, aged 26 months.

They have in live stock one cow, one ewe, one sow, three pigs and two fowls.

They have no dwelling and are going to live near Bedecq.

Joseph Henry dit le petit homme, native of l'Acadie, ploughman, aged 45 years, has been in the country two years and nine months.   Married to Catherine Pitre, native of l'Acadie, aged 40 years.

They have eight children, three sons and five daughters :—

 Joseph Henry, aged 17 years,
 Bazille, aged 13 years,
 Jean Baptiste, aged 6 years,
 Marie, aged 19 years,
 Sephorose, aged 14 years,
 Anne, aged 13 years,
 Margueritte Modeste, aged 2 years,
 Margueritte Joseph, aged 3 months

In live stock they have four oxen, one cow, one sheep, three sows and two pigs.

The land on which they are settled is situated on the north side, of the said Rivière du Ouest and was given to them verbally by Monsieur de Bonnaventure.

They have a clearing on which they have sown two bushels of wheat and one bushel of oats.

Charles Henry, ploughman, native of l'Acadie, aged 20 years, has been in the country nine months.   Married to Françoise Josèphe Terriaud, native of l'Acadie, aged 19 years.

Their live stock all told consists of two pigs.

The land on which they are settled is that of Joseph Terriaud, their father and father-in-law.   They have sown a bushel of wheat and hope to sow four more next spring.

Jean Pitre, ploughman, native of l'Acadie, aged 55 years, has been in the country fourteen months.   Married to Margueritte Terriaud, native of l'Acadie, aged 51 years.

They have six children, three sons and three daughters :—

 Jean Pitre, aged 20 years,
 Pierre, aged 18 years,
 Enselme, aged 14 years,
 Marie, aged 30 years,
 Elizabeth, aged 28 years,
 Anne, aged 15 years.

They have the following live stock : two oxen, two calves, one wether, three ewes, one sow and four pigs.

The land on which they are settled is situated as in the preceding case and was given to them verbally.   They have made a garden on it.

Baptiste Olivier, ploughman, native of l'Acadie, aged 24 years, has been in the country, fifteen months.   Married to Suzanne Pitre, native of l'Acadie, aged 22 years.

The have three daughters ;—

 Marie, aged 31 months,
 Margueritte, aged 18 months.
 Magdelaine, aged 15 days.

Live stock : two oxen, one cow, four heifers, one bull, one ewe, one sow, two pigs and one horse.

The land on which they are settled is situated on the north side of the Rivière du Ouest, and was given to them verbally by Monsieur de Bonaventure.   They have made a clearing on it for a garden only.

Jean Henry, junior, ploughman, native of l'Acadie, aged 24 years, has been in the country two years. Married to Marie Caret, native of l'Acadie, aged 30 years.

Margueritte Joseph, aged 9 years ;
Marie Roze, aged 8 years ;
Marie, aged 6 years ;
Margueritte, aged 4 years ;
Auzitte, aged 33 months ;
Annastazie, aged 4 months.

They have in live stock, two oxen, one wether, three sheep, two pigs, two sows and nine fowls.

The land on which they are settled is situated as in the preceding case, and has been given to them under similar conditions. On it they have made a clearing for the sowing of four bushels of wheat next spring.

Census of Rivière du Nord.

Census of the inhabitants of Rivière du Nord, in men, women, children, etc.

Francois Landry, ploughman, native of l'Acadie, aged 34 years, has been in the country two years. Married to Marie Babin, native of l'Acadie, aged 32 years.

They have six children, five sons and one daughter :—

Joseph Landry, aged 16 years ;
Jean Charles, aged 14 years ;
Germain, aged 12 years ;
Francois, aged 6 years ;
Claude Raphael, aged 5 weeks ;
Marie Joseph, aged 10 years.

Their live stock is as follows : Three oxen, five cows, three calves, one horse, two ewes, one sow, one pig and twenty-four fowls or chickens.

The land on which they are settled was given them verbally by Monsieur de Bonnaventure, Commandant for the King at Isle Saint-Jean. It is situated on the north side of the river of that name. They have made on it a clearing for the sowing of about sixteen bushels of wheat the coming spring.

Benjamin Landry, ploughman, native of l'Acadie, aged 54 years, has been in the country two years. Married to Margueritte Rabin, native of l'Acadie, aged 45 years.

They have three sons and three daughters :—

Jean Landry, aged 19 years ;
Mathieu, aged 16 years ;
Joseph, aged 8 years ;
Magdelaine, aged 13 years ;
Marie, aged 11 years ;
Genneviève, aged 4 years.

Living with them are, Cecille Melançon, mother of the said Benjamin, native of l'Acadie, aged 86 years ;
Daniel Le Jeune, native of l'Acadie, aged 30 years ;
Roze Landry, their niece, native of l'Acadie, aged 18 years ;
Magdelaine Dingle, native of Niganiche, aged 18 years.

They have the following live stock : Two oxen, two cows, two heifers, one bull, one calf, one ewe, one sow, three pigs and twenty-one fowls or chickens.

The land on which they are settled was given them verbally by Monsieur de Bonnaventure. They have made a clearing on it for the sowing of eight bushels of wheat next spring.

Augustin Landry, ploughman, native of l'Acadie, aged 26 years, has been in the country two years. Married to Margueritte Granger, native of l'Acadie, aged 23 years.

They have one son and one daughter :

Benjamin Landry, aged 18 months.
Margueritte, aged 3 months.

18—6½

5-6 EDWARD VII., A. 1906

They have the following live stock, two oxen, two cows, one bull, two ewes, two sows, one pig and fifteen fowls or chickens.

The land on which they are settled was given to them verbally by Monsieur de Bonnaventure. They have made a clearing on it for the sowing of two bushels of wheat next spring.

Charles Landry, ploughman, native of l'Acadie, aged 21 years, has been in the country two years. Married to Marie Granger, native of l'Acadie, aged 19 years.

They have Pierre Landry, their son, aged six days.

They have in live stock :—one ox, two cows, one ewe and eight fowls or chickens.

The land on which they are settled was given them verbally by Monsieur de Bonnaventure. They have made no clearing, having been but a short time on their land.

Amand Daigre, ploughman, native of l'Acadie, aged 40 years, has been in the country two years. Married to Elisabeth Vincent, native of l'Acadie, age 34 years.

They have six children, two sons and four daughters :

Simon Daigre, aged 15 years ;

Pierre, aged 4 years ;

Margueritte, aged 10 years ;

Magdelaine, aged 8 years ;

Auzitte, aged 6 years;

Marie Joseph, aged 10 months.

They have the following live stock : one cow, two calves, one sow and four pigs.

The land on which they are settled was given to them verbally by Monsieur de Bonnaventure. They have made a clearing on it for the sowing of four bushels of wheat.

Charles Daigre, ploughman, native of l'Acadie, aged 38 years, has been in the country for two years. Married to Cecille Landry, native of l'Acadie, aged 36 years.

They have two daughters :

Margueritte Cecille, aged 2 years ;

Marie, aged 9 months.

Living with them are :—Rémy Daigre, brother of said Charles, native of l'Acadie, aged 25 years ;

Marie Joseph, their sister, aged 10 years.

They have the following live stock : four oxen, three cows, one bull, two calves, one heifer, three sows, five pigs and twenty-two fowls or chickens.

The land on which they are settled was given them verbally by Monsieur de Bonnaventure. They have made a clearing on it for the sowing of six bushels of wheat.

Alexandre Daigre, ploughman, native of l'Acadie, aged 22 years, has been in the country one year. Married to Elisabeth Granger, native of l'Acadie, aged 20 years.

They have Charles Daigre, their son, aged 3 months.

In live stock they have : one ox, one cow and one sow.

The land on which they are settled was given to them verbally by M. de Bonnaventure. They have made no clearing, having been there only a short time.

CENSUS OF RIVIÈRE DU NORD-EST.

Census of the inhabitants of the Rivière du Nord-est, in men, women, children, etc. North side :—

Enselme Boudrot, ploughman, native of l'Acadie, aged 33 years, has been in the country two years. Married to Geneviève Giroir, native of l'Acadie, aged 31 years.

They have three sons and one daughter :—

Enselme, aged 7 years ;

Simon, aged one year ;

Henriette, aged 4 years.

Their live stock consists of four oxen, four cows, four ewes, and two pigs.

The land on which they are settled is situated on the north side of the said river, and was given to them verbally by M. de Bonnaventure. They have made a clearing on it for the sowing of twenty bushels of wheat next spring.

Denis Boudrot, ploughman, native of l'Acadie, aged 75 years, has been in the country two years. Married to Anne Vincent, native of l'Acadie, aged 60 years.

They have the following live stock : three oxen, two cows, two pigs, one sow and two fowls.

The land on which they are settled was given to them verbally by Monsieur de Bonnaventure. They have made a clearing on it for the sowing of 20 bushels of wheat.

Isidore Daigre, native of l'Acadie, aged 27 years, has been in the country two years. Married to Agatte Bariaud, native of l'Acadie, aged 21 years. They have one son, Firmain, aged one year.

Their live stock is as follows : two oxen, two cows, one mare, three ewes, two sows, three pigs and four fowls or chickens.

The land on which they are settled was given them verbally by Monsieur de Bonnaventure, and upon it they have made a clearing for the sowing of six bushels of wheat.

Marie Boudrot, widow of Pierre Richard, very poor, native of l'Acadie, aged 36 years, has been in the country two years.

She has six children, five sons and one daughter :—

Pierre Richard, aged 19 years ;
Paul, aged 17 years ;
Joseph, aged 13 years ;
Honoré, aged 10 years ;
Thomas, aged 6 years ;
Marie, aged 15 years.

They have no live stock.

The land on which she is settled is situated on the north bank of the said Rivière du Nord-Est. It was given to her verbally by Monsieur de Bonnaventure and he resumes possession as they have made no improvements.

Marie Madeleine Pitre, widow of Pierre Godet, poor, native of l'Acadie, aged 39 years, has been in the country two years.

She has six sons and three daughters :—

Etienne Godet, aged 23 years.
Pierre, aged 23 years.
Dominique, aged 19 years.
François, aged 14 years.
Cyprien, aged 12 years.
Joseph, aged 6 years.
Doratte, aged 16 years.
Anne, aged 9 years.
Marie, aged 12 years.

Live stock : she has two oxen, one cow, one ewe, one sow and one hen.

The land on which they are settled is situated as in the preceding case and was given to them verbally by M. de Bonnaventure. They have made a clearing for sowing thirty-two bushels of wheat.

Jean Blanchard, ploughman, native of l'Acadie, aged 40 years, has been in the country 14 months. Married to Anne Bourg, native of l'Acadie, aged 30 years.

They have one son and two daughters :—

Jean Grégoire, aged 7 years.
Anne, aged 5 years.
Cécile, aged 18 months.

They have live stock as follow : four oxen, one heifer, five sheep, one sow, four pigs, and three fowls.

The land on which they are settled was given to them verbally by M. de Bonneventure. They have made a garden on it.

Joseph Bourg, ploughman, native of l'Acadie, aged 41 years and 5 months. He has been in the country one year. Married to Françoise Dugast, aged 29 years.

They have four sons and four daughters :—

Joseph Bourg, aged 16 years.
Bernard, aged 10 years,

CANADIAN ARCHIVES

5-6 EDWARD VII., A. 1906

François, aged 40 months.
Jean Baptiste, aged 3 months.
Agnès, aged 14 years.
Isabelle, aged 12 years.
Marie Françoise, aged 8 years.
Margueritte Josephe, aged 6 years.

They have live stock as follows : four oxen, one cow, one calf, two sows and three pigs.

The land on which they are settled was given to them verbally by Monsieur de Bonnaventure. On it they have made a garden.

Paul Douaron dit le Grand Paul, native of l'Acadie, ploughman, aged 42 years, has been in the country two years. Married Marguerite Michel, native of l'Acadie, aged 46 years.

They have three sons and six daughters :—
Pierre Paul, aged 12 years.
Jean Baptiste, aged 8 years.
Joseph, aged 4 years.
Margueritte Joseph, aged 17 years.
Anne Appoline, aged 15 years.
Blanche, aged 10 years.
Auzitte, aged 6 years.
Roze, aged 2 years.
Helenne, aged 8 months.

His live stock consists of four bulls, three cows, two heifers, two sows, two pigs and twenty-five fowls or chickens.

The land on which they are settled was given to them verbally by M. de Bonnaventure. They have made a clearing on it where they hope to sow eight bushels of wheat next spring.

Claude Dugats, ploughman, native of l'Acadie, aged 40 years, has been in the country twelve months. Married to Marie Joseph Aucoin, native of l'Acadie, aged 43 years

They have five sons and three daughters :—
Joseph Dugats, aged 16 years.
Jean Baptiste, aged 14 years.
Victor, aged 8 years.
Théodore, aged 6 years.
Paul, aged 4 years.
Marie, aged 9 years.
Angélique, aged 7 years.
Anne, aged 5 years.

His live stock consists of two oxen, two cows, two heifers, three sows, four pigs and twelve fowls or chickens.

The land on which they are settled was given to them by M. de Bonnaventure. They have made a clearing on it for sowing two bushels of wheat.

Paul Aucoin, ploughman, native of l'Acadie, aged 41 years, has been 13 months in the country. Married to Marie la Blanche, native of l'Acadie, aged 37 years.

They have a son and three daughters :—
Joseph, aged 4 years.
Marie Joseph, aged 8 years.
Marguerite Suzanne, aged 6 years,
Terzille, aged 2 years.

They have the following live stock :—
One ox, one cow, one wether, one sow, four pigs and seven fowls or chickens.

The land on which they are settled was given to them verbally by Monsieur de Bonnaventure, and they have made a clearing on it for sowing a bushel of wheat.

Michel Aucoin, ploughman, native of l'Acadie, aged 75 years, has been in the country thirteen months. Married to Jeanne Bourg, native of l'Acadie, aged 69 years.

They have no children with them. They have in live stock, : one cow and one sow. They have no land but are settled on the land of Paul Aucoin and Claude Dugast their son and son-in-law.

Le Sr. Amand Bugeaud, senior, merchant and navigator, native of l'Acadie, aged 51 years, has been in the country four years. Married to Dame Claire Doussets, native of l'Acadie, aged 37 years. They have no children with them but Françoise Blanchard, mother of the said dame.

They have the following live stock : six oxen, four bulls, nine cows, six calves, one horse, one sow, three pigs, five sheep and twenty-five fowls ; and a vessel of twenty-five tons.

The land on which they are settled was granted to them by Messieurs de Bonnaventure and de Goutin, comprising————arpents of front and forty of depth. They have made a clearing on which they hope to sow twelve bushels of wheat next spring.

Le Sr. Pierre Gautier, navigator, native of l'Acadie, aged 24 years, has been in the country three years. Married to Jeanne La Forest, native of Louisbourg, aged 18 years.

He has in live stock, two oxen and six sheep.

The land on which they are settled is situated on the north side of the said Rivière du Nord-Est, and was given them verbally by M. de Bonnaventure. He has made no clearing.

Le Sr. Jean Bugeaud, ploughman, native of l'Acadie, aged 24 years, has been in the country two years. Married to Anne Douville, native of the harbour of Saint-Pierre, in the north of this island, aged 26 years.

They have no children.

In live stock they have two oxen, three cows, two calves, one horse, two wethers, three ewes, one sow, three pigs, seven geese, seven turkeys and thirty fowls or chickens.

The land on which they are settled was given to them by the Sr. Joseph Bugeaud, their father and father-in-law, on which the said Jean Bugeaud has made a clearing where he has sowed four bushels of wheat and five bushels of oats, and he hopes next spring to sow sixteen bushels.

Le Sr. Joseph Bugeaud, ploughman, native of l'Acadie, aged 53 years, has been three years in the country. Married to Marie Joseph Landry, native of l'Acadie, aged 48 years.

They have three sons and five daughters :—

Charles Bugeaud, aged 21 years ;
François Placide, aged 16 years ;
Mathurin, aged 10 years ;
Elizabeth, aged 19 years ;
Marie Roze, aged 17 years ;
Anne, aged 15 years ;
Marie, aged 11 years ;
Félicité, aged 6 years.

They have the following live stock : two oxen, two cows, one calf, two ewes and their young, one sow, two pigs and three fowls.

The land on which they are settled is situated on the north side of the said Rivière du Nord-Est, like the preceding, and was given to them by a permit from Monsieur de Bonnaventure. On it they have made a clearing where they have sowed six bushels of wheat and a half bushel of peas, and they hope next spring to sow twelve bushels more.

Joseph Gautier, senior, navigator, native of l'Acadie, aged 35 years, has been in the country three years. Married to Demoiselle Margueritte Bugeaud, native of l'Acadie, aged 24 years.

They have one son and one daughter :—

Joseph Gauthier, aged 3 years ;
Elisabeth, aged 11 months.

Baptiste Allain, native of l'Acadie, aged 12 years, lives with them.

5-6 EDWARD VII., A. 1906

In live stock they have three oxen, five cows, two heifers, one horse, four calves' four ewes, three sows, three pigs, eight geese, thirty fowls, and one vessel of 45 to 50 tons.

The land on which they are settled is situated as in the preceding case and was given to them verbally by Monsieur de Bonnaventure. They have made a clearing on which they have sown six bushels of wheat, and hope to sow twelve bushels next spring.

Paul Broussard dit Courtiche, ploughman, native of l'Acadie, aged 25 years, has been in the country 26 months. Married to Magdelaine Landry, native of l'Acadie, aged 23 years 8 months.

They have one son :—

Jean Baptiste, aged 2 years.

In live stock they have four oxen, one cow, three bulls, one horse, three ewes, four pigs and three fowls.

The land on which they are settled is situated as in the preceding case, and was given to them verbally by M. de Bonnaventure. They have made a clearing on it where they have sown eleven bushels of wheat and six of peas, and they hope to sow twenty-five bushels next spring.

Le Sr. Louis Amand Bugeaud, junior, navigator, native of l'Acadie, aged 23 years, has been in the country four years. Not married.

Living with him are :—

Antoine Amand Gautrot, native of l'Acadie, aged 20 years ;

Charles Gautrot, his brother, native of l'Acadie, aged 17 years, domestics.

His live stock consist of eleven cows, four calves, one sow, four pigs, one wether, ten ewes and 25 fowls.

The land on which he is settled is situated on the north side of the said Rivière du Nord-Est, and was granted him under a permit from Monsieur Benoist, dated 1749, comprising seven arpents frontage by forty in depth. This land is called "la source à Bellair." There is a clearing on which they have sown three bushels of wheat, two bushels of oats and three bushels of peas, and ploughed land for sowing ten bushels of wheat.

Dame Marie Allain, widow of the Sr. Nicolas Gautier, merchant, aged 58 years, and has been three years in the country.

She has two sons and two daughters :—

Joseph Gautier, aged 19 years ;

Jean, aged 11 years ;

Elisabeth, aged 15 years ;

Marie, aged 12 years.

In her employ is Guillaume Lagneau, of Indian nationality, native of Baston, aged 55 years.

She has the following live stock :—six oxen, four cows, three heifers, two bulls, three calves, two wethers, two ewes and 80 fowls.

The land on which they are settled is situated on the north side of the Rivière du Nord-Est at Source à Bellair, and was given them by permit from Monsieur Benoist dated 24th January, 1749. It comprises seven arpents frontage by forty arpents in depth. They have made a clearing and have sowed there seven bushels of wheat and one bushel of oats.

The said lady enjoys the possession of another piece of land, situated at the place de Brouillant, of four arpents frontage by forty in depth.

Jacques Langlois dit Jacqui, carpenter and ploughman, native of l'Acadie, aged 36 years, has been nine years in the country. Married to Marie Joseph Darambour, native of l'Acadie, aged 25 years.

They have two sons and one daughter :—

Aimable, aged 4 years 6 months.

Jacques Mathieu, aged 20 months.

Cecille, aged 6 years.

They have in live stock two oxen, two cows, one calf, three ewes, two sows, five pigs, and twelve fowls.

The land on which they are settled is situated as in the preceding case, and was granted to them verbally by Monsieur Duchambon. They have made a clearing and sowed on it ten bushels and a half of wheat, one bushel of oats, two bushels of peas, and ploughed land for sowing two bushels besides.

Joseph Michel, ploughman, native of l'Acadie, aged 24 years, and has been 18 months in the country. Married to Geneviève Du Rambour, native of Port St. Pierre, in the north of the island, aged 19 years.

They have Marie Joseph Michel, aged three months.

Their stock is as follows : one cow, two ewes, one sow, one pig and six fowls.

The land on which they are settled is situated as in the preceding case and was given to them verbally by Monsieur de Bonnaventure. They have made a clearing on it where they have sown three bushels and a half of wheat and half a bushel of peas.

Etienne Charles Philippe dit LaRoche, native of Paris, aged 37 years, and he has been in the country . . . . . years. Married to Marie Mazerolle, native of l'Acadie.

They have five children, all sons :—

Jean Baptiste Du Rambour, aged 15 years.

Jacques Du Rambour, aged 13 years.

Joseph Philippe, son of said Etienne.

Charles Philippe, aged 8 years.

Joseph, aged 5 years.

Jean Pierre, aged 3 years.

Of live stock they have two oxen, one cow, one calf, three ewes, one sow, two pigs and ten fowl.

The land on which they are settled is situated on the north side of the Rivière du Nord-Est, and was granted to them by Messieurs de Pensens and Dubuisson. They have made on it a clearing for sowing thirty-two bushels of grain and this year they have sown on it sixteen bushels of wheat, one of oats and two of peas.

Jean Helie, master tailor, native of the town of Poitiers, in Poitou, aged 46 years, and has been in the country three years. Married to Françoise Bonnevie, native of l'Acadie, aged 50 years.

They have one son of a previous marriage :

Jean Baptiste Olivier, aged 19 years,

Jeanne, native of l'Acadie, aged 30 years.

Their live stock consist of two cows, two oxen, one bull, two heifers, eight pigs and one cow in calf.

The land on which they are settled, is situated as in the preceding case and was given to them verbally by Monsieur de Bonnaventure. They have sown on it four bushels and a half of wheat, and have besides fallow land sufficient for the sowing of another eight bushels.

François Dugay, ploughman, native of the parish of Pluvigné, bishopric of Vannes, in Brittany, aged 50 years, and has been in the country 36 years. Married to Marie Bonnevie, native of l'Acadie, aged 48 years.

They have six children, four sons and two daughters :

Charles Dugay, aged 14 years ;

Jean Baptiste, aged 13 years ;

Olivier, aged 6 years ;

Jacques, aged 4 years ;

Margueritte, aged 10 years ;

Marie, aged 19 months.

Their live stock consist of two oxen, one horse, one ewe, one sow, four pigs and ten fowls.

The land on which they are settled is situated as in the preceding case. They have made a clearing for the sowing of five bushels of wheat in the coming spring.

François Haché Galland, ploughman, native of l'Acadie, aged 45 years, and has been 28 years in the country. Married to Anne Boudrot, native of l'Acadie, aged 33 years.

They have seven sons and one daughter:

François Silvestre Haché, aged 16 years ;

5-6 EDWARD VII., A. 1906

Louis, aged 14 years ;
Jasques Ange, aged 13 years ;
Jean François, aged 11 years ;
René, aged 9 years ;
Joseph, aged 4 years ;
Charles, aged 4 months ;
Marie Roze, aged 5 years.

They have the following live stock : four oxen, four cows, three heifers, two bulls, four sows, two pigs, three fowls : Also, a corn mill made of coarse stone, which is used at the most only half the year.

The land on which they are settled is situated on the North side of the Riviére du Nord-Est, and was given to them by grant from Monsieur Duvivier, under date of the first July, 1745. It comprises four arpents frontage by forty arpents in depth. They have sown ten bushels of wheat and two of peas and have fallow land sufficient for the sowing of sixteen bushels more.

Joseph Pretieux, ploughman, native of La Rochelle, aged 63 years, and he has been 28 years in the country. Married to Anne Haché Galland, native of l'Acadie, aged 48 years.

They have three sons and one daughter :
Pierre Pretieux, aged 15 years,
Joseph, aged 13 years,
Louis, aged 11 years,
Louise Margueritte, aged 18 years.

Of live stock they have four oxen, two heifers, one wether, five ewes, one sow and six pigs and two cows with four calves.

The land on which they are settled is situated as in the preceding case and is held by them under grant by Monsieur Duvivier, dated the first July, 1745. It is four arpents in depth. They have made a clearing and have sown seven bushels of wheat, two bushels of rye and have sufficient fallow land for sowing eighteen bushels more.

Augustin Doucet dit Justice, ploughman, native of Quebec, aged 29 years, and has been in the country eighteen years. Married to Anne Marie Pretieux, native of Port La Joye, of this island, aged 20 years.

The said Dousset has two sons by a previous marriage :
Joachim Dousset, aged nine years,
Joseph, aged 7 years.

In live stock they have : one bull, one heifer, one ewe and one sow.

The land on which they are settled is situated on the north shore of the Rivière du Nord-Est, and was given to them verbally by Monsieur de Bonnaventure. No clearing has been made, permission having been given them to go on the land only in the month of June.

François Haché Galland, son of Marie Genty, ploughman, native of Louisbourg, aged 25 years, has been in the country two years. Married to Françoise Olivier, native of l'Acadie, aged 20 years.

They have Marie Auzitte, their daughter, aged 17 months.

And in live stock they have two oxen, two cows, one ewe, nine fowls, and one cow in calf.

The land on which they are settled is situated as in the preceding case and was given to them by Monsieur Duvivier. They have made a clearing on it where they have sown seven bushels of wheat and they have fallow land besides for the sowing of fifteen bushels.

Jean Bte. Haché Galland, ploughman, native of l'Acadie, aged 32 years, has been 29 years in the country. Married to Anne Olivier, native of l'Acadie, aged 33 years.

They have one son and one daughter :
Pierre Paul Haché, aged 4 months,
Anne Marie, aged 22 months.

They have in live stock : four oxen, one cow, one horse, one wether, three ewes, one sow, one pig, and five fowls.

The land on which they are settled is situated as in the preceding case and is held under a grant accorded to them by Monsieur Duvivier.

They have made a clearing for the sowing of seventeen bushels of seed on which they have sown seven bushels of wheat.

Marie Genty, widow, very poor, of Jean Baptiste Haché Galland, native of l'Acadie, aged 48 years, and she has been 29 years in the country.

She has seven children, five sons and two daughters :—

Antonine Haché, aged 18 years ;

Michel, aged 16 years ;

Joseph, aged 14 years ;

Louis, aged 12 years ;

Georges, aged 10 years ;

Marie Joseph, aged 25 years ;

Margueritte Louise, aged 23 years.

Of live stock they have two oxen, one cow, one horse, one wether, two ewes, two sows, four pigs, five geese and ten fowls.

The land on which they are settled is situated as in the preceding case. They hold it by grant from Monsieur Duvivier. They have made a clearing for the sowing of thirty two bushels, but have only sown seven not having been able to procure more owing to their poverty.

Michel Deveau, ploughman, native of l'Acadie, aged 33 years. Has been in the country twenty years. Married to Marie Poirier, native of l'Acadie, aged 25 years.

They have one son and two daughters :—

Michel Deveau, aged 3 years ;

Marie, aged 5 years ;

Louise, aged 10 months.

In live stock, they have two oxen, one cow, one horse, one wether, four ewes, five sows, four pigs and nine fowls.

The land on which they are settled is situated as in the preceding case, and was given to them verbally by Monsieur de Bonnaventure   No clearing has been made on said land owing to its not being good for cultivation. They have made their clearing on land situated at the harbour Au Sauvage where they have sown six bushels of wheat, one bushel of oats, and one bushel and a half of peas and have fallow land for the sowing of ten bushels. They hold this land verbally as they do the other.

Charles Haché dit Charlit, ploughman, native of Port La Joye, aged 27 years. Married to Anne Desveau, native of the harbour Au Sauvage, aged 18 years. They have in live stock two oxen, one cow, one heifer, one calf, two wethers, three ewes, two sows, one pig and seven fowls.

The land on which they are settled is situated on the north shore of the Riviére du Nord-Est, at the part called La Grande Source. It was granted to them by Monsieur Dupont Duvivier. They made no clearing, finding the soil was poor in quality. They have made a clearing on the Crown lands where they have sown eight bushels of wheat.

Pierre Deveaux, ploughman, native of l'Acadie, aged 29 years, has been in the country 24 years. Married to Marie Haché, native of l'Acadie, aged 28 years.

They have two sons and one daughter :—

Blaise Deveaux, aged 5 years ;

Charles, aged 5 months ;

Marie Modeste, aged 2 years.

François Haché, his brother, native of l'Acadie, aged 21 years.

In live stock they have two oxen, two bulls, one heifer, two mares, one wether, four ewes, one sow, three pigs and seventeen fowls.

The land on which they are settled is situated as in the preceding case, and was granted to them by Monsieur Dupont Duvivier. They have made a clearing on it for the sowing of sixteen bushels and have sown eight.

Charles Poitier, ploughman, native of l'Acadie, aged 27 years and has been in the country three years. Married to Marie Blanche Caissy, native of l'Acadie, aged 26 years.

5-6 EDWARD VII., A. 1906

They have Modeste Poitier, their daughter, aged 3 years.

Rosalie Caissy, her sister, native of l'Acadie, aged 19 years.

In live stock they have two oxen, two bulls, one cow, one wether, two ewes, one sow, three pigs and seven fowl.

The land on which they are settled is situated as in the preceeding case and was given them by Monsieur Benoist. They have made no clearing on it for similar reasons to those already given in other cases. They have made a clearing in the Crown lands for sowing eight bushels of seed.

Census of Rivière du Nord-Est.

Census of the inhabitants of the south side of Rivière du Nord-Est, in men, women, children, etc.

Nicholas Bouchard, ploughman, native of the parish of St. Thomas, bishopric of Quebec, aged 29 years, has been three years in the country. Married to Marie Chias-son, native of l'Acadie, aged 29 years.

They have one son and one daughter :—

Nicolas Bouchard, aged 4 years ;

Marie, aged 2 years.

Their live stock consists of two oxen, two cows, two heifers, two bulls, two calves, four wethers, three ewes, three sows, one pig and ten fowls.

The land on which they are settled is situated on the south side of the Rivière du Nord-Est, and was given to them verbally by Monsieur de Bonnaventure. On it they have made a clearing in which they have sown five bushels of wheat, and fallow land for the sowing of another five bushels.

Pierre Haché, son of Marie Genty, ploughman, native of l'Acadie, aged 27 years, and has been in the country 16 years. Married to Marie Douaron, native of l'Acadie, aged 22 years.

They have no children, not being long married.

Magdelaine Douaron, native of Isle St. Jean, aged two years, lives with them.

Of live stock they have two oxen, one bull, one mare, two ewes, one sow and five fowls.

The land on which they are settled is situated as in the preceding case, and is held under grant, dated third January, 1745, from Monsieur Duvivier.

It comprises four arpents of frontage by forty in depth. They have made no clear-ing having been only a short time on the land.

François Vescot, ploughman, native of l'Acadie, aged 37 years, and has been in the country 34 years. Married to Anne Marie Arceneau, native of l'Acadie, aged 26 years.

They have two sons and one daughter :—

François Vescot, aged 7 years ;

Michel, aged 4 years ;

Marie, aged 2 years.

Their live stock consists of four oxen, four cows, four bulls, one heifer, one calf, one mare, eight wethers, three ewes, four sows, four pigs and twelve fowls.

The land on which they are settled is situated on the south side of the Rivière du Nord-Est. They hold it by grant from Monsieur Benoist. They have made a clearing on which they have sown fourteen bushels of wheat, two bushels of oats, and one bushel and a half of peas.

Charles Haché dit Galland, ploughman, native of l'Acadie, aged 53 years, and has been in the country 30 years. Married to Geneviève Lavergne, native of l'Acadie, aged 42 years.

They have two sons and three daughters :—

Joseph Haché, aged 8 years ;

Jean Baptiste, aged 2 years ;

Louise Geneviève, aged 22 years ;

Anne, aged 15 years ;

Anne, aged 12 years.

Damoiselle Louise Margueritte Poitier Dubuisson, native of Montreal, bishopric of Quebec, aged 42 years.

Their live stock is as follows : Five oxen, five cows, two heifers, three bulls, one calf, eight wethers, fourteen ewes, four sows, six pigs and five fowls.

The land on which they are settled is situated as in the preceding case and was granted as follows, to wit : One piece of land granted by Monsieur Duvivier in 1745 under date the first of July, comprising five arpents, five perches of frontage and forty arpents in length ; and another piece of land that the said Charles Haché has purchased from Joseph Haché, his brother, granted to said Joseph Haché by Monsieur Duvivier under date sixth July, 1745, comprising four arpents of frontage and forty arpents in depth, the two pieces of land lying contiguous to each other and forming one estate of nine arpents five perches frontage by forty arpents in depth. They have sown on it twenty-four bushels of wheat, three bushels of oats and three bushels of peas.

Pierre Haché Galland, widower, ploughman and navigator, native of l'Acadie, aged 51 years, has been 30 years in the country.

He has three sons and five daughters :—

Louis Haché, aged 25 years ;
Pierre, aged 23 years ;
Jean Baptiste, aged 17 years ;
Geneviève, aged 21 years ;
Marie Anne, aged 19 years ;
Louise, aged 15 years ;
Anne, aged 13 years ;
Marie Joseph, aged 8 years.

In live stock they have six oxen, four cows, two bulls, two calves, two mares, five wethers, eleven ewes, seven sows, two pigs and twenty-three fowls.

The land on which they are settled is situated on the south side of the Rivière du Nord-Est of Port La Joye. They hold it by grant, and have made a clearing on which they have sown thirty-two bushels of wheat, one bushel of oats, and have made fallow land for the sewing of sixteen bushels.

Pierre Duval, blacksmith and ploughman, native of the parish of Sougeal, bishopric of Rennes, aged 48 years, and has been 22 years in the country. Married to Marie Magdelaine Haché, native of l'Acadie, aged 42 years.

They have two sons and four daughters :—

Jean Pierre Duval, aged 10 years ;
Charles, aged 6 months ;
Marie Joseph, aged 17 years ;
Anne, aged 15 years ;
Margueritte, aged 7 years ;
Auzitte, aged 5 years.

François Mazierre, orphan, native of this island, aged 6 years.

They have in live stock, four oxen, four cows, two heifers, one bull, two calves, one mare with young, four wethers, ten ewes, two sows, five pigs, and fifty fowls or chickens.

The land on which they are settled is situated as in the preceding case, and was granted them by Messieurs Duvivier and Degoutin. On it they have made a clearing where they have sown sixteen bushels of wheat and eight bushels of oats, and made fallow land sufficient for the sowing of seventeen bushels more.

Charles Martin, ploughman, native of l'Acadie, aged 40 years, has been in the country 30 years. Married to Françoise Carré, native of l'Acadie, aged 30 years. No children.

Their live stock consists of four oxen, five cows, one calf, one mare, five wethers, two sows, fourteen pigs and sixteen fowls or chickens ; and a boat.

The land on which they are settled is situated as in the preceding case. They hold it under grant from Messieurs Duvivier and Degoutin. On it they have made a clearing where they have sown ten bushels of wheat, four bushels of oats, and two bushels of peas.

5-6 EDWARD VII., A. 1906

Barthélemy Martin, ploughman, native of l'Acadie, aged 42 years ; has been in the country 30 years. Married to Magdeleine Carret, native of l'Acadie, aged 38 years.

They have six sons and four daughters :—

Pierre Paul Martin, aged 20 years.

Charles Michel, aged 18 years.

François, aged 16 years.

Jacques Christophe, aged 14 years.

Joseph, aged 12 years.

Jean Foelix, aged one year.

Marie Joseph Martin, aged 13 years.

Euphrosinne, aged 9 years.

Marie Joseph, aged 7 years.

Jeanne, aged 3 years.

They have the following live stock : four oxen, four cows, four heifers, nine wethers, eleven ewes, five pigs, nine fowls.

The land on which they are settled is situated as in the preceding cases and was given to them by grant from Messieurs Duvivier and Degoutin. They have made a clearing on it where they have sown forty bushels of wheat, fifteen bushels of oats, and half a bushel of peas, and made fallow land for the sowing of twenty bushels more.

Joseph Martin, ploughman, native of l'Acadie, aged 50 years ; has been in the country 30 years. Married to Elizabeth Caret, widow of the late Dousset, native of l'Acadie, aged 32 years.

They have two sons and four daughters :—

Joseph Doucet, aged 12 years.

Pierre, aged 9 years.

Margueritte, aged 13 years.

Rose, aged 6 years.

Marie Joseph, aged 17 months.

Anne, aged 4 months.

Their live stock consists of five oxen, one cow, two calves, two wethers, three ewes, two sows, four pigs, and ten fowls or chickens.

Honnoré Bourgeois, ploughman, native of l'Acadie, aged 52 years, and has been two years in the country. Married to Marie Magdelaine Pichard, native of the parish of Saint-Léger, bishopric of Chartres, aged 48 years.

They have one son and one daughter :—

Margueritte Bourgeois, aged 17 years.

François, aged 15 years.

In live stock they have four oxen, four cows, four calves, one horse, six wethers, twelve ewes, two sows, four pigs and twelve fowls.

The land on which they are settled is situated on the south side of the Rivière du Nord-Est of Port La Joye, and they acquired it from Charles Hache as guardian and curator of the children, minor and major, of the late Renné Rassicot. They have made a clearing for the sowing of forty bushels of seed where they have sown twelve bushels of wheat, one bushel of barley, one bushel of sprat, four bushels of oats and six bushels of peas.

CENSUS.

Census of the settlers of the Rivière de Peugiguit, said river being situated on the south side of the Rivière du Nord-Est.

Jean Baptiste Rassicot, ploughman, native of Port La Joye.

His live stock consists of one ox, one sow and one pig.

The land on which he is settled is situated on the east side of the Rivière de Peugiguit. It was given to him under grant from Monsieur Benoist, and on it he has made a clearing sufficient for sowing ten bushels of seed of which he has sown four.

Pierre Galloa, ploughman, native of the parish of St Pierre Langers, aged 42 years, has been in the country 30 years. Married to Marguerite Montaury, native of Port Toulouse, aged 33 years.

They have three sons and two daughters.

Felix Galloa, aged 7 years.

Jean Baptiste, aged 5 years.

Joseph, aged 2 years.

Marie Françoise, aged 13 years.

Henriette, aged 11 years.

Their live stock consists of two oxen, two cows, two calves, one wether, six ewes, three pigs and one hen.

The land on which they are settled is situated as in the preceding case and was granted to them by Monsieur Benoist. They have made a clearing on it sufficient for the sowing of nine bushels of which they have sown three bushels of wheat and one of peas.

Paul Olivier, ploughman, native of l'Acadie, aged 25 years, has been in the country three years. Married to Margueritte Poyrier, native of l'Acadie, aged 27 years.

They have one son and one daughter :—

Jean Baptiste Olivier, aged 2 years.

Marie Magdelaine, aged 11 months.

Of live stock they have two oxen, one cow, one heifer, one sow, seven pigs and five fowls.

The land on which they are settled is situated as in the preceding case, and they hold it by permission of Monsieur Duchambon and M. Degoutin. They have made a clearing where they have sown eight bushels of wheat, and half a bushel of peas and have fallow land sufficient for seven bushels more.

Mathieu Glin dit Cadet, fisherman and ploughman, native of the town of Bayonne, aged 58 years, and has been in the country 34 years. Married to Marie Martin, native of l'Acadie, aged 54 years.

They have one son and three daughters :—

Jean François Montaudy, aged 25 years.

Anne Agathe, aged 27 years.

Marie Joseph, aged 19 years.

Marie Louise Glin, aged 16 years.

Their live stock consists of four oxen, three cows, three calves, four wethers, three ewes, five sows, one pig and two fowls.

The land on which they are settled is situated as in the preceding case. It was given to them by Monsieur Benoist. They have made a clearing where they have sown ten bushels of wheat, one bushel of peas and have fallow land for the sowing of six bushels besides.

Pierre Mathurin Girard dit Crespin, soldier of the former company of Monsieur de Bonnaventure, native of the parish of St. Coulombin, bishopric of Nantes, aged 31 years, and has been in the colony three years. Married to Marie Margueritte Closquinet. native of the country, aged 25 years.

Their live stock consists of two oxen, three cows, two calves, three wethers, three ewes, three sows, three pigs and eight fowls.

The land on which they are settled is situated as in the preceding case, and was granted by Messieurs Duvivier and Degoutin They have made a clearing for the sowing of twelve bushels of wheat next spring.

Jacques Haché dit Galland, ploughman, native of the country, aged 25 years. Married to Anne Boudrot, native of Port Toulouse, aged 25 years.

They have one son and two daughters :—

Pierre Haché, aged 4 years.

Marie, aged 30 months.

Geneviève, aged 10 months.

Louis Racicot, native of the island, aged 13 years.

Their live stock consists of the following : two oxen, five cows, four calves, six ewes, one wether, two sows and twelve fowls or chickens.

The land on which they are settled is situated as in the preceding case, and was granted to them by Monsieur Duvivier. On it they have made a clearing and have sown ten bushels of wheat and one bushel of peas, and have fallow land for fourteen bushels in addition.

Joseph Poirier, ploughman, native of l'Acadie, aged 31 years, has been in the country one year. Married to Ursulle Renauld, native of l'Acadie, aged 30 years.

They have Marie Poirier, their daughter, aged 2 years, Marie Lapierre, his mother.

Pierre Renauld, his brother, native of l'Acadie, aged 18 years.

Julict, native of the same, age 16 years.

Anne, aged 13 years.

Enselme, aged 8 years.

In live stock they have one cow with calf, two sows, one pig and seven fowls.

The land on which they are settled is situated as in the preceeding case. It was given to them verbally by Monsieur de Bonnaventure. They have made on it a clearing sufficient for the sowing of twelve bushels of seed the coming spring.

Census.

Census of Rivière de Peugiguit on the west side.

François Dousset, ploughman, native of l'Acadie, aged 26 years and has been in the country 12 years. Married to Margueritte Jacquemire, native of Louisbourg, aged 26 years.

In live stock they have one bull, one cow, one calf, one wether, seven ewes, and one sow.

The land on which they are settled is situated on the west side of the Rivière de de Peugiguit. It was given to them by a grant from Monsieur Duvivier. They have made a clearing on it on which they sowed eight bushels of wheat, and have fallow land for 12 bushels more.

Pierre Closquinet, ploughman, native of Louisbourg, aged 27 years. Married to Marie Joseph Boudrot, native of l'Acadie, aged 20 years.

They have the following live stock, two oxen, two cows, one calf, two wethers, nine ewes, two sows, seven pigs and six fowls.

The land on which they are settled is situated as in the preceding case. It was given to them by a grant from Messieurs Duvivier and Degoutin. On it they have made a clearing where they have sown sixteen bushels of wheat, six bushels of peas, six bushels of oats, and have fallow land for sixteen bushels additional.

Louis Closquinet dit Desmoulins, ploughman, native of France, aged 66 years, has been in the country 25 years. Married to Marguerite Longueépée, native of l'Acadie, aged 52 years.

They have four sons and one daughter :—

Louis Closquinet, aged 22 years.

Joseph, aged 19 years.

Jean Baptiste, aged 19 years.

Aimable, aged 13 years.

Louise Genneviève, aged 17 years.

Their live stock consists of the following : nine oxen, six cows, four heifers, one bull, one horse, one mare with colt, eight wethers, fifteen ewes, fourteen pigs, eight sows and twenty fowls or chickens.

The land on which they are settled is situated as in the preceding case. It was given to them by grant from Messieurs Duvivier and Degoutin. They have made a clearing on it for sowing sixty-four bushels of grain, where they have sowed thirty-two bushels of wheat, fourteen bushels of peas and ten bushels of oats.

Robert Hengo, ploughman, native of the parish of Carolle, bishopric of Avranche, aged 36 years, and has been 18 years in the country. Married to Margueritte Haché, widow of the late Jacquemin.

They have two sons and threee daughters ;

Jean François Hengo, aged 9 years ;

Michel, aged 7 years ;

Marianne Jacquemin, aged 18 years ;

Marie Louise Jacquemin, aged 16 years ;
Magdeleine Hengo, aged 11 years.

Their live stock consists of four oxen, four cows, three calves, one horse, twelve wethers, twelve ewes, three sows, seven pigs and ten fowls.

The land on which they are settled is situated as in the preceding case. It was given to him by grant from Monsieur Duvivier. He has made a clearing sufficient for sowing thirty-two bushels of grain, of which he has sown five in wheat and three in peas.

Louis Vallet dit Langevin, extremely poor, soldier formerly of the company of Monsieur Dangeac, native of the town of Angers, aged 47 years ; has been 19 years in the country. Married to Brigitte Pinet, native of Canada, aged 33 years.

They have one son and four daughters :
Louis Vallet, aged 18 months :
Margueritte, aged 17 years ;
Louise, aged 9 years ;
Rose, aged 7 years ;
Marie, aged 5 years.

The land on which they are settled is situated as in the preceding cases. They acquired it for the sum of 70 livres from Michel Hébert. They have made a clearing on it where they have sown six bushels of wheat and two bushels of peas, and have fallow land sufficient for the sowing of thirty bushels this coming spring.

In live stock they have five oxen, one cow, one calf, one mare with colt, three wethers, eight ewes, three sows, four pigs and ten fowls or chickens.

Jean Lucas dit Bergerac, soldier of the company of Montalembert.

He is alone, his wife having left him.

The land on which he is settled was given him by grant from Monsieur Duvivier. He has made a clearing on it for sowing thirty-two bushels of seed of which he has sown five in wheat and three in peas.

Jacques Leblanc, ploughman, native of l'Acadie, aged 57 years ; he has been four years in the country. Married to Cecille Dupuis, native of l'Acadie, aged 55 years.

They have four sons and two daughters :
Jean Pierre Le Blanc, aged 25 years ;
Joseph, aged 23 years ;
Dominique, aged 21 years ;
Cazimire, aged 19 years ;
Françoise, aged 26 years ;
Margueritte, aged 16 years.

Their live stock consists of eight oxen, six cows, one heifer, three calves, two bulls, two horses, five ewes, three sows, three pigs and twenty-five fowls.

The land on which they are settled is situated on the south side of the River du Nord-Est of Port La Joye. They have sown on it ten bushels of wheat, one bushel of oats and seven bushels of peas, and they have fallow land sufficient to sow twelve bushels of seed ; they also have a saw mill.

Abraham Landry dit Chaques, widower, inhabitant of l'Acadie, aged 52 years ; he has been four years in the country.

He has two sons :—
Charles Landry, aged 22 years ;
Joseph, aged 18 years.

They have in live stock : two oxen, one cow, three bulls, one sow, four pigs and eight fowls.

The land on which they are settled is situated as in the preceding case ; they have sown five bushels of wheat and three bushels of peas, and have fallow land for the sowing of six bushels of wheat.

CENSUS.

Census of the settlers of Rivière du Moulin-à-scie, situated on the south side of the Rivière du Nord-Est of Port La Joye.

18—7

5-6 EDWARD VII., A. 1906

Jacques Leblanc, proprietor of a saw mill, native of l'Acadie, aged 57 years; he has been in the country four years. Married to Cecille Dupuis, native of l'Acadie, aged 55 years.

They have four sons and two daughters :

Jean Pierre LeBlanc, aged 25 years ;

Joseph, aged 23 years ;

Dominique, aged 21 years ;

Casimire, aged 19 years ;

Françoise, aged 26 years ;

Margueritte, aged 16 years,

In live stock they have : eight oxen, six cows, one heifer, three calves, two bulls, two horses, five ewes, three sows, three pigs and 25 fowls.

The land on which they are settled is situated on the south side of the Rivière du Nord-Est ; it was given to them verbally by Monsieur de Bonnaventure. On said land they have made a clearing of six arpents in extent, where they have sown ten bushels of wheat, one bushel of oats, and seven bushels of peas.

Abraham Landry dit Jacquet, ploughman, native of l'Acadie, aged 52 years ; he has been in the country four years.

He has two sons :—

Charles Landry, aged 22 years ;

Joseph, aged 18 years.

His live stock consists of two oxen, one cow, three bulls, three ewes, five sows, four pigs and eight fowls.

The land on which he is settled is situated as in the preceding case, and was given to him verbally by Monsieur de Bonnaventure. He has made a clearing of three arpents in extent where he has sown five bushels of wheat and three bushels of peas.

Estienne Terriaud, ploughman, native of l'Acadie, aged 26 years ; he has been two years on the island. Married to Helenne Landry, native of l'Acadie, aged 28 years.

They have one son and one daughter :—

Joseph Terriaud, aged 4 years ;

Françoise, aged 10 months.

Their live stock consists of two oxen, two cows, two bulls, two heifers, five ewes, five sows, four pigs and seven fowl.

The land on which they are settled is situated as in the preceding case ; it was given to them verbally by Monsieur de Bonaventure.

They have made a clearing on it of three arpents in extent and have sown four bushels of wheat and four bushels of peas.

Enselme Landry, ploughman, native of l'Acadie, aged 34 years ; he has been two years in this country. Married Marie Magdelaine Leblanc, native of l'Acadie, aged 32 years.

They have Jean Pierre Landry, aged nine months.

Their live stock consists of six oxen, five cows, two bulls, one horse, three ewes, four sows, four pigs and fifteen fowls.

The land on which they are settled is situated as in the preceding cases ; it was given verbally to them by Monsieur de Bonaventure.

They have made a clearing of three arpents and a half in extent on it where they have sown five bushels of wheat and four bushels of peas.

Prosper Thibaudeau, ploughman, native of.l'Acadie, aged 27 years ; he has been in this country 22 months. Married to Helenne Bariaud, native of l'Acadie, aged 26 years.

They have three daughters :

Doratte Thibaudeau, aged 6 years ;

Margueritte, aged four years ;

Auzitte, aged 18 months.

Their live stock consists of four oxen, one cow with calf, two sows, four pigs and thirty fowls.

The land on which they are settled is situated on the south side of the Rivière du Nord-Est ; it was given to them verbally by Monsieur de Bonnaventure.   On this land they have made a clearing of four arpents in extent.

Joseph Tibaudeau, ploughman, native of l'Acadie, aged 53 years, has been in this island 22 months.   Married to Marie Joseph Bourgeois, native of l'Acadie, aged 50 years.

They have six sons and one daughter :

Olivier Thibaudeau, aged 23 years ;

Ustache, aged 20 years ;

Joseph, aged 18 years ;

Charles, aged 15 years ;

Firmain, aged 10 years ;

Roze, aged 8 years.

Live stock : four oxen, one sow and five pigs.

The land on which they are settled is situated as in the preceding case ; and it was given to them verbally by Monsieur de Bonnaventure.   They have made on it a clearing of six arpents in extent.

Antoinne Thibaudeau, ploughman, native of l'Acadie, aged 56 years ; he has been on this island only two months.   Married to Susanne Commeau, native of l'Acadie, aged 47 years.

They have five sons and five daughters :

Ambroise Thibaudeau, aged 26 years ;

Blaise, aged 23 years ;

Simon, aged 20 years ;

Silvain, aged 18 years ;

Bonnaventure, aged 15 years.

Marie Susanne, aged 13 years.

Elisabeth, aged 10 years.

Margueritte, aged 8 years.

Anne, aged 6 years.

Doratte, aged 2 years.

The land on which they are settled is situated as in the preceding case ; and it was given to them verbally by Monsieur de Bonnaventure.

Jacques Sellier, ploughman, native of l'Acadie, aged 55 years ; he has only been in the country two years.   Married to Blanche Hébert, native of l'Acadie, aged 25 years.

They have four sons :—

Pierre Sellier, aged 7 years.

Noel, aged 5 years.

Jasques, aged 4 years.

Jean, aged 18 months.

Two oxen are all there live stock.

The land on which they are settled is situated as in the preceding cases ; and it was given to them verbally by Monsieur de Bonnaventure.   They have not made any clearing.

Claude Gautrot, ploughman, native of l'Acadie, aged 35 years ; he has been in the country two years.   Married to Genevieve Hébert, native of l'Acadie, aged 35 years.

They have three sons and two daughters :—

Jean Baptiste, aged 7 years.

Joseph, aged 5 years.

Michel, aged 9 months.

Anastasie, aged 13 years.

Marie, aged 3 years.

They have in live stock, two oxen, two cows, two calves, three pigs and fifteen fowls.

The land on which they are settled is situated as in the preceding cases ; and it was given to them verbally by Monsieur de Bonnaventure.   On it they have made a clearing of four arpents in extent.

5-6 EDWARD VII., A. 1906

Jean Hébert, ploughman, native of l'Acadie, aged 30 years; he has been three years in the country.   Married to Marie Hébert dit Jolicœur, native of l'Acadie, aged 20 years.

They have one son and one daughter :—

Jean Baptiste, aged 3 months.

Marie, aged 5 years.

The land on which they are settled is situated as in the preceding cases; it was given to them verbally by Monsieur de Bonnaventure.   They have not made any clearing.

Louis Hébert dit Baguette, ploughman, native of l'Acadie, aged 58 years; he has been in the country three years.   Married to Marie la Bauve, native of l'Acadie, aged 60 years.

They have one son and two daughters.

Jean Hébert, aged 22 years.

Téotiste, aged 18 years.

Modeste, aged 15 years.

They have one horse.

The land on which they are settled is situated as in the preceding cases, it was given to them verbally by Monsieur de Bonnaventure.   On it they have made a clearing of two arpents in extent.

Allain Bugeauld, ploughman, native of l'Acadie, aged 24 years, he has only been on the island one month.   Married to Marie Granger, native of l'Acadie, aged 21 years.

They have one son, aged 9 months.

In live stock, they own four oxen, one cow, one heifer and one calf.

The land on which they are settled is situated as in the preceding cases, it was given to them verbally by Monsieur de Bonnaventure.

Allain Bugeaud, ploughman, native of l'Acadie, aged 48 years, has been in the colony one year.   Married to Magdeleine Boudrot, native of l'Acadie, aged 47 years.

They have two sons and seven daughters :

Pierre Bugeaud, aged 19 years ;

Simon, aged 11 years ;

Elisabeth, aged 21 years ;

Margueritte, aged 17 years ;

Anne, aged 15 years ;

Marie, aged 9 years ;

Joseph, aged 7 years ;

Ursulle, aged 5 years ;

Ozitte, aged 5 months.

Their live stock consists of : two oxen, two cows, two heifers, two horses, one sow, four ducks and twenty fowls.

The land on which they are settled is situated as in the preceding cases, it was given to them verbally by Monsieur de Bonnaventure.   On it they have made a clearing of six arpents in extent.

Joseph Sellier, ploughman, native of l'Acadie, aged 46 years, he has been three years in the country.   Married to Anne Hébert, native of l'Acadie, aged 32 years.

They have two sons and three daughters :

Amant Sellier, aged 8 years ;

Abraham, aged 6 years ;

Marie, aged 12 years ;

Elisabeth, aged 10 years ;

Margueritte, aged 3 years.

Of live stock they have : one ox, four cows, three heifers, four calves, one pig and nineteen fowls.

The land on which they are settled is situated as in the preceding cases, it was given to them verbally by Monsieur de Bonnaventure.   They have made a clearing on it of three arpents in extent.

Michel Aucoin, ploughman, native of l'Acadie, aged 48 years, he has been on the island one year. Married to Marie Joseph Henry, native of l'Acadie, aged 41 years.

They have six daughters :
Marie Joseph Aucoin, aged 22 years ;
Margueritte, aged 18 years ;
Magdeleine, aged 15 years ;
Geneviève, aged 11 years ;
Elisabeth, aged 8 years ;
Ozitte, aged 5 years.

For live stock, they have : five sheep, six pigs and nine fowls.

They have not yet fixed the extent of land on which to settle.

Michel Caissy, ploughman, native of l'Acadie, aged 38 years, he has been in this country two years. Married to Margueritte Henry, native of l'Acadie, aged 21 years.

They have two daughters :—
Marie Caissy, aged 3 years ;
Marie Geneviève, aged one year.

Their live stock consists of one heifer, one sow, three pigs and one hen.

The land on which they are settled is situated on the south shore of the Rivière du Nord-Est, and was given to them verbally by Monsieur de Bonnaventure. They have made a clearing on it of two arpents in extent where they have sown two bushels and a half of wheat and three bushels and a half of peas.

Pierre Boisseau, ploughman, native of l'Acadie, aged 30 years, and has been in the country two years. Married to Magdelaine Boudrot, native of l'Acadie, aged 28 years.

They have one son and one daughter :—
Pierre Boisseau, aged 11 months ;
Marie, aged 3 years.

Foelix, a relative, native of l'Acadie, aged 29 years.

They have in live stock : two oxen, two cows, one heifer, two ewes, two pigs and twelve fowls.

The land on which they are settled is situated as in the preceding case, and was given to them verbally by Monsieur de Bonnaventure. They have made a clearing on it two arpents in extent and sown eight bushels of wheat.

Thomas Douaron, ploughman, native of l'Acadie, aged 53 years, and has been in the country two years. Married to Anne Giroir, native of l'Acadie, aged 48 years.

They have ten children, four sons and six daughters :—
Paul Douaron, aged 21 years ;
Charles, aged 14 years ;
Alexandre, aged 12 years ;
Jasques, aged 10 years ;
Roze, aged 22 years ;
Magdelaine, aged 18 years.
Anne, aged 8 years ;
Marie Marthe, aged 6 years ;
Elizabeth, aged 5 years ;
Margueritte, aged 3 years.

In live stock they have one ox, one heifer, two sows, one pig and thirty-three fowls.

The land on which they are settled is situated on the south side of the Rivière du Nord-Est, and was given to them by Monsieur de Bonnaventure. On it they have made a clearing of two arpents in extent and have sown two bushels of wheat.

Bennony Douaron, ploughman, native of l'Acadie, aged 27 years, and has been in the country 2 years. Married to Margueritte Boisseau, native of l'Acadie, aged 26 years.

They have three sons :—
Simon Grégoire, aged——years ;
Pierre, aged 34 months ;
Ignasse, aged 6 weeks ;
François Boisseau, senior, native of Paris, aged 66 years ;

5-6 EDWARD VII., A. 1906

Jeanne Boisseau, native of l'Acadie, aged 21 years.

Their live stock consists of four oxen, one cow, one heifer, one calf, one sow, one pig and twenty-five fowls.

The land on which they are settled is situated as in the preceding case, it was given to them by Monsieur de Bonnaventure. On the said land they have made a clearing of three arpents in extent where they have sown two bushels and a half of wheat and a bushel of oats.

Michel Hébert, ploughman, native of l'Acadie, aged 50 years, and has been on this island three years. Married to Claire Boisseau, native of l'Acadie, aged 39 years.

They have eight sons and one daughter :—

Joseph Hébert, aged 22 years ;
Claude, aged 19 years ;
Pierre, aged 15 years ;
Benoist, aged 14 years ;
Aimable, aged 13 years ;
Jean, aged 10 years ;
François, aged 2 years ;
Joseph, aged 7 months ;
Marie Anne, aged 18 months ;

They have in live stock four oxen, two cows, two heifers, three ewes, four sows, three pigs and thirty fowls.

The land on which they are settled is situated as in the preceding cases. It was given to them verbally by Monsieur de Bonnaventure. On the said land they have made a clearing of eleven arpents in extent where they have sown thirty-six bushels of wheat and one bushel and a half of peas.

Paul Boudrot, ploughman, native of l'Acadie, aged 49 years, he has been two years in the colony. Married to Marie Joseph Duaron, native of l'Acadie, aged 40 years.

They have two sons and three daughters :—

Jean Charles Boudrot, aged 12 years ;
Bazille, aged 4 years ;
Margueritte, aged 17 years ;
Françoise, aged 14 years ;
Anne, aged 7 years.

Charles Douaron, their father, native of l'Acadie, aged 90 years and infirm. Married to Françoise Godet, native of l'Acadie, aged 85 years.

They have in live stock five oxen, four cows, one sow and four pigs.

The land on which they are settled is situated on the Rivière des Blancs, it has been given to them verbally by Monsieur de Bonnaventure. They have made a clearing on it of five arpents in extent where they have sown seven bushels of wheat and eight bushels of oats.

Pierre Barriaud, native of l'Acadie, aged 45 years, he has been in the country two years. Married to Véronique Giroir, native of l'Acadie, aged 44 years.

They have two sons and seven daughters :—

Jean Baptiste Barriaud, aged 19 years ;
Olivier, aged 15 years ;
Marie Blanche, aged 17 years ;
Anne, aged 13 years ;
Anastasie, aged 11 years ;
Pelagie, aged 9 years ;
Frozinne, aged 7 years ;
Marie, aged 5 years;
Helenne, aged one year.

And in live stock four oxen, one cow, one calf, one wether, five ewes, two sows, five pigs and twenty-five fowls.

The land on which they are settled is situated as in the preceding case, it was given to them verbally by Monsieur de Bonnaventure. They have made on it a clearing of eight arpents in extent where they have sown seven bushels of wheat and seven bushels of oats.

Pierre Boudrot, ploughman, nat've of l'Acadie, aged 40 years, he has been two years in the country.   Married to Marie Duaron, native of l'Acadie, aged 36 years.

They have two sons and seven daughters :—

Firmain Boudrot, aged 7 years ;

Jasques, aged 4 years ;

Marie Blanche, aged 18 years ;

Anne, aged 16 years ;

Marie, aged 14 years ;

Magdeleine, aged 12 years ;

Marie, aged 10 years ;

Nastazie, aged 8 years ;

Ufrozinne, aged 6 years ;

Judict, aged 12 days.

And in live stock four oxen, three cows, three heifers, five ewes, two calves, one sow, six pigs and ten fowls.

The land on which they are settled is situated on the Rivière des Blancs, it was given to them verbally by Monsieur de Bonnaventure.   On it they have made a clearing of eight arpents in extent and have sown five bushels of wheat, eight bushels of oats and one bushel of peas.

Jean Daigre, ploughman, native of l'Acadie, aged 54 years, he has been one year in the country.   Married to Marie Braud, native of l'Acadie, aged 46 years.

They have three sons and nine daughters :—

Jean Daigre, aged 22 years ;

Charles, aged 19 years ;

Paul, aged 11 years ;

Françoise, aged 24 years ;

Catherine, aged 23 years ;

Félicité, aged 18 years ;

Roze, aged 16 years ;

Marie, aged 13 years ;

Hursulle, aged 9 years ;

Margueritte, aged 8 years ;

Jeanne Joseph, aged 4 years ;

Elisabeth, aged 3 years.

In live stock, two oxen, five cows, one calf and two pigs.

The land on which they are settled is situated as in the preceding case, it was given to them verbally by Monsieur de Bonnaventure.   On the said land they have made a clearing of three arpents and a half in extent where they have sown half a bushel of wheat and half a bushel of oats.

Petit Paul Duaron, ploughman, native of l'Acadie, aged 39 years, he has been in the country two years.   Married to Marie Richard, native of l'Acadie, aged 40 years.

They have one son and four daughters :—

Paul Michel Duaron, aged 12 years.

Marie Joseph, aged 15 years.

Margueritte Modeste, aged 8 years.

Elizabeth, aged 5 years.

Judith, aged 7 months.

And in live stock one pig and six fowls.

The land on which they are settled is situated on the creek à Dubuisson, it was given to them verbally by Monsieur de Bonnaventure ; on which said land they have made a clearing of two arpents in extent.

Antoine Barriau, ploughman, native of l'Acadie, aged 26 years, he has been in the country two years.   Married to Marie Blanche, native of l'Acadie, aged 19 years.

They have in live stock, two oxen, one pig and one hen.

5-6 EDWARD VII., A. 1906

The land on which they are settled is situated as in the preceding case, it was given to them verbally by Monsieur de Bonnaventure, and on the said land they have made a clearing of one arpent and a half in extent.

Antoinne Barriau, senior, ploughman, native of l'Acadie, aged 55 years, he has been two years in the country.   Married to Angelique Thibaudeau, native of l'Acadie, aged 48 years.

They have three sons and four daughters :—

Simeon Barriau, aged 21 years.
Jean Charles, aged 16 years.
Hustache, aged 14 years.
Félicité, aged 24 years.
Marie, aged 19 years.
Marie Blanche, aged 12 years.
Margueritte Joseph, aged 10 years.
And in live stock, two oxen, two calves and one sow.

The land on which they are settled is situated as in the preceding case, it was given verbally to them by Monsieur de Bonnaventure, on which said land they have made a clearing of three arpents in extent on which they have sown five bushels of wheat.

Pierre Vincent dit Clément, ploughman, native of l' Acadie, aged 30 years, he has been 22 years in the country.   Married to Roze Barriot, native of l'Acadie, aged 30 years.

They have one son and one daughter :—

Hesidore Vincent, aged 4 years.
Anne, aged 8 years.

The land on which they are settled is situated as in the preceding cases, it was given to them verbally by Monsieur de Bonnaventure, on which said land they have made a clearing of two arpents in extent.

Joseph Savary, ploughman, native of l'Acadie, aged 33 years, he has been two years in the country.   Married to Françoise Barriaud, native of l'Acadie, aged 27 years.

They have one son and one daughter.

Joseph Savary, aged 4 years ;
Marie, aged 2 years.
They have in live stock, two oxen and four fowls.

The land on which they are settled is situated as in the preceding cases, it was given to them verbally by Monsieur de Bonnaventure, on which said land they made a clearing of three arpents in extent.

Jean Baptiste Duaron, ploughman, native of l'Acadie, aged 27 years ; he has been in the country two years.   Married to Elizabeth Boudrot, native of l'Acadie, aged 27 years.

They have one son and two daughters :

François Duaron, aged 3 years ;
Margueritte, aged 5 years ;
Gennevieve, aged 4 months.
And in live stock four oxen and one horse.

The land on which they are settled is situated as in the preceding cases, it was given to them verbally by Monsieur de Bonnaventure, on which said land they have made a clearing of three arpents in extent.

Jean Barriaud, ploughman, native of l'Acadie, aged 22 years, he has been two years in the country.   Married to Margueritte Duaron, native of l'Acadie, aged 20 years.

They have Marie Barriaud, their daughter, aged 21 days.
All their live stock consists of one pig.

The land on which they are settled is situated as in the preceding cases, it was given to them verbally by Monsieur de Bonnaventure, on which said land they have made a clearing of three arpents.

Charles Boudrot, ploughman, native of l'Acadie, aged 27 years, he has been two years in the country. Married to Marie Joseph Doucet, native of l'Acadie, aged 28 years.

They have three daughters :

Marie Boudrot, aged 4 years ;

Margueritte, aged 3 years ;

Nastazie, aged 18 months.

And in live stock, two oxen and three fowls.

The land on which they are settled is situated as in the preceding case, it was given to them verbally by Monsieur de Bonnaventure, and on it they have made a clearing of two arpents in extent.

Charles Terriaud, ploughman, native of l'Acadie, aged 60 years, he has been two years in the country. Married to Angelique Duaron, native of l'Acadie.

They have four sons and two daughters :

Honoré Terriaud, aged 22 years ;

Charles Terriaud, aged 22 years ;

Jean, aged 15 years ;

Joseph, aged 12 years ;

Anne, aged 25 years ;

Marie, aged 18 years.

In live stock they own four oxen, two heifers, one sow and one pig.

The land on which they are settled is situated on the Creek aux Morts, it was given to them verbally by Monsieur de Bonnaventure, and on it they have made a clearing of six arpents in extent and have there sown eleven bushels of wheat.

Honnoré Duaron, ploughman, native of l'Acadie, aged 38 years, he has been two years in the country. United in a second marriage to Bonne Savary, native of l'Acadie, aged 27 years.

They have eight children, three sons and five daughters :—

Joseph Duaron, aged 16 years.

Alexis, aged 14 years.

Claude Duaron (brother), aged 25 years.

Théodore Duaron, aged 12 years.

Cécille, aged 10 years.

Marie Joseph, aged 8 years.

Margueritte Savary, aged 23 years.

Margueritte Joseph, aged 19 years.

The land on which they are settled is situated as in the preceding case, it was given to them verbally by Monsieur de Bonnaventure, a d on it they have made a clearing of six arpents.

François Poirier, ploughman, native of l'Acadie, aged 33 years, he has been two years in the country. Married to Cécille La Bauve, native of l'Acadie, aged 35 years.

They have one son and four daughters :—

Pierre Poyrier, aged 20 months.

Marie, aged 6 years.

Clotilde, aged 4 years.

Marie Magdeleine, aged 3 years.

Anne Modeste, aged 5 months.

And in live stock, four oxen, three cows, one heifer, one calf, one sow, five pigs, nine ewes and seven fowls.

The land on which they are settled is situated in la Petitte Ascension. They acquired it by purchase for 300 livres from François Haché Galland, and have made on it a clearing of five arpents in extent.

Louis La Bauve, ploughman and navigator, native of l'Acadie aged 38 years, he has been two years in the country. Married to Marie Landry, native of l'Acadie, aged 35 years.

They have three sons and two daughters :—

Amant Labauve, aged 11 years.

5-6 EDWARD VII., A. 1906

Bazille, aged 8 years.

Estienne, aged 18 months.

Magdeleine, aged 19 years.

Helenne, aged 6 years.

And in live stock, two oxen, one cow, one ewe, one sow and four pigs.

They are settled on the same lot as that of François Poirier is. They have also made a clearing on it of five arpents in extent.

Olivier Daigre, ploughman, native of l'Acadie, aged 21 years, he has been two years in the country. Married to Ursulle Landry, native of l'Acadie aged 28 years.

They have Louis Daigre, their son, aged 6 months.

In live stock, two oxen, one calf, one horse, one wether, four ewes and eight fowls.

The land on which they are settled is situated on the south side of the Petitte Ascension. They have acquired it by purchase for the sum of 300 livres from François Haché Galland, and have made on it a clearing of four arpents in extent.

Bernard Savary, ploughman, native of l'Acadie, aged 40 years, he has been two years in the country. Married to Marie Michel, native of l'Acadie, aged 35 years.

They have eight sons and five daughters :

André Savary, aged 17 years ;

Jean Baptiste, aged 14 years ;

Isaac, aged 9 years ;

Charles, aged 3 years ;

Louis, aged 13 months ;

Agnesse, aged 10 years ;

Roze, aged 7 years ;

André Savary, his father, native of l'Acadie, aged 60 years, lives with them.

He has three sons and three daughters :

Charles Savary, aged 25 years ;

Jean Baptiste, aged 20 years ;

Charles Olivier, aged 13 years ;

Margueritte, aged 23 years ;

Margueritte Joseph, aged 21 years ;

François Anastazie, aged 18 years.

They have in live stock : two oxen, two cows, two pigs and eight fowls.

The land on which they are settled is situated as in the preceding case, it was given to them verbally by Monsieur de Bonnaventure. They have made a clearing on it of three arpents in extent.

Paul Hébert, imbecile, ploughman, native of l'Acadie, aged 35 years, he has been three years in the country. Married to Marie Michel, native of l'Acadie, aged 32 years.

They have two sons and two daughters :

François Hébert, aged 10 years ;

Louis, aged 8 years ;

Théotiste, aged 17 years ;

Margueritte, aged 6 months.

The land on which they are settled is situated on the Anse aux Pirogues, it was given to them verbally by Monsieur de Bonnaventure. On it they have made a clearing for the sowing of six bushels of wheat.

Jean Baptiste Marquis, ploughman, native of Saint-Malo, aged 50 years. Married to Marie Clément, widow of the late Paul Laruine, native of l'Acadie, aged 45 years.

They have four sons and four daughters :

Jean Baptiste Marquis, aged 20 years ;

Paul, aged 16 years ;

Jean Michel Laruine, aged 18 years ;

Pierre, aged 16 years ;

Marie Joseph Marquis, aged 18 years ;

Anne Margueritte Laruine, aged 15 years ;

Judict, aged 10 years.

Roze, aged 7 years.

The land on which they are settled is situated as in the preceding case, it was given to them verbally by Monsieur de Bonnaventure. On it they have made a clearing of two arpents in extent.

Paul Michel Hébert, ploughman, native of l'Acadie, aged 27 years, he has been two years in the country. Married to Roze Hébert, native of l'Acadie, aged 22 years.

They have Jean Michel, their brother, aged 19 years ;

Rose, their sister, age 10 years.

The land on which they are settled is situated as in the preceding case. It was given them verbally by Monsieur de Bonnaventure. On the said land, they have made a clearing for the sowing of eight bushels of wheat.

Jean Vincens, ploughman, native of l'Acadie, aged 40 years, he has been in the country two years. Married to Margueritte Hébert, native of l'Acadie, aged 25 years.

They have three sons and five daughters :

Jean Vincens, aged 18 years ;

Jeromme, aged 13 years ;

Joseph, aged 2 years ;

Margueritte, aged 20 years ;

Blanche, aged 15 years ;

Marie Joseph, aged 10 years ;

Anastasie, aged 9 years ;

Elisabeth, aged 6 years.

And in live stock, two pigs and eight fowls.

The land on which they are settled is situated as in the preceding case ; it was given to them verbally by Monsieur de Bonnaventure. On it they have made a clearing for the sowing of eight bushels of wheat.

Charles Hébert, ploughman, native of l'Acadie, aged 60 years, he has been two years in the country. Married to Catherine Saunnier, native of l'Acadie, aged 40 years.

They have five sons and two daughters :

Joseph Hébert, aged 19 years ;

Simon, aged 15 years ;

Jean, aged 13 years ;

Pierre, aged 7 years ;

François, aged 3 years ;

Marie, aged 20 years ;

Hursulle, aged 18 years.

In live stock they have, two oxen and three fowls.

The land on which they are settled is situated as in the preceding case, it was given to them verbally by Monsieur de Bonnaventure. On it they have made a clearing two arpents in extent.

CENSUS.

Census of the Anse au Comte Saint-Pierre.

François Gautrot, ploughman, native of l'Acadie, aged 67 years, he has been in the colony two years. Married to Marie Vincens, native of l'Acadie, aged 62 years.

They have three sons and three daughters :

François Gautrot, aged 28 years ;

Charles, aged 22 years ;

Pierre Maturin, aged 18 years ;

Magdelaine, aged 30 years ;

Marie, aged 26 years ;

Margueritte, aged 24 years.

Their live stock consists of : one ox, two cows, one horse, five pigs and three fowls.

The land on which they are settled is situated on the Anse au Comte St. Pierre, it was given to them verbally by Monsieur de Bonnaventure. On it they have made a clearing three arpents in extent.

5-6 EDWARD VII., A. 1906

Jean Gaudrot, ploughman, native of l'Acadie, aged 43 years, he has been in the country one year. Married to Elisabeth Sire, native of l'Acadie, aged 34 years.

They have one son and four daughters :—

Charles Gautrot, aged 2 years ;

Marie Joseph, aged 15 years ;

Anne, aged 13 years ;

Margueritte Tersille, aged 8 years ;

Françoise, aged 6 years.

Their live stock consists of three pigs and ten fowls.

The land on which they are settled is situated as in the preceding case, it was given to them verbally by Monsieur de Bonnaventure. On it they have made a clearing for the sowing of three bushels of wheat.

Jean Sire, ploughman, native of l'Acadie, aged 36 years, he has been in the country two years. Married to Marie Joseph Gautrot, aged 40 years.

They have four sons :—

Jean Sire, aged 13 years ;

Pierre, aged 11 years ;

Joseph, aged 4 years ;

Charles, aged 3 years ;

In live stock one horse, two pigs and four fowls.

The land on which they are settled is situated as in the preceding case, it was given to them verbally by Monsieur de Bonnaventure. They have made a clearing on it of one arpent.

Joseph Deschamps dit Cloche, ploughman, native of l'Acadie, aged 42 years, he has been in the country three years. Married to Judict Duaron, native of l'Acadie, aged 32 years.

They have five sons and three daughters :—

Philippe Deschamps, aged 16 years ;

Louis, aged 14 years ;

Augustin, aged 12 years ;

Jean Baptiste, aged 6 years ;

François, aaged 4 years ;

Eufrozinne, aged 18 years ;

La Blanche, aged 8 months ;

Elisabeth, aged 18 months.

Their live stock consists of : eight pigs and twenty fowls.

The land on which they are settled is situated as in the preceding case, it was given to them verbally by Monsieur de Bonnaventure. On it they have made a clearing for the sowing of three bushels of wheat.

CENSUS OF ANSE AU MATELOST.

Honoré Lavache, ploughman, native of l'Acadie, aged 26 years, he has been in the country two years. Married to Magdeleine Daigre, native of l'Acadie, aged 27 years.

They have one son and one daughter :—

Jean Baptiste Lavache, aged 5 years ;

Marie Modeste, aged 2 years.

The land on which they are settled is situated on Anse au Matelost, it was given to them verbally by Monsieur de Bonnaventure. They have made a clearing on it for the sowing of two bushels of grain.

Louis Sire, ploughman, native of l'Acadie, aged 60 years, he has been on the island three years. Married to Marie Joseph Michel, native of l'Acadie, aged 50 years.

The land on which they are settled is situated as in the preceding case, it was given to them verbally by Monsieur de Bonnaventure. On it they have made a clearing for a garden.

They have two sons and three daughters :—

Charles Sire, aged 26 years.

Paul, aged 21 years.

Marie Joseph, aged 28 years.

Margueritte, aged 25 years.

Marie Magdeleine Prince, native of l'Acadie, aged 30 years.

In live stock, one heifer, two sows and twenty fowls.

Joseph Vincens dit Clément, ploughman, native of l'Acadie, aged 38 years, he has been on the island two years. Married to Margueritte Hébert, native of l'Acadie aged 36 years.

They have three sons and three daughters :—

Joseph Vincens, aged 11 years.

Alexis, aged 8 years.

François, aged 6 years.

Margueritte, aged 10 years.

Agathe, aged 4 years.

Anne Geneviève, aged 20 months.

And in stock one horse, three pigs and three fowls.

The land on which they are settled is situated as in the preceding cases, it was given to them verbally by Monsieur de Bonnaventure. On it they have made a clearing for the sowing of eight bushels of wheat.

François Clément, ploughman, native of l'Acadie, aged 27 years, he has been in the country two years. Married to Marie Douaron, native of l'Acadie, aged 29 years.

They have one son and one daughter :—

Amant George, aged 4 years.

Marie, aged 18 months.

In stock, one pig and three fowls.

The land on which they are settled is situated as in the preceding cases, it was given to them verbally by Monsieur de Bonnaventure. They have made a clearing on it for a garden.

Jean Douaron, ploughman, native of l'Acadie, aged 23 years, he has been in the country one year. Married to Anne Cerié, native of l'Acadie, aged 17 years.

Their live stock consists of one pig and one hen.

The land on which they are settled is situated as in the preceding cases, it was given to them verbally by Monsieur de Bonaventure. They have made a clearing on it for a garden.

Philippe Douaron, ploughman, native of l'Acadie, aged 32 years, he has been in the country two years. Married to Ursulle Le Jeune, native of l'Acadie, aged 33 years.

They have one son and four daughters :—

Firmain Joseph, aged 6 years ;

Marie Joseph, aged 10 years ;

Gertrude, aged 8 years ;

Magdelaine, aged 4 years ;

Margueritte, aged 15 months.

In stock, two cows, three pigs and one horse.

The land on which they are settled is situated as in the preceding cases, it was given to them verbally by Monsieur de Bonnaventure. On it they have made a clearing of one arpent in extent.

Joseph Billerois, ploughman, native of Verny Fontaine, bishopric of Besançon, aged 26 years, he has been in the country three months. Married to Brigitte Forêt, native of l'Acadie, aged 23 years.

The land on which they are settled is situated as in the preceeding case, it was given to them verbally by Monsieur de Bonnaventure. On it they have made a clearing for the sowing of two bushels of wheat.

François Rullier, ploughman, native of the parish of Crideville, bishopric of Bayeux, aged 43 years, he has been in the country five years. Married to Anne Forest, native of l'Acadie, aged 43 years.

They have in live stock : two oxen, three cows, four calves, one heifer, five pigs and three fowls.

5-6 EDWARD VII., A. 1906

The land on which they are settled is situated as in the preceding cases, it was given to them verbally by Monsieur de Bonnaventure. On it they have made a clearing of five arpents in extent.

Pierre Aucoin, ploughman, native of l'Acadie, aged 44 years, he has been two years in the country. Married to Elizabeth Breaud, native of l'Acadie, aged 37 years.

They have three sons and five daughters :—

Pierre Aucoin, aged 16 years ;

Charles, aged 7 years ;

Jean Baptiste, aged 18 months ;

Marie Blanche, aged 18 years ;

Magdelaine, aged 17 years ;

Elizabeth, aged 13 years ;

————————, aged 10 years ;

Véronique, aged 5 years ;

In stock : one ox, one cow, four sows, one pig and six fowls.

The land on which they are settled is situated like the preceding, it was given to them verbally by Monsieur de Bonnaventure. On the said land they have made a clearing of one arpent in extent.

Claude Trahant, ploughman, native of l'Acadie, aged 58 years, he has been in the country two years.

He has two sons and seven daughters :—

Auguste Trahant, aged 17 years ;

Fiacre, aged 12 years ;

Auzitte, aged 25 years ;

Margueritte, aged 23 years ;

Blanche, aged 21 years ;

Magdelaine, aged 19 years ;

Anne, aged 15 years ;

Elisabeth, aged 10 years ;

Rozalie, aged 7 years ;

In stock, four oxen, three cows, one heifer, two calves, one horse, five pigs, and two fowls.

The land on which they are settled is situated as in the preceding cases, it was given to them verbally by Monsieur de Bonnaventure. On it they have made a clearing for the sowing of radishes.

François Lavache, ploughman, native of l'Acadie, aged 55 years, he has been in the country two years. Married to Marie Vincens, native of l'Acadie, aged 46 years.

They have three sons and two daughters.

Alexis Lavache, aged 21 years ;

Jean Charles, aged 12 years ;

Joseph, aged 7 years ;

Margueritte, aged 10 years ;

Anne, aged 4 years.

In stock, four oxen, eight cows, one bull, eight calves, two horses, four sows, three pigs and one hen.

The land on which they are settled is situated as in the preceding cases, it was given to them verbally by Monsieur de Bonnaventure. On it they have made a clearing for the sowing of eight bushels of wheat.

Joseph Trahant, ploughman, native of l'Acadie, aged 38 years, he has been in the country two years. Married to Anne Terriaud, native of l'Acadie, aged 33 years.

They have three sons and two daughters :—

Joseph Terriaud, aged 16 years ;

Mathurin, aged 8 years.

Jean, aged 3 years ;

Marie, aged 5 years ;

Margueritte, aged 3 months ;

In stock, four oxen, two cows, one bull and two pigs.

The land on which they are settled is situated as in the preceding cases, it was given to them verbally by Monsieur de Bonnaventure. On the said land they have a clearing for the sowing of three bushels of wheat.

Claude Guedry, ploughman, native of l'Acadie, aged 38 years, he has been in the country two years. Married to Anne Terriaud, native of l'Acadie, aged 38 years.

They have three sons :—

Jean Baptiste Guedry, aged 5 years ;

Joseph Marie, aged 2 years ;

Pierre Janvier, aged two months ;

And in stock, one cow, one calf, one bull, one sow and five pigs.

The land on which they are settled is situated as in the preceding cases, it was given to them verbally by Monsieur de Bonnaventure. On it they have made a clearing for the sowing of three bushels of wheat.

Joseph Lucas, ploughman, native of l'Acadie, aged 29 years, he has been two years in the country. Married to Margueritte Lejeunne, native of l'Acadie, aged 24 years.

They have one son and one daughter :—

Joseph Mary Lucas, aged 2 years ;

Margueritte Thérèse, aged 5 years.

They have in stock one mare and three pigs.

The land on which they are settled is situated as in the preceding cases, it was given to them verbally by Monsieur de Bonnaventure. On it they have made a clearing for a garden.

Paul Trahant, ploughman, native of l'Acadie, aged 49 years, he has been in the country two years. Married to Marie Boudrot, native of l'Acadie, aged 49 years.

They have two sons and five daughters :

Charles Trahant, aged 12 years ;

Estienne, aged 10 years ;

Marie, aged 16 years ;

Margueritte, aged 15 years ;

Brigitte, aged 8 years ;

Elizabeth, aged 6 years ;

Marie, aged 3 years ;

In stock, two oxen, one cow, one calf, three pigs and three fowls.

The land on which they are settled is situated as in the preceding cases, it was given to them verbally by Monsieur de Bonnaventure. On it they have made a clearing for a garden.

René Roy, ploughman, native of l'Acadie, aged 48 years, he has been in the country two years. Married to Marie Joseph Daigre, native of l'Acadie, aged 35 years.

They have one son and three daughters :

Jean Baptiste Roy, aged 3 months ;

Marie Joseph, aged 8 years ;

Margueritte, aged 4 years ;

Anne Magdelaine, aged 28 months.

In stock, one cow, one heifer, one calf, six pigs and two fowls.

The land on which they are settled is situated as in the preceding cases, it was given to them verbally by Monsieur de Bonnaventure. On it they have made a clearing for a large garden.

Jean Baptiste Trahant, ploughman, native of l'Acadie, aged 47 years, he has been in the country two years. Married to Catherine Boudrot, native of l'Acadie, aged 47 years.

They have two sons and six daughters :

Charles Joseph, aged 11 years ;

Pierre Helie, aged 7 years ;

Magdelaine, aged 16 years ;

Marie Monique, aged 14 years ;

Roze, aged 12 years ;

Radegonde, aged 9 years ;
Elizabeth, aged 6 years ;
Margueritte, aged 26 months.

In stock, two oxen, two cows, two calves, one horse, five pigs and fifteen fowls.

The land on which they are settled is situated as in the preceding cases, it was given to them verbally by Monsieur de Bonnaventure. On it they have made a clearing of two arpents in extent.

Joseph Daigre, ploughman, native of l'Acadie, aged 56 years, he has been two years in the country. Married to Magdelaine Goutrot, native of l'Acadie, aged 53 years.

They have three sons and two daughters :
Allain Daigre, aged 28 years ;
Jean Baptiste, aged 19 years ;
Simon Joseph, aged 13 years ;
Margueritte, aged 26 years ;
Anastazie, aged 17 years.

And in stock, two oxen, twelve pigs and nine fowls.

The land on which they are settled is situated as in the preceding cases, it was given to them verbally by Monsieur de Bonnaventure. They have made a clearing on it of two arpents in extent.

Claude Trahant, junior, native of l'Acadie, aged 34 years, he has been two years in the country. Married to Anne Leblanc, native of l'Acadie, aged 32 years.

They have three sons :
Jean Baptiste, aged 5 years ;
Joseph Firmain, aged 3 years ;
Joseph, aged 2 years.

In stock, two oxen, one c w and four pigs.

The land on which they are settled is situated as in the preceding cases. It was given to them verbally by Monsieur de Bonnaventure, and on it they have a clearing of two arpents.

Pierre Gautrot, native of l'Acadie, aged 58 years, living with the said Claude Trahant.

Claude Leblanc, native of l'Acadie, aged 56 years, widower with one son and two daughters :—
Paul Leblanc, aged 9 years.
Magdelaine, aged 20 years.
Geneviève, aged 11 years.

All living with the said Claude Trahant.

Jean Baptiste Lejeune, ploughman, native of l'Acadie, aged 30 years, he has been in the country two years, married to Margueritte Clémenceau, native of l'Acadie.

They have four sons and one daughter :—
Joseph Lejeune, aged 9 years.
Jean-Baptiste, aged 7 years.
François Olivier, aged 3 years.
Victor, aged 9 months.
Marie, aged 5 years.

And in stock, one cow, one calf and four sows.

The land on which they are settled is located as in the preceding cases, it was given to them verbally by Monsieur de Bonnaventure, and on it they have made a clearing for the sowing of two bushels of wheat.

Charles Benoist, ploughman, native of l'Acadie, aged 58 years, he has been two years in the colony. Married to Magdelaine Terriaud, native of l'Acadie, aged 58 years.

They have two sons and four daughters :—
Jean Charles Benoist, aged 6 years ;
Pierre, aged 10 months ;
Marie, aged 16 years ;

Anne, aged 13 years ;

Françoise, aged 11 years ;

Judict, aged 8 years.

They have in live stock one ox, one cow, one calf and four pigs.

The land on which they are settled is situated as in the preceding cases, he has been given to them verbally by Monsieur de Bonnaventure. On it they have made a clearing for sowing three bushels of wheat.

Abraham Benoist, ploughman, native of l'Acadie, aged 42 years, he has been in the country two years. Married to Marie Joseph Le Jeune, native of l'Acadie, aged 34 years.

They have two sons and five daughters :—

Jean Benoist, aged 18 years.

Joseph, aged two months.

Margueritte, aged 16 years ;

Marie Magdelaine, aged 12 years ;

Joseph, aged 14 years ;

Pelagie, aged 10 years ;

Marie, aged 5 years.

And in stock, two oxen, two cows, two heifers, five sows and five fowls.

The land on which they are settled is situated as in the last instance, and was given to them verbally by Monsieur de Bonnaventure. On it they have made a clearing of two arpents.

Claude Benoist, ploughman, native of l'Acadie, aged 31 years, he has been in this country two years. Married to Elizabeth Terriaud, native of l'Acadie, aged 27 years.

They have two sons and four daughters :

Gregoire Benoist, aged 8 years ;

Daniel, aged 4 years ;

Lablanche, aged 11 years ;

Anne, aged 6 years ;

Marie Joseph, aged 4 years ;

Margueritte, aged two months.

And in stock, one horse and one sow.

The land on which they are settled is situated in the Anse au Matelost. It was given to them verbally by Monsieur de Bonnaventure. They have made a clearing on it for the sowing of three bushels of wheat.

CENSUS

Census of the Inhabitants of the Grande Anse.

Jean Landry, ploughman, native of l'Acadie, aged 51 years, he has been in the country two years. Married to Marie Lablanche, native of l'Acadie, aged 24 years.

They have Charles Landry, their nephew, aged 19 years ;

Théodose Boudrot, their niéce, aged 15 years.

And in stock, three oxen, five cows, two heifers, one horse and one ewe.

The land on which they are settled is situated at the further end of the Grande Ance, it was given to them verbally by Monsieur de Bonnaventure. On it they have made a clearing for the sowing of four bushels of wheat.

Honoré Landry, ploughman, native of l'Acadie, aged 38 years, he has been on the island two years. Married to Magdelaine Gautrot, native of l'Acadie, aged 29 years.

They have two sons and two daughters :

Enselme Landry, aged 9 years ;

Honoré, aged 5 years ;

Magdelaine, aged 2 years.

Joseph, aged 8 days.

And in stock, seven oxen, two cows, one calf and four pigs.

The land on which they are settled is situated as in the preceding case. It was given to them verbally by Monsieur de Bonnaventure. On it they have made a clearing for the sowing of six bushels of wheat.

5-6 EDWARD VII., A. 1906

Estienne Melançon, ploughman, native of l'Acadie, aged 30 years, he has been in the country two years. Married to Françoise Grangerre, native of l'Acadie, aged 24 years.

They have one son and two daughters :

Joseph Melançon, aged 4 years ;

LaBlanche, aged 2 years ;

Elizabeth, aged 4 months ;

Paul Granger, aged 30 years, brother ;

Margueritte, aged 13 years, sister.

They have in live stock, two oxen, three ewes, two heifers, two calves and five pigs.

The land on which they are settled is situated as in the preceding cases. It was given to them verbally by Monsieur de Bonnaventure. On it they have made a clearing for the sowing of six bushels of wheat.

Prosper Landry, ploughman, native of l'Acadie, aged 26 years, he has been in the country two years. Married to Josette Boudrot, native of l'Acadie, aged 24 years.

They have Margueritte Landry, their daughter, aged 9 weeks ;

Joseph Landry, his brother, aged 20 years ;

Mathurin Boudrot, her brother, aged 10 years ;

And in stock, three oxen, three cows and two calves.

The land on which they are settled is situated as in the preceding cases. It was given to them verbally by Monsieur de Bonnaventure. On it they have made a clearing for the sowing of four bushels of wheat.

François Raimond, ploughman, native of l'Acadie, aged 32 years, he has been in the country two years. Married to Cecille Landry, native of l'Acadie, aged 28 years.

They have Paul Raimond, their son, aged 2 years.

Catherine Boudrot, native of l'Acadie, aged 8 years.

And in stock, two oxen, three cows, one calf, two ewes, two pigs and eight fowls.

The land on which they are settled is situated as in the preceding cases. It was given to them verbally by Monsieur de Bonnaventure. On it they have made a clearing for the sowing of two bushels of wheat.

Pierre Claude Herrement, ploughman, native of l'Acadie, aged 58 years, he has been in the country two years. Married to Marie Joseph Terriau, native of l'Acadie, aged 52 years.

They have two sons and one daughter :—

Pierre, aged 21 years ;

François, aged 17 years ;

Marie Joseph, aged 17 years.

And in stock, two oxen, one heifer and one pig.

The land on which they are settled is situated as in the preceding cases. It was given to them verbally by Monsieur de Bonnaventure. On it they have made a clearing for the sowing of three bushels of wheat.

Amant Pitre, ploughman, native of l'Acadie, aged 28 years, he has been one year in the country. Married to Geneviève Hertrement, native of l'Acadie, aged 28 years.

They have three sons and one daughter :—

Bazille Pitre, aged 15 years ;

Tranquille, aged 4 years ;

Ambroise, aged 3 years ;

Anne, aged one year.

They have in live stock two oxen, three cows, one calf, two pigs and three fowls.

The land on which they are settled is situated as in the preceding cases. It was given to them verbally by Monsieur de Bonnaventure. On it they have made a clearing for the sowing of three bushels of wheat.

Antoine Leprince, ploughman, native of l'Acadie, aged 32 years, he has been in the country two years. Married to Cecille Hertrement, native of l'Acadie, aged 25 years.

They have one son and five daughters :—

Firmain Leprince, aged 6 years.

Marie, aged 7 years.

Ozille, aged 5 years.

Magdelainne, aged 3 years.

They have in live stock, one cow and three pigs.

The land on which they are settled is situated as in the preceding cases. It has been given to them verbally by Monsieur de Bonnaventure. On it they have made a clearing for the sowing of three bushels of wheat.

Emilliant Segoilliot dit Sans Chagrin, formerly sergeant in the company of Monsieur Benoist, native of Casthelineau, in Bourgogne, aged 35 years. Married to Elizabeth Blanche Lavache, native of l'Acadie, aged 17 years.

They have in live stock, six oxen, four cows, two sows, five pigs and one hen.

The land on which they are settled is situated as in the preceding cases. It was given to them verbally by Monsieur de Bonnaventure, and on it they have made no clearing.

Antoinne Boudrot, ploughman, native of l'Acadie, aged 60 years, he has been in the country two years. Married to Cecille Brassaud, native of l'Acadie, aged 57 years.

They have two sons and three daughters :—

Joseph Boudrot, aged 31 years.

Prudent, aged 18 years.

Theodore, aged 17 years.

Anne, aged 22 years.

Ainesse, aged 13 years.

Ignace Boudrot, their nephew, orphan, without father or mother, aged 4 years, lives with them.

They have in live stock, two cows, two pigs and three fowls.

The land on which they are settled is situated like the preceeding. It was given to them verbally by Monsieur de Bonnaventure. On it they have made a clearing for a garden.

Alexis Breaud, widower, ploughman, native of l'Acadie, aged 30 years, he has been on the island one year.

He has four daughters.

Magdelainne, aged 6 years.

Anne, aged 5 years.

Marie Ozitte, aged 3 years.

Marie Victoire, aged 11 months.

They have in live stock, two oxen, one cow and two pigs.

The land on which they are settled is situated as in the preceding case. It was given to them verbally by Monsieur de Bonnaventure. On it they have made a clearing of one arpent square.

Jean Douaron, ploughman, native of l'Acadie, aged 25 years, he has been in the country two years. Married to Anne Thibaudeau, native of l'Acadie, aged 23 years.

They have in live stock, two oxen, one cow and six pigs.

The land on which they are settled is situated at the farther end of the Grande Anse and was given to them verbally by Monsieur de Bonnaventure. On it they have made a clearing of one arpent.

Alexis Douaron, widower, ploughman, native of l'Acadie, aged 29 years, he has been in the country two years.

He has three sons :—

Gregoire, aged 8 years.

Joseph, aged 6 years.

Theodore, aged 3 years.

And the following live stock : two oxen, one horse and two pigs.

The land on which he is settled is situated as in the preceding case. It was given to him verbally by Monsieur de Bonnaventure. He has made no clearing.

Margueritte Barriaud, his mother, native of l'Acadie, aged 58 years.

18—8½

5-6 EDWARD VII., A. 1906

Jean Hebert, ploughman, native of l'Acadie, aged 42 years, he has been two years on the island.   Married Veronique Sire, native of l'Acadie, aged 23 years.

They have three sons and four daughters :—

Pierre Hebert, aged 17 years.

Joseph, aged 4 years.

Jean Baptiste, aged 3 years.

Marie, aged 16 years.

Margueritte, aged 15 years.

Anne, aged 9 years.

Roze, aged 7 years.

And in stock six oxen, six cows, two calves and one pig.

The land on which they are settled is situated as in the preceding cases.   It was given to them verbally by Monsieur de Bonnaventure.   They have made a clearing on it of one arpent square.

Victor Boudrot, ploughman, native of l'Acadie, aged 24 years, he has been two years in the country.   Married to Catharine Hebert, native of l'Acadie.

They have Magdelainne Boudrot, an orphan, native of l'Acadie, aged 17 years, living with them.

Their land forms part of the homestead of Antoinne Boudrot their father.

Olivier Daigre, ploughman, native of l'Acadie, aged 34 years, he has been in the country two years.   Married to Angelique Duaron, native of l'Acadie, aged 32 years.

They have five sons and three daughters :—

—— —— Daigre, aged 8 years.

Charles, aged 6 years.

Paul, aged 3 years.

Joseph, aged 2 years.

Pierre, aged 2 months.

Margueritte, aged 12 years.

Ozitte, aged 7 years.

Roze, aged 5 years.

They have the following live stock : three oxen, three cows, four heifers, two calves, one mare and one sow.

The land on which they are settled is situated as in the preceding cases.   It was given to them verbally by Monsieur de Bonnaventure.   On it they have made a clearing for the sowing of three bushels of wheat in the coming spring.

Joseph Leprince, ploughman, native of l'Acadie, aged 38 years, he has been one year in the country.   Married to Marie Ozitte Pitre, native of l'Acadie, aged 23 years.

They have Joseph Olivier Prince, their son, aged 20 months.

And in stock, one cow, one calf, two sows, eight ducks and twelve fowls.

The land on which they are settled is situated as in the preceding cases.   It was given to them verbally by Monsieur de Bonnaventure.   On it they have made a clearing for the sowing of six bushels of wheat.

Alexandre Chauvel, ploughman, native of l'Acadie, aged 32 years, he has been in the country 26 months.   Married to Catherine Josette Prince, native of l'Acadie, aged 30 years.

They have two sons and one daughter :

Mathurin Chauvel, aged 5 years ;

Jean Baptiste, aged 3 years :

Margueritte, aged 14 months.

And in stock they have one sow, two pigs and one hen.

The land on which they are settled is situated as in the preceding cases.   It was given to them verbally by Monsieur de Bonnaventure.   On it they have made a clearing for the sowing of six bushels of wheat.

CENSUS.

Census of the settlers of the Grande Ascension.

Joseph Dugas, ploughman, native of l'Acadie, aged 50 years, and has been 15 months in the country.   Married to Anne Marie Hebert, native of l'Acadie, aged 50 years.

They have two sons and four daughters :
Joseph Dugas, aged 10 years ;
Jean, aged 8 years ;
Margueritte, aged 18 years ;
Françoise, aged 13 years ;
Anne, aged 5 years.
Their live stock consists of the following : five oxen, three cows, seven wethers, three ewes, four pigs and five fowls.
The land on which they are settled is situated east of the Rivière de la Grande Ascension, it was given to them verbally by Monsieur de Bonnaventure. On it they have made a clearing for the sowing of two bushels of wheat during the coming spring.
François Henry, ploughman, native of l'Acadie, aged 36 years, he has been in the country 13 months. Married to Marie Dugast, native of l'Acadie, aged 30 years.
They have two sons and three daughters :
Basille Henry, aged 11 years ;
Joseph, aged 9 years ;
Margueritte Joseph, aged 7 years ;
Elizabeth, aged 4 years ;
Victoire, aged 18 months.
And in stock, three oxen, two cows, four heifers, three ewes, one sow, three pigs and ten fowls.
The land on which they are settled is situated as in the preceding cases. It was given to them verbally by Monsieur de Bonnaventure. On it they have made a clearing for the sowing of two bushels of wheat in the coming spring.
Ambroise Dugast, ploughman, native of l'Acadie, aged 23 years, he has been 13 months in the country. Married to Margueritte Henry, native of l'Acadie, aged 23 years.
They have Ambroise Dugast, their son, aged 10 months.
And in stock two oxen, two cows, two heifers, one mare, three wethers, five ewes, one sow, two pigs and two fowls.
The land on which they are settled is situated as in the preceding cases. It was given to them verbally by Monsieur de Bonnaventure. On the said land they have made a clearing for the sowing of one bushel of grain in the coming spring.
Pierre Dugast, ploughman, native of l'Acadie, aged 20 years, he has been in the country 13 months. Married to Joseph Hebert, native of l'Acadie, aged 21 years.
In live stock they have only two cows.
The land on which they are settled is situated as in the preceding cases. It was given to them verbally by Monsieur de Bonnaventure, and on it they have made a clearing for a garden.
Claire Dugast, widow of the late Jean Hebert, aged 46 years, he has been in the country one year.
She has two sons and six daughters .—
Pierre Hebert, aged 17 years ;
Jean, aged 12 years ;
Françoise, aged 21 years ;
Elisabeth, aged 19 years ;
Anne, aged 15 years ;
Helene, aged 10 years ;
Marie Joseph, aged 8 years ;
Victoire, aged 5 years.
And in stock they have three oxen, one cow, one bull, three wethers, two sows and two pigs.
Jean Lejeune, ploughman, native of l'Acadie, aged 28 years, he has been in the country two years. Married to Margueritte Blanche, native of l'Acadie, aged 32 years.
They have one son and one daughter :—
Mathurin Lejeune, aged one year ;
Rozalie, aged 3 years.

5-6 EDWARD VII., A. 1906

And in stock, two oxen, one cow, one calf, two sows and one pig.

The land on which they are settled is situated as in the preceding cases. It was given to them verbally by Monsieur de Bonnaventure. On it they have made a clearing of two arpents in extent.

François Guerin, ploughman, native of l'Acadie, aged 34 years, he has been two years on the Island. Married to Geneviève Mieux, native of l'Acadie, aged 32 years.

They have two daughters :—

Margueritte Genneviève Guerin, aged 5 years.

Marie Roze, aged 3 years.

And in stock they have four pigs and twelve fowls.

The land on which they are settled, is situated on the west bank of the east river of the Grande Ascension, it was given to them verbally by Monsieur de Bonneventure.

They have made a clearing on it for the sowing of four bushels of wheat in the coming spring.

Eloy Lejeune, ploughman, aged 28 years, he has been two years in the country, native of l'Acadie. Married Rosalie Mieux, native of l'Acadie, aged 27 years.

They have two sons and one daughter :—

Françoise Lejeune, aged 5 years.

Jean Baptiste, aged 3 years.

Marie Joseph, aged 11 months.

And of stock, one cow, one calf, three pigs and fifteen fowls.

The land on which they are settled is situated as in the preceding cases. It was given to them verbally by Monsieur de Bonnaventure. On it they have made a clearing for the sowing of four bushels of wheat in the coming spring.

Paul Benoist, ploughman, native of l'Acadie, aged 48 years, he has been in the country two years. Married to Marie Vinet, widow of the late Corporon, native of l'Acadie, aged 43 years.

They have three sons and six daughters :—

Jean Charles Corporon, aged 19 years.

Antoine Benoist, aged 11 years.

Jean Benoist, aged 9 years.

Josette Benoist, aged 9 years.

Françoise, aged 17 years.

Marie, aged 15 years.

Elizabeth, aged 13 years.

Rose, aged 7 years.

Collastique, aged 5 years.

In stock they have three oxen, four cows, one calf and six pigs.

The land on which they are settled is situated on the west point of the Grande Ascension. It was given to them by Monsieur de Bonnaventure. On the said land they have made a clearing for the sowing of twelve bushels of grain during the coming spring

Paul Benoist, junior, ploughman, native of l'Acadie, aged 25 years, he has been 26 months in the country. Married to Marie Magdelaine Douaron, native of l'Acadie, aged 19 years.

They have one son and one daughter :—

Joseph Benoist, aged 3 years.

Agatte, aged 2 years.

And in stock one horse, three sows and three fowls.

The land on which they are settled is situated as in the preceding cases. It was given to them verbally by Monsieur de Bonnaventure. On the said land they have made a clearing for the sowing of six bushels of grain in the coming spring.

Pierre Carret, ploughman, native of l'Acadie, aged 25 years, he has been in the country three years. Married to Anne Gautrot, native of l'Acadie, aged 26 years.

They have Firmain Carret, their son, aged one year.

And in stock one cow, one calf, two sows and four pigs.

The land on which they are settled is situated as in the preceding cases. It was given to them verbally by Monsieur Bonnaventure. On it they have made a clearing for garden only.

CENSUS.

Census of the settlers of Pointe au Boulleau, situated to the east of the entrance of Rivière de la Grande Ascension.

Ambroise Guillot, ploughman, native of l'Acadie, aged 24 years, he has been in the country 26 months. Married to Theotiste Daigre, native of l'Acadie, aged 24 years.

They have Margueritte Blanche Guillot, their daughter, aged 5 months.

Paul Severain Bertrand, native of l'Acadie, aged 15 years.

And in stock, one heifer.

The land on which they are settled is situated on the Pointe au Boulleau. It was given to them verbally by Monsieur de Bonnaventure. They have made on it a clearing for the sowing of twelve bushels of grain in the coming spring.

François Daigre, ploughman, native of l'Acadie, aged 48 years, he has been in the country 26 months. Married to Marie Boudrot, native of l'Acadie, aged 40 years.

They have one son and five daughters :

François Marie Daigre, aged 16 years ;

Margueritte, aged 18 years ;

Anne, aged 15 years ;

Helenne, aged 13 years ;

Marie, aged 11 years ;

François, aged 9 years.

And in stock : three oxen, one cow, two sows, one pig and two fowl.

The land on which they are settled is situated as in the preceding cases. It was given to them verbally by Monsieur de Bonnaventure. They have made a clearing on it for the sowing of twelve bushels of grain in the coming spring.

Alexis Daigre, ploughman, native of l'Acadie, aged 24 years, he has been in the country 26 months. Married to Margueritte Douaron, native of l'Acadie, aged 19 years.

In stock they have : one ox, one cow and two pigs.

The land on which they are settled is situated as in the preceding cases, and was given to them verbally by Monsieur de Bonnaventure. On it they have made a clearing for the sowing of two bushels of grain the coming spring.

CENSUS.

Census of the family of Pierre Henry, settled at the Anse de la Boullotierre.

Pierre Henry, ploughman, native of l'Acadie, aged 46 years, he has been in the country 14 months. Married to Anne Aucoin, native of l'Acadie, aged 46 years.

They have five sons and four daughters :—

Pierre Henry, aged 19 years ;

Paul, aged 18 years ;

Antoinne, aged 16 years ;

Barthelemy, aged 7 years ;

Thimotée, aged 5 years ;

Jeanne, aged 14 years ;

Anastazie, aged 12 years ;

Elisabeth, aged 10 years ;

Marie Josette, aged 17 months.

In stock they have : two oxen, two cows, one heifer, one calf, four sows and five pigs.

The land on which they are settled is situated on the Ance de la Boulottiere. It was given to them verbally by Monsieur de Bonnaventure, and on it they have made a clearing for the sowing of twelve bushels of grain this coming spring.

Census.

Census of the settlers of the Pointe Prime.

François Douaron, ploughman, native of l'Acadie, aged 38 years, he has been in the country 26 months. Married to Magdelainne Tilliac, native of l'Acadie, aged 35 years.

They have two sons and four daughters :—

Ambroise Douaron, aged 6 years ;
François, aged 4 years ;
Ozitte Josette, aged 12 years.
Magdelaine Angelique, aged 10 years ;
Blanche, aged 8 years ;
Marie Joseph, aged 5 months.

Their live stock consists of one cow, one calf, one bull, one horse and one pig.

The land on which they are settled is situated at Pointe Prime. It was given to them verbally by Monsieur de Bonnaventure. On it they have made a clearing for the sowing of twelve bushels of grain in the coming spring.

Noël Douaron, ploughman, native of l'Acadie, aged 70 years, and has been in the country 26 months. Married to Marie Henry, native of l'Acadie, aged 72 years.

They have with them Jean Baptiste Douaron, their grandson, native of l'Acadie, aged 17 years.

And in stock, two cows with their calves.

The land on which they are settled is situated as in the preceding cases. It was given to them verbally by Monsieur de Bonnaventure. On it they have made a clearing for the sowing of twelve bushels of grain in the coming spring.

Joseph Douaron, ploughman, native of l'Acadie, aged 36 years, he has been in the country 26 months. Married to Marie Tilliard, native of l'Acadie, aged 38 years.

They have four sons and four daughters :—

Paul Helie Douaron, aged 17 years ;
Laurent, aged 10 years ;
Joseph, aged 8 years ;
Gregoire, aged 2 months ;
Magdelaine, aged 14 years ;
Marie Rose, aged 12 years ;
Anastazie, aged 6 years ;
Anne Marie, aged 3 years.

They have the following live stock : two oxen, four cows, four calves, two mares, two pigs and five fowls.

The land on which they are settled is situated as in the preceding cases. It was given to them verbally by Monsieur de Bonnaventure. They have made a clearing on it for the sowing of twenty-four bushels of grain during the coming spring.

Claude Leprince, ploughman, native of l'Acadie, aged 24 years, he has been 26 months in the country. Married to Magdelaine Douaron, native of l'Acadie, aged 23 years.

They have in live stock : two oxen, one cow, one calf and three pigs.

The land on which they are settled is situated as in the preceding cases. It was given to them verbally by Monsieur de Bonnaventure. They have made a clearing on it for the sowing of six bushels of grain in the coming spring.

Louis Mathieu, ploughman, native of Baston, aged 48 years, he has been 26 months in the country. Married to Magdelainne Pitre, native of Cap de Sable, bishopric of Quebec, aged 47 years.

They have Baptiste Olivier Douaron, their son, aged 18 years ;

Hemilienne Perpétuité Douaron, their niece, orphan, native of l'Acadie, aged 12 years.

In live stock, they have : four oxen, three cows, two calves, three sows and two pigs.

The land on which they are settled is situated as in the preceding cases. It was given to them verbally by Monsieur de Bonnaventure. They have made on it, a clearing for the sowing of 16 bushels of grain in the coming spring.

Paul Douaron, ploughman, native of l'Acadie, aged 43 years, he has been in the country 26 months. Married to Margueritte Benoist, native of l'Acadie, aged 42 years.

They have one son and one daughter. And,

Pre. Paul Douaron, aged 15 years, native of l'Acadie ;

Pelagie Benoist, native of l'Acadie, aged 11 years, their nephews, orphans.

And in stock they possess : two oxen, three cows, one calf, one bull, one sow and one pig.

The land on which they are settled is situated as in the preceding cases. It was given to them verbally by Monsieur de Bonnaventure. They have made a clearing on it for the sowing of 16 bushels of grain in the coming spring.

Charles Douaron, ploughman, native of l'Acadie, aged 24 years, he has been in the country 26 months. Married to Anne Gertrude Benoist, native of l'Acadie, aged 19 years.

They have in live stock one ox, two cows, two calves, one sow and one pig.

The land on which they are settled is the same as that of their father. They have made on it a clearing for the sowing of eight bushels of grain in the coming spring.

Jean Arcenaud, ploughman, native of l'Acadie, aged 27 years, and has been in the country two years. Married to Marie Joseph Douaron, native of l'Acadie, aged 26 years.

They have one son and two daughters :—

Alexis Arcenaud, aged 6 years ;

Margueritte Joseph, aged 3 years ;

Marie Blanche, aged 2 years.

And in stock : four oxen, one cow, three heifers, and three pigs.

The land on which they are settled is situated east-south-east of the said Ance de la Pointe Prime, and was given to them verbally by Monsieur de Bonnaventure. They have made on it a clearing for the sowing of eight bushels of wheat in the coming spring.

Jean Baptiste Henry, ploughman, native of l'Acadie, aged 44 years, and has been in the country two years, Married to Marie Magdelaine Mieux, aged 42 years.

They have eight sons :—

Joseph Henry, aged 19 years ;

Jean Baptiste, aged 17 years ;

Paul, aged 15 years ;

Louis, aged 11 years ;

Bazille, aged 9 years ;

Charles, aged 7 years ;

Clement, aged 4 years ;

Firmain, aged 10 months ;

Marie Boudrot, orphan, aged 21 years.

And in stock : four oxen, one cow, two calves, one sow and two pigs.

The land on which they are settled is situated as in the preceding cases. It was given to them verbally by Monsieur de Bonnaventure. On it they have made a clearing for the sowing of thirteen bushels of wheat, and four bushels of oats in the coming spring.

Michel Pitre, ploughman, native of l'Acadie, aged 46 years, and has been in the country two years. Married to Marie Magdelaine Douaron, native of l'Acadie, aged 44 years.

They have four sons and three daughters :—

François Pitre, aged 19 years ;

Charles, aged 17 years ;

Paul Michel, aged 14 years ;

Simon, aged 13 years ;

Theotiste, aged 21 years ;

Marie Magdelaine, aged 16 years ;

Eufrosinne, aged 8 years ;

And in stock : two oxen, one cow, and six pigs.

The land on which they are settled is situated as in the preceding cases. It was given to them verbally by Monsieur de Bonnaventure. On it they have made a clearing for the sowing of ten bushels of wheat and eight bushels of oats in the coming spring.

Claude Arcement, ploughman, native of l'Acadie, aged 26 years, he has been in the country two years. Married to Angelique Douaron, native of l'Acadie, aged 24 years.

They have one son and two daughters : —

Firmain, aged 2 years.

Susanne Angelique, aged 5 years.

Theotiste Helenne, aged 3 years.

And in stock, two oxen, one cow, one calf and two pigs.

The land on which they are settled is situated as in the preceding case. It was given to them verbally by Monsieur de Bonnaventure. On it they have made a clearing for the sowing of six bushels of wheat and six bushels of oats in the coming spring.

Herné Guillot, ploughman, native of Doix, bishopric of Angers, aged 59 years.

He has Marie Joseph Guillot, his daughter, aged 29 years.

Jean Baptiste Guillot, native of l'Acadie, aged 31 years.

He has one son and two daughters :—

Charles Olivier, aged 6 years.

Elisabeth, aged 4 years.

Marie Joseph, aged 2 years.

And in stock two cows and one calf.

The land on which he is settled is situated as in the preceding case. It was given to him verbally by Monsieur de Bonnaventure. On it they have made a clearing for the sowing of four bushels of wheat in the coming spring.

René Guillot, ploughman, native of l'Acadie, aged 26 years, he has been in the country two years. Married to Marie Roze Daigre, native of l'Acadie, aged 20 years.

They have in live stock one ox, one cow, one calf and six pigs.

The land on which they are settled is situated as in the preceding case and was given to them verbally by Monsieur de Bonnaventure. On it they have made a clearing for the sowing of six bushels of wheat and six bushels of oats in the coming spring.

Census.

Census of the settlers of Ance à Pinnet.

Olivier Boudrot, ploughman, native of l'Acadie, aged 41 years, he has been in the country two years. Married to Henriette Guérin, native of l'Acadie, aged 40 years.

They have two sons and three daughters :—

Bazille Boudrot, aged 6 years.

Mathurin, aged 3 years.

Margueritte Joseph, aged 10 years.

Magdelaine Joseph, aged 8 years.

Anne Marie, aged 7 years.

And in stock two oxen, four cows, two calves, one bull, one heifer, five pigs and twenty-three fowls or chickens.

The land on which they are settled is situated at the farther end of Ance à Pinet to the south of the said ance. It was given to them verbally by Monsieur de Bonnaventure. On it they have made a clearing for a garden only.

Charles Boudrct, ploughman, native of l'Acadie aged 42 years, he has been 14 months in the country. Married to Cecille Terriaud, native of l'Acadie, aged 45 years.

They have two sons and one daughter ;

Charles Olivier, aged 16 years.

François, aged 14 years.

Cecille, aged 6 years.

And in stock four oxen, five cows, one calf, one horse, one ewe, three sows, two pigs and four fowls.

The land on which they are settled is situated as in the preceding case. It was given to them verbally by Monsieur de Bonnaventure. On it they have made a clearing for alarge garden.

Jean Apart, ploughman, native of l'Acadie, aged 32 years, he has been two years in the country. Married to Margueritte Joseph Braud.

They have one son and one daughter ;

Joseph Baptiste, aged 2 years.

Margueritte Joseph aged 5 years.

And in stock two oxen, one cow, one calf, one sow and six fowls.

The land on which they are settled is situated as in the preceding cases. It was given to them verbally by Monsieur de Bonnaventure. On it they have made a clearing for a garden only.

François Michel, junior, ploughman, native of l'Acadie, aged 32 years, he has been in the country 14 months. Married to Marie Joseph Bourg, native of l'Acadie, aged 34 years.

They have in live stock two oxen, one cow, one heifer, two sows, four pigs and four fowls.

The land on which they are settled is situated as in the preceding cases. It was given to them verbally by Monsieur de Bonnaventure. On it they have made a clearing for the sowing of three bushels of wheat in the coming spring.

Jean Michel, ploughman, native of l'Acadie, aged 27 years, he has been in the country 14 months. Married to Martinne Bourg, native of l'Acadie, aged 28 years.

They have two daughters ;

Anne Agathe, aged 4 years.

Margueritte, aged 2 years.

And in stock one ox, one cow, three sows and three pigs.

The land on which they are settled is situated as in the preceding cases. It was given to them verbally by Monsieur de Bonnaventure. On it they have made a clearing for the sowing of three bushels of grain in the coming spring.

François Michel, senior, native of l'Acadie, aged 63 years, he has been in the country 14 months. Married to Elisabeth Le Jeuge, native of l'Acadie, aged 65 years.

They have two sons and five daughters :—

Joseph Michel, aged 17 years ;

Pierre, aged 14 years ;

Margueritte, aged 19 years ;

Catherine. aged 16 years ;

Félicité, aged 11 years ;

Françoise Perpétue, aged 9 years.

Anne Benoist, daughter of the said Elizabeth Le Jeuge, aged 22 years.

Their live stock consists of two oxen, one heifer, one sow, two pigs and one hen.

The land on which they are settled is situated as in the preceeding cases. It was given to them verbally by Monsieur de Bonnaventure. On it they have made a clearing for the sowing of four bushels of grain next spring.

Ambroise Naquin, native of l'Acadie, aged 27 years, he has been two years in the country. Married to Isabelle Bourg, native of l'Acadie, aged 20 years.

They have Isabelle Naquin, their daughter aged two years.

And in stock two oxen, two cows, one calf, one horse, one ewe, four pigs and two fowls.

The land on which they are settled is situated on the south side of Ance à Pinet. It was given to them verbally by Monsieur de Bonnaventure. On it they have made a clearing for the sowing of a bushel and a half of grain.

Jacques Naquin, ploughman, native of l'Acadie, aged 51 years, he has been one year in the country, widower of the late Jeanne Melançon.

He has three sons and three daughters :—

Jasques Naquin, aged 24 years ;

Joseph, aged 20 years ;

Pierre, aged 17 years ;

Margueritte, aged 25 years ;
Elisabeth, aged 19 years;
Marianne, aged 14 years.

Pierre Melançon, native of l'Acadie, aged 80 years, his father-in-law, lives with him. They have in stock, four oxen, two cows, one calf, one mare, seven ewes and four pigs.

The land on which they are settled is situated as in the preceeding case. It was given to them verbally by Monsieur de Bonnaventure. On it they have made a clearing for the sowing of two bushels of wheat in the coming spring.

François Naquin, ploughman, native of l'Acadie, aged 48 years, he has been in the country two years. Married to Angélique Blanchard, native of l'Acadie, aged 45 years.

They have four sons and six daughters :—
Jean Baptiste, aged 23 years ;
François, aged 19 years ;
Charles, aged 14 years ;
Joseph, aged 12 years ;
Angélique, aged 21 years ;
Anne, aged 18 years ;
Marianne Nastazie, aged 11 years ;
Ursulle, aged 7 years ;
Tersille, aged 4 years ;
Marianne, aged 2 years ;
Isaac Hébert, aged 3 years, his grand-son.

They have in stock four oxen, two cows, three calves, three ewes and five pigs.

The land on which they are settled is situated as in the preceding cases. It was given to them verbally by Monsieur de Bonnaventure. On it they have made a clearing for the sowing of three bushels of wheat in the coming spring.

Pierre Dugas, ploughman, native of l'Acadie, aged 43 years, he has been on the island one year. Married to Elizabeth Bourg, native of l'Acadie, aged 40 years.

They have three sons and five daughters :—
Jean Dugas, aged 16 years ;
Pierre, aged 6 years ;
Prosper, aged 1 year ;
Marie, aged 18 years ;
Marie Joseph, aged 15 years ;
Elizabeth, aged 13 years ;
Ainesse, aged 11 years ;
Ozitte, aged 10 years.

The land on which they are settled is situated on the south side of Ance à Pinet. It was given to them verbally by Monsieur de Bonnaventure. They have made a clearing on it for the sowing of two bushels of wheat in the coming spring.

Charles Pitre, ploughman, native of l'Acadie, aged 32 years, he has been one year on the island. Married to Anne Thibadeau, native of l'Acadie, aged 31 years.

They have one son and two daughters :—
Jean Baptiste, aged one year ;
Marie Martha, aged 6 years ;
Ozitte, aged 4 years.

They have in stock three oxen, five cows and four pigs.

The land on which they are settled is situated as in the preceding cases. It was given to them verbally by Monsieur de Bonnaventure. On it they have made a clearing for the sowing of four bushels of wheat in the coming spring.

Paul Henry, ploughman, native of l'Acadie, aged 29 years, he has been on the island one year. Married to Théotiste Thibaudeau, native of l'Acadie, aged 27 years.

They have two sons and one daughter :—
Athanase Henry, aged 6 years ;
Firmain, aged 2 years ;

Magdelaine Joseph, aged 4 years.

In stock they have two oxen, one cow, one ewe, one bull and five pigs.

The land on which they are settled is situated as in the preceding case. It was given to them verbally by Monsieur de Bonnaventure. They have made a clearing on it for the sowing of four bushels of wheat in the coming spring.

Alexandre Gautreau, native of l'Acadie, aged 34 years, he has been one year on the island. Married to Margueritte Hébert, native of l'Acadie, aged 27 years.

They have three sons and one daughter :—

François Hilaire, aged 7 years ;

Alexander, aged 3 years ;

Marin, aged 1 year ;

Jullienne, aged 5 years ;

Victor Gautreau, native of l'Acadie, aged 13 years, his nephew.

They have in stock one cow and four pigs.

The land on which they are settled is situated as in the preceding cases. It was given to them verbally by Monsieur de Bonnaventure. They have made a clearing on it for the sowing of two bushels of wheat in the coming spring.

François Gautreau, ploughman, native of l'Acadie, aged 74 years, he has been in the country one year. Married to Louise Aucoin, native of l'Acadie, aged 72 years.

They have Marie Magdelaine Gautreau, their daughter, aged 25 years.

Their live stock consists of one cow and four pigs.

François Gautreau, ploughman, native of l'Acadie, aged 28 years, he has been on the island one year. Married to Marie Leblanc, native of l'Acadie, aged 23 years.

They have three sons :

Jean Baptiste, aged 3 years ;

Joseph, aged 19 months ;

Charles Gautreau, orphan, aged 17 years, their nephew, lives with them.

In stock they have two oxen, one cow and five fowls.

The land on which they are settled is situated on the south side of Ance à Pinet. It was given to them verbally by Monsieur de Bonnaventure. They have made on it a clearing for the sowing of three bushels of wheat in the coming spring.

René Aucoin, ploughman, native of l'Acadie, aged 41 years, he has been 14 months on the island. Married to Magdelaine Michel, native of l'Acadie, aged 35 years

They have one son and five daughters :

François Marin, aged 8 months ;

Marie Magdelaine, aged 14 years ;

Ozitte, aged 12 years ;

Elisabeth, aged 9 years ;

Anne Lablanche, aged 6 years ;

Margueritte Joseph, aged 5 years.

They have in live stock two oxen, two cows, one heifer, three sows, four pigs and five fowls.

The land on which they are settled is situated as in the preceding cases. It was given to them verbally by Monsieur de Bonnaventure. On it they have made a clearing for the sowing of four bushels of wheat in the coming spring.

Pierre Gautreau, ploughman, native of l'Acadie, aged 44 years, he has been in the country 15 months. Married to Elisabeth Terriaud, native of l'Acadie, aged 42 years.

They have seven sons and three daughters :

Pierre Landry, aged 20 years ;

Theo, aged 14 years ;

Bazille, aged 11 years ;

Honoré, aged 9 years ;

Benoist, aged 3 years ;

Pierre Melançon, aged 17 years ;

Joseph, aged 15 years.

Aniesse Gautreau, aged 18 years ;

Marie Joseph, aged 7 years ;
Roze, aged 5 years.

They have in live stock : three oxen, two cows, two mares, one ewe, six pigs and three fowls.

The land on which they are settled is situated as in the preceding cases. It was given to them verbally by Monsieur de Bonnaventure. They have made a clearing on it for the sowing of three bushels of wheat and two bushels of oats in the coming spring.

Ance du Havre à Mathieu is situated on the south shore of the Isle Saint-Jean, three leagues from the peninsula of Trois-Rivières and six from Pointe de l'Est. It is formed by Cap à David lying to the south and Cap à la Soury to the north. The distance between these points is estimated at one league. The creek lies north and south and runs a half league inland to the west, having an almost uniform breadth throughout. At its extreme furthermost end it branches into two harbours. One of which is called Havre à Matthieu. It is void of any settler and lies to the north of the creek running west one league inland.

The width of this harbour is ascertained to be irregular, but is estimated at an average of 200 toises. In the middle of the creek there is a channel twenty toises in breadth, in which there is from eight to nine feet of water at low tide. The lands surrounding the harbour are covered with hardwood of every description.

At the other extremity of the said creek lies havre la Fortune. It runs south-west to a depth of a league and a half inland. Its breadth at the widest part is estimated to be from 300 to 350 toises, whilst the channel has seven to eight feet of water on the bar at high tide. The nature of the soil renders it profitable for cultivation, and the settlers who took refuge here at the time of the last war, praise it very highly.

The meadow lands are situated on the banks of these rivers. They yield a sufficiently large quantity of hay to serve as fodder for such live stock as the settlers have in possession at present, but it is thought that if the area was extended a large number of head of cattle might be raised and fed. All the surrounding lands are covered with different sorts of mixed timber, but the settlers have not yet discovered a quarry of any sort.

CENSUS.

Census of the settlers at Havre La Fortune, in men, women, children, &c. Namely :—

Joseph Le Prieur, navigator, native of Port Royal, in l'Acadie, aged 49 years, he has been in the country 30 years. Married to Marguerite Olivier, native of Beaubassin, aged 29 years.

By their marriage they have had three sons and one daughter :—

Emanuel Le Prieur, aged 9 years ;
Rocq, aged 7 years ;
Jean Baptiste, aged 5 years ;
Marie, aged 3 years.

In stock they have the following : six oxen, six cows, two heifers, four calves, five ewes, five pigs, and twenty fowls; as well as one schooner of 26 tons burden, and another of 15 tons.

The land on which they are newly settled is situated on the right bank of the harbour of La Fortune. Their only title is that of possession, and a verbal permission from Monsieur de Bonnaventure, the King's commandant in the isle Saint Jean. They have made a large clearing and could have sown 28 bushels of seed if they had had it, but have only sown nine bushels and a half of wheat, half a bushel of rye, half bushel of barley, four and a half bushels of peas, two bushels of oats, and they could have sown another eleven bushels.

Cristophle Delanne, ploughman, native of the the parish of Perier, bishopric of Avranche, Normandy, aged 47 years, he has been in the country 23 years. Married to Marguerite Caissy, native of Beaubassin, aged 25 years.

By their marriage they have five children, four sons and one daughter :—

Pierre Delanne, aged 13 years ;
Jean, aged 9 years ;
Jacques, aged 6 years ;
Jean, aged 30 months ;
Geneviève, aged 7 years.

In stock they have : four oxen, three cows, one calf, four ewes, four pigs and four fowls.

The land on which they are settled is contiguous to that of Joseph Le Prieur. They have made a large clearing on it where they have sown eight bushels of wheat, four bushels of oats, one bushel and a half of peas, half a bushel of barley, half a bushel of buck wheat and a piece of land sufficient for two bushels of seed sown with turnips, and they have sufficient land for the sowing of another eight bushels of seed.

Pierre Le Prieur, ploughman, native of St. Pierre in the north part of the island, aged 27 years. Married to Judict Chiasson, widow of the late Charles Lacroix dit Durel, native of l'Acadie, aged 39 years.

She has six children by her first marriage and two by the second, namely, two sons and six daughters :—

Charles Lacroix, aged 13 years ;
Pierre Le Prieur, aged 4 years ;
Marie Lacroix ;
Margueritte Lacroix, aged 21 years ;
Anne, aged 18 years ;
Judict, aged 16 years ;
Marie Anne, aged 7 years ;
Marie Le Prieur, aged 2 years ;

In stock they have three oxen. two cows, and one heifer.

The land on which they are settled is situated to the south-west of that of Joseph Le Prieur, his brother. They have made a clearing where they were only able to sow six bushels of wheat, having no more. Their land is sufficiently large to sow eighteen bushels of seed.

Joannis Laborde, ploughman, native of the parish of la Bastide, bishopric of Bayonne, aged 34 years, he has been in the country 12 years. Married to Marie Le Prieur, native of St. Pierre in the north of this island, aged 32 years.

They have five children by their marriage, three sons and two daughters :—

Guaillaume Laborde, aged 12 years ;
Charles François, aged 9 years ;
Jean Baptiste, aged 1 year ;
Marie, aged 6 years ;
Marguerite, aged 3 years ;

They have in live stock four oxen, five cows, four calves, one wether and nine fowls.

The land on which they are settled is situated on the left bank of the harbour of la Fortune. They have made a clearing on it and sown ten bushels of wheat and half a bushel of peas.

Joseph Leblanc, ploughman, native of l'Acadie, aged 40 years, he has been in the country one year. Married to Marie Bourg, native of l'Acadie, aged 35 years.

They have five children of their marriage, all sons ;—

Ambroise LeBlanc, aged 14 years ;
Simon Joseph, aged 12 years ;
Benony, aged 3 years ;
Charles, aged 4 months ;
Joseph, aged 8 years :

In live stock they have four oxen, six cows, five calves, one horse, six pigs and fourteen fowls or chickens.

The land on which they are settled was given to them verbally by Monsieur de Bonnaventure, commandant of this island, to the south-west of the dwelling of Joannis Laborde. They have made a clearing on it where they have sown four bushels of wheat.

5-6 EDWARD VII., A. 1906

Abraham Daigre, ploughman, native of l'Acadie, aged 47 years, he has been in the country two years. Married to Marie Boudrot, native of the parish of St. Charles, bishopric of Quebec, aged 44 years.

They have nine children of their marriage, seven boys and two girls :—

Aimable Daigre, aged 21 years ;
Jean , aged 20 years ;
Jean Eloy, aged 14 years ;
François Marie, aged 12 years ;
Pierre, aged 10 years ;
Joseph, aged 5 years ;
Nicolas, aged 2 years ;
Margueritte, aged 23 years ;
Marie Rosalie, aged 16 years ;

In live stock they they have two oxen, two cows, one calf, one ewe, three pigs and four fowls.

The land on which they are settled is situated on the right shore of the said harbour. It was given to them verbally by Monsieur de Bonnaventure, commandant of Isle Saint-Jean. They have made a clearing on which they have sown two bushels of wheat, two bushels of peas and one bushel of oats.

We left Havre de la Fortune on the 11th and took the route for Pointe de l'Est, situated, it is stated, six leagues from the harbour. After having doubled the point of Havre à Mathieu, we passed a little to seaward of the harbour la Souris and observed that it runs a league and a half inland to the north, throwing out an arm to the east. The entrance to the harbour is practicable only for boats and wood boats of the capacity of three to four cords. Next we noticed the little harbors that run, the one to the west and the other to the north-west, which are practicable for boats alone. In all this part of the country there is but little hay made. The land seems to be of a nature suitable for cultivation, and is covered with all kinds of hard wood fit for the construction of small vessels and boats. These two harbours lie a distance of one league apart and two leagues from the harbour of la Fortune. After having made another two leagues, we found ourselves crossing Havre de l'Echourie. Its entrance lies north and south, and is estimated at one hundred toises in length. Inside the entrance the harbour divides into two arms, running east and west so that that on the starboard side on entering may have a league in length, by a quarter of league of breadth, and that to the larboard three-quarters of a league. There is a great deal of grass on the banks of the harbour. The harbour is practicable only for boats. It is considered that this harbor would only have been a large creek but for the sand dunes thrown up by the wind, which sand dunes separate it from the sea. Next, after making another two leagues, we doubled Pointe de l'Est. This point has been reduced to a wilderness by a fire which has passed through this section, and the settlers have established themselves at a distance of two leagues from the point on the north side.

The land on which the people have settled is of the best for cultivation. Nevertheless they have sown no seed here, and the truth is that they lack seed to sow, and if the King does not make them a gift or loan of seed so that they can sow it next spring they will find it impossible to maintain themselves, being to-day at the last stage of poverty through the great mortality among their live stock.

Census.

Census of the settlers at Pointe de l'Est in men, women and children.

Noel Pinet, ploughman, native of l'Acadie, aged 70 years, he has been twelve years in the country. Married to Rose Henry, native of l'Acadie, aged 50 years.

They have with them one son and one daughter.

Charles Pinet, aged 18 years.
Anne, aged 13 years.

In live stock they have three oxen, two cows, one heifer, one mare, seven wethers and nine pigs.

The land on which they are settled was granted to them by Messieurs Duchambon and Dubuisson. They have made a clearing on it where they ordinarily sow forty bushels of grain yearly, and will sow that quantity next spring if they are given the seed.

Antoine Dechevery, fisherman and ploughman, native of Bayonne, aged 40 years; he has been 25 years in the colony. Married to Marie Pinet, native of Canada, aged 30 years.

They have six children, five sons and one daughter :

Denis Dechevery, aged 11 years.

Antoine, aged 10 years.

François, aged 8 years.

Pierre, aged 6 years.

Jean, aged 4 years.

Marie, aged 6 months.

In stock they have six oxen, one cow, one heifer, two calves, one mare, six ewes, four pigs and three hens.

The land on which they are settled was given to them by Noel Pinet, their father. They have made a clearing where they could sow 36 bushels of grain in the coming spring.

Jean Baptiste Pinet, fisherman and ploughman, native of Quebec, aged 41 years. Married to Jeanne Pillot, native of La Rochelle, aged 24 years.

They have three sons :

Charles Pinet, aged 4 years.

Bazille, aged 3 years.

Jean Baptiste, aged 2 years.

In stock they have : two oxen, one cow, one calf and four pigs.

The land on which they are settled is part of the homestead of their father. They have made a clearing where they could sow twenty bushels of grain if it were given to them.

Pierre Pinet, ploughman, native of Petit Degrat, aged 24 years. Married to Geneviève Trahant, native of l'Acadie, aged 22 years.

They have three sons :

Jean Pinet, aged 3 years.

Pierre, aged 2 years.

Paul, aged 6 weeks.

They have in live stock two oxen, two cows, one calf, one wether and one pig.

They are settled on the homestead of Noel Pinet, their father. They have made a clearing where they could sow thirty bushels of grain if they had it.

We left on the 13th and took the route for l'Etang du Noffrage, following the sea shore continually for the six leagues at which the distance from the Post at Pointe de l'Est to l'Etang du Noffrage is estimated.

In this distance we met with nothing worthy of notice. The land is a desert owing to the occurrence of the fire, but a short distance inland the country is covered with hardwood and the soil was good for the production of all kinds of grain and roots ; everything coming up in abundance. Owing to the lack of seed grain the settler here was unable to seed his land this year, but the small quantity of wheat which he was able to sow is amongst the finest in the island. The ears are long, large and well filled. The Etang du Noffrage runs a quarter of a league inland to the south-west. The breadth averages 80 toises. At the extremity of the étang, a long brook, which never dries up, discharges its water. This brook is supplied from two large springs lying at a distance of two leagues and a half inland to the west south-west. The brook contains sufficient water to run flour and saw mills, but as regards the latter they are considered useless as there is no timber suitable for sawing, all the hardwood, growing in the surrounding district being good at the best for the building of boats.

We left on the 14th for St. Pierre du Nord. We counted the distance between the two points as six leagues by the road. We saw nothing on the way that calls for description.

18—9

5-6 EDWARD VII., A. 1906

DESCRIPTION OF HAVRE ST. PIERRE.

The harbour of St. Pierre lies on the north coast of the Isle St. Jean. It is well suited for the pursuit of cod fishing, the fish being as a rule more abundant here than at Ile Royale ; but, in truth, of a quality much inferior to those of the latter island. A market for the cod is found at Louisbourg, as well as with the merchants of that town, for shipment with the consignments they make to the islands of America. The lands around St. Pierre are suitable for cultivation and the settlers successfully follow the occupations of fishing and of cultivating the soil.

The lands that have been seeded this year present one of the most beautiful scenes that anyone could desire to witness.

The entrance to the harbour is formed by sand dunes. It is estimated that the entrance is 350 toises across, the sand dunes lying east and west. The channel is navigable only for vessels having a draft of eight or nine feet, and at high tide the channel runs north and south with a depth everywhere of from 15 to 16 feet of water, and if it were not for the bar and shallows that have been thrown up by the different currents, vessels of 300 tons burden could make their passage without any difficulty. In order to enter the harbour it is necessary to follow the lines of the sand dunes at a distance of 100 toises, on the west side, afterwards passing at a distance of 20 or 30 toises at the utmost the fish-drying grounds of le Sieur Aubin.

It is believed that if an embankment were constructed from the foot of the sand dune on the east side of the harbour to the border of the channel, sufficiently high to force the currents to flow into and out of the harbour, of St. Pierre as well as the main body of the river to pass through the said channel from that point, the currents would be diverted from the flat ground, and become sufficiently rapid to clear away the bar which proves the greatest impediment to the navigation of the harbour. The settlement at the harbour of St. Pierre is deemed to be one of considerable importance now, as much because of the trade connected with the fisheries, as of that which might be carried on in the interior of the Isle, were it, as it seems likely to be, well settled. When one considers seriously all that might be accomplished to make this trade solid and durable, it becomes apparent that the cultivation of the land, and the raising of live stock of all descriptions must be regarded as the pivot on which the whole ought to turn. It must be remembered that so long as the fishermen are obliged to procure all their fishing equipment, supplies and food from the merchants of Louisbourg, or other itinerant traders, they will, owing to the excessive prices they have to pay for what merchandise they require, and the moderate prices they receive for their fish, always find themselves conducting their fishery operations at a loss.

On the other hand if the settlers had the power of making from their own produce the bread, butter, meat, clothes and linen, to supply their principal wants, and the fishermen were obliged to procure only their salt, lines, hooks, etc., from the aforesaid merchants, they would be able to sell their fish at the lowest price, and reap a substantial profit.

Census.

Census of the settlers at St. Pierre du Nord.

Louis Beaulieu, ploughman, native of—— ——————aged 54 years. Married to Margueritte Oudy, native of l'Acadie, aged 34 years.

They have seven children, three sons and four daughters :—

Pierre Beaulieu, aged 19 years ;
Jean Louis, aged 13 years ;
Jasques, aged 1 year ;
Marie Jeanne, aged 11 years ;
Helenne, aged 7 years ;
Marie Louise, aged 6 years ;
Margueritte, aged 3 years ;

They own the following live stock :—four oxen, three cows, two bulls, one sow, five pigs, one ram, twelve ewes and three fowls.

The land on which they are settled is situated on the north bank of the river St. Pierre. It was granted to them in 1736 by Messrs. Despiet de Pensens and Dubuisson. The grant has been homologated by Messieurs de Brouillant and Le Normand. It contains five arpents, eight perches, nine feet of front facing on the said river with a depth extending from the bank of said river to the dunes.

They have made on said grant a large piece of pasture land, with a clearing, on which they have sown twenty bushels of wheat, two bushels of peas, and there remains fallow land sufficient for the sowing of twenty-four bushels of seed which they have not seeded for want of grain.

Jean Oudy, fisherman and ploughman, native of l'Acadie, aged 29 years, he has been in the country 22 years. Married to Marie Blanchard, native of l'Acadie, aged 23 years.

They have Jean Baptiste, their son, aged 10 months.

Rosalie Blanchard, her sister, aged 9 years.

They have in live stock two cows, one mare, ten ewes, two sows and eleven fowls or chickens.

The land on which they are settled is situated on the north side of the river St. Pierre. They have been there since the month of August last by the verbal permission of M. de Bonnaventure.

They have made a clearing on it where they have sown two bushels and a half of wheat, one bushel of peas and half a bushel of oats.

Jean Lacroix dit Canniche, fisherman and ploughman, native of Bayonne, aged 40 years, he has been 26 years in the colony. Married to Cecille Oudy, native of l'Acadie, aged 39 years.

They have five children, three sons and two daughters :—

In live stock they have six oxen, four cows, one bull, fifteen ewes, one calf, six lambs, four pigs, two sows and five fowls.

The land on which they are settled is situated on the north side of the river Saint-Pierre. It contains, fronting on the said river————————arpents——-———— perches and—————feet and in depth extending the back to the dunes.

They have made a clearing on which they have sown nine bushels of wheat and one bushel of peas and there remains a piece of fallow land sufficient for the sowing of nine bushels.

Martin Tchiparé, fisherman and ploughman, native of Bayonne, aged 38 years, he has been 24 years in the colony. Married to Marie Oudy, native of l'Acadie, aged 36 years.

They have six children, three sons and three daughters :—

Jacques Martin, aged 14 years ;

Pierre, aged 8 years ;

Martin, aged 2 years ;

Marie Anne, aged 13 years ;

Cecille, aged 11 years ;

Magdelaine, aged 4 years ;

Guillaume Gallet, native of————————————aged 22 years, domestic to the said Tchiparé.

They have in live stock five oxen, one cow, two heifers, one calf, five wethers, three ewes, two lambs, two pigs, three sows, eight geese, ten hens, together with one boat.

The land on which they are settled is situated on the north side of the river Saint-Pierre. It was granted to them by deed but they were unable to produce the title to us having lost it. They have made a clearing on which they have sown twelve bushels of wheat and a bushel and a half of peas and they still have sufficient fallow land for the sowing of nine bushels.

Claude Oudy, fisherman and ploughman, poor, native of l'Acadie, aged 40 years, he has been in the country 30 years. Married to Angelique Potier, native of Beaubassin, aged 29 years.

They have eight children, two sons and six daughters :—

18—9½

5-6 EDWARD VII., A. 1906

Claude Oudy, aged 12 years ;

Jean Baptiste, aged 5 years ;

Marie Henriette, aged 8 years ;

Cecille, aged 6 years ;

Monique, aged 4 years ;

Marie Joseph, aged 3 years ;

Marie Anne, aged 2 years ;

Marie Magdelaine, aged one month.

They have in live stock one ox, six wethers, two ewes, one pig, and fifty-six fowls or chickens.

The land on which they are settled is situated on the north of the river Saint-Pierre. It was granted to them by Messieurs de Pensens and Dubuisson, and homologated by Messieurs de Brouillant and Lenormand. They have made a clearing on it in which they have sowed two bushels of wheat, and there remains fallow land in which they might sow twenty bushels.

The widow of Jacques Oudy, native of l'Acadie, aged 55 years, she has been in the country 24 years.

She has seven children, four sons and three daughters :—

Pierre Oudy, aged 28 years ;

Joseph, aged 20 years ;

Etienne, aged 16 years ;

Charles, aged 14 years.

Anne, aged 24 years.

Magdelaine, aged 17 years ;

Cecille, aged 12 years.

In live stock she has eight oxen, four sows, two bulls, two heifers, eight wethers, ten ewes, eight pigs, thirty geese and eight fowl.

The land on which she is settled is situated on the north side of the river Saint-Pierre. It was granted by Messieurs de Pensens and Potier Dubuisson, and homologated by Messieurs de Brouillant and Le Normant under date the 20th July, 1736. It contains 5 arpents, 6 perches facing on the said river with a depth including all to the dunes. They have made a clearing on it where they have sown twenty-four bushels of wheat, six bushels of peas, six bushels of oats and one of linseed, and still have sufficient fallow land for another twenty-two bushels.

Jacques Oudy, fisherman and ploughman, native of l'Acadie, aged 30 years, he has been on the island 24 years. Married to Magdelaine Dousset, native of l'Acadie, aged 26 years.

They have Marie Magdelaine, their daughter, aged 9 months.

In stock they have two cows, four ewes, one sow and three pigs.

The land on which they are settled is situated on the north of the river Saint-Pierre. The only title they have is that of possession, and permission from Monsieur de Bonnaventure, the King's Commandant on the Isle. On it they have made a clearing for the sowing of three bushels of wheat and one bushel of peas.

Jean Baptiste Vescot, ploughman, native of the parish of Saint Jouachim, bishopric of Quebec, aged 62 years, he has been in the country 24 years. Married to Marie Chiasson, native of Beaubassin, in the bishopric aforesaid.

They have six children, three sons and three daughters :

Jean Baptiste, aged 22 years ;

Pierre, aged 16 years ;

Joseph, aged 14 years ;

Angélique, aged 24 years ;

Anne, aged 20 years ;

Rosalie, aged 8 years.

In live stock they have the following : eight oxen, eight cows, eight calves, one horse, one mare, thirty ewes or wethers, seventeen pigs, twenty-one geese, eleven turkeys and twelve fowls and also a flour mill situated between Saint Pierre and the Pointe de l'Est.

The land on which they are settled is situated to the north-east of the harbour of Saint-Pierre. They have made a clearing on it where they have sown forty bushels of wheat, eleven bushels of oats, three bushels of peas and four bushels of rye, and there still remains fallow land sufficient for the sowing of thirty-two bushels. They hold the said land under grant from Messieurs de Pensens and Dubuisson, under date of the 18th of July, 1736. The said land contains five arpents frontage by a depth extending to the dunes, said to be ten arpents. They enjoy another piece of land which is a sort of a marsh, where they make their hay, situated at Grand Etang in the north part of this isle, under a certificate of the late Monsieur Potier Dubuisson, dated the 22nd July, 1738, in which it is stated that half of this land is given to them and the other half to Jacques Oudy and that with the consent of Monsieur de Pensens.

Pierre Bonnière, tailor and ploughman, native of parish of Raquiel, bishopric of Rennes, aged 43 years, he came from l'Acadie with his family to this isle two years ago. Married to Magdelaine Forest, native of Cobequit, in the said Acadia, aged 35 years.

They have six children—three sons and three daughters :—

Michel Joseph, aged 17 years ;
Jean Jacques, aged 16 years ;
Charles, aged 8 years ;
Marie Madelaine, aged 19 years ;
Rose, aged 14 years ;
Anne, aged 11 years.

They have the following live stock : three oxen, two cows, one calf, one sow, four ewes, eleven fowls.

The land on which they are settled is situated half a league in the interior of the lands in the south part of the settlement of said Pierre du Nord. It was given to them verbally by Monsieur de Bonnaventure. On it they have only made a clearing for a garden.

The said Sr. Bonnière occupies another piece of land that he has purchased from Anne Daigre, widow of the late Etienne Poitevin situated to the south of the farm of Sr. François Douville, at Pointe de St. Pierre. They have made a clearing on it on which they have sown eight bushels of wheat.

Pierre Bonnier, junior, ploughman, native of l'Acadie, aged 21 years, he has been in the country two years. Married to Anne Granger, native of l'Acadie, aged 21 years.

They have in stock, one ox, one cow and eight fowls.

The land on which they are settled is situated to the south-west of the property of Pierre Bonnière, their father. It was given to them verbally by Monsieur de Bonnaventure. On it they have made a clearing on which they have sown five bushels of wheat ; and they have fallow land besides sufficient for the sowing of another five bushels.

Mathurin Thenière, fisherman and ploughman, native of Avranches, Normandy, aged 60 years, he has been in the country 10 years. Married to Anne Daigre, native of l'Acadie, aged 80 years.

They have Anne Noyer, their grand-daughter, aged 8 years.

One cow with her calf.

The land on which they are settled is situated in the interior at half a league distance from the parish on the King's Highway to Grande Source. On it they have made a clearing on which they have sown one bushel and a half of wheat.

François Legendre, ploughman, native of Saint-Malo, Brittany, aged 27 years, he has been in the country two years. Married to Marguerite Labauve, native of l'Acadie, aged 25 years.

They have Henrietta Legendre, their daughter, aged 18 months.

They have in live stock two oxen, two cows, one pig and three fowls.

The land on which they are settled is situated on the south of the havre Saint-Pierre. It was given to them verbally by Monsieur de Bonnaventure. They have made on it a large clearing and sown two bushels and a half of wheat and one bushel and a half of peas.

5-6 EDWARD VII., A. 1906

Charles Emanuel, ploughman, native of l'Acadie, aged 45 years ; he has been in the country two years. Married to Claire Daigre, native of l'Acadie, aged 52 years.

They have five sons and one daughter :—

Jean Emanuel, aged 18 years ;
Marcel, aged 15 years ;
Pierre, aged 13 years ;
Alexis, aged 10 years ;
Paul, aged 8 years ;
Marie, aged 16 years.

In stock they have three oxen, three cows, one heifer, two calves and two pigs.

The land on which they are settled is situated to the south of the havre Saint Pierre, half a league in the interior. It was given to them verbally by Monsieur de Bonnaventure. They have made a clearing and sowed on it one bushel of peas, and they still have fallow land for the sowing of 24 bushels the coming spring.

Mr. Delaborde, merchant, native of Coulombe, archbishopric of Paris, aged 48 years, he has been in the country 11 years. Married to Anne Verrien, native of this place, aged 27 years.

They have by their marriage two sons :—

François, aged 8 years ;
Louis, aged 2 years.

They have in live stock four oxen, one horse, eleven ewes and eight fowls.

The land they occupy was given to them verbally by Messieurs Duchambon and Dubuisson, in 1742. They have made a clearing where they can sow thirty-two bushels of grain the coming spring.

The said Sr. Delaborde owns a boat.

Pierre Dubocq, ploughman, native of Rouen, aged 42 years ; he has been in the country twenty years. Married to Suzanne Lemercier, native of Saint-Machoux, bishopric of Rouen, aged 50 years.

They have four children, two sons and two daughters :—

Pierre, aged 16 years ;
Jacques, aged 9 years ;
Magdelaine, aged 16 years ;
Marie, aged 11 years.

Their live stock consists of two ewes and eight fowls.

The land on which they are settled was given to them verbally by Messieurs Duchambon and Dubuisson in 1743. They have made a clearing on it where they can sow ten bushels of grain, if they are given it for they appear to be in very great indigence.

Suzanne Berloin, widow of the late George Mansel, native of the town and parish of Saint-Jean d'Angelly, aged 45 years, she has been 33 years in the country.

She has the following live stock : seven oxen, two cows, eighteen ewes, six pigs, three sows, twenty-four geese, six turkeys and thirty-two fowls or chickens.

The land on which she is settled, was given to her verbally by Messieurs Duchambon and Dubuisson in 1741, the extent she does not know. She has made a clearing on which she has sown ten bushels of wheat, one bushel of peas, and one bushel of oats, and has sufficient land remaining for the sowing of twenty bushels of grain.

François Durocher, ploughman, native of the bishopric of Rennes, aged 80 years, he has been in the country 33 years. Married to Elizabeth Brunau, native of Sainte in Xaintonge, aged 69 years.

All their live stock consists of one cow with her calf.

The land on which they are settled was sold to them by the late Etienne Thomas in 1726, for the sum of 112 livres. They have made a clearing on which 24 bushels of wheat could be sown.

Guillaume Patris, fisherman and ploughman, native of Saint Brieux, aged 38 years, he has been in the country 20 years. Married to Françoise Chiasson, widow of the late Guillaume Gallet, native of l'Acadie, aged 46 years.

They have six children, four sons and two daughters :

Guillaume Gallet, aged 22 years ;

François Gallet, aged 12 years ;

George Patris, aged 8 years ;

Paul, aged 5 years ;

Françoise, aged 15 years ;

Angélique, aged 7 years.

They have in live stock : two oxen, two cows, one calf, six wethers, one pig, two geese and eight turkeys.

The land on which they are settled was granted to them in form by Messieurs Aubert and Dubuisson in 1723, but they cannot produce the deed, it having being burnt in the fire of 1724. They have made a clearing, where they have sown three bushels of wheat, and they have fallow land besides for the sowing of thirty-seven bushels.

Jean Le Breton, fisherman and ploughman, native of Saint Malo, aged 63 years, he has been in the country 28 years. Married to Marie Bertrand, native of l'Acadie, aged 50 years.

They have six children, five sons and one daughter :

Charles, aged 25 years ;

François, aged 23 years ;

Jean, aged 20 years ;

Joseph, aged 18 years ;

Bonnaventure, aged 12 years ;

Margueritte, aged 24 years.

In live stock they have two oxen, two cows, two calves, one heifer, five ewes, three sows, three pigs and six fowls.

The land on which they are settled was granted to them by Messieurs de Pensens and Dubuisson, but they have lost the deed. They have made a clearing where they have sown eight bushels of wheat and two bushels of peas.

Simon Billard dit la Valleur, locksmith, formerly soldier of the company of Monsieur de Bonnaventure, native of Paris, aged 43 years, he has been 23 years in the colony. Married to Marie Joseph Charpentier, native of Havre, Saint-Pierre du Nord, aged 28 years.

They have three children, one son and two daughters :—

Simon Billard, aged 11 months ;

Marie Rose, aged 5 years ;

Louise, aged 3 years ;

In live stock they have four oxen, two cows, two calves, four wethers, four ewes, one mare and her colt, one sow, four pigs ; and they also own one boat.

They have made a clearing on which they can sow ten bushels of grain.

The said Billard possesses another piece of land in the wood, where he has made a clearing for the sowing of eight bushels of wheat.

This last named homestead is situated on Rivière à Charles, one league from the harbour of St. Pierre.

In live stock they have thirteen geese and eighteen fowls.

Joseph Jacquet, fisherman, native of Grandville, in Normandy, aged 35 years, he has been 12 years in the country. Married to Elizabeth Boulanger, native of Havre Saint-Pierre du Nord on this island, aged 30 years.

They have five children by their marriage, three sons and two daughters :—

Joseph Jacquet, aged 8 years ;

Antoine, aged 3 years ;

Jacques, aged 8 months ;

Marie Françoise, aged 10 years ;

Thérèse, aged 5 years ;

In live stock they have two oxen, two cows, one heifer, two calves, two ewes and two pigs.

They bought their house for 50 livres from Pierre Gallon and have their land under a permit from Monsieur Degoutins under date the 13th November, 1750. They have made a clearing on it where they have sown two bushels of wheat, and have fallow land besides for sowing fourteen bushels in the coming spring.

Le Sr. Louis Bernard, fisherman and ploughman, native of Chartres in Beauce, aged 52 years, he has been — years in the country. Married to Magdelaine Simon, native of Louisbourg, aged 34 years.

They have five children, four sons and one daughter :—
Louis Bernard, aged 16 years ;
Pierre, aged 10 years ;
Hustache, aged 3 years ;
Simon, aged 9 months ;
Anne, aged 11 years ;
They have in live stock two oxen and two ewes.

They hold the land by purchase for the sum of 80 livres from Jean Chesnay, as appears by certificate from the said Chesnay under date of 1738. They have made a clearing for the sowing of twenty bushels and have sown nothing for three years, having no seed.

Nicolas Hango, fisherman, native of Verly, bishopric of Coutance, aged 36 years, he has been in the country — years. Married to Anne Gallais, native of Havre Saint-Pierre du Nord on this island, aged 23 years.

They have four children, three sons and one daughter :—
Vincent Hengo, aged 7 years ;
Simon, aged 5 years ;
Louis, aged 32 months ;
Marie Rose, aged 10 months.
They have in live stock three ewes, one sow and one pig.

The land on which they are settled was given to them verbally by Monsieur Deschambon, commandant of this Isle. They have made a clearing and sown four bushels of wheat and one bushel of peas, and have fallow land for the sowing of four bushels in the coming spring. Their homestead is situated on the river à Charles, one league from the harbour of St. Pierre du Nord.

André Renauld, poor, ploughman, native of the parish of Mattes, in Xaintonge, aged 60 years, he has been in the country 26 years. Married to Jeanne Roger, native of La Rochelle, aged 40 years.

They have two sons :—
Mathurin Renauld, aged 10 years ;
André, aged 8 years.
In live stock they have one cow and her calf, one heifer, two ewes and two pigs.

The land on which they are settled is situated at Havre Saint-Pierre. It was granted to them by deed from Messieurs de Pensens and Dubuisson. They have fallow land sufficient to sow twenty-four bushels. Nothing has been sown as they had no seed.

Le Sr. Emard de Thezen, from Dauphiné, merchant, aged 43 years, he has been in the country three years.

Jacques Meunier, native of Balle, Switzerland, an arrival from the British possessions, aged 18 years, domestic to the said Sr. Emard.

Bazille Boudrot, his farmer, native of l'Acadie, aged 30 years, he has been in the country two years. Married to Margueritte Giroire, native of l'Acadie, aged 30 years.

They have three children, one son and two daughters :—
Pierre Paul Boudrot, aged 8 years ;
Marie Joseph, aged 4 years ;
Euphrosinne aged 2 years.
In live stock they have three cows with their calves, four geese, one horse, five ewes and ten fowls.

The said Sr. Emard holds his land by purchase from Monsieur Saint-Villemay. He has made a clearing for the sowing of 96 bushels the coming spring.

Marie Ducloux, widow of the late Michel Loyal dit Mignet, native of Cap Breton, aged 38 years, left with five children, two sons and three daughters :—

Michel Loyal, their eldest son, aged 13 years ;

Jacques, aged 10 years ;

Marie Rose, aged 12 years ;

Charlotte, aged 7 years ;

Modeste, aged 4 years.

She has in live stock four oxen, three cows, two calves, one mare, one ram, six ewes, one sow, ten geese and eight fowls.

The land on which she is settled is situated at Havre of St. Pierre du Nord, on this Isle, where she has sown five bushels and a half of wheat, one bushel and a half of barley, one bushel of oats, half a bushel of peas, and has fallow land for the sowing of twenty-four bushels more.

The said widow holds her land under deed made by Messieurs de Pensens and Dubuison, dated the 20th July, 1736, and homologated by Messieurs de ⁀ ⁀illant and Le Normant.

Robert Mancel, fishermen, native of the parish of la Luzerne, bishopric of Avranches, aged 32 years, he has been three years in the country. Married to Jeanne Goupy, native of the same place, aged 32 years.

They have one son and one daughter :

Blaise, aged 3 years ;

Suzanne, aged 17 months.

Their live stock consists of the following : one cow with her calf, one wether, four ewes, one pig, one sow, twenty geese, five fowls ; with two boats and a share in a bateau.

They have no dwelling.

Marie Simon, widow of the late Dominique Duclaud, native of l'Acadie, aged 55 years. She has Simone, her niece, aged 18, and she lives with her son.

Jacques Dominique Duclaud, fisherman, native of this place, aged 31 years. Married to Marie Vescot, native of l'Acadie, aged 28 years.

They have two daughters :—

Marie Françoise, aged 2 years ;

Marie Joseph, aged 1 year.

In live stock they have : two oxen, six cows, five calves, fifteen ewes, one horse, ten pigs, twenty geese, three turkeys and forty fowls or chickens.

The land on which they are was granted to them by Messieurs Duchambon and Dubuisson. They have sown ten bushels of wheat. They share a boat with Joseph Dumont.

Joseph Dumont, fisherman and ploughman, native of Petit Degrat, aged 38 years.

He has four daughters :—

Anne, aged 13 years ;

Marie, aged 11 years ;

Helenne, aged 5 years ;

Suzanne, aged 18 months.

He has three oxen, three cows, two heifers, fifteen wethers, three pigs, ten geese and four fowls.

On the land on which he is settled, he has sown four bushels of wheat.

Marie Joseph Chenel, widow of the late Morel, native of l'Acadie, aged 50 years.

She has three sons :—

Joseph Charpentier, aged 22 years ;

Louis, aged 20 years ;

Joseph, aged 15 years.

In live stock, she has : four oxen, one cow, two calves, fifteen wethers, five pigs, fifteen geese, eighteen turkeys, thirty fowls or chickens.

Her land, which she has improved, is on the river. She has made a clearing on which she has sown some ten bushels of wheat, and has besides fallow land sufficient to sow twenty-four bushels ; and a second piece of land which she has improved for the fishery, on the point of Havre Saint-Pierre du Nord.

5-6 EDWARD VII., A. 1906

Le Sr. Charles Jousseaume, .merchant, native of Saint-Martin de Villeneuve bishopric of La Rochelle, in France, aged 30 years, he has been in the country three years. He has been married for one month to Demoiselle Magdelaine Bugeaud, native of l'Acadie, aged 16 years.

He is living in the house of the widow Morel, which he has rented.

They have in live stock, two oxen, three pigs, five geese, five fowls ; with two fishing boats and half of two other batteaus, one with Robert Mancel and the other with Jacques Galland and he is purveyor for seven boats.

The said Sr. Jousseaume has in his employ as a domestic a 36 months boy named Claude Duriand, native of Quentin, bishopric of St. Brieux in Brittany, aged 16 years.

The said Sr. Jousseaume has no land yet except thirty feet square that he has purchased from the widow Morel.

François Jolly, fisherman, native of Paramé, bishopric of St. Malo, aged 69 years.

Jean Le Vieux, native of Soubise, bishopric of Sainte, in Xaintonge, aged 60 years, both bachelors and partners.

In live stock they have two pigs and four fowls.

The land they occupy is situated to the south quarter-south-west of the bay of Saint-Pierre, it was given to them verbally by Monsieur————————

They have made a clearing on it where they have sown eight bushels of wheat, one bushel and a half of rye, three-quarters of a bushel of barley and four bushels of peas, and they have sufficient fallow land for the sowing of three bushels.

Magdelaine Poitevin, widow of Guillaume Prieur dit Dubois, native of l'Acadie, aged 50 years, and he has been in the country 32 years.

She has three sons :—

Pierre, aged 23 years ;

Guillaume, aged 19 years ;

Louis, aged 13 years ;

André Dugay, orphan, aged 7 years.

The land on which she is settled is situated at Havre Saint-Pierre in the north part of this Isle. She holds the said land under deed from Messieurs de Pensens and Dubuisson. She declares the said deed was burned at the time of the fire fourteen years ago.

Her live stock is as follows : three oxen, four cows, one calf, eight ewes, two pigs, five geese and five fowls.

She has made a clearing where she has sown two bushels and a half of wheat and has fallow land for the sowing of sixty bushels the coming spring.

The said widow and her sons enjoy in addition to the above land another piece of land situated up the rivière du Nord-Est of Port La Joye, where they have sown eight bushels of grain.

Jacques Le Prieur dit Dubois, her son, native of the Isles Michaud, near Ile Royale, fisherman and ploughman, aged 35 years and has been 32 years in the country. Married a short time ago to Marguerite Michel dite Laruine, native of l'Acadie, aged 20 years.

All the live stock they possess consists of but one wether and three fowls.

The land they occupy is situated near the source of the riviere du Nord-Est of the Port La Joye. On it they have made a clearing for the sowing of eight bushels of wheat.

Joseph Tricoud dit Picard, settler, (discharged) soldier in the company of Stimauville of the Department of Ile Royale, native of the burg of Au, province of Picardie, in the jurisdiction of the town of Eu, aged 30 years, he has been 15 years in the colony. Married to Margueritte Prieur, native of Havre Saint-Pierre, in Ile Saint-Jean, aged 20 years..

They have two sons :—

Joseph, aged 2 years ;

Jean Louis, aged 5 months.

In live stock they have two cows, one calf and two fowls.

They have their portions of the dwelling place of Magdelaine Poitevin, widow Prieur their mother.

Le Sr. Claude Antoine Duplessis, surgeon, native of Saint Quentin, in Picardie, aged 43 years, and has been ———— years in the country.   Married to Catherine Lejeune, native of l'Acadie, aged 49 years.

They have three children—one son and two daughters :—

François Marin, aged 3 years ;

Nastazie, aged 15 years ;

Marie Louise, aged 13 years.

Louis LaBauve, orphan, native of the east coast of l'Acadie, aged 12 years.

In stock they have one mare, one cow, one calf and six fowls.

Their dwelling is situated at Havre Saint-Pierre, Ile Saint Jean.   They hold it by virtue of an application they presented to Monsieur Prevost in 1750, which said application would have been sealed up among the papers of Monsieur Degoutins after his death.

Claude Chatel, fisherman, native of Saint-Michel des Loups in Lower Normandy, bishopric of Avranche, aged 38 years, he has been in the country 18 years.   The said Chatel is not married.

He has in live stock two oxen, one cow, one calf, ten wethers and one sow.

The land on which he is settled is situated on the before-mentioned harbour and he purchased it for the sum of 35 livres from Michael Duffaut, as it appears by the deed of sale made on the 17th day of May, 1743.   He has made a clearing on it where he has sown eleven bushels of wheat and a bushel and a quarter of peas, and has fallow land besides sufficient for the sowing of eight bushels more.

Jacques Montaury, fisherman and ploughman, native Havre Saint-Pierre on Isle Royale, aged 31 years, he has been in the country 25 years.   Married to Magdelaine Quimine, native of l'Acadie, aged 31 years.

They have four children—three sons and one daughter :—

Grégoire Montaury, aged 5 years ;

Jean Baptiste, aged 3 years ;

Joseph, aged one year ;

Marie Rose, aged 6 years.

Their live stock consists of the following : eight oxen, three cows, two calves, five ewes, seven pigs, five geese, six fowls and twelve chickens.

The land on which they are settled is situated on the aforesaid harbour of Saint Pierre of the Ile Saint Jean and they hold it in half shares with Mathieu Glain of Rivière de Peuguiguit.

The said Montaury has another piece of land at the place called les Etangs, where they have made a clearing and have sowed there eight bushels of wheat and four bushels of peas, and still have fallow land sufficient for the sowing of twelve bushels of grain.

Geneviève Poitevin, widow of David Despoyés, poor, native of l'Acadie, aged 36 years, left with six children, four sons and two daughters :—

Jean François, aged 11 years.

Charles, aged 9 years.

Jean, aged 6 years.

Ruffin, aged 2 years.

Marie Madelaine, aged 13 years.

Appolline, aged 5 years.

In live stock, she had two ewes, one heifer and two fowls.

The land in which she is settled is situated at the harbour of Saint-Pierre, on the Isle Saint-Jean and is hers by succession.

She enjoys another piece of land situated at the place called les Etangs and which was granted to her late husband by Messieurs de————and Dubuisson.   Dated———— The said widow cannot seed her land owing to her great poverty.   She had been in the country about thirty years.

Le Sr. Louis Aubin Lebuffe, fisherman, native of Saint-Michel des Loups, in Normandy, aged 36 years, he has been 22 years in the country.   Married to Anne Quimine, native of l'Acadie, aged 30 years.

They have two daughters :—

Modeste, aged 4 years.

Marie Françoise, aged 30 months.

In live stock, they have four oxen, three cows, two heifers, two calves, one mare with her colt, ten ewes, six pigs and three fowls.

The land on which they are settled is situated in that part of the harbour of Saint-Pierre du Nord of the Isle Saint-Jean called le Nigeagant. They hold said land by purchase from Sr. Charles LeBuffe, brother of said Aubin, as appears by a deed sale made under date of 1749; signed Bernard, Notary Royal.

A clearing has been made by them, on which they have sown eight bushels of wheat and they have fallow land besides for the sowing of sixteen bushels more. They hold another piece of land at les Etangs, where they have a clearing for the sowing of thirty-two bushels. They have one boat and have lost one within the past few days.

They also have working for them three thirty-six-months men, all of them natives of Brittany.

Also Margueritte Quimine sister and sister-in-law of Sr. Aubin and his wife, native of l'Acadie, aged 16 years.

Charles Fouquet, fisherman, native of Avranche in Normandy ; aged 50 years, he has been in the country 30 years. Married to Marie Poitevin, native of l'Acadie, aged 37 years.

They have nine children, five sons and four daughters :—

Louis Fouquet, aged 24 years.

Jean Aubin, aged 22 years.

Jean Martin, aged 14 years.

Simon, aged 6 years.

Charles, aged 8 months.

Marie Françoise, aged 16 years.

Anne, aged 12 years ;

Elisabeth, aged 8 years ;

Françoise, aged 4 years.

In live stock they have the following : four oxen, three cows, two heifers, four calves, twelve wethers or ewes, seven pigs, one mare and her foal and fifteen fowls or chickens.

They hold their land under grant made by Messieurs .... On it they have made a clearing where they have sown eight bushels of wheat and have fallow land for the sowing of another twenty-four bushels, none of which was seeded for lack of grain.

Le Sr. François Douville, fisherman, navigator and ploughman, native of St. Denis Le Gatz, bishopric of Coutance in Normandy, aged 62 years, he has been in the country 35 years. Married to Dame Marie Rogé, native of La Rochelle, aged 42 years.

They have four sons and three daughters :—

Jacques, aged 24 years;

François, aged 17 years ;

Philippe, aged 11 years ;

Pierre, aged 9 years ;

Françoise, aged 18 years ;

Louise, aged 16 years ;

Margueritte, aged 3 years.

In live stock they have eight oxen, eight cows, four heifers, eight calves, one horse, twenty-two ewes, nine pigs, four geese, fifty fowls or chickens and twenty turkeys or young turkeys.

The land where they are settled is situated at Nigeagant, on which they have made a clearing and sown sixty bushels of wheat, where they have fallow land for as much more.

They have another piece of land, situated at the place called le fond des Etangs, on which there is a flour mill. The said land where the flour mill is placed was given to them under a permit from Monsieur de Bonnaventure, dated 1750.

The first-named land and that which is hereinafter described were given to them by Messieurs de Pensens and Potier Dubuisson, of which they have the grant dated 1736.

The last-named piece of land belonging to them is situatèd at the place called la Pointe du Havre Saint-Pierre du Nord, where they have made a clearing for a garden, the remainder serving as a kind of beach for the cod fishery. They have a fishing bateau and two fishing boats. They have had a fire in which they lost all their effects and their house which were burnt.

Le Sr. Louis Talbot, fisherman, native of Bar le Duc, in Barrois, province of Lorraine, aged 45, he has been in the country twenty years. Married to Françoise Douville, native of Havre Saint-Pierre du Nord on this Isle, aged 30 years.

They have four sons :—
Charles Louis, aged 9 years ;
Joseph, aged 7 years ;
Jean François, aged 4 years ;
François, aged 7 months.

In live stock they have eight oxen, four cows, two heifers, four calves, one horse, sixteen ewes, seven pigs, thirty-four geese, twelve turkeys and sixty fowls or chickens.

The land on which they are settled is situated at the place called le Nigeagant, where they have a clearing for the sowing of forty bushels of grain which they have seeded this year. They have two fishing boats.

Jean Delaunois, fisherman and ploughman, native of the parish of Saint-Quast, bishopric of Saint Brieux, aged 50 years he has been in the country 28 years. Married to Marie Arcenaud, native of l'Acadie, aged 32 years.

They have seven children, four sons and three daughters :—
Hustache, aged 14 years ;
Jacques, aged 12 years ;
Paul, aged 6 years :
Jean, aged 3 years ;
Suzanne, aged 11 years ;
Marie, aged 5 years ;
Magdelaine, aged one year.

In live stock they have four oxen, one cow, one heifer, two bulls, one calf, seven ewes, six geese, twenty fowl or chickens.

The land on which they are settled is situated on the west side of the harbour aux Sauvages and was given to them by grant from Messrs. de Pensens and Dubuisson, homologated by Messieurs de Brouant and Le Normand, under date of the 20th of June, 1736. It contains four arpents frontage by forty arpents in depth. On it they have made a clearing where they have sown six bushels of wheat and they have fallow land besides sufficient for the sowing of another four bushels.

Jacques Devaux, senior, fisherman and ploughman, native of l'Acadie, aged 50 years, has been 28 years in the country. Married to Marie Potier, native of l'Acadie, aged 50 years.

They have two sons and one daughter :
Jean, aged 25 years ;
Joseph, aged 22 years ;
Marie, aged 18 years.

Their live stock consists of six oxen, five cows, two heifers, two bulls, three calves, twenty-eight wethers, twelve pigs and fifty fowls or chickens.

The land on which they are settled is situated on the west side of the harbour aux Sauvages and was given to them by a grant from Messieurs de Pensens and Potier Dubuison, in 1736, and homologated by Messieurs de Brouillant and Le Normand. It contains four arpents front by a depth of forty arpents. On it they have made a clearing and sown twenty-four bushels of wheat, and they still have fallow land sufficient for sowing of fifty-six bushels more.

Jean Baptiste Duvivier, extremely poor, native of St. Michel des Loups, bishopric of Avranches, aged 50 years, he has been 29 years in the country. Married to Madelaine Caissy, native of l'Acadie, aged 34 years.

5-6 EDWARD VII., A. 1906

They have six children, three sons and three daughters :—
Pierre, aged 15 years ;
Jacques, aged 8 years ;
Jean, aged 3 years ;
Marie, aged 13 years ;
Theotiste, aged 11 years ;
Henriette, aged 5 years.

They have in live stock six oxen, one cow, one calf, one horse, six ewes, six pigs and three fowls or chickens.

The land on which they are settled is situated on the west side of the harbour aux Sauvages, and was given to them by Messieurs de Pensens and Dubuisson in 1736, and homologated by Messieurs de Brouillant and Le Normand. On it they have made a clearing and sown three bushels of wheat and have fallow land in addition for the sowing of four bushels and a half.

Jacques Devaux, ploughman, native of l'Acadie, aged 26 years, he has been 24 years in the country. Married to Madelaine Robichaud, native of l'Acadie.

They have two oxen, one cow, one calf, one ewe and one sow.

The land on which they are settled is situated on the west side of the harbour aux Sauvages, and they hold it only by verbal permission of Monsieur de Bonnaventure. They have made a clearing in which they can sow eight bushels.

Christophe Potier, fisherman and ploughman, native of l'Acadie, aged 38 years, he has been in the country 31 years. Married to Anne Boudrot, native of Port Toulouse, aged 29 years.

They have five daughters :—
Marie, aged 11 years ;
Anne, aged 11 years ;
Charlotte, aged 8 years ;
Margueritte, aged 5 years
Marie, aged 18 months.

In live stock they have two oxen, two cows, two heifers, one bull, two calves, eight wethers, three pigs and ten fowls.

The land on which they are settled is situated on the east side of the harbour aux Sauvages, and was given to them under a grant from Messieurs de Pensens and Potier Dubuisson in 1736, and homologated by Messieurs de Brouillant and Le Normant. It contains four arpents frontage by forty in depth On it they have made a clearing and sown ten bushels of wheat, and they also have land in fallow for the sowing of another six bushels.

Julien Compagnon, fisherman and ploughman, native of the parish of Saint Michel des Loups, bishopric of Avranche in Normandy, aged 23 years, he has been in the country four years. Married to Cécille Nivrat, native of l'Acadie, aged 39 years.

They have six children :—
Jean Poitier, aged 22 years ;
Christophe, aged 18 years ;
Louis, aged 16 years ;
Henriette, aged 13 years ;
Suzanne, aged 5 years ;
Marie Compagnon, aged one year.

In live stock they have two oxen, two cows, two bulls, one heifer, one calf, six wethers, one mare, nine pigs and thirty fowls or chickens.

The land on which they are settled was granted to the late Louis Poitier, by Messieurs de Pensens and Dubuisson in 1736, and the grant was homologated by Messieurs de Brouillant and Le Normant. On this land they have made a clearing and sown twelve bushels of wheat, and they have besides fallow land sufficient for the sowing of another twenty-eight bushels.

Michel Ouvray, fisherman and ploughman, native of the parish of Vir, bishopric of Bayeux, aged 25 years, he has been in the country three years. Married to Elisabeth Poirier, native of l'Acadie, aged 23 years.

SESSIONAL PAPER No. 18

They have Jean François, their son, aged 10 months.

Their live stock consists of one cow, one calf, one pig and four fowls.

The land on which they are settled is situated on the border of the pond de Saint Pierre. They have it by permission of Monsieur de Bonnaventure. On it they have made a clearing and sown six bushels of wheat and a bushel of peas.

Jean Quimine, fisherman and ploughman, native of l'Acadie, aged 23 years, he has been ten years in the country. Married to Magdelaine Terriaud, native of l'Acadie, aged 23 years.

They have in live stock one cow, one pig and two geese.

They have no dwelling yet and are living with Jacques Quimine, father of said Jean.

Jacques Quimine, fisherman and ploughman, native of France, in feeble health, aged 60 years. Married to Marie Chiasson, native of l'Acadie, aged 58 years, they have been in the country ten years.

They have four children, one son and three daughters :—

Pierre Quimine, aged 26 years ;

Judicth, aged 20 years ;

Françoise, aged 18 years ;

Marguerite, aged 14 years.

Their live stock is as follows : four oxen, four cows, two calves, three heifers, four wethers, eight pigs, eight geese and eighteen fowls or chickens.

The land on which they are settled is situated to the east of the pond of Saint Pierre, and was granted to them by Messieurs de Pensens and Dubuisson. On it they have sown nine bushels of wheat and four bushels of peas, and there remains a piece of fallow land sufficient for the sowing of sixteen bushels. The said grant has been homologated by Messieurs de Brouillant and Le Normant.

Marie Chiasson, widow of Joseph La Foresterie, native of l'Acadie, aged 60 years, and has been in the country thirty years.

She has two sons :—

Joseph, aged 22 years ;

Jean, aged 20 years.

Their live stock is as follows : four oxen, four cows, four heifers, four calves, two horses, twenty wethers or ewes, five pigs, five turkeys and fifty fowls or chickens.

The land on which she is settled is situated on the road from Saint Pierre to the harbour aux Sauvages, and was granted to her by Messieurs Duchambon and Dubuisson, and homologated by Messieurs de Brouillant and Le Normand. She has had a clearing made where she has sown thirteen bushels of wheat and one bushel of oats, and has still a piece of fallow land sufficient for the sowing of thirty-two bushels.

Jean Arnauld, fisherman and ploughman, native of Rochefort, aged 48 years, he has been in the country 28 years. Married to Marie Poitier, native of l'Acadie, aged 32 years.

They have seven children, one son and six daughters :—

Jean Arnauld, aged 13 years ;

Marie, aged 18 years ;

Rose, aged 16 years ;

Colette, aged 13 years ;

Veronique, aged 5 years ;

Sevrienne, aged 3 years ;

Magdelaine, aged five months.

In live stock they have two oxen, three cows, one heifer, five wethers, three pigs and thirty fowls.

The land on which they are settled is situated on the road from the harbour of Saint Pierre to the harbour aux Sauvages, and was granted to them by Messieurs de Pensens and Dubuisson, and contains four arpents frontage by forty in depth. On it they have made a clearing for the sowing of ten bushels. They have sown nothing.

5-6 EDWARD VII., A. 1906

Pierre Grossin, fisherman and ploughman, native of the parish of Carolle, bishopric of Avranche, aged 44 years, he has been in the country 25 years. Married to Cécille Caissy, native of l'Acadie, aged 38 years.

They have eight children, three sons and five daughters :—

Michel Grossin, aged 18 years ;

Jacques, aged 8 years ;

Pierre, aged 7 years ;

Cécille, aged 15 years ;

Magdelaine, aged 14 years ;

Anne, aged 12 years ;

Marguerite, aged 6 years ;

Rose, aged 3 years.

Their live stock consists of two oxen, three cows, three bulls, two heifers, one calf one horse, eleven wethers, four pigs and three fowls.

The land on which they are settled is situated at les Etangs, and was granted to them by Messieurs de Pensens and Dubuisson and homologated by Messieurs Duquesnel and Bigot. It contains four arpents frontage by forty in depth. They have made on it a clearing for the sowing of forty-five bushels of seed, but they have only sown five bushels of wheat and eight bushels of peas.

François Chiasson, ploughman, native of l'Acadie, aged 60 years, he has been 25 years in the country. Married to Anne Dousset, native of l'Acadie, aged 48 years.

They have seven children, five sons and two daughters :—

Jean Chiasson, aged 25 years ;

François, aged 22 years ;

Joseph, aged 19 years ;

Louis, aged 13 years ;

Crisostôme, aged 3 years ;

Anne, aged 16 years ;

Marie, aged 12 years.

They have in live stock, six oxen, six cows, one bull, two heifers, five calves, twenty wethers, twelve pigs and twenty fowls or chickens.

The land on which they are settled is situated on the west side of the harbour aux Sauvages, and was granted to them by Messieurs de Pensens and Dubuisson. They have made a clearing on it for the sowing of sixty-eight bushels, and have sown twenty-four bushels of wheat.

Michel Grossin, fisherman and ploughman, native of Carolle, bishopric of Avranche, aged 47 years, he has been in the country 25 years. Married to Marie Caissy, native of l'Acadie, aged 44 years.

They have nine children, three sons and six daughters :—

Jacques Grossin, aged 13 years ;

Louis, aged 10 years ;

Michel, aged 6 years ;

Marie Louise, aged 18 years ;

Marie, aged 16 years ;

Henriette, aged 7 years ;

Brigitte, aged 4 years ;

Françoise, aged 3 years ;

Marie Magdelaine, aged 6 months.

They have in live stock two oxen, one cow, one calf, ten wethers, two pigs and six fowls.

The land on which they are settled is situated to the south of the ponds of Saint Pierre. On it they have made a clearing for the sowing of thirty-two bushels, one part of which they have sown with eight bushels.

Paul Caissy, bachelor, fisherman and ploughman, native of l'Acadie, aged 21 years, has been three years in the country.

In live stock he has two cows, one calf and five pigs.

The land he occupies is situated to the south quarter south-west of the ponds of Saint Pierre. He acquired the said land for the sum of 100 livres from Christophle Delanne, his brother-in-law on the 15th of May in the present year. There is a clearing on it for the sowing of twenty-four bushels of grain, but none has been sown, he not having any.

Joseph Tudal, fisherman, native of Saint Malo, aged 40 years, he has been 21 years in the country. Married to Anne Lebauve, native of l'Acadie, aged 42 years.

They have five children, two sons and three daughters :—

Joseph Tudal, aged 13 years ;

François, aged 2 years ;

Marie Joseph, aged 11 years ;

Pelagie, aged 7 years ;

Louise, aged 5 years.

The said Anne Lebauve has two sons with her of her first marriage :

Jean Beurit, aged 22 years ;

Pierre, aged 18 years.

In live stock they have one cow and her calf.

The land on which they are settled is situated at the harbour aux Sauvages, and was given to them by Messieurs Duchambon and Dubuisson. They have made a clearing on it for the sowing of fifteen bushels, but have sown nothing for want of seed.

Jean Chainay, fisherman, native of l'Acadie, aged 50 years, he has been in the country 25 years. Married to Anne Potier, native of l'Acadie, aged 40 years.

They have five children, three sons and two daughters :—

Jean Baptiste, aged 22 years ;

Joseph, aged 12 years ;

Charles, aged 9 years ;

Geneviève, aged 5 years ;

Marie, aged 4 years.

Their live stock consists of two oxen, two cows, two calves, twelve ewes and eight pigs.

The land on which they are settled is situated at the harbour aux Sauvages. They hold it under a grant from Messieurs Duchambon and Dubuisson.

They have made a clearing on it for sowing thirty-two bushels of seed, but have sown none.

Pierre Livois, fisherman and ploughman, native of the parish of Dargues, bishopric of Avranche, in Normandy, aged 30 years, of which he has been twelve in the country, widower of the late Marie Daigre.

He has Marie Anne Livois, his daughter, aged five months.

In live stock he owns two oxen, two cows, one calf, and three fowls.

The land on which he is settled is situated on the south side of the ponds of Saint Pierre. He acquired the land from Jouannis Laborde, and has sown on it five and a half bushels of wheat.

We left the harbour of Saint Pierre on the 17th of August for Tracadie. The distance between the two harbours is four leagues. We did not come across anything worthy of remark with the exception of the harbour of au Sauvage, and the sand dunes that occur all along the sea shore. On these dunes a considerable amount of hay is made, and behind them extensive meadows could be made at but small outlay, if grants of small parcels of land were made to those who may need them.

The harbour Au Sauvage lies on the north coast of the island and a league from Saint Pierre. It is suited to the pursuit of the cod fishing industry, but by boat only, and for the cultivation of the soil. It runs inland half a league to the south, afterwards dividing into two branches. The first branch runs south-south-east for a quarter of a league and then empties its waters into a stream by which a flour mill is run ; the other runs west-north-west for half a league. Several settlers are living on the banks of this second branch, and it is here that the finest wheat on the island is found.

5-6 EDWARD VII., A. 1906

THE HARBOUR OF TRACADIE.

Eight famlies are settled on the harbour of Tracadie, whilst two are settled at the Etang des Berges, three quarters of a league distant from Tracadie.

It is like the harbour of Saint Pierre, suitable for the cod fishery, and the cultivation of the soil. The settlers who have established themselves here follow both industries with success. The entrance to the harbour is formed by a break in the chain of sand dunes, and lies east and west, the width being estimated at 200 to 250 toises. In the middle of the entrances lies a channel, sixty fathoms in width running north-north-east by south-south-west, and having throughout its length a deposit of fifteen to sixteen feet of water at high tide.

A bar of sand lying partly across the outside of the entrance prevents the passage of vessels having a draft of more than eleven or twelve feet of water. The general course of this bar is nearly east and west.

The harbour is very capacious and runs inland for a distance of two leagues behind the dunes to the eastward, and a good league to the south, preserving the same width to its extreme limits. The inhabitants are settled on the west coast of the said harbour. The lands that have been improved by the settlers, are partly under seed this year, and, generally, the crops appear to be fair enough. The lands are covered with all kinds of wood, whilst on the east-south-east and south-south-east the shores of the harbour contain plenty of pasture lands with a very good supply of grass, and it would be a very easy task, without incurring any great expenditure of labour to extend the meadows so that more settlers could be located.

The most convenient method, for securing the extension of these meadowlands that could be adopted, would be to grant to each individual a portion of land sufficient for the keep of as many head of live stock as is necessary for the subsistence and requirements of each family. When, in the course of time, the settlers wish to maintain the increase of their live stock, they will find themselves under the necessity of enlarging the area of their pasturage and therefore of clearing the adjoining land. In proportion as the settlers increase the number of their live stock, they will be forced to extend their pastureland.

Census.

Census of the settlers at Tracadie, in men, women, children, etc.

Jacques Haché dit Galland, navigator and ploughman, native of l'Acadie, aged 40 years, he has been in the country 16 years. Married to Marie Joseph Boudrot, native of l'Acadie, aged 32 years.

They have seven children, four sons and three daughters :—

Jacques Phillippe, aged 14 years.
Joseph, aged 10 years.
Charles, aged 8 years.
Syprien, aged 4 years.
Marie Jeanne, aged 12 years.
Marie, aged 5 years.
Anne, aged 1 year.

Their live stock consists of six oxen, one cow, five ewes, four pigs, five geese and six fowls.

The land that they occupy was given to them verbally by Messieurs Duchambon and Dubuisson, on it they have made a clearing for the sowing of twenty-four bushels of grain, and they have sown fifteen bushels of wheat, three bushels of peas and half a bushel of oats.

Charles Boudrot, ploughman and navigator, native of l'Acadie, aged 40 years ; he has been in the country 39 years. Married to Marie Fougère, native of Port Toulouse, aged 29 years.

They have four children, one son and three daughters :—

Jean, aged 11 years.

Théotiste, aged 9 years,

Marie, aged 5 years.

In live stock, they have three oxen, four cows, six calves, two wethers, three ewes, three pigs and seven fowls.

The land on which they are settled was given to them verbally by Messieurs Duchambon and Dubuisson. On it they have made a clearing on which they have sown seven bushels and a half of wheat and one of peas.

Pierre Boudrot, fisherman and ploughman, native of Port Toulouse, aged 30 years. Married to Cecille Vescot, native of l'Acadie, aged 2 3 years.

They have one son and one daughter.

Foelix Boudrot, aged 2 months ;

Marie Joseph, aged 19 months.

The land on which they are settled was given to them verbally by Messieurs de Pensens and Dubuisson. On it they have made a clearing where they have sown ten and a half bushels of wheat and three bushels and a half of peas, and they still have fallow land for the sowing of eight bushels more.

Charles Bourg, fisherman and ploughman, native of l'Acadie, aged 58 years, he has been in the country 24 years. Married to Anne Boudrot, native of l'Acadie, aged 44 years.

They have twelve children, seven sons and five daughters :—

Charles, aged 25 years ;

Pierre, aged 21 years ;

Louis, aged 19 years ;

Paul, aged 11 years ;

Ange, aged 4 years ;

Joseph, aged 18 months ;

Anne, aged 17 years ;

Marguerite, aged 15 years ;

Elisabeth, aged 13 years ;

Magdelaine, aged 8 years ;

Gertrude, aged 5 years.

Their live stock consists of the following : four oxen, four cows, three heifers, two calves, eighteen ewes, nine pigs, seven geese, seven fowls ; together with one fishing boat.

The land on which they are settled was given to them verbally by Messieurs de Pensens and Dubuisson. On it they have made a clearing where they have sown twenty-five bushels of wheat and five bushels of peas, and they have fallow land for the sowing of twenty bushels.

Michel Bourg, fisherman and ploughman, native of l'Acadie, aged 60 years, and has been 24 years on the Isle. Married to Anne Boudrot, native of l'Acadie, aged 50 years.

They have seven children, four sons and three daughters :—

Michel, aged 30 years ;

Joseph, aged 25 years ;

Abraham, aged 23 years ;

Pierre, aged 13 years ;

Anne, aged 27 years ;

Marie, aged 19 years ;

Magdelaine, aged 14 years.

In live stock they have four oxen, four cows, three calves, eight ewes, fifteen pigs, two sows, seventeen fowls or chickens ; and one boat.

The land on which they are settled was given to them verbally by Messieurs de Pensens and Dubuisson. On it they have made a clearing for the sowing of sixty-four bushels of grain, they have sown one half of this quantity.

François Boudrot dit Manne, ploughman and fisherman, native of l'Acadie, aged 61 years, he has been 25 years in the country. Married to Jeanne Landry, native of l'Acadie.

18—10½

5-6 EDWARD VII., A. 1906

They have six children, three sons and three daughters :—
Joseph, aged 29 years ;
Charles, aged 18 years ;
François, aged 8 years ;
Judich, aged 20 years ;
Louise, aged 16 years ;
Elisabeth, aged 10 years.

In live stock they have four oxen, four cows, three heifers, one mare, twenty ewes, twenty-seven fowls ; and one fishing boat.

The land on which they are settled was given to them verbally by Messieurs de Pensens and Dubuisson. On it they have made a clearing for the sowing of eighty-six bushels of seed, and this year they have sown thirty-two bushels of wheat and six bushels of peas.

Louis Belliveaux, navigator and ploughman, native of l'Acadie, aged 44 years, he has been 23 years in the country. Married to Louise Haché native of l'Acadie, aged 36 years.

They have six children, three sons and three daughters :—
Jean, aged 16 years ;
Joseph, aged 10 years ;
Athanase, aged 5 years ;
Louise Félicité, aged 14 years ;
Anne, aged 12 years ;
Marie, aged 3 years ;

In live stock they have four oxen, four cows, two heifers, four wethers, one calf, six ewes, two sows, ten pigs and two fowls.

The land on which they are settled was given to them verbally by Messiéurs de Pensens and Dubuisson. They have made a clearing on it for the sowing of fifty bushels of seed, and have sown twenty-five bushels of wheat and five bushels of peas.

Claude Boudrot, fisherman and ploughman, native of l'Acadie, aged 50 years, he has been in the country 31 years. Married to Judich Belliveaux, native of l'Acadie, aged 46 years.

They have six children, three sons and three daughters :—
Claude, aged 20 years ;
Michel, aged 17 years ;
Pierre, aged 8 years ;
Marie, aged 16 years ;
Marguerite, aged 14 years ;
Louise, aged 11 years ;

They have the following live stock : three oxen, three cows, one bull, three calves, one mare, four pigs, one sow, five fowls and one boat.

The land on which they are settled was given to them verbally by Messieurs de Pensens and Dubuisson. On it they have made a clearing on which they have sown twenty-two bushels of wheat, two bushels of barley and four bushels of peas.

CENSUS.

Census of the settlers at Etang des Berges, in men, women, children, &c.

Joseph Boudrot, fiisherman and ploughman, native of Cap Breton, aged 33 years, he who has been in the country two years. Married to Margueritte Chiasson, native of l'Acadie, aged 25 years.

They have one daughter, Marie Boudrot, aged 2 years.

Their live stock consists of one ox, two cows, one heifer, three pigs, two hens, together with one boat.

The land on which they are settled is situated at the Etang des Berges, and was given to them verbally by Monsieur de Bonnaventure. On it they have made a clearing for the sowing of six bushels of grain.

Jacques Chiasson, fisherman and ploughman, native of l'Acadie, aged 69 years, he has been in the country two years. Married to Marie Arceneau, native of l'Acadie.

They have seven sons and two daughters :

Pierre, aged 27 years.

Paul, aged 25 years.

Jacques, aged 23 years.

Michel, aged 21 years.

Joseph aged 15 years.

Jean, aged 12 years.

Amand, aged 7 years.

Magdelaine, aged 18 years.

Elizabeth, aged 14 years.

Marie Joseph Hebert, native of l'Acadie, aged 6 years.

In live stock they have ten oxen, nine cows, seven calves, one mare, nine pigs and fifteen fowls.

The land on which they are settled is situated at the Etang des Berges and was given to them verbally by Monsieur de Bonnaventure.

We left Tracadie and took our way for Macpec. An hour after starting we found ourselves crossing the harbour of the petit Racica (Racicot). The entrance to the harbour lies north-north-east and south-south-west, and is only navigable by boats, and even then only at high tide, and in fine weather. The lands surrounding the harbour are covered with all kinds of hard wood fit for use in the construction of schooners, bateaux and boats ; whilst the soil is good in quality and fit for cultivation.

About six o'clock in the evening whilst passing the harbour of the Grand Racico in a strong wind we were forced to put into port there. This harbour lies on the north coast eight leagues from Saint-Pierre. We found that the entrance to the harbour lies north-east and south-west, that it is about one hundred toises in width and that it is only accessible to vessels of 30 to 40 tons burden. Inside the entrance the harbour divides into two arms. One runs inland three leagues to the east-south-east towards Petit Racicot.

The depth of the water has not been ascertained. The other runs half a league to the south-west and in it vessels anchor ordinarily in three to four fathoms of water whilst two rivers empty into this arm, the one in the centre and the other at the extremity.

Both these rivers take their rise three or four leagues inland to the west-north-west Their currents are rapid throughout and they are well fitted for the construction of flour and saw mills, especially as the surroundings of the harbour and of these rivers are full of all kinds of timber suitable for every description of building purpose.

We left this harbour on the 23rd but a contrary wind blowing from the north-north-west compelled us to take to rowing, and the wind growing stronger we had to put into port in the little harbour.

This harbour is situated similarly to the others on the north coast. It is eleven leagues from Saint Pierre and three leagues from the east entrance to the harbour of Macpec.

We found that its entrance lay north-north-east and south-south-west, with a breadth of 100 to 150 toises. A channel flowing in the centre is 30 to 40 toises in width with a depth of 10 to 11 feet of water at high tide.

We also found that formerly certain persons had prosecuted the fishing industry here by means of vessels.

The harbour is formed something like the gulf of a river, and so penetrates inland to the south-south-west for a distance of a league.

There are two rivers on the west side of said harbour. They take their rise in the interior to the west-south-west, and they resemble the foregoing rivers in character, fitted for the same purposes, and possessed of the same facilities.

The wind having veered to the south-west, we resumed our journey, and finally reached the harbour of Macpec towards five o'clock in the evening.

5-6 EDWARD VII., A. 1906

SKETCH OF THE HARBOUR OF MACPEC.

The harbour of Macpec lies on the north coast, at a distance of sixteen leagues from the harbour of Saint-Pierre.

Thirty-two families who follow the cultivation of the soil as a means of livelihood, are settled there. The harhour is also suitable for the prosecution of the cod fishery, and it is certain that too much encouragement to engage in the industry cannot be given to the settlers, especially as the conditions of the locality itself invite them to do so. The situation is one of the best adapted on the Island to the drying of codfish, owing to several small islands that lie directly in front of the harbour, and which give certainty of no lack of fresh air, whilst they also add to the security of the harbour.

We found that the harbour of Macpec has four distinct entrances. The first lies east and west, being formed by the south-west point of the mainland of Isle Saint-Jean, and the north-east point of the small isle at the eastern entrance. The distance between these points is estimated at 800 toises. They lie north-east and south-west, and between them there is a quarter of a league in which vessels drawing twelve or thirteen feet of water can tack, there being usually about three fathoms of water throughout the entrance at low tide.

The second entrance lies north-north-east, and south-south-west. It is formed by the west-north-west point of the aforesaid island at the eastern entrance, and the east-south-eastern point of the isle at the north-western entrance. This entrance is considered to be wider throughout its whole length than the former, with the difference, however, that the channel in this entrance is estimated to have a width of only 300 toises, in which there are from five to six fathoms of water at low tide, and six to seven at high tide. Only these two entrances are navigable for vessels of any kind. As regards the other two they are accessible by boats only.

THE ISLANDS WHICH LIE IN THE MIDDLE OF THE HARBOUR.

The Isle des Sauvages lying in the harbour of Macpec is half a league from the east and north-west entrances. Its position greatly facilitates the entrance of vessels into the harbour, as well as contributes to their finding safe anchorage in good water. In order to secure this when vessels at sea have reached a point at which they can take one or the other of the two entrances already mentioned, they have only to steer directly for the cape on Ile aux Sauvages, in order to be always certain that they are in the middle of the channels, for both channels run together from a distance from three to four hundred toises outside the two entrances to where they meet again some five hundred or six hundred fathoms from Ile aux Sauvages. After that point vessels can approach the land to the west as closely as they deem convenient, according to their draft, and anchor wherever they wish, there being a depth of six to seven fathoms of water throughout the harbour.

To the west-south-west of the Ile aux Sauvages lies a second isle which had been granted to the late Monsieur Courtin, Priest and Missionary to the Indians, from which fact it bears the name of Ile à Monsieur Courtin. It lies about eight hundred toises distant from the other island and to the west-north-west. Its circumference is estimated at one league, with a diameter of eight hundred toises. The lands are high and wooded with all sorts of hard timber, such as maples, red maples, black birch, oak, &c., but not much oak.

One sees at a glance that the harbour of Macpec is shut in by an island that lies directly facing the entrance, and which adds at once to its value as a harbour, and to the security of the shipping. As already stated the three entrances that the sea has made into three different parts of the island have subdivided it into three, that form with the two extremities of the harbour the four entrances that were referred to already.

There is yet another reason, and a better, for concluding that the currents of water caused by the rising and falling of the tide are very strong throughout the whole of the capacious harbour. The most westerly entrance was rendered impassable in 1750, when during a huricane, the said dunes were broken through, and the strength of the currents of water has prevented their becoming re-united since.

It is estimated that from the north-west point of the eastern entrance to the point west of the western entrance a distance of two leagues and a half, running east-south-east and west-north-west, together making the length of the isles and entrances to the harbour of Macpec. Then, from the entrances on the east and north-west to the further end of the bay, the distance is put at two leagues, in which vessels of 100 to 150 tons burden can make the passage, afterwards the harbour divides into two arms. One arm runs to the south-south east about one league, at the extremity of which a small stream that rises about half a league inland to the south, empties itself. The second arm runs inland three leagues to the west-south-west and is navigable by small vessels for two leagues.

From the west point of the harbour, a species of canal or river runs north-west to the harbour of Cachechampec, and is practicable only by boats. Notwithstanding that the distance between the two harbours is six leagues, there is inland communication between all parts of the two harbours.

The lands in the neighbourhood of the harbour of Macpec are superior in quality to those of St. Pierre and Rivière du Nord-Est, and even to all those we have visited up to the present time. Nevertheless those who have settled here have not been able to seed their lands this year, but it must be taken into consideration that this was due to the bad seasons, from which the unfortunate settlers have suffered, during three consecutive years. The first year the trouble was caused by field mice. These animals resemble in appearance those found in the rural districts of France, especially in Champagne, where during the fall, they store up, at a depth of two or three feet in the earth, grain for their comfortable subsistence, and then go to sleep for six months of the year. It is only in this foresight that the field mice of this country do not resemble those of the old land, for here, after they have devoured everything that they can find to their taste in the country, they throw themselves into the water where they are drowned in such prodigious numbers that their bodies form a kind of dam to the waters, by which they are carried down and accumulate, so that the shores of the lakes, rivers, creeks and streams are filled with them. A prejudiced, ignorant and vulgar people did not long hesitate in ascribing the coming of this plague to some evil spirit working against the island. Suspicion fell on a man named St. Germain dit Périgord. This suspicion coming to the knowledge of the Indians, they took the man Périgord, put him to death and buried him on the Isle of the Comte Saint Pierre, which lies to larboard as you enter Port la Joye.

The second bad season was caused by innumerable legions of locusts of a prodigious size. They were of so voracious a species that they ravaged all the growing grain, vegetables and even the grass and the buds on the trees.

The last year the wheat crop was totally scalded. These are the events of those three years of anguish, that have reduced these poor settlers to the depths of poverty, so that for at least six months the greater number amongst them had not even bread to eat, but subsisted on the shell fish they gathered on the shores of the harbour when the tide was out. It is certain that unless the King makes them a gratuity, or a loan of seed grain, to seed their land this coming spring, the settlers will be under the bitter necessity of abandoning the district, if they would escape death from hunger, as they have no other source of livelihood.

The condition to which the settlers on the harbour of Macpec have been actually reduced, demonstrates that it is an important and absolute necessity, that they should be permitted and encouraged to pursue the cod fishing industry. There has for a long time been a mistaken belief, founded on a lack of experience of the conditions, that the settlers who follow the fisheries, neglect the cultivation of the soil. The harbours of Saint-Pierre and of l'Acadie are a certain proof in evidence to the contrary. Witness the extensive clearings which the settlers have made in those places, and I venture to affirm that the fishery is an incontestable means of promoting the culture of the soil, because it enables settlers to employ domestics, and to raise cattle and live stock for lack of which land will be allowed to remain idle. This is not the only advantage that would accure to the settlers, for it can be stated as a certain fact verified by experience that if ever again the people suffer such hardship, as are said to return every ten years, in the form of a plague of locusts, followed the ensuring year, when beech nuts are plentiful, by one of field mice, they will be enabled to support the losses these animals occasion there, by means of the proceeds of the fisheries.

On the shore of the harbour of Macpec, a vein of clay has been discovered on land belonging to one Ambroise Barnabé. This clay is proved to be of the quality required for making bricks, being rich, soft, loamy and free from stones. A peck has been placed on board a vessel commanded by Joseph Boudrot, together with a log of cedar, to be carried to Louisbourg, to the address of Monsieur Pichon, secretary to Monsieur le Comte de Raymond.

The timber in the environs of the harbour of Macpec as well as of its rivers may be described as very fine, and in a general way as including well-nigh all the kinds found in this part of the island such as pine, spruce, maple, red maple, black birch, beech, ash, oak, white birch, cedar, &c.

Between the harbour of Cascampec, situated on the north coast, six leagues from Macpec and seven leagues from Pointe du Ouest and Grand Ance, situated on the south side of the Isle Saint-Jean at a distance of —— leagues from Pointe du Ouest and —— leagues from the harbour of Bedec, is a great cedar grove which is estimated to be two to three leagues in circumference and in which there are cedars of four feet in diameter and two toises and a half in circumference.

CENSUS.

Census of the settlers at Macpec in men, women and children.

Joseph Arceneau, ploughman and navigator, native of l'Acadie, aged 35 years, and has been twenty-three years in the country. Married to Margueritte Boudrot, native of Port Toulouse, aged 29 years.

They have five children, four sons and one daughter :—

Pierre Arcenaud, aged 10 years ;
François, aged 8 years ;
Cyprien, aged 6 years ;
Joseph, aged 4 years ;
Anne, aged 15 months.

Antoine Arcenaud, native of l'Acadie, aged 30 years, his brother lives with them. They have in live stock, two oxen, one cow, four ewes, one wether, three pigs six fowls, together with one bateau.

The land on which they are settled was granted to them by Messieurs Duchambon and Dubuisson, under date the fifth of September, 1742. On it they have made a clearing and sown twelve bushels of wheat and two bushels of peas and still have fallow land sufficient for the sowing of twenty-five bushels.

Abraham Arcenaud, ploughman, native of l'Acadie, aged 34 years, he has been in the country 23 years. Married to Marguerite Mirat, native of l'Acadie, aged 30 years.

They have three sons and two daughters :—

Joseph, aged 9 years ;
Pierre, aged 4 years ;
Jean, aged 4 years ;
Marguerite, aged 7 years ;
Rosalie, aged 2 years.

In live stock they have four oxen, two cows, one calf, three wethers, three ewes, four pigs and four fowls.

The land on which they are settled was granted to them by Messieurs Duchambon and Dubuisson. They have made a clearing on it and sown twelve bushels of wheat, one bushel of barley and one bushel of peas, and have fallow land for the sowing of about eighteen bushels.

Julien Desroches, ploughman, native of the parish of Carolle, bishopric of Avranche in Normandy, aged 35 years, he has been 21 years in the country. Married to Marie Arcenaud, native of l'Acadie, aged 27 years.

They have three sons :—

Julien, aged 7 years ;

Felix, aged 5 years ;

Joseph aged 2 years.

In live stock they have one ox, one cow, six wethers, ten ewes and one fowl.

They hold the land under a grant given by Messieurs Duchambon and Dubuisson, and homologated by Messieurs the Governor and the Intendant-Commissary of Ile Royale. On it they have made a clearing and sown four bushels of wheat and have fallow for the sowing of twelve bushels.

Louis Desroches, fisherman and ploughman, native of the same place as his brother above described, aged 40 years. Married to Marguerite Arcenaud, native of l'Acadie, aged 40 years.

They have eight children, three sons and five daughters :—

Eustache, aged 16 years ;

Alexandre, aged 12 years ;

Joseph, aged 9 years ;

Rosalie, aged 20 years ;

Marie Joseph, aged 14 years ;

Marie Anne, aged 10 years ;

Henriette, aged 5 years ;

Anne, aged 2 years.

In live stock they have two oxen, one cow, one calf, two wethers, ten ewes and four pigs.

They hold their land under a grant from Messieurs Duchambon and Dubuisson, and homologated by Messieurs the Governor and Intendant-Commissary of Ile Royale, but from whom they have only a certificate.

On said land they have made a clearing and sown two bushels of wheat and have fallow land for the sowing of twenty-one bushels.

Jean Arcenaud, son of Jacques, native of l'Acadie, aged 23 years, ploughman, he has been eleven years in the country. Married to Magdelaine Boudrot, native of Port Toulouse, aged 25 years.

They have Joseph, their son, aged one year.

In live stock they have one ox, two cows, one wether, one ewe, two pigs, one sow.

They hold their land upon verbal permission from Monsieur de Bonnaventure. On it they have made a clearing in which they have sown six bushels of wheat, one half bushel of oats and one bushel of peas.

Alexis Dugats, smith and ploughman, native of l'Acadie, aged 45 years, he has been in the country one year. Married to Marie Bourg, native of l'Acadie, aged 42 years.

They have nine children, five sons and four daughters :—

Pierre, aged 20 years ;

Jean, aged 15 years ;

Mathurin, aged 12 years ;

Regis, aged 5 years ;

Cyprien, aged 3 years ;

Elizabeth, aged 18 years ;

Magdelaine, aged 14 years ;

Victoire, aged 10 years ;

Marie, aged one year.

In live stock they have four oxen, two cows, two calves, one heifer, one wether, one ewe and one pig.

They hold their land upon verbal permission from Monsieur de Bonnaventure, but have not made any clearing on it.

Marguerite Richard, widow of the late Claude Arcenaud, native of l'Acadie, aged 45 years, she has been 15 years in the country.

She has nine children—four sons and five daughters :—

Claude Arcenaud, eldest son, aged 24 years ;
Paul, aged 20 years ;
Ambroise, aged 14 years ;
Joseph, aged 11 years ;
Magdelaine, aged 21 years ;
Anne, aged 18 years ;
Judich, aged 16 years ;
Rose, aged 9 years ;
Anastazie, aged 7 years.

She has in live stock, seven oxen, three cows, four heifers, one horse, seven wethers, eight ewes, two sows, one pig and one hen.

They hold their land under a grant given by Messieurs Duchambon and Dubuisson under date the 6th September, 1742, and homologated. On it they have made a clearing and sown nineteen bushels of wheat, one bushel of barley, three bushels of oats, one bushel of peas and have fallow land sufficient for the sowing of thirty-two bushels.

Pierre Arcenaud, son of Jacques, ploughman, native of l'Acadie, aged 27 years, he has been 11 years in the country. Married to Magdelaine Landry, native of l'Acadie, aged 25 years.

They have Marie Arceneau, their daughter, aged one year.

In live stock they have two oxen, one wether and two ewes.

They hold their land under a grant from Messieurs Duchambon and Dubuisson. On it they have made a clearing and sown six bushels of wheat, and three bushels of peas. They have no fallow land.

Pierre Arceneau, widower, ploughman, native of l'Acadie, aged 52 years, he has been 21 years in the country.

He has seven children, four sons and three daughters :

Pierre, aged 24 years ;
Claude, aged 21 years ;
Françoise, aged 17 years ;
Louis, aged 14 years ;
Marguerite, aged 15 years ;
Anne, aged 11 years ;
Henriette, aged 9 years.

In live stock they have two oxen, four heifers, three wethers, two ewes and one sow.

They hold their land under a grant made to them by Messieurs Duchambon and Dubuisson. On it they have made a clearing for the sowing of about fifty bushels of wheat, and have sown nothing this year, they not having the seed.

Pierre Poirier, ploughman, native of l'Acadie, aged 42 years, he has been in the country 11 years. Married to Louise Caissy, native of l'Acadie, aged 35 years.

They have eight children, three sons and five daughters :

Pierre, aged 18 years ;
François, aged 12 years ;
Joseph Isidore, aged 6 years ;
Marie, aged 15 years ;
Appollinne, aged 10 years ;
Magdelaine, aged 8 years ;
Anne, aged 4 years ;
Marie Modeste, aged 15 months ;

In live stock they have four oxen, four ewes, two calves, thirteen ewes, one sow, four pigs and eight fowls.

They hold their land upon verbal permission from Messieurs Duchambon and Dubuisson. On it they have made a clearing and sown fourteen bushels of wheat, two bushels of peas, and have fallow land for the sowing of twenty-four bushels.

SESSIONAL PAPER No. 18

Honoré Commeau, ploughman, native of l'Acadie, aged 37 years, he has been in the country 11 years. Married to Marguerite Poirier, native of l'Acadie, aged 38 years.

They have six children, one son and five daughters :

Joseph, aged 4 years ;

Marie, aged 15 years ;

Rose, aged 13 years ;

Anne, aged 10 yearz ;

Monique, aged 7 years ;

Marguerite, aged 18 months.

In live stock they have two oxen, two cows, three calves, eight wethers, two ewes and six pigs.

They hold their land under grant made by Messieurs Duchambon and Dubuisson, under date the 6th of September, 1742, and homologated by Messieurs the Governor and the Intendant Commissary of Ile Royale. On it they have made a clearing and sown ten bushels and a half of wheat and five bushels and a half of peas, and have fallow land for the sowing of eight bushels.

Alexandre Richard, ploughman, native of l'Acadie, aged 57 years, he has been in the country 11 years. Married to Magdelaine Thibaudeau, native of l'Acadie, aged 47 years.

They have three sons and three daughters :—

Jean Richard, aged 15 years ;

Joseph, aged 11 years ;

Victor, aged 5 years ;

Anne, aged 17 years ;

Catherine, aged 13 years ;

Jeanne Rosallye, aged 9 years.

In live stock they have four oxen, two cows, one heifer, six ewes, four pigs, seventeen geese, twenty hens.

They hold their land upon verbal permission from Messieurs Duchambon and Dubuisson. On it they have made a clearing where they have sown ten bushels and a half of wheat, and three bushels of peas, and have fallow land for the sowing of twenty bushels.

Ambroise Barnabé, widower, ploughman, native of l'Acadie, aged 49 years, he has been in the country ten years.

He has seven sons and two daughters :—

Ambroise, aged 18 years ;

Joseph, aged 16 years ;

Michel, aged 14 years ;

Pierre, aged 12 years ;

Jean, aged 10 years ;

François, aged 6 years ;

Paul, aged 4 years ;

Marguerite, aged 19 years ;

Marie, aged 8 years.

In live stock they have two oxen, one cow, one heifer, one wether, seven ewes and five pigs.

He holds his land under a grant made by Messieurs Duchambon and Dubuisson under date the ————, 1742, and homologated by Messieurs the Governor and the Intendant Commissary of Ile Royale. He has made a clearing on it, and sown sixteen bushels of wheat, one bushel of oats, one bushel of peas, and has ploughed land sufficient for the sowing of thirty-two bushels besides.

Paul Daigre, ploughman, native of l'Acadie, aged 29 years, he has been in this country two years. Married to Marie Hebert, native of l'Acadie, aged 22 years.

They have two daughters :—

Marie, aged 4 years ;

Agnes, aged 18 months.

In live stock they have two oxen, three cows, one bull, two calves, one horse, seven ewes, four pigs and four fowls.

5-6 EDWARD VII., A. 1906

They hold their land upon verbal permission from Monsieur de Bonnaventure.

They have sown eight bushels on a neighboring piece of ground, but have made no clearing of their own beyond cutting a little wood.

Jean Commeaux, ploughman, native of l'Acadie, aged 32 years, he has been in the country 2 years. Married to Marie Henry, native of l'Acadie, aged 29 years.

They have one son and one daughter:

Jean Baptiste, aged 7 years ;

Magdelaine, aged 2 years.

In live stock they have three oxen, one cow, one calf, two ewes and one sow.

They hold their land under a grant made by Messieurs Duchambon and Dubuisson, under date of ——— ——— 1742, and homologated by Messieurs the Governor and the Intendant Commissary of Ile Royale. On it they have made a clearing and sown nine bushels of wheat and have fallow land for the sowing of three bushels.

Michel Richard, ploughman, native of l'Acadie, aged 20 years, he has been in the country 11 years. Married to Marie Dugast, native of l'Acadie, aged — years.

They have no children yet.

In live stock they have one cow and her calf and two ewes.

They hold their land under verbal permission from Monsieur de Bonnaventure, but have not yet made any clearing, being newly settled on it.

Pierre Richard, ploughman, native of l'Acadie, aged 22 years, he has been in the country 11 years. Married to Margueritte Dugast, native of l'Acadie, aged 17 years.

They have no children, being only recently married.

In live stock they have one cow and her calf.

They hold their land under verbal permission from Monsieur de Bonnaventure. They have made no clearing.

François Blanchard dit Gentilhomme, native of Saint-Marc de Blanc, in Brittany aged 66 years, he has been in the country 40 years of which he passed 15 at Macpec, widower.

He has seven children, two sons and five daughters :—

François, aged 14 years ;

Jean, aged 10 years ;

Margueritte, aged 20 years ;

Catherine, aged 17 years and 6 months ;

Cecille, aged 12 years ;

Rosallie, aged 8 years ;

Agathe, aged 6 years.

In live stock they have four oxen, one cow, two heifers, one calf, thirteen ewes, two pigs and two sows.

They hold this land under a grant made by Messieurs Duchambon and Dubuisson. For lack of seed they have sown none of their land this year, but they have fallow land for the sowing of twenty-four bushels.

Abraham Arcenaud dit le petit Abraham, native of l'Acadie, aged 50 years, he has been in the country 11 years, ploughman. Married to Marie Joseph Savoyé, aged 42 years.

They have ten children, five sons and five daughters :

Jean Baptiste, aged 16 years ;

Jacques, aged 12 years ;

Joseph, aged 8 years ;

Hilarion, aged 4 years ;

Baptiste, aged 2 years ;

Anne, aged 20 years ;

Marie Joseph, aged 18 years ;

Anne Anastasie, aged 14 years ;

Marguerite, aged 10 years.

Martine, aged 6 years.

In live stock they have two oxen, two cows, two calves, five wethers, eight ewes and three pigs.

The land on which they are settled is situated to the west of the harbour of Macpec, and was given to them by Messieurs Duchambon and Dubuisson. On it they have made a clearing where they can sow thirty-two bushels of wheat. They have sown only six bushels and a half of wheat, having no more seed.

Charles Arceneau, ploughman, native of l'Acadie, aged 50 years, he has been in the country 24 years. Married to Cecille Braud, native of l'Acadie, aged 48 years.

They have four sons and one daughter :

Charles, aged 21 years ;
Claude, aged 16 years ;
Joseph, aged 14 years ;
Hurbain, aged 12 years ;
Auzide, aged —— years.

They have in live stock two oxen, three cows, three calves, one horse, three wethers, twelve ewes, one sow, ten pigs and six hens.

The land on which they are settled is situated to the west of the said harbour and was given to them by Messieurs de Pensens and Dubuisson. On it they have made a clearing and sown forty bushels of wheat and one bushel of peas, and they still have remaining fallow land sufficient for the sowing of forty-eight bushels that they were unable to sow for want of seed.

Joseph Boudrot, ploughman and navigator, native of Port Toulouse, aged 35 years. Married to Rose Arcenaud, native l'Acadie, aged 30 years.

They have six children, two sons and four daughters :—

Joseph Boudrot, aged 8 years ;
Charles, aged 5 years ;
Marie, aged 6 years ;
Anne, aged 4 years ;
Marguerite, aged 2 years ;
Marie Joseph, aged 3 months.

They have in live stock three oxen, one cow and her calf, five ewes, three pigs and one hen.

The land on which they are settled is situated as in the preceding case, and was given to them by Messieurs Duchambon and Dubuisson. They have made a clearing on it where they have sown four bushels of wheat and have fallow land sufficient for the sowing of twelve bushels.

Marie Poirier, widow of Jacques Arcenaud, native of l'Acadie, aged 50 years.

She has two sons :—

Alexander, aged 20 years ;
Paul, aged 15 years.

In live stock they have four oxen, three cows, one heifer, one calf, three wethers, three pigs and three hens.

The land on which they are settled is situated up the Rivière du Ouest, and had been granted to the late Jacques Arcenaud by Messieurs Duchambon and Dubuisson. They have made a clearing on it where they have sown ten bushels of wheat, two bushels of peas and one bushel of barley, and they have fallow land for the sowing of twenty bushels.

Jean Arcenaud, son of Charles, ploughman, native of Macpec, aged 23 years. Married to Magdelaine Boudrot, native of Port Toulouse, aged 22 years.

They have Andre Arecnaud, their son, aged 8 months.

And in live stock two oxen, one cow, two ewes and two pigs.

The land on which they are settled was given to them verbally by Monsieur de Bonnaventure in 1751. On it they have made a clearing where they have sown seven bushels of wheat.

Pierre Arcenaud, ploughman, native of Macpec, aged 23 years. Married to Judich Boudrot, native of Port Toulouse, aged 20 years.

In live stock they have two oxen, one cow, one heifer, five ewes, three pigs and two fowls.

The land on which they are settled is the same as that of Jean Arcenaud, his twin brother.

5-6 EDWARD VII., A. 1906

Jean Baptiste Hent, native of Isle d'Orléans, parish of Saint Jean, bishopric of Quebec, aged 19 years, he has only been one year in the country. Married to Thérèse Arcenaud, native of Macpec, aged 20 years. The whole of their live stock consists of one heifer, three ewes and three fowls.

They are settled on the land of Pierre Arcenaud, his wife's father.

Paul Richard, ploughman, native of l'Acadie, aged 27 years, he has been 11 years in the country. Married to Herre Boudrot, native of Port Toulouse, aged 23 years.

They have two sons and one daughter :

Joseph, aged 5 years ;

Charles, aged one year ;

Marie, aged two months.

In live stock they have one ox, two cows, two calves and five ewes.

The land on which they are settled was given to them verbally by Monsieur de Bonnaventure. On it they have made a clearing for the sowing of two bushels of wheat.

François Doucet, ploughman, native of l'Acadie, aged 58 years, he has been in the country 11 years. Married to Marie Lapierre, native of l'Acadie, aged 45 years.

They have eight children, four sons and four daughters :

Michel, aged 17 years ;

Cristophle, aged 9 years ;

Jean, aged 8 years ;

Marin, aged 3 years ;

Margueritte, aged 22 years ;

Marie Joseph, aged 16 years ;

Françoise, aged 12 years ;

Anniès, aged 5 years.

In live stock they have two oxen, one cow, one calf, two wethers, five ewes and three pigs.

The land they occupy was given to them by Messieurs Duchambon and Dubuisson. On it they have made a clearing where they have sown twelve bushels of wheat and still have remaining follow land sufficient for the sowing of fourteen bushels.

Charles Doucet, fisherman and ploughman, native of l'Acadie, aged 30 years, he has been in the country 11 years. Married to Jeanne Boudrot, native of Tracadie, aged 22 years.

They have two daughters :

Anne, aged 4 years ;

Marguerite, aged 2 years.

In live stock they have two oxen, one cow, one calf, four ewes and five pigs.

The land on which they are settled was given to them by Messieurs Duchambon and Dubuisson. On it they have made a clearing and sown ten bushels of wheat and one bushel-and-a-half of peas, and still have remaining fallow land for the sowing of eight bushels.

Jacques Arceneaux, ploughman, native of l'Acadie, aged 30 years, he has been 10 years in the country. Married to Marie Joseph ————, native of the same place, aged 20 years.

They have three daughters :

Rose, aged 3 years ;

Euphrozine, aged 4 years ;

Magdelaine, aged 2 years.

In live stock they have two oxen, two cows, one bull, two ewes and six fowls.

The land on which they are settled was given to them by Messieurs Duchambon and Dubuisson. On it they have made a clearing where they have sown eight bushels of wheat.

Louis Giroir, ploughman, native of l'Acadie, aged 36 years, he has been two years in the country. Married to Marie Thibaudeau, native of l'Acadie, aged 28 years

They have six children, three sons and three daughters :

Gervais, aged 8 years ;

Firmain, aged 3 years ;
Charles, aged 8 months ;
Marguerite, aged 15 years ;
Anne Theodose, aged 13 years ;
Marie Joseph, aged 6 years.
They have one pig for the whole of their live stock.

The land on which they are settled is situated on the north shore of Rivière de Macpec. They have only had it since the 25th of July last, and have made a clearing of about one arpent.

Joseph LeBlanc, ploughman, native of l'Acadie, aged 34 years, he has been in the country one year. Married to Magdelaine Giroir, native of l'Acadie, aged 33 years.

They have six children, two sons and four daughters :
Bazille, aged 11 years;
Joseph, aged 9 years ;
Marie, aged 7 years ;
Elizabeth, aged 5 years ;
Marguerite, aged 3 years ;
Magdelaine, aged 8 months.
They have no live stock.

The land on which they are settled since last autumn, is situated as in the preceding case. On it they have made a clearing of about two arpents in extent.

Joseph Arceneau, ploughman, native of l'Acadie, aged 27 years, he has been in the country 15 years. Married to Anne Doucet, native of l'Acadie, aged 27 years.

They have Anne, their daughter, aged 18 months.

Their live stock consists of five oxen, two cows, two calves, six ewes, one wether, five pigs, two geese and twelve fowls.

The land on which they are settled was granted to them by Messiers Duchambon and Dubuisson. They have made a clearing on it where they have sown fifteen bushels of wheat and two bushels of peas, and have fallow land for the sowing of fifteen bushels.

We left the harbour of Macpec in a canoe, crossed the three leagues of the bay and disembarked on a small stream. This streamlet, which is of little account, is maintain-ed by the filtration of the waters from the surrounding lands which are peaty and marshy. From the banks of this stream a road was taken running one league to the south. It is practicable for carts which can cross from one bay to the other. The lands are covered with all kinds of different woods, but the predominant is the hemlock.

THE HARBOUR OF BEDEC.

The harbour of Bedec is settled by eight families, and is situated on the south side of the Isle Saint-Jean, sixteen leagues distant from Pointe la Joye, and eight from Baye Verte. The lands around the said harbour are good for cultivation, and the shores of the harbour abound in pasturage.

The entrance is formed by the point of the Isle de Bedec lying on the east and by the point to the west-north-west lying on the west. They lie east-south-east and west-north-west, and are three quarters of a league apart. The channel lies north-east and south-west and is estimated at a quarter of a league in width, with four to five fathoms of water at low tide. After doubling the Isle de Bedec the harbour is found to be divided in two parts, one running to the north-east for about one league and a half ; and the other three quarters of a league to the south-east. Vessels can anchor on either the one or the other, in a depth of four, five or six fathoms of water at low tide, but for the greatest safety it is necessary to anchor in the south-east branch which is generally sheltered from all winds.

CENSUS.

Census of the settlers at Bedec, in men, women, children, &c.

Jean Robichaud dit Cadet, ploughman, native of l'Acadie, aged 59 years and a half, he has been in the country 14 months. Married to Marie Leger, native of l'Acadie, aged 53 years and a half.

5-6 EDWARD VII., A. 1906

They have seven children—five sons and two daughters :—
Joseph, aged 34 years.
Jean, aged 31 years ;
René, aged 26 years ;
Pierre, aged 22 years ;
François, aged 18 years ;
Marie Joseph, aged 16 years ;
Anne, aged 13 years.
René Blanchard, orphan, native of l'Acadie, aged 5 years.
In live stock they have four oxen, nine cows, one heifer, four calves, one bull, one wether, two ewes and five pigs.
The land on which they are settled is situated on the north shore of Rivière de Bedecq. On it they have made a clearing where they can sow sixteen bushels of wheat.
Jacques Guedry dit Grivoye, ploughman, native of l'Acadie, aged 28 years, he has been in the country 14 months. Married to Brigitte Le Jeune, native of l'Acadie, aged 34 years.
They have three daughters :
Marie Joseph, aged 6 years ;
Victoire, aged 4 years ;
Marie, aged 2 years.
In live stock they have one cow, one heifer and four pigs.
The land on which they are settled is situated as in the preceding case, and was given to them verbally by Monsieur de Bonnaventure. They have made a clearing and on it a large garden.
Alexis Terriaud, ploughman, native of l'Acadie, aged 26 years, he has been in the country two years. Married to Magdeleine Robichaud, native of l'Acadie, aged 26 years.
They have three children, two sons and one daughter :—
Pierre Alexis, aged 3 years ;
Louis, aged 17 months ;
Magdeleine Geneviève, aged 4 years.
In live stock they have two oxen, two cows, one calf, one horse and four pigs.
The land on which they are settled is situated as in the preceding case, and was given to them verbally by Monsieur de Bonnaventure. They have made no clearing having been constantly ill.
Joseph Terriaud dit le Bonhomme, ploughman, native of l'Acadie, aged 24 years, he has been in the country 13 months. Married to Marie Joseph Pitre, native of l'Acadie, aged 21 years.
They have one son :—
Pierre Paul, aged 7 months.
In live stock they possess two oxen, one cow, one horse, one wether and one pig.
The land on which they are settled is situated as in the preceding case, and was given to them verbally by Monsieur de Bonnaventure. They have made a clearing where they hope to sow three bushels next spring.
They have with them Paul Pitre, their brother, native of l'Acadie, aged 10 years.
Pierre Lejeune, senior, ploughman, native of l'Acadie, aged 70 years, he has been in the country two years. Married to Jeanne Benoist, native of l'Acadie, aged 60 years.
They have one son and one daughter :—
Joseph, aged 21 years ;
Marguerite, aged 24 years.
In live stock they have three oxen, one cow, and two pigs.
The land on which they are settled is situated on the south shore of Rivière de Bedecq, and was given to them verbally by Monsieur de Bonnaventure. On it they have made a clearing for the sowing of four bushels of wheat in the coming spring.
Pierre Le Jeune, ploughman, native of l'Acadie, aged 32 years, he has been in the country 21 months. Married to Marie Le Blanc, native of l'Acadie, aged 34 years.
They have four children, two sons, and two daughters :—

SESSIONAL PAPER No. 18

David, aged 7 years ;
Enselme, aged 6 years ;
Anne, aged 3 years ;
Marie Blanche, aged 8 months.
In live stock they have two oxen, one cow, two pigs and one hen.

The land on which they are settled is situated on the south shore of Rivière de Bedecq. They hold it verbally from Monsieur de Bonnaventure. On it they have made a clearing where they can sow four bushels of wheat.

Jean Fraiquingout, ploughman, native of Plouanne, bishopric of Saint Malo, aged 37 years, he has been in the country two years. Married to Anne Lejeune, native of l'Acadie, aged 35 years.

They have one son and two daughters :—
Joseph, aged 7 years ;
Véronique, aged 5 years ;
Anne Marie, aged 6 months.
In live stock they have one pig, having lost all besides, during the past winter.

They hold their land verbally from Monsieur de Bonnaventure, and have made a clearing for the sowing of three bushels of wheat.

Augustin Le Jeune, ploughman, native of l'Acadie, aged 26 years, he has been 21 months in the country. Married to Marie Joseph Chenois, native of l'Acadie, aged 27 years.

They have one daughter :—
Marie Joseph, aged one year.
They have no live stock.

The land on which they are settled is situated as in the preceding case. It was given to them verbally by Monsieur de Bonnaventure. On it they have made a clearing for sowing three bushels of wheat.

CENSUS.

Census of the settlers at La Traverse, in men, women, children, &c.

Pierre Blanchard, senior, ploughman, native of l'Acadie, aged 60 years, he has been in the country one year. Married to Françoise Braud, native of l'Acadie, aged 59 years.

They have three sons and one daughter :—
Jean Baptiste, aged 22 years ;
Joseph, aged 19 years ;
Charles, aged 16 years ;
Marie Magdelaine, aged 25 years.
In live stock they have six oxen, two cows, one calf, three pigs and one horse.

The land on which they are settled is situated on the north-west bank of Rivière de la Traverse. It was given to them verbally by Monsieur de Bonnaventure. On it they had made a clearing and out of that a large garden.

Pierre Blanchard, junior, ploughman, native of l'Acadie, aged 31 years, he has been in the country one year. Married to Marie Hebert, native of l'Acadie, aged 25 years.

They have one son :—
Jean Pierre, aged 20 months.
In live stock they have one ox, one cow and three pigs.

The land on which they are settled is situated as in the preceding cases. It was given to them verbally by Monsieur de Bonnaventure. On it they have made a clearing and out of that a garden.

Jean Baptiste Boudrot, ploughman, native of l'Acadie, aged 70 years, he has been in the country one year. Married to Louise Saunier, native of l'Acadie, aged 58 years.

They have three children, one son and two daughters :
Honoré, aged 24 years ;
Anastazie, aged 19 years ;
Marie Magdelaine, aged 16 years.
In live stock they have two oxen, two cows, one calf and two pigs.

18—11

5-6 EDWARD VII., A. 1906

The land on which they are settled is situated as in the preceding cases. It was given to them verbally by Monsieur de Bonnaventure. They have a clearing on which they have made a garden.

Zacharie Boudrot, ploughman, native of l'Acadie, aged 31 years, he has been one year in the country. Married to Margueritte Daigre, native of l'Acadie, aged 24 years.

They have one son and one daughter :—

Paul, aged one year ;

Marie, aged 3 years.

Margueritte Boudrot, orphan, native of l'Acadie, aged 10 years, lives with them.

In live stock they have four oxen, three cows, three calves, one horse and two pigs.

The land on which they are settled is situated as in the preceding cases. It was given to them verbally by Monsieur de Bonnaventure and on it they have made a garden.

Antoine Boudrot, ploughman, native of l'Acadie, aged 35 years, he has been one year in the country. Married to Brigitte Apart, native of l'Acadie, aged 25 years.

They have one son :

Jean Baptiste, aged 4 years.

Alexis Apart, infirm, brother of the said Brigitte, native of l'Acadie, aged 27 years, lives with them.

In live stock they have two heifers, one horse and one pig.

The land on which they are settled is situated on the north-west shore of Rivière de la Traverse. It was given to them verbally by Monsieur de Bonnaventure, and on it they have made a garden.

We left Rivière de la Traverse on the 31st of August and took the route for Rivière des Blonds, following the coast all the way to the mouth of Rivière des Blonds. It is estimated that from the mouth of one river to that of the other is three leagues. In this distance nothing remarkable was met with. The lands are covered with all kinds of mixed timber.

Rivière des Blonds runs four leagues into the land to the north. Families are settled on both sides of the river, and at a league from its entrance the lands that have been cleared promise well and the rest are covered with all descriptions of wood fit for construction purposes. There is a great deal of grass on the banks of the said river, which is navigable only by boat.

CENSUS.

Census of the settlers at Rivière des Blonds in men, women, children, etc.

François Reneauld, ploughman, native of l'Acadie, aged 25 years, he has been 21 months in the country. Married to Françoise Commeau, native of l'Acadie, aged 30 years.

They have three daughters :—

Marie Tompic, aged 15 years, daughter of a previous marriage of said Commeau ;

Theotiste Reneau, aged 20 months ;

Rose, aged 5 months.

In live stock they have two cows, two calves, three pigs and one hen.

The land on which they are settled is situated on the north-west shore of the said river. It was given to them verbally by Monsieur de Bonnaventure. They have made a clearing on it for the sowing of two bushels in the coming spring.

Pierre Robichaud dit Cadet, ploughman, native of l'Acadie, aged 45 years, he has been 21 months in the country. Married to Suzanne Brasseau, native of l'Acadie, aged 45 years.

They have eight children, three sons and five daughters :—

Pierre, aged 15 years ;

Olivier, aged 10 years ;

Phirmain Foelix, aged 19 months ;

Suzanne, aged 19 years ;

Marie Rose, aged 16 years ;

Marie Anne, aged 14 years ;

Anastasie, aged 8 years ;
Marie Joseph la Blanche, aged 3 years.

In live stock they have one ox, one bull, two cows, two heifers, four pigs and four fowls.

The land on which they are settled is situated as in the preceding cases. It was given to them verbally by Monsieur de Bonnaventure. On it they have made a clearing for the sowing of six bushels of wheat in the coming spring.

Alexandre Bourg, ploughman, native of l'Acadie, aged 43 years, he has been in the country 21 months. Married to Ursulle Hébert, native of l'Acadie, aged 36 years.

They have six children, three sons and three daughters :—

Joseph, aged 16 years ;
Raymond, aged 6 years ;
Grégoire, aged 30 months ;
Marie Magdelaine, aged 14 years ;
Anne Marguerite, aged 10 years ;
Anne Radegonde, aged 8 years.

In live stock, they have two oxen, one cow, two heifers, one calf and five pigs.

The land on which they are settled was given to them verbally by Monsieur de Bonnaventure. It is situated on the east bank of said river. They have made a clearing for the sowing of six bushels of grain in the coming spring.

François Bourg, ploughman, native of l'Acadie, aged 35 years, he has been in the country one year. Married to Marguerite Hébert, native of l'Acadie, aged 38 years.

They have five children, two sons and three daughters :—

Charles, aged 12 years ;
Jean, aged 10 years ;
Françoise, aged 6 years ;
Marguerite, aged 4 years ;
Marie, aged one year.

In live stock, they have two oxen, one cow, one heifer and four pigs.

The land on which they are settled is situated on the east bank of Rivière des Blonds. It was given to them verbally by Monsieur le Bonnaventure. They have made a clearing on it for the sowing of six bushels of wheat.

Jean Bourg, ploughman, native of l'Acadie, aged 45 years, he has been in the country one year. Married to Marie Pitre, native of l'Acadie, aged 46 years.

They have five children, three sons and two daughters :—

Jean, aged 17 years ;
François, aged 14 years ;
Charles, aged 6 years ;
Marguerite, aged 18 years ;
Marie, aged 8 years.

In live stock they have three oxen, one cow, three heifers and five pigs.

The land on which they are settled is situated as in the preceding cases. It was given to them verbally by Monsieur de Bonnaventure. On it they have made a clearing for the sowing of six bushels of wheat in the coming spring.

CENSUS.

Census of the settlers at the Rivière au Crapeau, in men, women, children, etc.

Louis Bourg, ploughman, native of Port Royal, in l'Acadie, aged 65 years, he has been 22 months in th country. Married to Cecille Michel, native of l'Acadie, aged 58 years.

They have seven children, three sons and four daughters :—

Eustache, aged 30 years ;
Louis, aged 22 years ;
Charles, aged 15 years ;
Marguerite, aged 25 years ;

5-6 EDWARD VII., A. 1906

Elizabeth, aged 24 years ;

Marie Magdelaine, aged 19 years ;

Anne Joseph, aged 8 years.

In live stock they have two oxen, four cows, one calf, four pigs and ten fowls.

The land on which they are settled is situated on the east bank of the said river. It was given to them verbally by Monsieur de Bonnaventure. They have made a clearing on it for the sowing of four bushels of wheat.

Jean Baptiste Bourg, ploughman, native of Acadie, aged 29 years he has been 22 months in the country. Married to Françoise Douaron, native of l'Acadie.

They have one son :

Jean Casimir, aged 7 months.

In live stock they have two cows and two pigs.

The land on which they are settled is situated as in the preceding cases. It was given to them verbally by Monsieur de Bonnaventure. On it they have made a clearing for the sowing of four bushels of wheat.

CENSUS.

Census of the settlers on the Anse du Nord-Ouest, in men, women and children.

François Nogues, ploughman, native of the parish of Piriac, bishopric of Nantes, aged 50 years, he has been in the country two years. Married to Magdelaine Douaron, native of l'Acadie, aged 47 years.

They have two sons and four daughters :

François, aged 15 years ;

François Joseph, aged 10 years ;

Marguerite, aged 22 years ;

Catherine Joseph, aged 19 years ;

Anne Théotiste, aged 12 years ;

Marie Magdelaine, aged 6 years ;

Marie Trahant, their mother, aged 80 years lives with them.

In live stock they have two oxen, three cows, two heifers, one calf one wether, one ewe, two pigs, one sow and one hen.

The land on which they are settled was given to them verbally by Monsieur De Bonnaventure. On it they have made a clearing where they can sow five bushels of wheat.

Mathieu Brasseux, ploughman, native of l'Acadie, aged 50 years, he has been in the country two years. Married to Anne Marie Pitre, native of l'Acadie, aged 45 years.

They have eleven children, five sons and six daughters :

Pierre, aged 21 years ;

François, aged 15 years ;

Mathurin, aged 13 years ;

François Xavier, aged 11 years ;

Jean Baptiste, aged 6 years ;

Anthiotiste, aged 24 months ;

Marguerite Joseph, aged 19 years ;

Brigitte, aged 17 years ;

Elizabeth Gertrude, aged 7 years ;

Marie Joseph, aged, 4 years ;

Pellagie, aged 2 months.

In live stock they have two oxen, one heifer, two wethers, six ewes, two pigs and one hen.

The land on which they are settled was given to them verbally by Monsieur de Bonnaventure. On it they have made a clearing where they have sown six bushels of wheat.

Jean Baptiste Godet, ploughman, always ill, and poor, native of l'Acadie, aged 50 years, he has been two years in the country. Married to Marie Joseph Darois, native of l'Acadie, aged 42 years.

They have six children, two sons and four daughters :

Joseph Ignasse, aged 9 years.

Paul Marie, aged 3 years.

Marguerite, aged 21 years.

Anne Joseph, aged 18 years.

Marie Blanche, aged 16 years.

Marie Magdelaine, aged 11 years.

In live stock they have one ox, two cows, one calf, one sow, four pigs, and one hen.

They hold their land as in the preceding case. They have made a clearing where they can sow two bushels of wheat.

CENSUS.

Census of the settlers on the Anse aux Sanglier, in men, women, children, &c.

François Tureaud, poor, nailer, not having the means of buying the requisites to work at his trade native of the parish of Saint Pierre du Doy, in Enjou, aged 24 years, he has been two years in the country. Married to Catherine Douaron, native of l'Acadie, aged 35 years.

They have four children, three sons and one daughter :

Annaclet, aged 9 years.

Jean Baptiste, aged 7 years.

François, aged 3 years.

Marie Joseph, aged 11 years.

In live stock they have one pig and twelve fowls or chickens.

They hold their land upon verbal permission from Monsieur de Bonnaventure. On it they have made a clearing for a large garden.

Michel Join, extremely poor, ploughman and formerly a soldier, native of the town of Saint Maslo in Britany, aged 46 ; he has been in the country 22 months. Married to Marie Impérisse, native of Port Royal, Acadia, aged 46 years.

They have no issue of that marriage.

Marie Marthe André, widow, daughter by a previous marriage of the said Marie Impérisse, aged 20 years ; and

François Marie Lecchis, son of the said Marthe, aged five months, lives with them. They have no live stock.

They hold their land upon verbal permission from Monsieur de Bonnaventure and on it have made a large garden.

INDEX

Doucet, François, Macpec, p. 158.
Doussett, *see also* Doucet.
Dousset, François, Rivière de Pengiguit, p. 96.
Douville, Sieur François, Pte de St. Pierre, p. 133.
Douville, Sieur François, St. Pierre du N., p. 140.
Duaron, see also Douaron.
Duaron, Honnoré, Rivière du Moulins à Scie, p. 105.
Duaron, Jean Baptiste, Riv. du Moul. à Scie, p. 101
Duaron, Petit Paul, Riv. du Moulins à Scie, p. 103.
Dubardier, Jean, Ance Darambourg, p. 66.
Dubocq, Pierre, St. Pierre du Nord, p. 134.
Duchambon, Sieur, page 5.
Ducloux, Marie, widow, St. Pierre du Nord, p. 137.
Ducland, Jacq. Dominique, St. Pierre du N., p. 137.
DuGas, see also Dugas and Dugast.
Dugas, Alexis, Macpec, p. 153.
Dugas, Claude, Port Toulouse, p. 19.
DuGas, Habraham, Port Toulouse, p. 16.
Dugas, Joseph, Grande Ascension, p. 116.
Dugas, Joseph, Port Toulouse, p. 17.
Dugas, Marguerite, widow, La Briquerie, p. 22.
Dugas, Pierre, Ance à Pierre, p. 124.
Dugast, Ambroise, Grande Ascension, p. 117.
Dugast, Pierre, Grande Ascension, p. 117
Dugast, Claire, widow, Grande Ascension, p. 117.
Dugats, Claude, Rivière du Nord Est, p. 86.
Dugay, François, Rivière du Nord Est, p. 89.
Dumont, Joseph, St. Pierre du Nord, p. 137.
Duplessis, le Sieur, Laurenbec, p. 73.
Duplessis, Sieur Claude Ant., St. Pierre du N., p. 139
Duport, Pierre, Bay of Gabarus, p. 6.
Durand, Julien, Petite Bras d'Or, p. 43.
Durocher, François, St. Pierre du Nord, p. 134.
Duval, Pierre, Rivière du Nord Est, p. 93.
Duvivier, Jean Baptiste, St. Pierre du Nord, p. 141.

E

Ebert, Charles, Pointe à la Jeunesse, page 40.
Ebert, François, Pointe à la Jeunesse, p. 40.
Ebert, Joseph, Pointe à la Jeunesse, p. 39.
Ecard, Nicolas, Petit Degrat, p. 29.
Emanuel, Charles, St. Pierre du Nord, p. 134.
Etang des Berges, p. 146.
Etang du Noffrage, p. 129.

F

Fausse Baye, page 57.
Fond, Sebastia, Anse Darambourg, p. 66.
Forin, Jean Baptiste, Isles Madame, p. 26.
Fougère, Jean, St. Esprit, p. 9.
Fougère, St. Joseph, Port Toulouse, p. 19.
Fouquet, Charles, St. Pierre du Nord, p. 140.
Fouré, Julien, Port Dauphin, p. 42.
Fraiquingout, Jean, Bedec, p. 161.
Friel, Pierre, Isles Madame, p. 26.
Froncak, p. 34.

G

Gabarus Bay, page 5.
Galland, François Haché, Rivière du Nord Est, p. 89-90.
Galland, Jean Bte, Haché, Riv. du Nord Est, p. 90.
Galland, Pierre Haché, Riv. du Nord Est, p. 93.
Gallet, Guillaume, St. Pierre du Nord, p. 131.
Gallou, Pierre, Rivière du Pengiguit, p. 97.
Gascot, Louis, Havre de la Baleine, p. 68.
Gation, le Sieur Silvain Jean Semidon, Ance Darambourg, p. 65.
Gaudrot, Jean, Anse au Comte Saint-Pierre, p. 108.
Gaultier, Simon, Laurenbec, p. 71.
Gautier, Joseph, senior, Rivière du Nord Est, p. 87.
Gautier, le Sieur, Pierre, Rivière du Nord Est, p. 87.
Gautreau, Alexandre, Ance à Pinet, p. 125.
Gautreau, François, Ance à Pinet, p. 125.
Gautreau, François, junior, Ance à Pinet, p. 125.

Gautreau, Pierre, Ance à Pinet, p. 125.
Gautrot Claude, Rivière du Moulins à Scie, p. 99.
Gautrot, François, Anse au Comte St.-Pierre, p. 107.
Gautrot, Pierre, Anse au Matelost, p. 112.
Gedry, *see also* Guedry.
Gedry, Pierre, Isles Madame, p. 26.
Genty, Marie, widow, Rivière du Nord Est, p. 91.
Girard dit Crespin, Pierre Mathurin, Rivière de Pengiguit, p. 95.
Giroir, Claude, Isles Madame, p. 25.
Giroir, Louis, Macpec, p. 158.
Giroir, Pierre, Petit Degrat, p. 31.
Glace Bay, p. 54.
Glin dit Cadet, Mathieu, Riv. du Pengiguit, p. 95.
Godet, Jean Baptiste, Anse du Nord-Ouest, p. 164.
Gouet, François, Petite Bras d'Or, p. 43.
Gouret, François, Rivière de Miré, p. 61.
Gosselin, Catherine, widow, Havre de la Baleine, p. 69.
Gracia, Joseph, Rivière de Miré, p. 60.
Grand Etang, p. 133.
Grand Nerichac, p. 34.
Grand Saint-Esprit, Story of, p. 62.
Grande Anse, p. 113.
Grande Ascension, p. 116.
Grande Baye, p. 13.
Grande Grave, p. 14.
Grand Montagne, p. 31.
Grande Rivière, p. 11.
Grandville, Louis, Ance Darambourg, p. 66.
Granne, Jean, St.-Pierre, p. 9.
Great Creek du Petit Degrat, p. 27.
Grossin, Michel, St. Pierre du Nord, p. 144
Grossin, Pierre, St.-Pierre du Nord, p. 144.
Gruneau, Théréyea, Rivière de Miré, p. 60.
Guedry, Charles, Pointe à la Jeunesse, p. 40.
Guedry, Claude, Anse au Matelost, p. 111
Guedry dit Grivoye, Jacques, Bedec, p. 160.
Guedry, Joseph, Baye des Espagnols, p. 46.
Guedry, Joseph, Rivière du Miré, p. 60.
Guedry, Paul, Baye des Espagnols, p. 46.
Guérin, Charles, Rivière du Ouest, p. 80.
Guérin, Dominique, Pointe à la Jeunesse, p. 40.
Guérin, François, Grande Ascension, p. 118.
Guérin, Jean Bte, Pointe à la Jeunesse, p. 39.
Guérin, Pierre, Baye de Mordienne, p. 56.
Guitant, Jacques, Rivière de Miré, p. 61.
Guillaume, Jean, Rivière de Miré, p. 58.
Guillot Ambroise, Pointe au Brulleau, p. 119.
Guillot, Herné, Pointe Prime, p. 122.
Guillot, Mathurin, Isle de Scatary, p. 64.
Guillot, René, Pointe Prime, p. 122.

H

Haché dit Charlit, Charles, Rivière du Nord-Est, page 91.
Haché dit Galland, Charles, Rivière du Nord-Est, p. 92.
Haché dit Galland, Jacques, Rivière du Pengiguit, p. 95.
Haché dit Galland, Jacques, Tracadie, p. 146.
Haché, Pierre, Rivière du Nord-Est, p. 92.
Hamet, Etienne, Isles Madame, p. 26.
Hango, Nicolas, St. Pierre du Nord, p. 136.
Harbour de Cheticamps, p. 66.
Havre à Mathieu, p. 126.
Havre aux Sauvages, p. 142.
Havre de Bedec, p. 152-159.
Havre de Cachechampené, p. 151.
Havre de Casampec, p. 152.
Havre de Fourché, p. 7.
Havre de l'Echourie, p. 128.
Havre de Malpie, p. 150.
Havre de Petit Laurenbec, p. 70.
Havre de la Baleine, p. 67.
Havre la Fortune, p. 126.

SESSIONAL PAPER No. 18

R

S

T

V

Y

APPENDIX A

PART II

GENEALOGY OF THE FAMILIES OF THE ISLAND OF ORLEANS.

Considerable importance is attached to the genealogy here printed, from the fact that descendants of families born on the Island of Orleans are to be found not only in the parishes in the immediate vicinity of Quebec, but reaching far beyond the bounds of the province. The manuscript, which represents much of the work of the best years of the late Abbé Michel Forgues (1), is the property of the Parish of St. Laurent, Island of Orleans, and it is now published with the authority and approval of His Grace the Archbishop of Quebec. A large number of students are engaged in genealogical research at the present time, and the work in its published form will greatly facilitate their labors in tracing numerous families to their source.

The parishes on the Island of Orleans are as follows :—

Sainte Famille.
St. François.
Saint Jean.
Saint Laurent.
St. Paul.
Saint Pierre.
Ste. Pétronille.

In the appendix will be found a summary of the Archives of the various parishes. The information therein given will be arranged systematically to form a part of the guide to the sources of Canadian history, which is now in the course of preparation

---

(1) Abbé Michel Forgues, ptre., born at St. Michel de Bellechasse, Feby. 13, 1811. Son of Michel Forgues and Marie Anne Denis.

Ordained priest, 23rd Sept., 1837.

Professor in Quebec Seminary, 1837.

Curate of St. Roch, 1837.

Parish Priest at Ste. Marguerite, Co. of Dorchester, 1840.

Parish Priest of Ste. Marie de la Beauce, 1845.

Assistant Bursar, Quebec Seminary, 1847.

Parish Priest of Ste. Monique (Nicolet), 1848.

Parish Priest of St. Gervais (Bellechasse), 1849.

Bursar of Quebec Seminay, 1849.

Parish Priest of St. Germain (Rimouski), 1859.

Retired from ministry, resided at St. Michel, 1861.

Parish Priest of St. Laurent, I. O., 1865.

Died Nov. 28th, 1882.

In 1854, he took an active part in the foundation of Laval University.

EXPLANATION OF ABBREVIATIONS IN GENEALOGY OF THE FAMILIES OF THE ISLAND OF ORLEANS.

A. G.	Ange Gardien
B.	Beaumont
Bpt.	Beauport
Bert.	Berthier
Chs. Brg.	Charlesbourg
C. R.	Château Richer
I	Islet
L.	Lévis
Q.	Québec
S. A.	Ste. Anne
S. Aug.	St. Augustin
S. Chs.	St. Charles
S. F.	Ste. Famille, I. O.
S. Frs.	St. François, I.O.
S. F. S.	St. François du Sud
S. G.	St. Germain
S. I	St. Ignace (Cap.)
S. J.	St. Jean, I. O.
S. Jos.	St. Joseph
S. L.	St. Laurent, I.O.
S. M.	Ste. Marie
S. P.	St. Pierre, I. O.
S. P. S	St. Pierre du Sud.
S. R.	St. Roch des Aulnais
S. T.	St. Thomas
S. V.	St. Valier

GENEALOGY OF THE FAMILIES OF THE ISLAND OF ORLEANS

Compiled by Rev. Michel Forgues.

NOTE—The original is preserved in the Archives of the parish of St. Laurent, Isle of Orleans.

P. M. O'LEARY, Priest.

ADAM.

1	Jean		Marie Mezerai.	
	Louise		Frs. Loquel.	Q 1712
	M. Anne		Guill. Couture	S.L. 1713
	René			
	Jean Baptiste			
2	René	(1)	Anne Maillou	B. 1696
	Ignace			
	René			
3	Jean Baptiste	(1)	Cath. Guillet, Batiscan.	1708
4	Ignace	(2)	Susanne Lacasse B.	1720
	M. Louise		J. B. Bissonnet B.	1751
	M. Marthe		Jos. André Samson.	1755
	Pierre			
	Joseph			
	Le même		Ursule Lefebvre S.M.	1754
	Joseph			
	Jacques			
	Pierre			
5	René	(2)	Marie Maupas. B.	1734
	Françoise		Aug. Fraser. B.	1763
	„		2° Jacq. Beaucher B.	1781
	Marguerite		Ant. Dutile B.	1764
6	Joseph (1°No.)	(4)	M. Jos. Plante S.M.	1753
7	Pierre (1° No.)	(4)	Aug. Bolduc S. V.	1753
	Marie		Aug. Polequin S.M.	1778
	Angélique		Michel Boilard S.M.	1789
	Françoise		Michel TurgeonS.M.	1782
	„		2° Ant.Gendreau S.M	1822
	„		3° Louis Roy S.M.	1830
	Josette		Jos. Lacasse S.M.	1782
			2° Pierre Deschesnes	S. V. 1820
8	Joseph (2dm)	(4)	Angé BissonnetS.M.	1775
9	Jacques	(4)	M.Mad.MichonS.Chs	1775
	„			
10	Pierre (2dm)	(4)	Marie Patoine S.Chs.	1787
	Rose		J.B.Quemeneau S.G.	1815
	Marguerite		Frs. Filteau S.G.	1820
	Pierre			
	Le même		Marguerite Fournier	S.G.1799
11	Jacques	(9)	Eliz Senechal S.G.	1796
	Jacques			
12	Pierre	(10)	M.Anne Nadeau S.G	1809
	Jean			
13	Jacques	(11)	Rosalie Roy S. V.	1819
14	Jean	(12)	JulieSimoneau S.F.S.	1837

AINSE.

1	Jean		Angelique Folkne	
	Joseph			
2	Joseph	(1)	Marie Posé S. Tho.	1712
	Frs. Marie			
	Clement			
3	Clement	(2)	Marie Proulx S.Tho.	1756

AINSE.

	Marie Anne		Joseph Boulet, S.P.S.	1778
	Marie Louise		Frs. Fournier	„ 1781
	Marguerite		Jean GourdeauS.Tho	1795
4	FrançoisMarie	(2)	Fse Clement S.M.	1761
	M. Françoise		Jos. Lecours S.G.	1780
	Elizabeth		Etn. Patouel	„ 1794
	Marguerite		Jos. Couture	„ 1794
	Louise		Ant. Patouel	„ 1795
	François			
	Jean			
5	François	(4)	M Ls. Blanchet S.G.	1787
	Marguerite		Chs. Monmeny	„ 1821
	Louise		Etn. Marseau	„ 1823
	Archange		Frs. Royer	„ 1826
	Stanislas			
	Charles			
6	Jean	(4)	Charlotte FortierS.G.	1796
7	Stanislas	(5)	Marie Asselin S.G.	1813
8	Charles	(5)	Marie Terrien S.G.	1819
9	François	(4)	M. L. Noel	
	Alexis			
10	Alexis	(9)	M. Jos. Fortier S.I.	1826
1	Jean Bernard		M. Mad. DeBure Q.	1666
	Marie		Frs. Milliet S.J.	1702
	Marie		2° Robert VermetS.F	1703
	Nicolas			
	Charles			
	Jean			
2	Nicolas	(1)	Marie Bruneau Q.	1707
3	Jean	(1)	Marie Bourbeau Cho. bourg	1712
4	Charles	(1)	Genev. Martin S.Foye	1697
	Marie		Ls. Gautier S. Foye	1726
	Charles			
			Charlotte Chevigny	
5	Charles	(4)		S. Foye 1726

ALAIRE—DALAIRE.

1	Sebastien		Pèrine Fleurissonne	
	Jean			
	Charles			
2	Jean	(1)	Périne Terrier Q.	1662
	François			
	Jean			
3	Charles	(1)	Cath. Lefebvre Q.	1663
	Marie		Pierre Dubeau S.Frs.	1684
	Catherine		Gab. Chamberlan „	1694
	Françoise		Jacq. Bidet „	1701
	Charles			
	François			
	Louis			
	Etienne			
	Joseph			
4	Jean	(2)	Fse. Simart Contr.	1688
	Louis			

ALAIRE—DALAIRE.

5	François	(2)	Marg. Eliz. Derome	Q.	1693
	Marg. Elizabeth		Simon Jolin	S.I.	1711
	François				
	Nicolas				
6	Charles	(3)	Marie Bidet	S.I.	1691
	Catherine		Jos. Lavoie	S.Frs.	1726
	"		2° Jos. Savard	S.Frs.	1727
	M. Thérèse		Simon Talbot	S.V.	1734
	Alexandre				
	Charles				
	Joseph				
	Jacques				
7	François	(3)	Anne Labbé	S.Frs.	1694
	M. Anne		Michel Gautron	B.	1714
	Angélique		Ls. Portelance	„	1725
	M. Charlotte		Chs. Paquet	„	1725
	Elizabeth		Pierre Albert	„	1727
	M. Josette		J. B. Lacasse	„	1734
	Françoise Bégis		Jos. Gauthier	„	1740
	Marguerite		Jean Turgeon	Q.	1723
	Louis				
	Joseph				
8	Etienne	(3)	M. Anne Bilodeau	S.Frs.	1705
9	Louis	(3)	Anne Asselin	S.F.	1706
	M. Josette		Raphael Gagné	S.Frs.	1729
	Marthe		Jos. Lemelin	„	1740
	Catherine		J. B. Gendreau	„	1742
	Genéviève		Michel Labbe	„	1749
	Ls. Sebastien				
	Pierre				
	Joseph				
10	Joseph	(3)	Mad. Bidet	S.I.	1706
	Marguerite		Pierre Valière	S.V.	1732
	Marie		Nic. Chamberlan	„	1734
	Françoise		Pierre Le Roy	„	1737
	Agathe		Etn. Carrière	„	1739
	Geneviève		Jos. Carrière		1737
	"		2° Frs. Couturier	S.M.	1751
	"		3° Etn.Corriveau	„	1755
	M. Josette		Jos. Daniau	„	1741
	Pierre				
	Joseph				
11	Louis	(4)	Genev.Racine	S.Jos.	1730
	Le même		Angè. Siselin	S.Frs.	1732
12	Nicolas	(5)	Genev. Moleur	B.	1723
13	François	(5)	M. Jos. Moleur	B.	1738
14	Alexandre	(6)	Cath. Bidet	S.M.	1708
	Pierre				
	Louis				
	François				
15	Charles	(6)	Marie Asselin	S.Frs.	1722
	M. Josette		Jos. Thibaut	S.F.S.	1744
16	Joseph	(6)	Anne Gagnon,	C.B.	1736
	M. Anne		Ls. Gautron	S.J.	1755
			2° Etn. Vallée	S.M.	1761
	M. Josette		Jos. Marie Pepin	S.F.	1757
	Etienne				
	Le même		Genev.Dufresne	S.L.	1746
	Jean Baptiste				
17	Jacques	(6)	Angé, Cloutier	S.M.	1724
	M. Madeleine		Ls. Delage	S.F.	1756
	François				
18	Louis	(7)	Marg. Provost	Q.	1738
	Le même		Marie Chamart	„	1745
19	Joseph	(7)	Charlotte Renaud	Chs. Brg.	1731
	Isabelle		Pierre Dion	B.	1761
	Charlotte		Pierre Roy	„	1760
	Josette		Pierre Bussière	S.R.	1771
	M. Anne		Bernard Boucher	„	1772
	Marguerite		J. B. Nadeau	„	1767

ALAIRE—DALAIRE

	Marguerite		2° Chs. Couture	S.Tho.	1784
	Pierre				
	Joseph				
	Louis				
20	Jean		M. Mad. Fontaine		
	François				
21	Ls. Sébastien	(9)	M. Jos. Marseau	S.Frs.	1727
	Louis				
22	Pierre	(9)	Marie Nolin	S.P.	1744
	Joseph				
	Marie				
	Michel				
	François				
	Le même		M. Ange. Monmeny	S.V.	1784
23	Joseph	(9)	Louise N.Labbé	S.Frs	1745
	M. Louise		Vic.Martineau	„	1770
	Joseph				
	Le même		Ange. Landry	„	1752
	Angelique		Ls. Nadeau	„	1775
	"		2° Frs. Martineau	S.J.	1709
	Marie		Ls. Coulombe	S Frs.	1803
	M. Catherine		Jacq. Blouin	„	1807
	M. Anne		Ls. Gagnon	„	1817
	Louis				
24	Pierre	(10)	Marthe Thibaut	S.M.	1743
	Marie		Jos. Lacasse	„	1773
	Ursule		Gaspard Lacasse	„	1782
	Joseph				
	Marie				
	Pierre				
25	Joseph	(10)	Dorothée Helie	S.V.	1735
26	Etienne		M. Chs. Lavoie	B.St.P.	1747
	Etienne				
27	François		Marie Chabot	„	1700
	Marie		Ant. Coté	S.H.	1785
	Pierre				
28	Pierre	(14)	Genev. Corriveau	S.V.	1733
	M Geneviève		Athanase Fradet	S.V.	1765
	Françoise		Aug. Couture	S. V.	1772
	Joseph				
	Charles				
	Le même		M. Anna Boissel	Bert.	1774
			V. de Jean Durand		
A	Louis	(14)	M. Jos. Thibaut	SV.	1736
	Le même		M. Anna Leraux Levis	St. Chs.	1762
29	François	(14)	Mad. Denis	S.M.	1743
	Françoise		Jos. Chs. Gagnon	SV	1762
30	Etienne	(16)	M. Jos. Boissonneau	S.Frs.	1766
	Josette		Olivier Frs. Assilin	S.J.	1794
	Etienne				
	François				
	Joseph				
	Henri				
31	JeanBaptiste	(16)	M. Anne Landry	S.J.	1784
32	François	(17)	M. Anne Delage	S.J.	1754
33	Joseph	(19)	Genev. Couillard	B.	1755
34	Louis	(19)	Fse. Couillard	S.M.	1768
	Généviève		Ign. Coté	B.	1791
	Françoise		Jean Le Roy	B.	1795
	Madeleine		Aug. Valière	B.	1800
	Cécile		J. B. Roy	B.	1801
	"		2° J. B. Gosselin	S.H.	1815
	M. Anne		Basile Fortier	S.Chs.	1807
	Louis				

ALAIRE—DALAIRE.

35 Pierre	(19)	Marg. Curadeau	S.F.1767
36 François	(20)	M. Genev. Mercier	S.F.S. 1766
M. Josette		Firmin Doison	S.F.S. 1787
Thérèse		Jacque Tangue	„ 1795
"		2° Pierre Noel Picard	„ 1821
Geneviève		Ant. Mercier	„ 1807
Louis			
Auguste			
Joseph			
Jean Baptiste			
37 Louis	(21)	Thérèse Deblois	S.Frs.1755
Le même		M. Ls. Fradet	S.M 1760
M. Josette		André Basquet	„ 1787
"		2° J. B. Marcoux	„ 1814
M. Louise		J. B. Bonneau	„ 1789
François			
38 Joseph Marie	(22)	Angé. Doré	S.M. 1773
M. Angelique		J. B. Langlois	S.F.S. 1805
Françoise		Jos. Martineau	„ 1806
Joseph			
Marie			
Ignace			
Le même		M. Marg. Buteau	S.F.S. 1796
Luce Marguerite		J. B. Beaudoin	„ 1825
Angèle		J. B. Baudoin	S.V. 1825
Thomas			
39 Michel	(22)	Marie Trahan	S.Chs. 1774
Marie		Jos. Audet	S.G. 1803
M. Pélagie		Ls. Clement	S. H. 1809
Etienne			
Joseph			
40 François	(22)	M. Jos. Edmond	S.F.S 1781
Josette		L. S. Genest	S.H. 1803
41 Joseph	(23)	M. Ls. Marseau	S.Frs. 1772
42 Louis	(23)	M. Ls. Pepin	S.Frs. 1803
Josette		Elie Gagnon	„ 1831
M. Louise		Etn. Magl. Fontaine	„ 1845
Reparate		Ls. Gagné	„ 1848
Catherine		J. B. Verret	„ 1846
Louis			
43 Jos. Marie	(24)	M. Jcs. Lacasse	S.M. 1777
Josette		Pierre Royer	S.G. 1821
Jean Marie			
Joseph			
44 Pierre	(24)	Natalie Chabot	S Chs 1778
Marie		Aug. Audet	S.G. 1801
Theotiste		Jean Royer	„ 1806
Marguerite		Pierre Audet	„ 1809
Thérèse		Frs. Genest	„ 1812
Athalie		Jacq. Baudoin	„ 1815
Judith		Michel Corriveau	„ 1818
Pierre			
45 Etienne	(26)	Osite Vict. Blouin St. Anne	1774
Etienne			
46 Pierre	(27)	Susanne Buteau	S.F.S. 1785
Louise		Ls. Tardif	S.H. 1810
47 Joseph	(28)	Veuve Pierre Roy	S.V. 1757
48 Charles	(28)	M. Jos. Bolduc	S.V. 1774
M. Louise		Jos. Gagnon	„ 1800
M. Geneviève		Frs. Dubord	„ 1817
M. Angélique		Ign. Hélie	„ 1824
Marguerite		Ls. Clavet	S. Tho. 1801
Charles			
49 Joseph		Marie Pouliot	S. L. 1780
50 Pierre Noel		Marie Pouliot	

ALAIRE—DALAIRE.

M. Josette		Jos. Roy	S.V. 1805
Geneviève		Etn. Langlais	„ 1819
Justina		Jac. Labrecque	S.G. 1812
51 Etienne	(30)	Genev. Hélène Emond	S.J. 1795
Marie		Jos. Picard	S.Frs. 1817
Justine		Prisque Paré	„ 1833
Geneviève		Ign. Trudel	„ 1840
Joseph			
Le même		M. Thècle Pepin	S.F. 1811
52 Joseph	(3o)	M. Chs. Emond	S. Frs. 1820
Marguerite		Jacq. Plante	S.J. 1825
Justine		Jean Emond	S.J. 1838
Joseph			
Etienne			
53 François	(30)	Josette Turcot	S.J. 1809
Catherine		Ed. Audibert	„ 1835
Madeleine		Frs. Martineau	„ 1841
M. Louise		Frs. Gosselin	S.L. 1847
M. Luce		Pierre Dion	„ 1848
Henriette		Ant. Helie	„ 1851
Josette		Magl. Blouin	„ 1858
Paul			
François Xavier			
Joseph			
54 Henri	(30)	Marg. Emond	S.J. 1812
Marguerite		Eloi Coulombe	S.Frs. 1846
Sophie		J. B. Cochon	„ 1856
Magloire			
55 Louis	(34)	Mad. Couture	S.Chs. 1802
56 Louis	(36)	Marg. Mercier	S.V. 1797
Celeste		Etn. Cadrin	„ 1825
Marguerite		Jos. Gendron	S.F.S. 1826
Joseph			
Louis			
Le même		Mad. Quemeneur	S.F.S. 1805
Julie		J. B. Boutin	S.V. 1841
57 Jean Baptiste	(36)	Cath. Morin	S.F.S. 1797
Emerina		Magl. Gontier	S.V. 1826
Luce		Hubert Gontier	„ 1829
Marcelline		Narcisse Gendron	S.V.1831
Augustin			
Louis			
Éphrem			
Jean Baptiste			
58 Joseph	(36)	Marie Doiron	S.F.S. 1797
Gertrude		Ant. Roy	S.G. 1830
Marguerite		Michel Roy	„ 1825
Augustin			
Joseph			
François			
59 François	(36)	M.Chs.Picard	S.F.S.1800
M. Charlotte		Antoine	S.V. 1820
Marguerite		Frs. Roby	„ 1823
Julienne		Germ. Jolin	„ 1833
Augustin			
Le même		M. Thècle Pepin	S.F.1811
60 François	(37)	Marie Couture	S.Chs.1788
Charlotte		Jacq. Helie	S.M. 1818
Geneviève		Jean Lefebvre	„ 1838
"		2° Ls. Blais	„ 1840
Reine		Frs. Fortier	„ 1840
Sophie		Paul Mercier	„ 1846
André			
Jean			
Pierre			
61 Ignace	(38)	Thérèse Buteau	S.F.S.1799
62 Joseph Marie	(38)	M. Angé Langlois	S.F.S. 1807
Apolline		Noel Campagna	S.F.S. 1831
Marguerite		Jean Cadrien	S.V. 1828
Brigitte		Frs. Buteau	„ 1862

ALAIRE—DALAIRE.

Olvier

63	Thomas	(38)	Angele Fradet S.F.S.1843
64	Etienne	(39)	Marie Clément S.H. 1809
	Louis		
65	Joseph	(39)	M. Anne Gosselin
			S.H. 1812
66	Louis	(42)	Cath. Dalaire S.Frs. 1850
67	Joseph	(43)	M. Anne Audet S.G. 1802
	M. Anne		Pierre Roy " 1818
68	Jean Marie	(43)	Mad. Mercier S.G. 1803
	Madeleine		Jos. Labbé S.G. 1825
	Jean		
69	Pierre	(44)	Angé.Lacroix S.Chs. 1804
	Archange		Chs. Corriveau " 1828
	Euphrosine		Dom. Mercier " 1830
	M. Anne		Jean Naud " 1836
	Angèle		Alexis Roy " 1839
	Romain		
	Pierre		
70	Etienne	(45)	Genev.ThiviergeS.J. 1797
71	Charles	(48)	M. Fse Bernard S.V. 1808
	M. Josette		Jos. Brochu " 1836
	Le meme		Marg. Bissonet S.V. 1826
	M. Desanger		Jos. Lemieux " 1856
	Cyrille		
72	Joseph	(51)	Anastasie Popin S.F. 1820
	Adelaid		Jean Foucher " 1842
	Catherine		Ls. Dalaire " 1850
	Joseph		
73	Joseph	(52)	Cath. Emond S.J. 1832
	M. Anne		Narcisse Audet " 1851
	Marcelline		F. X. Blouin " 1857
	Philomène		Jean Bernard " 1864
	Rose		Jos. Boissonneau " 1865
	Jean		
74	Etienne	(52)	Cath. Geguère S.J. 1835
75	Paul	(53)	Justine Blouin S.J. 1843
76	Frs. Xavier	(53)	Cath. Picard S.Roch.
77	Joseph	(53)	M. Anne Demeule
			S.J. 1857
78	Magloire	(54)	Marie Campagne
			S.Frs. 1846
79	Louis	(56)	Angile Quemenneur
			S.Chs. 1832

Pierre
Louis

80	Joseph	(56)	Genev. Langlois S.V. 1821
	Marie		Jos. Hudson Bert. 1844
	Joseph		
81	Augustin	(57)	Theotiste Gagnon
			S.V. 1829
82	Louis	(57)	" " 1830
83	Jean Baptiste	(57)	Julie Coté S.V. 1831
84	Ephrem	(57)	Adé Boulet Bert. 1833
85	Joseph	(58)	Louise Audet S.G. 1824
86	Augustin	(58)	Marie Audet S.G. 1825
87	François	(58)	Adé Roy S.G. 1826
88	Augustin	(59)	Marg. Mercier S.V. 1829
89	Jean	(60)	Félicité Métivier
			S.M. 1825
90	André	(60)	M. Jos. Cotin S.M. 1838
91	Pierre	(60)	Desanges Gagnon
			S.V. 1844
	Le même		M. Anne Eliz. Tur-
			geon S.M. 1849
92	Olivier	(62)	M. Philoméne Le-
			blanc S. Chs. 1858
93	Louis	(64)	Justine Labrecque
			S.Chs. 1844
	Le même		Marie Couture S.Chs.1852
94	Jean	(68)	Charlotte Cameron
			S.G. 1826
9	Romain	(69)	M. Esther Denis
	Pierre		S.Chs. 1852
	Louis		

ALAIRE—DALAIRE.

96	Pierre	(69)	Marie Trudel S.Chs. 1836
97	Cyrille	(71)	Eliza Odile Roy S.V. 1855
98	Joseph	(72)	M. Natalie Pepin
			S.Frs. 1844
99	Jean	(73)	Theotiste Giguère
			S.F. 1855
100	Joseph	(80)	Adé Roy S.V. 1839
101	Pierre	(95)	M. Elise Lebrun
			S. Chs. 1856
102	Louis	(95)	M. Herosias Marcou
			S. Chs. 1863
103	Jean		M. Chs. Carmail
	Sophie		René Chabot S.Chs. 1860

AMAURY—MAURY.

1	Jean		Marie Vigny
	Marguerite		J. B. Leblond S.Frs. 1711
	Françoise		2o Frs. Asselin S.F. 1719
	Michel		Nic. Leblond " 1725
2	"	(1)	M. Anne Guimon
			S.Anne 1713
	Marie		Dom. Dompierre
			S.Frs. 1739

ARBOUR.

1	Michel Marie		Coutansineau Q. 1671
	Jean Baptiste		
	Michel		
	François		
	August		
2	Jean Baptiste	(1)	M. Cath. Proulx
			Pte. Trembles 1700
3	Michel	(1)	M. Barbe Morin 1703
	"		
	Jean		
	Antoine		
4	Frs. Augustin	(1)	Mad. Proulx
			Pte. Trembles 1711
5	Michel	(3)	Genev. Fregeot Bert. 1728
	Geneviève		Ant. Pepin S.F.S. 1745
	Michel		
6	Jean	(3)	Cecile Lemieux,Bert. 1744
	M. Josette		Etn. Remillard S.V. 1782
7	Antoine	(3)	Marthe Lemieux
			Bert. 1744
8	Michel	(5)	M. Ls. Boutin S.F.S.1753
	Reine		Isaac Morin " 1804
	M. Josette		J. B. Remillard " 1807
	Barbe		Chs.Ducourberon " 1809
	Ls. Jerome		
	Pierre		
	Chrysostôme		
9	Michel	(8)	Ursule Proulx S.F.S. 1795
	Le même		M. Anne Labrecque
			S.G. 1807
	Simon		
10	Ls Jérome	(8)	M. Ls Remillard S.G.1796
	M. Marguerite		Ed. Terrien S.M. 1850
	Louis		
11	Pierre	(8)	Marie Brochu S.G. 1801
	M. Marguerite		Michel Quemenneur
			S.V. 1821
	Euphrosine		Etn. Vallée S.V. 1821
	Angèle		Alexandre Bélanger
			S.V. 1840
	Chrysostôme		
	Antoine		
	Eustache		
12	Chrysostôme	(8)	Frse Marseau S.F.S. 1808
13	Simon	(9)	M. Rose Mercier
			Bert. 1831
14	Louis	(10)	M. Mad. Leblond
			S.V. 1828

ARBOUR.

15	Eustache	(11)	Genev. Thibaut, Bert.		1832
16	Antoine	(11)	Sophie Jolin	S.V.	1845
	Michel				
17	Chrysostôme	(11)	Sophie Mercier	S.V.	1846
18	Michel				
	Le même		Marcelline Fradet		
				S.V.	1865
19	Michel	(16)	Victoria Thivierge		
				S.V.	1867

ARGUIN.

1	François		M. Anne Belleau		
	Marie		J. B. Deschamps		
				S.H.	1766
	Joseph				
2	"		M. Anne Boucher		
				S.H.	1775
	M. Anne		Jacq. Carbonneau		
				S.H.	1815
	M. Louise		Alexis Roy	"	1819
	Jean Baptiste				
	Joseph				
3	Jean Baptiste	(2)	Modest Labrecque		
				S.G.	1804
4	Joseph	(2)	Marie Fortier	S.G.	1811

ARRIVÉ—LARRIVÉ.

1	Jean		Jeanne Barberet		
	Jeanne		Jean Demers	S.F.	1696
	Joseph				
	Jean Baptiste				
2	Maurice		Jacquette Touraud		
				Q.	1654
	Le même		Fse Pednelle	S.F.	1670
	Marguerite		Olivier Levesque S.F.		1723
	Maurice				
	François				
	Simon				
3	Jean Baptiste	(1)	Cath Poiré	Levis	1700
	M. Anne		Claude Boilard	B.	1738
	M. Louise		Jacques Lis	B.	1753
	Jean Baptiste				
	Joseph				
4	"	(1)	Louise L'heureux S.F.		1716
	M. Josette		Ls Deblois	"	1743
	Louise		J B. Morisset	"	1747
	Joseph				
5	François		Marie Laine	S.Frs.	1703
	Hélène		Pierre Beneto	Bert.	1722
	M. Josette		Jean Lambert S.F.S.		1740
	M. Louise		Jean Dodier S.F.S.		1744
	François				
	Jean Baptiste				
6	Maurice	(2)	Anne Laine		1709
	M. Thérèse		Isidore Landry S.Frs.		1731
7	Simon	(2)	Cath. Garant S. Frs.		1704
8	Jean Baptiste	(3)	Marg. Lis.	B.	1745
	Marguerite		Jos. Gautier	S.M.	1772
9	Joseph	(3)	Thérèse Begin	Lévis	1744
	Catherine		Chs. Girard	S.R.	1769
	Etienne				
	Joseph				
	Michel				
10	Joseph	(4)	Marie Lefebvre	S.R.	1757
	Joseph				
11	François	(5)	M. Genev. Gaudin		
				Levis	1730
	M. Josette		Jean Montigny S.F.S.		1753
	M. Geneviève		Chs. Morin	"	1753
	Marguerite		Urbain Cadrin	S.M.	1774
	Jean				
	François				
	Joseph				

ARRIVÉ—LARRIVÉ.

12	Jean Baptiste	(5)	M. Jos. Paré S.F.S.		1742
13	Jean		Marg. Lemelin		
	Angélique		Pierre Drapeau S.Chs		1782
14	Jean		Marg. Gourdeau		
	Charles				
15	Joseph	(8)	M. Ls Bourget Lévis		1778
	Pierre				
16	Michel	(9)	Thècle Ratte	S.Chs.	1781
	Catherine		Jos. Lefrançois	B.	1809
	Thérèse		Abraham Boulet	B.	1815
	M. Josette		Jos. Blais	B.	1817
	Marie		Jos. Talbot		1824
	Abraham				
17	Etienne	(9)	Marg. Gontier S. Chs.		1780
	Charlotte		André Bissonnet	"	1801
	"	(20)	Etn. Lacroix	"	1814
	Etienne				
18	Joseph	(10)	Marg. Fradet	S.V.	1790
19	JeanFrançois	(11)	Thérèse Talbot S.F.S.		1761
	M. Josette		Jérome Richard, Bert.		1786
	Marthe		Michel Marcoux S.Chs		1788
	M. Madeleine		Frs Leclaire	"	1805
	Charlotte		Laurent Couture S.G.		1796
	M. Josette		Jean Frs Lacroix SM		1799
	Jean				
	François				
20	Joseph	(11)	M. Jos. Boutin S.P.S.		1764
	M. Josette		Pierre Noel Boulet		
				S.F.S.	1787
	Le même		M. Genev. Gosselin		
				S.M.	1788
21	Charles	(14)	M. Chs. Filteau		
				S. Chs.	1783
	M. Charlotte		J. B. Gosselin	B.	1822
	Joseph				
	Charles				
	Benoni				
22	Pierre	(15)	M. Ls Paradis S.H.		1812
23	Abraham	(16)	M. Ls Begin Lévis		1822
	M. Celelanire		Hubert Bourrassa B.		1847
	M. Louise		Michel Carrier	B.	1847
	Hombelin		Jacq. Shinek	B.	1854
	Lucie		Alexis Thérer	B.	1854
	Edward				
24	Etienne	(17)	Thérèse Royer S.Chs.		1804
	François Xavier				
	Ignace				
	Edward				
25	Jean François	(19)	M. Jos. Nadeau		
				S. Chs.	1789
	Thérèse		Ant. Plante S. Chs.		1819
	Josette		André Clement S.Chs		1826
	Archange		Jacq. Labrecque		
				S. Chs.	1826
	Jean François				
	Augustin				
	Charles				
	Michel				
26	Joseph	(21)	Judith Durand	B.	1815
27	Charles	(21)	Marg. Coüet	B.	1822
	Louis				
28	Bénoni	(21)	Genev. Bergeron	B.	1833
29	Edward	(23)	Flore McIntyre	B.	1857
30	Frs. Xavier	(24)	Charlotte Gosselin		
				S. Chs.	1829
31	Edward	(24)	Marg. Gaudin S.Chs.		1831
32	Innace	(24)	Ange Baron, Levis		1837
33	JeanFrançois	(25)	Frse. Roy	S.V.	1815
34	Michel	(25)	Basilisse Guilmet S.V.		1819
35	Augustin	(25)	Thérèse Baudoin Bert.		1831
36	Charles	(25)	M. Fse. Roy	S. G.	1812
37	Louis	(27)	Celina Boilard	B.	1853

ARSENEAU.

1	Charles		Marg. Poirier	
	Jean			
2	Abraham		Agnes Cyr	
	Marie		Jos. Cochon	S.M. 1772
	André			
3	Jean	(1)	Fse. Dumas	S.L. 1764
4	André	(2)	Marie Forgues	S.M. 1775
	Susanne		André Lacroix	S.G. 1797
	Françoise		Chs. Denis	S.G. 1804
	Françoise		2° Michel GautronSG1829	
	Angèle		Ant. Balan	S.M. 1816
	André			
5	André	(4)	Genev. Diers	S.G. 1807

ASSELIN.

1	David		Cath. Boudard	
	Pierre			
2	Jacques		Louise Roussin	S.R. 1662
	M. Madeleine		Guill Beaucher	S.F. 1694
	Louise		Jacq. Pichet	„ 1696
	Jacques			
	Pierre			
	Thomas			
	Nicolas			
	Michel			
3	Pierre	(1)	Louise Beaucher	S.F.1769
	M. Anne		Ls. Dalaire	„ 1706
	Louise		Nicolas Rioux	„ 1710
	Marguerite		Jean Letourneau	„ 1711
	Charles			
	Jacques			
	François			
4	Jacques	(2)	Marie Morisset	S.F. 1687
	Geneviève 1838		Jos. Gendron	S. Frs. 1715
	Madeleine		Pierre Mercier	„ 1718
	Françoise		Frs. Emond	„ 1727
	„		2° Aug. Marseau	„ 1737
	Jacques			
	Le même		Barbe Trudel	A.G. 1710
5	Thomas	(2)	Genev. Leclaire	SFrs1694
	Geneviève		Jean Mercier	„ 1715
	Marie		Chs. Dalaire	„ 1722
	„		2° Jean Boulet	„ 1727
	Angelique		Ls Dalaire	„ 1732
	Louis			
	Michel			
	Jean			
6	Nicolas	(2)	Marg. Gagnon	S.F. 1794
	Marguerite		Barth. Voyer	„ 1727
			2° Jos. Isabel	„ 1737
	Jean Baptiste			
	Jacques			
	Nicolas			
	Le même		M. Rene Turcot	SF 1703
	Josette		Simon L'heureux	„ 1747
	M. Thècle		Frs. Deblois	„ 1753
	Joseph			
	Louis			
7	Pierre	(2)	Eliz Jahan	S.F. 1695
8	Michel	(2)	Anne Gagnon	S.R. 1700
	Le même		Marthe LemieuxS.F.1730	
9	Chas. Jacques	(3)	Marg. Drouin	S.F. 1711
10	François	(3)	Marg. Amaury	S.F. 1719
	François			
	André			
	Basile			
11	Jacques	(4)	Anne Trudel	A.G. 1710
	Marthe		André Poire	S.V. 1747
	Thérèse		Chs. Bélanger	S.V. 1751
	François			
	Noël			
12	Jean	(5)	Cécile Trépanier	S.R.1723
	Cécile		Jean Guion	S. Frs 1745
	Claire		Jos. Roy	„ 1762

ASSELIN.

	Angélique		Jos. Lainé	S. Frs 1753
	„		2° Jean Marie Emond	S.J. 1761
	Jean			
	Joseph			
	Jacques			
13	Louis	(5)	M. Marthe Marseau	S. Frs 1728
	M. Josette		Claude Bélanger	„ 1751
	Marthe		Pierre Fabartier	„ 1759
	Elizabeth		J. B. Bibeau	S.J. 1748
	Louis			
14	Michel	(5)	MarieFournierS.Tho.1736	
	Geneviève		Jos. Mercier	S.F.S. 1751
15	Jean Baptiste	(6)	M. Marthe Maranda	S.P. 1724
16	Jacques	(6)	M. Mad. Audet S.J. 1725	
	Louise		Aug. Martel	S.F. 1752
	M. Madeleine		Jacq. Aveline	„ 1760
	Louis			
17	Nicolas	(6)	Marie Leblanc	S.J. 1732
18	François		M. Jos. Leblanc	
	M. Madeleine		Pierre Dorval	S.F. 1770
	M. Rose		Pierre Audet	„ 1770
	François			
19	Louis	(6)	Thérèse Ratte	S.P. 1734
	Thérèse		Pierre Paradis	„ 1784
	M. Angélique		Jean Bazin	S.V. 1774
	Marie		Jean Gosselin	S.F. 1767
	Geneviève		Ant. Morel	„ 1783
20	Joseph	(6)	Perpétue Audet S.L. 1746	
	Le même		M. Mad. Gobeil S.J. 1751	
	M. Madeleine		Jos. Turcot	S.F. 1781
	M. Angélique		Frs. Paschal	„ 1795
	M. Josette		Ls. Faucher	„ 1803
21	Jean Baptiste		M. Thérèse Bazin SV1728	
22	Joseph		M. Chs. Talbot	
	Le même		M. Mad. Mercier	Bert. 1739
	M. Josette		Jean Lainé	S. Frs. 1761
23	François	(10)	Dorothé FoucherS.F.1768	
	Le même		Marie Bilodeau	S.F. 1749
	M. Geneviève		Jos. Létourneau S.F.1771	
	M. Thècle		François Gagnon	„ 1791
	Marguerite		Etn. Drouin	„ 1799
	Rose		Julien Mercier	„ 1803
	André			
	François			
	Jean Baptiste			
24	André	(10)	M. Ls Drouin S.Frs. 1757	
	Marguerite		Jacq. Gagné	„ 1775
	M. Louise		Ls. Gagnon	„ 1781
	Thècle		Jos. Gagné	„ 1782
	Elizabeth		J. Marie Gagné	„ 1783
	M. Charlotte		Frs. Guion	„ 1782
	M. Josette		Jacq. Baudoin, S.F. 1791	
	Olivier Frs			
25	Basile	(10)	Anne Couture	S.F. 1756
	M. Anne		Jacq. Martineau S.F1797	
	Amand			
	François			
	Père Chryslogue			
	Pierre			
26	Phillippe		Genev. Toussaint	
	M. Anne		Jos. Beaudoin	S.M. 1789
	Phillippe			
27	François	(11)	M. Anne Gautron	S.M. 1751
	M. Anne		Michel Goulet	S.V. 1776
	M. Angélique		Frs. Bruneau	„ 1779
	M. Anne		J. B. Ruel	„ 1785
	Marguerite		Aug. ChamberlanS.V.1788	

ASSELIN.

Pierre		
Jacques		
28 Noël	(11)	M. Angé. Gautron S.M. 1756.
M. Josette		Frs. Denis, S.M 1782
M. Josette		2° Chs. Lacasse S.Chs.1785
M. Thérèse		J. B. Paré S.Ch. 1783
"		2° Jacq.GendronS.G.1785
Michel		
Jean Baptiste		
Pierre		
29 Jean	(12)	M. Genev. Lainé S.J.1753
M. Angélique		René Picard " 1783
Geneviève		Jos. Beaudoin, S.Frs1778
"		2° Etn. Couillard S.J 1788
30 Joseph		M. Jos. Martineau S. Frs. 1766
Geneviève		Jos. L'heureux " 1788
Joseph		
31 Jacques	(12)	Thècle Lainé S.J. 1767
"		
32 Louis	(13)	Marie Deblois, S.F. 1754
33 "	(16)	Perpétue Dorval S.F 1767
34 François	(18)	M. Rose Vaillancour S.F 1763
35 Louis	(19)	Louise Paquet S.F 1775
36 François	(23)	M. Abondante Loiseau S.F 1770
M. Abondante		Jos. Beaucher " 1806
M. Rose		J. B. Loignon " 1806
Marguerite		Jacq. Poulin " 1811
Ursule		Frs. Foucher " 1824
"		2° Frs. Penat " 1829
Marie Charles		Jacob Pedeak Q.
Jean Baptiste		
François		
37 Jean Baptiste	(23)	M. Jos. Deblois S.F. 1782
M. Josette		Jean Guion " 1814
Marie		Claude Guion " 1821
Marguerite		Isaïe Asselin " 1825
Geneviève		Jos. Asselin " 1828
David		
François		
Pierre		
Martin		
38 André	(23)	M. Brigitte Gaulin S.F. 1789
Marguerite		Prisque Paquet " 1813
André		
Louis		
Le même		Marie Faucher " 1797
M. Madeleine		Pierre Noël Gosselin S.F. 1816
M. Josette		J. B. Primont " 1830
Jacques		
39 Olivier Frs	(24)	M. Jos. Dalaire S.J 1794
40 Amand	(25)	Fse Robertson, S.F. 1792
Marguerite		Jos. Racine " 1827
M. Thècle		Ls Racine " 1831
Isaïe		
41 Pierre	(25)	Marie Drouin S.F. 1799
M. Louise		Tho. Tardif " 1847
Marie		Clément Plante. S.P. 1839
M. Josette		Frs. Dupont " 1842
Pierre		
Joseph		
François		
Ferdinand		
Régis		

ASSELIN.

42 François		Mad. Létourneau S.F. 1813
Le même		Ange Griffart " 1841
α Pre Chrysologue		M. Cath. Campagna S. Frs. 1804
M. Catherine		Germ. Baudoin " 1830
M. Adelaïde		Jean Zacharie Taillon S.P 1845
Joseph		
44 Philippe		M. Jos. Picard S.V. 1775
45 Pierre	(27)	M. Ls. Roy S.M. 1782
M. Rosalie		Amb. Aubé " 1806
"		2° Claude Audet S.M.1814
M. Françoise		Jos. Couture " 1809
M. Louise		Jean Philippe Filion S.M. 1814
Anastasie		Pierre Boucher " 1820
Antoine		
Louis		
46 Jacques	(27)	Josette Gosselin S.V. 1787
Josette		Michel Bétie S.M. 1813
"		2° Jos. Denis " 1836
Marie		Stanislas Ainée S.G. 1813
Jacques		
Le même		Fse Dupont " 1801
Françoise		Ant. Ouellet " 1829
47 Michel		Josette Gosselin
Michel		
48 Pierre	(28)	M. Fse. Boulet S.F. 1757
Geneviève		Jos. Boulet S.G. 1810
Marie		Aug. Ratte S.G. 1813
Marie		Frs. Verical S.G. 1814
Hélene		Abraham Baudoin S.G. 1820
Pierre		
Le même		Josette Bruneau S.G. 1828
		V. d'André Lavoie
49 Michel	(28)	Marie Bétil S.M. 1792
Michel		
Noël		
50 JeanBaptiste	(28)	M. Chs. Patry S.M. 1797
Geneviève		Michel Martineau S.M. 1831
"		2° Frs. Mercier " 1857
Julie		Paul Gautron " 1837
Charles		
Jean Baptiste		
Le même		M. Jos. Roy S.V. 1824
51 Joseph	(30)	M. Anne Gaulin S.Frs. 1800
Marie		Ls. Dompierre S.F. 1828
François		
52 Philippe	(31)	M. Ange Mimaux
M. Madeleine		Jean Viau S.V. 1778
53 Jacques	(36)	M. Jos. Bidet S.J. 1798
M. Anne		Ls Mercier S.L. 1840
54 François	(36)	M. Jos. Foucher S.F.1806
Marguerite		Aug. Beaucher S.F. 1834
Marie		Ant. Pepin S.F. 1837
Constance		Basile Canac S.F. 1841
François Xavier		
55 Jean Bapti'e	(36)	Luduvine Guérard S.F. 1813
M. Luce		Eustache Beaucher S.F. 1842
Adelaïde		Jos. Drouin S.F. 1846
Hombeline		F. X. Martineau S.F.1854
M. Josette		J. B. Lamoth S.F. 1855
Justine		Onésime Lamothe S.F. 1864
Abraham		

ASSELIN.

```
56 David          (37)  Marg. MartineauS.F.1811
   Marguerite          Frs. Asselin S.Frs. 1832
   David
57 François       (37)  Marie MartineauS.F.1813
   Le même             Theotiste Dion S.F. 1824
58 Pierre         (37)  M. Ls Pouliot  S.F. 1816
59 Martin         (37)  Ange Jolin     S.F. 1817
   Marie               Jean Beaucher  S.F. 1837
   M. Adelaïde         Edward Dion    S.F. 1841
   Julie               F. X. Gagnon   S.F. 1846
   Justine             F. X. Canac    S.F. 1854
   Martin
   Pierre
60 André          (38)  Reparate Guérard
                               S.F. 1820
   Justine             F. X. Gagnon   S.F. 1848
   François Xavier
   Joseph
   André
   Athanase
61 Louis          (38)  Marie Ouvrard
   M. Celina           Pierre Narcisse Dion
                               S.Frs. 1862
62 Jacques        (39)  Emilie Vézina  S.F. 1816
   Philomène           J. B. Giguère  S.F. 1860
   Celina              Joachim Letourneau
                               S.F. 1867
   Eusèbe
   François Xavier
63 Louis          (40)  Angèle Asselin Cap. S.
                            Ingnace
   M. Louise           Jacq.NicTradel S.M.1861
   Honorine
   Romuald
64 Isaïe               M. Marg. AsselinS.F.1825
   Le Même        (41)  Angèle Turcot  S.F. 1829
   Joseph
   Pierre
   Evariste
65 Pierre         (41)  M. Anne Martineau
                               S.F. 1824
   Mathilde            Jean Leblond   S.F. 1852
   Martin
   François Xavier
66 Joseph         (41)  Genev. Asselin S.F. 1828
   Geneviève           Jean Samuel Lang-
                            lois      S.P. 1851
   Joseph
67 François       (41)  M. Julie Lessard
                               S.Frs. 1836
68 Ferdinand      (41)  MarcellineCanacS.F.1851
69 Regis          (41)  Pétronille Martineau
                               S.F. 1855
70 Joseph(1ᵉʳm)   (43)  M. Anne TurcotteSJ.1813
71 Chrysostôme    (43)  M. Jos. Dubé, Lévis 1836
72 Joseph(2ᵐm)    (43)  Justine Drouin S.F. 1846
   Justine             F. X. Asselin  S.F. 1867
73 Joseph         (42)  A. Flavie Beaucher
                               S.F. 1837
   Philomène           Jos. Poiré     S.F. 1863
   Flavie              Geo. Gagné     S.F. 1868
74 Antoine        (45)  Cath. Balan    S.V. 1812
   Geneviève           Ls. Cotin      S.M. 1839
   Antoine
75 Abraham             Angèle Mathieu
                               S.P.S. 1822
   Elizabeth           Jos. Fournier S.P.S. 1840
76 Jacques        (46)  M. Jos. Patry S.Chs.1813
77 Michel         (47)  Ursule Brochu  S.G. 1828
78 Pierre         (48)  Marg. Roy      S.G. 1809
79 Michel         (49)  M. Vict. Mar-
                            coux       S.Chs. 1812
                       Jos. Lacroix S.Chs. 1839
   Angèle              Honoré Clément
                               S.Chs. 1853
   Hermine
   M. Victoire         Pierre Clement
                               S.Chs. 1855
```

ASSELIN.

```
   Pierre
   Charles
   Edmond
   Joseph
   Marc
80 Noël           (49)  M. Victor Lemelin
                               S. Chs. 1819
81 Charles        (50)  Fse. Bacquet   S.M. 1829
   M.Angel Florida     Eugene Lebrun  "  1856
82 Jean Baptiste(50)    M. Jos. Chamber-
                            lan        S.R. 1831
   Philomène           Geo. Theophite Trem-
                            blay       S.R. 1860
83 François       (51)  Marg. Asselin S.Frs. 1832
   Nicolas
84 François Xav-
   ier            (54)  M. Adé. Deblois S.F.1832
   Narcisse
   Paul
85 Abraham        (55)  Albine Lamothe
                               S.M. 1850
86 David          (56)  Adé. Emond    S.Frs. 1857
87 Florentin           Angè. Thibaut S.H.
   Jean Baptiste
88 Martin         (59)  Henriette Foucher
                               S.F. 1843
   Joseph
89 Pierre         (59)  Julie Létourneau
90 André Atha-                  S. F. 1860
   nasse          (60)  Henriette Poulin
91 Francois Xav-                S.F. 1847
   ier            (60)  Cath. Turcotte S.J. 1852
92 Joseph         (60)  Seraphiné Dion S.F. 1858
93 Eusèbe         (62)  Domitelle Ferland
94 Francois Xa-                 S.P. 1862
   vier           (62)  Justine Asselin S.F. 1867
95 Romuald        (63)  Hermine McNeil
                               S.M. 1858
96 Joseph         (64)  Philomène Canac'
                               S.F. 1860
97 Evariste       (64)  Justine Letourneau
                               S.F. 1860
98 Pierre         (64)  Adè Leblond    S.F. 1862
99 Francois Xa-  (65)   Claudine Letourneau
   vier                        F. 1850
100 Martin        (65)  Zoé MartineauS.S.F.1862
101 Joseph        (66)  Sarah Leclaire S.P. 1855
102 Antoine       (74)  Genev. Bacquet S.M. 1841
103 Pierre        (79)  Hélène Clement S.M.1841
104 Marc          (79)  Luce Lebrun    S.M. 1840
105 Charles       (79)  Ange Lacroix   S.M. 1845
106 Joseph        (79)  Zoé Roy        S.V. 1859
107 Edward        (79)  Felicité Lacroix S.V. 1859
108 Nicolas       (83)  M. Vict.Fortier S.Frs1857
    Désiré
109 Paul          (84)  Séraphine Foucher
                               S.F. 1863
110 Narcisse      (84)  Hombeline Drouin
                               S.F. 1864
111 Jean Baptiste(87)   Esther Lemelin S.Chs1824
112 Joseph        (88)  Celina Vaillancour
                               S.F. 1865
113 Désiré       (108)  Rose Rouleau   S.L. 1880
```

AUBÉ.

```
1 André (Anglais)      Genev. Fradet  S.V. 1713
   M. Geneviève        Jos. Beaucher  "  1735
   M. Agathe           Aug. Roy       "  1740
   M. Louise           Ls Langlois    "  1747
       "               2° Jos. Marie Rou-
                            leau       S.V. 1758
   M. Josette          Jos. Lemieux   "  1754
   M. Anne             Michel Lemieux "  1751
       "               2° Michel Balan
   André                   Bert 1759
```

AUBÈ

	Name		Spouse	Place	Year
	Augustin				
	Boniface				
	Pierre				
	François				
2	André	(1)	M. Anne Remillard	S.V.	1748
3	Augustin	(1)	M. Anne Lemieux	Bert.	1751
·	Guillaume				
	Joseph				
	Jean Baptiste				
4	Pierre	(1)	M. Jos. Blais	Bert.	1758
	M. Josette		Etn. Lebrun	S.V.	1774
5	Boniface	(1)	M. Mad. Blais	Bert.	1762
	Madeleine		Chs. Morisset	S.Chs.	1789
	Joseph				
	André				
	Boniface				
	André				
	Le même		M. Anne Beaucher	S.G.	1799
6	François	(1)	M. Judith Tangué	S.V.	1762
	Geneviève		Frs. Bolduc	"	1791
	M. Marguerite		Jean Blais	"	1798
	M. Josette		Jos. Jobin	"	1803
	M. Louise		André Blais	"	1808
	M. Charlotte		Jacq. Thivierge	"	1814
	Françoise		Michel Blais	"	1818
	Rose		Frs. Cochon	S.G.	1813
	François				
	Jean Baptiste				
7	Antoine		Vict. Letourneau		
	Pierre				
8	Guillaume	(3)	Marie Roy	S.V.	1786
	Marie		Fred. Daigle	S.Chs.	1851
9	Jean Baptiste	(3)	M. Anne Pouliot	S.G.	1786
	M. Anne		André Brochu	S.G.	1807
	Marguerite		Frs. Patry	S.G.	1818
	Angélique		Michel Labbé	S.G.	1826
	Rosalie		Ls. Vien	B.	1825
	Guillaume				
	Jean Baptiste				
	Prisque				
	François				
	Pierre				
10	Joseph	(3)	Louis Blouin	Bert.	1793
	Louise		Pierre Couture	S.G.	1818
	Archange		Amb. Limieux	S.G.	1821
	"		2° Pierre Boisson-neau	S.G.	1827
	Marcel				
	Gabriel				
	Raimond				
11	André	(5)	M. Jos. Gautron	S.M.	1792
	Le même		M. Ls Dussaut, Levis		1797
	M. Louise		F. X. Baudoin	S.Chs.	1821
	M. Charlotte		Ls Goulet	S.Chs.	1844
	M. Josette		Ls Leclaire	S.Chs.	1829
	André				
	Jean Baptiste				
	Etienne				
12	Boniface	(5)	Vict. Genest	S.Chs.	1793
	André				
	Le même		Julienne Pepin	S.Chs.	1799
	M. Anne		Pierre Lefebvre	S.G.	1823
	Judith		Jean Audet	S.G.	1828
	Marie		Magl. Morin	S.V.	1837
	Louis				
13	Joseph	(5)	M. Marthe Roy	S.M.	1796
14	Ambroise	(5)	Rosalie Asselin	S.M.	1806
15	François	(6)	Marg. Bolduc	S.V.	1799
	Marguerite		André Roby	S.V.	1823
	Jean Baptiste				
	Le même		Barbe Roby	S.V.	1820

18—13

AUBÉ.

	Name		Spouse	Place	Year
	Euphemie		F. X. Guilmet	S.V.	1849
	Francois Xavier				
	Pierre				
16	Jean Baptiste	(6)	M. Mad. Gosselin	S.V.	1807
17	André		Euphrosine Beaulieu	S. Marguerite	
	M. Angèle		Jos. Goupy	B.	1841
18	Pierre	(7)	Marie Couture	S.G.	1819
19	Jean Baptiste	(9)	M. Genev. Lacroix	S.G.	1811
	Michel				
20	Guillaume	(9)	Marg. Lacroix	S.G.	1816
21	Prisque	(9)	Marg. Bilodeau	S.Chs.	1828
22	François	(9)	Filicité Dangucuger	B.	1829
	François				
	Le même		Marie Couture	B.	1834
	Ferdinand				
23	Pierre	(9)	Augé.Couture	S.Chs.	1834
25	Raimond	(10)	Josette Lemieux	S.G.	1821
26	Gabriel	(10)	Marcelline Boissonneau	S.H.	1831
26	Marcel	(10)	Ursule Bouchard	S.V.	1832
27	André	(11)	Archange Leclaire	S. Chs	1825
	Eulalie		Hilaire Couture	S. Chs.	1852
28	JeanBaptiste	(11)	Henriette Marseau	S.V.	1827
29	Etienne	(11)	Cath. Chabot	S. Chs.	1827
	Adèle		Paul Boulet	S. Chs.	1853
	Catherine		Chs. Coté	S. Chs.	1853
	Virginie		Abraham Leblond	S. Chs.	1857
	Philomène		Pierre Leblond	S.Chs.	1860
	Etienne				
	André	(12)	Marthe Bisson	S.Chs.	1818
29	Louis	(12)	Marg. Charron	S.G.	1824
30	Amable		Fse. Lefebvre	S. Anselme	
	Mathilde		Nic. Boulet	S. Chs.	1856
	Calixte				
32	Jean Baptiste	(15)	Apolline Marseau	S.V.	1838
33	Francois Xavier	(15)	Luce Gautron	S.V.	1850
34	François Xavier	(15)	Mathilde Roy	S.V.	1858
35	Pierre	(15)	Agnès Guilmet	S.V.	1858
36	Michel	(19)	Eliz. Perrin	B.	1826
37	François	(22)	M. Ls Nadeau	B.	1852
38	Ferdinand	(22)	Gertrude Goupy	S.M.	1865
39	Etienne	(29)	Marg. Bourassa	S. Chs.	1858
40	Calixte	(31)	Octavie Bouffart	S.V.	1869
41					

AUBIN.

	Name		Spouse	Place	Year
1	Pierre		Marie Paradis	S.P.	1693
	Jean				
	Gabriel				
	Pierre				
	Charles		*11 children - jette*		
2	Jean		Eliz. Chesnay	S.P.	1724
3	Pierre		Marg. Marcoux	S.P.	1730
	Agathe		Philippe Noel	S.P.	1755
	M. Thérèse		J.B. Roy Audy	S.P.	1763
	Louis				
	Le même		Genev. Couture	S.P.	1752
4	Gabriel	(1)	M. Jos. Leclaire	S.P.	1741
	Thérèse		Ign. Roberge	S.P	1760
5	Charles	(1)	Genev. Blouard	S.P.	1767
6	Joseph		M. Anne Michaud		
	Jacques				

AUBIN.

7	Louis	(3)	Genev. Noel	S. P.	1767
	Marguerite		Pierre Bédard	„	1788
	M. Angélique		Ign. Roberge	„	1797
	Thérèse		Pierre Pichet	„	1798
	Agathe		Jos. Couture	„	1802
	Pierre				
	Louis				
8	Jacques	(6)	Marthe Rousseau	S.P S.	1763
	M. Marthe		Jos. Carrier	„	1794
	Le même		M. Mad.Gagné	„	1782
	Rose		LaurentBacquet	S.G.	1814
	Marguerite		Chs. Carbonneau	„	1816
	Angélique		Jacq. Labrecque	„	1820
	François				
9	Joseph		M.Chs.Frechet S.An.		
	„				
10	„	(9)	M.Chs.Leclaire	S.P.	1770
11	Pierre	(7)	Genev. Crépeau	„	1799
	Marguerite		Jean Godbout	S.F.	1819
	„		2°NarcisseTessier	„	1845
	Louis	(7)	Eliz. Mirand	S.P.	1807
12	Elizabeth		Aug. Nolin	„	1831
	„		2° Jean Collard	„	1840
	Henriette		Jean Jalbert	„	1841
	Isidore				
13	Jean Baptiste		Fse. Croteau		
	Charles				
14	François		Judith Audet	S.G.	1810
15	Louis	(11)	M. Anne Crepeau	S.P.	1826
16	Charles	(13)	M. Jos. Ferlant	„	1824
17	Louis		M. Jos. Miville S. André		
	Joseph				
18	Isidore	(12)	Henriette Gosselin	S.L.	1838
19	Leon	(12)	Scolastique Goulet	S.P.	1844
	M. Hombéline		Jean Pie Ferlant	„	1869
	Ignace				
	Leon				
20	Joseph	(17)	Marie Fortin	S.V.	1856
21	Ignace Leon	(19)	M. Demerine Poulin	S.P.	1867

AUDET—LAPOINTE.

1	Nicolas		Mad. Després	S.F.	1670
	Marie		MauriceCrepeau	S.J.	1702
	Nicolas				
	Pierre				
	Joseph				
	François				
	Innocent				
	Joachim				
2	Nicolas	(1)	M. Ls. Chabot	S.L.	1697
	M. Madeleine		Jacq. Turcot	„	1726
	Marie		Mathurin Boilard	„	1729
	M. Anne		PierreFrs.Pouliot	„	1730
	Genevieve		Aug. Dumas	„	1723
	Thérèse		Jacq. Gendron	B.	1743
	Jean				
	Louis				
3	Pierre	(1)	Marie Dumas	S.J.	1698
	M. Madeleine		Pierre Terrien	„	1726
	Genevieve		Pierre Letang	„	1758
	Guillaume				
	Pierre				
4	Joseph	(1)	Jeanne Pouliot	S.L.	1703
	M. Josette		Jos. Turcot	S.J.	1732
	„		2° Ign. Terrien	„	1750
	Catherine		Ant. Viger	„	1751
	Jean François				
	Joseph				
	Gabriel				

AUDET—LAPOINTE.

5	Jean Baptiste	(1)	M. Ls. Godbout	S.L.	1708
	Perpetue		Jos. Asselin	„	1746
	M. Angélique		Simon Lheureux	„	1750
	M. Madeleine		Jacq. Asselin	S.J.	1725
	M. Charlotte		Ls. Terrien	„	1751
	Pierre				
	Jean Baptiste				
6	François	(1)	Mary Bernard	S.L.	1709
	M. Marguerite		Jean Gaulin	„	1733
	M. Madeleine		Marc Dufresne	„	1738
	Jean François				
	François				
	Louis				
	Pierre				
7	Innocent	(1)	Genev. Lemelin	„	1710
8	Joachim	(1)	Louise Roberge	„	1716
9	Joseph		M. Chs. Jahan	S.J.	1725
	M. Charlotte		Ant. Fontaine	„	1753
	Joseph				
	Le même		M. Anne Terrien	„	1740
	Basilesse		Jean Marie Lainé	„	1764
	Guillaume				
	Le même		M. Jos. Plante	„	1761
10	Jean	(2)	M.AnneJoanne	S.L.	1726
	M. Anne		Alexis Picard	„	1750
	Marie		Ls. Coulombe	„	1757
	M. Geneviève		Chs. Diers	„	1757
	M. Madeleine		Florent Dubeau	„	1759
	M. Thérèse		J. B. Brunet	„	1761
	M. Cécile		Henry Roy	„	1763
	M. Louise		Laurent Lemelin	„	1770
	Jean				
	Pierre				
	Laurent				
11	Louis	(2)	Angé Drapeau	B.	1741
	Marie		Chs. Fortier	S.Chs.	1773
	Angélique		Pierre Royer	„	1777
	M. Louise		Pierre Gosselin	„	1778
	Catherine		Pierre Belleau	S.H.	1790
	Thérèse		Chs. Pepin	„	1790
	Louis				
12	Antoine		M. Jos. Pepin		
	M. Anne		Frs. Fontaine	S.J.	1771
	Louis				
	Charles				
	Barthe				
	Ignace				
13	Pierre	(3)	Marie Labrecque	S.L	1727
	François				
	Gabriel				
14	Guillaume	(3)	M. Mad. Turcot	S.F.	1742
	François				
	Gabriel				
15	Jean		Marie Dabret		
	M. Anne		Chs. Nadeau	S.Chs.	1776
	Louis				
	Le même		Marg. Emond	S.Chs.	1765
16	Jean François	(4)	Marie Joseph	S.J.	1743
17	Joseph	(4)	Marie Pepin	S.J.	1732
18	Gabriel	(4)	M. Félicite Hautbois	S.R.	1753
			Baie des Chaleurs		
	Louis				
	Jean Baptiste				
19	Jean Baptiste	(5)	Cath. Rondeau	S.J.	1732
20	Pierre	(5)	Angé Charlan	S.F.	1750
	Le même		2° M. Thérèse Thibaut	S.F.S.	1752
	Louis				
21	François	(6)	M. Mad. Baillargeon	S.L.	1736
	Marguerite		Jacq. LétourneauS.L.		1763
	Marie		Jean Leclaire	„	1763
	„		2° Pierre Beaucher	„	1777
	Jean François				

AUDET—LAPOINTE.

	Louis			
	Pierre			
	Augustin			
	Le même	M. Anne Gosselin	S.L.	1762
22	Jean François (6)	Génev. Leclaire	S.L.	1742
	François	Alexis Dumas	,,	1770
	Généviève	Ls. Lemelin	,,	1772
	M. Madeleine	Ant. Turgeon	,,	1773
	M. Josette	Jacq. Godbout	,,	1781
	Jean Baptiste			
	Marc			
	Françoise			
23	Pierre (6)	Fse. Mailly	S.L.	1749
	Françoise	Martin Dinhard	Bert.	1775
	Louis			
24	Louis (6)	Marg. Dumas	S.L.	1750
	Marie	Jean Shafer	S.L.	1784
	Geneviève	Nic. Meyer	,,	1785
25	Jean Baptiste	M. Agathe Greffart	Avant	1746
	M. Charlotte	Gab. Royer	S.J.	1769
	M. Anne	J. B. Paquet	,,	1789
	Pierre			
	François			
26	Joseph (9)	Marg. Thivierge	S.J.	1756
	Marguerite	Laurent Fortier	,,	1784
	M. Anne	Jean S. Pierre	,,	1786
	Benoit			
	Joseph			
	Guillaume			
	Nicolas			
	Jean Baptiste			
27	Guillaume (9)	M. Ange Delage	S.J.	1763
	M, Angélique	Laurent Thivierge	,,	1790
	M. Anne	J. B. Timblay	,,	1799
	Basilisse	Pierre Coulombe	,,	1801
	Michel Olivier			
	Louis			
	Antoine			
28	Jean (10)	Genev. Civadier	S.L.	1784
	Thérèse	Joachim Gosselin	S. Chs.	1781
	Angélique	Ant. Letourneau	,,	1793
	Agathe	Jos. Turgeon	,,	1793
	Nicolas			
	Jean			
29	Laurent (10)	Marg. Coulombe	S.L.	1763
	Marguerite	Jos. Leclaire	,,	1796
	Marie	Pierre Bernard	S.V.	1797
	Pélagie	J.B. Beaucher	S.F.S.	1801
	Laurent			
	Guillaume			
	Henri			
30	Pierre (10)	Genev. Létourneau	S.P.	1769
31	Louis (11)	Genev. Ferlant	S.Chs.	1762
32	Louis (12)	Hélène Langlois	S.L.	1770
	Hélène	Jos. Blouin	S.J.	1794
33	Charles (12)	M. AnneLanglois	S.L.	1773
	M. Anne	Jos. Dalaire	S.J.	1802
	Pierre			
34	Barthélemie (12)	M. Reine Boucher	S. Chs.	1773
	M. Anne	Jos. Fortier	S.G.	1809
	Euphrosine	Ls. Verieul	,,	1812
	Eustache			
	Jean Baptiste			
	Barthélemie			
	Pierre			
	Ignace			
35	Ignace (12)	Théotiste Bilodeau	S. Chs.	1774
	Marie	André Hélie	S.H.	1809
	François			
	Charles			
	Louis			

18—13½

AUDET--LAPOINTE.

	Joseph			
36	Antoine (12)	Marg. Lecours	S.Chs.	1774
	Marguerite	Etn. Gontier	,,	1797
	Catherine	Etn. Couture	,,	1797
	Françoise	Jos. Royer	,,	1803
	Elizabeth	Jos. Bisson	,,	1805
	Victoire	André Bernier	,,	1803
	Angélique	AlexandreDuquet	,,	1809
	,,	2° Ls. Morin	,,	1814
	Antoine			
	Jean Baptiste			
37	Antoine	Marg. Couture		
	Le même	Thérèse Couture	S.G.	1751
	Angèle	J. B. Paquet	S. Chs.	1817
	Luce	Aug. Picard	,,	1835
	Elie			
	Antoine			
	Marc			
	Marcel			
38	François (13)	M. Joseph Leblanc	S.J.	1764
39	Charles (13)	Marie Gobeil	S.F.	1765
40	François (14	M. Ange Pepin	S.J.	1773
	Le même	M. Jos. Drouin	,,	1782
	François			
41	Gabriel (14)	Fse. Vermet	S.H.	1794
	Le même	M. Angé. Guion	,,	1801
42	Louis (15)	M.Chs.Gosselin	S. Chs.	1778
	Charlotte	J. B. Fortier	S.G.	1818
	Marie	Germ. Dion	,,	1825
	Adelaïde	Frs. Dion	,,	1826
	Gabriel			
	Pierre			
	Le même	Reine Lamare	S.G.	1827
		v. d'Ignace Roy.		
43	Louis (18)	Genev. Nadeau	Bert.	1800
44	JeanBaptiste(18)	Marie Garont	S.G.	1787
45	Louis (20)	Angé. Lepage	S.Chs.	1782
46	Louis (21)	Thécle Fortier	S.G.	
	M. Geneviève	Jean Dumas	S.L.	1804
	M. Josette	Pierre Cinqmars	,,	1796
	Guillaume			
	Louis			
	Jean			
47	JeanFrançois(21)	Thérèse Létourneau	S.L.	1763
48	Pierre (21)	Angé. Fournier	S.Chs	1772
	Angélique	J. B. Garant	S.G.	1792
	Josette	Pierre Garant	,,	1798
	Marie	Ign. Nadeau	,,	1813
	Claude			
	Augustin			
	Louis			
	Pierre			
	Michel			
	Jean			
	Joseph			
49	Augustin (21)	Marie Nadeau	S.Chs.	1773
	Marie	Frs. Patouel	S.G.	1795
	Angélique	Frs. Moor	,,	1810
	Augustin			
	Jean			
	Guillaume			
50	JeanBaptiste(22)	Genev. Langlois	S.L.	1776
	M. Victoire	Jos. Chabot	,,	1804
	Françoise	Jos. Delisle	,,	1845
	Antoine			
	Pierre			
	Jean François			
51	Marc (22)	M. Anne Gendreau	S.L.	1778
	Charlotte	René Tangué	S.G.	1806
	Judith	Frs. Aubin	,,	1810
	Jean			
	François			

AUDET—LAPOINTE.

Gervais
52 François   (22)   M. Anne Godbout
                      S.L. 1786
    Jean
    François
    Pierre
53 Louis   (23)   Genev.Nadeau S.Frs.1800
54 Pierre   (25)   M. Rose Asselin S.F.1770
    M. Madeleine   Jos. Curadeau   S.J. 1801
55 François   (25)   M. Frse Delage, S.J.1789
    Marie   Julien Rousseau SL. 1819
    François
    Joseph
    Jean Baptiste
    Le même   Marg.Chatigny, S.J.1803
    Cécile   J. B. Morin   ''   1823
    Louis
56 Gabriel   Marie Desnoyers,Baie des
                     Chaleurs.
    Augustin
    Joseph
57 Joseph   (26)   M.Chs.Lebrun S.Chs.1789
    Le même   Scolastique Thibault
                          S.Chs. 1825
58 Nicolas   (26)   M.Jos.Audebert S.J.1787
59 Guillaume   (26)   Marie Goupy S.M. 1792
    Julie   Chrysostine Leclair
                          S.G. 1823
    Hubert
    Joseph
60 Benoit   (26)   Agathe Poulet S.P. 1791
    Marguerite   Ls. Servant   S.J. 1826
61 Jean Baptiste(26)   Brigitte Lebrun S.G. 1793
    Pierre
62 Antoine   (27)   Agathe Thibault ''   1789
63 Louis   (27)   Angé. Tremblay S.J. 1793
64 Michel Olivier
           (27)   M. Ls. Tremblay S.J. 1803
    M. Louise   Ant. Gosselin   S.J. 1825
    M. Louise   Ant. Fortier   S.J. 1830
    Marguerite   Abraham Royer S.J. 1830
    Julie   Frs. Pouliot
    Luce   Ls. Dion
    Narcisse
    Jean Baptiste
    Michel
    Joseph
65 Jean   (28)   Angé Baudin S.Chs. 1782
66 Nicholas   (28)   M. Fse. Vallée S.M. 1787
    Paul
67 Henri   (89)   M. Jos. Mercier S.V. 1785
    M. Charlotte   Ls. Lemieux   S.V. 1809
    M. Marguerite   Etn. Remillard S. V. 1814
    M. Angélique   Michel Bernard S.V. 1817
    Louise   Jean Roy   S.V. 1820
    Geneviève   Jos. Patoüel   S.V. 1821
    M. Josette   Jean Roy   S.V. 1831
    Michel
    Louis
    Henri
68 Laurent   (29)   M. Mad.GosselinS.L.1789
    M. Madeleine   Amb. Dumas   S.L. 1812
    Laurent
    Antoine
    Joseph
69 Guillaume   (29)   Marg. Roy   S.V.1801
70 Pierre   (33)   Marg. Buteau S.G. 1803
71 Eustache   (34)   M. Vict. LetellierS.V.1801
72 Pierre   (34)   Marie Baillargeon
                          S.G. 1803
    François
73 Ignace   (34)   M. Anne Baillargeon
                          S.G. 1803
74 Barthélemi   (34)   Angèle Boutin S.G. 1803
75 JeanBaptiste(34)   TheodisteBoutinS.V.1825
76 Joseph   (35)   Marie Dalaire S.G. 1803

AUDET—LAPOINTE.

    Marie   Ant. Roy   B. 1338
    Angèle   Jos. Turgeon   B. 1839
    ''   2" Pierre Terrier B. 1847
    Pierre
    Jean Baptiste
    François
77 François   (35)   M.Jos.MercierS.Chs.1818
    M. Josette   Pierre Labrecque
                          S.Chs. 1831
    Marguerite   Chs. Vien   S.Chs. 1840
    Marcelline   Pierre Vien   S.Chs. 1841
    François
78 Charles   (35)   Agathe Bedard S.G. 1813
    David
79 Louis   (35)   CésarieDuquetS.Chs.1829
80 Antoine   (36)   Ange Duquet S.Chs. 1803
81 Antoine   Mad. Boulet
    Le même   Charlotte Tangué
                          S.V. 1838
82 JeanBaptiste(36)   Anastasie Gosselin
                          S.Chs. 1810
    Anastasie   Jos. Mercier S.Chs. 1828
    Le même   M. Ls. PelchatS.Chs.1812
    M. Victoire   Ls. Goulet   S.Chs. 1825
    M. Emélie   Ls. Leclaire   S.Chs. 1850
    Jean
    Joseph
    Pierre
83 Charles   Josette St. Louis
    Marguerite   Louis Roy   S.G. 1825
84 Marc   (37)   Charlotte Campeau
                          S.G. 1818
85 Elie   (37)   Constance Gosselin
                          S.Chs. 1819
86 Antoine   (37)   Susanne Couture
                          S.Chs. 1823
87 Marcel   (37)   Marie Godbout S.G. 1829
88 François   (40)   M. Mad. Tremblay
                          S.J. 1799
    Julie   Frs. Bouchard S.J. 1825
    M. Madeleine   Ant. Fontaine S.J. 1826
    Cécile   Jos.MariePlante S.J.1827
    Barbe   Laurent Tremblay
                          S.J. 1835
    Emerence   Etn. Thivierge S.J. 1835
    François Isaac
89 Gabriel   (42)   M.Marg.Fortier S.V.1803
    Louis
    Gabriel
    Thomas
90 Pierre   (42)   Marg. Gnay   S.G. 1828
    Laurent
91 Louis   (46)   M. Chs. Gosselin
                          S.Chs. 1795
92 Guillaume   Vict. Baillargeon
                          S.L. 1807
    Justine   David Choret   S.L. 1838
    Pierre
    Louis
    David
    Guillaume
    François
93 Jean   (46)   Genev. Baillargeon
                          S.L. 1809
    Geneviève   Alexis Poliquin   B. 1839
    Angèle   Michel Turgeon S.M.1847
    Sophie   Jean Gualbert Martineau
                          S.M. 1850
    Jean
    George
    Pierre
    François Xavier
94 Pierre   (48)   Marg. Bouchard S.G.1799
    Antoine
95 Augustin   (48)   Marie Diers   S.G. 1800
    Marie   Alexis Leclaire S.G. 1820

AUDET—LAPOINTE.

	Barbe		Féreol Roy	S.G. 1824
	Geneviève		Frs. Gontier	S.G. 1826
	Augustin			
96	Louis	(48)	M. Ls. Pelchat S. Chs.1801	
	Tharsille		Vital Lemieux	„ 1855
	Marcelline		Jos. Roy	S.M. 1841
	Michel			
	Louis			
	François Xavier			
	Jean Baptiste			
	Etienne			
97	Michel	(48)	M. Chs. Frogue S.G. 1806	
	Cécile		Jacq. Gagnon	„ 1828
	Michel			
98	Claude	(48)	Rosalie Asselin S.M. 1814	
	Le même		Marie Quéset	S.G. 1826
99	Joseph	(48)	Archange Nadeau	
				S.G. 1808
	Le même		Cecile Lefebvre	
				S. Chs. 1818
	Cécile		Alexis Couture	„ 1840
100	Jean	(48)	ArchangeLasanteS.G.1807	
101	Jean	(49)	Louise Dalaire S.G. 1805	
	Louise		Jos. Alaire	„ 1824
	Louis			
102	Augustin	(49)	Marie Dalaire	S.G. 1801
	Marie		Lug. Alaire	„ 1825
	Marguerite		Pierre Gagnon	„ 1829
	Augustin			
	Pierre			
103	Guillaume	(49)	M. Ls. Genest	S.G. 1823
	Guillaume			
104	Antoine	(50)	Marg. Baillargeon	
				S.L. 1819
	Marguerite		Laurent Godbout	„ 1841
	Antoine			
105	Pierre	(50)	Vict. Fontaine	S.J. 1822
	M. Séraphine		Jos. Zoel Tremblay	
				S.L. 1864
	Zéphirin			
	François Xavier			
106	Jean	(51)	Marthe Ratté	S.G. 1802
	Marie		Pierre Caman	„ 1827
	Marguerite		Ant. Fournier	„ 1830
	Jean			
107	Gervais	(51)	M. Anne Chamberlan	
				S. G. 1811
	Marguerite		Pierre Guay	B. 1849
108	François	(51)	Vict. Thibaut	S.G. 1820
	Emilie Victoire		Isidore Fradet S.M. 1846	
109	Jean	(52)	M. Ls. Turcot S.F. 1814	
	Julie		Frs. Regis Dion	„ 1839
	Emilie		Moise Létourneau	
				S.F. 1843
	M. Esther		Jean Vaillancour	„ 1853
	Susanne		Chs Deblois	„ 1855
	Jean Elie			
	Jean			
	Pierre			
110	Pierre	(52)	Justine Guérard S.F. 1826	
111	François	(52)	Luce De Viller	
112	François	(55)	Angèle Audibert S.J.1812	
	Vénérande		Jos. Pepin	„ 1836
	M. Louise		Ls. Poulin	„ 1842
	Cécile		F. X. Thivierge	„ 1842
	Jérémie			
	Paul			
	François			
113	Joseph	(55)	M. Anne Hélie S.J. 1815	
114	Jean Baptiste	(55)	Mad. Gosselin S.J. 1823	
	La même		Constance Boissonneau	
				S.J. 1835
	Séraphine		Nazaire Pepin	„ 1858
115	Louis	(55)	Marie Labrecque	
				S.Chs. 1828
	Florence		Michel Lacroix S.V. 1856	

AUDET—LAPOINTE.

116	Magloire		Luce Lemieux, Lévis	
	Le même		Angèle Lepage	B. 1841
117	Augustin	(56)	Marie Pepin	S.J. 1819
118	Joseph	(56)	Marie Pepin	S.J. 1827
119	Joseph	(59)	Marie Leclaire S.G. 1822	
120	Hubert	(59)	Angé. Guay	S.G. 1827
121	Pierre	(62)	Cécile Leclaire S.G. 1822	
122	Michel	(64)	M. Cath. Ginchereau	
				S.Frs. 1832
123	JeanBaptiste	(64)	Cécile Pepin	S.J. 1845
124	Joseph	(64)	Marcelline Blouin	
				S.J. 1847
125	Narcisse	(64)	M.Anne Dalaire S.J. 1851	
126	Paul	(66)	Marg. Chabot S. Chs 1812	
	Marguerite		Ls. Fournier	„ 1838
	Catherine		Anselme Rouillard	
				S.Chs. 1840
	Olive		Pierre Pepin	„ 1845
	Hermine		Modiste Naud	„ 1849
	Charles			
127	Michel	(67)	Marg. Picard S.F.S. 1813	
	M. Marthe		Etn. Fréderic Cochon	
				S.M. 1841
	Marguerite		Ed. Carbonneau	„ 1848
	Soulange		Frs. Gontier	S.V. 1845
	Michel			
	Louis			
128	Louis	(67)	Cath.Rémillard S.V. 1814	
	M. Emilie		Adrien Marseau	„ 1835
	M. Luce		F. X. Herpe	„ 1835
129	Henri	(67)	Marg. Roy	S.G. 1829
	Sara		Basile Chabot S.Chs 1864	
130	Antoine	(68)	M. Jos. Beaulieu	
131	Laurent	(68)	Louise Pouliot S.L. 1813	
	Salomé		Jean Couture	
	Geneviève		Frs. Godbout	S.L. 1858
	Jérome			
	Le même		Marie Cinqmars S.L.1839	
132	Joseph	(68)	M.Anne Coulombe	
				S.L.1833
	Marguerite		Jos. Emond	„ 1871
	Cyrille			
	Joseph			
133	François	(72)	Hermine Corriveau	
				S.V. 1846
134	Pierre	(76)	Josette Turgeon B. 1839	
135	François	(76)	Adé Turgeon	B. 1841
136	Jean Baptiste	(76)	M. Ls. Turgeon B. 1844	
137	François	(77)	M. Ange Lacasse	
				S.Chs. 1834
138	David	(78)	Marcelline Coulombe	
				S.Chs. 1842
139	Jean	(82)	AnastasieCoté S.Chs.1840	
140	Pierre	(82)	Anastasie Chabot	
				S.Chs. 1840
141	Joseph	(82)	Caroline Turgeon	
				S.Chs. 1854
142	Jean Baptiste		M. Henriette Finley Q.	
	Jean Leon			
143	Prosper		Flore Gaumont	
	Le même		M.Eudoce RuelS.Chs1843	
144	Paul		Marg. Gosselin	
	Le même		Genev.Gosselin S.Chs1845	
145	Frs. Isaac	(88)	M. Chs. Hélie	S.J. 1826
	François Isaac			
146	Gabriel	(89)	Marg. Bilodeau S.G. 1827	
147	Thomas	(89)	Eliz. Boulet	S.G. 1830
148	Louis	(89)	SophieChabot S. Chs.1840	
149	Laurent	(90)	M.Anne Paquet	
				S.Chs.1862
150	Guillaume	(92)	Zoé Gagnon	Bert. 1842
151	Louis	(92)	Theodiste PichetS.L.1843	
	M. Aurélie		Damase Pouliot	„ 1864
	M. Sara		Frs. Dion	„ 1865
	M. Josephine		Ed. Maronda	„ 1865
	Louis			

AUDET—LAPOINTE.

152	Pierre	(92)	Adé Dumas	S.L. 1845
	Le même		M. Jos. Campeau "	1863
153	David	(92)	Apolline Beaudoin "	1854
154	François	(92)	M.Emélie Langlois "	1869
155	Jean	(93)	Genev.Poliquin S.M.1837	
	M. Luce Jeanne		Edmond Patry "	1864
156	Pierre	(93)	Emelie Méridie "	1838
	M. Genev.Arcad		Jos. Nap. Fraser "	1862
	M. Luce Olympe		PierreDamienCotin " 1865	
	Albert			
157	François Xavier			
		(93)	Renaud	
158	George	(93)	Luce Anastasie Beaucher	
				B. 1844
159	Antoine	(94)	MartheLemieux S.G.1826	
160	Augustin	(95)	Marg. Bruneau "	1826
161	Louis	(96)	M.Angèle Gontier "	1827
	M. Salomé		Frs. Plante S.Chs. 1859	
	Gervais			
162	Etienne	(96)	M.Chs Bernier S.Chs 1833	
163	Michel	(96)	M.Chantal Goupy	
164	François Xavier			S.M.1840
		(96)	M. Vict. Gautron " 1840	
165	JeanBaptiste	(96)	Emile Paquet " 1848	
166	Michel	(97)	SophieCoutureS.Chs.1835	
167	Louis	(101)	Sophie Maranda S.L.1859	
168	Pierre	(102)	Marg. Dalaire S.G. 1809	
	Marguerite		Prudent Talbot " 1829	
169	Augustin	(102)	Genev. Gagnon S.V. 1829	
160	Guillaume	(103)	Emélie Gagnon S.G. 1830	
171	Antoine	(104)	Marie Côté S.L. 1846	
172	Zephirin	(105)	Aurée Morisset S.L. 1861	
173	François Xavier			
		(105)	Marie Ruel " 1861	
174	Jean	(106)	Judith Aubé S.G. 1828	
175	Jean	(109)	Adé Ferland S.F. 1846	
176	Jean Elie	(109)	Philoméne Clusiau	
				S.P. 1860
177	Pierre	(109)	Justine Létourneau	
				S.F. 1862
178	Jérémie	(112)	Cécile Campeau S.L.1841	
	Le même		Marie Pouliot S.J.	
179	Paul	(112)	M.Caroline Plante	
				S.P. 1846
	M. Caroline		Ls. Jos. Conture " 1867	
180	François	(112)	Eliz. Pouliot S.J. 1845	
181	Charles	(126)	Leocadie Roy S.Chs.1847	
182	Michel	(127)	MarieBilodeau Bert. 1840	
183	Louis	(127)	Emérentienne Pilote	
				S.M. 1842
184	Jérome	(131)	Théotiste PichetS.L. 1864	
185	Cyrille	(132)	M. Eugénie Chabot	
				S.L. 1865
186	Joseph	(132)	Arthémise Pouliot	
				S.L. 1872
187	Jean Léon	(142)	Louise Flora Fraser	
				B. 1843
188	Frs. Isaac	(145)	Séraphine Labrecque	
				S.J. 1848
189	Louis	(151)	Salomé Audet S.L. 1876	
190	Albert	(156)	M. Olymphe Zéphirine	
			Roy	S.V. 1868

AUDIBERT—LAJEUNESSE.

1	Etienne		Cath. Bochon S.F. 1699	
	M. Madeleine		Claude Campeau S.F.1732	
	Dorothée		Chs. Plante " 1740	
	M. Josette		Claude Lefebvre 1742	
	Jean François			
	Etienne			
	Joseph			
2	Etienne	(1)	M.Mad.FontaineS.J.1739	
	M. Madeleine		Jean Vivier " 1763	
	M. Josette		Nicolas Audet " 1787	

AUDIBERT—LAJEUNESSE.

3	Jean François	(1)	M. Mad. Plante S.F. 1742	
	M. Charlotte		Ls. Baillargeon " 1779	
	Prisque			
	Pierre Noël			
	Jean Marie			
4	Joseph	(1)	M. Angé. Greffart	
				S.J. 1744
5	Prisque	(3)	M. Anne Letourneau	
				S.P. 1775
	Le même		Marie Dufresne S.L. 1792	
	Antoine			
	François			
	Joseph			
	Jean			
	Laurent			
	Edouard			
6	Pierre Noël	(3)	Marg. Curadeau S.J. 1778	
	M. Madeleine		Pierre Dufresne " 1809	
	M. Charlotte		Michel Turcot " 1812	
	Marguerite		Pierre Labresque " 1812	
	Angèle		Frs. Audet " 1812	
	Marie		Eméry Blouin " 1817	
	Jean Marie			
	Joseph			
7	Jean Marie	(3)	Eliz. Hélie S.J. 1782	
	Jean			
8	Antoine	(5)	Arehange Thivierge	
				S.L. 1821
9	François	(5)	Angé. Coulombe S.J. 1821	
10	Jean	(5)	Félicité Bernier S.P. 1830	
11	Laurent	(5)	M. Mad. Shoret S.P. 1831	
12	Joseph	(5)	Adé Gosselin S.L. 1834	
13	Edouard	(5)	Cath. Dalaire S.J. 1835	
	Euphémie		Fabien Frenet S.L.1861	
	M. Emma		Napoléon Rouleau " 1871	
	M. Octavie		J. B. Coulombe " 1877	
	Célestin			
	Damase			
	Nazaire			
14	Jean Marie	(6)	M. Thécle Coté S.F.1822	
	M. Angélique		Gatien Jolicœur " 1848	
	Flavie		Michel Cookson " 1848	
	Apolline		Marcel Noël " 1850	
	Jean			
15	Joseph	(6)	Marg. Hélie S.J. 1819	
	Le même		Genev. Brochu S.M. 1829	
16	Jean	(8)	Mad. Coulombe S.H. 1843	
	Jean			
17	Célestin	(13)	Delvine Blanchet S. Tho.	
18	Damase	(13)	Philomème Pouliot	
				S.L. 1865
19	Nazaire	(14)	M.Angèle Pepin S.L.1877	
20	Jean	(14)	Scolastique Crépeau	
				S.J. 1840
21	Jean	(16)	FélicitéGagnonS.Chs.1841	

BACON.

1	Gilles		Marie Fournier Q. 1647	
	Eustache			
2	Eustache	(1)	Louise Guimon	
	M. Angélique		Nic. Martin G.R.1696	
	Louise		Denis Constantin " 1703	
	M. Françoise		Guill. Thibaut	
	Jeanne		Zach. Cloutier	
	Eustache			
	Joseph			
	Noël			
3	Eustache	(2)	Mad. Cloutier S.G.1711	
4	Joseph	(2)	Dorothée Cloutier " 1716	
	Madeleine		Ls. Langlois " 1743	
	Dorothée		J. B. Talon " 1755	
5	Noël	(2)	M. Chs. Morin	
	M. Angélique		Isidore Coté S.P.S.1758	
	"		Jos. Frs.Munville " 1789	
	Thérèse		Ls. Campbell " 1763	

BACON.

	Joseph Marie		
	Alexis		
6	Jos. Marie	(5) M. Mad. Lavergne	S.P.S. 1752
7	Alexis	(5) M. Genev. Picard	S.P.S. 1766
	M. Geneviève	Laurent Picard "	1794
	M. Elizabeth	Charles Denis "	1794
	Alexis		
8	Eustache	M. Fse. Picard	
	Eustache		
9	Eustache	(8) M. Angé. Letourneau	S.P.S. 1780
	M. Angélique	Jean François Morin	S.P.S. 1803
	M. Charlotte	Ls. Blais "	1806
	M. Rosalie	Ls. Nicols "	1807
	M. Geneviève	Pierre Celestin Blanchet	S.P.S. 1823
	Eustache		
	Joseph		
10	Alexis	(7) Charlotte Couture	S.Chs. 1786
11	Eustache	(9) Flavie Gagne S.P.S. 1825	
	Le même	Mag. Guénet S.Chs. 1840	
12	Joseph	(9) M. Mag. Fournier	S.Tho. 1814

BACQUET—LAMONTAGNE.

1	François	Anne Philippe Q. 1671	
	François		
2	François	(1) M. Isabelle Guénet	S.M. 1710
	Marie	Ls. Lacroix S.M. 1739	
	M. Louise	Thomas Plante S.M. 1747	
	Hélène	Ths. Quéret S.M. 1750	
	Pierre		
	Joseph		
	Jean Baptiste		
	Simon		
	André		
3	François	M. Portelance	
	M. Josette	Ant. Bissonet S.M. 1763	
	M. Marcelline	Frs. Molleur S.M. 1773	
	M. Elizabeth	Chs. Michon S.M. 1775	
	Louise	Louis Terrien S.Chs. 1786	
	François		
	Le même	Agnès Cyr S.M. 1760	
4	François	(2) Mag. Monmény S.M.1741	
	Marguerite	Robert Leonard Roussel	S.M. 1771
	Pierre		
	Louis		
	Simon		
	François		
	Le même	Dorothé Brochu S.M.1776	
5	Joseph	(2) Agathe Goupy S.M. 1747	
	M. Anne	Jean Hélie S.M. 1783	
	Marie	Pierre Rousseau S.M.1786	
	Agathe	Céleste Lacroix S.M. 1787	
	Françoise	J. B. Bissonnet S.M. 1794	
	M. Josette	Michel Lacroix S.M. 1793	
	"	2° Chs. Hébert Gouillard	S.M. 1799
	Amable		
	André		
	Joseph		
	Pierre		
6	Jean Baptiste	(2) M.Angé Quéret S.M.1750	
	Angelique	Nicolas DanieauS.M.1775	
	Marie	Chs. Lacroix S.M. 1779	
	Judithe	Guill. Nadeau S.M. 1783	
	Françoise	Ant. Couture S.M. 1787	
	Jean Baptiste		
	Joseph		

BACQUET—LAMONTAGNE.

7	Simon	(2) Marcelle Gautron	S.M. 1750
	M. Marguerite	Paul Mercier S.M. 1781	
	M. Judithe	Jean François Trudel	S.V. 1776
	Simon		
	Le même	Mad. Gaboury S.H. 1773	
8	André	(2) Marg. Quéret S.M. 1758	
	Charlotte	Jos. LabrecqueS.Chs.1795	
	Natalie	J. B. Paquet S.Chs. 1797	
	Joseph		
	Jean		
	André		
9	François	(3) Angé Corriveau S.V. 1763	
	Marie	Chs. Drapeau S.Chs. 1795	
	François		
10	Pierre	M. Anne Balan Bert. 1766	
	Marie	Frs. Fradet S.M. 1795	
	M. Louise	Ls. Vien S.M. 1797	
	M. Anne	Jos. Dion S.M. 1798	
	M. Marguerite	Ls. Theverge S.M. 1799	
	Françoise	Paul Mercier S.M. 1804	
	Le même	Genev. Dion S.M. 1788	
	Geneviève	Jean Forgues S.M. 1806	
	Angèle	J. B. Lemieux S.M. 1828	
	Pierre		
	Jean		
	Jacques		
11	Simon	(4) M.Chs.Girard S.Chs.1779	
		V. de Pilippe Munso.	
	Le même	Marie GosselinS.Chs.1782	
	Marie	Amb. Goulet S.G. 1823	
	"	2° J. B. Tangué S.G. 1820	
	Catherine	Jos. Godbout S.G. 1817	
	Madeleine	J. B. Toussaint S.G. 1820	
	Marcelline	Pierre Corriveau S.G.1828	
	Simon		
	Pierre		
	Jean		
12	François	(4) Charlotte Morin	S.F.S. 1786
	Thérèse	Jean Lacasse S.G. 1816	
	Charlotte	Ls. Tangué S.G. 1808	
	"	2° Pierre Roy S.G. 1811	
	Magloire		
	Louis		
13	Louis	(4) Marie Lemelin S.M. 1794	
	M. Anne	Frs. Blouin S.J. 1827	
	"	2° J. B. Servant S.J. 1831	
	François		
	Le même	M. Ls. Plante S.J. 1803	
	Le même	Euphrosine Dubé	S.Chs. 1807
14	Pierre	(5) M. Jos. Lefebvre	S.M. 1780
	Pierre		
	Le même	Mad. Ratte S.Chs. 1798	
	Josette	Pierre Godbout S.G. 1825	
	Madeleine	Jacq. Nicole S.G. 1820	
15	Joseph	(5) M.Jos. Gosselin S.M.1776	
	M. Josette	Michel Roy S.M. 1800	
	"	2° Jos. Bacquet S.M. 1833	
	Catherine	Guill. Roy S.M. 1801	
	Joseph		
	Le même	Mad. Civadier S.M. 1786	
	Le même	Marie Collet S.M. 1820	
16	Amable	(5) M. Anne Patry S.M.1786	
	M. Josette	Louis Cotin S.V. 1808	
	Marguerite	Pre. Chrysostome Fortin	S.V. 1818
	Françoise	Pierre Queret S.V. 1819	
	Marie	Laurent Roy " 1821	
	M. Anne	Urbain Cadrin " 1831	
	Amable		
	Pierre		
	Augustin		

BACQUET—LAMONTAGNE.

17	André	(5)	M. Joseph Dalaire
			S.M. 1787
	André		
	Joseph		
	Pierre		
18	Jean Baptiste	(6)	M. Genev. Roy S.V. 1791
	M. Lucie		Jacq. Blais S.M. 1827
	M. Geneviève		Benj. Couët „ 1828
	Angèle		Marcel Nicole „ 1840
	Jean Baptiste		
	Joseph		
	Eustache		
19	Joseph	(6)	M. Thérèse Mercier
			S.M. 1795
20	Simon	(7)	M. Cath. Rousseau
			S.M. 1779
	Catherine		Aug. Thibaut S.G, 1807
	Marguerite		J. B. Balan „ 1815
	Simon		
	Jean		
	Guillaume		
	Laurent		
21	Joseph	(8)	M. Chas. Richard
			S.Chs. 1784
	Charlotte		Pierre Ballargeon
			S.G. 1812
	Louise		Jos. Godbout „ 1814
	Marguerite		Frs.Dessaint „ 1820
	Josette		Michel Dessaint „ 1822
	Marie		Jacq. Mercier S.M. 1820
	François		
	Joseph		
22	Jean	(8)	Reine Gontier S.Chs 1787
	Le même		M. Jos. Terrien „ 1794
23	André	(8)	Angé Gontier „ 1794
	Reine		Frs. Labrecque „ 1805
	M. Josette		Jos. Pelchat „ 1815
	André		
	Louis		
24	Françoise	(9)	M. Reine Lessart
			S.M. 1795
25	Pierre	(10)	M. Angé Racine „ 1812
	Angélique		Jos. Corriveau „ 1841
	Geneviève		Ant. Asselin „ 1841
	Marie		Augustin Roy „ 1842
	Anne		Pierre Corriveau „ 1847
	M. Angèle		Sam Richard Dominique
			S.M. 1849
	M. Josette		Nicl. McNeil „ 1856
	Ambroise		
26	Jean	(10)	M. Anne Gautron
			S.M. 1828
			V. de Robert Racine
	Luce		Edward Borlard S.M.1843
	Jean		
27	Jacques	(10)	Agathe Brochu S.V. 1836
28	Simon	(11)	Marie Roy S.G. 1810
	Françoise		Jean Chabot S. Chs. 1843
	Simon		
29	Pierre	(11)	Fse. Goulet S.G. 1812
30	Jean	(11)	Marg. Dessaint „ 1822
31	Louis	(12)	M. Angé GautronS.G.1843
32	Magloire	(12)	Marg. Gautron „ 1826
33	François	(13)	Angé Noel „ 1821
34	Pierre	(14)	Marie BrousseauS.M.1801
35	Joseph	(15)	Archange Belanger
			S.M 1806
	Ursule		Landry Poliquin „ 1834
	Archange		Frs. Modeste Bourassa
			S.M. 1836
	Cécile		Simon Marcoux „ 1839
	Emilie		Frs. Rousseau „ 1842
	M. Marcelline		Ignace Hallé „ 1849
	M. Malvina		Benj. Hallé „ 1850
	Julienne		Ls. Damas „ 1852
	Jean Baptiste		

BACQUET—LAMONTAGNT.

	Honoré		
	André		
	François		
	Joseph		
36	Amable	(16)	Fse. Dorval S.M. 1811
	Françoise		Chs. Asselin „ 1829
	„		2° Alexandre Chamberlan
			S.M. 1836
	Julie		Frs. Trépanier „ 1833
37	Pierre	(16)	Hélène Tangué „ 1816
	Marcelline		Ant. Gagnon S.V. 1848
	Emile		André Roy „ 1857
	Adélaïde		Chs. Domicile Cotin
			S.V. 1858
	Soulange		Anaclet Roy „ 1867
	Domitille		Jean Frs. Blais „ 1866
	Michel		
38	Augustin	(16)	Marie Lefebvre S.V. 1829
39	André	(17)	Genev. Coté S.M. 1812
40	Joseph		Françoise Gagnon
			S.M. 1813
	François		
	Joseph		
	Jean Baptiste		
	Michel		
	Honoré		
	Le même		Marie Paquet S.M. 1823
41	Pierre	(17)	Angèle Marcoux
			S.Chs. 1818
	Angèle		Magloire Gosselin
			S.M. 1839
	Ursule		Honoré Roy „ 1842
	Zoé		Edward Pouliot „ 1840
	Julienne		Jos. René Martineau
			S.M. 1848
	Sara		Jos. Martineau „ 1848
	M. Malvina		Pierre Dennis „ 1852
	Marie Aladie		Jos. Cyrille Samson
			S.M. 1859
	Emilie		J. B. Theotime Couture
			S.M. 1860
	M. Zephirine		Jean Denis
	Romuald		
42	Jean Baptiste		M. Mad. Morisset
			S.M. 1813
	Honoré		
43	Eustache	(18)	M. Angèle Tangué
			S.M. 1815
	Julie		Pierre Ruellan „ 1841
	M. Thècle		Prudent Dumas „ 1861
	Joseph		
	Honoré		
	Ferdinand		
	Le même		M. Ls. Patry S.M. 1845
44	Joseph	(18)	Adé Corriveau S.M. 1851
45	Simon		M. Anne Chamberlan
			S.M. 1803
	Le même		(20) Josette Carbonneau
			S.G. 1804
	Archange		Michel Tangué „ 1825
	Françoise		Ls. Pelchat „ 1828
	Le même		Génev. St. Félix „ 1820
46	Jean	(20)	Marg. Brochu S.G. 1809
	Reine		Ls. Fortier S.F.S. 1843
	Simon		
	André		
47	Guillaume	(20)	Marg. Pepin S.Chs. 1807
	Guillaume		
48	Laurent	(20)	Rose Aubin S.G. 1814
	Abraham		
49	Joseph	(21)	Marie Roy S.G. 1804
	Marie		Frs. Bruneau „ 1824
	Le même		Angé Leclaire „ 1823
50	François	(21)	M, Genev. Fradet
			S.M. 1817
51	André	(23)	M.Anne Ruel S.Chs. 1805

BACQUET- LAMONTAGNE.

	Marie		Jacq. Garant	S.G. 1826
52	Louis	(23)	Véronique Pelchat	S.G. 1816
			S. Anselm	
	Edward			
53	Ambroise	(25)	M. Thérèse Polequin	S.M. 1839
54	Jean	(26)	M. Mathilde Couët	S.M. 1853
55	Simon	(28)	Cath. Brodrique	B. 1839
			V. de Denis Favard	
56	Joseph	(35)	Genev.CorriveauS.M	1829
57	André	(35)	Adé Bétil	S.M. 1831
58	François	(35)	M. Anne Roussel	S.M. 1832
	M. Mathilde		Pierre Corriveau	" 1851
	M. Flore Délima		Romuald Bacqut	" 1857
	M. Jos. Philomène		Marjorique Roy	B. 1858
	Annibal			
59	JeanBaptiste(35)		M. Susanne Bélanger	F.S.M. 1843
	Marie Sally		André Hélie	S.M. 1862
	Delphine		Nap. Pacquet	" 1863
	Jacques			
60	Honoré	(35)	M. Angèle Philomène Lacroix	S.M. 1854
61	Michel	(37)	M. Sophronie Roy	S.V. 1858
62	Michel,fils de Jos et de Mad. Doriveau, dit Lafleur Luce		M. Anne Dabouville	G. 1884
63	Michel	(40)	Jean Jobin Marcelline Morin	B.B. 1844 S.M. 1815
64	Joseph	(40)	Mathilde Martineau	S.M. 1835
	Olympe		Damase Gagnon	S.M 1862
65	JeanBaptiste(40)		Constance Mercier	S.M. 1843
66	Honoré	(40)	M. Eudore Cotin	S.M. 1845
67	François	(40)	Zoé Herpe	S.V. 1846
68	Romuald	(41)	M. Flore Délina Bacquet	S.M. 1851
69	Honoré	(42)	M.Elie Ruellan	S.M. 1855
70	Joseph	(43)	M. Flaviè Denis	S. Chs. 1843
	Anne		Frs.Chs.Dumas	S.M 1865
	Philomène		Romuald Morrisset	S.M. 1864
71	Honoré	(43)	Anatole Ruellan	S M 1846
72	Ferdinand	(23)	M. Anne Ange Veau	S.M. 1850
72	Simon	(46)	Reine Tradet	S.V. 1842
73	André	(46)	Luce Langlois	S.V. 1834
A	Guillaume	(47)	M. Anne Fagot, Levis	1829
75	Abraham	(48)	M.Angé Ichard	S.M.1847
76	Edward	(52)	M. Zoé Couture	S.Chs. 1842
77	François	(58)	M. Henriette Odile H. Gautron	S.M. 1856
	Aug. Annibal.			
78	Jacques	(59)	M. Delphine Corriveau	S.V. 1870

BACTAELT—BARTHEL

1	Antoine		Angé Pole Hesse	
	Antoine			
2	Antoine	(1)	M.Anne Jolin	S.F.S. 1791
	M. Angèle		Chs. Richard	" 1815
	Antoine			
3	Antoine	(2)	Ursule Morin	S.F.S. 1824
	Godfroi			
4	Godfroi		Marie Naud	S.Chs. 1858

BAILLARGEON.

1	Jean		Marg. Guillebourday	Q. 1650
	Jeanne		Jean Labreque	C.R. 1664
	"		2° Pierre Burlon	S.F. 1674
	"		3° Ant.Mondaine	S.L1681
	Jean			
	Nicolas			
	Le même		Esther Gaudreau	Q. 1666
2	Jean	(1)	Jeanne Godbout	S L 1683
	M. Madeleine		Aug. Coté	L.L. 1710
	Marie		Pierre Coté	S.P. 1707
	Nicolas			
	Jean			
3	Nicolas	(1)	Anne Crépeau	S.P. 1683
	M. Angélique		Pierre Langlois	S.L. 1701
	Paul			
	Le même		Jeanne Rouleau	S.L. 1707
	Susanne		Pierre Dumas	" 1725
	Louis			
4	Nicolas	(2)	Marg. Leclaire	S.L. 1711
	M. Madeleine		Jacq. Létourneau	" 1739
	Marguerite		Théophile Greffart	" 1755
	"		2° Ignace Martel	" 1766
	Marie		Louis Chabot	" 1763
	Joseph			
	Louis			
	Antoine			
5	Jean	(2)	Marie Denis	S.L. 1723
	M. Madeleine		Frs. Audet	" 1736
	Geneviève		Jacob Belanger	" 1740
	Le même		Cath. Isabel	" 1725
	Cécile		Pierre Labresque	" 1755
	Madeleine		Antoine Gosselin	" 1762
	Marguerite		Jos. Godbout	" 1773
	Jean			
	François			
6	Paul	(3)	M. Mad. LeRoy	S.L. 1729
7	Louis	(3)	Marie Dumas	S.L. 1739
	Charles			
	Louis			
	Nicolas			
	Charles			
8	Louis	(4)	Thérèse Dorval	S.P. 1756
	Thérèse		J. B. Rousseau	S.L. 1786
	Louis			
9	Joseph	(4)	Hélene Noël	S.P. 1754
10	Antoine	(4)	Eliz Chabot	S.L. 1763
	Euphrosine		Jos. Thivierge	S.J. 1794
	"		2° Etienne Roy	" 1816
	Jean Baptiste			
11	Jean	(5)	Gertrude Labresque	S.L. 1761
	Le même		Louise Côté	S.Chs. 1767
	Le même		VéroniqueMarotte	" 1778
12	François	(5)	Pierre Audet	S.V. 1776
	Marie		Ignace Audet	S.G. 1803
	M. Anne		Frs. Goulet	" 1812
	Judith			
	Pierre			
	Paul			
13	Charles	(7)	Judith Rouleau	
	François			
	Jean			
	Simon			
14	Nicolas	(7)	Thérèse Létourneau	S.L. 1777
	M. Josette		Louis Pouliot	" 1813
	Victoire		Guill. Audet	" 1807
	Geneviève		Jean Audet	" 1809
	Angèle		Ls. Abraham Delisle	S.L. 1811
	Marguerite		Ant. Audet	" 1819
	Nicolas			
15	Louis	(7)	M.Chs.Audebert	S.J.1779
	Marguerite		Jos. Lefebvre	S.H. 1807
	Charlotte		Alexis Longchamp	" 1812

BAILLARGEON.

M. Françoise		Pierre Longchamp	,, 1816
Louis			
Nicolas			
16 Jean		Véronique Clement	
			S.Chs. 1812
Véronique			
Paul			
Charles			
17 Louis	(8)	Marie Nadeau S.Chs.	1785
Marie		J. B. Goulet	S.G. 1809
"		2° Ant. Coriveau	,, 1816
Madeleine		Paul Baillargeon	,, 1815
Rosalie		Léon Gosselin	,, 1827
Geneviève		J. B. Brisson	,, 1829
18 JeanBaptiste	(10)	Marg. Couture S.G.	1796
Marguerite		Frs. Roy	,, 1822
Pierre			
Jean			
Alexis			
Ambroise			
19 Pierre	(12)	CharlottePaquet S.G.	1812
Le même		Marie Clement	,, 1844
20 Paul	(12)	Mad. Baillargeon	,, 1815
21 Charles	(7)	Marie Canac	S.H. 1792
Jean			
Charles			
22 Louis		Marg. Charrier	S.H. 1815
Le même		Rose Vallière	S.G. 1829
A Nicolas	(15)	M. Jos. Canac	S.H. 1809
23 François	(13)	M. Ls. Langlois	
			Cap St. Ign. 1797
Charles François		Né le 26 avril 1798—Evê-	
			que de Quebec.
24 Simon	(13)	Judith Lepage S.Chs.	1806
25 Jean	(13)	Marg. Lepage	,, 1808
Marguerite		Jos. Tangué	,, 1827
Emélie		Pierre Cochon	,, 1831
Angèle		Ls. Roumillard	,, 1827
Sophie		Benj. Terrien	,, 1838
Jean Baptiste			
Le même		Susanne Terrien	
			S.Chs. 1827
Zoé		Jac. Couture	,, 1848
Magloire			
26 Nicolas	(14)	Marie Delisle	S.L. 1811
Marguerite		Bruno Létourneau	,, 1850
Marcelline		Cyprien Baudoin	,, 1853
M. Soulange		Adolphe Pepin	,, 1851
Benjamin			
Joseph			
Gilbert			
27 Paul	(16)	Marg. Gourgue S.M.	1805
Apolline		Théodule Gosselin	
			S.Chs. 1827
"		2° Léonard Brochu	,, 1823
M. Louise		Barth Leclaire	,, 1831
Marie		Jean Olivier Briart	,, 1832
"		2° Frs. Charrier	,, 1853
Paul			
Charles	(16)	Marg. Perron Levis	1821
28 Pierre	(18)	Angé Jolin	S.G. 1819
29 Jean	(18)	Marie Boutin	,, 1841
30 Alexis	(18)	Ursule Langlois S.G.	1874
31 Ambroise	(18)	Cécile Paquet	S.G. 1876
32 Jean	(21)	Charlotte Rousseau	
			S.G. 1870
A Charles	(21)	Fse. Dupile	S.H. 1814
33 Jean Baptiste	(25)	M. Ls. Couture SChs	1837
M. Caroline		Chs. Bolduc	,, 1862
34 Magloire	(25)	Marg. Catellier S.M.	1842
35 Benjamin	(26)	Genev. Turgeon S.L.	1849
36 Gilbert	(26)	M. Marthe Chatigny	
			S.P. 1847
M. Célanie		Geo. Bélanger	,, 1866
37 Joseph	(26)	Rose de Lima Pepin	
			S.J. 1850
38 Paul	(27)	Eudozie Ruel S. Chs.	1832

BALAN—LACOMBE.

1 Pierre		Renée Bisitte	Q. 1672
Marie		PierreBissonnet S.M.	1692
"		Noël Laforme	,, 1701
Henriette		Chs. Dussant	,, 1693
Marguerite		Mathieu Guay	Q. 1905
Jeanne		JeanCoulombeS.Tho.	1706
Jean Baptiste			
Etienne			
Pierre			
Michel			
2 Jean Baptiste	(1)	Jeanne Maillou	B. 1699
Jean Baptiste			
Le même		Marie Vandet	S.M. 1716
M. Anne		Jos. Goupy	,, 1749
Joseph			
Gabriel			
3 Michel	(3)	Mad. Turmel	Q.
Michel			
Le même		M. Chs. Savard	
			Chs. Bourg. 1726
4 Pierre	(1)	Eliz. Chartier S.Frs.	1708
Joseph			
Le même		Eliz. Pepin	S. Frs. 1715
Michel			
5 Etienne	(1)	Mad. Brassard	Q. 1710
6 Jean Baptiste	(2)	Marg. Hélie	S. V. 1729
7 Joseph	(2)	Hélène Chamberlan	
			S.M. 1748
Thérése		Ant. Gondreau	
			S. Tho. 1786
8 Gabriel	(2)	M. Fse. Goupy S.M.	1752
Marguerite		Frs. Coté	,, 1788
Françoise		Pierre Dion S. Chs.	1786
Madeline		Simon Bisson	,, 1787
Joseph			
Antoine			
9 Michel	(3)	Madeleine Pepin	
			S. Frs. 1752
10 Joseph	(4)	M. Anne Coulombe	
			Bert. 1736
M. Josette		J. B. Nadeau	,, 1761
M. Anne		Pierre Basquet Bert.	1766
Marguerite		Nicolas Fradet	,, 1771
Françoise			
Joseph			
Pierre			
Le même		M. Chs. Quéret Bert.	1756
M. Charlotte		Michel Patry	,, 1778
		2° Aug. Mercier S.M.	1787
Jean Baptiste			
Charles			
11 Michel	(4)	M. Anne Aubé Bert.	1759
Marie		Esidore Guilmet	,, 1794
Charles			
13 Joseph	(8)	M. Mad. Momeny	
			S.M. 1795
Le même		M. Fse. Rouleau	,, 1800
14 Joseph	(10)	M. Jos. Carbonneau	
			Bert. 1765
M. Josette		Jos. Gantron S.V.	1787
M. Marthe		Jos. Nadeau	,, 1787
M. Ursule		Pierre Roy	,, 1801
M. Victoire		Gab. Belanger	,, 1803
Marie		Frs. Roy	,, 1807
Marguerette		Pierre Veau	,, 1811
Françoise			
Joseph			
15 François	(10)	M. Anne Simart	
			S.M. 1771
M. Anne		Aug. Dorval S.V.	1794
M. Charlotte		Jos. Denis	,, 1796
M. Angélique		Etn. Roy	,, 1799
Le même		M. Ls. Leclair	,, 1788
M. Louise		Pierre Fortin S.V.	1813
16 Pierre	(10)	Mary Blais	Bert. 1783
Marie		Pierre Hebert	,, 1801
Charlotte		Isidore Bernier	,, 1815

BALAN--LACOMBE.

	Pierre			
17	Jean Baptiste(10)	Marie Chamberlan	S.M.	1789
	Jean Baptiste			
	Joseph			
19	Charles (10)	M. Mad. Fournier	S. Tho.	1778
	M. Elizabeth	Frs. Paquet Bert.	1798	
	M. Angéle	Ls. Mercier "	1812	
	M. Françoise	Jos. Talon "	1814	
	"	2° Marcel Kersack	S.P.S.	1817
20	Charles (11)	M. Hélène Gosselin	S.V.	1798
	Geneviéve	Frs. Delanteigne S.G.	1845	
	Hélène	Jos. Délanteigne "	1828	
	Adélaïde	Ls. Goulet "	1829	
21	Joseph (14)	M. Cath. Gautron	S.M.	1787
	M. Catherine	Ant. Asselin S.V.	1812	
	"	2° Prisque Fiset S.M.	1825	
	M. Archange	Laurent Fortier S.V.	1823	
	M. Victoire	Basile Blouin "	1823	
	Féréal			
	Françoise			
	Le même	M. Archange Bouten	S.V.	1812
	Barthélemi			
22	François (14)	M. Jos. Roy S.V.	1797	
	François Xavier			
23	Antoine (8)	Eliz. Lebel S.Tho.	1794	
	Antoine			
	Louis			
24	Charles	Marg. Turgeon		
	Julie	Flavien Letellier S.V.	1833	
	Edmond			
	Francois Xavier			
	Prudent			
25	Pierre (16)	Marg. Bernier S.F.S	1813	
26	Jean Baptiste(17)	Marg. Bacquet S.G.	1815	
27	Joseph (17)	Archange Dessaint	S.G.	1819
28	François (21)	Angèle Bouchard	S.V.	1820
29	Féréol (21)	Julie Bouchard "	1825	
30	Barthélemi (21)	Adé Cochon "	1838	
31	François Xa-(22)			
	vier	Sophie Turgeon	Beauce	1821
32	François Ré-(23)	Henriette Fortin		
	gis			
	Louis			
33	Antoine	M. Angèle Arseneau	S.M.	1816
	Flavie	Ed. Terrien "	1832	
	Le même	Marg. Cochon "	1821	
	Geneviève	Jos. Dion "	1846	
	Antoine			
34	Louis	M. Martha Plante	S.M.	1822
35	François Xa-(24)	Marg. Mercier S.P.S	1825	
	vier			
	M. Zoé	F. X. Belanger S.V.	1844	
	M. Esther	F. X. Morin "	1845	
	Hermine	Geo. Helie "	1849	
	Hélène	J. B. Huret "	1860	
36	Edouard (24)	Cecile Bouchard "	1835	
	Prudent (24)	Luce Mercier S.M.	1843	
	Louis (32)	Anastasie Terrien "	1857	
	Antoine (33)	Luce Voisin "	1854	

BARET.

1	Pierre	Mad. Bélenger C.R.	1689
	Marie	Jean Mercier S.Anne	1718
	Le même	Dorothée Vandal	

BARET.

Angélique	Ignace Emond	S.Anne	1734
"	2° Simon Turcot	S.Frs.	1759
Dorothée	Alexis Dompierre "	1746	
3 Pierre	M. Anne Compagna	S.Frs.	1775

BARILLAU.

2	Nicholas (1)	Ursule Gautron		
	M. Josette	Frs. Trahan S.Chs.	1759	
3	Antoine	Angé Thibodeau		
	Charles			
4	Charles (13)	Marie Bilodeau S.Chs	1761	
	Le même	Marg. Terrien S.G.	1792	
		V. de Guill. Fortier		
	Le même	Francoise Bolduc	S.G.	1801
		V. de Ls. Plante		

BAUDON--LARIVIÈRE.

1	Jacques	Marg Vericul S.F.	1690	
	Marie	Jacques Chrétien	S.Frs.	1713
	Jacques			
2	Jacques (1)	M.Fse. Buteau S.Frs	1731	
	Marguerite	J. B. Bidet "	1757	
	Marie	Jos. Coté S.P.	1755	
	François			
	Jean			
3	Francois (2)	Reine Chrétien S.Frs	1745	
4	Jean (2)	Hélène Pepin "	1754	
	Thérése	Jos. Martineau "	1778	
	Marie	Jacq. Gagné S.F.	1810	
	Jacques			
	Joseph			
5	Jacques (4)	Josette Asselin Q.	S.F.	1791
	Jean			
6	Joseph (4)	M. Ls. Terrien S.J.	1784	
	Jean (5)	Brigitte Dalaire Lévis	1827	

BAUDOIN.

1	Jacques	Fse. Durand		
	Françoise	Pierre Blais		
	Jacques			
	Louis			
	Marie			
2	Jacques (1)	Cath. Morin S.Tho.	1699	
	M. Françoise	Frs. Marseau Bert.	1729	
	Marguerite	Jacq. Marseau "	1730	
	Jacques			
	Joseph			
3	Louis (1)	Angé Roy S.M.	1705	
	Angélique	Gab. Blouin S.Frs.	1739	
	M. Madeleine	Jos. Frs. Dandurand	Bert.	1729
	Geneviève	Claude Coté Q	1728	
	Joseph			
4	Marc (1)	Eliz. Lapage S.Frs.	1711	
	M. Thécle	Jos. Buteau "	1736	
	Catherine	Frs. Turcot "	1742	
	Germain			
	Joseph			
5	Jacques (2)	Marg. Mercier	S.Anne	1727
	Jacques			
6	Joseph (2)	Mad. Leclaire S.L.	1730	
	M. Louise	Frs. Gaudin Bert.	1758	
	Marie	Chs. Rousseau "	1762	
	François			
	Jacques			
	Joseph			

BAUDOIN.

BAUDOIN.

Le même		Marg. Guay	B. 1744
François			
Le même		Marg. Lacasse S.Chs.1763	
7 Pierre		Genev. Talbot	
M. Fse. Osithe		J. B. Roy	S.F.S. 1762
Scolastique		Jos. Gendron	1773
Geneviève		Rém.i Fouillet	1781
Marie		Jos. Danian	1784
Jacques			
Jacques François			
Antoine			
Louis			
François			
Pierre			
8 Joseph	(3)	Marg. Boutin Bert. 1749	
Le même		Angé. Gaudin S.F.S. 1754	
M. Osite		Jos. Garant	„ 1784
"		2° Ign. Noël	„ 1813
M. Josette		Jacq. Garant	„ 1798
M. Louise		Ant. Morin	S.M. 1794
Joseph			
Jean Baptiste			
Antoine			
9 Germain	(4)	M. Ls. Thibault	
			S. Tho. 1739
Germain			
Joseph			
10 Joseph	(4)	M. Mad. Toupin S.R.1745	
Madeleine		Ls Gosselin	S.Frs.1763
Catherine		Jean Marie Talon „ 1775	
Ursule		Aug. Genchereau „ 1879	
Joseph			
11 Jacques		M. Angé. Picard	
			S.P.S. 1752
M. Josette		Jos. Boutin	S.F.S. 1779
Louis			
Le même		M. Genev. Vermet	
			Bert. 1759
M. Isabelle		Ant. Morin	S.F.S.1781
Marguerite		Ls. Boutin	„ 1788
"		2° Basile Dionne „ 1806	
M. Thérèse		Frs. Roy	1801
André			
Louis			
Jacques			
12 Joseph	(6)	M. Genev. Rolandeau	
			S.P.S. 1754
M. Josette		Pierre Isabel S.F.S. 1782	
Nicolas			
Jacques			
Joseph			
Le même		Genev. Picard S.F.S.1780	
M. Geneviève		Pierre Tangué „ 1798	
François			
Joseph			
13 Jacques	(6)	M. Thérèse Bois-	
		sonneau	S.E.S. 1761
M. Thérèse		Jos. Marie Que-	
		meneur	Bert. 1782
M. Catherine		Jacq. Rémillard „ 1789	
Madeleine		Pierre Mercier „ 1797	
M. Josette		Ls. M. Binnal „ 1798	
M. Elizabeth		Pierre Guilmet „ 1804	
Jacques			
François			
Le même		M. Ursule Tangué	
			Bert. 1804
14 François (1er M.)	(6)	Genev. Marcoux S.M.1765	
Alexandre			
François			
Jean Baptiste			
Le même		M. Pelaque Labrecque	
			S.H. 1791
15 François (2 m)	(6)	Marie Viger S.Chs. 1476	
Pierre			

François			
16 Pierre	(7)	Angé Paré	S.F.S.1765
M. Geneviève		Frs. Mathieu	„ 1798
M. Théotiste		André Rolandeau „ 1801	
Pierre			
Louis			
17 Antoine	(7)	M. Angé. Gagnon	
			S.F.S. 1772
Marguerite		J. B. Gagnon	„ 1819
M. Josette		Pierre Catellier	„ 1811
Joseph Marie			
Louis			
Pierre			
Jean Baptiste			
18 Jacques Fran-	(7)	M. Thérèse Thibault	
çois			S.F.S. 1773
Le même		M. Genev. Boutin	1779
M. Reine		Ls Isaac Turcot S.V. 1808	
Pierre			
Germain			
19 François	(7)	Fse. Fregeot S.F.S. 1775	
Marguerite		Jean Coté	„ 1805
François		J. B. Patry	1806
Louise		Jacq. Catellier	1808
Le même		M. Barbe Gaudin	1801
Joseph			
20 Louis	(7)	M. Ls. Lemieux	
			S.F.S. 1781
M. Louise		Pierre Leclair	1843
Louis			
21 Jean Baptiste	(8)	M. Ls Picard S.F.S. 1786	
Adelaïde		Jos. Noël	S.V.1815
M. Louise		Ant. Riciard	„ 1815
M. Françoise		Isidore Corriveau „ 1817	
Marguerite		Chs. Brochu	„ 1823
Rosalie		Isidore Boileau S.G. 1818	
M. Archange		Ls. Roy	S.F.S. 1831
Jean Baptiste			
22 Antoine	(8)	M. Jos. Blais S.F.S. 1789	
Marguerite		Jacq. Cochon	1833
Marie		Jacq. Roy	1841
Joseph			
23 Joseph	(8)	M. Anne Asselin S.M.1789	
24 Germain	(9)	M. Jos. Buteau Bert. 1770	
Germain			
Le même		M.Chs. Gosselin S.H.1777	
25 Joseph	(9)	Marg. Dumas S.F.S. 1781	
M. Thècle		Pierre Martineau	
			Bert. 1804
Marie		Jos. Mercier	„ 1807
Paul			
Jean Baptiste			
Joseph			
26 Joseph	(10)	Genev. Asselin S.Frs.1778	
Marie		Chs. Maranda	„ 1799
Catherine		Frs. Gosselin	„ 1799
M. Louise		Michel Emond	„ 1817
27 François		Susanne Hallé	
M. Louise		Pierre Hélie	S.H. 1806
Thérèse		Pierre Daniau S.H. 1802	
		2° Jean Ruel	„ 1819
Catherine		Isaac Fortier	„ 1819
François			
Germain			
Marc			
28 Louis	(11)	M. Ls. Jolivet S.F.S.1785	
M. Anne		Eustache Doiron S V 1819	
Louise		Jos. Roy	„ 1822
Joseph			
Louis			
29 Jacques	(11)	M. Anne Gautron	
			S. H. S.F.S. 1788
Pierre			
Jacques			
Jérome			
Abraham			

BAUDOIN.

Felix
Noël
30 Louis (2ᵐ m) (11) M. Anne Roy S.Tho. 1793
Charles
31 Andre (11) Cath. Roy S. V. 1795
Archange Amb. Gagnon ,, 1846
Louis
32 Jacques (12) M. Ls. Blais S.F.S. 1787
Françoise Aug. Roy S.V. 1812
  ,, 2° F.X.Boivin S.F.S. 1844
M. Louise Jos. Brousseau S.V. 1817
Marguerite Etn. Roy ,, 1845
Jean Baptiste
Jacques
33 Joseph (12) M. Agathe Terrien
  S.F.S. 1787
34 Nicolas (12) N. Ls. Guilmet S.V. 1797
Angèle Jean Boissonneau ,, 1839
M. Esther J. B. Roy ,, 1840
David
Nicolas
André
Florent
Hubert
35 Joseph (2ᵐ) (12) Angé Pouliot S.H. 1814
36 François (12) M. Julie Goupy S.M. 1809
Ls. Anselme
François
Le même Marg. Labreque
  S.Chs. 1825
37 François (13) Louis Langlois S.F.S.1698
Thérèse Aug. Larrivé Bert. 1831
Louise Ignac. Quemeneur
  Bert. 1837
Germain
38 Jacques (13) M. Anne Blais Bert. 1801
M. Adélaide Aug. Lessart ,, 1830
Paschal
Jacques
39 François (14) Marg. Pilote S.H. 1789
Le même Marg. Boulet S.V. 1810
40 Alexandre Marie Roy S.M. 1798
  S.H.
41 JeanBaptiste(14) Marie Polequin S.H. 1807
42 François Marg. Gosselin S.G. 1805
Marguerite Etn. Réaume S.Chs. 1832
43 Pierre (15) M.Anne Tailleur S.P.1817
Domitille Aug. Cantin ,, 1841
Edilise Aug. Nolin ,, 1843
44 Louis (16) Fse. Fournier S.F.S. 1797
M. Françoise Lambert Moren ,, 1816
M. Eléonore Jos. Fournier ,, 1826
Luce Marguerite Frs. Fradet ,, 1829
Anastasie Tho. Quemeneur ,, 1840
45 Pierre (16) M. Ange Mathieu
  S.P.S. 1797
Euphrosine Jules Isidore Blanchet
Anastasie S.P.S. 1832
46 Pierre (17) Susanne Chartier
  S.F.S. 1797
Claire Jos. Leclaire S.H. 1821
Le même Angé Gosselin ,, 1813
47 Louis (17) Angèle Talbot ,, 1811
48 Joseph Marie(17) M. Genev. Rémillard
  S.V. 1812
49 JeanBaptiste(17) Rosalie Quemeneur
  S.F.S. 1822
50 Pierre (18) Marie Thivierge
  S.F.S. 1803
Marcelline Hubert Jolin S.V. 1828
Rose Ls. Roy ,, 1822
Brigitte Frs. Gosselin ,, 1842
Fabien
Pierre
51 Germain (18) M. Adé Morin S.Tho 1810
Flavie Ephrem Jolin S.V. 1830

BAUDOIN.

M. Jeanne Ls. Bernard S.V. 1845
Germain
52 Joseph (19) Marie Morin S.F.S 1803
Marcelline Ls. Campagna ,, 1836
53 Louis (20) Marg. Paquet S Chs 1820
M. Angèle Pierre Lainé 1841
Le même Adé Couture 1845
54 JeanBaptiste(21) Angèle Dalaire S.V. 1825
Zoé Paschal Corriveau ,, 1853
55 Joseph (22) Archange Boutin
  S.F.S. 1827
56 Germain (24) Rosalie Gagné S.H. 1790
M. Rose J. B. Gosselin S.H. 1815
François Xavier
Ambroise
57 Joseph Marie(25) Fse. Létourneau
  S.P.S. 1803
Joseph
François Xavier
58 JeanBaptiste(25) M. Anne Dion Bert. 1809
François Xavier
59 Paul (25) Rosalie Talon S.Tho. 1819
Le même M. Anne Gosselin
  S.F.S. 1829
60 Germain (27) M. Archange Nadeau
  S.H. 1807
Le même Cath. Fortier S H. 1810
Le même Marg. Lacasse S.Chs,1830
61 François (27) Marie Nadeau S.H. 1805
62 Marc (27) M. Ls. Blouin S.H. 1815
63 Louis (28) Marg. Rousseau S.V.1812
Anastasie Michel Lacroix 1848
Michel
Hubert
64 Joseph (28) M. Genev. Gagnon
  S.V. 1823
65 Pierre (29) M. Jos. Catellier
  S.M. 1813
66 Jacques (29) Athalie Dalaire S.G. 1815
67 Noël (29) Reine Gagné S.H. 1815
Noël Prudent
Joseph
68 Abraham (29) Hélène Asselin S.G. 1820
69 Félix (29) Angé Roy S.G. 1830
70 Jérôme (29) Marie Gosselin
  S.Chs. S. Marie 1833
71 Charles (30) Thérèse Filteau B. 1834
72 Louis (31) Genev. Bolduc S.M. 1836
73 André Reine Patry S.H.
Nicolas
74 Joseph Angé Aubé
Honoré
75 Jacques (32) M. Anne Corriveau
  S.G. 1822
76 JeanBaptiste(32) Marie Jolin S.V. 1834
77 André (34) Marg. Quemenuer
  S.F.S. 1836
Louis
78 Florent (34) Marg. Morin S.V. 1836
79 Hubert (34) M. Zoé Dalaire S.V. 1840
80 Nicolas (34) Archange Jolin S.V. 1840
81 David (34) Marie Gagné S.V. 1843
23 LouisAnselm(36) Luce Clement S.M. 1842
83 François (36) M.AnneGagnonS.M.1845
84 Germain (37) Cath. Asselin S.Frs. 1830
85 Jacques (38) Marie Rosalie Bert. 1823
86 Paschal (38) Marie Paquet Bert. 1830
87 Fabien (50) Marcelline Martineau
  S.F.S 1844
88 Pierre (50) Marcelline Blanchet
  S.V. 1852
89 Germain (51) Isabelle McNeil
  S.V. 1840
90 Ambroise (56) Apolline Morriset
  S.H. 1820
Apolline David Audet S.L. 1854

BAUDOIN.

Vitaline		Frs. Pouliot	S.L. 1858
"		2·Frs. Coulombe	S.L.1867
Cyprien			
91 François Xavier	(56)	M. Ls. Aubé	S.Chs. 1820
92 Joseph	(57)	Mad. Labbé	S.Frs. 1829
93 François Xavier	(57)	Eulalie Blais	Bert. 1839
94 François Xavier	(58)	M. Mathilde Mercier	S.M. 1845
Le même		Adé Vien	S.M. 1855
95 Michel	(63)	Euphrosine Lemieux	S.V. 1840
96 Hubert	(63)	Luce Gontier	S.V. 1850
97 Joseph	(67)	Marie Marcoux	S.Chs. 1847
98 Noël Prudent	(67)	Henriette Labrecque	B. 1849
99 Nicolas	(73)	Marie Pénin	S.Chs. 1853
100 Honoré	(74)	Philomène Fournier	S.Chs. 1861
101 Louis	(77)	Philomène Bernier	S.Chs. 1862
102 Cyprien	(90)	Marcelline Baillargeon	S.L. 1853

BAZIN.

1 Pierre		Marg. Leblanc	Q. 1670
Marguerite		J. B. Roy	S.M. 1698
Angelique		Gull Roy	
François			
2 François	(1)	Fse. Cadrin	S.M. 1701
M. Thérèse		J. B. Asselin	S.V. 1728
Jean Baptiste			
Louis			
3 Jean Baptiste	(2)	Angé Ratté	S.P. 1744
M. Claire		Robert Robertson	S.V. 1764
Marie		Frs. Deblois	S.H. 1791
Jean			
Antoine			
4 Louis	(2)	Charlotte Ricasse	S.V.1744
M. Charlotte		Frs. Pouliot	S.Chs. 1769
Augustin			
Louis			
5 Jean	(3)	M. Angé. Asselin	S.V.1774
M. Angélique		Jos. Dorval	" 1798
M. Charlotte		Frs. Marceau	" 1798
6 Antoine		M. Chs. Roy	" 1779
M. Charlotte		Michel Clavet	" 1805
Rosalie		Jean Marie Roy	" 1805
M. Julie		Nic Bernard	" 1814
M. Anne		J. B. Turgeon	" 1814
M. Biliane		Pierre Leclaire	" 1842
Antoine			
7 Louis	(4)	Marie Gendreau	S.L. 1723
Thérèse		Olivier Bétel	S.Chs. 1800
8 Augustin	(4)	Genev. Quéret	" 1778
Catherine		Ls. Labrecque	" 1799
9 Joseph		Angé Gagné	
Le même		Marie Blouin	S.H. 1812
10 Antoine	(6)	M.Marg.Talbot	S.Tho.1801
M. Marguerite		Guill. Lemieux	Bert. 1831
M. Charlotte		Jos. Gaulin	S.V. 1835
Caroline		J. B. Dubreuil	" 1843
Anastasie		Aug. Morin	" 1846
11 Antoine		M. Marg. Blais	S.H.
12 M. Reine		Magl. Ferlent	S.P. 1849

BEAUCHER—MORENCY.

1 Guillaume	Marie Paradis	Q. 1656
Marie	Frs. Racine	S.F. 1676
Louise	Pierre Asselin	" 1674

BEAUCHER—MORENCY.

Louise		2° Nic Leblond	S.F. 1696
Marguerite		Chs. Leclaire	" 1696
Claire		Jean Clavet	" 1684
"		2° Jean Valière	S.P. 1700
Martin			
Guillaume			
Joseph			
2 Martin	(1)	Thérèse Gaulin	S.F. 1686
3 Guillaume	(1)	Marie Asselin	" 1694
Marie		Frs. Bilodeau	" 1717
Dorothée		Jean Trépanier	" 1728
Geneviève		Clement Fortier	S.J.1732
Guillaume			
Joseph			
Hilaire			
4 Joseph	(1)	Marthe Lemieux	Cap St. Ignace 1698
Marth		Jean Guion	S.F. 1719
Angéliq'ie		Jos. Gendron	" 1775
M. Brigitte		Jos. Guion	" 1730
M. Thècle		Jacq. Pichel	" 1733
M. Josette		Ls. Pichel	" 1733
Basile			
Joseph			
5 Guillaume	(3)	Eliz. Gendron	" 1726
Angélique		J. B. Premont	" 1756
Gertrude		Jacq. Drouin	" 1764
Joseph			
Le même		Genev. Duouin	" 1756
6 Hilaire	(3)	Fse. Simon	" 1728
Louise		Frs. Gagnon	" 1748
"		2° Ign Avase	" 1758
Augustin			
Le même		M. Jos. Gagnon	" 1749
7 Joseph	(3)	Genev. Huot	A.G. 1737
Angélique		Jos. Alex. Girard	B. 1759
Dorothée		Ant. Turgeon	" 1763
Geneviève		Frs. Turgeon	" 1764
Marguerite		J. B. Fournier	" 1785
M. Josette		Jean Couture	S.M. 1771
"		2° Jos. Patry	" 1783
Guillaume			
Joseph			
Jacques			
Michel			
8 Basile	(4)	M. Jos. Guion	S.F. 1734
Thérèse Gertrude		J. B. Cornelier	" 1763
M. Anne		Aug. Roy	Q. 1791
Alexandre			
Charles			
Pierre			
Basile			
9 Joseph	(4)	M. Genev. Aubé	S.V. 1735
Basile			
André			
10 Joseph	(5)	M. Marthe Loignon	S.F. 1758
M. Anastasie		Basile Deblois	" 1780
Louise		Ign. Faucher	" 1799
Thérèse		Frs. Deblois	" 1799
Pierre			
11 Augustin	(6)	M. Cath. Canac	" 1762
M. Catherine		Jos. Vericue	" 1807
Lazare			
Joseph			
François			
Jacques			
Le même		Marie Ruel	S.L. 1786
Ignace			
12 Joseph	(7)	M. Anne Turgeon	S.F. 1775
13 Guillaume	(7)	M.Angé.Turgeon	S.M.1772
M. Angélique		Jos. Abraham Danguenger	B. 1797
Marguerite		Ls. Provost	" 1805
Rosalie		Chs. Labresque	" 1805

BEAUCHER—MORENCY.

	Guillaume			
	Joseph			
	Gabriel			
14	Jacques		M. Fse. Adam	B. 1781
	M. Angélique		Michel Letellier	„ 1802
	Jacques			
15	Michel	(7)	M. Anne Turgeon	„ 1793
	Julie Eléonore		Ignace Fiset	B. 1814
16	Charles	(8)	Dorothée Drouin	S.F.1757
17	Basile		M.Fse.Picard	S.F.S. 1758
	M. Francoise		Jérome Paré	„ 1783
	M. Madeleine		Ls. Gagné	„ 1784
	Marguerite		Jos. Carbonneau	„ 1793
	Pierre Réné			
	Jacques			
	Basile			
	Jean Baptiste			
	Joseph			
	Louis			
18	Pierre	(8)	Marie Audet	S.L. 1777
19	Alexandre	(8)	M. Anne Leclaire	„ 1777
	M. Victoire		Basile Canac	S.F. 1807
	M. Josette		Pierre Faucher	„ 1877
	Alexandre			
	Jean			
20	André	(9)	Mad. Boutin	Bert. 1763
	Le même		Genev. Mercier	„ 1807
21	Basile	(9)	M. Genev. Morin	S.P.S. 1775
	M. Josette		Chs. Abraham Roy	S.V. 1807
	Geneviève		J. B. Bilodeau	Bert. 1808
	Marguerite		Jacq. Mercier	„ 1812
	Joseph			
	Basile			
	Louis			
	François Xavier			
22	Pierre		M. Jos. Roberge	S.P 1793
	Marguerite		Ign. Paradis	S F. 1824
	M. Josette		Frs. Gagnon	„ 1824
	Catherine		Frs. Gagnon	„ 1829
	M. Ludivine		Jos. L'heureux	„ 1832
	Henriette		Ls. L'heureux	„ 1840
	Thérèse		Ed. Lavoie	„ 1835
	Louise		Celestin Poulin	„ 1844
	Pierre			
	Joseph			
23	Pierre		Anastasie Asselin	S. Marie
	Le même		M. Mélanie Vaillancour	S.T. 1827
24	Francois	(11)	Genev. Foucher	S.F. 1795
	Marie		Michel Drouin	„ 1827
	Angèle		Barth. Deblois	„ 1831
	Francois			
	Joseph			
	Augustin			
25	Jacques	(11)	Cath. Foucher	S.F. 1800
			S. Marie	
26	Joseph	(11)	Abondance Asselin	S.F. 1801
27	Lazare	(11)	Angèle Paradis	S.P. 1845
28	Ignace	(11)	Reine Pichet	„ 1812
	Le même		Marg. Plante	„ 1821
	M. Léocadie		Ferd. Drouin	„ 1852
29	Guillaume	(13)	M. Ls. Dangucuger	S.Chs. 1803
	Le même		Agathe Labrecque	B 1805
	Emérance		F. X. Corriveau	„ 1839
	Magloire			
	Fabien			
	Joseph			
	Gabriel			
	Cyprien			

BEAUCHER—MORENCY.

30	Joseph	(11)	M. Archange Richard	B. 1815
	Flavie		Chs. Ed. Turgeon	„ 1841
	Mathild		Didase Patry	„ 1845
	Jos. Théophile			
31	Gabriel	(13)	M. Félicité Guay	Lévis. 1826
	M. Scholastique		Etn. Couture	B. 1846
32	Jacques	(14)	Marg. Turgeon	„ 1810
	Marguerite		Jos. Mercier	„ 1833
	M. Fermine		Philippe Vien	„ 1835
	M. Desange		Ludger Buellan	„ 1853
	Luce Anastasie		Geo. Audet	S.R. 1844
	Francois Apol-linaire			
	Jean Stanislas			
	Jacques Georges			
33	Basile	(17)	M. Jos. Chartier	S.F.S. 1785
	Pierre			
	Le même		M. Ls. Gagnon	„ 1799
	Jean Baptiste			
34	Pierre Réné	(17)	M. Judith Chartier	S.F.S. 1792
	M. Julie		Jos. Blais	S.P.S. 1815
35	Joseph	(17)	M. Ls. Rouleau	S F.S. 1795
	Joachim			
	Jacques			
36	Jacques	(17)	M. Marg. Denis	S.Chs. 1800
	Angèle		André Brochu	„ 1822
37	Jean Baptiste	(17)	Pélagie Audet	S.F.S 1801
	Pilagie		Ls. Tangué	S.V. 1829
	M. Angèle		Jos. Rémillard	„ 1829
	Jean Baptiste			
38	Angèle	(17)	Eliz. Boutin	Bert. 1808
39	Alexandre		Fébronnie Martineau	S.T. 1801
40	Jean	(19)	Hélène Martineau	S.F. 1807
	Flavie		Jos. Asselin	„ 1837
	Eustache			
	Jean			
	François			
41	Basile	(21)	M. Rosalie Blais	Bert 1806
42	Joseph	(21)	M. Anne Nadeau	S.V.1810
43	Louis	(21)	Sophie Proulx	Bert. 1828
44	François	(21)	Apolline Carbonneau	Bert. 1843
	Xavier			
45	Pierre	(22)	Marie Savoie	S.F. 1824
	Joseph			
	Pierre			
46	Joseph	(24)	Genev. Prémont	S.F.1846
	Justine		Abraham Letourneau	S.F. 1856
	„		2? Alexis Lamothe	S.F. 1863
	Anastasie		F. X. Faucher	„ 1856
	Léocadie		Jos. Drouin	„ 1819
	Adelaïde		Ls. Drouin	„ 1862
	François Xavier			
	Joseph			
47	François	(24)	M. Anne Boissonneau	S.F. 1820
	Mathilde		J. B. Drouin	„ 1848
	François Xavier			
48	Joseph	(24)	Scholastique Letourneau	S.F. 1831
49	Augustin	(24)	Marg. Asselin	„ 1834
	Philomène		Frs. Letourneau	„ 1857
	Le même		Luce Ferland	„ 1848
50	Joseph	(29)	Cécile Filteau	B. 1837
51	Gabriel	(29)	Hélène Turgeon	B. 1838

BEAUCHER—MORENCY.

52	Fabien	(29)	Hermine Turgeon B. 1841
53	Magloire	(29)	M. Angé. Labrecque B. 1846
54	Cyprien	(29)	M. Félicité Patry B. 1851
55	Jos.Théophile	(30)	M. Délima Couture S. Chs. 1851
56	JeanStanislas	(22)	Marie Thibault S.R. 1847
57	Jacques Georges	(32)	M. Séraphin Turgeon B. 1850
58	Frs. Apolli- naire	(32)	Eulalie Caroline Turgeon B. 1850
59	Pierre	(33)	M. Ls Bégin S.H. 1813
60	JeanBaptiste Marcelline	(33)	Ursule Boivin S.F.S.1823 Didace Naud S.Chs. 1850
61	Joachim	(35)	Marg. Nadeau Lévis 1825
62	Jacques	(35)	Cath. Campagna F.R.S. 1833
63	JeanBaptiste	(37)	Julie Daniau S.F.S. 1823
64	Jean	(40)	Marie Asselin S.F.1837
65	Eustache Le même Joséphine	(40)	Adé Letourneau „ 1839 Luce Asselin „ 1842 Phileas Leblond „ 1865
66	François	(40)	Mathilda Isabelle Letourneau S.F. 1842
	Joseph Le même		SéraphinLeblondS.F.1855
67	Pierre	(45)	Justine Drouin „ 1855
68	Joseph	(45)	MarcellineDeblois„ 1859
69	François Xa- vier	(46)	M. Justine Dion „ 1864
70	Joseph	(46)	Cécile Drouin „ 1858
71	François Xa- vier	(47)	M. Antoinette Leblond S.F. 1845
72	Joseph	(66)	Zenaide Leblond „ 1869

BÉCHARD.

1	Louis Réné		M. Anne Vaillan- court S.F. 1691
	Anne Jacques Louis		J. B. Lepage S.M. 1737
2	Jacques Joseph	(1)	Mad. Lecours S.M. 1743
3	Louis M. Louise M. Anne M. Josette		Marie Guénet B. 1718 Ls. Côté „ 1741 Jacq. Taillon „ 1742 Jean Jacq. Guay „ 1742
4	Joseph Louis Angélique Jean Le même	(2)	M. Ls. Custeau S.G.1781 Frs. Roy „ 1810 Frs. Chouinard „ 1813
5	Jean	(4)	Ursule Couturier „ 1791 Julie Doutile „ 1810

BEDARD.

1	Isaac Jacques		Marie Girard
2	Jacques Thomas Charles François	(1)	Isabelle Doucinet 1666
3	François	(2)	Marie Auclair Chs. Brg. 1696
	Pierre		
4	Thomas	(2)	Jeanne Fse Huppé, Beauport 1707
	Jacques Joseph Paul		
5	Charles Jean Baptiste	(2)	Eliz. HuppéBeauport 1712
6	Pierre	(3)	M. Ls. Garneau Chs. Brg. 1732
7	Jacques Jo- seph	(4)	Lse. Vachon Chs.Brg.1736

BEDARD.

	Alexis		
8	Paul	(4)	Genev. Niel S.P. 1757
9	Jean Baptiste	(5)	M. Mad. Paquet Chs. Brg. 1751
	Tho. Laurent Pierre		
10	François		M. Thérèse Leclair S.P. 1664.
10ᵃ	Louis Louis		Josette Berthiaume
10ᵇ	Jean Baptiste Jean Baptiste		Thérèse Levaux
10ᶜ	François François		Angé. Paradis
10ᵈ	François Gabriel		Josette Léonard
10ᵉ	Charles Etienne Charles		Mad. Berthiaume
11	Alexis	(7)	Fse. Cliche Chs. Bourg. 1770
	Le même		Thérèse Montigny S.P. 1801
12	Louis	(10ᵃ)	Genev. Ratel Chs. Berg. 1771
	Jacques		
13	Tho. Laurent	(9)	Gertrude Gendreau S.L. 1780
	Pierre Joseph François		
14	Jean Baptiste Ambroise Jean Pierre	(10ᵇ)	M. Thérèse Ratté Chs. Brg. 1773
15	Pierre	(9)	Marg. Aubin S.P. 1788
16	Jean Geneviève		Genev. Roy Ant. Patoine S.G. 1821
17	Jacques	(12)	Angé Langevin Chs. Brg. 1804
	François		
18	François	(10ᶜ)	Scholastique Bernard Chs. Brg. 1792
	François		
19	Etienne		M. Marg. Bédard Chs. Brg. 1784
	Marguerite Agathe Marie Angélique Etienne Ambroise		Pierre Rousseau S.G.1809 Chs. Audet „ 1813 Ant. Guay „ 1820 Jos. Morin „ 1824
20	Ambroise Le même	(14)	Marg. Naud S.H. 1801 M. Osalie Baudoin S.F.S. 1813
21	Jean Jean	(14)	Fse. Valiere S.H. 1803
22	Le même Pierre	(14)	Charlotte Coté S.H. 1815 M. Ange Lasante S.H. 1800
23	Pierre Pierre		Agathe Boissonneau
24	Pierre	(13)	Marie Hebert B. 1814
25	François François	(13)	M.Jos. Crépeau S.P. 1822
26	Joseph	(13)	Marie Coulombe S.J. 1824
27	François	(17)	Anatalie Pepin S.J. 1855
28	François	(18)	M. Ls. Villeneuve Chs.Brg. 1823
	Théodore		
29	Jean Gabriel	(10ᵈ)	Fse.Quéret Chs. Brg. 1828 S. Claire
	Le même		M. Flavie Coté S.F.S.1833
30	Etienne Charles Louis	(10ᵉ)	Mad. Parent, Beauport 1823

BEDARD.

31	Louis Simon		Charlotte Bourbeau	
	Etienne Simòn			
32	Etienne	(19)	Marg. Terrien S.G.	1813
33	Ambroise	(19)	Marie Noël "	1823
34	Jean	(20)	Théotiste Dessaint	
			S.V.	1838
	Stanislas			
35	Pierre	(33)	Marie Hébert S.Frs.	1833
36	François	(25)	Scholastique Vézina	
			S.P.	1850
	Le même		Henriette Lepage	
			S.Chs.	1855
37	Théodore	(28)	M. Célina Fournier	
			S.Chs.	1854
38	Louis	(30)	Sara Naud S.Chs.	1864
39	Etienne Ver-	(31)	M. Jos. Belzemire Couet	
	non		S.M.	1865
40	Stanislas	(34)	Marie Turgeon B.	1870

BÉGIN.

1	Louis		Jeanne Durand Q.	1668
	Jacques			
	Jean Baptiste			
	Etienne			
2	Jean Baptiste	(1)	Louise Carrier, Lévis.	1714
	Charles Louis			
	Joseph			
3	Etienne	(1)	M. Genev. Rochon, Lévis	
				1722
	Charles Etienne			
	Louis			
4	Jacques	(1)	Genev. Rochon, Lévis	
				1722
5	Charles Louis	(2)	Susanne Duquet, Lévis	
				1744
	Charles			
6	Joseph	(2)	M. Anne Huot, Lévis	
				1751
	François			
	Antoine			
7	Jean Baptiste		M. Ls. Bourassa	
	Jean Baptiste			
	Le même		Gertrude Pouliot S.L.	1750
	Louis			
8	Louis	(3)	M. Genev. Lacasse B.	1753
	M. Rose		Chs. Chenier S.H.	1789
	Hélène		J.B. Turcot "	1800
	M. Charlotte		André Pilet "	1801
	Pierre			
	Antoine			
	Michel			
	Etienne			
9	Charles Etien-	(3)	Marthe Turgeon	
	ne			B. 1756
10	Charles	(5)	M. Jos. Lacasse B.	1780
11	François	(6)	M. Chs. Boilard B.	1788
12	Antoine	(6)	Reine Roberge S.P.	1793
13	Jean Baptiste	(7)	Louise Couture Lévis	1778
	M. Angelique		Ls. Turgeon "	1807
	Marguerite		Germ. Brousseau S.M.	1834
14	Joseph	(7)	Véronique Carrier Lévis	
	Joseph			
15	Michel	(8)	M. Marg. Gouillard	
				S. H. 1787
16	Etienne	(8)	M. Jos. Dion S.H.	1788
17	Pierre	(8)	M. Vict. Chabot S.V.	1804
18	Antoine	(8)	M. Ange. Chabot S V.	1804
19	François		Véronique Crépeau	
	Le même		Agathe Poiré Lévis	1804
	Emérence		Benoit Jos. Létourneau	
				B. 1852
20	Joseph		Emélie Dumont	
	Le même		Ange Guay B.	1839
21	Joseph	(14)	Euphrosine Roberge	
				S. P. 1826

BÉGIN.

22	Charles		Rosalie Samson Lévis	1832
	Charles			
23	Charles		M. Rose Pouliot S.L.	1865

BELLAY.

1	Guillaume		Jeanne Repnel	
	François			
2	François	(1)	M. Genev. Daniau	
				S.V. 1747
	Le même		Marie Freyot S.F.S.	1749
	M. Félicité		Pierre Monmemy	
				S.V. 1768
	Françoise		J. B. Martin S.V.	1774

BÉLANGER.

1	François		Marie Guion Q.	1637
	Charles			
	Louis			
	Nicolas			
	Jean François			
	Jacques			
2	Nicolas	(1)	Marie Rinville Q.	1660
	Nicolas			
3	Charles	(1)	Barbe Cloutier S.R.	1663
	Charles			
4	Jean François	(1)	Marie Cloutier S.R.	1671
	Pierre Paul			
	Jean François			
	Charles			
	Ignace			
5	Louis	(1)	Marg. Lefrançois S. R.	1682
	François			
6	Jacques	(1)	Eliz. Thibault	
				Cap. S. Ign. 1691
	François			
7	Nicolas	(2)	Marie Magnan	
				Chs. Brg. 1699
	Ignace			
	Joseph			
8	Charles	(3)	Genev. Gagnon	
				S. Anne 1692
	Prisque			
	Charles			
	Pierre			
9	Jean François	(4)	Genev. Thibault	
				Cap. S. Ign. 1699
	Ignace			
	Louis			
	Le même		M. Ls. Caron	
				Cap. St. Ign. 1736
10	Charles	(4)	Jeanne Emond	
				Cap. S. Ign. 1713
11	Ignace	(4)	Jeanne Angé. Vaillan-	
			cour Islet.	1706
	Ignace			
12	Pierre Paul	(4)	Claire Fournier	
				Cap. S. Ign. 1742
13	François	(5)	Genev. Cloutier	
				Cap. S. Ign. 1711
	Geneviève		Jean Gaudreau Islet.	1733
	François		Jos. Gaudreau "	1734
	Jean Baptiste			
14	François	(6)	Genev. Doyon A.G.	1716
15	Joseph	(7)	Cath. Lefrançois S.F.	1735
	Le même		Genev. Baillargeon	
				S.L. 1740
16	Ignace	(7)	Genev. Gagné S.V.	1746
	M. Marguerite		Isaac Langlois	
				S.P.S. 1773
	Françoise		Aug. Morin S.P.S.	1779
	M. Anne		Alexis Morin "	1784
	M. Reine		Pierre Bélanger "	1786
	François			
	Jean Baptiste			

BÉLANGER.

BÉLANGER.

17	Pierre	Genev. Lessart	
	Jean Gabriel		
18	Alexis	Genev. Lessart	
		Isle aux Coudres	
	Le même	Susanne Paquet S.L.	1793
19	Pierre	(8) Marthe Couillard	
		S. Tho.	1716
	Genev. Régis	Ls. Thibault "	1750
20	Charles	(8) Eliz. Fournier S.Tho.	1723
	Elizabeth	Jos. Coté	
	Charles		
	Louis		
21	Presque	(8) Genev. Gosselin S.L.	1724
	Marie	Pancrace Catellier	
		S.V.	1749
	Geneviève	Pierre Lacroix "	1751
	Elizabeth	Paschal Corriveau "	1760
	Jacques		
22	Louis	(9) M. Angé Vaillancour	
		Islet	1734
	Le même	Genev. Nadeau Bert.	1753
23	Ignace	(9) Marie Desmoliers	
		Islet	1738
	Le même	Helène Pepin S. Frs.	1749
24	Ignace	(11) Marg. Thibaut Islet	1735
25	Jean Baptiste	(13) Brigitte Buteau S.F.	1742
26	Joseph	M. Anne Brisson Islet	
	Jean Baptiste		
27	Jean Gabriel	(17) M. Vict. Bernier	
		Cap.S.Ign.	1758
	J. B. Prosper		
	Pierre		
28	François	(16) M. Ls. Morisset S.M.	1786
	Archange	Jos. Baquet S.M.	1806
	Guillaume		
	François		
29	Jean Baptiste	(16) M. Reine Boulet	
		S.F.S.	1785
	Agathe	Bonaventure Morin	
		S.F.S	1826
	M. Reine	J. B. Prosper Bélanger	
		S.P.S.	1812
	M. Marguerite	Jos. MarcBlais S.P.S.	1818
	"	2° Aug. Simoneau	
		S.P.S.	1833
	Pierre		
	Jean Baptiste		
30	Charles	(20) Thérèse Asselin S.V.	1751
31	Louis	(20) M. Mad. Vallée S.V.	1752
	Charles		
32	Jacques	(21) M. Anne Bolduc S.V.	1764
	Le même	M. Ls. Rousseau S.M.	1768
	Marie	André Blais S.V.	1788
	M. Josette	Denis Roy S.V.	1795
	Marguerite	Jos. Marie Couture	
		S.V.	1804
	M. Angèle	Thomas Roy S.V.	1808
	Prisque		
	Jean Baptiste		
	Jacques		
	Gabriel		
	Pierre		
33	Jean Baptiste	(26) M. Clotilde Rousseau	
		S.P.S.	1777
34	Pierre	(27) M. Reine Bélanger	
		S.P.S.	1786
35	J. Bte. Pros-	(27) M. Reine Bélanger	
	per		
		S.P.S.	1812
36	Charles	(31) M.Reine AinseS.Tho.	1777
	Paschal		
	Charles		
37	François	(28) Marie Bétie S.M.	1810
	Flavie	Jean Blais S.M.	1828
	Apolline	Frs. Dubord S.M.	1837
	Marcelline	Ls. Cadron S.M.	1842

	Prudent		
	Joseph		
38	Guillaume	(28) M. Rosalie Blais	
			S.P.S. 1819
	M. Susanne	J. B. Basquet S.M.	1843
	François		
	François Xavier		
	Le même	Eliz. Sheen S.Chs.	1840
39	Pierre	(29) M. Adé Letellier B.	1819
40	Jean Baptiste	(20) Eléonore Bernier	
			S.P.S. 1833
41	Pierre	M. Angé Perron Grondines	
	M. Angélique	Jos. Beauchamp S.V.	1820
	Joseph		
42	Joseph	M. Fse. Daneau S.Tho.	
	Marie	Ant. Gontier S.Chs.	1820
	"	2° Etn. Couture	
			S.Chs. 1841
	Augustin		
43	Jacques	Thérèse Brochu S.V.	1788
	Angèle	J. B. Boulet S.G.	1816
	Basilisse	Pierre Fradet S.G.	1821
	Soulange	Laurent Lebrun S.G	1826
	Angélique	Pierre RémillardS.G.	1826
	Prisque		
	François Xavier		
	François		
	Jacques		
	Thérèse	J. B. Rousseau S.G.	1815
44	Prisque	(32) M. Ls. Roy S.V.	1795
	Françoise	Frs. Roy S.G.	1820
	Marie	Pierre Catellier S.G.	1826
	Clarisse	Pierre Roy	
	Magloire		
	Louis		
45	Pierre	(32) Marg. Roy S.V.	1797
	Soulange	Jos. Collet S.H.	1820
	François Xavier		
	Pierre		
	Le même	M. Angé Picard	
			S.P.S. 1811
	Flavien		
46	Jean Baptiste	(32) M. Genev. Roy S.V.	1800
	M. Angèle	Ls. Catellier S.V.	1825
	"	2° Jos. Fortier S.V.	1832
	Archange	Paul Gourgue S.V.	1823
	Tho. Léonard		
	Misael		
	Laurent		
	Damase		
47	Gabriel	(32) M. Vict. Balan S.V.	1803
	Adélaïde	Reine Leclaire S.V.	1823
	Julie	Jos. Gosselin S.V.	1827
	Edouard		
	Le même	M. Annie Talbot	
			S.P.S. 1811
	Caroline	Jos. Talbot S.P.S.	1846
	M. Julie Desan-	Tinbert Valier Lame	
	ges		
			S.V. 1850
	Carmel	Théodore Turgeon	
			S.V. 1853
	Prudent		
	Henri		
	Norbert		
	Gabriel		
	François		
48	Charles	M. Claire Mignot	
			S.Tho. 1801
	Le même	M.Genev. BlaisS.Tho.	1810
	Le même	M. Vict. Simoneau	
			S.P.S. 1813
49	Paschal	(37) M. Marthe Tangué	
			S.Chs. 1808
50	Prudent	Césarie Blais S.V.	1839
51	Joseph	(37) Helène MorissetS.M.	1844

BÉLANGER.

52 François	(38)	M. Zoé Balan S. V. 1844
Xavier		
53 François	(38)	Florence Cotin S.M. 1849
54 Joseph	(41)	M. Ange Blanchet
		S. Chs. 1814
55 Augustin	(42)	M. Claire Bernier
		S.P.S. 1811
56 Jacques	(43)	Marie Corriveau S.G.1819
57 Prisque	(43)	Emérence Goulet
		S.G. 1828
58 François	(43)	Emérentinne Roy
		S.V. 1831
Joseph		
59 François	(43)	M. Emile Gosselin
Xavier		S.V. 1847
60 Magloire	(44)	Adé Roy S. G. 1830
61 Louis	(44)	Sophie Dessaint S.G. 1830
62 Pierre	(45)	M. Anne Quemineux
		S.H. 1820
63 François	(4)	Mde. Gagnon S.Chs. 1833
Xavier		
64 Flavien	(45)	Mary Roussel S.V. 1845
65 Louis		
Joseph		S. Tho.
66 François		Fse. Langlois
Jos. Clovis		
67 Jean-Baptiste		Rosalie Grenier S.
fils de J.-B. et de		Marie 1812
M. Ls. Bédard		
Gaspard		
68 Pierre		Cath. Goulet
Pierre		
69 Thos. Léo-	(46)	Julie Brochu S.V. 1826
nard		
Flore		Ludger Lemieux " 1853
Célina		Ferd. Lemieux " 1854
Julie		Adolphe Blais " 1861
Elizabeth		Jos. Michel Paré " 1861
Agnès		F. X. Coulombe " 1866
Jacob		
70 Damase	(46)	Marg Martineau
		S.F.S. 1832
M. Symphorose		Paul Bouchard S.V. 1858
Agnès		Prophile Coté " 1865
M. Egyptienne		Hilaire Quémeneux
		S.V. 1867
Joseph		
71 Misaël	(46)	Rose Dumas S.M. 1837
Le même		Célarine Fournier
		S. Chs. 1846
72 Laurent	(46)	Angé Fontaine S.V. 1834
73 Edouard	(47)	Emérentienne Roy
		S.V. 1830
Etienne		
74 Henri	(47)	Marie Gourgue S.V. 1841
Marie		Jos. Bélanger " 1870
Henri		
Le même		Sophie Roy S.V. 1855
75 Gabriel	(47)	M. Vict. Dumas S.M.1844
Le même		M. Osite Roy S.V. 1848
Le même		M.Emérence Dion " 1855
76 Norbert	(47)	Cath. Harpe S.V. 1842
M. Honorine		Henri Bélanger " 1869
M. Elise		Emilien Ruel " 1870
77 François	(47)	M. Zoé Mercier S.V. 1843
78 Prudent	(47)	Macelline Veau S.V. 1851
79 Joseph	(58)	M.Cath.Garant S.V. 1870
80 Joseph	(65)	M. Jos. Bernier
		S.P.S. 1833
81 Jos. Clovis	(66)	Céleste Arch. Perras
		S. Chs. 1835
Le même		Marie Verret " 1852
82 Gaspard	(67)	Constance Dumas
		S. Chs. 1847
83 Pierre	(68)	Sophie Coûture S.P.1857
84 Jacob	(69)	M. Lucie Roy S. Chs.1862

18—14½

BÉLANGER.

85 Joseph	(70)	Marie Bélanger S.V. 1870
86 Etienne	(73)	Philomène Letellier
87 Henri	(74)	M. Honorine Bélanger

BERGERON.

1 André		Marie Dumay
André		
Jacques		
Jean		
2 André	(1)	Marie Guernon
		Pte Temble 1694
Pierre		
3 Jean	(1)	Marg Guéron
		Pte Temble 1699
Le même		M.Mde Ferland S.P. 1711
4 Jacques	(1)	M. Ls. Guernon
		Pte Tremble 1704
5 Pierre	(2)	M. Mde Poulet S.P. 1730
6 Joseph		Marie Croteau
Joseph		
Le même		Genev. Bussière S.P. 1749
7 Joseph	(6)	Cécile Turgeon S.M. 1761
M. Charlotte		Alexander Boilard B.1791
Jean		
Joseph		
8 Jean	(7)	M. Jos. Bossière B. 1797
M. Josette		Michel Guay 1823
Geneviève		Bénoni Larivé 1833
Bénoni		
Jean-Baptiste		
9 Joseph	(7)	Marie Hélie S. Chs. 1812
10 Jean-Baptiste		Marie Guénard
M. Charlotte		Ang. Mateau 1840
M. Angèle		Alexis Gosselin 1841
M. Christine		J. B. Nadeau 1841
"		2° Evariste Baugy 1856
Joseph		
11 Athanase		Flavie Bélanger
Salem		
12 Jean Baptiste	(8)	Henriette Fontaine
		B. 1836
Le Même		M. Rosalie Duperron
		B. 1846
13 Bénoni	(8)	M. Chs. Boilard B. 1839
14 Joseph	(10)	Emélie B. 1842
15 Salem	(11)	Sara Couillard, St-
		Chs. 1860

BERNARD.

1 André		Marie Giton Q. 1676
M. Anne		Frs. Paquet S.L. 1703
Marguerite		Frs. Audet S.L. 1709
2		
3		
4		
5 Mathurin		Marie Amiot
Pierre		
6 Pierre	(5)	Genev. Giroux, Beau-
		port 1730
Jacques		
7 Jacques	(6)	M. Thérèse Lefebvre
		Chs. Brg. 1753
M. Charlotte		Eustache Fortier S.V.1786
Marguerite		Jos. Bolduc S. V. 1787
Thérèse		J. B. Bolduc S. V. 1788
Le même		M.Marthe Fredet
		S. V. 1767
Geneviève		Michel Bolduc S.V. 1789
Basilisse		Pierre Catellier S.V. 1794
M. Françoise		Chs. Dallaire S.V. 1808
Céleste		Etn. Guenet S.G. 1804
Antoine		
Jacques		

BERNARD.

8	Pierre		M. Jos. Pageot	
	Scolastique		Frs Bédard, Chs. Bourg	1792
	Michel			
9	Pierre		M. Chs. Cotin	
	Godfroi			
	Pierre			
	François			
10	Antoine	(1)	M. Ls Dutile, Bert.	1801
	Louise		Pierre Labbé S.G.	1827
11	Jacques	(1)	Marie Boulet, Bert.	1800
12	Michel	(8)	Genev. Bonnet, S.V.	1788
	Marie		Luce Cotin	1820
	M. Geneviève		Ant. Fradet	1824
	Olivier		Michel François Xavier	
	Le même		M. Ange Audet, S.V.	1817
	Pierre François			
	Joseph			
13	Pierre	(9)	M. Anne Audet, S.V.	1797
	M. Anne		Magl. Bisson S.V.	1838
	Pierre			
14	François	(9)	M. Anne Beaucher, B.	1797
15	Godfroi	(9)	M. Agathe Cochon, S.V.	1802
	Michel			
	Louis			
16	Charles		M. Ange Faucher	
	M. Angélique		Aug. Larue, S.V.	1814
	Marguerite		Michel Richard	1815
	Nicolas			
	Guillaume			
	Louis			
	Le même		M. Fse. Tangué, S.V.	1814
17	Michel	(12)	M. Eliz. Blais, Bert.	1812
	Julie		Michel Mercier,S.V.	1834
	Elizabeth		Ls Mercier S.V.	1836
	"		2° Abraham Guay S.V.	1840
18	Francois X.	(12)	Marie Picard S.V.	1824
	M. Adelaide		Jos. Perrat S.V.	1843
19	Pierre Frs.	(12)	Reiné Roy S.V.	1839
	Elizabeth		Pierre Roberge S.V.	1870
	Michel			
	Pierre			
20	Olivier	(12)	Anastasie Garant S.Fs.	1833
21	Joseph	(12)	Clarisse Roy S.V.	1841
22	Pierre	(12)	Adé Chamberlan S.P.S.	1829
23	Guillaume		Genev. Guay	
	Ferd. Mathieu			
24	Rémi		Cécile Lacasse	
	Jean			
25	Michel	(15)	Sophie Lemieux S.V.	1837
26	Louis	(15)	M. Jeanne Baudoin S.V.	1845
27	Nicolas	(16)	Julie Bazin S.V.	1814
	Angélique		F. X. Tangué S.M.	1840
	Charles			
	Nicolas			
28	Louis		Archange Richard S.V.	1816
	Angélique		Jos. Leclaire S.F.S.	1841
	Le même		Marie Mercier S.V.	1820
	Esther		Pierre Boutin S.V.	1848
29	Guillaume	(16)	Archange Richard S.F.S.	1827
30	Michel	(19)	Virginie Mercier S.V.	1867
31	Pierre	(19)	M. Olympe Roy S.V.	1870

BERNARD.

32	Ferd Mathieu	(22)	Marg. Fortier S.V.	1854
33	Jean	(23)	Philomène Dalaire S.J.	1864
34	Charles	(26)	Emerence Thibaut S.V.	1835
35	Nicolas	(26)	Soulange Bouillard S.V.	1847

BÉTIL.

1	Charles		Angé. Greffart S.V.	1763
	Marie		Michel Asselin S.M.	1792
	Victoire		Jean (Plante) "	1794
	M. Angélique		Jos. Gourgue "	1794
	M. Reine		Pierre Mercier "	1805
	M. Josette		Pierre Fortin "	1791
	"		2° Chs. Pepin S.Chs	1806
	Marguerite		Jos. Goulet "	1803
	Olivier			
	Michel			
2	Michel	(1)	Marie McNeil S.M.	1784
	Marie		Frs. Belanger "	1810
	Le même		M. Fse. Mercier "	1801
	Adelaide		André Bacquet "	1831
	François		Michel Roy "	1831
	Pierre			
	Joseph			
	Edmond			
	Le même		Josette Asselin S.M.	1813
3	Olivier	(1)	Thérèse Bazin S.Chs	1800
	Luce		Ezéchiel Nolin "	1841
	Louis			
4	Joseph	(2)	Archange Roy S.Chs	1824
5	Edouard	(2)	Eliz. Pouliot S.G.	1830
	Rose		Jos. Lacroix S.M.	1857
	Elizabeth		Naz. Pouliot "	1865
6	Pierre	(2)	Anastasie Cosset "	1836
	Romuald			
7	Louis	(5)	M. Anne Mercier SG	1830
8	Romuald	(6)	Luce Lacroix S.M.	1861

BERNIER.

1	Jacques		Antoinette Grenier Q.	1656
	Philippe			
	Pierre			
	Charles			
	Jean Baptiste			
2	Pierre	(1)	Fse. Boulet S.Tho.	1689
	Pierre Basile			
	Jacques			
	Joseph			
	Jean Baptiste			
3	Charles	(1)	M. Anne Lemieux C.S.Ign.	169
	Alexandre			
	Isidore			
	André			
	Pierre			
	Charles			
4	Jean Baptiste	(1)	Genev. Caron S.Anne	1694
	Louise		Ls. Maurice Keroack C.S.Ign.	1732
5	Philippe	(1)	Ursule Caron S.Anne	1701
6	André		Jeanne Bourré Chs.Burg.	1693
	André			
7	Jacques	(2)	Eliz. Guay	
8	Jacques	(2)	Mad. Caron Islet	1738
	Madeleine		Pierre Carbonneau Islet	1757
9	Pierre Basile	(2)	M. Jos. Fortin "	1727

BERNARD.

10	Jean Baptiste (2)	Claire Fortin C.S.Ign 1734	
	Ursule	Ls. Vermet " 1764	
	Théotiste	Frs. Gagné " 1787	
11	Alexandre (3)	M. Ls. Fortin " 1723	
12	Isidore (3)	Ursule Belleau " 1726	
13	André (3)	Ange Buteau Bert. 1734	
14	Charles (3)	Genev Belanger Islet 1740	
	M. Victoire	Ls. Letourneau " 1764	
	Claire	Ls. Lemieux C.S.Ign 1761	
15	Pierre (3)	M. Ls. Guemont	
		C.S.Ign. 1742	
16	André (6)	M. Fse. Larivière Q. 1724	
	Joachim		
	Paul		
	Jacques		
17	Nicholas	Marg. Galarneau	
	Jean Baptiste		
18	Joseph	M. Cath. Bouchard S Tho	
	Véronique	Jos. Fournier S.Tho. 1759	
	Joseph		
	Charles		
19	Joseph Marie	M. Thérèse Dionne	
		C.S.Ign.	
	M. Claire	Martin Morin S.P.S 1814	
	Amable		
20	Albert	M. Genev. Adelaïde	
	Albert		
21	Basile	M. Anne Guion C.S.Ign.	
	M. Geneviève	Etn. Gaumont	
		S. Tho. 1795	
	Jean Baptiste		
22	Joachim (16)	Françoise Lis B. 1754	
	M. Anne	Ignace Ruel S.Chas. 1781	
	Françoise	Chs. Letourneau " 1785	
	Joachim		
	André		
23	Paul (16)	Thérèse Couture	
		S.Chs. 1763	
	Thérèse	Jos. Leroux " 1797	
	Françoise	Frs. Leblond " 1798	
	Marguerite	Alexis Pouliot " 1808	
	André		
	Paul		
24	Jacques (16)	Louis Reneaud	
		Chs. Brg. 1770	
	Madeleine	Berth. Terrien S.G. 1799	
	Charles		
	Jacques		
	Le Même	Marie Hébert S.G. 1801	
25	JeanBaptiste(17)	Marg. Cagnac S.T. 1756	
	M. Anne	Michel Fortier S.H. 1812	
	Marie	Frs. Dumas " 1814	
	Marguerite	Ls. Isabel " 1817	
26	Joseph (18)	M. Anne Blandeau	
		Bert. 1758	
27	Charles (18)	Thérèse Picard S.P.S.1770	
28	Amable (19)	M. Mad. Lepage	
		S.Frs. 1787	
29	Albert (20)	M. Ls. Bilodeau S.V. 1791	
30	Louis	M. Anne Chiasson	
	M. Marguerite	Gab. Bontin S.H. 1809	
	Joseph		
	Louis		
31	JeanBaptiste(21)	M. Vict. Roy S.V. 1794	
32	Joachim (22)	Louise Fortier S.Chs.1781	
	Louise	Chs. Ruel " 1801	
	Joachim		
	Paul		
	Le Même	M. Ls. Boutillet	
		S.Chs. 1793	
	Francoise	Jos. Couture " 1823	
	Charles		
33	André (22)	Marg.Turgeon S.Chs.1782	
	Marguerite	Jos. Lainé " 1810	
	"	Marg. Marcoux " 1819	

BEBNARD.

	Joachim		
	Bernard		
	Gervais		
	Nicolas		
34	Jean	M. Fse. Blais	
	Félix		
35	Paul (23)	Cath. Gosselin S.Chs.1796	
		S.H.	
36	André	Vict. Audet S.Chs. 1803	
	Victoire	Ign Fournier " 1876	
	Marie	Jacq. Royer " 1838	
	Luce	Marcel Chabot " 1840	
	M. Charlotte	Pierre Bouchard " 1845	
	Pierre		
37	Charles (24)	Marg. Valière S.G. 1791	
	Félicité	Frs. Dupile S.P. 1819	
38	Jacques (24)	Mad. Terrien S.G. 1799	
	M. Angélique	Jos. Chevanel S.Chs. 1831	
39	Charles (27)	M. Angé. Chartier	
		S.P.S. 1796	
	Louis (30)	M.Ls.Michon S.Frs.1806	
41	Joseph (30)	Marie Belleau S.H. 1811	
42	Paul (32)	Charlotte Surgeon	
		S.H. 1810	
	M. Charlotte	Etn. Audet S.Chs. 1833	
	M. Aussile	Jos. Gosselin " 1840	
	Angéle	Aug. Gautron " 1849	
	Paul		
	Le Même	Brigitte Vaillancour	
		S.F. 1836	
43	Joachim (32)	M. Jos. Samson S.H. 1819	
	Marie	Pierre Dupont S.Chs.1845	
	Perpetue	Vital Charier " 1848	
	Vitalene	Michel Emond " 1858	
	Philomène	Ls. Baudoin " 1862	
	Joachim		
44	Charles (32)	Scolastique Pelchat	
		S.Chs. 1828	
	Rosalie	Pierre Pelchat " 1856	
	Léocadie	Jos. Filteau " 1856	
	Diace		
	Cyprien		
45	Nicolas (33)	Marg. Samson S.H. 1817	
46	Joachim (33)	Marie Ruel S.G. 1820	
47	Bernard (33)	Charlotte Fournier	
		S.G. 1824	
48	Gervais (33)	M. Anne Boutillet	
		S.Chs. 1829	
49	Pierre		
	Isidore		
50	Amable	Vict. Couillard C.S. Ign.	
	Joseph		
51	Germain	Adé Blais S.P.S. 1817	
	M. Elizabeth	Chérubin Gagné " 1846	
	Didime Frédéric		
52	Félix (34)	Emerance Clavet	
		S.Thos. 1833	
	Le Même	Marie Colombe Bert. 1844	
53	Pierre (36)	Emelie Chabot S.Chs. 1843	
54	Paul (42)	Vitaline Samson	
		S.Chs. 1849	
55	Joachim (43)	M. Marg. Rousseau	
		S.Chs. 1846	
	Le Même	Agnes Couture " 1851	
56	Didace (44)	M. Dina Blais " 1852	
57	Cyprien (44)	Caroline Chabot " 1859	
58	Isidore (49)	Charlotte Balan Bert.1815	
59	Joseph (50)	Henriette Dion " 1840	
60	Didine Frederic		
	deric (51)	Archange Langlois	
		S.V. 1843	
61	Joseph	Adé Paré S.Thos.	
	Alphé		
62	" (61)	M. Jos. Roy S.V. 1856	

BIDET-DESRUSSEL.

1	Jacques	Fse. Desfossés	S.F 1669	
	Marie	Chs. Dalaire	S.J. 1691	
	Françoise	Pierre Hélie	„ 1692	
	Jeanne	Martin Dupas	„ 1700	
	Madeleine	Jos. Dalaire	„ 1706	
	Elizabeth	Antoine Pepin	„ 1739	
	Catherine	Louis Terrien	„ 1700	
	„	2° Alexandre Alaire		
			S.M. 1718	
	Jacques			
2	Jacques	(1)	Fse. Dalaire	S.M. 1701
	M. Françoise		Jos. Dion	S.V. 1729
	Louis			
	Jacques			
3	Jacques	(2)	Hélène Dion	S.V.1728
	M. Josette		Pierre Alexis Roy	„ 1751
	„		2° Etn. Paradis	„ 1790
	„		3° Aug. Roy	„ 1798
	M, Hélène		Pierre Roy	„ 1755
	„		2° Ant. Fortier	„ 1766
4	Louis	(2)	M. Jos. Drouin S.Frs 1742	
	M. Josette		Frs. Hébert	S.J. 1770
	Jacques			
	Jean Baptiste			
5	Jean Baptiste		Eliz Asselin	
	Le même		Marg. Baudoin S.Frs.1751	
6	Jean Baptiste	(4)	M. Mad. Lefebvre	
				S.J.1776
	M. Marguerite		Jos.Marie Plante	„ 1792
	M. Madeleine		Ign. Giguère	„ 1798
	M. Catherine		Jos. Pichet	„ 1803
	Françoise		Ls. Pichet	„ 1818
	M. Angèle		Jos. Lefebvre	„ 1819
	Jacques		M. Jos. Blouin	„ 1777
	M. Josette		Jacq. Asselin	„ 1798
8	Alexis		Marg. Mathurin	Q.

BILODEAU.

1	Jacques		Genev. Longchamps	
				Q. 1654
	Simon			
	Antoine			
	Jean			
2	Jean	(1)	Eliz. Leblanc	S.F. 1689
	Le même		Marg. Jehan	„ 1684
	M. Anne		Etn. Dalaire	S.Frs 1705
	Elizabeth		Ls. Morin	„ 1721
	Jean			
	Jacques			
3	Antoine	(1)	Genev. Turcot S.Frs.1685	
	Marie		Chs. Laignon	„ 1734
	Elizabeth		Pierre Deblois	„ 1720
	Françoise		Jos. Daniel	„ 1726
	Anne		J. B. Paquet	„ 1731
	Geneviève		Jean Emond	„ 1736
	François			
	Antoine			
	Jacques			
	Gabriel			
4	Simon	(1)	Anne Turcot	S.F. 1689
	Angélique		Frs. Langelier S.Frs.1721	
	Marie		Frs. Gendron	„ 1726
	Elizabeth		Gab. Gendron	„ 1728
	Hélène		Jos. Dompierre	„ 1736
	Agnès		Pierre Paquet	„ 1736
5	Jean	(2)	Marie Turgeon	B. 1716
	Marie		Frs. Asselin	S.Frs. 1749
	Louise		Réné Meneux	1747
	Jacques			
	Jean			
6	Jacques	(2)	Marie Morin S.Tho. 1720	
	Jean Valier			
	Gabriel			
	Le même		Angé. Boutin	Bert. 1730
	Marie		Jos. Daniau	„ 1758
	Geneviève		AndréCarbonneau	„ 1762

BILODEAU.

	Pierre			
	Joseph			
	Michel Domi-			
	nique			
	Augustin			
7	Gabriel		Eliz. Roy	
	Isabelle		Pierre Dodier	Bert. 1744
	Madeleine		Jean Valier Boutin	
				Bert. 1746
	M. Marthe		Pierre Boutin	1751
	Jean Baptiste			
	Jacques			
8	Antoine	(3)	Angé. Lepage S.Frs. 1713	
	M. Angélique		PierreSimoneau Bert.1735	
	M. Anne		Nicolas Hélie	„ 1744
	Madeleine		Pierre Hélie	„ 1751
	Françoise		Ls. Leroux	„ 1743
	„		2° Chs. Barilleau	
				S.Frs. 1761
9	François	(3)	Marg. Beaucher S.F.1717	
	Marie		Pierre Noël	„ 1748
	M. Madeleine		Jos. Marie Noël	„ 1749
	François			
10	Jacques	(3)	M. Fse. Paquet	B. 1741
	Gabriel			
	Louis			
	Jacques			
11	Gabriel	(3)	Suzanne Bissonnet	
				Bert. 1731
	Marguerite		Chs. Blanchet	„ 1754
	Marie		Pierre Isabel	S.H. 1788
	Pierre			
	Louis			
	Gabriel			
	Joseph			
12	Jean		Eliz. Gagné	S.Frs. 1742
	Théotiste		Ign. Audet	S.Chs. 1774
	Pierre			
	Joseph			
	Le même		Genev. RobergeS.Chs.1764	
	M. Anne		Etn. Leclaire	„
	Geneviève		Pierre Roy	„
	Euphresine		Jos. Daniau S. Chs. 1804	
	Zacharie			
	Jean Baptiste			
	Charles			
	Ignace			
	François			
13	Jacques	(5)	Marie Plante S.Frs. 1750	
	M. Louise		Barth. Gobiel S.J. 1776	
	François			
14	Jean Valier	(6)	M.Jos. Mercier Bert.1754	
	M. Marthe		Michel Lemieux	„ 1794
	M. Josette		Jacq.Carbonneau	„ 1799
	M. Elizabeth		AmableLemieuxS. V.1785	
	„		2° Aug. Morin Bert. 1809	
	Michel			
	Jean Baptiste			
	Augustin			
	Jacques			
15	Gabriel	(6)	M. Genev. Balan	
				S.Tho. 1764
	Geneviève		Ant. Coté	S.H. 1783
	M. Elizabeth		Ls. Boutin	„ 1788
	Pierre			
	Gabriel			
	Ignace			
16	Joseph	(6)	Genev.Clément Bert.1767	
17	Pierre	(6)	M. Mad. Vadboncœur	
				Levis 1768
	M. Louise		Albert Bernier S.V. 1791	
18	Michel Domi-	(6)	M. Anne Carbonneau	
	nique			Bert. 1771
	Le même		Thérèse Isabel S.Chs.1780	
	Marguerite		Germ. Gosselin S.H. 1812	
	Victoire		Jos. Filteau	„ 1816
	Thérèse		André Mercier	„ 1817

BILODEAU.

19	Augustin	(6)	M. Ls. Carbonneau	1785
	Marguerite		Simon Morin	1811
	Joseph			
	Augustin			
20	Jean Baptiste	(7)	M.Jos. Boucher Bert.	1742
	M. Josette		Ls. Nadeau "	1765
	M. Geneviève		Jacq. Boutin "	1787
	Louis Marie			
	Joseph Marie			
	Gabriel			
	Jean Baptiste			
21	Jacques	(7)	M. Claire Daniau S.F.S.	1749
	M. Claire		J. B. Guilmet Bert.	1795
	Gabriel			
	Jean Baptiste			
	Jacques			
22	François	(9)	Céleste Rochon S.F.	1756
23	Pierre		Marie Chartier	
	Alexis			
24	Jacques	(10)	M. Ls. Chartier S.V.	1751
	M. Louise		Michel Lefebvre S.M.	1794
	Victoire		Nic. Filteau S.Chs.	1796
	Joseph			
25	Gabriel	(10)	Eliz. Gosselin S.V.	1757
	Jean Baptiste			
	Antoine			
	Joseph			
	Le même		M. Anne Plante S.M.	1770
	Marie		Jos. Labrecque S.G.	1802
	Jean Baptiste			
	Gabriel			
	Louis			
26	Louis	(10)	Marg. Peltier S.F.S.	1775
	Marie		Jos. Gosselin S.G.	1827
27	Gabriel	(11)	M. Anne Morin Bert.	1753
28	Pierre	(11)	M.Mad.Lainé S.Chs.	1760
	Marcelline		Alexis Gagné "	1782
	Marie		Alexis Pouliot "	1790
	Pierre			
	Jean Baptiste			
	Le même		Louise Denis "	1782
	Louise		Michel Roy S.G.	1801
	Françoise		Pierre Thibault "	1804
29	Joseph	(11)	Cath. Paré S.Chs.	1777
	M. Catherine		Nic. Quéret S.G.	1799
	M. Anne		J. B. Guilmet S.H.	1809
	Le même		Agathe Fouquet "	1803
30	Louis	(11)	M. Mad. Guilmet Bert.	1768
31	Louis		Louise Chartier	
	Barthélémi			
32	Jean		Thérèse Faucher S.Fran.	
	Jean			
33	Joseph	(12)	M. Genev. Lemelin S.L.	1772
	Geneviève		Frs. Roy S.Chs.	1796
	M. Charlotte		Clément Bisson "	1804
	Charles			
	Joseph			
	Jacques			
34	Pierre	(12)	Susanne Samson S.G.	1783
	Angélique		Jos. Chabot "	1814
	Josette		Frs. Fortier "	1820
	Pierre			
	Joseph			
35	François	(12)	Genev. Fournier "	1793
	M. Anne		Etn. Gontier "	1811
	Justine		Jos. Ruel "	1820
	Geneviève		Henri Guay "	1821
	Marie		Ls. Duprat "	1826
	Pierre Edmond			
	Barnabé			
	Jean			
36	JeanBaptiste	(12)	Marg. Fortier S.Chs.	1795
	Marguerite		Ant. Plante	1827

BILODEAU.

	Marie		Tho. Gautron	1840
	Angé. Alice		Ls. Huert	1847
37	Charles	(12)	M. Chs. Lacasse S.Chs.	1800
	Angèle		Hyacinthe Rémillard S.G.	1845
	Marguerite		Gab. Audet	1827
	Charles			
	Joseph			
38	Zacharie	(12)	Marg. Lacasse S.Chs.	1800
	Marguerite		Presque Aubé "	1828
	Adélaïde		Jacq. Denis "	1833
	Anselme			
	Zacharie			
39	Ignace	(12)	Natalie Lacasse "	1804
40	François	(13)	M.Jos. Labbé S.Frs.	1783
	Marguerite		Anable Durand "	1821
	M. Josette		Chs. Demeule S.F.	1812
	François			
41	JeanBaptiste	(14)	M.Eliz.Marcoux Bert.	1783
	M. Elizabeth		Lambert Bilodeau S.F.S.	1815
	M. Thérèse		Gab. Bilodeau S.V.	1821
	Jean Baptiste			
42	Augustin	(14)	M. Anne Carbonneau Bert.	1789
	M. Thérèse		Joseph Marie S.F.S.	1812
	Julie		Michel Lee S.P.S.	1821
	M. Anne		Pierre Fradet S.G.	1825
	Michel			
	Jean			
	Ambroise			
	Joseph			
	Le Même		Marg. Patoine S.G.	1801
	Marguerite		Féréol Brochu "	1825
43	Jacques	(14)	M. Anne Denis S.V.	1794
	Luce			1842
	Michel J. B.,		Auguste, Joseph	
	Le Même		M. Angé Roy Bert.	1816
	Louis			
44	Michel	(14)	Marie Roy S.V.	1805
	M.Emérentienne		Jacq. McNeil "	1838
	Marie		Antoine Quéret "	1840
	Clotilde		Ant. Tangué "	1841
	Michel			
45	Gabriel	(15)	M Mad. Fradet B.	1797
46	Ignace	(15)	M.Marg.Plante S.H.	1800
47	Pierre	(15)	M. Angé "	1806
48	Augustin	(19)	M. Anne Menard Bert.	1806
49	Joseph	(19)	Vict. Nadeau "	1829
50	JeanBaptiste	(20)	M. Christine Boulet S.F.S.	1775
	Reine		Jos. Rouleau "	1799
	M. Reine		Frs. Pilote "	1808
	Madeleine		AmbroiseBédard "	1813
	M. Christine		Jean Frs. Thibault "	1814
	M. Louise		Germ. Gagné "	1818
	Jean			
	Joseph			
51	Jos. Marie	(20)	Thérèse Paré S.F.S.	1788
52	Gabriel	(20)	Fse. Daniau Bert.	1785
	Reine		Thos. Lemieux "	1822
	Angèle		Aug. Paré "	1841
	Gab. Toussaint			
	Joseph			
53	Louis Marie	(20)	M. Ls. Mercier Bert.	1791
	M. Josette		André Tangué "	1812
	Luce		Aug. Bilodeau "	1826
	Julie		Ls. Guilmet "	1826
	Marie		J. B. Tangué "	1834
	Thérèse		Jos.Carbonneau "	1843
	M. Riene		J.B. " S.V.	1820
	Louis			

BILODEAU.

54	JeanBaptiste(21)	Marie Mercier Bert.	1783
	Marie	Gug.Carbonneau „	1842
	Thérèse	HyacinthePicard „	1823
	M. Angèle	J. B. Bouchard „	1830
	Julie	Paschal Bilodeau „	1836
	Marguerite	Pierre Boulet S.F.S.	1834
	Charles		
	Jean Baptiste		
55	Gabriel (21)	Angé Daniau Bert.	1787
	Françoise	Jos. Boldue S.V.	1821
	Ursule	Frs. Guilmet „	1822
	Gabriel	Pierre Lambert	
56	Jacques (21)	M. Marthe	
		Guilmet „	1790
57	Alexis (23)	MarieBoucherS.Chs.	1785
58	Joseph (24)	M. Claire Moreau	
		S.Thos.	1778
	Marie	Aug. Guilmet S.Chs.	1804
	Le même	M. Anne Bourassa	
		Levis	1795
59	Joseph 25)	Marie Lacasse S.G.	1786
	Marie	Michel Blais „	1825
	Pierre		
60	JeanBaptiste(45)	Marie Gontier S.Chs.	1791
61	Michel	Théotiste Gontier	
	Jean Bte.		
62	Antoine (25)	Angé Couture S.G.	1795
	Geneviève	Chs. Clément S.Chs.	1830
	Charles		
	Antoine		
	François		
	Le même	Genev. Forgues S.M.	1827
63	Jean (25)	M. Anne Roy „	1803
	Baptiste(2°)		
64	Gabriel (25)	Josette Goulet S.G.	1804
	Charles		
	François		
65	Louis (25)	M. Fse. Labrecque	
		S.M.	1807
	Magloire		
	Le même	Marg. Brochu S.G.	1823
	M. Louise	Genev. Morin S.V.	1843
	Flaorie	Michel Roy S.M.	1849
66	Pierre (28)	Dorothée Morin	
		S. F. S.	1787
	Marie	Jos. Dion S. Chs.	1806
67	Jean Baptiste(28)	Cécile Thibault S.G.	1797
	Julie	Jacq. Gosselin „	1828
	Louis		
68	Barthélemie (31)	Josette Blanchet S.G.	1791
	Marie	Barnabé Shinck „	1724
	Victoire	Gab. Blais „	1821
	Louise	Jos. Pepin „	1825
	Josette	Jacq. Boutin „	1827
	Archange	Jos. Guilmet „	1829
	François		
69	Jean (32)	Marg. Perrot	
		S. Marie	1801
	Isaïe		
	François		
70	Charles (32)	Genev.Fontaine S. H.	1801
71	Joseph (33)	M. Jos. Morisset	
		S. Chs.	1804
	Reine	Pierre Paradis „	1835
	Marcel		
	Joseph		
72	Jacques (33)	Eliz. Dessaint S.Chs.	1812
	M. Françoise	Zéph. Turgeon B.	1846
	Esther	Geo. Carrier B.	1850
	Marie	Ls. Boilard „	1852
	Ignace		
73	Pierre (54)	Agathe Leclaire S.G.	1817
74	Joseph (34)	Marie Leclaire ,	1823
75	Barnabé (35)	Marg. Lepage „	1820
76	Jean (33)	M. Anne Royer „	1821

BILODEAU.

77	Pre. Edward (35)	Martine Hombeline	
		Couture Levis	1840
78	Pierre	M. Anne Blais	
	Marie	Ls. Lavoie S M.	1842
	Jérome		
	François Xavier		
79	Antoine	M. Chs. Alaire	
	M. Marcelline	Ant.Picard S. F. S.	1843
	Le Même	Fse. Langlois S V.	1821
80	Charles, fils de	Cath. Marcoux	
	Jacq.Françoise		S. Marie 1891
	et de Catherine		
	Marcoux		
	Charles		
81	Joseph (37)	Fs. Ruel S.G.	1829
82	Charles (37)	Angé. Paquet S.Chs.	1830
83	Zacharie (38)	M. Angé. Denis „	1830
	François Xavier		
	Charles		
84	Anselme (38)	ArchangeGosselin „	1850
85	François (40)	Thérèse Dion S.F.	1809
86	JeanBaptiste(41)	Genev.Boucher Bert.	1804
87	Michel (42)	Louise Blouin S.G.	1817
88	Jean (42)	M. Anne Gosselin „	1823
89	Ambroise (42)	M. Anne Pénin „	1824
90	Joseph (42)	Eliz. Bernier Levis	1825
91	Augustin (43)	Luce Bilodeau Bert.	1826
92	JeanBaptiste(43)	Cath. Guilmet „	1826
93	Michel (43)	M. Claire Devroy,	1830
94	Joseph (43)	Soulanges Roy „	1831
95	Louis (43)	Cath. Mercier „	1842
96	Michel (44)	M. Antoinette	
		Parant S.V.	1831
	Théodore		
97	Joseph (50)	Marie Marguerite	
		S. P. S.	1807
98	Jean (50)	M. Marg. Morin	
		S.F.S.	1812
99	Gabriël Tous-		
	saint (52)	M. Luce Roy Bert.	1819
100	Joseph (52)	M. Ls. Carbonneau	
		Bert.	1819
	Caroline	J. B. Mercier „	1845
101	Louis (53)	Julie Mercier „	1840
152	JeanBaptiste(54)	M. Mad. Blouin „	1817
	Le même	Euphémie Bilodeau	
		Bert.	1843
103	Charles (54)	Reine Blais Bert.	1823
104	Gabriel (55)	M. Thérèse Bilodeau	
		S. V.	1821
105	Pre.Lambert(55)	M. Eliz. Bilodeau	
		S. F. S.	1815
	Marie	Michel Audet Bert.	1840
	Euphémie	J. B. Bilodeau „	1821
	Restitul	Fred. Etn.Cochon „	1844
	Hubert		
106	Pierre (59)	Marie Boucher S.G.	1819
107	JeanBaptiste(61)	Marie Labreque S.G.	1812
108	Antoine (62)	Marie Gontier S.Chs.	1820
	Antoine		
109	Charles (62)	Angé Bourgue S.M.	1823
	M. Desanges	Jos. Hélie S.M.	1858
	Hermine	Naz. Gagnon „	1860
	Agnès	Jos. Lacroix „	1861
	Louis		
110	François (62)	Charlotte Renaud	
		S. G.	1824
	Marie	Jacq.Fournier S.Chs.	1848
111	Jean (63)	Louise Gagné Lévis	1830
112	Charles (64)	Phébée Turgeon B.	1841
113	François (64)	M. Anne Tessier S-L.	1842
114	Magloire (65)	Genev. Emond S.M.	1847
115	Louis (67)	Marg. James S.J.	1822
116	François (68)	Ange Marcoux S.J.	1830
117	François (69)	Adé Vallée S.G.	1827
118	Isaïe (69)	Sophie Pepin S.F.	1841
119	Joseph (71)	MarieBrousseau S.M.	1833

BILODEAU.

120	Marcel	(71)	Sophie Fraser B. 1838
121	Ignace	(72)	AnastasieTurgeon B. 1848
122	François-Xavier	(78)	Osite McNeil S.V. 1845
123	Jérôme	(78)	Mathilde Pepin S. Chs. 1854
124	Charles	(80)	Lorette Talbot S.F.S.1844
125	François-Xavier	(83)	Henriette Queret S. Chs. 1855
126	Jean		Ursule Bégin
	Le même		Angé Trudel S. Chs. 1855
127	Théodore	(96)	Lucie Tangué S.V. 1851
128	Hubert	(105)	M. Desanges Blair S.F.S. 1842
129	Louis	(109)	M. Osite Philomène Roy S. Chs. 1860
130	Antoine	(108)	Léonce Méthat S. Roch. 1855

BISSON.

1	Gervais		Marie Lerreau 1635
	Réné Gervais		
2	Réné Gervais	(1)	M. Mde Bouthet Q. 1664
	Simon		
3	Simon	(2)	Fse Labadie Pte Tremble 1702
	Charlotte		Ant. Hélie B. 1745
	Joseph		
4	Louis		Susanne Samson
	Susanne		Ls. Picard S. Chs. 1780
	Pachal		
	Joseph		
5	Joseph	(3)	Susanne Lacasse B. 1748
	M. Angélique		Ant. Boutin S.V. 1780
	Susanne		Frs. Taillon S.G. 1783
	Pachal		
	Simon		
	Charles		
	Joseph		
6	Melchior		M. Ls. Dubois
	Le même		M. Ls. Jabon S. Chs.1758
	Geneviève		Pierre Cadieu S.M. 1788
7	Joseph	(4)	Marg. Lemelin 1765
	Françoise		Frs. Lepage 1794
	"		Ant. Côté 1835
	Marie		Michel Dubé 1798
	Joseph		
	Jean-Baptiste		
8	Paschal	(4)	Marg. Terrien S.Chs. 1775
9	Charles	(5)	M. Chs. Terrien S. Chs. 1778
	Le même		Angé Gontier " 1791
	Le même		Angèle Beausoleil S.L. 1802
10	Joseph	(5)	Marie Terrien S.Chs. 1782
	M. Josette		Ant. Gaulin " 1811
	Marguerite		Jos. Naud " 1812
	Françoise		Frs. Rousseau " 1813
	Angélique		Julien Pigeon " 1817
	Marthe		André Aubé " 1812
	Judith		Ls. Mercier " 1820
	Geneviève		Bénoni Corriveau S. Chs. 1826
	Christine		Jos. Gontier " 1830
	Victoire		Frs. Cochon " 1842
	Bénoni		
	Antoine		
11	Simon	(5)	Mad. Balan S. Chs. 1787
	Marie		Etn. Labrecque S.G. 1819
	Pierre		
	Jacques		
	Simon		
	Le même		Mad. Gaudin S.G. 1820
12	Paschal	(5)	Marg. Pénin S. Chs. 1795

BISSON.

	Marguerite		Barth. Rosa S.J. 1837
	Elizabeth		Ls. Chrétien S.V. 1839
	David		
	Prosper		
	Paschal		
13	Louis		Dorothé Corriveau
	Clément		
14	Clément		M. Anne Raimond
	Clément		
15	Charles, fils de		Marg. Parent
	Jean et de M.		S. Marie 1797
	Jos. Bilodeau		
	Régis		
16	Joseph	(7)	Eliz. Audet S. Chs. 1805
	Magloire		
	Antoine		
	Pierre		
17	Jean-Baptiste	(7)	M. Anne Denis S.Chs.1809
	Charles		
18	Bénoni	(10)	Agathe Côté S. Chs. 1824
	Marie		Laurent Eugène Carrier S. Chs. 1848
	Angèle		Chs. Provost " 1864
	Hermine		Télesphore Drolet " 1852
19	Antoine	(10)	Charlotte Turgeon S. Chs. 1828
20	Simon	(11)	Angé Labrecque S.L.1810
21	Pierre	(11)	M.Ls. Monminy S.M.1819
22	Jacques	(11)	Théotiste Dessaint S.G. 1821
23	Paschal	(12)	M. Anne Carbonneau S.G. 1823
24	Prosper	(12)	M. Anne Blouin S.F. 1832
25	David	(12)	Louise Renaud S.P. 1845
26	Clément	(13)	Marie Côté S. Chs. 1800
	Amable		
27	Clement	(14)	M. Chs. Bilodeau S. Chs. 1804
28	Regis	(15)	Emérence Pepin S.J. 1836
29	Antoine	(16)	M. Jos. Leblond S.V. 1834
30	Pierre	(16)	M. Esther Ratté|S.V. 1836
31	Magloire	(16)	M. Anne Bernard S.V. 1838
32	Charles	(17)	Marg. Plante S.J. 1839
	Amable	(26)	Marg. Belan S.H. 1819

BISSONNET.

1	Pierre		Marie D'Albon Q. 1668
	Anne		Jos. Bonneau S.F. 1696
	"		2° Martin Leblond B. 1704
	Marie		Jos. Forgues S.M. 1696
	"		2° Jean Ouimet B 1705
	André		
	Jean		
	Jacques		
	Pierre		
2	Pierre	(1)	Marie Balan S.F. 1692
	Jean Baptiste		
	"		
3	Jean	(1)	Charlotte Davenne
	Charlotte		Chs. Filibot S.M. 1708
	Susanne		Gab. Briais B. 1714
	Charles		
4	André	(1)	Fse. Guilmet S.J. 1702
	Marie		J. B. Monmeny B. 1743
	M. Françoise		Jos. Goupy S.V. 1728
	"		2° Jean Marie Leblanc
	Susanne		Gab. Belodeau Bert. 1731
5	Jacques	(1)	Marie Vandet S.M. 1709
	Dorothée		Paul Boulet " 1730
	"		2° Jean Pilote S.V. 1734
	Susanne		Claude Lefebvre B 1736
6	Jean Baptiste	(2)	Genev. Chamberlan B1720

BISSONNET.

M. Josette	Ls. Plante	S.M. 1740
Marie	Simon Queret	„ 1750
M. Anne	Jean Guibert,	Bert. 1783
Jean		
Gabriël		
7 Jean Baptiste (2)	M. Thérèse Hélie	
		S.V. 1726
Marguerite	Jos. Quéret	S.M. 1754
Marguerite	2° Pierre Clément	
		S.M. 1760
M. Louise	Jos. Jolivet	„ 1754
Louis		
Antoine		
„		
Joseph		
Jean Baptiste		
8 Charles (3)	Marie Quemeneur	
		S. Frs. 1727
Marie	Pierre Martineau „	1746
Louise	Pierre Boivin	„ 1757
9 Gabriël (6)	M. Jos. Pepin S.M.	1748
	V. de Jean Landique	
Jacques Gabriël		
Le même	M. Mad. Mateau S.M. 1753	
	V. de Frs. Landique	
10 Jean (6)	M. Claire Queret S.M. 1748	
Le même	M. Félicité Fregeot	
		S.V. 1757
M. Rose	Frs. Guilmet	„ 1779
11 Jean Baptiste (7)	M. Ls. Adams	B 1751
M. Louise	J. B. Pepin	S.M. 1773
Le même	M. Eliz. Morin	„ 1768
	V. de Ls Marie Michon	
Jean Baptiste		
Le même	Angé Nadeau S.M. 1786	
12 Louis (7)	M. Angé Queret S.M. 1756	
M. Angélique	Jas. Adam	„ 1775
13 Antoine (7)	M. Mad. Frontigny	
		S.M. 1761
	V. de J. B. Chabot	
14 Antoine (7)	M. Jos. Bacquet S.M. 1763	
„		
Pierre		
„		
Michel		
André		
Jacques		
Le même	M. Chs. Terrien	
		S. Chs. 1799
15 Joseph (7)	Marie Pepin	S.M. 1763
M. Françoise	Jos. Guenet	„ 1793
M. Geneviève	Pierre Coté	„ 1796
Marie	Frs. Mercier	„ 1821
Louis		
Joseph		
Jean Baptiste		
16 Jacqs. Gabriël (9)	M. Anne Blais S.V. 1771	
17 Jn. Baptiste (11)	Fse Bacquet S.M. 1794	
Jean Baptiste		
Le même	Angile Roy S.M. 1833	
M. Philomène	Eloi Octave Tangué „ 1854	
18 Pierre (14)	Marie O'Neil Bert 1789	
M. Rose	Chs. Couture S.M. 1815	
M. Madeleine	Basile Faucher „ 1828	
Angèle	Jacques Bolduc „ 1825	
Marguerite	Chs. Dalaire S. V. 1826	
Jean Baptiste		
Pierre		
Le même	Eliz. Couture S.M. 1836	
	V. d'Etn. Pepin	
19 Pierre (14)	Marg. Labrecque S.M. 1796	
Angèle	Jacq. Gendron „ 1840	
Archange	F. X. Blais „ 1841	
Madeleine	Jos. Hubert Blais „ 1848	
Pierre		
Louis		
Thomas		

BISSONNET.

20 Michel (14)	M. Claire Lorandeau	
		S.M. 1799
21 Michel	M. Claire Aubin	
Marie	J. B. Guilmet S.M. 1821	
22 André (14)	M. Chs. Larrivé S. Chs. 1801	
Elizabeth	J. B. Lefebvre „ 1838	
André		
23 Jacques (14)	Cath. Lemelin S. Chs. 1810	
Julie	Jean Huart „ 1842	
Marguerite	Félix „	
Flavien		
24 Antoine (14)	M. Jos. Dodier S.V. 1798	
25 Joseph (15)	M. Cath. Furois S.M. 1787	
M. Catherine	Joachim Gosselin „ 1808	
Joseph		
26 Jean Baptiste (15)	Sr. S. Lanoue, veuve	
	de Jacq. Roy S.V. 1791	
Reine	J. B. Boutin, S.G. 1820	
Jean Baptiste		
Le même	M. Ls. Lacroix S.M. 1805	
27 Louis 15	Marg. Goupy S.M. 1802	
Marguerite	Frs. Roy S.G. 1826	
Basilisse	J. B. Sylvestre „ 1828	
Louis		
Gervais		
28 Pierre	M. Reine Rémillard	
Julie	Jos. Bolduc S.M. 1820	
29 Jean Baptiste (17)	Louise Gagnon „ 1819	
M. Louis	J. B. Blais „ 1845	
Le même	Olive Morin „ 1833	
Jean Baptiste		
30 Pierre (18)	M. Anne Catellier	
		S.V. 1819
Vilbon	Jos. Damase	
31 Jean Baptiste (18)	Basilisse Denis S.M. 1828	
32 Pierre (19)	Marg. Tangué „ 1820	
33 Thomas (19)	Julie Tangué „ 1834	
34 Louis (19)	Rose Gagnon „ 1839	
35 Joseph (25)	Marg. Keroack S.P.S. 1812	
Marguerite	Honoré Roger S.M. 1841	
M. Susanne	Ls. David Gautron „ 1851	
Joseph		
36 Jean Baptiste	Luce Emond	
Lucien		
Joseph		
Ferdinand		
37 André (22)	Marg. Leclaire S. Chs. 1828	
38 Flavien (23)	Marie Gontier „ 1826	
39 Jean Baptiste (26)	M. Fse. Lacroix S.M. 1819	
40 Louis (27)	Angé. Roberge S.G. 1828	
41 Jean Baptiste (29)	Constance Quéret	
		S.M. 1857
42 Vilbon (30)	M. Malvina Tangué „ 1854	
43 Joseph (30)	Susarie Mercier „ 1854	
Le même	Louise Gagné „ 1863	
44 Damase (30)	Eléonore Bolan S.V. 1849	
45 Louis (40)	Marg. Lecours S. Claire	
Le même	M. Célina Morisset	
		S.M. 1862
46 Joseph (35)	M. Angèle Catellier „ 1840	
47 Lucien (36)	Flavie Shinck B. 1852	
48 Joseph (36)	Marie Labbé S. J. 1857	
49 Ferdinand (36)	Philomène Leclaire	
		S.L. 1863

BIZEAU—LAROSE.

1 Jean	Mad. Bergerat	
		Montréal 1696
Jeanne	Jean Roy B. 1716	
Geneviève	Chs. Quenet 1721	
Le même	Cath. Gertrude Forgues	
		Montréal 1703
M. Charlotte	Jos. Plante 1733	
2 Jean Baptiste	Marie Bernier Lévis	
Jean Baptiste		
3 Jean Baptiste (2)	Marie Vermet Bert. 1751	

SESSIONAL PAPER No. 18

BLAIS.

→ 1	Pierre		Anne Perrat	S.F. 1669
	Pierre			
	Antoine			
	Jacques			
	Le même		Eliz Royer	S.J. 1689
	François			
2	Pierre	(1)	Fse. Baudoin	1695
	M. Anne		Guill. Lemieux	Bert.1726
	M. Josette		Jos.Marie Blouin	" 1734
	Jean Baptiste			
	Joseph			
	Augustin			
	Louis			
	Michel			
	Pierre			
3	Antoine	(1)	Jeanne Lamy	S.M. 1705
	Jeanne		Pierre Ménard	Bert. 1735
	Pierre			
	Antoine			
	Le même		Ambroise Fournier	S.M. 1716
	M. Anne		J.B. Leprince	Bert. 1738
	Marie		Nicholas Morisset	S.V. 1747
	Dorothée		Jean Thibaut	" 1750
	Jacques			
4	Jacques	(1)	Ang. Louise Cartier	3 Riv. 1713
5	François	(1)	M. Marthe Amelot	Q 1727
6	Jean Baptiste	(2)	Marg. Le Roy	S.V. 1726
	Marguerite		Jos. Boissonneau	Bert. 1747
	M. Françoise		Guill.Lemieux	" 1750
	M. Geneviève		Etn. Remillard	" 1757
	M. Madeleine		Boniface Aubé	" 1762
	M. Louise		Ls. Gégu	" 1765
	M. Reine		Pierre Blanchet	" 1867
	M. Josette		Pierre Gaudin	" 1755
	"		2° Ant. Marseau	" 1755
	Jean Baptiste			
	François			
	Augustin			
	André			
7	Pierre	(2)	Eliz. Bilodeau	
	M. Elizabeth		Aug. Picard	Bert. 1742
	M. Louise		Jacq. Chartier	" 1751
	M. Geneviève		Pierre Morin	" 1751
	M. Josette		Jean Fortin	" 1761
	M. Louise		Jos. Gagné	S.P.S. 1757
8	Augustin	(2)	Genev. Brocher	Bert 1730
	Françoise		J. B. Morin	" 1753
9	Louis	(2)	M. Anne Mercier	" 1733
	M. Louise		Jos. Toussaint Gagné	Bert. 1757
	Angélique		Frs. Talbot	" 1763
	M. Anne		Basile Bouchard	" 1763
	M. Françoise		Pierre Daniau	" 1773
	M. Madeleine		Ignace Fortin	" 1777
	Catherine		Jos. Morisset	" 1788
	M. Elizabeth		J. B. Morin	" 1790
	Françoise			
	Pierre			
	Augustin			
	Louis			
10	Joseph	(2)	M.Chs.Leblond	S.V. 1740
	M. Josette		J. B. Picard	S.P.S. 1761
	M. Françoise		Pierre Fournier	" 1764
	"		2° Frs. Hyacinthe Peltier	S.P.S. 1778
	M. Anne		Aug. Talbot	" 1778
	M. Reine		J. B. Martineau	" 1767
	Michel			
	André			
	Joseph			
	Louis			
	Pierre			

BLAIS.

	Jean			
	Augustin			
11	Michel	(2)	M. Fse Lizotte	S.Anne 1741
	Françoise		Ant. Talbot	S.P.S. 1763
	M. Louise		Simon Fournier	" 1782
	Michel			
	Louis			
	Joseph			
12	Jean Baptiste		Ange Dumont	Q.
	Jean Baptiste			
13	Augustin	(2)	M. Mad. Fortier	S.F.I.O. 1744
	M. Elizabeth		J. B. Mercier	Bert. 1757
	Marguerite		Amb. Gagné	" 1765
	M. Madeleine		Pre. Simon Corriveau	Bert. 1766
	M. Angélique		Michel Gagné	" 1771
	M. Josette		Pierre Aubé	" 1758
	"		2° Ls. Lemieux	S.V. 1789
	André			
	Augustin			
	Jean Baptiste			
	François			
	Pierre			
	Joseph			
14	Pierre	(3)	Eliz. Mercier	Bert. 1734
	Marie		Jean Boucher	S.V. 1761
	Elizabeth		Frs. Goulet	" 1763
	M. Anne		Pierre Guenet	" 1771
	Pierre Paul			
	Joseph			
15	Antoine	(3)	Marie Chartier	Bert. 1731
	Le même		M. Jos. Corriveau	S.V. 1743
	M. Anne		Jacq. Gab. Bissonnet	S.V. 1771
	Jacques			
16	Jacques	(3)	Louis Lacroix	S.V. 1747
	M. Josette		Ls. Barnabé Bouton	S.V. 1771
	Madeleine		Jacq. Labreque	" 1778
	Jacques			
	Etienne			
	Thomas			
17	Pierre		Mary Isabel	
	Michel			
18	Augustin	(6)	Angé Mercier	Bert. 1765
	Angélique		Jean Frs. Chrétien	Bert. 1790
	M. Charlotte		J. B. Dutile	" 1807
	Marguerite		Jacq. Lessart	" 1813
	M. Marthe		Jos. Boulet	" 1819
	M. Françoise		Andre Proulx	" 1844
	Augustin			
	Lazare			
	Michel			
	François			
	Louis			
	Jean Baptiste			
	Jean Baptiste			
	Joseph			
19	Jean Baptiste		Ange Mercier	
	André			
20	Jean Baptiste		M. Anne Mercier	Bert. 1771
	M. Anne		Aug. Mercier	" 1794
	Catherine		J. B. Gaulon	" 1797
	Marguerite		Pierre Mercier	" 1804
	Pierre			
	Augustin			
	Antoine			
	Michel			
	Jean Baptiste			
	Le même		Eliz. Buteau, Bert. 1788	

BLAIS.

21	André	(6) Marthe Blanchet S.P 1767
	Marthe	Ant. Talbot, Bert. 1789
	Geneviève	Aug. Lessart, „ 1791
	André	
	Le même	Marie Belanger, S.V 1788
	Charlotte	IsidoreCochon,S.P.S.1820
	Rosalie	Pierre Samson. „ 1825
	Fréderic	
	Joseph	
	Andre	
	Toussaint	
	Jacques	
22	François	(6) Marg. Blanchet Bert. 1772
	M. Roger	J. B. Guilmet, „ 1794
	Marguerite	Jos. Gaupy, „ 1797
	Madeleine	Eustache Plante, „ 1799
	Le même	Marg. Roy, S.Chs. 1780
	Marie	Ign. Lecours „ 1818
	Féréol	
	Augustin	
	François	
23	Jean Baptiste	Thérese Morin
	Thérese	Jos. Marie Carbonneau, Bert. 1769
	Reine	Chs. Blanchet, Bert. 1779
	Marguerite	Pierre Balan „ 1783
24	Pierre	Marg. Morin
	M. Louise	J. B. Gendron S.P.S. 1786
	Marguerite	Frs. Rocher, „ 1786
	Pierre Noël	
	Joseph	
	Alexis	
25	Louis	(9) Genev. Gaulin S.P.S. 1757
	Geneviève	Frs. Boulet, S. F. S. 1784
	M. Louise	Germ. Landry „ 1787
	Catherine	Jos. Quemeneur „ 1787
	M. Josette	Ant. Baudoin „ 1789
	Françoise	Jacq. Langlois „ 1795
	Louis	
	Le même	Vict. Quemeneur S.F.S. 1788
	Victoire	Ls. Savoie „ 1813
	M. Marthe	J. B. Dumas „ 1817
	Françoise	Jos. Guilmet, S.V. 1841
	Jean Baptiste	
	François	
	Joseph	
26	Aug. Louis	(9) M. Eliz. Beaupied S.P.S. 1779
	Michel	
	Augustin	
	Jean Baptiste	
27	François	(9) Thérese Dougot S.V. 1784
	Marie	Ant. Blais. Bert. 1803
28	Pierre	(9) M. Bonne Dessaint, S.P.S. 1786
29	Joseph	(10) M. Jos. Pare, S.F.S. 1773
	M. Josette	Abraham Rouleau „ 1795
	M. Francoise	Jos. Morin, „ 1799
	M. Reine	Chs. Goupy „ 1813
	Véronique	Frs. Boulet, S.P.S. 1816
	Joseph	
	Louis	
30	Michel	(10) Marg. Mercier S.F.S. 1775
	M. Françoise	Jean Olivier Bernier, S.P.S. 1803
	M. Adelaide	Germ. Bernier, S.P.S.1817
	Michel	
	Joseph	
31	Jean	(10) M. Fse. Fontaine, S.P.S. 1778
	M. Anne	Paul Côté, „ 1818
	Julie	Ls. Rousseau „ 1827
	Joseph Marie	
	Jean Baptiste	
	Thomas	

BLAIS.

	Félix	
32	Pierre	(10) M. Jos. Dessaint, S.P.S. 1780
	Jeanne Fse.	Paul Fournier, „ 1811
	M. Bibiane	Tho. Fournier „ 1823
	M. Angélique	Gab. Grégoire, „ 1823
	Jos. Théophile	
33	André	(10) M. Genev. Blanchet, S.P.S. 1781
	M. Geneviève	Aug. Gagné, S.P.S. 1801
34	Louis	(10) M. Roger Blanchet, S.P.S. 1784
	M. Roger Pélagie	Ls. Nicole, S.P.S. 1813
	M. Rosalie	Guill. Bélanger, „ 1819
	M. Charlotte	Jos. Couët „ 1822
	Joseph Marc	
	Benjamin	
	Louis	
35	Augustin	(10) M. Genv. Terriau, S.P.C. 1785
	M. Geneviève	André Vallée „ 1805
	M. Charlotte	Michel Picard, „ 1810
	Le même	Louise Paré, S.F.S. 1793
	Augustin Noël	
36	J. Baptiste	(12) Angé Monmeny S.M.1757
37	Pierre	(13) Rosalie Fournier, S.P.S. 1765
	M. Rose	Frs. Morin, S. H. 1787
	M. Reine	Chs. Demers, „ 1792
	M. Josette	Frs. Cantin „ 1794
	M. Geneviève	Ign. Paradis, „ 1804
	Michel	
	Louis	
38	J. Baptiste	(13) M. Jos. Rémillard, Bert, 1762
	M. Josette	J. B. Daniau, „ 1783
	M. Archange	Pierre Bouchard „ 1788
	M. Françoise	Aug. Bolduc, S. V. 1788
	Le même	M. Mad. Boucher, Bert. 1783
	M. Madeleine	Ls. Dessaint, „ 1802
	M. Thècle	Pierre Roy, S. V. 1808
	François	
39	André	(13) Marie Lecours S.Chs 1772
40	Joseph	(13) M. Eliz. Michon S.Tho. 1773
	Rose	André Ls. Blouin Bert. 1798
	„	2° Basile Beaucher Bert.1806
	M. Angélique	André Picard „ 1801
	M. Madeleine	Guill. Boucher „ 1802
	M. Archange	J. B. Belleau „ 1806
	M. Angèle	Chs Roy „ 1813
	M. Anne	J. B. Lecomte „ 1824
	Jean	
	Joseph	
41	Augustin	M. Anne Mercier S.F.S.1773
	M. Angélique	Pierre Fontaine „ 1806
	M. Anne	Jacq. Baudoin Bert. 1801
	Pierre	
	Louis	
	Le même	M. Jos. Coulombe Bert.1791
	Marie	Michel Denis „ 1885
42	François	(13) M. Bonne Gagné S.P.S. 1777
	Thérèse	Jean Paradis S.H.1807
	M. Josette	Jos. Couture „ 1808
	M. Bonne	Etn. Carrière „ 1809
	„	2° Pierre Bussière „ 1815
	M. Euphrosine	Charles Paschal Bussière S.H. 1815
	Ambroise	
	Augustin	

BLAIS.

43	Joseph	M. Ls Goulet S.Chs. 1762	
	M. Josette	Michel Guilmet S.V. 1804	
	Joseph		
	André		
	Jean		
	François		
	Louis		
	Michel		
44	Pierre Paul (14)	M. Amy Guenet	
		S.Chs. 1770	
	Le même	M. Marg. Dussault	
		S.Chs.1777	
	Marguerite	J. B. Terrien „ 1796	
	Geneviève	Jos. Nadeau „ 1799	
	Catherine	Pierre Terrien „ 1814	
	Marie	Jacq. Brochu „ 1817	
	M. Cécile	Pre. Michel Blanchet	
		S.F.S. 1821	
	Joseph		
	Guillaume		
	Pierre		
	Jean Baptiste		
45	Jacques (15)	M. Jos Ratté S.Chs.1773	
46	Jacques (16)	Brigitte Clément	
		S.V. 1780	
	M. Françoise	Etn. Viau „ 1804	
	Marguerite	Jos. Pepin S.M. 1801	
	Brigitte	Frs. Plante S.G. 1802	
47	Etienne (16)	M. Ls Corriveau	
		S.V. 1785	
	M. Elizabeth	Jacq. Bédard S.H. 1807	
	M. Angélique	Guill. Grenier „ 1814	
	Françoise	Ls Côté „ 1818	
	Jacques	.	
48	Thomas (16)	M. Angé.Dodier S.V.1794	
49	Michel (17)	M. Eliz. Tangué „ 1767	
50	Michel (11)	Charlotte Fournier	
		S.P.S.1769	
51	Joseph (11)	Marg. Mathieu „ 1774	
	M. Louise	Jos. Bossé „ 1804	
	M. Flavie	Gab. Maufait „ 1821	
	Michel		
	Joseph		
	Jean Baptiste		
	Louis		
	François Xavier		
	Angèle	Philippe Vineault	
	Marie	Louis Caseault	
	Calixte	Jos. Bernier	
52	Louis (11)	Gabriel Roy B. 1781	
	Le même	M. Anne Bossé, Cap St.	
		Ign. 1786	
	M. Marguerite	Chs. Aug. Vilbon Larue	
		S.P.S. 1831	
	Louis		
53	Jean Baptiste	Théotiste Beaulieu	
	Théotiste	Jos. Gravel Bert.1795	
	Joseph		
54	Augustin (18)	M. Jos. Mercier „ 1788	
55	François (18)	Brigitte Buteau „ 1801	
56	Jean Baptiste(18)	M. Jos. Corriveau „ 1801	
57	Jean Baptiste(18)	M.Marg. Mercier „ 1802	
	Marie	Aug. Buteau „ 1826	
	François		
	Le même	Genev.Marcoux Bert.1813	
	Catherine	J. B. Blais „ 1838	
	Julie	Jos. Buteau „ 1839	
	Léandre		
58	Joseph (18)	Marg. Picard S.Tho. 1807	
59	Michel (17)	Constance Côté Bert.1808	
60	Louis (18)	Marie Denis „ 1817	
61	Lazare (18)	Marie Boulet S.F.S. 1823	
62	André (19)	Marg. Bouchard S.V.1812	
	André Nazaire		
63	Jean Baptiste(30)	M. Thérèse Peltier	
		S.P.S. 1795	

BLAIS

	Marie	Aug. Carbonneau	
		Bert. 1823	
	Jean Baptiste		
64	Pierre (20)	M. Thècle Dutile	
		Bert. 1798	
65	Augustin	M. Ls Mercier „ 1800	
	Marguerite	Frs. Samson S.G. 1823	
	Louise	Mag. Lacroix „ 1827	
	Jean Baptiste		
	Augustin		
	Le même	Aug. Valière S.G. 1825	
66	Antoine (20)	Marie Blais Bert.1803	
	M. Rose	Jos. Joncas „ 1824	
	M. Anne	Jean Laurent Roy „ 1829	
67	Michel	Reine Corriveau Bert.1804	
	Marguerite	Simon Lessart „ 1838	
	Jean Baptiste		
	Antoine		
68	André (21)	M. Ursule Vernet	
		Bert. 1789	
	Geneviève	Jos. Guilmet „ 1822	
	Marguerite	Pierre Mercier „ 1830	
	Marie	Laurent Ratté S.V. 1822	
	Louis Emélie	Pierre Guénet S.F.S 1834	
	Toussaint		
	André		
	François		
69	Jean Baptiste	M. Fse. Vernet	
	Elizabeth	Michel Bernard Bert.1812	
	Françoise	Pierre Corriveau	
		S.F.S. 1812	
	Emelie	Pierre Roy S.G. 1822	
	Olivier		
	Jean Baptiste		
	Gabriel		
70	Jacques	Eliz. Letourneau	
		S.Tho. 1814	
	Le même	Adé Boulet S.F.S. 1826	
71	André Tous- (21)	M. Claire Fournier	
	saint	S.P.S. 1814	
	Catherine	Pierre Gagné „ 1840	
	M. Delphine	Frs. Daniau S.F.S. 1835	
	André		
72	Joseph (21)	Sophie Têtu S.Tho. 1818	
	Le même	M. Fse. Chamberlan	
		S.P.S. 1824	
73	Frédéric (21)	Perpétue Blanchet	
		S.P.S. 1839	
74	François (22)	Marie Hébert S.Chs.1810	
75	Augustin (22)	M. Chs. Paquet B. 1845	
76	Fériol (22)	Mad. Roy S.Chs. 1827	
79	Louis (29)	Marg. Harnois	
	M. Angèle	Jos. Mercier S.F.S. 1842	
	M. Céleste	Jos. Chabot „ 1844	
	Marguerite	F. X. Leroux „ 1825	
80	Pierre Noël (24)	M. Genev.Picard	
		S.P.S. 1777	
81	Alexis (24)	M. Genev. Proulx	
		S.Tho. 1786	
	Louis		
	Jean Baptiste		
82	Joseph (24)	M. Genev. Gagné	
		S.P.S. 1803	
	Marie	Félix Blais „ 1842	
	M. Desanges	Hubert Bilodeau	
		S.F.S. 1842	
	Joseph		
	Le même	Thérèse Gaudin S.P.S1834	
83	Louis (25)	M. Marthe Lemieux	
		S.F.S. 1793	
	E. Victoire	Jos. Buteau S.F.S. 1823	
	M. Rose	F. X. Pénin „ 1820	
	Françoise	J. B. Boulet 1831	
	Elizabeth	Ls Boutin S.F.S. 1837	

BLAIS.

BLAIS.

Jacques		
Joseph		
François Xavier		
84 François	(25)	M. Genev. Quemeneu
		Lotbinière S.F.S. 1814
85 Joseph	(25)	M. Julie Beaucher
		S.P.S. 1815
Adélaïde		Pierre Boulet S.F.S. 1842
M. Julie		Jos. Morin „ 1843
86 JeanBaptiste	(25)	Reine Mercier Bert. 1831
87 Augustin	(26)	M. Anne Dion „ 1804
M. Anne		Godfroi Guilnet „ 1826
Elizabeth		Jos. Carbonneau „ 1835
Flavie		Athanase Guilmet „ 1845
David		
Augustin		
88 JeanBaptiste	(26)	Marg. Mercier Bert. 1812
89 Michel	26)	Rose Wells „ 1825
Adolphe		
90 Joseph	(29)	M. Dorothée Robin
		S.F.S. 1801
Le même		Marie Lemieux „ 1843
91 Michel	(30)	M. Fse. Couillard
		S.Tho. 1800
Désan		Pierre Bonneau „ „
		S.P.S. 1829
Eliza		Ls. Morin S.P.S. 1829
Thérèse		Ls. Norbert Blanchet
		S.P.S. 1839
M. Françoise		Jos. Prudent Picard
		S.F.S. 1825
Télesphore		
Antoine Hubert		
Jean Baptiste		
92 Joseph	(30)	M. Genev. Couillard
		S.Tho. 1811
M. Eléonore		Aug. Morin S.F.S. 1836
M. Anne Saly		Frs. Quemeneu 1839
Alfred		
93 Joseph Marie	(31)	M. Cath. Fournier
		S.P.S. 1806
Catherine		André Talbot „ 1829
Angèle		Jacq. Garant S.Chs. 1827
Apolline		Jacq. Blais „ 1828
Le même		M. Ls. Pigeon „ 1843
94 JeanBaptiste	(31)	Fse. Côté S.P.S. 1814
95 Thomas	(31)	Sophie Côté „ 1828
96 Félix	(31)	Marie Blais „
97 Jos. Théo-	(32)	Marg. Durand „ 1820
phile		
Le même		M. Euphrosine Blanchet
		S.P.S. 1824
Louis Théophile		
98 Louis	(34)	M. Chs. Bacon „ 1806
M. Charlotte		Tho. Fournier „ 1834
Hubert		
François Xavier		
Etienne		
Frédéric		
99 Jean Baptiste		Cath. Belanger
Soter		
Eulalie		F. X. Baudoin Bert 1839
JeanBaptiste Sota		
100 Jos. Marc	(34)	M. Marg. Bélanger
		S.P.S. 1818
101 Benjamin	(34)	Césarie Coté S.P.S. 1838
102 Pierre Veuf de		
Le même		Marg.Leclaire S.Chs.1802
„		Angé Lepage „ 1822
103 Aug. Noël	(35)	Dorothee Delagrave
		S.P.S. 1822
104 Louis	(37)	M. Aime MorinS.H. 1794
M. Anne		Jos. Rousseau „ 1814
105 Michel	(37)	Angé Noël „ 1809
106 Français	(38)	Marie Marcoux Bert.1808
107 Jean	(40)	M. Marg. Roy S.H. 1807

108 Joseph	(40)	Rosalie Dubord
		S.Tho. 1815
Marcelline		F. X. Brochu S.V. 1842
Elizabeth		L. S. Mercier Bert. 1845
André		
Le même		M. Claire Morin
		S.F.S. 1824
109 Pierre	(41)	Marg. Boissel Bert. 1801
Reine		Chs. Bilodeau „ 1823
110 Louis	(41)	Marg Langlois S.F.S.1805
Marguerite		Frs. Brochu Bert. 1823
Le même		M.Jos. Gagné S.P.S. 1820
„		M. Vict. Dubé „ 1825
111 Ambroise	(42)	Roger Fontaine S.H. 1803
112 Augustin	(42)	Marie Gosselin „ 1813
113 Joseph	(43)	Genev. Guilmet S.V. 1791
M. Geneviève		F. X. Lapage „ 1825
M. Rose		Tho. Gautron „ 1834
Michel		
Louis		
Jacques		
Simon		
Joseph		
114 Michel	(43)	M. Vict. Lemieux
		Bert. 1798
Geneviève		Jac. Rouillard S.G. 1825
Angéle		Simon Mercier „ 1826
Marcelline		Marcel Théberge „ 1830
Jean		
Le Même		Marie Bilodeau S.G. 1825
115 Jean	(43)	M. Marg. Aubé S.V. 1798
Geneviève		Narcisse Tangué „ 1826
M. Josette		Jacq. Masseau „ 1834
Césarine		Prudent Belanger „ 1839
Françoise		Ant. Morin S.M. 1836
Michel		
Jean		
116 François	(43)	M. Marthe Guilmet
		S.V. 1802
François		
117 André	(43)	M. Ls. Aubé S.V. 1808
Le même		M. Barbe Chabot
		S.V. 1811
Narcisse		
118 Louis	(43)	Thérèse Brochu
		S.V. 1810
Le même		Sussane Gourgue „ 1815
119 Pierre	(44)	Marthe S.Chs. 1799
120 JeanBaptiste	(44)	M. Vict. Gautron
		S.V. 1812
Marie		J. B. Carrier S.Chs. 1843
Jean Baptiste		
Le même		Adé Roy S.Chs. 1826
M. Dina		Didace Bernier „ 1852
121 Guillaume	(44)	M. Jos. Lacroix
		S.Chs. 1820
122 Joseph	(44)	Josette Coté S.M. 1823
123 Jacques	(47)	M. Ls. Coté S.Chs. 1805
124 Joseph	(51)	Marg. Fournier
		S.P.S. 1799
Marg. Ma-		Ls. Genest „ 1838
thilde		
Prudent		
Charles		
François Xa-		
vier		
Le même		Marg. Guénet S.F.S. 1825
125 Michel	(51)	M. Ls. Fournier
		S.Tho. 1806
126 Louis		Anatholie Talbot S.Tho.
Le même		M. Adé Harmais
		S.P.S. 1815
Elizabeth		Pierre Joly S.F.S. 1836
Anselme, J.B.		W. Prétre Cure S.
		Lambert Q.Dec. 1882
Narcisse		Luce Quemineur S.F.S.

BLAIS.

Benjamin		Henriette Morin S.P.S.
Onézime		Pierre Picard "
Mélanie		Paul Samson "
Ceaulie		Phidime Rousseau "
127 JeanBaptiste	(51)	Charlotte Delagrave
		S.P.S. 1823
127ª Louis	(52)	Marie Genest S.J. 1818
128 Joseph	(53)	M. Jos. Larrivé B. 1817
129 Jean François		M. Chs. Cloutier
François Xavier		
130 François	(57)	Onesime Mercier
		Bert. 1845
131 Léandre	(57)	Célina Bolduc S.V. 1854
132 André Na-	(62)	Anastasie Guilmet
zaire		S.F.S. 1839
133 JeanBaptiste	(63)	M. Marthe Terrien
		Bert. 1825
134 Augustin	(65)	M.Ange Samson S.H.1818
135 JeanBaptiste	(65)	Genev. Roy S.G. 1826
136 Antoine	(66)	Mabor Bert. 1844
137 Antoine	(67)	Rosalie Roy Bert. 1838
138 JeanBaptiste	(67)	Cath. Blais " 1838
139 Toussaint	(68)	M. Soulange Joncas
		Bert. 1818
140 André	(68)	M. Ls. Blais " 1824
141 François	(68)	Reine Tangué " 1832
142 JeanBaptiste	(69)	Rosalie Picard " 1817
143 Gabriel	(69)	Vict. Bilodeau S.G. 1821
144 Olivier	(69)	Vict. Fortier S.G. 1823
145 André	(71)	Eliz. Guilmet Bert. 1845
146 Louis	(52)	Marie Genest S.J. 1818
Praxède		
Onésiphore		
Wenceslas		
Georges		
Sophronie		J. B. Pouliot S.P.S.
Odile		Aug. Casgrain "
Anselmie		Dr. Onésime Pelletier
		S.P.S
147 Louis	(81)	M. Ange Keroack
		S.P.S. 1822
148 JeanBaptiste	(81)	Genev. Morin S.P.S. 1829
149 Joseph	(82)	Josette Garant S.F.S.1824
150 Joseph	(83)	Marg. Turgeon S.G.1828
Prudent		
151 François Xa-	(83)	M. Reine Goupy
vier		
		S.F.S. 1832
152 Jacques	(83)	Emérence Dominque
		S.F.S. 1837
153 David	(87)	Archange Roy S.P.S. 1828
154 Augustin	(87)	Luce Bilodeau Bert. 1842
155 Antoine Hu-	(91)	M. Soulange Peltier
bert		S.P.S. 1828
156 Télesphore	(91)	M. Mad. Blanchet
		S.P.S. 1837
157 JeanBaptiste	(91)	M.Ls.Bissonnet S.M.1845
158 Alfred	(92)	Adèle Césairie Pepin
		S. M. 1852
159 Ls.Théophile	(97)	Angéle Gagnon S.V. 1849
160 Hubert	(98)	Marg. Roy S.V. 1841
André Albert		Ev. de Rimouski
Le même		Mad. Bissonet S.M. 1848
161 François Xa-	(98)	Archange Bissonnet
vier		S. M. 1846
162 Etn.Frédéric	(98)	Flavie Adéline Cor-
		riveau S.V. 1857
163 JeanBaptiste	(99)	Anastasie Bouillard
Soter		S.V. 1837
164 Adolphe	(89)	Julie Bélanger S.V. 1861
165 André	(108)	Mathilde Brochu
		S.V. 1842
166 Louis		Saly Blais
Le même		Anne Tangué S. V. 1858
167 Jean François		Eléonore Couture
Le même		Domitille Basquet " 1867

BLAIS.

168 Joseph	(113)	Marg. Bourassa S.V.1816
David		
Jean		
169 Michel	(113)	Fse. Aubé S.V. 1818
Le même		Mad. Mercier S.Chs. 1822
Luce		Jean Blais " 1846
170 Jacques	(113)	M. Luce Basquet
		S. Chs. 1827
Le même		Apolline Blais S.Chs.1828
Elizabeth		Ed. Marcoux " 1853
Louis		
Joseph		
171 Simon	(113)	Henriette Gautron
		S.V. 1829
Vilbon		
172 Louis	(113)	Henriette Pruneau
		S.G. 1829
173 Jean	(114)	Eliz. Gosselin S.G. 1824
174 Jean	(115)	Flavie Bélanger S.M. 1828
M. Césarie		Pierre Chabot S.V. 1857
Saly		Geo. Aug. Roy " 1765
Adolphe		
Jean Baptiste		
175 Michel	(115)	M. Désanges Tangué
		S.V. 1841
176 François	(116)	Marie Nadeau S.G. 1829
177 Narcisse	(117)	Flavie Talbot S.V. 1848
178 Jean Bap-	(120)	M. Ls.Pelchat S.Chs.1840
tiste		
179 François	(124)	Luce Picard S.V. 1844
Xavier		
180 Prudent	(124)	Ange. Conture Lévis 1837
M. Désanges		Honoré Marmen S.P.1868
M. Malvina		J. B. Octave Gour-
		deau S.P. 1863
Godfroi Prudent		
181 Charles	(124)	Flavie Chamberlan
		S.F.S. 1837
182 Michel	(125)	Marcelline Daniau
		S.Chs. 1836
183 Narcisse	(126)	Luce Quemeneur
		S.F.S. 1863
184 François	(129)	Marg. Cochon S.M. 1832
Xavier		
185 Prudent	(150)	Malvina Corriveau
		S.V. 1865
186 Jean	(168)	Luce Blais S. Chs. 1846
Le Même		Marcelline Gautron
		S. Chs. 1846
187 David	(168)	M. Chs. Gautron " 1848
188 Louis	(170)	Geneviève Dalaire
		S.M 1862
189 Joseph	(170)	Marcelline
		Turgeon S.M. 1862
190 Vilbon	(171)	M. Georgina
		Patouel S.V. 1862
191 Jean Bapt.	(174)	Desanges Roy S.V. 1857
192 Adolphe	(174)	Adélina Gautron
		S.V. 1864
193 Godfr.Prud.	(180)	Adé. Gourdeau S.P. 1860

BLANCHET.

1 Pierre		Marie Fournier Q. 1670
M. Madeleine		Vincent Chrétien
		S.Tho. 1699
"		2e Chs.Picard S.Tho. 1709
Pierre Alphonse		
Guillaume		
Jean		
Louis		
2 Pierre Alph.	(1)	Louise Gagné
		Cap St. Ign. 1699
M. Anne		Laurent Michon
M. Reine		Jos. Lessart
Noël		

5-6 EDWARD VII., A. 1906

BLANCHET.

Louis			
Pierre			
3 Guillaume	(1)	M.Anne Gagné S.M.	1705
M. Gertrude		Halin Boivin S.Tho.	1747
M. Marthe		Jos. Buteau	
		Cap S.Ign.	1749
4 Jean	(1)	M. Genév. Gagné	
		Bert.	1712
Geneviève		J. B. Morin	
"		2° Ls.Thibault S.F.S.	1761
Pierre			
Le Même		Genev. Rousseau	
Geneviève		J. B. Morin S.P.S.	1756
M. Claire		Michel Quemeneur	
		S.P.S.	1763
M. Louise		J.B. Thibault S.P.S.	1763
Charles			
André			
Alexis			
Jean Baptiste			
Augustin			
5 Louis	(1)	M. Ange Joby Bert.	1723
M. Louise		Jos. Couture S.P.S.	1749
Angélique		J. B. Morin S.P.S.	1751
M. Geneviève		Simon Talbot S.P.S.	1753
Marguerite		Prisque Mathieu	
		S.P.S.	1754
M. Angélique		Jos. Marie Picard	
		S.P.S.	1761
Pierre			
Jean Baptiste			
Louis			
6 Joseph		M. Jos Picard	
M. Angélique		Jos. Cloutier S.P.S.	1754
Pierre			
Jacques			
Joseph			
7 Pierre	(2)	M. Jos. Joly Bert.	1723
8 Noël	(2)	M. Xainte Fortin	
		Islet	1731
9 Louis	(2)	Génev. Fontaine	
Jacques			
Le même		M. Genev. Gagnon	
		S.F.S.	1761
10 Jean		M. Jos. Fournier	
M. Josette		Germ. Gaudreau	
		S.P.S.	1768
Joseph			
Jean Baptiste			
11 Simon		Frs. Bouchard	
M. Françoise		J. B. Huset S.P.S.	1766
12 Pierre		Cath. Rousseau	
Louise		Jos. Fontaine S.H.	1773
M. Hélène		Jos. Lefebvre S.H.	1792
Antoine			
13 Pierre	(4)	M. Gad. Gagné Islet	1740
Pierre Bernard			
Gabriel			
14 Augustin	(4)	M. Angé Gerbert	
		Cap S.Ign.	1752
M. Angélique		Jos. Marie Lévesque	
		S.P.S.	1774
Rosalie		Pierre Blanchet	
		S.P.S.	1780
M. Josette		Chs. Kiroack S.P.S.	1801
Hyacinthe			
15 Charles	(4)	Marg.Bilodeau Bert.	1754
Marguerite		Frs. Blais Bert.	1772
M. Josette		MichelGagnon S. V.	1784
"		2° Noël Gerbert	
		Bert.	1806
"		3° Frs. Pouliot Bert.	1823
Charles			
16 Alexis	(4)	M. Mad. Frégeot	
		S.F.S.	1765
M. Louise		Frs. Aime S.G.	1787

BLANCHET.

Josette		Berthe Bilodeau S.G.	1791
Reine		J. B. Guay S.G.	1797
Alexis			
17 André	(4)	Fse Buteau Bert.	1769
18 Jean Baptiste	(4)	Angé DessaintS.P.S.	1773
Marguerite		Ant. Fortin S.G.	1797
"		2° Ls. Cochon S.V.	1813
Angélique		Chs. Goulet S.G.	1800
Marie		Jos. Talbot S.G.	1801
19 Louis	(5)	M. Marg. Jalbert	
		Cap S.Ign.	1747
M. Marguerite		Ls. Lemieux S.P.S.	1779
Madeleine		J. B. Picard S.P.S.	1786
Paschal			
Joseph			
Pierre			
Louis			
20 Jean Baptiste	(5)	Genev. Picard S.P.S.	1760
M. Geneviève		André Blais S.P.S.	1781
M. Roger		Ls. Blais S.P.S.	1784
M. Pélagie		J. B. Morin S.P.S.	1790
M. Angélique		Ls. Couture S.P.S.	1792
Joseph Marie			
André			
21 Pierre	(5)	M. Blais Bert.	1767
Pierre			
Jean Baptiste			
Le même		Rosalie Blanchet	
		S.P.S.	1780
Rosalie		J. B. Peltier "	1799
M. Judith		Frs. Noël Cloutier "	1799
Pierre Michel			
Louis			
André			
Hubert			
22 Jacques		Mad. Vermet Bert.	1755
Marguerite		Julien Fontaine Bert.	1675
23 Joseph		Genev. Samson S.P.S.	1759
M. Angélique	(6)	Pierre Couture "	1793
Geneviève		Etn. Normandeau S.G.	1796
Abraham			
Pierre			
Jean Baptiste			
24 Pierre	(6)	M. Marthe Cloutier	
		S.P.S.	1761
25 Joseph		M. Jos. Quemeneur	
M. Josette		Ls. Fontaine S.P.S.	1776
Joseph Marie			
26 Alexandre		M. Ls. Pepin	
M. Louise		Frs. Cloutier S.P.S.	1777
Le même		M. Jos. Soucy "	1778
27 Jacques	(9)	M. Genev. Grondin	
		Vve St. Jos.Beauce	1764
Jacques			
28 Joseph	(10)	M. Mad. Cloutier	
		S.P.S.	1764
29 JohnBaptiste	(10)	M. Frs.Isabel "	1775
Louis Etienne			
30 Antoine	(12)	M. Agathe Roy S.V	1768
M. Louis		Lse. Gagné S.H.	1794
Louis			
Antoine			
Le même		Genev. Ferlant S.H.	1783
31 Gabriel	(13)	M. Thérèse Chamberlan	
		S.P.S.	1786
32 P. Bernard	(13)	M. Anne Gilbert Cap. S.	
		Ign.	1790
Pierre			
33 Hyacinthe	(14)	M. Eliz. Fournier	
		S.P.S.	1785
34 Charles	(15)	Reine Blais Bert.	1779
M. Reine		Pierre Boulet "	1803
Charles			
35 Alexis	(16)	Cécile Fournier S.G.	1793
Pierre			
François			

BLANCHET.

36	Louis Marie	(19)	M. Jos. Oucellet Islet 1773
	M. Archange		Jos. Lacroix S. M 1802
	Le même		Luce Bernier S.P.S 1834
37	Joseph	(19)	M. Eliz Garant S.M.1780
38	Paschal	(19)	Mad. Picard S.P.S. 1793
	Pierre		
39	Pierre	(19)	M. Ls. Chrétien S.P.S. 1794
40	Louis Marie		Marie Couillard
	Victoire		Jacq. Richard B. 1802
41	François		M. Thérèse Lamy S. Thos
	Charles		
42	André	(20)	M. Genev. Létourneau S.P.S. 1769
	Marcelline		J. B. Fontaine S.P.S.1831
	M. Natalie		Ls. Picard ,, 1832
	M. Geneviève		Aug. David Talon S P.S. 1832
	Perpétue		Frédéric Blais S.P.S.1839
	Le même		Genev. Chritien S.P.S. 1834
43	Jos. Marie	(20	M. Euphrosine Cloutier
	M. Euphrosine		Jos. Théophile Blais S.P.S. 1844
	Jules Isidore		
	Pie Célestin		
	Joseph		
44	Pierre	(21)	Claire Dambourgés S.P.S. 1790
	Joseph Felix		
	Augustin		
45	JeanBaptiste	(21)	M. Angé Samson S.P.S. 1795
46	Louis	(21)	M. Ls. Gosselin S. Chs. 1805
	Cidulie		Jos. Jolivet ,, 1854
	Albert		
	Louis		
	Damase		
	Godfroi		
47	André	(21)	Rosalie Roy S. Chs. 1821
48	Pierre Michel	(21)	M. Cécile Blais S.F.S. 1821
49	Hubert	(21)	Julie Provost S.Chs. 1846
	Julie Olive		Etn. Plante ,, 1840
	André		
	Magloire		
50	Thomas	(21)	M. Mad. Morin S.Roch des Aunets 1813
	M. Madeleine		Telesphore Blais S.P.S. 1837
	Louis Norbert		
51	Pierre	(23)	M. Vict. Morin S.P.S. 1784
52	JeanBaptiste	(28)	M. Ls. Turgeon S. Chs, 1789
	M. Angileque		Jos. Belanger S.V. 1814
	Jean Baptiste		
53	Abraham	(23)	M. Thérèse Fournier S.P.S. 1803
	Marcelline		Pierre Baudoin S. V. 1832
	Marie		Ls. Théberge ,, 1835
	Luce		Ls. Théberge ,, 1841
	Abraham		
54	Joseph Marie	(25)	Agathe Godbout B. 1780
	Agathe		Alexis Fluet S.G. 1806
55	Jacques	(27)	Susanne Tailleur S.P.1788
	Madeleine		Philippe Charet ,, 1809
56	LouisEtienne	(29)	Cath. Brousseau S.M.1821
57	Antoine	(30)	Genev. Ferlant S.H. 1783
58	Louis	(30)	Louise Gagné S.G. 1800
	Le même		Genev Godbout S.H.1805
59	Pierre	(32)	Cath.Clément S.Chs. 1817
60	Charles	(41)	M. Thérèse Talon S.P.S. 1811

18—15

BLANCHET.

61	Charles	(34)	Marg. Guilmet Bert. 1807
62	Pierre	(35)	Genev. Clément S.M.1826
63	François	(35)	Marg. Fradet ,, 1829
	François		
64	Zacharie, fils de Jacq.and deM. Agnès Dodier.		M. Anne Daniel Q. 1791 Riv. du Loup
	Zacharie		
65	Pierre	(38)	Marg. Gagnon S.V. 1817
66	Joseph	(43)	M.AnneTalbotS.P.S.1822
67	Pierre Celestin	(43)	M. Genev. Bacon S.P.S. 1823
68	Jules Isidore	(43)	Euphrosine Anastasie Baudoin S.P.S. 1832
69	Joseph Felix	(44)	Marg. Picard ,, 1820
70	Augustin	(44)	M. Luce Picard ,, 1821
71	Louis	(46)	M. Emélie Lavergne S.P.S. 1823
72	Damase	(46)	M. Anne Couture S.Chs. 1839
73	Godfroi	(46)	M. Caroline Turgeon S.Chs. 1846
74	Albert	(46)	Adéline Couillard B. 1848
75	André	(49)	Mélamie Turgeon S.Chs. 1861
76	Magloire	(49)	Marg. Mercier ,, 1863
77	Ls. Norbert	(50)	Thérèse Blais S.P.S. 1839
78	JeanBaptiste	(52)	M.Ange.Gosselin S.Chs. 1813
	Joseph		
79	Abraham	(53)	Marg. Dépont S.V. 1836
80	François	(63)	M. Vict. Jahan ,, 1862
81	Zacharie	(64)	Basillisse Couillard S.Tho. 1826
	Eulalie		Jos. Dorval S.M. 1851
82	Joseph	(78)	Vitaline Quemenneur S.V. 1857

BLEAU.

1			
2			
3	François		Bernier
	Le même		Frs. Lemoine S.M. 1760
4	Antoine		M. Mad. Bluteau
	M. Josette		Ls. Paquet S.M. 1765
	,,		2° Etn. Monmeny ,, 1776
	Le même		Mad. Monmeny ,, 1777
5	Jean		Marie Nolin
6	Le même		M. Anne Lacasse S.Chs. 1758

BLONDEAU.

1	Germain		Mad. Beauchamp Isle Verte 1730
	M. Agathe		Frs. Mercier Bert. 1754
	,,		2°Aug. Mathieu ,, 1798
	M Anne		Jos. Bernier ,, 1758
	M. Louise		Jos. Gautron S.V. 1766
	Germain		
2	Germain	(1)	Eliz.BonchardS.Tho.1765
	Le même		M.ReineLessartS.M.1773
	M. Reine		Jos. Lainé S. V. 1795
	M. Madeleine		Jos. Mareau ,, 1804
	M. Josette		Jos. Fortin ,, 1808

BLOUIN.

1	Médéric		Marie Carreau C.R. 1669
	Marie		Chs. Campagna S.J. 1662
	Geneviève		Jean Letarte ,, 1714
	,,		2° Pierre Tardif A.G.1722
	Anne		Ls. Letoureau S.J. 1796
	Catherine		Claude Guion ,, 1700
	Madeleine		Ant. Pepin ,, 1722

BLOUIN.

Gabriel		
Jean		
Jacques		
2 Jean	(1)	Mad. Langlois S.Tho.1700
Joseph Marie		
Gabriel		
Le même		Cath. Trudel A.G. 1725
3 Jacques	(1)	M. Genev. Racine
		S. Anne 1708
Joseph		
Le même		Genev. Plante S.J. 1715
Geneviève		Jos. Marie Thivierge
		S.J. 1746
"		2 Aug. Manseau " 1756
Angélique		Gervais Pepin " 1743
M. Josette		Jacq. Tremblay " 1756
M. Louise		Jos. Leblond " 1773
M. Anne		Jos. Boissonneau " 1777
Marguerite		Ignace Gosselin " 1787
Charles		
Jacques		
4 Gabriel	(1)	Cath. Jahan " 1713
Marguerite		J. B. Gaulin " 1742
Madeleine		Jos. Dion " 1752
Marie		Jos. Meneux " 1847
"		2 Jean Guion S.F. 1751
Jean Baptiste		
René		
Louis		
Jacques		
Gabriel		
François		
Paul		
5 Joseph Marie	(2)	M. Jos. Blais Bert. 1734
Geneviève		Basile Thivierge S.J. 1754
M. Josette		Jos. Lacroix S.J. 1755
M. Catherine		Frs. Blouin S.J. 1774
M. Marguerite		Jos. Perrot S.J. 1763
M. Anne		J. B. Coté S.P.S. 1771
Joseph		
Jean		
Charles		
Le même		Mad. Turcot S.F. 1751
6 Gabriel	(2)	Ange Baudouin S.Frs.1739
M. Angélique		André Picard Bert. 1774
Gabriel		
7 Joseph	(3)	M. Mad. Mercier
		S. Anne 1737
M. Josette		Jos. Gagnon 1763
Pierre		
8 Charles	(3)	M. Mad. Tremblay
		S.L. 1664
M. Madeleine		Jos. Boissonneau S.J.1785
9 Jacques	(3)	M. Cath. Gosselin
M. Geneviève		Frs. Leblond S.J. 1777
Jacques		
Charles		
Louis		
10 Gabriel	(4)	M. Mad. Perrot S.F. 1741
M. Madeleine		Berth. Terrien S.J. 1761
"		2 Ls. Bussière S.Chs.1791
Elizabeth		J. B. Fortier S.J. 1775
M. Catherine		Basile Plante S. J. 1776
11 Jean Baptiste		M. Anne Delage S.J.1754
M. Anne		Frs. Théberge S.F.S. 1783
M. Thérèse		Ls. Fontaine S.F.S. 1784
M. Louise		Frs. Fontaine S.F.S. 1787
Madeleine		Jacques Picard S.F.S.1889
Joseph		
12 Louis	(4)	Angé Roberge S.P. 1755
M. Charlotte		Barth. Pepin S.J. 1801
M. Josette		Jacq. Bidet S.J. 1777
"		2 Guil. Terrien S.J. 1793
Eméry		
Pierre		
13 François	(4)	Hélène Leclaire S.P. 1755
Marie		Jos. Bazin S.H. 1812

BLOUIN.

François		
Joseph		
Emery		
Gabriel		
Le même		M. Cath. Blouin S.J.1774
Louis		
14 René		M. Jos. Plante S.J. 1706
M. Angélique		J. B. Ferlant S.J. 1786
M. Elizabeth		Etn. Boissonneau S.J.1792
M. Anne		Chs. Blouard S.J. 1793
René		
Le même		M. Jos. Niel S.P. 1788
15 Jacques	(4)	M. Céleste Rochon
		S.F. 1761
Etienne		
16 Paul		Hélène Gagnon
		S. Anne 1775
Hélène		Ls. Pichet S.F. 1830
M. Josette		Michel Savoie S.Frs. 1817
Gabriel		
Jean Baptiste		
17 Gabriel		M. Angé Audebert
M. Angèle		Job. Fortier S.J. 1808
Joseph		
18 Joseph	(5)	M. Jos. Leclaire S.P.1764
M. Madeleine		Ant. Pepin S.J. 1795
Jean François		
Joseph		
Le même		M. Mad. Goupy S.M.1774
Barthélemi		
Paul		
19 Jean	(5)	M. Chs. Lescabut
		S.Frs. 1773
M. Jos. Natalie		Jacq. Blouin S.J. 1800
M. Marguerite		J. B. Turcot S.J. 1813
Jean François		
Joseph		
20 Charles	(5)	M. Jos.Tremblay S.J.1778
Le même		Ursule Blouin S.J. 1812
21 Gabriel	(6)	M. Genev. Mercier
		Bert. 1763
M. Geneviève		Jos. Lemieux Bert. 1786
M. Louise		Jos. Aubé Bert. 1793
M. Marguerite		Nicolas Pouliot Bert.1794
M. Geneviève		Frs. Bolduc Bert. 1815
André Louis		
22 Pierre	(7)	M. Dorothée Martineau
		S.F. 1764
Jacques		
23 Jacques	(9)	M. Mad. Leblanc S.J.1773
M. Madeleine		Jos. Blouin S.J. 1798
"		2 Jos. Lainé S.J. 1807
Elizabeth		Frs. Dessaint S.J. 1809
Jacques		
24 Charles	(9)	M.Chs.Thivierge S.J.1783
Charlotte		Chs. Leblanc S.J. 1813
M. Josette		Jos. Paquet S.J. 1826
M. Madeleine		Louis Pepin S.J. 1819
Charles		
Jacques		
Joseph		
François		
25 Louis	(9)	M. Jos. Drouin S.J. 1790
Sophie		Pierre Gautier S.J. 1819
Joseph		
26 Joseph	(11)	Mad. Angé Remillard
		S.V. 1784
Marie		Jos. Aubé S.H. 1811
François		
Pierre		
Joseph		
27 Emery	(12)	Josette S.J. 1786
M. Ursule		Chs. Blouin " 1816
Apolline		Frs. Campagna " 1820
M. Josette		Pierre Blouin " 1822
Julienne		Ls. Poulin " 1822
M. Thérèse		Jos. Lainé " 1827

BLOUIN.

M. Charlotte	Ls. Lainé	„	1827
Angèle	Ant. Turgeon	„	1836
Emery			
Pierre			
28 Pierre (12)	Marg. Moreau	S.G.	1794
Marguerite	Jos. Fournier	„	1817
Marie .	Ls. Plante	„	1820
Judith	J. B. Mercier	„	1823
Charles			
29 François (13)	Angé Pouliot	S.J.	1781
Joseph Marie			
Jean François			
30 Joseph (13)	M. Jos. Cochon	S.J.	1788
Alexis			
Gabriel			
A Emery (13)	Marg. Hélie	S.J.	1790
B Gabriel (13)	Gertrude Grenet	S.H.	1800
31 Louis (13)	M. Angèle Cochon	S.J.	1808
Le même	Ursule Fontaine	S.H.	1816
32 Réné (14)	Genev. Terrien	S.J.	1786
M. Josette	Frs. Pouliot	„	1808
Geneviève	Jos. Blouin	„	1809
Euphrosine	Pierre Labrecque	„	1822
Marie	Laurent Thivierge	S.J.	1814
Réné			
Emery			
Pierre			
François			
Jean			
Paul			
Guillaume			
33 Etienne (15)	M. Angé Roberge	S.P.	1787
M. Olive	Jacq. Gosselin	S.F.	1820
M. Anne	Prosper Bisson	„	1832
Geneviève	J. B. Gosselin	„	1832
Joseph			
Le même	Abondance Tremblay	S.F.	1815
34 Gabriel (16)	Marg. Dupuis	S.J.	1804
35 JeanBaptiste(16)	M. Ls. Martineau	S. Frs.	1807
36 Joseph (17)	Hélène Audet	S.J.	1794
M. Angèle	J. B. Giguière	„	1824
Angélique	Chs. Labrecque	„	1847
Hélène	Jérémie Turcot	„	1852
Guillaume			
Gabriel			
37 Joseph (18)	Mad. Blouin	S.J.	1798
38 JeanFrançois(18)	Véronique Roy	S.M.	1806
	V. de Chs. Dubord		
39 Paul (18)	Vict. Turcot	S.J.	1813
40 Barthelemi (18)	Marie Gosselin	S. Chs.	1805
M. Marguerite	Simon Gosselin	„	1822
41 Joseph (19)	Genev. Blouin	S. J.	1809
Paul			
42 JeanFrançois(19)	Marg. Turcot	S.J.	1810
Marguerite	Magl. Demeule	„	1836
Cécile	Frs. Blouin	„	1851
Jean			
43 Gabriel (21)	M. Jos. Lemieux	Bert.	1792
Amable			
Marie	Jean Brochu	S.G.	1813
Louise	Michel Bilodean	„	1817
Victoire	Jacq. Lefebvre	„	1816
44 Basile (21)	M. Anne Harpe	S.V.	1797
Marie	J. B. Bilodeau	Bert.	1817
M. Apolline	J. B. Bolduc	„	1824
Basile			
45 André Louis (21)	Rose Blais	„	1798
Rosalie	Michel Gosselin	Bert.	1818
Louise	Frs. Lefebvre	„	1823

18—15½

BLOUIN.

François			
Louis			
46 JeanBaptiste(21)	M. Cath. Corriveau	S.V.	1805
Catherine	J. B. Couillard	Bert.	1826
Le même	M. Angé Bergevin	Bert.	1816
Amable Nazaire			
47 Jacques (22)	M. Cath. Dalaire	S. Frs.	1807
48 Jacques (23)	Josette Natalie Blouin	S.J.	1800
Benjamin			
Jacques			
49 Charles (24)	M. Cath. Hébert	S.J.	1812
Charles			
Joseph			
Le même	M. Anne Lebrecque	S.J.	1819
Angèle	Ls. Pepin	„	1842
M. Anne	Tho. Theberge	„	1845
Cécile	Jos. Hébert	„	1857
Jean			
François			
Louis			
Paul			
Pierre			
Guillaume			
50 Jacques (24)	M. Anne Délage	S.J.	1812
Apolline	Geo. Turcot	„	1846
Marcelline	Paschal Langlois	S.J.	1849
51 Joseph (24)	Genev. Labrecque	„	1823
52 François (24)	M. Anne Bacquet	„	1827
53 Joseph (25)	Marie Turcot	S.F.	1831
54 François (26)	Angé Quéret	S.V.	1806
Le même	Mad. Tangué	„	1830
55 Pierre (26)	Cath. Plante	S.Chs.	1816
56 Joseph (26)	Marie Plante	„	1816
58 Emery (27)	Josette Terrien	S.J.	1838
58 Pierre (27)	Justine Leblanc	„	1839
59 Charles (28)	Louise Morisset	S.G.	1823
60 JeanFrançois(29)	Euphrosine Delisle	S.J.	1808
Justine	Paul Dalaire	„	1843
Françoise			
61 Joseph Marie(29)	M. Angé Paquet	„	1812
Jérémie			
Jean Baptiste			
Joseph			
Ferdinand			
62 Gabriel (30)	M. Angé Thivierge	S.J.	1810
Adelaïde	Frs. Dumas	„	1832
François			
Louis			
Paul			
Joseph			
Magloire			
63 Alexis (30)	Mad. Thivierge	S.J.	1818 Q
64 René (32)	Cécile Pepin	S.J.	1811
Christine	Frs. Blouin	„	1832
Emélie	Paul Blouin	„	1844
Charles			
65 Emery (32)	Marie Audibert	„	1817
Ursule	Jos. Fradet	„	1845
Julie	Chs. Lainé	„	1852
„	F. X. Terrien	„	1856
Marcelline	Frs. Hébert	„	1855
Eléonore	Nazaire Pepin	„	1857
Philomène	Michel Quemeneur	S.J.	1863
François			
Charles			
René			

BLOUIN.

66	Pierre	(32)	Frs. Gosselin	S.J.	1819
	Le même		M. Jos. Blouin	"	1822
	Marcelline		Jos. Audet	"	1847
67	Guillaume	(32)	Marg. Plante S.Frs.		1820
	François Xavier				
	Jean				
68	François	(32)	Julie Cotin	S.J.	1825
	Ferdinand				
	Le même		M. Barbe Roy S.V.		1837
	Antoine Hubert				
69	Jean	(32)	Esther Gosselin S.J.		1833
	Hubert				
70	Paul	(32)	Marg. Simard	"	1834
	Philomène		Jos. Pepin	"	1862
71	Joseph	(33)	Marie Lamothe S.F.		1831
	Marie		Bruno Prémont	"	1862
	Joseph				
72	Guillaume	(36)	M. Jos. Cochon S.J.		1819
	M. Josette		Samuel Fortier	"	1840
	Henriette		Jos. Dupuis	"	1851
	Luce		"	"	1852
	Philomène		Honoré Langlois	"	1856
	Guillaume				
	Joseph				
	Edouard				
	François Xavier				
73	Gabriel	(36)	Marie Emond	S.J.	1822
				S.H.	
74	Paul	(41)	Adé Simard	S.J.	1843
	Theophile				
75	Jean	(42)	Emélie Marseau		
				S.Frs.	1843
76	Basile	(44)	M. Vict. Balan S.V.		1823
	Le même		Rosalie Bolduc S.M.		1827
77	François	(44)	Louise Nadeau S.H.		1796
	Olivier				
78	François	(35)	Adé Brochu	S.V.	18:6
79	Louis	(45)	Mad.Brousseau Bert.		1823
80	Amable Na-	(46)	Delphine Fortin S.V.		1840
	zaire				
81	Jacques	(48)	M. Anne Fortin S.J.		1825
	Le même		Marie Gaulin	"	1841
82	Benjamin	(48)	Henriette Pepin	"	1845
83	Charles	(49)	Emérence Plante	"	1836
84	Joseph	(49)	Marie Pepin	"	1842
85	Jean	(49)	Marie Roberge	"	1850
86	François	(49)	Marie Hébert	"	1853
87	Paul	(49)	Julie Turcot	"	1855
88	Pierre	(49)	PhilomèneFortier	"	1857
89	Louis	(49)	Demerise Curadeau		
				S.J.	1858
90	Guillaume	(49)	Julie Turcot	"	1863
91	François	(60)	Cath. Gosselin	S.J.	1831
	Catherine		Chs. Langlois	"	1856
	Louis Adeline				
	Jean				
	François-Xavier				
92	Jérémie		Cath. Pichet	S.J.	1841
93	Joseph		Henriette Poulins	.J.	1841
94	J.-Baptiste	(61)	Ursule Pichet S.J.		1841
95	Ferdinand	(61)	Justin Thevierge	S.J.	1857
96	François	(62)	Christine Blouin	S.J.	1832
	Julie		Edouard Blouin	"	1854
	Delvina		Paul Litourneau	"	1861
	Marie		Jos. Paquet	"	1862
	Lumina		Jos. Pichet	"	1864
	Joseph				
97	Magloire	(62)	Josette GodboutS.L		1832
	Le même		Josette Dalaire, S. Croix		
					1858
98	Paul	(62)	Emelie Blouin	S.J.	1844
99	Louis	(62)	Angé Dupuis	S.J.	1844
	Le même		Marg. Jahan	"	1857
100	Joseph	(62)	Angé Labrecque		1848
101	Charles	(64)	Cécile Pouliot	S.J.	1852
102	François	(65)	Cécile Blouin	S.J.	1851

BLOUIN.

103	René	(65)	Marcelline Pepin	S.J.	1852
104	Charles	(65)	Mad. Pouliot	S.J.	1860
105	Jean	(67)	Marie Gaulin	S.F.	1849
106	François-Xa-	(67)	MarcellineDalaire	S.J	1859
	vier				
107	Ferdinand	(68)	Sara Pedeak	S.J.	1856
108	Ant. Hubert	(68)	Car. Hort. Verginie Roy		
	Honoré			S.V.	1864
109	Hubert	(69)	M. Anne Pepin S.J.		1865
110	Joseph	(71)	Caroline Drouin S.F.		1855
111	Guillaume	(72)	Séraphine PichetS.	J.	1846
112	Joseph	(72)	Odile Tangué	S.J.	1850
113	Edouard	(72)	Julie Blouin	S.J.	1854
	Joseph				
114	François Xa-(72)		Philomène Pouliot		
	vier			S.J.	1864
115	Théophile	(74)	Lea Picard	S.Frs.	1861
116	Olivier	(77)	Scolastique Tanqué		
				S.Chs.	1838
117	François Xa (91)		Henriette Noël S.L.		1854
	vier				
118	Louis Adeline				
			(91)	Adé Toussaint S.J.	1857
119	Jean	(91)	Adé Dion	S.J.	1865
120	Joseph	(113)	M. Aurelie Leclaire		
				S.L.	1878

BLOUARD.

1	Mathurin		Marg. Poulet	S.F.	1671
	Madeleine		J. B. Ratté	S.P.	1698
	Marquerite		Jean Goulet	"	1700
	Anne		Jean Roberge	"	1709
	"		2° Jean Cochon	"	1717
	Mathieu				
	Jean Baptiste				
2	Mathieu	(1)	Mad. Ferlant	S.P.	1707
3	Jean-Baptiste(1)		Marie Roberge	S.P.	1711
	Véronique		Pierre Leclaire	"	1751
	Marie		Jos. Asselin	"	1735
	Geneviève		Chs. Aubin	"	1767
	Charles				
4	Charles	(3)	Reine Montigny	S.P.	1761
	Thérèse		J. B. Volant de		
			Champlain	S.P.	1785
	Reine		Chs. Guay	S.P.	1793
	Charles				
5	Charles	(4)	M. Anne Blouin	S.J.	1793

BOILARD.

1	Jean		Jeanne Maranda	Q.	1680
	Claude				
	Jean-Baptiste				
	Mathieu				
2	Mathieu	(1)	Marie Audet	S.L.	1729
	M. Thérèse		Ls. Bourré	B.	1761
	M. Anne		J. B. Nadeau	"	1764
	Catherine		Jos. Guay	S.M.	1756
	"		2° Jos. Gosselin	"	1783
	Nicolas				
3	Jean-Baptiste(1)		Marg. Palin	Q.	1693
	Le même		M. Genev. ValiéreS.	P	1720
4	Claude		M. Anne Larrivé	B.	1738
	Claude				
5	Nicolas	(2)	M. Chs. Girard	B.	1756
	M. Josette		Jacq. Girard	"	1793
	Alexandre				
	Louis				
6	Claude	(4)	M. Fse. Bourré, Chs.		
				Bourg	1761
	Marguerite		Jos. Bourassa	B.	1785
	M. Charlotte		Frs. Begin	"	1788
	Josette		Pierre Valière	"	1796
	Claude				

BOILARD.

```
    Joseph
 7  Augustin
    M. Catherine        M. Vict. Tremblay
    Michel              J. B. Turgeon S.M. 1787
    Le Même             M. Jos. Bolduc S. V. 1764
 8  Alexandre      (5)  M. Chs. Bergeron B. 1791
    M. Charlotte        Charlemagne Couil-
                            lard          B. 1813
    Cecile              Jos. Amable Couil-
                            lard          B. 1813
 9  Louis          (5)  M. Ch. Labrecque B. 1798
    M. Josephine        Chs. Guay         B. 1831
    M. Charlotte        Bénoni Bergeron B. 1839
    Edouard
10  Claude         (6)  M. Eliz. Hélie Levis.1789
    Marguerite          Jos. Roy      S. G. 1819
    Marie               Ls. Lessard   S. G. 1847
    Isidore
    Antione
    Le Même             Ursule Boulet S. G. 1815
                        V. de Simon Talbot
11  Joseph         (6)  Susanne Girard   B. 1796
    M. Charlotte        J. B. Labrecque  ,, 1830
    François
    Etienne
    Joseph
    Charles
12  Michel         (7)  Angé Adam     S. M. 1789
13  Edouard        (9)  Luce Bacquet  S. M. 1843
14  Antoine       (10)  Judith Roy    S. G. 1828
15  Isidore       (10)  Rosalie Baudouin S.G.1818
16  François      (11)  M. Anne Filteau B. 1828
17  Etienne       (11)  M. Ls. Guay      B. 1829
18  Joseph        (11)  Marg. Guay    Levis. 1822
    Célina              Ls. Larrivé      B. 1853
    Henriette           Frédéric Rousseau ,, 1859
    Prudent
    Joseph
    Louis
 A  Charles       (11)  Vict. Gontier Lévis. 1831
19  Joseph        (18)  Cath. Turgeon    B. 1846
20  Prudent       (18)  Henriette Dubé   B. 1857
21  Louis         (18)  Marie Bilodeau   B. 1852
```

BOISSEL.

```
 1  Jacques
    Marguerite          Marie Herepel
                        Etn. Bouchard      1687
    ,,                  2° Julien Joyau    1687
    Noël
    Gilles
    Guillaume
 2  Noël           (1)  Marie Morin      Q. 1669
    François            Pierre Lefebvre  B. 1704
    Claude
    Louis
    Pierre Noël
 3  Claude         (1)  Louise Leblanc
 4  Gilles         (1)  Marg. Salois  S. F. 1697
 5  Claude         (2)  Marg. Morin        1693
    Marguerite          Ls. Bourbeau     Q. 1717
    Marthe              J. B. Levitre    ,, 1721
 6  Pierre Noël    (2)  Louise Gesseron    1707
    Louise              J. B. Labrecque  B. 1727
    Marie               Pierre Forgues   ,, 1737
    Madeleine           J. B. Caron      ,, 1745
    Joseph
    Louis
    Charles
 7  Louis          (2)  Genev. Coté   A. G. 1707
 8  Pierre              Ursule Caron
    Catherine           Ls. Pouliot   S. Chs. 1770
    ,,                  2° Frs. Coté     ,, 1798
    Jean Baptiste
 9  Joseph         (6)  Angé Gosselin S. V. 1763
10  Charles        (6)  Rosalie Doison S.Chs.1763
```

BOILARD.

```
    M. Charlotte        Ant. Gosselin    ,,  1789
    M. Josette          Jos. Valière     ,,  1802
    Catherine           André Dupont     ,,  1807
    Marie               J. B. Dupont     ,,  1807
    ,,                  2° Aug. Pilote   ,,  1817
    Joseph
    Antoine
11  Louis               Angé Lacasse      B. 1755
    M. Angélique        Ls. Canier       ,,  1786
    Françoise           Ls. Mariage      ,,  1797
    Le même             M.Marg.Plante S.M.1775
    Marguerite          Pierre Blais    Bert. 1801
12  Jean Baptiste (8)   Genev. Queret S. M. 1774
13  Antoine      (10)   Marg. Roy     S. Chs. 1794
    Marguerite          Timothé Garant S.G.1812
    Antoine
    Le même             Charlotte Valière
                                        S. G. 1799
    Charles
    Le même             M. Anne Gonthier
                                        S.G. 1813
14  Joseph       (10)   Marg. Bussière   B. 1801
    Marguerite          F. X. Couture   ,,  1829
    Françoise           J. B. Roy     S. Chs. 1835
    Marie               Michel Poliquin S.Chs1825
    ,,                  2° Pierre Quemeneur
                                        S.M. 1833
    Julie               Pierre Fortin   ,,  1839
    Charles
15  Antoine      (13)   Marguerite      S.G. 1842
16  Charles      (13)   Charlotte Gosselin
                                        S.G. 1830
17  Charles      (14)   Angé Labrecque
                                        S. Chs. 1835
```

BOISSONNEAU—ST. ONGE.

```
 1  Vincent             Anne Colin     S.F. 1669
    Isabelle            René Desloriers S.J. 1694
    Jeanne              J. B. Gélina    ''  1700
    Nicolas
    Jean
 2  Nicolas        (1)  Anne Jeanne Poisson
                                        S.L. 1685
    Thérèse             Chs. Lefebvre  S.J. 1741
 3  Jean           (1)  Marg Choret    S.F. 1707
    Elizabeth           Pre. Noël Plante S.J.1746
    ,,                  2° Claude Guion ,, 1783
    Nicolas
    Joseph
    Pierre
 4  Jean Baptiste       Josette Demeule
    Madeleine           Gab. Dufour    S.J. 1756
    M. Josette          Ls. Emond       ,, 1757
    M. Louise           Guill. Terrien  ,, 1764
    ,,                  2° Ant. Coulombe ,, 1772
    Joseph
 5  Nicolas             Anne Fse Tangué
                                        S.V. 1734
    Anne Françoise      Michel Philippe Daniau
                                        S.F.S. 1758
    M. Josette          J. B. Marseau S.F.S. 1758
    M. Thérèse          Jaq. Baudouin   ,, 1761
    M. Angélique        Noël Roy     Bert. 1767
    Pierre Nicolas
    Joseph
    Le même             Génév. Plante S.F.S. 1755
    Nicolas François
 6  Pierre         (3)  Génév. Gontier   B. 1740
    Marie               Gab. Duquet S.Chs. 1763
    Françoise           Jean Plante     ,, 1723
 7  Joseph         (3)  Marg. Blais   Bert. 1747
    Victoire            Frs. Thibaut S.F.S. 1787
    Marguerite          Ignace Fortier  ,, 1789
    M. Madeleine        Jean Marie Fradet
                                        S.F.S. 1791
```

BOISSONNEAU—ST. ONGE.

	Nicolas			
	Joseph			
	Michel			
	Jean Baptiste			
8	Joseph	(4)	Anne Mad. Blouin	S.J. 1785
	M. Marguerite		Jos. Demeule	S.J. 1809
	M. Anne		Pierre Terrien ,,	1801
	M. Josette		Ls. Abraham Del sle	S.J. 1819
	M. Anne		Frs. Beaucher	S.F. 1880
	Jean François			
	Amable			
	Pierre			
	Joseph			
9	Pierre Nicolas (5)		Thérèse Genderon	S.F.S. 1763
	Marguerite		Chrysostome Dumas	S.F.S. 1796
	M. Thérèse		Etn. Boulet ,,	1797
	M. Angélique		Frs. Morin ,,	1798
	Françoise		Pierre Canac	S.P. 1797
	Pierre			
	Louis			
10	Joseph	(5)	Mad. Boutin	S.F.S. 1765
	Geneviève		And. Thibaut ,,	1806
	Josette		Ls. Valière	S.H. 1807
11	Nicolas Frs.	(5)	Mad. Pilote	S.M. 1802
	Marguerite		Michel Mercier ,,	1822
12	Joseph Marie		M. Jos. Asselin	
	M. Louise		J. B. Bégin	S.H. 1795
	Madeleine		Claude Vaillancour	S.J. 1801
	Etienne			
	Louis			
13	Nicolas	(7)	Marie McNeil	S.V. 1789
	M. Anne		Firmin Bois ,,	1811
	Marcelline		Jos. Fortier ,,	1876
	Angile		Pierre Leblond ,,	1829
	Archange		Jacq. Fradet	S.M. 1818
	Nicolas			
	Jean			
	Prudent			
	Pierre			
	Joseph			
14	Jean Baptiste (7)		M. Eliz. Buteau	S.F.S. 1777
	Elizabeth		Jos. Jolin	
	Le même		M. Chaire Lamandeau	S.F.S. 1787
	Thomas			
	Louis			
	Augustin			
15	Joseph	(7)	M. Genev. Gagnon	S.F.S. 1775
	M. Geneviève		Michel Guilmet S.V.	1813
	M. Reine		Chas. Hébert ,,	1814
	Jacques			
16	Michel	(7)	Marie Bolduc	S.V. 1791
A	Joseph	(8)	Eliz. Helie	S.H. 1799
17	Jean François (8)		Julie Pouliot	S.J. 1803
	Julie		Frs. Hébert ,,	1832
	,,		2° Jean Plante ,,	1860
	Constance		J. B. Audet ,,	1835
	Madeleine		Magl. Pichet ,,	1838
18	Pierre	(8)	M. Angile Pepin ,,	1807
	Soulange		Frs. Curadeau ,,	1835
	Cécile		Jos. Terrien ,,	1839
	,,		2° PierreCoulombe ,,	1854
	Christine		F. X. Gagnon ,,	1843
	Damase			
	François Xavier			
19	Amable	(8)	Ursule Pichet	S.L. 1821
	François			
20	Pierre	(9)	Marg. Morin	S.F.S. 1789
	Pierre			

BOISSONNEAU—ST. ONGE.

21	Louis	(9)	M. Reine Mercier	S.F.S. 1798
	Marcelline		Gab. Aube	S.F.S. 1831
	M. Zoé		Jos. Canac ,,	1842
	M. Lorette		Magl. Morin ,,	1842
	Louis			
	Pierre			
	Vital			
23	Louis	(13)	M. Eliz. Morriset	S.M. 1792
	Le même		M. Eliz. Guérard	S.J. 1802
24	Etienne	(12)	M. Eliz. Blouin S.J.	1792
	Marguerite		Jean Charlan ,,	1816
	M. Elizabeth		Martin Giguère ,,	1827
	Angèle		Louis Moor ,,	1834
	Jean			
	Joseph			
	Pierre			
	Louis			
25	Nicolas	(13)	——Mathurin	Q.
26	Joseph	(13)	Cath. Buteau S.F.S.	1822
27	Prudent	(13)	Flavie Bolduc	S.V. 1825
28	Jean	(13)	Angèle Beaudouin	S.V. 1839
29	Pierre	(13)	M. Emélie McNeil	S.M. 1847
30	Jacques		Josette Gagnon S.V,	1839
31	Jacques		Josette Queret	
	Le même		Marcelline Richard	S.V. 1845
32	François-	(18)	Henriette Gagnon	S.J. 1843
	Xavier			
33	Damase	(18)	M. Hombeline Terrien	S.L. 1853
	Belzimire		Pierre Gosselin ,,	1879
34	François	(19)	Emélie Demeule S.J.	1850
35	Pierre	(20)	Marg. Rouleau S.R.	1810
	Marguerite		Jos. Gaulin S.F.S.	1831
	Elizabeth		Joseph Paré ,,	1835
	M. Angèle		Luc Boulet ,,	1841
	Pierre			
	Le même		Genev. Talbot ,,	1832
36	Pierre	(21)	Archange Aubé S.L.	1827
37	Vital	(21)	Constance Morin	S.F.S. 1835
38	Louis	(21)	Eliz. Turgeon	B. 1832
	M. Elizabeth		Jos. Gautron ,,	1851
39	Thomas	(14)	Marie Couture	S.P. 1833
40	Augustin	(14)	Thècle Noël	S.P. 1852
	M. Olive		Nazaire Chatigny ,,	1865
41	Louis	(14)	Cécile Rousseau S.P.	1825
42	Jean	(24)	Marie Giguère	S,J. 1827
	François Xavier			
	Joseph			
43	Joseph	(24)	M. Angèle Giguère	S.J. 1827
44	Pierre	(24)	Vict Labbé	S. Frs. 1837
45	Louis	(24)	Cath. Dompierre	S. Frs. 1853
46	Pierre	(35)	M. Restitut Couture	S. Frs. 1836
47	François-	(42)	Eléonore Labrecque	S.J. 1865
	Xavier			
48	Joseph	(42)	Rose Dalaire	S.J. 1865

BOIVIN

1	Pierre	Etiennette Fafart	3 Riv. 1664
	Marie	Jos. Simard S Anne	1702
	Augustin		
	Pierre		
	Jean		
	Charles		

BOIVIN.

2	Pierre	(1)	M. Anne Paré S. Anne 1710
3	Charles	(1)	Anne Aimee Poulin S. Anne 1714
4	Jean	(1)	Mad. Simard S. Anne 1825
5	Augustin	(1)	Barbe Gagné
	Pierre		
	Le même		Reine Simard S. Anne 1825
6	Pierre	(5)	Hélène Labbé S. Frs. 1747
	Le même		Louise Bissonnet " 1757
	Le même		M.Jos. Morin S.F.S. 1767
	Joseph		
7	Hélin		M. Gertrude Blanchet S. Tho. 1747
	Simon		
	Joseph		
8	Pierre		Josette Boutin
	Le même		Cath. Robitaille, Lorette 1743
	Catherine		Ls Létourneau S.V. 1781
	"		Etn. Corriveau " 1785
	Thérèse		J. B. Dorval " 1787
9	Joseph	(6)	Marie Deblois S.F. 1799
10	Simon	(7)	M. Genev. Gagnon S.F.S. 1767
	M. Euphrosine		Pierre Fortier S.F.S. 1790
	Geneviève		Jos. Gagnon " 1793
	Simon		
	Jean-Baptiste		
	François		
	Michel		
11	Joseph	(7)	M. Scolastique Chiasson S.F.S. 1773
	Marie		Toussaint Langlois S.M. 1707
12	Simon	(9)	Reine Gagnon S.F.S.1792
	Ursule		J. B. Beaucher " 1823
	Elizabeth		J. B Morin " 1837
	Marcelline		Jos. Samson " 1843
	Françoise		Chs. Langlois S.V. 1819
	Reine		Félix Bélanger " 1821
	M. Sophie		Ant. Mercier " 1829
	Antoine		
	François Xavier		
	Simon		
	Jérôme		
13	Jean Baptiste	(9)	Marg.MarseauS. F.S.1797
	Brigitte		Flavien Duchesneau S.F.S.1824
	Le même		Marg. Paquet " 1807
A	Michel		Reine Fse. Picard S.P.S. 1798
14	François	(9)	Vict. Gagnon S. F.S.1809
15	Antoine	(12)	Reine Fradet S.V. 1819
	Reine		Frs. Marseau S.F.S.1844
16	Simon	(12)	Archange Paré S.V.1832
17	Jérôme	(12)	Angé. Samson S.G.1828 V. d'August Blais.
18	François Xa-vier	(12)	Fse. Baudouin S.F.S.1844

BOLDUC.

1	Louis	(1)	Eliz. Hubert Q. 1668
	Louis		
	René		
2	Louis	(1)	Louis Caron S. Anne 1697
	Pierre		
	Joseph		
	Jean		
2A	René	(1)	M. Anne Gravel
	Zacharie		
3	Louis		Agnès Dufour
	Le même		Agnès Leblond S.F. 1728

BOLDUC.

	François		
	Paul		
4	Zacharie	(2)	G. Jeanne Meunier S. Joa. 1728
	Zacharie		
5	Louis		Marg. Poulin
	Marguerite		Pierre Forgues S.V. 1745
	Angélique		Pierre Adam " 1753
	M. Agathe		Jos. Pilote " 1764
	Louis		
	Jacques		
6	Pierre	(2)	M. Jos. Leblond S.F. 1728
	Marguerite		Aug. Pilote S.V. 1763
	M. Josette		Aug. Balard " 1764
	M. Josette		Ls. Plante " 1768
	"		2° Chs. Barillau S.G. 1806
	Pierre		
	Joseph		
7	Joseph	(2)	Thérèse Poulin S.Joa.1727
	M. Anne		Jacq. Bélanger S.V. 1764
	Pierre		
8	François	(3)	Fse. Filion S.Joa. 1741
	Agnès		Aug. Roy S.M. 1774
A	Paul	(3)	M.Anne Morin S.P.S.1773 S. Marie
9	Zacharie	(4)	M.Anne Poulin S.Joa.1756
	Le même		M. Jos. Plante S.Frs. 1789
10	Jean	(2)	M.Josette OtioS.Anne1733
	Jean Baptiste		
11	Louis	(5)	Angé. Mercier Bert. 1751
	Le même		M.Marthe Couture B.1754
	Le même		M.Jos.LabrecqueS.V.1760
	Catherine		Jos. Roy " 1790
	Marie		Michel Boissonneau " 1791
	Joseph		
	François		
	Michel		
12	Jacques	(5)	Eliz. Denis S.M. 1761
	Jacques		
	Charles		
	Michel		
13	Pierre	(6)	M.Genev.Guilmet S.V.175
	M. Josette		Chs. Dalaire " 1774
	"		2° Jean Gagné " 1789
	Pierre		
14	Joseph	(6)	M. Marg. Pilote S.M.1761
	Etienne		
	Joseph		
	Pierre		
15	Pierre	(7)	Eliz. Cloutier S.R. 1752
	Marguerite		Chs. Tangué S.V.1781
	Pierre		
	Jean Baptiste		
16	Pierre		M. Ls. Roy
	M. Louise		Michel Gautron S.V. 1790
	"		2° Pierre Denis S.G. 1828
	Michel		
	Louis		
	Augustin		
	François		
17	JeanBaptiste	(10)	Marg. Filion S.Joa.1760
	M. Josette		Aug. Bernard Marseau S.V. 1797
	Marie		J. B. Quemeneur " 1797
	Marguerite		Frs. Aubé " 1799
	Jean Baptiste		
	Paul		
18	Joseph	(11)	Marg. Bernard S.V.1787
	Marie		Pierre Corriveau " 1812
	M. Louise		J. B. Hélie " 1813
	François Xavier		
	Guillaume		
	Louis		
	Joseph		
	Pierre		
19	Michel	(11)	Genev. Bernard S.V.178

BOLDUC.

20	François		Genev. Blouin	Bert.1815
21	Jacques	(12)	M.Thérèse Cadrin	
				S.V. 1783
	Le même		Suzanne Roy	S.V. 1791
	Geneviève		Antoine Pigeon	S.M. 1820
	Rosalie		Basile Blouin	" 1827
	Alexis			
22	Charles	(12)	M. Ls. Voisin	S.V. 1791
	Marie		J. B. Dumas	" 1842
	Marguerite		J. B. Quemeneur	S.M.1840
	Antoine			
23	Michel	(12)	M. Anne Lacroix	S.M.1894
	Le même		M. Ls. Rémillard	" 1797
24	Pierre	(13)	Genev. Bruneau	S.V.1780
	M. Geneviève		J. B. Dépont	" 1802
	Marie		Jos. Mercier	" 1806
	Pierre			
	Le même		Eliz. Lorandeau	S.M.1793
	Elizabeth		Chs. Lainé	S.V.1814
	Marguerite		Jos. Cochon	" 1821
	Louise		Prudent Lefebvre	" 1824
	Flavie Julie		Prudent Boissonneau	
				S.V.1825
	"		2° Jean Morin	" 1834
	Jacques			
	Joseph			
	Augustin			
25	Étienne	(14)	Marie Cadrin	S.M. 1791
	Marguerite		Michel Roy	" 1837
	Etienne			
26	Joseph	(14)	Ursule Cadrin	S.M. 1802
27	Pierre	(14)	Reine Rémillard	S.F.S.1787
	Marguerite		Bénoni Tangué	S.Chs.1819
	Joseph			
	Jacques			
28	Pierre	(15)	M.Jos.Corriveau	S.M.1771
	M. Madeleine		Nicolas Roy	S.V.1795
	Madeleine		Frs. Rousseau	" 1801
	Pierre			
	Etienne			
	Jean Baptiste			
	Joseph			
29	JeanBaptiste	(15)	Thérèse Bernard	S.V.1788
30	Michel		Rosalie Roy	" 1783
	M. Marguerite		Jos Labbé	S.M. 1816
	Marie		J. B. Talbot	" 1807
	Michel			
31	Augustin	(16)	M. Fse. Blais	S.V.1788
	M. Archange		Paul Cadrin	" 1808
	Marguerite		Simon Talbot	" 1810
	M. Victoire		Paul Catellier	" 1828
	Jean Baptiste			
32	François	(16)	Genev. Aubé	S.V.1791
	M. Geneviève		Alexis Mercier	" 1814
	M. Louise		Louis Roy	" 1817
	François			
	Joseph			
	Louis			
	Pierre			
33	Louis	(16)	M. Jos. Roy	S.V.1794
	M. Josette		Jos. Goulet	" 1813
	Angèle		Nicolas Roy	" 1819
	Louis		Jos. Denis	" 1820
	Victoire		Ant. Roy	" 1823
	Luce		Stanislas Gosselin	" 1834
	M. Cécile		Isaac Fortier	" 1839
	Isidore			
	Louis			
	Joseph			
34	Paul	(17)	M. Ls. Paré	S.Joa. 1763
	Marie		Pierre Roy	S.V. 1794
	M. Louis		Paul Marseau	" 1797
	Pierre			
34ª	JeanBaptiste	(17)	Marg. Roy	S.M. 1797
	M. Josette		Jos. Tangué	" 1821
35	Louis		Josette Naud	

BOLDUC.

	Marguerite		Jacq. Morin	S.V. 1795
36	Joseph	(17)	Angèle Lessart	Bert. 1821
37	Louis	(18)	Eliz. Brochu	S.V. 1827
	Le même		Jeanne de Chantal Roy	
				Bert. 1837
38	Pierre	(18)	Luce Rémillard	S.G. 1828
	Pierre			
39	François Xa-	(18)	Luce Lessart	S.V. 1830
	vier			
40	Guillaume	(18)	Sophie Mercier	" 1841
41	Antoine	(22)	Marie Boulet	S.Ths. 1821
	Le même		Genev. Guibord	S.V. 1826
	Charles			
42	Alexis	(21)	Marie Lacroix	S.M.1817
43	Pierre	(24)	Genev. Ratté	" 1810
	Geneviève		Ls. Beaudoin	" 1836
	Sophie		Théodore Tangué	" 1839
	Emélie		Jacques Fradet	" 1843
	Archange		Tho. Abraham Lacroix	
				S.V 1846
	Michel			
	Louis			
	François Xavier			
	Jacques			
44	Jacques	(24)	Marie McNeil	S.V.1820
45	Joseph	(24)	Fse. Bilodeau	" 1821
46	Augustin	(24)	Mad. Mercier	" 1832
47	Etienne	(25)	Marie Roy	S.M.1822
	Marguerite		J. B. Baudouin	" 1850
48	Joseph	(27)	Julie Bissonnet	" 1820
	Antoine			
49	Jacques	(27)	Angèle Bissonnet	
				S.M. 1825
50	Pierre	(28)	M. Anne Richard	
				S.M. 1803
	Edouard			
	Joseph			
	Pierre			
	Antoine			
51	Etienne	(28)	Reine Lefebvre	S.M. 1814
	Le même		Angé Fortier	S.G. 1824
52	Jean Bapte.	(28)	Angé Rousseau	S.G. 1819
53	Joseph	(28)	Marcelline Dessaint	
				S.F.S. 1826
54	Michel		Genev. Gontier	
	Michel			
55	Michel	(30)	M. Jos Ratté	S.M. 1808
	Archange		Ant. Chamberlan	
				S.M. 1839
	Christine		Frs Pilote	S.M. 1839
	Michel			
	Le même		Olive Fradet	S.M. 1849
56	Louis, fils de			
	Ls. Marie et			
	d'Agnès Pepin		M. Placide Cunningham	
				S.Jos 1823
	M. Zéloide		Michel Carbonneau	
				S.P. 1837
57	Jacques		Marie Fafart	
	Emérentienne		Ant. Bolduc	S.M. 1851
	Jacques			
	Henri			
58	François		Génev. Audet	
	Nazaire			
59	Charles		Marg. Baudoin	
	Charles			
	Antoine			
60	Jean Bte	(31)	Apolline Blouin	Bert. 1824
	Célina		Léandre Blais	S.V. 1854
	Philomène		Jérôme Urbain Vézina	
				S.V. 1857
	Flore		Octave Corriveau	
				S.V. 1867
	Théophile			
	Siméon			

BOLDUC.

61	François	(32)	M. Louis Roy	S.V. 1818
	Émélie		Magl. Lemieux	S.V. 1844
	Désanges		Thos Boutin	S.V. 1853
	François Xavier			
	Pierre			
62	Joseph	(32)	M. Angèle Roy	S.M. 1821
	M. Marcelline		Olivier Corriveau	
63	Pierre	(32)	Félicité Dubord	S.M. 1827
64	Louis	(32)	M. Eliz. Théberge	
				S.G. 1827
	François Xavier			
65	Louis	(32)	M. Marg. Tangué	
				S.V. 1819
	Victoire		Nazaire Bolduc	S.Chs. 1845
66	Isidore	(33)	Julie Fse Lessart	
				S.M 1838
	Julie		Chs Hélie	
67	Joseph	(33)	Marg. Gagnon	S.V. 1835
68	Pierre	(34)	M. Thérèse Marseau	
				S.M. 1797
	Louise		Pierre Paquet	S.G. 1818
	Angélique		Ls Lemieux	S.G. 1822
	Pierre			
69	Pierre	(36)	Joséphine Lacroix	B. 1848
70	Pierre	(38)	M. Anne Mercier	
				S.Chs. 1853
71	Charles	(41)	M. Caroline Baillargeon	
				S.Chs. 1862
72	Michel	(42)	Sophie Talbot	S.M. 1839
73	Frs Xavier	(43)	Angé Quéret	S.M. 1842
74	Jacques	(43)	Marie Thivierge	S.M. 1843
75	Louis	(43)	Eliz. Quéret	S.V. 1869
76	Antoine	(48)	M. Emérentienne Bolduc	
				S.M. 1851
77	Pierre	(50)	Luce Fradet	S.G. 1828
78	Antoine	(50)	M. Marg. Roby	S.M. 1834
79	Joseph	(50)	Angèle Gasselin	
				S.Chs. 1835
80	Edouard	(50)	Sophie Langlais	S.V. 1839
81	Michel	(54)	Angé James	S.G. 1826
82	Michel	(55)	Anastasie Savoie	S.V. 1840
83	Jacques	(57)	Julie Cochon	S.M. 1842
84	Henri	(57)	Vitaline Roy	S.M. 1854
85	Nazaire	(58)	Vict. Bolduc	S.Chs. 1845
86	Charles	(59)	M. Luce Roy	S.V. 1857
87	Antoine	(59)	Vitaline Fournier	
				S.Chs. 1859
88	Théophile	(60)	Philomène Roy	S.V. 1866
89	Siméon	(60)	Cath. Emélie Forgues	
				S.M. 1866
	Le même		M. Arthemise Roy	
				S.V. 1870
90	Frs Xavier	(61)	Emélie Couët	S.M. 1847
91	Pierre	(61)	Philippine Roy	S.V. 1848
	M. Belzimire		Théophile Gourgue	
				S.V. 1870
92	Frs Xavier	(64)	M. Charles Roy	
				S.Chs- 1861
93	Pierre	(68)	Josette Rémillard	
				S.M. 1825

BONNEAU—LABÉCASSE

1	Joseph		M. Anne Lelong	S.F. 1670
	Joseph			
	Le même		Mad. Duchesne	S.Frs.1684
	Jean			
	Augustin			
	Dominique			
	Basile			
2	Joseph	(1)	Anne Bissonnet	S.F. 1696
				S.M.
3	Jean	(1)	Eliz. Gagné	S.Frs. 1708
4	Dominique	(1)	Fse. Gingras	Q. 1716
5	Augustin	(1)	Genev. Gagné	Q. 1713
	Marie		Jean Jolin	S.Frs. 1740

BONNEAU—LABÉCASSE.

	Marie	2°	Jos. Marie Boulet	
				S.F.S. 1757
	Thérèse		Ls. Véricol	S.Frs. 1753
	Zacharie			
	Jean Baptiste			
	Pierre			
6	Basile	(1)	Mad. Parent Beauport	1727
	M. Anne		André Turgeon	B. 1760
7	Jean Baptiste	(5)	Dorothée Coté	S.P. 1743
	M. Josette		Etn. Dalaire	S.Frs. 1766
	M. Victoire		Frs. Champagne	S.Frs.1769
	"		2° Jos. Emond	S.J. 1819
8	Zacharie		M. Jos. Noël	S.P. 1757
9	Pierre	(5)	M.Jos.Gosselin	S.Tho.1751
	M. Choquette		Roy	S.F.S. 1775
	Thérèse		Jean Frs. Mercier	
				S.F.S. 1782
	Louise		Jacq. Leclaire	S.F.S. 1783
	Reine		Pierre Morin	S.F.S. 1794
	Pierre			
	Basile			
10	Jean Baptiste		Judith Duchesne	
				S. Anne la Pocatiere
	Jean Baptiste			
11	Pierre	(9)	M. Anne Thibaut	
				S.F.S. 1791
	M. Francoise		Pierre Paré	S.V. 1809
	Julie		Jos. Langlais	1816
	M. Flavie		J. B. Morin	1835
	M. Archange		Jean Naud	1838
	Marguerite		Jean Lacasse	1843
	M.AnneRomaine		Chs. Lacasse	1843
12	Basile	(9)	M. Anne Morin	
				S.V. S.F.S. 1796
	Marie		Michel Cochon	S.V. 1830
	Jean Baptiste			
	Prudent			
	Basile			
	Pierre			
13	Jean Baptiste	(10)	Louise Dalaire	S.M. 1789
	M. Louise		Jacq. Durand	S.Frs. 1822
	Jean Baptiste			
	Pierre			
	Le même		M. Ls. Martel Isle aux	
				Coudres 1805
	Marie		Jacq. Quemeneur	S.L.1842
	M. Louise		Jos. Bouffard	S.L. 1827
	Judith		Chs. Coulombe	S.L. 1849
	"		2° Ls. Godbout	S.L. 1853
	Elizabeth		Jos. Coulombe	S.L. 1849
	Joseph			
14	Charles		Fse Vaillancour	
	Charles			
15	Basile	(12)	M. Genev. Morin	S.M.1837
	Joseph			
16	Jean Baptiste	(12)	Angèle Boulet	S.F.S. 1842
	Prudent			
17	Jean Baptiste	(13)	Marie Gagné	S.F. 1815
18	Pierre	(13)	Eliz. Genest	S.P. 1821
19	Joseph	(13)	Genev. Bouffard	S.L. 1835
20	Pierre	(12)	Désanges Blais	S.P.S. 1829
21	Pierre		M. Celeste Fournier	S.Tho.
	Le même		M. Genev. Samson	
				S.P.S. 1814
22	Charles	(14)	Theotiste Leblond	S.G.1828
23	Joseph	(15)	Emélie Marcoux	
				S.Chs. 1862

BOUCHARD.

1	Nicolas		Anne LeRoy	S. Anne
				S.Tho. 1670
	Angélique		Ls. Bossé	Cap.St.Ign. 1692
	Eliz. Agnès		Chs. Fournier	Cap.St.Ign. 1699
	Eliz. Agnès		2° Jos. Morin	Cap.St.Ign. 1701

BOUCHARD.

```
  Nicolas
  Charles
  Pierre
  Ignace
  Pierre
2 Ignace        (1) M. Jeanne Roy Bert. 1712
  Marguerite        Aug. Guimet     Bert. 1735
  M. Angélique      Pierre Terrien  Bert. 1739
  M. Josette        Jos. Pruneau    Bert. 1752
  Isabelle          Thos. Denis     Bert. 1766
  M. Claire         Pierre Pruneau  S.V. 1754
  Joseph
  Guillaume
  Basile
3 Nicolas       (1) Anne Viau       S.G. 1709
4 Pierre        (1) Marie Fournier S.Tho.1709
  Joseph
5 Pierre        (4) Marg. Caron
  Augustin
  Pierre
  Charles
  Joseph Marie
6 Charles       (1) M.Jos. Corriveau S.V.1749
  Angélique         J. B. Quemeneur S.V.1769
  Françoise         Paul Gougue     S.V. 1769
  Charles
7 Pierre        (1) Ursule Roy      S.V. 1750
  M. Ursule         J. B. Brochu    "   1783
  Nicolas
  Pierre
  Charles
8 Joseph        (2) M. Mad. Boutin Bert 1746
  M. Josette        Aug. Morin      "   1781
  Guillaume         Monique Boulet S.F.S.1750
  Ignace
  Augustin
10 Basile       (2) M. Anne Blais  Bert. 1765
  Le même           Cath. Minier    Islet. 1781
  Basile
11 Pierre       (5) Marie Talbot   S.P.S. 1761
12 Augustin     (5) Fse. Picard     "    1771
  M. Françoise      Chs. Samson     "    1790
  M. Madeleine      René Toussaint Morin
                                    S.P.S. 1791
  Le même           M. Mad. Morin   "    1784
  M. Madeleine      Ign. Létourneau "    1806
  M. Marguerite     Prosper Goudreau
                                    S.P.S. 1813
  M. Françoise      J. B. Lemieux S.F.S. 1821
  Pierre Augustin
  Augustin
13 Charles      (5) Angé Cloutier S.P.S. 1774
  Marie             Frs. Picard     "    1800
  Pierre
  Joseph
  Charles
14 Joseph Marie (5) Theotiste Gagné
                                    S.Tho. 1775
  Theotiste         Ant.Chamberlan S.M.1798
  Joseph Marie
15 Joseph       (4) Eliz. Couillard S.Tho 1744
  Le même           Marg. Coté      "    1749
  Jean Baptiste
16 René             Marie Cyr
  Louis
  Le même           Josette Quéret  S.G. 1795
17 Charles      (6) M.Angé Chretien S.V.1776
  M. Françoise      J. B. Hélie     "    1806
18 Charles      (6) Cécile Solien   "    1784
  Cécile            Frs. Turgeon    "    1804
  M. Ursule         Gab. Mercier    "    1808
  Julie             Féréol Balan    "    1829
  Barbe             Bénoni Roy      "    1833
19 Nicolas      (1) Marg. Brochu    "    1785
  Marguerite        André Blais     "    1812
  Angéle            Frs. Balan      "    1820
```

BOUCHARD.

```
   Nicolas
   Etienne
   Jérémie
   Pierre
20 Pierre       (7) M. Archange Blais
                                    Bert. 1788
   M. Archange      Pierre Roy      S.V. 1809
   Séraphine        Jacq. Fournier  "    1821
   M. Ursule        Ls. Pepin       "    1821
   "                2e Manuel Aubé  "    1832
   Sophie Adé       Abel Rousseau   "    1827
   Cécile           Ed. Balan       "    1835
   Pierre
   Jean Baptiste
21 Ignace       (9) Reine Langlois S.F.S. 1777
   M. Josette       Frs. Baudry         1804
   Ignace
22 Augustin     (9) Marg. Clément  S.H. 1785
   Jean Baptiste
23 Pre.Augustin(12) M. Marg. Denis S.Chs 1808
                                    S. Cleuré
   Le même          Angé Morin     S.F.S. 1832
24 Augustin    (12) M.Marg.Talbot  "    1817
25 Pierre      (13) M. Thérèse Picard
                                    S.P.S. 1801
   Emérentienne     Jos. Moudina    "    1827
   Théodore         Prudent Gendreau
                                    S.P.S. 1831
   Noël
26 Charles     (13) M. Dorothée Simoneau
                                    S.P.S. 1805
   Charles
   François Xavier
27 Joseph           Marg. Coté     S.Tho 1820
   Charles Thomas
   Paul
28 Joseph Marie(14) Cath.Chamberlan S.M.1793
   Marie            Frs. Ménard     "    1831
   Euphrosine       F. X. Brochu    "    1836
   Joseph
   Le même          M. Anne Gagnon  "    1875
   M. Hermine       Geo. Chamberlan "    1847
   Marcelline       Jos. Tangué     S.V. 1844
29 Jean Baptiste(15) M. Vict. Oresteille
                                    S.Tho. 1777
   Françoise        Chs. Frs. Simoneau
   Joseph
   Etienne
   Le même          Frs. Brousseau S.Tho 1801
   Alexis
31 Louis        (16) Marg. Lacasse S.Chs. 1778
   Marguerite       Pierre Audet    S.G. 1799
   Pierre
   Louis
   Réné
32 Nicolas      (18) Marie Guilmet  S.G. 1808
   Marguerite       Jos. Couture,  Levis 1839
   David
33 Pierre       (19 Vict. Roy       S.V. 1812
   M. Victoire      Michel Eustache
                    Letellier       S.V. 1833
   Pierre
34 Etienne      (19) Eliz. Searle   S.V. 1822
   Etienne
35 Jérémie      (19) M. Anne Kéroack S.P.S.
                                         1825
36 Pierre       (20) Eliz. Enouf    B. 1818
37 Jean Baptiste(20) M. Angèle Bilodeau Bert.
                                         1830
38 Ignace       (21) Marg. Morin  S.F.S. 1806
39 Jean Baptiste(22) M. Anne Baudoin S.H. 1820
40 Noël         (25) M. Ls. Henriette Berne
                                    S.P.S. 1840
41 Frs. Xavier  (26) M. Rose Coté  S.P.S. 1833
42 Charles      (26) Luce Picard   S.F.S. 1836
```

BOUCHARD.

43	Chs. Thomas	(27)	M. Edwidge Martineau S.F.S. 1844
44	Paul	(27)	M. Symphorose Belanger S.V. 1858
45	Joseph	(28)	Josette Pepin S.M. 1835
46	Joseph	(29)	M. Vict. Rousseau S.P.S. 1820
47	Alexis	(29)	M. Sophie Picard S.P.S. 1827
48	Etienne	(29)	M. Genev. Rousseau S.P.S. 1827
	Le même		Marg. Minville S.P.S. 1840
49	Basile	(10)	M. Jos. Demeule S.L. 1805
50	Réné	(31)	Marg. Rousseau S.F.S. 1804
51	Louis	(31)	Marg. Labrecque S.G. 1804
	Joseph		
52	Pierre	(31)	Marie Turgeon B 1814
53	David	(32)	Marie Samson, Levis 1837
54	Bernard		Félicité Tremblay
	François		
55	Louis		
	Pierre		
56	Pierre		Angele Leclaire
	Luce		Jos. Pepin S.Chs. 1852
	Marie		Ls. Couture „ 1857
57	Anselm		Josette Tremblay
	Gédéon		
58	Henri		Modeste Patry S. Croix
	Eleusippe		
59	Pierre	(33)	M. Ursule Mercier S.V. 1826
60	Etienne	(34)	M. Vitaline Gagnon S. Chs. 1852
61	Joseph	(51)	Marg. Baudry Levis 1837
62	François	(54)	Julie Audet S.J. 1825
63	Pierre	(55)	M. Chs. Bernier S.Chs. 1845
64	Gédéon	(27)	Marie Roger S.J. 1855
65	Eleusippe	(58)	Sara Labrecque S.L. 1861

BOUCHER.

1	Quatrin		Jeanne Denis
	Jean		
2	Elie		M. Mad. Boucherie
	Elie		
3	Jean	(1)	Mad. Pare S. Anne 1678
	Jean		
4	Elie	(2)	Thérèse Montambaut S.F. 1700
5	François		M. Anne Demers S. Nic
	Charles		
	François		
6	Ignace		Fse. Pouliot S. Nic
	Charles		
7	Jean	(3)	Mad. Gravel, Jacob Notau 1704
	M. Josette		J. B. Bilodeau Bert 1742
	Paschal		
	Joseph		
	Le même		Marg. Carbonneau Bert. 1726
	Catherine		Alexis Gagné Bert. 1743
	Marguerite		Joseph Isabel Bert. 1749
	Catherine		Jean Morel S.P.S. 1764
8	Charles	(6)	Marg. Filteau B. 1733
9	Charles	(5)	Marie Rémillard S.V. 1758
	Le même		M. Jos. Couture B. 1763
10	François	(5)	Eliz. Couture S.V 1760
11	Paschal	(7)	Genev. Vermet S.Chs. Bert. 1733
	M. Anne		Paul Gaumont „ 1766
	„		2° Boniface Aubé S. Chs. 1799
	Reine		Bart. Audet „ 1773
	Bernard		
	Jean		

BOUCHARD.

	Peirre		
	Le même		Marie Hélie S. Chs. 1755
	Marie		Alexis Bilodeau „ 1785
12	Joseph	(7)	M. Anne Picard S.F.S.1753
	M. Madeleine		J. B. Blais Bert. 1779
	Angélique		Jacq. Quirouet „ 1779
	Marguerite		J. B. Quéret „ 1793
	Joseph		
	Jean		
13	Jean		Marie Guilmet
	M. Josette		Ls. Chatigny S. Chs. 1772
	M. Charlotte		J. B. Lepage „ 1785
	Jean		
	Charles		
	Le même		Marie Roy S.V. 1770
	Marie		Ls. Paradis S.Chs. 1800
	Marguerite		Ls. Morisset „ 1812
	Louise		Ls. Rouleau „ 1822
	Augustin		
14	Etienne		Marg. Fréchet
	Josette		J. B. Nadeau B. 1786
15	Charles		Agathe Coté
	Charles François		
	Jean		
16	Jean	(11)	Marie Blais S.V. 1761
	Marie		Zach Couture S. Chs 1785
	Jean Marie		
17	Bernard	(11)	M. Anne Dalaire S.M. 1772
	Le même		Frs. Bernard „ 1797
	François		
18	Pierre		M. Théotiste Gontier S. Chs. 1785
	Marie		Nic. Gontier „ 1806
	Marguerite		Jos. Denis S.M. 1824
19	Joseph	(12)	M. Genév. Isabel Bert.1787
	Marguerite		Jos. Mercier „ 1826
	Marie		Frs. Pelchat S.F.S 1827
	Laurent		
	Le même		M. Anne Jolin S.F.S.1833
20	Jean	(12)	M. Eliz. Couture S.P.S. 1791
	Jean Baptiste		
	Le même		M. Anne Dumas S.H.1805
21	Jean Baptiste		M. Jos. Cloutier
	Guillaume		
22	Jean Baptiste		M. Rose Boivin
	Veuf de Fse Paré		S. Marie 1790
	Pierre		
	Le même		Mad. Lepage S.M. 1824
23	Jean	(23)	Marie Labrecque S. Chs. 1786
	Michel		
	Charles		
24	Charles	(13)	M. Reine Mimaux S.H. 1802
	Pierre		
25	Augustin		Judith Nadeau S. Chs. 1806
	Judith		Alexandre Couture S.Chs. 1832
	Augustin		
26	Charles François		Angé Bourrassa Levis 1785
	Le même		Mad. Brault S.P. 1807
27	Jean	(15)	Marie Deslisle S.H. 1804
28	Jean Marie	(16)	Marie Helie S.M. 1795
	Marie		Pierre Bilodeau S.G. 1819
	Marguerite		Adrien Remillard „ 1822
	Françoise		Jean Pouliot „ 1824
	Gervais		
	Jean		
	Charles		
29	François	(17)	M. Jos. Crepeau S.P. 1798
30	Pierre		Theotiste Fortier
	Josette		Jos. Lemieux S.G. 1824

BOUCHARD.

31	Michel fils de Prisque Marg. Huot	Marg. Viger, Marie	Beauce 1791
	Le même	Euphrosfme Diou	S. Frs. 1823
32	Jacques fils de Jacq. et Dorothée Alaire.	Fse. Guilbeau S. Joa. 1806	
	Louis		
33	Laurent	(19) Thède. Marcoux Bert. 1817	
39	J. Baptiste	(20) M. Mad. Patry S.H. 1820	
35	Guillaume	(21) M. Mad. Blais Bert. 1812	
36	Pierre	(22) Anastasie Asselin	S.M. 1820
37	Charles	(23) Fse. Couture S. Chs. 1813	
38	Michel	(23) M. Ls. Noel S.L. 1832	
39	Pierre	(24) Archange Nadeau B. 1846	
40	Augustin	(25) M. Fse. Coutere	S. Chs. 1830
	Angéle Alexandre	Oliver Peltier „ 1859	
41	Jean	(28) M. Cécile Gautron	S.V. 1818
	Le même	Luce Labrecque S.G. 1824	
42	Gervais	(28) Marg. Lemieux S.G. 1823	
43	Charles	(28) Agnès Thibaut S.G. 1824	
44	Louis	(32) Christine Gagné	S. Frs. 1843
45	Alexandre	(40) Hermine Labrecque	B. 1859

BOUFFART.

1	Jacques	Anne Leclaire S.P. 1680	
	Nicole	Guill. Couture S.L. 1703	
	Anne Catherine	Ant. Rousseau „ 1709	
	Marguerite	Pierre Couture „ 1727	
	Jean		
	François		
2	Jean	(1) M. Fse. De Caruel	S.L. 1709
	Geneviève	Jean Chabot „ 1637	
	M. Louise	J. B. Coté „ 1733	
	Jacques		
3	François	M. Anne Fournier	
	Pierre		
	Ignace		
	Jean Baptiste		
	Basile		
	Ambroise		
4	Jacques	(2) M. Genév. Gosselin	S.L. 1731
	M. Françoise	Frs. Morin S.L. 1753	
	Françoise	Chs. Paquet B. 1762	
	Elizabeth	Ant. Labrecque S.M. 1775	
	Pierre		
	Jacques		
	Antoine		
	Antoine		
5	Jean Baptiste	(3) Fse. Maranda S.L. 1756	
	Le même	Marg. Leclaire „ 1762	
	Basile		
	Louis		
6	Pierre	(3) M. Angèle Cochon	
	Jean		
	Jacques		
	Pierre		
	Louis		
7	Ignace	(3) Fse. Pouliot S.P. 1762	
	M. Françoise	Jean Godbout S.L. 1789	
	Ignace		
	Le même	Marie Gendreau „ 1775	
	Marie	Ls. Abraham Delisle	S.L. 1802
	Louise		

BOUFFARD.

8	Basile	(3) M. Thérèse Pouliot	S.V. 1773
	Louis Marie		
	Louis		
9	Ambroise	(3) Marie (Goulet) S.H. 1773	
	Thérèse	Jacq. Hélie „ 1808	
	Madeleine	Claude Lacroix „ 1809	
	François		
	Jacques		
	Ambroise		
	Le même	Mad. Belleau „ 1805	
10	Jacques	(4) Anne Dufaut S.P.S. 1763	
11	Antoine	(4) Genev. Fournier „ 1765	
	Joseph		
12	Pierre	(4) M Mad. Turcot S.J. 1769	
13	Antoine	(4) M. Jos. Guilmet	S. Tho. 1774
	Antoine		
14	Louis	Fse. Rouleau S.L. 1798	
	Scolastique	Jos. Clément „ 1833	
	Marguerite	Chs. Rousseau S.P. 1829	
	Jean		
	Elie		
	Pierre		
	Louis		
	Jude		
15	Basile	(5) M Susanne Labonté	S.P.S. 1807
	M. Susanne	Pierre Langlois „ 1838	
	Edouard		
16	Jean	(6) Marie Noël S.P. 1799	
17	Pierre	(6) Mad. Noël S.P. 1801	
	Françoise	Frs. Nolin S.L. 1826	
	M. Madeleine	Abraham Corriveau	S.L. 1830
	Apolline	Basile Corriveau „ 1836	
	Pierre		
18	Louis	(6) M. Jos. Lecours	S. Chs. 1804
19	Jacques	(6) M. Marthe Leroux	S.L. 1806
20	Ignace	(7) Véronique Maranda	S.L. 1798
	Charlotte	Abraham Simart „ 1841	
	Jacques		
	Ignace		
21	Louis	(7) Fse. Godbout S.L. 1798	
	Geneviève	Jos. Bonneau „ 1835	
	„	2° Frs. Cinqmars „ 1858	
	Joseph		
	Ignace		
	David		
22	Ls. Marie	(8) M. Mad. Fradet S.V. 1801	
	Thérèse	Raphael Tangué „ 1829	
	Marie	Pierre Corriveau „ 1838	
	David		
	Louis		
23	Louis	(8) M. Ls. Nadeau S.G. 1806	
24	Ambroise	(9) M. Mad. Hélie S.H. 1798	
25	Françoise	(9) Marg. Lacroix S.M. 1808	
26	Jacques	(9) Archange Fontaine	S.H. 1812
27	Joseph	(11) M. Théotiste Picard	S.P.S. 1791
	M. Théotiste	Pierre Morin S.H. 1818	
	Augustin		
	Joseph		
28	Antoine	(13) Marg. Wells Bert. 1798	
	Jean Baptiste		
	Charles		
29	Louis	(14) Marg. Mercier S.G. 1824	
	Le même	Angèle Corriveau S.L.1829	
30	Jean	(14) Michel Archange Lacroix	S.L. 1830
31	Pierre	(14) Fse. Prémont S.P. 1831	
	Anastasie	Frs. Alain S.L. 1854	

BOUFFARD.

	Etienne		
32	Jude	(14)	Anastasie Fleury S.P.S. 1838
33	Elie	(14)	Olive Rousseau S.M. 1839
34	Edouard	(15)	M. Chs. Picard S P.S.1835
35	Pierre	(17)	Marg. Crèpeau S.P. 1829 S. Croix
	Louis		
	François		
36	Ignace	(20)	Natalie Labrecque S.J. 1825
37	Jacques	(20)	Marie Pedeack S.F. 1840
	Marie		Ant. Carrier S.L. 1872
	M. Délima		Bonav. Vizina „ 1879
	David		
38	Joseph	(21)	M. Ls. Bonneau S.L. 1827
	Alexis		
	Louis		
39	Ignace	(21)	Angéle Pouliot S.L. 1837
	M. Célanire		Ferd. Labrecque „ 1858
	Louis Achille		
	George		
40	David	(21)	Fse. Chabot S.L. 1852
41	Louis	(22)	Marg. Gougne S.M. 1832
	Le même		Marie Gagnon „ 1837
	Philomène		Geo. Tangué S.V. 1865
42	David	(22)	Emérence Thivierge S.V. 1846
43	Augustin	(27)	Charlotte Gagné S.H. 1818
44	Joseph	(27)	M. Genev. Morin S.H. 1819
	Edouard		
45	Joseph		Marie Bilodeau
	Elzéar		
46	Féréal		Cath. Pouliot
	Octavie		Calixte Aubé S.V. 1869
47	JeanBaptiste	(28)	Archange Pruneau Bert 1826
48	Charles	(28)	Marg. Samson S.F.S. 1834
49	Elie	(31)	Philomène Foucher S.F. 1860
50	Louis	(35)	Marie Doncourt S.L. 1858
51	François	(35)	Ursule Guérard S.L. 1863
52	David	(37)	Philomène LabbéS.L. 1870
53	Alexis	(38)	Adé Pouliot S.L. 1864
54	Louis	(38)	Mathilde Coté Q. 1866
55	Ls. Achille	(39)	Cédulie CinqmarsS.L. 1877
56	Georges	(39)	Fse. Laroche Q. 1866
57	Edouard	(44)	M. Esther Goulet S.P. 1852
58	Elzéar	(45)	Sophie Marseau S.F. 1867

BOULET.

	Robert		Fse. Grenier	
	Jacqueline		Pierre Joncas	S.F. 1672
	Françoise		Pierre Bernier	S.Tho. 1689
	Jacques			
	Paul			
	Martin			
2	Jacques	(1)	Fse. Fournier	S.Tho. 1686
	Marie		Pierre Morin	„ 1707
	Guillaume			
	Paul			
	Jean Baptiste			
	Martin			
	Joseph			
	Louis			
	Louis			
3	Paul	(1)	Fse. Paquet	Q. 1695
	M. Françoise		Ant. Goupy	S.Tho. 1724
	Geneviève		Jos. Gaboury	S.V. 1740
	Louise Françoise		Ant. Gaboury	
	Elizabeth		Jean Courtois	Levis 1734
	„		2° Frs. Felant	„ 1755
	Pierre			
	Paul			
	Françoise			

BOULET.

	Augustin			
	Alexis			
	Louis			
4	Martin	(1)	Fse. Nolin	S.P. 1698
	Elizabeth		Jos. Denaut	S.P.S. 1728
	Angélique		Etne. Corbin	Q. 1733
	Alexis			
	Jacques			
5	Joseph	(2)	Monique Meunier S.Anne 1723
	Monique		Guill. Bouchard S.F.S.1750
	Marguerite		Jean Laurent Roy „ 1754
	M. Josette		Jean Fradet S.F.S. 1759
	M. Généviève		J. B. Jolin „ 1762
	Françoise		Alexandre Roy „ 1764
	M. Madeleine		Pierre Fontaine „ 1774
	Antoine		
	Augustin		
6	Jean Baptiste		Marie Asselin S.Frs. 1727
	M. Thérèse		Etn. Dion S.F.S. 1756
	Madeleine		Mathurin Gagnon „ 1760
	Geneviève		Mathurin Dubreuil „ 1766
	Jean Marie		
	Joseph Marie		
7	Guillaume	(2)	Mad. Miville S.P.S. 1727
	Geneviève		Laurent Cloutier S.Tho 1751
	Le même		M. Anne Dandurand S.Tho. 1734
	Jacques		
	François Xavier		
8	Louis	(2)	M. Eliz. Chiasson Bert1730
9	Louis		M.Genev.Daniau Bert1731
	Jacques		
10	Paul	(2)	M. Claire Minville S.Tho. 1731
	M. Claire		Guill.GaumontS.Thos.1767
	Paul		
11	Martin	(2)	Louise Lemieux Cap S. Ign. 1736
12	Paul	(3)	Dorothée Bissonnet S.M. 1830
13	François	(3)	M. Anne Dubois, Lévis 1732
14	Pierre	(3)	Cath. Albert Lévis 1733
15	Augustin	(3)	Susanne Samson „ 1732
16	Louis	(3)	Angé Samson „ 1739
17	Alexis	(3)	Génev. Samson „ 1745 S.H.
	Elizabeth		Ls. Goupy S.M. 1766
	Le Même		Fse. Ferland Levis 1756
	M. Françoise		Jos. Morel S.H. 1807
	Joseph		M. Jos. Chiason Bert. 1750
18	Jacques	(4)	Eliz. Fournier S.Tho. 1750
19	Alexis	(4)	Aug. Rousseau „ 1763
	Françoise		
	Alexis		
	Joseph		
20	Jacques		Agathe Morin
	M. Marthe		Jos. Caouet S.F.S. 1744
	M. Louise		Jos. Pepin „ 1750
	Agathe		Jacq. Marceau „ 1751
	Michel		
	Jean		
	Robert		
21	Jacques		Jeanne Terrien
	Le Même		Marg. Isabel S.F.S. 1751
22	Pierre		M. Ls. Langlois
	M. Thérèse		Ls. Pepin S.F.S. 1702
	M. Josette		Jos. Fradet „ 1764
	Jean Baptiste		
	Joseph		
	Pierre		
23	François		Véronique Morin, S.Tho.

BOULET.

Le Même	M. Jos. Rousseau,	S.P.S. 1766
M. Claire	J. B. Fortin,	Cap.St.Ign. 1807
24 Jean	(20) 2 M.Mad. Terrien S.J.1745	
M. Madeleine	Jacq. Quemeneur	S.T.S. 1764
Madeleine	Philippe Chartier " 1773	
M. Josette	Paschal Richard " 1784	
Guillaume		
Pierre		
Pierre Noel		
Jean Baptiste		
25 Robert	(20) M. Genev. Gendron,	Bert. 1748
M. Françoise	Pierre Asselin S.F.S. 1787	
M. Geneviève	Frs. Terrien " 1791	
Jean Baptiste		
Jacques		
Robert		
François		
26 Michel	(29) Genev. Audet, S.F.S. 1757	
27 Augustin	(5) M. Anne Tangué S.V.1752	
Marie	Jacq. Boulet S.F.S. 1781	
Pierre	Jos. Goupy S.Chs. 1788	
Françoise	Alexandre Couture B. 1804	
Joseph		
28 Antoine	(5) Génev. Jolin S.F.S. 1766	
Marguerite	Frs. Baudoin S.V. 1810	
Jean Marie		
François		
29 Louis	Ursule Rousseau	
Marie	Joachim Marois S.H. 1787	
Henri		
30 Louis	Jacobée Cloutier,	S.Tho.
Louis		
31 Lazare	Marie Langlu ?	
Jacques		
32 Jean Marie	(6) M. Anne Fortier	S.F.S 1756
M. Thérèse	J. B. Gagnon S.F.S. 1777	
M. Louise	Basile Roy " 1785	
M. Géneviève	Jos. Roy " 1786	
Françoise	Aug. Roy " 1786	
Marguerite	J. B. Gagnon " 1798	
Jean		
33 Jos. Marie	(6) Marie Bonneau S.F.S. 1757	
M. Josette	Eustache Morin " 1777	
Le Même	M. Angé Monmaeny	S.F.S. 1799
34 Jacques	(7) Angé Picard S.P.S. 1764	
Jean François		
Pierre		
35 Frs-Xavier	(7) M. Marg. Labonté,	S.Tho. 1775
M. Anne	Ant. Bolduc S.Tho. 1821	
François Gabriel		
36 Jacques	(9) M. Eliz. Morin S.Tho. 1763	
Jacques		
37 Paul	(10) Genev. Ruel S.Tho. 1762	
M. Geneviève	Jos. Fournier " 1782	
Ursule	Simon Talbot " 1782	
Euphrosine	Ls. Talbot " 1786	
Etienne		
38 Joseph	(17) Louise Couture S.H. 1787	
M Louise	Pierre Langlais " 1805	
Marguerite	Jacq. CarbonneauS.H.1807	
Joseph		
39 Alexis	(19) Héléne Coté S.Tho. 1776	
Marguerite	Etn. Fournier " 1817	
Alexis		
François		
40 Joseph	(19) M. Anne Ainse S.P.S. 1778	
Dorothée	Frs. Noël S.P. 1818	

BOULET.

41 Pierre	(22) M. Jos. Courteau,	S.Tho. 1743
M. Josette	Frs. Dutile S.F.S. 1770	
42 Jean Baptiste	Agathe Gendron	S.F.S. 1750
M. Christine	J. B Bilodeau S.F.S. 1775	
M. Agathe	Jean Frs. Daniau	S.F.S. 1777
Marguerite	Ant. Paré S.F.S. 1784	
Reine	J. B. Bélanger S.F.S. 1785	
M. Louise	Jacq. Talbot S.F.S. 1792	
Joseph Marie		
Pierre		
Jean Baptiste		
43 Joseph	(22) Marg. Paré S.F.S. 1762	
44 François	Genev. Morin	
François		
45 JeanBaptiste(24) Eliz. Rousseau S.F.S. 1780		
Elizabeth	Etn. Robin S.F.S. 1812	
M. Angèle	Ant. Ratté S.F.S. 1843	
Joseph		
François		
46 Pierre Noel	(24) M.Jos. Larrivé S.F.S. 1787	
M. Josette	J. B. Guilmet S.F.S. 1814	
François		
47 Pierre	(24) M. Ls. Gagnon S.P.S. 1787	
48 Guillaume	(24) Jeanne Lacasse S.Chs. 1788	
49 Robert	(25) Marie Fradet S.V. 1784	
M. Josette	Pierre Goulet S.M. 1811	
50 Jacques	(25) Marthe Guilmet S.V. 1779	
François	25) Genev. Blais S.F.S. 1784	
Geneviève	Etn. Cochon S.M. 1810	
Marguerite	Frs. Théberge S.M. 1817	
52 JeanBaptiste(25) M. Clotilde Cochon		
		S.M. 1796
Marguerite	Alexandre Cloutier	S.G. 1820
Jean		
53 Joseph	(27) Mad. Cloutier S.F.S. 1810	
54 Jean Marie	(28) M. Maud. Morin	S.F.S. 1802
55 François	Genev. Pigeon S.V. 1807	
Marguerite	Jérémie Champagna	S.F.S. 1841
Jacques		
56 Henri	(29) Josette Alaire S.H 1774	
Victoire	Michel Bourassa " 1803	
Thérèse	J. B. Carrier " 1804	
M. Catherine	Pierre Longchamps " 1804	
Josette	Pierre Lambert " 1804	
57 Louis	(30) M. Genev. Jacques	S.F.S. 1774
58 Jacques	(31) M. Rosalie Boulet	S.F.S. 1781
Rosalie	Jacq. Cote S.H. 1806	
Jean Baptiste		
Jacques		
60 Jean	(32) M.Anne Mercier S.H. 1812	
61 Pierre	(34) M. Reine Blanchet	Bert. 1803
62 JeanFrançois(34) M. Reine Guilmet		Bert. 1804
63 Frs. Gabriel (35) M. Marthe Campagna		S.Tho. 1801
Etienne Célestin		
64 Jacques	(36) M. Genev. Colin	S.P.S. 1788
65 Etienne	(37) M. Thérèse Boissonneau	S.F.S. 1797
66 Joseph	(38) Genev. Asselin S.G. 1810	
67 Alexis	(89) Genev. Fournier	S.Tho. 1807
Joseph Alexis		
68 François	(39) M.Marg.Pepin S.F.S. 1821	
69 JeanBaptiste(42) Marg Morin " 1782		
Louise	Aug. Mercier " 1799	

BOULET.

M. Rosalie	Frs. Roy	S.F.S. 1819
Julie	Michel Pelchat	,, 1824
Adélaïde	Jacq Blais	,, 1826
Marie	Pierre Bonneau	,, 1836
M. Agathe	Vita Gagnon	,, 1837
Joseph Prudent		
Jean Baptiste		
Pierre		
Le Même	Marie Morin	S.F.S. 1790
70 Pierre (42)	M. Chas. Rolandeau	S.F,S. 1784
M. Charlotte	Ls. Picard	S.F.S. 1807
Reine	Pierre Samson	,, 1808
Reine	2° Chas. Fournier	,, 1830
M. Louise	Jaq. Gagnon	,, 1821
Marie	Lazare Blais	,, 1823
Joseph		
Pierre		
Jacques		
François		
71 JosephMarie (42)	M. Roger Chartier	S.F.S. 1786
M. Soulange	PierreLecomte	S.F.S. 1841
Angèle	J. B. Prudent Bonneau	S.F.S. 1842
Marguerite	André Brochu	S.F.S. 1846
Luc		
72 Abraham	M. Archange Couillard	
Le Même	Thérèse Larrivé	B. 1815
73 François (44)	M. Thérèse Coulombe	S.P.S. 1787
M. Françoise	Ant. Plante	S. Chs 1800
François		
Jean Baptiste		
Joseph		
74 Joseph	M. Thérèse Coulombe	
Nicolas		
75 Joseph (45)	Louise Coté	S.G. 1823
76 François (45)	Julie Valcourt	S.F.S. 1834
77 François (46)	Eliz. Morin	,, 1842
78 Jean (52)	Marg. Cloutier	S.G. 1819
79 Jacques (55)	Esther Richard	S.V. 1855
80 Jacques (58)	M. Angé Simoneau	S.H. 1806
81 JeanBaptiste(58)	Angéle Belanger	S.G. 1816
Marguerite	Chs. Genest	S.V. 1833
82 Paul	Marie Mercier	
Michel		
83 Etn. Celestin(63)	M. Flavie Brousseau	S.F·S. 1843
84 JosephAlexis(66)	Hermine Lebrun	S.Chs. 1836
85 Joseph Pru-dent (69)	Marie Gendron	S.F.S 1825
86 JeanBaptiste(69)	Fse. Blais	,, 1831
87 Pierre (69)	Adé Blais	,, 1842
88 Pierre (70)	Julie Dessaint	,, 1808
Marguerite	Jacq. André Wells	,, 1831
Marie	Ed. Morisset	,, 1839
Pierre		
89 François (70)	VeroniqueBlais	S.P.S.1816
Constance	Jos. Prudent Gendron	S.F.S. 1839
M. Angélique	Tho. Samson	,, 1841
Le même	Théotiste Noyer	,, 1828
90 Joseph (70)	M. Marthe Blais	Bert 1819
91 Jacques (70)	Marg. Bernier	,, 1831
92 Luc (71)	M. Angèle Boissonneau	S.F.S. 1841
93 Joseph (73)	M. Anne Lainé	S.H. 1814
Damase		
Paul		
François Xavier		
94 Jean Baptiste	Eliz. Mercier	S.G. 1814
Elizabeth	Tho. Audet	,, 1830
Le même	M. Chs. Roger	S.Chs. 1816

BOULET.

95 Francois (73)	Judith Gontier	S.G. 1815
96 Nicolas (74)	M.Jos.Turgeon	S.Chs 1825
Nicolas		
97 Michel (82)	M. Emercé Roby	S.V 1859
98 Pierre (88)	Marie Nadeau	S.Chs. 1837
99 François Xa-vier (93)	M. Anne Tangué	,, 1845
100 Damase (93)	Hermine Fournier	
101 Paul (93)	Adé Aubé	S.Chs. 1853
102 Nicolas (96)	Mathilde Aubé	,, 1856

BOURASSA.

1 FrançoisModeste	M. Cath. Sénéchal	
FrançoisModeste		
2 FrançoisModeste	M. Judith Tangue	S.M. 1792
Archange	Aug. Goulet	S.Chs. 1836
Victoire	Frs. Cochon	,, 1852
FrançoisModeste		
3 François Mo-deste (2)	Archange Becquet	S.M. 1836

BOURGET.

1 François	Julie Sampson	
Charles		
François		
2 Pierre	Fse. Guay	
Pierre		
3 Charles	Marg. Sampson	
Charles		
4 François	M. Anne Ruel	S.L. 1781
5 Charles (1)	Genev. Paradis	Lévis 1793
M. Thérèse	Jos. Guay	B. 1816
Euphrosine	J. B. Guay	,, 1821
Charles		
François		
Féréal		
Jean		
6 Pierre (2)	Ursule Carrier-	Lévis 1756
Guillaume		
7 Guillaume (6)	Angé Ruel	S.L. 1781
8 Charles (3)	Félicité Begin	Lévis 1819
Pierre		
9 Charles (5)	Emmélie Turgeon	B. 1817
Marie	Eugéne Bilodeau	,, 1844
10 François (5)	Genev. Turgeon	,, 1823
M. Geneviève	Honoré Polequin	S.M.1846
François		
11 Fèréol (5)	M.MartheTurgeon	B. 1829
12 Jean (5)	JulieChamberlan	S.M.1831
13 Pierre (8)	M. Desanges Morin	S.M. 1845
14 Francois (10)	M. Eléonore Poliquin	S.M. 1848

BOUTIN.

1 Antoine	Genev. Gaudin	Q. 1665
Jean Baptiste		
Louis		
2 Jean Baptiste(1)	Jeanne Audibert	Q. 1692
M. Madeleine	Pierre Vermet	Bert. 1727
Angelique	Jacq. Bilodeau	,, 1730
Jean Baptiste		
Louis		
Jean Baptiste		
5 Louis (2)	Mad. Hélie	S.J. 1658
Le même	M. Chs. Chare	,,, 1720
M. Charlotte	Pierre Dumas	S.L 1747
Jean Valier		
Louis		
4 Jean Baptiste(2)	Cath. Rolandeau	S. Tho. 1717
Madeleine	Jos. Bouchard	Bert. 1746

5-6 EDWARD VII., A. 1906

BOUTIN,

Marguerite	2° André Beaucher	"	1763
Jean François	Jos. Baudoin Bert.		1749
Pierre			
Louis			
5 Louis	(2) M. Anne Mercier Bert.		1731
Thérèse	Jean Guibert	"	1771
M. Louise	Michel Arbour S F.S.		1753
Madeleine	Jos. Boissonneau	"	1763
M. Anne	Jos. Buteau	"	1766
Geneviève	Jacq. Baudoin	"	1779
M. Josette	Jos Larrivé S.P.S.		1764
Jean			
Louis			
Joseph			
6 Jean Baptiste	(2) Genev.Bousseau Bert.		1773
7 Louis	(3) Marie Ménaux S.F.		1746
M. Charlotte	Ls. Roy S.V.		1772
Ls. Barnabé			
Antoine			
Jacques			
Le même	M. Rose Gaudet S.V.		1767
8 Jean Valier	(3) Mad. Bilodeau Bert.		1746
Pierre			
Jean Baptiste			
Joseph			
Le même	M. Mad. Isabel Bert.		1769
M. Madeleine	Ant. Guillot S.V.		1793
M. Cécile	J. B. Lebrun	"	1807
M. Archange	Jos. Balan	"	1812
Marguerite	Etn. Coté	"	1800
"	2° Jos. Roy S.G.		1827
Paul			
François			
9 Jean François	(4) M. Anne Guignard Bert.		1746
Isabelle	Jos. Isabel Bert.		1783
"	2° Jos. Bonnet	"	1794
"	3° Ls. Boucher	"	1808
M. Anne	J. B. Campagna	"	1795
Nicolas François			
Jacques			
André			
10 Pierre	(4) M. Marthe Bilodeau Bert.		1751
M. Marthe	Jos. Gaumont B.		1772
M. Brigitte	Pierre Guilmet	"	17-9
11 Louis	(4) Eliz. Mercier Bert.		1757
M. Elizabeth	Jac Fournier	"	1788
Jean Baptiste			
Gabriel			
Louis			
Le même	Genev. Gagnon Bert.		1781
Le même	SusanneGagnonS.F.S.		1784
Susanne	J. B. Joly S.H.		1808
Joseph			
12 Pierre	Mad. Turcot		
M. Madeleine	Henri Nicole S.J.		1789
13 Louis	(5) M. Jos. Fortier S.F.S.		1761
Louis			
Le même	M. Ls. Mahneux	"	1766
Michel			
Joseph			
Basile			
14 Jean	(5) M. Fse. Peltier S.F.S.		1767
Françoise	Pierre Lefebvre	"	1795
Jean François			
15 Joseph	(5) M. Jos. Baudoin	"	1779
Louis			
16 Louis Barnabé	(7) M. Jos. Blais S.V.		1771
Paulette	Jos. Lacasse S.G.		1801
M. Anna	Eloi Roy	"	1802
Marguerite	Ls. Corriveau	"	1816
Louis			
Charles			
Jacques			
17 Jacques	(7) Théotiste Chabot S.Chs.		1778

BOUTIN.

Angèle	Barth. Audet S.G.		1803
Marguerite	Frs. Roy	"	1807
Angélique	Jos. Dupont	"	1817
Marie	Jean Baillargeon	"	1821
Théotiste	J. B. Audet S.V.		1845
Jacques			
Antoine			
Le même	Josette Bilodeau S.G.		1827
18 Antoine	(7) M.Angé Bisson S.V.		1780
Jacques			
Joseph			
Simon			
Antoine			
19 Pierre	(8) M.CécileGosselin S.V.		1787
	S. H.		
François			
Pierre			
20 Jean Baptiste	(8) M.Ursule Marseau SV		1796
M. Ursule	J. B. Hoffman	"	1819
M. Cécile	Eustache Gagné	"	1821
Archange	Julien Fleury	"	1823
Jean Baptiste			
21 Joseph	(8) M. Angé Coté S.V.		1798
M. Marguerite	Ls. Genest	"	1824
Joseph			
Thomas			
Paul	(8) M. Rose Marseau S.V.		1798
M. Rose	Pierre Garant S.V.		1832
Jean Baptiste			
Paul			
23 François	(8) M. Genev. Gosselin S.V.		1803
Céleste	Alexandre Ratté S.V.		1833
Sophie	Frs. Marcotte	"	1833
Geneviève	Jos. Roy	"	1837
M. Marthe	Félix Roy	"	1840
Anastasie	Jos. Faucher	"	1826
"	2° Frs. Gontier S.G.		1830
Louis			
24 Nicolas Fran- çois	(9) Jeanne Buteau Bert.		1778
Marie	Aug. Violette	"	1830
M. Reine	Moïse Beaulieu S.V.		1811
Lazare			
Charles			
25 Jacques	(9) M. Genev. Bilodeau Bert.		1787
Geneviève	Michel Queret S.V.		1812
Jacques			
26 André	(9) M. Jos. Picard S.P.S.		1793
Dorothée	Chs. Vincent Pepin S.F.S.		1835
François			
27 Louis	(11) Marie Bilodeau S.H.		1788
Antoine			
Pierre			
28 Jean Baptiste	(11) Véronique Duperron S.H.		1789
Véronique	Pierre Couture	"	1812
M. Françoise	Jos. Rouleau	"	1814
Jean Baptiste			
Le même	Marie Létellier	"	1813
29 Joseph	(11) M. Ursule Côté	"	1808
30 Gabriel	(11) M. Marg. Bernier	"	1809
31 Louis	Josette Roy		
Jean Baptiste			
32 Louis	Marie Moor		
François			
33 Louis	Marie Caron, (?) Garreau		
Marie	J. B. Bourbeau S.G.		1815
Rosalie	Frs. Plante	"	1821
Angélique	Frs. Campeau	"	1823
Louis			
Charles			
Jacques			
Jean Baptiste			

BOUTIN

34	Louis	(13)	Marg. Baudoin S.F.S.1788
	Françoise		J. B. Gagnon S.V. 1818
	Louis		
35	Basile	(13)	M. Jos. Dubé S.P.S. 1795
	Basile		
	Joseph		
36	Joseph	(13)	Fse. Morin S.V. 1796
37	Michel	(13)	M. Anne Dupont
			S.F.S. 1805
38	JeanFrançois(14)		M. Thérèse Roy S.F.S.1792
	Archange		Jos. Baudoin ,, 1827
	Rose		Chrysostôme Dumas
			S.F.S. 1827
	Jean François		
	Lazare		
	Louis		
39	Louis	(15)	M. Marg. Gaulin S.V.1815
40	Louis	(16)	Louise Corriveau S.G.1794
41	Charles	(16)	Louise Lacasse ,, 1799
	Louise		Chs. Valière ,, 1820
	Clémentine		Paschal Quemeneur
			S.G. 1829
	Joseph		
42	Jacques	(16)	Rosalie Terrien S.G. 1804
43	Jacques	(17)	Cath. Télémer ,, 1804
	Catherine		Eloi Lecours ,, 1826
	François		
44	Antoine	(17)	Marg. Mercier S.G. 1809
45	Antoine	(18)	Genev. Goupy S. Chs.1807
	Geneviève		Frs. Gaumont ,, 1829
	Julie		Laurent Morin ,, 1847
	Adélaïde		Godfroi Bégin Lévis 1839
	Louis		
	François		
46	Jacques	(18)	Eliz. Chabot S.Chs. 1812
47	Joseph	(18	M. Anne Naud ,, 1812
	Henriette		Jacq. Frs. Gravel B. 1845
	Le même		Marie Gaudin ,, 1824
48	Simon	(18)	M. Vict. Leclaire
			S.Chs. 1816
	Simon		
	Le même		Josette Fortier S.G. 1821
49	Pierre	(19)	M.Rose Morisset S.H.1820
	Pierre		
50	François	(19)	M. Anne Audet S.V. 1826
	M. Désanges		Théodore Rémillard
			S.V. 1857
51	JeanBaptiste(20)		M. Ls. Hearn ,, 1821
	Sophie		Michel Corriveau ,, 1848
52	Joseph	(21)	M. Anastasie Lemieux
			S.V. 1821
	M. Zoé		Frs. Félix de Valois Gau-
			tron S.V. 1841
	Delvina		Gaspard Tangué ,, 1844
	Aussile		Ls. Chabot ,, 1858
	Cyrille		
53	Thomas	(21)	Mathilde Lemieux
			S.V. 1829
	Emmélie		Geo. Fagot ,, 1863
	Jean		
	Thomas		
54	Paul	(22)	Marg. Roy S.F.S. 1834
55	Jean Baptiste(22)		Julie Alaire, S. V. 1841
56	Louis	(23)	Henriette Gourgue,
			S. V. 1843
57	Charles	(24)	Mad. Fortier Bert. 1808
	Marguerite		J. B. Turgeon ,, 1841
	Louis		
58	Lazare	(24)	M. Genev. Brousseau
			S.V. 1819
	Narcisse		
59	Jacques	(25)	Marie Cochon S.V. 1827
	Henriette		Geo. Roy ,, 1858
	Pierre		
60	François	(26)	Marie Morin S.P.S. 1822

BOUTIN.

61	Pierre	(27)	M. Genev. Coté S.H. 1816
62	Antoine	(27)	Charlotte Langlais
			S. P. 1817
	François		
	Le même		Eléonore Marcoux
			S.P. 1864
63	JeanBaptiste(28)		Thérèse Langlais S.H.1819
64	JeanBaptiste(31)		Vict. Guenet S.P. 1814
65	François	(32)	Marie Cameron S.G. 1829
66	Louis	(33)	Angéle Roy S.G. 1813
67	JeanBaptiste(33)		Reine Bissonnet S.G. 1820
68	Charles	(33)	Marie Labbé S.G. 1824
			M. Marg. Corriveau
69	Jacques	(33)	S. Chs. 1833
70	Louis		M. Ls. Mercier
	Jean Baptiste		
			Fils de Michel et de
			M. Agathe Boucher
71	Augustin		Marie Grégoire Ste.
			Marie St. Isidore 1821
	Joseph Godfroi		
	Abraham		
72	Augustin		M. Jos. Gagné
	Augustin		
73	Pierre		Marie Gosselin
	Jean Baptiste		
74	Henri		Agathe Lortie
	Henri Michel		
75	Charles		Marcelline Leclaire
	Le même		M. Chs. Carrier S.Chs.
			1857
76	Louis	(34)	Angé Corriveau S.V. 1817
77	Basile	(35)	M. Mad. Quemeneur
			S.H. 1817
78	Joseph	(35)	M. Marg. Corriveau
			S.V. 1822
79	JeanFrancois(38)		Eléonore Morin S.F.S.1828
80	Lazare	(38)	Marcelline Laurandeau
			S.F.S. 1829
81	Louis	(38)	Eliz. Blais S. F. S. 1837
82	Joseph	(41)	M. Marg. Corriveau
			S.V. 1839
83	François	(43)	Héloise Dessaint
			S.F.S. 1841
84	Louis	(45)	Angèle Fournier S.Chs.
			1836
85	François	(45)	Marg. Fournier S.Chs.
			1848
86	Simon	(48)	Theotiste Goulet
			S. Chs. 1841
87	Cyrille	(52)	Zélie Roy S. V. 1859
88	Thomas	(53)	Désanges Bolduc S.V.1813
	Le même		Séraphine Dion ,, 1870
89	Jean	(53)	Delphine Ratté S. V. 1863
90	François	(62)	Symphorienne Marcoux
			S. P. 1864
91	Pierre	(49)	Esther Bernard S.V. 1848
92	JeanBaptiste(70)		M. Ls. CorriveauS.V. 1848
			S. Anselme.
93	Joseph L.		
	Godfroi	(71)	Zoé Chabot S. Chs. 1850
94	Abraham	(71)	Perpétue Denis S.Chs. 1853
95	Augustin	(72)	Caroline Fournier
			S.Chs. 1851
96	JeanBaptiste(73)		Hortense Clément
			S. Chs. 1851
97	Henri Michel(74)		Emélie McNeil S.V. 1869
98	Louis	(57)	Sophie Tangué Bert. 1843
99	Narcisse	(58)	Angé Naud S. Chs. 1853
100	Pierre	(59)	M. Emélie Turgeon
			S.V. 1864

BOUTILLET.

1	Pierre		Jacqueline Vandandaigne
			Beauport 1699

BOUTILLET.

M. Françoise	Jos. Cyr. Isle Jésus 1725
M. Charlotte	Jean Berthiaume Chs.
Le même	Bourg 1775
	M. Anne Allard Chs.
2 Jacques	Bourg 1714
	Marie Deslorier
Joseph	
3 Joseph	(2) Genev. Fafart A. G. 1761
	Q
Pierre	
4 Pierre	(3) Marie Vérieul C. R. 1793
Le même	M. Jos. Fournier B 1796
5 Simon	M. Ls. Langlois
	Joachim Bernier S. Chs.
M. Louise	1795
"	2° Jos. Mercier " 1815
Françoise	Alexandre Lefebvre
	S. Chs. 1801
Charles	
Jacques	
Simon	
6 Charles	(5) Judith Fortier S. Chs. 1789
7 Jacques	(5) Marie Charrier " 1797
M. Anne	Gervais Bernier " 1829
Marie	Pierre Marcoux S. G. 1819
Simon	(5) Marie Voisin S. H. 1793

BRIDAUT.

1 Jean	Marie Crête Q. 1687
Jean Hilaire	
2 "	(1) M. Jos. Paquet Q. 1716
M. Louise	Jos. Lacroix S. M. 1739
M. Josette	Noël Roumillard " 1741
M. Elizabeth	Frs. Morin S. P. S. 1753
M. Angélique	Ls Valière 1772

BRIART—LEJEUNE.

1	
2 Joseph	(1)
Le même	Mad. Deblois S. Frs. 1757
3 Jean Baptiste	Marg. Beaulieu
Jean	
4 "	(3) M. Ls. Forgues S. Chs. 1766
5 François Olivier	Fse. Forgues
Charlotte	Aug. Nadeau S. G. 1807
Angélique	Guill. Labrecque " 1812
"	2' Pierre Lacasse " 1823
Marguerite	Ls. Gontier " 1821
François	
Antoine	
Le même	Josette Dutile " 1807
Jean Olivier	
6 François	(5) Charlotte Dutile " 1803
François	
7 Antoine	(5) Thérèse Gontier " 1810
Adélaide	Frs. Fradet " 1830
8 Antoine Olivier	Olive Baudoin
Le même	Domitille Plante
	S. Chs. 1855
9 Jean Olivier	(5) Marie Baillargeon
	S. Chs. 1832
Apolline	Dominique Morisset
	S. Chs. 1860
10 François	(6) M. Anne Vallée S. G. 1826

BRISSON.

1 René	Anne Vezina
Réné	
Charles	
2 René	(1) Genev. Testu A. G. 1696
François Joseph	
René	
3 Charles	(1) Marie Letartre " 1698
M. Françoise	Guill. Gravel C. R. 1783

BRISSON.

Charles François	
Ignace	
4 René	(2) M. Anne Doyon " 1719
5 Joseph François	
	(2) Marg. Perrot S. Anne 1720
6 Charles François	
	(3) Brigitte Tremblay
Marie	A. G. 1730
Jean Hilaire	Laurent Couture S. M. 1762
Michel	
François	
7 Ignace	(3) Marg. Lavoie Baie
	S. Paul 1731
8 Jean Hilaire	(6) M. Anne Roy S. M. 1773
M. Louise	Frs. Coté " 1794
Pierre Noël	
9 François	(6) Thérèse Fortier " 1764
M. Charlotte	Frs. Talbot S. V. 1814
Joseph	
10 François	M. Anne Fradet
François	
11 Michel	(6) M. Ls. Fradet S. M. 1778
François	
12 Pierre Noël	(8) Marie Coté " 1796
Marie	Jos. Coté S. G. 1820
Josette	Frs. Morin " 1826
Marguerite	Raphaël Lemieux " 1828
M. Anne	Frs. Leclaire S. V. 1834
Jean Baptiste	
13 Joseph	(9) M. Angé. Carbonneau
	Bert. 1814
14 François	(10) Genev. Comeau S. Chs. 1806
15 "	(11) M. Rose Gautron S. M. 1803
Marcelline	Edouard Roy " 1844
M. Anne	Damase Gautron " 1851
Jean	
Georges	
David	
16 Jean Baptiste	(12) Genev. Baillargeon
	S. G. 1829
17 Jean	(15) Angèle Roussel S. M. 1838
18 David	(15) Génev. Pouliot S. J. 1846
19 Georges	(15) Eulalie Mercier S. M. 1848

BROCHU.

1 Louis	René Gaschet
Jean	
2 Jean	(2) Nicole Saulnier S. F. 1669
Marie	Jean Tangué S. P. 1692
Anne	Noël Lebrun " 1696
Jean	
3 Jean	(2) Marie Delaunay Q. 1697
Geneviève	Aug. Blais Bert. 1730
Marguerite	J. B. Gagné " 1734
	2° Frs. Quemeneur S. V. 1739
Jean Baptiste	
4 Jean Baptiste	(3) Dorothée Alaire Q. 1724
Agathe	Michel Garant S. V. 1744
M. Josette	Jacques Roy " 1755
Dorothée	Clément Patry " 1744
"	2° Pierre Bacquet S. M. 1777
Pierre	
Louis	
Le même	Susanne Garant S. V. 1741
M. Louise	Olivier Nicole " 1765
M. Susanne	Jacq. Roy " 1765
M. Susanne	Jacq. Roy " 1771
5 Jean Baptiste	(4) M. Agathe Roy 1756
Marguerite	Nicolas Bouchard S V. 1785
Thérèse	Jacques Bélanger " 1788
Michel	
Jean Baptiste	
André	
Thomas	

BROCHU.

```
      Charles
      Joseph
 6  Pierre          (4) Genev. Roy      S.V. 1753
    M. Geneviève        J. B. Helie        "  1782
    M. Josette          Ignace Denis .     "  1793
    Marguerite          Michel Gagnon      "  1795
    André
    François
 7  Louis           (4) Marg. Roy       S.V. 1759
    Louis
 8  Jean Baptiste  (5) M. Ursule Bouchard
                                         S.V. 1783
    Marguerite          J. B. Lemieux      "  1809
    M. Anne             Paul Martineau     "  1812
    M. Apolline         Frs. Chabot        "  1820
    M. Ursule           Jos. Roy           "  1826
    Jean Baptiste
    Thomas
 9  Joseph         (5) M. Anne Poliquin
                                       S.Chs. 1786
    M. Charlotte        Pierre Rousseau    "  1822
    Louise '            Jean Chabot        "  1819
    M. Anne             Michel Rousseau    "  1812
    Jacques
    Jean
    Féréol
    Joseph
    Charles
10  André          (5) M. Anne Tangué S.M. 1793
    M. Lucie            Amable Paquet  S.V. 1818
    Julie               Tho. Léonard Bélanger
                                         S.V. 1826
    Sophie              Chs. Gourge        "  1833
    M. Anne             Vilmère Roy        "  1837
    Vilmère
    Luc
    André
    Féréol
    Léonard
    Pierre
    Le même             Ange Langlois  S.V. 1836
                        V. de Jos. Alaire
11  Thomas         (5) M. Euphrosime Lemieux
                                         S.V. 1800
    Adélaïde            Frs. Blouin        "  1826
    Elizabeth           Ls. Bolduc         "  1827
    Agathe              Jacq. Bacquet      "  1836
    Sophie              Frs. Régis Roy     "  1840
    Catherine           Edouard Genest     "  1842
    Mathilde            André Blais        "  1842
    Stanislas
    François Xavier
12  Michel         (5) Fse. Quirouet  Bert. 1803
    Eulalie             Chs. Penin     S.G. 1830.
    Pierre
13  Charles        (5) M. Ls. Herpe   S.V. 1802
    Stanislas
14  André          (6) Marie Roy      S.V. 1781
    Marie               Pierre Arbour  S.G. 1801
    Marie               Frs. Rémillard     "  1826
    Marguerite          Jean Bacquet       "  1809
            "           2° Ls. Bilodeau    "  1823
    Louise              Jean Quéret        "  1810
    M. Anne             Jos. Roby          "  1810
    Thérèse             Frs. Morin         "  1824
    Angèle              Frs. Langlois      "  1826
    Angélique           Basile Thibault    "  1827
    Louis
    Joseph
    André
    André
15  François       (6)        Marceau S.V. 1788
    Marguerite          Chs. Vien     S.M. 1814
    Victoire            Jean Quemeneur
                                        Bert. 1824
    Reine               J. B. Lepage  S.Chs. 1825
```

18—16½

BROCHU.

```
      Ursule          Michel Asselin  S.G. 1828
      Pierre
      Antoine
      François
      Michel
16  Louis           (7) Génev. Leclaire S.V. 1785
    Marguerite          Chs. Paquet    S.M. 1822
    Françoise           André Gosselin    "  1828
    Geneviève           Jos. Audibert     "  1829
    Pierre
    Jacques
    François Xavier
    Louis
17  Thomas         (8) M. Emélie Roy  S.V. 1812
    Emélie              Sévère Théberge   "  1868
    Aurélie             Frs. Morrisson    "  1869
    Narcisse
    Thomas
18  Jean Baptiste (8) N. Archange Roy S.V.1820
    Marcelline          Damasse Corriveau  M.
                                         S.V.1846
    Césaire             Jacq. Roy      S.V. 1852
    Lucie               Pierre Quéret     "  1853
    Delphine            F. X. Lainé       "  1858
    Adélaïde            Laurent Roy       "  1859
    Théodore
    Venceslas
19  Jean           (9) Marie Blouin   S.G. 1813
    Charles        (9) Marie Fortier  S.H. 1815
20  Jacques        (9) Marie Blais    S. Chs. 1817
21  Féréol         (9) Marg. Bilodeau S.G. 1825
22  André          (10) Angèle Beaucher
                                      S. Chs. 1822
    Zoé                 Jean Royer        "  1852
    Nazaire
    André
    Le même             Marg. Boulet   S.F.S. 1840
23  Féréol         (10) Adé Couture  S. Chs. 1832
24  Léonard        (19) Apolline Baillargeon
                                      S. Chs. 1833
25  Luc            (10) M. Zoé Chabot S.V. 1834
26  Vilmère        (10) Genev. Chabot S.V. 1844
27  Pierre         (10) Susanne Guénet S.G. 1819
28  Stanislas      (11) Emélie Roy    S.V. 1829
29  François-
        Xavier (11) Marceline Blais S.V. 1842
30  Pierre         (12) Natalie Naud S. Chs. 1850
31  Stanislas      (13) Sara Roy      Bert. 1843
32  André          (14) M. Anne Aubé S.G. 1807
    André
33  François            M. Génev. Aubé
    Charles
34  Joseph         (14) Marie Fradet  S.G. 1811
    Frédéric
    Léandre
    Joseph
35  André          (14) M.Anne Gontier S.G. 1819
36  Louis          (14) Emérentienne Langlois
                                         S.V. 1830
37  Antoine        (15) Apolline Fradet S.M. 1810
    Emélie              Léandre Brochu    "  1860
    Apolline            Marcel Pepin S. Chs. 1846
    Antoine
    Jean
    Michel
38  François       (15) Marg. Blais   Bert. 1823
39  Michel         (15) Sophie Guilmet Bert. 1824
40  Pierre         (15) Marg. Tangué  S.V. 1828
41  Pierre         (16) M. Ls. Lefebvre S.M. 1810
    Angèle              Pierre Labbé      "  1831
    Luce                Ls. Couture       "  1835
    Eulalie             Jean Fortin       "  1845
    Le même             Louise Clément    "  1830
42  Jacques        (16) Génev. Goupy  S.M. 1830
    Adéline             Jos. Gagnon       "  1864
    Jacques
```

BROCHU.

43 Louis	(13) Marg. Garant S. Chs. 1816	
44 François-Xavier	(16) Euphrosine Bouchard	S.M. 1836
Le même	Anastasie Turgeon	S.M. 1853
45 Joseph	(9) Brigitte Galbert S.H. 1810	
Joseph		
46 Etienne	Marg. Faneuf	
André		
47 Narcisse	(17) Emélie Tangué S.V. 1842	
48 Thomas	(17) Rose Catellier S.V. 1853	
49 Théodore	(18) M. Délima Tangué	S.V. 1857
50 Wenceslas	(18) Marie Lepage S.V. 1858	
51 Nazaire	(22) M. Angé Charrier	S. Chs. 1850
52 André	(22) Henriette Chabot	S. Chs. 1855
53 André	(32) Eliz. Labbé S.G. 1826	
54 Charles	(33) M. Marg. Baudouin	S.V. 1833
55 Joseph	(34) M. Jos. Dalaire S.V. 1836	
55 Joseph	(34) M. Jos. Dalaire S.V. 1836	
Philomène	Gaspard Vaillancour	S.V. 1865
Joseph		
56 Frédéric	(34) M. Marcelline Morisset	S.M. 1841
57 Léandre	(34) Emélie Brochu S.M. 1860	
58 Antoine	(37) Luce Chamberlan	S.M. 1838
59 Michel	(37) M. Eliz. Chamberlan	S.M. 1844
60 Jean	(37) Henriette Cochon	S.M 1849
61 Jacques	(42) Marie Pruneau S.Chs. 1854	
62 Joseph	(45) Genev.Théberge S.V. 1839	
63 André	(46) Philomène Nadeau	S. Chs. 1863
64 Joseph	(55) Cath. Lemelin S.V. 1863	

BROUSSEAU.

1 Pierre	M. Thérèse Bernard	Q. 1704
Pierre		
Antoine		
2 Pierre	(1) Genev. Parent, Beauport	1727
Simon		
Charles		
3 Antoine	(1) Louise Eliz. Gagnon Q.1746	
Louise Eliz.	Nicolas Morisset S.M. 1775	
Joseph		
Le même	M. Ls. Dalaire Q. 1756	
M. Anne	Paul Veau S.M. 1787	
Marie	Pierre Bacquet „ 1801	
Louise	Jacq. Naud S.Chs. 1783	
Marguerite	Thos. Corriveau S.V. 1790	
Pierre		
François		
4 Michel	Marg. Dussant	
Augustin		
5 Charles	(2) Félicite Spinard Q. 1773	
Marie	Pierre Pouliot S.L. 1783	
6 Simon	(2) Marie Rouleau S.L. 1773	
Joseph		
7 Antoine	Angé Moreau	
Angéle	Laurent Lacroix S.M.1804	
„	2° Jos. Gautron „ 1834	
Félicité	Jos. Fontaine „ 1810	
Catherine	André Lacroix „ 1812	
„	2° Etn. Blanchet „ 1821	
Germain		

BROUSSEAU.

8 Augustin	(4) Fse. Boulet S. Tho. 1763		
François	J. R. Bouchard „ 1801		
Augustin			
9 Joseph	(3) M. Cath. Lacroix S.M.1779		
Céleste	Ls. Tangué S.V. 1807		
M. Thérèse	Jos. Tangué „ 1813		
M. Josette	Aug. Vérieul „ 1816		
M. Geneviève	Lazare Boutin „ 1819		
M. Angélique	Ant. Talbot „ 1843		
Antoine			
Joseph			
François			
10 Joseph	(6) Genev. Dumas S.L. 1804		
M. Geneviève	Ant. Noël „ 1824		
Geneviève	Frs. Gosselin „ 1833		
Marguerite	Edouard Dumas „ 1836		
Magloire			
Joseph			
Pierre			
11 Pierre	(3) Marie Bacquet S.M. 1786		
Marie	Jean Bte. Ruel S.H. 1815		
Geneviève	Basile Plante „ 1819		
André			
Jean Baptiste			
12 François	(3) Marg. Couture S.Chs. 1795		
Marguerite	Aug. Roy S.G. 1820		
Jacques			
François			
13 Germain	(7) Angé Couture S.Chs. 1811		
Marie	Jos. Bilodeau S.M. 1833		
Marguerite	Michel Tangué „ 1839		
Le même	Marg. Bégin „ 1834		
Le même	M. Ls. Rebecca Gagné	S.M. 1847	
14 Augustin	(8) M. Mad. McKinnal,	Bert. 1798	
Madeleine	Ls. Blouin „ 1823		
Le même	Louise Carbonneau „ 1810		
15 François	(9) M. Jos. Alaire S.H. 1817		
Nazaire			
16 Antoine	(9) Pélagie Tangué S.V. 1807		
Simon			
Antoine			
Le même	Marie Roy S.V. 1818		
Lucie	Michel Quéret „ 1847		
17 Joseph	(9) M. Ls. Baudewin	S. Claire S.V. 1817	
M. Flavie	Etn. Célestin Boulet		
18 Magloire	(10) S.F.S. 1843		
	M. Anne Nadeau S.L.1840		
19 Joseph	(10) M. Jos. Labrecque	S.L. 1850	
20 Pierre	(10) Rose Gendreau S.L. 1855		
A Jean Baptiste	(11) Tharsill Cadoret S.H. 1820		
21 André	(11) M. Chs. Turgeon S.H.	B. 1823	
22 Jacques	(12) Marie Goulet S.G. 1827		
23 François	(12) Julie Roger S.G. 1825		
24 Nazaire	(15) M. Ls. Parent S.F.S.	S.V. 1849	
25 Simon	(16) Marg. Richard S.V. 1832		
26 Antoine	(16) Marie Thivierge S.M. 1841		

BRUNEAU.

1 René	Jeanne Anne Poitreau	Q. 1668
François		
Nicolas		
2 François	(1) Marie Provost	
François		
3 Nicolas	(1) Mad. Lafleur	
Le même	Anne Leroux, Chs. Bourg.	1721
4 François	(2) Mad. Bourgouin, Beauport	1702

BRUNEAU.

	Charles		
5	Charles	(4) M. Ls. Lamothé, Beauport	1744
	M. François	Guill. Corriveau S.V.	1773
	M. Louise	Louis Coté ,,	1775
	Marguerite	Frs. Roy ,,	1780
	Geneviève	Pierre Bolduc ,,	1780
	M. Josette	Jos. Terrien ,,	1792
	Joseph		
	Charles		
	François		
6	Charles	(5) M. Eliz. Corriveau	S.V.1772
	Marie	Jacq. Guilmet ,,	1807
	Joseph		
	Charles		
7	François	(5) M. Angé. Asselin S.V.1779	
	François		
	Charles		
	Jean Baptiste		
	Joseph		
8	Joseph	(5) Marie Ruel S.Chs.	1788
	Joseph		
9	François	(7) Genev. Létourneau	S.G. 1800
	Sophie	Chs. Ratté ,,	1826
	François		
10	Charles	(7) Marg. Cloutier S.G.	1806
	Marguerite	Aug. Audet ,,	1826
	Henriette	Ls. Blais ,,	1829
11	Jean Baptiste	(7) Marie Labrecque ,,	1807
	Françoise	Frs. Roy ,,	1828
12	Joseph	Angé. Philippe ,,	1810
	Le même	Louis Morin ,,	1825
13	Jean Baptiste	Adé Roy, S. Claire	
	Jean Baptiste		
14	Joseph	(8) Josette Gosselin S.G.	1824
15	François	(10) Marie Bacquet ,,	1824
16	JeanBaptiste(14)	Philomène Lemelin	S.Chs. 1862
	Charles	(6) M. Mad. Gagné S.P.S.1807	

BUSSIÈRE,

1	Jacques	Noelle Gossard S.F.	1671
	Jean		
2	Jean	(1) Ursule Rondeau S.P.1693	
	Madeleine	Pierre Roy ,,	1733
	Angélique	Frs. Lafrance ,,	1737
	M. Marthe	Maurice Michel Jean	S.P. 1744
	Jean		
	Augustin		
	François		
	Gabriel		
	Paul		
3	Jean	(2) Fse. Dupile S.P.	1716
	Véronique	Jacq. Rousseau ,,	1744
	,,	3° Pierre Gauvin S.L.	1773
	Marie	Jos. Cloutier S.P.	1747
	Geneviève	Jos. Bergeron ,,	1749
	Jean Baptiste		
	Le même	M. Chs. Nadeau B.	1758
4	Augustin	(2) M. Chs. Lecompte ,,	1726
5	François	(2) M. Anne Ferland S.P.1733	
	M. Thérèse	Michel Parent ,,	1769
	Louis		
	Le même	M. Anne Ruel S.L.	1745
	Le même	M. Anne Dufaut S.F.	1751
	Barbe	Amb. Roberge S.P.	1788
6	Gabriel	(2) M. Anne Paradis ,,	1734
	M. Louise	J. B. Perrot ,,	1769
	Louis		
7	Paul	(2) Cath. Ferlant S.P.	1744
8	Joseph	Genev. Parant	
	M. Charlotte	Pierre Crépeau S.H.	1778
	Pierre Paul		

BUSSIÈRE.

9	Jean Baptiste (3)	Josette Poiré, Lévis	1741
	M. Josette	Ls. Crépeau ,,	1770
	Pierre		
	François		
10	Louis	(5) Gertrude Ratté S.P.	1761
11	Louis	(6) Thérèse Leclaire ,,	1765
	M. Thérèse	Pierre Tardif S.H.	1786
	M. Josette	André Forgues ,,	1807
	Etienne		
	Louis		
	Léger		
	Le même	Mad. Blouin S.Chs.	1791
	Le même	M.Anne Déport S.G.1808	
12	Pierre Paul	(8) Fse. Fournier S.P.S.	1774
	M. Françoise	Ls. Lehoux S.H.	1807
	M. Louise	Alexandre Filteau ,,	1811
	Joseph Magloire	M. Paschal Lévis	
13	Pierre	(9) Josette Dallaire S.M.	1771
	M. Josette	Jean Bergeron B.	1797
	Marguerite	Jos. Boissel ,,	1801
	Françoise	Jos. Labrecque ,,	1806
	M. Charlotte	Ant. Blanchet S.H.	1796
	Rosalie	Pierre Paradis ,,	1797
	Pierre		
	Victor		
	Le même	Marie Gosselin S.Chs.	1825
14	François	(9) M. Fse. Fontaine S.M.1771	
15	Louis	(11) Mad. Roy B.	1792
	Louis		
16	Ludger	(11) Marg. Noël S.H.	1810
17	Etienne	(11) Judith Paradis S.G.	1822
18	Sévère	(12) Ursule Quemeneur	S.H. 1808
19	Charles Paschal	(12) M. Euphrosine Blais	S.H. 1815
20	Jos. Magloire(12)	M. Jos. Filteau B.	1815
	Joseph Magloire		
21	Pierre	(13) M. Agathe Poliquin	S.M. 1804
22	Victor	(13) Angé Gosselin S.Chs.	1811
23	Edouard	Angé Gosselin	
	Charles		
	Le même	Fse. Roy S.M.	1826
24	Charles	M. Anne Bacon Q.	
	Charles		
25	Louis	(15) Marie Turgeon B.	1819
26	Joseph	Marie Guilmet S.H.	
	Pierre		
27	Joseph Magloire	Mathilde Labrecque B.	(20) 1847
28	Charles	(23) M. Anne Mercier S.Chs.	1841
	Philomène	Wilmer Duquet S. Chs.	1861
29	Charles	(24) Genev. Langlois Bert.	1834
30	Pierre	(36) Olive Labrecque B.	1856
31	François	M. Jos. Genest	
	Le même	Marg. Leclaire S.Chs.	1863
32	Paul	Delphine Bochet	
	Le même	Damaris Pouliot S. J.	1865

BUTEAU.

1	Pierre	Perette Loriot S.F.	1671
	Madeleine	Pierre Duchesne S.Fro.	1701
	Madeleine	(2) Dominique Gagné S. Fro.	1704
	Claire	J. B. Gagné S. Chs.	1706
	Marguerite	Jos. Vericul ,,	1710
	,,	2° J. B. Leblond ,,	1710
	M. Françoise	Jacq. Baudon ,,	1740
	,,	2° Frs. Dupont ,,	1723
	Pierre		
	François		

BUTEAU.

2	Pierre	(1)	Marie Carbonneau	S.Frs. 1697
	Marie		Jacq. Corriveau	S.V. 1724
	Angélique		Aug. Bernier	Bert. 1734
	Pierre			
	Joseph			
3	François		Marie Ginchereau	S.Frs. 1715
	François			
	Joseph			
4	Joseph	(2)	M. Thècle Baudoin	S.Frs. 1736
	Le même		Ursule Guimont Cap.	S.Ign. 1742
	M. Ursule		J. B. Proulx	Bert. 1763
	M. Josette		Germ. Baudoin	,, 1770
	Jeanne		Nic. Frs. Boutin	,, 1778
	Elizabeth		J. B. Blais	,, 1788
	Lazare			
	Joseph			
	André			
5	Pierre	(2)	Brigitte Fournier	S.P.S. 1749
	M. Brigitte		Jean Moïse Morin	S.F.S.
	M. Susanne		Pierre Alaire	,, 1785
	M. Marguerite		Jos. Dalaire	S.F.S. 1796
	,,		2° Jacq. Plante	,, 1807
	Basile			
	Jacques			
6	Joseph	(3)	M. Marth Blanchet Cap	S.Ign, 1749
	M. Elizabeth		J. B. Boissonneau	S.F.S. 1777
7	Francois	(3)	M. Anne Tangué	S.V. 1744
	M. Françoise		André Blanchet	Bert. 1769
	Joseph			
8	Joseph		Ursule Dumas	
	Jacques			
9	Joseph	(4)	M. Anne Boutin	S.F.S.1766
	Joseph			
	Le même		M. Thérèse Fortin	S.F.S. 1771
	Thérèse		Ign. Dalaire	S.F.S. 1799
	,,		2° Ls. Proulx	,, 1805
	Marg. Reine		J. B. Labrecque	,, 1803
	Louis			
10	Lazare	(4)	Marg. Marcoux	Bert. 1780
11	André	(4)	Brigitte Brisson	S.Tho.1774
	Brigitte		Frs. Blair	Bert. 1801
	Jacques			
12	Jacques	(5)	Brigitte Fournier	S.Tho. 1786
	Lazare			
	Joseph			
13	Basile	(5)	M. Jos. Fortin	S.V. 1797
	Angèle		Isidore Bernier	S.F.S. 1825
	Marie		Guill. Lemieux	,, 1827
	M. Julie		Michel Litourneau	,, 1829
	Marguerite		Paschal Mercier	,, 1830
	Soulange		Mag. Valière	,, 1840
	Francois			
14	Joseph	(7)	Cath. Hall	Bert. 1794
	M. Christine		Jacq. Cochon	,, 1824
	Thècle		Jos. Hébert	,, 1837
	Augustin			
	Joseph			
15	Jacques		Marg. Chabot	S. Chs. 1783
	Marguerite		Pierre Audet	S.G. 1803
	Cecile		Pierre Filteau	,, 1807
	Jacques			
	Le même		Justine Roy	S.V. 1790
16	Joseph	(9)	Fse. Mercier	S.F.S. 1788
	Catherine		Jos. Boissonneau	,, 1822
	M. Françoise		Jos. Pepin	S.P.S. 1822
	Bénoni			
	Louis			
	Joseph			
	Jean Baptiste			

BUTEAU.

17	Louis	(9)	Marg. Daniau	S.F.S. 1798
	M. Reine		Pierre Gagnon	,, 1834
	Marguerite		Pierre Laine	,, 1835
	Angéle		Jos. Laine	,, 1837
	Pierre			
	Louis			
18	Jacques	(11)	Genev. Lemieux	S.H.1806
19	Joseph		Geneviève Théotiste Lemieux	S.P.S. 1815
	Genev.Théotiste.		Michel Godfroi Létourneau	S F.S. 1835
20	Lazare	(12)	MarcellineCadrin	S.V.1841
21	François	(13)	Brigitte Alaire	,, 1832 S.H.
22	Augustin	(14)	Marie Blais	Bert. 1826
23	Joseph	(14)	Julie Blais	,, 1839
24	Jacques	(15)	Marie Fortier	S.H. 1812
25	Joseph	(16)	M. Vict. Blais	S.F.S. 1823
	Joseph Honoré			
26	Louis	(16)	M. Honorée Turgeon	S.V. 1844
27	JeanBaptiste	(16)	M. Julie Langlais	S.F.S.1831
28	Bénoni	(16)	Euphémie Morin	,, 1836
	Bénoni			
29	Pierre	(17)	Thècle Picard	S.F.S. 1835
30	Louis	(17)	M. Olive Roy	,, 1838
31	Basile		M. Olive Gagné	
	Le même		Marg. Mercier	Bert. 1846
32	Joseph Honoré	(25)	Flore Letellier	S.V. 1855
33	Bénoni	(28)	Perpétue Corriveau	S.V. 1865

CADRIN.

1	Nicolas		Fse. Delaunay	S.F. 1679
	Anne		Micolas Morisset	,, 1709
	Claire		Nicolas Roy	S.M. 1701
	Françoise		Frs. Bazin	,, 1701
	Marie		Laurent Terreau	Q. 1715
	Marguerite		Robert Vermet	S.V. 1716
	,,		2° Pierre Gagné	Bert. 1742
	Pierre			
2	Pierre	(1)	Marthe Marseau	S.V.1727
	M. Marthe		Jos. LeRoy	S.M.1749
	,,		2° Frs. Mercier	" 1776
	M. Hélène		Pre. Arsène Daniau	,, 1754
	Marguerite		J. B. Tangué	,, 1772
	Urbain			
	Pierre			
	Paul			
3	Urbain	(2)	M.Thérèse Fortier	S.M. 1752
	Thérèse		Jacq. Bolduc	S.V.1783
	Le même		Marg. Larrivé	S.M.1774
4	Pierre Alexis	(2)	M. Chs. Fortin	S.M.1766
	M. Marthe		Frs. Mercier	,, 1777
	Elizabeth		Frs. Lafontaine	,, 1799
	M. Anne		Joseph Marseau	,, 1802
	Pierre			
	Etienne			
	Jean Baptiste			
5	Paul	(2)	Ursule Mercier	S.M.1765
	Marie		Etn. Bolduc	,, 1791
	M. Marthe		Chs. Dubord	,, 1802
	Ursule		Jos. Bolduc	,, 1802
	M. Madeleine		Frs. Alexis Roy	,, 1808
	,,		2° Ls. Gagnon	,, 1816
	Paul			
	Joseph			
6	Urbain		Marg. Morisset	
	Joseph			
7	Pierre Alex-andre	(4)	Genev. Bisson	S.M.1788
	Marie		Simon Jolin	S.M.1807
	Françoise		Laurent Guilhnet	,, 1825

CADRIN.

	Josette	Ant. Guilmet	S.M.1846
8	Etienne	(4) M. Ls. Roy	S.M.1797
	M. Louise	J. B. Langlois	S.V.1821
	M. Angèle	Jos. Chrétien	" 1834
	Marcelline	Lazare Buteau	" 1841
	Etienne		
	Jean		
9	Jean Baptiste	(4) Marie Lepage	S.Chs. 1807
10	Paul	(5) Archange Bolduc	S.V.1808
	Louis		
	Paul		
11	Joseph	(6) Marg. Lefebvre	S.M. 1802
	Soulange	J. B. Marseau	" 1842
12	Etienne	(8) Céleste Alaire	S.V.1845
	M. Céleste	F. X. Morin	S.F.S.1844
	Le même	M. Anne Rousseau	
			S.V.1834
13	Urbain	M. Anne Bacquet	" 1831
14	Jean	(8) Marg. Dalaire	" 1828
15	Louis	(10) Marcelline Bélanger	
			S.M. 1842
16	Paul	(10) Marie Pigeon	" 1844
	Marguerite	Telesphore Drolet	" 1864

CAMAN.

1	Pierre (1)	M.Chs. Daniau	S.P.S.1802
	Catherine	Pascal Corriveau	S.G.1825
	Charlotte	Jean Dalaire	" 1846
	Pierre		
2	Pierre	(1) Marie Audet	S.G.1827
	(1)Soldat écossais.		

CAMERON.

1	John	M. Anne Fraser, Ecosse	
	Thomas		
2	Thomas	(1) M. Fse. Roy	S.V. 1772
	M. Charlotte	Tho. Fitty Gibbon	" 1792
	M. Françoise	Gab. Dangueuger	" 1799
	"	2° Jos. Royer	S.Chs. 1816
	Jean Baptiste		
	Antoine		
3	Jean Baptiste	(2) Rosalie Roy	S.V. 1788
	Rosalie	Jean Jalbert	S.G. 1809
	"	2° Eustache Roy	S.V. 1811
	Angélique	Michel Couture	S.G. 1815
	Marguerite	Jean Henri	" 1820
	Archange	Alexandre Pouliot	" 1825
	Soulange	Jos. Bigaouette	" 1827
	Thomas		
	Prisque		
	Lazare		
	Jean Baptiste		
	Magloire		
4	Antoine	(2) M. Ls. Bourque	S.V. 1797
5	Antoine	M. Ls. Warren Labadie	
	Antoine		
6	Augustin	Angé Lemolleux	
	M. Françoise	Jos. Nadeau	B. 1832
7	Prisque	(3) Claire Flavie L'heureux	
			S.F. 1819
	Adelaïde	Jean Campagna	S.J. 1858
	Prisque		
8	Magloire	(3) Marg. Rouleau	S.L. 1831
9	Thomas	(3) Marie Canac	S.G. 1821
10	Lazare	(3) Marg. Giguère	S.Tho. 1838
11	Jean Baptiste	(3) Marie Houde	S.G. 1809
	Marie	Frs. Bouton	" 1829
	Le même	Marie Blanchet	" 1825
13	Antoine	(5) Julie Leclaire	B. 1826
	M. Alvina	Pierre Cochon	" 1853
14	Prisque	(7) Cath. Descombes	S.J. 1845

CAMPAGNA.

1	Charles	Mad. Blouin	S.J. 1692
	Marie	Louis Gaulin	S.Frs. 1717
	Geneviève	Noël Paquet	" 1728
	Joseph		
	Simon		
	Jacques		
2	Simon	(1) Hélène Lepage	S.Frs. 1739
	Le même	M. Anne Pepin	
	M. Anne	Pierre Barret	" 1775
3	Joseph	(1) M. Mad. Canac	S.F. 1745
	Angelique	Ls Gagnon	S.Frs. 1778
	Marie	J. B. Jean	" 1790
	M. Rose	Henri Nicole	" 1798
	Augustin		
	Jean		
3ᴬ	Jacques	Eliz. Morin	S.Tho. 1731
	Jacques		
4	Jacques	(3ᴬ) Marie Michon	S.Tho. 1754
	M. Rose	Jos. Carbonneau	" 1781
	Jacques		
	Jean Baptiste		
	François		
5	Augustin	(3) Genev. Landry	S.Frs.1778
	Le même	Susanne Charron	S.G. 1800
	Le même	Louise Henri	" 1811
		V. d'Amond Comeau	
6	Jean	(3) M. Mad. Gagnon	
	M. Catherine	Pre. Crysologue Asselin	
	M. Elizabeth	Pierre Picard	
	M. Louise	Chs. Guérard	
	M. Louise	Jean Pepin	
	M. Josette	Pierre Chatigny	
	Joseph		
	Augustin		
	François		
	Jean		
7	Jacques	(4) Agathe Roy	Bert. 1778
		V. de Jean Bouffert	
	M. Marthe	Frs. Gab. Boulet	
			S.Tho. 1801
8	Jean Baptiste	(4) M. Anne Boutin	Bert.1795
	M. Anne	Chs. Veau	S.G. 1813
	M. Anne	2° Paschal Mercier	" 1813
	Le même	Rosalie Patoüel	" 1799
	Marie	Jos. Quemeneur	" 1830
	Etienne		
9	François	(4) M. Marg. Marseau	
			S.F.S. 1795
	Jérémie		
	Noël		
	Louis		
	Hubert		
10	Jean	(6) M. Angé Boucher	
			S.Joa. 1806
	Catherine	Jacq. Beaucher	S.Frs.1833
	Marie	Magloire Dalaire	" 1846
	Michel		
	Jean		
11	Augustin	(6) M. Marg. Terrien	S.J 1820
12	François	(6) Appolline Blouin	" 1820
	Le même	Louis Marseau	S.Frs. 1825
	Henriette	Léandre Lepage	" 1845
	Sophie	Olivier Gagné	" 1849
	Louise	Ls. Gendreau	" 1855
	Marie	Jos. Marseau	" 1859
	Jean		
	Le même	Domitille Paradis	S.P.1856
13	Joseph	(6) Cath. Guion	S.F. 1818
14	Etienne	(8) Marg. Fournier	S.G. 1826
15	Noël	(9) Appolline Dalaire	
			S.F.S. 1831
16	Jérémie	Marg. Robin	" 1835
	Le même	(9) Marg. Boulet	S.F.S. 1841
17	Louis	(9) Marcelline Beaudoin	
			S.F.S. 1836

CAMPAGNA.

18	Michel	(10) Cath. Pepin	S.F.S.	1846
19	Jean	(10) Flore Lessart	„	1862
20	Jean	(12) Adé Cameron	S.J.	1858
21	Jean Baptiste	Marie Coté		
	Basilisse	Nap. Hudon	S.L.	1866
	Hubert	(9) Sophie Minville	S.P.S.	1834

CAMPBELL.

1	Louis (Ecosse)	Thérèse Bacon	S.P.S.	1763
	M. Thérèse	Jos. Simoneau	„	1784
	M. Angélique	Jos. Talbot	„	1787
	Jacques			
2	Jacques	(1) Thérèse Coté	S.P.S.	1802

CAMPEAU.

1	Etienne	Cath. Paulo Montréal		1663
	François			
2	François	(1) Mad. Brossard	„	1698
	Claude			
3	Claude	(2) Mad. Audebert	S.J.	1732
	Le même	Isabelle Fortier		
	Elizabeth	Frs. Pouliot	S.L.	1763
	Marie	Jos. Gosselin	„	1773
	Louise	Frs. Godbout	„	1778
	Louis Célestin			
	Antoine			
4	Louis Célestin(3)	Marie Crépeau	S.L.	1778
	M. Angélique	Ulric Tremblay	„	1815
	Cécile	Jérémie Audet	„	1841
	Louis			
	François			
	Michel			
5	Antoine	(3) Josette Couture	S.Chs.	1786
	M. Josette	Frs. Rousseau	S.G.	1815
	M. Charlotte	Marie Audet	„	1818
	Antoine			
	François			
	Charles			
6	Louis	(4) Archange Richard	B.	1809
	Julie	Barth. Nadeau	B.	1831
7	François	(4) M. Anne Coulombe		
			S.L.	1811
		Q.		
8	Michel	(4) M. Jos. Coulombe		
			S.L.	1820
	M. Josette	Pierre Audet	„	1863
	François			
	Louis			
	Michel			
9	Antoine	M. Perpétue Bigouette	Q.	
	M. Félicité	Fabien Blais	Q.	
	M. Felicité	2° Jean Frs. Martineau	Q.	
10	François	Angé Boutin	S.G.	1723
11	Charles	(5) Frs. Godbout	S.L.	1818
12	Michel	(8) Angèle Terrien	„	1853
13	Louis	(8) Célina Denis	„	1855
14	François	(8) Célina Denis	„	1858

CANAC—MARQUIS.

1	Marc Antoine (1)	Jeanne Nauric	S.F.	1688
	Reine	Tho. Chrétien	„	1710
	M. Thérèse	J. B. Genchereau	S.F.	1719
	M. Thérèse	2° J. B. L'heureux	„	1730
	Catherine	Frs. Drouin	S.F.	1719
	M. Josette	Pierre Drouin	„	1730
	Marc Antoine			
	Joseph			
	Jean Baptiste			
	François			
2	Marc Antoine(1)	Cath. Laignon	S.F.	1726
	Marie	Jos. Campagna	„	1745
	Le même	Cath. Boisjoly		
	Catherine	Aug. Beaucher	S.F.	1762

CANAC—MARQUIS.

	M. Monique	Aug. Martineau	S.F.	1770
	Charles			
3	Joseph	(1) M. Mad. Drouin	„	1730
	M. Madeleine	Jos. Giguère	„	1763
	M. Geneviève	Michel Giguère	„	1763
	M. Claire	Pierre Pichet	„	1767
	M. Claire	2° Jos. Lessart	„	1775
	M. Marguerite	Amador Turcot	„	1771
	M. Rose	Jos. Meneux	„	1775
	Pierre			
	Françoise			
4	Jean Baptiste	(1) Marg. Drouin	S.F.	1730
	Marguerite	J. B. Bernier	„	1756
	Catherine	Jean Marseau	„	1758
	Marie	Jos. Marie Pepin	„	1767
	M. Rose	Denis Vérieul	S.Frs.	1775
	Jean			
	Etienne			
5	François	(1) Marthe Paquet	S.F.	1744
6	Charles	(2) M. Mad. Fortier	„	1771
	Marie	Etn. Mad Drouin	„	1806
	Basile			
	Antoine			
	Pierre			
7	Pierre	(3) Genev. Leclair	S.P.	1767
	Geneviève	Ant. Gobeil	S.F.	1793
	Marie	Frs. Vaillancour	„	1800
	Pierre			
	François			
	Charles			
8	François	(3) Thérèse Gaulin	S.F.	1773
	Marguerite	Pierre Deblois	„	1812
	François			
	Joseph			
9	Jean	(4) Judith Pepin,	S.Anne	1763
	Judith	Jos. Giguère	S.F.	1797
	Jean			
	François			
10	Etienne	(4) Thérèse Colin	S.Frs.	1764
	Marie	Chs. Baillargeon	S.H.	1791
	Thérèse	Pierre Delenteigne	„	1791
	Thérèse	2° Frs. Naud	„	1799
	Marguerite	J. B. Bernier	„	1791
	Madeleine	Etn. Delâge	„	1800
	Françoise	Aug. Gautron	„	1800
	Josette	Nic. Baillargeon	„	1809
	Le même	Anne Lemieux	Bert.	1797
11	Basile	(6) Vict. Beaucher	S.F.	1807
	Victoire	Jos. Drouin	„	1826
	François Régis			
	Basile			
	Louis			
	François			
12	Pierre	(6) M. Anne Gaulin	S.F.	1816
13	Antoine	(6) Marie Pépin	„	1833
	Le même	Marie Guérard	„	1838
14	Pierre	(7) Frs. Boissonneau	S.P.	1797
	Françoise	J. B. Létourneau	S.F.	1845
	Apolline	Frs. Letourneau	„	1829
	M. Justine	Marc Turcot	„	1831
	Brigitte	Frs. Leblond	„	1833
	François Narcisse			
	Joachim			
15	François	(7) Marie Gosselin	S.G.	1803
	Marie	Tho. Cameron	„	1821
	Julienne	Joachim Plante	„	1828
	François			
16	Charles	(7) Charlotte Réaume	S.R.	1798
	Joseph			
	Etienne			
17	François	(8) M. Thècle Deblois		
			S.Frs.	1808
	Constance	Pierre Prémont	S.F.	1835
	Constance	2° Benj. Turcot	„	1843
	M. Ludivine	Edouard Poulin	„	1836
	M. Olive	Olivier Drouin	„	1844

CANAC—MARQUIS.

	François				
18	Joseph	(8)	Reine Paradis	S.P.	1811
19	Jean	(9)	Marie Lepage	S.F.	1791
	Marguerite		Aug. Côté	,,	1814
	M. Thècle		Pierre Demeule	,,	1827
	Jean				
	François				
	Pierre				
20	François	(9)	M. Thècle Lepage		
				S.Frs.	1802
	Julienne		Stanislas Ubald Duprat		
				S.F.	1838
	François				
21	Basile	(11)	Constance Asselin	,,	1841
	Pierre				
22	FrançoisRégis	(11)	M. Hombeline Lamothe		
				S.F.	1856
23	Louis	(11)	Martin Drouin	,,	1853
24	François	(11)	Sophie Bilodeau		
				S.Marie	1837
	M. Zoé		Ferd. Gosselin	S.F.	1863
	Anastasie		Ferd. Royer	,,	1868
	Démérise		Jos. Deblois	,,	1868
25	Joachim	(14)	Marg. Létourneau	,,	1825
26	François	(14)	HombelineGagnon	,,	1844
	Narcisse				
27	François	(15)	Archange Daniau		
				S.Chs.	1833
28	Joseph		M. Marg. Lizotte		
				Kamouraska	
	Edouard				
29	Joseph	(16)	Marg. Pouliot	S.G.	1820
	Joseph				
30	Etienne	(16)	Eliz. Fortier	,,	1828
31	François	(17)	Sophie Poulin	S.F.	1832
	Philomène		Jos. Asselin	,,	1860
	M. Eléonore		Frs.PhiliasGiguère	,,	1862
	François Xavier				
32	Jean	(19)	Thérèse Deblois	S.Frs.	1824
	Caroline		Gilbert Drouin	S.F.	1847
	M. Marcelline		Ferd. Asselin	,,	1857
	M. Thérèse		Olivier Drouin	,,	1858
	Marguerite		Pierre Racine	,,	1859
	François				
33	François	(19)	Hélène Foucher	S.F.	1824
34	Pierre	(19)	Basilisse Létourneau		
				S.F.	1831
	Basilisse		Paul Deblois	,,	1857
	Michel				
35	François	(20)	M. Jos. Lasalle	S.Frs.	1841
36	Pierre	(21)	Philomène Drouin		
				S.F.	1868
37	Edouard	(28)	M. Jos. Gosselin	S.V.	1827
38	Joseph	(29)	M. Zoé Bissonneau		
				S.F.S.	1842
39	François Xavier	(31)	Justine Asselin	S.F.	1854
40	François	(32)	Marg. Guérard	S.Frs.	1862
41	Michel	(34)	Philomème Paradis		
				S.F.	1859

CANTIN.

1	Nicolas		Mad. Roulois	Q.	1660
	Denis				
	Charles				
	Louis				
2	Denis	(1)	Ursule Gaudin	A. G.	1689
3	Charles	(1)	M. Mad. Vézina		
				A. G.	1703
4	Louis	(1)	Marie Mathieu	A. G.	1701
	M. Ursule		Pierre Paradis	S.P.	1744
	Louis				
	Charles				
	Ambroise				
5	Louis	(4)	Marg. Leclaire	S.P.	1739

CANTIN.

6	Charles	(4)	Ursule Leclaire	S.P.	1743
	Christine		Jean Vézina	A.G.	1778
	Ursule		Frs. Huot	A.G,	1782
7	Ambroise	(4)	M. Dorothée Leclaire		
				S.P.	1748
	M. Agathe		Pierre Langlois	S.P.	1781
	Marie		Jean Poulet	S.P.	1785
	Ambroise				
8	Michel (1)		Mad. Gosselin	S.H.	1785
	Michel				
9	Ambroise	(7)	M. Vict. Chabot	S.P.	1775
	Christine		Aug. Nolin	S.P.	1810
	Cécile		Jos. Marcoux	S.P.	1815
	Adrien				
	Joseph				
	Ambroise				
10	Joseph	(9)	Marg. Tessier	S.P.	1803
	Marguerite		Aug. Plante	S.P.	1818
	Clément				
	Le même		M. Angé Martel	S.P.	1837
A	Ambroise	(9)	Louise Simoneau	S.H.	1805
11	Adrien	(9)	Cécile Noel	S.P.	1807
	Justine		Ignace Paradis	S.P.	1838
	Victoire		Prosper Tailleur	S.P.	1841
	M. Esther		Magl. Ferland	S.P.	1845
	Firmine		Jean Bruno Paquet		
				S.P.	1848
	Vénéranda		Jean Bruno Goulet		
				S.P.	1848
	Cécile		Laurent Paquet	S.P.	1851
	Adrien				
	Joseph				
	Augustin				
12	Michel	(8)	Euphrosine Chabot	B.	1809
13	Clément	(10)	Rosalie Leclaire, Gentilly		
				S.P.	1831
14	Adrien	(11)	Marcelline Ferland		
				S,P	1841
15	Augustin	(11)	Domitille Baudouin		
				S.P.	1841
16	Joseph	(11)	M. Mad. Goulet	S.P.	1854

(1) Fils de Ls. et de Suz. Carrier.

CARBONNEAU—PROVENÇAL.

1	Hespery		Marg. Landry	S.F.	1672
	Marie		Pierre Buteau	S.Frs.	1678
	Thérèse		Pierre Menanteau		
				S.Frs.	1701
	Thérèse		2° Frs. Quenneville		
	Marguerite		J. B. Nadeau	Bert.	1721
	Marguerite		2° Jean Boucher	Bert.	1726
	Jean				
	Barthélemi				
	Jacques				
2	Jacques	(1)	Génév. Martin		
	Jacques				
	Jean Baptiste				
3	Jean	(1)	Gertrude Lepage		
				S.Frs.	1722
4	Barthélemi	(1)	Génev. Nadeau	S.V.	1726
5	Jacques	(2)	Jeanne Guimon		
				S. Anne	1725
	Augustin Michel				
	Jacques				
	André				
6	Jean Baptiste		Isabelle Lefebvre		
				Bert.	1729
	Marguerite		Jos Lessart	,,	1758
	M. Josette		Jos Balan	,,	1765
	Isabelle		Frs Letellier	,,	1771
	Joseph Marie				
	Pierre				
7	Jacques	(5)	M. Anne Chartier		
				Bert.	1751

CARBONNEAU—PROVENÇAL.

M. Anne	Michel Dominique Bilodeau	Bert. 1771
Reine Ursule	Jacque Prisque Corriveau	Bert. 1787
M. Louise	Aug. Bilodeau	S.V. 1785
Isidore		
Jacques		
André		
Joseph		
8 August.Michel (5)	Fse Ursule Lemieux	Bert. 1761
M. Anne	Aug. Bilodeau	" 1789
Le même	Mad. Gaulin	" 1778
M. Victoire	J. B. Ménard	" 1798
Joseph		
9 André (5)	Genev. Bilodeau	" 1762
M. Angélique	Jos Brisson	" 1814
Géneviève	Michel Guay	S.H. 1791
André		
Jacques		
10 Pierre (6)	M. Mad.Bernier	Islet 1757
Josette	Simon Basquet	S.G. 1804
Félicité	Ant. Godbout	" 1812
M. Géneviève	Clément Couillard	S.V. 1807
Joseph Marie		
Dieudonné		
Pierre		
Charles		
11 Joseph (7)	M. Rose Campagna	S.Tho. 1781
Rose	André Damiau	Bert. 1806
M. Josette	Louis Wabur	" 1808
Louise	Aug. Brousseau	" 1810
M. Anne	Aug. Mercier	Bert. 1812
M. Louise	Jacq. Lemieux	Bert. 1817
Archange	Jacq. Guilmet	Bert. 1823
Victoire	Laurent Lemelin	S.G. 1815
Jean Baptiste		
Le même	{ Angé Poiré S.G. 1813 { V. de P. Lacroix	
Le même	M. Anne Lemieux	Bert. 1815
12 Joseph Marie (6)	Thérèse Blais	Bert. 1769
Marie Josette	J. B. Mercier	Bert. 1801
M. Christine	Jean Bourgot	Bert. 1803
M. Marthe	Pierre Guilmet	Bert. 1805
Isabelle	Nicolas Pouliot	Bert. 1818
Catherine	Jean Pouliot	S.G. 1815
Joseph Marie		
Jean Baptiste		
Simon		
François		
Pierre		
13 Jacques (7)	M. Jos. Bilodeau	Bert.1779
M. Louise	J. B. Carbonneau	Bert.1805
M. Louise	2° Pre. Noel Quémeneur	Bert. 1833
M. Marguerite	Simon Carbonneau	Bert. 1808
M. Josette	Ls. Gautier	Bert. 1814
M. Marthe	Pierre Pigeon	S.V. 1821
Grégoire		
Jean Baptiste		
André		
Augustin		
14 Isidore (7)	M. Ls. Daniau	Bert. 1802
Luce	J. B. Patry	S.G. 1822
Adélaïde	J. B. Guay	S.G. 1825
Isidore		
15 André (7)	M.Marthe Lavoie	Bert.1804
André		
16 Joseph (8)	M. Vict. Rémillard	S.V. 1804
Olivier		
17 Jean Marie (10)	M. Ls. Quéret	S.V. 1795

CARBONNEAU—PROVENÇAL.

18 Dieudonné (10)	Mag. Monmeny	S.M. 1797
19 Pierre (10)	M. Eliz. Tangué	Bert.1792
Elizabeth	Chs. Cochon	S.G. 1802
M. Louise	Jos. Bilodeau	Bert. 1819
Le même	Angé Guénet	S.Chs. 1806
Madeleine	Edouard Dessaint	S.G.1830
20 Charles (10)	Marie Chamberland	S.G. 1796
M. Anne	Guill. Isabel	S.G. 1822
Charles		
Pierre		
Dieudonné		
Le même	Marie Nadeau	S.G. 1830
21 JeanBaptiste(11)	Angèle Carbonneau	Bert.1826
M. Adèle	Damase Cochon	S.V. 1862
Edouard		
22 Joseph Marie(12)	M. Barbe Roy	S.V. 1790
Le même	Marg.Beaucher	S.F.S.1793
Marie	Michel Picard	S.F.S. 1820
M. Marguerite	Jos. Lessard	Bert. 1824
Angèle	J.B. Carbonneau	Bert.1826
Joseph		
Augustin		
Le même	M. Thérèse Marcoux	Bert. 1808
M. Rose	Fabien Guilmet	Bert. 1830
Dieudonné		
23 Pierre (12)	Françoise Blais	S.F.S.1812
24 François (12)	M. Anne Pouliot	S.G.1821
25 JeanBaptiste(12)	M. Ls. Carbonneau	Bert. 1805
M. Louise	Ls. Fortier	Bert. 1830
Apolline	F. X. Beaucher	Bert. 1843
Catherine	Jos. Fournier	S.G. 1839
26 Simon (12)	M. Marg. Carbonneau	Bert. 1808
Soulange	Zacharie Nadeau	Bert.1840
Michel		
Jacques		
27 Jacques (9)	Marg. Boulet	S.H. 1807
Le même	M. Anne Arguin	S.H.1815
Le même	Eliz. Plante	S.J. 1820
28 André (9)	Genev. Guay	S.H. 1791
M. Anne	Paschal Bisson	S.G. 1823
André		
29 JeanBaptiste(13)	M. Reine Bilodeau	S.V. 1820
Le même	Ursule Chrétien	Bert. 1826
30 Grégoire (13)	Marie Bilodeau	Bert. 1822
31 Augustin (13)	Marie Blais	Bert. 1823
32 André (13)	Rosalie Chrétien	Bert. 1828
33 Isidore (14)	Françoise Lemelin	S.M. 1827
34 André (16)	Thècle Mercier	Bert. 1830
35 Olivier (16)	Soulange Dion	Bert. 1833
36 Charles (20)	Marg. Aubin	S.G. 1816
37 Pierre (20)	Agnès Thibaut	S.G. 1824
38 Dieudonné (20)	Marg. Pouliot	S.G. 1827
39 Augustin (22)	Constance Keroack	S.P.S. 1827
Joseph		
Le même	Reine Lessard	Bert. 1834
41 Jacques	Angèle Proulx	
Angèle	Samuel Minard	Bert. 1841
42 Edouard (21)	Marg. Audet	S.M. 1848
43 Joseph (22)	Genev. Lessard	Bert. 1824
Le même	Eliz. Blais	Bert. 1835
Le même	Thérèse Bilodeau	Bert. 1843
44 Dieudonné (22)	M. Delphine Guilmet	Bert. 1837
45 Michel (26)	M. Zeloïde Bolduc	S.P. 1837
46 Jacques (26)	M. Marthe Lessart	Bert. 1841

CARBONNEAU--PROVENÇAL.

47	André	(28)	Louis Nadeau S. Chs.	1815
48	Joseph	(39)	Constance Paquet S. Chs.	1849
49	Dieudonné		Sophie Coté	
	Le même		M. Anne Vien B.	1854

CARON.

1	Robert		Marie Crevet Q.	1637
	Robert			
	Pierre			
2	Michel		Jeanne Allard	
	Vital			
3	Robert	(1)	Marg. Cloutier S. Anne	1674
	Ignace			
	Augustin			
	Claude			
4	Pierre	(1)	Marie Bernier 2.	1768
	François			
5	Joseph		Eliz. Bernier	
	Louis			
6	Vital	(2)	Marg. Gagnon S.R.	1686
	Vital			
7	Ignace	(3)	Marie Gaulin S.F.	1707
	Marthe		Jos. Fortier Islet	1749
	Jean Baptiste			
8	Augustin	(3)	M. Mad. Gaulin S.F.	1712
	Ignace			
	Augustin			
9	Claude	(3)	M. Marthe Gaulin S.F.	1716
10	François	(4)	Genev. Domingo Cap. S. Ign.	1710
	François			
11	Louis		Marie Lemieux Cap. S. Ign.	1727
	Charles			
12	Claude		Mad. Pepin	
	Ignace			
A	Jean		Agnés Paulin	
	Jean			
13	Vital	(6)	Charlotte Joliette S.L.	1735
14	Joseph		Fse. Sausier	
	Joseph			
15	Jean Baptiste	(7)	Mad. Boissel B.	1745
16	Augustin	(8)	Thérèse Guion S.T.	1738
17	Ignace	(8)	M. Eliz. Roy-Audy S. Anne	1750
	Ignace			
18	François	(10)	Eliz. Cloutier Islet	1740
	Le même		M. Anne Coriveau S.V.	1753
19	Bonaventure		M. Claire Langelier Islet	1757
	Joseph			
20	Charles	(11)	M. Eliz. Picard Bert.	1762
21	Ignace	(17)	M. Eliz. Emond S.Frs.	1776
22	Pierre		M. Mad. Fortin Islet	1783
	Jean			
23	Joseph	(19)	Vict. Kérvack Cap. S. Ign.	1785
	Bonaventure			
24	Ignace	(12)	Josette Giguière S. Anne	1754
	Etienne			
25	Jean		Josette Paré S. Anne	1774
	Marie		Jacq. Roy S.G.	1795
26	Jean Baptiste		Théotiste Gauvin	
	Jean Baptiste			
27	Jean	(22)	Marg. Gosselin S.Chs.	1810
28	Bonaventure	(23)	M. Rosalie Martineau	1828
29	Etienne	(24)	Marie Taillon S.Anne	1809
	Pre. Ls. Gonzague			
	François Xavier			
30	François		Marg. Lemieux	

CARON.

	Edouard			
31	Jean Baptiste	(26)	M. Onésime Gagné S.P.S.	1838
32	Grégoire		Esther Vaillancour S. Bernard	
	Le même		M. Perpétue Couture S. Chs.	1845
33	Joseph	(14)	Pélagie Simard S.Joa.	1773
	Le même		Mad. Martineau S.Frs.	1804
34	François Xavier	(29)	Eliz. Pichet S.P.	1847
35	Pre. Ls. Gonzague	(29)	Marie Tailleur S.P.	1848
36	Edouard	(30)	Cédulie Couillard B.	1852

CARRÉ.

1	Pierre		Anne Thiery Acadie
	Josette		Pierre Carreau

CARREAU.

1	Joseph		Barbe Letarte A.G.	1696
	Geneviève		Louis Giroux ,,	1719
	Pierre			
	Joseph			
	Le même		Marie Pouliot S.L.	1721
2	Pierre	(1)	Jeanne Pouliot S.L.	1723
	Jeanne		Pierre Charier ,,	1746
	Pierre			
3	Joseph	(1)	Mad. Pouliot ,,	1725
4	Pierre	(2)	M. Josette Carré ,,	1763
	Marie		Louis Coulombe ,,	1785
	Le même		M.Louis Demeule S J.	1771

CARRIER.

1	Jean		Barbe Hallé Q	1670
	Charles			
2	Charles	(1)	Marie Gesseron Lévis	1699
	Charles			
3	Charles	(2)	Véronique Quay Lévis	1727
	Véronique		J. B. Paradis ,,	1755
	Joseph			
	Charles			
4	Jean Baptiste		Susanne Duquet	
	Jean Baptiste			
5	Charles	(3)	M. Anne Pichet S.P.	1752
	Geneviève	(3)	Michel Rousseau S.H.	1791
	M. Louise		Jos. Bourassa ,,	1794
	Ignace			
	Joseph			
	Louis			
	Antoine			
6	Joseph	(3)	Véronique Drapeau Levis	1766
	Marguerite		J. B. Ignace Roy B.	1792
	Geneviève		Jean Rouleau ,,	1795
	Françoise		Jos. Jolivet ,,	1807
	François			
	Le même		Thècle Coté ,,	1797
	Le même		M. Angé Lefebvre ,,	1810
	Germain			
7	Jean Baptiste		Cath. Bégin	
	Jean Ignace			
8	Pierre		Angé Amiot	
	Le même		Ursule Agnès Denis S.M.	1765
9	Jean Baptiste		M. Anne Poiré	
	Jean Baptiste			
10	Jean Baptiste	(4)	M. Angé Lacasse SM	1778
	Joseph			
11	Louis	(5)	M. Angé Boissel B.	1786
12	Ignace	(5)	Marg. Patry S.M.	1798
13	Joseph	(5)	M. Jos. Paris S.V.	1799

CARRIER.

14	Antoine	(5) M. Thérèse Fontaine	S.H. 1805
15	Ignace	Genev. Huart	
	François		
	Le même	Marie Belleau	S.H. 1789
16	François	(6) Genev. Paquet	B. 1793
17	Germain	(6) Hermine Pelchet	S.Chs. 1836
18	Etienne	Charlotte Begin	
	Jean Baptiste		
19	Jean Ignace	(7) Cécile Filteau	B. 1795
	Jean Baptiste		
20	Jean Baptiste	(9) Genev. Gendron	S.H. 1805
	Le même	M. Angé Gautron	B. 1839
21	Joseph	(10) M. Archange Nadeau	S.H. 1808
22	François	(15) Marg. Carrier	Levis 1811
	François		
23	JeanBaptiste(18)	M. Frs. Guénet	" 1810
	Jean Baptiste		
		Christine McPhee	
24	Joseph		Q
	Le même	Henriette Moreau	B. 1831
A	Joseph	Thérèse Crête	
	Jean		
	Joseph		
25	Jean Baptiste	Genev. Lemieux	Lévis 1815
	François		
26	Frederic	Marg. Brulot	
	Michel		
27	Jean	A. Véronique Demers	S. Marie 1821
	Jean		
		A. M. Chs. Labrecque	S. Marie 1819
28	Joseph	(24)	
	Georges		
29	JeanBaptiste(19)	Angèle Nadeau	B. 1823
30	François	(22) Angèle Fortin	S.Chs. 1845
31	JeanBaptiste(23)	Marie Blais	" 1843
32	François	(25) M. Domitille Turgeon	B. 1850
33	Michel	(26) M. Ls. Larrivé	" 1847
34	Jean	(27) M. Sara Turgeon	" 1849
35	Georges	(28) Esther Bilodeau	" 1850

CARRIÈRE—LEBRUN

1	Noël	Anne Brochu	S.J. 1696
	M. Anne	Michel Gautron	S.V. 1716
	Angélique	Joseph Gautron	" 1725
	Marguerite	Etn. Veau	" 1727
	Elizabeth	Joseph Mercier	" 1729
	M. Thérèse	Pierre Dodier	" 1730
	Joseph		
	Etienne		
	Noël		
2	Joseph	(1) M. Genev. Alaire	S.V. 1737
	Geneviève	Guill. Guion	S.M. 1765
	Pierre		
	Jean		
3	Etienne	(1) Agathe Alaire	S.V. 1739
	Le même	Marg. Boldue	S. Joa. 1742
	Marguerite	Louis Fontaine	S.P.S.1773
	Louis		
	Jean Baptiste		
	Joseph		
4	Noël	M. Ursule Roy	S.V. 1743
	Etienne		
	Joseph		
5	François	Mad. Dupuis	S. Marie
	Le même	Gertrude Deblois	S.F. 1765
6	Jean Baptiste	M. Mad. Pellerin	
	Armand		

CARRIÈRE—LEBRUN.

7	Pierre	(2) Reine Roy	S.V. 1772
	Angélique	Pierre Chartier	S.G. 1804
	Pierre		
8	Jean	(2) Brigitte Couture	S.Chs. 1771
	Charlotte	Joseph Audet	S.G. 1789
	Brigitte	J. B. Audet	" 1793
	Josette	Pierre Roberge	" 1793
	Céleste	Louis Roberge	" 1796
	Monique	Joseph Goulet	" 1804
	Jean		
9	Louis	(3) M. Anne Mercier	S.M. 1771
	Françoise	Michel Lacroix	" 1824
	Marie	Jacques Nicole	" 1825
	M. Anne	Michel Gagné	S.H. 1809
	Paschal		
	Jean		
	Etienne		
10	Jean Baptiste	(3) Catherine Sampson,	Lévis 1781
a	Joseph	(3) Dorothée Lemelin	S.P.S. 1765
11	Joseph	(4) M. Chs. Denis	S.Chs. 1769
	Marie	Nicolas Morriset	S.Chs. 1794
	Angélique	Jos. Fournier	" 1801
	Reine	Thomas Roy	" 1807
	M. Geneviève	Pierre Roy	" 1812
	Pierre		
	Jean Baptiste		
12	Etienne	(4) M. Joseph Aubé	S.V. 1774
	Le même	M. Reine Paré	S.F.S. 1778
13	Armand	(6) Marg. Gourdeau	S.P. 1770
14	Pierre	(7) Marg. Lasante	S.G. 1800
	Marguerite	Jean Thibaut	" 1920
	Archange	André Lacroix	" 1820
15	Jean	(8) Marg. Goulet	S.G. 1800
	Brigitte	Pierre Pouliot	S.G. 1821
	Archange	Isidore Létourneau	S.G. 1822
	Margueritte	Michel Talbot	" 1826
	Monique	Etienne Rémillard	" 1826
	Etienne		
	Jean Baptiste		
a	Etienne	(9) M. Bonne Blais	S.H. 1809
16	Paschal	(9) Marg. Lessart	S. M. 1812
17	Jean	(9) M. Marg. Denis	S.M. 1815
	Luce	Marc Asselin	" 1840
	Romain		
	Joseph		
	Charles		
	Louis		
	Le même	Angé Chabot	S.M. 1827
	Soulange	Aug. Mercier	" 1863
18	Pierre	(11) Marg. Tangué	S.Chs. 1803
	Marguerite	J. B. Turgeon	" 1827
	Michel		
19	Jean Baptiste(11)	M. Cécile Boutin	S.V.1807
	Marcelline	Louis Gautron	S.Chs. 1836
	Marie Louise	Anselme Prosper Tangué	S. Chs. 1841
	M. Charlotte	Charles Boutin	" 1851
20	Etienne	Félicité Samson	
	Angèle	Thomas Roy	S. Chs. 1833
	Hermine	Jos. Alexis Boulet	S. Chs. 1836
	Laurent	Soulange Biloyer	S.G. 1826
21	Charles	M. Genev. Dessaint	
	Joseph		
22	Jean Baptiste(15)	Genev. Fauchon	S.G. 1823
23	Etienne	(15) Thérèse Nadeau	S.G. 1830
24	Joseph	(17) Marie Couture	S. Chs. 1841
25	Charles	(17) Natalie Sénécal	S.Chs. 1844
26	Romain	(17) Sophie Chabot	S.M. 1848

CARRIÈRE—LEBRUN.

27 Louis	(17)	Constance Couture S. Chs. 1855
28 Michel	(18)	Angé Pouliot S.Chs. 1829
Narcisse		
Le même		M.Anne Pigeon S.M. 1845
29 Laurent	(20)	Soulange Bélanger S.G. 1826
Soulange		Laurent Justinien Gagnon S. Chs. 1852
M. Elise		Pierre Dalaire S. Chs. 1856
Laurent Eugène		
Octave		
30 Joseph	(31)	Angèle Lemelin S.V. 1827
31 Narcisse	(28)	AngèleiLacroix S.Chs. 1862
32 L. Eugène	(29)	Marie Bisson S. Chs. 1848
Le même		M. Angèle Floride, Asselin S.M. 1856
33 Octave	(29)	AngèleMarcouxS.Chs.1852 S. Vital
34 Amable		Lucie Dubuc
Lucie		François Guay S.Chs.1859
Virginie		Laurent Gosselin „ 1862

CARSONNE.

Henri		Eliz. Jean
Robert		
Le même	(1)	Genev. Gobeil S.P. 1821 Dorothée Martineau S.F. 1848

CARUEL.

1 Charles		Marie Dubuc
Marie		Jean Bouffart S.Q. 1709
		2° Pierre Gosselin „ 1717
Marie Louise		J. B. Ducas „ 1715

CATELLIER.

1 Pancrace		M.Mad.Bélanger S.V.1749
Prisque		
Jacques		
Pierre		
Joseph		
2 Prisque	(1)	M.Judith MivilleS.V.1780
3 Jacques	(1)	Marie Goupy „ 1788
M. Josette		Pierre Baudouin S.M. 1813
Angèle		Ant. Létourneau „ 1813
Paul		
Jacques		
Pierre		
4 Pierre		M.Mad VrigneauS.V.1788
Le même		Basilisse Bernard „ 1794
Joseph		
Pierre		
5 Joseph	(1)	M. Anne Roy „ 1796
M. Anne		Pierre Bissonnet „ 1819
Prisque		
Louis		
Joseph		
Pierre		
6 Jacques	(3)	Louise Baudouin S.F.S. 1808
Marie		Laurent Noël S.M. 1839
M. Angèle		Joseph Bissonnet „ 1840
Constance		André Côté „ 1844
Julie		Jean Gourgue „ 1845
Lucie		J. B.Roy „ 1848
Michel		
Paulin		
7 Pierre	(3)	M. Jos. Baudouin S.F.S. 1811
Angélique		Louis Gagnon S.M. 1840
Marguerite		Magl.Baillargeon „ 1842
Madeleine		Paul Goupy S.Chs. 1847

CATELLIER.

Pierre		
Antoine		
Le même		M. Ls. Quemeneur S.F.S. 1825
Caroline		David Goupy S.M. 1846
8 Paul	(3)	M. Vict. Bolduc S.V. 1828
9 Joseph	(4)	CharlotteGodboutS.L.1823
10 Pierre	(4)	Marie Bélanger S.G. 1826
11 Prisque	(5)	Marg. Masseau S.V. 1824
Le même		M. Cath. Roy B. 1846
		V. d'Ant. Roy
Adolphe		
12 Joseph	(5)	MarieQuemeneur S.V.1824
Catherine		Ant. Hubert Roy „ 1857
Caroline		Frédéric Roy „ 1860
M. Philomène		Jos. Leger Corriveau S.V. 1863
Théodore		
Napoléon		
13 Louis	(5)	M. Angèle Bélanger S V. 1825
Marie Sara		Jean François Lamare S.V. 1844
Rose		Thomas Brochu „ 1853
14 Pierre	(5)	Marg. Lemieux „ 1835
Pierre		
15 Paulin	(6)	Marg. Chamberlan S.M. 1835
Philomène		Florent Gagnon „ 1858
Le même		Constance Pouliot „ 1843
16 Michel	(6)	„ Chamberlan S.M. 1839
17 Pierre	(7)	Clotilde Tangué „ 1838
18 Antoine	(7)	Adelaïde Dion „ 1846
19 Adolphe	(11)	Luce Roy S V. 1868
20 Napoléon	(12)	M. Délima Mercier S.V. 1861
21 Théodore	(12)	M. Malvina Corriveau S.V. 1862
22 Pierre	(14)	M. Poméla Corriveau S.V. 1866

CASAULT.

1 Jean		Marie Dubosque
Jean		
Jean	(1)	M. Mad. Voyer S.V. 1721
Jean		
3 Jean Baptiste		Rosalie Michon S.Tho.1767
Rose Angèle		J. B. Talbot „ 1789
M. Geneviève		Charles Faucher „ 1795
Jean Baptiste		
François		
4 Pierre		Marie Dion Q.
Clément		
5 Jean	(2)	Fse Ruel S.L. 1765
Le même		Genev. Chabot „ 1793
6 Jean Baptiste	(3)	Mad. Mathieu S.V 1804
		Susanne Bernier S. Tho. 1803
A François	(3)	M. Angé Morin S.P.S. 1806
7 Clément	(4)	Pre Féréol Gagné S.F.S. 1836
Olive		Marie Blais S.P.S. 1807 ou 1808
Louis		

CHABOT.

1 Mathurin		Marie Mésange Q. 1661
Marie		Charles Pouliot S. L. 1689
M. Louise		Antoine Pouliot „ 1696
M. Louise		Nicolas Audet „ 1697
Marguerite		André Pouliot „ 1699
Antoine		Curé de Ste. Anne

CHABOT.

CHABOT.

Michel
Joseph
Jean
François
2 Michel   (1) Thérése Legardeur
M. Thérése   Frs. Larchevéque   1706
Michel
Le même   Angé Plante   C.R. 1690
François
Joseph
3 Joseph   Francoise Pouliot
Joseph
Pierre
4 Jean   Eléonore Enaut S.P. 1692
M. Louise   Charles Delengré S.L.1727
Anne   Julien Gendreau S.L. 1728
Jeanne   Ant. Frs. Dorloge ,, 1741
Antoine
Jean
Jean Baptiste
5 François   (1) Marg. Noël   S. L. 1698
    Mad. Charron Lorette
6 Michel   (2)   1703
7 François   (2) Ursule Ferlant S. P. 1730
M. Josette   Augustin Coté   ,, 1764
Augustin
8 Joseph   (2) Ursule Crépeau S. P. 1734
M. Reine   Chs. Labrecque   ,, 1769
M. Véronique   Frs. Julien   ,, 1769
M. Victoire   Amb. Cartin   ,, 1775
M. Josette   Pierré Nolin   ,, 1780
Joseph
9 Joseph   (3) Mad. Coulombe S. L. 1733
Isabelle   Ant. Baillargeon ,, 1763
Louis
10 Pierre   (3) Cécile Jeanne   S. L. 1741
11 Jean   (4) Marie Dufresne S. L. 1718
Marie   François Pouliot ,, 1735
Pierre
Le même   Génév. Bouffart S. L. 1737
M Geneviève   Ant. Couture   ,, 1767
Marie Louise   Francois Pouliot S.L. 1775
M. Françoise   Charles Pouliot   ,, 1777
Joseph
12 Antoine   (4) Mad. Leclaire S. L. 1741
Madeleine   Eustache Roy   ,, 1763
Marie Anne   Basile Dion   ,, 1767
Cécile   Gabriel Paradis ,, 1781
Geneviève   Jean Cazeau   ,, 1793
Antoine
François
Pierre
13 Jean Baptiste (4) Mad. Frontigny S.L. 1746
Madeleine   Charles Giguére S.Chs 1769
M. Geneviève   Jos. Paquet   S. M. 1773
Francois
Jean Baptiste
Gabriel
    Dorothé Cochon
14 Michel   S. Joa. 1730
Jean Baptiste
    M. Anne Gendron
15 Michel   S. F. S. 1740
    Mathurin Gagnon
Marguerite   S. F. S. 1768
16 Augustin   (7) M. Marg. Noel S. P. 1764
François
17 Joseph   (8) Cath. Paquet   S. P. 1764
18 Louis   (9) Marie Baillargeon S.L.1763
19 Pierre   (11) Thérése Leclaire S.L. 1752
Thérése   Victor Hébert S.Chs. 1773
Theotiste   Jacques Boutin ,, 1778
Natalie   Pierré Dalaire   ,, 1778
Marguerite   Jacques Buteau   ,, 1783
Agathe   Laurent Poiré   ,, 1790

Jean
Pierre
Basile
Louis
    M. Thérése Gosselin
20 Joseph   (11)   S. L. 1773
Marie   Louis Rouleau   ,, 1798
M. Catherine   Ant. Gosselin   ,, 1801
Véronique   Francois Gosselin ,, 1804
Joseph
Le même   M. Angé Paquet S.J. 1782
21 Antoine   (12) M. Josette Ruel S.P. 1770
22 Pierre   M. Ursule Tangué SV 1770
Ursule   Joseph Leclairé ,, 1795
M. Angélique   Ant. Bégin   ,, 1804
M. Victoire   Pierre Bégin   ,, 1804
M. Barbe   André Blais   ,, 1811
Le même   M. Ls. Dorval   ,, 1797
Félicité   Amable Baudet   ,, 1818
Anastasie   Michel Roy   ,, 1821
Lucie   Hubert Roy   ,, 1846
Pierre
André
23 François   (12) M. Fse Pepin S.J. 1784
Angélique   Jean Ruel   S.L. 1810
Cécile   Etn. Pelchat S. Chs. 1812
Françoise   Laurent Genest   ,, 1814
Catherine   Etn. Aubé   ,, 1827
Justine   Bénoni Marcoux   ,, 1831
Pierre
François
Alexis
Ambroise
Gabriel
Julien
Laurent
24 Jean-Baptiste   M. Luce Fortin
Marie   Pierre Labrecque
    S. Chs. 1805
Marguerite   Paul Audet   ,, 1812
Euphrosine   Michel Cantin   B. 1809
Emélie   Frs Nadeau   ,, 1818
Jean-Baptiste
25 JeanBaptiste(13) Genev. Lafontaine
    Lévis 1766
Geneviève   Etn. Nadeau S. Chs. 1791
Geneviève   Jos. Fontaine S.H.1800
Marie   Michel Rousseau
    S. Chs. 1793
Jean-Baptiste
Le même   Marie Lacasse S.Chs. 1782
Louis
François
Joseph
26 Gabriel   (13) Marie Lucas S. Chs. 1768
27 François   (13) M. Brigitte Fortier
    S.M. 1783
François
28 Jean-Baptiste
    (14) M. Thérése Dupont
    S.F.S. 1762
Michel
29 François   (16) M. Mad. Turcot S.P. 1803
M, Madeleine   Louis Pichet   ,, 1823
François
30 Jean   (19) M. Marg. Lacasse
    S. Chs. 1781
M. Josette   Amb. Vien   S. Chs. 1815
Jean-Baptiste
Louis
Joseph
Pierre
Landry
Antoine
Le même   M.Anne Cochon
    S. Chs. 1789

CHABOT.

Elizabeth	Jacques Boutin	"	1812
Marie Anne	Charles Charrier	"	1863
Angélique	Jean Lebrun	S.M.	1827
30 Pierre	(19) Marg. Lamothe		
		S. Chs.	1785
M. Charlotte	Joseph Fournier	"	1811
Marguerite	François Nolin	"	1811
Marie	Joseph Genest	"	1813
Luce	F. X. Genest	"	1823
Jean			
François			
32 Basile	M. Jos. Provost		
		S. Chs.	1787
M. Josette	J. B. Leclaire	S. Chs.	1811
Marguerite	Etn. Couture	"	1814
Marie	J. B. Fournier	"	1816
Angélique	Jos. Lacasse	"	1817
Geneviève	Louis Couture		
		S.Chs.	1822
Pierre			
Louis			
Charles			
33 Louis	(19) Marg. Naud	S. Chs.	1790
34 Joseph	(20) Victoire Audet	S.L.	1804
François	David Bouffart	"	1852
Joseph			
Pierre			
Bernard			
35 Pierre	(22) M. Thibé Roy	S.V.	1850
36 Gabriel	(23) Marie Lemieux	Lévis	1815
M. Anne	Michel Roy	"	1836
37 Pierre	(23) Marg. Enouf	B.	1821
38 François	(23) Agathe Fournier	B.	1821
		S. Isidore	
Césarie Marguerite			
39 Laurent	(23) Louise Samson,	Lévis	1827
40 Ambroise	(23) Archange Moreau	S.L.	1829
Ambroise			
Henri			
41 Julien	(13) Susanne Carrier	Lévis	1830
42 Alexis	(23) Marg. Lemelin	S.Chs.	1834
Marie	Edouard Huart	"	1854
Caroline	Cyp. Bernier	"	1859
43 Jean-Baptiste			
	(24) M. Jos. Guay	B.	1821
Marie Louise	Frs Rémidion	"	1843
Jean Baptiste			
Pierre			
44 Jean-Baptiste	Thérèse Couture		
(25)		S. Chs.	1805
		S. Claire	
Le même	Marg. Trahan	S.L.	1812
M. Marguerite	Denis Naud	S. Chs.	1840
45 Louis	(25) Marie Pénin	S. Chs.	1804
46 François	(25) Charlotte Lacasse		
		S. Chs.	1805
François			
Jean			
47 Joseph	(25) M. Jos. Gontier		
		S. Chs.	1812
M. Josette	Amable Coté	"	1832
Marcelline	Marcel Leclaire	"	1839
Emélie	Pierre Bernier	"	1843
Henriette	André Brochu	"	1855
Caroline	Philippe Fournier	"	1855
François			
Joseph			
Joseph			
48 André	(22) Eliz. Herant Dominique		
		S. Tho.	1811
Marie Zoé	Luc. Brochu	S.V.	1834
Geneviève	Vilmére Brochu	"	1844
M. Josephine	Jean Fortin	"	1845
Elizabeth	F. X. Marseau	"	1851

CHABOT.

Célina	Simon Fortin	S.V.	1857
Samuel			
Louis			
André			
Pierre			
49 François	(27) Marie Turgeon	S.Chs.	1809
50 Michel	(28) M.Anne Dodier	S.F.S.	1798
51 François	(29) Genev. Couture	S.P.	1829
Marie	Héliodore Ulric Plante		
		S.P.	1867
52 Pierre	(30) Genev. Gosselin	S.Chs.	1810
		S.Lazare	
M. Madeleine	Tho. Samson	S.Chs.	1845
Pierre			
Le même	Esther Genest	S.G	1830
53 Jean Bapt.	(30) Marg. Marcoux	S.Chs.	1813
		S.H.	
Esther	J. B. Theotime Couture		
		S.Chs.	1842
Anastasie	Pierre Audet	S.Chs.	1843
Sophie	Romain Lebrun	S.M.	1848
54 Louis	(30) M. Anne Richard		
		S.Chs.	1813
M. Hermine	Jacques Fournier	B.	1840
Romain			
Louis			
Marcel			
Delphine			
Rémi			
55 Joseph	(30) Angèle Bilodeau	S.G.	1814
Suz. Marcelline	Chs. Fournier	S.Chs.	1839
Scolastique	Pre. Narcisse Turgeon		
		S.Chs.	1839
Sophie	Louis Audet	S.Chs.	1840
M. Angèle	Hubert Couture	"	1853
56 Landry	(30) Ménalie Nolin	S.Chs.	1819
57 Antoine	(30) Barbe Labrecque	"	1827
		S.Claire	
58 Jean	(31) M. Ls. Brochu	S.Chs.	1819
Marie Louise	Ant. Pacquet	"	1843
Zoé	Jos.Godfroi Boutin	"	1850
Eudoxie	Antoine Plante	"	1856
Emélie	Damase Paquet	"	1858
Charles			
Luc			
Laurent			
59 François	(31) M. Apol. Brochu	S.V.	1820
		S.Claire	
Le même	Angèle Ruel	S.Chs.	1826
60 Pierre	(32) Marg. Couture	S.Chs.	1820
Elizabeth	Olivier Morin	"	1852
Basile			
61 Louis	(32) Emérence Couture		
		S.Chs.	1827
Joseph			
62 Charles	(32) Marie Paquet	S.Chs.	1827
Ferdinand			
63 Pierre	(34) Marg. Petitgrew		
		Isle Verte	
64 Joseph	(34) M. Ls. Denis	S.L.	1840
M. Athanïse	Zeph. Denis	"	1860
Marie Luce	Malcolm Blackburn	"	1876
Joseph			
65 Bernard	(34) Natalie Labrecque	SL.	1842
M. Eugénie	Cyrill Audet	S.L.	1865
Natalie	François Denis	"	1869
66 Ambroise	(40) Scolastique Leclaire		
		S.Chs.	1852
67 Honoré	(40) Leonie Poulet	S.Chs.	1861
68 Antoine	Josette Hamel		
Adèle	Alexandre Lefebvre		
		S.Chs.	1854
69 Antoine	Caroline Boutin		
Le même	Marie Gaumon	S.Chs.	1864
70 Jean Bapt.	(43) Marcelline Nadeau	B.	1847
71 Pierre	(43) Angèle Roy	B.	1855

CHABOT.

72	François	(46) Angé Couture S.Chs. 1830	
73	Jean	(46) Fse. Bacquet S.Chs. 1843	
		S.Claire	
74	Joseph	(47) M.-Céleste Blais	
		S.F.S. 1844	
75	Joseph	(47) Marg. Marcoux S.Chs. 1855	
76	François	(47) Emile Paquet S.Chs. 1861	
77	Samuel	(48) M. Adé Roy S.V. 1857	
78	Pierre	(48) M. Césarie Blais S.V. 1857	
79	Louis	(48) Osite Boutin S.V. 1858	
80	Andre Narc.	(48) Soulange Fortin S.V. 1846	
81	Pierre	(52) Adé Trudel S.Chs. 1846	
82	Marcel	(54) Luce Bernier S.Chs. 1840	
83	Louis	(54) M. Anne Leroux	
		S.Chs. 1841	
84	Delphin	(54) Marg. Terrien S.Chs. 1850	
85	Romain	(54) Anastasie Nadeau B. 1857	
86	Rémi	(54) Sophie Dalaire S.Chs. 1860	
87	Charles	(58) Louise Alice Fournier	
		S.Chs. 1857	
88	Luc	(58) Rosalie Fournier	
		S.Chs. 1857	
89	Laurent	(58) Hélène Marcoux	
		S.Chs. 1858	
90	Basile	(60) Sara Audet S.Chs. 1864	
91	Joseph	(61) Léocadie Gosselin	
		S.Chs. 1855	
92	Ferdinand	(62) Cédulie Couture	
		S.Chs. 1863	
93	Jos. Hermé-négilde	(64) Séraphine Cédulie Pepin	
		S.L. 1872	

CHAMBERLAN.

1	Simon	Marie Boileau S.F. 1669	
	Catherine	Michel Chartier S.Frs. 1688	
	Marie	Frs. Quemeneur „ 1700	
	Simon		
	Gabriel		
	Ignace		
2	Simon	(1) Eliz. Rondeau S.F. 1692	
	Angélique	Aimé Lecompte Q. 1716	
3	Gabriel	Cath. Dalaire S.Frs. 1694	
	Marie	Pierre Mercier S.F. 1717	
	Jean Baptiste		
	Etienne		
4	Ignace	(1) M. Mad. Rondeau S.J.1699	
	M. Madeleine	Jean Frs. Lemoine	
		S.M. 1736	
	M. Catherine	J. B. Monmény S.M. 1749	
	Geneviève	Jean Bissonnet B. 1720	
	Jean		
	Pierre		
	Ignace		
	Nicolet		
5	Jean Baptiste	(3) M. Marg. Lumina,	
		V. de Jos. Peltier S.F.1723	
	Jean Baptiste		
6	Etienne	(3) Mad. Laignon S.F. 1731	
7	Pierre	(4) M. Jos. Filteau S.V. 1727	
	M. Josette	Aug. Thibaut B. 1748	
8	Ignace	(4) Marie Gautron S.V. 1727	
	Hélène	Jos. Balan S.M. 1748	
	Michel		
	Le même	M. Jos. Terrien S.J. 1741	
9	Jean	(4) Marg. Lefebvre S.V. 1729	
	Marie Anne	Jean Frs. Pilote S.M. 1754	
	Joseph		
	Joseph		
	Le même	Fse. Mateau S.M. 1757	
10	Nicolas	(4) M. Mad. Alaire S.V. 1734	
	M. Josette	Pierre Maupas S.M. 1764	
	Joseph Marie		
	Pierre Marie		
11	Michel	(5) Françoise Garant S.M.1750	

CHAMBERLAN.

12	Jean Baptiste (5)	Ursule Lemieux	
		Cap.S.Ign. 1753	
	Joseph Marie		
13	Joseph	(9) M. Angé Lepage S.M. 1753	
14	Joseph	(9) Genev. Morin S.P.S. 1759	
	Marie Thérèse	Gabriel Blanchet S.P.S. 1786	
	Augustin		
	Charles		
	Jean Baptiste		
	Joseph		
15	Joseph Marie (10)	M. Anne Fradet S.M. 1765	
	Catherine	Jos. Marie Bouchard	
		S.M. 1798	
	Marie Anne	Simon Bacquet „ 1803	
	Marie	J. B. Balan „ 1789	
	Marie	2° Chs. Carbonneau	
		S.G. 1796	
	Laurent		
	Joseph		
	Antoine		
	Le même	Ursule Roy S.M. 1810	
16	Pierre Marie (19)	M. Anne Goupy „ 1782	
	Marie	Pierre Ouimet B. 1815	
	Joseph Marie		
	Jean		
	Louis		
A	Joseph Marie (12)	M. Rose Gaudin	
		S.P.S. 1790	
17	Charles	(14) Thérèse Sénéchal	
		S.P.S. 1787	
	M. Charlotte	Ant. Bouffart „ 1817	
	Thérèse	J. B. Lecomte „ 1829	
	M. Françoise	Jos. Janvier Blais	
		S.P.S. 1824	
	Rose	Ignace Chartier „ 1826	
	Adélaïde	Pierre Bernard „ 1829	
	Charles		
18	Jean Bapt.	(14)M. Julienne Sénéchal	
		S.P.S. 1792	
	M. Thérèse	Benoit Pellerin „ 1819	
	Marguerite	Vital Gagné „ 1827	
19	Augustin	(14) Marg. Asselin S.V. 1788	
	Marie Anne	Roch Nadeau S.Chs. 1815	
	Alexandre		
	Joseph		
	Felix		
	Jean		
20	Joseph	(14) Marie Fortier S.P.S. 1810	
21	Joseph	(15) Hélène Forgues S.M. 1791	
	Marie Anne	Gervais Audet S.G. 1811	
	Hélène	Chas. Morisset S.M. 1818	
	Joseph		
22	Antoine	M. Théotiste Bouchard	
		S.M. 1798	
	Marguerite	Simon Corriveau „ 1829	
	Marguerite	2° Paulin Catellier „ 1835	
	Constance	Michel Catellier „ 1839	
	Adélaïde	Proper Roy „ 1843	
	Antoine		
23	Laurent	(15) Apolline Gosselin	
		S.M. 1808	
	Luce	Ant. Brochu S.M. 1838	
	Apolline	Olivier Morin „ 1844	
	M. Elizabeth	Michel Brochu „ 1844	
	Antoine		
	Jean		
	Le même	M. Agathe Vien B. 1822	
	Le même	Reine Bilodeau S.M.1845	
24	Joseph Marie(16)	Josette Forgues „ 1805	
	Josette	J. B. Asselin „ 1831	
	Julie	Jean Bourget „ 1831	
	Adélaïde	Majorique Rousseau	
		S.M. 1846	
	Hubert		
	Joseph		
	George		

CHAMBERLAN.

25	Jean	(16) Marg. Gautron	S.M.1803
	Marie	Féréol Dorval	„ 1831
	Marguerite	Michel Jahan	„ 1820
	Vital		
	Jean		
26	Louis	(16) M. Anne Plante	S.V. 1812
27	Charles	(17) Julie Gagné	S.P.S. 1830
28	Joseph	(19) Archange Penin	
			S.Chs. 1822
29	Jean	(19) Genev. Nadeau	S.G. 1827
30	Felix	(19) Louise Couture	S.Chs.1831
31	Alexandre	(19) François Bacquet	S.M.1836
32	Joseph	(21) M. Marthe Nadeau	
			S.M. 1818
33	Charles	Genev. Gagnon	
	François Xavier		S. Roch de Q.
34	Antoine	(22) Angèle Mercier	S.M.1828
	Marie Célina	J. B. Toussaint	„ 1854
	Euphrosine	F. X. Roy	„ 1861
	Narcisse		
	Elzéar		
35	Antoine	(23) Archange Bolduc	S.M.1839
36	Jean	(23) Henriette Langlois	
			S.V. 1848
37	Joseph	(24) M. Jos. Gautron	S.M.1832
38	George	(24) M.Hermine Bouchard	S.M
39	Hubert	(24) Anastasie Dion	S.M.1839
40	Vital	(25) Genev. Forgues	„ 1833
41	Jean	(25) Céleste Labbé	S.G. 1829
	Adelaïde	François Tangué	S.M.1854
	Jean		
42	François Xavier	(33) M. Rose Lemieux	S.M.1845
43	Narcisse	(34) Victoire Gosselin	„ 1854
44	Elzéar	(34) Henriette Faucher	„ 1861
45	Jean	(41) Agathe Molleur	S.L. 1861

CHANTAL.

1	Pierre	Angé. Martin	S.P. 1696
	Marie Claire	Frs. Barbin	„ 1778
	Marie Claire	2° Jos. Godbout	„ 1748
	Marie Claire	3° Chs. Roberge	„ 1762
	M. Angélique	Pierre Charlan	„ 1733

CHARLAN—FRANCŒUR.

1	Claude	Jacqueline Desbordes	
			Q. 1652
	Noël		
	Denis		
	Le même	Jeanne Peltier	Q. 1661
	Marie Anne	Jacq. Gendron	S.F. 1681
	Anne	René Beaucher	„ 1688
	Michelle	Pierre Paris	„ 1691
	Geneviève	Louis Bluteau	„ 1702
	Marie	Pierre Paquet	„ 1694
	Marie	2° Jean Filiau	Q. 1711
	Jean		
	Joseph		
	Gabriel		
	Gabriel		
2	Denis	(1) M. Anne Létourneau	
			S.F. 1681
	Elizabeth	Ls.Aug. Gagné	S.Tho.1707
	Pierre		
	Le même	Marie Gautier	S.F. 1688
3	Noël	(1) Marie Turcot	„ 1682
	Marie	Jean Paquet	S.J. 1708
	Marie René	Pierre Rouillard	Q. 1719
	Joseph		
4	Jean	(1) Anne Paré	S.F. 1691
5	Joseph	(1) M. Angé. Arbour	Q. 1710
6	Gabriel	(1) Eliz. Testu	S.F. 1708
7	Gabriel	(1) Marg. Drouin	„ 1715
	Marguerite	Ignace Ratté	„ 1747
	Joseph Marie		
	Jean Baptiste		

18—17

CHARLAN—FRANCŒUR.

8	Pierre	M. Jeanne Guilmet	
	Marie Josette	Pierre Coté	S.F. 1734
	Félicité	Joseph Turcot	„ 1740
	Angélique	Pierre Audet	„ 1750
	Marie Thérèse	Jacques Hélie	„ 1758
	Marie Thérèse	2° Frs. Godbout	„ 1783
	Pierre		
9	Joseph	(5) M. Anne Gagnon	S.F.1707
10	François		
	Marie Thècle	J. B. Paquet	S.J. 1760
	Pierre		
11	Joseph Marie	(7) Véronique Ratté	S.P, 1746
	Le même	Marg. Thivierge	S.F. 1760
	Julienne	Louis Pichet	S.P. 1801
	Marguerite	J. B. Chatigny	„ 1802
	Marguerite	2° Pierre Letellier	S.P.1816
12	Jean Baptiste	(7) Félicité Guion	S.F.1756
	Le même	M.Thècle Marseau	„ 1810
13	Pierre	(8) M. Angé. Chantal	S.P.1733
14	Pierre	(10) M. Anne Defoy	S.F. 1751
	Marie Anne	Jean Vermet	S.J. 1783
	Pierre		
15	Pierre	(14) Cath. Gendreau	S.L. 1772
	Marie	Claude Vaillancour	S.J.1804
	Jean		
16	Jean	(16) Marg. Boissonneau	„ 1816
	Marguerite	Firmin Tangué	„ 1841

CHARRIER.

2	Etienne	Marthe Bourassa	
	Pierre		
3	Pierre	(2) Jeanne Carreau	S.L. 1746
	Marie Jeanne	Michel Delanteigne	
			S.Chs. 1766
	Pierre		
	Le même	M. Jeanne Poliquin	
			S.Chs. 1758
	Claire	Pierre Fortin	„ 1786
	Judith	François Leblanc	„ 1792
	Cécile	Alexis Langlois	„ 1792
	Marguerite	Ignace Roy	„ 1799
	Marie	Joseph Morin	„ 1803
	Laurent		
	Charles		
4	Pierre	(3) Cath. Gosselin	S.Chs. 1772
	Catherine	Ignace Lecours	„ 1790
	Le même	Véronique Fortier	„ 1775
	Véronique	Joseph Couture	„ 1794
	Marie	Jacques Boutillet	„ 1797
	Marie Anne	J. B. Delanteigne	„ 1808
5	Laurent	(3) Cath. Lefebvre	„ 1796
	Marguerite	Louis Baillargeon	S.H.1815
	Madeleine		
6	Charles	(3) M. Rose Begin	S.H.1789
	Charles		
	Le même	M. Genev. Dessaint	
			S.Tho. 1797
	Félicité	Joachim Plante	S.Chs. 1835
	Pierre		
	François		
	Bénoni		
8	Charles	(6) M.Anne Chabot	S.Chs.1813
9	Pierre	(6) M, Angé. Leclaire	„ 1822
	Marie Angélique	Nazaire Brochu	„ 1850
	Restitut	Laurent Nadeau	„ 1753
	Vital		
10	Bénoni	(6) M. Olive Leclaire	„ 1831
11	François	(6) M.Marg. Baillargeon	„ 1853
12	Vital	(9) Perpétue Bernier	„ 1843

CHARRON—LAFERRIÈRE.

1	Jean Baptiste	Anne d'Anneville	Q 1669
	M. Madeleine	Michel Chabot Lorette	1703
	M. Madeleine	2° Alexis Bleau	1710

- 5-6 EDWARD VII., A. 1906

CHARRON—LAFERRIÈRE.

Jean Baptiste
2 Jean Baptiste (1) Genev. Dupile S.Aug.1710
M. Angélique   Alexandre Blanchard
                                 S.P. 1727
Geneviève   Simon Pradet   „ 1730
Madeleine   Jean Fleuret   „ 1730
Madeleine   Etienne Samson   B. 1739
Marie Louise   Louis Dechaune   „ 1739
Marie Cécile   Joseph Mimaux   S.M. 1746
Marie Thècle   Joseph Ouellet   „ 1749
Marguerite   François Vigneau „ 1751
Jean
3 Jean   (2) M. Jos. Samson Levis 1739
Marie Susanne   J. B. Forgues   S.M.1775
Marie Susanne   2° Olivier Campagna
                                 S.G. 1800
Jean
Michel
Le même   M. Jos. Picard S.P.S.1766
Marguerite   Etn Roy   S.G. 1829
Marie Claire   Jean Gervais S.P.S. 1789
4 Michel   (3) Marie Jos. Proulx
                                 S.Tho. 1791
Luce   Antoine Dubé S.P.S. 1819
5 Jean   (3) M. Mad. Clément
                                 S.M.1765
Marie Anne   J. B. Plante   S.G.1765
Angélique   Louis Noël   „ 1811
Jean
6 Jean   (4) Marie Jos. Lacroix
                                 S.V.1790
7 Joseph   Marg. Marcoux
Marguerite   Louis Aubé   S.G. 1824
Angèle   Michel Louineau „ 1830
Joseph
8 Joseph   (7) BrigitteLouineau S.V.1827

CHARTIER.

1 Michel   Marie Magnié
Michel
Charles
2 Michel   (1) Cath. Chamberlan
                                 S.Frs. 1688
Elizabeth   Pierre Balan   „ 1708
Charles
Gabriel
Le même   Anne Picard S.Tho. 1704
Marie   Antoine Blais Bert. 1731
Isabelle   Pierre Gagnon   „ 1734
Philippe
Louis
François
Le même   Jeanne Grondin   Q. 1722
Le même   Marie Shinck S.Frs. 1734
3 Charles   (1) Louise Lemaitre Q. 1694
4 Charles   (2) Marie Carrier Lévis 1720
Michel
5 Gabriel   (2) M. Jeanne Cosance Q.1727
Joseph
6 Louis   (2) Mad. Lefebvre Bert.1728
Marie Louise   Jacques Bilodeau S.V.1751
Marie Louise   2° J. B. Custeau S.G.1789
Thérèse   Jean Hébert   S M.1764
M. Catherine   Pierre Plante   „ 1771
Louis
7 Philippe   (2) Eliz. LeRoy   Bert.1730
                 V. de Gab. Bilodeau
Marie Anne   Jacq. Carbonneau Bert.1751
Le même   Angé Boulet S.F.S.1733
8 François   (2) Thérèse Chartré Bert.1738
Marie   Michel Dubord   „ 1761
François
Joseph
Jean

CHARTIER.

9 Jacques   Mad. Blanchet
Reine   Chrysostôme Langlois
                                 S.P.S.1763
Jacques
Le même   Rose Guillet
                             Cap St. Ign.1737
Rosalie   Joseph RouleauS.P.S.1764
10 Jacques   M. Eléz. Thibaut
M. Madeleine   JosephBlanchetS.P.S 1764
12 Michel   Marg. Morin S.P.S.1761
Marguerite   Basile Gagnon S.F.S.1784
Marie Josette   Basile Beaucher „ 1785
Marie Roger   Jos. Marie Boulet
                                 S.F.S.1792
Susanne   Pierre Beaudoin „ 1797
Reine   Paschal Corriveau
                                 Bert.1793
Reine   2° Pierre Rémillard
                                 S.G.1808
Ignace
13 Jean-Baptiste Marie Jos. Morin
M. Françoise   Gab. Thibaut S.P.S..1788
Philippe
Jean-Baptiste
André
Joseph
14 Joseph   (5) Eliz. Dufour   S.M.1761
15 Jacques   (9) Marie Louise Blais
                                 Bert.1751
16 Louis   (6) Mad. Talbot   Bert.1753
17 François   (8) Marie Ls. Fondiami
                                 Bert.1774
18 Joseph   (8) M. Eléz. Guignard
                                 Bert. 1774
19 Jean   (8) Thérèse Hill   Bert.1778
20 Jean-Baptiste Marie Angé Cloutier
M. Angélique   Charles BernierS.P.S.1796
21 Ignace   12 Génév. Picard S.F.S.1788
M. Marguerite   Michel Vital Létourneau
                                 S.F.S.1809
M. Marguerite   2°Louis Quemeneur
                                 S.F.S.1810
Marie Louise   Jean Frs. Morin   1815
Le même   Susanne Roy S.F.S.1837
22 Pierre   Véronique Fortier
Pierre
23 JeanBaptiste(13) M. Genev. Picard
                                 S.F.S.1787
Adélaïde   Aug. Etn. Morin
                                 S.P.S.1812
Adélaïde   2° Jos. Caron   „ 1816
Marie Angèle   Joseph Simoneau „ 1813
Emérentienne   Antoine Talbot „ 1839
Ignace
24 André   (13) M. Anne Picard „ 1792
M. Geneviève   Louis Gontier S.H.1815
25 Philippe   (13) Marg.LemieuxS.F.S.1795
26 Joseph   (13) Rosalie Fontaine
                                 S.P.S.1796
27 Pierre   Marg. Gagné.. ... ...
Narcisse
28 Pierre   (22) Angé. Lebrun S.G.1804
29 Ignace   (23) Rose Chamberlan
                                 S.P.S.1826
30 Narcisse   (27) Marie Zoé Mercier
                                 S.M 1850

CHATIGNY.

1 Pierre   M. Angé Martin S.P.1710
Françoise   François Jahan S.P.1736
M. Catherine   Joseph Drouin „ 1748
Pierre
Louis
2 Pierre   (1) Marg. Ratté   S.P.1742
Marie   Pierre Thivierge„ 1767

CHATIGNY.

Charlotte	Joseph Racine	"	1784
Charlotte	2° François Pichet	"	1811
Agathe	François Vérieul	"	1797
Marguerite	François Audet	S.J.	1801
Marie	Gabriël Pepin	"	1785
Geneviève	Louis Rouleau	S.L.	1786
Jean-Baptiste			
Louis			
Pierre Laurent			
François			
3 Louis	(1) Marie Anne Leclaire		
		S.P	1750
Angélique	Jacques Hélie	S.J.	1785
Louis			
Pierre			
Paul			
Régis			
4 Pierre Laurent(2)	M. Reine Paradis	S.P.	1783
Reine	Pierre Dufresne	"	1812
Angèle	Antoine Marcel	"	1816
Pierre			
5 François	(2) Cath. Roberge	S.P.	1786
Catherine	Ignace Pichet		1816
Marguerite	Pierre Côté		1821
Marie	Pierre Alain		1822
Angéle	Jean Racine	S.P.	1828
Pierre			
6 Jean Baptiste	(2) Marg. Charlan	S.P.	1802
Marguerite	J. B. Gagné	S.G.	1827
7 Louis	(2) Géneviève Giguère		
		S.F.	1787
Jean			
8 Louis	(3) Marie Jos Boucher		
		S.Chs.	1773
Josette	François Royer	S.H.	1808
9 Pierre	(3) Cath. Viger	S.Chs.	1777
Marie Anne	Raphaël Landry	S.G.	1808
Madeleine	Laurent Gosselin	"	1809
Françoise	Joseph Dorval	"	1812
Elizabeth	Louis Hizoir	S.G.	1813
Pierre			
Pierre			
10 Paul	(3) M, Génev. Hayot		
		S.Chs.	1778
Le même	Eliz. Lacroix	S.M.	1797
A Frs Régis	(3) M. Anne Clément		
		S.H.	1784
Louise	Charles Carrier	"	1817
Géneviève	Antoine Tangué	"	1820
Louis			
11 Pierre	(9) Eliz. Badeau	Q.	1819
Charlotte	Michel Moreau	S.G.	1819
12 Pierre	(4) Constance Paradis		
		S.P.	1812
Angèle	Louis Couture	"	1842
Constance	Louis Pepin	"	1843
Théotiste	Joseph Dupile	"	1844
Marie Marthe	Gilbert Baillargeon	"	1847
Soulange Arthé	Ls Elz. Gendreau	"	1861
Marcelline	Jos Ed. Gosselin	S.F.	1839
François			
13 Pierre	(5) Marie Roberge	S.P.	1816
Timothé			
Nazaire			
A Jean	(7) Charlotte Gaudreau		
		S. H.	1804
Le même	M. Roger Fontaine		
		S.H.	1819
14 Pierre	(9) Joseph Campagna		
		A.G.	1810
Pierre			
15 François	(12) Françoise Bonne	S.P.	1859
16 Timothé	(13) Marie Louise Deblois		
		S.P.	1860
47 Nazaire	(13) M. Olive Boissonneau		
		S.P.	1865

18—17½

CHATIGNY.

18 Pierre	(14) Luce Labbé	S.Frs.	1834
Louis	(10a) Marie Tangué	S.H.	1821

CHEVANEL.

1 François	Marie Claimont		
Pierre			
2 Pierre	(1) M. Ange Malbœuf		
		S.P.S.	1757
M. Angélique	Pierre René Morin		
		S.P.S.	1791
Geneviève	Joseph Dumas	S.F.S.	1801
Pierre			
3 Pierre	(2) Marie Anne Lepage		
Geneviève	Antoine Dubé	S.G.	1830
Augustin			
Joseph			
Pierre			
4 Pierre	(3) Marg. Roy	S.G.	1817
Le même	Victor Picard	S.F.S.	1824
5 Augustin	(3) Mad. Lacroix	S.G.	1823
6 Joseph	(3) M. Ange Bernier		
		S.Chs.	1831

CHISSON—GIASSON.

1 Jean	Jeanne Bernard		
Michel			
Le même	Mad. Martin	Q.	1683
2 Michel	(1) Marg. Mourier	S.J.	1706
M. Elizabeth	Louis Foulet	Bert.	1730
Marie Josette	Jacq. Boulet	"	1730
Marie Hélène	Frs. Gaudreau	"	1731
Louis			
3 Louis	(2) Génev. Quemeneur		
		S.F.S.	1745
M. Scholastique	Jos Boivin	"	1773
Marie Louise	Benj. Langlois	"	1780
Marie	Basile Thibaut	S G.	1788
Jean Baptiste			
Pierre			
4 Jean Baptiste (3)	M. Eliz. Langlois		
		S.F.S.	1776
Thérèse	Jean Guillot	S.G.	1821
Michel			
5 Pierre	(3) Angèle Dutile	"	1787
6 Michel	(4) Ange Paquet	"	1815

CHORET.

1 Mathieu	Sébastienne Veillon		
Joseph			
Jean			
2 Joseph	(1) M. Ange Loignon	S.F.	1676
Jean			
3 Jean	(1) Claire Boucher	"	1684
Marguerite	Jean Boissonneau	S.L.	1707
4 Jean	(2) Thérèse Trudel	A.G.	1711
Pierre			
5 Pierre	(4) M.Anne Paradis	S.P.	1741
Le même	Thérése Nolin		1745
Agathe	Jac. Girardin		1794
Ignace			
6 Ignace	M. Thècle Noël	S.P.	1778
Marie Louise	Ignace Paradis	S.P.	1810
Marie Louise	2° Frs. Poulet	S.P.	1824
Judith	Pierre Roberge	S.P.	1815
Geneviève	Nicolas Dumas	S.L.	1807
Philippe			
Jean			
Pierre			
7 Philippe	(6) Mad. Blanchet	S.P.	1809
Madeleine	Laurent Audibert	S.P.	1831
8 Jean	(6) Mad. Paradis	S.P.	1816
9 Pierre	(6) Genev. Gagnon	S.F.	1807
Adélaïde	François Gosselin	S.L.	1827

CHORET.

David				
10 David	(9)	Marie Bédard	Chs. Bourg.	1830
Le même		Justine Audet	S.L.	1838

CHRETIEN.

1 Jacques		Cath. Chrétien Niverd		
Michel				
Vincent				
2 Michel	(1)	Marie Meunier	Q.	1665
Jean Charles				
Michel				
Jean Baptiste				
3 Vincent	(1)	Anne Leclaire		1668
Anne		Nicolas Groinier	S.E.	1687
Marie Madeleine		Charles Guérard	S.E.	1697
Vincent				
Jacques				
Jean				
Thomas				
François				
4 Michel	(2)	Mag. Coeur	Chs. Bourg.	1692
Jean Baptiste				
5 Jean Charles	(2)	Marg. Roy	Chs. Bourg.	1694
		Jacques Choret	Chs. Bourg.	1718
Madeleine				
Geneviève		Jean Michel Parent	Chs. Bourg.	1728
6 Jean Baptiste	(2)	Cath. Roy	Chs. Bourg.	1703
Louis				
Louis				
7 Vincent	(3)	Mad. Blanchet	S.Tho.	1699
Vincent				
8 Jean		M. Mad. Louineau	Chs. Bourg.	1701
Joseph				
9 Thomas		Reine Canac	S.F.	1710
Reine		Frs. Baudon	S.Tho.	1748
Joseph				
10 François	(3)	Louise Migneron		1713
11 Jacques	(3)	Marie Baudon	S.Frs.	1713
12 Jean Baptiste	(4)	Jeanne Eliz. Bédard	Chs. Brg.	1723
13 Louis		Eliz. Hélie	S.H.S.V.	1761
M. Elizabeth		François Terrien	S. V.	1784
Antoine				
14 Vincent	(7)	Marie Lefebvre	S.Tho.	1716
15 Joseph	(8)	Marie Paquet	S.M.	1740
16 Joseph	(9)	M. Gertrude Jolin	S.Frs.	1750
17 Jean (S. Malo)		Thérèse Fse. Behier	S.V.	1741
18 Jacques		Julienne Moisie	Ev.d'I.	
Charles François				
19 Louis	(6)	Marie Angé Cotin	Q.	1744
M. Angélique		Chs. Bouchard	S.V.	1776
Louis				
20 Antoine	(13)	M.Chs.Rémillard	S.V.	1792
21 Charles François	(18)	Ursule Guimont V. de Jos. Buteau	Bert.	1765
Jean François				
22 Louis	(19)	Mad. Daniau V. de Pre. Gautron	S.V.	1780
Le même		Cath. Roy	S.V.	1782
Marie Céleste		Jacques Roy	S.V.	1808
Joseph				
Louis				
23 JeanFrançois(21)		Angé Blais	Bert.	1790
Ursule		J. B. Corriveau	Bert.	1826
Rosalie		André Corriveau	Bert.	1828
François				
24 Louis	(22)	Marguerite Roy	S.M.	1810
Louis				

CHRETIEN.

25 Joseph	(22)	M.AngèleCadrin	S.V.	1834
26 Jacques		Marie Ruel	Q.	
Pierre				
27 François	(23)	Rosalie Corriveau	Bert.	1818
Fabien				
François				
28 Louis	(24)	Eliz. Bisson	S.V.	1819
Pierre				
29 Pierre	(26)	M. Délima Guay	B.	1854
30 François	(27)	Marie Naud	S.Chs.	1850
31 Fabien	(27)	Odile Fournier	S.Chs.	1818
32 Pierre	(28)	M. Célina Plante	S.M.	1864
33 Pierre		Eléonore Pruneau		
Cecile		Vital Létourneau	S.Chs.	1863

CHYSTOPHE—SAUVAGE.

1 Thomas(Sauvage)		Anne Denis Acadie		
Jacques (Chysostophe)				
2 Jacques (Chystophe)	(1)	Genev. Couture	S.V.	1758
		V. de Jacq. Rémillard		
Jacques				
3 Jacques	(2)	Ange. Richard	S.V.	1784
Angélique		Jos. Asselin	S.F.	1814
Jacques				
Joseph				
Julien				
Michel				
4 Jean		Susanne Nadeau		
Marie Anne		Louis Clément	S.Chs.	1815
Marie Anne		2° Chs. Gagné	"	1824
5 Jacques	(6)	Ange. Daniau	S.G.	1806
Le même		Josette Quemeneur	"	1807
Marie		Joseph Gautron	"	1823
6 Julien	(3)	Marg. Fontaine	S.G.	1810
7 Michel	(3)	M. Louis Turcot	S.F.	1815
8 Joseph	(3)	Marg. Lebrecque	S.G.	1821

CINQMARS—GOBLIN DIT ST. MARS.

1 Marc. Antoine		Cath. Boisandré	Q	1663
Le même		Fse. Chapelain	S.L.	1692
Pierre				
2 Pierre	(1)	Genev. Bélanger	C.R.	1727
Marie Louise		Jacq. Denis	S.P.	1764
Pierre				
Charles				
Guillaume				
3 Charles	(2)	Angé. Isabel	S.L.	1762
4 Guillaume	(2)	Eliz. Ruel	S.L.	1765
Pierre				
François				
Guillaume				
5 Pierre	(2)	Thérèse Ferlant	S.P.	1782
Marguerite		Louis Roberge	"	1807
6 Pierre	(4)	Marie Audet	S. L.	1796
Geneviève		Louis Labrecque	"	1845
Marie		Laurent Audet	"	1839
Pierre				
François				
7 Guillaume	(4)	M.Anne Gadbout	S.L.	1796
Elizabeth		Amb. Coulombe		
Marie Anne		Charles Gosselin		
Marie Louise				
(2 Noces)		Frs. Chouinard		
Guillaume				
Pierre				
8 François	(4)	M.Anne Langlois	S.L.	1803
Marie Louise		Greg. Labrecque	"	1840
François				
Pierre				
David				

CINQMARS—GOBLIN DIT ST. MARS.

	Charles				
9	Pierre	(6)	Marie Noël	S.L.	1838
			S. Féréol		
10	François	(6)	Génev. Bouffart	S.L.	1858
11	Pierre	(7)	Marg. Fournier S. Chs.		
12	Guillaume	(7)	Judith Rouleau	S.L.	1824
	Salomé		Pierre Denis	S.L.	1854
	Julie		Pre. Celestin Lefran-		
			çois	S.L.	1854
	M. Anne Celanire		Joseph Plante	S.L.	1855
	Marie Louise		Julien Gravel	„	1866
	Damase				
	Pierre Billarmin				
13	François	(8)	Charlotte Poulhot	S.J.	1836
14	Pierre	(8)	Angèle Labrecque	S.L.	1837
	Angèle		François Denis	„	1867
	Rosalie		François Paradis	„	1869
	Caroline		Jean Cyrille Grenier	„	1869
	Marie Sophie		Pierre Roberge	„	1870
	Adélaïde		Edouard Leclaire	„	1876
	David				
15	David	(8)	Marcelline Noel	S.L.	1848
16	Charles	(8)			
17	Pierre Bellar-				
	min	(12)	Adéline Plante	C.R.	1869
18	Damase	(12)	Philoméne Curodeau		
				S.J.	1870
19	David	(14)	M. Adeline Gadbout		
				S.L.	1875

CIVADIER.

1	Louis		Agnés Olivier	S.F.	1669
	Jeanne		Joachim Molleur	S.L.	1693
	M. Françoise		Michel Molleur	S.L.	1694
	Marie		Jacq. Laneuville	„	1702
	Anne		Jean Ginchereau	„	1703
	Antoine				
2	Antoine	(1)	Marie Domingo	Q.	1707
	Marguerite		Philippe Benoit	S.L.	1732
	Marie		Pierre Roberge	„	1747
	Geneviève		Jean Audet	„	1754
	Louise		Michel Roberge	„	1757
	Joseph				
	Ignace				
	Antoine				
3	Joseph	(2)	Marie Gosselin	S.L.	1746
4	Antoine	(2)	M. Mad. Couture	S.L.	1746
	Madeleine		Pierre Clément	S.Chs.	1779
	Madeleine		2° Jas. Bacquet	S.M.	1786
5	Ignace	(2)	Gertrude Roberge	S.L.	1753
	Marie Anne		J. B. Rousseau	S.L.	1807

CLAND.

1	Jean Baptiste		Marie Peltier Allemagne.		
	Jean Baptiste				
2	Jean Baptiste	(1)	M. Louise Langlois		
				S.F.S	1793
	M. Angélique		Chs. Mercier	S.V.	1815
	Jean Baptiste				
3	Jean Baptiste	(2)	M. Reine Roy	S.P.S	1828

CLAVET.

1	Jacques		Marg. Fontaine		
	Michel				
2	Michel		Cath. Thibaut	S.V.	1760
	Simon				
	Louis				
	Michel				
3	Simon	(2)	M. Angé Hamel		
				S.Tho.	1799
	M. Martine		Tho. Couillard	„	1833
	Narcisse				
4	Louis	(2)	Marg. Dalaire	S.Tho.	1801
	Emérence		Felix Bernier	„	1833

CLAVET.

	Henriette		Jean Labrecque	Bert.	1836
	Julie		Magl. Gaumont	„	1846
	M. Marcelline		J. B. Mercier	S.M.	1844
5	Michel	(2)	M. Chs. Bazin	S.V.	1805
	Charlotte		Pierre Pepin	S.J.	1835
	Marguerite		Cyriac Soucy	S.M.	1839
6	Ignace		Adé Boulet		
				S. Roch de Q	
	Fabien				
8	Narcisse	(3)	M. Anne Turgeon		
				S.M.	1841
9	Fabien	(6)	M. Rose Roy	S.M.	1847

CLÉMENT—LABONTÉ.

1	Léonard		Jeanne Morisset	S.F.	1699
	Marie		Jos. Denis	B.	1722
	Marie Josette		Pierre Gosselin	S.V.	1728
	Jeanne		Jos. Plante	S.M.	1732
	Marie Anne		J. B. Forgues	„	1749
	Ignace				
	Louis				
	André				
2	Louis	(1)	Marie Mad. Plante		
				S.J.	1733
	Marie		Noel Simart	S.M.	1761
	M. Catherine		Ignace Pilote	„	1765
	Madeleine		Jos. Forgue	„	1773
	Louis				
	Pierre				
	Ignace				
	Joseph François.				
	Joseph				
	Michel				
3	André	(1)	Marie Fse. Dubeau		
				S.V.	1738
	M. Angélique		Augustin Roy	„	1757
	M. Angélique		2° Jacq. Labrecque		
				S. V.	1770
	M. Brigitte		Jacq. Blais	„	1780
	M. Madeleine		Jean Charron	S.M.	1765
	Marie Louise		Nicolas Gontier	S.Chs.	1776
4	Ignace	(1)	M. Véronique Fleuret		
				S.M.	1749
	M. Geneviève		Joseph Roy	„	1768
	Marguerite		Pierre Forgue	„	1773
	Félicité		Joachim Lainé	S.H.	1788
	Michel				
	Ignace				
	Pierre				
5	Louis	(2)	Genev. Gosselin	S.M.	1758
	Marie Anne		Regis Chatigny	S.H.	1784
	Geneviève		Aug. Gautron	S. Chs.	1774
	Thérèse		Pierre Delenteigne		
				S.H.	1788
	Louis				
	Augustin				
6	Pierre	(2)	Marg. Bissonnet	S.M.	1760
	Le même		Genev. Pouliot	„	1764
	Le même		Marie Fournier	S.Chs.	1769
	Le même		Françoise Fortin	S.M.	1771
	Le même		Mad. Civadier	S. Chs.	1779
7	Joseph	(2)	Marie Goupy	S.M.	1762
	Marguerite		Aug. Bouchard	S.H.	1785
	Louise		Jean Jolin	S.Chs.	1779
	Joseph				
8	Joseph François		M. Angé Forgue	S.M.	1771
	Louis				
	Joseph				
	Charles				
	François				
9	Michel	(2)	Mad. Cochon	S.M.	1773
	Madeleine		Louis Roy	„	1805
	Louise		Pierre Brochu	„	1830
	Judith		Michel Lefebvre		
				S.Chs.	1819

CLÉMENT—LABONTÉ.

	Joseph		
10	Ignace	(2)	M. Anne Couture
			S.Chs. 1777
	Joseph		
	François		
	Ignace		
11	Pierre	(4)	Agathe Gontier S.Chs.1789
	Judith		Jos. Couture „ 1810
	Agathe		Pierre Vien „ 1815
	Marie		Antoine Gosselin „ 1821
	Geneviève		Jos. Richard „ 1830
	Jean Baptiste		
12	Ignace	(4)	Genev. Fradet S.M. 1790
	Judith		Magl. Tangué „ 1836
	Geneviève		Pierre Blanchet „ 1826
	Charles		
	Joseph		
	François		
	Michel		
	Jean		
	Marc		
13	Michel	(4)	Cécile Gontier S.Chs. 1794
14	Jacques		M. Thècle Balan
	Geneviève		Jos. Bilodeau Bert. 1767
15	Louis		M. Thècle Balan
	Jacques		
16	André		Mad. Boissel
	André		
17	Henri		M. Anne Montigny
	Marie Anne		Louis Cochon S.V. 1798
18	Paul		M. Anne Guénet
	Louis		
19	Augustin	(5)	Louise Fortier S.H. 1794
	Augustin		
20	Louis	(5)	M. Anne Fortier „ 1783
	Marie Anne		Nic. Tangué „ 1806
	Marie		Etn. Dalaire „ 1809
	Marguerite		Denis Collet „ 1820
	Louise		Jean Monmeny „ 1820
	Louis		
	Le même		Genev. Lefebvre
			S.Chs.1803
	Joseph		
21	Joseph	(7)	M. Marg. Pilet S.H. 1791
22	François	(8)	M. Anne Terrien „ 1792
23	Joseph	(8)	Ursule Gautron „ 1804
	Marie		Pierre BaillargeonS.G.1824
24	Charles	(8)	Marie Moresset S. H. 1811
	Hortence		J. B. Bouton S.Chs. 1857
	Augustin		
	François Xavier		
25	Louis	(8)	M. Anne Bodfil „ 1815
26	Joseph	(9)	M. Anne Hélie S.M. 1806
	Luce		Ls. Anselme Baudoin
			S.M. 1842
	Vitaline		Jean Dion „ 1859
	Michel		
	Jean Baptiste		
27	Jacques	(15)	M. Louis Corriveau
			S.V. 1784
28	Ignace	(10)	Marg. Pouliot S.Chs. 1804
	Charles		
	Le même		M. AnneMarseau S.G. 1812
29	Joseph	(10)	Marie Fortier S.G. 1807
	Le même		M. Jos. Goulet S.Chs. 1813
30	François	(10)	M. Euphrosine Roy
			S.G. 1818
	M. Archange		Antoine Albert S.V. 1850
31	JeanBaptiste	(11)	Olive Gosselin S.Chs. 1829
	François		
32	Charles	(12)	Mad. Forgue S.M. 1820
	François		J. B. Clément „ 1843
33	Joseph	(12)	Angéle Gagnon „ 1821
34	Michel	(12)	Luce Morisset „ 1822
35	François	(12)	Angèle Coté „ 1828
			Rosalie Veau „ 1835

CLÉMENT—LABONTÉ.

36	Jean	(12)	S. Claire
			M. Anne Coté S.M. 1839
37	Marc	(12)	S. Claire
38	André	(16)	BasilisseGoulet S.Chs.1797
	Archange		Aug.Goupy „ 1831
	Angelique		Pierre Lacroix S.M. 1819
	Elizabeth		PierreGuilmet „ 1820
	Hélène		Pierre Asselin „ 1841
	Marguerite		Paul Goupy „ 1826
	Marguerite		2° J. B. Dorval S.Chs. 1845
	Pierre		
	Joseph		
	André		
	Le même		Josette Larrivé S.G. 1826
	Honoré		
39	Louis	(18)	Genev. Dion „ 1799
40	Augustin	(19)	Angèle Couture S.H. 1820
			M. Pelagie Dalaire
41	Louis	(20)	S.H. 1809
42	Joseph	(20)	Marie Morin S.Chs. 1840
43	François Xavier		Angèle Daigle „ 1840
	ier	(24)	
44	Augustin	(34)	M.´Jos. Lecours „ 1846
			Emérentienne Pepin
45	Michel	(26)	S.M. 1838
			Françoise Clément
46	JeanBaptiste	(26)·	S.M. 1843
47	Charles	(28)	Genev. BilodeauS.Chs.1830
48	François	(31)	M. Angé Leblanc „ 1863
49	Joseph	(32)	M. Justine Veau „ 1859
50	Joseph	(38)	Louise Ruel S.G. 1825
51	André	(38)	Luce Rousseau S.Chs. 1830
52	Pierre	(38)	M. Vict. Asselin „ 1835
	Pierre		
53	Honoré	(38)	Hermine Asselin „ 1853
54	Pierre	(52)	Louise Faucher S.M. 1862

CLOUTIER

1	Zacharie		Xainte Dupont
	Charles		
	Jean		
	Zacharie		
2	Jean	(1)	Marie Martin Q. 1648
	Jean		
3	Zacharie	(1)	Mad. Barbe Aymant
	Pierre		
	Charles		
4	Charles	(1)	Louise Morin Q. 1659
	Jean		
	Zacharie		
5	Jean	(2)	M.Eliz. Morisset C.R. 1679
	François		
6	René	(3)	Marie Leblanc
	Louis		
	Jean Baptiste		
7	Charles	(3)	Anne Thibaut C.R. 1685
	Angélique		Jacq. Alaire „ 1724
	Basile		
	Charles		
8	Jean	(4)	Anne Morisset S.F. 1702
9	Zacharie	(4)	Jeanne Bacon S.R. 1708
	Zacharie		
10	Louis	(6)	M. Anne Thibault
			Cap.S.Ign. 1703
11	Jean Baptiste	(6)	Marie Gerbert
			Cap.S.Ign. 1706
	Pierre Paul		
	Pierre		
12	Joseph		Eliz. Morin
	Laurent		
	Jean Baptiste		
	Joseph		
	Le même		M. Mad. Lefebvre
			S.Tho. 1733
	Marie Marthe		Pierre Blanchet S.P.S.1763

CLOUTIER.

	Eustache			
	François			
	Alexis			
	Charles			
13	Gabriel		M. Fse. Toupin	
	Charlotte		Jos. Gosselin	S.P.S. 1760
	M. Françoise		Jos. Marie Letourneau	S.P.S. 1766
	Angélique		Chs. Bouchard "	1774
	Charles			
14	François	(5)	M. Anne Filion	S.Joa. 1752
	François			
15	Charles	(7)	Marg. Gravel	C.R 1721
	Louise		Etn. Réaume "	1751
	Charles			
16	Basile	(7)	Marie Moreau	S.L. 1735
	Pierre		M. Hélène Alaire	S.J. 1739
17	Zacharie	(9)	Agnés Bélanger	C.R. 1737
	Jean Baptiste			
18	Pierre Paul	(11)	Genev. Gaudreau	S.Tho. 1741
	Le même		Angé. Turcot	S.Fras. 1743
19	Pierre	(11)	Genev. Langelier	Islet 1746
	André			
20	Joseph	(12)	Marie Bussiére	S.P. 1747
21	Laurent	(12)	M. Genev. Boulet	S.Tho. 1751
	M. Angelique		Ant. Rousseau	S.P.S. 1781
	Marguerite		Pierre Gagné "	1797
	"		2° Olivier Jacq. Mondena	S.P.S. 1800
	Laurent			
	François			
22	François	(12)	Marie Morin "	1753
23	Jean Baptiste	(12)	Angé Blanchet "	1754
24	Alexis	(12)	M. Mad. Picard "	1766
25	Eustache	(12)	Eliz. Gagné "	1773
26	Michel		M. Angé Thibault	
	Pierre			
	Michel			
27	Charles	(12)	M. Marg. Bélanger	Cap. S.Ign. 1765
	Marie Pélagie		Jos. Fortier	S.H. 1785
	M. Elizabeth		Ant. Létourneau	S.P.S. 1795
28	Charles	(13)	M. Marthe Picard	S.P.S. 1765
	Marie Marthe		Louis Keroack "	1788
29	François	(14)	Marg. Faucher	S.F. 1780
30	Charles	(15)	Genev. Moreau	C.R. 1748
	Le même		Françoise Dion "	1760
	François			
31	François Noël		Cath. Peltier	
	M. Euphrosime		Jos. Blanchet	S.P.S. 1793
	François Noël			
32	Jean Baptiste (17)		Louise Gagnon	S.Anne 1774
	Jean			
33	André	(19)	M. Reine Morin	S.P.S. 1778
34	François	(21)	M. Louise Blanchet	S.P.S. 1777
35	Laurent	(21)	Marg. Vermet	S.H. 1792
	Angèle		Gervais Pepin	S.G. 1820
	Marguerite		Joseph Gagné	S.P.S. 1823
36	Michel	(26)	Charlotte Morin	Islet 1786
	Marguerite		Charles Bruneau	S.G. 1806
	"		2° François Lainé "	1822
	Marie		Marc Garant "	1806
	"		2° Jean Labbé "	1819
	Michel			
37	Pierre	(26)	Mad. Fortin	Islet 1786
	Marguerite		Jean Boulet	S.G. 1819
	Alexis			
	Ambroise			
38	François	(30)	Rose Réaume	C.R. 1799
	François			

CLOUTIER.

39	François Noël (31)		M. Judith Blanchet	S.P.S. 1799
	Euphrosine		Charles Leclaire "	1822
	François Noël			
40	Jean	(32)	Rose Simard	C.R. 1801
	Zacharie			
41	Michel	(36)	Vict. Gontier	S.G. 1813
42	Ambroise	(37)	Marie Geneviève	S.P.S 1818
43	Alexis	(37)	Marg. Goulet	S.G. 1820
44	François	(38)	M. Anne Noël	S.G. 1823
45	François Noël (39)		M. Gertrude Picard	S.P.S. 1827
	M. Philomène		Honoré Dion	S.Frs. 1861
46	Zacharie	(40)	Philomène Drouin	S.F. 1853
47	Joseph		Perpétue Girard	
	Joséphine		Louis Lefebvre	S.L. 1840
48	Jean		Marie Maranda	Q.
	Edouard			
49	Prisque		Josette Dufresne	
	Prisque			
50	Edouard	(48)	M. Esther Corriveau	S.V. 1846
51	Prisque	(49)	Emelie Gincherau	S. Frs. 1849

CLUSIAU.

1	Augustin		Marc. Lucas, Levis	
	Geneviève		François Dupile	S.P. 1799
	Marguerite		François Leclaire "	1811
	Joseph			
2	Joseph	(1)	M. Joseph Pculiot	S. Chs. 1792
	Joseph			
3	Joseph	(2)	Genev. Paradis	S.P. 1813
4	Joseph		Zoe Binet	
	M. Philomène		Jean Eliz. Audet	S.P. 1860

COCHON—LAVERDIÈRE.

1	Jacques		Jeanne Abraham	
	Jacques			
2	René		Charlotte Estole	
	René			
3	Jacques		Burte Delphine Tardif	S.R. 1661
	Jacques			
4	René		Anne Langlois	S.F. 1670
	Anne		Egn. Terrien	S.J. 1706
	Louis			
	René			
	François			
5	Jacques	(3)	Jeanne Verreau	S.R. 1703
	Joseph			
6	Louis	(4)	Cath. Dumas	S.J. 1688
	Véronique		Louis Plante "	1732
	Marguerite		Pierre Plante "	1726
	Joseph Marie			
	Louis			
	Pierre Noël			
7	René		Jeanne Dubeau	S.J. 1710
	Véronique		Jean Frs. Noël	S.V. 1733
	Agnés		Pierre Labbé "	1741
	M. Françoise		J. B. Labbé "	1744
	René			
	Henri			
8	François	(8)	Jeanne Plant	S.J. 1711
9	Joseph	(5)	Agnes Malbœuf	C.R. 1729
	Marie		Ant. Nadeau	S.H. 1732
	Madeleine		Julien Mercier	S.V. 1786
10	Louis	(6)	Cath. Marchand	S.J. 1732
	Geneviève		Jos. Drouin "	1755
	Louise		Pierre Gautron "	1755

COCHON—LAVERDIERE.

M. Catherine	J. B. Blouin	„	1773
M. Madeleine	Michel Clément S.M.		1773
François			
Joseph			
Louis			
Le même	Rose Coulombe	S.L.	1773
11 Joseph Marie (6)	M. Mad. Denis	B.	1738
Marie Josette	Pierre Tangué	S.V.	1759
Marguerite	Pierre Ferlant S.Chs.		1764
Joseph			
12 Pierre Noël (6)	Marie Le Roy	S.V.	1746
Françoise	Michel Quéret S.Chs.		1781
Marguerite	Jacq. Lavoie	„	1791
Charles			
Louis			
Joseph			
13 René (7)	M. Genev. Thebaut		
		S.M.	1744
Marie Josette	Joseph Roy	S.V.	1770
Marie	Joseph Couture	„	1780
14 Henri (7)	M. Ls. Loriaux ? Glorieux ?		
		S.V.	1761
M. Charlotte	Pierre Joncas	S.H.	1808
Louis Henri			
François			
15 Louis (10)	M. Jos. Guerard S.J.		1765
Marie Josette	Joseph Blouin	„	1788
Cécile	Joseph Giguère	„	1794
Marie Thécle	Antoine Fortier	„	1794
Marie Thécle	Laurent Marcoux	„	1818
Marie Louise	J. B. Giguère	„	1798
Angélique	Joseph Emond	„	1799
Angélique	2° François Turcot	„	1810
Madeleine	Martin Giguère	„	1801
Angéle	Louis Blouin	„	1808
Louis			
16 Joseph (10)	Marie Arseneau S.M.		1772
17 François (10)	Cath. Patry S.M.		1773
Catherine	Gab. Pichet	S.J.	1810
Marie	François Lefebvre S.J.		1815
Joseph			
Jean			
Le même	M. Jos. Demeule S.J.		1807
18 Joseph (11)	Françoise Roy	S.V.	1767
M. Clotilde	J. B. Boulet	S.M.	1796
Joseph			
19 Etienne (Laverdière)	Cath. Gontier S.Chs.		1775
Catherine	Ant. Gautron S.M.		1816
Etienne			
Le même	Marie Guillot	S.V.	1792
Marguerite	Ant. Balan	S.M.	1821
Louise	Joseph Lacroix	„	1821
Madeleine	Joseph Terrien	S.M.	1827
Marie	Ant. Thivierge	„	1837
Joseph			
20 Joseph	M. Agnés Beausoleil		
Marie	J. B. Chabot S.Chs.		1789
M. Elizabeth	Jean Marie Ruellan		
		S.M.	1792
21 Charles (12)	Marie Habran	S.V.	1783
Marie	Féréol Turgeon S.Chs.		1809
Barbe	Ant. Plante	„	1810
Barbe	2° Michel Marcoux	„	1832
Charles			
Jacques			
Noël			
Jean Baptiste			
Michel			
22 Joseph (12)	Marthe Marseau S.V.		1783
Marie Agathe	Godfroi Emond	„	1802
Le même	Genev. Coulombe	„	1789
Le même	M. Rose Fortin	„	1790
23 Louis (12)	Françoise Habran	„	1787
Françoise	J. B. Vermet	„	1810
Marguerite	François Fortier S.V.		1824

COCHON—LAVERDIERE.

Michei			
Augustin			
Louis			
Julien			
Jacques			
Isidore			
Olivier			
24 Louis Henri (14)	M. Hélène Deschamps		
		Levis	1795
Le même	M. Anne Clément S.V.		1798
25 François (14)	M. Victor Roy S.V.		1798
Marie Louise	Amb. Pelchat S.Chs.		1825
François			
Pierre			
Le même	Rose Aubé	S.G.	1813
26 Louis (15)	Marie Emond	S.J.	1794
Josette	Guill. Blouin	„	1819
Ursule	Jos. Guérard	„	1821
M. Archange	Jos. Pepin	„	1828
Jean Baptiste			
27 Joseph (17)	M. Jos. Labreqne S.L.		1794
Joseph			
28 Jean (17)	M.Cath. Lepage S.Frs.		1804
29 Louis	Marg. Ragagnon ?		
		S.V.	
Louis			
30 Joseph (18)	M. Reine Roy S.V.		1791
Reine	Etienne Roy	„	1820
Marie	Jacq. Bouten	„	1827
Julie	Pierre Fortier	„	1828
Françoise	Frs. Morin S.F.S.		1823
Joseph			
Jacques			
31 Etienne (19)	Genev. Boulet S.M.		1810
Marguerite	F. X. Blais	„	1832
M. Mélanie	Tho. Duquet	„	1839
Julie	Jacq. Bolduc	„	1842
Etn. Frédéric			
32 Joseph (19)	Marg. Turgeon S.M.		1823
33 Charles (21)	Eliz. Carbonneau S.G.		1808
34 Jacques (71)	Véronique Baillargeon S.Chs.		1813
M. François (1)	Chrysostome Roy	„	1831
Hermine	Etn. LeClaire	„	1831
35 Noël (21)	Angé. Pouliot	„	1821
36 Michel (21)	Veronique Daniau		
		S.G.	1823
37 Jean Baptiste (21)	Marie Pouliot S.Chs.		1825
38 Louis (23)	M.Marg.Blanchet		
		S.V.	1813
Adélaïde	M. Marg. Blanchet	„	1813
M. Hermine	Hilaire Masseau	„	1840
Esther	J. B. Thibaut	„	1841
Seraphine	Damase Thibaut	„	1850
Nazaire			
Damase			
39 Jacques (23)	M. Christine Buteau		
		Bert.	1824
40 Michel (23)	Marie Bonneau S.V.		1830
Philomène	Guill. Mercier	„	1857
Nazaire			
41 Augustin (23)	Marie Dupont S.M.		1833
42 Julien (23)	Marie Guilmet Bert.		1843
43 François (25)	Marg-Tangué S.Chs.		1819
Julie	Jos. Pouliot	„	1854
Olive	F. X. Pilote	„	1856
Michel			
Le même	Vict. Bisson	„	1842
Le même	M. Jos. Dorval	„	1851
Le même	Vict. Bourassa	„	1852
44 Pierre 25	Eliz. Pepin S. Chs.		1823
Julie	André Dupont	„	1841
Le même	Em. Baillargeon	„	1831
Emelie	Edouard Rousseau	„	1862
45 Jean Baptiste (26)	M. Archange Turcot		
		S.J.	1824

COCHON—LAVERDIERE.

	Henriette	Jos. Dompierre S.J. 1859
	Jean Baptiste	
46	Joseph	(27) M. Jos. Terrien S.J. 1826
	Joseph	
47	Louis	(29) Rose Pepin S.M. 1839
48	Joseph	(30) Marg. Bolduc S.V. 1821
	Désanges	Pierre Séverin Joncas
		S.V. 1849
	Henriette	Jean Brochu S.M. 1849
49	Jacques	(30) Marg. Baudouin S.F.S.1833
50	Etn. Frédéric(31)	M. Marthe Audet S.M.1841
	Le même	Restitut Bilodeau Bert.
		1844
51	Pierre	Clarisse Fradet
	Le même	M. Alvine Cameron B. 1853
52	Damase	(38) Genev. Rochet S.V. 1855
53	Nazaire	(38) M. Tharsile Roy S.V.1842
54	Nazaire	(40) M. Césarie Pigeon S.V.1856
55	Isidore	Charlotte Blais
	M. Cédulie	Ludger Marseau S.V. 1868
56	Michel	(43) Léocadie Roy S.Chs. 1856
57	Jean Baptiste(45)	Sophie Dalaire S.Frs. 1856
58	Joseph	(46) Adé Langlois S.J. 1856
59	Isidore	(23) M. Chs. Blais S.P.S. 1820
	Marie Cédulie	Ludger Marseau S.V. 1868
60	Olivier	(23) Clotilde Picard S.P.S. 1838

COLLARD.

	Thomas	Marie Louise Crépin
1	Thérèse	Henri Avare S.P. 1844
	Jean	
	Le même	M. Félicité Jobidon
		S.P. 1825
2	Jean	(1) Eliz. Aubin S.P. 1840

COLLET.

1	Alix	Marie Mau Ev. de Lyon
	François	
2	François	(1) M.Marg. Tangué S.V 1762
	Marie	Jos. Bacquet ,, 1820
	Josette	François Leclaire S. Chs.
		1794
	M. Geneviève	Jos. Marie Gaulin
		S.F.S. 1800
	Denis	
	François	
3	Denis	(2) Marie Leclaire S.Chs. 1792
	Denis	
	Joseph	
	Le même	Genev. Couture S.H. 1815
4	François	(2) Ursule Duquet S.Chs. 1794
	Marguerite	Alexis Coulombe ,, 1821
	Marie	Pierre Nolin ,, 1824
5	Charles	(3) Rosalie Genest S.H. 1830
		Soulange Bélanger
6	Joseph	(3) S.H. 1820
7	Denis	(3) Marg. Clément S.H. 1820

COMEAU

1	Amand	Marie Coulombe,
		Bert. 1767
	Le même	M. Anne Taillon
		S. Chs. 1772
	Marie Anne	Louis Pénin ,, 1800
	Geneviève	Frs. Brisson ,, 1806
	Victoire	Louis Terrien S.M. 1821
	Joseph	
	Jean Baptiste	
	Le même	Marie Louise Jacques
		S.F.S 1806
2	Amand	Marie Babineau
	Marie	Aug. Lacroix S.Chs. 1783

COMEAU.

3	Joseph	(1) Agathe(Pénen) S.Chs.
		1801
	Marguerite	Abraham Marseau
		S.Chs. 1849
	Joseph	
4	Jean Baptiste	Marie Jos. Mercier
		S. Chs. 1807
5	Joseph	M. Marth. Pepin
		S. Chs. 1823

CORNELIER—GRANDCHAMP.

1	Pierre	Marie Certain
	Cécile	Charles Dubé S.F. 1721
	Pierre	
2	Pierre	(1) Marie Louise Lehoux
		S.F. 1720
	Geneviève	Michel Morin ,, 1757
	Thérèse	Jacq. Turcot ,, 1762
	Marie Anne	Jean Leclaire ,, 1764
	Pierre	
	Jean Baptiste	
3	Pierre	(2) Agathe Leclaire S.P. 1752
4	Jean Baptiste	(2) M. Thérèse Gertrude
		Beaucher S.F. 1763
	Thérèse	Chs. Loiseau S.F. 1792

CORRIVEAU.

1	Etienne	Catherine Bureau S.F.1669
	Jacques	
	Etienne	
	Pierre	
	Guillaume	
2	Jacques	(1) Fse. Gaboury S.M. 1693
	M. Angélique	Jacques Badeau Q. 1725
	Jacques	
	Le même	M. Mad. Larcheveque
		Q. 1728
3	Etienne	(1) Louise Fse. Gaboury
		S.M. 1700
	Le même	Jeanne Rabouin S.F. 1703
	Madeleine	Philippe Martineau
		S.V. 1727
	Geneviève	Pierre Allaire ,, 1733
	Marguerite	Aug. Marceau ,, 1737
	Marie Anne	Louis Canuel ,, 1741
	Jacques	
	Jean-Baptiste	
	Etienne	
	Pierre	
4	Pierre	(1) Anne Gaboury S.M. 1702
	Anne Louis	Etienne Veau S.V. 1724
	Marguerite	Louis Terrien ,, 1726
	Joseph	
	Le même	Ambroise Fournier
		S.V. 1741
5	Guillaume	(2) Marie Rémillard S.M. 1709
	Marie	Joseph Hélie S.V. 1727
	M. Susanne	Aug. Boulet ,, 1733
6	Jean	Françoise Hélie (1)
	Marguerite	Ignace Isabel S.V. 1738
	Marie	Antoine Blais ,, 1743
	Marie	2°Louis Labrecque ,, 1771
	Marie Anne	(2) François Caron ,, 1753
	Geneviève	Charles Pouliot ,, 1761
	Angélique	François Bacquet ,, 1762
	François	
7	Jacques	(2) Marie Buteau S.V. 1724
	Catherine	Pierre Pacaud S.V. 1761
	(1) Epouse e n	
	2° noce	J. B. Monmeny
	M. Basilisse	Jos. Gaboury S.V. 1761
	M. Basilisse	2° André Poiré ,, 1785
	Jean Guillaume	
	Pierre Simon	

CORRIVEAU.

Joseph
Paschal
Jacques
8 Jacques (3) Ange Gautron S.V. 1747
9 Pierre (3) M. Eliz. Fortin
　　　　　　　Cap. S. Ign. 1751
　M. Elizabeth 　Charles Bruneau S.V. 1772
　Marie Louise 　Etienne Blais　 ,, 1785
　Théotiste 　　François Roy　 ,, 1791
　Etienne
10 Jean Baptiste 　M. Brigitte Clouet ,, 1754
　Marie 　　　　Ignace Veau　 ,, 1779
　Jean Baptiste
11 Etienne (3) M.Genev. DalaireS.M.1755
　Marie Josette 　Pierre Bolduc　 ,, 1771
12 Joseph (4) M. Fse Bolduc S. Jos. 1727
　Josette 　　 Charles Bouchard S.V.1749
　Josette 　　 2° Louis Dodier ,, 1761
13 François (6) Eliz. Courteau　 ,, 1747
14 Jacques (7) Louise Jeanne Dupéré
　　　　　　　　　　　　Bert. 1752
　M. Angélique 　Jos. Roberge S.V. 1783
　Marie Louise 　Jacq. Clément S.V. 1784
　Basile
　Charles
　Michel
　Jacques
　Le même 　　M. Genev. Falardeau
　　　　　　　　　　　　S.V. 1783
　M. Françoise 　J. B. Tangué　 ,, 1803
　Marguerite 　 Frs Guilmet　 ,, 1820
15 Joseph (7) M. Jos. Tangué S.V. 1754
　M. Angélique 　Amb. Goulet　 ,, 1787
　Joseph
　Louis
　Thomas
　Le même 　　M. Rose Roy S.V. 1773
　Elizabeth 　　Pierre Gautron ,, 1791
　Marie Cécile 　Paul Gourgue ,, 1803
　M. Basilisse 　Raphael Tangué ,, 1813
　Marie 　　　 Ant. Fleury S.V. 1815
　Isidore
　Antoine
16 Paschal (7) Eliz. Bélanger S.V. 1760
　M. Elizabeth 　Frs. Gagné Bert. 1791
　Marie Josette 　J. B. Blais　 ,, 1801
　Reine 　　　 Michel Blais　 ,, 1804
　Marie Reine 　Jos. Morceau　 ,, 1794
　Marie Reine 　2°Jacq. Baudouin S.J.1822
　Jacq. Prisque
　Paschal
17 Pierre Simon 　Mad. Blais Bert. 1766
　Le même 　　M.Chas. Tangué S.V. 1769
　M. Françoise 　Hyacinthe Rémillard
　　　　　　　　　　　　S.V. 1796
　M. Victoire 　 J. B. Corriveau ,, 1796
　M. Victoire 　 2° Frs. Parant　 ,, 1815
　Marie 　　　 Pierre Denis S.M. 1787
　Marie Josette 　Jos. Lemelin　 ,, 1796
　M. Catherine 　J. B. Fradet　 ,, 1800
　M. Basilisse 　Michel Goupy　 ,, 1800
　M. Barbe 　　Pierre Goupy　 ,, 1803
　Marguerite 　 Jos. Paquet　 ,, 1803
　Madeleine 　 Jacq. Fleury　 ,, 1810
　Simon
　Etienne
　Le même 　　Josette Lacroix ,, 1789
　Bénoni
　Joseph
18 Jean Guill- (7) M. Genev. Gagnon
　aume 　　　　　　　　　　S.M. 1768
　Le même 　　M.Fse Bruneau S.V. 1773
　Marie Anne 　Antoine Harpe　 ,, 1803
　M. Catherine 　J. B. Blouin　 ,, 1803
　Françoise 　　J. B. Harpe　 ,, 1803
　Joseph

CORRIVEAU.

　Louis
　Guillaume
19 Etienne (9) M. Cath. Boivin S.V. 1785
20 JeanBaptiste(10) M. Vict. Corriveau
　　　　　　　　　　　　S.V. 1796
21 Jacques (14) Thérèse Nadeau
　　　　　　　　　　　　S. Chs. 1781
22 Basile (14) M. Joseph Hélie S.V. 1785
　Marie Louise 　Jacq. Roy S.V. 1803
　Marie Louise 　Michel Veau　 ,, 1804
23 Michel (14) M. Anne Fortier S.M. 1793
　Marie 　　　 Frs. Couture S.Chs. 1821
　Marie 　　　 Guill. Turgeon S.G. 1823
　Angèle 　　 Louis Bouffard S.L. 1829
　Marguerite 　Ant. Forgues B. 1832
　Abraham
　Basile
　Bénoni
　Michel
　Le même 　　Marie Marseau S.L. 1829
24 Charles (14) Ange Tangué S.G. 1797
　Geneviève 　 Ls. Gangné　 ,, 1826
　M. Françoise 　Clément Royer S.Chs. 1827
　M. Marguerite 　Jacq. Boutin　 ,, 1833
　Angélique 　 Louis Boutin S.V. 1817
　Charles
　Le même 　　Marie Quéret S.G. 1794
25 Pierre 　　 Louise Demeule
　Louise 　　 Louis Boutin S.G. 1794
26 Joseph (15) M. Jos. Roy S.V. 1785
　Marie Josette 　Michel Maurice ,, 1816
　Pierre
　Joseph
　Alexis
27 Louis (15) Marthe Gosselin
　　　　　　　　　　　　S.Chs. 1734
　Le même 　　M. Ls. Morisset S.H. 1796
　Nicolas
28 Isidore (15) Cécile Roy S.V. 1796
　Marie Cécile 　Raphael Tangué　 ,, 1816
　Marie Josette 　J. B. Thibaut　 ,, 1827
　M. Marguerite 　Jos. Boutin　 ,, 1830
　Pierre
　François-Xavier
　Thomas
　Le même 　　M. Fse. Baudouin
　　　　　　　　　　　　S.V. 1817
　Marie Louise 　André Langlois S.V. 1839
　Marie Esther 　Ed. Cloutier　 ,, 1841
　Marie Louise 　J. B. Bouton　 ,, 1848
　Alexis
29 Thomas (15) Marg. Brousseau S.V.1790
30 Antoine (15) 　Génev. Baillargeon
　　　　　　　　　　　　S.G. 1816
31 Jacq. Prisque(16) M. Ursule Carbonneau
　　　　　　　　　　　　Bert. 1787
　Rosalie 　　 Frs. Chrétien Bert. 1819
　Marie Luce 　Frs. Mercier　 ,, 1824
　M. Marguerite 　Jos. Boutin S.V. 1822
　François
　Jean
32 Paschal (16) Reine Chartier Bert. 1793
　Marie 　　　 Jacq. Bélanger S.G. 1819
　Reine 　　　 Ign. Quéret　 ,, 1824
　Paschal
　Pierre
33 Simon (17) Mad. Mercier S.M. 1799
　Madeleine 　 Jean Racine　 ,, 1821
　René
　Pierre
　Simon
34 Etienne (17) Marg. Couture S.G. 1813
35 Joseph (17) Marg. Gendron S.M. 1814
36 Bénoni (17) Louise Couture S.G. 1816

CORRIVEAU.

#	Name	(p)	Spouse		
37	Joseph	(18)	M. Marg. Tangué	S.V.	1797
	Marguerite		Jos. Gagnon	S.V.	1821
	Adélaide		Jean Herpe	"	1832
	Marie Angéle		J. B. Quemeneur	S.M.	1839
	Benoni				
	Joseph				
38	Guillaume	(18)	Marg. Rouillard	S.M.	1797
	M. Marguerite		Michel Dessaint	"	1821
	Géneviève		Joseph Bacquet	"	1829
	Géneviève		2° Jean Forgues	"	1861
	Adélaide		Joseph Bacquet	"	1851
	François				
	Guillaume				
	Joseph				
	Frédéric				
39	Louis		M. Cécile Roy	S.V.	1803
	Cécile		Jean Roy	"	1823
	Emérentienne		Ign. Létourneau	"	1839
	Louis				
	François-Xavier				
	Jean Baptiste				
40	Michel	(23)	Judith Dalaire	S.G.	1818
41	Bénoni	(23)	Génev. Bisson	S.Chs.	1826
42	Abraham	(23)	Mad. Bouffard	S.L.	1830
43	Basile	(23)	Apolline Bouffard	S.L.	1836
44	Charles	(24)	Archange Dalaire	S.Chs.	1828
45	Pierre	(26)	Marie Bolduc	S.V.	1812
	Marie Emelie		Elise Dangueur	"	1842
	M. Marguerite		Jean Mercier	"	1843
	Hermine		Frs. Audet	"	1846
	Olivier				
	Pierre				
	Michel				
	Frs. Anaclet				
46	Joseph	(26)	Marg. Turgeon	S.G.	1820
47	Alexis	(26)	M. Euphrosine Dorval	S.F.S.	1820
49	Louis	(27)	Marg. Boutin	S.G.	1816
50	Thomas	(28)	Marcelline Théberge	S.F.S.	1831
51	Frs Xavier	(28)	M. Dina Patry	B.	1835
	François Xavier				
	Le même		Emérence Beaucher	B.	1839
52	Pierre	(28)	Marie Bouffart	S.V.	1838
53	Alexis	(28)	Desanges Lainé	"	1850
54	François	(31)	Cécile Lavoie	Bert.	1816
55	Jean	(31)	M. Angèle Nadeau	Bert.	1818
56	Pierre	(32)	Thérèse Tanguè	S.V.	1819
	Thérèse		Hubert Habar	Bert.	1846
	Paschal				
	Le même		Marcelline Bacquet	S.G.	1828
57	Paschal	(32)	Cath. Cameron	S.G.	1825
58	René	(33)	M. AngéGagnon	S.M.	1824
	Jean				
	Pierre				
59	Pierre	(33)	Sophie Gagnon	S.M.	1828
	Pierre				
	Le même		Adé Gourgue	S.M.	1835
	Adélaïde		Telesphore Roy	"	1862
60	Simon	(33)	Marg. Chamberlan	S.M.	1829
61	Joseph	(37)	M. Fse Cagnon	S.M.	1821
	Pierre				
62	Bénoni	(37)	Marg. Gagnon	S.M.	1840
63	Guillaume	(38)	Louise Morisset	"	1819
64	François	(38)	Angèle Couillard	B.	1825
	Soulange		Flavien Golet	S.L.	1847
65	Joseph	(38)	Angé Bacquet	S.M.	1841
66	Frédéric	(38)	M. Marg. Mercier	S.M.	1854

CORRIVEAU.

#	Name	(p)	Spouse		
67	Louis	(39)	M. Marg. Marseau	S.V.	1827
	Damase				
	Le même		Adé Herpe	S.V.	1839
68	Frs Xavier	(39)	Flavie Dessaint	S.F.S.	1830
	Flavie Adéline		Etn. Frédéric Blais	S.V.	1857
	M. Malvina		Théodore Catelier	S.V.	1862
	Joseph Léger				
	Ferdinand				
69	JeanBaptiste	(39)	Perpétue Dessaint	S.F.S.	1837
	Délima		Eusébé Roy	S.V.	1860
	Délima		2° Jacq. Lainé	"	1866
	Malvina		Prudent Blais	"	1865
	Perpétue		Benoni Buteau	"	1866
	M. Poméla		Piérre Catellier	"	1866
	M. Valine		Uldéric Fortin	"	1870
	M. Mathilde		Stanislas Roy	"	1870
	Louis Nazaire				
	Octave				
	Elzéar				
	Philéas				
70	Michel	(45)	Sophie Boutin	S.V.	1848
71	Frs Anaclet	(45)	Emélie Helie	"	1848
	Delphine		Jacq. Bacquet	"	1870
72	Olivier	(45)	M. Marcelline Bolduc	S.M.	1850
73	Pierre	(45)	Archange Helie	S.V.	1857
74	Nicolas	(27)	Brigitte Lacroix	S.G.	1828
75	Frs Xavier	(51)	M. Eliza Turgeon	B.	1857
76	Paschal	(56)	Zoé Baudouin	S.V.	1853
77	Jean	(58)	M. Belzemire Letellier	S.M.	1856
78	Pierre	(58)	M. Mathilde Bacquet	S.M.	1856
79	Pierre	(59)	Julie Helie	S.M.	1853
80	Pierre	(61)	M. Fse Roy	S.M.	1840
	Le même		Anne Bacquet	S.M.	1847
81	Damase	(67)	Marcelline Brochu	S.V.	1846
82	Ferdinand	(68)	Sophie Talbot	S.V.	1854
83	Jos. Ludger	(68)	M. Philomène Catellier	S. V.	1863
84	LouisNazaire	(69)	Eulalie Roy	S.V.	1801
85	Octave	(69)	Flore Bolduc	"	1867
86	Elzéar	(69)	Marcelline Fleury	"	1869
87	Philéas	(69)	Sara Lamare	"	1870
88	Paschal	(69)	Sophie Audet		
	Le même		Marcelline Vien	S.Chs.	1860

COTÉ.

#	Name	(p)	Spouse		
1	Jean		Anne Martin	Q.	1635
	Simone		Pierre Soumande	"	1649
	Louise		Jean Grignon	"	1663
	Louise				
	Martin				
	Mathieu				
	Noël				
	Jean				
2	Louis	(1)	Eliz. Langlois	Q.	1667
	Madeleine		Louis Lemieux	Cap.S.Ign.	1682
	Louis				
3	Jean	(1)	Anne Couture	Q.	1667
	Jean Baptiste				
	Noel				
	Guillaume				
	Pierre				
	Le même		Genev. Verdon	Q.	1686
	Marie		André Allier	"	1733
	M. Charlotte		Francois Tinon	S.P.	1705
	Geneviève		Louis Boissel	A.G.	1709

COTÉ.

Joseph
Jean
Ignace
Gabriel

4	Martin	(1)	Susanne Pagé	C.R.	1667
	Marie		Guill. Couture	S.P.	1691
	Elizabeth		Pierre Pichet	"	1703
	Marguerite		André Parent	"	
	Marguerite		2° Noël Marcoux, Beauport		
	Pierre		·		1701
	Jean				
5	Noël		Hélène Graton		
	Louise		Annette Jaladon	S.P.	1698
	Anne		François Posé	"	1710
	Jacques				
	Augustin				
6	Mathieu	(1)	Eliz. Gravel		1669
	M. Charlotte		François Gosselin	S.P.	1688
	Marie Anne		Louis Pichet	"	1710
	Mathieu				
	Pierre Mathieu				
	Martin				
7	Louis	(2)	Génév. Bernier	Cap. S.Ign.	1691
	Joseph				
	Paul				
	Isidore				
	Joseph				
	Jean				
8	Jean Baptiste	(3)	Françoise Choret	S.P.	1695
	Seignuer de l'Isle Verte				
9	Noël	(3)	M. Mad. Drouin	S.F.	1696
	Pierre				
10	Pierre	(3)	M. Chs. Rondeau	S.P.	1707
	Ursule		Louis Langlois	"	1735
	Augustin				
11	Guillaume		Clotilde Amelot	L.	1719
12	Joseph	(3)	Thérèse Huot	A.G.	1711
	Joseph				
	Le même		Jeanne Roussin	A.G.	1730
	Gabriel				
13	Jean	(3)	Mad. Huot	A.G.	1716
	Ignace				
14	Ignace	(3)	Véronique Hébert	A.G.	1733
	Marie		Jacq. Poliquin	S. Chs.	1751
	Véronique		J. B. Valière	"	1757
	Angélique		Joseph Goulet	"	1775
	Thècle		Etienne Turgeon	"	1775
	Thècle		2° Joseph Carrier	Q.	1797
	Joseph				
	Louis				
	Augustin				
15	Gabriel		Cecile Gosselin	Q.	1739
16	Jean		M. Anne Langlois	Beauport	1694
	Marie Anne		Louis Pichet	S.P.	1710
	M. Madeleine		Charles Roberge	"	1720
	Marie Thérèse		Jean Leclaire	"	1720
	Marie Hélène		François Leclaire	Q.	1732
	Marie Louise		Charles Lerreau	Q.	1740
	Pierre				
	Jean				
17	Pierre		Marie Baillargeon	S.P.	1707
	Madeleine		Augustin Dupile	S.P.	1748
	Ursule		François Paradis	"	1749
	Joseph				
18	Jacques	(5)	Mad. Rondeau	S.P.	1706
19	Augustin	(5)	M. Mad. Baillargeon	S.L.	1720
	Marie Josette		J. B. Rousseau	S.P.	1751
	Marie Josette		2° Jean Godbout	S.L.	1762
	M. Madeleine		Ign. Leclaire	S.P.	1748
	François				
	Joseph				
	Pierre				

COTÉ.

20	Martin	(6)	Marg. Ferlant	S.P.	1698
	Marguerite		Joseph Lacasse	B.	1740
	Jean Francois				
	Etienne				
	Michel				
	Louis				
	Jean				
21	Pierre Mathieu	(6)	Genev. Ferlant	S.P.	1707
	Marie Anne		Pierre Coulombe	"	1739
	Madeleine		J. B. Poulet	"	1740
	Marie Josette		Louis Goulet	"	1740
	Geneviève		Charles Dorval	"	1746
	Joseph				
22	Mathieu	(6)	Françoise Dupile	S.P.	1710
	Pierre				
23	Joseph	(7)	Eliz. Couillard	S.Tho.	1716
24	Joseph	(7)	Marg. Couillard	B.	1726
25	Isidore	(7)	M. Génév. Bouchard		
	Thérèse		Germ. Morin	S.P.S.	1760
	Joseph				
	Jean Baptiste				
	Le même		M. Anne Bacon	S.P.S.	1758
26	Jean	(7)	Marthe Fortin	Cap S.Ign.	1729
	Jean Baptiste				
27	Paul	(7)	Genev. Langlois	S.Tho.	1734
	Véronique		Charles Couillard	"	1761
	Joseph				
28	Pierre	(9)	Dorothée Marseau	S.Frs.	1720
	Dorothée		J. B. Bonneau	S.P.	1743
	M. Angélique		Michel Emond	"	1753
	Jean Marie				
	Antoine				
	Joseph				
	Jacques				
29	Augustin	(10)	M. Jos. Chabot	S.P.	1764
	M. Angélique		Ant. Couture	"	1788
30	Joseph	(12)	Anne Jobidon	C.R.	1740
	Michel				
A	Gabriel	(12)	Hélène Pichet	S.P.	1768
31	Ignace	(13)	M. Jos. Paradis	"	1753
	Marie Josette		François Hébert	A.G.	1782
	Marie Josette		2° Charles Fortier	S.J.	1794
	Le même		Mad. Riopel	A.G.	1758
	Madeleine		Jean Huot	"	1783
	Joseph				
32	Louis	(14)	M. Angé. Valière	S.Chs.	1757
	Marie		Pierre Vincent	"	1782
	Marie Anne		Joseph Leclaire	"	1785
	Louis				
	Le même		Marie Noël	S.M.	1770
	Angélique		Jacques Schink	S.Chs.	1791
	Le même		M. Ls. Bruneau	S.V.	1775
	Marie Josette		Augustin Nadeau	S.Chs.	1804
	Marie Louise		Jacques Blais	"	1805
	Abraham				
	Joseph				
33	Augustin	(14)	M.Jos. Couture	S.Chs.	1762
	Marguerite		Paschal Gendron	"	1789
	Ignace				
	Jean				
	Louis				
34	Joseph	(14)	Marie Turgeon	S.M.	1768
	Joseph				
	Jean Baptiste				
	Louis				
	Le même		Cath. Côté	S.Chs.	1797
	Le même		Angé. Guay	B.	1817
35	Jean	(16)	Genev. Trépanier	C.R.	1721
36	Pierre	(16)	Marg. Délage	S.L.	1726
	Marie Louise		André Provost	S.P.	1769
	Geneviève		François Crépeau	"	1769

COTÉ.

Marguerite			
Joseph			
Pierre	J. B. Langlois	„	1769
37 Joseph	(17) Marie Paradis	S P.	1750
Thérèse	Amb. Leclaire	„	1765
Thérèse	2° Gab. Rouleau	„	1777
Marie Josette	Louis Pichet	„	1774
Marie	Germ. Ratté	„	1779
Geneviève	Pierre Roberge	„	1787
Angélique	François Hallé	„	1810
Pierre			
Joseph			
38 François	Hélène Thivierge		
Louis			
Jean Baptiste			
39 Claude	M. Genev. Baudouin	Q.	1728
Charles Claude			
40 François	(19) Agnès Rousseau	S.L.	1751
François			
41 Pierre	(19) Genev. Godbout	S.L.	1762
42 Joseph	(19) Thérèse Dorval	„	1763
Joseph			
Jean			
François			
43 Jean Baptiste(20)	M. Ls. Bouffart	S.L.	1733
Marie	Laurent Gosselin	S.Chs.	1757
Geneviève	François Guénet	„	1759
Thérèse	Claude Drapeau	„	1762
Louise	Jean Baillargeon	„	1767
M. Josette	Amb. Coulombe	„	1780
44 JeanFrançois(20)	M. Cath. Paquet	S.L.	1737
Marie	Chas. Provost	S.Chs.	1764
Catherine	Gab. Renaud	„	1769
Catherine	2° Joseph Côté	„	1797
Marie Josette	Augustin Tangué	„	1775
François			
45 Etienne	(20) Marie Gontier	B.	1739
Joseph			
46 Louis	(20) M. Ls. Béchard	B.	1741
47 Michel	(20) Eliz. Gontier	„	1747
François			
48 Joseph	(21) Marie Baudon	S.P.	1735
Jean Baptiste			
49 Pierre	(22) Josette Charlan	S.F.	1734
50 Joseph	(25) Véronique Mathieu	S.P.S.	1770
Monique	Aug. Proulx	„	1798
Thérèse	Jacq. Campbell	„	1802
Jean Baptiste			
Joseph			
François			
Isidore			
Etienne			
51 JeanBaptiste(25)	M.Anne Blouin	S.P.S.	1771
Geneviève	Jacq. Talbot	„	1798
Marie Anne	Jacq. Bernier	„	1800
JeanPaul Isidore			
52 JeanBaptiste(26)	M. Marthe Boulet	S.Tho.	1751
Augustin			
53 Joseph	(27) Eliz. Bélanger	S.Tho.	1767
Joseph			
54 François	Genev. Plante		
Marie Françoise	Frs. Noël	S.P.	1780
Agathe	J. B. Paradis	„	1781
Thècle	Pierre Noël Fortier	„	1784
Angélique	Jacq. Gourdeau	„	1787
Jean Baptiste			
Gabriel			
François			
55 Jean Marie	(28) Marie Marthe Ruel	S.L.	1747
56 Joseph	(28) Marie Thècle Emond	S.Frs.	1753

COTÉ.

Marie Françoise	Frs. Dupuis	S.H.	1783
Marie Charlotte	Ls. Lacasse	„	1790
Marie Louise	Pierre Noël Quemeneur	S.H.	1795
Marie Angélique	Jos. Boutin	S.V.	1798
Marie Anne	Pierre Fortier	„	1799
Michel			
Le même	Marie Suzor	S.Chs.	1791
Le même	Marie Eliz.Hélie	S.H.	1801
57 Antoine	(28) Marie Ange Terrien	S.J.	1757
Antoine			
58 Jacques	Marg. Gendron	S.F.S.	1762
Marguerite	Jos. Morin	S.H.	1787
Marie Geneviève	Jean Baptiste Cantin	S.H.	1791
Madeleine	Ls. Curadeau	„	1801
Jean Marie			
Augustin			
Jacques			
Ambroise			
59 Michel	(30) Brigitte Thibaut	S.Aug.	
Jean Bte.			
60 Joseph	(31) Marie Huot	A.G.	1811
Ignace			
61 Louis	(32) Marie Vincent	S.G.	1784
Bonaventure			
Louis			
62 Joseph	(32) Genev. Forgue	S.M.	1808
63 Abraham	(32) Marie Fse. Tangué	S.Chs.	1808
Françoise	Pierre Inconnu	„	1830
64 Ignace	(33) Genev. Dalaire	B.	1791
Marie	Chs. Auclair	S.Henri	1820
Ignace			
Louis			
65 Louis	(33) Fse. Pilote	S.Henri	1798
Angèle	Philippe Pelchat	S.G.	1821
Louise	Jos. Boulet	„	1823
Archange	Chs. Pouliot	„	1821
66 Jean	(33) Marie Anne Gautron	S.H.	1806
67 Louis	Genev. Carrier		
Le même	Thérèse Pouqueville	S. Marie	1776
Marie	J.Bte. Simoneau	S.H.	1805
Amable			
Jacques			
68 Joseph	(34) Genev. Claisse	B.	1790
69 Louis	(34) Louise Munro	„	1793
Françoise	Chs. Tangué	„	1816
Le même	Marie Ls. Turgeon	S.M.	1803
Luce	J. Bte. Hélie	B.	1829
Luce	2° Benoni Roy	„	1836
Bénoni			
Thomas			
70 JeanBaptiste(34)	Marie Chs. Munro	B.	1794
Marie	Nic. Pouliot	„	1824
Pierre			
Jean Baptiste			
George			
François Xavier			
71 Pierre	(36) Marg. Barbel	S.P.	1752
72 Joseph	(36) Thérèse Ferland	„	1765
Thérèse	Ign. Paquet	„	1786
Angélique	Basile Thivierge	S.P.	1792
Madeleine	Frs. Simard	„	1794
Marie Josette	Barth. Paquet	„	1803
Joseph			
73 Joseph	Marie Fse. Morin		
Jean Marie			
Paul			
74 Joseph	(37) Marie Reine Crépeau	S.P.	1793
Scolastique	Jacq. Roberge	„	1833

COTÉ.

COTÉ.

	Euphrosine	Frs. Régis Roberge	S.P.	1836
	Charles			
75	Pierre	(37) Thérèse Roberge	„	1803
76	Louis	(38) Charlotte Normand	S.Tho.	1775
	Le même	Véronique Cornelier	S.Tho.	1781
	Alexis			
77	JeanBaptiste(38)	Marie Roger Aubin	S.Tho.	1793
	François			
78	Charles	(39) Eliz. Proulx	„	1754
	Claude			
	Marie Madeleine	Ls. Roy	S.Michel	1794
79	François	(40) Fse. Morisset	S.M.	1774
	Marie Françoise	Pierre Dupont	„	1804
	Jean			
	François			
	Abel			
80	Louis	Angé Lacasse		
	Antoine			
81	Joseph	(42) Marg. Gosselin	S.Lr.	1790
	Cécile	Ant. Rouleau	„	1824
	Marguerite	Etn. Paradis	„	1842
	Antoine			
	Joseph			
82	Jean	(42) Marg. Godbout	S.G.	1794
	Jean			
	Noël			
	Joseph			
	Etienne			
83	François	(42) Marie Ls. Brisson	S.M.	1794
	Louise	Chs. Lecours	S.G.	1823
	Françoise	Isaac Filion	„	1830
84	François	(44) Louis Nadeau	S.Chs.	1768
	Joseph			
	Le même	Marie Hélène Tangué	S.M.	1778
	Marie	Clément Bisson	S.Chs.	1800
	Catherine	Alexis Couture	„	1803
	Angélique	Chs. Pouliot	„	1809
	Angélique	2° Michel Roy	„	1812
	Le même	Cath. Boissel	„	1798
85	Joseph	(45) Eliz. Lemelin	S.M.	1778
	Marie	Pierre Noël Brisson	„	1796
	Geneviève	André Bacquet	„	1812
	Louis			
	Joseph			
86	François	(47) Marie Ls. Proulx	S. Chs.	1775
	Joseph			
	Le même	Marg. Balan	S.M.	1788
	Josette	Jos. Blais	„	1823
87	JeanBaptiste(48)	Marie Ls. Turgeon	„	1767
	Louise	Chs. Couture	S.Chs.	1787
	Elizabeth	Michel Gagnon	„	1802
	Etienne			
	Jean			
	Pierre			
88	Joseph	(50) MarieLs.Gagné	S.P.S.	1801
	Marie Josette	J. Bte. Harnais	„	1823
	Sophie	Thomas Blais	„	1828
	Julie	Jos. Simoneau	„	1834
	Césarie	Benj. Blais	„	1838
89	François	(50) Marie Genev. Lefebvre	S.Tho.	1802
	Marie Flavie	Ls. Langlois	S.P.S.	1827
90	Isidore	(50) Véronique Mercier	S. Tho.	1811
	Marie Rose	Frs.-X. Bouchard	S.P.S.	1835
91	Étienne	(50) Josette Coulombe	S. Tho.	1812
	Olive	Frs.-Xavier Caron	S.P.S.	1838

92	JeanBaptiste(50)	Félicité Roy	S. Valier	1815
93	Jean Paul	(51) Marie Thérèse Talon		
	Isidore		S.P.S.	1793
	Thérèse	Etn. Proulx	„	1820
	Françoise	Pierre Poitras	„	1837
	Chs. Théophile			
94	Augustin	(52) Angé. Joncas	S.Tho.	1784
	Geneviève	Jos. Gagné	„	1812
	Augustin			
95	Joseph	(53) Eliz. Fournier	„	1788
	Elizabeth	Ls. Gaumont	„	1813
	Le même	Marie Marg. Morin	„	1811
96	François	(54) Mad. Fortier	S.Pierre	1798
	Marie	Ls. Vermet	„	1801
	Hélène	Gab. Bureau	„	1808
	Marie	Aug. Nolin	„	1817
	Thècle	Jean Marie Audibert	S. Jean	1812
	Euphrosine	Jean Roger	„	1822
	Augustin			
	François			
97	JeanBaptiste(54)	Mad. Rouleau	S.Pierre	1794
	Pierre			
98	Gabriel	(54) Genev. Prémont	S.Frs.	1798
99	Antoine	(57) Marie Genev. Bilodeau	S.Henri	1783
	Le même	Marie Alaire	„	1785
	Marie	Etn. Guillot	„	1814
	Marie Anne	Chs. Maranda	„	1820
100	Antoine	Génev. Couillard		
	Marie	Chs. Tremblay	S. Henri	1804
	Marie Victoire	Aug. Verieul	„	1808
	Marie Louise	Jean Frs. Martin	„	1819
	Marguerite	Jos. Bouchard	S.Tho.	1820
101	Ambroise	(58) Marie Thècle Pichet	S. Pierre	1795
	Marie Thècle	Etn. Roberge	S.Henri	1816
102	Jacques	(58) Rosalie Boulet	„	1806
103	Augustin	(58) Marg. Pepin	„	1810
104	Jean Marie	(58) Susanne Cantin	„	1813
105	JeanBaptiste(59)	Josette Thibaudeau	Cap Santé	1809
	Le même	Marie Marchand	Grondines	1838
106	Ignace	(60) Ange Drouin	S.F.	1838
107	Louis	(61) Genev. Hélie	S.G.	1793
108	Bonaventure(61)	Marg. Leclaire	„	1819
109	Ignace	(64) Marg. Fortier	S. Henri	1814
110	Louis	(64) Fse. Blais	„	1818
111	Jacques	(67) Marie Ls. Dubois	„	1807
112	Amable	(67) Charlotte Fontaine	S. Henri	1809
	Le même	Marie Julien	S. Pierre	1828
113	Bénoni	(69) Marie Reine Théberge	S.M.	1829
114	Thomas	(69) Marie Ange Fontaine	S.P.S.	1830
115	Michel	(56) Cécile Morin	S.Henri	1788
	Marie Ursule	Jos. Boutin	„	1809
	Marie Louise	Chs. Lemelin	„	1811
	Josette	Pierre Ferlant	„	1814
	Marie Geneviève	Pierre Boutin	„	1816
	Marie Angélique	Michel Quéret	S. Valier	1812
	Christine	Pierre Sylveste	„	1820
116	JeanBaptiste(70)	Ange Pénin	Lévis	1823
	Flavie	Pierre Turgeon	B.	1847
	Thomas			
	Jean Baptiste			
117	François	(70) Marie Ls. Turgeon		
	Xavier		S. Chs.	1825
118	Pierre	(70) Angèle Shinck	S. Michel	1825
	Le même	Julie Roy	B.	1831
119	Georges	(70) Marie Jos. Martin	B.	1827

COTE.

	Marie Célina		Honoré Turgeon	B.1859
120	Joseph	(72)	Marie Martel S. Pierre	1800
	Théotiste		Pierre Leroux ,,	1830
	Marthe		Ls. Gencheau ,,	1837
	Joseph			
	Magloire			
121	Paul	(73)	Genev. Lemieux	
				S.Tho. 1772
	Paul			
122	Jean Marie	(73)	Marg. Daillet S. Tho.1777	
	Constance		Michel Blais Bert.1808	
123	Charles	(74)	Rosalie Gendreau S.L.1831	
	Scolastique		Romule Christophe Racine	
				S. Pierre 1858
124	Alexis	(76)	Angé Gendreau S.L.1819	
125	Jean-Baptiste		Marie Ls. Nadeau	
	Sophie		Jean-Baptiste Guay B.1830	
	Marguerite		Chs. Goulet B.1830	
	Adélaïde		Éd. Girard B.1837	
126	Joseph		Eliz. Baron	
	Julie		J.-Bte. Alaire S.Valier1831	
	Josette		Frs. Roby ,, 1836	
127	Louis		Genev. McNeil	
	Amable			
128	Jean-Baptiste		Marie Chs. Dubé 3 Pistoles	
	Marie Rose		Chs. Paquet B.1835	
129	Jean-Baptiste		Brigitte Ratté	
	Jean-Baptiste			
130	Jean-Baptiste		Marie Jos. Jacques Québec	
	Le même		Théotiste Tangué	
				S. Chs.1833
131	Amable			
	Edouard			
132	François	(77)	Emélie Létourneau	
				S.P.S.1829
133	François	(79)	Marg. Leclaire S. Chs.1800	
134	Jean	(79)	Marg.Beaudoin S.F.S.1805	
135	Abel	(79)	Marie Angé Pilet	
				S. Henri 1802
136	Antoine	(80)	Marie Marcoux S.G.1802	
	Le même		Marie Fse. Bisson	
				S. Chs.1835
137	Joseph	(81)	Marie Brisson S.G.1820	
	Marie		Ant. Audet S.Laurent 1846	
	Mathilde		Ls. Bouffart Québec 1866	
138	Antoine	(81)	Eliz. Huot S.Laurent 1826	
139	Jean	(82)	Mad. Fortier S.G.1819	
	Charles			
140	Joseph	(82)	Fse Boulet S.G.1825	
141	Etienne	(82)	Cath. Goulet ,, 1826	
142	Noël	(82)	Angé Couture ,, 1827	
143	Joseph	(84)	Marie Chs.Roy S.Chs.1798	
	Apolline		Marcel Monmeny ,, 1831	
	Marie Charlotte		J.-Bte Côté ,, 1836	
	Marie Charlotte		2°Jos. Mercier ,, 1842	
	Anastasie		Jean Audet ,, 1840	
	Martin			
	Marcel			
	Joseph			
144	Joseph	(85)	Marie Angé Gagnon	
				S.M.1802
	Angèle		Frs. Clément S.M.1825	
	Pierre			
	Le même		Marie Anne Fradet	
				S.G.1812
	Anne		Marc Clément S.M.1839	
	Zoé		Nicolas Roy ,, 1846	
	Louise		Antoine outure ,, 1844	
	Euphrosine		Paul Lacroix ,, 1858	
	André			
145	Louis	(85)	Ange Tangué S.G.1809	
	François			
146	Joseph	(86)	Fse. Trahan S. Chs.1807	
147	Pierre	(87)	Marie Genev. Bissonnet	
				S.M.1796
	Agathe		Bénoni Bisson S. Chs.1824	

COTÉ.

	Marie Geneviève		Jos. Gagnon S. Chs.1825	
	Marie		Jean-Baptiste Couture	
				S. Chs.1840
	Flavie		Jos Damase Provost	
				S. Chs.1847
	Michel			
	Jean			
	Pierre			
148	Jean	(87)	Hélène Forgue S.M.1797	
	Marie		Jacq. Quéret S.G.1821	
	Félicité		Gab. Terrien S.G.1822	
	Olive		Frs. Gosselin S.G.1825	
	Benoni			
	Jean			
149	Etienne	(87)	Marg.Boutin S.Valier 1800	
	Marguerite		Ant. Couture S.G.1824	
	François			
150	Augustin	(94)	Cath. Couillard S.Tho.1815	
	Norbert			
151	Augustin	(96)	Marg. Canac S. Frs.1814	
	Marcelline		Jean Damase Godbout	
				S. Pierre 1852
152	François	(96)	Marie Anne Maupas	
				S. Pierre 1807
153	Pierre	(97)	Marg. Chatigny	
				S. Pierre 1821
154	Charles Théo-	(93)	Marie Ange Picard	
	phile			S.P.S.1833
	Théophile			
155	Joseph		Angé Roy	
156	Paul		Mathilde Gagnon	
				Isle Verte
	Joseph Valère			
157	Louis		Marie Ange Fabas S. Tho.	
	Françoise		Jean Baptiste Blais	
				S.P.S. 1814
158	Thomas	(116)	Marie Vien B. 1851	
159	Jean Bapt.	(116)	Marie Célanire Talbot	
				B. 1851
160	Joseph	(120)	Scolastique Gosselin	
				S. Pierre 1830
	Génev. Adèle		Jean Basile Goulet	
				S. Pierre 1855
	Marie Philomène		Narcisse Drouin	
				S. Pierre 1862
	Marie Célina		Narcisse Nap. Roberge	
				S. Pierre 1869
	Joseph Octave			
	Edouard			
161	Magloire	(120)	Marie Marthe Goulet	
				S. Pierre 1846
	Marie Célina		Victor Ferland	
				S. Pierre 1867
162	Paul	(121)	Marie Anne Blais	
				S.P.S. 1818
	Thomas			
163	Amable	(127)	Marie Jos Chabot	
				S.Chs. 1832
164	Jean Bapt.	(129)	Marie Chs Coté	
				S.Chs. 1836
165	Edouard	(131)	Pauline Létourneau	
				S.F. 1838
166	Charles	(131)	Cath. Aubé S.Chs. 1853	
167	Joseph	(143)	Véronique Gosselin	
				S.Chs. 1825
	Angèle		Jean Durand S.Chs. 1853	
	Le même		Julie Turgeon S.Chs. 1841	
	Léocadie		Jos Couture S.Chs. 1861	
168	Martin	(143)	Damasile Gagnon	
				S.M. 1843
169	Marcel	(143)	MarieGontier S.Chs. 1848	
170	Pierre	(144)	Marie Jos Marcoux	
				S.M. 1832
	Le même		Emérence Gagnon	
				S.M. 1862

COTÉ.

171 André (144) Constance Catellier
S.M. 1844
Le même Henriette Ratté S.M. 1858
172 François (145) Philomène Couture
S.Chs. 1862
173 Pierre (147) Marg. Paquet S.Chs. 1826
174 Michel (147) Constance Mercier
S.Chs. 1830
Marie Constance Tho. Picard S.Chs. 1853
Léocadie Frs Guénet S.Chs. 1861
175 Jean (147) Julie Couture S.Chs. 1840
176 Jean (148) Génev. Marcoux S.G. 1821
177 Bénoni (148) Marg. Couture S.Chs. 1836
178 François (149) Fse Dion S.G. 1829
179 Norbert (150) Génev. Thibault
S. Valier 1840
180 Théophile (154) Agnès Bélanger
S. Valier 1865
181 Joseph (155) Angèle Turgeon B. 1853
182 Joseph Va- (156) Philomène Noël
lère S. Laurent 1856
183 Joseph Oc- (160) Apoline Célina Goulet
tave S.P. 1862
184 Edouard (160) Luce Dion S.Frs. 1862
185 Thomas (162) Euphrosine Shinck
B. 1849

COTIN—DUGAL

1 Jugal Etiennette Baudon
Que. 1672
Elizabeth Jean Pénisson S.Aug. 1707
Marie Jean Béland S. Aug. 1710
Françoise Ant.Gaboury S. Aug. 1713
Mathieu
Louis
Joseph
Jean Baptiste
Charles
2 Louis (1) Jeanne Béland
Pte Tremble 1709
3 Mathieu (I) Charlotte Meunier
S. Aug. 1709
Marie Thérèse Ls Chrétien Que. 1744
Le même Marie Sévigny 1749
4 Joseph (1) Marie Chs. Gaboury
S. Aug. 1709
5 Charles (1) Thérèse Gaboury
S. Aug. 1720
6 Jean Baptiste (1) Mad. Bourbeau
S. Aug. 1722
7
8 Pierre Marie Thivierge S.F.S.
Géneviève Gab' Frs Ferland
S. Valier 1780
9 Augustin Charlotte Fluet ? Turet ?
Chs Bourg.
Madeleine Pierre Maupas B. 1783
Pierre
10 Louis Mad. Bernard
Marie Anne Aug. Morin S.M. 1803
Julie Barth. Pepin S.M. 1822
Julie 2° Frs Blouin S. Jean 1825
Michel
Louis
Pierre
François Xavier
11 Pierre (9) Fse Lacroix S. Michel 1789
Marie Claire Jean Bte Langlois
S.F.S. 1819
Luc or Elie
12 Louis (10) Marie Jos Bacquet
S. Valier 1808
Soulanges Ant.Pouliot S. Michel 1835
Marie Josette André Dalaire
S. Michel 1838

COTIN—DUGAL.

Florence Frs Bélanger
S. Michel 1849
Charles Domicile
Louis
David
François
13 Pierre (10) Pélagie Picard
S. Michel 1812
Marie Pélagie Paul Lacroix
S. Michel 1847
Marie Eudoce Honoré Bacquet
S. Michel 1845
Josette Paul Turcot S. Jean 1845
Narcisse
Pierre
Louis
Le même Euphrosine Paquet
S. Michel 1842
14 François Xa- (10) Marie Ls. Roussel
vier S. Jean 1830
Rose Ls. Pepin S. Jean 1855
15 Michel (10) Sophie Gautron S. M. 1835
16 Luc ou Elie (11) Marie Bernard S.V. 1820
Charles
17 Louis (12) Genev. Asselin
St. Michel 1839
Marie Honorine Romuald Alphonse Gagne
Olympe St. Michel 1865
18 David (12) Marg. Martineau
St. Michel 1843
Le même Julie Roy " 1846
19 François (12) Anastasie Martineau
S.M. 1842
20 Charles Domi-(12) Adé. Bacquet
cille St. Valier 1858
21 Pierre (13) Fsé.Gontier S.Laurent1841
Pierre Damien
22 Narcisse (13) Caroline Dion
St. Michel 1845
23 Louis (13) Henriette Trépanier
St. Valier 1845
24 Charles (16) Marie Paquet B. 1851
25 Pierre Da- (21) Marie Luce Olympe
mien Audet St. Michel 1865

COUET.

1 Michel Marie Mauger
Marie Jean Leclaire S.F. 1669
2 Louis Mad. Deleugré
Catherine Aug. Tangué
St. Michel 1791
Louis
3 Louis (2) Marie Marg. Fortin
S.M. 1784
Marie Joachim Valière S.M. 1812
Louis
André
Benjamin
Michel
Joseph
4 Louis (3) Thérèse Gautron
St. Michel 1810
Anastasie Pierre Bêtel " 1836
Emélie Jos. Roy " 1839
Elisabeth Nazaire Marcouse
St. Michel 1842
Jacques
Louis Prosper
5 André (3) Louise Roy S.M. 1819
6 Joseph (3) MarieChs. Blais S.P.S.1822
7 Benjamin (3) Marie Génév. Bacquet
S.M. 1828
Emélie Fs. Xavier Bolduc
St. Michel 1847
Marie Mathilde Jean Bacquet " 1853

COUET.

8	Michel	(3)	Eliz. Nadeau St.Mich 1831
9	Jean Baptiste		Marie Rose Chouinard
	Marguerite		Chs. Larrivé B. 1822
10	Prosper	(4)	Cath. Turgeon S.M. 1841
	Marie Jos. Bel-		Etn. Semin Bedard
	zémire		S.M. 1865
11	Louise	(5)	Euphrosime Marcoux S.M. 1843
	Le même		Marie Eliz. Fradet S.M. 1852
12	Jacques	(4)	Reiné Coté St. Valier 1854

COUILLARD.

1	Guillaume		Guillemette Hebert Que. 1621
	Charles		
	Guillaume		
2	Guillaume	(1)	Génév. Després Que. 1653
	Louis		
	Jacques		
3	Charles Tho-	(1)	Marie Paquet Que. 1668
	mas		
	Charles Marie (1)		
	Le même		Louise Couture 1688
	Marie		Alexandre Morel B. 1724
	Marguerite		Jos. Coté B. 1726
	Marie Anne		Jean Bte. Gérard B. 1727
	Marie Françoise		Ls. Turgeon B. 1758
	Joseph		
	Pierre		
	Louis Charles		
4	Louis (2)	(2)	Marie Vandry Que. 1680
	Le même		Marie Fortin Que. 1688
	Elizabeth		Jos. Coté S. Tho. 1716
	Paul		
5	Jacques (3)	(2)	Eliz. Lemieux S.Tho. 1691
	Marthe		Pierre Belanger S. Tho. 1716
	Marie Madeleine Ls. Chs. Couillard S.Tho. 1728		
	Clement		
	Joseph		
6	Charles Marie (3)		Fse. Couture B. 1726
	Charles		
7	Louis Charles (3)		Marie Mad. Couillard S.Tho. 1728
	Charles		
8	Pierre	(3)	Eliz. Nadeau B. 1727
	Marie Anne		Jean Bte. Guenet B. 1753
	Isabelle		Jean Maurice B. 1761
	Louise		Augustin Roy S.Chs. 1765
	Marie		Henri Roy St. Michel 1767
	François		
9	Joseph He-	(3)	Genev. Turgeon B. 1729
	bert		
	Geneviève		Jos. Dalaire B. 1755
	Marguerite		Jean Guay B. 1761
	Cécile		Tho. Guenet B. 1766
	Marie		Jean Bte. Gosselin S.Chs. 1759
	Françoise		Ls. Dalaire St. Michel 1768
	Joseph Hebert		
10	Paul	(4)	Marie Jos. Couture B. 1732
11	Joseph	(5)	Génév. Caron Islet 1733
	Joseph		
12	Clement	(5)	Marie Cath. Denaut S. Tho. 1738
	Clement		
	Etienne		

(1) Souche des Couillard de Beaumont.
(2) Souche des Couillard Dupuis.
(3) Seigneur de l'Islet et de St. Jean Port Joly.
Souche des Couillard Des Prés.

18—18

COUILLARD.

13	Charles	(6)	Marie Fse. Boilard B. 1757
	Marie Françoise		Nicolas Pénin B. 1781
	Charlotte		Jean Bte. Lacasse B. 1785
	Thérése		Claude Dubord B. 1791
14	Charles	(7)	Véronique Coté S. Tho. 1761
	Jean Baptiste		
15	Jacques		Marie Jos. Blanchet
	Marie Reine		Frs. Vallée S. Henri 1782
	Marie Louise		Ls. Hallé S. Henri 1783
	M. Marguerite		Michel Bègin S. Henri 1787
	Francois		
16	Francois	(8)	Marie Jos. Molleux B. 1756
17	Joseph Hebert(9)		Mad. Filteau B. 1763
	M. Madeleine		Jos. Couture B. 1785
	Francoise		Ant. Turgeon B. 1796
	Francoise		2° Ls. Couture S.Chs. 1803
	Charles Hebert		
18	Joseph	(11)	Marie Fournier S.Tho.1763
	M. Madeleine		Gab. Thibault S. Tho. 1786
	M. Geneviève		Aug. Mathieu S. Tho. 1789
	Joseph		
	Jean Baptiste		
19	Jacques		Marie Chs. Fournier
	Jacques		
20	Clément	(12)	Marie Fse. Dubeau S. Valier 1778
	Marie Josette		Michel Roy S. Chs. 1817
	Clément		
21	Etienne	(12)	Marie Genev. Asselin S. Jean 1788
	M. Madeleine		Ls. Guèrard S. F. 1815
	Marie Josette		Ls. Marie Pepin S.F. 1823
22	Jean Baptiste(14)		Marie Chs. Couillard S. Tho. 1788
	Jean Baptiste		
23	Charles		Fse. Dessaint
	Julie		Jean Bte. Marcoux S. Michel 1809
	Emérentienne		Frs. Gosselin S. Michel 1822
	Flavien		
	Hilaire		
	Joseph		
24	Francois	(15)	Marie Cath. Judith Tangué S. Michel 1787
	Véronique		Jean Emond S. Henri 1811
25	Charles Hébert		Marie Apolline Nadeau B. 1787
	Marie Apolline		Claude Nollet S. Chs. 1805
	Marie Apolline		2° Pierre Bédard B. 1814
	Joseph		
	Charles		
	Le même		Marie Jos. Baecquet S. Michel 1799
	Archange		Jacq. Richard S. Michel 1834
	Angéle		Frs. Corriveau B. 1825
	Marie Josette		Jean Roy B. 1826
	Jean		
26	Joseph	(18)	Marie Mathieu S.P.S. 1786
27	Jean Baptiste(18)		Marie Ls. Vézina Cap S. Ign. 1798
	Jean Baptiste		
28	Jacques	(19)	Marie Roger Damour S. Tho. 1789
	Le même		Fse. Laberge S. Tho. 1797
	Le même		Marie Claire Bernier S.Tho. 1800
	Abraham		
	Thomas		
29	Clément	(20)	Marie Genev. Carbon- neau S. Valier 1807
	Marie Angéle		Jos. Lepage S. Chs. 1830
	Marie		

COUILLARD.

30	JeanBaptiste(22)	Theodore Bernier	
		S. Tho. 1818	
	Charlemagne		
	Joseph Amable		
30	Joseph	(23) Genev. Ménard	B. 1813
32	Flavien	(23) Genev. Morisset S.	
		Michel 1822	
33	Hilaire	(23) Fse. Lacroix S. Michel 1831	
	Sara	Salem Bergeron SChs. 1860	
34	Charles	(25) Angéle Roy	B. 1808
35	Joseph	(25) Cécile Turgeon	B. 1816
36	Jean	(25) Marie Turgeon	B. 1827
37	Michel	Marie Jos. Vigneau	
	Michel		
38	Michel	(37) Marg. Dion Cap S. Ign 1801	
	Eusébe		
39	JeanBaptiste(27)	Cath. Blouin	Bert. 1826
40	Thomas	(28) Martin Clavet S.Tho. 1833	
	Auguste		
41	Abraham	(28) Anastasie Dion S.	
		Michel 1845	
42	Marie	(29) Justine Gagnon SChs. 1841	
43	Charlemagne	(30) Marie Chs. Boilard B.1813	
44	Joseph	(30) Cécile Boilard	B. 1813
	Amable		
	Flavie	Thomas Roy	B. 1836
	Caroline	Jos. Ménard	B. 1846
	Adéline	Albert Blanchet	B. 1848
	Cédulie	Ed. Caron	B. 1852
	Henriette	Frs. Etn. Hudon B. 1852	
	Thaiselle	Jos. Prudent Fournier	
		B. 1856	
	Maxime		
45	Paul	Marie Jos. Chamberlan	
	Le même	Marie Angé McCarthy	
		Kamouraska B. 1831	
46	Augustin	Réine Lessart Bert.	
	Jean Baptiste		
47	Rémi	Scolastique Caron	
	Marie Zoé	Pre. Celestin Lavergne	
		Bert. 1844	
48	Eusèbe	(38) Julie Gosselin St. Valier 1833	
49	Thomas Pre(40)	Anne Aurélie Gautier	
	Auguste	St. Michel 1855	
50	Maxime	(44) Marie Adélina Enouf B.1858	
51	Jn. Baptiste(46)		

COULOMBE.

1	Louis	Jeanne Boucand S.F. 1670	
	Jeanne	Chs.Paquet St.Laurent 1694	
	Marie Marthe	Pierre Labrecque	
		St. Laurent 1694	
	Marguerite	Pierre Bouvet	Que. 1703
	Marguerite	2° Tho. Foru	Que. 1727
	Angélique	Claude Bernard	Que. 1713
	Catherine	Pierre Prudhomme Que.1716	
	Louis		
	Jean		
	Nicolas		
2	Nicolas	(1) Anne Maillou	B. 1794
3	Jean	(1) Jean Balan	S Tho. 1706
	Marie	Jacq. Nollet	B. 1727
	Alexis		
	François		
	Le même	Marie Leblond	
		St. Michel 1716	
	Marie Anne	Jos. Balan	Bert. 1736
4	Louis	(1) Hélène Poulet St. Pierre1710	
	Madeleine	Jos. Chabot St. Laurent 1733	
	Catherine	Ls. Rouleau " 1738	
	Marguerite	Jean Bte. Vaillancour	
		St. Laurent 1743	
	Elisabeth	Michel Magnan " 1748	
	Hélène	Laurent Moreau " 1748	
	Rosalie	Ign. Noël " 1763	

COULOMBE.

	Rosalie		2° Ls. Cauchon	
			St. Laurent 1773	
	Marie		Michel Vallée " 1752	
	Pierre			
	Louis			
	Antoine			
5	Alexis	(3)	M.Mad. Groissart Bert.1733	
	Marie		Amand Comeau	Bert. 1767
	Geneviève		Pierre Quéret	Bert. 1669
	Geneviève		2° Jos. Couchon	S.V. 1789
	M. Madeleine		J. B. Picard	S.P.S. 1758
	M. Madeleine		2° Jos. Daigle	S.P.S. 1774
	Augustin			
	Louis			
	Jean Baptiste			
	François			
6	François	(3)	M. Jos. Lavoie	Bert. 1746
	Joseph			
	François			
7	Louis	(4)	Marg. Pouliot	S.L. 1734
	Marguerite		Laurent Audet	S.L. 1763
	Louis			
8	Pierre	(4)	M. Anne Coté	S.P. 1739
9	Antoine	(4)	Genev. Magnan Chs. Bourg	
			1748	
	Geneviève		Jean Marie GontierS.L.1787	
	Antoine			
	Louis			
	Pierre			
	Le même		Anne Gendreau	S.L. 1767
	M. Anne		Frs. Campeau	S.L. 1811
	Jacq.Christophe			
10	François	(8)	Susanne Valière S.P.S 1756	
	M. Susanne		J. B. Monmeny S.P.S. 1778	
	Marie		Isaac Zach. Tondreau	
			S.P.S. 1784	
	M. Thérèse		Frs. Boulet	S.P.S. 1787
	M. Roger		Sylvestre Sylvestre	
			S.P.S. 1791	
	Joseph			
11	Jn. Baptiste	(5)	M. Mad. Cyr.	S.F.S. 1766
12	Augustin	(5)	Genev. Guignard Bert. 1776	
13	Louis	(5)	M. Angé Lessart Bert. 1779	
	Marguerite		Ls. Morin	Bert. 1813
	M. Sophie		J. B. Vernet	Bert. 1823
	M. Josette		Andre Picard	Bert. 1824
	M. Charlotte		Prudent Guilmet Bert. 1833	
	François			
14	Joseph		M. Genev. Morin	
	Louis			
15	François	(6)	Mad. Gendron S.F.S. 1767	
	M. Josette		Aug. Blais	Bert. 1791
16	Joseph	(6)	M. Eliz. Fournier Bert. 1783	
	M. Josette		Chs.Frs.Simoneau Bert.1808	
	M. Josette		2° Etn. Coté	S. Tho. 1812
	Marguerite		Chs. Thibault	Bert. 1823
	M. Luce		Hilarion Thibault Bert.1825	
	Joseph			
17	Louis	(7)	Marie Audet	S.L. 1757
	Marie		Jos. Ruel	S.L. 1780
	M. Louise		Philippe Braün	S.L. 1784
	Ambroise			
	Louis			
	Pierre			
	Antoine			
18	Jacq. Chrys-	(9)	M. Ls. Pouliot	S.L. 1805
	tophe			
	M. Louise		Jean Denis	S.L. 1831
19	Antoine	(8)	M. Ls. Boisonneau S.J.1772	
	M. Anne		Jean Marie Pepin S.J. 1798	
	Madeleine		Pierre Noel Gosselin	
			S.J. 1802	
	Euphrosine		Laurent Marcoux S.J. 1825	
	Bénoni			
	Pierre			
20	Louis	(9)	Josette Dufresne S.L. 1780	

COULOMBE.

	M. Louise		Ant. Langevin	S.L.	1801
	Geneviève		J. B. Leblond	S. L.	1814
	M Josette		Michel Campeau	S. L.	1820
	Thérese		Frs. Réaume	S.L.	1820
	Louis				
21	Pierre		Mad. Godbout	S.L.	1785
	M. Anne		Prisque Métayer	S.L.	1823
	Madeleine		Jean Audibert	S.H.	1813
	Joseph				
22	Joseph	(10)	Marie Gaudreau	S.P.S.	1790
	M. Louise		Jos. Gagné	"	1818
	M. Brigitte		Jos. Létourneau	"	1821
	Marie		Jos. Guilmet	"	1827
	Rose		Alexis Picard	"	1830
	M. Marguerite		Jos. Langlois	S.F.S.	1810
	Jean Baptiste				
23	François	(13)	Marie Sénéchal	S.F.S.	1812
24	Louis	(14)	M. Anne Gaumont		
				S.P.S.	1796
25	Joseph	(16)	Marie Hébert	Bert,	1817
	Marie		Felix Bernier	"	1844
	François Xavier				
26	Ambroise	(17)	M. Jos. Coté	S. Chs.	1780
	M. Josette		Frs. Métivier	S. Chs.	1815
	Marguerite		Chs. Gosselin	S. Chs.	1826
	"		2° Ferd. Morin	S. Chs.	1840
	Ambroise				
	Etienne				
	Laurent				
	Alexis				
	Le même		Ursule Duquet	S.Chs.	1833
27	Louis	(17)	M. Ls. Carreau	S.L.	1785
	Angélique		Frs. Godbout	S.L.	1808
	"		2° Frs. Audibert	S.L.	1828
	Marguerite		Jos. Pouliot	S.L.	1821
	Ambroise				
	Le même		Marie Dalaire	S.Frs.	1803
	M. Anne		Jos. Audet	S.L.	1833
	Fille adoptive				
	Charles				
	Joseph				
28	Antoine	(17)	Cath. Lepage	S.J.	1795
	M. Catherine		Prisque Metayer	S.L.	1816
	Elizabeth		Chas. Dumas	"	1813
	M. Louise		Chs. Labrecque	"	1815
	Geneviève		Michel Henri Peltier		
				S.L.	1829
	Antoine				
	François				
	Olivier				
29	Pierre	(17)	M. Anne Labrecque		
				S.L.	1806
30	Pierre	(19)	Basilisse Audet	S.J.	1801
	Marie		Jos. Bedame	"	1824
	Alexis				
31	Bénoni	(19)	Marie Gosselin	"	1815
32	Louis	(20)	Cath. Fontaine	"	1812
	Pierre				
	Jean				
33	Joseph	(21)	Marg. Labrecque	S.J.	1838
34	Jean Baptiste	(22)	Emélie Mercier	Bert.	1831
35	François Xa-	(25)	Agnès Bélanger	S.V.	1866
	vier				
36	Ambroise	(26)	M. Anne Gosselin		
				S. Chs.	1807
	Anastasie		Frs. Marseau	S.Chs.	1838
	M. Marcelline		David Audet	S.Chs.	1842
	Angèle		Aug. Pigeon	S.M.	1847
	Louis				
	Charles				
	Le même		Marie Goulet	S.Chs.	1829
37	Alexis	(26)	Marg. Collet	S.Chs.	1821
	Restitut Salomé		J. B. Naz. Gautron		
				S.Chs.	1862

18—18½

COULOMBE.

38	Laurent	(26)	Marg. Guay	B.	1823
39	Etienne	(26)	M. Ls. Denis	S.L.	1827
	Louise		Jean Noël	"	1847
40	Ambroise	(27)	Eliz. Cinqmars	"	1824
	Eléonore		Elie Ouimet	"	1850
	Elisabeth		Ls. Langlois	"	1850
	Ambroise				
	François				
	Pierre				
41	Charles	(27)	Cécile Curadeau	S.L.	1831
	Charles				
	Le même		Judith Bonneau	S.L.	1849
42	Joseph	(27)	Eliz. Bonneau	"	1849
43	Antoine	(28)	Fse. Denis	"	1823
	Eléonore		Luc. Terrien	S.Chs.	1843
44	François	(28)	Marie Gosselin	S.L.	1831
	M. Catherine		Gev. Ruel	"	1861
	Françoise		Olivier Coulombe	S.L.	1861
	M. Adelaide		Eugène Jalbert	S.L.	1865
45	Olivier		Fse. Gontier	S.J.	1836
	Olivier				
46	Alexis		Marg. Ginchereau	S.B.	1827
47	Eloi		Marie Boucher	S.L.	
	Frs. & Suz. Lavoi			"	1809
	Eloi				
48	Joseph		Marg. Morisset	S.	Isidore
	Michel				
49	Pierre	(32)	Justine Pouliot	S.L.	1845
	Le même		Cécile Boissonneau		
				S.J.	1854
50	Jean	(32)	Mathilde Gosselin	S.L.	1851
	M. Mathilde		Jean Maranda	S.L.	1875
	M. Lumina		Michel Gosselin	S.L.	1878
	Jean Baptiste				
51	Louis	(36)	Cath. Lacroix	S.M.	1851
52	Charles	(36)	Ursule Lacroix	S.M.	1859
53	Ambroise	(40)	Sophie Langlois	S.L.	1852
54	Pierre	(40)	Cécile Giguère	S.Frs.	1861
55	François	(40)	Vitaline Baudoin	S.L.	1867
	Le même		Philomène Turcot	S.F.	1881
56	Charles	(41)	Marie Godbout	Que,	——
57	Olivier	(45)	Fse. Coulombe	S.L.	1861
	Le même		Anne Labrecque	S.L.	1856
58	Eloi	(47)	Marie Dalaire	S.Frs.	1846
59	Michel	(48)	Olive Plante	S.Chs.	1854
60	Jean Bapt.	(50)	M. Octavie Audebert		
				S.L.	1877

COUTURE.

1	Guillaume		Anne Aymard	Que.	1649
	Charles				
	Guillaume				
	Jean Baptiste				
	Joseph				
	Eustache				
2	Joseph. (a)	(1)	Anne Marret	A.G.	1686
	Jean Bte-Jos?				
3	Charles (B)	(1)	Marie Huart	Levis.	1690
	Marie		Pierre Ruel	B.	1709
	Geneviève		Guill. Le Roy	B.	1712
	Jeanne		Jos. Le Roy	B.	1716
	M. Louise		Ign. Labrecque	B.	1724
	Marguerite		Pierre Le Roy	B.	1730
	Joseph				
4	Guillaume	(1)	M. Mad. Coté	S.P.	1691
	Guillaume				
	Joseph				
	Augustin				
	Jean Baptiste				
	Pierre				
	Le Même		Nicole Bouffard	S.L.	1703

(a) Souche des Couture Lamonde.
(B) Souche des Couture Lafresnoy.

COUTURE.

Marguerite	Gab. Gosselin	S.L.	1732
M. Madeleine	Ant. Civadier	S.L.	1740
Geneviève	Pierre Aubin	S.P.	1752
Clément			
Le même	M. Anne Adam	S.L.	1713
Françoise	Pierre Fournier	B.	1743
Laurent			
Alexis			
Louis			
5 Eustache (c) (1)	Marg. Bégin	Levis.	1695
Marie	Jacq. Guay	B.	1723
Elisabeth	Frs. Suzor	B.	1733
Philippe Olivier			
Le Même	Fse. Huart	Levis.	1701
Angélique	Ls. Turgeon	B.	1728
M. Josette	Paul Couillard	B.	1732
M. Louise	Chs. Forgues	B.	1746
Joseph			
Charles			
Louis			
Nicolas			
6 Joseph (1)	Jeanne Huart	Levis.	1695
Charles			
7 Jean Baptiste (2)	Marg. Leclaire	S.P.	1720
Marguerite	Ign. Létourneau	S.P.	1744
Le Même	Éliz. Gosselin	S.P.	1732
M. Thécle	Pierre Jobin	S.P.	1762
M. Anne	Basile Asselin	S.F.	1736
Thérèse	J. B. Bigaouët		
		Chs.Bourg.	1768
Thérèse	2° Jean Roy		
		Chs.Bourg.	1772
8 Joseph (2)	Génev. Leclaire		
Josette	Pierre Godbout	S.P.	1747
Geneviève	Aug. Langlois	S.P.	1747
Dorothée	Jacq. Jobin	S.P.	1749
Agathe	J. B. Jolin	S.P.	1754
Véronique	Nic. Alexis Jacques		
		S.P.	1771
Joseph			
Augustin			
9 Joseph (3)	Angé Roy	B.	1731
Thérèse	Paul Bernier	S.Chs.	1763
M. Charlotte	Ant. Gosselin	S.Chs.	1765
Madeleine	Frs. Gosselin	S.Chs.	1767
Brigitte	Jean Lebrun	S.Chs.	1771
Angélique	Ls. Gosselin	S.Chs.	1771
Catherine	Jean Gosselin	S.Chs.	1782
Alexandre			
Etienne			
10 Jean Baptiste (4)	Mad. Lacasse	B.	1722
Marie	Ls. Gontier	B.	1745
Elisabeth	Pierre Lecours	B.	1746
Catherine	J. B. Gosselin	S.Chs.	1751
Cécile	Pierre Jos. Mercier		
		S.Chs.	1761
Cécile	2° Chs. Fournier	Bert.	1780
Joseph			
11 Guillaume (4)	Charlotte Turgeon	B.	1722
M. Marthe	Ls. Bolduc	B.	1754
M. Josette	Chs. Boucher	B.	1763
Elisabeth	Frs. Boucher	S.V.	1760
Thérèse	Jean Fournier	S.M.	1759
Guillaume			
Jean			
12 Augustin (4)	Eliz. Turgeon	B.	1723
Elizabeth	Jos. Roberge	"	1742
Marthe	Marc Isabel	"	1742
Angélique	Jean Goulet	"	1748
Geneviève	Jacq. Naud	"	1749
Alexandre			
Louis			
Augustin			
13 Pierre (4)	Marg. Bouffard	S.L.	1727

(c) Souche des Couture Bellerive.

COUTURE.

Marie	Prisque Bélanger		
		S.M.	1750
Marie	2° Frs. Fradet	S.M.	1754
Geneviève	Jacq. Rémillard	S.M.	1754
Geneviève	2° Jacq. Chrystophe		
		S.V.	1758
Geneviève	3° Pierre Rouleau		
		S.Chs.	1767
14 Joseph (4)	Susanne Turgeon	B.	1732
M. Josette	Aug. Coté	S.Chs.	1762
M. Anne	Ign. Clement	S.Chs.	1777
Alexandre			
Etienne			
Charles			
15 Clément (4)	Mad. Gosselin	S.L.	1733
Antoine			
Guillaume			
Clément			
16 Louis (4)	Fse. Girard	B.	1744
M. Françoise	Bénoni Fournier	B.	1771
Régis	Etn. Gontier	S.M.	1775
17 Alexis (4)	M. Anna Fournier		
		L.S.	1748
Le même	M, Fse. Langlois	S.P.	1786
18 Laurent (4)	M. Jos. Grandier	S.M.	1759
Laurent			
Le même	Marie Brisson	S.M.	1762
Marie	Frs. Delaire	S.Chs.	1788
Susanne	Laurent Fortier	"	1793
Jean			
19 Antoine	Marie Morin		
Jacques			
20 Alexis	M. Mad. Morin		
André			
Joseph			
21 Phil. Olivier (5)	Angé Guay	B.	1728
Le Même	Eliz. Bonrassa	Lévis	1733
Joseph			
Etienne			
22 Joseph (5)	Génev. Fournie	B.	1756
M. Josette	Guill. Couture	"	1763
Joseph			
23 Louis (5)	M. Jeanne Valière	B.	1737
Marie (3)	Nic. Gosselin	S.Chs.	1757
Pierre			
Charles			
Louis			
24 Charles (5)	Charlotte Girard	B.	1739
25 Nicolas (5)	Eliz. Joncas	S.Tho.	1749
Elizabeth	Ls. Isabel	S.Chs.	1773
Louise	Jos. Boulet	S.H.	1787
Etienne			
Charles			
Le même	Thérèse Pichet	Levis	1760
Thérèse	Etn. Coutiure	S.Chs.	1787
Marguerite	Chs. Couture	"	1797
M. Josette	Alexandre Turgeon		
		S.Chs.	1803
Michel			
Louis			
Jean Baptiste			
Joseph			
26 Charles (6)	Marie Poliquin		
Marie	Chrysostome Langlois		
		S.P.S.	1765
Joseph			
27 Augustin (8)	Genev. Jobin		
		Chs. Bourg	1764
28 Joseph (8)	M. Jos. Rousseau	S.P.	1772
M. Madeleine	Jacq. Roberge	"	1802
Joseph			
29 Joseph (9)	Thérèse Girard	S.M.	1766
Thérèse	Ant. Audet	S.G.	1791
Angèle	Ant. Bilodeau	"	1795
Marguerite	J. B. Baillargeon	"	1796
Etienne			

COUTURE.

30	Alexandre	(9)	Maud. Mercier	S.Chs. 1782
	Madeleine		Ls. Dalaire	,, 1802
	Madeleine		2° Ed. Marseau	B. 1842
	Alexandre			
31	Joseph	(10)	Marg. Gosselin	S.Chs. 1753
	Joseph			
	Jean			
	François			
	Le même		Ange Huart	S.Chs. 1761
	M. Charlotte		Jos. Marcoux	,, 1784
	M. Charlotte		2° Pierre Vernet	
				S.F.S. 1815
	Zacharie			
	Pierre			
32	Guillaume	(11)	M. Jos. Dangueuger	B. 1758
	M. Josete		Jean Poulet	B. 1796
	Angélique		Jos. Gosselin	S.P. 1801
	Jacques			
	Louis			
33	Jean	(11)	M. Jos. Beaucher	S.M. 1771
	Josette		Pierre Guay	B. 1793
	Jean Baptiste			
34	Augustin	(12)	M. Fse. Rancour	B. 1752
	Joseph			
	François			
	Le Même		Anastasie Doison	S.Chs. 1766
	M. Charlotte		Alexis Bacon	S.Chs. 1786
	Anastasie		Michel Dubé	S.Chs. 1800
	Le même		Fse. Alaire	S.V. 1772
	Thérèse		Alexandre Terrien	S.Chs. 1798
35	Alexandre	(12)	Cath. Frontigny	S.Chs. 1758
36	Louis	(12)	M. Ls. Huart	S.M. 1759
37	Charles	(14)	M. Jos. Gosselin	S.Chs. 1759
	Angélique		J. B. Toussaint	S.Chs. 1785
	M. Josette		Ant. Campeau	S.Chs. 1806
	M. Charlotte		Pierre Turgeon	S.Chs. 1795
	Alexandre			
	Charles			
	Le Même		M. Jos. Nolin	S.Chs. 1784
38	Alexandre	(14)	Louise Pouliot	S.L. 1763
	Marguerite		Frs. Brousseau	S.Chs. 1757
	M. Louise		J. B. Couture	S.Chs. 1797
	M. Josette		Jos. Turgeon	S.Chs. 1799
	Alexandre			
	Charles			
	Jos. Paschal			
	Joseph			
39	Etienne	(14)	Ange Paquet	S.Chs. 1753
	Angélique		Frs. Nolin	S.Chs. 1789
	M. Josette		Amb. Lemieux	S.Chs. 1797
	Cécile		Jean Goulet	S.Chs. 1799
	Thérèse		J. B. Chabot	S.Chs. 1805
	Marguerite		J. B. Roy	S.Chs. 1814
	Etienne			
	Joseph			
	Pierre			
	Antoine			
40	Clément		Marie Dangueuger	B. 1762
	M. Marguerite		Frs. Xavier Turgeon	S.Chs. 1798
	Pierre			
	Etienne			
	Alexis			
	Jean Baptiste			
	Guillaume			
41	Guillaume		M. Jos. Couture	B. 1763
	M. Josette		Ls. Letellier	B. 1789
42	Antoine		Genev. Chabot	S.L. 1767
	Marie		Jean Leclaire	S.L. 1796

	Marguerite		Pierre Huot	S.L. 1800
	Cécile		Amb. Leclaire	S.L. 1820
	Antoine			
	Joseph			
	Alexis			
43	Augustin		M. Ls. Boulet	
	Augustin			
44	Laurent	(18)	Madeleine (Boulet)	S.Chs. 1784
	Le même		Marie Pouliot	S.G. 1786
	Marie		Ls. Fortier	S.G. 1811
	Laurent			
	Le même		Charlotte Larrivé	S.G, 1796
	Rosalie		Ls. Quéméneur	S.G. 1827
	Antoine			
45	Jean	(18)	M. Jos. Royer	S.Chs. 1796
	Sophie		Michel Audet	S.Chs. 1835
	Hubert			
	Jean Baptiste			
	Alexis			
46	Jacques	(19)	Angé Gagné	S.P.S. 1751
47	Joseph	(20)	M. Ls. Blanchet	S.P.S. 1749
	M. Elizabeth		Jean Boucher	S.P.S. 1791
	Joseph			
	Le même		M. Ls. Lemieux	S.Tho. 1766
48	André	(20)	M. Fse. Picard	S.P.S. 1766
49	Joseph	(21)	Marg. Turgeon	B. 1753
	Marguerite		Frs. Valière	B. 1780
	Charles			
	Joseph			
	Etienne			
	Paul			
	Louis			
50	Etienne	(21)	M. Mad. Turgeon	B. 1761
	M. Josette		Jos. Poiré	B. 1786
	Elizabeth		Alexandre Filteau	B, 1788
51	Joseph	(22)		
52	Pierre	(23)	M. Jos. Turgeon	S.Chs. 1763
	Angélique		Jean Rousseau	S.Chs. 1789
	Marguerite		Frs. Genest	S.Chs. 1795
	Pierre			
53	Louis	(22)	Marie Guénet	S.Chs. 1763
54	Charles	(23)	Génév. Marchand	Levis 1771
	Charles			
	Le même		M. Ls. Poiré	Levis 1781
	Joseph			
	Jean			
55	Etienne	(25)	Génév. Nolin	S.Chs. 1783
	M. Angèle		Frs. Fortier	S.Chs. 1817
	Susanne		Ant. Audet	,, 1823
	M. Josette		J. B. Lacasse	,, 1828
	Jean Baptiste			
	Francois Xavier			
	Etienne			
	Charles			
	Antoine			
	Joseph			
	Pierre			
56	Charles	(25)	Marg. Dalaire	S.Chs. 1784
	Charles			
	Etienne			
57	Joseph	(25)	Marg. Ainse	S.G. 1794
	Marguerite		Etn. Corriveau	,, 1813
	Louise		Bénoni Corriveau	,, 1816
58	JeanBaptiste	(25)	M. Ls. Couture	S.Chs. 1797
59	Louis	(25)	Fse. Couillard	S.Chs. 1803
	Louise		Felix Chamberlan	,, 1831
	Rosalie		Fréderic Lainé	,, 1843
	Charles			
	Louis			
60	Michel		Fse. Gosselin	S.G. 1809
	M. Angèle		Ls. Ed. Turgeon	S.Chs. 1830

COUTURE.

Angélique	Pierre Aubé	,,	1834
M. Louise	J. B. Baillargeon	,,	1837
Julie	Jean Coté	,,	1840
M. Rose	Prisque Vien	,,	1842
M. Délima	Théophile Beaucher	S.Chs.	1851
Perpétue	Marcel Labbé	,,	1855
Jean Baptiste			
Louis			
61 Joseph	(26) Susanne Guay	S.Chs.	1771
Joseph			
62 Joseph	(28) M. Agathe Aubin	S.P.	1802
Geneviève	Frs. Chabot	,,	1829
Elizabeth	Pierre Rouleau	,,	1830
Marie	Tho. Boissonneau	,,	1833
M. Olive	Ls. Rousseau	,,	1837
Basilisse	Frs. Crépeau	,,	1840
Sophie	Magl. Tessier	,,	1841
M. Emélie	Firmin Rousseau	,,	1845
Olivier			
Louis			
Jean			
63 Étienne	(29) Cath. Audet	S.Chs.	1797
64 Alexandre	(30) M. Fse Ruel	,,	1809
M. Françoise	Aug. Boucher	,,	1830
M. Françoise	2° Amb. Naud	,,	1862
M. Restitut	Pierre Boissonneau	S.F.S.	1836
M. Angèle	Ls. Turgeon	B.	1837
Alexandre			
65 Joseph	(31) Genev. Royer	S.Chs.	1779
M. Angélique	Victor Olivier Sénéchal	S.H.	1803
Geneviève	Denis Collet	,,	1815
Angèle	Aug. Clément	,,	1820
Joseph			
66 François	(31) M. Chs. Dion	B.	1787
Elizabeth	Raphaël Corbeau	S.G.	1808
Joseph			
67 Jean	(31) Cécile Roy	S.Chs.	1790
68 Zacharie	(31) Marie Boucher	S.Chs.	1785
Scholastique	Pierre Gautron	S.G.	1824
Michel			
Jean			
Zacharie			
Pierre			
69 Pierre	(31) M. Anne Godbout	S.G.	1802
70 Louis	(32) M. Jos. Lacroix	S.Chs.	1793
71 Jacques	(32) Thérèse Roberge	S.P.	1798
72 Jean Baptiste	(32) M. Chs. Paquet	B.	1808
M. Louise	Noël Fontaine	,,	1835
Sophie	Michel Turgeon	,,	1837
Adélaïde	Ls. Baudoin	S.Chs.	1843
Adélaïde	2° Frs. X. Turgeon	S. Chs.	1860
Jean Baptiste			
Le même	M. Angé Dion	B.	1831
73 François	(34) Genev. Couillard	S.H.	1801
74 Joseph	(34) M. Mad. Valière	S.H.	1801
75 Charles	(37) M. Ls. Coté	S.Chs.	1787
M. Josette	Flavien Lambert	S.H.	1812
Charles			
Pierre			
76 Joseph	(37) Véronique Charier	S.Chs.	1794
Véronique	Chs. Drapeau	S.M.	1816
Angélique	Noel Coté	S.G.	1827
77 Alexandre	(37) M. Ls. Lacroix	S.M.	1793
M. Louise	Chs. Labrecque	S.Chs.	1813
78 Joseph	(38) Thérèse Leclaire	S.V.	1786
Alexandre			
Jean Baptiste			
François Xavier			
André			
Benoit			

COUTURE.

79 Alexandre	(38) M. Angé Guay	S.Chs.	1787
Le même	Fse. Boulet	B.	1804
80 Charles	(38) Marg. Couture	S.Chs.	1797
81 Joseph Paschal	(38) Marie Lecours	S.G.	1802
82 Etienne	(39) Thérèse Couture	S.Chs.	1787
M. Josette	Ambr. Naud	,,	1811
Marguerite	Etn. Lemelin	,,	1814
Angèle	Alexandre Marcoux	S.Chs.	1815
Louise	Théophile Turgeon	S.Chs.	1834
Etienne			
83 Antoine	(39) Fse. Bacquet	S.M.	1787
Françoise	Chs. Boucher	S.Chs.	1813
Marie	Etn. Couture	,,	1817
Marguerite	Pierre Royer	,,	1825
François			
Charles			
Gervais			
Joseph			
Etienne			
84 Pierre	(39) M. Ls. Ruel	S.G.	1792
Marie	Pierre Aubé	,,	1819
Pierre			
85 Joseph	(39) Isabel Ruel	S.Chs.	1793
Antoine			
Jean Baptiste			
86 Pierre	(40) Thérèse Molleur	B.	1786
87 Etienne	(40) Marie Drapeau	S.Chs.	1790
Scolastique	(40) Jean Bte. Paquet	,,	1821
M. Josette	Jean Lacasse	,,	1834
Etienne			
Le même	M. Anne Gosselin	,,	1812
François			
88 Guillaume	(40) Scolastique Thibault	S.P.S	1794
Scolastique	Jos. Naud	S.Chs.	1814
Marguerite	Pierre Chabot	,,	1820
89 Alexis	(40) Cath. Coté	S.Chs.	1803
Marie	Frs. Aubé	B.	1834
90 Jean Baptiste	(40) Rosalie Quéret	S.Chs.	1803
91 Michel	Marie Pouliot		
Michel			
92 Antoine	(42) M. Angé Coté	S.P.	1788
93 Alexis	(42) Julie Rouleau	S.L.	1800
Scolastique	Olivier Couture	,,	1827
94 Joseph	(42) M. Anne Fortier	S.L.	1816
95 Augustin	(43) Véronique Bégin	S.H.	1802
Augustin			
96 Laurent	(44) Marthe Lainé	S.G.	1817
97 Antoine	(44) Marie Quemeneur	S.G.	1829
98 Jean Baptiste	(45) M. Anne Leclaire	S.Chs.	1825
99 Hubert	(45) Marg. Girard	S.Chs.	1826
Marguerite	René Gagné	,,	1857
Marc			
Joseph			
Hubert			
Romain			
100 Alexis	(45) Cécile Audet	S.Chs.	1840
Philoméne	François Côté	S.M.	1862
101 Joseph	(47) M. Barbe Cochon	S.V.	1780
M. Barbe	Jos. Morisset	,,	1805
Félicité	Jos. Roy	,,	1812
Euphrosine	Prudent Proulx	,,	1827
Joseph Marie			
102 Joseph	(49) M. Mad. Couillard	B.	1785
Madeleine	Jos. Turgeon	,,	1809
M. Josette	Ls. Patry	,,	1822
Charles			
Etienne			
Bénoni			
Joseph			

COUTURE.

103	Charles	(49)	Josette Filteau	B.	1790
	M. Josette		Frs. Octeau	"	1819
	Marguerite		Barthe Paquet	"	1838
104	Louis	(49)	Angé. Blanchet S.P.S.		1792
	M. Angélique		Germ. Brousseau		
				S.Chs.	1811
	Le même		Thérèse Gosselin	"	1796
	Emérence		Ls. Chabot	"	1827
	Olive		Chs. Fortier	S.M.	1826
	Joseph				
	Louis				
105	Etienne	(49)	Eliz. Pouliot	S.Chs.	1792
	Stanislas				
	Etienne				
106	Paul	(49)	M. Jos. Beaucher		
				S.P.S.	1804
	Marguerite		Chs. Leclaire	S.Chs.	1831
	Adelaïde		Féréol Brochu	"	1832
	Olivier				
	Vital				
107	Pierre	(54)	M. Angé. Blanchet		
				S.P.S.	1793
108	Charles	(54)	M. Désanges Morin		
				S.Chs.	1799
	Angélique		Frs. Chabot	"	1830
	Madeleine		Chs. Couture	"	1831
	Martin Obiline		Pre. Ed. Bilodeau		
				Lévis	1840
	Victoire		Florent Fournier	B.	1847
	Le même		Marg. Ruel	S.Chs.	1822
109	Joseph	(54)	Angé. Gourdeau	S.P.	1810
110	Jean	(54)	Monique Gourdeau	"	1831
111	Pierre	(55)	M. Anne Fortier	S.H.	1809
112	JeanBaptiste	(55)	M. Angèle Mercier		
				S.Chs.	1812
	M. Angéle		Nic. Pouliot	"	1831
	M. Zoé		Ed. Bacquet	"	1842
	Marie		Ls. Dalaire	"	1852
	J. B Théotine				
	Hubert				
	Joseph				
113	Etienne	(55)	Marie Hizoir	S.G.	1816
114	Charles	(55)	Marie Hizoir	"	1817
	Charles				
115	Joseph	(55)	Angé. Gosselin	S.G.	1841
116	François Xa-	(55)	Marthe Mercier	S.Chs.	1823
	vier				
117	Antoine	(55)	Marg. Côté	S.G.	1824
	Jean				
	Le même		Louise Côté	S.M.	1844
118	Etienne	(56)	M. Anne Forgues	"	1816
	Marie		Jos. Lebrun	S.Chs.	1841
	Constance		Ls. Lebrun	"	1855
	Hermine		Frs. Leblanc	"	1855
	M. Anne		Jos. Turgeon	"	1856
	Angèle		Pierre Lacroix	"	1864
	Magloire				
	François				
	Le même		Marie Bélanger	S.Chs.	1841
119	Charles	(56)	Martiane Rémillard		
				S.V.	1812
120	Louis	(59)	Louise Brochu	S.M.	1835
121	Charles	(59)	Archange Gautron		
				S.Chs.	1840
122	JeanBaptiste	(60)	Marie Côté	"	1840
123	Louis	(60)	Marie Bouchard	"	1857
124	Joseph	(61)	Fse. Asselin	S.M.	1809
125	Olivier	(62)	Scholastique Couture		
				S.L.	1827
126	Louis	(62)	Angèle Chatigny	S.P.	1842
	Louis Jos.				
127	Jean	(72)	Constance Roussin		
				S.P.	1846
128	Alexandre	(64)	Judith Boucher	S.Chs.	1832
129	Joseph	(65)	Judith Clément	"	1810
	Le même		Céleste Denis	S.G.	1823

COUTURE.

130	Joseph	(66)	Genev. Dompierre	S.F.	1819
131	Jean	(68)	Thérèse Labrecque		
				S.G.	1814
132	Michel	(68)	Angé. Cameron	"	1815
133	Zacharie	(68)	Adé Lemieux	"	1825
	Adelaïde		Maxime Goulet	S.V.	1850
	Le même		M. Mad. Lemieux	S.M.	1830
134	Pierre	(68)	Archange Fleury	S.G.	1826
135	JeanBaptiste	(72)	Marie Fortin	B.	1834
136	Pierre	(75)	Véronique Boutins		
				S.H.	1812
137	Charles	(75)	M. Rose Bissonnet		
				S.M.	1815
	Emélie		Pierre Quéret	S.Chs.	1835
	Le même		Marg. Denis	S.M.	1829
138	Alexandre	(78)	Félicité Dangueger	B.	1820
	M. Zoé				
	Alexandre				
139	Bénoit	(78)	Angèle Lacroix	S.Chs.	1814
140	André	(78)	M. Marg. Lacasse	"	1821
	Marie		Léon Patry	"	1846
	André				
	Louis				
	Le même		Fse. Picard	"	1847
141	JeanBaptiste	(78)	Angèle Dangueuger	B.	1824
142	Frs. Xavier		Marg. Boissel	"	1829
143	Etienne	(82)	Marg. Chabot	S.Chs.	1814
	M. Anne		Damase Blanchet	"	1839
	Elizabeth		Frs. Roy	"	1850
	Julie		Ant. Fournier	"	1851
	Frédéric				
144	François	(83)	Marie Corriveau	"	1821
	Flavie		Stanislas Couture	"	1856
	Etienne				
145	Joseph	(83)	Agathe Leblanc	S.G.	1821
146	Gervais	(83)	Angé Royer	"	1825
147	Charles	(83)	Mad. Couture	S.Chs.	1831
148	Etienne	(83)	Basilisse Pénin	S.G.	1830
149	Pierre	(84)	Louise Aubé	"	1818
150	Antoine	(85)	Ange Monmeny	S.Chs.	1819
	Louise		Jos. Fournier	B.	1844
151	JeanBaptiste	(85)	Genev. Gosselin	S.Chs.	1821
	Abraham				
152	Etienne	(87)	Cath. Duquet	"	1825
153	François	(87)	M. Reine Pilote	"	1839
154	Louis		Angé Dumont	Lévis	1817
	Le même		Marie Giguère	S.F.	1829
155	Michel	(91)	Marg. Leclaire	S.G.	1820
156	Augustin	(95)	Reine Roberge	S.P.	1827
157	Antoine		Marie Marteau (Mataut)		
	Marguerite		Chs. Frs. Lizotte	B.	1857
158	Alexis		Marg. Mateau		
	Le même		Marg. Dion	S.M.	1847
159	Jean		Marie Veau		
	Jacques				
	Jenjamin				
160	Joseph		Thérèse Doyons	S.Jos.	1822
	"		Jos. et Pélagie Lemieux		
				Lévis	Beauce
	Hilaire				
161	Jean		Rosalie Côté		
	Jean				
162	Marc	(99)	M. Célinar Gagnon		
				S.M.	1858
163	Hubert	(99)	M. Angèle Chabot		
				S.Chs.	1853
164	Romain	(99)	Emélie Pepin	"	1859
165	Joseph	(99)	Léocadie Côté	"	1861
166	Jos. Marie	(101)	Marg. Bélanger	S.V.	1804
	Frédéric				
167	Joseph	(102)	Marie Moor	B.	1822
	Domitille		Tho. Paquet	"	1852
168	Charles	(102)	Lucie Goupy	S.M.	1827
	M. Alviné		Geo. Monmeny	B.	1858
169	Etienne	(102)	Véronique Letang	"	1858
	Onésime				

COUTURE.

170	Benoni	(102)	M. Ls. Goupy	S.M. 1839
	Charles			
171	Joseph	(104)	Fse. Bernier	S.Chs. 1822
172	Louis	(104)	Genev. Chabot	„ 1822
173	Etienne	(105)	Marie Couture	„ 1817
	Marguerite		Jacq. Lainé	„ 1843
	Marie		Ls. Naud	„ 1846
	M. Perpétue		Greg. Caron	„ 1845
	Geneviève		Pierre Charrier	„ 1857
	M. Zoé		Ovide Voisin	„ 1852
	Etienne			
174	Stanislas		M. Flavie Lefebvre	
				S.Chs. 1829
	Stanislas			
	Etienne			
175	Olivier	(106)	Genev. Labrecque B. 1839	
176	Vital	(106)	Luce Gaumont S.Chs. 1843	
177	J. B. Théotine	(112)	M. Esther Chabot „ 1842	
	Le même		Emilie Bacquet S.M. 1860	
178	Charles	(114)	Marg. Patry S.Chs. 1844	
179	Jean	(117)	Salomé Audet S.L 1856	
	Salomé		Adolphe Cantin S.L. 1879	
180	Ignace		Anastasie Lefebvre Lévis	
	George			
181	François	(118)	Angé Duquet S.Chs. 1822	
182	Magloire	(118)	Angèle Naud „ 1841	
	Pierre			
183	Louis Joseph	(126)	M.Caroline Audet S.P.1867	
184	Alexandre	(138)	Vict. Voisin S.M. 1843	
185	André	(140)	M. Désanges Mercier	
				S.Chs. 1847
186	Louis	(140)	Marie Nadeau S.Chs. 1859	
187	Frédéric	(143)	M. Ls Rosalie Naud	
				S.Chs. 1840
	Virginie		Chs. Pépin „ 1861	
	Cédulie		Ferd. Chabot „ 1863	
188	Etienne	(144)	M. Scolastque Beaucher	
				B. 1846
189	Abraham	(151)	Hombéline Mercier	
				S.V. 1840
190	Binjamin	(159)	Fse. Poliquin S.Chs. 1848	
191	Jacques	(159)	Zoé Baillargeon „ 1848	
192	Hilaire	(160)	Eulalie Aubé „ 1852	
193	Jean	(161)	Eliz. Marseau S.V. 1861	
194	Frédéric	(166)	Eliz. Côté S.F.S. 1836	
195	Onésime	(169)	Apolline Plante S.L. 1854	
	Anne		Jos. Tessier „ 1874	
196	Charles	(170)	Anastasie Fortier S.V.1864	
197	Etienne	(173)	Emelie Mercier S.Chs.1839	
198	Etienne	(174)	Sophie Genest „ 1853	
199	Stanislas	(174)	Flavie Couture „ 1856	
200	Georges	(180)	Marie Roy „ 1846	
201	Pierre	(182)	Marie Mercier S.M. 1861	

CRÉPEAU.

1	Maurice		Marg. Laverdure	
	Anne		Nic Baillargeon S.P. 1683	
	Marguerite		Geo. Plante „ 1685	
	M. Madeleine		Pierre Dufresne „ 1692	
	Geneviève		Jean Pichet „ 1700	
	„		2° Chs. Pouliot „ 1703	
	Maurice			
	Robert			
2	Maurice	(1)	Marie Audet S.J. 1702	
	Geneviève		Gab. Gosselin S.P. 1726	
	Hélène		J. B. Ferlant „ 1732	
	Ursule		Joseph Chabot „ 1734	
	Basile			
	Joseph			
	Jean Baptiste			
	Louis			
	Pierre			

CRÉPEAU.

3	Robert	(1)	Mad. Lémelin	S L. 1703
	Marguerite		Ant. Gosselin	„ 1726
	Françoise		Jos. Maranda	„ 1734
	Marie		Ant. Gosselin	„ 1748
	Marie Anne		Ant Béleau	„ 1758
	Geneviève		J. B. Dorval	S.P. 1732
	M. Hélène		Pierre Ratté	„ 1732
	Joseph			
4	Guillaume		Marg. Labadie	
	Pierre			
5	Basile	(2)	Marg. Ratté	„ 1725
	Le même		Eliz. Mateau	
	M. Louise		Jean Langlois	„ 1777
	M. Elizabeth		Ant. Cadoret	„ 1783
	M. Josette		Ls Plante	C.R. 1746
	„		2° Jos. Pépin	„ 1777
	Thérèse		Dominique Poulin	„ 1754
			2° Ls Hélie	S.Joa. 1769
6	Louis	(2)	M. Jos Leclaire	S.P. 1739
7	Joseph	(2)	Genev. Turcot	S.F. 1736
	Geneviève		Laurent Gosselin	S.P. 1765
	M. Angélique		Ign. Martel	„ 1773
	Marie Anne		Jos. Letourneau	„ 1774
	Marie Thérèse		J. B. Drouin	„ 1780
8	Jean Baptiste	(2)	M. Anne Goulet	„ 1735
	Marie Anne		J. B. Faucher	„ 1763
	Marie Louise		Ls Tremblay	„ 1783
	Louis			
	Jean			
	Charles			
	François			
9	Pierre	(2)	Josette Dorval	„ 1752
	Michel			
	Joseph			
	Pierre			
10	Joseph	(3)	Marg. Dorval	„ 1746
	Marie Rose		Ls Célestin Campeau	
				S.L. 1778
	Hélène		Jos.Chs.Jeanjoux	„ 1790
	Marie Anne		Jos.Marie Gagnon	„ 1791
11	Pierre	(4)	M. Fse. Martel	S.P. 1777
	Geneviève		Pierre Pichet	S J. 1809
	Marie		Frs. Fortier	„ 1830
	Pierre			
12	Louis	(8)	M.Jos.Bussière Lévis 1770	
	Marie Josette		Frs. Boucher	S.P. 1798
	Marie		Pierre Gendreau	„ 1801
	Jean			
	Pierre			
13	Jean	(8)	M. Thècle Ratté	„ 1764
14	Charles	(8)	M. Reine Ratté	„ 1769
	Marie		Jos. Côté	„ 1793
	Geneviève		Pierre Aubin	„ 1799
	Angélique		Jos. Poulin	„ 1808
15	François	(8)	Gene. Côté	1769
	Marie		Michel Patry	„ 1793
	Marie Reine		Chs. Goulet	„ 1796
	Geneviève		Pierre Valière	„ 1803
	Thérèse		Pierre Gariépy	„ 1804
	François			
16	Pierre	(9)	Charotte Bussière S.H.1778	
	Archange		Jacq. Nicole	„ 1802
	Marie		Gab. Royer	S.G. 1810
	Joseph			
	Maurice			
17	Joseph	(9)	Véronique Carrier	
				Lévis 1781
18	Michel	(9)	Mad. Baugy	S.V. 1784
19	Pierre	(11)	Euphrosine Thivierge	
				S.J. 1813
	Scolastique		Jean Audet	S.J. 1840
	Flavie		Maurice Pépin	S.J. 1844
	Florence		Timothie Tremblay	
				S.J. 1848
	Clavie		Jos. Tremblay	S.J. 1851

CRÉPEAU.

```
   Alexis
   Pierre
20 Jean          (12) M. Anne Turcot S.P. 1838
   Marie Anne         Ls. Aubin        S.P. 1826
   Marguerite         Pierre Bouffart  S.P. 1829
   Thérèse            Pierre Pichet    S.P. 1831
   Léocadie           Chs. Alexis Godbout
                                       S.P. 1847
   Basilisse          J. B. Leclaire   S.L. 1843
   Pierre
   Francois
21 Pierre        (12) Marie Noël       S.P. 1810
   Marguerite         Pierre Tourdeau Q
22 Francois      (16) M. Jos. Pichet   S.P. 1800
   Marie Josette      Frs. Bedard      S.P. 1822
   Ignace
23 Joseph        (16) Riene Quemeneur
                                       S.F.S. 1809
 ° Maurice       (16) M. Genev. Métivier
                                       S.H. 1812
24 Alexis        (19) Cath. Martineau S.J. 1843
25 Pierre        (19) Marg. Labrecque
                                       S.Chs. 1839
26 Pierre        (20) Rosalie Pichet   S.P. 1839
27 François      (20) Basilisse CoutureS.P. 1840
28 Ignace        (22) Sophie Marcoux   S.P. 1841
```

CURODEAU.

```
 1 Pierre            Fse. Huot         A.G. 1733
   Pierre
   Le même           Marie Gosselin    IQ 1740
   Marguerite        Pierre Dalaire    S.J. 1767
 2 Pierre       (1)  Marg. Gosselin    S.J. 1754
   Marguerite        Pierre Noël Audebert
                                       S.J. 1778
   François          Issac Timothée Delisle
                                       S.J. 1780
   Marie             Abraham Delisle S.J. 1787
   Madeliene         Aug. Bornais      S.J. 1795
   M. Charlotte      Aug. Gobeil       S.J. 1798
   François
   Joseph
   Louis
   Pierre
 3 Pierre       (2)  Genev. Bornay     Q 1787
 4 François           Chs. Euphrosine Delisle
                                       S.J. 1787
   Marguerite        Jos. Labrecque    S.J. 1821
   Madeleine         Pierre Mercier    S.J. 1822
   Marie Ursule      Jos. Pouliot      S.J. 1822
   Cécile            Chs. Coulombe     S.L. 1831
   Archange          Jos. Leclaire     S.L. 1850
   Soulange          Frs. Ruel         S.P. 1828
   François
   Pierre
 5 Joseph       (2)  Mad. Audet        S.J. 1801
   François
 6 Louis        (2)  Mad. Coté         S.H. 1801
 7 François      (4)  M. Soulange Thivierge
                                       S.J. 1813
 8 Pierre       (4)  Angéle Labrecque S.J.1815
   Pierre
 9 François      (5)  M. Soulange Boissonneau
                                       S.J. 1835
   Demerise          Ls. Blouin        S.J. 1858
   François
10 Pierre       (8)  Agnés Royer       S.J. 1846
   Eugéne
11 François      (9)  Marg. Pepin       S.J. 1858
12 Eugéne       (10) M. Céline Pepin S.J.
```

CUSTOS.

```
 1 Pierre Jacques    Marie Bonnier         1694
   Jean
 2 Jean        (1)   Cath. Fauteux
```

CUSTOS.

```
   Jean Baptiste
 3 Jean Baptiste (2) Mad. Falardeau
                                    Chs. Bourg 1754
   Jean Baptiste
   Le même            Ursule Caron S.Chs. 1763
                                   V. de P. Boissel
   Marie Louise       Jos. Béchard    S.G. 1781
   Le même            M. Mad. Gontier
                                       S.Chs. 1768
   Le même            Louise Chartier S.Chs 1789
 4 Jean Baptiste (3) Catherine Leclair
                                       S.Chs. 1780
```

CYR.

```
 1 Jean               M. Jos. Gottereau, Acadie
   Pierre
   Jean
 2 Paul               Marg. Daigle
   Le même            Marie Dubois S. Chs 1758
 3 Pierre             Marg Hébert, Acadie
   N. Madeleine       J. B. Coulombe S.F.S.1766
   Marie              JeanMarieFradetS.V.1770
 4 Pierre       (1)  Zith Trahan     S.F.S. 1760
 5 Jean               Fse. Malboeuf S.P.S. 1761
```

DAIGLE.

```
 1 André              Thérèse Proulx
                                   Pte. Trembles 1711
 2 Joseph             Mad. Gottereau, Acadie
   Anastasie          Pierre Naud      S.V. 1760
   Joseph
 3 René               Mad. Hébert, S. Roche
   Joseph
 4 Jean Baptiste      Blanche Trahan, Acadie
   Le même            Marie Trahan S.Chs. 1759
 5 Charles            M. Anne Royer St.Antoine
   Jean Baptiste
 6 Joseph        (2) Marg. GuilbeauS.F.S.1762
 7 Joseph        (3) MarieCoulombeS.P.S.1771
 8 Jean Baptiste (5) Thérèse Tangué S.V. 1781
   Jean Marie
   André
   Pierre
 9 Jean Marie    (8) Marie Lepage    S.V. 1802
   Françoise         FlavienTerrien S.Chs. 1835
   Jean
   Le même           Marg. Leblond S.Chs. 1841
10 André         (8) Apolline Gosselin
                                       S.Chs. 1813
   Angele            F. X. Clement S.Chs. 1843
11 Pierre        (8) Angé. Gosselin S.Chs. 1821
   Ferdinand
   André
12 Jean          (9) Louise Thibaut  S.G. 1827
13 André         (11) M. Zoé Couture S.Chs.1845
14 Ferdinand     (11) Marie Aubé     S.Chs. 1837
```

DANDURAND.

```
 1 Antoine            Marie Vérieul    S.F. 1696
   Elizabeth          Jacq.Gendreau S.Tho.1722
   Marie Anne         Guill Boulet    "    1734
   Joseph Frs.
   Antoine
 2 Joseph Frs.   (1) M. Mad. Baudouin
                                    Bert. 1729
 3 Antoine       (1) Véronique Proulx
                                       S.Tho. 1738
   Marie Louise      Frs. Fortin    S.P.S. 1766
   Jacques
   Charles
   Jean Baptiste
 4 Jean Baptiste      Eliz. Morin    S.Tho. 1763
                                       S.Tho.
```

5-6 EDWARD VII., A. 1906

DANDURAND.

```
    Jean Baptiste
    Charles
 5  Jacques          (3) ·M. Reine Morin S. Tho 1777
                         S. Tho.
    Marie Reine          Pierre Bernier S.F.S. 1810
    Judith               Jos. Larrivé      B. 1815
    Marie Pélagie        Joachim Gosselin S.H.1816
    Madeleine            Jos. Mercier     „  1820
    Marie Anne           Pierre Mercier   „  1820
    Jacques
 6  Jean Baptiste (4) M. Mad. Rousseau
                                   S.P.S. 1796
 7  Charles       (4) M. Mad. Rousseau
                                   S.P.S. 1802
 8  Charles       (3) Josette Morin S.Tho. 1782
                         S. Tho.
    Geneviève         Jos. Théophile Blais
                                   S.P.S. 1820
    Charles
    Pierre
    Felix
 9  Jacques       (5) Marg. Lacasse S.Chs. 1801
10  Charles       (8) Fse. Marseau S.F.S. 1808
11  Pierre        (8) M. Rosalie Picard
                                   S.F.S. 1820
12  Felix         (8) M. Rosalie Proulx
                                   S.F.S. 1825
```

DANGUEGUER.

```
 1  Jean              Ange Roulois
    Marie Josette     Guill. Couture    B. 1758
    Angélique         Jos. Dam. Poliquin B. 1752
    Marie             Clément Couture   B. 1762
    Jean
    Pierre
 2  Jean          (1) Thérèse Terrien S.J. 1763
    Généviève         Ant. Ratté        B. 1788
    Louise            Guill. Beaucher S.Chs. 1803
    Jos. Abraham
    Gabriel
 3  Pierre        (1) M.Marg. Lacroix S.M.1779
 4  Jos. Abraham (2) M. Angé Beaucher B. 1797
    Félicité          Alexandre Couture B. 1820
    Félicité          2° Frs. Aubé      B. 1829
    Angéle            J. B. Couture     B. 1824
    Adelaïde          F. X. Turgeon     B. 1833
    Jean
    Gabriel
    Germain
    Elisé
 5  Gabriel       (2) M. Fse. Cameron S.V. 1797
 6  Jean          (4) Clotilde Fournier B. 1829
 7  Germain       (4) Marg. Vict. Turgeon
                                   B. 1831
 8  Gabriel       (4) Henriette Labrecque
                                   B. 1839
 9  Elisé         (4) M. Emélie Corriveau
                                   S.V. 1842
```

DANIAU—LAPRISE.

```
 1  Jean              M. Ls. Michaud   S. 1670
    Marguerite        Armand Lavergne
                                   S.M. 1693
    M. Françoise      Frs. Picard      S.M. 1700
    Jacques
    Le même           Fse. Rondeau     S.J. 1686
    Jean
    Joseph
    Guillaume
 2  Jacques       (1) Louise Picard S.Tho. 1702
    Marguerite        Ant. Morin    S.P.S. 1734
    M. Marthe         Etn. Fontaine S.P.S. 1737
    M. Geneviève      Ls. Boulet    Bert. 1731
    Jean Baptist
```

DANIAU—LAPRISE.

```
 3  Jean          (1) Marthe Lamy
    Le même           Fse. Guilmet    S.M, 1711
    Louise Mad.       Pierre Rouleau  S.M. 1741
    M. Madeleine      Pierre Patry    S.M. 1748
    Jean
    Joseph
    Le même           Marg. Malboeuf S.M. 1748
                         V. de Pre Gagné
    Le même           Marg. Guenet
    M. Louise         Michel Tangué  S.M. 1778
 4  Guillaume     (1) Genev. Lamy    Bert. 1723
    M. Geneviève      Frs. Belloy    S.V. 1747
    Pierre Arséne
    Guillaume
    Le même           Susanne Dumont Bert.1736
    Le même           Jeanne Guimon Bert. 1743
 5  Joseph        (1) Ange Lepage    Bert. 1730
    Le même           Marie Bilodeau Bert. 1758
    M. Génévieve      Jean Valière Nadeau
                                   Bert. 1780
    Françoise         Gab. Bilodeau  Bert. 1788
    Ursule            Pierre Guilmet Bert. 1797
    M. Thécle         Pierre Emond   Bert. 1798
 6  Jean Baptiste     Claire Blanchet
    M. Claire         Jacq. Bilodeau S.F.S. 1749
    Jean François
    Joseph
    Michel Philippe
 7  Joseph            M. Jos. Greffart
    Marie Josette     J. B. Gagné   S.F.S. 1751
 8  François          Marie Rousseau
    Marie             Pierre Morin  S.P.S. 1756
    Reine             Jos. Talbot   S.P.S. 1762
    Prisque
    Pierre
    Jean Baptiste
 9  Jean Baptiste (2) Mad. Plante    S.J. 1747
    M. Madeleine      Pierre Gautron S.F.S. 1767
    M. Geneviève      Jean Mercier  S.F.S. 1771
    Rose              Frs. Gagnon   S.F.S. 1786
    Pierre
    Réné
10  Jean          (3) Thérèse Guénet   B. 1740
11  Joseph        (3) M. Jos. Dalaire S.M. 1741
    Marie Josette     André Forgues  S.M. 1766
    Joseph
    Nicolas
12  Pierre Arsène (4) M. Héléne Cadrin
                                   S. M. 1754
    Marguerite        Chs. Girard    B. 1797
    Pierre
    Jean Baptiste
    Joseph
13  Guillaume     (4) Isabett Noël   S. M. 1762
14  François           Genev. Morin
    Madeleine          J. B. Rousseau S.P.S. 1772
    Pierre
    Joseph
    François
15  Michel Phi-   (6) Anne Fse. Boissonneau
      lippe                        S. F. S. 1758
    François          Fse. Plante   S.Chs. 1786
    Thérèse           Pierre Fradet S. Chs. 1815
    Joseph
16  Joseph        (6) Ursule Richard S.F.S. 1762
    Le même           Véronique Tangué
                                   S. G. 1804
    Véronique         Michel Cochon S. G. 1823
17  Jean François (6) Marg. Morin S. F. S. 1767
    Le même           Agathe Boulet S.F.S. 1777
    Marie Reine       Jean Garant S. F. S. 1804
    Jean Baptiste
18  Jean Baptiste (8) M. Jos. Morin Bert. 1753
    M. Josette        Ant. Gagné  S. P. S. 1780
    Joseph
```

DANIAU—LAPRISE.

Le même		M. Euphrosine Lizotte	S. P. S. 1775
	M. Louise	Ant. Dassylva S.P.S. 1797	
	M. Charlotte	Pierre Caman S.P.S. 1802	
	Jean Baptiste		
19	Prisque	(8) Genev. Plante S.F.S. 1762	
	Le même	M. Claire Rolandeau	S. M. 1793
20	Pierre	(8) M. Genev. Rousseau	S.P.S. 1770
	M. Reine	Pierre Guilmet S.P.S. 1792	
	Thérèse	Alexis Langlois S. H. 1802	
	Généviève	Ls. Duperron S. H. 1805	
	Angéle	Olivier Duperron S.H.1817	
	Pierre		
21	Pierre	(9) Fse. Blais Bert. 1773	
	Marguerite	Ls. Buteau S. F. S. 1798	
	René Abraham		
	Jean Baptiste		
22	René	(9) M. Gertrude Quéret	S. V. 1800
23	Joseph	(11) M.Ange Pelletier S.M.1772	
24	Nicolas	(11) M. Angé Bacquet	S. M. 1775
25	Pierre	(12) Rose Furois S. M. 1791	
	Marie Louise	Michel Vien S. M. 1807	
	Le même	M. Reine Richard	S. M. 1802
	Pierre		
26	Joseph	(12) M. Ls. Jolin S. H. 1794	
27	JeanBaptiste	(12) M. Jos. Arguin S. H. 1808	
28	François	(14) Véronique Gaudreau	S. Tho. 1775
	Angélique	Jacq. Sauvage S. G. 1806	
	Jean Marie		
	François		
	Le même	M. Pélagie Labonté	S. P. S. 1818
29	Pierre	(14) Thérése Garant S.F.S.1780	
30	Joseph	(14) Marie Baudoin S.F.S.1784	
31	Joseph	(15) Euphrosine Bilodeau	S. Chs. 1804
	Archange	Frs. Canac S. Chs. 1835	
	Marcelline	Michel Blais S. Chs. 1836	
	Adé. Euphrosine	Amb. Naud S. Chs. 1839	
	Michel		
	Jacques		
32	JeanBaptiste(17)	M. Claire Lemieux	S.F.S. 1816
	Marie Claire	J. B. Marseau S.F.S. 1842	
33	Joseph	(18) M. Jos. Pellerin	S.P.S. 1782
	Françoise	Greg. Filteau S. H. 1812	
	Josette	Frs. Nollet S. H. 1816	
	Pierre		
34	JeanBaptiste(18)	M. Jos. Blais Bert. 1783	
	M. Françoise	Frs. Germ. Gaumont	S. P. S. 1803
	M. Josette	Marcel Thibault	S. P. S. 1806
	Euphrosine	Jacq. Bernier S.P.S. 1811	
	Angéle	Abraham Antil S.P.S.1823	
	Geneviève	Jos. Fontaine S. P. S. 1824	
	Marie Julie	Chs. Lemieux S.P.S. 1826	
35	Charles	M. Ls. Picard	
	Louise	Isidore Carbonneau	Bert. 1802
	André		
	Jacques		
36	François	Julie Garneau (?)	
	Julie	J. B. Boucher S.F.S. 1826	
37	Pierre	(20) Thérése Baudoin S.H. 1802	
	Louis		
	Pierre		
38	René Abra-ham	(21) M. Marg. Morin S.M. 1802	

DANIAU—LAPRISE.

	Pierre		
39	JeanBaptiste(21)	Marg. Morin S. F. S. 1803	
	Jean Baptiste		
40	Pierre	(25) Rosalie Duchesne	S.F.S. 1834
41	Jean Marie	(28) M. Barbe Vallée	S.P.S. 1812
	Marie	Abraham Leclaire	S.P.S. 1838
42	Francois	(28) M. Delphine Blais	S. F. S. 1835
43	Michel	(31) Eudore Poliquin	S. Chs.1836
44	Jacques	(31) Natalie Monmeny	S. Chs. 1842
45	Pierre	(33) Marie Leclaire S. H. 1813	
	Le même	Angé Gagnon S. Chs. 1815	
	Pierre		
46	Jacques	(35) M. Vict. Mercier Bert. 1807	
	Le même	Josette Godbout S.G. 1816	
47	André	(35) Rose Carbonneau Bert. 1806	
48	Louis	(37) Marcelline Noel S.P. 1841	
49	Pierre	(37) Huméland Martel S.P. 1841	
	Pre. Siméon		
50	Pierre	(38) M. Anne Pouliot S.M. 1833	
51	Jn. Baptiste(39)	Genev. Gagnon S.F.S. 1832	
52	Pierre	(45) Adéline Denis S.L. 1855	
53	Pre. Siméon (49)	Belzémire Genest S.P. 1866	

DANIEL.

1	Thomas	Barbe Poisson	
	Joseph		
	Le même	Susanne Lefebvre, V. de Jean Plante S.J. 1715	
	M. Geneviève	Frs. Prudhomme S.P. 1747	
2	Joseph	(1) Fse. Bilodeau S. Frs. 1726	
	Joseph		
3	François	Agathe Terrien	
	Marie	Pierre Verpillot	S. Chs. 1763
	Marie	Jos. Roy S. Chs. 1765	
	Joseph		
	Le même	M. Cath. Turgeon B. 1756	
4	Joseph	(2) M. Ls. Lamare S.P.S. 1756	
5	Joseph	(3) M. Fse. Dion S.F.S. 1774	

DARVEAU.

1	François	Marie Savard Pte. Tremble	
	Jean		
2	Jean	(1) Reine Gagnon S.F.S. 1803	
	Marie	Pierre Gontier S.G. 1821	
	Archange	F. X. Patoüel S.G. 1829	
	Angéle	Michel McCarthy S.G.1830	
	Le même	M. Marg. Fortier S.V.1810	
	Fréderic		
	Le même	Scolastique Patry S.V.1844	
3	Fréderic	(2) Eléonore Théberge	S. V. 1842

DEBLOIS.

1	Grégoire	Fse. Viger S.R. 1662	
	Reine	Sixte Lerreau S.F. 1694	
	Marie	J. B. Dupont S. F. 1695	
	Jean Baptiste		
	Joseph		
	Germain		
	Jean		
2	Joseph	(1) Marg. Rousseau S.F. 1686	
	Madeleine	Etn. Bluteau S.F. 1709	
	Anne	Noel Couët S. Frs. 1717	
	Marguerite	Jean Paquet	
	Simon		
	Joseph		

DEBLOIS.

Jean Baptiste		
Le même	Marie Lefort	S. Frs. 1718
3 Jean	(1) Fse. Rousseau	S. Frs. 1688
Françoise	Jacq. Labbé	S. Frs. 1709
Claire	Chs. Paradis	S. Frs. 1714
M. Marthe	Mathieu Parent	S.Frs.1721
Le même	Genev. Lemaitre	Q. 1706
Le même	Marg. Meunier	S.Frs.1719
4 Germain	(1) M. Mad. Dupont	S.F.1696
M. Marthe	Chs. Laignon	S.F. 1732
M. Madeleine	Pierre Drouin	S.F. 1734
Marie	Chs. Loiseau	S.F. 1746
Angélique	Pierre Serand	S.F. 1752
Angélique	2° Jean Rocray	S.F. 1760
Germain		
Pierre		
5 Jean Baptiste (1)	Louise Peltier	S.F. 1703
Le même	M. Mad. Labbé	S.Frs.1710
Madeleine	Ant. Gagnon	S. Frs. 1760
Claire	Chs. Poulin	S. Frs. 1744
Catherine	Chs. Landry	S. Frs. 1746
Félicité	Aug. Landry	S. Frs. 1748
Pierre		
Jean Baptiste		
Joseph		
François		
Agathe	Michel Morisset	S.F. 1745
Marie	Ls. Asselin	S.F. 1754
François		
Charles		
Pierre		
Le même	Gertrude Vérieul	S. Frs. 1723
Marie	Frs. Dubé	S. Frs. 1757
M. Gertrude	Frs. Lebrun	S.F. 1765
Basile		
7 Simon	Marg. Guérard	S.Frs. 1716
Thérèse	Ls. Dalaire	S. Frs. 1753
Madeleine	Jos. Lejeune	S. Frs. 1757
Louis		
Charles		
François		
Le même	Marthe Marseau	
8 Jean Baptiste (2)	Angé Dumont	Que. 1719
9 Joseph (2)	Veronique Martineau	S. Frs. 1724
10 Germain (4)	Cath. Lehoux	S. F. 17378
11 Pierre (4)	M. Cath. Letourneau	S.F. 1745
Anastasie	Urbain Thibodean	S.F. 1777
Catherine	Jos. Perrot	S.F. 1777
Chs. Maxine		
Pre Chrysologue		
12 Jean Baptiste(5)	Cath Gagné	S. Frs. 1737
Marie Anne	Jean Gagnon	S. Frs. 1755
Jean Baptiste		
62 Joseph (5)	Marie Fournier	S.Frs.1742
Le mêne	M. Dorothée Coté	,, 1774
14 Pierre (5)	Angé Fugère	,, 1747
A Louis (5)	Ursule Levasseur	,,
Etienne		
15 François (6)	Marie Guion	S.F. 1747
Abondance	Michel Tremblay	,, 1774
Josette	J. B. Asselin	,, 1782
François		
16 Charles (6)	Marthe Asselin	S.F. 1749
Basile		
Charles		
17 Pierre (6)	Marie Guérard	S.Frs. 1749
18 Basile (6)	Marie Lehoux	S.F. 1762
Charlotte	Jos Laurent	,, 1794
Marie	Jos. Boivin	,, 1799
Basile		
François		
Ambroise		

DEBLOIS.

19 Charles	(7) Eliz. Fugère	S.Frs. 1741
Marie	Jos. Martineau	,, 1776
Charles		
20 Louis	(7) M. Jos. Larrivé	S.F. 1743
Le même	Hélène Gagnon	,, 1745
Louise	Hyacinthe Martineau	S.Frs. 1764
Marie Victoire	Jos. Lerreau	,, 1779
21 François	M. Thérèse Asselin	F.S. 1753
Le même	Marie Bazin	S.H. 1791
22 Chs. Maxime(11)	Thérèse Tringue	S.F. 1776
23 Pre. Chryso-(11)	M. Angé Giguère	,, 1780
logue		
24 Jean Bap- (12)	Mad. Gagnon	S.Frs. 1759
tiste		
25 François	(15) Marg. Poulin	S.F. 1776
Marguerite	Jos. Martineau	,, 1807
Marie	Etn. Drouin	,, 1812
26 Charles	(16) M. Jos.Baudon	S.Frs. 1773
M. Thécle	Frs. Canac.	,, 1808
Jean Marie		
Pierre		
Basile		
François		
Joseph		
Le même	M. Mad. Pepin	S.F. 1791
M. Josette	Frs. Dorval	,, 1815
Madeleine	Ls. Guérard	,, 1826
27 Basile	M. Anastasie Beaucher	S.F. 1780
28 Pierre	Marie Avare	S. Marie
Pierre		
29 Basile	Sussanne Deblois	
Louis	Louis	
30 Pierre	Fse. Baudouin	Bert.
Pierre		
31 Basile	(18) M. Abondance Avare	S.F. 1792
32 François	(18) Thérèse Beaucher	,, 1799
M. Marthe	Jean Lheureux	,, 1827
M. Adelaide	F. X. Asselin	,, 1832
Olive	J. B. Martineau	,, 1841
Thérèse	Jean Canac	S.Frs. 1823
Barthelemi		
Paul		
33 Ambroise	(18) Marg. Faucher	S.F. 1807
34 Charles	(19) Thécle Gagnon	S.Frs. 1760
35 François	(26) Cath. Morel	,, 1704
	V. de Frs. Dompiere	
Catherine	Edouard Guérard	S.Frs. 1829
Le même	Thérèse Pouliot	S.L. 1847
36 Basile	(26) M. Jos. Pepin	S.Frs. 1801
A Etienne		S: Marie 1780
Etienne		
37 Joseph	(26) M. Ls. Lemelin	S.Frs. 1808
38 Jean Marie	(26) M. Angé Dorval	S.F. 1812
39 Pierre	(26) Marg. Canac	S.F. 1812
Ludivine	Jos. Hébert	S.Frs. 1842
Marguerite	Chs. Guérard	,, 1845
Pierre		
Charles		
Marcel		
40 Pierre	(28) Marie Parent	B. 1793
41 Joseph	Marg. Parent	Que. 1785
Julienne	Jos. Jolin	S.F. 1821
Joseph	Est-ce le même No. 40.	
42 Louis	(29) M. Marg. Savoie	S.Frs.1817
	Kamouraska.	
43 Pierre	(30) Eliz. Belo0eau	S.Frs. 1820
44 Barthélemi	(32) Angéle Beaucher	S.F. 1831
Marie	Eliz. Drouin	,, 1856
Marcelline	Jos. Beaucher	,, 1859

DEBLOIS.

	Barthélemi			
45	Paul	(32)	Genev. Drouin S.F.	1831
	Géneviève		Pierre Demeule ‖	1852
	Marie		Anselme Drouin ‖	1858
	Paul			
	Joseph			
46	Pierre	(39)	Marie Lepage S.Frs.	1846
47	Marcel	(39)	Eliz. Gosselin S.L.	1852
48	Charles	(39)	Susanne Audet S.F.	1855
49	Joseph	(41)	Euphrosine Pouliot	
			S.J.	1815
	Joseph			
50	Etienne	(36ᵃ)	M. Ls. Faucher S.M.	1825
	Olive		Célestin Montigny	
			S.P.	1853
	Marie Louise		Timothée Chatigny ‖	1860
51	Barthélemi	(44)	Angéle Pepin S.F.	1864
52	Paul	(45)	Basilisse Canac ‖	1857
53	Joseph	(49)	Cath. Hélie ‖	1839
54	Joseph	(45)	Démerise Canac ‖	1868

DELAGE

1	Nicolas		Marie Petit S.F.	1669
	Charles			
2	Charles	(1)	Marie Manseau S.L.	1697
	Charles			
	Le même		Marg. Plante S.J.	1706
	Marguerite		Pierre Coté S.L.	1726
	Marie Anne		Ls. Labrecque ‖	1730
	Geneviève		Jos. Pepin ‖	1730
	Geneviève		2° Gab. Filteau S.J.	1744
	Jean			
3	Charles	(2)	Mad. Pouliot S.L.	1723
	Le même		M. Jos. Plante S.J.	1725
	Madeleine		Basile Fortier ‖	1751
	Marie Anne		Frs. Dalaire ‖	1754
	M. Marianne		Jean Blouin ‖	1754
	Elizabeth		Jacq. Gaudreau ‖	1761
	M. Angélique		Guill Audet ‖	1763
	Marie Louise		Jos. Drouin ‖	1783
	Louis			
4	Louis	(3)	Mad. Dalaire ‖	1753
	Marie		Etu. Turcot ‖	1794
	Joseph			
	Charles			
	Etienne			
5	Jean	(2)	M. Blanche Doucet	
			Que.	1761
	M. Françoise		Frs. Audet S.J.	1789
6	Joseph	(4)	Mad. Lefebvre ‖	1786
7	Charles	(4)	M. Ls. Thivierge ‖	1789
	Le même		M. Anne Huot ‖	1792
	Marie Anne		Jacq. Blouin ‖	1812
	Marie		Jos. Dupuis ‖	1822
	Charles			
A	Etienne	(4)	Mad. Canac S.H.	1800
8	Charles	(7)	Marie Picard S.Frs.	1822

DELANTEIGNE—LANTAGNE

1	Jean Nicolas		Marie Gérard	
			Ev. d'Avranches	
	Jean Michel			
2	Jean Michel	(1)	M. Jeanne Charier	
			S.Chs.	1766
	Pierre			
	Le même		Agathe Ouimet S.M.	1770
	Marie		Frs. Vallée ‖	1790
	Marie Anne		Gab. Thibaut ‖	1802
	François			
	Jean Baptiste			
	Joseph			
3	François	(2)	Marie Anne Fortin	
			S.V.	1804
	Marie Anne		Féréal Labreque S.G.	1827

DELANTEIGNE—LANTAGNE.

	François			
	Joseph			
4	Jean Baptiste	(2)	Marie Anne Charier	
			S.Chs.	1808
	Le même		Constance Gaudreau	
			S.M.	1813
5	François	(3)	Genev. Balan S.G.	1825
6	Joseph	(3)	Hélène Balan ‖	1828
7	Pierre	(2)	Thérèse Clement S.H.	1788
	Le même		Thérèse Canac ‖	1791
	Angélique		André Hélie ‖	1815
8	Joseph	(2)	Cath. Fortier ‖	1802
	Catherine		Jos. Turcot ‖	1820

DELAUNAY

	Jacques		Cath. Bernard	
	Catherine		Jean Larchevèque C.R.	1683
2	Nicolas		Antoinette Durand	
			Que.	1661
	Françoise		Nicolas Cadrin S.F.	1679
	Madeleine		Frs. Morvent ‖	1694
	Nicolas			
3	Simon		Jeanne Ceillier	
	Claude			
4	Gilles		Louise Dubois	
	Pierre			
5	Pierre	(4)	Frs. Pinguêt Que.	1645
	Henri			
A	Claude	(3)	Denise Leclaire S.F.	1669
6	Henri	(5)	Frs. Crête Beauport	1679
	M. Françoise		Jean Brochu Que.	1697
	M. Françoise		2° Jacq. Griffart	
	Marguerite		Pierre Belanger	
			Beauport	1700
7	Nicolas	(2)	Eliz. Rainville Que.	1695
8	Julien		Fse. Perreau Ev. de Dole	
	Nicolas			
9	Nicolas	(9)	Angé Roy Bert.	1729
	M. Angélique		Baptiste Rogerie ‖	1749

DELEUGRE

1	Jacques		Marie Taupier Que.	1661
	Mathurine		Jean Plante S.F.	1687
	Jacques			
2	Jacques	(1)	Cath. Gendreau C.R.	1688

DEFOURNEAU

1				
2	Jean Baptiste	(1)	Véronique Cochon	
	Véronique		J. B. Roy S.V.	1753
	Elizabeth		J. B. Remillard ‖	1764

DELISLE.

1	Louis		Louise des Granges	
			Que.	1669
	Marie Louise		Chs. Robitaille	
			Pte. Trembles	1705
	Antoine			
2	Antoine	(1)	M. Cath. Faucher	
			Pte. Trembe	1694
	M. Catherine		Jean Amiot ‖	1722
	M. Catherine		2° Jean Renaud	
			Pte. Tremble	1734
	Ls. Joseph			
3	Louis Joseph	(2)	M. Mad. Toupin	
			Pte. Tremble	1724
	Louis Joseph			
	Jean Baptiste			
4	Louis Joseph	(3)	M. Gertrude Lemieux	
			Cap. S. Ign.	1749
			Lévis	
	M. Françoise		Aug. Dion S.J.	1774
	Marguerite		Pierre Fontaine ‖	1780

DELISLE.

Marguerite	2° Jean Boucher	S.H.	1804
Geneviève	Louis Gobeil	S.J.	1784
Chs. Euphrosine	Frs. Curodeau	"	1787
Chs. Euphrosine	2° Frs. Blouin	"	1808
Isaac Timothée			
Louis Abraham			
Joseph			
A Jean Baptiste (3)	Genev. Lemieux		
	Cap. S.	Ign.	1751
5 Joseph	(4) Eliz. Leblanc	S.J.	1777
6 Isaac Tim-	(4) Fse. Curodeau	S.J.	1784
othée			
Angélique	Joseph Ratté	S.H.	1802
Marie Louise	Pierre Dutile	"	1807
Archange	Louis Roberge	"	1809
Madeleine	Joseph Tardif	"	1810
Joseph			
7 Louis Abra-	(4) Marie Curodeau	S.J	1787
ham			
Marie	Nicolas Baillargeon		
		S.L.	1811
Louis Abraham			
Le même	Marie Bouffart	"	1802
Théotiste	Ant. Noël	S.J.	1825
Marguerite	Frs. Maranda	S.L.	1831
Alexis			
Joseph			
Le même	Marie Noël	"	1811
Emélie	Félix Maranda	"	1839
Jean Baptiste			
Le même	M. Jos. Boissonneau		
		S.J.	1819
François Xavier			
8 Joseph	(6) M. Anne Lemieux		
		Lévis	1808
9 Louis Abra-	(7) Angèle Baillargeon		
ham		S.L.	1811
10 Joseph	(7) Marie Maranda	S.L.	1829
Félix			
Le même	Fse. Audet	"	1845
11 Alexis	(7) Josette Pepin	S.J.	1831
Léocadie	Paul Paquet	"	1854
Sara	Aug. Lemieux	"	1859
Adélaïde	Ls. Hébert	"	1860
12 Jean Baptiste (7)	Marie Godbout	S.L	1839
Angélique Del-	F. X. Grenier	"	1873
phine			
Ismael			
Désiré			
Zéphirin			
13 François Xa-	(7) Henriette Gosselin		
vier		S.J.	1842
14 Ismael	(12) Louise Roberge	S.L.	1870
15 Désiré	Caroline Labrecque		
		S.L.	1870
16 Zéphirin	(12) Dina Duchesne	S.L.	1876

DEMEULE.

1 Joseph	Marie Dubeau	S.J.	1707
Angélique	Pierre Moreau	"	1742
M. Monique	Ls. Tremblay	"	1751
Marie Louise	Frs. Moor	"	1753
Marie Louise	2° Jean Carreau	"	1771
Josette	J. B. Boissonneau		
François			
Jean Baptiste			
2 Françoise	Fse. Petrot	S.F.	1748
Marie Anne	Jos. Loignon	S.J.	1778
Françoise	Pierre Pichet	"	1792
Louise	J. B. Landry	"	1798
Josette	Frs. Cochon	"	1807
François			
Joseph			
Charles			
3 Jean Baptiste (1)	Cath. Poulin	C.R.	1741

Q

DEMEULE.

Le même	Ange Pepin	S.J.	1780
4 François	(2) Eliz. Denis	S.L.	1773
Marie Josette	Basile Bouchard	"	1805
5 Joseph	(2) Mad. Pepin	S.J.	1785
Madeleine	Pierre Descombes	"	1813
Joseph			
François			
Pierre			
6 Charles	(2) M. Anne Labrecque		
		S.L.	1788
Le même	Josette Bilodeau	S.F.	1812
7 Joseph	(5) M. Marg. Boissonneau		
		S.J.	1809
Marie Anne	Marcel Letellier	"	1850
Marie	Laurent Gosselin	"	1760
Magloire			
Joseph			
8 François	(5) Mad. Giguère	S.J.	1814
9 Pierre	(5) M. Thècle Canac	S.F.	1827
Emélie	Frs. Boissonneau	S.J.	1850
Marie Anne	Jos. Dalaire	"	1857
Pierre			
Le même	Marie Fortier	"	1841
10 Joseph	(7) Théotiste Pepin	S.J.	1836
11 Magloire	(7) Marg. Blouin	S.J.	1836
12 Pierre	(9) Genev. Deblois	S.F.	1852

DENIS-LAPIERRE.

1 Pierre	Marie Gaudin	A.G.	1687
Marie	Jean Baillargeon	S.L.	1718
Anne	Jean Pouliot	S.L.	1724
Marguerite	Ls. Rouleau	S.L.	1730
Charles			
Joseph			
Jacques			
2 Charles	(1) Mad. Pichet	S.V.S.L.	1719
M. Madeleine	Jos. Marie Cochon		
		S.V.	1738
Marguerite	J. B. Racine	S.V.	1746
Marie	Nicolas Herpe	S.V.	1796
Charles			
Etienne			
3 Joseph	(1) Marie Clément	S.M.B.	1722
Madeleine	Frs. Alarie	S.M.	1743
Madeleine	2° Aug. Rémillard		
		S.V.	1746
Marie Josette	Jos. Forgue	S.M.	1745
Thérèse	Ant. Gontier	S.M.	1754
Ursule Agnès	Jacq. Allard	S.M.	1750
Ursule Agnès	2° Pierre Carrier	S.M.	1765
Clotide	Jos. Rémillard	S.M.	1755
Marguerite	J. B. Labbé	S.M.	1756
Elizabeth	Jacq. Bolduc	S.M.	1761
Elizabeth	2° Jos. Saillard	S.M.	1775
Pierre			
4 Jacques	(1) Véronique Mathieu		
		A.G.	1725
Véronique	Ls. Fortier	S.L.	1746
Marie Anne	Pierre Godbout	S.L.	1751
Isabelle	Thomas Moor	S.L.	1763
Isabelle	2° Frs. Demeule	S.L.	1773
Marie Anne	Michel Lacroix	S.L.	1760
Marie Anne	2° Jos. Lemelin	S.M.	1871
Geneviève	Nicolas Lefebvre	S.M.	1769
Nicolas			
Jacques			
Jos. Marie			
François			
5 Charles	(2) M. Ls. Fradet		
		S.Chs.S.V.	1749
M. Charlotte	Jos. Lebrun	S.Chs.	1769
Elizabeth	Chs. Letlaire	S.Chs.	1770
Geneviève	Chs. Beaulieu	S.Chs.	1780
Louise	Pierre Bilodeau	S.Chs.	1782
M. Marguerite	Jos. Létourneau	S.Chs.	1785

DENIS—LAPIERR

M. Marguerite		2ᵈ Jacq. Beaucher		S.Chs. 1800
Etienne				
Charles				
Le même		Désanges Matte		
		V. de Phil. Picard		S.Chs.1797
6	Etienne	(2)	Eliz. Leclaire	S.M. 1765
	Marie		Nicolas Tangué	S.V. 1787
	Marie Anne		Jacq. Bilodeau	S.V. 1794
	Elizabeth		Ant. McNeil	S.V.1795
	Judith		J. B. Roy	S.V. 1803
	Etienne			
	Le même		M. Eliz. Bacon	S.P.S.1794
7	Pierre	(3)	M. Anne Fortier	S.M.1753
	Françoise		Louis Guay	S.M. 1782
	Geneviève		Jacq. Ratté	S.M. 1783
	Marie Anne		Gab. Gagnon	S.M. 1785
	Marie		Ls. Leclaire	S.M. 1786
	Marguerite		Philippe Leclaire	S.M.1793
	Marguerite		2ᵈ Frs. Nic. Roy	S.G. 1800
	Joseph			
	Pierre			
	Ignace			
	Michel			
8	Nicolas	(4)	Charlotte Isabel	S.L. 1762
	François			
	Joseph			
	Louis			
9	Jacques	(4)	M. Ls. Cinqmars	S.P.1764
	Marie		Guill. Turgeon	S.L. 1786
	Thérèse		Pierre Pouliot	S.L. 1800
	Geneviève		Ant. Godbout	S-L. 1804
	Jacques			
	Charles			
	Pierre			
10	Joseph Marie	(4)	Hélène Quéret	S.M. 1771
	M. Hélène		Ant. Goupy	S.M. 1794
	Marie Anne		Michel Forgue	S.M. 1801
	Joseph			
	Pierre			
11	François	(4)	M. Jos. Asselin	S.M. 1782
12	Joseph		M. Anne Moyen ?	
	Le même		Cécile Hebert	S.G. 1792
	Marguerite		Chs. Couture	S.M. 1829
	Angèle		Jean Marie Tangué	S.Chs.1832
	Augustin			
	Joseph			
13	Charles	(5)	M. Genev. Leclaire	S.Chs. 1780
	Marguerite		Pre. Aug. Bauchard	S.Chs. 1808
	Marie Anne		J. Bisson	S.Chs. 1809
	Etienne			
	Charles			
14	Etienne	(5)	Angé Ferlant	S.Chs. 1782
	M. Angélique		J. B. Pelchat	S.Chs. 1804
	M. Louise		Chs. Tardif	S.Chs. 1806
	Etienne			
	Le même		M.Mad. Picard	S.F.S.1800
15	Etienne	(6)	Marie Roy	S.V. 1800
16	Joseph	(7)	Mag. Marseau	S.V. 1782
	Marguerite		Jean Lebrun	S.M. 1815
	Marie Anne		Ls. Leclaire	S.M. 1817
	Marie Reiné		Jean Voisin	S.M. 1820
	Céleste		Jos. Couture	S.G. 1823
	Victoire		Aug. Roy	S.G. 1827
	Joseph			
	Charles			
	Augustin			
17	Pierre	(7)	Marie Corriveau	S.M. 1787
	Charlotte		Jean Paquet	S.M. 1806
	Marie		Ls. Voisin	S.M. 1809
	Marie		2ᵈ Jacq. Kéroack	S.M.1825
	Marie Angèle		Paul Marseau	S.M. 1813

DENIS--LAPIERRE.

Catherine		Jacq. Gendron		S.M. 1816
Madeleine		Magloire Forgue		S.M.1821
Pierre				
Joseph				
Le même		Louise Bolduc		S.G.1828
Le même		Scolastique Thibault		S.Chs.1839
18	Ignace	(7)	M. Jos. Brochu	S.V.1793
	Marie		Ls. Blais	Bert.1817
	Françoise		Ant. Quemeneur	„ 1818
19	Michel	(7)	Marie Blais	„ 1808
20	Louis	(8)	Josette Turgeon	S.Chs.1796
	Josette		Aug. Morin	S.G.1819
21	Erançois	(8)	Cécile Gosselin	S.L.1799
	Cécile		Ignace Roberge	„ 1831
	Soulange		Jos. Gosselin	„ 1836
	Flavie		J. B. Gosselin	„ 1842
	Jean			
	Joseph			
	Nicolas			
	Pierre			
22	Joseph	(8)	Angé Labrecque	S.L.1818
	M. Zoé		Jacq. Fournier	S.Chs.1839
	M. Zoé		2ᵈEtn. Labrecque	„ 1840
	M. Flavie		Jos. Bacquet	„ 1843
	Hermine		Chs. Picard	„ 1843
	Dominique		Gev. Gagnon	„ 1847
	Pierre			
	Jean			
23	Charles	(9)	Louise Godbout	S.L 1798
	M. Françoise		Ant. Carlombe	„ 1828
	Marie Louise		Etn. Coulombe	„ 1827
	Angèle		Chs. Terrien	„ 1830
	Elizabeth		Pierre Pouliot	S.J.1826
24	Jacques	(9)	Marie McDonnel	S.L.1800
25	Pierre	(9)	Genev. Blackburn	
	Charlotte		Noël Couture	
	Geneviève		Etn. Gosselin	Lévis 1833
	Marie Louise		Jos. Chabot	S.L.1840
	Pierre			
26	Joseph	(10)	M. Chs. Balan	S.V.1796
	Marie		Paul Fradet	S.M.1824
	Basilisse		J. B. Morisset	„ 1828
	Marie Anne		André Gosselin	„ 1831
	Joseph			
	Le même		Marg. Boucher	S.M.1824
27	Pierre	(10)	M. Rosalie Dodier	S.V.1803
	Pierre			
28	Augustin	(12)	Anne Philippe	Lévis 1830
29	Joseph	(12)	Genev. Guay	„ 1833
30	Charles	(13)	Fse. Arseneau	S.G.1804
	Françoise		Félix Gautron	„ 1830
31	Etienne	(13)	M. Angé Morrisset	S.Chs.1805
	Angélique		Zacharie Bilodeau	„ 1830
	M. Esther		Romain Dallaire	„ 1832
	Perpétue		Abraham Boutin	„ 1853
	Jacques			
	Cyprien			
32	Etienne		M. Genev, Cantin	
	M. Geneviève		Benoni Gosselin	S.Chs.1822
33	Etienne	(14)	M. Marg. Demers	Lévis 1819
34	Joseph	(16)	M. Mad. Mercier	S.M.1814
	Le même		Josette Asselin	„ 1836
35	Charles	(16)	Vict. Furois	„ 1815
	Victoire		Frs. Thivierge	„ 1838
	Charles			
36	Augustin	(16)	Marie Quéret	„ 1821
37	Pierre	(17)	Angèle Forgue	„ 1817
38	Joseph	(17)	Louise Bolduc	S.V. 1820
	Louise		Alexis Leclaire	S.M.1842

DENIS—LAPIERRE.

	Flavie	Michel Ed. Gautron	S.M.1848
	Le même	Soulange Mercier „	1834
	Le même	Sophie Tangué S.Chs.1851	
39	Jean	(21) M. Ls. Coulombe S.L.1831	
	M. Célina	Ls. Campeau „	1855
	Jean-Baptiste		
	François		
	Zéphirin		
	Pierre		
40	Nicolas	(21) Marie Maheux S.Roch 1836	
	M. Adéline	Pierre Daniau S.L.1855	
	Philomène	Marg. Gosselin „ 1858	
	Soulange	Frs. Pouliot „ 1858	
	Agnès	Jos. Maranda „ 1865	
	François		
	Jean		
	Louis		
	Isaïe		
	Didase		
41	Joseph	(21) Marg. Genest S.L.1832	
	Philomène	F.X. Turcot S.F.1867	
42	Pierre	(21) M. Salomé Cinqmars	S.L.1854
43	Pierre	(22) M. Malvina Bacquet	S.M.1812
44	Dominique	(22) Philomène Samson	S.Chs.1859
45	Jean	(22) M. Zéphirine Bacquet	S.M.1860
46	Pierre	(25)	
47	Joseph	(26) Marie Gontier S.M.1836	
48	Pierre	(27) Marg. Bédard Lévis 1829	
49	Jacques	(31) Adé Bilodeau S.Chs.1823	
50	Cyprien	(31) M. Jos. Naud „ 1842	
51	Charles	(35) M. Henriette Perrot	S.M.1850
52	Zéphirin	(39) M. Athanaïse Chabot	S.L.1860
53	François	(39) Natalie Chabot S.L. 1869	
54	Jean Baptiste	(39)	
55	Pierre	(39) M.Mélanie Pouliot „ 1871	
56	François	(40) Angèle Cinqmars „ 1867	
57	Jean	(40) Adèle Labrecque „ 1868	
58	Didase	(40)	
59	Louis Isaïe	(40)	

DEPORT

1	Laurent	Claude Mariette	
		Ev. de Coutances	
	Jean		
2	Jean	(1) M. Mad. Guignard	Bert. 1739
	Marie Anne	Frs. Plante S.V.1770	
	Marie Anne	2° Ls. Bussière S.G. 1808	
	M. Josette	Frs. Thibault S.F.S. 1796	
	Jean Noël		
3	Jean Noël	(2) M. Claire Chouinard	S.Tho. 1768
	Marguerite	Alexandre Roy S.F.S.1783	
	Françoise	Jacq. Asselin S.G.1801	
	Jean Noël		
	Le même	M.Fse.Marseau S.F.S.1781	
	Marie Anne	Michel Boutin S.F.S.1805	
	Marie Anne	2° J. B. Doiron S.F.S.1810	
	M. Barbe	Pierre Théberge S.V. 1821	
	Félix		
	Jean Baptiste		
4	Jean Noël	(3) LouiseFontaine S.F.S.1795	
	Marguerite	Aug. Théberge S.G. 1827	
	Louise	Jos. Théberge „ 1830	
	Ignace		
5	Jean Baptiste	(3) M.Genev. Bolduc S.V.1802	
	Marguerite	Abraham Blanchet „ 1836	
	Jean Baptiste		

DEPORT.

6	Félix	(3) Reine Mercier S.V. 1821	
7	Ignace	(4) M.Chs.Pelchat S.Chs.1839	
8	Jean Baptiste	(5) Marg. Langlois S.V. 1839	

DESCOMBE

1	Pierre	Marie Roux	Bordeau
	Pierre		
2	Pierre	(1) Mad. Demeule S.J. 1813	
	Catherine	Prisque Cameron „ 1845	
	Emélie	Gab. Dupuis „ 1857	
	Pierre		
	François		
3	Pierre	(2) SoulangeThivierge „ 1844	
4	François	(2) Domitille Létourneau	S.F. 1855

DESRUISSEAUX

1	Joseph	Adé Lebrun	
	Catherine	Chs. Fournier S.P. 1821	
	Julie	Frs. Pepin S F. 1820	
2	Joseph	Angé Bélanger	
	Marguerite	Jos. Jolin S.V. 1822	

DESSAINT—DE SAINT-PIERRE

1	Pierre	Marie Gerbert S.F. 1672	
	Marie Anne	Jacq. Soulard	Riv.Ouelle 1699
	Madeleine	Philippe Ancelin „ 1701	
	Elizabeth	Adrien Thiboutot „ 1710	
	M. Barbe	Chs. Pelletier „ 1711	
	Marie Louise	Jean Gauvin „ 1712	
	M. Ursule	Jos. Peltier S.Anne 1728	
	Alexandre		
	Pierre		
	Ignace		
2	Pierre	(1) Marie Gagnon	Riv.Ouelle 1712
	Le même	M. Hélène Leclaire	Islet 1727
3	Alexandre	(1) Marie Chouinard „ 1728	
	Louis Henri		
4	Ignace	M. Mad. Peltier	
	Ignace		
5	Louis Henri	(3) M.AnneDenaut S.P.S.1766	
6	Ignace	(4) Marie Proulx S.Tho. 1745	
	Joseph		
	Ignace		
	Le même	M. Mad. Morin S.Tho. 1753	
	Le même	M. Mad. Proulx „ 1769	
	Marie	Chs. Charier „ 1797	
	M. Modeste	Chs. Gaudreau „ 1806	
	M. Victoire	Ant. Morin S.Chs. 1804	
	Elizabeth	Jacq. Bilodeau „ 1812	
	Louis		
	Charles		
	Thomas		
7	Jean Chrysos-tôme	Ange Richard	
	Angélique	J. B. Blanchet S.P.S. 1773	
	Françoise	J. B. Dubé „ 1774	
	Marguerite	Guill. Lemieux „ 1776	
	M. Josette	Pierre Blais „ 1780	
	M. Bonne	Pierre Blais „ 1786	
	Marie Anne	J. B. Gagné „ 1791	
	M. Madeleine	Michel Toussaint Talbot	S.P.S. 1816
	Charles Pie		
	Michel		
8	Joseph Marie	M. Mad. Saucier	S.Roch.
	Pierre		
9	Ignace	(6) M. Thérèse Talbot	S.P.S. 1763

DESSAINT—DE SAINT-PIERRE.

	Name		Spouse		Year
	M. Marguerite		Frs. Talbot	S.F.S.	1798
	M. Françoise		Jacq. Roy	„	1791
	Thérèse		Ign. Dalaire	„	1799
	Marie Reine		Pierre Dion	„	1804
	Michel				
	Ignace				
10	Joseph	(6)	Mad. Pepin	„	1773
	Marie		Ls. Gosselin	S.G.	1803
	Françoise		J. B. Talbot	„	1816
	Ignace				
	Augustin				
11	Louis	(6)	M. Mad. Blais	Bert.	1802
12	Charles	(6)	Marg. Boulet	S.Tho.	1790
	Julie		Pierre Boulet	S.F.S.	1808
13	Charles Pie	(7)	M. Angé. Lavergne	S.P.S.	1794
14	Michel	(7)	Fse. Pouliot	S.G.	1794
	Rose		Barnabé Lainé	„	1820
	Marguerite		Jean Bacquet	„	1822
	Françoise		Pierre Letourneau	„	1825
	Sophie		Louis Bélanger	„	1830
	Flavie		Pierre Turgeon	„	1830
	Simon				
	Joseph				
	Michel				
15	François		Archange Labbé		
	Archange		Jos. Balan	S.G.	1819
	Edmond				
	François				
	Michel				
	Le même		Marg. Bacquet	S.G.	1820
16	Pierre	(8)	M.Claire Morin	S.P.S.	1788
17	Ignace	(9)	M. Rose Morin	„	1788
18	Michel	(9)	M. Vict. Marseau	S.V.	1801
	M. Marcelline		Jos. Bolduc	S.F.S.	1826
	M. Flavie		F. X. Corriveau	„	1830
	M. Perpétue		J. B. Corriveau	„	1837
	Théotiste		Jean Bédard	S.V.	1838
	Eloïse		Frs. Boutin	S.F.S	1841
	Marcel				
	Didace				
	François Xavier				
19	Thomas	(6)	Marie Anne Beaucher	Que.	1797
	Prudent				
20	Augustin	(10)	VéroniquePelchat	S.G.	1811
21	Ignace	(10)	Marg. Penin	S.Chs.	1821
22	François		Eliz. Blouin		
			S. Antoine de Tilly		
	Jean				
23	Michel	(14)	M. Marg. Corriveau	S.M.	1821
24	Simon	(14)	Celeste Roy	S.G.	1826
25	Joseph	(14)	Olympiade Picard	S.P.S.	1838
26	François	(15)	M. Anne Lacroix	S.G.	1821
27	Michel	(15)	Joseph Bacquet	„	1830
28	Edouard	(15)	Mad. Carbonneau	„	1830
29	Marcel	(18)	Julie Morin	S.F.S.	1835
30	François Xavier	(18)	M. Henriette Proulx	S.F.S.	1841
31	Didase	(18)	M.Angèle Gagnon	„	1843
32	Prudent	(19)	Marg. Picard	„	1833
33	Michel		Salomé Peltier	S.J.	1840
34	Jean	(22)	Marg. Leclaire	S.M.	1841
35	Augustin		Scolastique Goulet		
	Marie Eloïse		Ls. Turgeon	S.Chs.	1855

DESTROISMAISONS—PICARD.

	Name		Spouse		Year
1	Philippe		Martine Grosnier	C.B.	1669
	Angélique		Alphonse Morin	Cap S. Ign.	1692
	Angélique		2°JeanLanglois	S.Tho.	1714
	Françoise		Chs. Langelier	Cap S. Ign.	1692

18—19

DESTROISMAISONS—PICARD.

	Name		Spouse		Year
	Marguerite		J. B. Malbœuf	Cap S. Ign.	1692
	Marie		Jean Rousseau	Cap S. Ign.	1699
	Louise		Jacq. Daniau	S.Tho.	1702
	Geneviève		Robert Vaillancour	S.Tho.	1704
	Anne		Michel Chartier	„	1704
	Agathe		Pierre Proulx	„	1711
	François				
	Charles				
	Jacques				
2	Philippe		Hélène Maranda		
	Geneviève		J. B. Blanchet	S.P.S.	1760
	Philippe		Jacq. Boulet	„	1764
3	François	(1)	Marie Daniau	S.Tho.	1700
	M. Geneviève		J.B. Morel	S.P.S.	1764
	François				
4	Charles	(1)	Mad. Blanchet	S.Tho.	1709
	Marguerite		Ant. Létourneau	„	1736
	Augustin				
	Charles				
5	Jacques	(1)	M.Mad. Peltier	S.P.	1710
	Angélique		Jacq. Beaudoin	S.P.S.	1752
	Alexis				
	Louis				
	Jean Baptiste				
6	Pierre		Mad. Picard	S.Tho.	1711
	Madeleine		Pierre Gagné	S.P.S.	1764
7	François	(3)	Eliz. Ursule Rousseau	Islet	1730
	Ursule		JulienBeaupied	S.P.S.	1752
	M. Josette		Jean Marie Michon	„	1757
	Pierre				
	Gabriel				
	François				
8	René		Fse. Morin		
	M. Françoise		Eustache Bacon	S.F.S.	1752
	M. Françoise		J. B. Rousseau	„	1754
	René				
9	Louis		Ann Proulx		
	M. Madeleine		Simon Mercier	S.P.S.	1751
	M. Madeleine		2° Ls. Gagnon	„	1661
	Thérèse		Alexandre Nadeau	„	1757
	Anne		Aug. Gendron	„	1757
	Marie Louise		Chs. Daniau;	„	1760
	M. Thérèse		Aug. Talbot	„	1781
	Jean François				
	Louis				
	Gabriel				
	Augustin				
10	Jacques Frs.		Marie Anne Morin		
	Marie Anne		Jos. Boucher	S.F.S.	1753
	M. Marthe		Pierre Noël Terrien	S.F.S	1755
	M Françoise		Basile Beaucher	„	1758
	Madeleine		Basile Morin	„	1771
	„		2° Michel Gagnon	„	1786
	Marie Josette		Ign. Gagné	„	1780
	Geneviève		Jos. Coupard	„	1780
	„		2° Frs. Cloutier	„	1784
	Augustin				
	Jacques				
	Philippe				
	Joseph				
11	Charles	(4)	Marthe Bouchard	S.Tho.	1732
	Marie Marthe		Chs. Cloutier	S.P.S.	1765
	Françoise		Aug. Bouchard	„	1771
	Joseph Marie				
	Jean Baptiste				
	Charles				
	Le même		Eliz Nolin	„	1752
12	Augustin	(4)	M. Eliz. Blais	Bert.	1742
	Elisabeth		Chs. Caron	„	1762
	Geneviève		Jean Boulière	„	1768

DESTROISMAISONS—PICARD.

13	Marie Marthe	Paul Mercier Bert. 1796	
	Pierre Noël	M. Mad. Morin	
	M. Geneviève	Jos. Thibaut S.F.S. 1768	
	Pierre Noël		
14	Jacques	M. Genev. Gagné	
	M. Geneviève	Ls Pruneau S.P.S. 1762	
	Augustin		
15	Augustin	M. Fse. Langlois	
	M. Madeleine	Alexis Cloutier S.P.S.1766	
	Marie Josette	J. B. Charron „ 1766	
	M. Françoise	André Couture « 1766	
	M. Geneviève	Pierre Noël Blais „ 1777	
	Augustin		
16	Joseph	M. Genev. Isabel	
	M. Geneviève	Jos. Thibaut S.F.S. 1768	
	Madeleine	Ant. Marseau „ 1778	
17	Alexis (5)	M. Anne Audet S.L. 1750	
	Louis		
	Le même	M. Ls Morin S.P.S. 1773	
	M. Angélique	Pierre Bélanger „ 1811	
18	Louis Marie (5)	Marie Talbot „ 1751	
	Thérèse	Chs. Bernier „ 1770	
	Louis Marie		
	André		
	Jean Baptiste		
19	Jean Baptiste (5)	M. Jos. Blais „ 1761	
	Charlotte	Ant. Forꞇier S.Chs. 1785	
	Marie	Frs. Goyer „ 1790	
	M. Françoise	Frs. Terrien „ 1796	
	Augustin		
20	Philippe (2)	Marg. Huret S.P.S. 1759	
	Marguerite	Ant. Gagné „ 1784	
	M. Françoise	Jean Frs. Hopper „ 1787	
	M. Théotiste	Jos. Bouffart „ 1791	
	M. Madeleine	Paschal Blanchet „ 1793	
	M. Geneviève	André Proulx „ 1804	
	Philippe		
	Louis		
	Jean Baptiste		
	François		
21	Pierre (7)	M.Jos.Mercier S.F.S.1754	
	Geneviève	Jos. Baudoin „ 1780	
	„	2° Ign. Chartier „ 1788	
	Marie Josette	Philippe Asselin S.V. 1775	
22	François (7)	M. Marthe Michon	
		S.Tho. 1761	
	Jos. Marie		
	Jean Baptiste		
23	Gabriel (7)	M. Genev. Martin	
		S.F.S. 1766	
24	Réné (8)	Thècle Pichet S.F. 1755	
	M. Geneviève	Ign.Létourneau S.F.S.1779	
	M. Françoise	Jos.Noël Gagnon „ 1790	
	M. Marguerite	Pre. Basile Létourneau	
		S.F.S. 1790	
	Michel		
	René		
	Jacques		
	Pierre Noël		
	Le même	M. Mad. Gagnon „ 1777	
25	Augustin (15)	M.Jos.Gosselin S.Tho.1760	
	M. Madeleine	Ls Vallée S.P.S. 1786	
26	Jean François (9)	M. Fse.Terrien S.F.S.1756	
	Marie Louise	J. B. Baudoin „ 1786	
	M. Geneviève	Pierre J. Bte. Chartier	
		S.F.S. 1787	
	Marie Josette	Michel Picard „ 1790	
	Françoise	Jos. Bacquet S.Chs. 1784	
	Jean Françoise		
27	Gabriel (9)	Marie Morin S.P.S. 1762	
28	Louis (9)	Genev. Mathieu „ 1763	
	M. Geneviève	Ls Toussaint „ 1790	
	M. Barbe	Chs. Guay „ 1794	
	Marie Josette	André Picard „ 1807	
	Marguerite	Étienne Roy S.G. 1809	

DESTROISMAISONS—PICARD.

	Michel		
	Jean Baptiste		
	Joseph		
29	Augustin (9)	M. Chs. Marotte	
			S.P.S. 1775
30	Joseph (10)	M.Chs.Drapeau S.Chs.1769	
	Le même	Marg. Pelchat „ 1811	
	Angèlique	J. B. Gautron „ 1835	
	Marguerite	Jos. Mercier „ 1840	
	Jacques		
	Joseph		
31	Jacques (10)	M. Reine Gendron	
			S.F.S. 1770
	Marie Josette	André Boutin S.P.S. 1793	
	Marie Josette	2 Jos. Fontaine S.P.S.1815	
	Reine Françoise	Michel Boivin „ 1798	
	Marie Rose	Pierre Quemeneur	
			S.P.S. 1801
	Marguerite	Jos. Fontaine „ 1800	
	Marie Thérèse	Pierre Bouchard S.P.S1801	
	Marie Charlotte	Jos. Marie Gagné „ 1803	
	Jacq. Siméon		
32	Augustin (10)	Reine Morin S.F.S. 1771	
33	Philippe (10)	Angé Matté S.Chs. 1775	
34	Pierre René Fils	M. Jeanne Alain Bert.1765	
	de Jacq.—Neuv.		
	et Pre. Noël		
	Marie Anne	André Chartier S.P.S.1792	
	M. Madeleine	Frs. Ruel „ 1796	
	M. Françoise	Aug. Daniau „ 1799	
	M. Marguerite	Etn. Denis S.F.S. 1800	
	Jos. Thomas		
	Laurent		
35	Pierre	M. M. Georgine Ouel	
	M. Georges	Jean Emond S.J. 1791	
	Marie Anne	Jacq. Plante S.Frs. 1801	
	Yves		
	Pierre		
	Michel		
36	Jean Baptiste(11)	M. Mad. Coulombe	
			S.P.S. 1758
37	Joseph Marie(11)	M. Anne Lavoie „ 1761	
38	Charles (11)	M. Jos. Talbot „ 1769	
	M. Charlotte	Aug. Alaire S.F.S. 1800	
39	Augustin (12)	Marg. Guilmet Bert. 1780	
	Marguerite	Ls. Pellerin „ 1805	
	M. Archange	Gab. Fortier „ 1815	
	M. Madeleine	Frs. Fortier „ 1819	
	Augustin		
40	Pierre Noël (13)	Agathe Gagnon S.P.S.1768	
	M. Madeleine	Frs. Fortier S.F.S 1788	
	M. Agathe	Simon Paré „ 1787	
	Pierre Noël		
41	Augustin (14)	M. Genev. Sylvestre	
42	Louis (17)	Susanne Bisson S.Chs.1780	
43	Louis Marie (18)	M. Genev. Bélanger	
			S.P.S. 1773
	Marie Anne	Jos. Fournier „ 1802	
	Marie Modeste	J. B. Fontaine „ 1803	
	M. Marguerite	Frs. Peltier „ 1804	
	Pélagie	Pierre Cotin S.M. 1812	
	Julie Josette	J. B. Fournier S.P.S. 1823	
	Louis Marie		
	Antoine		
	Le même	M.Mad. Peltier S.P.S.1800	
44	André (18)	Angé Blouin „ 1774	
	M. Marguerite	Etn. Samson „ 1800	
	M. Angélique	Ant. Talbot „ 1814	
	Julie	Ls. Roberge „ 1834	
	André		
	Le même	M. Jos. Picard „ 1807	
	M. Angélique	Chs. Théophile Coté	
			S.P.S. 1833
	Clothilde	Olivier Cochon „ 1838	
	André		

DESTROISMAISONS--PICARD.

```
        Joseph
45  JeanBaptiste(18)  Mad. Blanchet S.P.S. 1786
46  Augustin    (19)  Cath. Pénin    S. Chs. 1808
    Françoise         André Couture      "    1847
    Rose              Jean Duguet    S.Chs.  1862
    Charles
    Augustin
47  JeanBaptiste(20)  Marg. Fournier S.P.S.1792
    M. Anastasie      Pierre Mercier     "    1822
48  Philippe    (20)  Rosalie Fournier   "    1793
    Rosalie           Frs. Thibaut       "    1813
    Marguerite        Jos.Felix Blanchet "    1820
    Marie Luce        Aug. Blanchet      "    1821
    M. Gertrude       Frs. Noël Cloutier "    1827
    Joseph
49  François    (20)  Marie Bouchard     "    1800
50  Louis       (20)  Marg. Talbot       "    1825
51  Jos. Marie  (22)
52  JeanBaptiste(22)  Mad. Guilmet   Bert. 1788
    Rosalie           J. B. Blais        "    1817
    Alexis
53  René        (24)  M. Angé Asselin S.J. 1783
    Le même           M. Albondante Guérard
                                       S.F. 1786
    M. Angélique      J. B. Drouin   S.Frs. 1811
    Frs.RemiFlavien
    Le même           Marg. Perrot    S.F. 1799
    Marguerite        Jean Ginchereau S.F. 1826
54  Jacques     (24)  Mad. Blouin    S.F.S. 1789
    Michel
55  Michel      (24)  M. Jos. Picard S.F.S. 1791
56  Jean Fran-  (26)  Louise Belanger    "    1792
    çois
    Adélaïde          Pierre Morin       "    1815
    Archange          Guill. Bernard     "    1827
    Jean François
    Jean Baptiste
57  Pierre Noël (24)  M. Marthe Caron
                                St. Roch 1788
    Marguerite        Michel Audet  S.F.S. 1813
    Marie Marthe      Jos. Morin         "    1821
    Marie Marthe      2° Abraham Fournier
                                 S.F.S. 1830
    Marie Cécile      Jos. Morin         "    1822
    Marie Josette     Amb. Vien          "    1824
    Thècle            Pierre Buteau      "    1835
    Jos. Prudent
    Noël
58  Augustin          Théotiste Thibaut
    Victoire          Pierre Chevanel
                                 S.F.S. 1824
    Madeleine         J. B. Talbot       "    1824
    Basile

59  JeanBaptiste(28)  Marie Pruneau   Bert 1809
60  Michel      (28)  M. Chs. Blais  S.P.S. 1810
    Charlotte         Ed. Bouffart   S.P.S. 1835
    Olympiade         Jos. Dessaint  S.P.S. 1839
    Geneviève         Frs. Coté      S.P.S. 1836
    Le même           Fse. Blais     S.P.S  1832
61  Joseph      (30)  Sophie Labrecque B. 1842
62  Jacques     (30)  Hermine Dalaire
                                 S.Chs. 1796
63  Jacq. Simeon(31)  Marguerite   S. Chs. 1796
    Angélique         Ls. Nollet   S. Chs; 1831
64  Jos. Thomas (34)  M. Reine Rouleau
                                 S.F.S. 1791
    M. Marguerite     Amb. Fortier   S.H. 1815
65  Laurent     (34)  M. Genev. Bacon
                                 S.P.S. 1794
66  Pierre      (35)  M. Chs. Emond S.J. 1792
    Marie             Chs. Delage  S. Frs. 1822
    Michel
    Jean
    Pierre
67  Yves        (35)  Isabelle Gagné  S.J. 1795
```

18—19½

DESTROISMAISONS—PICARD.

```
    Le même           Modeste Verieue S-F. 1808
68  Michel      (35)  M. Vict. Gagné
                                  S. Frs. 1800
    Marie Emélie      J. B. Forceville
                                  S. Frs. 1852
69  Augustin    (39)  Rose Guilmet  Bert. 1812
    Mathilde          J. B. Dorval  S. Chs. 1835
    Magloire
    Thomas
    Le même           Luce Audet   S. Chs. 1835
    Amélie            Magloire Roy S.Chs. 1864
70  Pierre Noël (40)  M. Rosalie Brie
                                  S. Tho. 1796
    Marie Agathe      J. B. Daneau  S.P.S. 1820
    Marie Sophie      Alexis Bouchard
    M. Constance      Pierre Guénet S.P.S. 1837
    Marie Rosalie     Pierre Dandurand
                                   S.F.S. 1820
    Françoise         Jean Frs. Létourneau
                                   S.F.S. 1820
    Marie Louise      Ls. Thibaut   S.F.S. 1836
    Le même           Thérèse Alaire S.F.S. 1821
71  Antoine     (43)  Angé Bernier S. Tho. 1797
    Marie Luce        F. X. Blais   S.P.S. 1824
    Le même           M. Angé Lavergne
                                   S.P.S. 1816
72  Joseph      (28)  Marg. DessaintS.Tho.1807
    Marguerite        Prudent Dessaint
                                   S.P.S. 1833
    Flavie            Marcel Talbot S.P.S. 1834
    Geneviève         Frs. Narcisse Bouchard
                                   S.P.S. 1835
    Louis
73  Louis Marie (43)  Fse. Harnais  S.P.S. 1802
    M. Catherine      Ls. Greg. Kéroack
                                   S.P.S. 1825
    Le même           M. Chs. Boulet
                                   S.F.S. 1807
    Louis
74  André (1$^n$m)(44)  M. Angé Blais Bert. 1801
    André
75  André (2$^n$m)(44)  Vict. Guénet S.P.S. 1835
76  Joseph      (44)  Eliz. Talbot  S.P.S. 1839
77  Hyacinthe   (44)  M. Adé Normand
    Hyacinthe
    Le même           Thérèse Bilodeau Bert.
78  Charles     (46)  Rosalie Denis S. Chs. 1843
79  Augustin    (46)  Marg. Roy      S.M. 1846
80  Joseph      (48)  Marie Létourneau
                                   S.P.S. 1827
81  Alexis      (52)  Rose Coulombe S.P-S.1830
82  Joseph      (53)  Marie Dalaire S. Frs. 1817
    Catherine         F. X. Dalaire S. Roch.
83  Frs. Réné   (53)  M. Vict. Lepage
                                   S.F.S. 1817
    Flavien
    Madeleine         Paul Gosselin S.J. 1842
    Hombeline         Pierre Plante S.J. 1842
    Marie Lousie      Paul Pouliot  S.J. 1847
    Désanges          Jos. Pouliot  S.J. 1854
    Rose de Lima      Jos. Désiré Proulx
                                    S.J. 1861
    Marie             Cyp. Langlois S. Frs. 1838
    Réparate          Etn. Turcot  S. Frs. 1845
    Moïse
    Réni
84  Michel      (54)  Marie Carbonneau
                                   S.F.S. 1820
85  JeanFrançois(56)  M. Jos. Gendron
                                   S.F.S. 1815
    Antoine
86  Jean Baptiste(56  Emérence Morin
                                   S.F.S. 1830
87  Noël        (57)  M. Fse. Morin S.F.S. 1820
88  Joseph      (57)  M. Fse. Blais S.F.S. 1825
    Prudent
89  Basile      (58)  Reine Roy     S.F.S. 1812
```

DESTROISMAISONS—PICARD.

90	Jean	(66)	Cath. Hélie	S.J. 1813
	Marie Anne		Jos. Gosselin	S.J. 1850
	François Régis			
	Joseph			
91	Pierre	(66)	Eliz. Campagna S. Frs.1820	
	Marie		Flavien Marseau	
				S.Frs. 1850
	Joseph			
92	Michel	(66)	Marie Dompierre	
				S.Frs. 1820
	Modeste		René Labbé	S.Frs. 1845
	Olivier			
	Pierre			
	Joseph			
	François Xavier			
93	Magloire	(69)	M. Ls. Lacasse S.Chs.1846	
94	Thomas	(69)	Constance Coté S.Chs.1853	
95	Louis	(72)	Olympiad Proulx	
				S.P.S. 1836
96	Louis	(73)	M. Natalie Blanchet	
				S.P.S. 1732
97	André	(74)	M. Jos. Coulombe	
				Bert 1824
98	Hyacinthe	(77)	Clarisse Guilmet Bert 1846	
99	Moïse	(83)	Jules Lepage S. Frs. 1852	
100	Antoine	(85)	Marcelline Bilodeau	
				S.F.S 1843
101	Frs. Régis	(90)	Marg. Gosselin S. Frs.1846	
102	Joseph	(90)	Marie Louise S.J. 1833	
103	Joseph	(91)	M. Marcelline Rouleau	
				S.L. 1853
104	Olivier	(92)	Lucie Lepage S. Frs. 1853	
105	Pierre	(92)	Clémentine Gagnon	
				S. Frs. 1855
106	Joseph	(92)	M. Genev. Pepin	
				S. Frs. 1858
107	Frs. Xavier	(92)	Pétronille Lepage	
				S. Frs. 1861
108	René	(83)	Josette Labbé S.Roch 1839	
	Léa		Théophile Blouin	
				S. Frs. 1861

DICK

1	Amable		Julie Mignot	
				Kamouraska
	Joseph			
2	Joseph	(1)	Marie Terrien	S.J. 1818
	Joseph			
	Gabriël			
	Thomas			
3	Joseph	(2)	Ursule Hélie	S.J. 1842
4	Gabriël	(2)	Emélie Noël	S.J. 1842
5	Thomas	(2)	Adé Pépin	S.J. 1852

DIERS ? DIARS ?

1	Pierre		Charlotte Mondain Q. 1714	
	Charles			
2	Charles		Genev. Audet	S.L. 1757
	Charles			
4	Charles	(2)	Genev. Denis S. Chs. 1780	
	Marie		Aug. Audet	S.G. 1800
	Genetiève		André Arseneau S.G. 1807	
	Marie		Jean Fournier	S.G. 1823
	Charles			
	Etienne			
	Jean			
	Joseph			
	Le même		M. Ls. Leclaire S. Chs. 1806	
5	Charles	(4)	Hélène Goulet	S.G. 1802
6	Etienne	(4)	M.Anne TellemerS.L.1806	
	Charles			
7	Jean	(4)	Cécile Lacasse	S.G. 1810
8	Joseph	(4)	M. Mad. Monmeny	
				S. Chs. 1811
9	Charles	(6)	Marie Roy	B. 1849

DION—GUYON.

1	Jean		Mathurine Robin	
	Marie		Frs. Bélanger	Q. 1637
	Jean			
	François			
	Simon			
	Claude			
	Denis			
	Michel			
2	Jean	(1)	Eliz. Couillard	Que. 1645
	Guillaume			
3	Simon	(1)	Louise Racine	Que. 1653
4	Claude	(1)	Cath. Colin	Que. 1655
	Madeleine		Gervais Rochon	S.F. 1671
	Louise		Pierre Racine	S.F. 1682
	Catherine		Etn. Racine	S.F. 1683
	Rénée		Jean Pepin	S.F. 1688
	Françoise		Chs. Gravel, S. Anne 1689	
	Claude			
	Jean			
	Gervais			
	Le même		Marg.Remodière S.F. 1688	
5	Denis	(1)	Eliz. Boucher	Que. 1659
6	Michel	(1)	Genev. Marsolet Que. 1662	
7	François	(1)	Mad. Marsolet	Que. 1662
8	Guillaume	(2)	Jeanne Toupin	C.R. 1688
	Joachim			
9	Claude	(4)	M. Mad. Lehaux S.F. 1688	
	M. Madeleine		Bertrand Perrot S.F. 1715	
	Jean			
	François			
	Le même		Cath. Blouin	S.J. 1700
	Catherine		Pierre Guinard	S.F. 1717
	Anne		Chs. Giguère	S.F. 1726
	M. Josette		Basile Beaucher S.F. 1734	
	Elizabeth		Frs. Patenotre	S.F. 1734
	Elizabeth		2° Théophile Greffart	
				S.F. 1748
	Thérèse		Aug. Caron	S.F. 1738
	Claude			
	Joseph			
10	Jean	(4)	Marie Pepin	S.F. 1688
	M. Madeleine		Ls.Saint-Jean S. Frs. 1708	
	Angélique		Denis Gagné S. Frs. 1715	
	Angélique		2° Aug.Landry S. Frs. 1729	
	Marie Anne		Frs. Marseau S. Frs. 1718	
	Marie Anne		2° Etn.Bluteau S.Frs. 1734	
	Marie Josette		Ls. Malet	S. Frs. 1728
	Hélène		Jacq. Bidet	S.V. 1728
	Claude			
	Joseph			
11	Gervais	(4)	Cath. Lehoux	S.F. 1695
	Catherine		Prisque Gagnon S.F. 1719	
	M. Madeleine		Pierre Loignon	S.F. 1724
	Agathe		Ls. Létourneau	S.F. 1727
	M. Françoise		Ant.Jacq.Perrot S.F. 1729	
12	Joachim	(8)	Eliz. Agnès Morin	
				S.P.S. 1727
	Elizabeth		Pierre Gagnon S. Frs. 1751	
13	Joachim		M. Jeanne Fontaine	
	M. Jeanne		Jos. Gendron S.F.S. 1762	
	M. Catherine		Jos. Marie Gaulin	
				S.F.S. 1763
	M. Françoise		Frs. Godbout S.F.S. 1764	
	M. Françoise		2° Chrysostôme	
			Morin	S.F.S. 1765
	M. Françoise		3° Jos. Daniel S.F.S. 1774	
	Etienne			
14	Jean	(9)	Marthe Beaucher S.F.1719	
	Marie		Frs. Deblois	S.F. 1747
	Marie Anne		Jos. Drouin	S.F. 1751
	Thècle		Etn. Drouin	S.F. 1756
	Félicité		J. B. Charlan	S.F. 1756
	Elisabeth		Basile Turcot	S.F. 1751
	M. Madeleine		Laurent Turcot	S.F. 1765
	M. Charlotte		Jacq. Plante	S.F. 1771
	Jean			

DION–GUYON.

	Joseph			
15	Joseph	(9)	M. Brigitte Beaucher	S.F. 1730
	Marie Josette		Ls. Jos. Mercier	Bert. 1750
	Marie Thècle		Pierre Frechet	Bert. 1754
	Marie		Louis Roy	Bert. 1766
	Claude			
	Jean Baptiste			
	Guillaume			
	Basile			
	Louis			
	Joseph			
15	François	(9)	Marg, Lessart	S. Anne
	Françoise		Chs. Cloutier	C.R. 1760
	Pierre			
16	Claude	(9)	Brigitte Gaulin	S.F. 1741
	Claude			
17	Claude	(10)	Fse. Gagnon	
	Claude			
	Joseph			
	Jean			
	François			
	Benjamin			
18	Joseph	(10)	M. Fse. Bidet	S.V. 1729
	Marie Louise		Ant. Fontaine	S.F.S. 1775
	Augustin			
	Louis			
19	Etienne	(13)	Thérèse Boudet	S.F.S.1756
	Marie Josette		Etienne Bégin	S.H. 1788
	M. Angélique		Gabriel Audet	S.H. 1801
	M. Thérèse		Frs. Lefebvre	S.H. 1803
	Joachim			
20	Jean	(14)	M. Cath. Blouin	S.F. 1751
	Jean			
	Jacques			
	Le même		M. Jos. Lacroix	S.F. 1794
21	Joseph	(14)	M. Mad. Blouin	S.J. 1752
22	Joseph	(15)	Marthe Roy	S.V. 1751
	Marthe		Guill. Lemieux	Bert. 1773
23	Jean Baptiste	(15)	Genev. Morisset	S.M. 1754
	Le même		Mad. Paré	S.F.S. 1770
	Marguerite		Michel Couillard Cap.	
				S. Ign. 1801
24	Guillaume	(15)	M. Genev. Lebrun	
				S.M. 1765
	M. Geneviève		Pierre Bacquet	S.M. 1788
	M. Marguerite		Ls. Fournier	S.M. 1803
	Marie		Jos. Dodier	S.M. 1807
	Joseph			
	Eloi			
	Pierre			
	Prisque			
	Jean Baptiste			
25	Basile	(15)	M. Anne Chabot	S.L. 1767
	Marie Anne		Aug. Blais	Bert. 1804
	Joseph			
	Basile			
26	Louis	(15)	M. Marg. Racine	S.M.1772
	M. Marguerite		Henri Marie Lemieux	
				Bert. 1793
	Marie Barbe		Pierre Gosselin	Bert. 1805
	Marie Anne		J. B Baudouin	Bert. 1809
	M. Geneviève		Frs. Gaudreau	Bert. 1822
	Thécle		J. B. Rèmillard	Bert. 1830
	Louis			
	Thomas			
	Joseph			
27	Claude	(15)	M. Jos. Rémillard	
				S.V. 1758
28	Claude	(16)	Marie Gagné	S.Frs. 1782
	M. Brigitte		Jean Lescabiet	S.Frs. 1800
	M. Catherine		Ls. Letourneau	S.F. 1807
	Marie		Martin Martineau	
				S.F. 1818
	Joseph			

DION—GUYON.

	Jean			
	Claude			
29	Claude	(17)	Génev. Martineau	S.Frs. 1744
	Marie Thécle		J. B. Emond	S. Frs. 1776
	Geneviève		Ls. Clément	S.G. 1799
	Geneviève		2° Michel Terrien	
				S.Chs. 1814
	Joseph			
	François			
	Louis			
	Le même		M. Eliz. Boissonneau	S.J. 1783
30	Jean	(17)	Cécile Asselin	S.Frs. 1745
31	Joseph	(17)	M. Félicité Martineau	S. Frs. 1745
	Félicité		Jos. Dompierre	S.Frs. 1770
	M. Brigitte		Ls. Emond	S. Frs. 1778
	Joseph			
	François			
32	François	(17)	Thécle Martineau	S.Frs. 1757
A	François		M. Claire Durand	
	François			
33	Benjamin	(17)	Mad. Landry	S.Frs. 1766
34	Jean		Marg. Rambuse Ev. de Hanovre	
	Pierre			
35	Pierre	(15)	A Eliz. Dalaire	B. 1761
	M. Charlotte		Frs. Cantin	B. 1787
	Marie Anne		Jos. Girard	B. 1790
	Marie Elisabeth		J. B. Tangué	B. 1790
	Marie Elisabeth		2° Ls. Fleury	S.M. 1802
	Charles			
	Joseph			
	Pierre			
	Le même		Charlotte Morin	S.G. 1808
			V. de Michel Cloutier	
36	Augustin	(18)	Thérèse Delisle	S.J. 1774
	M. Geneviève		Ls. Gagné	S.J. 1792
	Thérèse		Frs. Bilodeau	S.F. 1809
	Catherine		Jos. Campagna	S.F. 1818
	Amand			
	Jacques			
37	Louis	(18)	M. Angé Loignon	S.F. 1776
	M. Angèlique		Jos. Emond	S.Frs. 1789
	Marie Louise		Ant. Levasseur	S.Frs. 1820
	M. Euphrosine		Michel Boucher	S.Frs. 1823
38	Joachim	(19)	Marg. Terrien	S.Chs. 1792
39	Jean	(20)	M. Ls. Filteau	S.F. 1782
	Marie Louise		Amb. Létourneau	S.F. 1806
	Le même		Mad. Létourneau	S.F. 1810
40	Jacques	(20)	Mad. Gagné	S.F. 1786
	M. Madeleine		Michel Turcot	S.F. 1811
	Jacques			
41	Joseph	(24)	M. Anne Bacquet	S.M. 1878
	'			S.G.
	Marie Anne		Pierre Tangué	S.G. 1886
	Germain			
	Le même		M. Agathe Marseau	S.V. 1808
42	Eloi	(24)	M. Jos. Tangué	S.M. 1801
	Josette		Ant. Fournier	S.G. 1822
	Angélique		Pierre Roy	S.G. 1823
	Le même		Angèle Leblanc	S.Chs. 1821
	Angèle		Ferd. Fortier	S.M. 1847
	Eloi			
43	Pierre	(24)	M. Fse. Forgues	S.M. 1803
	Françoise		Jos. Ruel	S.G. 1825
	Françoise		2° Frs. Coté	S.G. 1829
44	Prisque	(24)	M. Agathe Leclaire	S.V. 1808
	M. Emérence		Gab. Bélanger	S.V. 1855
	Séraphine		Tho. Boutin	S.V. 1870

DION—GUYON.

	Marie Esther	J. B. Lemieux	S.M.	1846
	Emélie	Isaac Marcoux	S.M.	1846
45	Jean Bapt.	(24) Marg. Racine	S.M.	1810
46	Joseph	(25) Marie Bilodeau	S.Chs.	1806
	Marie	Pierre Vallée	S.Chs.	1825
47	Louis	(26) M. Marthe Roy	S.V.	1803
	Soulange	Olivier Carbonneau		
			Bert.	1833
	Henriette	Jos. Bernier	Bert.	1840
	Etienne			
48	Thomas	(26) Marg. Tellemer	S.M.	1806
	Thomas			
49	Joseph	(26) Marg. Lemieux	S.F.S.	1810
	Scolastique	Ed. Mercier	Bert.	1846
	Nazaire			
	Joseph			
	Jean Baptiste			
	George			
50	Joseph	(28) M. Ls. Mercier	S.M.	1812
	Marie	Pierre Lemieux	S.M.	1840
	Anastasie	Herbert Chamberlan		
			S.M.	1839
	Anastasie	2° Abraham Couillard		
			S.M.	1845
	Marcelline	J. B. Goupy	S.M.	1841
	Caroline	Narcisse Cotin	S.M.	1846
	Esther	Jos. Lacroix	S.M.	1846
51	Jean	(28) Josette Asselin	S.F.	1814
	Marie	Laurent Vaillancour		
			S.F.	1843
	Génevière	Pierre Paquet	S.F.	1845
	Frs. Régis			
	Pierre			
52	Claude	(28) Marie Asselin	S.F.	1821
	Le même	Emélie Létourneau		
			S.F.	1840
	Séraphine	Jos. Asselin	S.F.	1858
	Justine	F. X. Beaucher	S.F.	1864
53	Joseph	(29) Mad. Guérard	S.Frs.	1771
	M. Madeleine	Jos. Hebert	S.F.	1793
	Marie	Frs. Lemelin	S.F.	1812
	Jean Marie			
	François			
	Joseph			
54	François	(29) M. Chs. Asselin	S.Frs.	1782
55	Louis	(29) Josette Plante	S.J.	1785
	Josette	Ls. Jolin	S.G.	1809
	Louis			
	Le même	M. Mad. Ratté	S.M.	1816
56	Joseph	(31) Thérèse Racine		
			S.Anne.	1774
	M. Madeleine	Frs. Dupont	S.Frs.	1810
	M. Théotiste	Frs. Asselin	S.Frs.	1824
57	François	(31) M. Ls. Martineau		
			S.Frs.	1788
	M. Angélique	Michel Tremblay	S.F.	1818
	François			
A	Louis	Josette Boirard		
	Charles			
58	Pierre	Marg. Lescabiét		
	Marguerite	Jos. Queret	S.G.	1803
59	Pierre	(34) Fse. Balan	S.Chs.	1786
	Pierre			
	Joseph			
60	Pierre	(35) Thérèse Gosselin	S.G.	1790
	Joseph			
	Le même	M. Reine Dessaint		
			S.F.S.	1804
	François			
	Bénoni			
	Protais			
61	Charles	(35) Cath. Lacroix	S.M.	1797
	Catherine	Ant. Goupy	S.M.	1822
	Julie	Jos. Lefebvre	S.M.	1826
	Charles			
	Jean Baptiste			

DION—GUYON.

62	Joseph	(35) M. Thérèse Dessaint		
			S.F.S.	1799
	Marie Angèie	J. B. Couture	B.	1831
	Archange	Ls. Oct. Paquet	B.	1832
	M. Marguerite	Etn. Patouel	B.	1836
	Frs. Remi			
	Joseph			
	Ignace			
63	Amand	(35) Marg. Lemelin	S.Frs.	1807
	Catherine	René Labbé	"	1844
	Jacques			
	Louis			
	Joachim			
64	Jacques	(36) Mad. Lemelin	S.Frs.	1819
65	François	Thérèse Dion		
	François			
66	Joseph	Marg. Jobin		
		Lorette		
	Joseph			
	Louis			
67	Basile	(25) Maud. Couillard		
			S.Tho.	1807
	Madeleine	Jean Lemelin	S.G.	1828
68	Jean Baptiste	Marie Campagna		
	Jean Baptiste			
69	Jacques	(40) Louise Giguère		
			S.Anne	1820
	Edouard			
	Le même	Marie Pichet	S.F.	1837
	Rose de Lima	F. X. Vaillancour	"	1860
	Honoré			
70	Germain	(41) Marie Audet	S.G.	1825
71	Eloi	(42) Marg. Morin	S.M.	1843
72	Etienne	(47) Henrietta Proulx		
			Bert.	1837
73	Thomas	(48) Marie Dupont	S.Chs.	1826
74	Joseph	(49) M. Flavie Morin	Bert.	1745
75	Georges	(49) Césaire Roy	S.V.	1846
76	Jean Bapt.	(49) Adelaïde Lemieux		
			Bert.	1846
77	Nazaire	(49) Déline Roy	S.V.	1855
78	Frs. Régis	(51) Julie Audet	S.F.	1839
79	Pierre	(51) Luce Dalaire	S.L.	1848
80	Joseph	(53) Louise Morel	S.Anne	1797
	Marie Angèle	Chs. Guérard	S.Frs.	1830
	Marie Emélie	Jos. Marseau	S.Frs.	1838
	Marie Céleste	Nic. Mathieux	S.Frs.	1839
	François			
	Joseph			
81	Jean Marie	(53) M. Marg. Morel	S.Frs.	1808
82	François	M. Thécle Drouin		
			S.F.	1800
	Scolastique	Jean Lasalle	S.Frs.	1831
	Thècle	Michel Emond	"	1840
	Lucie	Frs. Lessart	"	1842
	Ignace			
	Jean Baptiste			
	Le même	Marie Emond	S.Frs.	1822
	Angéle	Aug. St. Hilaire		
			S.Frs.	1845
83	Louis	(55) Angele Dodier	S.G.	1816
84	François	(57) M. Luce Guérard	S.F.	1818
	Justine	Ls. Larrivé	S.Frs.	1852
	Pierre Narcisse			
	David			
85	Pierre	(49) M. Ls. Guilmet	S.M.	1817
86	Joseph	(59) Angèle Terrien	"	1823
	Marguerite	Alexis Couture	"	1845
	Joseph			
87	François	(32)a Fse. Guimon		
			Cap.S.Ign.	1814
	François			
88	Charles	(57)a Ursule Cloutier	S.Tho.	
	Rose	Tho. Fournier	S.F.S.	1840
89	Jean Baptiste	Marie Lasanté	St. Ant.	
	François Xavier			

DION—GUYON.

90	Joseph	Marie Lebel	
	Odilon		
91	Joseph	Mad. Fournier S.M.	
	Margurite	Pierre Richard S.M. 1858	
	Eusèbe		
	Le même	Genev. Balan S.M. 1846	
	Constance	Michel Menard S.V. 1865	
92	Joseph	(60) Fse. Mercier S.G. 1822	
	Le même	Rosalie Sylvestre ,, 1828	
	Jean		
93	François	(60) Adé Audet S.G. 1826	
	Abraham		
94	Bénoni	(60) Genev. Fournier S.G. 1828	
95	Protais	(60) Marie Paquet S.Chs. 1849	
96	Charles	(61) M. Anne Forgue S.M. 1825	
	Julienne	Nicolas Fortin ,, 1851	
	Charles		
	Napoléon		
97	Jean Bapt.	(61) Sophie Enoeuf B. 1831	
98	Joseph	(62) Marie Pepin B. 1826	
99	Ignace	(62) Théotiste Patouel B. 1829	
	Chs. Théophile		
	Jean Baptiste		
100	Frs. Remi	(62) M. Ls. Chabot B. 1843	
101	Jacques	(63) Marie Emond S.Frs. 1835	
102	Louis	(63) Luce Audet S.J. 1842	
103	Joachim	(63) M. Léocadie Lamothe	
		S.F. 1847	
104	François	(65) Mad. Racine S.Anne 1821	
	Jean		
105	Joseph	(66) Mad. Emond S.J. 1827	
	Julie	André Paquet S.J. 1850	
	Marie	Léandre Pouliot S.J. 1851	
	Cécile	Magloire Pepin S.J. 1861	
	Adélaïde	Jean Blouin S.J. 1865	
106	Louis	(66) Agnès Victoire S.J. 1834	
107	Jean Baptiste	(68) M. Jos. Lemelin S.F. 1828	
108	Edouard	(69) Adé Asselin S.F. 1845	
109	Honoré	(69) Marie Vaillancour S.F. 1864	
110	François	(80) Cath. Lasalle S.Frs. 1826	
	Luce	Edouard Coté ,, 1862	
	Eléonore	Ls. Ginchereau ,, 1862	
	François		
	Basile		
	Honoré		
	Jean Baptiste		
111	Joseph	(80) M. Angé Guérard S.F.1825	
112	Ignace	(82) Cath. Langlois S.Frs. 1828	
	François Xavier		
113	Jean Baptiste	(82) M. Hombéline Lepage	
		S.Frs. 1842	
114	Pierre	(84) M. Céline Asselin S.Frs.	
	Narcisse	1862	
115	David	(84) Ludivine Gosselin S.P.1864	
116	Joseph	(86) Marg. Maindel S.M. 1847	
117	Francois	(87) Anastasie Lessart Bert.1837	
118	Francois	(89) Léonie Toussaint S.J. 1858	
	Xavier		
119	Odilon	(80) Caroline Racine S.M. 1860	
120	Eusebé	(91) Eliz. Richard S.V. 1864	
121	Abraham	(93) Julie Cochon C.R. 1857	
	Le même	Perpétue Turcot S.F. 1868	
122	Jean	(92) Vitaline Clément S.M.1859	
123	Charles	(96) Belzémire Forgue	
124	Napoléon	(96)	
125	Chs.	(99) M. Célina Roy B. 1858	
	Théophile		
126	Jean Baptiste	(99) Rosalie Gontier S.Chs.1863	
127	Jean	(104) Delima Pepin S.Frs. 1856	
128	Basile	(110) Anastasie Pepin S.Frs.1854	
129	Jean	(110) M. Ls. Guérard S.Frs. 1861	
130	Honoré	(110) Philomène Cloutier S.Frs.	
		1861	
131	Francois	(110) Sara Audet S.L. 1865	
132	Francois	(112) Mathilde Lessart S.Frs.	
	Xavier	1855	

DIONNE.

1	Antoine		Cath. Yvory	
	Anne		Bernard Lainé Que. 1665	
	M. Madeleine		Chs. Lenormand ,, 1691	
	Marie		Pierre Benoit S.Frs. 1694	
	Anne		Barth. Gobeil ,, 1697	
	Catherine		Jos. Michaud ,, 1702	
	Jean			
2	Jean	(1)	M. Chs. Mignot C.R. 1694	
	Augustin			
3	Augustin	(2)	Marie Paradis S.P. 1726	
A	Joseph		M. Mad. Meneur	
	Germain			
4	Germain	(A)	Thérèse Fournier S.Tho.	
				1776
	Basile			
5	Basile		Marg. Boudouin S.F.S.	
				1806

DODIER.

1	Jacques		Cath. Caron C.R. 1662	
	Angé			
2	Angé	(1)	Marg. Paré S.Anne 1699	
	Pierre			
	Jean			
3	Pierre	(2)	M. Thérèse Lebrun S.V.	
				1730
	Marie		Alexis Fauchon S.V. 1762	
	Marie		Frs. Gagné S.M. 1750	
	Joseph			
	Louis			
	Le même		Isabelle Bilodeau Bert.1744	
	Elizabeth		Frs. Wells ,, 1761	
	Elizabeth		2° J. B. Thibaut ,, 1776	
4	Jean	(2)	M. Ls. Larrivé S.F.S. 1744	
5	Francois		Marie Robert, Diocèse	
			du Temple	
	Nicolas			
6	Joseph	(3)	Fse. Molleur B. 1758	
	Le même		Chrystine Roy S.V. 1769	
	Chrystine		Germain Roy ,, 1794	
	M. Angèlique		Thomas Blais ,, 1794	
	Marie Josette		Ant. Bissonnet ,, 1798	
	Marie Josette		2° Henri Peltier ,, 1809	
	Marie Rosalie		Pierre Denis ,, 1803	
	Joseph			
	Jean Baptiste			
	Pierre			
7	Louis	(3)	M. Jos. Corriveau S.V.1761	
8	Nicolas	(5)	Genev. Lemoine S.M. 1765	
	Antoinette		Jos. Lacroix S.F.S. 1794	
	Marie Anne		Michel Chabot S.F.S.1798	
9	Pierre	(6)	M Eliz. Letellier S.V.1794	
	M. Françoise		Paul Roy S.V. 1808	
	Mari		Jacq. Alexis Roy S.V. 1810	
	Marie		2° Rémi Rémillard	
				S. Fr. 1843
	Le même		Angé Royer S.G. 1795	
	Angélique		Ls. Dion S.G. 1816	
	Françoise		Frs. Moreau S.G. 1821	
	Marguerite		Jacq. Labbé S.G. 1821	
	Marguerite		André Gontier S.G. 1826	
10	Joseph		Marie Dion S.M. 1807	
11	Jean Baptiste	(6)	Marie Lacroix S.V. 1817	

DOIRON.

1	Honoré		Fse. Boudreau
	Alexis		
2	Joseph		Fse. Foret
	Rosalie		Chs. Boissel S. Chs. 1703
	Anastasie		Aug. Couture S. Chs. 1766
	Joseph		
3	Philippe		Ursule Lejeune
	Anne		Etn. Roy S. Chs. 1761
4	Paul		Marie Richard
	Marguerite		Frs. Jolivet B. 1765

DOIRON.

Elisabeth	Aug. Morin	B.	1767
Pierre			
5 Honoré	Bonne Savary		Acadie
Amand			
Jean Baptiste			
Firmin			
6 Alexis	(1) Natalie Michel S.Chs.		1761
7 Joseph	(2) Marie Forgue S. Chs.		1767
8 Pierre	(4) Thérèse Terrien	B.	1792
Amand	M. Angé Gagnon		
		S.F.S.	1774
Ignace Marie	Jos. Alaire	S.F.S.	1797
10 Jean Baptiste (5)	M. Genev. Gagné		
Jean Baptiste			
Ignace			
11 Firmin	(5) M. Jos. Alaire S.F.S.		1787
Marie Anne	André Roy	S.G.	1827
Eustache			
Joseph			
Basile			
Firmin			
12 Ignace	(10) Mad. Fradet	S.F.S.	1801
Madeleine	Ls. Théberge	S.V.	1824
13 Jean Baptiste (10)	M. Anne Dépont		
		S.F.S.	1810
14 Basile	(11) Fse. Fradet	S.G.	1814
15 Eustache	(11) M. Anne Baudoin S.V.		1819
Le même	Cath. Grubell	S.M.	1822
16 Firmin	(11) Marie Gontier	S.G.	1819
17 Joseph	(11) Genev. Guilmet S.G.		1827

DOMPIERRE.

1 Charles	Agnes Latouche S.F.		1669
Catherine	Robert Emond S.Frs.		1694
René			
2 René	(1) Marie Duchesne		
		S. Frs.	1699
Marc			
Joseph			
Dominique			
Alexis			
3 Marc	(2) M. Chs. Emond S.Frs.		1727
Charlotte	Pierre Longchamp		
		S. Frs.	1748
Scolastique	Aug. Landry S. Frs.		1750
Thérèse	Pierre Desbiens S.Frs.		1759
4 Joseph	Héléne Bilodeau		
		S. Frs.	1736
Geneviève	Toussant Dupont		
		S. Frs.	1761
Joseph			
5 Dominique	(2) Marie Maury S. Frs.		1739
Le même	Genev. Fugère S. Fs.		1742
Joseph			
6 Alexis	(2) Dorothée Barret S.Frs.		1746
7 Joseph	(4) M. Jos. Pepin S.Frs.		1757
Marie Josette	Pierre Lerreau S.Frs.		1781
Joseph			
8 Joseph	(5) Félicité Guion S.Frs.		1770
Marie Josette	Chs. Guérard S. Frs.		1803
Louise	Ls. Gagné S. Frs.		1833
Louise	2ᵉ J.B. Drouin S.Frs.		1855
Marie	Tho. Loyd	S.F.	1822
Joseph Marie			
François			
9 Joseph	(7) Thérèse Guérard		
		S. Frs.	1786
Le même	Marg Gaulin S.Frs.		1798
10 François	(8) M. M. Guérard S.F.		1793
Marie	Jos. Pepin S. Frs.		1833
Charles			
Joseph			
Louis			
François			

DOMPIERRE.

11 Joseph Marie (8)	Marie Vérieul	S.F.	1796
Geneviève	Jos. Couture	S.F.	1819
Marie	Michel Picard S. Frs.		1820
Catherine	F.X. Bourbeau S.Frs.		1831
Angélique	Jos. Jubeau S. Frs.		1849
Joseph Marie			
Charles			
Louis			
Joseph			
12 Joseph	M. Mad. Pepin	S.F.	1822
Catherine	Ls. Boissonneau		
		S. Frs.	1853
Delphine	Chs Gaulin	S. Frs.	1848
13 François	(10) Marie Pepin	S.F.	1824
14 Charles	(10) M. Vict. Emond		
		S. Frs.	1827
Le même	Christine Pepin		
		S. Frs.	1847
15 Louis	(10) Marie Asselin S. Frs.		1828
16 Jos. Marie	(11) Marg. Turcot	S.J.	1829
Marguerite	Pierre Pepin S. Frs.		1852
Joseph			
17 Charles	(11) Flavie Pepin S. Frs.		1845
18 Louis	(11) M. Luce Gagnon		
		S. Frs.	1851
19 Joseph	(11) Marie Pepin	S.F.	1825
20 Joseph	(16) Henriette Cochon S. F.		1859

DORVAL—BOUCHARD.

1 Jean	M. Mad. Cloutier C.R.		1679
M. Madeleine	Gab. Nolin	S.P.	1704
M. Madeleine	2º Jos. Godbout S.P.		1720
Hélène	Ign. Ratté	S.P.	1705
Marguerite	Pierre Paradis	S.P.	1711
Marie Thérèse	J. B. Gaulin	S.P.	1720
Geneviève	Frs. Turcot	S.P.	1714
Geneviève	2º Gervais Faucher		
		S.F.	1731
Jean Baptiste			
Pierre			
Charles			
Le même	Antoinette Chouart		
		Montréal	1695
2 Jean Baptiste (1)	Eliz. Paradis	S.P.	1705
Marie Rose	Pierre Nolin	S.P.	1743
Jean Baptiste			
Pierre			
3 Pierre	(1) M. Anne Paradis S.P.		1709
Marie Anne	Ignace Ratté	S.P.	1730
Marie Josette	Alexis Langlois	S.P.	1745
Marie Josette	2º Gab. Ferland S.P.		1750
Marie Josette	3º Pierre Crépeau S.P.		1752
Marie Josette	4º Ant. Nadeau S.P.		1791
Marguerite	Jos. Crépeau	S.P.	1746
Pierre			
Ignace			
Louis			
Le même	Dorothée Langlois		
		S.P.	1730
Thérèse	Bazile Paquet	S.P.	1749
Marie Rose	Chs. Ratté	S.P.	1761
Marie Rose	2º Barth. Gobeil	S.P.	1764
Pélagie	Benoit Ferland	S.P.	1772
4 Charles	(1) M.Mad.Gosselin S.P.		1712
Josette	J. B. Ratté	S.P.	1744
Catherine	Aug. Roy	S.P.	1750
Geneviève	Pierre Roy	S.P.	1750
Thérèse	Ls. Baillargeon	S.P.	1750
Thérèse	2º Jos. Coté	S.L.	1763
Françoise	Pierre Dubeau	C.R.	1741
Charles			
Joseph			
Jean Baptiste			
5 Jean Baptiste (2)	Genev. Crépeau	S.P.	1732
Geneviève	Ls. Nadeau	S.P.	1755

DORVAL—BOUCHARD.

```
 6 Pierre        (2) Cécile Ratté       S.P. 1737
   Marie Reine       Paul Comtois       S.P. 1760
   Pierre
 7 Pierre        (3) Agathe Ratté       S.P. 1737
   M. Perpétue       Ls. Asselin        S,F. 1767
   M. Jos. Monique   Etn. Racine        S.F. 1767
   M. Jos. Monique   2° Jos. Griffart   S.F. 1774
 8 Ignace        (3) M. Ls. Crépeau     S.P. 1741
 9 Louis         (3) M. Anne Langlois
                                        S.P. 1749
   Madeleine         Frs. Pichet        S.P. 1784
10 Charles       (4) Genev. Coté        S.P. 1746
   Marie             Frs. Pichet        S.P. 1768
   Marie             Ign. Gosselin      S.P. 1778
   François
11 Joseph        (4) Ange Thibault      S.V. 1762
   M. Geneviève      André Roy          S.V. 1797
   Marie Louise      Pierre Chabot      S.V. 1797
   Augustin
   Joseph
12 Jean Baptiste (4) Mad. Garneau
                                      Chs. Bourg 1762
   Jean Baptiste
13 Pierre        (6) Mad. Gosselin      S.F. 1770
   Marie Pélagie     Frs. Gagné         S.F. 1802
   Madeleine         Ls. Martel         S.F. 1804
   Pierre
14 Françoise    (10) M.Eliz.Godbout     S.F. 1787
   M. Angélique      Jean Marie Deblois
                                        S F. 1812
   François
15 Augustin     (11) M. Anne Balan      S.V. 1794
   Marie Josette     Frs. Cochon        S. Chs. 1851
   Marie Louise      Jos.LabrecqueS. Chs. 1860
   Augustin
   Antoine
   Pierre
   Jean Baptiste
   Jean Baptiste
16 J. Baptiste  (12) Thésèse Boivin     S.V. 1787
   M. Françoise      Amable Bacquet S.M. 1811
   Louis
   Le même           M. Ls. Gousse      S.V. 1798
   Féréol
   Jean Baptiste
   Le même           Thérèse Taillon    S.V. 1813
17 Joseph       (11) Euphrosine Lefebvre
                                        S. Tho. 1790
   M. Euphrosine     Alexis Corriveau
                                        S.F.S. 1820
   Joseph
   Ignace
   Le même           M. Anne Bazin      S.V. 1798
18 Pierre       (13) Thérèse Dupile     S.P. 1800
19 François     (14) M. Jos. Deblois    S.F. 1815
   Frs. Xavier
20 Augustin     (15) Marg. Fortier S.Chs. 1822
21 Pierre       (15) Angéle Fournier  "  1884
22 Jean Bap-    (15) Mathilde Picard
   tiste                              S.Chs. 1835
23 Jean Bap-    (15) Marg. Clément
   tiste                              S.Chs. 1845
24 Antoine      (15) Archange Lacasse "  1847

25 Louis        (16) Marie Goupy   S.M. 1820
   Louis
   Joseph
26 Féréol       (16) Marg. Chamberlan
                                      S.M. 1831
27 Jean Bap-    (16) Angé Levasseur B.  1842
   tiste
28 Joseph       (17) Fse. Chatigny S.G. 1812
29 Ignace       (17) Josette Roberge  " 1819
30 Frs. Xavier  (19) Marie Drouin S.F.   1851
31 Louis        (25) Dina Filteau   B-   1850
32 Joseph       (25) Eulalie Blanchet    1851
```

DRAPEAU.

```
 1 Antoine            M. Chs. Joly   S.F. 1669
   Marie              Jean Hallé   Lévis. 1695
   M. Charlotte       Clément Le SieurQué. 1716
   Jean Baptiste
   Pierre
 2 Jean Baptiste (1)  Ursule Bolduc Lévis 1740
   Le même            Périnne Lacroix  B. 1708
   Jean Baptiste
 3 Pierre        (1)  Anne Lacroix     B. 1710
   Jean Baptiste
   Le même            Marie Lis        B. 1718
   Angélique          Ls. Audet        B. 1741
   Elizabeth          Ls. Gosselin     B. 1755
   M. Charlotte       Pierre Guénet    B. 1748
   M. Charlotte       2°Jos. Picard S.Chs. 1769
   Claude
   Antoine
 4 Jean Baptiste (2)  M. Ls. Bégin  Lévis 1741
 5 Antoine       (3)  M. Anne Guénet B.  1748
   Marie              J. B. Paquet   S.L. 1788
   Joseph
   Pierre
   Le même            Marg. Naud     S.V. 1773
 6 Jean Baptiste (3)  M. Rose Ferlant S.P. 1752
 7 Claude        (3)  Thérèse Coté S.Chs. 1762
   Marie              Etn. Couture   "    1790
   Claude
 8 Joseph        (5)  Mad. Guilmet   "    1776
   Pierre
   Le même            Angé Forgues   S.H. 1809
 9 Pierre        (5)  Angé Larrivé S.Chs. 1782
   Marie Josette      Laurent PoliquinS.V.1814
   Pierre
   Charles
   Michel
   Le même            Marie Bacquet S.Chs. 1795
10 Claude        (7)  Génév. Gagnon S.Chs.1785
 A Pierre        (8)  M.Vict. Leclaire S.H. 1803
11 Pierre        (9)  M. Ls. Lacroix S.Chs. 1802
12 Michel        (9)  Agathe Lacroix "    1804
13 Charles       (9)  Véronique Couture
                                      S.M. 1806
   Catherine          Frs. Lessart   S.V. 1860
   Julien
14 Julien       (13)  Marcelline Turgeon B. 1848
```

DROUIN.

```
 1 Robert             Marie Chapelier Que. 1649
   Marie              Nicolas Label  C.R. 1662
   Marguerite         Jean Gagnon    "   1674
   Catherine          Michel Roulois "   1676
   Catherine          2° Guill Simon "   1688
   Nicolas
   Etienne
 2 Nicolas       (1)  Marie Loignon C.R. 1674
   M. Madeleine       Noël Coté      S.F. 1696
   Jeanne             Hypp Lehoux    "   1699
   Elizabeth          Guill. Leduc   "   1704
   Catherine          Jos. Leblond   "   1706
   Marguerite         Chs. Jacq.Asselin S.F.1711
   Marguerite         Gab. Charlan   "   1715
   Pierre
   Nicolas
   François
   Joseph
   Etienne       (1)  Cath. Loignon  S.F. 1682
   Marie              Pierre Crête   C.R. 1709
   Catherine          André Poulin   "   1718
   Agnès              Jean Poulin    "   1714
   Etienne
 4 Pierre        (2)  Louise Létourneau " 1704
   Marie              Jos. Canac     S.F. 1730
   Marguerite         J. B. Canac    "   1730
   Marie Louise       J. B. Leblond  "   1731
   Catherine          Simon Lheureux "   1734
```

DROUIN.

Dorothée	Jos. Martineau	"	1743
Dorothée	2°Chs. Beaucher	S.F.	1757
Brigitte	Frs. Perrot	"	1743
Pierre			
Etienne			
5 Nicolas	(2) Genev. Perrot	S.F.	1717
Catherine	Aug. Defoi	"	1754
Geneviève	Guill. Beaucher	"	1756
Marie	Chs. Defoi	"	1757
M. Françoise	Jos. Trudel	"	1762
Joseph			
Etienne			
Jacques			
6 François	(2) Cath. Canac	"	1719
Marie Josette	Ls. Bidet	S.Frs.	1742
Marie Louise	André Asselin	"	1751
Joseph			
Le même	Eliz. Fontaine	S.J.	1756
7 Joseph	(2) M. Chs. Aubert	C.R.	1719
Catherine	Pierre Roy	Que.	1768
Joseph			
8 Etienne	(3) Cécile Paré	S. Anne	1716
9 Pierre	(4) M. Jos. Canac	S.F.	1730
Le même	M. Mad. Deblois	"	1734
Marie	Jos. Perrot	"	1767
M. Madeleine	Aug. Marseau	"	1775
Chs. Amable			
Jérôme			
Jean-Baptiste			
Joseph			
Félix			
10 Etienne	(4) Marg. Rochon	S.F.	1744
M. Marguerite	Jean Simart	"	1764
M. Pauline	J. B. Simart	"	1770
M. Madeleine	J. B. Martineau	"	1777
Marie Anne	J. B. Turcot	"	1782
Etienne			
Joseph			
11 Joseph	(5) M. Angé Chaussé	S.F.	1745
	V. de J. B. Lehoux		
Julienne	Vincent Rioux	S.F.	1766
M. Madeleine	Frs. Létourneau	"	1767
Le même	M. Anne Guion	"	1751
Jos. Maxime			
Jean Baptiste			
12 Etienne	(5) Thècle Guion	S.F.	1756
Marie Thècle	Jos. Faucher	"	1775
Geneviève	Jacq. Martineau	"	1782
13 Jacques	(5) Gertrude Beaucher	"	1764
Geneviève	Michel Turcot	"	1786
Thècle	Jos. Pepin	"	1790
Jacques			
Joseph			
Michel			
14 Joseph	(6) Genev. Cochon	S.J.	1755
Marie Josette	Frs. Audet	"	1782
Marie Josette	2°Ls. Blouin	"	1790
Catherine	Pierre Lefebvre	"	1790
M. Angélique	Frs. Painchaud	S.Frs.	1782
Geneviève	Jean Marie Labbé	"	1798
M. Madeleine	Etn. Samson	S.H.	1801
Le même	M. Ls. Delâge	S.Frs.	1783
15 Joseph	M. Anne Langlois		
Angélique	Frs. Guirard	S.F.	1799
16 Joseph	(7) M. Chs. Chatigny	S.F.	1748
17 Jean Baptiste	(9) Thérèse Goulet	S.P.	1767
Pierre			
François			
Le même	Josette Roberge	S.P.	1793
M. Josette	Chs. Loignon	S.F.	1801
M. Josette	2°Frs. Pepin	S.F.	1806
M. Mathilde	Jos. Terrien	S.F.	1802
Etienne			
18 Jérôme	(9) Genev. Prémont	S.F.	1771
Jérôme			
19 Chs. Amable	(9) Marie Perrot	S.F.	1771

DROUIN.

Chs. Amable			
Joseph			
20 Etienne	((10 M. Angé Loiseau	S.F.	1768
Etienne			
21 Joseph	(10) Marie Prémont	S.F.	1777
Marie	Pierre Asselin	"	1799
Marguerite	Jos. Lemelin	"	1808
Jean Baptiste			
Joseph			
François			
Pierre			
22 Jean Baptiste	(11) M. Thècle Crépeau	S.P.	1780
Marie Thècle	Frs. Dion	S.F.	1800
Geneviève	Laurent Gosselin	"	1805
Joseph			
Jean Baptiste			
Le même	Marie Guérard	S.Frs.	1799
Archange	Jos. Trudel	S.F.	1825
M. Henriette	Frs. Plante	"	1828
23 Jos. Maxime	(11) M. Ls. Bélanger	"	1780
Marie Louise	J. B. Roberge	S.F.	1818
Angélique	Jos. Hébert	"	1815
Marie Anne	Michel Pichet	"	1821
24 Jacques	(13) M. Anne Létourneau	S.F.	1795
25 Joseph	(13) Vict. Dufresne	S.L	1798
Joseph			
Jacques			
Flavien			
Edmond			
Etienne			
26 Michel	(13) Fse. Dufresne	S.L.	1798
Françoise	Frs. Lemieux	S.F.	1828
Michel			
27 Jos. Félix	(9) M. Anne Paré	S.Jos.Beauce	1780
Joseph			
Jean			
Pierre			
28 Pierre	(17) Genev. Giguère	S.F.	1788
29 Etienne	(17) Marg. Asselin	S.F.	1799
Marguerite	Frs. Marcoux	S.F.	1827
Etienne			
Le même	Marie Deblois	S.F.	1812
30 François	(17) Marie Loignon	S.F.	1804
31 Jérome	(18) Mad. L'heureux	S. Marie S.F.	1799
32 Joseph	(19) Josette Gagné	S.F.	1798
33 Chs. Amable	(19) Louise Cantin	Lévis	1821
34 Etienne	(20) Josette Poulin	S.F.	1792
M. Veneranda	Abraham Letourneau	S.F.	1827
Catherine	Gervais Pepin	S.Frs.	1813
Josette	Michel Pepin	S.Frs.-	1813
Marguerite	Jos. Pepin	S.Frs.	1820
Etienne			
Le même	Marie Canac	S.F.	1806
Geneviève	Paul Deblois	S.F.	1831
Angèle	Ed. Lefrançois	S.F.	1838
Josette	Michel Morin	S.F.	1849
35 Joseph	(21) Marie Plante	S.Frs.	1809
Marie	F. X. Létourneau	S.F.	1832
Adelaïde	Etn. Parant	S.F.	1845
Martine	Ls. Canac	S.F.	1853
Caroline	Jos. Blouin	S.F.	1855
Hombeline	Narcisse Asselin	S.F.	1864
Narcisse			
Marcel			
36 François	(21) Angèle Plante	S.Frs.	1809
Justine	Ed. Drouin	S.F.	1836
Philomène	Zach. Cloutier	S.F.	1853
François Xavier			
37 JeanBaptiste	(21) M. Fse. Loignon	S.F.	1819
Gilbert			
Jean Baptiste			

DROUIN.

	Elie			
	Olivier			
	Alexis			
38	Pierre	(21)	Marie Lasalle	S.Frs. 1819
39	Joseph	(22)	M. Thérèse Ferlant	
				S.Frs. 1811
	M. Clotilde		Frs. Hébert	S.F. 1846
	M. Hombéline		Ls. Prémont	S.F. 1846
	Geneviève		Pierre Plante	S.F. 1846
	Olivier			
40	JeanBaptiste	(22)	Angé Picard	S.Frs. 1811
	Vénéranda		Jean Vaillancour	S.F.1835
	Angélique		Ignace Coté	S.F. 1838
	Justine		Jos. Asselin	S.F. 1846
	Philomène		Benj. Thivierge	S.F. 1856
	Célestin			
	Ferdinand			
41	Joseph	(25)	Vict. Canac	S.F. 1826
	Marie		F. X. Dorval	S.F. 1851
	Séraphine		Jos. Lamothe	S.F. 1863
	Philomène		Pierre Canac	S.F. 1868
	Célestin			
	Jacques			
42	Flavien	(25)	M.SophieLeblond	S.F.1831
	Flavien			
43	Edouard	(25)	Justine Drouin	S.F. 1836
44	Etienne	(25)	Cath. Emond	S.Frs. 1837
45	Jacques	(25)	Justine Letourneau	
				S.F. 1840
	Le même		Angèle Hébert	S.F. 1847
46	Michel	(26)	Marie Beaucher	S.F. 1827
	Justine		Pierre Beaucher	S.F. 1855
	Anselme			
	Louis			
47	Joseph	(27)	Marg. Tremblay	S.F. 1810
48	Jean	(27)	M. Reine Martel	S.F. 1813
49	Pierre	(27)	M. Angèle Gagnon	
				S.F. 1819
50	Etienne	(29)	Genev. Savoie	S.F. 1827
51	Etienne	(34)	Marie Létourneau	S.F.1820
	Marie		Frs. Emond	S.F. 1843
	Anastasie		Pierre Letourneau	S.F.1846
	Julie		Onésime Turcot	S.F. 1853
	M. Archange		Ant. Morin	S.F. 1853
	Cécile		Jos. Beaucher	S.F. 1858
	Joseph			
52	Marcel		Marie Mercier	S.Anne1846
	Marie		Bruno Marseau	S.F. 1869
53	Narcisse		M. Philomène Coté	
				S.P. 1862
54	François		Marie Gagnon Veuve	
			de Marie Cardinal	
				S. Marie 1820
	Thomas			
55	François		Marie Audet	S. Anselme
	Angélique		René Pelchat	B. 1834
	Emérence		Ls. Turgeon	B. 1834
56	Pierre		M. Ls. Fress	
	Pierre			
57	Jean Baptiste		Marie Lamothe	
	Le même		Louise Dompierre	
				S.Frs. 1855
58	Joseph		Angèle Drouin	
	Célina		F. X. Royer	S.F. 1864
59	Gilbert	(37)	Caroline Canac	S.F. 1847
60	JeanBaptiste	(37)	Mathilde Beaucher	
				S.F. 1848
61	Elie	(37)	Marie Deblois	S.F. 1856
62	Olivier	(37)	M. Thérèse Canac	S.F.1858
63	Alexis	(37)	PhilomèneFerlant	S.F.1858
64	Olivier	(39)	M. Olive Canac	
	Le même		Martine Gagnon	
65	Ferdinand	(40)	Léocadie Beaucher	
				S.P. 1852
66	Célestin	(40)	Mad. Goulet	A.G. 1855
	Le même		Cécile Turcot	S.J. 1858

DROUIN.

67	Célestin	(41)	Elise Leblond	S.F. 1855
68	Jacques	(41)	Justine Hélie	„ 1857
69	Flavien	(42)	HombelineGiguère	„ 1860
70	Anselme	(46)	Marie Deblois	„ 1858
71	Louis	(46)	Adé Beaucher	„ 1862
72	Joseph	(51)	Adé Asselin	„ 1846
	Le même		Léocadie Beaucher	„ 1857
73	Thomas	(54)	M. Ls Trudel	„ 1857
74	Pierre	(56)	Marie Paquet	S.M. 1843
75	Frs. Xavier	(36)	M. Brigitte Faucher	
				S.F. 1842
	Marie Célina		F. X. Paradis	„ 1862

DUBÉ.

1	Mathurin		Marie Campion	S.F. 1676
	Mathurin			
	Louis			
2	Mathurin	(1)	Anne Miville, Riv.	
				Ouelle 1691
3	Louis	(1)	Angé Boucher, Riv.	
				Ouelle 1697
4	Joseph		Marie Morin	Islet
	François			
5	Jean Baptiste		M. Rose Morin	
	M. Madeleine		J. B. Thibaut	S.P.S. 1773
	Marie Rose		Jacq. Langlois	„ 1777
	Marie Reine		Jos. Gilbert	„ 1786
	Marie Josette		Basile Boutin	„ 1795
	Antoine			
	Jean Baptiste			
	Jean Baptiste			
6	François	(4)	Marie Deblois	S.Frs. 1757
	Euphrosine		Ls Bacquet	S.Chs. 1807
	„		2e J. B. Fortier	„ 1821
7	Michel		Fse. Fournier	
	Rosalie		Chs. Plante	S.J. 1805
	Le même		Marie Bisson	S.Chs. 1798
	Louis			
8	Michel		Anastasie Couture	
	Le même		M.Jos.Pouliot	S.Chs. 1811
9	Jean Baptiste	(5)	Fse. Dessaint	S.P.S. 1774
	Euphrosine		LsMarieHudon	S.F.S.1807
	Geneviève		Frs. Fradet	S.G. 1818
	Marie Josette		J. B. Gosselin	S.V. 1819
	Antoine			
10	Antoine	(5)	Vict. Létourneau	
				S.P.S. 1784
	Marie Victoire		Ls Blais	„ 1825
	Louis			
	Joseph			
	Antoine			
11	Jean Baptiste	(5)	M. Jos. Simoneau	
				S.P.S. 1801
12	Louis	(7)	M. Angèle Pouliot	
				S.Chs. 1819
13	Antoine	(9)	Angé Goulet	S.G. 1804
	Angélique		Jean Lainé	„ 1822
	Thérèse		Jos. Lainé	„ 1826
	Antoine			
14	Antoine	(10)	Luce Charron	S.P.S. 1819
15	Joseph	(10)	M.Marg.Gaumon	„ 1824
16	Louis	(10)	Cath. Wells	Bert. 1833
17	Antoine	(13)	Genev. Chevanel	S.G.1830
18	Antoine		Luce Lapièrre	
	Henriette		Prudent Boilard	B. 1851
19	Laurent		Pétronille Dessaint	
				S.Luce
	Séraphine		Jean Lacroix	S.J. 1861

DUBEAU.

1	Toussant		Marg. Dami
	Pierre		
	Le même		Anne Jousselat	Qué. 1678
	Jacques		

DUBEAU.

```
2 Pierre          (1) M. Fse. Alaire  S.Frs. 1684
  Angèlique           Pierre Gagné       „    1725
  Marie               Jos. Demeule     S.J. 1707
  Jeanne              René Cochon        „   1710
  Jean
  Louis
  Pierre
3 Jacques         (1) Cath. Bédard
                              Chs. Bourg 1704
4 Jean            (2) Angé Gravel     C.R. 1728
  Florent
5 Louis           (2) M. Jos. Filteau  S.V. 1729
6 Pierre          (2) M.Angé Réaume C.R.1716
  M. Françoise        André Clément   S.V. 1738
  Pierre
7 Pierre          (6) Fse. Dorval      C.R. 1741
  M. Françoise        Frs. Fleury      S.V. 1762
     „                2° Clement Couillard
                                       S.V. 1778
8 Florent         (4) Marie Audet      S.L. 1759
  Madeleine           Jos. Leclaire    S.P. 1798
```

DUBOIS.

```
1 Jacques             Cath. Veillot    Qué. 1667
  Pierre
  Francois
  Clément
2 François        (1) Marie Guay       Qué. 1695
3 Pierre          (1) M. Anne Maillou  B. 1699
4 Clement         (1) Cath. Labrecque S.L. 1700
  Le même             Anne Jonin          B. 1706
                      V. de Pre Rondeau
5 Jean                Marie Plante
  Philippe
6 Philippe        (5) Génév. Ferlant S. P. 1746
7 Jean                Anne Vincent
  Marie               Paul Cyr      S. Chs. 1758
8 Augustin            M. Anne Rousseau
  Patrice             S. Gillie
9 Patrice         (8) Marie Martel   S. P. 1832
```

DUBORD.

```
1 Joseph              Marie Laviolette
  Joseph
2 Joseph          (1) Genev. Marand S. P. 1719
3 Jean Baptiste       Marie Lamothe Que.
  Michel
4 Michel          (3) Marie Chartier Bert. 1761
  Claude
  Le même             M. Anne Ménard  B. 1794
5 Charles             Félicité Doré
  Charles
  François
6 Jean Baptiste       M. Fse. Choret
  Jean Baptiste
7 Claude          (4) Thérèse Couillard B. 1791
8 Charles         (5) M. Marthe Cadrin
                                     S. M. 1794
  Marguerite          J. B. Lacroix  S. M. 1826
  Félicité            Pierre Bolduc  S. M. 1827
  Emélie              Olivier Morin  S.M. 1830
9 François        (5) Marg. Herpe    S. V. 1800
  Marie               Jos. Royer     S. G. 1830
  François
  Le même             M. Genev. Dalaire
                                     S. V. 1817
10 Jean Baptiste  (6) Marie Leclaire S. L. 1795
11 François       (9) Apolline Bélanger
                                     S. M. 1837
```

DUBREUIL.

```
1 Jean                Isabelle Martineau
                                Montreal 1682
  Le même             Marg. Gautier  S. F. 1686
```

DUBREUIL.

```
2 Jean Baptiste       Génév. Blanchet
  M. Geneviève        Ls. Marie Gendreau
                                     S. F. S. 1754
  Mathurin
  Jean Baptiste
3 Jean Baptiste   (2) M. Angé Gagnon
                                    S.F.S. 1759
  Marie Thérèse       Jacq. Fradet S. F. S. 1790
  M. Marguerite       Aug. Guilmet S.F.S. 1796
4 Mathurin        (2) Genev. Boulet S.F.S. 1766
  Génévieve           Clément Fradet
                                    S.F.S. 1785
  Le même             Genev. Coupart
                                    S.F.S. 1776
  Le même             Louise Gagnon S.F.S.1784
  Blaise
  Jean Baptiste
5 Blaise          (4) M. Claire Guilmet
                                    S. V. 1816
  Jean Baptiste
6 Jean Baptiste (4) M. Marg. Guilmet
                                    S. F. S. 1818
7 Jean Baptiste (5) Caroline Bazin S. V. 1843
```

DUCHESNE.

```
1 Pierre              Cath. Rivet   S. Frs. 1684
  M. Madeleine        Jos. Bonneau S. Frs. 1699
  Marie               René Dompierre Bert 1712
  Rosalie             Tho. Laforet
  Pierre
2 Pierre          (1) Mad. Buteau  S. Frs. 1701
```

DUCROT-LATERREUR.

```
1 Antoine             M. Jeanne Pierre Jean
                        de Boulogne Qué. 1725
2 Pierre          (1) M. Jos. Dube
  Marie Josette       Michel Roy   S. Chs. 1808
  Marie Josette       2° Pierre Naud S.Chs 1835
  Joseph
3 Joseph          (2) Théoliste Keroack
                                    S. F. S. 1817
  Le même             S. Marie
  Henriette           Vict. Gourgue S.Chs. 1821
                      Pierre Pilote S. Chs. 1856
```

DUFAUT.

```
1 Gilles              Fse. Simon
  Gilles
2 Gilles          (1) Véronique Plante S.G.1723
  Marie Anne          Frs. Bussière   S. F. 1751
  Basile
  Charles
3 Basile          (2) Mad. Leclaire   S. P. 1771
4 Charles         (3) M. Ls. Jolin    S. Frs. 1778
```

DUFRESNE.

```
1 Pierre              Anne Patin
  Anne Françoise      Jean Létourneau S.F.1673
  Jeanne              René Miniau    S. L. 1682
  Jeanne              2° Gab. Rouleau S. L. 1687
  Catherine           Guill. Rouleau S. L. 1688
  Catherine           2° Claude Plante S.L. 1706
  Pierre
  Guillaume
2 Pierre          (1) Mad. Crépeau  S. L. 1692
  Marie               Jean Chabot   S.L. 1718
  M. Madeleine        Frs. Mailly     „   1727
  Jeanne              J. B. Braconnier „  1730
  Marie Anne          Chs. Michon     „   1735
  Geneviève           Jos. Dalaire    „   1746
  Louis
  Augustin
```

DUFRESNE.

	Marc		
3	Guillaume	(1) Genev. Ruel	S.L. 1702
	Marie	Ls. Proulx	" 1730
	Thérèse	Jos. Morin	" 1730
	Thérèse	2° Chs. Mathieu	" 1735
	Geneviève	Amand Gaumon	" 1735
	Joseph		
4	Louis	(2) M. Aîne Lemelin	" 1732
	Marie Anne	Pierre Godbout	" 1755
	M. Madeleine	Ls. Godbout	" 1757
	Marie	Guill. Gillet Serindac Bert.	
	Augustin		
5	Marc	(2) Mad. Audet	" 1738
	M. Madeleine	Ant. Gobeil	" 1773
	Marie Louise	Chs. Gobeil	S.J. 1780
	Jean François		
	Louis		
6	Augustin	(2) Agnès Leclaire	S.L. 1749
7	Joseph	(3) M. Jos. Leclaire	" 1753
	Josette	Ls. Coulombe	" 1780
	Geneviève	Laurent Labrecque	
			S.L. 1785
	Marie	Prisque Audibert	" 1792
	Françoise	Michel Drouin	" 1798
	Victoire	Jos. Drouin	" 1798
	Thérèse	Etn. Faucher	" 1810
	Guillaume		
8	Augustin	(4) Marie Royer	S.Chs. 1784
9	Jean François	(6) M. Angé Gobeil	S.J. 1774
	Pierre François		
10	Louis	(6) M. Ls. Bésillau	S.L. 1779
	Joseph		
	Louis		
11	Guillaume	(7) Josette Létourneau	
			S.L. 1791
	Marie Josette	Etn. Royer	" 1820
	Thérèse	Pierre Goulet	" 1815
12	Pierre Fran-	(9)	
	çois	Mad. Audibert	S.J. 1809
	Pierre		
	Le même	Reine Chatigny	S.P. 1812
13	Louis	(10) M. Anne Pichet	" 1809
14	Joseph	(10) Marg. Labbé	S.L. 1813
15	Pierre	(12) M. Désanges Gobeil	
			S.P. 1832
16	Marc	Louis Carrier	
	Marc		
17	Toussaint	Eliz. Benoit	
	Candide		
18	Marc	(16) Constance Noël	S.L. 1848
19	Candide	(17) M. Narcisse Trudel	
			S.M. 1857

DUMAS.

1	Charles	Anne Lemaire	
	François		
2	Antoine	Anne Dubornais	
	Pierre		
3	François	(1) Marg. Foy	1668
	Catherine	Ls. Cochon	S.J. 1688
	Jeanne	Ls. Marseau	" 1697
	Marie	Pierre Audet	" 1698
	François		
	Charles		
4	Pierre	(2) Louise Vailllancour	
			S.F. 1698
5	François	(3) Marie Gervais	S.L. 1689
	Madeleine	Guill. Fortier	" 1711
	Marie Jeanne	Ls. Baillargeon	" 1739
	François		
	Pierre		
	Augustin		
	Charles		
	George		
	Le même	Jeanne Rouleau	" 1717

DUMAS.

	Nicolas		
6	Charles	(3) Fse. Rondeau	S.P. 1693
	M. Françoise	Jean Fournier	
			Cap. S. Ign. 1718
	Le même	Marie Guignard	S.M. 1702
	Le même	Marthe Garant	B. 1712
7	François	(5) Marg. Rouleau	S.L. 1717
	Marguerite	Laurent Labrecque	
			S.L. 1741
	Marguerite	2° Ls. Audet	" 1750
	Catherine	Ls. Gaulin	" 1746
	François		
	Pierre		
	Laurent		
8	Pierre	(5) Susanne Baillargeon	
			S.L. 1725
9	Augustin	(5) Genev. Audet	" 1733
	Joseph		
10	Georges	(5) M. Anne Godbout	" 1725
11	Charles	(5) Ursule Gaudin	" 1733
	Alexis		
12	Nicolas	(5) M. Anne Fortier	S.J. 1754
13	François	(7) Fse. Ruel	S.L. 1757
	M. Francoise	Jean Arseneau	" 1764
	Charlotte	Alexis Grenier	" 1775
	François		
	Louis		
14	Pierre	(7) Charlotte Boutin	" 1747
15	Laurent	(7) Gertrude Ruel	S.L. 1751
	Marguerite	Jean Poliquin S. Chs.	1707
	Claire	Jean Fournier S. Chs.	1775
	Laurent		
	François		
16	Joseph	(9) M. Genev. Morin	
	M. Marguerite	Jos. Beaudouin	S.F.S. 1781
	Joseph		
	Le même	Marg. Bourque	S.F.S. 1768
	Marie Josette	J. B. Talon	S.F.S. 1787
	Reine	Amable Paré	S.F.S. 1798
	Chrysostine		
	Augustine		
17	Alexis	(11) Fse. Audet	S.L. 1770
	Françoise	Guill. Petitgros	S.L. 1799
	Jean		
	Ambroise		
	Nicolas		
	François		
	Charles		
	Chrysologue		
18	François	(13) Thérèse Rousseau S L.1773
	M. Geneviève	Jos. Brousseau	S.L. 1804
	Antoine		
	François		
	Laurent		
19	Louis	(13) Mad. Rousseau	S.L. 1783
	Madeleine	Pierre Pichet	S.H. 1810
	Félicité	J. B. Demers	S.H. 1815
	Alexis		
20	François	(15) Marie Gautron S.Chs.1780
	Marie Anne	J. B. Boucher	S.H. 1805
	François		
	Jean Baptiste		
21	Laurent	(15) Mad. Roy	S.V. 1781
	Charles	Enfant adoptif	
22	Joseph	(16) Mad. Marseau	S.F.S. 1792
	Jean Baptiste		
	Le même	Genev. Chevanel	
			S.F.S. 1801
	Antoine		
23	Chrysostim	(16) Marg. Boissonneau	
			S.F.S. 1796
	Marguerite	Pierre Paré	S.F.S. 1818
	Chrysostim		
24	Augustin	(16) M. Fse.Picard	S.P.S. 1799
	Antoine		
	Joseph		

5-6 EDWARD VII., A. 1906

DUMAS.

25	Jean	(17) Génev. Audet	S.L. 1804
26	Nicolas	(17) Génev. Choret	S.L. 1807
	Henriette	Ant. Godbout	S.L. 1844
	Adelaïde	Pierre Audet	S.L. 1845
	Nicolas		
	Edouard		
27	François	(17) Vict. Langlois	S.L. 1809
	Rose	Misaël Bélanger	S.M. 1837
	Victoire	Gab. Bélanger	S.M. 1841
	Adelaïde	F. X. Larue	S.V. 1845
	François		
28	Ambroise	(17) M. Eliz. Avoine	S.L. 1809
	Le même	Mad. Audet	S.L. 1812
29	Jean Chry-sostim	(17) Susanne Coté Isle Verte	
30	Charles	(17) Eliz. Coulombe	S.L. 1813
31	François	(18) Marie Langlois	S.L. 1808
	François		
	Le même	M. Ls. Patry	S.L. 1817
32	Antoine	(18) Thérèse Bourget	
	Cécile		Lévis 1809
	Emélie	J. B. Hallé	Lévis 1835
	Thérèse	Prudent Morin	Lévis
	Antoine	Frs. Dumont	
	Louis		
33	Laurent	(18) Josette Roberge	S.P. 1816
	Marie	Jean Forgue	S.L. 1855
	Olivier		
	Eloi		
	A. Alexis	(19) Susanne Gosselin	S.H. 1817
34	François	(20) Marie Bernier	S.H. 1813
	François		
35	Charles	(21) Josette Nadeau	S.Chs.1809
	Marie Josette	Jos. Leclaire	S. Chs. 1833
	Angèle	Jacq.Lefebvre	S. Chs. 1833
	Constance	Gaspard Bélanger	
			S. Chs. 1847
	Charles		
	Joseph		
	Laurent		
	Augustin		
36	Jean Bap-tiste	(22) M. Marthe Blais	
			S.F.S. 1817
	Prudent		
37	Antoine	(22) Marie Langlois	S.F.S. 1826
38	Chrysostim	(23) Rose Boutin	S.F.S. 1827
39	Antoine	(24) Osite Thibaut	S.V. 1838
40	Joseph	(24) Fse.Martineau	S.F.S. 1841
41	Nicolas	(26) Thérèse Pouliot	S.L. 1884
	Célestin		
	Jos. Napoléon		
42	Edouard	(26) Marg.Brousseau	S.L. 1836
43	François	(27) Constance Morin	S.M.1841
	M.Constance	Tho. Nicole	S.M. 1863
	Frs. Charles		
44	Louis	Josette Langlois	
			S.H.
	Louis		
45	Jean Bap-tiste	(20) Fse. Chouinard	S.H. 1807
		S. Isidore	
	Le même	Marie Bolduc	S.V. 1842
46	François	(31) Adé Blouin	S.J. 1832
	Eléonore	Pierre Langlois	S.L.1859
	Marcelline	F. A. Terrien	„ 1860
	Marie	Jean Leclaire	„ 1869
	Philomène	Nazaire Dumas	„ 1875
47	Antoine	(32) M. Anne Bourget	Lévis
48	Louis	(32) Samson	„
49	Eloi	(33) Marie Disputeau	
50	Olivier	(33) Zoé Vien	S.L. 1866
51	François	(34) Marg. Lecours	S.Chs.1840
52	Charles	(35) Josette Gosselin	„ 1832
53	Laurent	(35) M. Chs. Leclaire	„ 1833
54	Joseph	(35) Hermine Gontier	„ 1835
55	Augustin	(35) M. Mad. Gosselin	„ 1853

DUMAS.

56	Prudent	(36) M.ThécleBacquet	SM.1861
57	Jos.Napoléon	(41) Genev. Godbout	S.L.1864
58	Célestin	(41) Marie Roberge	„ 1872
59	Frs.Charles	(43) Anne Bacquet	S.M.1865
60	Louis	(44) Julienne Bacquet	„ 1852

DUMET-DEMERS.

1	Jean	Jeanne Redie	
	Jean		
	Nicolas		
2	Jean	(1) Jeanne Larrivé	S.F.1696
3	Nicolas	(1) Anne Rochon	„ 1700
4	Jean	M. Anne Dussaut	
	Jean		
5	Jean	(4) Véronique Roberge	
			Lévis 1764
	Marie Anne	Joseph Genest	S.H.1786
	Jean		
	Charles		
6	Jean	(5) M. Hélène Leclaire	
			S.P. 1794
A	Charles	(5) M. Reine Blais	S.H.1792
7	Louis	Thérèse Gagnon	S.Nic.
	Jos.Marie		
	Louis		
8	Etienne	M. Jos. Simonneau	
			CapS.Ign.1791
	Louis Etn.	M.Marg. Demers	
	Louis		
9	Jos.Marie	(7) M.Mad.Paquet	S.M.1761
10	Louis	(7) Genev. Huart	Lévis 1752
	Le même	Fse. Paquet	S.J. 1761
11	Louis	(8) M. Jos Nadeau	B. 1824
12	Louis	Marie Blais	
	M.Eugénie	Chs. Leclaire	S.Chs.1860

DUMONT-LAFLEURE.

1	Jean	Cath. Topsan	
	Marie Anne	Jean Nadeau	S.J.1691
	Catherine	Jean Royer	
	Julien		
2	Julien	(1) Anne Journeroch	S.J.1702
	Susanne	René Pruneau	S.M.1716
	M. Madeleine	Michel Masson	S.V.1632
	M. Susanne	Guill. Daniau	Bert.1736
	François		
	Joseph		
	Julien		
3	François	(2) Pierre Lacroix	B. 1724
4	Julien	(2) Louise Guichard	S.V.1727
	Marie Josette	Drapeau	
	Marie Josette	2° Jos. Plante	S.P.S.1753
	Julien		
5	Joseph	(2) Mad. Lacasse	B. 1733
6	Julien	(4) M.Jos.Goulet	S.Chs.1752

DUPAS.

1	Guillaume	Jeanne Cailler	
	Mathurin		
2	Mathurin	(1) Jeanne Bidet	S.J. 1700
	M. Françoise	Ant. Fortier	„ 1732
	Charlotte	Ls. Delage	
	Charlotte	2° Ignace Gosselin	„ 1749

DUPERRON-LAVERTU.

1	Jean Guillaume	Josette Alaire	
	Josette	Etn. Couture	S.H.1786
	Marie Rose	J.B. Huart	„ 1783
	Véronique	J. B. Boutin	„ 1789
	M. Françoise	J. B. Forcade	„ 1787
	Marie Reine	Frs. Roberge	„ 1791
	M. Marguerite	Ls. Marie Gaudreau	
			S.H. 1802
	Jean Guillau		
	Pierre		

DUPERRON--LAVERTU.

2	Jean Guillaume	(1) M. Mad. Simoneau	S.H.	1784
	Josette	Jos. Goulet	S.G.	1810
	M. Madeleine	Jos. Labrecque	S.M.	1818
3	Pierre	(1) Marg. Couture Lévis		1805
	M. Rosalie	J.B. Bergeron	B.	1846
4	Louis	Marie Vermet		
	Marie Josette	Frs. Roberge	S.H.	1810
	Jean			
	Louis			
	Olivier			
5	Louis	(4) Genev. Daniau	S.H.	1805
6	Jean	(4) Thècle Ferland	"	1809
	Reine	Ant. Godbout	S.L.	1859
	Reine	2º Régis Leblond	S.L.	1870
	Le même	Louis Ruel	S. Chs.	1824
7	Olivier	(4) Angèle Daniau	S.F.	1817

DUPILE.

1	René	Anne Lajoue Pte. Tremble		1682
	René	Jacq. Vermet S. Aug.		1706
	Geneviève	J.B. Charron	"	1710
	Françoise	Mathieu Coté	S.P.	1710
	Le même	2º Jean Bussière	"	1716
	Thérèse	Jean Gosselin	"	1721
	M. Françoise	J.B. Michaud		
	Augustin			
2	Augustin	(1) Fse. Hébert	S.P.	1719
	Marie Dorothie	Frs. Langlois	"	1741
	Thérèse	Frs. Tailleur	"	1749
	Marguerite	Pierre Tailleur	"	1749
	Madeleine	Jacq. Noël	"	1757
	Augustin			
	Pierre			
3	Augustin	(2) Angé Coté	S.P.	1748
	Angélique	Jos. Nolin	"	1776
	Marie	Prisque Plante	"	1776
	Thérèse	Ant. Paradis	"	1782
	Augustin			
	Le même	Agathe Nolin	"	1768
	François			
4	Pierre	(2) Genev. Tailleur Que.		1751
	Geneviève	Pierre Richard	S.P.	1779
	Madeleine	Ls. Noël	S.L.	1788
	Augustin			
5	Augustin	(3) Thérèse Nolin	S.P.	1776
	Thérèse	Pierre Dorval	"	1800
	Cécile	Jean Quemeneur	"	1818
	Augustin			
	Joseph			
6	François	(3) Genev. Clussau	S.P.	1799
	Thérèse	Ls. Noël	"	1820
	Marguerite	Chs. Maranda	"	1824
	M. Henriette	Frs. Aubre	"	1820
	Angélique	Isaac Gourdeau	"	1833
	Le même	Felicité Bernier	"	1819
	Joseph			
7	Augustin	(4) M. Ls. Forgue S.F.B.		1808
	Marguerite	Chs. Couture S.H. Lévis		1828
	Françoise	Chs. Baillargeon S.F.		1814
8	Augustin	(5) M. Fse. Noël	S.P.	1804
	Françoise	Jos. Maranda	"	1822
	Sophie	Jean Gourdeau	"	1829
9	Joseph	(5) M. Mad. Greffart S.F.		1809
10	Joseph	(6) Théotiste Chatigny	S.P.	1844
	Marie Célina	J.B. Tremblay	"	1865

DUPONT.

1	François	Susanne Jarel	C.R.	1663
	Marie	Germain Deblois	S.F.	1696
	François			
	Jean Baptiste			

DUPONT.

	Louis			
2	François	(1) Marg. Rousseau	S.F.	1688
	M. Madeleine	Chs. Cochon	"	1715
3	Jean Baptiste	(1) Marie Deblois	"	1695
	Jean Baptiste			
	François			
4	Louis	(1) Jeanne Paradis	S.P.	1701
	Marie Anne	J.B. Martineau S.Frs.		1728
	Marc			
	Jean Baptiste			
5	François	(3) Marie Buteau	S.Frs.	1726
	Madeleine	Jean Baron	"	1754
	Toussaint			
	François			
6	Jean Baptiste	(3) Marie Leblond	S.Frs.	1723
7	Jean Baptiste	(4) Genev. L'heureux	S.F.	1736
	Geneviève	Aug. Vériel	S.F.S.	1755
	Marie Thérèse	J.B. Chabot	"	1762
	Marie Josette	Clement Langlois	"	1765
	Joseph			
	Jean Baptiste			
8	Marc	(4) Marthe Gagné	S.Frs.	1731
	Louis			
9	Jean Baptiste	M. Mad. Guignard		
	Madeleine	J.B. Girard	S.M.	1769
10	François	(5) Mad. Marseau	S.Frs.	1758
	Marguerite	Jos. Gagné	S.F.	1804
	François			
11	Toussaint	(5) Genev. Dompierre	S.Frs.	1761
12	Jean Baptiste	(7) Josette Théberge	"	1773
	M. Marguerite	J.B. Marseau	S.M.	1808
	Pierre			
	François			
	André			
	Joseph			
	Le même	Marie Boissel	S.Chs.	1807
	Marie	Thomas Dion	S.Chs.	1808
13	Joseph	(7) Marie Labrecque	"	1775
14	Louis	(8) Josette Caron S. Anne		1765
	Jean Baptiste			
15	François	(10) Mad. Dion	S.Frs.	1810
	François			
16	Pierre	(12) M. Fse. Coté	S.M.	1804
17	André	(12) Cath. Boissel	S.Chs.	1807
	André			
18	François	(12) Marie Fradet	S.M.	1809
	Marie	Aug. Cochon	"	1833
	Sophie	(12) Jean Gagnon	S.M.	1841
	Pierre			
	François			
19	Joseph	(12) Angé Boutin	S.J.	1818
20	Jean Bapt.	(14) Susanne Racine	S.Anne.	1832
	Philomène	Ed. Elz Métayer	S.F.	1869
21	François	(15) Josette Asselin S.Frs.		1842
22	André	(17) Julie Cochon	S.Chs.	1841
23	François	(18) Lucie Gautron	S.M.	1844
24	Pierre	(18) Angèle Fortier	S.M.	1845

DUPRAC--DUPRAT.

1	Jean Robert	Marg. Cochon		
	René			
2	René	(1) Genev. Gosselin	S.P.	1716
3	Etienne	M. Ls. Dupart		
	Louis			
	Le même	Reine Provost		
4	Louis	(3) Marie Bilodeau	S.G.	1826
5	Stanislas	Julienne Canac	S.F.	1838

DUPRÉ.

1	Jean Baptiste	Cath. Brouage		
	Catherine	Juchereau Duchesnay		
			S.P.	1778

DUPRÉ.

2 Martinal	Marie Solège-Bayonne	
Sauveur		
3 Sauveur	(2) Angèle Gautron S.M.	1840
Le même	Marg. Gagnon S.M.	1845

DUPUIS—ST. MICHEL.

1 Louis	M. Chs. Fontaine S.J.	1778
Marguerite	Gab. Blouin S.J.	1804
M. Charlotte	Etn. Turcot S.J.	1819
Louis		
Joseph		
François		
2 Louis	(1) Marg. Turcot S.J.	1808
Angélique	Ls. Blouin S.J.	1844
Marguerite	Geo. Hélie S.J.	1844
Marie Louise	Michel Fradet S.J.	1858
Louis		
Joseph		
François		
3 Joseph	(1) M. Ls. Lefebvre S.J.	1812
Le même	Marie Delage S.J.	1822
Cécile	F. X. Théberge S.J.	1860
Julie	Ls. Bourbeau S.J.	1862
Joseph		
Paul		
Gabriel		
4 François	(1) M. Jos. Lefebvre S.J.	1825
5 Louis	(2) Eliz. Jahan S.J.	1839
Elisabeth	Jean Plante S.J.	1863
6 François	(2) Flavie Lemelin S.Frs.	1844
Le même	Cécile Hélie S.J.	1855
7 Joseph	(2) Henriette Blouin S.J.	1851
8 Joseph	Judith Grondin	
		S.Marie. 1811
François	M. Pre. Coté	
Thomas		
9 Joseph	(3) Luce Blouin S.J.	1852
10 Paul	(3) Vitaline Gontier S.J.	1857
11 Gabriel	(3) Marie Descombe S.J.	1857
12 Thomas	(8) Eliz. Pouliot S.J.	1854

DUQUET.

1 Jean	Cath. Ursule	
	Amiot Pte. Trembs.	
Rosalie	Ign. Carrier Lévis.	1712
Jean Baptiste		
Gabriel		
2 Jean Baptiste	(1) Genev. Hallé Lévis.	1710
3 Gabriel	(1) Genev. Hallé Lévis.	1722
Gabriel		
Le même	M. Mad. Grondeau	
		Lévis. 1737
4 Gabriel	(3) Marie Lis B.	1739
Geneviève	Jean Rouleau S.Chs.	1760
Gabriel		
Joseph		
Etienne		
4 Gabriel	(4) M. Genev. Boissonneau	
		S.Chs. 1763
Louise	J. B. Fortier S.Chs.	1786
Ursule	Frs. Collet S.Chs.	1794
Ursule	2° Frs. Nolin S.G.	1814
Ursule	3° Amb. Colombe	
		S.Chs. 1835
Marie	Pierre Roger S.Chs.	1798
Angélique	Amb. Audet S.Chs.	1803
Angélique	2° Gervais Lacasse	
		S.G. 1812
Joseph		
6 Joseph	(4) Cécile Gontier S.Chs.	1767
Marguerite	Jacq. Lefebvre S.H.	1780
Joseph		
François		
Le même	M. Ls. Poliquin S.Chs.	1781

DUQUET.

Cécile	Chs. Morin S H.	1803
Ignace		
Roch		
7 Etienne	(4) Marie Gontier S.Chs.	1767
Catherine	J. B. Mercier S.Chs.	1810
Alexandre		
Gabriel		
Thomas		
Etienne		
8 Joseph	(5) Angé Gosselin S.Chs.	1812
Le même	Mad. Terrien S.Chs.	1828
A François	(6) M. Reine Jalbert S.H.	1800
9 Joseph	(6) Marg Mimaux S.Chs.	1796
Marguerite	Prudent Lainé S.H.	1819
Joseph		
10 Ignace	(6) Eliz. Pouliot S.Chs.	1817
Henriette	Jos. Rouleau S.Chs.	1847
Pierre		
Ignace		
A Roche	(6) Marie Morisset S.H.	1810
11 Etienne	(7) Marg. Gosselin S.Chs.	1796
Marguerite	Jean Royer S.Chs.	1822
Mathilde	Ant. Turgeon S.Chs.	1822
Catherine	Etn. Gouture S.Chs.	1825
Césarie	Ls. Audet S.Chs.	1829
Delphine	Jacq. Labrecque	
		S.Chs. 1837
Archange	Frs. Paquet S.Chs.	1850
Alexandre		
Isidore		
12 Gabriel	(7) Marg. Marseau S.M.	1814
Marguerite	Laurent Noël S.M.	1852
Vilmère		
Jean		
13 Alexandre	(7) Angé Audet S.Chs.	1809
Angélique	Frs. Gouture S.Chs.	1832
14 Thomas	(7) Mélanie Cochon S.M.	1839
15 Joseph	(9) Adé Guénet Lévis	1829
16 Pierre	(10) Marie Bernier S.Chs.	1845
17 Ignace	(10) Marg. Lemelin S.Chs.	1852
18 Alexandre	(11) Rosalie Nadeau S.Chs.	1822
19 Isidore	M. Anne Pepin S.Chs.	1834
20 Pierre	Marie Languedor	
Le même	Euphrosine Bacquet	
		S.Chs. 1840
21 Vilmère	(12) Philomène Bussière	
		S.Chs. 1861
22 Jean	(12) Rose Picard S.Chs.	1862

DURAND.

1 Pierrre	M. Jos. Robichard	
		Cap.S.Ign.
Jacques		
Abraham		
Amable		
2 Jacq. Abr'm	(1) M. Agathe Roy S.V.	1791
Amable		
Jacques		
3 Amable	(1) M. Fse. Roy S.V.	1793
4 Amable	(2) Marg. Bilodeau	
		S.Frs. 1821
Amable		
5 Jacques	(2) M. Ls. Bonneau S.Frs.	1822
6 Amable	(4) M. Jos. Rosseau S.P.	1859
7 François	Marie Gaudin Montreal	
François		
8 Jean	Josette Coté St. Lazare	
Jean		
9 François	(7) Mad. Marseau S.V.	1826
Sophie	André Ratté S.V.	1865
Antoine		
10 Jean	(8) Angèle Coté S.Chs.	1853
11 Antoine	(9) Désanges Roy S.V.	1849

DUSSAUT—LAFLEUR.

1 Elie		Mad. Nicolet	Que. 1663
Pierre			
Charles			
Jean			
François			
2 Pierre	(1)	Marie Rouleau	Que. 1687
3 Jean François	(1)	Mad. Bourassa	Levis 1692
Madeleine		F. X. Couture	
Pierre			
Jean			
4 Charles	(1)	Henriette Balan	S.M. 1693
5 Pierre	(3)	Genev. Huart	
6 Jean	(3)	Ange Huart	Levis 1728
Geneviève		Jacq. Leclair	Levis 1758
Françoise		Jos. Poiré	S.Chs. 1778
7 Jean		Marie Balan	
Marguerite		Paul Blais	S.Chs. 1777
8 Jean Baptiste		Elénore Pagé	
Malvina		Aug. Lepage	S.Frs. 1856
9 Marcel		Adé Talbot	
Charles			
10 Charles	(9)	Césarie Pigeon	S.V. 1860

DUTILE.

1 Antoine	(1)	Genev. Delisle	
Antoine			
2 Antoine	(1)	Ursule Lefebvre	E.M. 1740
Marie		Frs. Gosselin	B. 1763
Marie Anne		Michel Garant	S.M. 1773
Antoine			
François			
Michel			
3 Antoine	(2)	Marg. Adam	B. 1764
Angèle		Pierre Chiasson	S.G. 1787
Madeleine		Jean Pouliot	S.G. 1795
Marie		Jos. Rousseau	S.G. 1808
Julie		Jean Béchard	S.G. 1810
Math.			
Antoine			
Jean			
Jacques			
Pierre			
4 Michel	(2)	Marie Gosselin	S.M. 1772
5 Francois	(2)	M. Jos. Boulet	S.F.S. 1770
Marie Thécle		Pierre Blais	Bert. 1798
Marie Louise		Ant. Bernard	Bert. 1801
Charlotte		Frs. Lejeune	S.G. 1803
Charlotte		2° Jean Labbé	S.G. 1827
Josette		Frs. Lejeune	S.G. 1807
Jean Baptiste			
6 Antoine	(3)	Josette Guay	S.G. 1797
Marguerite		Etienne Roy	S.G. 1820
A Jacques	(3)	Marie Gagné	S.H. 1806
7 Jean		Marie Giguère	S.G. 1799
Marguerite		Pierre Mercier	„ 1828
A Pierre	(3)	M. Ls. Delisle	S.H. 1807
8 Marth	(3)	Ange Monmeny	S.G. 1810
9 Jean Baptiste	(5)	M. Chs. Blais	Bert. 1807
Le même		Julie Goulet	S.Chs. 1810
10 Joseph		Rosalie Daniau	

EMOND.

1 René		Marie La Fay	Qué. 1663
M. Madeleine		Nicolas Dupuis	Qué. 1681
Susanne		Jean Pruneau	S.Frs. 1691
Anne		Frs. Bretonnet	S.F. 1706
Robert			
René			
2 Robert	(1)	Cath. Dompierre	S.Frs.1694
François			
Michel			
Gervais			
Jean			
Ignace			

18—20

EMOND.

3 René	(1)	Louise Senelle	1697
M. Charlotte		Marie Dompierre	S.Frs.
			1727
3A René		Louise Picard	
François		Jos. Gendron	Bert. 1730
4 Jean	(2)	Anne Guimon	S.Frs. 1717
Jean			
François			
5 François	(2)	Fse. Asselin	S.Frs. 1727
Joseph			
Louis			
Jean Marie			
6 Michel		Agathe Ginchereau	
			S.Frs. 1728
Thècle		Jos. Coté	S.Frs. 1753
Louise		Jos. L'heureux	„ 1755
Madeleine		Ls. Gagnon	„ 1762
Michel			
Le même		Marg. Gagnon	S.Frs. 1762
7 Gervais	(2)	Louise Guimon	S.Anne1731
Marie Louise		Denis Gagné	S.Frs. 1746
Le même		Mad. Mercier	„ 1764
8 Ignace	(2)	Angé Barret	S.Anne 1734
Jean			
9 Jean	(4)	Genev. Bilodeau	S.Frs.
			1736
Madeleine		Louis Pepin	S.Frs. 1757
Genevieve		Ls. Boissieu	„ 1761
Le même		Genev. Gendron	„ 1748
Marie Josette		Jean Lescabiet	„ 1775
M. Elizabeth		Ignace Caron	„ 1776
Charlotte		Pierre Picard	S.J. 1792
Jean Baptiste			
10 Francois	(4)	Eliz. Gendron	S.Frs. 1741
Isabelle		Jos. Plante	„ 1765
Marie Louise		Ls. Miray	„ 1770
Marie Josette		Frs. Dalaire	S.F.S 1781
Joseph			
Louis			
11 Jean		Marie Blanchard	Acadie
Pierre			
12 Joseph	(5)	Marie Jolin	S.Frs. 1755
Le même		Marg. Gagnon	„ 1756
13 Louis		M. Jos.Boissonneau	S.J.
			1757
Louise		Jos. Lainé	S.J. 1782
Marie Josette		Frs. Turcot	„ 1785
14 Jean Marie	(5)	Ange Asselin	S.J. 1761
Geneviève		Michel Paquet	„ 1790
Marie		Ls. Cochon	„ 1794
Le même		Cécile Leclaire	S.L. 1773
Joseph			
15 Michel	(6)	Angé Coté	S.P. 1753
Angélique		Ls. Baugy	S.Frs. 1787
Jean Baptiste			
Michel			
16 Jean	(8)	Félicite Gagnon	S.Frs.1765
17 Jean Baptiste	(9)	M.Thécle Guion	S.Frs.1776
M. Charlotte		Aug. Labbé	S.Frs.1799
François			
Le même		Georgine Picard	S.J. 1791
18 Joseph		M. Jos. L'heureux	S.Frs.
			1765
M. Charlotte		Jos. Dalaire	S.Frs. 1800
Marie		Jos. Potin	S.J. 1793
Geneviève		Etn. Dalaire	„ 1795
Joseph			
Augustin			
Le même		M. Vict. Bonneau	S.J.1819
19 Louis	(10)	M. Bugitte Guion	S.Frs.
			1778
20 Jean Pierre	(11)	Thérèse Fradet	S.V. 1767
Marie Josette		Jos. Gautron	S.M. 1788
Thérèse		Jos. Paquet	Bert. 1793
Françoise		Felix Gautron	„ 1798
Marguerite		J. B. Letourneau	„ 1800

EMOND.

	Pierre				
21	Michel	(15)	Eliz. Gosselin	S.H.	1781
	Marie Louise		Frs. Leblanc	S.Frs.	1804
	Marie		Frs. Dion	„	1822
	Pierre				
	Jean Baptiste				
	Michel				
	Augustin				
22	Joseph	(14)	M. Angé Cochon	S.J.	1799
	Marie		Gab. Blouin	„	1822
	Madeleine		Jos. Dion	„	1827
	Catherine		Jos. Dalaire	„	1832
	Joseph				
	Jean				
23	Jean Baptiste	(15)	M. Fse. Plante	S.J.	1794
24	François	(17)	M. Mad. L'heureux	S. Frs.	1805
	M. Victoire		Chs. Dompierre	„	1827
	Veneranda		Pierre Réaume	„	1833
	Catherine		Etn. Drouin	„	1837
	Luce		Magl. Morin	„	1843
	Ursule		J. B. Laurent	„	1853
	Marie		J. B. Ginchereau	„	1859
	François				
	Le même		Eliz. Giguère S. Anne 1837		
	Le même		M. Ls. Unity McLean	S.Frs.	1840
25	Joseph	(18)	M. Angé Guion	S.Frs.	1789
	M. Victoire		Jos. Verret	S.J.	1826
	Augustin				
26	Augustin	(18)	Cath. Marseau	S.J.	1794
	Marguerite		Henri Dalaire	„	1812
	Catherine		Frs. Plante	S.F.	1818
	Le même		Marie Gaulin	S.Frs.	1804
	Joseph				
27	Pierre	(20)	Thècle Daniau	Bert.	1798
	Luce		Jean Baptiste	„	1830
	Pierre				
	Joseph				
	Basile				
28	Pierre	(21)	Brigitte Gaulin	S.Frs.	1806
	Brigitte		Ed. Filion	„	1835
	Marie		Jacq. Dion	„	1835
	Hombeline		Ls. Marseau	„	1843
	Emérentienne		Jean Marseau	„	1853
	Augustin				
29	Michel	(21)	M. Ls. Baudouin	S. Frs.	1807
	Marie Julie		Amable Hébert	„	1840
	Michel				
30	Jean Baptiste	(21)	Josette Pepin	S.F.	1814
	Adélaïde		David Asselin	S.Frs.	1857
	François Xavier				
31	Augustin	(21)	Thérèse Lemelin	S.L.	1822
32	Jean Baptiste		Angé Miville	Cap. St. Ign.	
	Henri				
33	Pierre		Julie Dessaint	S.P.S.	
	Geneviève		Magloire Bilodeau	S.M.	1847
34	Joseph	(22)	Eliz. Fauchon	S.J.	1835
	Joseph				
35	Jean	(22)	Justine Dalaire	S.J.	1838
36	François	(24)	Marie Drouin	S.F.	1843
37	Augustin	(25)	Louise Plante	S.Frs.	1828
38	Joseph	(26)	Marie Marseau	S.Frs.	1831
39	Pierre	(27)	Reine Roby	S.G.	1824
40	Basile	(27)	Sophie Wells	Bert.	1830
	Michel				
40	Joseph	(27)	Angéle Wells	Bert.	1833
42	Augustin	(28)	Marie Lemelin	S.Frs.	1843
	François				
43	Michel	(29)	Thècle Dion	S.Frs.	1840

EMOND.

44	François Xavier	(30)	Eléonore Lepage	S. Frs.	1856
45	Henry	(32)	Eliz. Morin	S.F.S.	1841
46	Joseph	(34)	Eulalie Peltier	S.L.	1858
	Le même		Marg. Audet	„	1871
47	Michel	(40)	Vitaline Bernier	S.Chs.	1858
48	François	(42)	Cath. Gagnon	S.F.	1849
49	Jean Baptiste		Séraphine Hamel		
	Le même		Emélie Gobeil	S.J.	1856

ENOUF.

2	Charles		Louis Fournier		
	Elizabeth		Pierre Bouchard	B.	1818
	Marguerite		Pierre Chabot	„	1821
	Louise		Jean Marie Maupas	B.	1827
	Adélaïde		Pierre Roy	„	1829
	Sophie		J. B. Dion	„	1831
	Jean				
	Charles				
	Abraham				
3	Charles	(2)	Esther Labrecque	B.	1832
	M. Adélaïde		Maxime Couillard	„	1858
4	Abraham	(2)	Seconde Fiset	B.	1838
5	Jean	(2)	M. Desneiges Turgeon	S.M.	1838

FALARDEAU.

1	Guillaume		Ambroise Bergevin	Beauport	1694
	Jean				
	Guillaume				
	René				
	Louis François				
2	Jean	(1)	Marie Bélanger	Chs. Bourg	1781
3	Guillaume		Jeanne Renaud	Chs. Bourg	1718
	Madeleine		Ls. Jacques	Chs. Bourg	1762
	Jean				
	René				
4	Réné		M. Chs. Renaud	Chs. Bourg	1727
	Madeleine		J. B. Custos	Chs. Bourg	1721
5	Louis François		Eliz. Gervais	Chs. Bourg	1721
6					
7	Jean	(3)	Mad. Bédard	Chs. Bourg	1744
	Madeleine		Alexis Boivin	S.P.	1788
8	Réné	(3)	Marie Beaumont	Chs. Bourg	1740
	M. Geneviève		Jacq. Corriveau	S.V.	1783
	M. Geneviève		2º Jean Frs. Hélie	S.V.	1788

FAUCHER.

1	Charles		Louis Cotin		
	Marguerite		Pierre Tangué	S.M.	1793
	Charles				
2	Joseph		Mad. Morin Beauport		
	Basile				
3	Charles	(1)	M. Genev. Casault	S. Tho	1795
	Marie Julie		Jos Furois	S.M.	1823
	M. Geneviève		Frs. Talbot	S.M.	1824
	Marie Louise		Eustache Forgues	S.M.	1824
	M. Sophie Emélie		Ls Fontaine	S.M.	1827
	M. Sophie Emélie		2º Paul Latouche	S.M.	1839

FAUCHER.

Charles			
George			
Narcisse			
4 Basile	(2) Mad. Bissonnet S.M.	1820	
5 Charles	(3) Hélène Dignard S.M.	1825	
	Vve de Geo. Coté		
6 Georges	(3) M. Ls. de Viller		
Henriette	Elzéar Chamberland		
		S.M	1861
Louise	Pierre Clément S.M.	1862	
7 Narcisse	(3) Mercier Qué.		

FAUCHON.

1 Jean	Anne Lereau, év.		
	d'Avranches		
Alexis			
2 Alexis	(1) Marie Dodier S.V.	1762	
Marie Josette	Jos. Chouinard S.P.S.	1780	
Marie Josette	2° Jos. Quemeneur		
		S.P.S.	1792
Geneviève	Jos. Quemeneur		
		S.P.S.	1792
Marguerite	Frs. Pelchat S.P.S.	1792	
Marguerite	2° Jos. Leblond S.P.S.	1806	
Joseph			
3 Joseph	(2) Genev. Fournier		
		S.F.S.	1800
Geneviève	J. B. Lebrun S.G.	1823	
Françoise	Frs. Lebrun S.G.	1827	
Elizabeth	Jos. Emond S.J.	1835	
Joseph			
Louis			
4 Joseph	(3) Anastasie Boutin S.V.	1826	
5 Louis	(3) Théotiste Fradet S.G.	1828	
Marie			

FERLAND.

1 François	Jeanne Fse Milois		
		S.F.	1679
Marguerite	Martin Coté S.P.	1698	
Geneviève	Pierre Coté S.P.	1707	
Madeleine	Mathieu Blouard S.P.	1707	
Madeleine	2° Jean Bergeron S.P.	1711	
Ursule	Jean Peltier S.P.	1715	
Ursule	2° Frs. Chabot S.P.	1730	
Jean Baptiste			
Gabriel			
François			
2 François	(1) Anne Goulet S.P.	1708	
Marie Anne	Frs. Bussière S.P.	1733	
Catherine	Paul Bussière S.P.	1744	
Marie Rose	J. B. Drapeau S.P.	1752	
Pierre			
Joseph			
Gabriel			
François			
Jean			
3 Jean Baptiste	(1) Genev. Goulet S.P.	1710	
Madeleine	Michel Montigny		
		S.P.	1730
Geneviève	Phil. Dubois S.P.	1746	
Jean Baptiste			
4 Gabriel	(1) Marg. Goulet S.P.	1719	
Gabriel Frs.			
Gabriel			
Gabriel			
Pierre			
Le même	M. Jos. Pichet S.P.	1740	
Agathe	Jos. Gosselin S.P.	1765	
M. Madeleine	Alexis Gosselin S.P.	1773	
Louis			
5 Pierre	(2) Genev. Goulet S.P.	1742	
Angélique	Jos. Goupy S.Chs.	1772	
Geneviève	Aug. Mercier S.Chs.	1775	

FERLAND.

Pierre	Jos. Gontier S.Chs.	1782	
Etienne			
6 Jean	(2) Marie Paquet S.F.	1741	
Thérèse	Frs. Gosselin S.L.	1773	
Benoit			
7 François	(2) M. Fse Fortier S.J.	1735	
		S.H.	
Geneviève	Ls. Audet S.Chs.	1762	
Geneviève	2° Ant. Blanchet S.H.	1783	
Le même	Eliz. Boulet Lévis	1755	
8 Gabriel	(2) Mad. Goulet S.P.	1747	
9 Joseph	(2) M. Anne Ratté S.F.	1753	
10 Jean Baptiste	(3) Hélène Crépeau S.P.	1732	
Rénée	Jean Noel S.P.	1754	
Marie Thérèse	Jos. Coté S.P.	1765	
Marie Thérèse	2° Pierre Cinqmars		
		S.P.	1782
Marie Hélène	Jos. Grenier S.P.	1770	
Marie Thècle	Frs. Simart S.P.	1772	
Jean			
Pierre			
11 Gabriel	(4) Josette Dorval S.P.	1750	
12 Pierre	(4) Josette Roberge "	1785	
Marie Josette	Bénoni Fontaine S.H.	1804	
Thècle	Jean Duperron "	1809	
Reine	Pierre Isabel "	1815	
Joseph			
Pierre			
13 Frs. Gabriel	(4) Genev. Cotin S.V.	1780	
14 Louis	(4) Angèle Montigny S.P.	1773	
Jean			
15 Gabriel	(4) Thérèse Guay Lévis	1786	
Marguerite	Chs. Vérieul S.H.	1806	
François			
Gabriel			
16 Pierre	(5) Marg. Cochon S.Chs.	1764	
17 Etienne	(5) Marg. Gontier "	1774	
Marie	Frs. Terrien "	1794	
18 Benoit	(6) M. Pélagie Dorval S.P.	1772	
19 Jean	(10) M. Josette Noël "	1761	
Pierre			
Jean Baptiste			
Louis			
20 Pierre	(10) M. Jos. Plante S.P.	1771	
Agathe	Paul Paradis "	1806	
Josette	Jos. Marie Gagnon "	1808	
Catherine	Olivier Goulet "	1812	
M. Angélique	Prisque Roberge "	1819	
Laurent			
Ambroise			
Louis			
Romain			
Olivier			
Pierre			
A Pierre	(12) Josette Côté S.H.	1814	
B Joseph	(12) Genev. Nadeau "	1814	
21 Guillaume	Angé Matte		
Angèlique	Etn. Denis S.Chs.	1782	
22 Jean	Genev. Gosselin S.P.	1803	
Dorothée	Ls. Gendreau "	1831	
Marie Reine	Etn. Poulet "	1835	
Jean			
Edouard			
A Gabriel	(15) M. Anne Joncas S.H.	1810	
23 JeanBaptiste	(19) M. Angé Blouin S.J.	1786	
Josette	Chs. Paradis S.P.	1810	
Josette	2° Chs. Aubin "	1824	
Angélique	Pierre Trudel "	1811	
Marie Anne	J. B. Langlois "	1815	
Rose	Jos. Gosselin "	1818	
Théotiste	Laurent Gosselin "	1818	
Etienne			
Jean Baptiste			
24 Louis	(19) Marg. Deblois		
Marie Thérèse	Jos Drouin S.Frs.	1811	
Alexis			

FERLAND.

Louis
25 Pierre   (19) Marg. Mirand   S.P. 1803
Marie Edilire   Moïse Poulin   „ 1843
Victor
François
26 François   (15) Anastasie Nadeau
                 S.Marguerite S.H. 1808
François
27 Laurent   (20) M. Thérèse Paradis
                          S.P. 1808
Marie Esther   Jean Roberge   „ 1852
Flavien
28 Louis   (20) Marie Goulet   „ 1819
29 Romain   (20) Angé Thivierge „ 1824
30 Olivier   (20) Marie Vézina   „ 1825
Pre. Chrysologue
31 Ambroise (20) Angèle Vézina   „ 1831
M. Domitille   Eusèbe Asselin „ 1862
Narcisse
32 Pierre   (20) Angèle Plante
Marcelline   Adrien Cantin S.P. 1841
33 Jean   M. Félicite Gendreau
                          S.P. 1832
Angé Colette   Pre. Chrysologue Ferlant
                          S.P. 1852
M. Delphine   Chs. Alfred Maranda
                          S.P. 1856
Marie   Frs. Paradis   „ 1857
Jean Pie
34 Edouard   (22) Marcelline Paradis
                          S.P. 1840
35 Jean Baptiste(23) M. Anne Poulin S.F. 1823
Marie Anne   Ignace Plante S.P. 1846
M. Apolline   Frs. Pichet   „ 1855
Théophile
Phydime Aug.
Jean Baptiste
36 Etienne   (28) Appolline Gosselin
                          S.P. 1828
37 Louis   (24) Luce Pepin   S.J. 1815
Adélaïde   Jean Audet   S.F. 1846
Luce   Aug. Beaucher „ 1848
Le même   M. Angé Goulet S.P. 1836
Philomène   Alexis Drouin S.F. 1858
Alexis
38 Alexis   (24) Marie Goulet   S.P. 1821
Marie   Pierre Godbout „ 1846
Alexis
39 François   Soulange Turcot S.F. 1835
Luce   Pierre Pouliot S.J. 1859
Sérénus
40 Victor   (25) Rosalie Goulet S.P. 1839
M. Rosalie   Frs. Leclaire   S.P. 1864
Delphine Célina Jos. Eustache Plante
                          S.P. 1867
Pierre Victor
41 François   (26) Cath. Talbot S.F.S. 1840
42 Flavien   (27) M. Ange Vézina S.P. 1840
Ange Elvine   Ls. Phéléas Gagnon
                          S.P. 1866
Flavien
43 Pre. Chry- (30) Angé Colette Ferlant
sologue   S.P. 1852
44 Narcisse (31) M. Zéloïne Goulet
                          S.P. 1860
45 Jean Pie (33) M. Célina Gosselin
                          S.P. 1862
Le même   M. Hombeline Aubin
                          S.P. 1869
46 Jean Bap- (35) Flavie Gosselin S.P. 1846
tiste
47 Phydime (35) Luce Philine Gosselin
Aug.   S.P. 1855
48 Jos. Théo- (35) M. Adéline Godbout
phile   S.P. 1862

FERLAND.

49 Alexis   (37) M. Lumena Lamothe
                          S.F. 1857
50 Alexis   Archange Desroches
                          S. Stan.
M. Adelaïde   Frs. Marcellin Noel
                          S.P. 1855
Alexis
51 Alexis   (38) M. Anne Godbout
                          S.P. 1846
52 Serenus (39) M.Caroline Montigny
                   Sault aux Récollet 1865
53 Pierre Victor(40) M. Célina Coté S.P. 1867
54 Flavien   (42) Julie Philomène
                   Gagnon   S.P. 1865
55 Alexis   (50) M. Aglaé Paradis S.P. 1856

FILTEAU.

1 Nicholas   Gillette Savard Que. 1666
Marguerite   Yves Durocher Que. 1719
Susanne   Jean Mimaux   S.J. 1698
Nicholas
Gabriel
Pierre
Jean Baptiste
Joseph
2 Nicholas   (1) Susanne Mourier S.J. 1699
Le même   Fse. Maillou   B. 1699
Marie Josette Pierre Chamberlan
                         S.V. 1727
Marie Josette 2° Ls. Dubeau S.V. 1729
Marie Josette 3° Chs. Lacasse S.V. 1734
M. Angélique Jean Polequin S.M. 1735
Louise   Pierre Paquet S.M. 1738
Geneviève   Jos. Roy   S.M. 1739
M. Françoise Ls. Paquet   S.M. 1742
Susanne   Julien Lavigne Que. 1739
Catherine   Claude Chauveau Que. 1747
Pierre
3 Gabriel   (1) Marg. LeRoy   1712
Gabriel
4 Pierre   (1) Marie LeRoy
Marie   Chs. Boucher   B. 1733
Marguerite   Jos. Brunel   B. 1754
Marie Marthe Pierre Guay   B. 1754
5 Jean Baptiste (1) M. Fse. LeRoy   B. 1721
François
Jean Baptiste
6 Joseph   (1) Marie Rainville Que. 1736
7 Pierre   (2) Marg. Noel   S.P. 1749
M. Marguerite André Forgue S.M. 1776
Louise   Ls. Fortier   S.Chs. 1782
Pierre
Nicholas
8 Gabriel   (3) Génév. Délage S.J. 1744
9 François (5) Marie Guay   B. 1750
A François   M. Fs. Choret
Jean Baptiste
Charlotte   Chs. Larrivé   S.M. 1783
Josette   Chs. Couture   S.M. 1790
10 Jean Baptiste (5) Marg. Guay S. H. B. 1760
Thérèse   Jos. Turgeon   B. 1797
Cécile   Jean Carrier   B. 1795
Alexandre
Joseph
Jean Baptiste
11 Jean   Marg. Fréchet S. Nicolas
Madeleine   Jos. Couillard B. 1763
Madeleine   2° Ant. Gendreau B. 1779
12 Antoine   M. Jos. Melote
Marguerite   Jos. Pichet   S.J. 1775
Marie Louise Jean Dion   S.F. 1782
13 Pierre   (7) Angé Pouliot S.Chs. 1783
14 Nicolas (7) Vict. Bilodeau S.H.
                          S.Chs. 1796

FILTEAU.

15	Pierre	Angé Guillet		
	Pierre			
16	Joseph	(10) Charlotte Roy	B.	1795
	Marie Josette	Jos. Magl. Bussiére	B.	1815
	Catherine	Simon Octeau	B.	1821
	Marguerite	Gab. Girard	B.	1823
	Charlotte	Jacq. Lainé	B.	1824
	Théotiste	Chs. Baudouin	B.	1834
	Hubert			
	Joseph			
	Jean Baptiste			
17	Alexandre	(10) Eliz. Couture	B.	1788
	François			
	Jean Baptiste			
	Alexandre			
	Joseph			
	Antoine			
	Le même	M. Ls. Bussière	S.H.	1811
18	Jean Bap-	(10) Fse. Paquet	S.Chs.	1792
	tiste			
	Marguerite	Jean Labrecque	B.	1828
	Cécile	Jos. Beaucher	B.	1837
19	Jn. Baptiste	9A M. Anne Turgeon	Que.	1798
	Marie Anne	J. B. Talbot	B.	1826
	Marie Anne	2° Frs. Boilard	B.	1828
	Jean Baptiste			
20	Pierre	(15) Cécile Buteau	S.G.	1807
	Le même	Angé Mercier	S.H.	1813
21	Alexandre	(17) Mad. Rousseau	S.G.	1817
A	Joseph	(17) Vict. Bilodeau	S.H.	1816
B	Antoine	(17) Angèle Morin	S.H.	1819
22	François	(17) Marg. Adam	S.G.	1820
23	Jn. Baptiste	(17) M. Anne James	S.H.	1816
	Le même	Marie Roy	S.G.	1826
24	Jn. Baptiste	(16) M. Ls. Fortin		
	Philomène	Benoni Roy	B.	1852
	Joseph			
25	Joseph	Josette Orteau	Lévis	1823
	Dina	Ls. Dorval	B.	1850
	Marcelline	Damase Labrecque	B.	1851
	Marie Zoé	J. B. Roy	B.	1855
	Louis			
26	Hubert	(16) Angèle Roy	B.	1827
27	Michel	Marg. Labrecque		
	Angèle	Jean Patry	S. Chs.	1844
	Damase			
28	Jn. Baptiste	(19) Euphrosine Maupas	B.	1826
29	Joseph	(24) Léocadie Bernier		
			S. Chs.	1858
30	Louis	(25) M. Tharsile Fournier		
			B.	1856
31	Damase	(27) Marie Marcoux		
			S. Chs.	1858

FISBACK.

1	Charles	Marie Ménage		
	Le même	Genev. Nadeau	S.M.	1795
2	Charles	Marg. Bourassa		
	Antoine			
3	Antoine	(2) Angèle Turgeon	S.M.	1816

FISET.

1	Frs. Abraham	Denise Savard	C.R.	1664
	Jean			
	Joseph			
	Charles			
	François			
	Louis			
2	Jean	(1) M. Renée Bezeau		
3	Joseph	(1) Aimée Jolivet	A.G.	1671
4	Charles	(1) M. Fse. Grenier	A.G.	1682
	Marie	Jean Valière	A.G.	1726
5	François	(1) M. Anne Page		
		Pte.	Trembles	1708

FISET.

6	Louis	M. Anne Voyer	C.R.	1711
7				
8				
9	Louis	M. Mad. Bon....		
	Pierre			
10	Jérôme Chs.	M. Mad. Moreau		
	Ange Dupuis	S.	Foy	1751
	Louis			
11	Pierre	(9) Félicité Lacroix	S.M.	1781
12	Louis	(10) Angé Coté	A.G.	1786
	Marie Louise	Frs. Quemeneur		
			S. Tho.	1824
	Ignace			
	Louis			
13	Charles	Ange Ouvrard Qué.		
	Prisque			
14	Louis	(12) Mary Cantin	A.G.	1814
	Abraham			
15	Ignace	(12) Julie Eleonore Beaucher		
			B.	1814
	Seconde	Abraham Enouf	B.	1838
	Julie Eléonore	Frs. Turgeon	B.	1839
16	Prisque	(13) Cath. Balan	S.M.	1825
	M. Elizabeth	Pierre Rosseau	S.M.	1855
	Marie Délima	Tho. Grenier	S.M.	1853
	Michel			
17	Barnabé Olivier	Lucie Jourdain		
	Le même	Julie Calixt Frechet		
			S.M.	1848
18	Abraham	(14) Délina Patry	B.	1845
19	Michel	(16) Julie Leroux	S.M.	1850

FLEURY.

1	Richard	Louise Lahaudé Normandie		
	André			
	François			
2	André	M. Jos. Tangué	S.V.	1760
	Marie Josette	J. B. Gautron	S.V.	1782
	Marie Rose	Alexis Leclaire	S.V.	1787
	Marie Rose	2° Michel Letellier		
			S.V.	1803
	Jacques			
	Félix			
	André			
	Antoine			
	Julien			
	Le même	M. Anne Morin		
			S.F.S.	1795
3	François	Fse. Dubeau	S.V.	1762
	M. Françoise	Olivier Nicole	S.V.	1797
	François			
	Louis			
4	Antoine	(2) Louise Gautron	S.V.	1790
	Le même	Louise Lessart	S.M.	1793
	Le même	Marie Corriveau	S.V.	1815
	Anastasie	Judes Bouffart	S.P.S.	1838
5	Félix	(2) Génév. Rémillard	S.V.	1794
	M. Geneviève	J. B. Racine	S.V.	1813
	Ursule	Ignace Plante	S.J.	1835
	Félix			
	Jacques			
	André Olivier	Thibot		
	Julien			
	Le même	M. Thérèse Gagné		
			S.V.	1812
6	André	(2) Marie Marseau	"	1794
	Le même	M. Chs. Vallée	"	1801
7	Jean	(2) Marie Rémillard	"	1804
	Archange	Pierre Couture	S.P.	1826
	Julien			
8	Jacques	(2) Mad. Corriveau	S.M.	1810
9	François	Margt. Forgue	"	1788
	François	Paul Racine	"	1818
10	Louis	(3) Eliz. Dion	S.M.	1802
		V. de J. B. Tangué.		

5-6 EDWARD VII., A. 1906

FLEURY.

11 Félix	(5) Archange Gautron	S.V.	1882
Marcelline	Pierre Tangué „		1859
Marcelline	2° Elzear Corriveau		
		S.V.	1869
12 Julien	(5) Archange Boutin	S.V.	1823
13 Jacques	(5) Fse. Thibaut	S.G.	1827
14 André Olivier	(5) M. Olive Beaucher		
		Bert.	1828
15 Julien	(7) Théotiste Turgeon		
		S.G.	1829

FLÉBOT.

1 Charles	Anne Geoffroy	S.F.	1670
Le même	Marg. Bousselot „		1673
Jean			
Charles			
Le même	Isabelle Roy	S.J.	1683
	V. d'Ant Leblanc.		
1 Jean	(1) Marie Selle	S.J.	1701
	V. de Nic. Guilmet.		
3 Charles	(1) M. Chs. Bissonnet		
		S.M.	1718

FONTAINE.

1 Etienne	Marie Conile	S.L.	1683
Marie	Philippe Paquet	S.J.	1700
Madeleine	Jean Pepin	S.J.	1703
Marguerite	2° Barth. Ferrin	S.J.	1721
Marguerite	3° Pierre Lepage „		1744
Marguerite	4° Jacq. Ouimet „		1752
Geneviève	Pierre Moreau „		1710
Angélique	Jean Frs. Thivierge		
		S.J.	1714
Elizabeth	Ls. Fortier	S.J.	1717
Elizabeth	2° Frs. Drouin „		1756
Jeanne	Gervais Pepin „		
Jeanne	2° Jacq. Griffart	S.J.	1732
Jeanne	3° J. B. Monmeny	S.J.	1764
Etienne			
Antoine			
Pierre			
2 Etienne	(1) Anne Mineau	S.L.	1706
Angélique	Frs. Nollet	S.V.	1754
M. Jeanne	Joachim Dion		
M. Jeanne	2° Jacq. Frégeot		
		S.F.S.	1771
Philippe			
Etienne			
A Etienne	Mad. Fournier		
Cécile	Denis Morin	S.P.S.	1750
Cécile	2° Jos. Blanchet „		1784
Marguerite	Pre. Noel Malboeuf		
		S.P.S.	1761
3 Pierre	(1) Mad. Pepin	S.J.	1722
M. Madeleine	Etn. Audibert „		1739
Le même	M. Jos. Gosselin „		1739
François			
4 Antoine	(1) Angé Godbout	S.L.	1726
Angélique	Claude Fortier	S.J.	1749
Joseph Marie			
Antoine			
Jean Baptiste			
Le même	M. Ls. Guion	S.Frs.	1775
Louise	Jos. Hamel	S.P.	1809
Etienne			
5 Philippe	(2) Anne Fse. Terrien		
		S.V.	1736
Philippe			
6 Etienne	(2) M. Marthe Daniau		
		S.F.S.	1737
6 A Etienne	Cath. Gaudin		
Joseph Louis			
7 François	(3) M. Ls. Plante	S.J.	1763
Le même	M. Anne Audet „		1771
8 Antoine	(4) M. Chs. Audet „		1753

FONTAINE.

M. Charlotte	Ls. Dupuis	S.J.	1778
Pierre Noel			
9 Jean Baptiste (4)	Fse. Fortier	S.J.	1754
M. Françoise	Frs. Bussière	S.M.	1771
M. Françoise	2° Jean James	S.H.	1785
Joseph			
10 Joseph Marie (4)	Angé Pouliot	S.L.	1756
11 Etienne	(4) Gertrude Turcot	S.J.	1800
12 Philippe	(5) Ursule Montigny	S.V.	1763
13 Joseph	(6 A) Eliz. Huart		
Louis			
Elizabeth	Chs. Gerbert	S.P.S.	1777
M. Françoise	Jean Blais „		1778
M. Françoise	Jos. Rousseau „		1785
Julien			
Louis			
Pierre			
Joseph			
René			
Le même	M. Jos. Blanchet		
		S.P.S.	1776
Marie Louise	Paul Lacroix	S.M.	1820
Guillaume			
Louis			
Jean Baptiste			
14 Pierre Noël (8)	Marg. Delisle	S. J.	1780
Marguerite	Jos Tremblay	S. J.	1806
Catherine	Ls. Coulombe	S. J.	1812
M. Victoire	Pierre Audet	S. J.	1822
Louis Abraham			
Pierre Joseph			
Antoine			
A Joseph	(9) Génèv. Chabot	S. H.	1800
15 Louis	(13) Marg. Lebrun	S.P.S.	1773
	Jean Marie Turgeon		
Marguerite		S. H.	1796
Angélique	Frs. Gagné	S. H.	1800
Roger	Amb. Blais	S. H.	1803
Victoire	Frs. Labrecque	S. H.	1811
Ursule	Ls. Blouin	S. H.	1816
Louis			
Joseph			
16 Julien	(13) Marg. Blanchet	Bert.	1775
17 Joseph	(13) Rose Gerbert	S. P. S.	1775
Rosalie	Jos. Chartier	S. P. S.	1796
M. Angélique	Ant. Langlois	S.P.S.	1798
Joseph			
	Marie Simonneau		
Le même		S.P.S.	1782
Le même	M. Jos. Picard	S.P.S.	1815
Edouard			
18 René	(13) Marie Valière	S.P.S.	1778
19 Pierre	(13) Marg. Lanoue	S.F.S.	1783
20 Jn. Baptiste (13)			
	M. Jos. Patry	S. M.	1804
	M. Ls. Longchamp		
Le même		S. H.	1813
21 Guillaume	(13) Fse. Lacroix	S. M.	1819
Flavien			
	(2 m) Angéle Gosselin		
		S. M.	1825
22 Louis	(13)		
23 Louis	M. Jos. Blanchet		
	M. Mad. Peltier		
Le même		S. Tho.	1777
Archange	Aug. Talbot	S. P. S.	1799
Archange	2 Frs. Ratté	S.H.	1803
Marie Josette	Noel Roy	S. P. S.	1801
Jean Baptiste			
Bénoni			
24 Pierre			
	(14) Marg. Mercier	S. J.	1788
Archange	Jacques Bouffart	S.H.	1812
Marguerite	Julien Sauvage	S. G.	1810
Josette	Isidore Bernier	S. H.	1815
25 Louis	(14)		
Abraham	Marg. Thivierge	S.J.	1819

FONTAINE.

	Louis				
26	Antoine	(14)	M. Mad. Audet	S.J.	1826
	Pierre				
			Félécite Brousseau		
27	Joseph	(15)		S. M.	1810
			M. Emélie Sophie		
28	Louis	(15)	Faucher	S.M.	1827
	Louis		parti en Australie		
			M. Marg. Picard		
29	Joseph	(17)		S P.S.	1800
	M. Angélique		Thomas Coté	S.P.S.	1830
	Marguerite		Ls. Blanchet S. F.	S.	1826
	Henriette		J. B. Bergeron	B.	1836
	Felix				
	Noël				
	Etienne Magloire				
	Joseph				
	Jean Baptiste				
			Desanges Gagnè		
30	Edouard	(17)		S.P.S.	1838
			Hombeline Lefebvre		
31	Flavien	(21)		S. Frs.	1850
32	Jn. Baptiste	(23)			
			Modeste Picard S.P.S.		1803
	Jean Baptiste				
	Joseph				
A	Bénoni	(23)	Marie Cotè	S.H.	1804
33	Pierre		M. Angè Blais		
	M. Angélique		Laurent Belanger S.V.		1834
	Prudent				
			Sophie Ginchereau		
34	Louis	(25)		S. Frs.	1849
35	Pierre	(26)	Cècile Gobeil	S. J.	1851
36	Joseph	(29)	Génèv. Daniau S.P.S.		1824
37	Félix	(29)	Angéle Labrecque B.		1831
38	Jn. Baptiste	(29)	Maicelline Blanchet		
				S.P.S.	1831
39	Noël	(29)	M. Ls Couture	B.	1835
40	Etienne				
	Magloire	(29)	M. Ls. Dalaire S.Frs.		1839
41	Jn. Baptiste	(32)	Henriette Gautron		
				S. V.	1841
42	Prudent	(33)	Anastasie Lainè S.V.		1844

FORGUE.

1	Jean Pierre		Marie Robineau Qué.		1668
	Anne		Jean Portelance Levis		1683
	M. Francoise		Bernard Gontier	B.	1698
	Cath. Gertrude		J. B. Bizeau Montréal		1703
	Joseph				
	Jacques				
2	Joseph	(1)	Marie Bissonnet S.M.		1696
	M. Angèlique		Jos. Monmeny S. M.		1715
	Joseph				
3	Jacques	(1)	M. Anne Le Roy	B.	1705
	Marie		Frs. Marinier	B.	1761
	Marie Anne		J. B. Dutartre	B.	1744
	Charles				
	Pierre				
4	Joseph	(2)	Marg. Paquet	B.	1717
	Marie Josette		Jos. Maupas	S. M.	1740
			2 Jean Marie Bolduc		
				S. M.	1760
	Marie Josette				
	Marguerite		Jean Lacroix	S. M.	1745
	Thérèse		Jean Pruneau	S. M.	1745
	Marie Louise		Pierre Gosselin	S. M.	1753
	Marie Louise		2 Jean Lefebvre S.M.		1777
	Marie Anne		Jos. Mimaux	S.M.	
	Joseph				
	André				
	Jean Baptiste				
	Michel				
	Pierre				
	Le même		Cath. Pruneau	,,	1744
5	Pierre	(3)	Marie Valière	B.	1732

FORGUE.

	Le même		Marie Boissel	B.	1737
6	Charles	(3)	M. Ls. Couture	,,	1746
				S.Chs.	
	Marie Louise		Jean Briart	S.Chs.	1766
	Marie		Jos. Doiron	,,	1767
	Elisabeth		Ant. Hélie	,,	1770
	Françoise		Frs. Ratté	,,	1773
	Catherine		Jos. Guay	Levis	1781
	Charlotte		Ls. Turgeon	,,	1787
	Antoine				
7	Joseph	(4)	M. Jos. Denis	S.M.	1745
	M. Madeleine		Nicolas Monmeny	,,	1771
8	Pierre	(4)	Marg. Bolduc	S.V.	1745
	M. Angélique		Frs. Clément	S.M.	1771
	M. Angélique		2° Jos. Drapeau	S.H.	1809
	Marguerite		J. B. Paré	S.M.	1785
	Marie		Pierre Lepage	,,	1785
	Pierre				
	André				
	Joseph Marie				
	Louis Marie				
	Jean François				
	Jean				
	Michel				
9	Jean Baptiste	(4)	M. Anne Clément		
				S.M.	1749
	Marie		André Arseneau	,,	1775
	Marie Anne		Ls. Bertrand	,,	1782
	Marguerite		Frs. Fleury	,,	1788
	Marie Louise		Aug. Dupile	B.	1788
	Jean Michel				
	François				
	Le même		M. Susanne Charron		
				S.M.	1775
	Susanne		J. B. Roy	S G.	1801
	Victoire		Ed. Auclair	,,	1810
10	Michel	(4)	M. Jos. Gosselin S.M.		1751
11	André	(4)	M. Jos. Daniau	,,	1766
A 11	Antoine	(6)	Cath. Gesseron	B.	1803
	Marie		Frs. Rousseau	,,	1830
	Julie		Jean Nadeau	,,	1834
	Antoine				
12	Pierre	(8)	Marg. Clément	S.M.	1773
	Charlotte		Michel Audet	S.G.	1806
	Marie		Michel Rémillard	,,	1808
	Judith		Michel Gautron	,,	1814
	Pierre				
	Jean				
13	Joseph	(8)	Mad. Clément	S.M.	1773
	Marie		Ls. Lacroix	S.Chs.	1819
14	André	(8)	Marg. Filteau	S.M.	1808
	Marie Louise		Jos. Guilmet	S.H.	1802
	André				
15	Louis Marie	(8)	Dorothée Labrecque		
				B.	1780
	Le même		Marie Lacroix	S.M.	1819
16	Jean Baptiste	(8)	M. Mad. Ruel	,,	1780
	Françoise		Jos. Terrien	S.G.	1812
	Euphrosine		Frs. Terrien	,,	1829
	Angèle		Pierre Patoüel	,,	1830
	André				
	Le même		Mad. Godbout	,,	1810
17	Jean François	(8)	M. Genev. Hélie S.M.		1788
	Geneviève		Jos. Coté	,,	1808
	Geneviève		2° Ant. Bilodeau	,,	1827
	Madeleine		Chs. Clément	,,	1820
	François				
18	Michel	(8)	M. Anne Lacasse	B.	1790
	Le même		Marg. Girard	S.Chs.	1816
19	Jean Michel	(9)	M. Hélène Roy S.V.		1773
	Hélène		Jos. Chamberlan S.M.		1791
	Hélène		2° Jean Coté	,,	1797
	Susanne		Elie Gontier	,,	1797
	M. Françoise		Pierre Dion	,,	1803
	Marie Anne		Etn. Couture	,,	1806
	Josette		Jos. Chamberlan	,,	1809

FORGUE.

	M. Geneviève		Alexis Poliqun S.M.	1812
	M. Angèle		Pierre Denis ,,	1817
	Michel			
	Jean Baptiste			
	Charles			
	Magloire			
20	François	(9)	M. Angé Fortin S.V.	1783
21	Jean	(12)	Marthe Rémillard S.G.	1809
22	Pierre	(12)	Marg. Gautron S.V.	1814
	Pierre			
A	André	(16)	M. Jos. Bussière S.H.	1807
23	François	(17)	M. Mad. Masseau	
			S.Frs.	1815
24	Antoine	(11)	ª Marg. Corriveau B.	1832
25	Michel	(19)	M. Anne Denis S.M.	1801
	Marie Anne		Chs. Dion ,,	1815
	Eustache			
	Pantaléon			
26	Jean	(19)	Genev. Bacquet ,,	1806
	Angèle		Jos. Paquet ,,	1832
	Geneviève		Vital Chamberlan ,,	1833
	Marcelline		Ursine Mercier ,,	1844
	Simon			
	Guillaume			
27	Charles	(19)	Barret Malbaie	
28	Magloire	(19)	Mad. Denis ,,	1821
29	Jean		Luce Couture	
	Pierre			
30	Pierre	(22)	Marie Plante S.J.	1841
31	André	(14)	Angé. Couture Levis	1803
			V. de Ls. Cadoret	
32	Alexis		Louise Théberge	
	Jean			
33	Eustache	(25)	M. Ls. Faucher S.M.	1824
	Emélie		Soter Ruellan ,,	1852
	Julie Sophie		Himère Ruellan ,,	1853
	Euphrémie		Jean Morisset ,,	1866
	Luce			
	Narcisse			
34	Pantaleon	(25)	Cath. Emélie Turgeon	
			S.G.	1842
	Emélie		Siméon Bolduc S.M.	1866
	Belzémire		Chs. Dion ,,	1872
	Amedine			1880
	Léocadie			1882
	Adélard			
	Solyme			
35	Jean		Céleste Thibaut	
	Le même		Marie Dumas S.L.	1855
	Le même		Genev. Corriveau S.M.	1861
36	Siméon	(26)	Marie Paquet ,,	1839
37	Guillaume	(26)	Genev. Martineau	
38	Pierre	(29)	Henriette Couture S.G.	1824
39	Jean	(32)	M. Bibiana Roy S.Chs.	1863
			S.Lazare	
40	Narcisse	(33)		
41	Adélard	(34)		
42	Solyme	(34)		

FORTIER.

1	Antoine		Mad. Cadieu	
	Madeleine		Gervais Pepin S.L.	1698
	Antoine			
	Jean Baptiste			
	Charles			
	Michel			
	Pierre Noël			
	Guillaume			
	Louis			
	Joseph			
2	Antoine	(1)	Mad. Noël S.L.	1706
	Marie Anne		Jean Chs. Pepin S.J.	1744
	Angélique		Jean Frs. Gosselin ,,	1749
	Dorothée		J. B. Martel ,,	1750
	Jean François			

FORTIER.

	Jos. Marie			
	Antoine			
	Claude			
3	Jean Baptiste	(1)	Mad. Ruel	S.L. 1708
	Jean François			
	Jean François			
	Clément			
	Jean Baptiste			
	Basile			
4	Michel	(1)	Ange Manseau	S.L. 1708
5	Pierre Noël	(1)	Anne Leclaire ,,	1710
				S. Antoine
	M. Madeleine		Thomas Isabel	S.L. 1731
	Marie Anne		Frs. Roy	S.V. 1734
	Marie Louise		Pascal Mercier	Bert. 1736
	Marie Thérèse		Urbain Valier Cadrin	
				S.M. 1752
	Pierre Noël			
	Louis			
6	Guillaume	(1)	Mad. Dumas	S.L. 1711
	Marie Josette		Jean Frs. Pouliot S.J.	1753
	Angélique		Pierre Noël Laforme	
				S.J. 1753
	Elizabeth		Jos. Gosselin ,,	1759
	Marie Anne		Frs. Labrecque ,,	1770
	Geneviève		Ls. Lacroix	S.M. 1750
	Guillaume			
	Joseph			
7	Louis	(1)	Eliz. Fontaine	S.J. 1717
	Marie Anne		Nicolas Dumas ,,	1754
	Brigitte		Pierre Jahan	
			(Voir B. 11 Féb. 1755)	
	Pierre Noël			
8	Joseph	(1)	Susanne Plante S.J.	1721
	(Notaire)			
	M. Madeleine		Frs. Mercier ,,	1747
	Marie Josette		Rosalie Gosselin ,,	1749
	Jean			
	Joseph			
	Ambroise			
	Le même		M. Jos. Filteau	
	M. Françoise		J. B. Fontaine	S.J. 1754
	Catherine		Ls. Goupy ,,	1762
	M. Geneviève		Jean Plante	S.M. 1765
	Thérèse		Frs. Brisson ,,	1764
	Nicolas			
	Antoine			
9	Charles	(1)	Fse. Blouin	
	M. Charlotte		Laurent Thivierge S.J.	1756
	Charles			
	François			
	Nicolas			
10	Antoine	(2)	Fse. Dupas	S.J. 1732
	M. Françoise		Basile Plante ,,	1753
	M. Françoise		2º Jos. Lacroix	S.M. 1760
11	Jean François	(2)	Brigitte Pepin	S.J. 1739
	Marguerite		Frs. Gaulin ,,	1771
	M. Brigitte		Jos. Gourgue	S.V. 1774
	M. Brigitte		2º J.B. Morin	S.M. 1813
	François			
	Le même		Fse. Jahan	S.J. 1757
	Marie		Ls. Gosselin	S.H. 1787
	Alexis			
	Jacques			
	Pierre			
	Antoine			
	Laurent			
	Ignace			
12	Claude	(2)	Angé Fontaine	S.J. 1747
13	Joseph Marie	(2)	Marg. Pouliot	S.J. 1754
	Marie Anne		Jos. Couture	S.L. 1816
	Guillaume			
	François			
	Charles			
	Joseph			
	Jean			

FORTIER.

```
    Louis
14  Clément        (3) Génev. Beaucher S.J. 1732
                                        S.F.S.
    Le même            Fse. Labrèque    S.L. 1733
    Marie Anne         Jean Marie Boulet
                                        S.F.S. 1776
    Marie Josette      Ls. Boutin       S.F.S. 1761
    Marie Thècle       Paschal Mercier
                                        S.F.S. 1766
    Marie Thérèse      Jos. Buteau      S.F.S. 1771
    Angèlique          Ls. Paré         S.F.S. 1775
    Joseph
15  Jean Baptiste (3) Thècle Plante     S.J. 1739
    Thècle             Ls. Audet        S.J.
    M. Madeleine       Ignace Gravel    S.J. 1769
    Jean Baptiste
    Louis
    Joseph
    François
16  Jean François (3) M. Clotilde Talbot
                                        S.F.S. 1745
    M. Marguerite      Valier Lepage    S.F.S. 1790
    Antoine
    Jacques
    Pierre
    Pierre
    François
    Jean Baptiste
17  Basile         (3) Mad. Delage      S.J. 1751
    Angèlique          J. B. Roy        S.F.S. 1788
    François
    Joseph
    Félix
18  Louis          (5) Véronique Denis S.L. 1747
                                        S.Chs.
    Veronique          Pierre Charrier S.Chs.1775
    Véronique          2° Ls. Jolin     S.Chs. 1782
    Véronique          3° Pierre Quénet S.G. 1819
    Louise             Joachim Bernier
                                        S.Chs. 1781
    Judith             Chs. Boutiller S.Chs. 1789
    Marie              Pierre Turgeon S.Chs. 1794
    Marie Anne         Louis Clément    S.H. 1783
    Charles
    Louis
    Pierre
19  Pierre Noël    (5) Génev. Poulet    S.P. 1752
                                        S. Antoine.
20  Guillaume      (6) Marg. Thivierge

21  Joseph         (6) Marg. Roy        S.V. 1739
    Le même            Eliz. Noël       S.P. 1749
    M. Geneviève       Jos. Hélie       S.M. 1768
    Louis
22  Pierre Noël    (7) Mad. Turcot      S.J. 1761
23  Ambroise       (8) Brigitte Tremblay
                                        S.J. 1750
    Geneviève          Amb. Nadeau S.Chs. 1790
    Marguerite         J. B. Bilodeau S.Chs. 1795
    M. Brigitte        Frs. Chabot      S.M. 1783
    Marie Anne         Michel Corriveau S.M.1793
    Ambroise
    Joseph
    Pierre
    Jean Baptiste
24  Jean           (8) Louise Tremblay S.J. 1755
    M. Madeleine       André Helie      S.M. 1785
    Jean Baptiste
    Le même            Cécile Nadeau    S.M. 1771
25  Antoine        (8) M. Genev. Fradet
                                        S.V. 1762
    Marie Anne         J. B. Monmeny S.M. 1795
    Le même            Louise Queret    S.M. 1775
    M. Marguerite      Gab. Audet       S.V. 1803
    M. Archange        Frs. Guay        S.V. 1809
    Marie Louise       Eustache Fortin S.V. 1815
```

FORTIER.

```
    Thomas
    Pierre
    Louis
    Laurent
    Gabriel
    Joseph
    Antoine
26  Joseph         (8) M. Anne Racine S.M. 1757
    Marie Anne         Philippe Richard S.M. 1785
    M. Madeleine       Ls. Lessard      S.M. 1790
27  Nicolas        (8) M. Ls. Garant    S.M. 1772
28  Pierre             Genev. Clément Qué.

    Pierre
29  Charles        (9) Genev. Noel      S.P. 1743
    M. Madeleine       Chs. Canac       S.F. 1771
    Marie Anne         Jean Marie Plante
                                        S.F.S. 1780
    Le même            M. Agnès Pacquet
                                        S.J. 1768
    François
    Louis
    Le même            Marie Martel     S.P. 1777
    Guillaume
30  Jean François (9) M. Jos. Martel    S.P. 1744
    M. Madeleine       Frs. Coté        S.P. 1778
    Marie Josette      Pierre Noël Plante
                                        S.J. 1776
    Marie Rose         Jean Frs. Gobiel S.J. 1773
    M. Françoise       Jos. Pacquet     S.J. 1782
    Geneviève          Jos. Plante      S.J. 1794
    Laurent
    Antoine
    Charles
    François
31  Nicolas        (9) Agathe Ratté     S.F. 1751
32  François      (11) Josette Jahan    S.J. 1767
33  Ignace        (11) Marie Coupard S.F.S. 1784
    Marguerite         Ls. Louineau     S.V. 1837
    Ignace
    Le même            Marg. Boissonneau
                                        S.F.S. 1789
    M. Marguerite      Jean Darveau     S.V. 1810
    Françoise          Pierre Gagnon    S.V. 1810
    Louis
    François
34  Antoine       (11) Charlotte Picard
                                        S.Chs. 1785
    Marie              Jos. Arguin      S.G. 1811
    Antoine
    François
35  Laurent       (11) Susanne Couture
                                        S.Chs. 1793
    Susanne            Michel Terrien   S.G. 1816
36  Alexis        (11) M. Angé Monmeny
                                        S.M. 1796
    M. Angélique       Michel Roussel S.M. 1842
    M. Angélique       2° Pierre Dupont S.M. 1845
    Oliver
    Alexis
37  Pierre        (11) M. Anne Coté     S.V. 1799
38  Jacques       (11) M. Jos. Lacroix S.M. 1809
39  François      (13) Madeleine Amiot
                                        Qué. 1787
    François
    Le même            Mad. Beatrice Poulin
    Richard
    Octave
    Romuald
    Felix
40  Charles       (13) M. Ls. Flanagain
                                        Qué. 1795
A   Joseph        (13) Rose Laurent     Qué. 1785
B   Guillaume     (13) Cath. Duprat     Qué. 1789
C   Jean          (13) Eliz. Borne      Qué. 1798
```

FORTIER.

D Louis	(13)	M. Anne Contant	Qué. 1801
41 Joseph	(14)	M. Anne Masseau	S.F.S. 1776
Marie Anne		Frs. Fradet	S.F.S. 1793
42 François	(15)	Cath. Patry	S.M. 1773
Marie Anne		Jean Frs. Naud	S.H. 1801
Marie Anne		2° Pierre Couture	S.H. 1809
François			
Le même		Marie Jolin	S.H. 1791
43 Jean Bapt.	(15)	Eliz. Blouin	S.J. 1775
44 Louis	(15)	M. Fse. Thivierge	S.J. 1776
Helène		Jacq. Plante	S.J. 1809
Rosalie		Frs. Gagné	S.J. 1818
M. Françoise		J. B. Roy	S.M. 1799
Louis			
45 Joseph	(15)	Eliz. Thivierge	S.J. 1776
Job			
46 Pierre	(16)	Marie Gagné	S.P.S. 1775
47 Françoise	(16)	M. Anne Gagné	S.P.S. 1779
Marie Anne		Jos. Lebrun	S.H. 1796
Geneviève		Ignace Gagnon	S.H. 1800
M. Madeleine		Paul Roy	S.H. 1815
Marie Anne		Chas. Fortier	S.H. 1817
48 Jean Bapt.	(16)	Hélène Leclaire	S.H. 1782
Le même		Marg. Paradis	S.H. 1786
Marie		Chs. Brochu	S.H. 1815
Pélagie		Jean Miller	S.G. 1828
Pierre			
Jean Baptiste			
49 Ant. Jacques	(16)	M. Agathe Quémeneur	S.F.S. 1787
Marie		Michel Morisset	S.F.S. 1809
M. Clotilde		Amb. Pouliot	S.F.S. 1817
François			
50 Pierre	(16)	M. Euphrosine Boivin	S.F.S. 1790
Le même		Marg. Fourrier	S.Tho. 1792
Marguerite		André Gagnon	S.G. 1821
51 Guillaume		Marg. Terrien	
Jean Charles			
52 Joseph	(17)	Pelagie Cloutier	S.H. 1785
Marguerite		Ign. Coté	S.H. 1814
Basile			
Joseph			
Isaac			
Michel			
53 François	(17)	Mad. Picard	S.F.S. 1788
. M. Marguerite		Alexis Leclaire	S.V. 1815
Marie Agathe		Pierre Tangué	S.V. 1816
M. Archange		Aug. Guilmet	S.V. 1831
Pierre			
Françoise			
Joseph			
54 Felix	(17)	Cath. Létourneau	S.H. 1789
Catherine		Germ. Boudoin	S.H. 1810
Marie		Jacq. Buteau	S.H. 1812
Marguerite		F. X. Lefebvre	S.H. 1813
Victoire		Olivier Blais	S.G. 1823
Antoine			
55 Charles	(18)	Marie Audet	S.Chs. 1703
Angelique		Guill. Prosper Mercier	S.H. 1793
Marie		Ls. Bougy	S.H. 1794
Louise		Aug. Clément	S.H. 1796
Catherine		Jos. Délenteigne	S.H. 1802
Thérèse		Frs. Lainé	S.H. 1806
Véronique		Ls. Morin	S.H. 1814
Louis			
Ambroise			
Pierre			
Charles			

FORTIER.

56 Louis	(18)	Louise Filteau	S.Chs. 1782
57 Pierre	(18)	Claire Charier	S.Chs. 1786
Marie		Adrien Rémillard	S.G. 1811
Judith		Michel Roy	S.G. 1815
Madeleine		Jean Coté	S.G. 1819
Pierre			
Charles			
Louis			
58 Louis	(21)	M. Jos. Boucher	Bert.1779
M. Marguerite		J. B. Mercier	" 1802
Madeleine		Chas. Boutin	" 1808
Julie		Denis Gagné	" 1821
Rose		Aug. Guilmet	" 1823
Le même		M. Marg. Roy	S.V. 1845
59 Ambroise	(23)	Charlotte Queril	S.M. 1777
Charlotte		Jean Ainse	S.G. 1796
Marie Anne		Jacq. Tangué	S.V. 1807
Marie		Jos. Chamberlan	S.P.S. 1810
60 Jean Baptiste	(23)	M. Ls. Duquet	S.Chs.1786
Marie		Jos. Clément	S.G. 1807
Josette		Simon Boutin	S.G. 1821
Charlotte		Etn. Turgeon	S.G. 1822
Marie Anne		Chs. Samson	B. 1820
Charles			
Jean Baptiste			
61 Joseph	(23)	Fse. Lepage	S.Chs. 1791
Joseph			
Pierre	(23)	M. Jos. Bétel	S.M. 1791
Francoise		Ant. Gosselin	S.Chs. 1821
Marguerite		Aug. Dorval	S.Chs. 1822
Michel			
Joseph			
63 Jean Baptiste		Félicité Gagnon	
M. Françoise		Jacq. Langlois	S.G. 1811
Basilisse		Etn. Thivierge	S.G. 1812
Paschal			
Jean Baptiste		M. Jeanne Langlois	S.V. 1812
Le même		Jos. Pilote	S.V. 1836
Marie		Euphrosine Dubé	S.Chs. 1821
Le même		Marg. Perrot	S.G. 1830
Vitaline		F. X. Mercier	S. M. 1855
64 Jean	(24)	Thérèse Nadeau	Levis 1786
Baptiste			
Jean Baptiste			
65 Joseph	(25)	M. Jos. Blondeau	S.V.1808
66 Thomas	(25)	Marie Roy	S.M. 1808
Joseph			
67 Pierre	(25)	M. Brigitte Nadeau	S.M. 1808
Emélie		Jos. Turge n	B. 1833
Luce		Pierre Turgeon	B. 1835
Pierre			
68 Laurent	(25)	M. Archange Balan	S.V. 1814
69 Gabriel	(25)	M. Archange Picard	Bert. 1815
70 Louis			
71 Pierre	(28)	M. Chs. Girard	Bert. 1792
72 Louis	(29)	M. Ls. L'heureux	S.F.1784
73 François	(29)	M. Jos. Pichet	S.J. 1799
François			
Le même		Marie Crepeau	S.J. 1830
74 Guillaume	(29)	Vict. Lainé	S.Frs. 1819
M. Victoire		Jean Ginchereau	S.Frs.1841
M. Victoire		2° Nic Asselin	S.Frs.1840
Le même		Marie Ginchereau	" 1822
75 François	(30)	M. Eliz. Plante	S.J. 1776
Marie Josette		Ls. Genest	" 1801
Madeleine		Alexis Fortier	S.M. 1821
Joseph			
François			

FORTIER.

76	Laurent	(30)	Marg. Audet	S.J.	1784
	M. Elizabeth		Simon Mercier	"	1821
	Julie		Michel Lemieux	"	1825
	Marie Josette		Alexis Ainsé	"	1826
	Marguerite		Jos. Gautron	S.M.	1819
	Laurent				
77	Charles	(30)	M. Jos. Coté	S.J.	1794
78	Antoine	(30)	M. Thècle Cochon	S.J.	1794
	Marguerite		Etn. Simart	"	1813
	Marie Josette		J. B. Turcot	"	1814
	Justine		Pierre Toussaint	"	1818
	Antoine				
	François				
79	Ignace	(33)	Rose Leblond	S.V.	1830
80	François	(53)	Marg. Cochon	S.V.	1824
	Marguerite		Ferd. Mathias Bernard	S.V.	1854
	Anastasie		Chs. Couture	"	1864
	Louis				
81	Louis	(33)	Vict. Gagnon	S.V.	1830
	Le même		Reine Bacquet	S.F.S.	1843
82	Antoine	(34)	Marie Roger	S.Chs.	1809
83	François	(35)	M. Angé Couture	S.Chs.	1817
84	Alexis	(36)	Mad. Fortier	S.M.	1821
85	Olivier	(36)	Marcelline Gagné	S.M.	1830
	M. Rose de Lima		F. X. Mercier	"	1854
	M. Octavie		Paul Racine	"	1857
86	François	(39)	Angé Olympe Penot	Que.	
	EléonoreOlympe		Ed. Sév. Belleau	S.M.	1845
	Hermine Emélie		Gab. N.S. Fortier	"	1849
87	Richard	(39)	Julie Louise Taschereau	S.Marie	1827
	Achille				
88	Octave	(39)	Henriette Emélie Ruel	Bert.	1833
89	Félix	(39)	Sara Prendergast	Que.	
	Le même		Amanda Belleau	S.M.	
90	Romuald	(39)	Caroline Mayrand		
91	François	(42)	M. Marthe Chamberlan	S.H.	1806
92	Louis	(44)	Geneviève Therien	S.J.	1815
93	Job	(45)	M. Angèle Blouin	S.J.	1808
	Emélie		Jos. Béland	"	1836
	Marie		Pierre Demeule	"	1841
	Samuel				
	Job				
	Le même		M. Mad. Pepin	S.J.	1848
94	Pierre	(48)	Marg. Gautron	S.M.	1820
95	JeanBaptiste	(48)	Vict. Lainé	S.J.	1846
96	François	(49)	Ursule Terrien	S.H.	1816
97	Jean Charles	(51)	Josette Leclaire	S.G.	1790
	Angélique		Etn. Bolduc	S.G.	1824
	Elizabeth		Etn. Canac	S.G.	1828
	Philippe				
	Charles				
98	Basile	(52)	M. Anne Dalaire	S.Chs.	1807
99	Joseph	(52)	M. Anne Audet	S.G.	1809
100	Michel	(52)	M. Anne Bernier	S.H.	1812
	Le même		Cécile Roy	S.H.	1820
101	Isaac	(52)	Cath. Baudoin	S.H.	1819
	Le même		Cecile Bolduc	S.V.	1839
102	François	(52)	Mad. Picard	Bert.	1818
	Le même		Reine Dalaire	S.M.	1840
103	Pierre	(53)	Julie Cochon	S.V.	1828
104	Joseph	(53)	Marcelline Boissonneau	S.V.	1826
105	Antoine	(54)	Marg. Roy	S.H.	1818
106	Charles	(55)	Eliz. Jalbert	S.H.	1782
107	Louis	(55)	Ursule Nadeau	S.H.	1810
108	Ambroise	(55)	M. Marg. Picard	S.H.	1815
109	Pierre	(55)	Marg. Darziel	S.H.	1816
110	Pierre	(57)	Marie Godbout	S.L.	1810
	Marie		Ls. Filion	S.G.	1829
111	Louis	(57)	Marie Couture	S.G.	1811

FORTIER.

112	Charles	(57)	Olive Couture	S.M.	1826
112	JeanBaptiste	(60)	Charlotte Audet	S.G.	1818
114	Charles	(60)	Luce McIntyre	S.Chs.	1820
	Le même		Thècle Servant	S.Chs.	1841
115	Joseph	(61)	Marg. Lacasse	S.Chs.	1821
116	Michel	(62)	Genev. Quemeneur	S.M.	1824
117	Joseph	(62)	Marg. Pouliot	S.Chs.	1824
118	JeanBaptiste	(63)	M. Agathe Langlois	S.V.	1815
119	Paschal	(63)	Fse. Gagné	S.G.	1822
120	JeanBaptiste	(64)	Brigitte Morin	S.H.	1808
121	Charles		Marie Blouin		
	Charles				
122	André		Angé Lemieux		
	Majorique				
123	Joseph	(66)	Esther Turgeon	S.V.	1848
124	Pierre	(67)	Angé Gontier	Levis	1838
125	François	(73)	Luce Hélie	S.J.	1837
	Le même		Marie Boissonneau	S.J.	1848
126	Joseph	(75)	Marg. Thivierge	S.J.	1812
	Luce		Ls. Poulin	S.J.	1838
	Apolline		F. X. Labbé	S.J.	1864
	Léandre				
127	François	(75)	Josette Bilodeau	S.G.	1820
	Rose de Lima		Frs. Rousseau	S.G.	1841
128	Laurent	(76)	Mad. Pepin	S.J.	1808
	Marcelline		Jacq. Boutin	S.J.	1840
	Scolastique		Léandre Fortier	S.J.	1849
	Antoine				
129	François	(78)	Marg. Lainé		
	Damase				
	François				
130	Antoine	(78)	M. Ls. Audet	S.J.	1830
	Marie		Narcisse Leblanc	S.J.	1854
	Philomène		Pierre Blouin	S.J.	1857
131	Louis	(80)	Sophie Goupy	S.M.	1855
	Le même		Adelina Fortier	S.V.	1867
132	Achille	(87)	Hermine Fortier	S.M.	1849
133	Job	(93)	Archange Terrien	S.J.	1834
134	Samuel	(93)	M. Jos. Blouin	S.J.	1840
135	Charles	(97)	M. Anne Fortier	S.H.	1817
136	Philippe	(97)	Ursule Talbot	S.G.	1821
137	Charles	(121)	M. Célanire Hélie	B.	1853
138	Majorique	(122)	M. Ls. Roy	B.	1854
139	Léandre	(126)	Scolastique Fortier	S.J.	1849
140	Antoine	(128)	Leocadie Servant	S.J.	1854
141	François	(129)	Chrestine Racine	S.J.	1853
142	Damase	(129)	M. Dina Lepage	S.Frs.	1860

FORTIN.

1	Julien		Genev. Gamache	Que.	1652
	Barbe		Pierre Gagnon	C.R.	1669
	Barbe		2° Pierre Lessard	S. Anne	1690
	Geneviève		Noël Gagnon	S. Anne	1690
	Charles				
	Jacques				
	Eustache				
	Joseph				
	Pierre				
2	Charles	(1)	Xainte Cloutier	C.R.	1681
	Geneviève		Ls. Lemieux	Islet	1705
	Elizabeth		Frs. Guimont	"	1714
	Marie Anne		Joseph Caron	"	1711
	Louis				
	Charles				
3	Jacques	(1)	Cath. Biville	Qué.	1689
			Baie St. Paul		
	Joseph				
	Jacques				
4	Joseph	(1)	Agnès Cloutier	C.R.	1691
	Louis Marie				

FORTIN.

```
Louis
5 Eustache      (1) Louis Cloutier
                        Cap. S. Ign. 1693
  Claire            J. B. Bernier  „    1734
  Marie Louise      Alexandre Bernier
                        Cap. S. Ign. 1723
  Geneviève         Jos. Lemieux  „     1729
  Marthe            Jean Coté     „     1729
  Marthe            2° J. B. Langlois
                        S. Tho. 1734
  Jos. Eustache
  François
  Pierre
  Jean Baptiste
  Louis
6 Pierre         (1) M. Gertrude Hudon
                        Riv. Ouelle 1697
  Marie Josette     Basile Bernier  Islet 1727
  Marie Anne        Jean Dorval     „    1729
  M. Madeleine      Jos. Bouchard   „    1734
  Reine             Julien Chouinard „   1741
  Pierre
  Jean Baptiste
  Joseph
  Louis
7 Charles        (2) Louise Guimont
                        Cap. S. Ign. 1712
8 Louis          (2) Anne Bossé
                        Cap. S. Ign. 1714
  Le même           Mad. Langelier „    1735
  M. Madeleine      Pierre Fournier S.Tho.1766
9 Jacques        (3) Genev. Lacroix
                        S. Anne 1721
10 Joseph        (3) Marg.Letourneau S.F.1727
  Joseph
11 Louis         (4) Dorothée Gaulin
                        S. Anne 1728
  Marie             Jos. Barth. Richard
                        S.V. 1752
  Le même           M. Marthe Plante S.J.1734
  Marie Anne        Jos. Taillon    S.V. 1766
  Catherine         Ls. Voisin      „    1773
  M. Madeleine      Jean Isabel     „    1777
  Marie Rose        Jos. Cochon     „    1790
  Eustache
12 Louis Marie   (4) Marg. Leblond  S.V. 1728
  M. Charlotte      Pierre Cadrin   S.M.
  Marie Anne        Pierre Denis    „
  Marie Anne        2° Alexis Roy
  Françoise         Pierre Clément
  Geneviève         Eustache Roy
  Ignace
  Antoine
13 François       (5) Mad. Richard
  Reine             Pierre Morin
                        Cap. S. Ign. 1742
14 Pierre         (5) Louise Caron
                        Cap. S. Ign. 1719
15 Jos. Eustache (5) Marth. Bernier
                        Cap. S. Ign. 1725
16 Louis          (5) Marie Blanchet
                        Cap. St. Ign. 1730
17 Jean Baptiste (5) Angé Richard
                        Cap. St. Ign. 1751
18 Pierre         (6) Marg. Chouinard
                        Islet 1730
19 Jean           (6) Marthe Richard
                        Cap. S. Ign. 1734
  Le même           M. Jos. Blais  Bert. 1761
A René              Charlotte Normand
  Jean Baptiste
20 Louis          (6) Marie Préjean  Islet 1742
21 Joseph         (6) Marthe Caron   Islet 1749
  M. Madeleine      Pierre Cloutier  „    1786
22 Eustache      (11) Chs. Bernard S.V.1786
  Marie             Ls. Fortier     „    1811
  M. Charlotte      Ls. Labrecque   „    1821
```

FORTIN.

```
  Eustache
  Pierre Chrysol-
   ogue
23 Antoine      (12) Hélène Bidet    S.V. 1766
  M. Angélique      Frs. Forgue      „    1783
  M. Françoise      J. B. Gautron    „    1787
  M. Victoire       Eustache Roy     „    1793
  M. Josette        Basile Buteau    „    1797
  Marie Anne        Frs. Delenteigne „    1804
  Antoine
  Le même           M. Chs. Queret   „    1808
24 Ignace       (12) M. Mad. Blais  Bert. 1777
  M. Madeleine      Frs. Marseau     S.M. 1800
  M. Madeleine      2° Pierre Pelchat S.G. 1816
  Le même           M. Eliz. Plante  S.J. 1789
  Nicolas
  Jean
  Ignace
  Pierre
25 Claude            M. Jeanne Méthot
                        Isle aux Grues
  Marie Josette     Ant. Simart      S.V. 1777
26 Michel           Genev. Bélanger
  M. Marguerite     Ls. Cotiet       S.M. 1780
  Joseph Marie
  Louis Michel
27 Joseph           Genev. Fortin
  Louise            Jos. Pepin       S.J. 1812
  Marie Anne        Jacq. Blouin     „    1825
A Joseph        (10) Genev. Fournier
                        S. Tho. 1751
28 Charles           Angé. Fournier
                        S.J. Port Joly
  Marie Claire      Ant. Gaudreau S.R S.1819
29 Jean Baptiste(19) A Genev. Fournier
                        S.Tho. 1792
  Madeleine         Jos. Theberge    S.V. 1824
  Barthiaume
  Le même           M. Claire Boulet
                        Cap S.Ign. 1817
  Marie             Pierre Théberge S.V. 1828
  Marguerite        Frs. Deschamps   „    1840
  Le même           Josette Morin    „    1828
  Le même           Marie Louineau   „    1837
30
31 Pre Chrysolo-(22) Marg. Bacquet   „    1813
   gue
  Frs. Régis
32 Eustache      (22) M. Ls. Fortier  „    1815
  Marie             Jos. Aubin       „    1850
  Adéline           Ls. Fortier      „    1867
  Eustache
  Jean
33 Antoine       (23) Marg. Blanchet S.G.1797
  Marguerite        Jean Roy         S.V.1817
  Eustache
  Joseph
  Joseph Prosper
  Antoine
34 Louis Michel (26) M. Jos. Terrien  S.J.1789
35 Joseph Marie(26) Fse. Goupy       S.M.1799
  Pierre
36 Ignace Pierre(24) M. Ls. Balan    S.V.1813
  Marie             Noël Tangué      S.M.1824
  Adélaïde          Magl. Lacroix    „    1848
  Pierre
  Jean
  Le même           Félicité Métivier „   1839
37 Nicolas       (24) M. Jos. Turgeon „    1821
  Nicolas
38 Jean          (24) M. Marianne Morrisset
                        S.M.1828
  Jos. Edouard
39 Barthélémi    (29) Marg. Jolin    S.V.1841
40 François Ré- (31) Luce Roy        S M.1851
   gis
```

FORTIN.

41	Jean Baptiste		Cath. Lémelin	
	Angèle		Frs. Carrier	S.Chs.1845
	Marie		Pierre Roy	" 1846
42	Eustache	(32)	Rose Bazin	S.V.1842
43	Jean	(32)	Philomène Thivierge	S.V.1863
44	Eustache	(33)	M. Vict. Roy	S.V.1817
	Delphine		Amable Naz. Blouin	S.V.1840
	Soulange		André Narcisse Chabot	S.V.1846
	Marie Zoé		Praxède Roy	S.V.1847
	Simon			
	Jean			
45	Joseph	(33)	M. Ursule Roy	" 1831
			S. Anselme.	
46	Joseph Pros-per	(33)	Angèle Bélanger	S.V.1832
	Marie Léonce		Télesphore Vien	S.V.1869
	Octave			
	Uldéric			
	Ludger			
47	Antoine	(33)	Flavie Talbot	S.V.1834
48	Pierre	(35)	Vict. Plante	S.G.1828
49	Pierre	(36)	Julie Boissel	S.M.1839
50	Jean	(36)	Eulalie Brochu	" 1845
51	Nicolas	(37)	Julienne Dion	" 1851
52	Jos. Edouard	(38)	M. Rose Gosselin	" 1861
53	Jean	(44)	M. Jos. Chabot	S.V.1845
54	Simon	(44)	Célina Chabot	" 1857
55	Octave	(46)	Delphine Roy	" 1860
56	Ludger	(46)	Philomène Tangué	" 1869
57	Uldéric	(46)	M. Valine Corriveau	S.V.1870

FOUCHER.

1	Gervais		Eliz. Gerbert	S.F.1689
	Gervais			
	Jacques			
	Gabriel			
	Augustin			
2	Gervais	(1)	Genev. Dorval	S.F.1731
	M. Dorothée		Frs. Asselin	" 1748
	Jean Baptiste			
3	Gabriel	(1)	Marie Gendron	S.F.1734
	M. Angélique		Chs. Chala	" 1763
	Gabriel			
	Jean Baptiste			
4	Jacques	(1)	Thérèse Meneux	S.F.1737
	M. Marguerite		Frs. Cloutier	" 1780
	Jacques			
	Joseph			
5	Augustin	(1)	Angé Giguère	S.F.1745
6	Jean-Baptiste	(2)	M. Anne Crépeau	S.P.1763
	Marie Anne		Jos. Giguère	S.F.1792
	Louis			
	Jean-Baptiste			
	Le même		M. Ls. Huot	S.F.1774
	Julienne		J. B. Martineau	" 1809
	Pierre			
7	Gabriel	(3)	M. Gertrude Pichet	S.P.1762
8	Jean-Baptiste	(3)	Mad. Rousseau	S.F.S.1773
9	Jacques	(4)	Genev. Turcot	S.F.1763
	Angélique		Jos. Poulin	" 1786
	Angélique		2°Jean Leclaire	" 1804
	Thérèse		Jacq. Prémont	S.F.1894
	Geneviève		Frs. Beaucher	" 1795
	Marie		André Asselin	" 1797
	Catherine		Jacq. Beaucher	" 1800
	M. Madeleine		Pierre L'heureux	" 1808
	M. Madeleine		2° Frs. Canac	" 1824
	Josette		Frs. Asselin	
	Ignace			
10	Joseph	(4)	M. Thècle Drouin	" 1775
	Marguerite		Amb. Deblois	" 1807

FOUCHER.

	Etienne			
	Pierre			
	François			
11	Jean Baptiste	(6)	M. Dorothée Godbout	S.F.1797
12	Louis	(6)	M. Jos. Asselin	" 1803
13	Pierre	(6)	Reine Provost	" 1801
	Archange		Frs. Lasalle	" 1824
	Jean			
14	Ignace	(9)	Louise Beaucher	" 1799
	Marie Marthe		J. B. Lamothe	" 1825
	Marie Louise		Magl. Savare	" 1827
	M. Geneviève		Jean Pichet	" 1831
	Thérèse		Frs. Guérard	" 1831
	M. Adelaïde		F. X. Giguère	" 1839
	M. Brigitte		F. X. Drouin	" 1842
	M. Brigitte		2°Jean Vaillancour	" 1858
	Henriette		Martin Asselin	" 1843
	Jacques			
15	Etienne	(10)	Thérèse Dufresne	S.L.1810
16	Pierre	(10)	Josette Beaucher	S.F.1823
17	François	(10)	Ursule Asselin	" 1824
18	Joseph		Genev- Fournier	
	Elisabeth		Jos. Emond	S.J.1835
19	Jean	(13)	Adé Dalaire	S.Frs.1842
20	Jacques	(14)	Josette Gosselin	S.J.1829
	Josette		Régis Gagnon	S.F.1848
	Philomène		Elie Bouffart	" 1860
	Séraphine		Paul Asselin	" 1863
	Joseph			
	François Xavier			
	Jacques			
21	Joseph	(10)	Adé Létourneau	S.F.1855
22	François Xa-vier	(10)	Anastasie Beaucher	S.F.1856
23	Jacques	(10)	Philomène Létourneau	S.F.1857

FOUGÈRE.

1	Simon		Anne Gensay	
	Pierre			
2	Pierre	(1)	M. Ls. Vérieul	S.F.1703
	Angélique		Pierre Deblois	S.Frs.1741
	Angélique		2° Jean Lefebvre	" 1751
	Geneviève		Dominique Dompierre	S.Frs.1742

FOURNIER.

1	Gilles		Noëlle Gagnon	Normandie
	Guillaume			
2	Guillaume	(1)	Fse. Hébert	Que. 1651
	Marie		Pierre Blanchet	" 1670
	Agathe		Ls. Gesseron	" 1671
	Jacquette		Jean Proulx	" 1673
	Françoise		Jacq. Boulet	S.Tho.1786
	Joseph			
	Jean			
	Simon			
	Pierre			
	Charles			
	Louis			
3	Hugues		Jeanne Huguet	Larochelle
	Nicolas			
4	Nicolas	(3)	Marie Hubert	Que. 1670
	Françoise		Pierre Lefebvre	S.F.1697
	Françoise		2° Ant. Blais	S.M.1716
	Françoise		3° Pierre Corriveau	S.V.1741
	Jean			
	Jacques			
	Michel			
5	Joseph	(2)	Barbe Girard	1685
	Anne		Jean Gagné	S.Tho.1729
	Françoise		Claude Guimont	

FOURNIER.

FOURNIER.

Françoise	2° Phil. Ign. Gravel		
		Cap S.Ign. 1738	
Joseph			
Jean			
François			
6 Jean	(2) Marie LeRoy	Que. 1687	
Cécile	Ls.Thibault		
		Cap S. Ign. 1716	
Anne	J. B. Durand	„ 1726	
Nicolas			
Jean			
Ambroise			
Augustin			
Charles			
7 Simon	(2) Cath. Rousseau S.P. 1791		
	Pierre Bouchard		
Marie		S.Tho. 1709	
Simon			
Joseph			
8 Louis	(2) Marie Caron		
		Cap S.Ign. 1796	
Louis			
9 Pierre	(2) Marie Isabel	S.Tho. 1795	
M. Charlotte	Nic Thivierge	S Tho. 1725	
Angélique	J. B. Gosselin	„ 1729	
Marie	Jos. Lepage	„ 1729	
10 Charles	(2) Eliz. Bouchard		
		Cap. S. Ign. 1799	
Elisabeth	Chs. Bélanger S.Tho. 1723		
Joseph			
Charles			
Basile			
11 Guillaume	Mad. Poirrier V. de Blais		
Pierre			
12 Michel	(4) Marie Bariaut	Que. 1702	
13 Jacques	(4) Marie Blanchon	B. 1708	
Geneviève	Jos. Couture	„ 1736	
Marie	Jacq. Turgeon	„ 1742	
Marie Anne	Jos. Turgeon	„ 1750	
Jean			
Jacques			
Etienne			
Antoine			
Alexandre			
Augustin			
14 Jean	(4) M. Mad. Fradet	„ 1711	
Geneviève	Jos. Monmeny S.M. 1739		
François			
15 Joseph	(5) Eliz. Gagné		
		Cap. S. Ign. 1710	
Elisabeth	Alexis Boulet S.Tho. 1740		
16 Jean	(5) M. Ls. Joncas	„ 1717	
Genev. Salomé	J. B. Hélie	S.P.S. 1750	
Pierre			
17 François	(5) Eliz. Bélanger S.Tho. 1727		
Geneviève	Frs. Gosselin	„ 1750	
Thomas			
18 Nicolas	(6) Barbe Thibault		
		Cap. S. Ign. 1714	
19 Charles	(6) Louise Gravel		
		Cap. S. Ign. 1708	
20 Jean	(6) M. Fse. Dumas		
		Cap. S. Ign. 1718	
21 Augustin	(6) Eliz. Gravel	„ 1727	
Le même	M. Fse. Bélanger		
		Cap. S. Ign. 1735	
22 Ambroise	Genev. Guillet Islet 1729		
Le même	Genev. Gamache		
		Cap. S. Ign. 1734	
Prisque			
23 Simon	(7) Marthe Bouchard		
Brigitte	Pierre Buteau S.P.S.1749		
24 Joseph	M. Angé Ruel	S.L. 1732	
25 Louis	(8) Angé Bossé		
		Cap. S. Ign. 1722	

Marie Marthe	Ign. Dersaint S. Tho. 1758		
Marie Thérèse	Germ. Dionne	„ 1766	
Benoni			
26 Jean	M. Fse. Talbot		
M. Ursule	Aug. Mathieu S.P.S. 1764		
Charlotte	Michel Blais S.P.C. 1769		
Simon			
27 François	Marie Talbot		
Pierre			
28 Joseph	Dorothé Plante		
Geneviève	J. B. Malboeuf S.P.S. 1754		
Rosalie	Pierre Blais	„ 1765	
Geneviève	Ant. Bouffart	„ 1765	
Marie Reine	Aug. Valière	„ 1772	
Rosalie	Jos. Valière	„ 1772	
Françoise	Pre. Paul Bussière		
		S.P.S. 1774	
29 Charles	(10) Angé Langlois S.Tho. 1725		
Geneviève	Jos. Fortin	„ 1751	
Pre. Basile			
Joseph			
30 Joseph	(10) Marg. Joanne S.Tho. 1734		
Elisabeth	Frs. Gosselin S.Chs. 1769		
31 Pierre Basile	(10) M. Mad. Langlois „ 1736		
Thérèse	Pierre Morin S.P.S. 1771		
M. Madeleine	Pre. Noel Gromelin		
		S.V. 1777	
Marguerite	Jos. Gaulin S.P.S. 1796		
Rosalie	Jos. Valière	„ 1798	
Pierre Basile			
Pierre Paul			
32 Joseph	Marie Joliet S.Tho.		
M. Elizabeth	Jos. Coulombe Bert. 1783		
Guillaume			
33 Augustin	(13) Marie Boutillet S.G. 1749		
Marie	Chs. Labrecque S.M. 1772		
Marguerite	J. B. Paquet S.M. 1783		
Angélique	Jean Turgeon B. 1780		
Marie Anne	Mathurin LabrecqueB.1799		
Marie Josette	Chs. Guay Lévis 1799		
Augustin			
Antoine			
34 Jacques	Cath. Turgeon Lévis.		
Louise	Amb. Nadeau S.Chs. 1785		
Françoise	J. B. Moreau „ 1789		
Jacques			
Charles			
35 Pierre	(11) Fse. Couture B. 1743		
36 Antoine	(13) M. Fse. Guay B. 1751		
M. Charlotte	J. B. Turgeon B. 1792		
Josette	Pierre Boutillet B. 1796		
Jean Baptiste			
Joseph			
Le même	M. Chs. Labrecque		
		S.Chs. 1770	
Françoise	Ls. Baudoin S.F.S. 1797		
François			
Joseph			
37 Jean	(13) Marie Gosselin B. 1742		
Angèle	Pierre Audet S.Chs. 1772		
Angèle	2° Pierre Adam „ 1799		
Marie	Pierre Clément „ 1769		
Jean François			
Joseph			
38 Jacques	(13) Eliz. Roy B. 1746		
39 Alexandre	(13) Marie Turgeon Levis 1761		
Marie	Michel Bois B. 1796		
Joseph			
Jacques			
Antoine			
Alexandre			
40 Etienne	(13) Josette Paquet S.M. 1766		
41 Jean Baptiste	Cath. Létourneau		
Jacques			
Jean Baptiste			
42 François	(14) Ursule Thibault S.M. 1749		

FOURNIER.

43	Pierre Basile (16)	M. Mad. Morin	S.Tho.	1743
	Françoise	J. B. Gaumont	,,	1781
	Victoire			
	Pierre			
	François			
	Joseph			
44	Thomas	(17) M. Mad. Morel	S.Tho.	1752
	M. Madeleine	Chs. Balan	,,	1778
	Marie Josette	J. B. Thibault	,,	1788
	Marie Roger	Jean Pruneau	,,	1789
	Charles			
	François			
	Pierre			
	Le même	M. Anne Pouliot	S.V.	1779
45	Joseph	M. Jos. Dumontier	S.Tho.	1751
	Le même	M. Ls. Robin	,,	1754
	Le même			
	Louis			
	Joseph			
	Thomas			
46	Charles	Joseph Lambert		
	Le même	Cath. St. Laurent	Levis	1787
	Le même	Marg. Tangué	S.G.	1818
47	Prisque	22 Thérèse Simoneau	Cap. S. Ign.	1764
	M. Thérèse	Jos. Marie Pinot	S.P.S.	1786
	Aug. Magl.			
48	Bénoni	(25) Louise Damour	S.Tho.	1761
	Marie Louise	Genev. Gagné	,,	1788
	Le même	M. Fse. Couture	B.	1771
49	Simon	(26) Eliz. Thibault	S.Tho.	1753
	M. Elizabeth	Hyacinthe Blanchet	S.P.S.	1785
	Marguerite	J. B. Picard	S.P.S.	1792
	Rosalie	Philippe Picard	,,	1793
	M. Geneviève	Jos. Girard	S.P.S.	1798
	Simon			
	Pierre	(27) M. Fse. Blais	S.P.S.	1764
51	Joseph	(29) Marie Rousseau	,,	1755
52	Pre. Basile	(29) Fse. Robin	S.Tho.	1754
	Brigitte	Isidore Morin	,,	1778
	M. Françoise	Jos. Dubé	S.P.S.	1783
	Pre. Basile			
53	Pierre Basile (31)	M. Ls. Simoneau	S. Tho.	1775
	Antoine			
54	Pierre Paul	(31) M. Ls. Talbot	S.P.S.	1791
	Le même	PélagieGautron	S.F.S.	1795
	Le même	Louise Turgeon	S.H.	1811
55	Guillaume	(32) Marie Rouillard	S.V.	1766
56	Augustin	(33) Marie Roy	B.	1786
	Cécile	Jos. Gravel	B.	1815
	Apolline	Joachim Paquet	B.	1818
	Agathe	Frs. Chabot	B.	1821
	Clothilde	Jean Dangueuger	B.	1829
	Michel			
	Augustin			
57	Antoine	(33) M. Chs. Roy	B.	1802
58	Jacques	(34) Marie Guenet	S. Chs.	1776
	Jacques			
	Jean Baptiste			
	Le même	Marie Labbé	S.G.	1785
	Charles			
59	Charles	(34) Cath. Gontier	S. Chs.	1783
	Catherine	Prisque Quemeneur	S. Chs.	1803
	Josette	Lazare Trahan	,,	1810
	Angèle	Pierre Dorval	,,	1824
	Louis			
	Jacques			
	Joseph			

FOURNIER.

60	JeanBaptiste(36)	Marg. Beaucher	B.	1785
	Angèle	Frs. Turgeon	B.	1818
	Françoise	Pierre Guay	B.	1831
	Marguerite	Michel Fournier	B.	1837
	Germain			
	Jean Baptiste			
61	Joseph	(36) Angé Turgeon	S.Chs.	1787
	Pierre			
	Joseph			
	Antoine			
62	Françoise	(36) Thécle Morin	S.Chs.	1809
63	Joseph(2ᵈ m.)(36)	Marie Louise	,,	1813
	Marguerite	Frs. Boutin	,,	1848
	Caroline	Jos. Nolin	,,	1848
	Louise Alice	Chs. Chabot	,,	1857
	Marie Rosalie	Luc. Chabot	,,	1857
	Vitaline	Ant. Bolduc	,,	1859
	Philomène	Honoré Baudoin	,,	1861
64	Joseph	(37) Hélène Goulet	,,	1768
	Geneviève	Frs. Bilodeau	S.G.	1793
	Cécile	Alexis Blanchet	,,	1793
	Hélène	Etn. Turgeon	,,	1797
	Rose	Frs. Rousseau	,,	1804
	Augustin			
65	JeanFrançois(37)	Thérèse Couture	S.M.	1769
	Jean			
	Joseph			
	Etienne			
	Louis			
	Charles			
	Le même	Genev. Leclaire	S.Chs.	1789
	Geneviève	Lazare Patry	,,	1810
	Le même	CharlotteGosselin	,,	1796
66	Joseph	M. Jos. Plante	S. Jean Port Joly	
	Olivier			
67	Alexandre	(39) Marg. Turgeon	B.	1794
	Honoré	Frs. Bellay	B.	1817
	Marguerite	Ign. Levesque	B.	1819
	Germain			
	Jean Baptiste			
	Léon			
68	Joseph	(39) M. Eliz. Roy	B.	1800
69	Antoine	Judith Nadeau	B.	1802
	Judith	Thomas Roy	S.G.	1826
	Antoine			
70	Jacques	(39) Genev. Roy	B.	1802
	Apolline	Ls. Godbout	S.L.	1851
	Amable			
	Guillaume			
	Le même	M. Hermine Chabot	B.	1840
71	JeanBaptiste(41)	M. Marthe Gagné	S.Tho.	1779
	Marie Thérèse	Abraham Blanchet	S.P.S.	1803
	M. Catherine	Jos. Marie Blais	S.P.S.	1806
	M. Victoire	Jos. Gosselin	S.P.S.	1820
	Jean Baptiste			
	Joseph			
72	Jacques	(41) M. Eliz. Boutin Bert.		1788
73	Pierre	(43) M. Mad. Fortin	S.Tho.	1766
	Le même	M. Jos. Proulx	,,	1769
	Marguerite	Pierre Fortier	,,	1792
	Marie Josette	Jos. Blanchet	,,	1800
	Marie Claire	André Toussaint Blais	S.Tho.	1814
	André			
	Pierre			
	Louis			
74	François	(43) M. Mad. Boulet	S.Tho.	1777
	Marguerite	Jos. Blais	S.P.S.	1799
75	Joseph	(43) Genev. Boulet	S.Tho.	1782
	Marie Louise	Michel Blais	,,	1806

FOURNIER.

	Paul		
	Etienne		
	Joseph		
76	François	(44)	Genev. Laberge S.Tho.1775
	M. Geneviève		J. B. Fortin " 1792
	Le même		M. Jos. Ainse S.P.S. 1781
77	Charles	(44)	Cécile Couture Bert. 1780
	Charles		
	Le même		Thérèse Lemieux Bert.1816
78	Pierre		M. Mad. Lefebvre
			S.Tho. 1792
	Pierre		
79	Joseph	(45)	Thérèse Nicole S.Tho.1784
	Thomas		
80	Louis	(45)	Genev. Proulx S.Tho. 1797
	Thomas		
81	Thomas	(45)	M. Hélène Proulx
			S.Tho. 1804
	Thomas		
82	Joseph		Marie Proulx
	Joseph		
83	Frs. Felix		M. Anne Bélanger
	Augustin		
84	Charles		M. Jos. Aubert
	Geneviève		Jos. Faucher S.F.S. 1800
85	Antoine		Marie Guénet
	Jacques		
86	Auguste	(47)	M. Susanne Guay S.H.1799
	Magloire		
87	Simon	(49)	M. Ls. Blais S.P.S. 1782
88	Pre. Basile	(52)	M. Marg. Morin S.P.S.1792
89	Antoine	(53)	Apolline Gautron S.M.1816
90	Augustin	(56)	Louise Turgeon B. 1814
	Anastasie		Jos. Raimond Patry B.1835
	Hermine		Maxime Paquet B. 1845
	Samuel		
91	Michel	(56)	M. Vic. Turgeon B. 1831
	Le même		Marg. Fournier B. 1837
	Le même		Genev. Turgeon B. 1846
92	Jacques	(58)	Angé Couture S.H. 1803
93	JeanBaptiste	(58)	Josette Couture Levis 1810
	Émélie		Geo. Quemeneur S.P. 1845
	Sophie		Pierre Gobeil S.J. 1848
	Barthélemi		
94	Charles	(56)	Cath. Desruisseaux
			S.P. 1821
95	Louis	(59)	Marg. Gosselin S.Chs. 1815
	Hermine		Marc Pepin S.Chs. 1839
	M. Desneiges		Chs. Marcoux S.Chs. 1843
	M. Célina		Théodore Bedard S.Chs1854
	M. Apolline		J. B. Jos. Eugène
			Gosselin S.Chs. 1856
	Ls. Frédéric		
	Firmin		
96	Joseph	(59)	Marg. Blouin S.G. 1817
	Le même		M. Anne Morisset S.G.1828
97	Jacques	(59)	Marie Roy S.Chs. 1820
	Rosalie		Prosper Naud S.Chs. 1842
	Marie Louise		Benoni Naud S.Chs. 1847
	Hermine		Damase Blanchet
			S.Chs. 1851
	Constance		Frs. Plante S.Chs. 1853
	Odile		Fabien Chrétien S.Chs. 1858
98	JeanBaptiste	(60)	Marie Chabot S.Chs. 1816
	Marie Louise		Raimond Naud B. 1844
	M. Marcelline		Féréol Ed. Turgeon B.1848
	M. Thassile		Ls. Filteau B. 1856
	Florent		
	Jean Baptiste		
	Louis		
99	Germain	(60)	M. Marg. Turgeon B.1828
	Rose		David Ouimet B. 1850
	Edouard		
100	Joseph	(61)	Charlotte Chabot
			S.Chs. 1811
	M. Charlotte		Jos. Naud S.Chs. 1836

FOURNIER.

	M. Célanire		Misael Bélanger S.Chs.1846
	Joseph		
	Le même		Louise Paré S.Tho. 1826
101	Antoine	(61)	Marg. Paré S.Tho. 1815
	Angèle		Ls. Boutin S.Chs. 1836
	Marguerite		Marg. Prevost S.Chs. 1836
	Bisane		Jos. Proulx S.Chs. 1846
	M. Christine		Herménégilde Plante
			S.Chs. 1863
	Philomène		Damase Voisin S.Chs.1864
	Jos. Prudent		
	Antoine		
102	Pierre	(61)	M. Anne Morisset
	Marie		Marcel Hébert S.Chs. 1847
	Caroline		Aug. Boutin S.Chs. 1851
	Philomène		Telesphore Morisset
			S.Chs. 1864
	Joseph		
103	Augustin	(64)	Agathe Goupy S.M. 1797
	Augustin		
	Joseph		
	Ignace		
104	Jean	(65)	Claire Dumas S.Chs. 1795
	Charlotte		Ben. Bernier S.G. 1824
	Restitut		Ignace Ruel S.G. 1828
	Jean		
105	Joseph	(65)	Angé Lebrun S.Chs. 1801
	Sophie		Germ. Ruel S.G. 1825
	Geneviève		Bénoni Dion S.G. 1828
	Angélique		Ls. Patouel S.G. 1829
106	Louis	(65)	M. Marg. Dion S.M. 1803
	Marguerite		Etn. Campagna S.G. 1826
	Louis		
107	Étienne	(65)	Marie Patry S.Chs. 1808
108	Charles	(65)	Véronique Terrien
			S.Chs. 1814
	Joseph		
109	Olivier	(66)	Angèle Caron
	Le même		M. Fse. Morin S.P.S.1822
110	JeanBaptiste	(67)	Marg. Roy S.M. 1803
	Jacques		
	Jean Baptiste		
	Antoine		
111	Germain	(67)	Marg. Shink B. 1821
112	Léon	(67)	Adé Turgeon B. 1831
113	Antoine	(69)	Marg. Audet S.G 1830
114	Guillaume	(70)	M. Ls. Labrecque
			S.L. 1840
115	Amable	(70)	M. Ls. Laliberté S.L. 1854
116	Joseph	(71)	Eléonore Baudoin
			S.F.S. 1826
117	Jean Bap-	(71)	M. Jos. Gosselin S.M. 1828
	tiste		
118	Joseph		Louise Rafou?
	Le même		Agathe Gosselin S.P. 1803
119	Joseph		Angé Carrier
	Joseph		
120	Jacques		Marg. Langevin S.Tho.
	Jacques		
121	Alexandre		Marg. Fournier
	Charles		
122	André		Agathe Pilote
	Louis		
123	Abraham		M. Marthe Picard
			S. Claire
	Philippe		
124	Antoine		Sophie Hoffman Que.
	Honoré		
			Thérèse Labrecque
125	Pierre	(73)	S.Chs. 1801
			M. Rose Dessaint
126	Louise	(73)	S.P.S. 1816
127	André	(73)	M. Jos. Dion S.G. 1822
128	Paul	(75)	Jeanne Blais S.P.S. 1811
129	Etienne	(75)	Marg. Boulet S.Tho. 1817
	Joseph		

FOURNIER

130 Joseph	(75) M. Marg. Morin	S.P.S. 1821
131 Charles	(77) Véronique Quirouet	Bert. 1807
Emélie	Ant. Talbot	Bert. 1828
132 Pierre	(78) Génév. Morin	S.P.S. 1820
133 Thomas	(79) M. Chs. Flavie Blais	S.P.S. 1834
134 Thomas	(80) Bibiane Blais	S.P.S. 1823
135 Thomas	(81) Eliz. Asselin	S.P.S. 1840
136 Joseph	(82) M. Anne Picard	S.P.S. 1802
137 Augustin	(83) M. Fse. Fournier	Cap. S. Ign. 1802
Jean Baptiste		
138 Jacques	(85) Judith Tangué	S.Chs. 1807
139 Samuel	(90) Zephérine Patry	B. 1845
140 Barthélemi	(93) Sophie Gourdeau	L.P. 1851
141 Ls. Fréderic	(95) Judithe Tangué	S.Chs. 1840
142 Firmin	(95) M. Anne Gagnon	S.Chs. 1848
143 Florent	(98) Vict. Couture	B. 1847
144 Jean Baptiste	(98) Marie Turgeon	S.Chs. 1848
145 Louis	(98) Constance Lacasse	B. 1852
146 Edouard	(99) M. Eliz. Vien	B. 1859
147 Joseph	(100) Delphine Naud	S.Chs. 1841
148 Antoine	(101) Constance Rippon	S.Chs. 1844
149 Jos. Prudent	(101) Tharsile Couillard	B. 1866
150 Joseph	(102) Eulalie Tangué	S.Chs. 1860
151 Joseph	(103) Adé Gontier	S.G. 1821
Jacques		
152 Ignace	(103) Vict. Bernier	S.Chs. 1826
153 Augustin	(103) M. Euphrosine Goupy	S.M. 1830
Le même	M. Anne Morisset	S.M. 1865
154 Jean	(104) Marg. Denis	S.G. 1823
Le même	Josette Dalaire	S.Chs. 1827
155 Louis	(106) Marg. Audet	S.Chs. 1838
Thomas		
156 Joseph	(108) Angèle Rémillard	S. Chs. 1842
157 Jean Baptiste	(110) Brigitte Pelchat	S.G. 1827
Jean		
158 Jacques	(110) Zoé Denis	S.Chs. 1839
159 Antoine	(110) Julie Couture	S.Chs. 1851
160 Joseph	(119) Flavie Lainé	S.G. 1830
161 Jacques	(120) Séraphine Bouchard	S.V. 1821
162 Charles	(121) Joséphine Turgeon	B. 1836
163 Louis	(122) Genev. Martineau	S.F. 1845
164 Philippe	(123) Caroline Chabot	S.Chs. 1855
165 Honoré	(124) Aurélie Roy	S.V. 1865
166 Joseph	(129) Félicité Leblanc	S.Chs. 1848
167 Jean Baptiste	(137) Genev. Gagnon	S.V. 1836
Jacques	(151) Marie Bilodeau	S Chs. 1848
Thomas	(155) Rosalie Quéret	S.Chs. 1863
Jean	(159) Luce Robitaille	S.Frs. 1853

FRADET

1 Thomas	Anne Roussé Bordeaux	
Jean		
2 Jean	(1) Jeanne Hélie	S.P.1692
Geneviève	André Aubé	S.V.1713
Agathe	Jos. Roy	" 1729
Marie Josette	Jean Métivier	" 1738

FRADET

M. Madeleine	Jean Fournier	B.1711
Augustin		
Le même	Mad. Gosselin	Qué. 1715
M. Isabelle	Aug. Roy	S.V.1735
Marie Reine	Etn. Roy	" 1742
Cécile	Jacq. Roy	" 1746
Marie Louise	Chs. Denis	" 1749
François		
Jacques		
3 Augustin	(2) Genev. Leclaire	S.L.1730
Marie Louise	Ls. Dalaire	S.M.1760
Marie Louise	2°Michel Brisson	" 1778
Marie Anne	Jos. Chamberlan	" 1765
M. Geneviève	Ant. Fortier	S.V.1762
Augustin		
Joseph		
Jean		
Jacques		
Le même	M. Ls. Lemieux	Bert.1754
Guillaume		
4 Jacques	(2) Eliz. Leclaire	S.L.1725
Marguerite	J. B. Guilmet	S.V.1751
Marie Anne	Aug. Roy	" 1753
Marie Louise	J. B. Guilmet	" 1753
Geneviève	J. B. Guilmet	" 1757
Jacques		
Le même	Thérèse Ayot	" 1736
Marie Marthe	Jacq. Bernard	" 1767
Marie Thérèse	Pierre Emond	" 1764
Marie	Robert Boulet	" 1784
Athanase		
Jean Marie		
Jean François		
Nicolas		
5 François	(2) M.Marg.Couture	S.M.1754
Marie Louise	Michel Leclaire	S.M.1778
Marie Louise	Michel Morisset	S.M.1785
Marie Anne	Jean Jos.Lacroix	S.M.1788
Geneviève	Ign. Clément	S.M.1790
Joseph		
François		
Le même	Fse. Jahan	S.M.1793
6 Augustin	Isabelle Tangué	S.V.1752
Marie Josette	J. B. Jolin	S.F.S.1790
Etienne		
Augustin		
Jacques		
Clément		
François		
Joseph		
Le même	Agathe Langlois	S.F.S.1786
7 Jean Baptiste	(3) M. Jos. Boulet	S.F.S.1759
Marie	Jos. Gontier	S.G.1797
Marie Anne	Jos. Lemieux	" 1813
André		
Joseph		
Pierre		
Antoine		
Jean Baptiste		
8 Joseph	(3) M. Jos. Boulet	S.F.S.1764
Pélagie	Etn. Roy	S.M.1786
9 Jacques	(3) M. Rose Cirier	S.Chs.1767
M. Madeleine	Gab. Bilodeau	B.1797
François		
Jacques		
Guillaume		
10 Guillaume	(3) M. Ls. Gautron	S.M.1781
Apolline	Ant. Brochu	" 1810
Marie Louise	J. B. Roy	" 1812
M. Catherine	Aug. Marseau	" 1812
Marie Anne	Jos. Gagnon	" 1824
Laurent		
Paul		
11 Jacques	(4) M. Thérèse Jolin	S.F.S.1762

FRADET

12 Athanase	(4)	M. Genev. Dalaire	S.V.1765
Le même		Marie Gontier	S.Chs.1871
13 Jean Marie	(4)	Marie Cyr	S.V.1770
Marie Louise		Théodore Langlois „	1791
M. Madeleine		Ls. Marie Bouffart „	1801
Marie Julie		Michel Paquet „	1812
M. Charlotte		Julien Mercier „	1818
Le même		M. Mad. Boissonneau	S.F.S.1799
14 Nicolas	(4)	Marg. Balan Bert.	1771
Marguerite		Jos Larrivé	S.V.1790
15 Jean François	(4)	M. Judithe Bacquet	S.V.1776
Marie		Jacq. Roby	S.M.1799
16 François	(5)	M. Jos. Lacroix „	1779
17 Joseph	(5)	M. Jos. Pruneau „	1789
Marie		Frs. Dupont „	1809
M. Geneviève		Frs. Bacquet „	1817
Jacques			
18 Augustin		M. Ls. Langlois	S.F.S.1779
M. Madeleine		Ignace Doiron „	1801
M. Madeleine		2ᵉ Ant. Gagnon „	1803
Marguerite		Basile Gagnon „	1805
Marie Reine		Ant. Boivin	S.V 1819
Marie		Jacq. Langlois „	1838
Augustin			
19 Clément	(6)	M. Genev. Dubreuil	S.F.S.1785
Françoise		Pierre Morin	S.G.1810
Françoise		2ᵉBasile Doiron „	1814
Marie		Jos. Brochu „	1811
Louise		Michel Gontier „	1817
Marguerite		J. B. Caron	S.P.S.1816
Pierre			
Antoine			
Clément			
20 Jacques	(6)	Thérèse Dubreuil	S.F.S.1790
Marguerite		Aug. Nadeau	S.G.1830
21 Joseph	(6)	M. Anne Marseau	S.F.S. 1790
Le même		M. Vict. Chouinard	S.F.S. 1795
Le même		M. Thècle Greffart	S.F.S. 1800
22 François	(6)	M. Anne Fortier	S.F.S.1793
Luce		Pierre Bolduc	S.G. 1828
Marie		Michel Gautron „	1828
Marguerite		Pre. Romain Trahan	S. Chs. 1843
François			
23 Etienne	(6)	Genev. Rousseau	S.F.S.1799
24 Antoine	(7)	M.Marg. Hélie	S.M. 1795
Marguerite		Frs. Blanchet „	1829
Antoine			
Joseph			
Michel			
Le même		Monique Guay	Lévis 1813
25 Jean Baptiste	(7)	Cath. Corriveau	S.M. 1800
26 Joseph	(7)	M. Anne Mercier „	1786
Archange		Jos. Gautron „	1822
Marie		Jos. Labreque	B. 1816
Marie Anne		Jos. Coté	S.G. 1812
Joseph			
Le même		M. Genev. Roy	S.G. 1801
Jean			
François			
Pierre			
Ambroise			
27 André	(7)	Marie Labbé	S.G. 1795
Jean Baptiste			

François			
André			
28 Pierre	(7)	Thérèse Daniau	S.Chs. 1815
29 François	(9)	Marie Bacquet	S.M. 1795
30 Jacques	(9)	Frs. Labbé	S.G. 1803
31 Guillaume	(9)	Eliz. Lecours „	1809
Théotiste		Ls. Fauchon „	1828
32 Laurent	(10)	M. Eliz. Jolin	S.V. 1812
Reine		Simon Bacquet „	1842
Angéle		Thomas Dalaire	S.F.S 1843
Olive		Michel Bolduc	S.M. 1849
Jacques			
Paul	(10)	M. Anne Denis	S.M. 1824
M. Clarisse		Pierre Cochon „	1847
M. Elizabeth		Ls. Coüet „	1852
Paul			
34 Jean		M. Mad. Fradet	
Marguerite		Jean Roy	S.V. 1770
35 Joseph		Ursule Lemieux	
Joseph			
36 Joseph	(35)	Marie Quéret	S.G. 1814
37 Jacques	(17)	Archange Boissonneau	S.M. 1818
38 Augustin		M. Celeste Mercier	S.V. 1809
39 Clément	(19)	Cath. Morin	S.H. 1813
Catherine		Jos Roy	S.G. 1830
Le même		Marie Roy	S.H. 1817
40 Pierre	(19)	Basilise Bélanger	S.G. 1821
Le même		Angé Pouliot „	1830
41 Antoine	(19)	M. Genev. Bernard	S.V. 1824
42 François	(22)	Eliz. Patouel	S.G. 1821
Le même		Luce Marg. Boudouin	S.F.S. 1829
43 Antoine	(24)	M. Marthe Aubé	S.M. 1817
Angéle		Laurent Guilmet „	1851
44 Michel	(24)	Josette Paquet	S.J. 1832
Hombéline		Frs. Gosselin „	1852
Le même		Archange Terrien „	1841
Le même		Louise Dupuis „	1858
45 Joseph	(24)	Ursule Blouin „	1845
Le même		Marie Sucrard	S.F. 1853
46 Joseph	(26)	Marg. Lemieux	S.G. 1813
Marcelline		Ant. Thibaut	S.V. 1844
Marie Osite		Jos. Louineau „	1841
Jean Baptiste			
47 Jean		Josette Roy	S.G. 1822
48 Pierre	(26)	M. Anne Bilodeau	S.G. 1825
49 Ambroise	(26)	Angé Gontier „	1829
50 François	(26)	Adé Briart „	1830
51 JeanBaptiste	(27)	Ursule Leclaire	S. Chs. 1819
52 André	(27)	Angé Gautron	S.G. 1818
53 François	(27)	Genev. Dubé „	1818
Marie		Etn. Duchesneau	B. 1845
Isidore			
François			
Le même		Marg. Morisset	S.M. 1825
54 Jacques	(32)	Emelie Bolduc „	1843
55 Paul	(33)	Marie Roussel „	1846
A Joseph	(35)	Marie Quéret	S.G. 1814
56 Jacq. Nic.	(37)	M. Ls. Honorine Asselin	S.M. 1861
57 JeanBaptiste	(46)	M. Eudoce Thibaut	S.V. 1848
58 Isidore	(53)	Emélie Vict. Audet	S.M. 1846
59 François	(53)	Soulange Quemeneur	S.V. 1847

FRASER.

1 Thomas		Eliz. Fraser	Ecosse
Augustin			

FRASER.

2 Augustin	(1) Fse. Adam	B.	1763
Geneviève	Simon Talbot	B.	1791
Angélique	Jos. Beaucher	B.	1799
François	Jos. Mercier	S.F.S.	1792
Thomas			
Joseph			
3 ,,	(2) M.Cath.Talbot	S.P.S.	1792
Catherine	Jos. Prudent Paré		
		S.F.S.	1821
Marie Anne	Louis Ruel	,,	1828
M. Henriette	Jacq. Isidore Morin		
		S.F.S.	1834
Jean Olivier			
Urbain Narcisse			
4 Thomas	(2) Marie Lagueux	Lévis	1802
Caroline	Maurice Soucy	B.	1829
Marie Lorette	F. X. Mercier	B.	1830
Marine	Bath. Pouliot	B.	1835
Anastasie Luce	Jos.Achile Chinique	B.	1838
Sophie	Marcel Bilodeau	B.	1838
Louise Flore	Jean Léon Audet	B.	1843
Thomas			
Joseph			
Alexandre			
Ferdinand			
5 Urbain Narc.	(3) Claire Gosselin	S.V.	1831
6 Jean Olivier	(3) Angèle Eléonore Paré		
		S.P.S.	1839
7 Thomas	(4) M.RosaliePoiré	Lévis	1837
Le même			
8 Alexandre	(4) M. Eliz. Gosselin	S.V.	1833
M. Anne Flore	Edmond Tétu	,,	1865
Jos. Napoléon			
Le même	Anna Gosselin	,,	1868
9 Joseph	(4) Johanna Ryan	B.	1848
10 Ferdinand	(4) CarolineSt.Germain	B.	1849

FREGEOT.

1 Daniel	Anne Posé	S.Tho.	1699
Marie	Michel Morin	Bert.	1727
Geneviève	Michel Arbour	,,	1728
Marie Josette	Frs.Quemeneur	S.F.S.	1745
Félicité	Frs. Belloy	,,	1749
Pierre Noël			
Jacques			
2 Jacques	(1) Marie Carrier	,,	1739
Le même	M. Jeanne Fontaine		
		S.F.S.	1771
3 Pierre Noël	(1) M. Ls. Quemeneur		
		S.F.S.	1744
M. Madeleine	Alexis Blanchet	,,	1765
Françoise	Frs. Baudouin	,,	1775
Marie Reine	J. B. Normand	,,	1786
Marguerite	Chs. Frs. Labbé	,,	1789
Jean Baptiste			
4 JeanBapttiste	(3) M. Jos. Lamie	,,	1779

FRONTIGNY.

1 Pierre	Mad. Lajoue	Que.	1715
Madelaine	J. B. Chabot	S.L.	1746
,,	2 Ant.Bissonet	S.M.	1761

FUROIS.

1 Jean	Jacqueline Ev. d'A.		
Jacques			
2 Jacques	(1) M.Mad. Plante	S.M.	1753
M. Françoise	Jacques Patry	,,	1773
M. Catherine	Jos. Bissonnet	,,	1787
Marie Rose	Pierre Daniau	,,	1791
Marie Thérèse	Jos. Queret	,,	1792
Marie Josette	Aug. Jolin	,,	1793
Charles			

FUROIS.

Jacques			
Joseph			
3 Charles	(2) M. Anne Quéret		
		S.M.	1789
Victoire	Chs. Denis	,,	1815
4 Jacques	(2) Susanne Guay	Lévis	1794
Cécile	Pierre Martineau	S.M.	1824
Joseph			
5 ,,	(4) M. Julie Faucher	,,	1823
Cécile Flore	John Mie	,,	1856
Aug. Annibal			
Stanislas			
Léger			
6 Aug. Annibal	(5) Julie Cath. Eliz. Pepin		
		S.M.	1857
7 Joseph	(2) Marie Hallé	S.H.	1810
Stanislas	(5) Mathilde Morin	,,	

GABOURY.

1 Louis	Nicole Soulard		
Anne	Frs. Rémillard	Islet	1681
,,	2° Pierre Corriveau		
		S.M.	1702
Françoise	Jacq. Corriveau	,,	1693
Marie	Ant. Goupy	,,	1698
,,	2° Pierre Naud	,,	1700
Louise Fse.	Etn. Corriveau	,,	1700
Jeanne	Isaac Laurent Savant		
		Lévis	1692
Joseph			
2 Antoine	Jeanne Mignot		
Marguerite	Pierre Valière	S.Aug.	1698
M. Charlotte	Jos. Cotin	,,	1709
Thérèse Angé	Chs. Cotin	,,	1791
Antoine			
3 Joseph	(1) M. Susanne Happé		
	Repentigny		1707
Marie Anne	J. B. Gosselin	S.V.	1734
M. Geneviève	Jos. Martin	,,	1743
Le même	Genev. Boulet	,,	1740
4 Antoine	(2) Fse. Cotin	S.Aug.	1713
5 Joseph	Mad. Fortier		
Joseph			
6 Jean Baptiste	Eliz. Couture		
Jacques			
7 Joseph	(5) M. Basilisse Corriveau		
		S.V.	1761
8 Jacques	(6) Marg. Rouleau	S.L.	1775

GAGNE.

1 Pierre	Marg. Rosée		
Louis			
2 Louis	Marie Michel		1641
Pierre			
Ignace			
Louis			
Olivier			
Joachim			
3 Louis	(1) Louise Picard	S. Anne	1673
Marie Anne	Guill. Blanchet	S.M.	1705
Geneviève	Jean Blanchet	Bert.	1712
Alexis			
Louis			
4 Pierre	(2) Louise Faure-Planchet		
Marie Anne	Denis Proulx		
		Cap S. Ign.	1699
Elizabeth	Jos. Fournier		
		Cap S. Ign.	1710
Pierre			
Jean François			
5 Louis	(2) Marie Gagnon	C.R.	1678
Pierre			

GAGNÉ.

Denis		
6 Olivier	(2)	Isabelle Pepin S.F. 1679
Elisabeth		Jean Bonneau S. Frs. 1708
Geneviève		Aug. Bonneau, Que. 1713
Marie		Paschal Poulin
M. Madeleine		Jos. Malboeuf C.R. 1721
Dominique		
Jean Baptiste		
Joseph		
7 Ignace	(2)	Barbe Dodier S. Anne 1680
Le même		Louise Tremblay A.G.1689
Raphael		
8 Joachim	(2)	Louise Marcoux Beauport 1682
9 Alexis	(3)	Cath. Cloutier Islet 1702
Jean		
10 Louis	(3)	M. Thérèse Lessart Islet 1714
11 Jean	(4)	Mad. Langlois Cap S. Ign. 1679
Jean		
12 Pierre	(4)	Louise Proulx S. Tho. 1700
13 François	(4)	Eliz. Langlois Islet 1709
Joseph		
Antoine		
François		
14 Pierre	(5)	Marg. Poulin S. Anne 1705
Jos. Marie		
15 Denis		Angé Dion S. Frs. 1715
Marthe		Julien Landry S. Frs. 1748
Pierre		
Jean		
Denis		
16 Dominique	(6)	Mad. Buteau S. Frs. 1706
Madeleine		Ant. Marseau S. Frs. 1731
Pierre		
17 Jean Baptiste	(6)	Claire Buteau S. Frs. 1706
Marthe		Marc Dupont S. Frs. 1731
Catherine		J. B. Deblois S. Frs. 1737
Elisabeth		Jean Bilodeau S. Frs. 1742
Jacques		
Jean Baptiste		
18 Raphael	(7)	M. Jos. Dalaire S. Frs. 1729
Thérèse		Jacq. Guérard S. Frs. 1761
Marie Josette		Aug. Marseau S. Frs. 1768
Pierre		
Louis		
Joseph		
19 Pierre		Marie Dufour
Le même		Angé Dubeau S. Frs. 1725
Marie Anne		Jacq. Paquet B. 1751
20 Pierre		Genev. Fournier
Geneviève		Jean Bélanger S.V. 1746
Toussaint		
Pierre		
Alexis		
Barthiaume		
21 Jean	(9)	M. Fse. Barthelot S.P.S. 1749
22 Jean Baptiste	(11)	Anne Fournier S. Tho. 1729
Anne		Jacq. Gendreau S.F.S.1751
Jean Baptiste		
23 François	(13)	Marie Métivier S. Tho. 1757
M. Madeleine		Jacq. Aubin S.P.S. 1782
24 Antoine	(13)	M. M. Marotte S.Tho.1751
Marie Thérèse		Ls. Langlois S.P.S. 1775
M. Madeleine		Jos. Isabel S.P.S. 1778
25 Joseph	(13)	M. Ls. Blais S.P.S. 1759
François		
Joseph		
26 Pierre		Marg. Boeuf
Marie Josette		Jean Moïse Morin S.M. 1750

GAGNÉ.

François		
27 Pierre		Angé Bouchard
Angélique		Jacq. Couture S.P.S. 1751
28 Ambroise		M. Genev. Picard
Bénoni		
Alexis		
A Joseph Marie	(14)	M. Jos. Perrot S.F. 1741
29 Denis	(15)	M. Ls Emond S.Frs. 1746
Le même		Marthe Vérieul S.Frs. 1749
Marthe		Pierre Lepage S. Frs. 1771
30 Jean	(15)	M. Ls. Guérard S. Frs. 1749
Marie Louise		J.B. Martineau S.Frs.1781
Joseph		
Le même		Dorothée Langlois S. Frs. 1762
François		
31 Pierre	(15)	Dorothée Emond S. Frs. 1756
M. Madeleine		Pierre Pepin S.F. 1792
Joseph Marie		
Le même		M. Jos. Plante S.Frs.1773
Marie		Basile Lasalle S.F. 1797
François		
32 Pierre	(16)	Marthe Lepage S.Frs.1840
33 Pierre		Mad. Plante
Le même		M. Mad. Plante S. J. 1770
34 Etienne		Mad. Gravel
Etienne		
35 Noël		M. Marthe Marotte
Elisabeth		Eustache Cloutier S. P. S. 1773
36 Jean Baptiste	(17)	Marg. Brochu Bert. 1734
Joseph		
Jean Baptiste		
37 Jacques	(17)	M. Anne Gagnon S. Joa. 1743
Marie Anne		Chs- Martineau S.Frs.1773
Marie Louise		Pierre Martineau S.Frs. 1775
Marie		Claude Dion S. Frs. 1782
Madeleine		Jacq. Dion S. F. 1786
Josette		Jos. Drouin S. F. 1798
Jean		
Jacques		
38 Louis	(18)	Isabelle Guérard S. Frs. 1754
Isabelle		Yves Picard S. J. 1795
Marie Victoire		Michel Picard S.Frs.1800
Jacques		
Louis		
39 Joseph	(18)	M. Ls. Guérard S Frs.1773
Marie		Pre. Noel Meiner S.G. 1799
Louise		Ls. Blanchet S. G. 1800
Joseph		
Le même		M. Jos. Martineau S. Frs. 1785
Catherine		J. B. Hélie S G. 1805
Pierre		
Le même		Charlotte Terrien S. Chs. 1814
40 Pierre	(18)	M. Anne Landry S. Chs. 1773
Marie Louise		Alexis Gourdel S. H. 1791
41 Pierre	(20)	Génév. Létourneau S. L. 1738
Marie		Pierre Fortier S.P.S. 1775
Marie Bonne		Frs. Blais S. P. 1777
Marie Anne		Frs. Fortier S. P. S. 1779
Michel		
Jean Baptiste		
Ambroise		
Alexis		

GAGNÉ

42 Alexis	(20)	M. Cath. Boucher	Bert. 1743
Alexis			
Ignace			
Antoine			
42A Barthélémi	(20)	M. Marthe Malboeuf	S. P. S. 1750
Barthélemi			
43 Jos. Toussaint	(20)	M. Ls. Blais	Bert. 1757
Marie Louise		J. B. Morin	S. P. S. 1788
M. Judith		Ls. Talon	S. P. S. 1782
M. Judith		2° J.B. Harnais	S.P.S.1820
M. Geneviève		Aug. Morin	S. P. S. 1794
Marie Rose		Ls. Barth. Levasseur	S. P. S. 1804
44 Jean Baptiste	(22)	M. Jos. Daniau	S.F.S.1751
45 Jean Marie		M. Chs. Picard	S. Tho.
Thérèse Marie		Nic. Bernatchez	S. P. S. 1775
M. Angélique		Chs. Gourdel	S. H. 1789
Jean Marie			
Jean			
Augustin			
46 Pierre		M. Mad. Picard	S. P. S. 1764
M. Madeleine		Michel Morisset	S.H. 1786
Marie Rosalie		Germ. Baudoin	S.H. 1790
Marie Josette		Ls. Gosselin	S. H. 1791
Joseph			
Pierre			
Louis			
François			
Michel			
Le même		Génév. Gosselin	S.H.1814
47 Augustin		M. Ls Lavergne	
Marie Marthe		J.B. Fournier	S.Tho. 1779
Augustin			
48 Joseph		Marie Landry	
		S. Marie	
Louis			
Jacques			
Bernard			
Antoine			
Germain			
49 Joseph	(25)	M. Eliz. Joncas	S. Tho. 1784
Marie Louise		Jos. Coté	S.P.S. 1801
50 François	(25)	M. Jos. Bernier	S. Tho. 1804
Julie		Chs. Chamberlan	S.P.S. 1830
Eléonore		Pierre Létourneau	S. P. S. 1839
Louis George			
Charles			
Joseph			
51 François	(26)	Marie Dodier	S.M. 1750
52 Bénoni	(28)	M. Ursule Fournier	S. Tho. 1764
Reine		Abraham Gagnon	Bert. 1812
François			
Le même		M. Anne Picard	Bert.1792
Le même		Genev. Ferlant	S.H.1816
53 Alexis	(28)	M. Claire Marotte	S.P.S. 1771
54 Joseph	(30)	Thècle Asselin	S.Frs. 1782
55 François	(30)	Reine Rousseau	S.H. 1794
56 Jos. Marie	(31)	Eliz. Asselin	S. Frs. 1783
57 François	(31)	M. Pélagie Dorval	S. F.1802
58 Etienne	(34)	Judith Fortin	Cap.S.Ign. 1774
François			

GAGNÉ

59 Joseph	(36)	Marie Langlois	S.F.S. 1763
M. Geneviève		J. B. Dorion	S.F.S. 1787
Marie		Jacq. Marceau	S.F.S. 1792
M. Elisabeth		Amb. Théberge	S.F.S. 1794
Jacques			
Le même		Scolastique Marie	S.F.S. 1795
60 Jean Bapt.	(36)	M. Génev. Loineau	S.F.S. 1766
M. Geneviève		J. B. Guay	S.P.S. 1804
Marie Thérèse		Felix Fleury	S.V. 1812
Pierre			
Jean Baptiste			
61 Jean	(37)	Cath. Lescabiet	S.Frs. 1775
62 Jacques	(37)	Marg. Asselin	S.Frs.1775
63 Louis	(38)	M.Genev.Guion	S.J. 1792
Marie		J. B. Bonneau	S.F. 1815
Josette		Isaac Fortin	S.F. 1822
M. Madeleine		J. B. Duchette	S.Frs.1829
Ls. Raphaël			
X. François			
Le même		Louise Dompierre	S.Frs. 1833
64 Jacques	(38)	Marie Baudon	S.F. 1810
65 Joseph	(39)	Marg. Dupont	S.F. 1804
66 Pierre	(39)	Thérèse Royer	S.G. 1813
67 Ambroise	(41)	Marg. Blais	Bert. 1765
Marguerite		Jos. Morisset	S.H. 1786
Ambroise			
Jean Baptiste			
Le même		Josette Malboeuf	S.H.1773
Josette		J. B. Langlois	S.H. 1802
Marie		Jacq. Dutile	S.H. 1806
Marie Anne		J. B. Nadeau	S.H. 1807
M. Archange		Chs. Lemieux	S.H. 1813
Rosalie		Frs. Blouin	S.H. 1815
Pierre			
François			
Jean Baptiste			
68 Michel	(41)	M. Ange Blais	Bert. 1771
Michel			
69 Jean Bapt.	(41)	M. Anne Pellerin	S.P.S. 1774
Marie Anne		J. B. Langlois	S.P.S. 1798
M. Geneviève		Jos. Blais	S.P.S. 1803
M. Madeleine		Chs. Bruneau	S.P.S. 1807
Marie Josette		J. B. Harnais	S.P.S. 1820
Pierre			
Jean Baptiste			
70 Alexis	(41)	Mad. Bilodeau	S.Chs. 1782
Charles			
71 Alexis	(42)	M. Anne Létourneau	S.P.S. 1774
72 Ignace	(42)	Josette Picard	S.P.S. 1780
Jean Baptiste			
73 Antoine	(42)	M. Jos. Daniau	S.P.S. 1780
François			
Joseph			

A

74 Barthélemi	(42)	M. Ls. Mélançon	S.F.S. 1785
75 Augustin	(45)	M. Claire Sylvestre	S.P.S. 1786
Denis			
76 Joseph		M. Ls. Miville	
Jos. Marie			
77 Jean	(45)	M. Jos. Bolduc	S.V. 1789
Marie Josette		J. B. Lepage	S.V. 1824
Eustache			
78 Pierre	(46)	M. Agathe Blanchet	S.H. 1791
79 Louis	(46)	M. Ls. Blanchet	S.H. 1704
M. Archange		Amb. Fréchet	S.H. 1820
80 François	(46)	Angé Fontaine	S.H. 1800
81 Michel	(46)	M. Ls. Samson	S.H. 1803

GAGNÉ.

82	Joseph	(46) Marg. Roy	S.M. 1799
			S.Anselme.
	Pierre		
82	Augustin	(47) Marie Duchesneau	
			S.P.S. 1781
	M. Madeleine	J. B. Mercier	S.M. 1811
	Angèlique	Eustache Vérieul	S.M.1819
	Thérèse	Ls. Lessard	S.M. 1825
	Marie Anne	Jean Veau	S.M. 1832
	Guillaume		
	Joseph		
84	Louis	(48) Marg. Viger	S.Chs. 1780
85	Jacques	(48) M. Mad. Morin	S.F.S. 1782
	Prosper		
86	Antoine	(48) Marg. Picard	S.P.S. 1784
87	Bernard	(48) M. Jos. Morin	S.P.S. 1788
88	Germain	(48) M. Ls. Fournier	
			S.Tho. 1788
	Germain		
	Le même	Rose Langlois	S.F.S. 1798
89	Jean Marie	(45) M. Eliz. Fournier	
			S.Tho. 1771
	Marie Rosalie	Frs. Talbot	S.Tho. 1800
	Augustin		
90	Pierre	Marie Duquet	
	Le même	M. Marg. Cloutier	
			S.P.S. 1798
91	Ambroise	Marie Marotte	
	Ambroise		
92	Joseph	M. Jos. Thibaut	
			Islet.
	Joseph		
93	Jacques	M. Hélène Labonté	
	Joseph		
94	Joseph	(50) Sophie Lemieux	
			Cap.S.Ign. 1826
		Isle aux Grues.	
	Olivier		
95	Louis George	(50) Fse. Létourneau	
			S.P.S. 1839
96	Charles	(50) Emélie Hoffman	Bert. 1845
97	François	(52) M. Eliz. Corriveau	
			Bert. 1791
	Reine	Noel Baudoin	S.H. 1815
98	Joseph	(93) M. Genev. Beauchamp	
			S.Tho. 1779
	M. Catherine	Marc Eustache Létourneau	
			S.P.S. 1820
99	François	(58) Christine Blanchet	
			Cap. S. Ign. 1801
	Françoise		
100	Jacques	(59) Thérèse Gosselin	
			S.F.S. 1797
101	Jean Bapt.	(60) Christine Langlois	
			S.F.S. 1796
	Christine	Ign. Bourget	S.G. 1824
102	Pierre	(60) Fse. Langlois	S.F.S. 1807
	Marcelline	Olivier Fortier	S.F.S. 1830
	Marcelline	2° Aug. Poliquin	
			S.F.S. 1842
	Françoise	Pierre Gagné	S.V. 1831
	Marie	David Baudoin	S.V. 1843
	Joseph		
	Pierre		
103	Ls. Raphael	(6) Marg. Verret	S.J. 1815
	Christine	Ls. Boucher	S.Frs. 1843
	Ferdinand		
	Louis		
104	François	(63) Cath. Verret	S.J. 1825
105	Ambroise	(67) Thérèse Gosselin	S.H. 1789
106	Jean Bapt.	(67) M. Anne Dessaint	
			S.B.S. 1791
	Jean Baptiste		
	Le même	M. Anne Demers	S.H. 1815
107	François	(67) Cécile Pouliot	S.G. 1802
108	Pierre	(67) Marg. James	S. H. 1805

GAGNÉ.

109	JeanBaptiste	(67) Marg. Chatigny	S.G. 1827
		(2d m.)	
110	Joseph	M. Scolastique Gagnon	
	Françoise	Paschal Fortier	S.G. 1822
	Prosper		
	François		
111	Louis	Rosalie Quéret	
	Marie	Jacq. Labbé	S.G. 1826
	Louis		
112	Pierre	M. Eléonore Leblanc	
	Marie Anne	Ant. Bernier	S.P.S. 1834
	Emélie	Jean Rouillard	S.V. 1855
	André		
	Edouard		
113	Michel	(68) M. Anne Lebrun	S.H. 1809
	Marie Anne	Denis Allen	S.M. 1833'
	Le même	Ursulle Coulombe	
			S.H. 1815
114	Jean Bapt.	(69) Thérèse Roy	S.P.S. 1802
	M. Désanges	Ed. Fontaine	S.P.S. 1838
	Vital		
	Le même	Marg. Jolivet	S.F.S. 1839
	Pierre		
115	Pierre	(69) Archange Couillard	
			S.P.S. 1805
	Flavie	Eustache Baron	
			S.P.S. 1825
	M. Onésime	J. B. Caron	S.P.S. 1838
	Cherubin		
	Amable		
116	Charles	(70) M. Anne Chrystophe	
			S.Chs. 1824
117	Jean Bapt.	(72) Genev. Roy	S.P.S. 1812
118	Joseph	(73) Genev. Coté	S.Tho. 1812
	Le même	Marg. Cloutier	S.P.S. 1823
119	François	(73) Adé Bernier	S.P.S. 1822
120	Denis	(75) Julie Fortier	Bert. 1821
121	Pierre Noël	Marg. Gagnon	
	René		
122	Louis	Jos. Eliz. Bolduc, Scolas-	
		astique Lessart, S. Jos.	
		Beauce	
	Louis		
123	Michel	Louise Dorval	
	M. Louise Re-	Germ. Brousseau	S.M. 1847
	becca		
	M. Louise Re-	2° Jos. Bissonnet	S.M. 1863
	becca		
124	Louis	Amb. & Mad. Verreau,	
		Marie Hébert S. Marie,	
		1823, S. Marie	
	Romuald Alph-		
	onse		
125	Odilon	Lucrèce Soucy.	S.Anne
	Louis		
126	JosephMarie	(76) M. Chas. Picard	
			S.P.S. 1803
127	Eustache	(77) M. Cécile Boutin	S.V. 1821
	Isabelle	Pierre McNeil	S.V. 1849
	Julie	Jos. Gautier	S.V. 1850
	Sophie	F. X. Roy	S.V. 1860
	Thomas		
128	Pierre	(82) Fse. Gagné	S.V. 1831
129	Guillaume	(93) Fse. Roy	S.G. 1824
130	Joseph	(83) Luce Mercier	S.M. 1833
131	Prosper	(85) Marg. Jolin	S.H. 1820
132	Germain	(88) M. Ls. Bilodeau	S.F.S.1818
133	Augustin	(89) M.Genev. Blais	S.P.S. 1801
134	Ambroise	(91) Apolline Nadeau	S.G. 1808
135	Joseph	(92) M. Angèle Mathieu	
			S.P.S. 1812
	Le même	M. Ls. Coulombe	
			S.P.S. 1818
136	Olivier	(94) Sophie Campagna	
			S.Frs. 1849
137	François	(99) Ange Paquet	S.Chs. 1831

GAGNÉ.

138	Joseph	(102) Archange RattéS.F S.1834
139	Pierre	(102) Fse. Gagnon S.V. 1832
140	Louis	(103) Reparate Dalaire S.Frs. 1848
141	Ferdinand	(103) Vict.Thivierge S.Frs. 1855
142	Jean	(106) Luce Roy Levis 1816
	Baptiste	
	Marguerite	Narcisse Turgeon B. 1844
143	François	(110) M. Thérèse PerrotS.V.1820
144	Prosper	(110) M. Anne Lepage S.Chs. 1824
145	Louis	(111) Genev. Corriveau S.G.1826
146	Edouard	(112) Emérentienne Gaudreau S.P.S. 1831
147	André	(112) Anastasie Keroack S.F.S. 1838
148	Vital	(114) M. Chamberlan S.P.S.1827
149	Pierre	(114) Cath. Blais S.P.S. 1840
150	Amable	(115) Anastasie TalbotS.P.S. 1836
151	Romuald	(124) M. Honorine Olympe
	Alphonse	Cotin S.M. 1865
152	Louis	(125) Artèmise Bérubé S.V.1866
153	Thomas	(127) Anastasie GagnonS.V.1848
154	Chérubin	(115) M. Eliz. BernierS.P.S.1840
155	René	(121) M. Marg. Couture S Chs. 1847
156	Louis	(122) M. Mad. Beaucher S.F.S. 1784

GAGNON.

1	Pierre	Reneé Royer Tourauvre
	Mathurin	
	Jean	
	Pierre	
2	Jean	Marie Gestray-Ventrouse
	Robert	
3	Jean	(1) Marg. Cochon Q. 1640
	Jean	
4	Pierre	(1) Vincente Desvarieux Que. 1642
	Jean	
	Pierre	
	Noel	
	Pierre Paul	Ordonné le 21 Dec. 1677
5	Mathurin	(1) Fse. Boudreaa Que. 1647
	Mathurin	
	Pierre	
	Joseph	
6	Robert	(2) Marie Parenthel Que. 1657
	Elizabeth	Ls. Moreau S.F. 1678
	Elizabeth	2° Jean Baril S.F. 1684
	Anne	Hyppolite Thivierge S.F. 1695
	Anne	2° Jos. Charlan S.F. 1707
	Jacques	
	Jean	
	Pierre	
	Joseph	
7	Jean	(3) Marg. Drouin R.C. 1670
	Marguerite	Etn. Veau C.R. 1693
	Jean	
	Pierre	
8	Jean	(4) Marg. Racine C.R.
	Marguerite	Nicolas Asselin C.R. 1694
	Anne	Michel Asselin C.R. 1700
	Jean	
	François	
	Prisque	
9	Pierre	Barbe Fortin C.R. 1669
	Marie	René Lepage S.Anne 1686
	Joseph	
	Pierre	
	Charles	
	Alexandre	
	Jean Baptiste	

GAGNON.

10	Noël	Génév. Fortin S. Anne 1683
	Le même	Barbe Cloutier C.R. 1705
11	Mathurin	(5) Charlotte Cochon C.R.1686
	Jean	
	Pierre	
	Mathurin	
12	Pierre	(5) Hélène Cloutier C.R. 1696
	Pierre	
	Jean	
13	Joseph	(5) Marie Cloutier C.R. 1699
	Marie	Bertrand Perrot S.F. 1731
	Hélène	Ls. Deblois S.F. 1745
	Marie Josette	Hilaire Beaucher S.F. 1749
	Joseph	
	François	
	Basile	
	Jean	
	Pierre	
14	Jean	(6) Jeanne Loignon Que. 1686
	M. Angèlique	J. B. Hudon Riv. Ouelle 1713
	M. Charlotte	Jean Bernard Hudon Riv. Ouelle 1718
	Jean	
	Antoine	
	François	
	Le même	Fse. Doré Que. 1718
15	Jacques	(6) M. Mad. Rochon S.F. 1695
	Catherine	Jos. Gilbert Riv. Ouelle 1718
16	Joseph	(6) Anne Louineau Que. 1699
	Elizabeth	Ant. Brousseau, Que. 1746
17	Pierre	(6) L. Létourneau S.F. 1700
18	Jean	(7) Anne Mesny S. Frs. 1699
	Marie	Jean Lepage " 1723
	Anne	Pierre Giroux " 1733
	Marie Josette	Jean Guichard " 1744
	Marguerite	Michel Emond " 1744
	Jean	
	Antoine	
19	Pierre	(7) Marie Lacroix S.Anne1704
	Joseph	
	Joseph	
20	François	(8) Marg. Bèlanger C.R. 1704
	Jean François	
	Joseph	
21	Jean	(8) Thérèse Rochon S.F. 1704
22	Prisque	(8) Cath. Guion " 1719
23	Joseph	(9) Agathe Bélanger C.R. 1700
	Jean	
24	Pierre	(9) Isabelle Lacroix " 1701
25	Charles	(9) Anne Bélanger " 1706
	Gabriel	
	Pierre	
26	Alexandre	(9) Angé Caron S. Anne 1711
27	Jean Baptiste	(9) Fse. Ouellet Riv. Ouelle 1714
28	Mathurin	(11) Marg. Crétien 1716
	Marguerite	Jos. Laurandeau S.V. 1747
	Marguerite	2° Pierre Rouleau S.F.S. 1757
	M. Madeleine	J. B. Quemeneur " 1753
	M. Geneviève	Simon Boivin " 1767
	Mathurin	
	Pierre	
	Michel	
	Jean	
	Le même	Gertrude Blanchet S.P.S. 1756
	Basile	
29	Jean	(11) Marg. Lavoie S. Joa. 1731
	Louis	
30	Pierre	(11) Anne Racine
	Marie Anne	Jacq. Gagné S. Joa. 1743
	Augustin	

GAGNON.

31	Pierre	Eliz. Fortier		
	Geneviève	Ls. Blanchet	S.F.S.	1761
32	Pierre (12)	Marie Charier	C.R.	1721
33	Jean (12)	Josette Lavoie	"	1733
	Le même .	Louise Jobidon	"	1739
	Hélène	Paul Blouin	S.Anne	1775
	Hélène	2° J. B. Roberge	S.F.	1789
	Berthiaume			
	Noël			
34	Joseph (13)	M. Jos. Pepin	S.Frs.	1732
	M. Angèlique	J. B. Dubreuil	S.F.S.	1759
	M. Angèlique	2° Armand Doiron	"	1774
	Thérèse	J. B. Roy	"	1774
	Louise	Mathurin Dubreuil	S.F.S.	1784
	Joseph			
	Jacques			
	Michel			
	Louis			
35	Pierre (13)	Isabelle Chartier	Bert.	1734
	M. Madeleine	Simon Turcot	S.Frs.	1773
	Susanne	Ls. Boutin	"	1784
	Clément			
36	François (13)	Thècle Déblois	S.F.	1739
	Thècle	Chs. Déblois	S. Frs.	1760
	Le même	Louise Beaucher	S.F.	1748
37	Basile (13)	Marie L'heureux	"	1743
38	Jean (13)	Marg. Morisset	"	1745
39	Jean (14)	Genev. Gamache	Islet	1713
40	Antoine (14)	Reine Ouellet	S.Anne	1727
41	François (14)	Cath. Morel	Kamouraska	1730
42	Jean (18)	M. Jeanne Marseau	S. Frs.	1731
	M. Madeleine	J. B. Déblois	"	1759
	Angèlique	Germain Landry	"	1762
	Félicité	Jean Emond	"	1765
	M. Thècle	Pierre Fréchet	"	1775
	Jean			
	Louis			
43	Antoine (18)	Mad. Déblois	"	1740
	Marguerite	Jos. Emond	"	1756
	Le même	Marg. Peltier	S.P.	1767
44	Joseph (19)	Mad. Caron	S. Anne	1738
	Ignace			
45	Joseph (19)	Cath. Dalaire	C.R.	1741
	Jos. Marie			
46	Jean Fran-	M. Reine Mercier		
	çois (20)		S. Anne	1732
	Louis			
47	Joseph (20)	Marg. Poulin	S. Joa.	1733
	Joseph			
48	Jean (23)	Mad. Boutillet	A.G.	1730
	Marie Agathe	Pierre Noël Picard	S.P.S.	1768
	Thérèse	Michel Sénéchal	"	1777
	M. Madeleine	René Picard	S.F.S.	1777
	Geneviève	Ls. Boutin	Bert.	1781
	Jos. Charles			
49	Pierre (25)	Genev. Routier	S. Foye	1745
	M. Geneviève	Jean Guill Corriveau	S.M.	1768
	Marguerite	Jos. Mercier	"	1783
	Marie Marthe	Ignace Ratté	"	1783
	Marie Félicité	J. B. Fortier	"	1783
	Charles			
	Jean Baptiste			
	Gabriel			
50	Gabriel (25)	M. Reine Gravel	C.R.	1751
	Elizabeth	Chs. Claude Nadeau	S.M.	1774
	Marie	Jean Goulet	"	1780
	Catherine	Ant. Turgeon	"	1795
	Gabriel			

GAGNON.

	Joseph			
51	Mathurin (28)	Angé Laurandeau		
	M. Angèlique	Ant. Baudouin	S.F S.	1772
	Mathurin			
	Le même	Mad. Boulet	"	1760
52	Michel (28)	Marg.Quemeneur	"	1750
	M. Madeleine	J B. Langlois	"	1788
	Marie Louise	Frs. Quéret	"	1792
	Michel			
53	Pierre (28)	Eliz. Dion	"	1751
54	Jean (28)	M. Angé Vérieul	"	1762
	Françoise	Chs. Labrecque	S.G.	1823
	Joseph			
	Pierre			
	Michel			
55	Basile (28)	Marg. Chartier	"	1784
	Marguerite	Aug. Labrecque	S.G.	1808
	Josette	André Brochu	"	1818
	Basile			
	Ambroise			
	André			
56	Louis (29)	Genev. Parent	S.P.	1762
57	Augustin (30)	Josette Boucher	S.Joa	1756
	Augustin			
58	Joseph	M. Ls. Boucher		
	M. Geneviève	Jos Boissonneau	S.F.S.	1775
	Marie Louise	Basile Beaucher	"	1799
	"	2° Jos. Fournier	"	1806
	Jean Baptiste			
	Joseph			
	Joseph Noël			
	François			
59	Jean	M. Chs. Boucher		
	Ignace			
60	Noël (33)	M. Abondante Létour-		
		neau	S.F.	1776
61	Barthéléme (33)	M. Jos. Plante	S.Frs.	1782
62	Louis (34)	M. Mad.Picard	S.P.S	1761
	Marie Louise	Pierre Boulet	"	1787
63	Joseph (34)	M. Genev. Morin		
			S.F.S.	1762
	Reine	Simon Boivin	"	1792
	Geneviève	Pierre Guilmet	"	1796
	Victoire	Frs. Boivin	"	1809
	Joseph			
	Antoine			
	Jean Baptiste			
64	Michel (34)	Mad. Picard	"	1786
	Euphrosine	Aug. Leblond	S.V.	1829
65	Jacques (34)	M. Rose Thibaut		
			S.F.S.	1788
	Marie Rose	J. B Morin	S.M.	1809
	Clotilde	J. B. Pigeon	"	1816
	Jacques			
66	Clément (35)	M. Reine Pruneau	Bert.	1785
	Reine	Jean Darveau	S.F.S.	1803
	Marguerite	Pierre Blanchet	S.V.	1817
	Abraham			
	Joseph			
	Pierre			
	Pierre			
	Antoine			
67	Jean (42)	M.AnneDeblois	S.Frs.	1755
68	Louis (42)	Thècle Lepage	"	1756
	Louis			
	Le même	Mad. Emond	"	1762
	Madeleine	Jean Campagna	"	1777
	Le même	Angé Campagna	"	1778
69	Ignace (44)	Genev. Bruneau	Bert.	1765
	Geneviève	ClaudeDrapeau	S.Chs.	1785
	Josette	Frs. Ouel	"	1802
		2° Jos. Lavoie	S.V.	1806
	Ignace			
	Pierre			

GAGNON.

70	Jos. Marie	(5)	M. Ls. Martineau S.F.	1767
	Jos. Marie			
	Louis			
	Le même		M. Anne Crépeau S.L.	1791
71	Louis	(46)	Cath. Meneux S.F.	1771
72	Joseph	(47)	M. Jos. Blouin S. Anne	1761
	Joseph			
73	Joseph			
	Charles	(48)	Fse. Dalaire S.V.	1762
	Françoise		J. B. Marcoux S.M.	1788
	Marie Jeanne		Jos. Guilmet ,,	1797
	Marie Rosalie		Pierre Roy ,,	1802
	Michel			
	Joseph			
	Pierre			
74	Louis		M. Mad. Daniau S.P.S.	
	Jacques			
75	Charles	(49)	Marguerite Roy S V.	1779
76	Gabriel	(49)	Angé Mercier S.Chs.	1784
	M. Angélique		Jos. Côté S.M.	1802
	Marguerite		Jos. Morisset ,,	1813
	Françoise		Jos. Bacquet ,,	1813
	Louise		J. B. Bissonnet ,,	1819
	Marie Olive		Paul Bacquet ,,	1820
	Angéle		Jos. Clément ,,	1821
	Archange		Jos. Gagnon ,,	1829
	Jean Paul			
	Pierre			
	Jen			
	Benjamin			
	Pierre		M. Rose Gamache	
	Pierre			
77	JeanBaptiste	(49)	M. Vict. Bonneau S.V.	1793
78	Gabriel	(50)	M. Anne Denis S.M.	1785
	Marie Anne		Jos. Bouchard S.M.	1815
	Marie Anne		2° Frs. Gosselin S.M.	1829
	Reine		Chs. Labrecque S.M.	1816
	Marguerite		Jos. Queret S.M.	1820
	Marguerite		2° Sauveur Dupré S.M.	1845
	Louis			
	Joseph			
	Jacques			
79	Mathurin	(51)	Marg. Chabot S.F.S.	1768
80	Michel	(52)	M. Jos Blanchet S.V.	1784
81	Joseph	(54)	M. Jos. Queret S.M.	1793
	M. Geneviève		Jos. Baudouin S.V.	1823
	Josette		Jacq. Boissonneau S.V.	1839
	Joseph			
82	Pierre	(54)	Vict. Terrien S.G.	1805
	Celeste		J. B. Langlois S.V.	1836
	Pierre			
83	Michel	(54)	Marie Royer S.G.	1808
84	Basile	(55)	Marg. Fradet S.F.S.	1805
	Angéle		Didace Dessaint S.F.S.	1843
	Marguerite		Aug. Roy S.G.	1829
	Marie Sophie		Jos. Plante S.V.	1851
	Basile			
85	André	(55)	Marg. Fortier S.G.	1821
86	Ambroise	(55)	Archange Boudouin S.V.	1826
87	Augustin	(57)	Josette Clouthier S. Joa.	1787
	Elie			
88	JeanBaptiste	(58)	M. Thérèse Boulet S.F.S.	1777
	Joseph			
	Jean Baptiste			
89	François	(58)	Eliz. Vivier S.P.S.	1777
90	Joseph Noël	(58)	Frs. Picard S.F.S.	1790
91	Ignace	(59)	Agathe Mercier Bert.	1783
92	Joseph	(63)	Genev. Boivin	
	Marguerite		Frs. Lemieux	

GAGNON.

	Marguerite		2° Pierre Samson	
	Théoliste		Aug. Alaire	
	Geneviève		Aug. Audet	
	Victoire		Ls. Fortier	
	Jean Baptiste			
	Laurent			
	Joseph			
	Pierre			
	Hubert			
	Vital			
93	JeanBaptiste	(63)	Marg. Boulet S.F.S.	1795
	Marie Josette		Ant. Morin S.F.S.	1829
	Antoine			
94	Antoine	(63)	Mad. Fradet S.F.S.	1803
	Louise		Ant. Simard S.V.	1829
	Théotiste		Ls. Leclaire S.V.	1832
	Francoise		Pierre Gagné S.V.	1832
	Cyprien			
95	François		Charlotte Deblois	
	M. Geneviève		Pierre Choret S. F.	1807
	Charlotte		Jos. Turcot S.F.	1811
	Angélique		Jos. Gosselin S.F.	1817
	François			
	Le même		Thècle Asselin S.F.	1791
96	Pierre	(69)	Mad. Mercier S.H.	1794
	Le même		Marg. Leclaire S.Chs.	1796
97	Etienne		M. Jos. Drouin	
	Josette		Jean Martineau S.F.	1812
	Marie Angéle		Pierre Drouin S.F.	1819
	Etienne			
98	Francois			
99	Jacques	(65)	M. Ls. Boulet S.F.S.	1821
	M. Damasile		Martin Coté S.M.	1843
	Barnabé			
	Gilbert			
100	Pierre	(66)	Fse. Fortier S.V.	1810
	Emélie		Guill. Audet S.G.	1830
101	Abraham	(66)	Reine Gagné Bert	1812
	Zoé		Guill. Audet Bert	1842
	Henriette		F.X. Boissonneau S.J.	1843
	Frs. Xavier			
102	Joseph	(66)	M. Marg. Roy S.V.	1814
	Angélique		Frs. Regis Ménard S.V.	1837
	Margueritte		Michel Paquet S.V.	1837
	Francois Xavier			
	Joseph			
103	Pierre	(66)	M. Ls. Tangué S.V.	1815
104	Antoine	(66)	Mad. Langlois S.V.	1824
	Angéle		Ls. Théophile Blais S. V.	1849
	Antoine			
105	Louise	(68)	M. Ls. Asselin S.Frs.	1781
	M. Madeleine		Jean Labbé S. Frs.	1826
	M. Louise		Ls. Langlois. S. Frs.	1840
	Marie		Jos. St. Jean S.J.	1825
	Louis			
	François			
	Joseph			
106	Ignace	(69)	M. Anne Leclaire S. Chs.	1787
	Marie Anne		Alexandre Marcoux S.Chs.	1809
	Angelique		Pierre Daniau S.Chs.	1815
	Le même		M. Genev. Fortier S.H.	1800
	Le même		M. Reine Savoie S.V.	1804
	Madeleine		F. X. Bélanger S.Chs.	1833
	Justine		Marc Couillard S.Chs.	1841
	Felicite		Jean Audibert S.Chs.	1841
	Marcelline		Frs. Lebrecque S.Chs.	1846
107	Louis	(70)	Marie Cazeau C.R.	1806
	Louis			
108	Jos. Marie	(70)	Josette Ferlant S.P.	1808
109	Joseph	(72)	Genev. Perrot S.A.	1787

GAGNON.

110	Joseph	(73) M. Aug. Marcoux	S.M.1791
	Geneviève	Ls. Morin	„ 1820
	M. Françoise	Jos. Corriveau	„ 1821
	Archange	Michel Paré	„ 1824
	Archange	J. B. Guilmet	
	Rose	Ls. Bissonnet	„ 1839
	Joseph		
111	Michel	(73) Marg. Brochu	S.V. 1795
	Marguerite	Pierre Gagnon	S.M. 1818
	Françoise	Louren Turgeon	„ 1819
	Michel		
	Le même	Eliz. Coté	S.Chs. 1802
	M. Angélique	René Corriveau	S.M. 1824
	Sophie	Pierre Corriveau	„ 1828
	Marie	Ls. Bouffart	„ 1837
	Athanase		
	Joseph		
	Vital		
112	Pierre	(73) Marg. Patry	S.M. 1803
	Marguerite	Jos. Labrecque	B. 1830
	Archange	Chs. Hébert	B. 1841
	Pierre		
	Charles		
113	Jacques	(74) M. Susanne Morin	S.F.S. 1788
114	Pierre	Marg. Naud	
	Bénoni		
115	Pierre	Jos. Geneviève Boucher	
	Le même	Agnès Paré, St. Joa., Que.,	1785
	François		
116	Pierre	(76) A. M. Reine Fournier	Cap St. Ig. 1800
	Julie	J. B. Morin	S.F.S. 1827
	Geneviève	J. B. Daniau	„ 1832
	Pierre		
117	Pierre	Fse. Fortier, S. Marie	
	Marguerite	Jos. Bolduc	S.V. 1835
118	Jean Baptiste	M. Anne Bazin	„ 1814
	Marie	Aug Roy	„ 1833
	Susanne	Barnabé Tangué	„ 1840
	Archange	Pierre Dalaire	„ 1844
	Cyprien		
	Jean		
119	Pierre	(96) Marg. Gagnon	S.M. 1818
	Marguerite	Bénoni Corriveau	„ 1840
	Marcelline	Honoré Morin	„ 1842
	Sara	Majorique Mercier	„ 1854
	M. Célina	Marc Couture	„ 1858
	Ferdinand		
	Narcisse		
	Frédéric		
120	Jean	(76) Archange Morisset	S.M. 1819
121	Jean Paul	(76) M. Anne Lemelin	S.M.1821
	Marie Anne	Frs. Baudouin	„ 1845
	Laurent		
122	Benjamin	(76) Eléonore Mercier	S.M.1835
123	Louis	(78) Mad. Cadrin	S.M. 1816
			S. Anselme
	Le même	Marg. Catellier	S.M. 1840
124	Joseph	(78) Genev. Coté	S.Chs. 1825
	Sophie	Rigobert Lessart	S.M.1851
	Flavie	F. X. Queret	„ 1854
	M. Philomène	Léon Mercier	„ 1856
	Antoine		
125	Jacques	(78) Cécile Audet	S.G. 1828
126	Joseph	(81) M. Anne Fradet	S.M. 1824
	Anastasie	Tho. Gagné	S.V. 1848
127	Pierre	(82) Angé Lepage	
	Chs. François		
128	Basile	(84) Marg. Lemieux	S.G. 1830
	Joseph		
	Le même	Josette Gosselin	S.Chs.1842
129	Elie	(87) Josette Dalaire	S.Frs.1831
130	Joseph	(88) M. Ls. Dalaire	S.V. 1800

GAGNON,

131	Jean Baptiste(88)	Marg. Baudouin	S.F.S.1809
	Le même	M. Reine Langlois	S.V.1814
132	Jean Baptiste(92)	Fse. Boutin	„ 1818
	Le même	M. Reine Lemieux	S.F.S 1823
133	Joseph (92)	M. Eulalie Marseau	S.V. 1821
134	Laurent (92)	Marg. Marseau	„ 1828
135	Pierre (92)	Marg. Audet	S.G. 1829
136	Hubert (92)	Césarie Garant	S.F.S. 1832
137	Vital (92)	M.AgatheBoulet	„ 1837
138	Antoine (93)	ArchangeGuilmet	S.G.1828
139	Cyprien (94)	Marie Langlois	S.V. 1832
140	Chs.François(95)	M. Anne Gosselin	S.F.1814
	Hombeline	Frs. NarcisseCanac	„ 1844
	Marie	Pierre Magl. Premont	S.F. 1846
	Martine	Olivier Drouin	„ 1847
	Pierre		
	François Xavier		
141	Etienne (97)	Mad. Gaulin	„ 1811
	Marguerite	Jacq. Martineau	„ 1836
	Marcelline	Jos. Paquet	„ 1841
	Adélaïde	Frs. Vaillancour	., 1848
	Catherine	Frs. Emond	„ 1849
	Olive	Stanislas Paquet	„ 1860
	Abraham		
	François Xavier		
	Régis		
142	François (97)	Josette Beaucher	S.F. 1844
143	Barnabé (99)	Marg. Pilote	S.M. 1848
144	Gilbert (99)	Delphine Pigeon	S.V. 1855
145	Frs. Xavier (101)	Christine Boissonneau	S.J. 1843
146	Frs. Xavier (102)	Soulange Dalaire	S.V. 1837
147	Joseph (102)	Fse. Minard	„ 1846
148	Antoine (104)	Mathilde Lemieux	Bert. 1847
149	Louis (105)	M. Anne Dalaire	S.F. 1817
	M. Constance	Pierre Marseau	S.Frs.1840
	Luce	Ls. Dompierre	„ 1851
	Clémentine	Pierre Picard	„ 1855
	Ls. Prosper		
	Pierre Célestin		
150	François (105)	M. Ls. Lefebvre	S.J. 1822
	Le même	Fse. Turcot	„ 1828
	Marcelline	Geo. Thivierge	„ 1859
	Célina	Léon Létourneau	„ 1863
	Jérémie		
	François		
151	Joseph (105)	Rose Lefebvre	Beauport 1831
	Le même	M. Ls. Laurent	S.Frs. 1837
152	Louis (107)	Vénérande Gosselin	S.P. 1835
	Flavie	Elz. Aug. Plante	„ 1862
	Julie Philoméne	Flavien Ferlant	„ 1865
	Vénéranda	Pierre Nap. Leclaire	S.P. 1865
	Ls. Philéas		
	Joseph		
153	Joseph (110)	Marg. Corriveau	S.V. 1821
	Emérence	Pierre Coté	S.M. 1862
	Nazaire		
	Joseph		
	George		
A	Michel (111)	M. Genev. Rouillard	S.M. 1820
154	Vital (111)	Archange Gagnon	„ 1829
	Marie Odile	Martial Roy	„ 1855
	Jos. Florent		
	Damase		
155	Vital (111)	Constance Morin	S.M.1834
156	Athanase (111)	Anastasie Poliquin	S.M. 1838
157	Charles (112)	Cécile Gravel	B. 1855

GAGNON.

158	Pierre	(112)	Théotiste Leblond S.Chs. 1833
	Le même		Marcelline Roy S.M. 1854
159	Bénoni	(114)	Eliz. Gautron S.G. 1828
160	François	(115)	Cath. Beaucher S.F. 1829
161	Pierre	(116)	M. Reine Buteau S.F.S. 1834
162	Jean	(119)	Sophie Dupont S.M. 1841
163	Cyprien	(118)	Marie Thivierge S.V. 1863
164	Fréderic	(119)	Dina Labrecque B. 1849
165	Ferdinand	(119)	Marcelline Lefebvre S.M. 1849
166	Narcisse	(119)	M. Cleophie Agnès Roy S.M. 1858
167	Laurent	(121)	Rosalie Quèret S.Chs. 1852
168	Antoine	(124)	Marcelline Paquet S.V. 1848
169	Charles Frs.	(127)	
170	Joseph	(128)	Vict. Terrien S.M. 1855
171	Pierre	(140)	Cath. Paradis S.P. 1847
	Le même		Marie Paré S.F. 1866
172	Frs. Xavier	(140)	Justine Asselin " 1848
	Le même		Anne Turcot S.J. 1854
	Le même		HombelineTurcot S.F.1857
173	Roger		Esther Lajoie Baie S. Paul 1848
	Marie Anne		Firmin Fournier S.Chs.
174	Frs. Xavier	(141)	Julie Asselin S.F. 1846
175	Régis	(141)	Josette Foucher " 1848
176	Abraham	(141)	Désanges Vaillancour S.F. 1852
177	Louis Prosper	(149)	
178	Pierre Célestin	(149)	M.Flavie Pepin S.Frs.1847
			M. Ls. Ginchereau S.Frs. 1859
179	François	(150)	Judith Pepin S.G. 1853
180	Jérémie	(150)	M. Anne Royer S.J. 1862
181	Louis Phil.	(152)	Angé Elvine Ferland S.P. 1866
182	Joseph	(152)	Philomène Roberge S.V.1861
183	Georges	(153)	Hermine Denis S.Chs.1847
184	Nazaire	(153)	Hermine Bilodeau S.M. 1860
185	Joseph	(153)	Adé Brochu " 1864
186	Joseph Florent	(154)	Philomène Catellier S.M. 1858
187	Damase	(154)	Olympe Bacquet " 1864

GARANT

1	Pierre		René Chamfrin S.F. 1669
	Marie		Pierre Naud S.L. 1692
	Marthe		Chs. Branchaud " 1694
	Marthe		2° Chs. Dumas B. 1712
	M. Catherine		Jean Martin C.R. 1706
	M. Catherine		2° Simon Larrivé S.Chs. 1709
	Pierre		
	Le même		Cath. Labrecque S.L. 1684
	Jeanne		Nic. Menanteau S.Tho. 1708
	Jean		
	Pierre		
2	Pierre (1ᵉʳ m)		Jeanne Molleur B. 1759
	Jeanne		Jos. Boivin B. 1738
	Marguerite		Frs. Aubert B. 1751
	Susanne		Jean Brochu S.V. 1741
	Pierre		
	Joseph		
	Michel		
3	Pierre (2ᵈ m)		M. Mad. Marson S.Tho. 1714
	Catherine		Ls. Grefford S.F.S. 1738
	Marie		Jacq. Henri S.F.S. 1738

GARANT.

	M. Madeleine		Frs. Clement Doucet S.F.S. 1750
	M. Thérèse		Julien Pigeon S.F.S. 1753
	M. Thérèse		2° Pierre Daniau S.F.S. 1780
	M. Geneviève		Hubert Letarte S.F.S.1760
	M. Geneviève		2° Charles Pel S.F.S. 1762
	Marie Claire		Jos. Vivier
	Marie Claire		2° Jacq. Chs. Lahaye S.F.S. 1760
	Alexandre		
4	Jean	(1)	Angé Tourneroche S.M. 1716
			V. de Julien Dumont
	Marie		Ign. Lefebvre S.M. 1748
	Françoise		Michel Chamberlan S.M. 1750
	Jean		
	Le même		Louise Lefebvre S.V. 1742
5	Joseph	(2)	Marie Veau S.V. 1752
6	Michel	(2)	Agathe Brochu S.V. 1745
	Marie Louise		Nicolas Fortier S.M. 1772
	Michel		
7	Pierre	(2)	Cath. Mimaux S.M. 1746
	Le même		M. Fse. Gendron S.F.S. 1749
8	Alexandre	(3)	Marie Gendron Bert. 1749
	Françoise		Ls. Théberge S.F.S. 1775
	M. Marguerite		Félix Théberge S.F.S. 1785
	Louise		Pierre Labbé S.F.S. 1777
	Joseph		
	Frs. Timothée		
9	Jean	(4)	M. Anne Monmeny S.M. 1747
	M. Elisabeth		Jos. Blanchet S.M. 1780
	Le même		Mad. Pepin S.M. 1781
10	Jean Baptiste		Marie Dumas
	Marie		J. B.Audet S.G. 1787
	Jean Baptiste		
	Jacques		
	Pierre		
11	Michel	(6)	M. Anne Dutile S.M. 1773
12	Frs. Timothée	(8)	Thérèse Théberge S.F.S. 1785
	Angèle		Marc Terrien S.F.S. 1824
	M. Archange		Jacq. Fournier S.F.S. 1826
	Timothée		
13	Joseph	(8)	M. Aussile Baudouin S.F.S. 1787
	Basile		
14	Jean Baptiste	(10)	Angé Audet S.G. 1792
	Marguerite		Ls. Brochu S.Chs. 1816
	Jean		
	Le même		M. Reine Daniau S.F.S. 1804
15	Jacques	(10)	Josette Baudouin S.F.S. 1798
	Jacques		
16	Pierre	(10)	M. Jos. Audet S.G. 1798
	Josette		Jos. Blais S.F.S. 1824
	Marie Olive		Ant. Tangué S.F.S. 1832
	Joseph		
	Jacques		
	Pierre		
17	Jean		Marie Lainé
	Marc		
18	Marc	(17)	Marie Cloutier S.G. 1806
19	Timothée	(12)	Marg. Boissel S.G. 1812
20	Basile	(13)	Génév. Pelchat S.V. 1813
	Césarie		Hubert Gagnon S.F.S.1832
	Anastasie		Olivier Bernard S.F.S. 1833
	Hubert		

GARANT.

21	Ambroise		M. Roger Bourassa
	M. Théotiste		Nicolas Godbout
			S.F.S. 1833
22	Jean	(14)	Fse. Thibaut S.G. 1821
	Sophie		Valère Plante S.V. 1847
23	Jacques	(15)	Marie Bacquet S.G. 1826
24	Jacques	(16)	Angèle Blais S.Chs. 1827
25	Joseph	(16)	Marg. Ménard S.V. 1829
	M. Catherine		Jos. Bélanger S.V. 1870
	Joseph Job		
26	Pierre	(16)	M. Rose Boutin S.V. 1832
27	Hubert	(20)	M. Sophie Pigeon
			S.F.S. 1844
28	Jos. Job	(25)	Luce Gontier S.V. 1850

GAUDIN.

1	Charles		Marie Boucher Que. 1656
	Marie		Ls. Goulet A.G. 1682
	Marie		2ᵉ Pierre Denis A.G. 1657
	Charlotte		Vincent André Guillot
			A.G. 1718
	Pierre		
	Charles		
	François		
	Alexis		
2	Pierre		Jeanne Rousselière
			Montréal
	Gabriel		
	Pierre		
3	Charles	(1)	M. Mad. Perron A.G. 1789
4	Pierre	(1)	Anne Mathieu A.G. 1704
5	François	(1)	Génév. Lefrançois
			C.R. 1705
6	Alexis	(1)	Mad. Jacob A.G. 1706
7	Pierre	(2)	Jeanne Cochon C.R. 1689
8	Gabriel	(2)	André Angé Cochon Qué.
			1690
9	Pierre		Cath. Pellerin S.F.S.
	Geneviève		Frs. Larrivé Bert. 1730
	Ursule		Chs. Dumas S.L. 1733
	Pierre		
10	Pierre		Ange Proulx
	Angélique		Jos. Boudoin S.F.S. 1754
	Joseph		
	Augustin		
	Pierre		
	François		
	Jean Marie		
11	Jacques		M. Anne Bergeron
	Hélène		Jean Martin S.F. 1767
12	Pierre	(9)	Marg. Audet S.L. 1733
13	Jean Marie	(10)	Claire Fse. Greffart S.F.S.
			1751
	Le même		M. Ursule Lamy S.F.S.1757
14	Pierre	(10)	M. Jos. Blais Bert. 1753
	Marie Josette		Jacq. Morin S.F.S. 1769
15	François	(10)	M. Ls. Baudoin Bert. 1758
	Marie Rose		Jos. Marie Chamberlan
			S.P.S. 1790
	Marie Louise		Chs. Jolivet S.F.S. 1796
	Marguerite		Philippe Richard S.V. 1800
16	Joseph	(10)	M. Ls. Martin S.F.S. 1765
17	Augustin	(10)	Eliz. Masseau ,, 1783
18	Ignace Fils de		M.Anne Fournier
	Jean et Marg.		Cap. S. Ign. 1773
	Audet		
	Marie Anne		Jocq. Louineau S.G. 1802
	M. Charlotte		Pierre Jacques S.F.S. 1807
19	Ignace		Marg. Coté Islet 1793
	Marguerite		Ed. Larrivé S.Chs. 1831
	Le même		M. Claire Morin S.V. 1812
20	Jean Baptiste		Angé Leveillé
	Félicité		Pierre Louineau S.G. 1797
	Marie		Jos. Boutin B. 1824

GAUDIN.

21	Etienne		Félicité Patry
	Thérèse		Jos. Blais S.P.S. 1834

GAUDREAU—GODREAU.

1	Jean		Marie Boucher
	Gilles		
	Jean		
2	Gilles	(1)	Anne De la Vieille S.F.1671
	Anne		Pierre Caouet Cap. S. Ign.
			1693
	Marguerite		Jacq. Marchand Cap.
			S. Ign. 1699
	Jeanne		Frs. Boucher Cap. St. Ign.
			1701
	Gabriel		
3	Jean	(1)	Marie Roy Qué. 1679
	Charles		
	Jean		
4	Gabriel	(2)	Eliz. Domingo Qué. 1700
	Joseph		
5	Charles	(3)	Mad. Thibaut Cap. S. Ign.
			1741
	M. Geneviève		Pre. Paul Cloutier S. Tho.
			1741
	Marie Reine		Ant. Langlois S.Tho. 1750
	François		
	Germain		
	Ignace		
	Charles		
	Joseph		
	Joseph		
6	Jean	(3)	Genev. Bernier Cap. S. Ing.
			1700
	Jean		
7	Joseph	(4)	M. Anne Gendreau S. L.
			1730
8	François	(5),	M. Hélène Chiasson Bert.
			1732
9	Joseph	(5)	M. Fse. Bélanger Islet 1734
	Le même		
10	Joseph	(5)	M. Ls. Vaillancour Islet
			1739
	Germain		
11	Charles	(5)	Marie Ruel S. Tho. 1748
	Le même		
12	Germain	(5)	M. Anne Thibault S.P.S.
			1752
	Marie Anne		Jos. Coulombe S.P.S. 1790
	Marie Roger		Michel Paul Labonté
			S.P.S. 1792
	Madeleine		Clément Luc Fortin
			S.P.S. 1796
	Jean Baptiste		
	Antoine		
13	Jean Baptiste	(5)	Ursule Morin S.P.S. 1758
	Ursule		Ls. Morin ,, 1795
14	Augustin		Eliz. Guimont
	Prosper		
15	Charles		Marie Bouchau
	Le même		Anne Bourque S.Chs. 1758
16	Jacques		Marie Desbiens
	Le même		Eliz. Delage S.J. 1761
17	Jean	(6)	M. Genev. Bélanger Islet
			1773
	Marie Claire		André Duchesneau S.P.S.
			1773
18	Joseph	(9)	M. Jos. Morin S.P.S. 1754
	François		
19	Germain	(10)	M. Jos. Blanchet S.P.S.
			1768
	Michel		
	Germain		
20	Charles	(11)	Marg. Durepos S.Tho. 1778
	François		
	Charles		

GAUDREAU—GODREAU.

21	JeanBaptiste(12)	M. Ls. Blais	S.P.S. 1786
22	Antoine	(12) Thérèse Balan	S.Tho. 1786
	Antoine		
23	Prosper	(14) Marg. Gagné S.	Tho. 1777
	Le même	Mad. Gagnon	S.Tho. 1780
	Prosper		
	Charles		
		Marg. Fse. Peltier	
24	Ignace		Islet 1787
	M. Constance	Jean Délanteigne	S.M.1819
25	François	(18) M. Genev. Gaumont	
			S.P.S. 1792
26	Germain	(19) Marg. Jolin	S. H. 1795
27	Michel	(19) Josette Parant S.	H. 1804
28	Francois	(20) Thérése Rousseau	
			S.P.S. 1814
	Le même	M. Genev. Dion Bert	1822
29	Antoine	(22) M. Claire Fortin	
			S. P. S. 1819
30	Charles	(20) Modeste Dessaint	
			S.Tho. 1804
	Emérentienne	Ed. Gagné S. P. S.	1831
	Elisabeth	Olivier Roy S. P. S.	1835
31	Charles	Génév. Fortin	
	Charles		
32	Joseph Marie	Constance Fortin	
	Pierre		
33	Prosper	(23) M. Marg. Bouchard	
			S. P. S. 1813
34	Charles	(31) Archange Létourneau	
			S.P.S. 1831
35	Pierre	(32) Adé Pepin	S. J. 1835

GAULIN.

1	François	Marie Rochon	Que. 1659
	M. Madeleine	Ign. Pepin	S. F. 1687
	Marie Thérése	Martin Beaucher	S.F.1786
		2° Nicolas Martin	
	Marie Thérése		S. Frs. 1703
	Simon		
	Robert		
2	Simon	(1) Fse. Létourneau	S.F. 1685
3	Robert	(1) Eliz. Létourneau	S.F. 1688
	Marie	Ign. Caron	S.F. 1707
	Marie Marthe	Aug. Caron	S.F. 1716
	Marie Dorothé	Ls. Fortin S.	Anne 1725
	Marie Josette	Chs. Caron	Islet 1731
	Robert		
	Louis		
	Jean Baptiste		
4	Robert	(3) M. Anne Soucy S. F.	1716
5	Louis	(3) Marie Campagna	
			S. Frs. 1717
	Michel		
	Louis		
	Joseph		
	Le même	Gertrude Vérieul	S.F.1753
6	Jean Baptiste	(3) Thérése Dorval	
	M. Thérése	Ign. Paradis	
	M. Brigitte	Claude Guion	
	Jean Baptiste		
7	Antoine	Brigitte Gagné	
	Geneviève	Ls. Blais S. P. S.	1757
	Joseph Marie		
8	Louis	(5) Cath. Dumas S. L.	1741
	M. Madeleine	J.B. Gourgue S. Frs.	1773
	Francois		
	Jean Baptiste		
	Ambroise		
9	Jean Baptiste	(6) Marg. Blouin S. J.	1742
	Thérése	Frs. Canac S. F.	1773
10	Jos. Marin	(5) Barbe Gagnon Islet	1753
	Madeleine	Aug. Michel Carbonneau	
			Bert. 1778
	Marie Barbe	Frs. Baudouin S.F.S.1801	

GAULIN.

	Marie Barbe	2° André Laurandeau	
			S. F. S. 1813
	Marie Josette	Jean Marie Langlois	
			S. Tho. 1783
	Joseph		
11	Jos. Marie	(7) M. Cath. Dion	S.F.S. 1763
			S.H.
	Le même	M. Eliz. Thivierge	
			S. Tho. 1767
	Pierre		
	Jean Baptiste		
	Antoine		
12	François	(8) Marg. Fortier S. J.	1771
	Marguerite	Jos. Dompierre	S.Frs.1798
	Marie	Aug. Emond S. Frs.	1804
	Marie	2° Jean Forceville	
			S. Frs. 1819
	Marie Josette	Ls. Lémelin S. Frs.	1806
	Brigitte	Pierre Emond S. Frs.	1806
	Marie Anne	Jos. Asselin S. Frs.	1800
	Marie Anne	2° Pierre Canac S. F.	1816
	Francois		
	Jean		
13	Jean Baptiste	(8) M. Jos. Jahan S. J.	1774
14	Ambroise	(8) Genev. Euphrosine	
			Pepin S. J. 1780
	Le même	Angé Martineau Que.	1783
	Madeleine	Etn. Gagnon S. F.	1811
15			
16	Joseph	(10) M. Marg. Fournier	
			S. P. S. 1796
	M. Marguerite	Ls. Boutin S. V.	1815
	Le même	M. Genev. Collet	
			S. F. S. 1800
	Adélaïde	Jacq. Rémillard	S.V. 1840
	Joseph		
	Le même	Félicite Roy S. Chs.	1834
17	Jean Baptiste(11)	Cath. Blais	Bert. 1797
18	Pierre	(11) Marie Guilmet S. V.	1805
	Marie	Jacq. Blouin S. J.	1841
	Pierre		
19	Antoine	(11) M. Jos. Bisson	S.Chs. 1811
20	Francois	(12) M. Chs. Plante	S.Frs. 1800
21	Jean	(12) Marie Doyon	C.R. 1807
	Marguerite	Frs. Régis Picard	
			S. Frs. 1846
	Marie	Jean Blouin S. Frs.	1849
	Charles		
	Jean Baptiste		
22	Joseph	(16) Marg. Boissonneau	
			S. F. S. 1831
	Le même	Charlotte Bazin	S.V. 1835
	Joséphine	Aug. Morin	S.V. 1869
23	Pierre	(18) Reine Talbot	S.F.S. 1831
24	Jean Bapt.	(21) Justine Toussaint	S.J. 1844
25	Charles	(21) Delphine Dompierre	
			S.Frs. 1848
26	Pierre	Marg. Gignac	
	Le même	Marie Pouliot	S.J. 1856
	Michel	(5) M. Jos. Vermet	S.H. 1776

GAUMONT.

1	Robert	Louise Robin	Que. 1671
	Germain		
2	Germain	(1) Marie Balard	S.Tho. 1700
	Anne	Aug. Gendron	S.Tho. 1740
	Amand		
	Joseph		
	Etienne		
3	Amand	(2) Félicité Robin	S.Tho. 1732
	Le même	M. Fse. Gosselin	S.L. 1735
	Le même	Génév. Dufresne	
	Germain		

GAUMONT.

4 Joseph	(2) Dorothée Lefebvre	S.Tho. 1728
Angélique	Chrysostome Langlois	S.P.S. 1769
François		
5 Germain	(3) Thérèse Proulx S.Tho. 1761	
Marguerite	Frs. Hyacinthe Peltier	S.P.S. 1827
Jean Baptiste		
6 François	(4) M. Réine Hervé	S.P.S. 1766
7 Etienne	(2) M. Jos. Pepin S.Tho. 1738	
Paul		
François		
Joseph		
8 Paul	(7) M. Anne Boucher	Bert. 1762
François		
Etienne		
9 François	(7) M. Anne Langlois	S.P.S. 1769
M. Geneviève	Frs. Gaudreau S.P.S. 1792	
Marie Anne	Ls. Chamberlan	S.P.S. 1796
10 Joseph	(7) M. Marthe Boutin	Bert. 1772
Marie Anne	Guill. Gaumont Bert. 1802	
Prosper		
Etienne		
Pierre		
11 Guillaume	(3) Claire Boulet S.Tho. 1767	
Marie	Simon Morin S.P.S. 1793	
Guillaume		
12 Jacques Veuf de	M. Marg. Morin	
Thérèse Gau-		S.Tho. 1787
chon.		
Julie	Chs. Mathieu S.P.S. 1812	
13 Jean Gabriel	Reine Ursule Lemieux	
Frs. Germain		
14 Jean Baptiste (5)	Fse. Fournier S.Tho. 1781	
M. Marguerite	Jos. Dubé S.P.S. 1821	
Geneviève	Laurent Racine S.G. 1826	
Jean Baptiste		
Louis		
15 Etienne	(8) M. Génev. Bernier	S.Tho. 1795
Geneviève	Ant. Rousseau S.G. 1821	
16 François	(8) Fse. Samson S.P.S. 1802	
Céleste	Ls. Vallée S.P.S. 1827	
François		
Le même	Agathe Vien S.G. 1815	
Luce	Vital Couture S.Chs. 1842	
17 Pierre	(10) M. Ls. Hélie Bert. 1808	
Marguerite	Honoré Roy Bert. 1842	
Magloire		
Pierre		
18 Etienne	(10) Marg. Mercier S.M. 1804	
Dorothée	Fréderic Quéret S.M. 1841	
19 Prosper	(10) Marg. Ouel Bert. 1828	
Samuel		
20 Guillaume	(11) M. Anne Gaumont	Bert. 1802
21 Frs. Germain (13)	M. Fse. Daniau S.P.S. 1803	
22 Louis	(14) Eliz. Coté S.Tho. 1813	
Laurent		
23 François	Vict. Dubé	
Marie Sara	J. B. Roy S.V. 1844	
24 Jean Bapt.	(14) Marg. Quemeneur	S.G. 1808
25 François	(16) Genev. Boutin S.Chs. 1829	
Marie	Ant. Chabot S.Chs. 1864	
26 Pierre	(17) Thérèse Langlois Bert. 1830	
27 Magloire	(17) Julie Clavet Bert. 1846	
28 Samuel	(19) Marcelline Gosselin	S.V. 1855
29 Laurent	(22) Soulange Carrier	

GAUMONT.

Justine	S.Chs. 1855	

GAUTRON—LAROCHELLE.

1 Joseph	Cath. Poisson Que. 1673	
Le même	Mad. Bissonnet	
Jeanne	Renaud Lavergne	S.M. 1714
Jeanne	2° Jos. Portelance B. 1714	
Marie	Claude Lefebvre B. 1705	
Marie	2° Ign. Chamberlan	S.V. 1727
Angélique	Jos. Quéret B. 1726	
Michel		
Pierre		
Joseph		
2 Michel	(1) M. Anne Alaire B. 1714	
Le même	M. Anne Lebrun S.V. 1716	
Marie Josette	Michel Lacroix S.M. 1748	
Marie Catherine	J. B. Lacroix S.M. 1749	
Marie Anne	Frs. Asselin S.M. 1751	
Marie Anne	2° Philippe Leclair	S.V. 1788
Michel		
Joseph		
Jean		
Augustin		
Louis		
3 Pierre	(1) Marie Marseau S.V. 1720	
Marie Josette	Théo. Plante S.M. 1748	
Marie Marcelle	Simon Bacquet S.M. 1750	
Marie Anne	J. B. Pilote S.M. 1759	
Marie Louise	Pierre Dupuis S.M. 1760	
Madeleine	Jean (Inconnu) S.M. 1761	
M. Elisabeth	Pierre Rousselot S.M. 1755	
M. Elisabeth	2° Michel Frs. Magnac	S.M. 1757
M. Elisabeth	3° Chs. Frs. De la Hamsay	S.M. 1759
Joseph		
Ignace		
Pierre		
Augustin		
4 Joseph	(1) Angé Lebrun S.V. 1721	
Thérèse	Jos. Veau S.V. 1746	
Angélique	Jacq. Corriveau S.V. 1747	
Marie Thérèse	Jos. Veau S.V. 1750	
Marie	Pierre Roy S.V. 1750	
Marguerite	Aug. Marseau S.V. 1765	
M. Geneviève	Pierre Gosselin S.V. 1762	
M. Geneviève	2° Aug. Roy S.V. 1784	
Joseph		
Louis		
Pierre		
5 Michel	(2) Angé Lacroix S.M. 1739	
M. Angélique	Noel Asselin S.M. 1756	
Jean Baptiste		
Le même	M. Genev. Gosselin	S.V. 1775
6 Joseph	(2) Fse. Régis Delaire B. 1740	
7 Jean	(2) Agathe Morriset S.M. 1747	
Jean		
8 Augustin	(2) M. Cath. Lacroix	S.M. 1754
M. Catherine	Jos. Balan S.M. 1787	
Marie Josette	André Aubé S.M. 1792	
Joseph		
Augustin		
Michel		
9 Louis	(2) M. Anne Delaire S.J. 1755	
Marie	Frs. Dumas S.Chs. 1780	
10 Joseph	(3) Fse. Goupy S.M. 1746	
Joseph		
11 Ignace	(3) M. Ls. Terrien S.M. 1750	
Marie Louise	Chs. Poiré S.V. 1776	

GAUTRON—LAROCHELLE.

Laurent				
Louis				
Ignace				
12 Pierre	(3)	Louise Cochon	S.J.	1755
Marie Louise		Guill Fradet	S.M.	1781
Marguerite		Pierre Quéret	S.M.	1790
Jean Baptiste				
Michel				
13 Augustin	(3)	Genev. Simort	S.M.	1765
14 Joseph	(4)	Eliz. Roy	S.V.	1744
Joseph				
15 Louis	(4)	M. Claire Isabel Bert.		1765
Marguerite		Raphael Tangué	S.V.	1792
Ignace				
Louis				
Jean				
16 Pierre	(4)	M. Mad. Daniau	S.F.S.	1767
Marie Anne		Jaq. Baudouin	S.F.S.	1788
M. Madeleine		Frs. Roy	S.F.S.	1792
Pélagie		Pierre Fournier	S.F.S.	1795
Pierre				
17 Jean Bapt.	(5)	Josette Fleury	S.V.	1782
Marie Rose		Frs. Brisson	S.M.	1803
Marie Josette		J. B. Goupy	S.M.	1805
Apolline		Ant. Fournier	S.M.	1816
Michel				
Augustin				
Le même		M. Angé Roy	S.M.	1804
Julie		Jacq. Mercier	S.M.	1845
Paul				
Charles				
18 Jean Baptiste	(7)	Ursule Roy	S.V.	1775
Thérèse		Ls. Coüet	S.M.	1810
Thérèse		2° J. B. Gosselin	S.M.	1832
Marguerite		J. B. Chamberlan	S.M.	1803
Marguerite		2 Frs. Forbes	S.M.	1843
Marie Anne		Robert Racine		
Marie Anne		2° Jean Bacquet	S.M.	1823
Marie		Laurent Noel	S.G.	1806
Ursule		Jos. Clément	S.H.	1804
19 Joseph	(8)	M. Jos. Balan	S.V.	1787
Marie Josette		Ignace Ruel	S.M.	1804
Victoire		J. B. Blais	S.V.	1813
Joseph				
Le même		Angèle Brousseau	S.M.	1834
20 Augustin	(8)	Genev. Clément	S.Chs.	1774
Marie Anne		Jean Coté	S.M.	1805
Angelique		Ant. Labrecque	S.H.	1 09
Augustin				
Joseph				
21 Pierre		Marie Clément	Qué.	
Joseph				
Pierre				
22 Michel	(8)	M. Ls. Bolduc	S.V.	1790
Marguerite		Pierre Forgue	S.V.	1814
Marie Cécile		Jean Boucher	S.V.	1818
Marie		Ls. Roberge	S.V.	1818
Archange		Michel Tangué	S.V.	1825
Michel				
Joseph				
23 Joseph	(10)	M. Angé Lacroix	S.M.	1775
Felix				
Le même		M. Jos. Emond	S.M.	1788
Louise		Chs. Terrien	S.G.	1806
Marguerite		Etn. Terrien	S.G.	1829
Joseph				
24 Ignace	(11)	Louise Guenet	S.Chs.	1784
25 Laurent	(11)	Marthe Gosselin	S.V.	1787
26 Louis	(11)	M. Fse. Roy	»	1792
M. Marguerite		Etn. Mercier	»	1816
Le même		Marg. Langlois	»	1814

GAUTRON—LAROCHELLE.

27 Michel	(12)	M. Anne Pilote	S.H.	1794
Marie Anne		Henri Labrecque	S.G.	1819
Charlotte		Aug. Monmeny	»	1824
Michel				
28 Jean Bap- tiste	(12)	M. Fse. Fortin	S.V.	1787
M. Françoise		Jos. Roy	S.M.	1809
Marguerite		Pierre Fortier	S.M.	1820
Josette		Frs. Gosselin	»	1821
Christine		Michel Lacroix	»	1831
Angèle		Sauveur Dupré	S.M.	1840
Antoine				
Joseph				
François				
Jean Baptiste				
29 Joseph	(14)	M. Ls. Blondeau	S.V.	1766
Marie Louise		Ant. Fleury	S.V.	1790
30 Ignace	(15)	M. Archange Tangué	S.V.	1802
Archange		Félix Fleury	S.V.	1823
Henriette		Simon Blais	»	1829
Henriette		2° J. B. Fontaine	S.V.	1841
M. Marcelline		Ign. Gosselin	»	1835
Séraphine		Jean Marie Roy	»	1840
Ignace				
Thomas				
François Régis				
31 Louis	(15)	M. Jos. Roy	S.M.	1805
Laurent				
32 Jean	(15)	Euphrosine Tangué	S.V.	1807
Archange		Frs. Couture	S.Chs.	1840
Marcelline		Jean Blais	»	1846
M. Charlotte		David Blais	»	1848
33 Pierre	(16)	Eliz. Corriveau	S.V.	1791
Angélique		André Fradet	S.G.	1818
Elizabeth		Benoni Gagnon	»	1828
Pierre				
34 Michel	(17)	Marg. Helie	S.M.	1823
Désanges		Chs. Lacasse	»	1839
Michel Edouard				
35 Augustin	(17)	Josette Isabel	S.V.	1824
Luce		F. X. Aubé	S.V.	1850
Euphrosine		Tho. Marseau	S.V.	1853
Augustin				
36 Paul	(17)	Julie Asselin	S.M.	1837
37 Charles	(17)	Ursule Roy	S.M.	1839
ⁿ Augustin	(20)	Fse. Canac	S.H.	1800
38 Joseph	(20)	Genev. Labrecque	B.	1819
ⁿ Pierre	(21)	Genev. Nadeau	S.H.	1812
39 Joseph	(21)	Marg. Fortier	S.L.	1819
40 Joseph	(19)	M. Jos. Mercier	S.M.	1812
Marie Josette		Jos. Chamberlan	S.M.	1832
Sophie		Jos. Lebel	S.M.	1832
Sophie		2° Michel Cotin	S.M.	1835
Abeline		Laurent Goupy	S.M.	1840
Honoré				
Le même		M. Théotiste Goupy	S.M.	1833
41 Michel	(22)	Judithe Forgue	S.G.	1814
Le même		Fse. Arseneau	S.G.	1829
42 Joseph	(22)	Marie Rouleau	S.G.	1823
Sophie		Ls. Mercier	S.V.	1851
Catherine		Jos. Gosselin	S.V.	1854
Constance		Alexandre Pouliot	S.V.	1854
Philomène		Etn. Labrecque	S.V.	1854
43 Félix	(23)	Fse. Emond	Bert	1798
Angélique		Ls. Bacquet	S G.	1823
Marguerite		Mag. Bacquet	S.G.	1826
Félix				
Antoine				
44 Joseph	(23)	M. Angé Guay	Lévis	1816
45 Michel	(27)	Marie Fradet	S.G.	1828
46 Antoine	(28)	Cath. Cochon	S.M.	1816

GAUTRON—LAROCHELLE.

47 François   (28) Lucie Marseau S.V. 1818
   Luce   Frs.Dupont   S.M. 1844
   M. Marg.   F.X. Turgeon S.M.1854
   Désanges
   Louis David
   Jos. Philibert
   Joseph
49 Joseph   (28) Archange Fradet S.M.1822
49 Augustin   (28) Adé Samson S.H.
   François
   Augustin
50 JeanBaptiste(28) Marg. Roy   S.M. 1810
   Marie   Ls. Tangué   S.Chs. 1848
   François Xavier
   Jean Baptiste
   Louis
   Thomas
51 Ignace   Olive Rémillard S.V. 1831
52 Thomas   (30) M.Rose Blais S.V. 1834
53 Frs. Félix de
   Valois (30) M.Zoe Boutin S.V. 1841
54 Laurent   (31) Henriette Pepin S.M. 1839
   Anne Aurélie   Tho. Pre Aug. Couillard
                                   S.M. 1856
   M. Henriette
   Odile Héloise Frs. Aug.Annibal
                        Bacquet 1856
55 Pierre   (33) Scolastique Couture S.G.
                                   1824
56 Michel   (34) Flavie Denis S.M. 1848
   Edouard
57 Augustin   (35) Archange Fleury S.V.1852
58 Honoré   (40) Josette Leclaire S.M. 1851
59 Antoine   (44) Anastasie Hamel S.G.1827
60 Félix   (44) Fse. Denis   S.G. 1830
61 Ls. David   (47) M. Suzarie Bissonnet S.M.
                                   1851
62 Joseph   (47) M. Eliz. Boissonneau B.
                                   S.H. 1821
63 Jos. Philibert(47) M. Irmine Turgeon B. 1852
64 François   (49) Philomène Labrecque B.
                                   1858
65 Augustin   (49) Angèle Bernier S.Chs. 1849
66 Jean   (50) Angé Picard S.Chs. 1835
   Baptiste
   J. B. Nazaire
67 Louis   (50) Marcelline Lebrun S.Chs.
                                   1836
68 Thomas   (50) Marie Bilodeau S.Chs.1840
69 Frs. Xavier (50) Emélie Roy   S.M. 1845
70 Laurent   (54) M. Marg. Eliz. Gourdeau
   Edouard   S.M. 1864
71 J. B. Nazaire(66) Restitut Salomé Coulombe
                                   S.Chs. 1862

GENDREAU.

1 Pierre   Jeanne Grenier C.R. 1665
  Catherine   Jacq. Deleugré C.R. 1688
  Jacques
2 Jacques   (1) M. Anne Dalret S.P. 1691
  Marie Anne   Jos. Gaudreau S.L. 1730
  Genev. Louise   Pierre Moor   S.L. 1724
  Julien
  Jean Baptiste
  Jacques
  Pierre
3 Jacques   (2) Isabelle Dandurand S.Tho.
  Jacques   1722
  Louis
A Pierre   (2) Louise Rolandeau S.Tho.
                                   1724
4 Julien   (2) Anne Chabot   S.L. 1728
  Marie Anne   Ant. Coulombe S.L. 1767
  Marie Jeanne   Ign. Bouffart S.L. 1775
  Gertrude   Pierre Noël Turcot S.L.1774
  Gertrude   2° Ls. Pichet S.J. 1794

GENDREAU.

  Julien Louis
  Antoine
5 Jean Baptiste(2) M. Cath. Dalaire S.Frs.
                                   1742
  M. Catherine   Pierre Noël Charlan S.L.
                                   1772
  Marie   Louis Bazin   S.L. 1773
  Marie Anne   Marc. Audet   S.L. 1778
  Joseph
  Louis
  Jean
6 Jacques   (3) M. Anne Gagné S.F.S.1751
7 Louis   (3) M. Genev. Dubreuil S.F.S.
                                   1754
  Le même   M. Anne Terrien S.F.S.
                                   1758
8 Julien Louis (4) Marg. Leclaire S.L. 1765
  Marguerite   Ign. Lefrançois S.L. 1786
  Gertrude   Tho. Laurent Bédard S.L.
                                   1786
  Marie   Jos. Langlois S.L. 1791
  Marie Cécile   Pierre Hébert S.L. 1792
  Julien
  Pierre
9 Antoine   (4) Mad. Filteau   B. 1779
10 Joseph   (5) Marie Lepage S.Frs. 1778
   Catherine   Guill. Pepin   S.L. 1810
   M. Madeleine   J. B. Lessart S.L. 1812
   Le même   Marie Marseau S.J. 1796
11 Louis   (5) Louise Pepin
12 Jean   (5) M. Angé Nolin S.L. 1790
   Marie Félicité Jean Ferlant   S.P. 1852
   Louis
13 Julien   (8) M. Angé Pichet S.P. 1791
   Angélique   Alexis Coté   S.L. 1819
   Rosalie   Chs. Cote   S.L. 1831
   Julien
   Louis
14 Pierre   (8) M. Anne Crépeau S.P.1801
15 Louis   (12) Dorothée Ferlant S.P. 1831
   Le même   Marthe Coté   S.P. 1837
16 Julien   (13) Marie Pouliot S.T. 1823
   Marie   Jean Goulet   S.L. 1847
   Marie   2° F. X. Hudon
   Rose   Pierre Brousseau S.L. 1855
   Cécile   Theophile Leclaire S.L.
                                   1865
   Julien
   Pierre
17 Julien   (13) Ursule Leclaire S.L. 1825
   Marie Esther   David Gosselin S.L. 1847
   Ursule   Frs. Ferd. Thivierge S.L.
                                   1852
   Scolastique   Damase Guay   S.L. 1855
   Louis
18 Julien   (16) Eugénie Leclaire S.L. 1854
   M. Delphine   Jos. Onésime Plante S.L.
                                   1880
   Julien
19 Pierre   (16) Marie Pouliot S.J. 1857
20 Louis   (17) Louise Campagna S.Frs.
                                   1855
21 Julien   (18) Desneiges Plante S.L. 1881
22 Jacques   Marth. Thips
   Jean Baptiste
23 Jean   (23) M. Modeste Proulx S.Tho.
   Baptiste   1802
   Prudent
   Prudent   (23) Théodore Bouchard S.P.
                                   1837

GENDRON.

1 Nicolas   Marie Hubert   Que. 1656
  Marie Marthe   Pierre Sylvestre S.F.1685
  Jacques
  Pierre

GENDRON.

```
 2 Jacques        M. Anne Charlan      S.F.1686
   Anne           Jean Létourneau      S.J.1715
   Joseph
   François
   Gabriel
   Augustin
 3 Pierre         Marie Thivierge      S.F.1694
   Elizabeth      Guill. Beaucher   "  1726
   Marie          Gab. Faucher      "  1734
   Marguerite     Aug. Turcot       "  1741
   Joseph
 4 Joseph     (2) Genev. Asselin      S.F.S.1715
   Elizabeth      Jean Emond          S.F.S.1741
   Geneviève      Jean Emond          S.Frs.1748
   Marie Anne     Michel Chabot       S.F.S.1740
   Marie Anne     2°Jacq. Alexandre "  1763
   Hélène         F.X. Peltier        S.F.S.1750
   Agathe         J. B. Boulet      "  1750
   Jacques
   Joseph
   Le même        Fse. Emond     Bert. 1730
   M. Françoise   Pierre Garant       S.F.S.1749
   Augustin
 5 François    (2) Marie Bilodeau     S.Frs.1726
   Marie Agnès    Robert Boulet   Bert.1748
   Marie          Alexandre Garant "  1749
   Marie Claire   Ls. Leroux          S.F.S.1764
   Louise         Chs. Jolivet     "  1765
   Jacques
   Joseph
 6 Gabriel        Eliz. Bilodeau      S.Frs.1728
   Elizabeth      Jos. Meneux         S.F.1744
 7 Joseph      (3) Angé Beaucher      S.Frs.1725
   Marie          Pierre Turcot    "  1749
   Angélique      Frs. Godbout     "  1751
 8 Augustin    (2) M. Anne Gaumont
                                     S.Chs.1740
   Marguerite     Jacq. Côté          S.F.S.1762
   Marie Agathe   Jos. Martin      "  1762
   M. Madeleine   Frs. Coulombe    "  1767
   Joseph
 9 Joseph      (4) M. Jos. Ainse      S.Tho.1742
   Isaac
10 Jacques     (4) Thérèse Audet      B.1743
   Marie Thérèse  Pierre Vic. Boissonneau
                                     S.F.S.1763
   Marie Anne     Jacq. Morin      "  1765
   Marie Reine    Jacq. Picard     "  1770
   Jacques
   François
11 Augustin    (4) Anne Picard        S.P.S.1757
12 Jacques     (5) Fse. Mercier       S.F.S.1761
   Paschal
   Jacques
   Joseph
13 Joseph      (5) M.Jeanne Dion      S.F.S.1762
14 Joseph      (8) Marg. Ternien   "  1761
   Le même        Scolastique Baudoin
                                     S.F.S.1773
   Modeste        Pierre Guenet       S.H.1800
   Geneviève      J. B. Carrier    "  1805
15 Frs. Isaac  (9) Fse. Proulx        S.Tho.1775
   Joseph
16 Jacques    (10) M. Angé Morin      S.F.S.1774
   Marie          Jacq. Lessart    "  1799
   Jacques
17 François   (10) Claire Thivierge "  1783
   Le même        M. Jos. Simoneau "  1794
18 Jacques    (12) Thérèse Asselin    S G.1785
   Marguerite     Jos. Corriveau      S.M.1814
   Angèle         Ls. Kéroack      "  1815
   Jacques
19 Paschal    (12) Marg. Côté         S.Chs.1789
   Marguerite     Jean Parant         S.H.1819
   Laurent
   Pierre
18—22
```

GENDRON.

```
20 Joseph     (12) M. Marthe Talbot
                                     S.P.S.1793
   M. Françoise   Frs. Rouleau        S.F.S.1813
   Marie Josette  Jean Frs. Picard "  1815
   Marie Anne     Jos. Picard      "  1817
   Marie Olive    Simon Prudent Lecomte
                                     S.F.S.1824
   Narcisse
   Jacques
   Joseph
   Le même        M. Ls. Thibault S.F.S.1813
21 Joseph     (15) Fse. Proulx        S.Tho.1808
   Joseph
22 Jacques    (16) M. Anne Ruel       S.Chs.1800
   Marie Anne     René Morin          S.F.S.1823
   Marguerite     Jos. Prudent Boulet
                                     S.F.S.1825
   Soulange       Simon Paré       "  1827
   Restitut       Benoit Morin     "  1834
   Jos. Prudent
   Jean
   François Xavier
23 Antoine        Mad. Filteau
   Le même        Fse. Adam           S.M.1822
24 Jacques    (18) Cath. Denis     "  1816
   Marcelline     Jean Samson      "  1841
   Jacques
25 Pierre     (19) Cath. Mercier      S.H.1814
26 Laurent    (19) Marg. Proulx       S.F.S.1844
27 Jacques    (20) Genev. Goulet      S.G.1823
28 Joseph     (20) Marg. Alaire       S.F.S.1823
29 Narcisse   (20) Marcelline Alaire  S.V.1831
30 Joseph     (21) Reine Fournier     S.F.S.1843
31 Jean       (22) Julie Bernier   "  1839
32 Jos Prudent (22) M. Constance Boulet
                                     S.F.S.1839
33 François Xa-(22) M. Edna Eliz. Domini
   vier                              S.F.S.1844
34 Jacques    (24) Angèle Bissonnet   S.M.1840
```

GENEST-LABARRE

```
 1 Jacques        Cath. Doribeau
   Anne           Ls. Ouimet          S.F. 1693
   Marie          J. B. Martin        S.P. 1710
   Pierre
   Charles
   Jacques
 2 Charles     (1) Marie Mourier      S.J. 1699
   Marie          François Langlois dit St-
                    Jean              S.J. 1719
   Josette        Jos. Jahan       "  1747
   Louise         Barth. Terrien   "  1748
   Laurent
 3 Jacques     (1) M. Fse. Huot
 4 Pierre      (1) Marie Maury
   Laurent
 5 Pierre      (2) Rose Marchand
   Marie Louise   Jos. Morisset       S.J. 1759
   M. Madeleine   Jean Perrot      "  1775
   Marie Josette  Jos. Leblond        S.M. 1765
   François
 6 Laurent     (2) Louise Riopel      A.G. 1749
   Marie Louise   Jos. Leclaire       S.J. 1772
   Marie Anne     Laurent Mauvide  "  1781
   Marguerite     Jos. Mercier     "  1786
   Laurent
   François
   Jean Baptiste
   Jacques
   Joseph
 7 Louis          Eliz. Miraux
   Elizabeth      Jacq. Genest        S.J. 1799
   Louis
   Le même        M. Jos. Pepin    "  1787
   Marguerite     J. B. Paradis       S.P. 1811
```

GENEST—LABARRE.

	Joseph		
8	François	(5) M. Vict. Leclaire	S.J. 1768
	Victoire	Boniface Aubé	S.Chs.1791
	Angélique	Ant. Gosselin	„ 1796
	M. Madeleine	Jacq. Pénin	„ 1815
	François		
	Jacques		
	Joseph		
	Louis		
	Le même	Marg. Couture	S.Chs.1795
	Marie Anne	Frs. Gontier	„ 1821
	Geneviève	F. X. Roy	„ 1831
	Marie	Philippe Vien	B. 1848
	Michel		
	Le même	Marie Lemelin	S.Chs.1815
9	Laurent	(6) Eliz. Mercier	„ 1777
	Le même	Fse. Chabot	„ 1814
10	Joseph	(6) M. Anne Demers	S.H. 1786
	Marie Anne	Frs. Turcot	S.J. 1831
	Laurent		
	Joseph		
11	Jean Baptiste	(6) Genev. Turgeon	S.Chs.1793
12	François	(6) Josette Turgeon	„ 1793
	Marie	F. X. Larue	S.J. 1814
	Marie	2° Ls. Blais	„ 1818
	Marguerite	Ant. Lefebvre	S.H.
	Josette	Etn. Vermet	„
	Angèle	Ign. Roberge	„
	Rosalie	Chs. Collet	„
	Laurent		
	François		
	Antoine		
	Joseph		
	Charles		
	Louis		
13	Jacques	(6) Éliz. Genest	S.J. 1799
	Elizabeth	Pierre Bonneau	S.P. 1821
14	Louis	(7) M. Jos. Fortier	S.J. 1801
	Madeleine	Jos. Létourneau	„ 1841
	Adelaïde	Isaac Tremblay	S.F. 1831
15	Joseph	(7) Marie Gourdeau	S.P. 1825
16	François	(8) Marg. Mercier	S.M. 1801
	Marguerite	Jos. Denis	S.L. 1832
	Amable		
	François		
	Le même	Thérèse Dalaire	S.G. 1812
17	Louis	(8) Josette Dalaire	S.H. 1803
	Louis		
18	Joseph	(8) Josette Samson	
			Lévis 1819
19	Jacques	(8) Delphine Vien	S.Chs.1821
	Sophie	Etn. Couture	„ 1853
	Jacques		
20	Michel	(8) Reine Marcoux	„ 1832
	M. Eléonore	Ferd. Naud	„ 1856
	Le même	Agnès Pelchat	„ 1856
21	Joseph	(10) Marie Chabot	„ 1813
	Edouard		
22	Laurent	(10) Angé Patoine	S.G. 1820
23	Pierre	Justine McNeil	
	Angèle	Chs. Gauvreau	S.M. 1844
	Edouard		
24	Joseph	Marg. Hallé	
	Louis		
25	Pierre	Vict. Lafond	
	Esther	Pierre Chabot	S.G. 1830
26	François Xa-vier	(12) Luce Chabot	S. Chs. 1823
27	Charles	(12) Marg. Boulé	S.V. 1833
28	Louis	(12) Angèle Lacasse	B. 1834
29	Antoine	(12) Archange Collet	
30	Joseph	(12) Césarie Collet	
31	Laurent	(12) Olympe Nadeau	
32	François	(16) Constance Noël	S.M. 1842
	Le même	Marg. Morisset	S.M. 1850
33	Amable	(16) Rebecca Vaillancour	
			S.M. 1842

GENEST—LABARRE.

34	Louis	(17) M.Marg. Boutin	S.V. 1824
35	Jacques	(19) Adé Roy	S. Chs. 1843
36	Edouard	(21) Cath. Brochu	S.V. 1842
37	Edouard	(23) Brigitte Noël	S.P. 1840
	M. Philomène	Chs. Geo. Honoré Gourdeau	S.P. 1866
	M. Belzémire	Pre. Siméon Daniau	S.P. 1866
38	Louis	(24) Delphine Simard	S.J. 1861

GIGUÈRE.

1	Robert	Aimée Miville	Que. 1652
	Anne	Pierre Poulin	S.Anne 1689
	Agnès	Chs. Canac	S. Anne 1698
	Agnès	2 Jos. Bilodeau	
	Joseph		
2	Joseph	(1) Angé Mercier	S.Anne 1698
	Chrétien		
	Joseph		
	Charles		
3	Joseph	(2) Marg. Racine	S.Anne 1722
	Angélique	Aug. Faucher	S.F. 1745
	M. Madeleine	Ls. Nadeau	S.F. 1757
	Marguerite	André Lombard	S.F. 1762
	Marguerite	2° J.B. Lamothe	S.F. 1792
	Michel		
	Joseph		
	Etienne		
4	Charles	(2) Anne Guion	S.F. 1720
	Pierre		
	Charles		
A	Chrétien	(2) Dorothée Racine	S. Anne 1752
	Josette	Ignace Caron	S. Anne 1754
	Ignace		
5	Joseph	(3) Marie Turcot	S.F. 1753
	Joseph		
	Le même	M. Mad. Canac	S.F. 1763
	Pierre		
6	Etienne	(3) M. Cath. Ratte	S.P. 1756
	Angélique	Pre. Chrysostome Deblois	S.F. 1780
	Martin		
	Joseph		
	Ignace		
	Jean Baptiste		
7	Michel	(3) M. Genev. Canac	S.F.1763
	Geneviève	Ls. Chatigny	S.F. 1787
	Geneviève	2° Pierre Drouin	S.F. 1788
	Marie-Louise	Jos. Létourneau	S.F. 1798
	Marie Claire	Jos. Leblond	S.F. 1828
	Le même ?	Thérèse Chatigny	S.P.1779
	François		
8	Pierre	(4) M. Fse. Quéret	S.M. 1773
	Marie	Jean Dutile	S.G. 1799
9	Charles	(4) Mad. Chabot	S. Chs. 1769
10	Ignace	(4) a M. Mad. Morel	S. Anne 1777
	Joseph		
11	Joseph	(5) M.Anne Faucher	S.F.1792
	Marie Anne	Pierre Leroux	S.P. 1819
	Le même	M.Judithe Canac	S.F.1797
	Benoit		
	Joseph		
12	Pierre	(5) Genev. Pageot	S.F. 1792
	Geneviève	Ant. Gérard	S.F. 1815
	Marie	Ls. Couture	S.F. 1829
	Pierre		
13	Joseph	(6) Cécile Cochon	S.J. 1794
	Madeleine	Frs. Demeule	S.J. 1814
	Angèle	Jos. Pepin	S.J. 1817
	Archange	Jean Marie Labbé	S.J. 1826
	Catherine	Etn. Dalaire	S.J. 1835
	Justine	Jean Pepin	S.F. 1825
	Pierre		
	Joseph		
	François		

GENEST—LABARRE.

14	Jean Baptiste (6)	M. Ls. Cochon	S.J.	1798
	Marguerite	Ls. Lamothe	S.F.	1847
	Isaac			
	Jean Baptiste			
	Etienne			
	François			
15	Ignace (6)	M. Mad. Bidet	S.J.	1798
16	Martin (6)	Mad. Cochon	S.J.	1801
	Madeleine	Ls. Plante	S.J.	1823
	Marie	2° Lazare Cameron		
			S. Frs.	1838
	Marie	Jean Boissonneau	S.J.	1827
	Marie Angèle	Jos. Boissonneau	S.J.	1827
	Magloire			
	Martin			
	Joseph			
17	François (7)	Marie Vaillancour	S.F.	1811
	François Xavier			
	Edouard			
	Joseph			
18	Joseph (10)	Marie Mercier	S.Anne	1814
	Côme			
19	Joseph (11)	Marg. Gosselin	S.F.	1826
20	Benoit (11)	Sophie Roberge	S.P.	1848
21	Pierre (12)	Genev. Thivierge	S.J.	1826
	Le même	Théotiste Hélie	S.F.	1832
	Théotiste	Jean Dalaire	S.F.	1855
	Louis Cyrille			
	François Xavier			
22	Joseph (13)	Cath. Pepin	S.F.	1825
23	François (13)	Angèle Labbé	S.Frs.	1828
24	Pierre (13)	Marie Lessard	S.Frs.	1836
	Cécile	Pierre Coulombe	S.Frs.	1861
25	Jean Baptiste (14)	Angèle Blouin	S.J.	1824
	Bruno			
	Jean Baptiste			
26	Etienne (14)	Scolastique Racine		
			S.F.	1833
	Hombeline	Flavien Drouin	S.F.	1861
27	Isaac (14)	Angèle Turcotte		
			S.Joa.	1834
	François Philéas			
	Jean Baptiste			
28	François (14)	Soulange Lainé	S.J.	1835
29	Martin (16)	M. Eliz. Boissonneau		
			S.J.	1827
	Anatalie	Jos. Royer	S.J.	1846
30	Joseph (16)	Adé Plante	S.J.	1832
	Clément			
31	Magloire (16)	Marg. Paradis	S.F.	1836
32	François (17)	Adé Foucher	S.F.	1839
	Xavier			
	Philomene	F. X. Létourneau	S.F.	1858
	Philomène	2° Frs. Pouliot	S.F.	1863
	Adélaide	F. X. Pouliot	S.F.	1866
	François Xavier			
33	Edouard (17)	Adé Roberge	S.F.	1840
34	Joseph (17)	Henriette Leclaire		
			S.V.	1847
35	Côme (18)	Josette Guérard		
			S.Anne	1838
	Chrysostome			
36	François (21)	Marie Pouliot	S.J.	1864
	Xavier			
37	Louis Cyrille (21)	M. Délima Turcot	S.F.	1869
38	Bruno (25)	Justine Lamothe	S.F.	1854
39	Jean Baptiste (25)	Luce Lamothe	S.F.	1850
40	Jean Baptiste (27)	Philomène Asselin	S.F.	1860
41	François (27)	M. Eléonore Canac		
	Philéas		S.F.	1862
42	Clément (30)	Adé Moor	S.J.	1853
43	François (32)	M. Malvina Létour-		
	Xavier	neau	S.F.	1866
44	Chrysostome (35)	Rosalie Couture	S.Frs.	1861

18—22½

GINCHEREAU.

1	Louis	Marie Marié	S.F.	1673
	Isabelle	Jacq. Marseau	S.Frs.	1694
	Pierre			
	Jean Baptiste			
2	Pierre (1)	Hélène Paquet	Qué.	1698
3	Jean Baptiste (1)	M. Marg. Buisson		
			Qué.	1698
	Dorothée	J. B. Gatien	S.Frs.	1723
	Agathe	Michel Emond	S.Frs.	1728
	Le même	Anne Civadier	S.L.	1703
4	Jean Baptiste	M. Thérèse Canac	S.F.	1719
	Joseph			
5	Joseph (4)	Thérèse Lheureux	S.F.	1749
	Augustin			
6	Augustin (5)	Ursule Baudoin	S.Frs.	1779
	Victoire	Pierre Lainé	S.Frs.	1812
	Ursule	Frs. Nadeau	S.Frs.	1814
	Catherine	Ls. Lemelin	S.Frs.	1817
	Madeleine	Jos. Lemelin	S.Frs.	1822
	Marie	Guil. Fortier	S.Frs.	1822
	Marguerite	Alexis Coulombe	S.J.	1827
	Augustin			
	Joseph			
	Jean			
7	Augustin (6)	M. Jos. Nadeau	S.Frs.	1802
	Josette	Ls. Maufait	S.Frs.	1834
	Emélie	Prisque Cloutier	S.Frs.	1849
	Marie Louise	Pre. Célestin Gagnon		
			S.Frs.	1859
	Jean Baptiste			
8	Joseph (6)	Marg. Lainé	S.J.	1811
	Julie	Frs. Lepage	S.Frs.	1841
	M. Catherine	Michel Audet	S.Frs.	1841
	Sophie	Ls. Fontaine	S.Frs.	1849
	M. Madeleine	Ls. Renvoigé	S.Frs.	1856
	Jean			
	Louis			
9	Jean (6)	Marg. Picard	S.F.	1826
	Jean			
10	Jean Baptiste (7)	Marie Emond	S.Frs.	1859
11	Jean (8)	M. Vict. Fortier	S.Frs.	1841
12	Louis (8)	Eléonore Dion	S.Frs.	1862
13	Jean (9)	Eléonore Noël	S.L.	1855

GIRARD.

1	Joachim	Marie Hallé	Qué.	1660
	Jacques			
	Le même	Jeanne Chalu	Qué.	1676
	Joachim			
2	Jacques (1)	Mathurin Poiré		1692
	Catherine	René Patry	B.	1721
	M. Charlotte	Chs. Couture	"	1739
	Françoise	Ls. Couture	"	1744
	Charles François			
	Louis			
	Joseph			
	Claude			
	Jean Baptiste			
3	Joachim (1)	M. Ls. Lefebvre	Qué.	1708
	Le même	Cath. Guay	"	1745
4	Jean Baptiste (2)	M. Anne Couillard	B.	1727
	Geneviève	Frs. Berlinguet	"	1749
	M. Charlotte	Nic. Boilard	"	1756
	Thérèse	Etn. Couture	"	1766
	Charles			
5	Charles Fran- (2)	Louise Duquet	Lévis	1733
	çois			
	Antoine			
	Charles			
6	Claude (2)	Susanne Guay	"	1736
	Joseph			
	Charles			
7	Louis (2)	M. Chs. Jourdain	"	1750
	Marie Josette	Pierre Roy	S. Chs.	1773

GIRARD.

Louis				
Le même		Marie Guénet	„	1764
8 Joseph	(2)	Mad. Marchand Lévis		1729
Françoise		Jean Marie Rouleau		
			S. Chs.	1773
Jean Baptiste				
9 Charles	(4)	M. Jos. Roy	B.	1750
Angélique		Nicolas Séguin	„	1782
Jean Baptiste				
10 Etienne Mot dit	Adrienne Mahan			
Girard			Ev. de Besançon	
Jos. Alexis				
11 Joseph Alexis	(10)	Angé Beaucher	B.	1759
Angélique		Aug. Cuvilier	„	1778
Joseph				
Jacques				
12 Charles	(5)	Susanne Aubert Lévis		1762
13 Antoine	(5)	Cath. Nadeau	„	1763
Marie		Marc Turcot	„	1795
Catherine		Jos. Gosselin S. Chs.		1795
14 Joseph	(6)	Marie Labrecque	B.	1763
Susanne		Jos. Boilard	„	1796
M. Charlotte		Etn. Paquet	„	1797
Marie		Pierre Patry	„	1782
Geneviève		Pierre Leclaire	S.G.	1791
Le même		Angé Leclaire	„	1796
15 Charles	(6)	Cath. Larrive	S.M.	1769
16 Jean Baptiste	(8)	Mad. Dupont	„	1769
17 Louis	(7)	Angé Guénet S. Chs.		1774
Marguerite		Michel Forgue	„	1816
Louis				
18 Antoine		Procule Lavoie		
			Eboulements	
Joseph				
19 Charles		M. Chs. Roy		
			Eboulements	
M. Charlotte		Pierre Fortier	B.	1792
20 Charles		Mad. Carrier		
			Lévis	
Charles				
Le même		Marie Fournier Lévis		1782
21 Jean Baptiste	(9)	Fse. Maranda	S.L.	1792
22 Joseph	(11)	Chs. Angé Roy	B.	1785
M. Chs. Angèle		Murdock McKenzie	B.	1807
Julie		Michel Turgeon	„	1812
Joseph				
Le même		M. Gén. Fournier		
			S.P.S.	1798
Geneviève		Chs. Turgeon	B.	1817
Madeleine		Jacq. Turgeon	„	1822
Héliodore				
23 Jacques	(11)	M. Jos. Boilard	„	1793
Adelaïde		Ant. Turgeon	„	1816
Adelaïde		2° Hubert Guay	„	1831
Jos. Benjamin		Jos. Prudent		
24 Louis	(17)	Marg. Gontier	S.G.	1800
Marguerite		Hubert Couture S.Chs.		1826
Susanne		Jos. Goulet	„	1835
Edouard				
Louis				
Ignace				
Le même		Josette Roy	S.M.	1822
25 Joseph	(18)	M. Anne Dion	B.	1790
Marie Anne		Basile David	S.J.	1812
26 Charles	(20)	Marg. Daniau	B.	1797
27 Joseph	(22)	M. Fse. Turgeon S.M.		1810
28 Héliodore	(22)	M. Mad. Mercier	B.	1830
Genev. Emelin		F. X. Paquet	„	1846
Célina		Honoré Nadeau	„	1858
29 Joseph Benjamin	(23)	Angé Turgeon	„	1815
Marie Luce		Jean Langlois	„	1835
30 Jos. Prudent	(23)	Louise Paquet	„	1838
31 Edouard	(24)	Adé Coté	„	1837
32 Ignace	(24)	Charlotte Lacroix S.G.		1830
33 Louis	(24)	M. Olive Nadeau	B.	1855

GIRARD.

34 Etienne		Angèle Ouvrand		
Célina		Etn. Roy	S. Chs.	1855
35 Joseph		Marg. Ménard		
M. Catherine		Jos. Bélanger	S.V.	1870
36 Gabriel		M. Fse. Turgeon		
Le même		Marg. Filteau	B.	1823

GOBEIL.

1 Jean		Jeanne Guiet		
Marie		Robert Vaillancour		1668
Françoise		Philippe Paquet		
Marguerite		Guill. Monmeny S.J.		1688
Barthélemi				
2 Barthélemi	(1)	Anne Dionne	S.F.	1697
Catherine		Michel Gosselin	S.J.	1717
Catherine		Jean Legaudie	S.J.	1745
Jean François				
Joseph				
Antoine				
Barthélemi				
3 Jean François	(2)	M. Fse. Gosselin	S.L.	1735
M. Françoise		Jos. Lepage	S.J.	1758
Jean François				
Louis				
Antoine				
Charles				
4 Joseph	(2)	M. Jos. Fortier	S.J.	1739
Barthélemi			S. Marie	
5 Antoine	(2)	M. Fse. Dupas		
M. Catherine		Jos. Terrien	S.J.	1768
6 Barthélemi	(2)	Marg. Thivierge		
M. Madeleine		Jos. Asselin	S.J.	1751
Marguerite		Jean Frs. Dufresne		
Marie		Gab. Audet	S.L.	1774
Barthélemi				1765
Antoine				
7 Antoine	(3)	Mad. Dufresne	S.L.	1778
Angèle		Ant. Pouliot	S.J.	1803
Antoine				
8 Jean François	(3)	M. Rose Fortier	S.J.	1773
9 Charles	(3)	M. Ls. Dufresne	S.J.	1780
10 Louis	(3)	Genev. Delisle	S.J.	1784
Marie		Henri Tardif	S.H.	1855
Marie Louise		Eustache Gautron		
			S.H.	1819
Jean				
Louis				
11 Barthélemi	(4)	M. Ls. Bilodeau	S.J.	1776
12 Barthélemi	(6)	M. Rose Dorval	S.P.	1764
Antoine				
13 Antoine	(6)	Angé Pouliot	S.J.	1772
Marie		Jos. Pouliot	S.J.	1800
Marie Josette		Ls. Terrien	S.J.	1800
Antoine				
14 Antoine	(7)	Marg. Pouliot	S.J.	1797
15 Jean	(10)	Romaine Belleau		
			Lévis	1817
A Louis	(10)	Angé Belleau	S.H.	1810
16 Antoine	(12)	Genev. Canac	S.F.	1793
Geneviève		Robert Carsonne	S.P.	1821
Marie Désanges		Pierre Dufresne	S.P.	1832
Antoine				
17 Antoine	(13)	Charlotte Curodeau		
			S.J.	1798
Josette		Pierre Pouliot	S.J.	1830
Antoine				
Jean				
Pierre				
18 Antoine	(16)	Scolastique Vaillancour		
			S.F.	1818
19 Antoine	(17)	Cécile Pepin	S.J.	1826
Cécile		Pierre Fontaine	S.J.	1851
Emélie		J.B. Emond	S.J.	1856
Antoine				

GOBEIL.

20	Jean	(17) Charlotte Gosselin	S.J. 1835
	Philomène	Félix Delisle	S.J. 1859
	Jean		
21	Pierre	(17) Justine Langlois	S.J. 1837
	Le même	Sophie Fournier	S.J. 1848
22	Antoine	(19) Eléonore Pouliot	S.J. 1850
23	Jean	(20) Flore Mignault	S.J. 1861

GODBOUT.

1	Nicolas	Marthe Bourgou^	Qué. 1662
	Marie	Jean Baillargeon	S.L. 1683
	Nicolas		
	Joseph		
	Antoine		
2	Nicolas	(1) Marg. Angé Lemelin	S.L. 1685
	Marie Louise	J. B. Audet	S.L. 1708
	Françoise	Jos. Gosselin	S.L. 1710
	M. Madeleine	Pierre Langlois	S.L. 1717
	Marie Anne	Geo. Dumas	S.L. 1725
	Marg. Angélique	Ant. Fontaine	S.L. 1728
	Geneviève	Jean Alexis Chevalier	S.L. 1729
	Marguerite	Ls. Pichet	S.P. 1730
	Thérèse	Ls. Pichet	S.P. 1757
	Jean		
	Joseph		
	Pierre		
	André		
	Louis		
	François		
3	Antoine	Marg. Labrecque	S.P. 1691
	Marguerite	Ign. Gosselin	S.L. 1714
	Antoine		
4	Joseph	(1) Marg. Manseau	S.L. 1700
	Marg. Angélique	Nic. Lefebvre	S.L. 1725
	Geneviève	Chs. Pouliot	S.L. 1727
	Madeleine	Nic. Marchand	S.L. 1736
	Jean		
5	Joseph	(2) M. Mad. Dorval	S.P. 1720
	Marie Josette	J.B. Manseau	S.P. 1751
	Pierre		
	Le même	M. Claire Chantal	S.P. 1743
6	Pierre	(2) Cath. Labrecque	S.L. 1723
	M. Madeleine	Chs. Lessart	S.L. 1752
	Geneviève	Pierre Coté	S.L. 1762
	Pierre		
	Jean		
	François		
7	Jean	(2) Louise Gautier	S.L. 1725
8	François	(2) M. Ls. Joly	Qué. 1733
	Louis		
9	André	(2) Mad. Choret	Qué. 1743
	Thècle Fse.	Ls. Nollet	Qué. 1775
10	Louis	(2) Agathe Lainé	Qué. 1760
11	Antoine	(3) Genev. Rouleau	S.L. 1721
	M. Geneviève	Vincent Jolicœur	S.L. 1752
	Marie Anne	Jean Labrecque	S.P. 1764
	Antoine		
	Pierre		
	Louis		
	François		
	André		
12	Jean	(4) Marie Pouliot	S.L. 1735
	Marie	Frs. Ruel	S.L. 1765
	Geneviève	Jean Gosselin	S.L. 1774
	Jean		
	Joseph		
	François		
13	Pierre	(5) Josette Couture	S.P. 1747
	Marie Thérèse	J. B. Beaulieu	S.P. 1762

GODBOUT.

	Pierre		
14	Pierre	(6) M. Anne Denis	S.L. 1751
	Agathe	Jos. Marie Blanchet	B. 1780
	Louise	Jacq. Greffart	S.G. 1787
	Pierre		
	Jacques		
15	François	(6) Angé Gendron	S.F. 1751
	Elisabeth	Frs. Dorval	S.F. 1787
	Marie Dorothée	J. B. Faucher	S.F. 1797
	Louise	Jean Frs. Réaume	C.R. 1794
	Joseph		
	Le même	Thérèse Charlan	S.F. 1783
	Le même	Fse. Tessier	S.L. 1798
16	Jean	(6) M. Jos. Ruel	S.L. 1753
	Marie Marthe	Jacq. Leroux	S.L. 1773
	Le même	M. Jos. Coté	S.L. 1775
17	Louise	(8) Josette Lacasse	S.Chs. 1771
	Le même	Angé Nadeau	S.Chs. 1792
		V. de Jos. Bissonnet	
18	Antoine	(11) M. Anne Leclaire	S.L. 1750
	Marie Anne	Ant. Langlois	S.L. 1773
	Geneviève	Pierre Pouliot	S.L. 1774
	Marie	Pierre Labrecque	S.L. 1785
	Charlotte	Ls. Labrecque	S.L. 1789
	Jean		
19	Pierre	(11) M. Anne Dufresne	S.L. 1755
	Marie Louise	Frs. Létourneau	S.L. 1783
	Marie Anne	Frs. Audet	S.L. 1786
	Françoise	Ls. Bouffart	S.L. 1799
	Geneviève	Ant. Rouleau	S.J. 1793
	François		
20	Louis	(11) Mad. Dufresne	S.L. 1757
	Madeleine	Pierre Coulombe	S.L. 1785
	Geneviève	Jos. Marie Pouliot	S.L. 1788
	Marie Anne	Guill. Cinqmars	S.L. 1796
	Marie Louise	Chs. Denis	S.L. 1798
	Antoine		
21	François	(11) M. Fse. Dion	S.F.S. 1764
22	André	(11) Marie Rousseau	Lévis 1776
	Josette	an Bte. Renaud	S.H. 1800
	Geneviève	Louis Blanchet	S.H. 1805
	Marguerite	Etienne Roberge	S.H. 1820
	Ignace		
23	François	M. Angé Brunet	Qué.
	François		
24	Jean	(12) Mad. Gosselin	S.L. 1773
	Marie Anne	Pierre Couture	S.G. 1802
	Madeleine	Jean Forgue	S.G. 1812
	Pierre		
	Jean Charles		
25	Joseph	(12) Marg. Baillargeon	S.L. 1773
	Marguerite	Jean Coté	S.G. 1794
	Marie	Etn. Roy	S.G. 1801
	Agathe	Etn. Rouillard	S.G. 1803
	Joseph		
26	François	(12) Louise Campeau	S.L. 1798
	Marie	Pierre Fortier	S.L. 1810
	Pierre		
	François		
27	Pierre	(13) M. Anne Leclaire	S.P. 1786
	Marie Anne	Louis Noël	S.P. 1809
	Pierre		
	Joseph		
	Jean		
	Alexis		
	Ambroise		
28	Pierre	(14) M. Jos. Pouliot	S.L. 1778

GODBOUT.

29 Jacques	(14)	M. Jos. Audet	S.L 1781
Marie Josette		Jacq. Daneau	S.G. 1816
Marie Josette		2° Jos. Lacasse	S.G. 1825
Antoine			
Joseph			
Pierre			
30 Joseph	(15)	M. Mad. Leclaire	
			S.L. 1786
31 Jean	(18)	Fse. Bouffart	S.L. 1789
Françoise		Chs. Campeau	S.L. 1818
Charlotte		Jos. Catellier	S.L. 1823
Cécile		Paul Pouliot	S.L. 1836
Jean			
Louis			
Antoine			
Pierre			
32 François	(19)	Angé Coulombe	S.L. 1808
33 Antoine	(20)	Génév. Denis	S.L. 1804
Marie Josette		Magl. Blouin	S.L. 1832
Scolastique		Gilbert Pouliot	„ 1846
Louis			
Antoine			
Laurent			
Jacques			
34 Ignace	(22)	Mad. Curodeau Lévis 1823	
35 François	(23)	M. Marg. Lemieux	
			S.V. 1808
Edouard			
Thomas			
36 Pierre	(24)	Marie Shinck	S.G. 1802
Marie		Marcel Audet	„ 1829
Pierre			
37 Jean Charles	(24)	Marg. Shinck	
Marguerite		Dieudonné Sylvestre	
			S.G. 1825
Jean			
Charles			
Pierre			
38 Joseph	(25)	Marie Goulet	„ 1809
39 François	(26)	Mad. Noël	S.L. 1810
Marie		J. B. Delisle	„ 1839
Louis			
Marc			
François			
40 Pierre	(26)	Fse. Labrecque	„ 1818
Françoise		Ed. Labrecque	„ 1846
Angélique		Isidore Labrecque	„ 1855
Pierre			
41 Pierre	(27)	Marg. Paradis	S.P. 1816
Marguerite		Laurent Gosselin	„ 1842
Marie Anne		Alexis Ferlant	„ 1846
Charles Alexis			
Pierre			
Joseph			
42 Jean	(27)	Marg. Aubin	„ 1819
Marie Emélie		Pierre Plante	„ 1844
Marguerite		Marcelline Vézina	„ 1847
Marie Célinie		Jos.Ferd.Leclaire	„ 1856
Jean Damase			
43 Joseph	(27)	Genev. Gosselin	„ 1831
			S.H.
Marie Adéline		Jos. Théophile Ferlant	
			S.P. 1862
44 Alexis	(27)	Julie Gauvreau	S.L. 1830
45 Ambroise	(27)	Eliz. Paradis	S.P. 1838
			S.H.
46 Antoine	(29)	Félicité Carbonneau	
			S.G. 1812
47 Joseph	(29)	Louise Bacquet	„ 1814
Louise		Gab. Lemelin	S.M. 1837
Le même		Cath. Bacquet	S.G. 1818
48 Pierre	(29)	Genev. Boulet	„ 1815
49 Jean	(31)	Marie Gosselin	S.L. 1818
50 Pierre	(31)	Cécile Gosselin	S.L. 1819
51 Louis	(31)	Angé Pouliot	„ 1823
52 Antoin	(31)	Thérèse Langlois	„ 1838

GODBOUT.

Le même		Mad. Lainé	S.J. 1848
Le même		Reine Lavertu	S.L. 1859
53 Louis	(33)	Marie Pouliot	„ 1835
		Lévis	
Marie		Chs. Coulombe	
Le même		Judith Bonneau	„ 1853
54 Laurent	(33)	Marg. Audet	„ 1841
55 Antoine	(33)	Henriette Dumas	„ 1844
Le même		Thérèse Goulet	„ 1848
Le même		Eliz. Théberge	S. Raphael
56 Jacques	(33)	Julie Terrien	S.J. 1849
57 Edouard	(35)	Louise Tangué	S.V. 1842
58 Thomas	(35)	Louise Tangué	Bert. 1842
59 Pierre	(36)	Josette Bacquet	S.G. 1825
60 Jean	(37)	Angé Patouel	„ 1824
61 Nicolas	(37)	M. Theotiste Garant	
			S.F.S. 1833
62 Pierre	(37)	Basilisse Goupy	S.M. 1859
63 François	(39)	Genev. Audet	S.L. 1838
Geneviève		Napoléon Dumas	„ 1864
Marie		Pierre Leclaire	„ 1868
Agnès		Théophile Leclaire	„
François Xavier			
David			
64 Louis	(39)	Apolline Fournier	„ 1851
M. Adéline		David Cinqmars	„ 1875
Le même		Cécile Roy	A.G. 1865
65 Marc	(39)	Olive Quemeneur	S.L. 1883
66 Pierre	(40)	Rosalie Langlois	„ 1850
67 Pierre	(41)	Marie Ferlant	S.P. 1846
68 Chs. Alexis	(41)	M. Léocadie Crépeau	
			S.P. 1847
69 Joseph	(41)	M.AdelinePichet	S.P. 1843
70 Jean Damase	(42)	Marcelline Coté	„ 1852
71 Jean		Caroline Rousseau	
			S. Roch
Le même		Mélanie Vézina	S.V. 1855
72 François	(63)	Martine Leclaire	S.L. 1864
Xavier			
73 David	(63)	M. Délima Leclaire	
			S.L. 1869

GONTIER.

1 Bernard		Marg. Paquet	Que. 1676
Marguerite		Ant. Hébert	„ 1701
Hélène		Tho. Lefebvre	„ 1707
Denis			
Jean Baptiste			
Le même		M. Fse. Forgue	B. 1698
2 Jean Baptiste	(1)	Genev. Le Roy	B. 1708
M. Geneviève		Chs. Lacasse	B. 1733
Geneviève		Pierre Boissonneau	B. 1740
Geneviève		2° J. B. Monmény	
			S.Chs. 1750
Pierre			
Jean Baptiste			
Etienne			
François			
Louis			
3 Denis	(1)	Ange Nadeau	B. 1714
Louise		Chs. Le Roy	B. 1734
Marie		Etn. Coté	B. 1739
Elizabeth		Michel Coté	B. 1747
M. Madeleine		Jos. Roy	B. 1741
M. Madeleine		2° Jean Custeau	S.Chs. 1768
Joseph			
Antoine			
4 Pierre	(2)	Marg. Lacasse	B. 1734
Marguerite		Chs. Roy	S.Chs. 1757
Marie		Etn. Duquet	„ 1767
Angélique		Gab. Duquet	„ 1773
Angélique		2° André Bacquet	„ 1781
Catherine		J. B. Paquet	„ 1773
Catherine		2° Paschal Mercier	
			S.G. 1796

GONTIER.

	Pierre			
5	Jean Baptiste	(2) Marie Lacasse	B.	1736
	Cécile	Jos. Duquet	S.Chs.	1767
	Véronique	J. B. Valière	„	1767
	Angélique	Etn. Guenet	„	1772
	Marguerite	Etn. Ferlant	„	1774
	Marguerite	2" Etn. Larrivé	„	1780
	Jean François			
	Joseph			
	Le même	Cath. Jourdain	S.Chs.	1759
	Le même	Cath. Leroux	„	1767
6	Louis	(2) Marie Couture	B.	1745
	Marie	Athanase Fradet		
			S.Chs.	1771
	Catherine	Ls. Nadeau	„	1774
	Catherine	2° Etienne dit Laverdiére		
			S.Chs.	1775
	Cécile	Frs. Turgeon	„	1783
	Théotiste	Pierre Boucher	„	1785
	Apolline	Chs. Nadeau	„	1788
	Louis			
	Jean			
	François			
7	Etienne	(2) M. Ls. Lis	B.	1746
	Louise	Frs. Gosselin	S.Chs.	1775
	Catherine	André Lemelin	„	1783
	Marie	J. B. Bilodeau	„	1791
	Gabriel			
	Etienne			
8	François	(2) M. Jos. Lis	B.	1747
	Le même	Reine Lemieux	S.Chs.	1753
	Reine	Jean Bacquet	„	1753
	Angélique	Chs. Bisson	„	1787
	François		„	1791
	Jean Baptiste			
	Etienne			
9	Nicolas	M. Jos. Turgeon·		
	Marie	Jean Lepage	S.Chs.	1786
	Charles			
	Nicolas			
	Le même	Fse. Goupy	S.M.	1765
	Le même	Agnès Thibaut	S.Chs.	1786
10	Joseph	Marie Leroux		
	Joseph			
11	Joseph	(3) M. Anne Lacrpix	S.M.	1749
12	Antoine	(3) Thérèse Denis	„	1754
13	Pierre	(4) Marie Paquet	S.Chs.	1779
	Marie	Jos. Nadeau	S.G.	1798
	Judith	Frs. Boulet	„	1815
	Adélaïde	Jos. Fournier	„	1821
	Pierre			
14	Jean François	(5) Cath. Guenet	S.Chs.	1761
	Catherine	Chs. Fournier	„	1783
	Agathe	Chs. Clément	„	1789
	Cécile	Michel Clément	„	1794
	Marguerite	André Labbé	„	1796
	Elie			
	Antoine			
15	Joseph	(5) Marg. Larrivé	S.M.	1772
	Marguerite	Ls. Girard	S.G.	1800
	Victoire	Michel Cloutier	„	1813
	Joseph			
	Jean			
	Pierre			
	Louis			
16	Louis	(6) Marie Marseau	S.Chs.	1777
17	Jean	(6) M. Jos. Rousseau		
			S.Chs.	1787
	Angèle	Ls. Audet	S.G.	1827
	Jean Baptiste			
	Michel			
	Louis			
	François			
	Magloire			
18	François	(6) M. Anne Hélie	S.M.	1802
	François			

GONTIER.

19	Gabriel	(7) M. Jos. Hélie	S.M.	1772
	Marie Josette	Jos. Chabot	S.Chs.	1812
	Antoine			
	François			
	Laurent			
20	Etienne	(7) Régis Couture	S.M.	1775
	Thérèse	Ant. Bréart	S.G.	1810
	Louise	Ls. Terrien	„	1811
	Etienne			
21	François	(8) M. Chs.Terrien	S.Chs.	1782
	Joseph			
22	Jean Baptiste	(8) Marie Goulet	S.Chs.	1786
	Marguerite	Amb. Lacasse	S.Chs.	1812
	Susanne	Barth. Rosa	S.J.	1888
	Rémi			
	Louis			
	Jacques			
	Ambroise			
	Pierre			
23	Etienne	(8) Marg. Audet	S.Chs.	1797
	François			
	Etienne			
24	Nicolas	(9) M. Ls. Clément		
			S.Chs.	1776
	Marie Marthe	Jos. Plante	S.Chs.	1801
	Nicolas			
	Le même	Angé Terrien	S.Chs.	1790
	Geneviève	Chs. Hélie	S.M.	1828
	Pierre			
	André			
25	Charles	(9) Agathe Goupy	S.M.	1778
	Catherine	Gab. Terrien	S.G.	1801
	Catherine	2° Etn. Gontier	S.G.	1812
	Jeanne	J. B. Monmény	S.G.	1809
	Jeanne	2° Ant. Bissel	S.Chs.	1813
	Etienne			
	Le même	M. Jos. Plante	S.M.	1823
26	Joseph	(10) Génev. Ferland	S.Chs.	1782
27	Pierre	(13) Marie Darveau	S.G.	1821
28	Elie	(14) Susanne Forgue	S.M.	1797
	M. Charlotte	Ls. Poulin	S.Chs.	1819
	Marie	Ant. Bilodeau	S.Chs.	1820
	Marie	2° Jos. Méthot	S.Roch.	
	Thérèse	J. B. Pepin	S.Chs.	1824
	Angèle	Ed. Pouliot	S.Chs.	1826
	Susanne	Ls. Pepin	S.Chs.	1829
	Julie	Frs. Turgeon	S.Chs.	1840
	Françoise	Olivier Coulombe	S.J.	1836
	Françoise	2° Pierre Cotin	S.L.	1841
	Emérence	Frs. Leblanc	S.J.	1841
	Jean Elie			
	Joseph			
	Antoine			
29	Antoine	(14) M. Mad. Lacroix	S.M.	1801
	Madeleine	Jos. Goulet	S.Chs.	1829
	Charles			
	Elie			
	Antoine			
	Le même	Marie Bélanger		
			S.Chs.	1820
	Marie	Marcel Coté	S.Chs.	1848
30	Joseph	(15) Marie Fradet	S.Chs.	1797
	Marie	Firmin Dorion	S.G.	1819
	Marie Anne	André Brochu	S.G.	1819
	Magloire			
	Hubert			
	Joseph			
31	Pierre	(15) Angé. Morin	S.G.	1803
	Angélique	Amb. Fradet	S.G.	1829
32	Jean	(15) M. Anne Morin	S.G.	1806
A	Louis	(15) M. Génev. Chartier		
			S.H.	1812
33	Jean Bapt.	(17) M. Félicité Parent		
			S.V.	1813
34	Michel	(17) Louise Fradet	S.G.	1817
35	Louis	(17) Marg. Briart	S.G.	1821

GONTIER.

36	François	(17) Marg. Jolivet	S.G. 1823
37	Magloire	(17) Cath. Jolivet	S.G. 1827
38	François	(18) Génev. Audet	S.G. 1826
39	Antoine	(19) Christine Jolin	S.Chs. 1807
	Hermine	Jos. Dumas	S.Chs. 1835
40	Laurent	(19) Angé. Royer	S.Chs. 1812
	Angélique	Pierre Fortier	Lévis. 1838
41	François	(19) M. Anne Genest	
	Marie		S.Chs. 1821
		Flavien Bissonnet	
			S.Chs. 1846
	Le même	Eustasie Boutin	S.G. 1830
42	Etienne	(20) Cath. Gontier	S.G. 1812
43	Joseph	(21) M. Chs. Paquet	
			S.Chs. 1812
44	Rémi	(22) Cécile Lacasse	S.Chs. 1818
	Jérémie		
45	Pierre	(22) Sophie Blouin	S.J. 1819
46	Jacques	(22) Marie Pouliot	S.Chs. 1845
	Rémi		
47	Ambroise	(22) Josette Plante	S.Chs. 1826
48	Louis	(22) Marg. Lepage	S.Chs. 1829
	Le même	Marie Nadeau	S.J. 1843
49	Etienne	(23) Angèle Pepin	Lévis. 1825
50	François	(23) Mad. Marseau	S.G. 1826
51	Nicolas	(24) Marie Boucher	S.Chs. 1806
	Marie	Jos. Denis	S.M. 1836
52	Pierre	(24) Angé. Terrien	S.G. 1819
53	André	(24) Marg. Dodier	S.G. 1826
54	Etienne	(25) M. Anne Bilodeau	
			S.G. 1811
	Le même	Fse. Hélie	S.G. 1821
	Zoé	Cyrille Thivierge	
			S.M. 1855
55	Joseph	(28) Christine Bisson	
			S.Chs. 1830
56	Jean Elie	(28) Marguerite	S.G. 1822
57	Antonin	(28) Marg. Naud	S.Chs. 1833
	Marguerite	Damase Plante	S.Chs. 1859
	Rosalie	J. B. Dion	S.Chs. 1863
	Antonin		
58	Elie	(29) M. Chs. Gosselin	
			S.Chs. 1832
	Joseph		
59	Charles	(29) Marie Labrecque	
			S.Chs. 1832
	Marie Julie	Pierre Roy	S.Chs. 1853
60	Antoine	(29) M. Fse. Roy	S.Chs. 1853
61	Joseph	(30) Angé. Mercier	S.G. 1825
62	Magloire	(30) Emérence Alaire	S.V. 1826
63	Hubert	(30) Luce Alaire	S.V. 1829
	Luce	Jos. Job Garant	S.V. 1850
64	Jean Baptiste	Marg. Poiré	
	François		
65	Louis	M. Jos. Carbonneau	
	Marie Josette	David Gingras	S.J. 1824
66	Guillaume	Genev. Guay	
	Luce	Hubert Baudoin	S.V. 1850
67	Louis	M. Jos. Isoir	
			S.J.
	Joseph	Agathe Brochu	
68	Gervais	Hermine Gosselin	
			S.Chs. 1863
	Le même	Mad. Naud	S.J. 1849
69	Jérémie		
70	Rémi	(46) Marie Tangué	S.Chs. 1854
71	Antoine	(57) Philomène Plante	
			S.Chs. 1862
72	Joseph	(58) M. Adéline Roy	S.M. 1863
73	François	(64) Soulange Audet	S.V. 1845
74	Joseph	(67) Julie Gagné	S.V 1850

GOSSELIN.

1	Gabriel	Fse. Lelièvre	Qué. 1653
	Gabriel		

GOSSELIN.

	Ignace		
	Michel		
	François		
	Amable		
	Jean		
	Le même	Louise Guillot	S.F. 1677
	Pierre		
	Louis		
2	Ignace	(1) Marie Ratté	S.P. 1683
	M. Madeleine	Jean Leclaire	S.L. 1720
	Geneviève	Prisque Bélanger	S.L. 1724
	Joseph		
	Michel		
	François		
	Ignace		
	Gabriel		
	Gabriel		
	Antoine		
	Guillaume		
3	Michel	(1) Marie Minville	S.P. 1684
	Louise	Pierre Noël	S.P. 1703
	M. Charlotte	Jean Dupuis	Qué. 1712
	M. Madelaine	Jean Fradet	Qué. 1715
	Pierre		
	Joseph		
	Gabriel		
	Jean Baptiste		
4	Gabriel	(1) M. Mad. Pichet	
	M. Madeleine	Chas. Dorval	S.P. 1712
	Geneviève	René Dupas	S.P. 1716
	Jean		
5	François	(1) Charlotte Coté	S.P. 1688
	M. Charlotte	Jean Peltier	S.P. 1714
	M. Madeleine	Pierre Poulet	S.P. 1729
	Elisabeth	J. Couture	S.P. 1732
	François		
	Joseph		
6	Frs. Amable	(1) M. Fse. Labrecque	
			S.P. 1690
	Geneviève	Jacq. Bouffart	S.L. 1731
	M. Madeleine	Clément Couture	S.L. 1733
	Ignace		
	François		
	Antoine		
	Pierre		
7	Jean	(1) Jeanne Tardiff	
	Le même	Marie Cadieu	Qué. 1644
	Jean Baptiste		
8	Pierre	(1) M. Mad. Garinet	
			Rimouski 1701
9	Louis	(1) Jeanne Duroy	Qué. 1682
	Le même	Eliz. Bosset	Qué. 1756
10	Joseph	(2) Fse. Godbout	S.L. 1710
	Josette	Pierre Fontaine	S.J. 1739
	Madeleine	Michel Huot	S J. 1747
	M. Françoise	Lambert Cohornon	
			S.J. 1753
	M. Françoise	2° Pierre Laforce	S.J. 1757
	Marguerite	Pierre Curodeau,	
			fils.S.J. 1754
	Marie	Pierre Gurodeau,	
			père.Qué. 1740
	Marie	2° Frs. Saint Laurent	
			S.J. 1756
	Jean François		
	Ignace		
	Pierre		
	Gabriel		
	Joseph		
11	Ignace	(2) Marg. Godbout	S.L. 1714
	Geneviève	Pierre Ruel	S.L. 1744
	Ignace		
	Antoine		
	Louis		
	Jean Baptiste		

GOSSELIN.

12 François	(2)	Fse. Lemelin	S.L.	1716
M. Madeleine		Ignace Noël	S.L.	1735
M. Françoise		Jean Frs. Gobeil	S.L.	1735
Dorothée		Nicolas Gautier	S L.	1742
Marie Louise		Etn. Papillon	S.L.	1751
Ignace				
Joseph				
13 Gabriel	(2)	M. Anne Renaud	S.F.	1716
14 Gabriel	(2)	Marg. Lemelin	S.L.	1718
Marie		Jos. Civadier	„	1746
Marie Anne		Frs. Audet	„	1762
François				
Gabriel				
Louis				
Joseph				
Le même		Marg. Couture	S.L.	1732
Geneviève		Chs. Rouleau	S.L.	1753
Marguerite		Jean Langlois	„	1765
Jean				
Antoine				
Nicolas				
Laurent				
Guillaume				
15 Guillaume	(2)	Genev. Gravel	Que.	1718
Basile				
16 Michel	(2)	M. Cath. Gobeil	S.J.	1717
Madeleine		Nic. Thivierge	S.J.	1755
Catherine		Jacq. Blouin		
17 Antoine	(2)	Marg. Crépeau	S.L.	1726
Geneviève		Michel Gautron	S.V.	1775
Geneviève		2'Jos. Larrivé	S.M.	1788
Amable				
François				
18 Pierre	(3)	Fse. Caruel	S.L.	1717
		V. de Jean Bouffart		
Pierre				
19 Gabriel	(3)	Genev. Crépeau	S.P.	1726
Véronique		Clément Rochon	S.F.	1750
Véronique		2'Ls. Létourneau	„	1763
Joseph Marie				
Jean				
20 Joseph	(3)	Mad. Leclaire	S.P.	1732
Joseph				
Laurent				
Ambroise				
Alexis				
Louis				
21 Jean Baptiste	(3)	Angé Fournier	S.Tho.	1729
Le même		M. Anne Gaboury	S.V.	1734
Marie Josette		Aug. Picard	S.Tho	1760
Genev. Régis		Aug. Thibaut	S.P.S.	1778
22 Jean	(4)	Thérèse Dupile Beaumont	S.P.	1721
Marie		Jean Fournier	B.	1742
Thérèse		Chs. Turgeon	„	1749
Marguerite		Jos. Couture	„	1753
Marie Josette		Chs. Couillard	„	1759
Joseph				
23 François	(5)	Angé Noël	S.P.	1720
Marie Josette		Pierre Bonneau	S.Tho.	1751
Joseph				
François				
24 Joseph	(5)	M. Cath. Blouard	S.P.	1735
Thérèse		Amb. Gagnon	S.H.	1789
Françoise		Zacharie Nadeau	B.	1763
Marie Charlotte		Germ. Baudoin	S.H.	1777
Ignace				
Alexis				
25 Antoine	(6)	M. Jos. Lajoue	S.L.	1724
Marie Josette		Jacq. Labrecque	„	1763
Le même (?)		Marie Crépeau	„	1748
Marie Thérèse		Jos. Chabot	„	1773
M. Madeleine		Jean Godbout	„	1773
Geneviève		Jos. Pouliot	„	1780
Joseph				
26 Ignace	(6)	Mad. Isabel S.V.	„	1727

GOSSELIN.

Marie Félicité		Jos. Marie Lefèvre	S.V.	1752
Elizabeth		Gab. Bilodeau	S.V.	1757
M. Marguerite		Jos. Marie Tangué	„	1757
Angélique		Jos. Boissel	„	1763
Pierre				
Joseph				
27 Pierre	(6)	M. Jos. Clément S.M.	„	1728
Marie Josette		Michel Forgue	S.M.	1751
Pierre				
Le même		Eliz. Lacasse	B.	1732
Elizabeth		Denis Nadeau	S.M.	1753
Elizabeth		2'Michel Dutile	„	1772
M. Geneviève		Ls. Clément	„	1758
M. Geneviève		2'Pierre Gagné	S.H.	1814
Marie Anne		Jos. Quéret	S.M.	1763
Marie Anne		2'Ls. Lemelin	„	1785
François				
28 François	(6)	Genev. Rousseau	S.L.	1734
Geneviève		Michel Turgeon	B.	1750
Charlotte		Ls. Vien	S.M.	1770
29 Jean	(7)	Marie Lemieux	Cap. S. Ign.	1723
Salomé		Frs. Richard	Cap. S. Ign.	1752
30 Jean François	(10)	Angé Fortier S.Chs.	S.J.	1749
Angélique		Eustache Royer	S.Chs.	1752
Marie Josette		Jos. Bacquet	S.M.	1776
Marie		Simon Bacquet	S.Chs.	1782
Pierre				
François				
31 Ignace	(10)	M. Chs. Dupas	S.J.	1749
Le même		Marg. Blouin	„	1787
32 Pierre	(10)	M. Anne Fortier	„	1752
M. Marguerite		Jos. Paquet	„	1773
Marie		Chs. Pinet	„	1785
Pierre Noël				
33 Gabriel	(10)	Angé Coursol Verchères		
Antoine				
Joseph				
34 Joseph	(10)	Marg. Labrecque	S.L.	1754
Le même		Eliz. Fortier	S.J.	1759
Elizabeth		Michel Emond	S.H	1781
35 Ignace	(11)	Marie Rousseau	S.L.	1738
M. Françoise		Jos. Marie Plante	S.L.	1771
M. Catherine		Jos. Terrien	S.J.	1768
François				
Pierre				
Antoine				
Louis				
36 Antoine	(11)	M. Anne Leclaire	S.L.	1743
Antoine				
François				
37 Jean Bap-tiste	(11)	Cath. Couture	S. Chs.	1751
Catherine		Pierre Charier	S. Chs.	1772
Jean				
Le même		Marie Couillard	S.Chs.	1759
Charlotte		Jos. Nadeau	S. Chs.	1787
Joseph				
François				
38 Louis	(11)	M. Marg. Labrecque	S.L.	1754
Elizabeth		Jos. Guay	S.L.	1781
Jean				
39 Ignace	(12)	M. Anne Pouliot	S.L.	1750
40 Joseph	(12)	M. Jos. Turcot	S.J.	1752
41				
42 François	(14)	M. Anne Lis	B.	1746
Marie		Jos. Lacasse	S. Chs.	1773
Joachim				
Jean Baptiste				
François				
Gabriel				

GOSSELIN.

43	Gabriel	(14)	Thérèse Lacasse	B.	1751
	M. Charlotte		Ls. Audet	S. Chs.	1778
	M. Charlotte		2° Jean Fournier	S. Chs.	1796
44	Joseph	(14)	Jeanne Vallière	S. Chs.	1751
	Le même		Cath. Boilard	S.M.	1783
45	Louis	(14)	M. Eliz. Drapeau	B.	1755
				S. Denis	
	Marie Anne		Jos. Plante	S. Chs.	1781
	Jean				
	Le même		Angé Couture	S. Chs.	1771
46	Nicolas	(14)	Marie Couture	S.Chs.	1757
	Marie		André Nadeau	S.Chs,	1793
	Catherine		Paul Bernier	S. Chs.	1796
	Marguerite		Etn. Duquet	S. Chs.	1796
	Nicolas				
	Jean				
	Le même		M. Jos. Morin	S.F.S.	1803
47	Laurent	(14)	Marie Côté	S. Chs.	1757
	Marguerite		Charles Rouleau	S.H.	1793
	Laurent				
	Louis				
	Joachim				
48	Antoine	(14)	Mad. Baillargeon	S.L.	1762
	Madeleine		Laurent Audet	S.L.	1789
	Marguerite		Jos. Côté	S.L.	1790
	Cécile		Frs. Denis	S.L.	1799
	Antoine				
	François				
	Louis				
49	Guillaume	(14)	Thérèse Nadeau	S. Chs.	1763
	Charlotte		Guill. Nolin	S. Chs.	1787
	Thérèse		Ls. Couture	S. Chs.	1796
	Marguerite		Pierre Pouliot S.	Chs.	1798
	Guillaume				
	Jean Baptiste				
50	Jean	(14)	Genev. Godbout	S.L.	1774
	Geneviève		Frs. Pouliot	S. Chs.	1797
	Joachim				
	Jean				
	Etienne				
	Le même		Marg. Trahan S.	Chs.	1782
51	Basile	(15)	M. Jos. Fortier	S.J.	1749
	Ignace				
52	Amable	(17)	Isabelle Maranda	S.L.	1765
	Elizabeth		Ls. Huot	S.L.	1798
	Marguerite		Jos. Hébert	S.L.	1800
	François				
53	François	(17)	M. Cécile Roy	S.V.	1765
	Marie Josette		Jacq. Asselin	S.V.	1787
	Marie Cécile		Pierre Boutin	S.V.	1787
	Marie Marthe		J. B. Rémillard	S.V.	1792
	Marie Hélène		Chs. Balan	S.V.	1798
	M. Madeleine		Pierre Ménard	S.V.	1803
	M. Geneviève		Frs. Boutin	S.V.	1803
	Marie Louise		Frs. Hélie	S.V.	1813
	Antoine				
54	Pierre	(18)	M. Benjamin Nolin	S.P.	1750
55	Joseph Marie	(19)	M. Jos. Létourneau	S.F.	1763
	Marie Josette		Jean Moor	S.F.	1798
	Joseph				
56	Jean	(19)	Marie Asselin	S.F.	1767
57	Louis	(20)	Mad. Baudouin	S.Frs.	1763
	M. Madeleine		Michel Cantin	S.H.	1785
	Marie Anne		Ls. Nadeau	S.H.	1789
	Marguerite		Ls. Cantin	S.H.	1803
	Marie Hélène		Germ. Roberge	S.H.	1898
	Josette		Jos. Paradis	S.H.	1808
	Ursule		Etn. Dussaut	S.H.	1810
	Marie Louise		Frs. Hébert	S.H.	1810
	Laurent				

GOSSELIN.

	Louis				
	Germain				
	Joseph				
	François				
	Jean				
58	Joseph	(20)	Agathe Ferland	S.P.	1765
59	Laurent	(20)	Genev. Crepeau	S.P.	1765
	Le même		Pélagie Martel	S.P.	1773
	Thècle		Jean Vézina	S.P.	1800
	Agathe		Jos. Fournier	S P.	1803
	M. Geneviève		Jean Ferland	S.P.	1803
	Laurent				
	Joseph				
60	Ambroise	(20)	Thérèse Montigny	S.P.	1765
61	Alexis	(20)	Mad. Ferland	S.P.	1773
	Agathe		Jos. Plante	S.P.	1790
	Marguerite		Ign. Noël	S.H.	1808
	Marie Josette		Chs. Cadoret	"	1815
	Le même		M. Fse. Fouquet	Lévis	1791
	Marie		Aug. Blais	S.H.	1813
	M. Madeleine		Pierre Demers	"	1814
	Susanne		Alexis Dumas	"	1817
62	Joseph	(22)	M. Chs. Cloutier	S.P.S.	1760
	M. Charlotte		Alexandre Paquet	S.Chs.	1782
	Angélique		Jos. McIntyre	"	1795
	Angélique		2° Jos. Duquet	"	1812
	Cécile		Etn. Labrecque	"	1798
	Joseph				
63	François	(23)	Thérèse Fournier	S.Tho.	
	Le même		Barbe Roy	S.G.	
64	Joseph	(23)	Thérèse Lacroix	S.Tho.	1757
	Thérèse		Jacq. Gagné	S.F.S.	1797
	Pierre				
	Joseph				
65	Alexis	(24)	M. Jos. Gagné	S.Tho.	1776
	Apolline		Laurent Chamberlan	S.M.	1808
	Marie Josette		J. B. Fournier	"	1828
	Thomas Alexis				
	Michel				
	Jean Baptiste				
	Joseph				
66	Ignace	(24)	Louise Pepin	S.F.S.	1779
	M. Charlotte		J. B. Bonneau	"	1822
	Marie Anne		Paul Baudoin	"	1829
	Marie Louise		Pierre Tardif	S.H.	1812
67	Joseph	(25)	Marie Campeau	S.L.	1773
	Marie		Frs. Canac	S.G.	1803
	Laurent				
	Joseph				
68	Pierre	(26)	M. Genev. Gautron	S. V.	1762
	Marguerite		Aug. Terrien	"	1796
	M. Madeleine		J. B. Aubé	"	1807
	Geneviève		Amb. Pouliot	"	1794
	Geneviève		2° Pierre Bussière	S.Chs.	1825
	Geneviève		Frs. Goulet	"	1790
	Joseph				
	Pierre				
69	Joseph	(26)	Marg. Marseau	S.V.	1762
	Antoine				
	Le même		M. Marthe Guilmet	S.V.	1767
	Marthe		Laurent Gautron	"	1787
	Marie		Frs. Vallée	"	1802
	Jacques				
	Ignace				
70	Pierre	(27)	M. Ls. Forgue	S.M.	1753
71	François	(27)	Marie Dutile	B.	1763
72	Joseph		Mad. Gosselin		
	Angélique		J. B. Mailhot	S.Chs.	1806
73	Guillaume		Marie Lemieux		
	M. Angélique		Jos. Turgeon	S.Chs.	1808

GOSSELIN.

74	François	(30)	Louise Gontier S.Chs.	1775
	Louise		Chs. Provost „	1792
	M. Angélique		J. B. Blanchet „	1813
	Marie		Pierre Goulet „	1815
	Marie Josette		Robert Rippea „	1818
	Joachin			
	Antoine			
75	Pierre	(30)	M. Ls. Audet „	1778
	M. Angélique		André Lacroix „	1802
76	Pierre Noël	(32)	Marg. Lefebvre S.J.	1783
	Marie		Bénoni Coulombe „	1815
	Françoise		Pierre Blouin „	1819
	Marguerite		Noël Beaupré „	1819
	Josette		Jacq. Foucher „	1829
	Pierre Noël			
	Laurent			
	Le même		Marg. Coulombe S.J.	1802
	M. Madeleine		J. B. Audet „	1823
	Esther		Jean Blouin „	1833
	Antoine			
77	Antoine	(33)	Clémence Adam Verchères	1789
	Le même		Cath. Vaudry Verchères	1791
	Antoine		Curé de St. Jean	
78	Joseph	(33)	Marie Lamoureux	
	Adélaïde		Anselme Turcot S.J.	1855
	Eléonore		Delphine Pouliot „	1864
	Paul			
79	François	(35)	M. Thérèse Ferlant S.L.	1793
	Thérèse		Pierre Dion S.G.	1790
	Geneviève		Alexandre Ruel „	1795
	Marie		Jos. Roy „	1798
	Françoise		Michel Couture „	1809
	Josette		Jos. Bruneau „	1814
80	Pierre	(35)	Genev. Pouliot S.L.	1774
	Louis			
	Antoine			
81	Louis	(35)	M. Chs. Vien S.M.	1778
	Angélique		Jos. Couture S.G.	1821
	Jean Baptiste			
	Antoine			
	Louis			
	Joseph			
82	Antoine	(35)	M. Jos. Pouliot S.L.	1780
	Geneviève		J. B. Roy S.G.	1812
	Angélique		Pierre Goulet S.G.	1812
	Antoine			
83	Antoine	(36)	M. Chs.Couture S.Chs.	1765
	Marie		Jos. Turgeon „	1795
	Charlotte		Ls. Audet „	1795
	Marguerite		Chs. Jalbert S.H.	1805
	Marie Anne		Jos. Dallaire „	1812
	Joseph			
	Antoine			
84	François	(36)	Mad. Couture S.Chs.	1767
	Marthe		Ls.Corriveau „	1794
	Angélique		J. B. Roy S.Chs.	1803
	Madeleine		Aug. Lefebvre S.Chs.	1815
	Marguerite		Frs. Baudoin S.G.	1805
	Charles			
85	Jean	(37)	Marg. Labrecque S.Chs.	1778
	Marguerite		Frs. Plante S.Chs.	1801
	Marie		Barth. Blouin S.Chs.	1806
	Marie Anne		Etn. Couture S.Chs	1812
	Marie Josette		J. B. Plante S.Chs.	1822
	Geneviève		J. B. Roy S.Chs.	1828
	Geneviève		2° Paul Audet S.Chs.	1845
	Laurent			
86	Joseph	(37)	Angé Leclaire S.Chs.	1792
	Le même		Cath. Girard S.Chs.	1795
	Marguerite		Frs. Naud S.Chs.	1825
87	François	(37)	Angé Lacroix S.Chs.	1792
	Angélique		Gab. Naud S.G.	1821

GOSSELIN.

	Catherine		Jos. Lepage S.G.	1821
	Angèle		Ignace Ruel S.G.	1827
	Françoise			
88	Jean	(38)	Genev. Nolin S.P.	1788
89	François	(42)	Eliz. Fournier S.Chs.	1769
	Le même		Mad. Nolin S.Chs.	1771
	Marie		Frs. Roy S.Chs.	1794
	Françoise		Mathieu Labrecque S.Chs.	1801
	Geneviève		Pierre Chabot S.Chs.	1810
	Apolline		André Daigle S.Chs.	1813
	Joachim			
90	Joachim	(42)	Thérèse Audet S.Chs.	1781
91	Jean Baptiste	(42)	Angéle Nolin S.Chs.	1784
	Angélique		Chs. Gosselin S.Chs.	1803
	Marie Anne		Amb. Coulombe S.Chs.	1807
	Marguerite		Jean Carson S.Chs.	1810
	Françoise			
	Jean Baptiste			
	Le même		M. Claire Morisset S.Chs.	1795
	Constance		Elie Audet S.Chs.	1819
	M. Geneviève		J. B. Couture „	1821
	Théodule			
	Bénoni			
	Charles			
92	Gabriel	(42)	Marie Pruneau S.Chs.	1786
	Angèle		Jos. Bolduc S.Chs.	1835
	Angélique		Aug. Nadeau S.Chs.	1845
	Barnabé			
	François			
93	Jean	(45)	Cath. Couture S.Chs.	1782
94	Nicholas	(46)	Félice Nadeau S.G.	1794
	Elisabeth		Alexandre Marcoux S.Chs.	1835
	Jacques			
	Françoise			
	Nicolas			
95	Jean	(46)	Marie Pilote S.Chs.	1796
	Joseph			
	Jean			
	Joseph			
	Laurent	(47)	Marie Racine S.Chs.	1783
	Angélique		Pierre Daigle S.Chs.	1821
	Marie		Jos. Terrien S.H.	1820
	Simon			
	Ignace			
	Le même		Genev. Nadeau S.Chs.	1807
97	Louis	(47)	Marie Fortier S.H.	1787
	Angélique		Ant. Baudoin S.H.	1813
	Joachim			
	Louis			
98	Joachim	(47)	Cath. Bégin S.H.	1798
99	Louis	(48)	Marie Leclaire S.P.	1794
	Marie		Jean Godbout S.L.	1818
	Marie		2° F. X. Ménard S.L.	1837
	Cécile		Pierre Godbout S.L.	1819
100	Antoine	(48)	Cath. Chabot S.L.	1801
	Catherine		Jean Labrecque S.L.	1829
	Marie		Frs. Coulombe S.L.	1831
	Adelaide		Jos. Audibert S.L.	1834
	Henriette		Clément Rouleau S.L.	1842
	Mathilde		Jean Coulcombe S.L.	1851
	Etienne			
	Francois Xavier			
	Edouard			
101	François	(48)	Véronique Chabot S.L.	1804
	Véronique		Jos. Coté S.L.	1825
	Marie		Marcel Provost S.Chs.	1828
	Magloire			
	François			
102	Guillaume	(49)	Fse. Pouliot S.Chs.	1788

GOSSELIN.

GOSSELIN.

103	Jn. Baptiste	(49)	Marg. Angé Morisset	S.Chs.	1796
	Marguerite		Ls. Fournier	S.Chs.	1815
	Thérèse		Pierre Marcoux	S.Chs.	1818
	Olive		J. B. Clément	S.Chs.	1829
	Charlotte		Elie Gontier	S.Chs.	1832
	Joseph				
104	Jean	(50)	M. Anne Roy	S.G.	1798
	Marie Anne		Jean Bilodeau	S.G.	1823
	Elisabeth		Jean Blais		
	Marguerite		Eustache Roy		
	Louise		Guill Amiot		
	Charlotte		Chs. Boissel		
			Cyp. Blanchet		
	Jean				
	Léon				
105	Etienne	(50)	Marie Goulet	S.G.	1801
	Marie		Murdock McKenzie	S.G.	1819
106	Joachim	(50)	Marg. Roy	S.G.	1805
107	Ignace	(51)	Marie Dorval	S.P.	1778
108	François	(52)	Cath. Baudoin	S.Frs.	1799
	Elizabeth		Marcel Deblois	S.L.	1852
	Henriette		Isidore Aubin	S.L.	1838
	Michel				
	François				
	Jean Baptiste				
	Joseph				
	Antoine				
	Le même		Cath. Hébert	S.Frs.	1823
	Magloire				
109	Antoine	(53)	M. Jos. Roy	S.V.	1811
	Marguerite		Michel Thivierge	„	1832
	Julie		Jean Raphaël Guilmet	S.V.	1865
	Josette		Basile Gagnon	S.Chs.	1842
	Antoine				
110	Joseph	(55)	Marie Pageot	S.F.	1788
	Marie Anne		Frs. Gagnon	„	1814
	Marguerite		Jos. Giguère	„	1826
	Jacques				
	Joseph				
	Jean Baptiste				
111	Louis	(57)	M. Jos. Gagné	S.H.	1791
112	Germain	(57)	Thècle Langlois	S.P.	1800
	Le même		Marg. Bilodeau	S.H.	1812
113	Joseph	(57)	Thérèse Roberge	„	1803
	Le même		Rose Ferlant	S.P.	1818
			Genev. Labrecque	B.	1821
114	Françoise	(57)	Josette Paradis	S.H.	1808
115	Jean	(57)	Angèle Talbot	„	1811
116	Laurent	(57)	Théotiste Ferlant	S.P.	1818
117	Laurent	(59)	Vict. Roberge	„	1800
	Le même		Genev. Drouin	S.F.	1805
	Apolline		Etn. Ferlant	S.P.	1828
	Scolastique		Jos. Côté	„	1830
	Geneviève		Jos. Godbout	„	1831
	Veneranda		Ls. Gagnon	„	1835
	Reine		Michel Gosselin	„	1845
	Flavie		J. B. Ferlant	„	1846
	Laurent				
	Jean				
118	Joseph	(59)	M. Angé Couture	„	1801
119	Joseph	(62)	Louise Ruel	S.Chs.	1787
	Marie Louise		Ls. Blanchet	„	1805
120	Joseph	(64)	M. Anne Richard	S.V.	1789
	Josette		Marc Turgeon	B.	1826
	Charlotte		F. X. Larrivé	S.Chs.	1829
	Alexis				
	Joseph				
	Antoine				
121	Pierre	(64)	M. Jos. Morin	S.F.S.	1798
122	Tho. Alexis	(65)	Angé Julie Evans	S.V.	1808
	Josette		Ed. Canac	„	1827
	Claire		Urbain Narcisse Fraser	S.V.	1831

	M. Elisabeth		Alexandre Fraser	„	1833
	Julie		Eusèbe Couillard	„	1839
	Alexis				
123	Michel	(65)	Rosalie Blouin	Bert.	1818
124	JeanBaptiste	(65)	M. Jos. Dubé	S.V.	1819
125	Joseph	(65)	M. Vict. Fournier	S.P.S.	1820
	Victoire		Narcisse Chamberlan	S.M.	1854
	Anne		Alexandre Fraser	S.V.	1868
	Joseph				
126	Joseph	(67)	Marie Viger	S.G.	1802
127	Laurent	(67)	Mad. Chatigny	„	1809
128	Pierre	(68)	M. Barbe Dion	Bert.	1805
	Marie Thècle		Jacq. Lainé	S.V.	1830
	Pierre				
	Ignace				
129	Joseph	(68)	Marie Bilodeau	S.G.	1827
130	Antoine	(69)	Charlotte Boissel	S.Chs.	1789
	M. Charlotte		Laurent Lemieux	„	1816
	Antoine				
	Le même		Marg. Raps	„	1812
131	Jacques	(69)	M. Jos. Roy	S.V.	1795
	Angèle		Ls. Fontaine	S.M.	1825
	François				
	Jacques				
	André				
	Jean Baptiste				
	Joseph				
132	Ignace	(69)	Marg. Poirier	S.Chs.	1798
133	Joachim	(76)	Cath. Bissonnet	S.M.	1808
	François				
134	Antoine	(74)	Marie Plante	S.Chs.	1818
	Le même		Fsᵉ. Paquet	S.M.	1819
135	Laurent	(76)	Charlotte Thivierge	S.J.	1811
	Catherine		Frs. Blouin	„	1831
	Charlotte		Jean Gobeil	„	1835
	Marie Anne		Laurent Paquet	„	1838
	Marie Anne		2° Pierre Pepin	„	1842
	Henriette		F. X. Delisle	„	1842
	Luce		J. B. Thivierge	„	1848
	Marcelline		Pierre Paquet	„	1857
	Paul				
	François				
	Le même		Marie Demeule	„	1860
136	Pierre Noël	(76)	M. Mad. Asselin	S.F.	1816
	Josette		Ant. Garneau	S.J.	1837
	Marguerite		Régis Poulin	„	1839
	Adelaïde		Pierre Pepin	„	1848
	Pierre				
	Joseph				
	Ferdinand				
137	Antoine	(76)	M. Ls. Audet	„	1825
138	Paul	(78)			
139	Louis	(80)	M. Ls. Letourneau	S.L.	1813
	Pierre				
	Joseph				
140	Antoine	(80)	M. Ls. Lainé	S.J.	1822
141	Louis	(81)	Marie Dessaint	S.G.	1803
	Alexandre				
	Jean				
142	Antoine	(81)	Genev. Roy	„	1817
	Le même		Marie Clément	S.Chs.	1821
143	JeanBaptiste	(81)	M. Chs. Larrivé	B.	1822
144	Joseph	(81)	Louise Roy	S.G.	1824
145	Antoine	(82)	Cécile Monmény	S.Chs.	1807
146	Antoine	(83)	Angé Genest	„	1796
	Joseph				
147	Joseph	(83)	Thècle Morin	„	1805
148	Charles	(84)	Angé Gosselin	„	1803
	Stanislas				
	Charles				
	Le même		Marg. Coulombe	„	1826

GOSSELIN.

```
        Marguerite        Isidore Provost S.Chs.1852
149 Laurent        (85)  Monique Plante   "    1815
    Marie Perpétue       Ant. Turcot      "    1837
150 François       (87)  Olive Côté       S.G. 1823
151 Joachim        (89)  Genev. MorissetS.Chs.1802
    Scolastique          Pierre Leclaire  "    1826
    Marie                Jérôme Baudoin   "    1833
    Joachim
    Le même              Genev. Roy       S.G. 1813
    Emerence             Frs. Pelchat     S.Chs.1845
    Le même (?)          M. Jos. Patry    S.M. 1829
152 JeanBaptiste(91)     M. Rose Baudoin S.H.1815
153 François       (91)  M. Eliz. Lacroix S.M.1818
154 Bénoni         (91)  M.Genev.DenisS.Chs.1822
155 Théodule       (91)  Apolline Baillargeon
                                          S.Chs.1827
156 Charles        (91)  Marie Labrecque  "    1831
157 François       (92)  Josette Gautron S.M. 1821
    Marie Rose           Jos. Ed. Fortin  "
    Philomène            Prudent Mousset  "    1861
158 Barnabé        (92)  Hermine Veau S.Chs.1829
159 Nicolas        (94)  Véronique Martin
                                          S.F.S.1825
160 Jacques        (94)  Julie Bilodeau   S.G. 1828
161 François       (94)  Zoé Martin       S.M. 1838
162 Jean           (95)  Marie Roy        S.G. 1820
163 Joseph         (95)  Julie Bélanger   S.V. 1827
164 Joseph         (95)  M. CélesteTangué "    1833
165 Ignace         (96)  Angèle Tangué    S.G. 1815
166 Simon          (96)  M. Marg. Blouin
                                          S.Chs.1822
    M. Marguerite        Amable Lacasse   "    1847
    M. Madeleine         Aug. Dumas       "    1853
    Hermine              Gervais Gontier  "    1863
167 Louis          (97)  M. Thérèse LainéS.H.1812
168 Joachim        (97)  M. Pélagie Dandurand
                                          S.H. 1816
169 Etienne        (100) Genev. Denis Lévis1833
    Geneviève            Jos. Noël        S.L. 1853
170 Edouard        (100) Henriette Parker
171 François       (100) Henriette Pepin S.L. 1844
    Xavier
    Marie Auxilia        Léon Labrecque   "    1881
172 Amable               Marg. Gagné
    Marguerite           F. X. Roy        S.V. 1831
    Soulange             F. X. Hélie      "    1838
    Marie Émélie         F. X. Bélanger   "    1847
173 Jean Baptiste        Josette Quéret
    Josette              Chs. Dumas     S.Chs.1832
    Le même (?)          Fse. Hélie       "    1836
174 Gabriel              Angé Verret
    Antoine
175 Joseph               Adé Nollet
    Le même              M. Aussile Bernier
                                          S.Chs.1840
176 Charles              M. Rose Gendreau
    Hermine              Hubert Chatenay
                                          S.Chs.1843
177 François       (101) Angèle Pepin     "    1842
178 Magloire       (101) Angèle Bacquet S.M. 1839
    Philomène            J. B. Plante S.Chs.1860
    Angèle               Frs. Labrecque   "    1862
179 Benoit         (104) Perpétue Talbot
    Philomène            Léon Goupy       S.M. 1858
180 Joseph         (103) Angèle Naud S.Chs.1842
181 Jean           (104) Baselisse Talbot S.G. 1826
182 Léon           (104) RosalieBaillargeon "  1827
183 François       (108) M. Adé Choret   S.M. 1827
    François
    Le même              Genev. Brousseau "    1833
    Adelaide             Félix Parant     "    1881
    Simon Jonas
    Jean Baptiste
    Le même              Louise Dalaire   "    1847
    Eugène
    Joseph
```

GOSSELIN.

```
    Amable
184 Joseph         (108) Soulange Denis  S.L. 1836
    Frs. Régis
185 Jean Bap-      (108) Flavie Denis     "    1842
    tiste
    Flavie               J. B. Maranda S. L. 1869
    François
    Magloire
186 Antoine        (108) Brigitte Turgeon
    Elizabeth            Chs. Dutile     S. H. 1862
    Antoine
    François
187 Michel         (108) Reine Gosselin S. P. 1845
    Marie                Omer Lemay      S. P. 1878
    Rose                 Frs. Gosselin   S. P. 1874
    Philoméne            Jos. Siméon Desrocher
                                         S. P. 1882
    Michel
188 Magloire       (108) Philoméne Denis
                                         S.L. 1858
189 Antoine        (109) Rose Roy        S. V. 1835
    Régis
    Joseph
190 Joseph         (110) Angè Gagnon     S.F. 1817
    Joseph Edouard
    Le même              M. Jos. Martel S. P. 1826
191 Jacques        (110) M. Olive Blouin S.F. 1820
192 Jean Bap-      (110) Genev. Blouin S. F. 1832
    tiste
193 Jean           (117) Luce Nolin      S. P. 1835
    Luce Philine         Phydime Auguste
                                         Ferlant S.P. 1855
    Philoméne            Onésime Turcot  S. P. 1858
    Marie Célina         Jean Pie Ferlant S.P. 1862
    Ludivine             David Dion      S. P. 1864
    Genev. Flamine       Pierre Epiphane
                                         Ferlant S.P. 1867
    Laurent
    Nicodème
194 Laurent        (117) Marg. Godbout S. P. 1842
    Pierre Olivier
195 Joseph         (120) Euphrosine LacasseB. 1819
    Cyprien
196 Antoine        (120) Marg. Quéret S.Chs. 1838
197 Alexis         (120) M. Angéle Bergeron
                                              B. 1841
198 Alexis         (122)
199 Joseph         (125) Cath. Gautron  S. V. 1854
200 Pierre         (128) Julie Roy      S. V. 1830
    M. Désanges          Benjamin Roy S. V. 1851
201 Ignace         (128) M. Marcelline Gautron
                                         S. V. 1835
    Marcelline           Samuel Gaumont S.V.1855
202 Antoine        (130) Marie Fortier  S. Chs. 1821
203 Jean Baptiste        Marie Boissonneau
    Laurent
204 Jean                 Julie Asselin
    Le même              Séraphine Thivierge
                                         S.J. 1863
205 Pierre               Théotiste Jacques
                                         S. Isidore
    Pierre
206 Jacques        (131) Marie Hélie   S. M. 1817
    Jean Baptiste
207 François       (131) Emérentienne Couillard
                                         S.M. 1822
    Constance            Didace Morisset S.M. 1846
    Le même              Marie Gagnon S. M. 1829
    Marie Flore          Edouard Samson S.M.1857
208 André          (131) Fse. Brochu    S.M. 1828
    Le même              M. Anne Denis S.M. 1831
209 Jean Baptiste
                   (131) Thérèse Gautron S.M.1832
210 Joseph         (131) M. Jos. Pichet S. M. 1832
    Le même (?)          Julie Guilmet  S. M. 1852
211 François       (133) Brigitte Baudoin S.V.1862
```

GOSSELIN.

212	Paul	(135)	Mad. Picard S. J.	1842
213	François	(135)	Hombéline Fradet S.J.	1852
214	Pierré	(136)	Luce Verreau S.J.	1841
215	Joseph	(136)	M. Anne Picard S.J.	1850
216	Ferdinand	(136)	M. Zoé Canac S. F.	1863
217	Pierre	(139)	Cécile Pepin S. L.	1844
	Le même		Rose de Lima Noël	
			S. J.	1851
	Marie Alice		Elzéar Roberge S. L.	1879
218	Joseph	(139)	Réparate Pichet S.L.	1848
219	Alexandre	(141)	Sophie Turgeon B.	1840
220	Jean	(141)	Marg. Morisset S.M.	1845
221	Joseph	(146)	Julie Plante B.	1827
	M. Virginie		Jean Raphaël Hill	
	Georgina		S. Chs.	1853
	Léocadie		Jos. Chabot S. Chs.	1855
	Célanire		J.B. Marcoux S.Chs.	1858
	Ant. J.B. Jos.			
	Eugéne			
222	Charles	(148)	M. Anne Cinqmars	
			S.L.	1834
			S. Claire	
223	Stanislas	(148)	Luce Bolduc S. V.	1834
224	Joachim	(151)	Marthe Terrien	
			S. Chs.	1832
	Le même		Eliz. Roy S. Chs.	1835
225	Antoine	(174)	Angéle Nadeau B	1845
226	Amable	(183)	Georgina Samson S.L	1882
227	Joseph		M. Caroline Hudon	
			S. L.	1881
228	François	(183)	Fse. Létourneau S.F.	1850
	Pierre			
	François Xavier			
229	Simon Jonas	(183)	M. Zoé Dion	
230	Jean Bapt.	(183)	Anne Ruellan S. M.	1866
231	Eugéne	(183)	Odile Labbé S. L.	1871
	Le même		Sophie Charbonneau	
232	François	(184)	M. Anne Natalie O'Neil	
	Régis			
233	François	(185)	Rose Gosselin S.L.	1874
234	Magloire	(185)	Marie Langlois S.P.	1878
235	Antoine	(186)	Célina Dutile S.Anselme	
				1862
236	François	(186)	Cédulie Duquet S.Chs.	1868
237	Michel	(187)	M. Lumena Coulombe S.L.	
				1878
238	Régis	(189)	M. Agnès Fournier S.M.	
				1865
239	Joseph	(189)	M. Jos. Hizoir S.V.	1847
240	Jos.	(190)	Marc. Chatigny S.F.	1839
	Edouard			
	Joseph			
	François Xavier			
241	Laurent	(193)	M. Eulalie Plante S.P.	1863
	Nicodime			
242	Pierre	(194)	Eliz. Adélina Leclaire	
	Olivier		S.P.	1867
243	Laurent	(203)	Virginie Lebrun S.Chs.	
				1862
244	Pierre	(205)	Vénérande Vaillancour	
			S.F.	1855
245	Jean	(206)	Marg. Guilmet S.Chs.	1845
	Baptiste			
246	Ant. J. B.	(221)	M. Apolline Fournier	
	Jos. Eug.		S.Chs.	1856
	Genev.			
247	François	(228)	Delima Roberge S.L.	1875
	Xavier			
248	Pierre	(228)	Belzémire Boissonneau	
			S.L.	1879
249	Joseph	(240)	M. Elise Gourdeau	
			S.P.	1866
250	François	(240)	Julie Leblond S.F.	1869
	Xavier			
251	Cyprien	(195)	M. Ls. Nadeau B.	1849

GOULET.

1	Jacques		Marg. Maillier	
	René			
	Louis			
	Nicolas			
	Antoine			
	Joseph			
2	René	(1)	Cath. Leroux C.R.	1670
3	Nicolas	(1)	Xainte Cloutier C.R.	1672
	Geneviève		J. B. Ferlant S.P.	1710
	Marguerite		Gab. Ferlant S.P.	1719
	Jean			
	Louis			
4	Louis	(1)	Marie Gaudin A.G.	1692
	Louis			
5	Antoine	(1)	Mad. Guion A.G.	1692
	Joseph			
6	Joseph	(1)	Anne Julien A.G.	1692
	Antoine			
	Louis			
7	Jean	(3)	Marg. Blouard S.P.	1700
	Angélique		Chs. Frs. Lemieux S.P.	
				1727
	Marie Louise		Ant. Roberge S.P.	1730
	Pierre			
	Louis			
	François			
	Jean Baptiste			
8	Louis	(3)	Anne Cantin A.G.	1712
	Marie Anne		J. B. Crépeau S.P.	1735
	Geneviève		Pierre Ferlant S.P.	1742
	Madeleine		Gab. Ferlant S.P.	1747
	Marguerite		Chs. Paradis S.P.	1750
	Jean			
9	Louis	(4)	Thérèse Roussin A.G.	1712
10	Joseph	(5)	Genev. Ratté S.P.	1722
11	Louis	(6)	M. Jos. Huot A.G.	1733
	Louis			
12	Antoine	(6)	Marie Laberge A.G.	1744
	Agnès		Ant. Noël S.P.	1775
13	Jean Baptiste	(7)	Marie Lemieux Cap.	
			S.Ign.	1727
	Marie Josette		Julien Dumont S.Chs.	1752
	Jean			
14	François		Hélène Ratte S.P.	1734
	Marie Salomé		Pierre Filian S.P.	1760
	Marie Agathe		Prisque Roberge S.P.	1766
	Thérèse		J. B. Drouin S.P.	1767
	Hélène		Jos. Fournier S.Chs.	1768
	Pierre			
	Charles			
	Michel			
	André			
	Jean			
	Ambroise			
15	Louis	(7)	Josette Coté S.P.	1740
16	Pierre	(7)	Génév. Paradis S.P.	1741
	Marie Louise		Jos. Blais S.Chs.	1762
	François			
	Pierre			
	Joseph			
	Jean			
17	Jean	(8)	Thérèse Paradis S.P.	1750
	Jean			
	Ignace			
	Pierre			
	Gabriel			
18	Louis	(11)	Marie Cantin A.G.	1759
	François			
19	Jean	(13)	Angé Couture B.	1748
20	Pierre	(14)	Hélène Noël S.P.	1771
	Charles			
	Pierre			
21	Charles	(14)	M. Mad. Noel S.P.	1774
	Hélène		Chs. Diers S.G.	1802
	Marguerite		Michel Valiére „	1802

SESSIONAL PAPER No. 18

GOULET.

Angélique	Ant. Dubé	S.G.	1804
Marie	Jos. Godbout	„	1809
François	Pierre Bacquet	„	1812
François			
Louis			
Joseph			
Charles			
Jean			
Pierre			
22 Michel (14)	M. Anne Asselin	S.V.	1776
Marie Josette	Chs. Guay	S.M.	1798
Geneviève	J. B. Henri	S.G.	1800
23 André	M. Anne Pilote	S.M.	1779
Marie Anne	Chs. Penin	S.G.	1800
Marguerite	Jean Lebrun	„	1800
Marie	Etn. Gosselin	„	1801
Josette	Gab. Bilodeau	„	1804
Archange	Jos Patouel	„	1817
André			
Joseph			
24 Jean (14)	Marie Gagnon	S.V.	1780
Jean Baptiste			
François			
Charles			
25 Ambroise (14)	M. Angé Corriveau	S.V.	1787
Pierre			
Jean			
Ambroise			
Le même	M. Anne Patouel	S.V.	1801
26 François (16)	M. Eliz. Blais ‡	„	1763
François			
Joseph			
27 Pierre (16)	M. Genev. Valiére	S.Chs.	1767
	V. de Chs. Dorion		
Marie	J. B. Gontier	S. Chs.	1786
Marguerite	Gab. Terrien	„	1792
Le même	Marg. Lépnèlin	„	1794
28 Joseph (16)	M. Angé Coté	„	1775
Basilisse	André Clément	„	1797
Isabelle	Pierre Terrien	„	1804
Marie	Aug. Tangué	„	1808
Charlotte	Céleste Lacroix	„	1810
Josette	Jos. Clément	„	1843
Pierre			
Joseph			
29 Jean (16)	M. Ls. Turgeon	„	1775
Marguerite	Aug. Alaire	S.V.	1815
Jean			
Pierre			
30 Jean (17)	Thérèse Paradis	S.P.	1783
Marie	Ls. Ferlant	„	1819
Thérèse	Zach. Amable Taillon	S.P.	1820
Olivier			
Louis			
31 Ignace (17)	Marie Langlois	„	1785
Marie Thérèse	Ls. Poulin	„	1834
Jean			
Ignace			
32 Pierre (17)	M. Anne Plante	„	1794
Rosalie	Victor Ferlant	„	1839
Pierre			
33 Gabriel (17)	M. Jos. Grivrau	„	1798
34 François (18)	Marie Marois	A.G.	1796
Marguerite	Dominique Carrier	Lévis	1836
Louis			
35 Charles (20)	M. Reine Crépeau Q.	S.P.	1796
36 Pierre (20)	Marie Gourdeau	„	1800
Marie	Alexis Ferlant	„	1821
Marie Angélique	Ls. Ferlant	„	1836

‡ Vérifier s'il est fils de Pre. ou de Jean.

GOULET.

37 Charles (21)	Angé. Blanchet	S.G.	1800
38 François (21)	M. Ls. Marseau	S.V.	1804
Louise	Nicolas Pouliot	S.G.	1824
Anastasie	Chs. Roy	„	1827
François			
Le même	Vict. Toussaint	„	1818
39 Joseph (21)	Monique Lebrun	„	1804
Monique	Abraham Turgeon	S.G.	1819
Catherine	Etn. Coté	„	1826
Maxime			
40 Jean (21)	Judith Nadeau	„	1809
Esther	Pierre Boivin	S.M.	1852
Louis			
41 Pierre (21)	Angé. Gosselin	S.G.	1812
42 Louis (21)	Charlotte Aubé	S.Chs.	1824
43 André (23)	Fse. Labreque	S.G.	1809
Françoise	Gab. Labreque	„	1828
44 Joseph (23)	Josette Duperron	S.G.	1810
45 JeanBaptiste(24)	Marie Baillargeon	S.G.	1809
Marie	Jacq. Brousseau	„	1827
Jean Baptiste			
46 François (24)	Judith Baillargeon	S.G.	1812
47 Ambroise (25)	Marie Paquet	„	1813
48 Pierre (25)	Thérèse Dufresne	S.L.	1815
Thérèse	Ant. Godbout	„	1848
Flavien			
Jean			
49 Jean (25)	Marg. Tangué	S.G.	1818
50 François (26)	Genev.Gosselin	S.Chs.	1790
Marie	Chs. Vaillancour	S. Chs.	1826
Marguerite	Jean Pender	„	1835
Joseph			
Augustin			
Charles			
51 Joseph (26)	M. Ls. Goupy	S.M.	1800
Marie	Amb.Coulombe	S.Chs.	1829
Félicité	Céleste Lacroix	S.Chs.	1832
Théotiste	Simon Boutin	S. Chs.	1841
Geneviève	Pierre Lacroix	S.Chs.	1850
Joseph			
Augustin			
52 Joseph (28)	Marg. Bêtel	S. Chs.	1803
Joseph			
Charles			
53 Pierre (28)	M. Jos. Boulet	S.M.	1811
54 Jean (29)	Cécile Couture	S.Chs.	1799
	S.H,		
Daniel			
55 Pierre (29)	Angé Leroux	S. Chs.	1802
Le même	Marie Gosselin	S.Chs	1815
Louis			
56 Louis (30)	Charlotte Huard	Lévis S.H.	1789
Luce	Ls. Shinck	B.	1830
Marie Claire	Ant. Nadeau	S.H.	1817
Josette	An. Noël	S.H.	1818
Angèle	Pierre Gagné	S.H.	1819
Jean Baptiste			
Louis			
57 Olivier (30)	Cath. Ferlant	S.P.	1812
Flavie	Frs. Pichet	S.P.	1840
Marie Noflette	Ant. Nolen	S.P.	1847
Félix			
Le même	Josette Paquet	S.P.	1851
58 Jean (31)	Thérèse Paquet	S.P.	1812
M. Marguerite	Jos. Cantin	S.P.	1854
Jean Bruno			
Jean Basile			

GOULET.

59	Ignace	(31)	Genev. Martel S.P. 1814
	Geneviève		Laurent Létourneau S. P. 1841
	Scolasticque		Leon Aubin S. P. 1844
	Marie Marthe		Mag. Coté S.P. 1846
	Marie Esther		Ed. Bouffart S.P. 1852
	Flavie		Isaac GuillMorinS.P. 1855
	Ignace		
60	Pierre	(32)	Apolline Nolin S.P. 1840
	Appolline Célina		Jos. Octave Coté S.P. 1662
	Pie. Epiphane		
61	Charles	(24)	Genev. Talbot S.Tho. 1807
	Geneviève		Jacq. Gendron S.G. 1823
	Emerance		Prisque BélangerS.G. 1828
	François		
62	Joseph		Louise Goulet
	Julie		Jos. Dutile S.Chs. 1840
63	Pierre		Josette Robert
	Joseph		
	Jean Baptiste		
64	Louis	(34)	M. Vict. AudetS.Chs 1835
65	François		Angèle Langlois S.G. 1830
66	Maxime	(39)	Adé Couture S.V. 1850
67	Louis	(40)	M. Vict. AudetS.Chs 1835
68	Jean Batiste	(45)	M.AngéTalbot S.F.S. 1831 St. Anselme
69	Jean	(48)	Marie Gendreau S.L. 1847
70	Flavien	(48)	Soulange Corriveau S.L. 1847
71	Charles	(50)	Angé Paquet B. 1825
72	Joseph	(50)	Mad. Gontier S.Chs. 1829
73	Augustin	(50)	Anastasie Rousseau S.Chs. 1830
74	Joseph	(51)	Emérence Rousseau S.Chs. 1830
75	Augustin	(51)	Archange Bourassa S.Chs. 1836
76	Charles	(52)	Marg. Coté B. 1830
77	Joseph	(52)	Susanne GirardS.Chs. 1835
78	Daniel	(54)	Marie Trahan S.Chs. 1827
79	Louis	(55)	Marg. Genest S.Chs. 1842
A	Louis	(56)	Marg. Nadeau S.H. 1819
80	JeanBaptiste	(56)	M. Ls. Labadie Lévis 1828
81	Félix	(57)	Marie Leclaire S.P. 1836
	Marie Zéloïve		Narcisse Ferlant S.P. 1860
	Jean Félix		
82	Jean Bruno	(58)	VénérandeCantinS.P.1848
	Marie Emérence		Jacq. Octave Plante S.P. 1867
83	Jean Basile	(58)	Genev.Adéle CotéS.P.1855
84	Ignace	(59)	Henriette Noël S.P. 1848
85	Pre.Epiphane	(60	Genev. Flamine Gosselin S.P. 1867
	Le même		Georgiana PlanteS.P. 1887
86	François	(61)	Marcelline Richard S.V. 1849
87	Joseph	(63)	Célina Terrien S.M. 1861
A	JeanBaptiste	(63)	Martine Plante S.M. 1862
88	Jean Félix	(81)	M. Octave Leclaire S.P. 1864

GOUPY.

1	Antoine		Marie Gaboury S.M. 1698
	Elisabeth		Frs. Duval Islet 1732
	Antoine		
	Louis		
	Joseph		
2	Antoine	(1)	Marie Boulet S.Tho. 1724
	Elisabeth		André Lacroix S.M. 1745
	Françoise		Jos. Gautron S.M. 1746
	Françoise		2°Gab. Balan S.M. 1752
	Agathe		Jos. Bacquet S.M.1747
	Brigitte		Claude Lefebvre ,, 1749
	Marie Marthe		J.B. LeRoy ,, 1753

GOUPY.

	Marie Louise		Pierre LeRoy S.M. 1759
	Marie Louise		2° Louis Marseau ,, 1763
	Marie Louise		3° Jos. Nadeau ,, 1768
	Pierre		
	Louis		
3	Joseph	(1)	Fse. Bissonnet S.V.1729
	Françoise		Nicolas Gontier S.M.1767
	Laurent		
	Pierre		
	Joseph		
	Le même		M. Anne Balan S.M 1749
	Agathe		Chs. Gontier ,, 1778
	Marie Anne		Pierre Chamberlan S.M.1782
	Catherine		Aug. Mercier ,, 1782
	M. Geneviève		Jos. Roy ,, 1796
	Marguerite		Ant. Rémillard ,, 1788
	Gabriel		
4	Louis	(1)	Eliz. Agnès Thibault S.V.1736
	Elizabeth		J.B. Poliquin S.M.1762
	Marie Louise		Jos. Gosselin ,, 1765
	Marie		Jos. Clément ,, 1762
	Marie		2° Jos. Lepage S.Chs.1778
	M. Madeleine		Jos. Blouin S.M 1774
	M. Madeleine		2° Frs. Pouliot S Chs.1791
	Louis		
	Paul		
	Augustin		
5	Louis	(2)	Cath. Fortier S.M.1762
6	Pierre	(2)	Marg. Roy ,, 1761
	Marie		Guill. Audet ,, 1792
	Agathe		Aug. Fournier ,, 1797
	Françoise		Jos. Marie Fortin ,, 1799
	Marguerite		Ls. Bissonnet ,, 1802
	Antoine		
	Pierre		
	Michel		
7	Pierre	(3)	M. Eliz. Gravel S.M.1766
	Marie		Jacq. Catellier S.V.1758
	Le même		M. Reine Labbé B.1779
8	Joseph	(3)	Angé.Ferlant S.Chs.1772
	M. Angélique		Nicolas Pouliot ,, 1799
	Victoire		Frs. Jolivet S.M.1797
	M. Judith		Frs. Baudoin ,, 1709
	Le même		Thérèse Boulet S.Chs.1788
	Charles		
9	Laurent	(3)	M. Jos. Tangué S.V.1782
	Marie		Jacques Quéret S.H. 1818
	Laurent		
10	Gabriel	(3)	M. Thérèse Peltier S.M.1777
	Marie		Ant. Leclaire ,, 1820
	Gabriel		
11	Louis	(4)	Eliz. Boulet S.M.1766
	Le même		Dorothée Lemelin ,, 1769 V. de Jos. Lebrun
	Louis		
	Joseph		
12	Augustin	(4)	M.Ls.Thivierge S.M.1775
	Marie Louise		Jos. Goulet ,, 1800
	M. Brigitte		Jos. Lacroix ,, 1804
	M. Geneviève		Aut. Boutin S.Chs.1807
	Augustin		
	Jean Baptiste		
13	Paul	(4)	M. Félicité Roy S.M.1797
	Paul		
	Augustin		
14	Antoine	(6)	M.Héléne Denis S.M.1794
	Marie		Ls. Dorval ,, 1820
	Lucie		Chs. Couture ,, 1827
	Marie Louise		Bénoni Couture ,, 1839
	Marie Chantal		Michel Audet ,, 1840
	Julie		Colomban Turgeon B.1834
	Françoise		Jean Couture ,, 1837
	Antoine		

GOUPY.

	Joseph				
15	Michel	(6)	Basilisse Corriveau		S.M.1800
	Basilisse		Pierre Godbout	"	1829
	Michel				
	Prudent				
16	Pierre	(6)	M. Barbe Corriveau		S.M.1803
	Michel				
	Pierre				
17	Charles	(8)	M. Reine Blais	S.F.S.	1813
	Marie Reine		F.X. Blais	"	1832
A	Laurent	(9)	M. Pelagie Cadoret		S.H.1816
18	Gabriel	(10)	M. Genev. Langlois		S.V.1805
	Euphrosine		Aug. Fournier	S.M.	1830
	Marie Désanges		Michel Leblanc	"	1843
	M. Anastasie		Ed. Letellier	"	1851
	Martial				
	David				
	Le même		Félicité Métivier	S.M.	1851
19	Louis	(11)	Marg. Guénet	S.Chs.	1794
20	Joseph	(11)	M. Marg. Blais	"	1797
	Joseph				
21	JeanBaptiste	(12)	M.Jos. Gautron	S.M.	1805
	Françoise		Etn. Pazuet	B	1827
	M. Elizabeth		Claude Paquet	"	1834
22	Augustin	(12)	M. Théotiste Métivier		S.V.1804
	Geneviève		Jacq. Brochu	S.M.	1830
	M. Theotiste		Jos. Gautron	"	1833
	Marie Sophie		J. B. Samson	"	1851
	Marie Sophie		2° Ls. Fortier	"	1855
	Laurent				
	Jean Baptiste				
23	Paul	(13)	Marg. Clément	B.	1826
	Paul				
24	Augustine	(13)	Archange Clément		S.Chs.1831
	Marc				
25	Antoine	(14)	Cath. Dion	S.M.	1822
	Luce		Etn. Quéret	"	1851
	Marie Clarisse		Gervais Pouliot	"	1852
	Gertrude		Fred. Aubé	"	1865
	Ephrem				
	Le même		Constance Guay	B.	1848
26	Joseph	(14)	Genev. Turgeon	B.	1829
	Marie Anne		Walden Roy	S.M.	1853
	Léon				
27	Prudent	(15)	Félicité Roy	"	1841
28	Michel	(15)	M. Rose Tangué	"	1835
29	Pierre	(16)	Cecile Leclaire	S.G.	1827
30	Michel	(16)	Christine Grégoire	Lévis	1836
31	David	(18)	Caroline Catellier	SM	1846
32	Martial	(18)	Soulange Roy	"	1858
33	Joseph	(20)	M. Augé Aubé	B.	1841
	Le même		Angéle Gontier	B.	1859
			V. de Pre. Fortier		
34	Pierre Noël		Christine Samson	B.	
	Pierre				
35	Laurent	(22)	Abéline Gautron	S.M.	1846
36	JeanBaptiste	(22)	Marcelline Dion	"	1841
37	Paul	(23)	Mad. Catellier	S.Chs.	1847
38	Louis		Marie Ouillet		S. Malache
	Marie		Frs. Lefebvre	S.V.	1861
39	Marc	(24)	Marcelline Hélie	S.M.	1864
40	Ephrem	(25)	¹ Rose de Lima Schambier		S.M. 1871

¹ Fille de Michel Schambier et d'Anastasie Furois de S.H.

18—23

GOURDEAU.

41	Léon	(26)	Philomène Gosselin		S.M. 1858
42	Pierre	(34)	Angèle Naud	S.Chs.	1847
1	Jacques		Eléonore de Grandmaison		
	Jeanne René		Chs. Macard	Qué.	1686
	Antoine				
	Jacques				
2	Antoine	(1)	Vve Fse. Taché	"	1685
3	Jacques	(1)	Marie Bissot	"	1691
	Jacques				
4	Jacques	(3)	Marie Barbel	"	1733
5	Pierre		Marg. Robichaud		
	Marguerite		Amand Greg. Lebrun		S.P. 1770
	Stanislas				
	Isidore				
	Isaac				
	Marien				
6	Stanislas	(5)	M.Jos.Leblanc	Miray	1779
	Marie Josette		Frs. Savard	S.P.	1777
	Ignace				
	Edouard				
7	Isidore	(5)	Mad. Dugas	Miray	1779
	Monique		Pierre Pichet	S.P.	1801
	Joseph				
	Jean				
8	Isaac	(5)	Natalie Miraux	Que.	1767
	Natalie		Pierre Savard	S.P.	1801
	Jacques				
	Isaac				
	Le même		Marcoux		
9	Marin	(5)	Marie Foret	Que.	1767
	Marie		Stanislas Moor	S.P.	1796
	Marie		2° Pierre Goulet	"	1800
	Pierre				
10	Isaac	(6)	Louise Forbes	Que.	1792
	Elisabeth		David Morin	S.P.	1825
	Marie		Jos. Genest	"	1825
	Julie		Frs. Julien	"	1829
	Angélique		Ls. Julien	"	1829
	Isaac				
	Jean				
	Pierre				
11	Jean Edouard	(6)	Marg. Ainse	S.Tho.	1795
	Marguerite		Olivier Grenier	S.P.	1822
	Julie		James Robertson		
	Edouard				
	Pierre				
12	Joseph	(7)	M. Thècle Noël	"	1783
	Monique		Jean Couture	"	1831
13	Jean	(7)	Ange Forbes	"	1802
A	Isaac	(8)	Josette Lemère	Qué.	1793
14	Jacques	(8)	Angé Coté	S.P.	1787
	Angélique		Jos. Couture	"	1810
	Monique		Frs. Félicien Noël	"	1813
	Marie Anne		Pierre Bonn	"	1818
	Rosalie		Pierre Plante	"	1820
	Rosalie		2° Chs. Guérard	"	1837
	François				
A	Pierre	(9)	Rose Desrocher	S.Tho.	1795
15	Jean	(10)	Sophie Dupile	S.P.	1829
	Sophie		Barth. Fournier	"	1851
16	Isaac	(10)	M. Angé Dupile	"	1833
	AngéleJosephine		Chs.Alex.Guérard	"	1869
	Isaac Octavien				
	Chs.Geo. Honoré				
17	Pierre	(16)	Adé Faucher		
	Adélaïde		Godfroi Prudent Blais		S.P. 1860
	J. B. Octave				
18	Edouard	(11)	DorothéeMontigny	SP.	1841
19	Pierre	(11)	M. Marg. Crepéau	Qué.	
	M. Mag. Eliza		Edmond Gautron	SM	1864
20	François	(14)	Genev. Paradis	S.P.	1811
	Geneviève		Pierre Leclaire	"	1837

GOURDEAU.

Pierre
François
Le même   Marg. Bégin   Lévis 1820
Rosalie   Jean Marcoux   S.P. 1843
Flore   Pierre Jobin   "   1853
Justine Eugènie   Isaac Octav. Gourdeau
        S.P. 1858
Chs. Eugène
21 Pierre   (20) Adé Noël   "   1840
Adelaïde   Ls. Fidèle Pichet   "   1864
Marie Elise   Jos. Gosselin   "   1866
Marie Artémise   Ls. Trudel   "   1872
Marie Joséphine   Jos. Oct. Côté S.Pétronille
22 François   (20)
23 Chs. Eugène (20)   M. Cath. Noël   S.P. 1851
Le même   Clementine Picard
24 Isaac Octa– (16)   Justine Eugenie
   vien   Gourdeau   S.P. 1858

25 Chs. Geo.   (16) M. Philomène Genest
Honoré   S.P. 1866
26 J. B. Octave (17)   M. Malvina Blais   "   1863

GOURGUE.

1 Paul   Susanne Lacoste Gascogne
Paul
2 Paul   (1) Jositte Ratté   SP. 1744.
Marie   Jos. Plante   S.M. 1770
Jean Baptiste
Paul
Joseph Paul
3 Paul   (2) Fse. Bouchard   S.V. 1769
Marie Josette   Jacq. Roy   "   1805
M. Françoise   Maurice McNeil   "   1806
M. Susanne   Ls. Blais   "   1815
Joseph
Charles
Paul
4 Joseph Paul   (2) M.Brigitte Fortier   "   1774
Marguerite   Pierre Guenet   S.M. 1802
Marie   Paul Baillargeon   "   1805
Joseph
5 Jean Baptiste(2) M. Mad. Gaulin S.Frs.1775
6 Charles   (3) Marie McNeil   S.V. 1802
Adelaïde   Prosper Roy   "   1840
Marie   Henri Bélanger   "   1841
Charles
7 Paul   (3) M. Cécile Corriveau
        S.V. 1803
Marguerite   Jacq. Langlois   "   1831
Victoire   Jos. Morisset   "   1837
Adelaïde   Vital Quéret   "   1842
Henriette   Ls. Boutin   "   1843
Paul
8 Joseph   (3) M. Anne Queret S.M. 1805
9 Joseph   (4) Vict. Tangué   "   1796
Victoire   Jos. Ducrot   S.Chs. 1821
Le même   M. Angé Bétil   S.M. 1799
Reine   Michel Turgeon   "   1821
Angélique   Chs. Bilodeau   S.M. 1823
Marguerite   Ls. Bouffart   "   1832
Adelaïde   Pierre Corriveau   "   1835
Charles
Joseph
Jean
10 Charles   (6) Sophie Brochu   S.V. 1833
11 Paul   (7) ArchangeBélanger "   1833
Delphine   F. X. Bilodeau   "   1865
Philomène   Jean Martineau   "   1870
Hyppolite
Urbain Cyriac
Théophile
Damase
12 Charles   (9) Marg. Clavet   S.M. 1839
       V. d'Ign. Hélie

GOURGUE.

13 Jean   (9) Julie Catellier   S.M. 1845
14 Joseph   (9) Marg. Turgeon S.Chs.1822
Angèle   Pierre Naud   S.M. 1846
Vitaline   Alexis Rousseau   "   1847
15 Hyppolite   (11) Florence Eliza Delima
       Gagnon   S.V. 1861
16 Urbain   (11) Séraphine Richard "   1862
Cyriac
17 Damase   (11) Genev. Richard   "   1867
18 Théophile   (11) M. Belzémire Bolduc
       S.V. 1870

GOUSSE.

2 Jean Baptiste (1) Marg. Boulet
Marguerite   Frs. Lainé   S.V. 1793
Marie Louise   J. B. Dorval   "   1798
Joseph
Louis
3   "   (2) Marie Patry   S.M. 1797
4 Joseph   (2) M. Marthe Leclaire
       S.V. 1800

GRAVEL.

1 Marie Joseph   Marg. Tavernier Que. 1644
Claude
Charles
2 Claude   (1) Jeanne Cloutier C.R. 1687
Marguerite   Chs. Cloutier   "   1721
Ignace
3 Ignace   (2) M. Mad. Braconnier
       C.R. 1737
Madeleine   Guill. Roy   B. 1764
M. Angélique   Jos. Chs. Rouillard
       S.M. 1768
M. Angélique   2° Frs. Mercier   "   1786
Ignace
4 Charles   (1) Fse. Guion   S.Anne 1689
Angélique   Jean Dubeau   C.R. 1728
Guillaume
5 Guillaume   (4) M. Fse. Brisson C.R. 1733
M. Elisabeth   Pierre Goupy   S.M. 1766
6 Claude   Angélique Roy   C.R.
Joseph
7 Ignace   (3) M. Mad. Fortier S.J. 1768
Marg. Vict.   Ls. Turgeon   B. 1799
M. Madeleine   J. B. Bélanger   "   1820
Jos. Clément
8 Joseph   (6) Théotiste Blais Bert. 1798
9 Jos. Clément (7) Cécile Fournier   B. 1815
Cécile   Chs. Gagnon   "   1855
Jacques Frs.
Jos. Clément
Simon
10 Simon   (9) M.Hermine NadeauB. 1840
11 Jacq. François(9) Henriette Boutin   "   1845
12 Joseph Clé– (9) M. Flavie Roy   "   1858
   ment

GREFFART.

1 Louis   Louise Gautier   S.F. 1648
Louis
Jacques
2 Louis   (1) Fse. Claire Mourier
       S.J. 1710
Angélique   Jos. Audibert   "   1744
Geneviève   Jos. Paquet   "   1744
Elisabeth   PierreVaillancourS.F.1748
Elisabeth   2° Chs. Guérard S.Frs.1767
Claire Françoise   Jean Marie Gaudin
       S.F.S. 1751
Joseph
Louis
3 Jacques   (1) Jeanne Terrien
Perpétue   Paul Plante

GREFFART.

Le même	Marie Delaunay			
	Vve. Jean Brochu			
Théophile				
Joachim				
Le même	Jeanne Fontaine	S.J.	1732	
Gabriel				
François				
4 Joseph	(2) Angé Pepin		"	1745
5 Louis	(2) Cath. Garant	S.F.S.	1738	
Marie Claire	Jos. Marie Thivierge			
		S.F.S.	1763	
Le même	M.Genev.Rouleau	"	1749	
Marie Thècle	Jos. Fradet		"	1800
6 Joachin	(3) Angé Simard	S.M.	1746	
Angélique	Chs. Bétil	S.V.	1763	
Le même	Mad. Pepin	S.J.	1751	
Antoine				
François				
Jacques				
7 Théophile	(3) Eliz. Guion	S.F.	1748	
Marie Victoire	Frs. Vaillancour	"	1771	
Joseph				
Le même	Marg. Baillargeon			
		S.L.	1755	
8 François	(3) M. Angé Quéret	S.M.	1757	
Le même	Marg. Guénet	"	1763	
9 Gabriel	(3) Mad. Eliz. Thivierge			
		S.J.	1753	
Gabriel				
10 François	(6) M. Hélène Chevalier			
	Q.	S.M.	1772	
Louise	J. B. Lainé	S.Chs.	1796	
11 Antoine	(6) M. Anne Tangué	S.M.	1787	
12 Jacques	(6) Louise Godbout	S.G.	1787	
13 Joseph	(7) Monique Dorval	S.F.	1774	
Marie Madeleine	Jos. Dupile		"	1809
Angélique	Frs. Asselin		"	1841
14 Gabriel	(9) M. Genev. Rousseau			
		S.Tho.	1786	

GROMELIN-LAFORME.

1 Noël	Marie Balan	S.M.	1701	
Marie	Pierre Hélie	B.	1722	
Marie Louise	Jacq. Guénet		"	1723
Joseph Noël				
2 Joseph Noël	(1) Susane Labrecque	S.V.	1727	
Marguerite	Jean Patry	S.M.	1748	
Marguerite	2° Laurent Couture		"	1750
Pierre Noël				
Le même	Josette Plante		"	1780
3 Pierre Noël	(2) Angé Fortier	S.J.	1753	
Le même	M. Mad. Fournier		1777	

GROINIER.

1 Nicolas	Marie Boette	Que.	1676	
M. Madeleine	Michel Masson	S.Frs.	1693	
Marguerite	Alphonse Martel	S.F.	1701	
Le même	Anne Chrétien		"	1687
Jean Baptiste				
2 Jean Baptiste	(1) Genev. Pepin	S.Frs.	1719	

GROISSART.

1 Jean Ignace	Jeanne Guignard			
M. Madeleine	Alexis Coulombe	Bert.	1733	
Geneviève	Frs. Jouet		"	1737

GUAY.

1 Jacques	Marg. Chauveau		1693	
Marie Josette	Ls. Paré	B.	1719	
Angélique	Olivier Couture		"	1728
Susanne	Jos. Miville		"	1736
Marguerite	Jos. Baudoin		"	1744

18—23½

GUAY.

Jacques				
Jean				
2 Louis	M. Anne Bégin			
Le même	Susanne Samson	Lévis	1692	
Louis				
Charles				
3 Jacques	(1) Marie Couture	B.	1723	
Marie	Frs. Filteau		"	1750
M. Françoise	Ant. Fournier		"	1751
Thérèse	Jean Molleur		"	1756
Geneviève	Jean Roy		"	1759
Marguerite	J. B. Filteau		"	1760
4 Jean	(1) Angé Plassant	B.	1730	
Joseph				
Jean				
Pierre				
5 Charles	(2) Mad. Labrecque		"	1733
Charles				
6 Louis	(2) M. Thérèse Duquet			
François				
Louis				
7 Etienne	Susanne Labrecque			
Marguerite	Chs. Roy	S.M.	1769	
8 Etienne	Susanne Naud			
Susanne	Jos. Couture		"	1771
Angélique	Jos. Coté	B.	1817	
9 Joseph	Angé Turgeon			
Joseph				
10 Charles	Cath. Samson			
Charles				
11 André	Genev. Poiré			
Jean Baptiste				
Henri				
Augustin				
12 Louis	(6) Genev. Bourget	Lévis	1744	
Joseph				
Louis				
13 François	(6) Marg. Lacasse	B.	1752	
14 Pierre	(4) M. Marthe Filteau		"	1754
Marie Anne	Chs. Lecours		"	1797
Louis				
Pierre				
François				
Joseph				
Charles				
15 Jean	(4) Marg. Couillard	B.	1761	
Marguerite	Pierre Ménard		"	1780
Marie Anne	Pierre Roy		"	1787
Marie Josette	Ant. Dutile	S.G.	1797	
Joseph				
Jean Baptiste				
16 François	Genev. Verret			
Jean Baptiste				
17 Joseph	(4) Cath. Boilard	S.M.	1763	
Catherine	Ant. Lacasse	B.	1781	
Angélique	Alexandre Couture			
		S.Chs.	1787	
18 Charles	(5) Génév. Carrier	Lévis	1769	
Ignace				
19 Joseph	(9) Cath. Forgues	Lévis	1781	
François				
20 Charles	(10) M. Claire Thivierge			
		Lévis	1783	
Le même	M. Jos. Goulet	S.M.	1798	
21 Jean	(11) M. Jos. Naud	Lévis	1784	
Baptiste				
Ambroise				
Jean Baptiste				
22 Henri	(11) Marg. Poiré	Levis	1800	
Le même	Genev. Bilodeau	S.G.	1821	
23 Thimothée	Louise Lemieux	Lévis	1781	
Le même	Louise Lefebvre		"	1791
Michel				
Charles				
Etienne				

GUAY.

24	Jean	Susanne Samson	
	Louis Prosper		
25	André	M. Chs. Naud	
	Joseph		
	Jean Baptiste		
	André		
26	Augustin	(11) Genev. Poiré	Lévis 1802
	Geneviève	Frs. Turgeon	B. 1829
	Angèlique	Etn. Bégin	„ 1839
	Euphrosine	Pierre David Roy	„ 1840
	Edouard		
27	Joseph	(12) Eliz. Gosselin	S.L. 1781
28	Louis	(12) Fse. Denis	S.M. 1782
	François		
29	François	(14) Euphrosine Naud S.Chs.	
			1791
	Euphosine	Jean Turgeon	B. 1828
	Marguerite	Jos. Turgeon	S.G. 1828
	Pierre		
	Le même	M. Ls. PoliquinS.Chs.1813	
30	Pierre	(14) Josette Couture	B. 1793
	Marie Josette	J. B. Chabot	B. 1821
	Abraham		
	Hubert		
31	Charles	(14) M. Barbe Picard S.P.S	
			1794
	Marguerite	Pierre Audet	S.G. 1828
	Charles		
32	Joseph	(14) Marg. Turgeon S.Chas.	
			1803
	Marguerite	Chs. Provost	B. 1827
	Sophie	Raimond Turgeon	B. 1830
33	Louis	(14) Marg. Alary	Bert. 1803
34	Charles	M. Jos. Fournier	
	Marie Louise	Etn. Boilard	B. 1829
	Geneviève	Frs. Labrecque	B. 1820
	Sophie	Jos. Labrecque	B. 1831
	Charles		
35	Jean	(15) Reine Blanchet S.G. 1797	
	Baptiste		
	Angélique	Hubert Audet	S.G. 1827
	Héléne	J. B. Guilmet	S.G. 1828
	François		
	Jean Baptiste		
36	Joseph	(15) Génév. Lacroix S.Chs.1798	
	Marguerite	Laurent Coulombe B. 1823	
	Geneviève	Hilaire Roy	B. 1827
	Pierre		
	Joseph		
	Thomas		
37	JeanBaptiste(16) Marg. Rèaume Chs.		
		Bourg. 1785	
	Geneviève	Guill Gautier	S. V. 1826
	Le même	Marg. Fongamy C.S.	
			Ign. 1801
	Le même	M. Genev. Gagné	
			S. P. S. 1804
38	Ignace	(18) Marg. Queret S.Chs. 1804	
39	François	(19) Archange Fortier S.V.1809	
	Scolastique	Chs. Labrecque	B. 1840
	Constance	Ant. Goupy	B. 1848
	Magloire		
40	Antoine	Genev. Crépeau Levis 1815	
	Le même	Marie Bédard S. G. 1820	
42	Pierre	Emélie Chabot	
			B.
	Marie Flavie	F. X. Nadeau S.Chs.	
			1847
43	JeanBaptiste(21) Sophie Coté	B. 1830	
44	Ambroise	(21) Eliz. Turgeon	B. 1835
45	Jérome	Thérése Foucher	
	Apolline	Etn. Paré	S. F. 1860
	Jacques		
46	Michel	(23) M. Jos. Bergeron B. 1823	
47	Charles	(23) Rose Robitaille	B. 1824
48	Etienne	(23) M. Chs. Paquet	B. 1830

GUAY.

49	LouisProsper(24) Félicite Bégin Lévis 1794		
	Jean		
50	André	(25) Genev. Paradis Lévis 1814	
	Damase		
	Joseph	(25) Thivierge Bourget B.1816	
52	JeanBaptiste(25) Euphrosine BourgetB.1821		
	Hubert		
	Edouard		
53	Michel	M. Anne Coté	
	Alexis		
54	Pierre	M. Eliz. Ouellet	
	Le même	Marg. Audet	B. 1849
55	François	Luce Bégin	
	Le même	M. Anne Racine S.M.1851	
56	Edouard	(26) M. Délina Nadeau B. 1840	
57	François	(28) Luce Samson, Levis 1830	
	François		
58	Pierre	(29) Fse. Fournier	B. 1831
59	Hubert	(30) M. Adé Girard	B. 1831
	Marie Délima	Pierre Chrétien	B. 1814
60	Abraham	(30) Eliz. Bernard S. V. 1840	
61	Charles	(31) M. Anne Dessaint	
			S. G. 1824
62	Charles	(34) M. Jos. Boilard B. 1831	
63	JeanBaptiste(35) Adé Carbonneau S.G.1825		
64	François	(35) Angéle Guilmet S.G.1828	
65	Joseph	(36) Rosalié Labrecque B. 1839	
66	Thomas	(36) Emerence Lacasse B. 1848	
67	Pierre	(36) Vitaline Lacroix B. 1848	
68	Magloire	(39) Emerence Labrecque	
			B. 1841
69	Jacques	(45) Adé Paradis	S. F. 1854
70	Jean	(49) Marg. Noel S. Chs. 1843	
71	Damase	(50) Scolastique Gendreau	
			S L. 1855
72	Hubert	(52) Hombéline Maranda	
			S.L. 1855
73	Edouard	(52) M. Sara Maranda S.L.1855	
			S.F. 1867
74	Alexis	(53) Damarise Létourneau	
75	François	(57) Lucie Lebrun S.Chs. 1859	

GUÉNET.

1	Pierre	Cath. Veullot S. F. 1675	
	Thomas		
	Le même	Eliz. Paquet	S. L. 1689
	Elisabeth	Frs. Bacquet	S. M. 1710
	Marie	Ls. Bechard	B. 1718
	Anne	Jean Le Roy	B. 1725
	Elisabeth	Jos. Jolivet	B. 1728
	Charles		
	Jacques		
	Pierre		
2	Thomas	(1) M. Anne Maheux B. 1705	
	Marie Anne	Paul Marotte	B. 1762
	Geneviève	Gregoire PoirierS.Chs.1759	
	Thomas		
3	Charles	(1) Génév. Larose	B. 1721
	Marie	Ls. Couture S Chs. 1763	
4	Pierre	(1) Marie Le Roy	B. 1723
	Marie Anne	Ant. Drapeau	B. 1748
	Marie	Ls. Gerard S. Chs. 1764	
	Pierre		
	Jean Baptiste		
	Etienne		
	François		
	Le même	Marie Lis S. Chs. 1768	
5	Jacques	(1) Louise Gromelin B. 1723	
	Thérése	Jean Daniau	B. 1740
6	Thomas	(2) Cath. Leroux S. M. 1738	
	M. Catherine	Jean Frs. Gontier	
			S. Chs. 1761
	Marie	Pierre Blais S. Chs. 1770	
	Angélique	Ls. Girard	„ 1774
	Marie	Jacq. Fournier	„ 1776

GUÉNET.

Thomas
Etienne
Pierre
7 Pierre   (4) M. Chs. Drapeau   B. 1748
8 Pierre   Marie Ratté
Marie   Eustache Royer   S. Chs. 1791
Josette   Ls. Vallerand   „ 1794
Pierre
Joseph
Gabriel
Le même   Susanne Mesteau   S.G. 1800
   V. de Ls. Vallerand
Le même   Véronique Fortier   S.G. 1819
   V. de Ls. Jolin
9 Jean Baptiste (4) M. Anne Couillard B. 1753
Elisabeth   Jos. Noël   S. Chs. 1778
Véronique   René Tangué   „ 1778
Angélique   Basile Leclaire   „ 1784
Louise   Ign. Gautron   „ 1784
Marie Anne   Laurent Lemelin   „ 1793
Marguerite   Ls. Goupy   „ 1794
Marie Josette   Gab. Lemelin   „ 1802
Angélique   Pierre Carbonneau   S. Chs. 1806
Jean Baptiste
Pierre
Le même   Mad. Ratté   „ 1795
10 Etienne   M. Jos. Lacasse   „ 1754
11 François   Genev. Coté   „ 1759
Le même   Louis Dejardon Lévis 1763
12 Thomas   (6) Cécile Couillard   B. 1766
12 Pierre   (6) M. Anne Blais S.V. 1771
14 Etienne   (6) Ange Gontier S.Chs. 1772
Angélique   Hyppolite Leclaire   S.G. 1794
Marie Louise   Guill. Audet   „ 1803
Victoire   J. B. Boutin   „ 1814
15 Charles   Genev. Couet, Que.
Joseph
16 Joseph   (8) Susanne Vallerand   S. Chs. 1796
Susanne   Pierre Brochu   S.G. 1819
17 Pierre   (8) Marg Gourgue S.M. 1802
Marguerite   Jos. Blais   S.F.S. 1825
   2° Eustache Bacon   S.P.S. 1840
Louise   Frs. Jolivet   „ 1833
Victoire   André Picard   „ 1835
Pierre
Louis
18 Gabriel   M. Angé Pilchat   S. Chs. 1814
Marguerite   Ls. Goulet   „ 1842
Marie Angélique Bernard Massé   B. 1838
Marie Hermine Ant. Labrecque   „ 1839
19 Jean Baptiste (9) Thérèse Leclaire   S. Chs. 1789
Marie Victoire Chs Morin   „ 1812
Marie Anne   Jean Pouliot   „ 1833
Barnabé
Thomas
Le même   (5) Thérèse Paquet   „ 1808
Félicité   Etn. Girard   Levis 1837
20 Joseph   (15) Fse. Bissonnet S.M. 1793
Joseph
Antoine
21 Jacques
Le même   Marie Goupy
   Angé. Lacasse   S.G. 1821
22 Pierre   (17) Louise Emélie Blais   S.F.S. 1834
Le même   M. Constance Picard   S.P.S. 1837

GUÉNET.

23 Louis   (17) Marg. Mathilde Blais   S.P.S. 1838
24 Barnabé   (19) Genev. Carrier Lévis 1814
25 Thomas   (19) Louise Lemieux   „ 1829
26 Joseph   (20) Marg. Hallé   „ 1823
Rigobert
François
27 Antoine   (20) Natalie Turcot   „ 1825
28 François   (26) Léocadie Coté S. Chs. 1861
29 Rigobert   (26) Sophie Provost   „ 1864
Pierre   (9) Modeste Gendron   S.H. 1860

GUÉRARD.

1 Charles   Mad. Chrétien   S.F. 1697
M. Madeleine   Chs. Landry S. Frs. 1715
Marguerite   Simon Deblois   „ 1716
Charles
François
Alexis
Joseph
2 Charles   (1) Mad. Lepage   S. Frs. 1722
Marie   Pierre Deblois   „ 1749
Hélène   Barth. Rosa   „ 1756
Isabelle   Ls. Gagné   „ 1764
Louis
Charles
Jacques
Le même   Eliz. Greffart   „ 1767
Marie Elizabeth Ls. Boissonneau S.J. 1802
3 François   (1) M. Jos. Lepage   S. Frs. 1727
Marie Louise   Jean Gagné   „ 1749
Josette   Ls. Cochon   „ 1765
Madeleine   Jos. Guion   „ 1771
Marie Louise   Jos. Gagné   „ 1773
François
Joseph
Charles
4 Joseph   (1) Genev. Langlois   S. Foye 1738
5 Alexis   (1) Véronique Martineau   S. Frs. 1726
Le même   Marthe Marseau S.J. 1757
6 Louis   (2) Louise Jobin   S. Frs. 1752
7 Charles   (2) M. Jos. Poulin S.Frs. 1760
8 Jacques   (2) Thérèse Gagné   „ 1761
Marie Lousie   Pierre Laurent   „ 1782
Marie Louise   2°Pierre Lheureux   S. Frs. 1808
Thérèse   Jos. Dompierre   „ 1786
M. Madeleine   Frs. Dompierre   S.F. 1793
M. Geneviève   Simon Lheureux   „ 1808
Louis
Charles
Jacques
9 François   (3) Julie Meneux   „ 1762
M. Abondance   Remi Picard   „ 1787
Marie Louise   Chs. Amable Primont
M. Madeleine   J. B. Marineau   S.F. 1806
Françoise
Louis
10 Joseph   Marie Meneux   „ 1763
M. Madeleine   Frs. Nadeau   S.Frs. 1798
Marie   J. B. Drouin   „ 1799
Marie Louise   Pierre Nadeau   „ 1802
Catherine   Jean Pepin   S.F. 1812
Françoise
Jean
11 Charles   (3) Marie Nadeau S.Frs. 1782
12 Jacques   (8) M. Ls. Pepin   „ 1787
Marie Louise   Michel Lessart   „ 1812
Josette   André Morisset   „ 1825
Charles
Louis

GUÉRARD.

	Joseph			
13	Louis	(8)	Brigitte Paré	S.F. 1792
	Marie		Ant. Canac	S.Frs. 1838
	Marie		2°Jos. Fradet	S.F. 1853
	Catherine		Pasome Hamel	S.Frs. 1840
	Marie Louise		Frs. Trudel	S.P. 1838
	Josette		Come Giguère	
				S. Anne 1838
	Louis			
	Jacques			
	Charles			
14	Charles	(8)	M. Jos. Dompierre	
				S.Frs. 1802
	Le même		M.Ls.Champagne S.F.1808	
15	Françoise	(9)	M. Pélagie Turcot S.F.1792	
	Ludivine		J. B. Asselin	" 1813
	Marie Luce		Frs. Guion	" 1818
	Marie Luce		2°J. B. Lemelin S.Frs.1847	
	M. Reparate		Andre Asselin	S.F. 1820
	Marie Colette		Jos. Poulin	" 1824
	Françoise			
16	Louis	(9)	M. Jos. Doyon S.Frs. 1798	
	Marie Josette		Jos. Rouleau	S.F. 1819
	Justine		Pierre Audet	" 1826
17	Françoise		M. Jos. Pepin	" 1792
	Le même		Angé Drouin	" 1799
	Marie Angélique		Jos. Dion	" 1825
	Edouard			
18	Jean	(10)	Genev. Pepin	" 1796
19	Charles	(12)	Angéle Guion	S.Frs. 1830
	Le même		Marg. Deblois	" 1845
20	Joseph	(12)	Ursule Cochon	S.J. 1821
	Luce		Jean Royer	S L. 1858
	Ursule		Frs. Bouffart	S.L. 1863
	Ursule		2°F. X. VilleneauS.P.1867	
	Célestin			
21	Louis	(12)	M. Mad. Couillard	
				S.F. 1815
22	Louis	(13)	Mad. Deblois	" 1826
	Sophie		Michel Martineau	
				S.Frs. 1848
	Marguerite		Frs. Canac	" 1862
23	Jacques	(13)	M. Henriette Loignon	
				S. F. 1829
	Anastasie		Honoré Déry	S.Frs. 1855
	Louis			
24	Charles	(13)	Rosalie GourdeauS.P. 1837	
	Chs, Alexandre			
25	Françoise	(15)	Thérèse Faucher S.G. 1831	
26	Edouard	(17)	Cath. Deblois	S.Frs. 1829
	Marie Louise		J. B. Dion	" 1861
27	Célestin	(20)	Marie Labrecque S.L. 1865	
28	Louis	(23)	Cécile Pépin	S.F. 1856
29	Chs. Alex-andre	(24)	Angéle Jos. Gourdeau	
				S.P. 1869

GUICHARD.

1	Jean		Marg. Gerbeau Montréal	
2	Pierre		Cath. Forgue	
	Louise		Julien Dumont S.V. 1727	
3	Jean Baptiste		Marie Aubry Poitau	
	Jean Baptiste			
4	Jean Baptiste	(3)	Josette GagnonS.Frs.1744	
5	Bernard		M. Chs. Gagnon	
	Marie Olive		Jos. Louineau	S.V. 1838

GUIGNARD.

1	Nicholas		Isabelle Lainé	
	Pierre			
2	Pierre	(1)	Jeanne Guilmet S.J. 1683	
	Marie		Chs. Dumas	S.M. 1702
	Augustin			
	Noël			
	Pierre			

GUIGNARD.

3	Augustin	(2)	M. Anne Nadeau Bert	
				1712
	Marie Anne		Frs. Peltier	Bert 1744
4	Noël	(2)	M. Anne Mercier	
				S. Anne 1719
	M. Madeleine		Jean Dupont	Bert 1739
	Marie Anne		Jean Frs. Boutin Bert 1746	
	Le même		Marg. Guimon S.Anne1726	
	Marguerite		Ant. Peltier	Bert 1747
	Marie Marthe		Lazare Richard	Bert 1751
5	Pierre	(2)	M. Jos. Paré S. Anne 1722	
	Jean Baptiste			
6	Jean Baptiste	(5)	Eliz. Nadeau	Bert. 1750
	M. Elizabeth		Jos. Chartier	" 1774
	Geneviève		Aug. Coulombe	" 1776

GUILLOT.

1	Nicolas		Mad. Doribel	
	Vincent			
2	Vincent		Jeanne Sicard	
	Vincent			
	André			
	Le même		Josette Blais	S.F.1677
	M. Madeleine		Paul Martel	" 1698
	Anne		Guill. Guérin	S.P.1704
	Marguerite		Paul Vaillancourt	" 1705
	Catherine		Ant. Martel	" 1706
3	Vincent	(2)	SusanneRodrigue Qué.1699	
	Jacques			
4	Mathieu		Marie Peltier	
				S.J. Port Joly
	Louis			
5	Jacques	(3)	Cath.Giroux Beauport 1728	
	Joseph			
6	Louis	(4)	Fse. Labbé	S.Frs.1754
7	Joseph	(5)	Justine Fradet	S.V.1761
	Marie		Etn. Cochon	" 1793
	Jacques			
	Antoine			
8	Jacques	(7)	M. Anne Lebœuf S.V.1789	
	Jean			
	Antoine			
	Pierre			
	Le même		Josette Trahan	S.G.1723
9	Antoine	(7)	M.Mad. Boutin S.V.1793	
	Antoine			
10	André	(2)	Charlotte Gaudin S.G.1718	
	Le même		M. Louis Lamothe Beau-	
				S.Marie port 1751
	Etienne			
11	Antoine	(8)	M.Anne Hallé Lévis 1816	
12	Pierre	(8)	M. Angé. Bisson	" 1820
13	Jean	(8)	ThérèseChiasson S.G.1821	
14	Antoine	(9)	Charlotte Quéret	" 1829
	Le même		Genev. Lefebvre S.M.1828	
15	Etienne	(10)	Josette Chabot S.Chs.1807	
	Le même		Marie Côté	S.H.1814
16	Michel		Marie Tremblay	S.J.1840

GUILMET.

1	Nicolas		Marie Selle	Qué.1667
	Barte		Frs. Lemoine	S.J.1694
	Agnès		Nicolas Maupas	" 1698
	Jeanne		Pierre Guignard	" 1683
	Jeanne		2° Raimond Dalmace	
				S.M.1703
	Françoise		André Bissonnet S.J.1702	
	Françoise		2° Jean Daniau S.M.1711	
	Anne		Fierre Charlan	
	Jean			
2	Jean	(1)	M. Anne Blais Bert. 1696	
	Augustin			
	Jean Baptiste			
	Guillaume			

GUILMET.

Pierre
3 Jean Baptiste (2) M. Anne Lefebvre
                                        Bert. 1729
    Marie   Jos. Morisset   S V. 1749
    M. Geneviéve   Pierre Bolduc   " 1751
    Marie Marthe   Jos. Gosselin   " 1767
    Marie Marthe   2° Jacq. Bilodeau " 1790
    Jean Baptiste
    Pierre
    Jacques
    Joseph
    Le même   Marg. Fradet   S.V. 1751
    Marguerite   Michel Lemieux " 1791
    Madeleine   Chs. Lainé   " 1799
    Augustin
    François
    Isidore
4 Pierre   (2) Dorothée Guimon
                               S.Anne 1727
    Jean Baptiste
5 Augustin   (2) Marg. Bouchard Bert.1735
6 Guillaume (2) M.Théodore Roy S.V.1738
    Marie Josette Ant. Bouffart S.Tho.1774
    Joseph
    François
    Le même   M. Mad. Pepin S.M.1773
7 Augustin   Mad. Lavoie
    M. Madeleine   Ls. Bilodeau Bert.1768
    M. Madeleine   2° Jos. Mercier S.Chs.1776
    M. Madeleine   3° Jos. Drapeau " 1776
    Marie Josette   Jacq. Thivierge Bert.1772
    Marguerite   Aug. Picard   " 1780
    Jean Baptiste
    Pierre
    Augustin
8 Jean Baptiste (3) Genev. Fradet S.V.1759
    Geneviève   Jos. Blais   " 1791
    Marie Louise   Nic. Baudoin " 1797
    Marie Reine   Jos. Lainé   " 1798
    Marie Josette   Michel Thivierge " 1805
    Jean Baptiste
    Michel
    Augustin
9 Pierre   (3) M. Genev. Roy S.V.1761
    Marie Marthe   M. Blais   " 1802
    Marie   Pierre Gaulin " 1805
    Jean Baptiste
    Joseph
    Ignace
    Michel
    Pierre
10 Jacques   (3) M. Mad. Peltier
                                S.Chs. 1762
11 Joseph   (3) Mad. Nollet S.Chs.1770
    Madeleine   Chs. Leclaire S.H. 1793
    Josette   Jean Ratté   S.H. 1804
    Joseph
12 Augustin   (3) M. Marthe Poulin
                                S.V. 1778
    Marie Louise   Pierre Dion   S.M. 1817
    Marthe   Joachim Valière
                               S.Chs. 1831
    Augustin
    Le même   Marie Nadeau S.Chs. 1804
13 François   (3) M. Rose Bissonnet
                                S.V. 1779
    Marie Rose   Ls. Roy   S.V. 1810
    Catherine   J. B. Bilodeau S.V. 1826
    Jacques
    François
    Michel
14 Isidore   (3) Marie Balan Bert. 1794
    Le même   Bridgitte Nadeau S.G.1800
    Julie   Pierre Hélie   S.G. 1820
    Angéle   Frs. Guay   S.G. 1828
    Isidore
    Jean Baptiste

GUILMET.

15 Jean Baptiste   M. Ls. Fradet S.V. 1753
    Marie Marthe   Jacq. Boulet S.V. 1779
    Marie   Etienne Roy   S.V. 1787
    Jean Baptiste
16 François   (6) M. Mad. Thébaut
                               S.P.S. 1763
    Madeleine   J. B. Picard   Bert. 1788
    M. Elisabeth   Jos. Mercier Bert. 1798
    Françoise   Aug. Mercier Bert. 1798
    Rose   Aug. Picard   Bert. 1812
    Joseph
    Pierre
    François
    Louis
17 Joseph   (6) Marie Lacroix S.M. 1773
    Joseph
    Pierre
    Le même   Josette Terrien S.M. 1787
18 Jean Baptiste (7) M. Genev. Pruneau
                                Bert. 1768
    Marie   Abraham (Monminy)
                                Bert. 1796
    Marie Reine   Jean Frs. Boulet Bert. 1804
    Jean Baptiste
    Pierre
19 Pierre   (7) M. Brigitte Boutin
                                Bert. 1780
    Augustin
    Jacques
    Jean Baptiste
    Louis
20 Augustin   (7) Reine Pruneau Bert. 1781
    Marguerite   Chs. Blanchet Bert. 1807
    Sophie   Michel Brochu Bert. 1824
    Angéle   Amable Lemieux
                                Bert. 1825
    Joseph
    Augustin
21 Jean Baptiste (8) Marg. Lepage S.V. 1790
    Geneviève   Ant. Bolduc   S.V. 1826
    Eulalie   Jos. Vital Royer S.G. 1827
    Le même   M. Anne Bilodeau
                                S.H. 1809
    Le même   Marg. Vallée   S.G. 1830
22 Augustin   (8) M. Marg. Dubreuil
                                S.F.S. 1796
    Luce   Jos. Marseau S.V. 1835
    Marie Adélaïde Magl. Jolin   S.V. 1838
    Isidore
    Augustin
    Jean Baptiste
23 Michel   (8) M. Jos. Blais   S.V. 1804
    Le même   M. Jos. Boissonneau
                                S.V. 1813
24 Pierre   (9) M. Reine Daniau
                                 S.P S. 1792
    Le même   Genev, Gagnon S.F.S.1796
    Le même   Ursule Daniau Bert. 1797
    Pierre
    Antoine
    Le même   M. Reine Leclaire
                                S.M. 1804
    Laurent
25 Jean Baptiste (9) M. Claire Bilodeau
                                Bert. 1795
    Marie Claire   Blaise Dubreuil S.V. 1816
    M. Marguerite J. B. Dubreuil S.P.S. 1818
    Le même   M. Agathe Jolivet
                                S.F.S. 1807
    Pierre
    Le même   M. Jos. Boulet S.F.S.1814
26 Joseph   (9)M. Jeanne Gagnon
                                S.M. 1797
    Angéle   Vital Leclaire S.V. 1828
    Joseph

GUILMET.

27 Ignace	(9) Génév. Labrecque	S.G.	1803
Génévieve	Jos. Doiron	S.G.	1827
Archange	Ant. Gagnon	S.G.	1828
28 Michel	(9) M. Anne Pouliot	S.Chs.	1820
29 Joseph	(11) M. Ls. Forgues	S.A.	1802
30 Augustin	(12) Marie Jolivet	S.V.	1806
31 François	(13) Josette Laviolette	S.Chs.	1806
32 Jacques	(13) Marie Bruneau	S.V.	1807
33 Michel	(13) Rosalie Isabel	S.V.	1811
Julie	Jos. Gosselin	S.M.	1852
Jacques			
34 Isidore	(14) Mad. Quéret	S.G.	1822
35 Jean Baptiste	(14) Hélène Guay	S.G.	1828
36 Jean Baptiste	(15) M. Jos. Roy	S.V.	1779
Marie	Nic. Bouchard	S.V.	1808
Basilide	Michel Larrivé	S.V.	1819
François			
Etienne			
37 François	(16) M. Claire Pruneau	S. Tho.	1795
Marie Olive	F. X. Bonneau	Bert.	1831
Godfroi			
François			
Fabien			
38 Joseph	(16) M. Genev. Lacroix	S.M.	1792
39 Louis	(16) Marg. Fournier	S.Tho.	1802
Marcelline	David Quemeneur	Bert.	1845
Louis			
Joseph			
40 Pierre	(16) M. Eliz. Baudoin	"	1804
Marie Judith	André Tangué	"	1831
Marie Delphine	Dieudonné Carbonneau	Bert.	1837
Athanase			
Pierre Prudent			
Le même	M. Vict. Thibaut	S.F.S.	1830
41 Pierre	(17) Marie Labrecque	S.G.	1804
Marie	Julien Richard	"	1830
Pierre			
42 Joseph	(17) Mad. Labrecque	"	1804
43 JeanBaptiste(18)	M. Royer Blais	Bert.	1794
Marguerite	J. B. Thibault	"	1812
Marie	Ls. Thibault	"	1823
Marie Luce	Jos. Talbot	"	1831
Michel			
Jean			
44 Pierre	(18) M. Marthe Carbonneau	Bert.	1805
"			
Jean Baptiste			
45 Augustin	(19) Marg. Turcot	"	1816
Elisabeth	André Blais	"	1845
Le même	Reine Morin	"	1829
46 Jn. Baptiste (19)	Marie Bissonet	S.M.	1821
Marguerite	Tho. Ménard	Bert.	1843
47 Jacques (19)	Archange Carbonneau	Bert.	1823
48 Louis (19)	Julie Bilodeau	"	1826
49 Joseph (20)	Genev. Blais	"	1822
50 Augustin (20)	Rose Fortier	"	1823
51 Isidore (22)	Julie Lemieux	"	1829
52 Augustin (22)	M. Archange Fortier	S.V.	1831
53 JeanBaptiste(22)	Marg.Théberge	S.F.S.	1844
54 Pierre (24)	Eliz. Clément	S.M.	1820
Marguerite	J. B. Gosselin	S.Chs.	1845
Marie Desanges	Chs. Poliquin	"	1847
Pierre			
Joseph			

GUILMET.

55 Laurent	(24) Fse. Cadrin	S.M.	1825
Laurent			
56 Antoine	(24) Josette Cadrin	"	1826
57 Pierre	(25) Genev. Marseau	S.V.	1834
58 Joseph	(26) Fse. Blais	"	1821
59 Jacques	(33) Marg. Richard	"	1841
60 Joseph	Mad. Labbé		
Joseph			
61 Pierre	Julie Verret		
Georges			
62 François	(36) Marg. Corriveau	"	1820
Jean Baptiste			
François Xavier			
63 Etienne	(36) Marg. Ménard	"	1831
Agnés	Pierre Aubé	"	1858
64 François	(37) Ursule Bilodeau	"	1822
Ursule	J. B. Talbot	Bert.	1843
65 Godfroi	(37) M. Anne Blais	"	1826
66 Fabien	(37) M. Rose Carbonneau	Bert.	1830
67 Louis	(39) Basilisse Wabah	"	1833
68 Joseph	(39) MarieCoulombe	S.P.S.	1827
69 Fse. Prudent (40)	Sophie Poirier	S.Tho.	1828
Le même	M. Chs. Coulombe	Bert.	1833
70 Athanase	(40) Flavie Blais	"	1845
71 Pierre	(41) Angé Patoine	S.G.	1828
72 Jean	(72) Anastasie Roy	S.F.S.	1815
Anastasie	André Naz.Blais	"	1839
Marie	Julien Cochon	Bert.	1843
Clarisse	Hyacinthe Picard	"	1846
73 Michel	(43) Luce Lemieux	"	1824
74 JeanBaptiste(44)	Geneviève	"	1829
75 Pierre	(44) Thérèse Rousseau	S.G.	1829
76 Laurent	(55) Angéle Fradet	S.M.	1851
77 Pierre	(54) Constance Marseau	S.Chs.	1847
78 Joseph	(54) Christine Naud	"	1852
79 Joseph	(60) Archange Bilodeau	S.G.	1829
80 Georges	(61) M. Hermine Leclaire	S.Chs.	1859
81 François	(62) Euphémie Aubé	S.V.	1849
Xavier			
82 JeanRaphael(62)	Julie Gosselin	"	1865
83 Jean Baptiste	Archange Gagnon		
	V. de Michel Paré		

HABRAN—LANGEVIN.

1 Jean	Marg.Plaisan	Ev.d'Angers	
Jean			
2 Jean	(1) M. Jos. Larrivé	S.V.	1762
	V. de J. B. Montigny		
Marie	Chs. Cochon	S.V.	1783
M. Françoise	Ls. Cochon	S.V.	1787
Marie Josette	Michel Tangué	"	1789
Jacques			
3 Jacques	(2) Marg. Tanqué	S.M.	1789
Marguerite	Pierre Pouliot	S.G.	1814
Ursule	Bénoni Patry	Lévis	1836
François			
4 François	(3) Fse. Fauchon	S.G.	1827

HARNAIS.

1 Isaac	Marg. Blaïse		1669
Laurent			
Eustache			
Joseph			
2 Laurent	(1) M. Anne Gilbert	S. Aug.	1706
Marie	Amb. Nadeau	S.Chs.	1756
3 Joseph	(1) Angé Petit	Que.	1707
4 Eustache	(1) Thérèse Chabot	"	1711
Le même	Marg. Thérèse Lamarre		
5 Jean	Marg. Pinet		

HARNAIS.

Le même	M. Marthe Mercier		S.P.S.	1749
Marie Josette	Laurent Morin	"		1775
Jean Baptiste				
6 Jean Baptiste (5)	M. Fse. Richard	S.V.		1774
M. Françoise	Ls. Marie Picard	S.P.S.		1862
Marie Victoire	Ls. Thibaut	,		1802
M. Adelaide	Ls. Blais	"		1815
Marie Céleste	David Roy	"		1819
Jean Baptiste				
Le même	M. Jos. Gagné	"		1820
7 Jean Baptiste (6)	M. Jos. Marseau	S.P.S.		1810

HAUTBOIS-ST. JULIEN.

1 Julien	Jeanne Mey			
Michel				
Charles				
2 Michel	(1) Fse. Marchand	Que.		1725
3 Charles	(1) M. Anne Morin	"		1728
M. Anne	Jos. Lepage	S.M.		1753
Marie Félicite	Gab. Audet	"		1753
M. Louise	Fse. Nadeau	"		1762
M. Geneviève	Jean Nadeau	"		1766
M. Geneviéve	2° Jacq. Poliquin	S.G.		1799
M. Geneviève	3° Jacq. Shinck	"		1814
Charles.				
4 Charles	(3) Scolastique Mateau		S.M.	1753

HAVARD.

1 Gabriel	Fse. de Girard			
Pierre				
2 Pierre	(1) Louise Gautier	S.J.		1690
	V. de Ls. Griffart			
Angélique	Pierre Plante	S.J.		1717
Ignace				
3 Ignace	(2) M. Louise Beaucher		S.F.	1758
M. Charlotte	Michel Savoie	"		1784
Ignace				
Jean Baptiste				
4 Ignace	(3) Reine Provost	"		1796
5 Jean Baptiste (3)	Vict. Routier S. Marie			1801
	S. Marie			
Henri				
6 Henri	(5) Thérèse Collard	S.P.		1844

HAYOT.

1 Jean	Anne Xainte Grondin			
	Riv. Ouelle			1695
Thérèse	Jacq. Fradet	S.V.		1736
2 Jean François	M. Jos. Rousseau			
Le même	M. Mad. Lefebvre	"		1748
3 Jean	Marie Vaillancour			
Genevieve	Paul Chatigny	S.Chs.		1778
Modeste	Geo. Shinck	S.G.		1784
Catherine	Jos. Labrecque	"		1785
Catherine	2° Jacq. Pénin	"		1799
Josette	Jos. Vérieux	"		1786
M. Anne	Ant. Rousseau	S.F.S.		1802

HÉBERT-LECOMPTE.

1 Guillaume	Anne Roussin	A.G.		1691
Véronique	Ign. Coté	"		1733
Guillaume				
François				
Louis				
2 Guillaume	(1) Mad. Laberge	"		1715
3 François	(1) Scolastique Trudel			
		A.G.		1727

HÉBERT—LECOMPTE.

4 Louis	(1) Cantin	A.G.		1732
M. Anne	Ls. Huot	"		1770
François				
5 Pierre	M. Anne Poiré			
Charlotte	Aug. Bussiere	B.		1726
6 François	Anne Baury Acadie			
Joseph				
7 Charles	Cath. Saulnier Acadie			
Simon				
8 Etienne	M. Jos. Boudreau Acadie			
Jean				
9 François	Marg. Bourque Acadie			
Victor				
10 François	(4) M. Jos. Bidet	S.J.		1770
Josette	Jos. Laviolette	S.P.		1787
Le même	Josette Coté	A.G.		1782
M. Catherine	Chs. Blouin	S.J.		1812
Pierre				
Joseph				
Simon				
François				
11 Joseph	(6) Chs. Bénoni Poulin		S.Frs.	1762
Catherine	Frs. Gosselin	S.Frs.		1823
Marie	Etn. Lessart	S.F.		1794
Joseph				
12 Simon	(7) Mad. Poirier	S.Chs.		1758
Le même	Marie Thicy	"		1761
13 Jean	(8) Thérèse Pouliot	"		1761
Le même	Thérèse Chartier	"		1764
Marie	Chs. Poliquin	"		1785
Marie	2° Jacq. Bernier	S.G.		1801
Cécile	Jos. Denis	"		1792
14 Victor	(9) Thérèse Chabot	S.Chs.		1773
Marie	· Frs. Blais	"		1810
Charles				
François				
15 Pierre	(10) M. Cécile Gendreau		S.L.	1792
M. Marguerite	Paul Langlois	S.P.		1818
Justine	Jacq. Roberge	"		1832
Marie Honorat	Olivier Paquet	"		1840
Pierre				
16 Joseph	(10) Angé Drouin	S.F.		1815
Angèle	Jacq. Drouin	"		1847
Sophie	Frs. Hébert	"		1864
Marcelline	Ferd. Labbé	S.J.		1864
François				
17 Simon	(10) M. Mad. Letourneau		S.F.	1824
Marie	Frs. Blouin	S.J.		1853
François				
Joseph				
Louis				
Pierre				
18 François	(10) Julie Boissonneau	S.J.		1832
Cécile	Gab. Pepin	"		1856
Julie	Célestin Pouliot	"		1860
Joseph				
François				
19 Joseph	(11) M. Mad. Guion	S.F.		1793
Le même	Marg. Gosselin	S.L.		1800
Marie	Pierre Bédard	S.Frs.		1833
Marie Louise	René Labbé	"		1839
Amable				
Joseph				
20 François	(14) M. Ls. Gosselin	S.H.		1810
Le même	Vict. Lacasse	S Chs.		1813
Le même	Angé Lecours	"		1817
Geneviève	Cléophas Cyp. Tangué		S.Chs.	1854
Marcel				
21 Charles	M. Reine Boissonneau		S.V.	1814
Emélie	Octave Levasseur		S.Chs.	1852

HÉBERT—LECOMPTE.

	Marie Lucie	Pantaléon Patry	,,	1855
	Charles			
22	Pierre	(15) Genev. Roberge	S.P.	1825
23	François	(16) Clotilde Drouin	S.F.	1846
24	François	(17) Marcelline Blouin	S.J.	1855
25	Joseph	(17) Cécile Blouin	,,	1857
26	Louis	(17) Adé Delisle	,,	1860
27	Pierre	(17) Marie Pouliot	S.L.	1865
28	Joseph	(18) Marg. Pepin	S.J.	1856
29	François	(18) Sophie Hébert	S.F.	1864
30	Marcel	(20) Marie Fournier	S.Chs.	1847
31	Amable	(19) Julie Eimond	S.Frs.	1840
32	Joseph	(19) Ludivine Deblois		
			S.Frs.	1842
33	Charles	(21) Archange Gagnon	B.	1841
	Mathilde	Jules Michaud	S.Chs.	1863
	Marie Desanges	Ouésime Morin	,,	1863

HÉLIE–BRETON.

1	Jean	Anne Labbé	S.F.	1669
	Jeanne	Jean Fradet	S.J.	1692
	M. Madeleine	Ls. Boutin	,,	1698
	François			
	Pierre			
	Jacques			
2	Pierre	M. Mad. Jean	Qué.	1688
	Léonard			
3	François	(1) Fse. Bidet	S.J.	1692
	Isabelle	Ls. Nadeau	S.V.	1734
	Angélique	Laurent Amiot	,,	1734
	Joseph			
	Jean Baptiste			
4	Pierre	(1) M. Rosalie Pepin	Qué.	1700
	Françoise	Frs. Rémillard	S.V.	1720
	Thérèse	J. B. Bissonnet	,,	1726
	Marguerite	J. B. Balan	,,	1729
	Dorotée	Jos. Alaire	,,	1735
	Angélique	Pierre Thibaut	,,	1737
	Catherine	Jacq. Tangué	,,	1737
	Marie Anne	Gab. Royer	,,	1740
	Antoine			
	Joseph			
	Pierre			
	Le même	Marie Gromelin	B.	1722
	Marie Josette	Basile Corriveau	S.V.	1785
	Pierre			
	Jean Baptiste			
	Jérome			
	André			
5	Jacques	(1) Louise Lacasse	B.	1715
	Marie	Paschal Boucher		
			S.Chs.	1755
	Joseph			
	Jacques			
	Nicolas			
6	Léonard	(2) Jeanne Bourbon		
			Chs. Bourg.	1725
	Louis			
7	Joseph	(3) Isabelle Tangué	S.V.	1729
	Jean François			
8	Jean Baptiste	(3) M. Isabelle Nadeau		
			Bert.	1734
	Elizabeth	Ls. Chrétien	S.V.	1761
	Elizabeth	2° Jos. Marie Côtés.	H.	1801
	M. Marguerite	Eustache Plante	S.M.	1775
	Jean Baptiste			
9	Joseph	M. Jos. Morrisset		
	M. Françoise	Ant. Pepin	S.V.	1749
10	Pierre (1ᵉʳm)	(4) Louis Lefebvre	Bert.	1725
	Pierre			
11	Joseph	(4) Marie Gauvreau	S.V.	1727
	Marie Josette	J. B. Lebel	,,	1752
	Madeleine	Frs. Lainé	S.M.	1764
	Catherine	Chs. Balan	Bert.	1765
	Jacques			

HÉLIE—BRETON.

12	Antoine	(4) M. Chas. Buisson	B.	1745
13	Antoine	M. Eliz. Forgues		
	M. Elizabeth	Claude Boilard	Lévis	1784
14	Pierre (2ᵈm)	(4) La veuve Dubeau	S.V.	1747
15	Pierre	Marie Dorval		
	Josette	Gab. Gontier	S.M.	1772
	Marie Louise	Chs. Pepin	S.V.	1774
	Pierre			
16	Jean Baptiste	(4) Genev. Salomé Fournier		
			S.F.S	1750
	Genev. Ursule	Pierre Valière	S.V.	1774
	Joseph			
	Le même	M.Mad. Pouliot	Lévis	1758
	Marie Anne	Jos. Ferd. Spilheimer		
			S.V.	1783
	Marie Anne	2° Frs. Gontier	S.M.	1802
	Françoise	Amb. Lacroix	,,	1789
	M. Marguerite	Ant. Fradet	,,	1795
	Pierre			
	Jean Baptiste			
17	Jérôme	(4) M. Marthe Meneux		
			S.V.	1751
	Marie Louise	Alexandre Nadeau	,,	1773
	Le même	M. Jos. Quéret	S.M.	1766
18	André	(4) M. Marg. Roy	S.V.	1762
	M. Geneviève	Frs. Forgues	S.M.	1788
	Marie	Jean Marie Boucher		
			S.M.	1795
	Marie Anne	Ls. Vien	S.M.	1805
	Michel			
	André			
	Ignace			
	Pierre			
19	Jean	M. Jos. Garant		
	Marie Josette	J.B. Ménard	S.V.	1773
	Jean François			
20	Nicolas	(5) M. Anne Bilodeau		
			Bert.	1744
	Le même	Genev. Nadeau	B.	1748
21	Joseph	(5) Mad. Thivierge	S.J.	1744
	M. Madeleine	Basile Plante	,,	1772
	Elizabeth	Jean Marie Audibert		
			S.J.	1782
	Marguerite	Emery Blouin	S.H.	1790
	Basile			
	Joseph			
22	Jacques	(5) M. Thérèse Charland		
			S.F.	1758
23	Louis	(6) Josette Légaré		
			Chs. Bourg	1763
	Geneviève	Ls. Coté	S.G.	1793
24	Jean François	(7) M. Angé. Vallée	S.V.	1753
25	Jean Baptiste	(8) M. Frs. Roy	S.M.	1769
	M. François	Royer Renaud	,,	1801
	Ignace			
	Jean Baptiste			
	Le même	Marie Plante	S.Chs.	1782
	Le même	M. Anne Bacquet	S.M.	1783
	Marie Anne	Jos. Clément	,,	1806
	Marie	Jacq. Gosselin	,,	1817
	Marguerite	Michel Gautron	,,	1823
	Jacques			
	François			
	Pierre			
26	Pierre	(10) Mad. Bilodeau	Bert.	1751
	Pierre			
A	Jacques	(11) Angé. Chatigny	S.H.	1785
	Françoise	Jean Gosselin	S.Chs.	1836
	Le même	Marg. Mercier	S.H.	1794
	Le même	Thérèse Bouffart	,,	1808
27	Pierre	(15) Madeleine (Royer)		
			S.Chs.	1774
	Marguerite	Jean Lepage	,,	1804
	Pierre			
	Le même	Marg. Terrien	S.Chs.	1787
	Françoise	Etn. Gontier	S.G.	1821

HÉLIE—BRETON.

28	Pierre	Geneviève Deschamps		
	Jean Baptiste			
29	Joseph	(16)	Mad. Plante	S.V.1775
	Elizabeth		Jos.Boissonneau S.H.1799	
	Pierre			
	Le même		Susanne Hallé	" 1817
30	Jenn Baptiste	(16)	M.Genev.Brochu S.V.1782	
	M. Geneviève		J. B. Lessart	" 1804
	Le même		M. Fse. Bouchard	" 1806
31	Pierre	(16)	M.Genev.Vallée S.M.1803	
32	André	(18)	M.Mad. Fortier	" 1785
	Marguerite		Jean Pouliot	S.G.1824
	Madeleine		Barthe Guénet	S.H.1809
	Reine		Frs. Dion	" 1820
	Cécile		Jean Maréchal	" 1820
	André			
	André			
33	Michel	(18)	M. Hélène Patry S.M.1793	
	Marthe		Pierre Plante	" 1829
	Angèle		Jacq. Plante	" 1831
	Marie Anne		Philippe Plante	" 1831
	Charles			
	Etienne			
	Le même		M. Jos. Terrien S.M.1827	
34	Ignace	(18)	M. Ls. Tangué	" 1797
A	Pierre	(18)	Josette Morin	S.H.1805
35	Jean Frs.	(19)	Genev.Falardeau S.V.1788	
	François			
	Jean Baptiste			
36	Joseph	(21)	M. Jos. Plante	S.J. 1770
	Joseph			
37	Basile	(21)	Mad. Turcotte	S.J. 1790 S.H.
38	Louis (Léonard)		Rose Leclaire	
	Marie		Jos. Bergeron S.Chs. 1812	
	Jacques			
39	Jean Bte.	(25)	M. Claire Labrecque B. 1796	
	Marie Louise		Honoré Paquet	B. 1836
	Jean Baptiste			
	Joseph			
40	Ignace	(25)	Marg. Roy	S.M. 1806
	Georges			
	Le même		M.Angé.Dallaire S.V.1824	
41	Pierre	(25)	Marie Labrecque S.G.1810	
42	François	(25)	M. Ls. Turgeon	B. 1816
43	Jacques	(25)	Charlotte Dallaire S.M. 1818	
44	Pierre	(26)	Marie Lepage	S.G. 1797
	Pierre			
45	Pierre	(27)	Genev.Thivierge S.M. 1801	
	Christine		Michel Terrien	S.V. 1843
46	Jean Bte.	(28)	Cath. Gagné	S.G. 1805
47	Pierre	(29)	M. Ls. Baudoin S.H. 1806	
48	André	(32)	Marie Audet	S.H. 1808
49	André	(32)	Angé. Delenteigne S.H. 1815	
50	Etienne	(33)	Marg. Terrien S. Chs. 1821	
51	Charles	(33)	Genev. Gontier S.M. 1828	
	Sara		Ed. Lessart	S.M. 1854
	Julie		Damase Quemeneur S.M. 1856	
	Marcelline		Marc Goupy	S.M. 1864
	Charles			
52	François	(35)	M. Ls. Gosselin S.V. 1813	
	Adélaïde		Michel Roy	S.V. 1840
	Emélie		Frs. Anadet Corriveau S.V. 1848	
	Emérence		Anaclet Roy	S.V. 1852
	Archange		Pierre Corriveau S.V. 1857	
	André			
	François Xavier			
	Charles			
	Nazaire			
	Sifroi			
	Thomas			

HÉLIE—BRETON.

53	Jean Bte.	(35)	M. Ls. Bolduc	S.V. 1813
54	Joseph	(36)	Anne Jos. Potin	S.J. 1790
	Marie Josette		Laurent Paquet	S.J. 1810
	M. Catherine		Jean Picard	S.J. 1813
	Marie Anne		Jos. Audet	S.J. 1815
	Marguerite		Jos. Audibert	S.J. 1819
	Cécile		Pierre Paquet	S.J. 1825
	Marie Charlotte		Frs. Isaac Audet S.J. 1826	
	Marie Ursule		J. B. Pichet	S.J. 1831
	Marie Luce		Frs. Fortier	S.J. 1837
	Joseph			
	George			
	Jean Baptiste			
55	Jacques	(38)	M. Cécile Lepage S. Chs. 1820	
56	Jean Bte	(39)	Luce Coté	B. 1829
	Marie Célanire		Chs. Fortier	B. 1853
57	Joseph	(39)	M. Chs. Paquet	B. 1831
58	Georges	(41)	Hermine Balan	S.V. 1849
59	Pierre	(44)	Julie Guilmet	S.G. 1820
60	Charles	(51)	Julie Bolduc	S.M. 1863
61	Frs. Xavier	(52)	Soulange Gosselin S.V. 1838	
62	Charles	(52)	Emélie Roy	S.V. 1846
63	Nazaire	(52)	M. Marg. Roy	S.V. 1848
64	Thomas	(52)	M. Archange Roy S.V. 1848	
65	Sifroi	(52)	Séraphine Tangué S.V. 1855	
66	André	(52)	M.Saly.Bacquet S.V. 1862	
67	Joseph	(54)	M. Jos. Paquet	S.J. 1810
	Christine		Honoré Pichet	S.J. 1841
	Ursule		Jos. Dick	S.J. 1842
	Cécile		Frs. Dupuis	S.J. 1855
	Théotiste		Pierre Giguère	S.F. 1832
	Théotiste		2° Jean Letourneau S.F. 1850	
	Catherine		Jos. Deblois	S.F. 1839
	Paul			
68	Georges	(54)	Genev. Lainé	S.J, 1822
	Antoine			
	Georges			
69	Jean Bte	(54)	Marg. Poulin	S.J. 1833
	Julie		Pierre Corriveau S.M. 1853	
70	Ignace		Marg. Clavet	
	Joseph			
	Joseph			
71	Jacques		Archange Célanire Talbot S.H.	
	M.Louise Genev.		Geo. Martineau S.M. 1854	
72	Joseph		M. Jos. Quemeneur S.R.	
	Justine		Jacq. Drouin	S.V. 1838
73	Paul	(67)	M. Zoé Turcot	S.F. 1854
74	Georges	(68)	Marg. Dupuis	S.J. 1844
	Le même		Eléonore Létourneau S.J. 1848	
75	Antoine	(68)	Henriette Dalaire S.L. 1851	
76	Joseph	(70)	M. Désanges Bilodeau S.M. 1858	
77	Joseph	(70)	M. Philomène Pouliot S.M. 1864	

HENRY.

1	Mathieu		Cath. Hely Ev. de Kimpe	
	Jacques			
2	Jacques	(1)	Susanne Garant S.F.S.1738	
5	Jean Baptiste		Josette Bouchard	
	Jean Baptiste			
	Le même		Génev. Goulet	S.G. 1800
6	Georges		Sara Meloney	
	Cécile		Pierre Noël	S.P. 1818
7	Jean		Génev. Ouellet	
	Jean			

HENRY.

8 Jean Baptiste (5)	Genev. Goulet	S.G.	1800
Généviéve	Ls. Tangué	S.G.	1825
Marie	Guill. Roy	S.G.	1830
9 Jean	(7) Marg. Cameron	S.G.	1820

HERPE—HARPE.

1 Nicolas	Charlotte Guérin		
	Ev. d'Avranche.		
Nicolas			
2 Nicolas	(1) Marie Denis	S.V.	1766
Marie Anne	Basile Blouin	S.V.	1797
M. Marguerite	Frs. Dubord	S.V.	1800
Marie Louise	Chs. Brochu	S.V.	1802
Antoine			
Jean Baptiste			
3 Antoine	(2) M. Marg. Corriveau		
		S.V.	1803
Martine	Jos. Lemieux	S.V.	1826
Adélaïde	Ls. Corriveau	S.V.	1839
Catherine	Norbert Belanger S.V.		1842
Flavien			
4 Jean Baptiste (2)	Fse. Corriveau	S.V.	1803
Seraphine	Pierre Marseau	S.V.	1822
Jean			
François Xavier			
5 Flavien	(3) Esther Herpe	S.V.	1848
6 François Xav. (4)	M. Esther Marseau		
		S.V.	1830
Esther	Flavien Herpe	S.V.	1848
Aug. Nazaire			
Le même	Luce Audet	S.V.	1835
Marie Césaire	Samuel Lemieux S.V.		1869
7 Jean	(4) Adé Corriveau	S.V.	1832
8 Aug. Nazaire (6)	Reine Désanges Marseau		
		S.V.	1860

HIZOIR—PROVENCAL.

1 Antoine	M. Thérèse Rainville		
		Beauport.	1699
Jean			
2 Jean	(1) Angé. Giroux		
		Beauport.	1728
Etienne			
3 Etienne	(2) Louise Leroux		
		Chs.Bourg.	1763
Le même	Brigitte Dery		
		Chs.Bourg.	1767
Etienne			
Louis			
4 Etienne.	(3 M. Anne Lepage		
		S.Chs.	1795
Marie Anne	J. B. Roy	S.G.	1817
Hubert			
Etienne			
5 Louis	(3) Angé. Nadeau	S.G.	1795
Marie	Chs. Couture	S.G.	1817
Angéle	J. B. Pepin	S.G.	1824
Louis			
6 Etienne	Brigitte Roy		
Le même	Josette Terrien	S.G.	1806
	V. de Jos. Guilmet.		
7 Etienne	Brigitte Denis		
Marie	Etn. Couture	S.G.	1816
8 Etienne	(4) Josette Langlois S.G.		1822
Marie Josette	Jos. Gosselin	S.V.	1847
9 Hubert	(4) Ursule Roy	S.G.	1826
10 Louis	(5) Eliz. Chatigny	S.G.	1813

HOLLERY.

1 Michel	Barte Aaron		
Barbe	Adam Phalmer S.Chs.		1763
Marguerite	Balthasa Moutarde		
		S.Chs.	1764
Catherine	Ant. Valiere	S.Chs.	1766

HUARD—DESILETS.

1 Jean	Marie Amiot		
Marie	Charles Couture		
Marie Jeanne	Joe Couture		
Françoise	Eustache Couture		
		Lévis.	1695
Marguerite	J. B. Grenet	Lévis.	1708
Marguerite	2° Pierre Naud Lévis.		1716
Marie Anne	Ignace Noël	Lévis.	1707
Angélique	Pierre Girard	Lévis.	1710
Geneviève	Ls. Levasseur	Lévis.	1716
Généviéve	2° Pierre Dussart		
Jean			
Etienne			
Mathieu			
Jacques			
2 Jean	(1) Angé. Jourdain		1704
3 Mathieu	(1) Jeanne Jourdain		
4 Jacques	(1) Angé. Beaucher		
Marie Louise	Ls. Couture	S.M.	1759
Jacques			
5 Etienne	(1) M. Thérèse Dolbec		
		S.Aug.	1719
6 Jacques	(4) M. Jos. Turgeon	B.	1749

HUOT.

1 Mathurin	Marie Letartre A.G.		1671
Jean			
Jacques			
2 Jean	(1) Mad. Roussin	A.G.	1701
Jean			
François			
Pierre			
3 Jacques	(1) M. Angé Trudel A.G.		1711
Michel			
4 Jean	(2) Fse. Fiset	A.G.	1733
Jean			
5 François	(2) M. Ls. Maheu	A.G.	1754
Marie Louise	J. B. Foucher	S.F.	1774
François			
6 Michel	(3) Mad. Gosselin	S.J.	1747
Jacques			
A Pierre	(2) Cath. Racine S. Anne 1747		
Jean			
7 Jean	(4) M. Anne Ruel S.L.		1766
Louis			
Pierre			
8 Louis	M. Anne Hébert S.J.		
fils de Nic. &			
Louise Daneau	A.G.		1770
Marie Anne	Chs. Delage	S.J.	1792
9 François	(5) M. Chs. Leblond S.F.		1780
10 Jacques	(6) Cath. Plante	S.P.	1780
11 Louis	(7) Eliz. Gosselin	S.L.	1798
Marie	Jean Leclaire	S.L.	1830
Elisabeth	Ant. Coté	S.L.	1820
Louis			
12 Pierre	(7) Marg. Couture	S.L.	1800
Le même	Viet Marseau	S.L.	1806
13 François	Frs. Marie Herbert		
	Ursule Cantin	A.G.	1782
Pierre			
14 Jean	(5ᵃ) Mad. Coté	A.G.	1783
	C.R.		
Joachim			
François			
15 Pierre	(13) M. Vict Richard	B.	1821
	Q.		
16 Louis	(11) Adé Leroux	S.L.	1855
17 François	(14) Julie Tangué	B.	1822
18 Joachim	(14) M. Vict Tangué	B.	1831

HURET—ROCHEFORT.

1 Jean	Marie Fiset	Qué.	1690
Jean Baptiste			

HURET—ROCHEFORT.

2	Jean Baptiste (1)	Fse. Métivier S.Tho.	1736
	M. Geneviève	Jacq. Malboeuf S.F.S.	1750
	Marguerite	Philippe Picard S.P.S.	1759
	Marie Louise	Jos. Quemeneur S.F.S.	1761
	Jean Baptiste		
3	Jean Baptiste (2)	M. Fse. Blanchet	
		S.P.S.	1767

ISABEL.

1	Jean		Marie Adam	
	Adrien			
	Michel			
2	Adrien	(1)	Cath. Poitevin S.F.	1669
	Marc			
3	Michel	(1)	Marie Bidon C.R.	1673
	Marie		Pierre Fournier	
			S. Tho.	1695
	Louis			
4	Marc		Marg. Lémelin S.L.	1698
	Françoise		Ls. Giroux S.L.	1725
	Catherine		Jean Baillargeon S.L.	1725
	Marguerite		Jean Morin S.L.	1725
	Marguerite		2° Jacq. Boulet S.F.S.	1751
	Madeleine		Ignace Gosselin S.L.	1727
	Jeanne		Innocent Pouliot S.L.	1735
	Thérèse		Chs. Pouliot S.L.	1743
	Thomas			
	Ignace			
	Marc			
	Louis			
	Louis			
5	Louis	(3)	M. Barbe Proulx S.Tho.	1704
	Joseph			
6	Louis		Mad. Blanchet S.P.S.	
	Joseph			
7	Thomas	(4)	M. Mad. Fortier S.L.	1731
	Angélique		Chs. Cinqmars S.L.	1762
	Charlotte		Nicolas Denis S.L.	1762
	Louis			
8	Ignace	(4)	Marg. Corriveau S.V.	1738
	Marie		Ls. Gautron Bert.	1765
	M. Madeleine		Jean Valier Boutin	
			Bert.	1769
	M. Geneviève		Jos. Baucher Bert.	1787
	Jean			
	Joseph			
9	Marc	(4)	Marthe Couture B.	1742
	Marie		Chs. Trahan S. Chs.	1766
	Marie Josette		Barth Terrien S. Chs.	1773
	Marc			
10	Louis	(4)	Josette Pouliot S.L.	1743
11	Louis	(4)	Thérèse Moreau S.L.	1746
	Thérèse		Michel Bilodeau	
			S. Chs.	1780
	M. Théotiste		Cyriac Soucy S.H.	1795
	Pierre			
	Louis			
12	Joseph	(5)	Marg. Boucher Bert.	1749
	Joseph			
13	Joseph	(6)	Marg. Asselim S.F.	1737
14	Jean		Charlotte Bacon	
	Marie Françoise		J. B. Blanchet S.P.S.	1775
	Marie		Jos. Marie Dessaint	
			S.P.S.	1781
	Jean			
15	Louis	(7)	M. Anne Quéret S.M.	1782
16	Jean	(8)	Mad. Fortin S.V.	1777
	Rosalie		Michel Guilmet „	1811
	Rose		Frs. Joncas „	1822
	Josette		Aug. Gautron „	1824
17	Joseph	(8)	Isabelle Boutin Bert.	1785
19	Marc	(9)	Marie Nadeau S.G.	1786
	Guillaume			
20	Louis	(11)	Eliz. Couture S.Chs.	1773

ISABEL.

21	Pierre	(11)	M. Jos. Baudoin S.F.S.	1782
	Le même		Marie Bilodeau S.H.	1788
	Marie		Augustin Roy „	1809
	Louis			
22	Joseph	(12)	M. Mad. Gagné S.P.S.	1778
23	Jean	(14)	Angé Gerbert „	1780
24	Louis	(21)	Cath. Roy S.M.	1815
	Le même		Marg. Bernier S.H.	1817
25	Guillaume	(19)	M. Anne Carbonneau	
			S.G.	1822

JACQUES.

1	Louis		Antoinette Leroux	
			Qué.	1688
	Nicolas			
	Pierre			
	Louis			
2	Nicolas	(1)	M. Jos. Bédard Chs.	
			Bourg	1712
	Louis			
	Le même		Cath. Alard Chs.	
			Bourg	1719
3	Louis	(1)	Marg. Séguin Chs.	
			Bourg	1719
4	Pierre	(1)	M. Ambroise Chalifou	
			Chs. Bourg	1720
5	Louis	(2)	M. Chs. Glinel	
			Chs. Bourg	1730
	Nicolas Alexis			
	Louis			
6	Henri		Marie Garant	
	Marie Josette		Ls. Marie Louineau	
			S.F.S.	1765
	M. Geneviève		Ls. Boulet „	1774
	Henri			
	Jean Baptiste			
7	Nicolas Alexis	(5)	Véronique Couture	
			S.P.	1771
8	Louis	(5)	Marg. Falardeau	
			Chs. Bourg	1762
	Marie		Aug. Nolin S.P.	1790
	Marie Anne		Paul Pichet S.P.	1803
9	Henri	(6)	Marie Anne Louineau	
			S.F.S.	1765
10	Jean Baptiste	(6)	M. Jos. Bouchard S.V.	1774
	Marie Josette		Jos. Quemeneur S.F.S.	1798
	Marie Louise		Amand Comeau S.F.S.	1806
	Pierre			
11	Pierre	(10)	M. Chs. Gaudin S.F.S.	1807
12	Jean		Marie Ruel	
	Marguerite		Jos. Patouël S.G.	1825

JAHAN—LA VIOLETTE.

1	Jacques		Marie Ferra Qué.	1658
	Marie		Jean Bilodeau S.F.	1684
	Elisabeth		Pierre Asselin S.F.	1695
	Jacques			
2	Jacques	(1)	Anne Trépanier S.F.	1686
	Marie Anne		Guil. Terrien S.J.	1712
	Catherine		Gab. Blouin „	1713
	Jacques			
	François			
	Augustin			
3	François	(2)	Marie Bourassa Lévis	1729
	Le même		Fse. Chatigny S.F.	1736
4	Augustin	(2)	Louise Martin Que.	1730
5	Joseph		Marg. Roy	
	Isabelle		Dominique Dassilva	
			S.J.	1747
	Françoise		Jean Frs. Fortier „	1757
	Françoise		2° Frs. Fradet S.M.	1793
	Marie Josette		Frs. Fortier S.J.	1767
	M. Angélique		Jos. Blanchard „	1803
	Joseph			
	Pierre			

JAHAN—LAVIOLETTE.

	Le même		Cath. Pruneau	S.M. 1764
6	Jacques	(2)	Anne Loriat	Lévis 1758
	Louise		Melchior Bisson	S.Chs.
	Joseph			
7	Joseph	(5)	M. Jos. Genest	S.J. 1747
	Marie Josette		J. B. Gautier	S.J. 1774
	Laurent			
8	Pierre	(5)	Brigitte Fortier, Bapt. de	
				S. Jean 1757
9	Joseph	(6)	Genev. Ruel	S.L. 1753
	Joseph			
	François			
10	Laurent	(7)	Genev. Marseau	S.J. 1730
	Geneviève		Jean Terrien	„ 1813
	Adélaïde		Basile Thivierge	„ 1822
	Josette		Jean Redman	„ 1831
	Michel			
	Joseph			
11	François		Josette Gosselin	S.L. 1785
	Josette		Frs. Guilmet	S.Chs. 1806
12	Joseph	(9)	M. Jos. Hébert	S.P. 1787
13	Joseph	(10)	Archange Pepin	S.J. 1814
	Rosalie		Pierre Pouliot	„ 1835
	Elisabeth		Ls. Dupuis	„ 1839
	Henriette		Gab. Pichet	„ 1842
	Marguerite		Ls. Blouin	„ 1851
	Joseph			
	Gabriel			
14	Michel	(10)	Marg. Chamberlan	
				S.M. 1820
15	Joseph	(13)	Luce Pepin	S.J. 1840
	Marie Victoire		Frs. Blanchet	S.V. 1862
	Luce		Michel Letellier	„ 1862
16	Gabriel	(13)	Rosalie Thivierge	S.J. 1853

JAMES.

1	Jean		Fse. Lancteau	
	Jean			
2	Jean	(1)	Fse. Fontaine	S.H. 1785
	Marguerite		Pierre Gagné	„ 1805
	Marie Anne		J. B. Filteau	„ 1816
	Jean Baptiste			
3	Joseph		Hélène Crépeau	
	Marguerite		Ls. Bilodeau	S.G. 1822
	Angèle		Michel Bolduc	„ 1826
	Joseph			
4	Joseph	(3)	Mad. Cloutier	„ 1819
5	Jean Baptiste	(2)	Cath. Nadeau	S.H. 1809

JOANE.

1	Jean		Anne Grimbaut	S.F. 1670
	Anne		Chs. Manteau	S.L. 1701
	Anne		2° Pierre Roberge	„ 1710
	Marc			
2	Robert		Fse. Savard	Que. 1665
	Marie Louise		Ant. Samson	Lévis 1707
	M. Genev. Chs.		Etienne Rochon	
	M. Genev. Chs.		2° Jacq. Morin	
3	Marc	(1)	M. Thérèse Poisson	
				S.J. 1699
	Le même		M. Anne Plante	
	Marie Anne		Jean Audet	S.L. 1726
	Marie Thérèse		André Pouliot	„ 1730
	Cécile		Pierre Chabot	„ 1741
	Marguerite		Jos. Fournier	S. Tho. 1734

JOLIN.

1	Jean		Marie Boileau	S. Frs. 1690
	Simon			
2	Simon	(1)	Eliz. Dalaire	„ 1711
	Angélique		Amb. Vériene	„ 1730
	Elizabeth		Ls. Lepage	„ 1743
	Marie Gertrude		Jos. Chrétien	„ 1750

JOLIN.

	Louise		Ls. Guérard	S. Frs. 1752
	Louise		2° Chs. Dufour	„ 1778
	Marie		Jos. Emond	„ 1755
	Jean			
	Joseph			
3	Jean	(2)	Marie Bonneau	„ 1740
	Marie Thérèse		Jacq. Fradet	S.F.S. 1762
	M. Geneviève		Ant. Boulet	„ 1766
	Jean Baptiste			
	Pierre			
4	Joseph	(2)	Thérèse Meneux	S.F. 1743
				S.H.
	Thérèse		Etn. Canac	S. Frs. 1764
	Marie Victoire		Chs. Lémelin	„ 1779
	Marie		Frs. Fortier	„ 1791
	Joseph			
	Louis			
	Jean			
5	Jean Baptiste	(3)	M. Genev. Boulet	
				S.F.S. 1764
	Marie Anne		Ant. Bactaelt	„ 1791
	Marie Anne		2° Jos. Boucher	„ 1833
	Marie Anne		3° J. B. Menard	„ 1837
	Marie Reine		Aug. Morin	„ 1798
	Jean Baptiste			
	Joseph			
6	Pierre	(3)	Ursule Proulx	S P. S. 1774
	Simon			
	Joseph			
7	Joseph	(4)	M. Jos. Racine	S.M. 1763
	Le même		M. Ls. Goupy	„ 1765
	Marie Louise		Jos. Danian	S.H. 1794
	Marguerite		Germ. Gaudreau	„ 1794
	Augustin			
	Joseph			
8	Louis		Joseph Plante	
	Louis			
9	Jean	(4)	Louis Clément	S.Chs. 1779
	Louise		René Pelchat	„ 1802
	Christine		Ant. Gontier	„ 1807
10	Louis	(4)	Véronique Fortier	
				S. Chs. 1782
	Angélique		Pierre Baillargeon	S.G. 1819
	Joseph			
	Pierre			
11	Jean Baptiste	(5)	M. Jos. Fradet	S.F.S. 1790
	Marie Elizabeth		Laurent Fradet	S.V. 1812
	Le même		Genev. Thibaut	S.F.S. 1796
	Geneviève		Jos. Marseau	S.V. 1822
	Marie		J. B. Baudoin	„ 1834
	Archange		Nic. Baudoin	„ 1840
	Ephrem			
	Germain			
12	Joseph	(5)	M. Eliz. Boissonneau	
				S.F.S. 1797
	Pierre			
	Joseph			
	Hubert			
	Magloire			
	Antoine			
	Le même		Marg. Desruisseaux	
				S.V. 1822
	Marguerite		Barth. Fortier	„ 1841
	Sophie		Ant. Arbour	„ 1845
13	Joseph	(6)	M. Jos. Aubé	„ 1803
	Louise		Joseph Turgeon	„ 1824
14	Simon	(6)	Marie Cadrin	S.M. 1807
15	Pierre		Marg. Lebrun	
	Angélique		Martin Asselin	S.F. 1817
	Elizabeth		Jean Marie Létourneau	
				S.F. 1818
16	Augustin	(7)	M. Jos. Furois	S.M. 1793
	Marguerite		Prosper Gagné	S.H. 1820
A	Joseph	(7)	Thérèse Thivierge	
				S.H. 1820
17	Louis	(8)	Josette Dion	S.G. 1809

JOLIN.

18	Pierre	(10)	Marg. Roberge	S.G.	1819
19	Joseph	(19)	Julienne Deblois	S.F.	1821
20	Ephrem	(11)	Flavie Baudoin	S.V.	1830
21	Germain	(11)	Julienne Alaire	S.V.	1833
22	Pierre	(12)	M. Olive Louineau	S.V.	1826
23	Antoine	(12)	M. Genev. Théberge	S.V.	1826
24	Hubert	(12)	Marcelline Baudoin	S.V.	1828
25	Joseph	(12)	Marg. Perrot	S.V.	1832
26	Magloire	(12)	Adé Guilmet	S.V.	1838

JOLIVET-MITRON.

1	Aimé		Anne Fiset		
	Marguerite		Nic. Vézina	A.G.	1715
	Joseph				
2	Joseph	(1)	Eliz. Guénet	B.	1728
	Thérèse		J. B. Bauseron	S.Chs.	1760
	Marie Marthe		Ign. Poulin	S.V.	1761
	Joseph				
	Charles				
	François				
3	Joseph	(2)	M. Ls. Bissonnet	S.M.	1754
4	François	(2)	Marg. Dairon	B.	1765
	François				
	Le même		Fse Plante	S.G.	1807
5	Charles	(2)	LouiseGendron	S.F.S.	1765
	Marie Louise		Ls. Baudoin	S.F.S.	1785
	Marie Agathe		J. B. Guilmet	S.F.S.	1807
	Marguerite		J. B. Gagné	S.F.S.	1819
	Charles				
6	Joseph		Marie Gontier (¹)		
	Marie		Aug. Guilmet	S.V.	1806
	Marguerite		Frs. Gontier	S.G.	1823
	Joseph				
7	Charles	(5)	M. Ls. Gaudin	S.F.S.	1796
	M. Françoise		Simon Clavet	S.F.S.	1826
8	Etienne		Louise Gaudin		
	François				
9	Joseph	(6)	Fse. Lebrun	B.	1807
	Catherine		Mag. Gontier	S.G.	1827
10	Joseph		Angèle Dessaint		
	Joseph				
11	François	(8)	Louise Guénet	S.P.S.	1833
12	Joseph	(10)	M. Cédulie Blanchet	S. Chs.	1854

¹ Elle épouse Jos. Roy S. Chs. 1801.

JOLY.

1	Vital		Marie Ginchereau	Qué.	1698
	Marie Anne		Aug. Mercier	Qué.	1747
	Marie		Ls. Blanchet	Bert.	1723
	Marie Josette		Pierre Blanchet	Bert.	1725
	Claire		J. B. Proulx	Bert.	1727

JONCAS.

1	Pierre		Jacqueline Boulet	S.F.	1672
	Pierre				
2	Pierre	(1)	Louise Nolin	S.P.	1696
	Louise		Jean Fournier	S.Tho.	1717
	Pierre				
3	Pierre	(2)	Marthe Fournier	S. Tho.	1719
	Elisabeth		Nic. Couture	S. Tho.	1749
	Jacques				
	Jean Baptiste				
4	Joseph		M. Eliz. Bernier		
	Louis				
5	Jacques	(3)	Mad. Couillard	S.Tho.	1755
	Angélique		Aug. Coté	S. Tho.	1784
	Le même		M. Marg. Rousseau	S. P. S.	1784

JONCAS.

6	Jean Baptiste	(3)	Marg. Daillet	S. Tho.	1765
	Jean Baptiste				
7	Pierre		M. Jos. Martin		
	Marie Anne		J. B. Roy	S.V.	1776
	Pierre				
	Pierre				
8	Louis	(4)	LouiseCouillard	S Tho	1760
	Joseph				
9	Jean Baptiste	(6)	M. Genev. Métivier	S. Tho.	1788
	Marie Soulange		Toussaint Blais	Bert.	1849
	Théodore				
	Joseph				
	Etienne				
10	Pierre	(7)	Genev. Cloutier	Islet	1778
	François				
11	Pierre	(7)	M. Chs. Cochon	S. H.	1788
	Louis		M. Vict. Peltier	S.P.S.	1805
12	Joseph	(8)	Vict. Rémillard	S.V.	1823
13	Pierre				
	Pierre Séverin				
14	Joseph	(9)	M. Rose Blais	Bert.	1824
15	Etienne	(9)	M. Chs. Baudry	Bert.	1828
16	Théodore	(9)	Brigitte Kiroack	Bert.	1832
17	François	(10)	Rose Isabel	S.V.	1822
18	Louis	(11)	Marie Tardif	S. H.	1818
19	Pre Séverin	(13)	Désanges Cochon	S.V.	1849

JOURDAIN.

1	Guillaume		Jeanne Constantin	Q.	1678
	Marie Angélique		Jean Huard		1704
	Jeanne		Mathieu Huard		
	Joseph				
2	Joseph		Cath. Duquet	Lévis	1718
	Catharine		Jean Gontier	S. Chs.	1759
	Le même		M. Thérèse Boucher,	Lévis	1739
	Jeanne		Jacq. Pénin	S. Chs.	1758

JUIN.

1	Pierre		Jeanne Beau Jean		
	Marie		Jean Ouinet	S. Frs.	1702
	Pierre				
2	Pierre	(1)	Marg. Lefebvre	„	1698
	Susanne		Ant Viger	S.V.	1739

JULIEN.

1	Nicolas		Marie Brisson	A.G.	1695
	Jean				
2	Jean	(1)	Louise Trudel	„	1717
	François				
	Joseph				
3	Jean	(2)	Mad. Laberge	„	1752
	Jean				
4	Joseph	(2)	M. Mad. Jacob	S.R.	1765
	Madeleine		Michel Tremblay		
	Nicolas				
5	François	(2)	Véronique Chabot	S.P.	1769
	Véronique		Pierre Rosa	„	1800
	Marie		Amable Côté	„	1828
6	Jean	(3)	M. Anne Vézina	A.G.	1782
	Jean				
	François				
7	Nicolas	(4)	Mad. Paradis	S.P.	1813
8	Jean	(5)	Thérèse Martineau	S.P.	1816
9	Jean	(6)	Angé Gourdeau	„	1829
10	François fils de	(6)	Julie Gourdeau	„	1829
	Pre. et Josette				
	Mercier				

JULIEN.

11 Joseph	Marie Paré	S.R. 1825
Le même	Genev. Pelchat	B. 1831

LABBÉ.

1 Pierre	Cath. Bernard	S.F. 1672
Le même	Marg. Meunier	
		S. Anne 1674
Anne	Frs. Dalaire	S. Frs. 1694
M. Madeleine	J. B. Deblois	„ 1710
Geneviève	Pierre Martineau	„ 1718
Marie	Pierre Ducuron	„ 1699
Marie	2° Claude Poliquin	B. 1718
Jean		
Jacques		
Pierre		
2 Jacques	(1) Fse. Deblois	S.F. 1709
Marthe	Pierre Paquet	S. Frs. 1740
Françoise	Guill. Paquet	„ 1740
Françoise	2° Ls. Guillot	„ 1754
Pierre		
Jacques		
3 Pierre	(1) Reine Garinet	„ 1715
Marie	Louise Marseau	B. 1747
Pierre		
Jean Baptiste		
4 Jean	(1) Marie Lepage	S. Frs. 1724
Louise	Jos. Delaire	„ 1745
Hélène	Pierre Boivin	„ 1747
Marie	Pierre Lefebvre	„ 1756
Michel		
Jean		
Joseph		
5 Jacques	(2) M. Fse. Mercier	
		Bert 1743
6 Pierre	(2) Angé. Martineau	S.F.1746
7 Pierre	Agnès Cochon	S.V. 1741
Reine	Pierre Goupy	B. 1779
Angélique	Barth. Paquet	S.G. 1787
Marie	Jacq. Fournier	„ 1785
Marie	2° André Fradet	„ 1795
Pierre		
8 Jean Baptiste	(3) M. Fse. Cochon	S.V. 1744
Jean Baptiste		
Le même	Cécile Fiset	A.G. 1752
Le même	Marg. Denis	S.M. 1755
9 Michel	Genev. Dalaire	S. Frs. 1749
10 Jean	M. Jos. Asselin	„ 1761
Marie Josette	Frs. Bilodeau	„ 1783
Marie Victoire	Frs. Lepage	S.J. 1794
Augustin		
11 Joseph	(4) Mad. Marseau	S. Frs. 1762
M. Françoise	J. B. Lamothe	S.F. 1807
Madeleine	Frs. Labbé-Lemelin	
Jean Marie		
Augustin		
12 Pierre	(7) Louise Garant	S.F.S. 1777
Marie	Eustache Roy	S.G. 1798
Françoise	Jacq. Fradet	„ 1803
Joseph		
André		
Jacques		
Jacques		
Le même	M. Fse Dessaint	
		S.F.S. 1809
13 Jean Baptiste	(8) Marie Lefebvre	S. V. 1767
André		
Jean		
Le même	Genev. Noël	S. Chs. 1798
14 Augustin	(10) Josette Réaume	S.A. 1787
Marguerite	Jos. Dufresne	S.L. 1813
Marie Josette	Frs. Noël	„ 1812
Victoire	Frs. Létourneau	„ 1815
Jean		
Le même	Mad. Lepage	S. Frs. 1799
Angèle	Frs. Giguère	„ 1828

LABBÉ.

Madeleine	Jos. Baudoin	S. Frs. 1829
Julie	Jos. Kéroack	„ 1837
René		
15 Joseph	Josette Dorion	
Olivier		
16 Jean Marie	(11) Genev. Drouin	S.M. 1798
Luce	Pierre Chatigny	„ 1834
Victorine	Pierre Boissonneau	
		S. Frs. 1837
Josette	René Picard	S.Roch 1839
M. Madeleine	Frs. Lasalle	S.J. 1841
Josette	René Picard	
Jean Marie		
Joseph		
René		
François		
17 Augustin	(11) M. Chs. Emond	S.Frs.1799
Marie	Jos. Lepage	S.F. 1823
18 Joseph	(12) M. Marg. Bolduc	S.M.1806
Céleste	Jean Chamberlan	1829
Pierre		
Michel		
19 André	(12) M. Anne Moreau	S.G. 1818
Pierre		
20 Jacques	(12) Marg. Dodier	S.G. 1821
21 Jacques	(12) Marg. Gagné	„ 1826
Marie	Jos. Bissonnet	S.J. 1857
Marie	Pierre Ouimet	S.L. 1848
Odile	Eugène Gosselin	„ 1871
Philomène	David Bouffart	„ 1870
François Xavier		
Thomas		
Norbert		
Ferdinand		
22 Jean	(13) M.Jos.Lemieux	S.F.S. 1791
Elisabeth	André Brochu	L.G. 1826
Michel		
Jean		
Pierre		
Gabriel		
Le même	Marie Dutile	S.G. 1827
23 Frs. Germain	M. Anne Dessaint	
François		
24 André	(13) Marg. Gontier	S.Chs. 1796
Marie	Chs. Boutin	S.G. 1824
Angéle	Féréol Patry	S.G. 1829
André		
Louis		
Michel		
Paschal		
Joseph		
Le même	M. Angèle Rousseau	
		S.Chs. 1815
25 Jean	Mad. Gagnon	S.Frs. 1826
26 René	(14) M. Ls. Hébert	S.Frs. 1839
Le même	(16) Cath. Dion	S. Frs. 1844
		S. Sylvestre
27 Jean Marie	(16) Archange Giguère	S.J.1826
28 François	(16) M. Ls. Lepage	S.Frs. 1828
29 Joseph	(16) Marg. Lemelin	„ 1837
Marguerite	Jos. Blouin	„ 1863
30 René	(16) Modeste Picard	„ 1845
31 Olivier	(15) M.Mad. Nadeau	S.F. 1825
32 Pierre	(18) Angèle Brochu	S.M. 1831
33 Michel	(18) M.Ls. Réaume	S.Chs. 1831
34 Pierre	(19) Marie Leclaire	S.Frs. 1662
35 Jean	(22) Soulange Clouticr	S.G.1719
36 Michel	(22) Angé Aubé	„ 1826
Marcel		
37 Pierre	(22) Louise Bernard	„ 1827
38 Gabriel	(21) M. Chantal Roy	1828
39 Norbert	(21) Genev. Pouliot	S.M. 1853
40 Frs. Xavier	(21) Apolline Fortier	S.J. 1664
41 Ferdinand	(21) Marcelline Hébert	„ 1864
42 Thomas	(23) M.Adeline Fortier	„ 1871

LABBÉ.

43 François	(23)	Rosalie Labrecque	B. 1842
44 André	(24)	M. Anne Paquet	S.M.1822
41 Michel	(24)	Angèle Paquet	" 1825
46 Louis	(24)	Marguerite Pacquet	S.M. 1825
47 Pierre Pasqual	(24)	Marie Paquet	S.M. 1827
48 Joseph	(24)	Mad. Dalaire	S.G. 1825
49 Marcel	(36)	PerpétueCouture	S.Chsl855

LABONTÉ-BOILEAU.

1			
2 Jean	(1)	Josette Aubin	
Joseph			
3 Joseph	(2(	Marg. Morel	S.P.S. 1787
Marie Pélagie		Frs. Daniau	" 1817
Jean Baptiste			
4 Michel Paul		Susanne Valiére	
Marie Susanne		David Bouffart	" 1807
Le même		M. Roger Gaudreau	S.P.S. 1792
Marie Flavie		J. B. Langlois	" 1832
Joseph			
5 Jean Baptiste	(3)	M. Julienne Morin	S.P.S. 1824
6 Joseph	(4)	Scolastique Bouffart	S.P.S. 1833

LABRECQUE.

1 Jacques		Jeanne Baron	
Pierre			
Jean			
2 Pierre	(1)	Gabriel Barré	
Le même		Jeanne Chotar	C.R. 1663
Catherine		Pierre Garant	S.L. 1684
Catherine		2° Clement Dubois	S.L. 1700
Anne		Gilles Laurent	S.L. 1691
Mathurin			
Pierre			
3 Jean	(1)	Jeanne Baillargeon	C.R. 1664
Françoise		Frs. Gosselin	S.P. 1690
Marguerite		Ant. Godbout	S.P. 1691
Jacques			
4 Mathurin	(2)	Marthe Lemieux	Lévis 1693
M. Madeleine		Chs. Guay	B. 1733
Marie Louise		Ant. Molleur	B. 1739
Susanne		Ls. Lacroix	B. 1714
Susanne		2° Noël Gromelin	S.V. 1727
Jean Baptiste			
Pierre			
Joseph			
Louis			
Ignace			
François			
5 Pierre	(2)	M. Marthe Coulombe	S.L. 1694
Marie		Pierre Audet	S.L. 1727
Marguerite		Jos. Gosselin	S.L. 1756
Joseph			
François			
Louis			
6 Jacques	(3)	Marg. Paquet	S.L. 1693
Catherine		Pierre Godbout	S.L. 1723
Jeanne		Ls. Beaulieu	S.L. 1729
M. Madeleine		Frs. Beaulieu	S.L. 1729
Françoise		Clément Fortier	S.L. 1733
Thérèse		Nic. Létourneau	S.L. 1736
Marguerite		Jos. Chalifour	Que. 1726
Laurent			
Louis			
7 Ignace	(4)	M. Ls. Couture	B. 1724
Louis			

18—24

LABRECQUE.

8 Jean Baptiste	(4)	Louise Boissel	B. 1727
Louise		Etn. Veau	B. 1756
Louise		2° Noël Simart	S.V. 1767
Louise		3° Jos. Pouliot	S.M. 1781
Marie Charlotte		Ant. Fournier	S.M. 1770
Marie Josette		Ls. Bolduc	S.V. 1760
Charles			
Joseph			
9 Pierre	(4)	Marie Paquet	B. 1734
Marthe		Claude Petitclerc	B. 1781
Mathurin			
Etienne			
Charles			
Louis			
Joseph			
François			
10 Joseph	(4)	M. Ls. Roy	B. 1734
Marie		Jos. Girard	B. 1763
Dorothée		Ls. Forgues	B. 1780
11 Louis	(4)	M. L. S. Roy	B. 1745
Mathurin			
Louis			
Joseph			
12 François	(4)	Louise Nadeau	B. 1748
Marie		Jos. Dupont	S.Chs. 1775
13 Joseph	(5)	Genev. Poulet	S.L. 1722
Marguerite		Ls. Gosselin	S.L. 1754
Marie Angélique		Jean Ruel	S.L. 1753
Gertrude		Jean Baillargeon	S.L. 1761
Pierre			
14 Louis	(5)	M. Anne Delage	S.L. 1730
Jean Baptiste			
Jacques			
15 François	(5)	M. Anne Fortier	S.J. 1770
Marie Anne		Chs. Demeule	S.L. 1788
Marie Josette		Jos. Cochon	S.L. 1794
16 Charles		Marg. Grenet	
Marie Angélique		Frs. Turgeon	S.M. 1768
Marguerite		Frs. Turgeon	B. 1772
Antoine			
17 Louis	(6)	M. AngéRéaume	S.V. 1728
Le même		V. de Pierre Dubeau	
18 Laurent (1)	(6)	Marg. Dumas	S.L. 1741
Marguerite		Jean Gosselin	S'L. 1778
Marie		Jean Boucher	S L. 1786
Laurent			
Jean			
Jacques			
Joseph			
Pierre			
19 Joseph		Marie Jacques	
Joseph			
Louis			
Pierre			
20 Louis	(7)	Cécile Roy	S.Chs. 1759
Pélagie		Pierre Lainé	S.Chs. 1775
Pélagie		2° Frs. Baudoin	S H. 1791
Le même		M. Anne Royer	S.J. 1762
Marie		Ls. Labrecque	S.Chs. 1796
Marie Anne		Chs. Lacasse	S.Chs. 1808
Gabriel			
Louis			
François			
21 Charles	(8)	Marie Fournier	S.M. 1772
Claire		J. B. Hélie	B. 1796
Charles			
22 Joseph	(8)	Genev. Fse. Mercier	S.M. 1775
M. Marguerite		Pierre Bissonnet	S.M. 1796
M. Françoise		Ls. Bilodeau	S.M. 1807
23 Etienne	(9)	Angé Quéret	S.M. 1764

(1) S'est marié sous le nom de Laurent et non sous celui de Joseph.

LABRECQUE.

24	Louis	(9) M. Anne Quéret S.M. 1766	
	Modeste	J. B. Arguin S.G. 1804	
	Mathurin		
	Louis		
	Jean Baptiste		
25	Joseph	(9) M. Anne Lacasse S.M.1770	
	Marguerite	Pierre Lacroix S.G. 1802	
	Marie Anne	Michel Arbour S.G. 1807	
	Augustin		
	Joseph		
26	François	(9) Genev. Petitclerc S.Chs. 1775	
	Marie	Pierre Guilmet S.G. 1804	
	Marie	Pierre Hélie S.G. 1810	
	François		
	Joseph		
27	Charles	(9) Angé Lainé S.Chs. 1777	
	Geneviève	Ign. Guilmet S.G. 1803	
	Madeleine	Jos. Guilmet S.G. 1804	
	Marguerite	Ls. Bouchard S.G. 1804	
	Angélique	Pierre Quemeneur S.G. 1819	
	François		
	Le même	Fse. Gagnon S.G. 1823	
28	Mathurin	(9) M. Marthe Nadeau S.M. 1793	
	François		
29	Mathurin	(11) M. Mad. Patry S.M. 1774	
	Marie	Ls. Thibaut S.G. 1802	
	Le même	M. Anne Fournier B. 1799	
	Joseph		
30	Louis	(11) Louise Mercier S.Chs.1788	
	Françoise	Ls. Goulet S.G. 1809	
	Marie	J. B. Bilodeau S.G. 1812	
	Louis		
	Le même	M. Anne Pilote S.G. 1816	
31	Joseph	(11) Charlotte Bacquet S.Chs. 1795	
	Joseph		
32	Pierre	(13) Cécile Baillargeon S.L.1755	
	Louis		
	Charles		
	Pierre		
33	Jacques	(14) M. Jos. Gosselin S.L. 1763	
34	Jean	(14) M. Anne Godbout S.P.1764	
	Marie Anne	Pierre Coulombe S.L. 1806	
35	Jean Baptiste	Cath. Gendron	
	Pierre		
36	Antoine	(16) Eliz. Bouffart S.M. 1775	
	Agathe	Guill. Beaucher B. 1808	
	Geneviève	Jos. Gautron B. 1819	
	Charles		
	Joseph		
	François		
	Antoine		
37	Jacques	M. Angé Clément S.V.1770	
	fils de Jos. Labrecque et Margt. Dumas Qué. 1743		
	Jacques		
	Louis		
	Le même	Mad. Blais S.V. 1778	
	Marie	Etienne Roy S.G. 1821	
	Jean Baptiste		
	Charles		
38	Jean	Marie Roy S.M. 1785	
	Joseph		
39	Laurent	(18) Genev. Dufresne S.L. 1785	
	Marie	Gab. Thivierge S.J. 1819	
	Laurent		
40	Joseph	(18) Thérèse Naud S.Chs. 1776	
	Thérèse	Pierre Fournier S.Chs.1801	
	Marguerite	Frs. Baudoin S.Chs. 1825	
	Barbe	Ant. Chabot S.Chs. 1827	
	Pierre		
	François		

LABRECQUE.

41	Pierre	(18) Marie Naud S.Chs. 1786	
	Marie	J. B. Bruneau S.G. 1807	
	Marie	2° Ls. Monmeny S.G. 1819	
	Marie	3° Tho. Quemeneur S.G.	
	Thérèse	Jean Couture S.G 1814	
	Charles		
	Etienne		
	Joseph		
42	Joseph	(19) Cath. Hayot S.G. 1785	
	Henri		
	Joseph		
	Gabriel		
43	Pierre	(19) M. Jos. Quéret S.G. 1786	
		V. de Jérôme Hélie	
	Angélique	Simon Bisson S.G. 1810	
44	Louis	(19) Judith Lepage S.G. 1791	
	Etienne		
	Jacques		
45	Etienne	Genev. Fournier	
	Marie Anne	Jos. Tangué S.Chs. 1808	
	Geneviève	Jos. Gosselin B. 1821	
	Joseph		
	Etienne		
46	Joseph	Susanne Girard	
	Charlotte	Ls. Boilard B. 1798	
	Marguerite	Claude Paquet B. 1799	
	Joseph		
	Etienne		
47	François	Ursule Lanouette	
	Jean Baptiste		
48	Guillaume	Genev. Samson	
	Angélique	Barnabé Tangué S.G. 1812	
	Susanne	Jean Lemelin S.G. 1822	
	Guillaume		
49	Pierre	M. Anne Royer	
	Jacques		
50	Jean	M. Anne	
	Françoise	Fse. Leblond S.G. 1816	
	Angélique	Frs. Roy S.G. 1816	
51	Etienne	(46) Fse. Valière B. 1803	
	Geneviève	Olivier Couture B. 1839	
	Charlotte	Delphin Provost B. 1841	
	Julien		
52	Gabriel	(20) Louise Leroux S.Chs.1797	
	Marguerite	Jos. Rouleau S.G. 1821	
	Louise	Jos. Roy „ 1823	
53	Louis	(20) Cath. Bazin S.Chs.1799	
	Catherine	Jos. Terrien „ 1834	
	Rosalie	Magl. Pouliot „ 1834	
	Angélique	Chs. Boissel „ 1835	
	Louis		
54	François	(20) Fse. Pouliot S.G. 1803	
	Françoise	Jean Monmeny S.G.1827	
55	Charles	(21) M. Ls. Couture „ 1813	
	Marguerite	Pierre Crépeau „ 1839	
	Marie Rose	Célestin Pepin „ 1847	
	Charles		
	François		
56	Louis	(24) Charlotte Nadeau S.G.1791	
	Marie Charlotte	Jos. Carrier S.Marie 1819	
57	Mathurin	Fse. Gosselin S.Chs.1801	
58	Jean Baptiste	(24) Marg. Reine Buteau S.F.S. 1806	
59	Joseph	(25) Marie Bilodeau S.G. 1802	
	Marie	Chs. Gontier S.Chs.1832	
	Jean Baptiste		
60	Augustin	(25) Charlotte Morin S.G. 1806	
	Le même	Marg. Gagnon „ 1808	
	Germain		
61	François	(26) Reine Bacquet S.Chs.1805	
	Reine	Pierre Terrien „ 1840	
	Hermine	Ignace Nadeau „ 1842	
62	Joseph	(26) Reine Rousseau S.G. 1813	
63	François	Angé Roy „ 1820	
64	Jean	Fse. Théberge	
	Françoise	Jos. Pelchat S.G. 1821	

LABRECQUE.

65	François	(27) Marie Leblond	S.Chs.	1821
66	François	(28) Marg. Turgeon	B.	1810
	Angèle	Félix Fontaine	,,	1831
	Sophie	Jos. Picard	,,	1842
	Godfroi			
67	Joseph	(29) Marg. Gagnon	,,	1830
	Marguerite	Pierre Pouliot	S.Chs.	1860
68	Louis	(30) M. Chs. Fortin	S.V.	1821
69	Joseph	(31) Charlotte Pepin	S.G.	1815
70	Pierre	(32) Marie Godbout	S.L.	1785
	Charlotte	Jos. Thivierge	S.J.	1812
	Angèle	Pierre Curodeau	,,	1815
	Marie Anne	Chs. Blouin	,,	1819
	Geneviève	Jos. Blouin	,,	1823
	Marguerite	Pierre Pepin	,,	1824
	Natalie	Ign. Bouffart	,,	1825
	Natalie	2° Jos. Royer	,,	1834
	Natalie	3° Zeph. Myrand	,,	1849
	Joseph			
	Antoine			
	Pierre			
71	Louis	(32) Charlotte Godbout	S.L.	1789
	Cécile	J. B. Jarnas	,,	1811
	Charlotte	Pierre Laberge	,,	1814
	Françoise	Pierre Godbout	,,	1818
	Marie	Aug. Noël	,,	1822
	Josette	Jos. Brousseau	,,	1850
	Grégoire			
72	Charles	'(32) Thérèse Noël	,,	1790
	Thérèse	Paul Langlois	,,	1812
	Angélique	Jos. Denis	,,	1818
	Marie	Jean Langlois	,,	1823
	Madeleine	Jean Leclaire	,,	1834
	Angèle	Pierre Cinqmars	,,	1837
	Natalie	Bernard Chabot	,,	1842
	Louis			
	Charles			
	Jean			
73	Pierre	(35) Genev. Girard	S.G.	1791
74	Charles	(36) Rosalie Beaucher	B.	1808
	Henriette	Gab. Dangueuger	,,	1839
	Elisabeth	J. B. Lainé	,,	1840
	Rosalie	Frs. Labbé	,,	1842
	Mathilde	Jos. Magl. Bussière	,,	1847
	Olive	Pierre Bussière	,,	1856
	Charles			
	Joseph			
75	François	(36) M. Angé Patry	B.	1809
	Angèle	Ls. Marc Turgeon	,,	1832
	Esther	Chs. Enouf	,,	1832
	Isabelle	Damase Turgeon	,,	1846
	Henriette	Noël Prudent Baudoin	B.	1849
	Célina	Jean Turgeon	,,	1853
	François			
76	Antoine	(36) Ange Gautron	S.H.	1808
	Emérence	Magl. Guay	B.	1841
	Antoine			
77	Joseph	(36) Marie Fradet	,,	1816
	Marie Rosalie	Jos. Guay	,,	1839
	Angélique	Magl. Beaucher	,,	1846
	Dina	Fréderic Gagnon	,,	1849
78	Jacques	(37) Josette Leblond	S.Chs.	1795
	Marie	Louis Audet	,,	1828
	Jacques			
79	Louis	(37) Marie Labrecque	,,	1796
80	Jean Baptiste	(37) Thérèse Pouliot	,,	1807
	Jean			
	Le même	Mad. Aubin	S.G.	1819
81	Charles	(37) Angé Blouin	S.J.	1847
82	Joseph	(38) Françoise Pouliot	S.Chs.	1822
	Anastasie	Aug. Leblond	,,	1837
83	Laurent	(39) M. Basilisse Thivierge	S.J.	1815

LABRECQUE.

	Laurent			
	Cyrille			
	Hubert			
	Octave			
84	Pierre	(40) Marie Chabot	S.Chs.	1805
	Marie	Chs. Gosselin	,,	1831
	Justine	Ls. Dalaire	,,	1844
	Pierre			
	Jacques			
85	François	(40) Vict. Fontaine	S.F.	1811
	Michel			
	François			
	Le même	Angé Turgeon	B.	1828
86	Charles	(41) Reine Gagnon,	S.M.	1817
87	Étienne	(41) Louise Patouel	S.G.	1820
88	Joseph	(42) Archange Nadeau	,,	1821
89	Joseph	(42) M. Mad. Duperron	S.M.	1821
90	Henri	(42) M. Anne Gautron	S.G.	1819
91	Gabriel	(42) Fse. Ruel	,,	1825
	Le même	Fse. Goulet	,,	1828
	Etienne			
92	Etienne	(44) Marie Bisson	S.G.	1819
	Eléonore	F. X. Boissonneau	S.J.	1854
93	Jacques	(44) Angé Mathieu	S.G.	1819
94	Etienne	(45) Cécile Gosselin	S.Chs.	1798
	Madeleine	Frs. Blais	,,	1840
	Cécile	Frs. Leclaire	S.G.	1821
	Luce	Jean Marie Beaucher	S.G.	1824
95	Joseph	(45) Mad. Nadeau	,,	1811
96	Joseph	(46) Fse. Bussière	B.	1806
	Adélaïde	Jos. Roy	B.	1842
	Bénoni			
	Joseph			
	Pierre			
	Magloire			
	Damase			
	François Xavier			
97	Jean Baptiste	(47) Marie Fontaine	S.G.	1809
98	Guillaume	(48) Angé Briart	,,	1812
	Etienne			
99	Jacques	(49) Justine Dalaire	S.G.	1812
100	Antoine	Eliz. Bourassa		
	Jean			
101	Louis	Cath. Morin	S.Chs.	
	Féréol			
102	Pierre	Marg. Audet		
	Marguerite	Jos. Coulombe	S.J.	1838
103	Julien	(51) Luce Turgeon	B.	1840
104	Louis	(53) Angéle Leblond	S.M.	1821
195	Charles	(55) Marie Hudon	S.Chs.	1849
106	François	(55) Angéle Gosselin	,,	1862
107	Jean Baptiste	(59) M. Chs. Boilard	S.	1830
	Félicité	Didase Rouleau	S.L.	1866
108	Germain	(60) Marg. Lacasse	S.Chs.	1834
109	Godfroi	(66) Anastasie Turgeon	B.	1856
110	Pierre	(70) Marg. Audibert	S.J.	1812
	Marguerite	Jos. Coulombe	,,	1838
	Le même	Euphrosine Blouin	,,	1822
	Scolastique	Frs. Pepin	,,	1845
	Angéle	Jos. Blouin	,,	1848
	Séraphine	Frs. Audet	,,	1848
	Ferdinand			
	Joseph			
111	Joseph	(70) Marg. Curodeau	S.J.	1821
	Anatalie	Henri Théophile Grenier	S.J	1854
	Marie	Cyp. Tangué	,,	1863
	Clément			
112	Antoine	(70) Pétronille Rouleau	S.L.	1833
113	Grégoire	(71) Genev. Poulin	,,	1835
	Le même	Marie Cinqmars	,,	1840
	Marie	Célestin Guérard	,,	1865

LABRECQUE.　　　　　　　　　　　LABRECQUE.

	Marcelline	Delphis Arel	S.L. 1870
	Adélaïde	Paul Pouliot	„ 1876
	Cyprien		
114	Charles	(72) Louise S. Norbert	
		Coulombe	S. L. 1815
	Marie Louise	Guill. Fournier	„ 1840
	Isidore		
	Edouard		
115	Louis	(72) Genev. Cinqmars S.L. 1825	
	Désiré		
	Léon		
116	Jean	(72) Cath. Gosselin	S.L. 1829
	Marie Zoé	Isidore Plante	„ 1855
	M. Emélandre	Guill. Lachaine	„ 1857
	Anatalie	Jean Simart	„ 1865
	Anatalie	2° Ls. Grenier	„ 1872
	Caroline	Désiré Delisle	„ 1870
	M. Catherine	Etn. Simart	S.P. 1850
117	Charles	(74) Scolastique Guay	B. 1840
118	Joseph	(74) Cévilie Turgeon	B. 1856
119	François	(75) Marcelline Gagnon	
			S.Chs. 1846
120	Jacques	(78) Angé Aubin	S.G. 1820
	Julie	Ant. Leblond	S.Chs. 1846
	Jacques		
	Le même	Archangé Larrivé S.G. 1826	
	Euphrosine	Ign. Terrien	S.Chs. 1847
121	Jean	(80) Henriette Clavet	
			Bert. 1836
	Adèle	Jean Denis	S.L. 1868
	Marie	Désiré Labrecque	
			S.L. 1873
122	Hubert	(83) Justine Cochin	C.R. 1844
123	Laurent	(83) Josette Paquet	S.J. 1845
	Le même	Marg. Mercier	S.J. 1852
124	Octave	(83) Marie Taupin	C.R. 1854
125	Cyrille	(83) M. Olimpe Nolin S.P. 1866	
126	Pierre	(84) M. Jos. Audet S.Chs. 1831	
127	Jacques	Delphine Duquet	
			S.Chs. 1837
	Le même	M. Onésime Morin	
			S.F.S. 1843
128	Etienne	(91) Philomène Gautron	
			S.V. 1854
129	Joseph	(96) Sophie Guay	B. 1831
130	Bénoni	(96) Marine Turgeon	B. 1840
131	Pierre	(96) M. Maxime Turgeon	
			B. 1846
132	Magloire	(96) Léocadie Turgeon B. 1846	
133	François	(96) Louis Roy	B. 1850
	Xavier		
134	Damase	(96) Marcelline Filteau B. 1851	
135	Etienne	(98) Zoé Denis	S.Chs. 1840
	Marie Zoé	Gervais Audet S.Chs. 1862	
136	Joseph	Marie Couture	
	Le même	M. Ls. Dorval S.Chs. 1860	
137	Jean	(100) Marg. Filteau	B. 1828
	Dina	Abraham Rouleau B. 1850	
138	Féréol	(101) M. Anne Delanteigne	
			S.S. 1827
139	Joseph	(110) M. Anne Raimond	
			S.J. 1851
140	Ferdinand	(110) M. Célanire Bouffard	
			S.L. 1858
141	Clément	(111) Eliz Royer	S.L. 1848
	Marie Anne	Olivier Colombe S.L. 1865	
	Antoinette	Barth. Pouliot	S.L. 1872
142	Cyprien	(113) Alvine Vézina	Que.
143	Edouard	(114) Fse. Godbout	S.L. 1846
	Léon		
144	Isidore	(114) Angé. Godbout S.L. 1855	
145	Léon	(115) Caroline Terrien S.L. 1853	
146	Désiré	(115) Marie Labrecque S.L. 1873	
147	Antoine	(76) M. Hermine Guénet B. 1839	
	Philomène	Frs. Gautron	B. 1858
	Hermine	Alexandre Boucher B. 1859	

148	Michel	(85) Analole Turgeon	B. 1844
149	François	(85) Emélie Lemelin S.M. 1844	
150	Jacques	(120) M. Marcelline Leblond	
			S.M. 1847
151	Léon	(143) M. Auxilia Gosselin	
			S.L. 1881

LACASSE.

1	Antoine	Fse. Pitié-Piloy C.R. 1665	
	M. Charlotte	Denis Nadeau	B. 1695
	Catherine	Rémi Valière	B. 1701
	Marguerite	Pierre Jahan	
	Jeanne Thérèse	Noel Le Roy	
	Charles		
	Joseph		
2	Joseph	(1) Marie Bazin	
	Louise	Jacq. Hélie	B. 1715
	Susanne	Ignace Adam	B. 1720
	M. Françoise	Ls. Le Roy	B. 1722
	M. Madeleine	J. B. Couture	B. 1722
	Marie Anne	Chs. Poirier	B. 1730
	Elisabeth	Pierre Gosselin	B. 1732
	Marie Josette	Ls. Ouellet	B. 1733
	Marguerite	Pierre Gontier	B. 1734
	Marguerite	2° Jos. Baudoin	
			S.Chs. 1763
	Marie	Jacq. Paquet	B. 1735
	Antoine	Etn. Le Roy	B. 1709
	Charles		
	Joseph		
	Jean Baptiste		
3	Charles	(1) Fse. Paquet	B. 1703
	Madeleine	Jos. Dumont	B. 1735
	Le même	M. Jos. Filteau S.V. 1734	
	Joseph		
4	Antoine	(2) Marie Bourget	B. 1718
	Marie	J. B. Gontier	B. 1736
	Susanne	Jos. Bisson	B. 1748
	Thérèse	Gab. Gosselin	B. 1751
	Marguerite	Frs. Guay	B. 1752
	Angélique	Ls. Boissel	B. 1765
	Etienne		
5	Charles	(2) M. Genev. Gontier B. 1733	
	M. Geneviève	Ls. Bégin	B. 1753
	Le même	Angélique Garneau	
			A.G. 1744
	Thérèse	Jacq. Tangué	B. 1757
	Marie Marthe	Amb. Pénin	S.M. 1772
	Charles		
6	Jean Baptiste	(2) Marie Alaire	B. 1734
	Marie Anne	Jean Bleau	S.Chs. 1758
	Marie Josette	Etn. Guénet	S.Chs. 1757
	Joseph		
	Jean		
7	Joseph	(2) Marg. Coté	B. 1740
	Joseph		
8	Joseph	Jossete Maufait	
	Marie Anne	Jos. Labrecque S.M. 1770	
	Marie Anne	2° Michel Forgue S.M. 1790	
	Josette	Ls. Godbout	S.Chs. 1771
	Le même	Marie Roy	S.Chs. 1749
	Marguerite	Jean Chabot	S.Chs. 1781
	Marie	Jean Chabot	S.Chs. 1782
	Joseph		
9	Etienne	(4) Marg. Roy	B. 1745
	Marie Louise	René Pelchat	S.Chs. 1772
	Marguerite	Ls. Bouchard	S.Chs. 1778
	Véronique	Jos. Pelchat	S.Chs. 1788
	Marie	Jos. Bilodeau	S.G. 1786
	Rose	J. B. Lefebvre	S.G. 1786
	Joseph		
	Charles		
	Jean		
	Le même	Marie Tangué S.Chs. 1781	
	Joseph		

LACASSE.

10	Charles	D'Angélique Garneau	
		M. Jeanne Renaud	
			Chsbourg
	Marie Josette	Jos. Marie Dalaire	
			S.M. 1777
	Gaspard		
	Joseph		
11	Joseph	(3) Josette Adam	S.M. 1782
	Josette	Pierre Théberge S.G. 1812	
	Jacques		
12	Antoine	(4) M. Jos. Huot	
	M. Angélique	J. B. Carrier	S.M. 1778
	Marie Josette	Chs. Bégin	B. 1780
	Ignace		
	Antoine		
13	Charles	(5) Marie Pénin S.Chs. 1765	
	Jeanne	Guill. Poulet S.Chs. 1788	
	Marguerite	Jacq. Dandurand	
			S.Chs. 1801
	Ambroise		
	Charles		
14	Jean	(6) Josette Copin S. Chs. 1757	
	Jean Baptiste		
15	Joseph	(6) Apollonix Lacroix	
16	Joseph	(7) Ursule Confulant S.M.1786	
17	Joseph	(8) Marie Gosselin S.Chs. 1773	
	Charlotte	Chs. Bilodeau S.Chs. 1800	
	Marguerite	Zach Bilodeau S.Chs. 1800	
	Marguerite	2ᵉ Gem. Baudoin	
			S.Chs. 1830
	Natalie	Ign. Bilodeau S.Chs. 1804	
	Victoire	Frs. Hébert S. Chs. 1813	
	Marie	Chs. Nadeau	S.G. 1798
	René		
	Joseph		
	Jean Baptiste		
18	Joseph(1er m.)	)(9) Cécile Noël	S.M. 1778
	Cécile	Jean Diers	S.G. 1810
	Angélique	Jacq. Guénet	S.G. 1821
	Joseph		
	Jean		
	Amable		
	Gervais		
	Le même	M. Marg. Chouinard	
			S.H. 1807
19	Jean	(9) Marie Pilote	S.V. 1773
20	Charles	(9) Genev. Mercier S.Chs.1778	
	Le même	Josette Asselin S.Chs.1785	
	Josette	André Rémillard	
	Charles		
	Charles		
	Joseph		
21	Joseph (2d m.)	)(9) Marg. Mercier S.Chs. 1804	
	Marguerite	Germ. Labrecque	
			S.Chs. 1834
	Marie Louise	Magl. Picard S.Chs. 1846	
	Archange	Ant. Dorval S.Chs. 1847	
	Françoise	Pierre Turgeon	B. 1840
	Joseph		
22	Joseph	Marie Dalaire	S.M. 1773
	Marie Louise	Chs. Boutin	S.G. 1799
	Marie	Jos. Moor	S.G.
	Barthéléme		
	Joseph		
23	Gaspard	(10) Ursule Dalaire S.M. 1782	
24	Jacques	(11) Louise Roby S.G. 1816	
25	Ignace	(12) M. Genev. Patry S.M.1779	
26	Antoine	(12) Cath. Guay	B. 1781
	Euphrosine	Jos. Gosselin	B. 1819
	Josette	Ls. Rousseau	S.H. 1819
	Marie Anne	Joseph Moisan S.H.	
	Antoine		
	Louis		
	Joseph	prêtre Curé de St-Henri	
27	Ambroise	(13) M. Marthe Thibaut	
			S.Chs. 1794

LACASSE.

	Cécile	Rémi Gontier S.Chs. 1818	
	Marguerite	André Couture	
			S.Chs. 1821
	Le même	Marg. Gontier S.Chs. 1812	
	Henriette	Phydime Vizina S.M.1847	
	Marie	Ed. Turgeon	S.M. 1849
	Emérence	Thomas Guay	S.M. 1848
	Constance	Ls. Fournier	S.M. 1852
	Charles		
28	Charles	(13) M.Mad. Roy S.Chs. 1801	
	Le même	Rosalie Leclaire	
			S.Chs. 1816
29	Jean Baptiste	(14) Charlotte Couillard B.1785	
	Charlotte	Frs. Chabot	S.Chs. 1805
	Marie Louise	Ls. Nollet	S.Chs. 1813
	Marguerite	Jos. Fortier	S.Chs. 1821
	Ignace		
	Jean		
	Le même	Angé Roy	S.Chs. 1806
	M. Angélique	Frs. Audet	S.Chs.1834
30	René (¹)	(17) Genev. Roy	S.Chs. 1807
31	Joseph	17 Angé Chabot S.Chs. 1817	
	Marthe	Michel Leclaire	
			S.Chs. 1842
	Joseph		
	Louis		
32	Jn. Baptiste	(17) M. Jos. Couture	
			S.Chs. 1828
33	Joseph	(18) Marie Labrecque S.G. 1804	
			S. Anselme
	Amable		
34	Jean	(18) Louise Lemieux	" 1807
35	Amable	(18) Marg. Moreau	" 1808
36	Gervais	(18) Angé Duquet	" 1812
	Le même	M. Genev. Roy S.P.S 1819	
37	Charles	(20) M. Anne Labrecque	
		S.H.	S.Chs. 1808
	Le même	Angé Patry S.Chs. 1816	
	Le même	M. Anne Romaine	
		Bonneau	S.V. 1843
38	Charles	(20) M. Jos. Tangué S.Chs.1816	
39	Joseph	(20) Josette Godbont S.G. 1825	
40	Charles	Josette Gautron	
	Pierre		
41	Joseph	(21) M. Jos.Couture S.Chs.1834	
42	Joseph	(22) Josette Boutin S.G. 1801	
	Josette	Ls. Roberge	" 1821
	Louis		
	Joseph		
43	Barthélemi	(22) Barbe Roy	" 1806
	Le même	Josette Leclaire	" 1819
44	Louis	(26) M. Anne Tangué	" 1814
45	Antoine	(26) Rose Caouet	" 1808
	Angèle	Ls. Genest	B. 1834
	Antoine		
46	Charles	(27) DésangesGautronS.M.1839	
47	Jean	(29) Thérèse Bacquet S.G. 1816	
48	Ignace	(29) M. Anne Turcot	" 1822
49	Jean Damase	(31) M. Euphrosine Ruel	
			S.Chs. 1843
50	Louis	(31) Marg. Naud	" 1853
51	Amable	(33) M.Marg.Gosselin	" 1847
52	Jean	(34) Mad. Langlois S.G. 1827	
	Le même	Archange Tangué S.V.1836	
53	Pierre	(40) Angé Briart S.G. 1823	
54	Joseph	(42) Marg. Roberge	" 1824
55	Louis	(42) Marie Roberge	" 1828
56	Antoine	(45) M. Sophie Roy	B. 1834

(¹) René Lacasse. No. 30 est dit dans son acte
de mariage, fils de Marie Roy et non de Marie
Gosselin.

LACROIX.   LACROIX.

1 François	Anne Gagné	S.Anne	1670
Agathe	Jacq. Tremblé	„	1696
Marie	Pierre Gagnon	„	1704
Claire	Frs. Paré	„	1704
Anne	Etn. Paré	„	1716
Geneviève	Jacq. Fortier	„	1721
Pierre			
2 Joseph David	Antoinette Bluteau	Qué.	1671
Le même	Barth. Maillou	Islet	1681
Périnne	J. B. Drapeau	B.	1708
Périnne	2° Frs. Dumont	B.	1724
Anne	Pierre Drapeau	B.	1710
André			
Louise			
Gabriël			
3 Pierre	(1) JeanneBarette	S. Anne	1723
Thérèse	Jos. Gosselin	S.Tho.	1757
Pierre			
4 André	(2) Mad. Marchand	B.	1701
Catherine	Jos. Marie Lefebvre	S.M.	1736
Marie Anne	Jos. Quéret	„	1742
Elizabeth	Ls.Josué Dulignon	„	1750
Elizabeth	2° Pierre Pouliot	„	1764
Marie Josette	Michel Monmeny	„	1750
Nicolas			
Jean			
André			
Michel			
Joseph			
5 Louis	(2) Susanne Labrecque	B.	1714
Marie	Michel Patry	S.M.	1743
Madeleine	J. B. Vérieul	„	1743
Louis			
Joseph			
Charles			
6 Gabriel	(2) Agnes Cloutier	C.R.	1716
Angélique	Michel Gautron	S.M.	1739
Marie Louise	Jos. Leblond	„	1744
Marie Louise	2° Jacq. Blais	S.V.	1747
Geneviève	J. B. Ruel	S.M.	1750
M. Catherine	Aug. Gautron	„	1754
Joseph			
7 Pierre	(3) M. Genev. Bélanger	S.V.	1758
Marie Anne	Ls. Royer	S.Chs.	1773
Louise	Clément Roy	„	1786
Angélique	Frs. Gosselin	„	1792
Pierre			
8 Nicolas	(4) M. Angé Leroux	S.M.	1736
Angélique	Jos. Gautron	„	1775
Elizabeth	Paul Chatigny	„	1797
Jean Baptiste			
Céleste			
Ambroise			
Claude			
9 Jean	(4) Marg. Forgue	„	1745
M. Catherine	Jos. Brousseau	„	1779
Félicité	Pierre Fiset	„	1781
Jean Joseph			
André			
Michel			
10 André	(4) Eliz. Goupy	„	1745
Marie	Louis Forgue	„	1801
André			
Antoine			
11 Michel	(4) M. Jos. Gautron	S.M.	1748
Marie	Jos. Guilmet	„	1773
M. Geneviève	Michel Roy	„	1808
Le même	Marie Denis	S.J.	1760
Louis			
12 Joseph Marie	(4) M. Anne Ouimet	S.M.	1757
Marie Anne	Pierre Tangué	S.M.	1785
Marie Josette	Simon Corriveau	„	1789
Marie Josette	2° Jacq. Fortier	„	1809

Catherine	Chs. Dion	„	1797
Joseph Marie			
13 Joseph	(5) M. Ls. Brideau	S.M.	1739
M. Françoise	Jos. Plante	S.V.	1778
Marie Josette	Jean Charron	„	1794
Charles			
Joseph			
14 Louis	(5) Marie Bacquet	S.M.	1739
Joseph			
Le même	Genev. Fortier	S.M.	1750
15 Charles	(5) M. Anne Patry	S.M.	1750
Marie	Jos. Lacroix	„	1782
Madeleine	Jos. Lessard	S.V.	1786
Charles			
16 Joseph	(6) M. Jos. Blouin	S.J.	1755
M. Marguerite	Pierre Dangeuger	S.M.	1779
Marie Josette	Frs. Fradet	„	1779
Apollonie	Jos. Lacasse	„	1780
Françoise	Pierre Coten	„	1789
Marie Louise	Alexandre Couture	S.M.	1790
M. Geneviève	Jos. Guilmet	„	1792
Jean Joseph			
Joseph			
17 Pierre	(7) M. Jos. Nolin	S.Chs.	1775
Geneviève	Jos. Guay	„	1798
Josette	Ls. Couture	„	1793
Josette	2° Pierre Dalaire	„	1795
Angélique	Pierre Dalaire	„	1804
Marie Victoire	Ls. Pepin	„	1806
Angèle	Benoit Couture	„	1814
Etienne			
18 Augustin	(8) M. Geneviève Monmeny	S.M.	1763
Le même	M. Ls. Roy	S.V.	1775
Marie Louise	Pierre Drapeau	S.Chs.	1802
Marie Louise	2° Jos. Rémillard	S.M.	1804
Etienne			
Le même	Marie Comeau	S.Chs.	1783
Marie	André Lemelin	„	1805
Josette	Guil. Blais	„	1820
Josette	2° J. B. Gagné	S.F.S.	1835
Augustin			
19 Jean Baptiste	(8) M. Marthe Leclaire	S.V.	1772
20 Claude	(8) Marie Morriset	S.M.	1777
Marie Louise	J. B. Bissonet	„	1805
Marguerite	Frs. Bouffart	„	1808
M. Elizabeth	Frs. Gosselin	„	1818
M. Françoise	J. B. Bissonnet	„	1819
Ambroise			
Louis			
Pierre			
Jean Baptiste			
Claude			
21 Céleste	(8) Agathe Bacquet	S.M.	1787
Agathe	Michel Drapeau	„	1804
Marguerite	Jean Tangué	„	1819
Pierre			
Joseph			
Céleste			
22 Ambroise	(8) M. Fse. Hélie	S.M.	1789
Marguerite	Jos. Pilote	„	1810
Françoise	Guil. Fontaine	„	1819
Paul			
23 Jean Joseph	(9) M. Anne Mercier	„	1772
M. Madeleine	Ant. Gontier	„	1801
Marie Anne	Michel Roussel	„	1805
Marie	Alexis Bolduc	„	1817
André			
Jean François			
François			
Joseph			
Laurent			
Michel			

LACROIX.

24	André	(9)	M. Anne Fortier S.M.	1777
	Le même		Cath. Rousseau "	1812
	Germain			
	André			
25	François		M. Anne Fortier	
	Marie Anne		Frs. Dessaint S.G.	1821
26	Michel	(9)	M. Jos. Bacquet S.M.	1793
27	André	(10)	M. Anne Mousset S.M.	1772
	Marie Anne		Michel Bolduc "	1794
	Marguerite		J. B. Royer "	1802
	Joseph			
	François			
	André			
28	Antoine	(10)	Brigitte Robin S.Tho.	1787
	Marie		J. B. Dodier S.V.	1817
	Marie Marthe		Ls. Thivierge "	1830
	Marie Anne		Ant. Thivierge S.M.	1827
	Jean Baptiste			
29	Louis	(11)	M. Eliz. Michon S.M.	1786
30	Joseph Marie	(12)	Claire Bernier S.Tho.	1801
	Magloire			
	Jean			
31	Joseph	(13)	Marie Roy S.V.	1771
	Marie Renée		J. B. Thibaut S.M.	1797
	Marguerite		Guil. Aubé S.G.	1816
	Marguerite		2° Jos. Leclaire "	1824
	Adélaïde		Jos. Roberge "	1820
	Françoise		Jos. Shink "	1821
	Joseph			
	Joseph			
	Joseph			
	Paul			
	Michel			
	Magloire			
32	Charles	(13)	Marie Bacquet S.M.	1779
	Geneviève		J. B. Aubé S.G.	1811
	Pierre			
33	Joseph	(14)	M. Fse. Fortier S.M.	1760
34	Charles	(15)	M. Ls. Dalaire "	1778
			V. d'Ant. Brousseau	
	Madeleine		J. B. Tangué S.M.	1798
	Le même		Louise Ratté "	1814
35	Joseph	(16)	Marie Lacroix "	1782
36	Jean Joseph	(16)	M. Anne Fradet "	1785
37	Etienne	(17)	Marie Pepin S. Chs.	1806
38	Etienne	(18)	M. Chs. Larrivé "	1814
39	Augustin	(18)	Marie Mercier "	1840
	Angèle		Narcisse Carrière S. Chs.	1862
	Louis			
	Augustin			
40	Charles		Louise Roy	
	Marie Louise		Jean Richard	
41	Jacques		Brigitte Roy	
	Jacques			
42	Joseph		M. Antoinette Desmarais S.M.	
	Marie		J. B. Leblond "	1815
43	Ambroise	(20)	M. Genev. Quemeneur "	1817
	Marie		Ls. Quemeneur "	1842
	Marie Anne		Damase Ruel "	1847
	Marie Anne		Victoire Roy "	1833
44	Pierre	(20)	Mad. Marcoux S.F.S.	1817
A	Jean Bap- tiste	(20)	M. Anne Bouffart S.H.	1809
45	Louis	(20)	Marie Forgue S.Chs.	1819
	Claude	(20)	Mad. Bouffart S.H.	1809
46	Céleste	(21)	Charlotte Goulet S.M.	1810
	Charlotte		Ls. Coulombe S.M.	1851
	Félicité		Ed. Asselin "	1859
	Ursule		Chs. Coulombe "	1859
	Pierre			
	Joseph			
	Le même		Félicité Goulet S.Chs.	1832

LACROIX.

47	Pierre	(21)	Angé Clément S.M.	1819
	Angèle		Michel Asselin "	1841
	Angélique		Chs. Asselin "	1845
	Michel			
	Pierre			
48	Joseph	(21)	Louise Cochon "	1821
	Philomène		David Terrien "	1862
	Anthyme			
	Paul			
	Joseph			
49	Paul	(22)	M. Ls. Fontaine "	1820
50	Jean Fran- çois	(23)	M. Jos. Larrivé "	1799
51	Joseph	(23)	Archange Blanchet S.M.	1802
	Marie Olive		Pierre Morisset "	1828
	Archange		Ed Rousseau "	1834
	Sophie		Flavien Richard "	1841
	Michel			
52	André	(23)	M. Angé Gosselin S. Chs.	1802
53	Laurent	(23)	Angé Brousseau S.M.	1804
	Laurent			
54	Michel	(23)	M. Fse. Vien B.	1808
	Marie Anne		Philippe Journeau "	1834
	Joséphine		Pierre Bolduc "	1848
	Michel			
	Jean Baptiste			
55	François	(23)	M. Chs. Shinck S.M.	1821
	M. Aglaé		Jos. Levasseur B.	1846
	Vitaline		Pierre Guay "	1848
	Dorothée		Ant. Nadeau "	1850
	Louise		Richard Vachon "	1856
56	Germain	(24)	Marcelline Rousseau S. Chs.	1834
	Léocadie		Amable Lainé "	1852
57	André	(24)	M. Chs. Marie (*) Qué.	
58	André	(27)	(¹) M. Susanne Arseneau S.G.	1797
	Madeleine		Aug. Chevanel S.G.	1823
	Charlotte		Ign. Girard "	1830
	Françoise		Hilaire Couillard "	1831
	André			
59	Joseph	(27)	M. Brigitte Goupy S.M.	1804
	Brigitte		Nic. Corriveau S.G.	1828
	Joseph			
60	François	(27)	Angèle Vallée S.M.	1808
61	Magloire	(30)	Adé Fortin "	1848
62	Jean	(30)	Séraphine Dubé S.J.	1861
63	Joseph	(31)	Marie Roy S.M.	1794
64	Joseph	(31)	Antoinette Dodier S.F.S.	1794
65	Paul	(31)	Marie Roy S.M.	1797
	Marie		Ls. Mercier "	1820
	Madeleine		Jean Racine "	1846
	Michel			
	Paul			
66	Michel	(31)	M. Anne Roy	1804
	Marguerite		David Lemelin "	1841
	Marie Anne		Jos. Nicole "	1845
	Paul			
	Charles			
	Michel			
	Le même		Fse. Lebrun "	1824
67	Joseph	(17)	Agathe Roberge S.G.	1813
68	Magloire	(31)	Louise Blais "	1827
69	Pierre	(32)	Marg. Labrecque "	1802
	Marguerite		Etn. Roy "	1828
	Reine		Nic. Pouliot "	1830
	Tho. Abraham			
	Pierre			
70	Louis	(39)	Sophie Pilote S.M.	1845
71	Augustin	(39)	M.Marg.Quéret "	1847

(¹) Ella épousa Magloire Garon S.M. 1839.

LACROIX.

72	Jean Baptiste(28)	Marg. Dubord	S.M.	1826
73	Jacques	(41)	M. Jos. Thibaut S.V.	1821
	M. Eudmie		Pierre Louineau	„ 1851
74	Joseph	(46)	Angèle Asselin S.Chs.	1829
	Joseph			
75	Pierre	(46)	Genev. Goulet	„ 1850
79	Pierre	(47)	M. Angèle Lessart S.M	1847
77	Michel	(47)	Florence Audet S.V.	1856
78	Joseph	(48)	Esther Dion	S.M. 1846
79	Anthyme	(48)	Marie Terrien	„ 1853
80	Paul	(48)	Euphrosine Côté	„ 1858
	Le même		Angèle Couture SChs	1864
81	Michel	(51)	Christine Gautron	
				S.M. 1830
	M. Angéle Philo-mène	·	Honoré Bacquet	„ 1854
	Luce		Romuald Bétil	„ 1861
	M. Belzimire		Simon Néré Marcoux	
				S.M. 1865
	Joseph			
82	Laurent	(53)	Adé Patry	„ 1836
83	Jean Baptiste(54)		Angèle Morisset	„ 1832
84	Michel	(54)	Marg. Tangué	„ 1841
	Marie		Ls. Narcisse Turgeon	
				B. 1857
85	André	(58)	Archange Lebrun S.G	1828
86	Joseph	(4)	Marg. Pigeon S.F.S.	1830
87	Michel		Julie Talbot	
	Le même		Anastasie Baudoin S.V	1848
88	Hubert Joseph		Mad. Dontaille	
	M. Catherine		Jos. Turgeon	B. 1859
89	Michel	(65)	Mad. Paquet	S.M. 1841
90	Paul [1]	(61)	M. Cath. Martineau	
				S.M. 1832
	Le même		M. Pélagie Cotin	„ 1841
91	Paul [2]	(66)	Angéle Leclaire SChs	1836
92	Michel	(66)	Luce Lemelin	S.M. 1839
93	Charles	(66)	Séraphine Morisset	
				S.M. 1844
94	T. Abraham	(69)	Archange Bolduc S.V	1846
95	Pierre	(69)	Angé Roy	S.G. 1823
96	Joseph	(74)	Agnès Bilodeau S.M.	1861
97	Joseph	(8)	Rose Bétil	„ 1857

LAFONTAINE DE BELCOUR.

1	Jacques		Charlotte Joliette Buissot	
	Joseph Nicolas			
	Le même		Genev. Lambert Lévis	1751
	Geneviève		J. B. Chabot	„ 1766
2	Joseph Nicolas(1)		M. Fse. Couillard B.	1781
	Marie		Ls. Chabot	S.Chs. 1804
	Marguerite		Ignace Dessaint	„ 1821
	Angélique		Pierre Vermet	„ 1821
	Archange		Jos. Chamberlan	„ 1822
	Josette		J. B. Bernard	S.G. 1819
	Alexis			
	François Xavier			
	Jacques			
3	Jacques	(2)	M. Mad. Genest S.Chs	1815
4	Alexis	(2)	Angèle Ruel	„ 1879
5	François Xav-(2)		M. Rose Blais S.F.S.	1825

LAINÉ–LALIBERTÉ.

1	Bernard		Anne Dionne	
	Marie		Fse. Larrivé	S.Frs. 1703
	Pierre			
2	Pierre	(1)	Marg. Plante	S.J. 1720
	Geneviève		Jean Asselin	„ 1753
	Thècle		Pierre Moreau	„ 1760
	Thècle		2° Jacq. Asselin	„ 1767
	M. Madeleine		Pierre Bilodeau S.Chs	1760

---

[1] L'acte le dit fils de Paul et de M.Chs. Roy
[2] L'acte le dit fils de Paul et de M. Anne Roy

LAINÉ-LALIBERTÉ.

	Jean Marie			
	Pierre			
	Joseph			
3	François		Marie Delay Ev. de Coutance	
	François			
4	Pierre	(2)	M. Angé. Dalaire S.J.	1750
				S.H.
	Angélique		Chs. Labrecque S.Chs	1777
	Madeleine		Chs. Quemeneur S.H.	1793
	Louis			
	Joseph			
	Pierre			
	Jean Baptiste			
	Joachim			
5	Joseph	(2)	Angé. Asselin	S.Frs. 1753
	Jean Marie			
	Joseph			
6	Jean Marie	(2)	Basilisse Audet S.J.	1764
	Basilisse		Ant. Trahan S.Chs.	1811
	Jean Baptiste			
	Le même		Fse. Lefebvre	„ 1775
	Françoise		Jos. Nadeau	„ 1802
	Catherine		Jos. Terrien	„ 1822
	Marie		Jos. Nadeau	B. 1809
	Jean			
	François			
7	François	(3)	Mad. Hélie	S.M. 1764
	Charles			
	François			
8	Pierre	(4)	Pélagie Labrecque	
				S. Chs. 1775
	Marie Anne		Nicolas Valiere S.H.	1801
	Félicité		Ls. Royer	S.H. 1810
	Pierre			
	Joseph			
9	Louis	(4)	M. Mad. Marcoux	
				S.M. 1778
	Angélique		Chs. Roy	S.H. 1802
	M. Madeleine		Jacq. Lefebvre	S.H. 1810
	Marie Thérèse		Ls. Gosselin	S.H. 1812
	Marguerite		Laurent Dumas S.H.	1814
	Marie Anne		Jos. Boulet	S.H. 1814
	Prudent			
10	Joseph		M. Reine Blondeau	
				S.V. 1795
	Le même		M. Reine Guilmet	
				S.V. 1798
	Reine		Ignace Toussaint S.V.	1822
	Anastasie		Prudent Fontaine	
				S.V. 1844
	Joseph			
	Jacques			
A	Joachim	(4)	Félicité Clément S.H.	1788
	Le même		M. Thérèse Morin	
				S.H. 1792
11	Jean	(4)	Marthe Roy	S.G. 1791
	Marthe		Gab. Nadeau	S.G. 1812
	Marthe		2° Laurent Couture	
				S.G. 1818
	Flavie		Jos. Fournier	S.G. 1830
	François			
	Joseph			
	Jean			
12	Joseph	(5)	M. Ls. Emond	S.J. 1782
	Marie Louise		Jos. Ratté	„ 1809
	Marie Louise		2° Ant. Gosselin	„ 1822
	Marguerite		Jos. Ginchereau	„ 1811
	M. Angélique		Basile Thivierge	„ 1817
	M. Angélique		J. B. Turcot	„ 1821
	Pierre			
	Joseph			
13	Jean Marie	(5)	M. Vict. Pepin S. F.	1790
	Josette		Frs. Morisset	„ 1826
	Marguerite		Frs. Fortier	S. J. 1820

LAINÉ—LALIBERTÉ.

	Marie Victoire		Hyacinthe Paquet	S. Frs. 1819
	Victoire		Guill. Fortier S. Frs. 1819	
	Joseph			
	Louis			
14	Jean Baptiste	(6)	Louise Greffart S.Chs.1796	
	Marie Louise		Ls. Shinck	B. 1844
	Marie		Michel Letellier	B. 1834
	Barnabé			
15	Jean	(6)	M. Angé Boutin Lévis 1819	
16	François	(6)	Thérèse Fortier S. H. 1800	
17	François	(7)	Marg. Gousse S. V. 1793	
18	Charles	(7)	Mad. Guilmet ,, 1799	
	M. Madeleine		Ant. Quemeneur S.V. 1821	
	Frédéric			
19	Pierre	(8)	Théotiste Royer S. G. 1802	
20	Joseph	(8)	Marg. Bernier S.Chs. 1810	
	Etienne			
	Joseph			
21	Charles	(9)	Eliz. Bolduc S. V. 1814	
22	Prudent	(9)	Marg. Duquet S. H. 1819	
	Amable			
23	Jacques		M. Julie Gagnon S.H.	
	Férdéric			
	Jacques			
	Le même		M. Chs. Filteau B. 1824	
24	Joseph	(10)	Vict. Tangué S. V. 1824	
25	Jacques	(10)	Brigitte Létourneau S. G. 1826	
	Le même		M. Thècle Gosselin S. V. 1830	
	Désanges		Alexis Corriveau S.V. 1850	
	François Xavier			
	Jacques			
26	François		Marg. Cloutier S. G. 1822	
	Le même		Marg. Théberge S. V. 1835	
27	Jean	(11)	Angé Dubé S. G. 1822	
28	Joseph	(11)	Thérèse Dubé ,, 1826	
29	Louis	(11)	Marie Gautron	
	Le même		Marie Morisset S. H. 1802	
	Angèle		Jos. Turgeon B. 1831	
	Emérence		Gab. Nadeau B. 1842	
	Pierre			
	Jean Baptiste			
30	Charles		Pélagie Bernier S. Anselme	
	Le même		Emélie Quéret S. M. 1849	
	Le même		M. Anne Richard S.V.1866	
31	François		Marie Blanchet	
	Damase			
A31	Pierre		Fse. Nadeau S. Anselme	
	Le même		Marg. Buteau S.F.S. 1835	
32	Joseph	(12)	M. Mad. Blouin S.J. 1807	
	Madeleine		Ant. Godbout ,, 1848	
	François			
	Charles			
	Le même		Barbe Mercier S.J. 1824	
	Pierre			
33	Pierre	(12)	M. Vict. Ginchereau S. Frs. 1812	
	Marie Soulange		Frs. Giguère S. J. 1835	
	Marie Luce		Ovide Pepin S.J. 1845	
	Marie Victoire		J. B. Fortier ,, 1846	
	Joseph			
	Pierre			
	Alexis			
	Le même		Marie Vaillancour S F. 1834	
	Damase			
	Nathalie		Chs. Maranda	
A33	Joseph	(13)	M.Thècle Blouin S.J.1827	
34	Louis	(13)	M Chs. Blouin ,, 1843	
35	Barnabé	(14)	Rose Dessaint S.G.1820	
36	Frédéric	(18)	Marie Roy S.M.1831	
37	Joseph	(20)	Angèle Buteau S.F.S.1837	

LAINÉ—LALIBERTÉ

38	Etienne	(20)	Christine Quéret S.M.1848	
39	Frédéric	(23)	RosalieCouture S.Chs.1843	
40	Jacques	(23)	Marg. Couture ,, 1843	
41	François Xa-	(25)	Delphine Brochu S.V.1858	
	vier			
42	Jacques	(25)	Adélina Corriveau S.V.1866	
43	JeanBaptiste	(29)	Eliz. Labrecque B.1840	
44	Pierre	(29)	M. Angèle Baudoin S.Chs.1841	
45	Amable	(22)	Léocadie Lacroix ,, 1852	
46	Damase	(31)	Philomène Leclaire S.Chs.1863	
47	François	(32)	Marcelline Turcot S.J.1851	
48	Charles	(32)	Julie Blouin ,, 1852	
49	Pierre	(32)	Eléonore Terrien ,, 1853	
50	Joseph	(33)	Marie Pepin ,, 1850	

LAJOUE (DE LA JOUE.)

1	François	M. Anne Ménage Qué.1689	
	M. Madeleine	Pierre Frontigny ,, 1715	
	Marie Josette	Jacq. Manseau S.L.1716	
	Marie Josette	Ant. Gosselin ,, 1724	

LAMOTHE.

1	Jean Baptiste		Marie S. Croix	
	Jean Baptiste			
2	Pierre		Angé. Doyon	
	Angélique		Pierre Morin S.P.S.1774	
3	Jean Baptiste	(1)	Marg. Giguère S.F.1792	
	Le même		Marg. Poulin ,, 1800	
	Marie		Jos. Blouin ,, 1831	
	Marguerite		Florian Tremblay ,, 1826	
	Louis			
	Jean Baptiste			
	Le même		M. Fse. Labbé S.F.1807	
4	Louis	(3)	Luce Loignon ,, 1824	
	Luce		J. B. Giguère ,, 1850	
	Marie Albine		Abraham Asselin ,, 1850	
	Justine		Bruno Giguère ,, 1854	
	Le même		Constance Vézina ,, 1837	
	Le même		Marg. Giguère ,, 1847	
5	Jean Baptiste	(3)	M. Marthe Foucher S.F.1845	
	M. Hombeline		Frs. Régis Canac ,, 1845	
	Marie Léocadie		Joachim Dion ,, 1847	
	Marie Lumina		Alexis Ferlant ,, 1857	
	Jean Baptiste			
	Joseph			
	Alexis			
	Le même		Marcelline Létourneau S.F.1844	
6	Pierre		Marie Bélanger	
	M. Séraphine		Jos. Terrien S.M.1864	
7	Onésime		Philomène Labrecque	
	Le même		Justine Asselin S.F.1864	
8	Jean Baptiste	(5)	M. Joséphine Asselin S.F.1855	
9	Joseph	(5)	Séraphine Drouin ,, 1863	
10	Alexis	(5)	Justine Beaucher ,, 1863	

LAMY.

1	Jean		Marie Savard	
	Jean			
2	Clément		Anne Thibaut	
	Pierre			
3	Pierre	(2)	Renée Picard Cap S.Ign. Isle aux Oies 1680	
	Jeanne		Ant. Blais S.M.1705	
	Geneviève		Guill. Daniau Bert.1723	
4	Jean	(1)	Marg. Salois S.L.1697	
5	Louis		M. Ls. Terrien S.F.S.	
	Marie Rose		Jos. Théberge S.M.1788	
	Antoine			

LAMY.

6 Antoine	(5) Thérèse Pouliot S.V.1781
	V. de Bazile Bouffart

LANDRY.

Guillaume	Gabriel Barret Qué.1659
Marguerite	Esprit Carbonneau
	S.F.1672
Claude	
2 Claude	(1) Angé. Vérieul S.F.1688
Claude	
Charles	
Augustin	
Isidore	
3 Charles	(2) M. Mad. Guérard
	S.Frs.1715
Angélique	Jos. Dallaire " 1752
Geneviève	Jean Rosen " 1760
Madeleine	Benj. Guion " 1766
Marie Anne	Pierre Gagné " 1773
Germain	
Julien	
Charles	
4 Claude	(2) Susanne Tareau S.Frs.1728
5 Augustin	(2) Angé. Guion " 1729
Augustin	
Le même	Félicité Deblois S.Frs.1748
Barthélemi	
Le même	Scolastique Dompierre
	S.Frs.1750
6 Isidore	M. Thérèse Larrivé
	S.Frs.1731
7 Charles	(3) Cath. Deblois " 1746
Geneviève	Aug. Campagna " 1778
Marie Anne	J. B. Dalaire S.J. 1784
8 Julien	(3) Marthe Gagné S.Frs. 1748
François	
9 Germain	(3) Angé. Gagnon " 1762
	S. Marie
Louise	Eustache Royer S.G. 1810
Raphael	
Germain	
10 Augustin	(5) M.Thècle Pepin S.Frs.
	S. Marie 1764
11 Barthélemi	(5) M. Mad. Langlois
	S.Frs. 1768
12 Jean Baptiste	Genev. Jourdain
	S. Marie
Le même	M. Ls. Demeule S.J. 1798
13 Raphael	(9) M.Anne ChatignyS.G.1808
14 Germain	(9) M. Ls. Pigeon S.Marie
	S.F.S. 1777
15 François	(8) Genev. Rousseau S.H.1786

LANGLOIS.

1 Noël	Frs. Grenier Qué. 1634
Anne	Jean Peltier Qué. 1649
Marguerite	Paul Vachon Qué. 1653
Jeanne	René Chevalier Qué. 1656
Marie	Frs. Miville Qué. 1660
Elisabeth	Ls. Coté Qué. 1662
Elisabeth	2° Guill. Lemieux Qué.1669
Jean	
Jean	
Noël	
Le même	Veuve de Robert Caron
Marie Anne	Jean Côté Beauport 1694
2 Philippe	Marie Binet
	S.Sulpice de Paris 1670
Anne	René Cochon S. Frs. 1670
3 Jean	(1) M. Chs. BélangerC.R. 1665
Geneviève	Guil. Levitre S.P. 1690
Marie Madeleine	Jean Leclaire " 1691
Elisabeth	Frs. Gagné Islet 1709

LANGLOIS.

Jean	
Joseph	
Pierre	
Clément	
4 Jean	(1) Marie Cadieu Cap S. Ign.
Marie Madeleine	Jean Gagné
	Cap S. Ign. 1699
Marguerite	Jean Blouin S. Tho. 1700
Madeleine	
Louis	
5 Noël	(1) Aimé Caron Qué. 1672
	Beauport
Marie Anne	Jean Côté Beauport 1694
François	
Le même	Genev. ParentBeauport1686
Geneviève	René Taupin " 1708
Louise Catherine	Jean Huppé " 1714
Jean	
6 Jean	(3) Genev. Rousseau S.L. 1692
	S. Tho.
Le même	Charlotte Laplante
	S. Tho. 1709
Jean Frs.	
Le même	Angé Picard S. Tho. 1714
7 Pierre	(3) M. Angé Baillargeon
	S. L. 1701
Geneviève	Ign. Ratté S. P. 1729
Dorothée	Pierre Dorval " 1730
Marthe	Jean Frs. Thivierge
	S.F. 1729
Louise	Nic. Turcot " 1743
Pierre	
Jean	
Alexis	
Louis	
Le même	M. Mad. Godbout
	S. L. 1717
Marie Anne	Ls. Dorval S.P. 1749
Marie	Chs. Paradis " 1775
Marie	2° Alexis Couture " 1786
Prisque	
Paul	
François	
Augustin	
Gabriel	
Joseph	
8 Clément	(3) M.Anne Provost C.R. 1704
Louis	
9 Joseph	(3) Louise Nolin S. Tho. 1705
Marie Angélique	Chs. Fournier S. Tho. 1725
Marie Claire	Pierre Morin S. Tho. 1732
Jean Baptiste	
10 Louis dit St.	(4) Mad. Dion
Jean	Isle aux Grues
Le même	M. Fse. Gabrielle Demant
	Bert. 1711
Marie Anne	Aug. Talbot S.P.S. 1769
Marguerite	Basile FournierS.Tho. 1736
Chrysostôme	
Louis	
Antoine	
11 François	(5) Jne. Baugy Beauport 1696
12 Jean	(5) Mad. Bisson S.Foy 1712
A Jean François	(6) Marie Voyer Qué 1725
13 Pierre	(7) Marg. Turcot S.P. 1731
Perpétue	Jean Leclaire " 1770
Thérèse	Ls. Paradis " 1782
Marie	Ign. Goulet " 1785
Marie Thècle	Jean Leclaire " 1789
Jean Baptiste	
Pierre	
14 Louis	(7) Ursule Côté S.P. 1735
	S. H.
Jean	
Gabriel	
Alexis	

LANGLOIS.

15	Jean	(7)	Hélène Nolin	S.P. 1739
	Hélène		Ls. Audet	S.L. 1770
	Marie Anne		Chs. Audet	" 1773
	Marie Geneviève		Jean Audet	" 1775
	Antoine			
	François			
	Jean Baptiste			
16	François	(7)	Dorothée Dupile	S.P. 1741
	Marie Dorothée		Jean Gagné	S. Frs. 1762
	M. Madeleine		Barth. Landry	S. Frs. 1768
	Marie Elizabeth		J. B Chiasson	S.F.S.1776
	Louise		Aug. Fradet	" 1779
	Louise		2° J. B. Clang	" 1793
	Agathe		Aug. Fradet	" 1786
	Benjamin			
	François			
17	Prisque	(7)	M. Jos. Alaire	S.J.1738
18	Alexis	(7)	M. Jos. Dorval	S.P.1745
	Jean-Baptiste			
19	Augustin	(7)	Genev. Couture	" 1747
20	Gabriel	(7)	Hélène Leclaire	" 1750
21	Joseph	(7)	Marthe Turcot	S.F.1753
	Geneviève		Jérémie Plante	S.P.1817
	Joseph			
22	Paul	(7)	Mad. Poulet	S.P.1754
23	Joseph	(8)	Rose Gagnon	Chat. 1735
	Marie		Jos. Gagné	S.F.S.1763
	Reine		Ign. Bouchard	" 1777
	Reine		2° Ls. Marseau	" 1788
	Clément			
	Jacques			
	Jean-Baptiste			
24	Charles François		Mad. Ainée	S.Tho.1747
	Jean François			
25	Jean-Baptiste		Charlotte Guimont	Cap. S.Ign.1749
	Jean Bte Pascal			
26	Louis	(8)	Mad. Bacon	C.R.1743
	Jean Marie			
	Etienne			
	Jean-Baptiste			
27	Jean		Josette Boulet	
	Le même		M. Anne Rousseau	S.P.S.1765
28	Jean		M. Ls. Morin	
	Le même		Monique Bélanger	Cap S.Ign.1766
	Théodore			
29	Jean Baptiste	(9)	Marthe Fortin	S.Tho. 1734
	Louis			
30	Louis	(10)	M. Ls. Aubé	S.V.1747
	André			
	Louis			
31	Antoine	(10)	M. Reine Gaudreau	S.Tho.1750
	Isaac			
32	Chrysostôme	(10)	Reine Chartier	S.P.S.1763
	Le même		Marie Couture	" 1765
	Le même		Angé Gaumont	" 1769
	Marie Angélique		Martin Morin	" 1797
	Joseph Magloire			
	Jean Baptiste			
	François			
33	Jean Baptiste	(13)	Thècle Plante	S.P.1772
	Thècle		Germ. Gosselin	" 1800
	Marguerite		Ls. Hallé	" 1808
	Joseph			
	Jean Baptiste			
34	Pierre	(13)	Agathe Cantin	S.P.1781
35	Jean	(14)	M. Ls. Crépeau	" 1777
	Louise		Jacq. Pepin	" 1803
	Charlotte		Ant. Boutin	" 1817
	Paul			
	Louis			
	Jean			
36	Gabriel	(14)	M. Mad. Parent	S.P.1779

LANGLOIS.

37	Alexis	(14)	Cécile Charier	S.Chs.1792
	Cécile		Frs. Roy	S.G.1812
	Angélique		Etn. Roy	" 1818
	Angélique		2° Frs. Goulet	" 1830
	Louis			
38	Jean Baptiste	(15)	M. Marg. Gosselin	S.L.1765
39	François	(15)	Cath. Raby	Que.1798
40	Antoine	(15)	M.Anne Godbout	S.L.1773
	Marie Anne		Frs. Cinqmars	" 1803
	Marie		Frs. Dumas	" 1808
	Marie Victoire		Frs. Dumas	" 1809
	Paul			
	Jean			
41	François	(16)	Thérèse Pepin	S.Frs.1771
	Catherine		Ignace Dion	" 1828
	Jean			
	Louis			
42	Benjamin	(16)	M.Ls.Chiasson	S.F.S.1780
	Louise		Frs. Beaudoin	" 1798
	Marguerite		Ls. Blais	" 1805
	Agathe		J. B. Fortier	S.V.1815
	Madeleine		Ant. Gagnon	" 1824
	M. Geneviève		Simon Thibaut	" 1811
	M. Geneviève		2° Jos. Alaire	" 1821
	M. Geneviève		3° Chs. Bussière	Bert.1834
	Euphrosine		Etn. Morin	Bert.1816
	Basile			
	Joseph			
	François			
43	Jean Baptiste	(18)	Marg. Côté	S.P.1769
	Marguerite		Ls. Paradis	S.H.1791
	Marie Josette		Basile Demers	" 1794
	Hélène		Ls. Bélanger	" 1820
	Alexis			
	Pierre			
	Jean Baptiste			
44	Joseph	(21)	Marie Gendreau	S.L.1791
	Joseph			
45	Clément	(23)	M. Jos. Dupont	S.F.S.1765
	Jeanne		Jos. Pelchat	" 1793
	Christine		J. B. Gagné	" 1796
	Le même		Rose Quemeneur	" 1781
	Françoise		Pierre Gagné	S.F.S.1807
	Josette		Pierre Mercier	" 1818
	Marguerite		Michel Leclair-	" 1810
	Ursule		Alexandre Baillargeon	S.F.S.1824
	Marie		Cyp. Gagnon	S.V. 1832
	Joseph			
	Jacques			
	Charles			
	Jean Baptiste			
46	Jacques	(23)	Marie Théberge	S.F.S.1768
	Jacques			
	Le même		Rose Dubé	S P.S.1776
	Angélique		Jos. Dalaire	S.F.S.1807
	Rose		Germ. Gagné	" 1798
	Angèle		Jacq. Rousseau	S.V.1812
	Marie Reine		J. B. Gagnon	" 1814
	Jean Baptiste			
47	Jean	(23)	M.Mad.Gagnon	S.F.S.1788
	Baptiste			
	M. Madeleine		Frs. Chouinard	" 1806
48	Jean François	(24)	Marg.Simoneau	S.Tho.1779
	Jean François			
49	Jean Bte.	(25)	M. Jos. Jacques	" 1782
	Paschal			
	Etienne			
	Jean Baptiste			
50	Jean Marie	(26)	M. Jos. Gaulin	S.Tho.1783
	Marie Josette		Jean Frs. Langlois	S.P.S.1805
	Louis			

LANGLOIS.

51 Jean Baptiste	(26)	M. Anne Gagné	„ 1798
52 Etienne	(26)	Cath. Talon	S.Tho.1804
Le même		Genev. Dalaire	S.V.1819
53 Théodore	(28)	M. Ls. Fradet	„ 1791
Marie Josette		René Roy	„ 1816
54 Louis	(29)	M. Chs. Simoneau	S.Tho.1765
Jean Baptiste			
55 André	(30)	Marg. Rolandeau	S.P.S.1775
M. Geneviève		Gab. Goupy	S.V.1805
Marguerite		La. Gautron	„ 1814
Marguerite		2° Etn. Pepin	S.M.1835
Toussaint			
André			
Pierre			
56 Louis	(30)	M. Thérèse Gagné	S.P.S.1775
Elisabeth		Ant. Roy	Qué.1801
57 Louis		Eliz. Chartier	
Jacques			
58 Isaac	(31)	M. Marg. Bélanger	S.P.S.1773
M. Marguerite		Basile Lefebvre	„ 1817
Isaac			
Antoine			
59 Charles		M. Angé Gagnon	
Prisque			
60 Joseph	(32)	M. Jos. Valière	S.P.S.1796
Magloire			
61 François	(32)	M. Eliz. Mondina	S.Tho.1797
Jean Baptiste			
62 Jean Baptiste	(32)	M. Jos. Roy	S.M.1803
Josette		Etn. Hizoir	S.G.1822
Madeleine		Jean Lacasse	„ 1827
Jean			
63 Jean Baptiste	(33)	M. Marg. Morin	S.F.1803
Scolastique		Jos. Noël	S.P.1827
Archange		Benj. Roberge	„ 1829
Alexis			
Jean Baptiste			
Le même		M. Anne Ferlant	S.P.1815
64 Joseph	(33)	M. Ls. Hallé	S.H.1803
65 Jean	(35)	M. Thècle Noël	S.P.1808
Emélie		Ed. Marcoux	„ 1834
66 Louis	(35)	Marg. Noël	„ 1811
67 Paul	(35)	Marg. Hébert	„ 1818
68 Louis	(37)	Sophie Roy	S.G.1820
Alexis			
69 Paul	(40)	Thérèse Labrecque	S.L.1812
Thérèse		Ant. Godbout	S.L.1838
Flavie		Paul Pouliot	„ 1844
Rosalie		Pierre Godbout	„ 1850
Sophie		Amb. Coulombe	„ 1852
Marie Emélie		Frs. Audet	„ 1869
Honoré			
Louis			
Paul			
Pierre			
70 Jean	(40)	Marie Labrecque	S.L.1823
71 Jean	(41)	M. Vict. L'heureux	S.F.1814
72 Louis	(41)	M. Cath.Lessard	S Frs 1833
Le même		M. Ls. Gagnon	„ 1840
73 Joseph	(42)	Marg.Coulombe	S.F.S.1810
Marguerite		J. B. Dépont	S.V.1839
Pierre			
74 Basile	(42)	Brigitte Roy	S.G.1825
Vitaline		Honoré Thibaut	S.V.1853
Antoine			
75 François	(42)	Angèle Brochu	S.G.1826

LANGLOIS.

76 JeanBaptiste	(43)	Josette Gagné	S.H.1802
77 Alexis	(43)	Thérèse Daniau	„ 1802
78 Pierre	(43)	M. Ls. Boulet	„ 1805
79 Joseph	44	Marie Rosa	S.P.1845
Marie		Magl. Gosselin	„ 1878
80 Joseph	(45)	Julie Bonneau	S.V.1816
81 Charles	(45)	Fse. Boivin	S.V.1819
Françoise		Ant. Marseau	S.V.1842
82 Jean Baptiste	(45)	M.Claire Cotin	S.F.S.1819
83 Jacques	(45)	Marg. Pellerin	S.P.S.1830
84 Jacques	(46)	Fse. Blais	S.F.S.1795
Françoise		Ant. Bilodeau	S.V.1821
Prudent			
Jean Baptiste			
Le même		Marie Fradet	S.V.1838
85 Jean Baptiste	(46)	M. Angé Dalaire	S.F.S-1805
Marie Julie		J. B. Buteau	S.F.S.1831
86 Jean Fran-çois	(48)	M. Jos. Langlois	S.P.S.1805
Pierre			
87 JeanBaptiste	(49)	Genev. Richard	Cap, S. Ign.1815 Isle aux Grues
Pascal			
88 Etienne	(49)	Louise Q.Quéret	S.M.1817
Le même		Thérèse Laurent	S. Frs.1822
89 Louis	(50)	M. Claire Kervack	S.P.S.1812
90 JeanBaptiste	(54)	Louise Roussin	S. Chs.1795
Jean Baptiste			
91 Toussaint	(55)	Marie Boivin	S.M.1807
Sophie		Ed. Bolduc	S.V.1839
42 André	(55)	Scolastique Patry	S.V.1808
Anastasie		Jacq. Lavoie	S.V.1838
Archange		Didime Ferd. Bernier	S.V.1843
Henriette		JeanChamberlan	S.V.1848
Raimond			
André			
93 Pierre	(55)	Marie Nadeau	Bert.1820
94 Jacques	(57)	M. Fse. Fortier	S.G.1811
Emérentienne		Ls. Brochu	S.V.1830
Luce		André Bacquet	S.V.1834
Jean Baptiste			
95 Antoine	(58)	M. Marg. Lecomte	S.P.S.1793
Le même		M. Angé Fontaine	S. P. S.1798
Louis			
96 Isaac	(58)	M. Anne Lecomte	S.P.S.1804
97 Prisque	(59)	Marg. Fortin	Cap. S. Ign.1798
Justine		Pierre Gobeil	S.J.1837
Joseph			
Cyprien			
98 JeanBaptiste	(61)	M. Flavie Labonté	S.P.S.1832
99 Jean	(62)	M. Luce Gérard	B.1835
100 JeanBaptiste	(63)	Josette Roberge	S.P.1825
Marie Josette		Jos. Maranda	S.P.1857
Jean Samuel			
101 Alexis	(63)	Dorothée Roberge	S.P.1829
102 Jacques	(63)	Marg. Gourgue	S.V.1831
103 Charles		Hélène Wilson	
Charles			
104 Alexis	(68)	Euphrosine Guay	S.F.1843
105 Paul	(69)	Marie Laberge	S.L.1843
Marie Virginie		Paul Pouliot	S.L.1867
Marie		Jos. Ephrem Bacquet	S.L.1868
Le même		Henriette Vien	S.L.1877

LANGLOIS.

106	Louis	(69)	Eliz. Coulombe S.L. 1850
107	Honoré Gil-bert	(69)	Philomène Blouin
			S.J. 1856
108	Pierre	(69)	Eléonore Dumas S.L. 1859
109	Pierre	(73)	Marg. Quémeneur S.F.S.
110	Antoine	(74)	Eliz. Quéret S.V. 1862
111	JeanBaptiste(84)		M. Ls. Cadrien S.V. 1821
112	Prudent	(84)	Sophie Morin S.F.S. 1830
113	Pierre	(86)	M. Susanne Bouffert
			S.P.S. 1838
114	Paschal	(87)	Marcelline Blouin S.J.1849
115	Jean Baptiste		M. Cazalie Boutin
	Marie		Jos. Quéret S.V. 1870
116	JeanBaptiste(90)		Angèle Michon S.Tho.1823
	Jean Baptiste		
117	André	(92)	M. Ls.Corriveau S.V. 1839
118	Raimond	(92)	Osite Lemieux S.V. 1845
119	JeanBaptiste(94)		Céleste Gagnon S.V. 1836
120	Louis	(95)	M. Flavie Côté S.P.S. 1827
121	Joseph	(97)	Emélie Tremblay S.J. 1831
	Adelaïde		Jos. Cochon S.J. 1856
	Joseph		
122	Cyprien	(97)	Marie Picard S. Frs. 1838
	Marie		Moïse Pépin S.J. 1861
123	JeanSamuel(100)		Genev. Asselin S.P. 1851
124	Charles	(103)	Cath. Blouin S.J. 1856
125	Jean Bap-tiste	(116)	Emélie Côté S.V. 1865
126	Joseph	(121)	Vitaline Létellier S.J. 1864

LAIGU—LANOUE.

1			
2	Charles	(1)	M. Jos. Larivière
	Louis Marie		
3	Louis Marie	(2)	M. Ls. Terrien S.F.S. 1748
	Louise		Jacq. Roy S.F.S. 1774
	Louise		2° J. B. Bissonnet S.V.1791
	Marie Josette		Frégeat S.F.S. 1779

LARUE.

1	Augustin		Marie Jean-Maurice
	François Xavier		
2	Augustin		M. Ursule Borne
	M. Anne Emélie		Ed. Rouleau S.V. 1840
	Ursule		Nazaire Roy S.V. 1862
	Vilbon		
	Nazaire		
	Le même		M. Angé Bernard
			S.V. 1814
	Henriette		Nazaire Roy S.V. 1845
	Sivibert		
	François Xavier		
3	François	(1)	Marie Genest S.J. 1814
	Xavier		
4	Abraham No-taire		M. Sophie Talbot
			S.P.S. 1809
5	Chs. Aug.	(2)	M. Marg. Blais S.P.S. 1831
	Vilbon		
6	Nazaire	(2)	Adé Roy S.V. 1831
7	François	(2)	Adé Dumas S.V. 1845
	Xavier		
8	Sivibert Va-lier	(2)	M. Julie Désanges Be-langer S.V. 1850

LASALLE—SANSCHAGRIN.

2	Basile		Marie Gagnon S. Anne
	Basile		
3	Basile	(2)	Marie Gagné S.F. 1797
	Marie		Pierre Drouin S.Frs. 1819
	Catherine		Frs. Dion S.Frs. 1826
	Josette		Frs. Canac S.Frs. 1841
	François		
	Jean		

LASALLE—SANSCHAGRIN.

	Le même		Marie Marseau
	Justine		Frs. Lemelin S.Frs. 1842
5	François	(3)	Archange Foucher
			S.F. 1824
	Le même		M. Mad. Labbé S.J. 1841
6	Jean	(3)	Scholastique Dion
			S.Frs. 1831

LATOUCHE.

1	Pierre		Marie Galet
	Marie Agnès		Chs. Dompierre S.F. 1669
	Marie Agnès		2° Frs. Guérinet
			S.Frs. 1690
2	Louis		Marie Couture Qué.
	Paul		
3	Paul	(2)	Sophie Faucher S.M. 1839

LAURENT—LASOUDE LORTIE.

1	Simon		Françoise Ev. de Nimes
	Gilles		
2	Etienne		Marg. Viger Ev de Périgueux
	Pierre		
3	Etienne		Périne Lefebvre Ev de St. Malo
	Pierre		
4	Gilles	(1)	Anne Lebrecque S.L. 1692
5	Pierre	(2)	Constance Guérinet
			S.Frs. 1699
6	Pierre	(3)	Eliz. Thibaut S.V. 1736
7	François		Josette Laroche Que. 1747
	Le même		Marie Gosselin S.J. 1756
			V. de Pierre Curodeau
8	Pierre		Jeanne Griaut
	(Lasonde)		
	Pierre		
	Le même		M. Rose Turcot S.F. 1762
	Rose		Jos. Fortier Que. 1785
	Joseph		
9	Pierre	(8)	M. Ls. Guérard S.Frs, 1782
	Thérèse		Etn. Langlois S.Frs. 1822
	Marie Louise		Jos. Gagnon S.Frs. 1837
	Georges		
	François		
10	Joseph	(8)	Charlotte Deblois
			S.Frs. 1794
11	Pierre	(Lortie)	M. Thérèse Baugy
	Dominique		
12	Jean		Barbe Chalifour, Beauport Beauport
	Charles		
13	Georges	(9)	Cath. Laignon S.F. 1830
	Marie Désanges		Magloire Pepin S.Frs. 1862
	Jean Baptiste		
14	Dominique	(11)	M. Thérèse Marseau
			S.J. 1789
A	François	(9)	Cath. Couillard S.H. 1809
15	Charles	(12)	Justine Lemelin
			S.Frs. 1849
16	Jean Bap-tiste	(13	M. Ursule Emond S.Frs. 1853

LAVERGNE.

1	François		Fse. Lafrançois Que. 1671
	Renaud		
2	Renaud	(1)	Marg. Daniau S.Tho. 1693
	Le même		Jeanne Gautron S.M. 1711
3	Joseph		M. Ls. Peltier
	Marie Madeleine		Jos. Marie Bacon
			S.P.S. 1752
4	Joseph		Mad. Charron
	Joseph Marie		
5	Joseph Marie	(4)	M. Angé Blanchet
			S.P.S. 1774

LAVERGNE.

Marie Angélique Chs. Pie Dessaint S.P.S. 1794
Marie Angélique 2° Ant. Picard S.P.S. 1816
Joseph
Augustin
Jean Baptiste
6 Joseph (5) M. Anne McNeil S.P.S. 1803
Donatille Germ. Samson S.P.S. 1828
Marie Emelie Ls. Blanchet S.P.S. 1833
Rosalie Gualbert Lavergne S.P.S. 1837
Pierre Celestin
Noël
7 Augustin Génév. Talbot S.P.S. 1806
Gualbert
Edouard
8 Jean Baptiste (5) Mélanie Delagrosse S.P.S. 1833
9 Noël (6) Marcelline Samson S.P.S. 1830
Pre. Célestin (6) M. Zoé Couillard Bert. 1844
Edouard (7) Eliz. Talbot S.P.S. 1834
Gualbert (7) Rosalie Lavergne S.P.S. 1837

LAVOIE.

1 Pierre Constance Duchesne
Le même Mad. Tourneroche S.M. 1716
V. de Julien Dumont
M. Geneviève J. B. Monmeny S.V. 1742
Marie Josette Frs. Coulombe Bert. 1746
2 René Anne Gaudin
Joseph
3 Joseph (2) Fse. Guimon S.Anne 1701
Le même Cath. Dalaire S.Frs. 1726
4 Basile Jeanne Tremblay
Le même Marie Martineau S.Frs. 1759
5 Nicolas Angé. L.
Joseph
6 Jacques M.Chs.LefebvreS.Tho.1728
Pierre
Jacques
André
7 Joseph (5) M. Marthe Roy S.M. 1767
8 Jacques (6) M. Ls. Roy S.V. 1765
Marie Anne Jos. Quéret S.V. 1803
Marie Reine Ign. Gagnon S.V. 1804
Marie Josette Ls. Vermet S.V. 1808
Jacques
Joseph
Jean Baptiste
9 Pierre (6) M. Angé Poiré S.V. 1773
Angélique Aug. Mercier S.V. 1796
Marie Marthe André Carbonneau Bert. 1804
Elizabeth Jos. Wabar Bert. 1808
Cécile Frs. Corriveau Bert. 1816
Pierre
André
10 André M. Jos. Bonnet S.V. 1780
V. de Jean Blondin
11 Pierre M. Mad. Ruais Rimouski
Le même Eliz. Lefebvre B. 1801
12 Jacques (8) Marg. Cochin S.V. 1791
Le même M. Jos. Plante S.V. 1830
Honoré
13 Joseph (8) M. Jos. Gagnon S.V. 1806
14 Jean Baptiste (8) M. Jos. Savoie S.F.S. 1797
15 André (9) M. Angé Savoie Bert. 1803
16 Pierre (9) M. Thérèse Marseau S.V. 1810
Jacques

LAVOIE.

17 Honoré Marcelline Bolduc S.V. 1848
18 Jean Baptiste Angé Langevin
Napoléon
19 Jacques (16) Anastasie Langlois S.V. 1838
20 Napoléon (18) Basilisse Vaillancour S.F. 1860

LEBLANC.

1 Antoine Eliz. Le Roy S.F. 1670
V. de Pierre Paillereau
Marie Nicolas Sustier S.J. 1691
Joseph
2 Joseph (1) Marie Thibaut 1697
Marie Nicolas Asselin S.F. 1732
Marie Anne Michel Monmeny S.P. 1743
Joseph
Jean
3 Joseph (2) M. Angé Thivierge S.J.
Marie Madeleine Jacq. Blouin S.J. 1773
Elizabeth Jos. Delisle S.J. 1777
Jean Baptiste
Joseph
François
4 Jean (2) M. Jos. Boissonneau S.J. 1737
Marie Josette Frs. Audet S.J. 1764
5 Jean Baptiste (3) M. Ls. Roy S.J. 1772
V. de Jean Royer
Charles
François
6 Joseph (3) M. Ls. Blouin S.J. 1773
Louise Jean Royer S.J. 1791
7 François M. Génév. Blouin S.J. 1777
Josette Gab. Lemelin S.Chs. 1812
Angélique Jean Lemelin S.Chs. 1826
François
Le même JudithCharrier S.Chs. 1792
Angèle Eloi Dion S.Chs. 1821
8 François (5) M. Ls. Emond S. Frs. 1804
Justine Pierre Blouin S.J. 1839
Narcisse
François
9 Charles (5) M. Chs. Blouin S.J. 1813
Le même M. Désanges Goupy S.M. 1843
10 François (7) Angé Lemelin S.M. 1809
Hermine Pierre Leclaire S.Chs. 1845
Laurent
Gabriel
Prosper
François
11 François (8) Emérence Gontier S.J.1841
12 Narcisse (8) Marie Fortier S.J. 1854
13 Laurent (10) Angé Leclaire S.Chs.1834
M. Philomène Olivier Dalaire „ 1858
Marie Angélique Frs. Clément „ 1863
14 Gabriel (10) Marie Leclaire „ 1839
15 Prosper (10) Hermine Terrien „ 1843
16 François (10) Hermine Couture „ 1855

LEBLOND.

1 Nicolas Marg. Leclaire C.R. 1661
Catherine Jean Rioux S.J. 1678
Marie Madeleine Nicolas LeRoy „ 1686
Marie Pierre Martineau „ 1691
Nicolas
Jean Baptiste
Martin
Joseph
2 Nicolas (1) Louise Beaucher Vve de Pierre Asselin S.F. 1696
Nicolas
Jean Baptiste

LEBLOND.

3	Jean Baptiste (1)	Cécile Rochon	S.F.	1702
	Le même	ThérèseLétourneau	„	1703
	Marie	J. B. Dupont	„	1723
	Agnès	Ls. Bolduc	„	1728
	Marie Josette	Pierre Bolduc	„	1728
	Le même	Marg. Maury	S.Frs.	1711
	Marguerite	Jacq. Meneux	S.F.	1740
4	Martin (1)	Anne Fse. Bissonnet	B.	1704
	Marguerite	Ls. Marie Fortin	S.V.	1728
	Marie Charlotte	Jos. Blais	„	1740
	Marie Anne	Ant. Létourneau	„	1749
	Louis			
	Joseph			
5	Joseph (1)	Cath. Drouin	S.F.	1706
6	Nicolas (2)	Fse. Maury	„	1725
	Marie	Ign. Létourneau	„	1762
	Jean			
7	Jean Baptiste (2)	M. Ls. Drouin	„	1731
	Le même	Marg. Buteau	S.Frs.	1740
8	Louis (4)	M. Marthe Morisset	S.M.	1742
9	Joseph (4)	M. Ls. Lacroix	„	1744
	Marie Louise	Frs. Roy	S.V.	1763
	Joseph			
10	Jean (6)	M. Chs. Létourneau	S.F.	1753
	Marie Charlotte	Frs. Huot	„	1780
	Jean Baptiste			
	Joseph			
	François			
11	Joseph (9)	M. Jos. Genest	S.M.	1765
	Josette	Jacq. Labrecque	S.Chs.	1795
	Marie	Etn. Parant	„	1798
	François			
12	Jean Baptiste	Mad. Gautron	S.M.	1761
	Madeleine	J. B. Mercier	„	1784
	Marguerite	J. B. Pruneau	„	1795
	Marie Anne	Jos. Pruneau	S.Tho.	1799
	Jean François			
	Augustin			
	Joseph			
	Jean Baptiste			
13	JeanBaptiste(10)	Judith Perrot	S.F.	1780
	Angélique	Jos. Turcot	„	1833
	François			
	Jean Baptiste			
14	Joseph (10)	Genev. Martineau	„	1807
	Sophie	Flavien Drouin	„	1831
	Martin	Jos. Pepin	„	1846
	Régis			
	Le même	M. Claire Giguère	„	1828
15	François (10)	Félicité Pepin	S.Frs.	1814
16	François (11)	Fse. Fernier	S.Chs.	1798
17	JeanBaptiste(12)	M. Jos. Roy	S.M.	1788
	Angèle	Ls. Labrecque	„	1821
	M. Madeleine	Ls. Arbour	S.V.	1828
	Marie Josette	Ant. Bisson	„	1834
	Marie Théotiste	Pierre Gagnon	S.Chs.	1833
	Marguerite	Jean Daigle	„	1841
	Soulange	Chs. Pruneau	S. Tho.	1827
	François			
	Jean Baptiste			
	Magloire			
	Augustin			
18	JeanFrançois(12)	M. Thérèse Leclaire	S.M.	1797
	Marie	Frs. Labrecque	S.Chs.	1821
	Marie Anne	André Lacroix	„	1821
	Théotiste	Chs. Bonneau	S.G.	1828
	François			
	Charles			
19	Augustin (12)	Fse.Quemeneur	S.F.S.	1797
	Rose	Ignace Fortier	S.V.	1830
	Françoise	Ls. Benj. Delagrave	S.V.	1836
	Pierre			
	Augustin			

LEBLOND.

20	Joseph (12)	M. Marg. Fauchon	S.F.S.	1806
21	JeanBaptiste(13)	Marie Coulombe	S.L.	1814
	MarieAntoinette	F. X. Beaucher	S.F.	1845
	Adelaïde	Pierre Asselin	„	1862
	Julie	F. X. Gosselin	„	1865
	Jean Baptiste			
	Jean			
22	François (13)	Brigitte Canac	„	1833
	Elise	Célestin Drouin	„	1855
	Séraphine	Frs. Beaucher	„	1855
	Marie	F. X. Paradis	„	1865
	Zénaïde	Jos. Beaucher	„	1869
	Phélias			
23	Régis (14)	Reine Lavertu	S.L.	1870
24	François (18)	Fse. Labrecque	S.G.	1816
	François			
25	Charles (18)	Victoire Royer	S.Chs.	1823
	Abraham			
	Pierre			
26	Jean Bte (17)	Marie Lacroix	S.M.	1815
27	Magloire (17)	Louise Lessart	S.M.	1821
	Marie Marcelline	Jacq. Labrecque	S.M.	1854
	Marie Constance	Nap. Lefebvre	S.M.	1854
	Marie	Romain Tangué	S.M.	1860
	Antoine			
	Le même	M.Jos. Lemelin	S.M.	1854
28	François (17)	M. Ls. Roy	S.Chs.	1831
29	Augustin (17)	Anastasie Labrecque	S.Chs.	1837
30	Augustin (19)	Euphrosine Gagnon	S.V.	1829
31	Pierre (19)	Angèle Boissonneau	S.V.	1829
32	Jean Bte. (21)	Agathe Vézina	S.P.	1844
33	Jean (31)	Mathilde Asselin	S.F.	1852
34	Philéas (22)	Joséphine Beaucher	S.F.	1865
35	François (24)	Restitut Rouillard	S.M.	1839
36	Abraham (25)	Virginie Aubé	S.Chs.	1835
37	Pierre (25)	Philomène Aubé	S.Chs.	1860
38	Antoine (27)	Julie Labrecque	S.Chs.	1846

LEBŒUF.

1	Nicolas	Marie Désert év.de Coulanses.		
	Jean			
2	Jean (1)	Agathe Roy	S.V.	1762
	Marie Anne	Jacq. Guillot	S.V.	1789

LE BRICE DE KÉROACK.

A	Frs. Hyacinthe	Véronique Mad- de Seuillac		
	Louis Maurice			
B	Ls Maurice (A)	Louise Bernier	Cap S.Ign.	1732
	Louis			
1	Louis (B)	M. Cath. Méthot	Cap S.Ign.	1757
	Marie Victoire	Jos.Caron	Cap S.Ign.	1785
	Marie Louise	Jos. Marie Lepage	S.P.S.	1790
	Louis			
	Joseph			
	Pierre			
2	Louis (1)	M. Marthe Cloutier	S.P.S.	1788
	Brigitte	Théodore Joncas	Bert.	1832
3	Joseph (1)	M. Marg. McDonnell	S.P.S.	1794
	Marguerite	Jos. Bissonnet	S.P.S.	1812

LE BRICE DE KÉROACK.

```
4 Jacques              M. Claire Fortin
  Marie Claire         Ls. Langlois   S.P.S. 1812
  Marcel
  Louis
  Jacques
  Le même              M. Hélène Roy S,M. 1814
                         v. de Michel Forgue
5 Charles              Théotiste Miville
  Marie Théotiste      Jos. Ducrot    S.F.S. 1817
  Le même              M. Jos. Blanchet
                                      S.P.S. 1801
  Marie Angélique  Ls. Blais          S.P.S. 1822
6 Pierre           (1) M. Anne Joncas
                                      S.Tho. 1797
  M. Constance         Aug. Carbonneau
                                      S.P.S. 1827
  Marie Brigitte       Jos. Létourneau
                                      S.P.S. 1828
  Anastasie            André Gagné  S.F.S. 1838
  Chs. Frédéric
  Louis Grégoire
  Joseph Marie
  Le même              M. Cath. Lepage
                                      S.Frs. 1817
7 Joseph               M. Ls. Poiré
  Marie Anne           Jérémie Bouchard
                                      S.P.S. 1825
  Le même              MarieGesseron S.P.S. 1806
8 Louis            (4) Angèle GendronS.M. 1815
9 Marcel           (4) M. Fse. Balan S.P.S. 1818
  Frs. Napoléon        curé de S. Guillaume
10 Jacques         (4) Marie Denis    S.M. 1825
11 Joseph              Marie Gagnon
  Marie Rufine         Pierre MétivierS.P.S. 1832
12 Ls. Grégoire    (6) M.Cath.PicardS.P.S. 1845
13 Joseph Marie   (6) Nathalie Lecompte
                                      S.P.S. 1829
  Le même              Julie Labbé    S.Frs. 1837
14 Chs. Frédéric  (6) M.Sophie VoisinS.M. 1835
```

LECLAIRE.

```
1 Antoine              Michelle Rubel
  Jean
2 Jean                 Périne Merceron
  Denis                Claude Delauny S.F. 1669
  Denis                2° Marie Dalret  S.L. 1703
3 Jean                 Marie Blanquet
  Marguerite           Clément Ruel  S.F.S. 1677
  Anne                 Jacq. Bouffard  S.P. 1680
  Madeleine            René Peltier    S.P. 1691
  Adrien
  Jean Charles
  Pierre
4 Jean            (1) Marie Couet     S.F. 1669
  Geneviève            Tho. Asselin  S.Frs. 1694
5 Jean            (2) Mad. Langlois   S.P. 1691
                           Islet
  Pierre               Isabelle RondeauS.P. 1690
  Anne                 Pierre Noel Fortier
                                      S.L. 1710
  Marguerite           Nic. Baillargeon S.L. 1711
  Marie                Alexis Le Roy   S.L. 1716
  Elizabeth            Jacq. Fradet    S.L. 1725
  Marie Madeleine      Jos. Baudoin    S.L. 1730
  Geneviève            Aug. Fradet     S.L. 1730
  Marie Anne           Ant. Gosselin   S.L. 1743
  Marie Anne           2° Jean ValièreS.Chs. 1760
  Agnès                Aug. Dufresne   S.L. 1769
  Jean
  Pierre
  Jacques
  Joseph
  Ignace
7 Adrien          (3) Genev. Paradis  S.P. 1694
  Marie Madeleine  Jos. Gosselin      S.P. 1732
```

LECLAIRE.

```
  Marguerite           Ls. Cantin     S.P. 1739
  Adrien
  Joseph
8 Charles         (3) Marg. Beaucher  S.F. 1696
  Marguerite           J. B. Couture   S.P. 1720
  Geneviève            Philippe Noël   S.P. 1729
  Marie Josette        Ls. Crépeau     S.P. 1739
  Pierre
  Jean
  François
9 François        (8) Hélène Côté     Que. 1732
  Hélène               Frs. Bloun      S.P. 1755
  Thérèse              Ls. Bussiere    S.P. 1765
  Marie Josette        Jos. Blouin     S.P. 1764
  Marie Victoire       Frs. Genest     S.J. 1768
  François
  Pierre
  Joseph
  Louis
  Le même              M. Marthe NolinS.P. 1763
10 Jean           (6) Mad. Gosselin   S.L. 1720
  M. Madeleine         Ant. Chabot     S.L. 1741
  Geneviève            Jean Audet      S.L. 1742
  Judith               J. B. Paquet    S.L. 1746
  Marie Anne           Ant. Godbout    S.L. 1750
  Marie Thérèse        Pierre Chabot   S.L. 1752
  Marie Josette        Jas. Dufresne   S.L. 1753
  Marguerite           Jean Bouffart   S.L. 1762
  Cécile               Jean Emond      S.L. 1773
  Jean
11 Pierre          (6) M. Jos. Mimaux S.V. 1724
  Phillipe
  Jean Baptiste
  Le même              M. Claire Allier S.V. 1739
12 Jacques        (6) Eliz. Turgeon    B. 1730
  Elisabeth            Etn. Denis      S.M. 1765
  Marie Josette        Jos. Patry      S.V. 1774
  François
  Charles
  Jacques
13 Joseph         (6) Ursule Noel     S.L. 1734
  Marguerite           Julien Gendreau S.L. 1765
  Cécile               Chs. Maranda    S.L. 1763
  Marie                André Tremblay S.P. 1769
  Laurent
  Jean Baptiste
14 Ignace         (6) M. Mad. Coté    S.P. 1748
  Marguerite           Gab. Tessier    S.L. 1771
  Marie Anne           Alexandre Beaucher
                                      S.L. 1767
  M. Madeleine         Jos. Godbout    S.L. 1786
15 Adrien          (7) Ursule Roy      S.P. 1722
  Marie Ursule         Frs. Cantin     S.P. 1743
  Josette              Aug. Valière    S.P. 1744
  Josette              2° Prisque Plante S.P. 1747
  Madeleine            Guill. Nolin    S.P. 1746
  Madeleine            2 Basile Dufaut S.P. 1771
  Madeleine            3° Amb. Roberge S.P. 1777
  Marie Dorothée       Amb. Cantin     S.P. 1748
  Marie Dorothée       2° J. B. Bras   S.P. 1763
  Agathe               Pierre Cornellier S.P. 1752
  Le même              Thérèse Valière S.P. 1744
16 Joseph          (7) Marie Bélang-r A.G. 1739
  Marie Charlotte      Jos. Aubin      S.P. 1770
  Joseph
17 Jean           (8) M. Thérèse CôtéS.P. 1720
  Marie Josette        Gab. Aubin      S.P. 1741
  Marie Josette        2° Jean Trudel  S.P. 1761
  Marie Thérèse        Ignace Ratté    S.P. 1747
  Hélène               Gab. Langlois   S.P. 1750
  Marie Anne           Ls. Chatigny    S.P. 1750
  Marie Thècle         Michel Morin    S.P. 1763
  François
  Pierre
  Jean
18 Pierre         (8) Angé Vigneau    S.P 1724.
```

LECLAIRE.

19	Ambroise	Genev. Loignon	
	Marie Thérèse	Frs. Bédard	S.P. 1764
	Geneviève	Pierre Canac	S.P. 1767
	Ambroise		
20	Jacques	M. Jos. Tangué	
	Alexis		
21	François (9)	M. Jos. Nolin	S.P. 1755
	Marie	Pierre Lemieux	
			S.Chs. 1782
	Thérèse	J. B. Guénet	S.Chs. 1789
	Hyppolite		
	Basile		
	François		
	Joseph		
22	Pierre (9)	M. Anne Noël	S.P. 1757
	Hélène	J. B. Fortier	S.H. 1782
	Marie Geneviève	Jean Couture	S.H. 1791
	Marie Anne	Ign. Tremblé	S.H. 1797
	Marie	J. B. Gravel	S.H. 1801
	Joseph		
	Pierre		
23	Louis (9)	Ursule Noël	S.P. 1765
	Hélène	Jean Demers	S.P. 1794
	Marie Claire	J. B. Pichet	S.P. 1797
	Marie Claire	2º Pierre Turcot	S.P. 1812
	Marie Thérèse	Ant. Vermet	S.P. 1803
	Marguerite	Ls. Pichet	S.P. 1807
	Louis		
	Joseph		
	François		
24	Joseph (9)	Genev. Paradis	S.P. 1765
25	Jean (10)	Marie Audet	S.L. 1763
	M. Anne	Michel Tremblay	" 1789
	Marie	J. B. Dubord	" 1795
	Madeleine	J. B. Turcot	" 1797
	Jean Baptiste		
26	JeanBaptiste(11)	Cath. Gautron	S.M. 1749
	Monique Hélène	Jean Pouliot	" 1779
	Thérèse	Jos. Couture	S.V. 1786
	Catherine	J. B. Custeau	S.Chs. 1780
	Josette	Jean Chs.Fortier	S.G. 1790
	Angélique	J. B. Girard	" 1796
	Michel		
	Louis		
	Philippe		
	Jean Baptiste		
	Le même	M. Angé Roy	S.V. 1774
	Marie Thérèse	JeanFrs.Leblond	S.M.1797
	Marie Reine	Pierre Guilmet	" 1804
	Marie Anne	Frs. Pouliot	" 1808
	Antoine		
	Louis		
27	Philippe (11)	M. Ls. Thibaut	S.V. 1748
	M. Marthe	J. B, Lacroix	" 1772
	Marie Marthe	2º Jos. Gousse	" 1800
	M. Thérèse	Nicholas Roy	" 1773
	M. Françoise	Michel Roy	" 1784
	Geneviève	Ls. Brochu	" 1785
	M. Louise	Frs. Balan	" 1788
	Philippe		
	Rémi		
	Jacques		
	Le même	M. Anne Gautron	" 1788
28	Jacques (12)	Genev. Dussaut Lévis	1758
	Geneviève	Chs. Denis	S.Chs. 1780
	Marguerite	Frs. Coté	" 1800
	Marie Louise	Chs. Diers	" 1806
	Etienne		
	François		
	Pierre		
	Joseph		
29	Charles (12)	Eliz. Denis	" 1770
	Marie	Denis Collet	" 1792
	Marguerite	Pierre Gagnon	" 1796
	Marie Victoire	Pierre Drapeau	S.M. 1803

18—25

LECLAIRE.

	Charles		
30	François (12)	Genev. Racine	S.M. 1789
31	Laurent (13)	M. Jos. Samson Lévis	1764
32	Jean Baptiste(13)	Josette Pepin	S.Frs. 1775
	Joseph		
33	Joseph (16)	M. Ls. Genest	S.J. 1772
	Marie	Ls. Gosselin	S.P. 1794
	Joseph		
	Le même	Mad. Dubeau	" 1798
	Le même	Rose Pichet	" 1808
34	François (17)	M. Anne Turgeon	B. 1749
35	Pierre (17)	Véronique Blouard	S.P.
	Geneviève	Jean Fournier	S.Chs. 1789
	Véronique	Barth. Terrien	" 1785
	Marie Anne	Ign. Gagnon	" 1787
	Angélique	Jos. Gosselin	" 1792
	Joseph		
	Jean Baptiste		
36	Jean (17)	M.AnneCornellier	S.F.1764
	Marie Anne	Pierre Godbout	S.P. 1786
	Marie Susanne	J. B. Jolin	" 1788
	Jean		
	Le même	Perpétue Langlois	" 1770
37	Ambroise (19)	Thérèse Coté	" 1768
	Josette	Amb. Plante	" 1797
	Ambroise		
38	Alexis (20)	Rose Fleury	S.V. 1787
	Marie Rose	Frs. Roy	" 1810
	Elizabeth	Ls. Lefebvre	" 1823
	Alexis		
39	Basile (21)	Angé Guénet	S.Chs. 1784
	Marie Josette	Victor Sénécal	" 1812
	Salomé	Jos. Pouliot	" 1829
	Charles		
	Le même	Rosalie Leclaire	" 1828
40	Joseph (21)	M. Anne Coté	" 1785
	Marie Victoire	Simon Boutin	" 1816
	Marie Anne	Jos. Leroux	" 1817
	Ursule	J. B. Fradet	" 1819
	Joseph		
	François		
41	Hyppolite (21)	Angé Guénet	S.G. 1798
	Josette	Barth. Lacasse	" 1819
	Angélique	Jacq. Bacquet	" 1823
	Le même	Louise Valière	" 1825
42	François (21)	M.Mad.Larrivé	S.Chs 1805
	Marguerite	André Bisonnet	" 1828
	Salomé	Jean Lemelin	" 1840
	Julie	Ant. Cameron	B. 1826
43	Joseph (22)	M. Ls. Morin	S.P. 1794
			S.H.
	Joseph		
A 43	Pierre (22)	Mad. Vermet	S.H. 1793
44	Louis (23)	Mad. Turcot	S.P. 1805
	M. Madeleine	Ls. Jobidon	" 1834
	Marie	Felix Goulet	" 1836
	Emélie	Jacq. Martel	" 1849
	Alexis Norbert		
	Pierre		
	Jean Sylva		
45	Joseph (23)	Thècle Leclaire	" 1811
46	François (23)	Marg. Clussare	" 1811
47	JeanBaptiste(25)	Marie Couture	S.L. 1796
	Ursule	Ls. Gendreau	" 1825
	Le même	Angé Foucher	S.F. 1804
	Jean Baptiste		
	François		
	Michel (26)	M. Ls. Fradet	S.M.1778
	Susanne	Jean Paquet	S.G.1812
	Marguerite	Bonaventure Côté	" 1819
	Michel		
	Jean Raptiste		
49	Jean-Baptis- (26)	Marie Roy	S.Chs.1780
	te		
	Pierre		

LECLAIRE.

No.	Name	Spouse / Event	Date
50	Louis (1er m.)(26)	Marie Denis	S.M.1786
	Hélène	J. B. Quemeneur	S.G.1810
	Marguerite	Michel Couture	,, 1820
	Cécile	Pierre Audet	,, 1822
	Marie	Jos. Audet	,, 1822
	Marie Anne	Jos. Bilodeau	,, 1823
	Marie Anne	2e Ls. Turgeon	,, 1825
	Chrysostôme		
51	Philippe (26)	Marg. Denis	S.M.1793
	Agathe	Pierre Bilodeau	S.G.1817
	Alexis		
52	Antoine (26)	Cécile Mercier	S.Chs.1809
	Cécile	Pierre Goupy	S.G.1827
	Le même	Marie Goupy	S.M.1820
53	Louis (2e m.) (26)	M. Anne Denis	S.M.1817
54	Philippe (27)	M. Genev. Roy	S.V.1775
	Marguerite	Pierre Blais	S.Chs.1802
	Le même	Marie Pepin	,, 1808
	Angèle	Paul Lacroix	,, 1836
55	Rémi (27)	M. Agathe Brochu	S.V.1785
	Marie Agathe	Prisque Dion	S.V.1808
	Marie Marguerite	Eustache Letellier	,, 1809
	Rémi		
56	Jacques (27)	M.Ls. Bonneau	S.F.S.1783
	Marie Louise	Michel Roy	S.V.1810
	Françoise	Michel Parant	,, 1822
	Vital		
57	Etienne (28)	Josette Racine	S.Chs.1790
	Le même	M. Anne Bilodeau	S.Chs.1796
	Marie Anne	J. B. Couture	,, 1825
	Michel		
58	François (28)	Josette Collet	S.Chs.1794
59	Pierre (28)	M. Jos. Lacroix	,, 1795
	M. Geneviève	Benoît Létourneau	,, 1825
	Josette	J. B. Fournier	,, 1827
	Charlotte	Laurent Dumas	,, 1833
	Charles		
60	Joseph (28)	Ursule Chabot	S.V.1795
	Archange	André Aubé	S.Chs.1825
	Etienne		
	Joseph		
60A	Charles (29)	Mad. Guilmet	S.H.1792
	M. Madeleine	Frs. Morisset	,, 1814
61	Joseph (32)	Josette Rouleau	S.L.1809
	Marie Josette	Jos. Poliquin	,, 1847
	Le même	Louise Pepin	S.Frs.1835
	Philomène	Ferd. Bissonnet	S.L.1863
	Le même	Archange Curodeau	S.L.1850
62	Joseph (33)	Marg. Audet	S.L.1796
	Maurice		
	Alexis		
	Isidore		
63	Joseph (35)	M. Angé Terrien	S.J.1790
	M. Angélique	Pierre Charier	S.Chs.1822
	Marie Olive	Benoni Charier	,, 1831
	Marguerite	Frs. Bussière	,, 1833
	Joseph		
	Pierre		
	Louis		
	Barthélemi		
	Marcel		
64	Jean Baptiste (35)	M. Jos. Chabot	S.Chs.1811
	Marie Josette	Jos. Morin	,, 1823
	M. Angélique	Laurent Leblanc	,, 1834
	Marie	Gab. Leblanc	,, 1839
	Pierre		
	Jean		
65	Jean (36)	M. Thècle Langlois	S.P.1789
	Thècle	Jos. Leclaire	,, 1811
	Julie	Frs. Montigny	,, 1816

LECLAIRE.

No.	Name	Spouse / Event	Date
	Marie Anne	J. B. Rousseau	,, 1828
	Rosalie	Clément Cantin	,, 1831
	Jean		
66	Ambroise (67)	Félicité Bazin	S.P.1801
	Le même	Cécile Couture	S.L.1820
	Jean		
67	Raphaël	Marie Roy	
	Philippe		
68	Joseph	M. Ls. Naud	
	Le même	M. Genev. Nadeau	S.V.1812
69	Alexis (38)	Marg. Fortier,	S.V.1815
	Marguerite	Jean Dessaint,	S.M.1841
	Josette	Honoré Gautron	S.M.1821
	Alexis		
70	Charles	Ursule Clément	S.Chs.1824
	Napoléon		
71	Joseph (40)	Rosalie Roy	S.G.1812
	Joseph		
	Benjamin		
	Le même	Marg. Lacroix	S.G.1824
72	François (40)	Cécile Labrecque	,, 1821
A	Joseph (43)	Louise Paradis	S.H.1819
73	Pierre (44)	Genev. Gourdeau	S.P.1837
	Genev. Octavie	Jos. Ignace Paradis	S.P.1865
	Eliz. Adelina	Pre. Olivier Gosselin	S.P.1867
	Pierre Napoléon		
74	Alexis Norbert (44)	Locadie Rousseau	S.P.1856
75	Jean Sylva (44)	M. Justine Paradis	S.P.1869
76	Jean (47)	Marie Huot	S.L.1830
	Le même	Mad. Labrecque	S.L.1834
	Eugénie	Julien Gendreau	S.L.1854
	Le même	Basilisse CrépeauS.L.1843	
	Martine	F. X. Godbout	S.L.1864
	Caroline	Ls. Achille Pouliot	S.L.1865
	Basilisse Emire	Frs. Turcot	S.L.1869
	Marie Célanire	Flavien Bacquet	S.L.1878
	Emilie	Ls. Achille Pouliot	S.L.1881
77	Jean		
	François (47)	M.Anne Brisson	S.L.1834
	Marie Délima	David Godbout	S.L.1869
	Marie Aurélie	Jos. Blouin	S.L.1878
	François		
	Théophile		
	Cléophas		
	Pierre		
	Edouard		
	Jacques		
78	Guillaume	Genev. Samson	
	Marguerite	Michel	S.L.1820
79			
80	Basile	Hélène Olivier	
	Marie	Frs. Protin	S.J.1826
81	Joseph	M. Rose Pierrejean	S. H.
	Le même	Cath. Vaillancour	S.F.1836
82	JeanBaptiste	Eliz. Bélanger	Islet, Islet
	Louis Olivier		
83	Louis	Justine Martineau	Que.
	Marie Octavie	Jean Félix Goulet	S.P.1864
84	Pierre	Adé Fortier	Frampton
	Marie	Pierre Labbé	S. Frs. 1862
85	Abraham	Marie Daniau	S.P.S. 1838
86	JeanBaptiste(48)	Marie Vincent	S.G.1804
	Jean		
87	Michel (48)	Marg. Langlois	S.L.1810
88	Pierre (49)	M.Ls.Baudoin	S.Chs.1823

LECLAIRE.

	Le même		M. Bibiane Bazin	S. V. 1842
89	Chrysostôme	(50)	Julie Audet	S.G. 1823
90	Alexis	(51)	Marie Audet	S.G. 1820
91	Rémi	(55)	Adé Bélanger	S.V. 1823
	Henriette		Jos. Giguère	S.V. 1847
	François			
92	Vital	(56)	Angèle Guilmet S.V. 1828	
93	Michel	(57)	Marthe Lacasse S.Chs.1832	
94	Charles	(59)	Marg. Couture S.Chs. 1831	
	Marie Anne		Pierre Leclaire S.Chs. 1859	
	Marie Désanges		Ls. Leclaire S. Chs. 1859	
	Charles			
95	Etienne	(60)	Hermine Cochon	S. Chs. 1831
	Marie Hermine		Geo. Guilmet S. Chs. 1859	
	Philoméne		Damase LainéS. Chs. 1863	
	Pierre			
	Louis			
96	Joseph	(60)	M.Jos.Dumas S. Chs. 1833	
97	Maurice	(62)	Félicité Paradis S.P. 1830	
	Marie Rose		Prudent Roberge S-P. 1858	
	Julie Celeste		Jean Roberge S.P. 1865	
	François			
98	Alexis	(62)	Adé Vézina	S.P. 1840
99	Isidore	(62)	Marg. Tessier	S.P. 1849
	Clement		Prêtre	
	Pierre		Prêtre	
	Paul			
100	Joseph	(63)	Marg.Turgeon S.Chs. 1821	
	Le même		M. Salomé Pouliot	S. Chs. 1852
101	Pierre	(63)	Scolastique Gosselin	S.Chs. 1826
	Scolastique		Amb. Chabot S.Chs. 1852	
	Louis			
102	Louis	(63)	M. Jos. Aubé S.Chs. 1829	
103	Barthélémi	(63)	M. Ls. Baillargeon	S.Chs. 1831
104	Marcel	(63)	Marcelline Chabot	S.Chs. 1839
105	Pierre	(64)	Hermine Leblanc	S.Chs. 1845
106	Jean	(64)	Marg. Tangué S.Chs. 1847	
107	Jean	(65)	Jos. Asselin S.P. 1855	
	Marie Sara		Tho. Cépin S.P. 1856	
	Marie Elise			
	Joseph Ferdinand			
108	Jean	(66)	Marcelline Royer S.L.1844	
109	Philippe	(67)	Modeste Shinck S.G. 1808	
110	Alexis	(69)	Louise Denis S.M. 1842	
111	Napoléon	(70)	Flavie Ratté S.M. 1860	
112	Pierre Napoléon	(73)	Vénérande Gagnon	S.P. 1865
113	Jean	(76)	Marie Dumas S.L. 1869	
114	François	(77)	Rose Pouliot S.L. 1762	
115	Théophile	(77)	Cécile Gendreau S.L. 1865	
	Le même		Agnès Godbout S.L. 1875	
116	Cléophas	(77)	Marie Terrien S.L. 1867	
117	Pierre	(77)	Marie Godbout S.L. 1868	
118	Edouard	(77)	Adé Cinqmars S.L. 1876	
119	Jacques	(77)	M. Desneiges Montigny	S.P. 1880
120	Benjamin	(7)	M. Anne Duchesneau	Lévis 1835
121	Joseph	(71)	Angé Bernard S.F.S. 1841	
122	Pierre dit Leclaire		M. Ls. Lemelin S.Chs.1852	
123	Louis Olivier	(82)	Eléonore TurgeonS.M.1851	
124	Jean	(86)	Agathe Rouillard S.G.1823	
125	François	(91)	Déline Roy S. V. 1855	
126	Charles	(94)	M. Eugenie Demers	S.Chs. 1860
127	Pierre	(95)	M. Anne Leclaire S.Chs.	1859

18—25½

LECLAIRE.

128	Louis	(95)	M. Desanges Leclaire	S.Chs. 1859
129	François	(97)	M. Rosalie Ferlant	S.P. 1864
130	Louis	(101)	M. Emélie Audet	S.Chs. 1850
131	Jos. Ferdin.	(107)	M. Célinie Godbout	S.P. 1856

LECOMTE.

1	Pierre		Louise	Normandie
	Jean Baptiste			
2	Jean Baptiste	(1)	Marg. Talbot S.P.S. 1770	
	Marie Marg.		Ant. Langlois S.P.S. 1793	
	Marie Anne		Isaac Langlois S.P.S. 1804	
	Pierre			
	Jean Baptiste			
3	Jean Baptiste	(2)	Marg. Samson S.P.S. 1796	
	Natalie		Jos. Marie Kéroack	S.P.S. 1829
	Jean Baptiste			
4	Pierre	(2)	Marie Balan Bert. 1807	
	Pierre			
5	Jean Baptiste		M. Anne Langlois	
	Marie		Jos. Coulombe Bert. 1817	
	Pacien			
	Joseph			
	Jean Baptiste			
6	Jean Baptiste	(3)	Thérèse Chamberlan	S.P.S. 1820
7	Pierre	(4)	M. Soulange Boulet	S.F.S. 1841
8	Jean Baptiste	(5)	M. Anne Blais Bert. 1824	
9	Pacien	(5)	Sophie Gottier Bert. 1833	
10	Joseph	(5)	Thècle Buteau Bert. 1837	

LECOURS.

1	Michel		Louise Ledron Lévis 1683	
	Michel			
	Charles			
	Joseph			
2	Michel	(1)	Louise Fse. Lemieux	
3	Charles		M. Anne Poliquin	Lévis 1708
	Marie Josette		Chs. Le Roy B. 1728	
	Cécile		Alexandre Turgeon B. 1744	
	Marie Louise		Jean Turgeon B. 1754	
	Charles			
	Jean			
	Pierre			
	Ignace			
4	Joseph	(1)	M. Anne Morel B. 1726	
5	Charles	(3)	Marg. Roy B. 1742	
	Marie Josette		Gilles Turgeon S.M. 1771	
6	Jean	(3)	M. Angé Nadeau B. 1742	
	Marie Anne		Jean Tangué S.Chs. 1771	
	Marie		André Blais S.Chs. 1772	
	Marguerite		Ant. Audet S.Chs. 1774	
	Ignace			
7	Pierre	(3)	Eliz. Couture B. 1746	
8	Ignace	(3)	M. Jos. Turgeon B. 1750	
	Marie Josette		Jos. Roy S.M. 1778	
	Charles			
	Ignace			
9	Charles		Louise Lévis Guay	
	Le même		M. Anne Guay B. 1787	
	Le même		Josette Turgeon B. 1794	
10	Joseph		M. Anne Samson	
	Ambroise			
	Joseph			
11	Pierre		Angé Carrier Levis 1815	
	Félix			
12	Ignace	(6)	Cath. Charier S.Chs. 1790	

LECOURS.

```
13 Ignace          (8) M. Jos. Lepage    S.G.   1781
   Marie Josette       Ls. Bouffart      S.Chs. 1804
   Angèlique           Frs. Hébert       S.Chs. 1817
   Marie Louise        Jos. McIntyre     S.Chs. 1820
   Rosalie             J. B. Letarte     S.H.   1820
   Ignace
   Éloi
   Laurent
·14 Charles         (8) M. Jos. Morisset  S.M.   1793
   Charles
   Joseph
15 Joseph         (10) M. Fse. Ainse     S.G.   1780
   Marie              Jos. Paschal Couture
                                         S.G.   1892
   Elizabeth          Guill. Fradet      S.G.   1809
   Le même            Louise Pouliot     S.Chs. 1812
16 Ambroise       (10) Marie Noël        S.P.   1784
17 Laurent        (13) Fse. Roy          S.H.   1812
   Marguerite         Frs. Dumas         S.Chs. 1840
   Marie Josette      Aug. Clément       S.Chs. 1846
18 Félix          (11) Marie Vachon      S.M.   1850
19 Ignace         (13) Marie Blais       S.Chs. 1818
20 Éloi           (13) Cath. Boutin      S.G.   1826
21 Joseph         (14) M. Mad. Dumas     S.F.   1818
22 Charles        (14) M. Ls. Coté       S.G.   1823
23 Pierre             Reine Morin
                      S. Claire
   Le même            Marie Marcoux      S.Chs. 1836
```

LEFEBVRE—BOULANGER.

```
1 Claude             Marie Arcular      S.F.   1669
  Maguerite          Pierre Juin        S.Frs. 1698
  Susanne            Jean Plante        S.Frs. 1699
  Pierre
  Charles
  Claude
2 Thomas             Génév. Peltier            1669
  Pierre
  Thomas
3 Pierre             Marg. Gagné, La-
                                        prairie 1673
  Jean
4 Jean               Reine Mesnil              1696
  Dorothée           Jos. Gaumont       S.Tho. 1798
  Isabelle           J. B. Carbonneau
                                        Bert.  1729
  Madeleine          Jos. Cloutier      S.Tho. 1733
  Claude
  Jean
  Joseph
5 Pierre         (1) Fse. Fournier      S.F.   1697
                     Aubain
  Louise             Pierre Hélie       Bert.  1725
  Louise             2° Jean Garant     S.V.   1742
  Madeleine          Ls. Chartier       Bert.  1728
  Madeleine          2° Jean Frs. Hayot
                                        S.V.   1748
  Marie Anne         J. B. Guilmet      Bert.  1729
6 Claude         (1) Marie Gautron      S.M.   1705
  Marie Anne         Pierre Quéret      S.M.   1736
  Ursule             Ant. Dutile        S.M.   1740
  Ursule             2° Ignace Adam     S.M.   1754
  Marguerite         Jean Chamberlan
                                        S.V.   1729
  Jean Baptiste
  Ignace
7 Charles        (1) Marie Plante       S.J.   1711
  Madeleine          Jean Marie Thivierge
                                        S.J.   1750
  Joseph Marie
  Pierre
  Charles
8 Pierre         (2) Marie Savard       Qué.   1696
                     V. de Jean Lefebvre
  Le même            Françoise Boissel  B.     1704
```

LEFEBVRE—BOULANGER.

```
9 Thomas         (2) Hélène Gontier     Que.   1707
  Le même            Marg. Girard       Que.   1718
10 Jean          (3) Marie Crête, Beauport    1685
   Marie             Etn. Parant Beauport      1730
11 Joseph        (4) Génév Lorandeau
                                        S.Tho. 1726
   Augustin
12 Claude        (4) Susanne Bissonnet  B.     1736
                                        S. Tho.
   Charles
13 Claude            M. Mad. Lacroix
   Michel
   Claude
   Le même           Josette Audebert   S.J.   1742
   Marie Geneviève   Jos. Roy           S.M.   1772
   Nicolas
14 Adrien            Cath. Racine Normandie
   Pierre
15 Jean Baptiste (6) M. Jos. Marseau
                                        S.Frs. 1730
   Marie Charlotte   Pierre Parant      S.M.   1764
   Marie Charlotte   2° Robert Boulet
                                        S.F.S. 1791
   Marie             Jos. Larrivé       S.M.   1757
   Marie             2° Frs. Vallée     S.M.   1771
   Joseph Marie
   Jean
   Pierre
16 Ignace        (6) Marie Gavant       S.M.   1748
17 Joseph Marie  (7) Cath. Lacroix      S.M.   1736
   Catherine         J. B. Quéret       S.M.   1764
   Marie Josette     Jean Bacquet       S.M.   1780
   Marie             J. B. Labbé        S.V.   1767
   Joseph
   Jean
   Le même           Angé Quéret        S.M.   1752
18 Charles       (7) Thérèse Boissonneau
                                        S.J.   1741
   Marie             Michel Pénin       S.V.   1778
   François
   Pierre
19 Pierre        (7) Marie Labbé        S.Frs. 1756
   Marie Madeleine   J. B. Bidet        S.J.   1776
   Marguerite        Pierre Noël Gosselin
                                        S.J.   1783
   Madeleine         Jos. Delage        S.J.   1786
   Pierre
20 Augustin      (11) M. Mad. Poirier
                                        S.Tho. 1773
   Marie Madeleine   Pierre Fournier
                                        S.Tho. 1792
   Augustin
21 Charles       (12) Marg. Tangué      S.V.   1787
22 Claude        (13) Brigitte Goupy    S.M.   1749
   Le même           M. Jos. Asselin    S.Frs. 1751
23 Michel        (13) M. Mad. Plante    S.M.   1754
   Le même           M. Ls. Bilodeau    S.M.   1794
   Marie Louise      Pierre Brochu      S.M.   1810
   Michel
24 Nicolas       (13) Genev. Denis      S.M.   1769
   Génévieve         Gilles Turgeon     B.     1797
   Elisabeth         Pierre Lavoie      B.     1801
   Angélique         Jos. Carrier       B.     1810
   Alexandre
25 Pierre        (14) M. Anne Tangué    Bert.  1756
26 Jean          (15) Eliz. Fougère     S.Frs. 1751
   Le même           M. Ls. Parant, Lévis      1761
27 Joseph Marie  (15) M. Félicité Gosselin
                                        S.V.   1752
   Elisabeth         Frs. Létellier     S.Chs. 1782
   Elizabeth         2° Jos. Rouleau    S.F.   1785
   Marie             Pierre Poliqun     S.Chs. 1787
   Joseph
   Jacques
   Jean Baptiste
```

LEFEBVRE—BOULANGER.

	Louis			
	Pierre			
28	Pierre	(15)	M. Genev. Roy	S.V. 1771
	Marguerite		Jos. Cadrien	S.M. 1802
	Geneviève		Ant. Guillot	,, 1828
	Pierre			
29	Jean		Marie Langelier,	
	Alexandre & M.		S. Jos. Beauce 1761
	Genev. Parant			
	Alexandre			
30	Joseph	(17)	Thérèse Pouliot S.Chs.1767
	Marie		Amb. Nadeau	S.G. 1809
	Joseph			
	François			
31	Jean	(17)	Louise Forgue	S.M. 1777
	Le même		Cath. Roy	S.V. 1789
	Catherine		Jean Patry	S.M. 1805
	Reine		Etn. Bolduc	,, 1814
	Marie Anne		Pierre Quéret	,, 1817
	Jean			
32	François	(18)	M.Mad.Thivierge S.J.1785
	Françoise		Jean Nadeau	S.L. 1821
	François			
	Joseph			
33	Pierre	(18)	Cath. Drouin	S.J. 1790
	Catherine		Pierre Pepin	S.H. 1813
	Pierre			
34	Pierre	(19)	M. Ls. Pepin	S.J. 1787
	Marie Louise		Jos. Dupuis	,, 1812
	Marie Louise		Frs. Gagnon	,, 1822
	Marie Josette		Frs. Dupuis	,, 1825
35	Augustin	(20)	Cath. Mercier	Bert. 1797
36	Michel	(23)	Judith Clément S.Chs.1819
37	Alexandre	(24)	Fse. Boutillet	,, 1801
	Prudent			
	Alexandre			
38	Joseph	(27)	M. Cath. Mousset	
				S.M. 1774
	Marguerite		J. B. Turgeon	S.M. 1815
	Catherine		Laurent Charier	
				S.Chs. 1796
	Geneviève		Ls. Clément	,, 1803
	Augustin			
	Joseph			
	Le même		Cath. Poliquin S.Chs. 1800
	Marie Flavie		Stanislas Couture ,, 1829
	Jean Baptiste			
	Jacques			
39	Pierre	(27)	Monique Leclaire	
	Pierre			
40	Jean Baptiste	(27)	Rosalie Lacasse	S.G. 1786
41	Louis	(27)	Mad. Mommeny S.M.1793
42	Jacques	(27)	Marg. Duquet	S.H. 1787
	Cécile		Jos. Audet	S.Chs. 1818
	Marguerite		Jos. Pouliot	,, 1825
	Jacques			
	Le même		M. Marg. Lainé S.H. 1810
	Anastasie		Pierre Nadeau S.Chs. 1841
	Pierre			
43	Pierre	(28)	Fse. Boutin	S.F.S. 1795
	Joseph			
	François			
44	Jean Baptiste		Fse. Filteau	
	François			
45	François		Angé. McKinnal	
	Adélaïde		Olivier Lemieux S.V. 1825
	Marie		Aug. Bacquet	,, 1829
	François			
46	Alexandre	(29)	Genev. Labranche	
				S. Jos. 1799
	Anselme			
	Louis			
47	Joseph	(30)	M. Hélène Blanchet	
				S.H. 1792
48	François	(30)	M. Thérèse Guion	
				S.H. 1803

LEFEBVRE—BOULANGER.

49	Jean	(31)	Vict. Quéret	S.M. 1816
50	François	(32)	Marie Cochon	S.J. 1815
51	Joseph	(32)	Angèle Bidet	,, 1819
	Hombéline		Flavien Fontaine	
				S.Frs. 1850
52	Pierre		Eliz. Ami	Jersey
	Jean			
53	Pierre	(33)	Marie Pepin	S.F. 1816
54	Prudent	(37)	Louise Bolduc	S.V. 1824
55	Alexandre	(37)	Rose Pouliot	S.G. 1826
	Léocadie		Jos. Pruneau	S.Chs. 1834
	Alexandre			
56	Augustin	(38)	Mad. Gosselin S.Chs. 1815
	Marc			
	Le même		M. Théodore Beaudoin
57	Joseph	(38)	Marg. Baillargeon	
				S.H. 1807
58	Jacques	(38)	Vict. Blouin	S.G. 1826
59	Jean Baptiste	(38)	Eliz. Bissonnet S.Chs.1838
60	Pierre	(39)	M. Anne Aubé	S.G. 1823
61	Jacques	(42)	Angèle Dumas S.Chs. 1833
62	Pierre	(42)	Flavie Paquet	B. 1848
63	François	(43)	M. Eliz. Leclaire S.V.1823
64	Joseph	(43)	M. Julie Dion	S.M. 1826
65	François	(44)	Genev. Guay	B. 1820
66	François	(45)	M. Ls. Blouin	Bert. 1823
	Esther		David Lemieux	S.V. 1854
	Emélie		Michel Roy	,, 1855
	Louise Zéphirine		Frs. Thivierge	,, 1862
	François			
	Ludger			
	Eusèbe			
	Napoléon			
67	Louis	(46)	Joséphine Cloutier	
				S.L. 1840
68	Anselme	(46)	Apolline Racine S.P. 1843
69	Jean	(52)	Genev. Dalaire S.M. 1838
70	Augustin	(38)	Théodore Baudoin	
	Marcelline		Frs. Gagnon	S.M. 1849
	Louis			
71	Alexandre	(55)	Adèle Chabot	S.Chs. 1854
72	Marc	(56)	Marg. Pepin	,, 1846
73	François	(66)	Marie Goupy	S.V. 1861
74	Ludger	(66)	Cath. Ménard	,, 1862
75	Eusèbe	(66)	Joséphine Voisin	,, 1863
76	Napoléon	(66)	M. Constance Leblond
				S.M. 1854
77	Louis	(70)	Philomène Provost	
				S.Chs. 1856

LEHOUX.

1	Jean		Eliz. Drugeon	Que. 1659
	Marguerite		Jos. Renaud	S.F. 1680
	Marguerite		2° Pierre Salier	,, 1699
	Elizabeth		Jean Bilodeau	,, 1682
	Marie Madeleine		Claude Guyon	,, 1688
	Catherine		Gervais Guyon	,, 1695
	Hyppolite			
	Jean			
2	Hyppolite	(1)	Jeanne Drouin	,, 1699
	Marie Anne		Pierre Cornelier	,, 1720
	Le même		Marg. Vérieul	,, 1713
3	Jean	(1)	Jeanne Gerbert	,, 1701
	Catherine		Germain Déblois	,, 1738
	Hyacinthe			
	Joseph			
	Jean Baptiste			
4	Hyacinthe	(3)	Fse. Morisset	,, 1741
5	Joseph	(3)	Marthe Asselin	,, 1746
	Marthe		Basile Déblois	,, 1762
6	Jean Baptiste	(3)	M. Angé Chaussé Qué.1741
	Angélique		Aug. Turcot	S.F. 1762

LEMELIN.

1	Jean		Marg. Brassart	Qué. 1656
	Marguerite		Marc Lebel	S.L. 1698

LEMELIN.

Marg. Angélique	Nicolas Godbout	S.L.	1685
Marie Madeleine	Robert Crépeau	„	1703
Louise Marie	André Dechaune	Qué.	1676
Jeanne	Tho. Moor	„	1690
Jean François			
Louis			
Guillaume			
2 Jean François (1)	Marg. Lauzet	„	1689
3 Louis (1)	M. Anne Delaunay		
		S.L.	1691
Geneviève	Innocent Audet	„	1710
Jeanne	Chs. Joliet	„	1714
Marie Madeleine	Jos. Roberge	„	1715
Françoise	Frs. Gosselin	„	1716
Marguerite	Gab. Gosselin	„	1718
Marie Anne	Ls. Dufresne	„	1732
Marie Thérèse	Nic. Pouliot	„	1742
Louis Thomas			
Jos. Laurent			
4 Guillaume (1)	Genev. Voyer	Qué.	1715
Le même	Louise Cath. Cosance		
		Que.	1720
5 Louis Thomas (2)	Genev. Pouliot	S.L.	1725
Françoise	Etn. Roy	S.V.	1752
Dorothée	Jos. Lebrun	S.P.S.	1765
Louis			
6 Laurent (2)	M. Jos. Doyon		
7 Joseph (2)	M. Marthe Dalaire		
		S.Frs.	1740
Marie	Jos. Bilodeau	S.L.	1772
Marie	2º Frs. Genest	S.Chs.	1815
Laurent			
Louis			
Joseph			
Charles			
André			
François			
8 Louis (5)	Marthe Veau	S.V.	1749
Marguerite	Jos. Bisson	S.Chs.	1765
Marguerite	2º Pierre Goulet	„	1794
Elisabeth	Jos. Coté	S.M.	1778
Louis			
9 Laurent (7)	Louise Audet	S.L.	1770
Louise	Henri Morin	S M.	1799
Angélique	Frs. Leblanc	„	1809
Laurent			
Jean Baptiste			
Gabriel			
François			
Charles			
10 Joseph (7)	Marie Denis	„	1771
Marie	Ls. Bacquet	„	1794
Marie Anne	Michel Patry	„	1797
Michel			
Joseph			
Le même	M. AnneGuénetS.Chs.1793		
11 Louis (7)	Genev. Audet	S.L.	1772
Louis			
Louis			
Charles			
12 Charles (7)	M. Vict. Jolin	S.Frs.	1779
Marie Louise	Jos. Deblois	S.M.	1808
Joseph			
André			
13 André (7)	Cath. Gontier	S.Chs.	1783
Catherine	Jacq. Bissonnet	„	1810
Catherine	2º J. B. Asselin	„	1824
Marie Victoire	Noël Asselin	„	1819
André			
Etienne			
Jean			
Flavien			
14 François (7)	Mad. Labbé		
Marguerite	Armand Dion	S.Frs.	1807
Marie	Frs. Nadeau	„	1819
Madeleine	Jacq. Dion	„	1819

LEMELIN.

Catherine	Ls. Voyer	S.Frs.	1832
Josette	J. B. Dion	S.F.	1825
François			
Joseph			
Jean Baptiste			
15 Louis (8)	M. AnneGosselinS.M.1785		
	V. de Jos. Quéret		
16 Laurent (9)	Agathe Roy	S.M.	1792
Laurent			
Jean			
Pierre			
17 Jean Baptiste (9)	M. Fse. Quéret	S.M.	1798
Françoise	André Ratté	„	1819
Marie Anne	Jean Paul Gagnon	„	1821
Angèle	Jos. Lebrun	„	1827
Julie	Jos. Ruel	„	1830
Josette	Flavien Ruel	„	1838
Emélie	Frs. Labrecque	„	1844
Jean			
Le même			
18 Gabriel (9)	M. Jos. Guenet	S.Chs.	1802
Le même	Josette Leblanc	„	1812
Gabriel			
Magloire			
Laurent			
19 François (9)	Marie Quemeneur	S.H.	1800
Angèle	Jean Roy	S.Chs.	1843
Pierre			
François			
20 Charles (9)	Louise Côte	S.H.	1811
André			
Jean			
21 Joseph (10)	M. Jos. Corriveau	S.M.	1796
Marie Josette	Jos. Marseau	„	1719
Marie Josette	2º Mag. Leblond	„	1854
Françoise	Isidore Carbonneau		
		S.M.	1827
Marie Madeleine	Zach. Couture	„	1830
Gertrude	Philippe Richard	„	1832
Luce	Michel Lacroix	„	1839
Romain			
Joseph			
David			
François Xavier			
22 Michel (10)	Agathe Roy	S.M.	1803
Marie	Etn. Duchesneau		
		S.F.S.	1832
23 Louis (11)	Thérèse De Champlain		
		S.L.	1803
24 Louis (11)	M. Jos. Pouliot	„	1803
Le même	M. Jos. Gaulin	S.Frs.	1806
Marie	Ed. Maranda	S.L.	1833
Le même	Cath. Ginchereau	S.M.	1817
25 Charles (11)	Judith Ruel	S.L.	1816
		Qué.	
26 Joseph (12)	Marg. Drouin	S.F.	1808
		Qué.	
M. Adelaide	Chs. Chalifour	S.F.	1832
Marie	Pierre Vaillancour		
		S.Frs.	1835
Flavie	Frs. Dupuis	„	1844
Justine	Chs. Lortie	„	1849
Joseph			
27 Joseph (12)	Justine Dion		
Le même	Eléopole Mercier	S.J.	1849
28 André (13)	Marie Lacroix	S.Chs.	1805
André			
Le même	Josette Royer	S.Chs.	1812
29 Etienne (13)	Marg. Couture	„	1814
Marguerite	Alexis Chabot	„	1834
Marguerite	2º Ign. Duquet	„	1852
30 Jean (13)	Suzanne Labrecque		
		S.G.	1822
31 Flavien (13)	Marie Lemieux	„	1828
32 François (14)	Marie Guion	S.F.	1822
Marguerite	Jos. Labbé	S.Frs.	1827

LEMELIN.

Marie	Aug. Emond	„	1743
Mathilde	Evariste Marseau	„	1825
Adelaïde	Pierre Déry	„	1846
François			
33 Jean Baptiste (14)	Véronique Couture S. Roch		
Le même	Luce Guérard S.Frs.1847		
34 Joseph (14)	M. Mad. Ginchereau S. Frs.1822		
35 Laurent (15)	Vict. Carbonneau S.G.1815		
36 Pierre (16)	Marg. Pouliot	„	1823
37 Jean (16)	Mad. Dion	„	1828
38 Jean (17)	Josette Roy S.M.1828		
Philomène	J.B. Bruneau S.Chs.1862		
Jean			
39 Laurent (18)	Marie Ruff S.M.1835		
Flavie	Jos. Letellier	„	1861
40 Gabriel (18)	Louise Godbout	„	1837
41 Magloire (18)	Eléonore Marcoux	„	1844
42 François (19)	Rose Pouliot S.G.1826		
43 Pierre (19)	M. Ls. Roy S.M.1825		
Marie Louise	Pierre Leclaire S.Chs. 1852		
44 Jean (20)	Salomé Leclaire S. Chs. 1840		
45 André (20)	Eliz. Nadeau S. Chs. 1841		
46 David (21)	Marg. Lacroix S. M. 1841		
47 Joseph (21)	Angé Marseau S. M. 1822		
48 Romain (21)	Marie Paquet S. M. 1848		
49 Joseph (26)	M. Fse. Lepage S.Frs.1842		
50 André (28)	Sophie McIntyre S. Chs. 1838		
51 François (32)	Justine Lasalle S.Frs. 1842		
52 Jean (38)	Archange Ratté S. Chs. 1855		
53 François	Cath. Godbout S. Raphaël		
Catherine	Jos. Brochu S. V. 1863		
54 Frs. Xavier (21)	Cath. Bélanger Beauport 1834		

LEMIEUX.

1 Guillaume	Eliz. Langlois Que. 1669	
Elisabeth	Jacq. Couillard S.Tho.1691	
Geneviève	Gab. Paradis Cap. S. Ign. 1698	
Marthe	Jos. Beaucher Cap. S. Ign. 1698	
Marthe	2° Michel Asselin S.F.1730	
François		
Joseph		
Le même	Louise Picard Cap. S. Ign. 1699	
Guillaume		
2 François (1)	M. Anne Paradis S.P.1698	
Marie	Jean Gosselin Cap. S. Ign. 1723	
Charles François		
Louis		
3 Joseph (1)	Eliz. Franquelin Qué. 1712	
Cécile	Jean Arbour Bert. 1744	
Marthe	Jean Arbour Bert. 1744	
Charles Prisque		
Guillaume		
4 Guillaume (1)	Mad. Belanger Islet 1723	
Guillaume		
Le même	M. Anne Deblois Bert 1726	
Marie Josette	Jean Marcoux Bert. 1749	
Marie Anne	Aug. Aubé Bert. 1751	
Françoise Ursule	Aug. Michel Carbonneau Bert. 1761	
Marie Louise	Aug. Fradet Bert. 1754	
Marie Louise	2° Pierre Lepage S.V. 1760	
Michel		
Joseph		
5 Joseph (2)	Genev. Fortin Cap. S. Ign. 1723	
Louis		

LEMIEUX.

6 Charles François			
	(2) Angè Goulet	S. P.	1727
Reine	Frs. Gontier	S. Chs.	1753
Ursule	J. B. Chamberlan	Cap. S. Ign.	1753
7 Michel	M. Anne Bégin		
Michel			
Claude			
8 Guillaume	(3) M. Fse Blais	Bert.	1750
Thérèse	Chs. Fournier	Bert.	1816
Joseph			
Guillaume			
Germain			
Louis			
Jean Baptiste			
9 Charles Prisque			
	(3) M. Eliz. Boulet	S.Tho.	1754
Marie Victoire	Michel Blais	Bert.	1798
Marie Josette	Jos. Terrien	Bert.	1803
Henri Marie			
Jean Baptiste			
10 Guillaume	(4) M. Ls. Marcoux	Bert.	1749
Marie Louise	Ls. Baudoin	S. F. S.	1781
Marie Josette	Jean Labbé	S. F. S.	1791
Guillaume			
Joseph			
Pierre			
Ambroise			
François			
11 Michel	(11) M. Anne Aubé	S. V.	1751
Marie Anne	Etn. Canac	Bert.	1797
Marie Anne	2° Jos. Carbonneau	Bert.	1815
Amable			
Michel			
12 Joseph	(4) M. Jos. Aubé	S.V.	1754
Marie Josette	Gab. Amable Blouin	Bert.	1792
Marie Anne	Chs. Abraham Roy	Bert.	1799
Michel			
Joseph			
François			
Guillaume			
13 Louis	(5) Louise Gamache	Cap. S. Ign.	1734
Louis			
14 Michel	(7) Marie Huart	Lévis	1767
Laurent			
15 Joseph	(8) M. Genev. Blouin	Bert.	1786
16 Guillaume	(8) Marie	Lévis	1781
17 Louis	(8) M. Jos. Blais	S.V.	1789
18 Germain	Marg. Roy	S. G.	1797
19 Jean Baptiste (8)	Marg. Roy	S. G.	1798
Marguerite	Gervais Boucher	S.G.	1823
Adélaïde	Zach. Couture	S. G.	1825
Joseph			
20 Henri Marie	(9) M. Marg. Dion	Bert.	1793
21 Jean Baptiste (9)	M. Jos. Mercier	Bert.	1801
Marie Josette	J. B. Roy	Bert.	1823
Marie Adélaïde	J. B. Dion	Bert.	1846
22 Marie Marthe (10)	Marthe Dion	Bert.	1773
Marie Marthe	Ls. Blais	S. F. S.	1793
Le même	Marg. Dessaint	S.P.S	1776
Marguerite	Philippe Chartier	S. F. S.	1795
Louis			
Pierre			
Augustin			
Joseph			
23 François	(10) Marg. Proulx	S.Tho.	1779
Marie Louise	Ls. Morin	S.F.S.	1798
Marguerite	Jos. Dion	S.F.S.	1810
Marie Reine	J. B. Gagnon	S.F.S.	1823
Genev. Théotiste	Jos. Buteau	S.P.S.	1815

LEMIEUX.

	François				
24	Pierre	(10)	Marie Leclaire S.Chs. 1782		
	Joseph				
25	Joseph	(10)	M. Ls. Paré	S.F.S.	1783
	Louise		Jean Lacasse	S.G.	1807
	Marguerite		Jos. Fradet	S. G.	1813
	Elizabeth		Jos. Petitclerc	S.G.	1822
	André				
	François				
	Joseph				
26	Ambroise	(10)	Thérèse Proulx S.F.S.1786		
	Le même		M.Jos. Couture S.Chs.1797		
	Josette		Raimond Aubé S.G. 1821		
	Marie		Flavien Lémelin S.G. 1828		
	Raphaël				
	Ambroise				
	Guillaume				
27	Amable	(11)	Eliz. Bilodeau	S.V.	1785
	Marthe		J. B. Monmeny Bert. 1811		
	Marie Elizabeth		Jos. Jean Bte. Mercier		
				Bert.	1816
	Amable				
	Jacques				
28	Michel	(11)	Marg. Guilmet	S.V.	1791
	Marguerite		Ign. Patry	S.G	1810
	Marie		Ls. Thibault	S.G.	1819
29	Joseph	(12)	M. Basilisse Roy S.V.		1780
	Euphrosine		Tho. Brochu	S.V.	1800
	Marie Margue-				
	rite		Frs. Godbout	S.V.	1808
	Marie		Jean Valier Roy S.V.		1809
	Anastasie		Jos. Boutin	S.V.	1821
	Jean Baptiste				
30	Françoise	(12)	Marg. Roy	S.V.	1785
	Marguerite		Ed. Marseau	S.V.	1818
	Louis				
	Le même		M. Anne Royer S.G.		1810
31	Michel	(12)	M. Marthe Bilodeau		
				Bert.	1749
	Marthe		Ant. Audet	S.G.	1826
	Michel				
32	Guillaume	(12)	M. Reine Mercier Bert 1805		
	Guillaume				
33	Louis	(13)	M. Claire Bernier Cap. S.		
				Ign.	1761
	Le même		M. Marg. Blanchet		
				S.P.S.	1779
	Jean Baptiste				
34	Claude	(7)	M. Ls. Bélanger		
				Beauport 1782	
	Michel				
	Antoine				
35	Guillaume		Fse. Nolin		
			Lévis		
	Guillaume				
36	Louis		Josette Levasseur		
			Lévis		
	Joseph				
37	Augustin		M. Jos. Dion		
	Marie Luce		Michel Guilmet Bert. 1824		
	Julie		Isidore Guilmet Bert. 1829		
	Marie		Ls. Quemeneur Bert. 1834		
	Marie		2° Jos. Blais	S.F.S.	1843
	Olivier				
	Thomas				
	François Xavier				
38	Laurent	(14)	M. Chs. Gosselin		
				S.Chs.	1816
39	Joseph	(19)	Martine Harpe S.V.		1826
	Samuel				
40	Louis	(22)	M. Chs. Audet	S.V.	1809
	Marie Archange		F. X. Roy	S.V.	1832
	Emérentienne		Jean Lin Roy	S.V.	1834
	Marguerite		Jos. Roby	S.V.	1837
	Sophie		Michel Bernard S.V.		1837
	Euphrosine		Michel Baudoin S.V.		1840

LEMIEUX.

	Soulange		Hubert Mercier S.V.		1843
	Osite		Raimond Langlois		
				S.V.	1845
	Michel				
	Louis				
41	Joseph	(22)	Josette Roy	S.G.	1808
	Marguerite		Basile Gagnon	S.G.	1830
42	Pierre	(22)	Agathe Roy	S.G.	1810
	Joseph				
43	Augustin	(22)	Mad. Roy	S.Chs.	1822
44	François	(23)	Marg. Gagnon	S.V.	1819
45	Joseph	(24)	Marthe Roy	S.G.	1819
	Marie Ursule		Chs. Roy	S.V.	1846
46	Joseph	(25)	M. Anne Fradet S.G.		1813
	Amable				
47	André	(25)	M. Agathe Morin		
				S.F.S.	1820
48	François	(25)	Fse. Drouin	S.F.S.	1828
49	Ambroise	(26)	Archange Aubé S.G.		1821
50	Guillaume	(26)	Marie Buteau S.F.S.		1827
51	Raphaël	(26)	Marg. Brisson	S.G.	1828
52	Joseph		Josette Boucher S.G.		1824
53	Jacques	(27)	M. Ls. Carbonneau		
				Bert.	1817
	Le même		Louise Ménard Bert.		1844
54	Amable	(27)	Angé Guilmet	Bert.	1825
	Marie Margue-		Etn. Mercier	Bert.	1844
	rite				
55	Noël		Josette Leclaire		
	Marie Claire		J. B. Daniau S.F.S.		1861
	Charles				
56	JeanBaptiste(29)		Marg. Brochu	S.V.	1809
	Mathilde		Tho. Catellier	"	1829
	Marguerite		Pierre Boutin	"	1835
	Marie Rosalie		F.X.ChamberlanS.M.1845		
	Eléonore		Jean Mercier	S.M.	1856
	Magloire				
	David				
	Jean Baptiste				
57	Louis	(30)	Ange Bolduc	S.G.	1822
58	Michel	(31)	Vict. Roy	"	1819
	Le même		Julie Fortier	S.J.	1825
59	Guillaume	(32)	Susanne Paquet S.G.		1830
60	JeanBaptiste(33)		M. Fse. Bouchard		
				S.F.S.	1821
61	Michel	(34)	Fse. Morin	S.H.	1816
	Augustin				
62	Antoine	(34)	Cath Morin	"	1819
63	Guillaume	(35)	Marg. Pouliot	S.G.	1813
	Mathilde		Ant. Gagnon	Bert.	1847
	Le même		M. Marg. Bazin Bert		1831
64	Joseph	(37)	Agathe Roberge S.G.		1817
65	Thomas	(37)	Reine Bilodeau	Bert	1822
	Reine		Frederic	Bert	1824
	Ludger				
	Edouard				
	Ferdinand				
66	Olivier	(37)	Adé Lefebvre	S.V.	1825
	Valéry				
e	François	(37)	M. Julie Morisset	"	1835
	Xavier				
67	Jean Baptiste		Zoé Paquet		
			Islet		
	Joseph				
68	Samuel	(39)	M. Césaire Harpe	"	1869
69	Louis	(40)	Archange Quemeneur		
				S.V.	1843
70	Michel	(40)	Vict. Roy	"	1844
71	Joseph	(42)	M.Marg.Paquet S.M.		1840
72	Amable	(46)	M. Mad. Ratté	"	1847
73	Charles	(55)	Marie Rousseau S.V.		1822
74	Magloire	(56)	Emelie Bolduc S.V.		1844
75	JeanBaptiste(56)		M. Ester Dion S.M.		1846
76	David	(56)	Esther Lefebvre S.V.		1854
77	Augustin	((61)	Sara Delisle	S.J.	1859

LEMIEUX.

78 Ludger	(65) Flore Bélanger	S.V.	1853
79 Ferdinand	(65) Celina Bélanger	„	1854
80 Edouard	(65) Philomène Roy	„	1864
81 Valery	(66) Mérisse Levisque	„	1860
82 Joseph	(67) M. Desanges Delaire		
		S.V.	1856
83 Pierre	Marie Noël		
Le même	Marie Dion	S.M.	1840
84 Jean François	M. Mad. Morin		
Le même	M. Vict. Marseau		
		S.F.S.	1843
85 Vital	Adé Drapeau		
Le même	Tharsile AudetS.Chs.		1855

LEMOINE-JASMIN.

1 François	Barbe Guilmet	S.J.	1694
Jean François			
2 Jean François(1)	Anne Mailloux	B.	1718
Le même	M. Mad. Chamberlan		
		S.M.	1736
Francoise	Frs. Bleau	„	1750
Marie Geneviève	Nic Dodier	„	1765

LEPAGE.

1 Etienne	Nicola Bertholot		
Germain			
Louis			
2 Germain	(1) Reine Lamy		
René			
3 Louis	(1) Sébastienne Laignon	1667	
Marie	Gab. Thivierge S.Frs.	1688	
Marguerite	Ls. Turcot	„	1706
Rose	Ant. Pepin	„	1707
Elizabeth	Marc Baudoin	„	1711
Madeleine	Chs. Guérard	„	1722
Angélique	Ant. Bilodeau	„	1713
Angélique	2° Jos. Danieau Bert.	1730	
Pierre			
Joseph			
Jean			
Jean Baptiste			
4 René	(2) M. Mad. Gagnon		
	St. Anne	1686	
Louis	Caida Terrebonne		
5 Pierre	(3) M. Mad. Turcot S.F.	1700	
Gertrude	JeanCarbonneau SFrs.	1722	
Marie	Jean Labbé	„	1724
Madeleine	Jean Marseau	„	1731
Le même	Cath Choret	S.J.	1736
Le même	Marg. Fontaine	„	1744
6 Joseph	(3) Claire Racine S.Anne	1707	
Marie Josette	Frs. Guérard S.Frs.	1727	
Louise	Ls. Pepin	„	1729
Hélène	Simon Campagna	„	1739
Marthe	Pierre Gagné	„	1740
Louis			
Le même	Marie Fournier S.Tho.	1729	
Thécle	Ls. Gagnon	S.Frs.	1756
Joseph			
7 Jean	(3) Marie Gagnon	„	1723
Marie Angélique	Jos. ChamberlanS.M.	1753	
Jean Baptiste			
Joseph			
Pierre			
8 Jean Baptiste(3)	M. Anne Béchard		
		S.M.	1737
9 Louis	(6) Eliz. Jolin	S.Frs.	1743
Pierre			
Joseph Marie			
10 Joseph	(6) M. Fse. Gobeil	S.J.	1758
Marie Catherine	Ant. Coulombe	S.J.	1795
Marie	Jos. Gendreau S.Frs.	1778	
Marie Madeleine	Amable Bernier S.Frs.	1787	
Marie Madeleine	2° J. B. Boucher S.M.	1824	

LEPAGE.

Joseph Marie			
François			
11 Jean Baptiste (7)	M. Genev. Leroux		
		S.M.	1749
Angèlique	Ls. Audet	S.Chs.	1782
Marie	Pierre Chevanel		
		S.Chs.	1786
Marie	Simon Mercier S.Chs.	1786	
Jean			
Charles			
12 Joseph	(7) M. Anne Hautbois		
		S.M.	1753
Marie Madeliene	Ign. Lecours	S.G.	1781
Marie Madeliene	2° Jacq. Létourneau		
		S.Chs.	1818
Marie	J. B. Royer	S.Chs.	1786
Françoise	Jos. Fortier	S.Chs.	1791
Marie Anne	Etn. Hizoir	S.Chs.	1795
Joseph			
Michel			
Jean Baptiste			
Gabriel			
François			
Pierre			
13 Pierre	(7) Louise Lemieux S.V.	1760	
Marie Louise	Jos. Turgeon	S.V.	1787
Marguerite	J. B. Guilmet	S.V.	1790
Catherine	Jos. Ruel	S.V.	1796
Marie	Jean Marie Daigle		
		S.V.	1802
Valier			
14			
15 Pierre	(9) Marthe Gagné S.Frs.	1771	
Marie Madeleine	Aug. Labbé	S.Frs.	1799
Marie Thècle	Frs. Canac	S.Frs.	1802
Marie Louise	Ant. Vallée	S.Frs.	1802
Marie Catherine	Pierre Keroack S.Frs.	1817	
Marie	Jean Canac	S.F.	1791
Josette	Ls. Pepin	S.F.	1819
Louis			
16 Joseph Marie (9)	M. Ls. Labbé.		
Marie Catherine	Jean Cochon	S.Frs.	1804
Marie Josette	Jos. Paquet	S.Frs.	1805
Joseph Marie			
17 Jean	(11) Marie Gontier S.Chs.	1772	
Judith	Ls. Labrecque	S.G.	1791
Marie	Pierre Hélie	S.G.	1797
Marie	2° Etn. Gaudin	S.G.	1811
Jean			
18 Charles	(11) Marg. Poulin	S.Chs.	1792
Cécile	Jacq. Hélie	S.Chs.	1820
Angélique	Basile Thibaut S.Chs.	1820	
Angélique	2° Pierre Gagnon S.V.	1827	
Angélique	3° Pierre Blais S.Chs.	1832	
Marie Anne	Prosper GagnéS.Chs.	1824	
Marguerite	Ls. Gontier	S.Chs.	1829
Angèle	Magloire Audet	B.	1841
Jean Baptiste			
Joseph			
19 Joseph	(12) Marie Goupy S.Chs.	1778	
20 Michel	(12) Marie Roy	S.Chs.	1782
Judith	Simon Baillargeon		
		S.Chs.	1806
Marguerite	Jean Baillargeon		
		S.Chs.	1808
21 Gabriel	(12) Marie Petiteclerc		
		S.Chs.	1704
Marie	J. B. Cadrin	S.Chs.	1807
Le même	Thérèse Patry	S.H.	1817
22 Jean Bapt.	(12) Charlotte Boucher		
	S.H.	S.Chs.	1785
Jean			
23 François	(12) Fse. Bisson	S.Chs.	1794
24 Pierre	(12) Marie Forgue	S.M.	1795

LEPAGE.

25	Valier	(13)	M. Marg. Fortier	S.F.S.	1790
	Marie Louise		Amb. Naud	S.V.	1822
	Marie Louise		Vincent Baudoin	S.V.	1826
	Ursule		Ls. Tangué	S.G.	1826
	Thomas				
	Jean Baptiste				
	François Xavier				
	Joseph				
26	Joseph Marie		M. Ls. Kéroack	S.P.S.	1790
	Germain				
27	François	(10)	M. Vict. Labbé	S.J.	1794
	Marie Victoire		Frs. René Flavien Picard	S.Frs.	1817
	Marie Catherine		Chrysostôme Pepin	S.Frs.	1825
	Marie Louise		Frs. Labbé	S.Frs.	1828
	Moïse		Josette Vallée	S.Frs.	1812
	Joseph		Etn. Marseau	S.Frs.	1840
28	Louis		Moïse Picard	S.Frs.	1852
	Julie		J. B. Dion	S.Frs.	1842
	Julie		Pierre Déblois	S.Frs.	1846
	M. Hombéline		Olivier Picard	S.Frs.	1833
	Marie		F. X. Picard	S.Frs.	1861
	Marie Lucie				
	Marie Pétronille				
	Athanase		Marg. Lheureux	S.Frs.	1808
	François Xavier		Jos. Pepin	S.Frs.	1834
29	Joseph Marie	(16)	Jean Frs. Racine	S.Frs.	1846
	Marguerite				
	Catherine				
	Léandre		Marg. Hélie	S.Chs.	1804
	François		Barnabé Bilodeau	S.G.	1820
30	Jean	(17)	Marg. Hélie	S.Chs.	1804
	Marguerite		Barnabé Bilodeau	S.G.	1820
31	Jean Bapt.	(18)	Reine Brochu	S.Chs.	1825
32	Joseph	(18)	M. Angèle Couillard	S.Chs.	1830
	Henriette		Frs. Bédard	S.Chs.	1855
	Célina		Jos. Alfred Moreau	S.Chs.	1860
	Charlotte Caroline		Prosper Naud	"	1862
33	Thomas	(25)	Marie Malbœuf	S.V.	1811
34	Joseph	(25)	Cath. Gosselin	S.G.	1821
35	Jean Baptiste	(25)	M. Jos. Gagné	S.V.	1824
36	François Xavier	(25)	M. Genev. Blais	S.H.	1825
	Marie		Wenceslas Brochu	"	1858
	François Xavier				
37	Germain	(26)	Marie Coté	S.P.S.	1820
38	Joseph	(27)	Marie Labbé	S.F.	1823
	Marie Françoise		Jos. Lemelin	S. Frs.	1842
	Marie Madeleine		F. X. Plante	"	1847
	Marie Victoire		F. X. Lepage	"	1853
	Marie Vénéranda		Etn. Légaré	"	1854
	Marie Eléonore		F. X. Emond	"	1856
	Augustin				
39	Moïse	(27)	Isabelle Filion	S. Joa.	1833
	Marie Dina		Damase Fortier	S. Frs.	1860
40	François Xavier	(28)	M. Vict. Lepage	"	1853
41	François	(29)	Julie Ginchereau	"	1841
42	Léandre	(29)	Henriette Campagna	S. Frs.	1845
43	François Xavier	(36)	Emélie McNeil	S.V.	1857
44	Augustin	(38)	Malvina Dussaut	S. Frs.	1856
	Jean	(22)	Marie Chrétien	S.H.	1819

LERREAU—L'HEUREUX.

1	Simon		Susanne Jarousel	Qué.	1655
	Marie		Jean Guy	S.F.	1671
	Anne		Frs. Frechet	"	1680
	Sixte				
	Pierre				
2	Pierre	(1)	M. Marg. Badeau	Qué.	1689
	Louise		Jos. Larrivé	S.F.	1716
	Simon				
3	Sixte	(1)	Reine Deblois	"	1694
	Marie		Yves Defleure	"	1724
	Geneviève		J. B. Dupont	"	1736
	Simon				
	Jean Baptiste				
4	Simon	(2)	Cath. Drouin	"	1734
5	Simon	(3)	Marg. Loignon	"	1722
	Marie		Basile Gagnon	"	1743
	Thérèse		Jos. Ginchereau	"	1749
	Thècle		Alexis Aucouin	"	1763
	Marie Josette		Jos. Emond	S. Frs.	1765
	Joseph				
	Le même		Josette Asselin	S.F.	1747
	Le même		M. Angé Audet	S.L.	1750
6	Jean Baptiste	(3)	Thérèse Canac	S.F.	1730
7	Joseph	(5)	Louise Emond	S. Frs.	1755
	Marie Louise		Ls. Fortier	S.F.	1784
	Joseph				
	Pierre				
	Pierre				
	Augustin				
	Simon				
	Jean Baptiste				
	Le même		M. Claire Plante	S. Frs.	1767
	Marie Josette		Aug. Martineau	S.F.	1796
	Madeleine		Jérome Drouin	"	1791
8	Joseph	(7)	M. Vict. Deblois		
	Marie Madeleine		Frs. Emond	S. Frs.	1805
	Marguerite		Jos. Marie Lepage	"	1808
	Marie Victoire		Jean Langlois	S.F.	1814
	Le même		Genev. Asselin	S. Frs.	1788
9	Pierre	(7)	M. Jos. Dampierre	"	1781
	Claire		Prisque Cameron	S.F.	1819
	Victoire		Aug. Martineau	"	1832
	Louise		Ign. Trépanier	C.R.	1815
	Joseph				
	Jean				
	Pierre				
10	Augustin	(7)	Hélène Rosa	S.F.	1792
11	Pierre	(7)	M. Ls. Guérard	S. Frs.	1818
12	Jean Baptiste	(7)	M. Louise Rosa	"	1786
13	Simon	(7)	M. Genev. Guérard	S.F.	1808
14	Pierre	(9)	M. Mad. Faucher	"	1808
	Geneviève		Jean Rancourt	"	1838
	Josette		Jean Turcot	"	1839
	Joseph				
	Louis				
15	Joseph	(9)	Marg. Charlack	"	1808
16	Jean	(9)	M. Marthe Deblois		
			S. Marie	S.F.	1827
17	Joseph	(14)	M. Ludivine Baucher	S.F.	1832
18	Louis	(14)	Henriette Beaucher	"	1840

LEROUX.

1	Jean		Angé Plante	S.J.	1715
	Angélique		Nicolas Lacroix	S.M.	1736
	Catherine		Tho. Guenet	"	1738
	Catherine		2° Jean Gontier	S. Chs.	1767
	Madeleine		Jacq. Bédard	S.M.	1743
	Marie Geneviève		J. B. Lepage	"	1749
	Marie Anne		Jos. Gontier	"	1749
	Marie Anne		2° Ls. Dalaire	S. Chs.	1762
	Louis				

LEROUX.

2 Louis	(1)	Fse. Bilodeau	Bert. 1743
Jacques			
Joseph			
Louis			
3 Louis	(2)	M. Claire Gendron	S.F.S. 1764
4 Jacques	(2)	M. Marthe Godbout	S.L. 1773
Marie Marthe		Jacq. Bouffart	S.L.1806
Françoise		Pierre Noël	„ 1816
Pierre			
Jacques			
Prudent			
5 Joseph	(2)	M. Anne Maupas	S. Chs. 1785
Le même		Thérèse Bernier	„ 1797
Marie		Chs. Pouliot	„ 1842
Joseph			
François-Xavier			
André			
6 Joseph		M. Fse. Grandmaison	
Louise		Jab. Labrecque S.Chs.1797	
Marie Angélique		Pierre Goulet	„ 1802
7 Jacques	(4)	Mad. Hébert	A.G.1808
8 Pierre	(4)	M. Anne Giguère S.P.1819	
Le même		Théotiste Coté	„ 1830
Adelaïde		Ls. Huot	S.L.1855
Pierre			
9 Prudent	(4)	Pelagie Boucher S.H.1820	
10 Joseph	(5)	M. Anne Leclaire	S.Chs.1817
Marie Anne		Ls. Chabot	„ 1841
Julie		Michel Fiset	S.M.1850
11 André	(5)	M. Anne Leblond	S.Chs.1821
12 François Xav.	(5)	Marg. Blais	S F.S.1825
13 Pierre	(8)	M.Clémentine Martineau	S.Nic.1869

LESCABICT—CANICHON.

1 Jean		Charlotte Chevery	Qué. 1749
Catherine		Jean Gagné	S.Frs.1775
Marie Charlotte		Jean Blouin	„ 1773
Jean			
2 Jean	(1)	M. Jos. Emond	„ 1775
Jean			
3 Jean	(2)	M. Brigitte Dion	„ 1806

LESSART.

1 Etienne		Marg. Sevestre	Qué. 1856
Prisque			
Joseph			
Etienne			
2 Charles		M.Anne Caron S. Anne1686	
Charles			
3 Etienne		Marie Poulin	„ 1679
Etienne			
4 Prisque		Marie Jacob	S.G.1699
Prisque			
5 Joseph	(1)	Marg. Racine S. Anne1700	
Ignace			
6 Charles	(2)	M. Cath. Paquet	Chs.Bourg.1721
Charles			
7 Etienne	(3)	Mad. Pepin S Anne 1732	
François			
8 Prisque	(4)	M. Jos. Parent	Beauport 1727
Marie		Jean Vermet	Bert.1751
Joseph			
9 Ignace	(5)	M.Reine Boluc S.Joa.1743	
Marie Reine		Germ. Blondeau S.M.1775	
Marie Louise		Jean Chs. Racine	„ 1780

LESSART.

Marie Louise	2°	Ant. Fleury	S.M. 1793
Louis			
Jean Baptiste			
10 Bonaventure		M. Eliz. Paré	
Jos.et Mad.Paquet			S.Anne 1741
Joseph			
11 Charles	(6)	Mad. Godbout	S.L. 1752
12 François	(7)	Mad. Morel	S.Anne 1758
Jean			
Augustin			
13 Joseph	(8)	Marg.Carbonneau Bert1758	
Angélique		Ls. Coulombe	„ 1779
Marie Élisabeth		J. B. Denaut	„ 1797
Augustin			
Joseph			
Jacques			
14 Etienne		M. Angé Guion	
Michel			
Jean Baptiste			
Etienne			
15 Louis	(9)	M. Mad. Fortier S.M.1790	
Louis			
16 Jean	(9)	M. Agathe Ratté	„ 1774
Baptiste			
Marie Reine		Frs. Bacquet	„ 1795
Marguerite		Paschal Lebrun	„ 1812
Marie Louise		Mag. Leblond	„ 1821
Pre. Noël			
Jean Baptiste			
17 Joseph	(10)	M. Claire Canac S.F.1775	
A 17 Augustin		Marie Saillart	
François			
18 Jean	(12)	Louise Racine S. Anne1785	
Jean			
19 Joseph	(13)	Mad. Lacroix	S.V. 1786
20 Augustin	(13)	Genev. Blais	Bert.1790
Geneviève		Jos. Carbonneau	„ 1824
Marguerite		Chs. Gautier	„ 1830
Reine		Aug. Carbonneau	„ 1834
Marie Marthe		Jacq. Carbonneau	„ 1841
Marie Angèle		Jos. Bolduc	„ 1821
Marie Angèle		2° Frs. Morin	S.V.1851
Marie Luce		F.X. Bolduc	„ 1830
Joseph			
Augustin			
21 Jacques	(13)	Marie Gendron S.F,S.1799	
Reine		Geo. Ouel	„ 1840
Françoise		Luc Ouel	Bert.1824
Simon			
Louis			
Jacques			
Le même		Marg. Blais	Bert. 1813
Jean Baptiste			
22 Etienne	(14)	Marie Hébert	S.F. 1794
Catherine		Jean Langlois	S.Frs. 1833
François			
François Xavier			
23 Michel	(14)	M. Ls. Guérard	S.F. 1812
Marie Julie		Frs. Asselin	S.Frs. 1836
Marie		Pierre Giguère	„ 1836
Mathilde		F. X. Dion	„ 1855
24 JeanBaptiste	(14)	Mad. Gendreau	S.L. 1812
25 Louis	(15)	Thérèse Gagné	S.M. 1825
Marie Adèle		Jean Ferd. Veau	„ 1852
Rigobert			
26 JeanBaptiste	(16)	M. Genev. Hélie	S.V. 1804
27 Pierre Noël	(16)	M. Fse. Roy	S.M. 1806
Françoise		Isidore Bolduc	„ 1838
Marie Angèle		Pierre Lacroix	„ 1847
Sophie		Aug. Mercier	„ 1851
Pierre			
Edouard			
Benjamin			
Joseph			

LESSART.

28 Jean Urbain	(18) Luce Simard S.Anne 1826
29 François	Angé Goulet
	S. Isidore 1835
François	
30 Joseph	(20) M. Marg. Carbonneau
	Bert. 1824
31 Augustin	(20) M. Adé Baudoin „ 1830
32 Louis	(21) Marie Boilard S.G. 1827
33 Jacques	(21) Scolastique Roy S.F.S.1832
34 Simon	(21) Marg. Blais Bert. 1838
35 JeanBaptiste	(21) Julie Tangué „ 1841
36 François	(22) Luce Dion S.Frs. 1842
37 François Xavier	(22) Justine Plante „ 1843
38 Pierre	(27) M. Désanges Quemeneur
	S.M. 1844
39 Edouard	(27) Sara Hélie „ 1854
40 Joseph	(27) M. Anne Johnston
	S.V. 1847
41 François Flore	(17)A Christine Pepin S.Joa.1831
42 Rigobert	(25) Sophie Gagnon S.M. 1851
43 Urbain	(28) Henriette Turgeon
	S. Anne B. 1846
44 François	(29) Cath. Drapeau S.V. 1860
45 Benjamin	(27) Domitille Quemeneur
	S.M. 1854

LÉTANG.

1 Jean Pierre	Claude Blésimont
2 Pierre	(1) Genev. Audet S.J. 1758
3 Antoine Véronique Hyppolite	M. Anne LaMadeleine
	Etn. Couture B. 1828
	Jean Turgeon B. 1828

LETELLIER.

1 Michel François	Marie Thélégne Noyan
2 Eustache Nicolas	Marie Cuissine S. Ouen
3 François	(1) M. Jos. Larivé
Le même	M. Fse. Peltier Que. 1743
Marie Françoise Michel	Geo. Borne S.V. 1762
François Pierre	
5 Nicolas	(3) Marie Renvaizé Que. 1758
Louis	Que.
6 François	(3) M. Eliz. Carbonneau
	Bert. 1771
Marie Elizabeth	Pierre Dodier S.V. 1790
Marie Françoise	Ant. Roy „ 1798
Marie Victoire Michel	Eustache Audet „ 1801
Le même	Eliz. Lefebvre S.Chs. 1782
Marie François Pierre	J. B. Boutin S.H. 1813
7 Michel	(3) M. Ls. Moreau S.V. 1774
Marie Louise	J. B. Têtu „ 1793
Eustache Michel François	
Le même	M. Hélène Quéret S.M.1808
8 Louis	(5) M. Jos. Couture B. 1789
Emérentienne	Etn. Valière B. 1814
Marie Adélaïde Charles	Pierre Bélanger B. 1819
9 Michel	(6) M. Rose Fleury S.V. 1803
Marie	Benjamin Roy S.V. 1831
	V. d'Alexis Leclaire
Michel	
10 François	(6) M. Jos. Monmeny
	S.Chs. 1809

LETELLIER.

11 Pierre	(6) Marg. Charlan S.G. 1816
12 Michel	(7) M. Angé Beaucher B. 1802
Marie Flavien Frédéric Edouard	Nazaire Roy S.V. 1834
13 Eustache	(7) M. Marg. Leclaire S.V.1809
Michel Eustache	
14 François	(7) Sophie Casgrain
	Riv. Ouelle 1814
Luc Oratio	
15 Charles	(8) M. Chs. Martin-Lepire
	.B. 1820
Charles	
16 Michel Michel	(9) Marie Lainé S.V. 1834
17 Flavien	(12) Julie Balan S.V. 1833
Marie Belzemire	Jean Corriveau S.M. 1856
Philomène Joseph	Etn. Bélanger S.M. 1857
18 Fréderic	(12) Adé Mercier S.F.S. 1829
Le même	M. Marg. Martineau
	S.F.S. 1840
19 Marcel	Adé Paquet S.J. 1837
Vitaline	Jos. Langlois S.J. 1864
Sara	Fidele Ballantyne
Le même	M. Anne Demeule
	S.J. 1850
20 Edouard	(12) Henriette Tétu S.Tho.1825
Flore	Jos. Honoré Buteau
	S.V. 1755
Elizabeth	André Quéret S.V. 1866
Joseph	
Le même	M. Anastasie Goupy
	S.M. 1851
21 Michel Eust.	(13) M. Vict. Bouchard
	S.V. 1833
22 Luc Oratio	(14) Eugénie Laurent,
	Riv. Ouelle
23 Charles	(15) M. Célina Turgeon B. 1832
24 Michel	(16) Luce Jahan S.V. 1862
25 Joseph	(17) Flavie Lemelin S.M. 1861
26 Joseph	(20) M. Florida Trépanier
	S.V. 1856

LÉTOURNEAU.

1 Jean Jean David	Sébastienne Guéry
2 David	(1) Fse. Chapelain C.R. 1664
Marie Anne	Denis Charlan S.F. 1681
Françoise	Simon Gaulin S.F. 1685
Elizabeth	Robert Gaulin S.F. 1688
Catherine	Pierre Morisset S.F. 1698
Louise	Pierre Gagnon S.F. 1700
Louise	2° Pierre Droiun S.F. 1704
Thérèse	J. B. Leblond S.F. 1703
Bernard Jean Louis	
3 Jean Jean	(1) Anne Dufresne S.F. 1673
4 Louis	(2) Anne Blouin S.J. 1896
Geneviève	Pierre Gagné S.L. 1738
Jeanne Louis Jacques Nicholas Ignace Antoine	Alexis Delounay S.L. 1739
5 Bernard	(2) Marie Rochon S.F. 1698
Le même	Hélène Gagne S.Frs. 1703
6 Jean	(2) Marg. Caron S.Anne 1706
Marie Françoise	Jean Pichet S.F. 1731
Marguerite	Jos. Fortin S.F. 1722

LÉTOURNEAU.

	Marthe	Jacq. Perrot	S.F. 1737
	Angélique	J. B. Loignon	S.F. 1743
	Geneviève	André Lombert	S.F. 1753
	Joseph		
	Jean		
7	Jean	(3) Marg. Asselin	S.F. 1711
	Le même	Anne Gendron	S.J. 1715
8	Louis	(4) Agathe Dion	S.F 1727
	Catherine	Pierre Deblois	S.F. 1745
	Louis		
	Le même	Marthe Deblois	S.F. 1735
	Charlotte	Jean Leblond	S.F. 1753
	Marie Josette	Jos. Marie Gosselin	S.F. 1763
	Marie Rosalie	Jacq. Pichet	S.F. 1767
	MarieAbondante	Noël Gagnon	S.F. 1776
	Madeleine	Pierre Turcot	S.F. 1781
	Madeleine	2° Jean Guion	S.F. 1810
	Joseph		
	François		
9	Nicholas	(4) Thérèse Lebrecque	S.L. 1736
	Thérèse	Frs. Audet	S.L. 1763
	Marie	Michel Monmeny	S.L. 1764
	Geneviève	Pierre Audet	S.P. 1769
	Marie Anne	Prisque Audibert	S.P. 1775
	Jacques		
10	Jacques	(4) Mad. Baillargeon	S.L. 1739
	Marie Geneviève	Jos. Valière	S.L. 1777
	Marie Madeleine	Jean Pouliot	S.L. 1786
	Marie Josette	Guill Dufresne	S.L. 1791
	Thérèse	Nic. Baillargeon	S.L. 1777
	Marie Anne	Ant. Rouleau	S.L. 1778
	Catherine	Felix Fortier	S.H. 1789
	Jacques		
	Charles		
	François		
11	Ignace	(4) Marg. Couture	S.P. 1744
	Marguerite	Etn. Simart	S.F. 1773
	Jean Baptiste		
	Ignace		
	Joseph		
12	Antoine	(4) Marthe Picard	S.Tho. 1736
	M. Marguerite	Amb. Samson	S.P.S. 1765
	Joseph Marie		
	Louis		
	Le même	M. Anne Leblond	S.V. 1749
	Marie Anne	Alexis Gagné	S.P.S. 1774
	Marie Charlotte	Chs. Mathieu	S.P.S. 1773
	Marie Angélique	Eustache Bacon	S.P.S. 1780
	Pierre Basile		
	Ignace		
	Antoine		
13	Joseph	(6) Mad. Montigny	S.P. 1756
14	Jean	(6) M. Anne Montigny	S.P. 1753
15	Louis	(8) Véronique Gosselin	S.F. 1763
16	François	(8) M. Mad. Drouin	S.F. 1767
17	Joseph	(8) Genev. Asselin	S.F. 1771
	Joseph		
	Le même	M. Anne Crépeau	S.P.1774
	Marie Anne	Jacq. Drouin	S.F. 1795
	Marie Anne	2° Ls. Poulin	1798
	Marie	Michel Tremblay	1806
	David		
	Louis		
	Jacques		
	Jean Moïse		
18	Jacques	(9) Marg. Audet	S.L. 1763
	Antoine		

LÉTOURNEAU.

	Le même	——Meunier	S.Chs. 1777
19	Jacques	(10) Marthe Naud	1777
	Geneviève	Frs. Bruneau	S.G. 1800
	Geneviève	2° Pierre Carbonneau	S.G. 1824
	Michel		
	Jac ues		
	Le même	Mad. Lepage	S.Chs. 1818
20	François	(10) Louise Godbout	S.L. 1782
	Marie Louise	Ls. Gosselin	1813
	François		
	Jean		
21	Charles	(10) Fse. Bernier	S.Chs. 1785
22	Jean Baptiste	(11) M. Jos. Poulin	S.F. 1775
	Marguerite	Jacq. Létourneau	1803
	Jean Baptiste		
23	Ignace	(11) Brigitte Gaulin	1795
	Brigitte	Jos. Vaillancour	1800
	Brigitte	2° Pierre Prémont	1809
	Madeleine	Jos. Racine	1804
	Madeleine	2° Frs. Asselin	1813
	Marie Louise	Jos. Paquet	1811
	Ignace		
	Ambroise		
24	Joseph	(11) Marg. Denis	S.Chs. 1785
	Elizabeth	Jacq. Blais	1814
	Joseph		
25	Louis	(12) M. Vict. Bernier	Islet 1764
	Marie Victoire	Ant. Dubé	S.P.S. 1784
	Angélique	Ant. Roy	1787
	Antoine		
	Jean Baptiste		
	Le même	Cath. Boivin	S.V. 1781
26	Joseph Marie(12)	Fse. Cloutier	S.P.S. 1766
	Joseph		
	Joseph		
27	Ignace	(12) M. Genev. Picard	S.F.S. 1779
	Marie Geneviève	André Blanchet	S.P.S. 1799
	Marie Françoise	Jos. Marie Baudoin	S.P.S. 1806
	Jeanne	Michel Talbot	1813
	Ignace		
	Joseph Basile		
28	Antoine	(12) M. Fse. Talbot	1784
	Marie Françoise	Ls. Boulotte	1813
	Michel Vital		
	Antoine		
	Le même	M. Eliz.Cloutier	1795
	Marie	Pierre Morin	1820
	Jean François		
	Marc Eustache		
29	Pierre Basile(12)	M. Marg. Picard	S.F.S. 1790
30	Joseph	(17) M. Ls. Giguère	S.F. 1798
	Marie	Etn. Drouin	1820
	Marie Louise	Jean Martineau	1827
	Geneviève	J. B. Martineau	1827
	Basilisse	Pierre Canac	1831
	Emélie	Claude Dion	1840
	Marcelline	J. B. Lamothe	1844
	Abraham		
31	Jacques	(17) Marg. Létourneau	1803
	Marie Josette	Simon Hébert	1824
	Justine	Jacq. Drouin	1840
	Joseph		
	François Xavier		
32	Louis	(17) M. Cath. Dion	1807
	Scolastique	Jos. Beaucher	1831
	Adélaïde	Eustache Beaucher	S.F. 1839
	Mathile Isabelle	Frs. Beaucher	1842
	Claudine	F. X. Asselin	1851
	Olivier		

LÉTOURNEAU.

Firmin			
33 David	(17)	Christine Pepin S.Frs.1815	
34 Jean Moïse	(17)	Eliz. Jolin	S.F. 1818
Elizabeth		Hubert Pepin	S.J. 1846
Eléonore		Geo. Hélie	1848
Paul			
Léon			
Jean			
Joseph			
35 Antoine	(18)	Angé Audet	S.Chs. 1793
Benoit			
Antoine			
36 Jacques	(19)	Brigitte Morin	S.G. 1801
Brigitte		Jacq. Lainé	„ 1826
Isidore			
Pierre			
37 Michel	(19)	Cath. Morin	„ 1812
Le même		M.Julie Buteau S.F.S.1829	
Vital			
38 François	(20)	Vict. Labbé	S.L. 1815
39 Jean	(20)	M. Chs. Marcoux	
			S.F.S. 1842
40 Jean Bap-	(22)	Cécile Dorval	S.F. 1799
tiste			
Marguerite		Joachim Canac	„ 1825
Pauline		Ed. Coté	„ 1838
Jacques			
François			
Jean Baptiste			
41 Ignace	(23)	Dorothée Poulin S.F. 1804	
Dorothée		Robert Kersonne „ 1848	
Jean Baptiste			
Ignace			
42 Ambroise	(23)M.	Ls. Guion	„ 1806
Marie Scolasti-		Prisque Plante	„ 1835
que			
Marie		Frs. Pouliot	„ 1840
Marie Désanges		Pierre Giguère	„ 1859
Laurent			
Ambroise			
Marie			
François Xavier			
Joseph			
43 Pierre Noël		M. Adé Picard	
Adélaïde		Ant. Pepin S. Frs. 1829	
Le même		M. Fse. Samson	
			S.P.S. 1812
44 Joseph	(21)	Josette Veau S. Chs. 1814	
45 Antoine	(25)	M. Fse. Mercier	
			Bert. 1796
46 JeanBaptiste(25)		Marg. Émond	„ 1800
47 Joseph	(26)	Genev. Talon S.P.S. 1791	
Marie Geneviève		J. B. Duchesneau	
			S.P.S. 1822
Le même		Angé Blanchet	
			S. Tho. 1803
Emérence		Jos. Denaut S.P.S. 1822	
Archange		Chs. Gaudreau „ 1831	
48 Joseph	(26)	M. Thérèse Gamache	
			S.P.S. 1801
Geneviève		Aug. Chs. Morin	
			S.P.S. 1818
Thérèse		Ancelle Mathieu „ 1824	
Sophie		Chs. Nicole „ 1829	
Emélie		Frs. Coté „ 1829	
Tertulle		Michel Létourneau	
			S.P.S. 1836
Joseph			
49 Ignace	(27)	M. Mad. Bouchard	
			S.P.S. 1806
Michel Godfroi			
Ignace			
50 Joseph Basile(27)		Mad. Daniau	
Michel			

LÉTOURNEAU.

Le même		M. Brigitte Coulombe	
			S.P.S. 1821
51 Antoine	(28)	M. Jos. Morin „ 1807	
Marie		Jos. Picard „ 1827	
Marie Rosalie		Ed. Talbot „ 1830	
Françoise		Ls. Geo. Gagné „ 1838	
Pierre			
Antoine			
52 Michel Vital (28)		Marg. Chartier	
			S.F.S. 1809
53 JeanFrançois(28)		Fse. Picard S.P.S. 1820	
54 Marc	(28)	M. Cath. Gagné „ 1820	
Eustache			
55 Abraham	(30)	Véneranda Drouin	
			S.F. 1827
Julie		J. B. Létourneau „ 1851	
Domitille		Frs. Descombes „ 1855	
Théotiste		Frs. Vaillancour „ 1858	
Abraham			
Vital			
56 François	(31)	Marie Drouin „ 1832	
Xavier			
Justine		Evariste Asselin „ 1860	
Julie		Pierre Asselin „ 1860	
François Xavier			
57 Joseph	(31)	Justine Prémont „ 1852	
58 Firmin	(32)	Martine Paradis „ 1851	
59 Olivier	(32)	Cécile Létourneau	
			S.F. 1855
60 Jean	(34)	Théotiste Helie „ 1850	
61 Paul	(34)	Delimna Blouin S.J. 1861	
62 Joseph	(34)	Caroline Pepin S.Frs. 1861	
63 Léon	(34)	Célina Gagnon S.J. 1863	
64 Louis	(34)	Philomène Poulin „ 1865	
65 Antoine	(35)	Angèle Catellier	
			S.M. 1842
66 Benoit	(35)	M. Genev. Leclaire	
			S. Chs. 1825
Benoit			
Le même		Louise Poiré, Lévis 1833	
67 Isidore	(36)	Archange Lebrun	
			S.G. 1822
68 Pierre	(36)	Fse. Dussaut „ 1825	
69 Vital	(37)	Cécile Chrétien	
			S. Chs. 1863
70 JeanBaptiste(40)		Fse. Canac S.F. 1825	
Marie Françoise		Frs. Gosselin „ 1850	
Philomène		Jacq. Faucher „ 1857	
Pierre			
Jean Baptiste			
Joachim			
François Xavier			
Joseph			
71 François	(40)	Apolline Canac „ 1829	
72 Michel	(50)	Tertulle Létourneau	
			S.P.S. 1836
74 Jacques	(40)	Marcelline Vaillancour	
			S.F. 1834
75 Ignace	(41)	Scolastique Prémont	
			S.F. 1832
Adelaïde		Jos. Faucher „ 1855	
Cécile		Olivier Létourneau	
			S.F. 1855
Scolastique		Pierre Paradis „ 1856	
Marie Elizabeth		Jos. Létourneau „ 1862	
Justine		Pierre Audet „ 1862	
Marie Anastasie		Pre. Octave Paradis	
			S.F. 1867
Marie Virginie		Frs. Nap. Paradis	
			S.P. 1866
Ignace			
76 JeanBaptiste(41)		Susanne Nadeau S.F. 1835	
77 Ambroise	(42)	Archange Paradis	
			S.P. 1831
78 Laurent	(42)	Genev. Goulet „ 1841	
79 Joseph	(42)	Mad. Genest S.J. 1841	

LÉTOURNEAU.

80 Moïse	(42)	Amélie Audet	S.F.1843
Marie Malvina		F. X. Giguère	„ 1866
Doméris		Alexis Guay	„ 1867
81 François Xa-	(42)	Flavie Montigny	S.P.1854
vier			
82 Joseph	(48)	M. Brigitte Kéroack	S.P.S.1828
83 Ignace	(49)	Emérentienne Corriveau	S.V.1839
84 Michel God-	(49)	Genev. Théotiste Buteau	S.F.S.1835
froi			
85 Antoine	(51)	Cath. Morin	„ 1839
86 Pierre	(51)	Eléonore Gagné	S.P.S.1839
87 Abraham	(55)	Justine Beaucher	S.F.1856
88 Vital	(55)	Appolline Vaillancour	S.F.1864
89 François Xa-	(56)	Philomène Giguère	S.F.1858
vier			
90 Benoit	(66)	Emérentienne Bégin	B.1852
91 Pierre	(70)	Anastasie Drouin	S.F.1846
92 JeanBaptiste	(70)	Julie Létourneau	„ 1851
93 François Xa-	(70)	Philomène Beaucher	S.F.1857
vier			
94 Joseph	(70)	M. Eliz. Létourneau	S.F.1862
95 Joachim	(70)	Célina Asselin	„ 1867
96 Ignace	(76)	Philomène Poulin	„ 1862

LIS—LISLE.

1 Zacharie		Eliz. Maranda	Qué.1673
Jeanne		Michel Molleur	B.1703
Marguerite		Ls. Nollet	„ 1710
Marie Anne		Pierre Drapeau	„ 1713
Marie Thérèse		Gab. Davenne	Lévis 1697
Jacques			
2 Jacques	(1)	M. Fse. Charet	S.P.1718
Marie		Gab. Duquet	B.1739
Marie		2° René Hardy	S.Chs.1761
Marguerite		J. B. Larrivé	B.1745
Marie Louise		Etn. Gontier	„ 1746
Marie Anne		Frs. Gosselin	„ 1746
Marie Josette		Frs. Gontier	„ 1747
Françoise		Joachim Bernier	„ 1754
Jacques			
3 Jacques	(2)	M. Ls. Larrivé	B.1753

LOIGNON.

1 Pierre		Fse. Roussin	Qué.1652
Anne		Jos. Charet	S.F.1676
Anne		2° Ant. Pouliot	S.P.1685
Françoise		Pierre Roberge	S.F.1679
Catherine		Etn. Drouin	„ 1682
Charles			
2 Charles	(1)	M. Mad. Mousset	„ 1695
Pierre			
Le même		M. Marg.Roulois	C.R.1701
Marguerite		Simon L'heureux	S.F.1722
Catherine		Ant. Canac	„ 1726
Madeleine		Etn. Chamberlan	„ 1731
Charles			
Jean Baptiste			
Le même		Marie Bilodeau	S.F.1734
3 Pierre	(2)	M. Mad. Guion	„ 1724
4 Charles	(2)	M.Marthe Deblois	„ 1732
Marthe		Chs. Loiseau	„ 1751
Marthe		2° Jos. Beaucher	„ 1758
5 Jean Baptiste	(2)	Angé. Létourneau	„ 1743
Marie Angélique		Ls. Guion	„ 1776
Charles			
Augustin			
Pierre			
Joseph			
6 Charles	(5)	Pierre Desmoliers	S.F.1774
Marie		Frs. Drouin	„ 1804
Marie Madeleine		Ls. Noël	„ 1814

LOIGNON.

Charles			
7 Pierre	(5)	Mad. Rouleau	S.P.1809
8 Joseph	(5)	M. Anne Demeule	S.J.1778
Marie Françoise		J. B. Drouin	„ 1819
Jean Baptiste			
9 Augustin	(5)	M. Ls. Dumont	S.F.1800
10 Charles	(6)	M. Jos. Drouin	„ 1901
Luce		Ls. Lamothe	„ 1824
11 Jean Baptiste	(8)	M. Rose Asselin	„ 1806
Marie Henriette		Jacq. Guérard	„ 1829
Adelaïde		Magl. Savoie	„ 1829
Catherine		Geo. Laurent	„ 1830
Le même		M. Jos. Pepin	„ 1815

LOISEAU.

1 Charles		Genev. Simon	S.F.1729
Charles			
Le même		Marie Deblois	„ 1746
Angélique		Etn. Drouin	„ 1768
Angélique		2° Ls. Poulin	„ 1794
2 Charles	(1)	Marthe Loignon	„ 1751
Marie Abondante		Frs. Asselin	„ 1775
3 Charles	(2)	Thérèse Cornelier	„ 1792

LOUINEAU.

1 Pierre		Marie Préval	S.F.1678
Pierre			
André			
Henri			
2 Pierre	(1)	Apolline Bisson	Qué.1699
Marie Anne		Nicolas Patouel	„ 1723
Jean Baptiste			
3 André	(1)	Suzanne Savaria	„ 1713
4 Henri	(1)	M. Ls. Lambert	„ 1714
5 Jean Baptiste	(2)	M. Ls Mathé	„ 1725
6 Henri		Hélène Chiasson	
Madeleine		Pierre Colin	S.F.S.1758
Marie Anne		Henri Jacques	„ 1765
Geneviève		J. B. Gagné	„ 1766
Louis			
7 Louis Marie	(6)	M. Jos. Jacques	„ 1765
Marie Margue-		Pierre Quemeneur	„ 1787
rite			
Jacques			
Louis			
8 Louis		Josette Henri	
Pierre			
9 Louis	(7)	Genev. Nicole	S.F.S. 1787
Marie		J. B. Fortier	S.V. 1837
Joseph			
Louis			
Michel			
10 Jacques	(7)	M. Anne Gaudin	S.G. 1802
Amélie		Jean Labelle	S.V. 1828
Marie Luce		Pierre Deschamps	„ 1840
Catherine		Frs. Ducourbereau	„ 1848
Joseph			
11 Pierre	(8)	Félicité Gaudin	S.V. 1797
Le même		M. Olive Côté	S.F.S. 1806
Marie Olive		Pierre Jolin	S.V. 1826
12 Louis		Genev. Morin	
Brigitte		Jos. Charron	S.V. 1827
13 Michel	(9)	Agathe Charron	S.G. 1830
14 Joseph	(9)	M. Olive Guichard	S.V. 1833
15 Louis	(9)	Marg. Fortier	„ 1837
16 Joseph	(10)	M. Osité Fradet	„ 1841
17 Pierre		M. Chs. Gagnon	
Le même		M. Eudémie Lacroix	S.V. 1851

MAILLOU.

1 Jacques		Claire Armand
Pierre		
Michel		

MAILLOU.

2 Pierre	Anne Delaunay Que. 1661		
Noël			
3 Michel	(1) Jeanne Mercier		
Anne	Nic. Coulombe	B.	1694
Anne	2° René Adam	B.	1696
Anne	3° Jean Frs. Lemoine		
		B.	1718
Marie Anne	Pierre Dubois	B.	1699
Jeanne	J. B. Balan	B.	1699
Françoise	Nic. Filteau	B.	1699
4 Noël	(2) Louise Marcoux		
		Beauport 1690	
Jean Baptiste			
Noël			
5 Jean Baptiste	(4) Genev. Chevalier		
		Beauport 1727	
Jean Baptiste			
6 Noël	(4) Charlotte Chevalier		
		Beauport	
Marie Charlotte	Ls. Vallée Beauport 1761		
Charles			
7 Jean Baptiste	(5) M. Agathe Boulet S. V. 1772		
	V. de Jacq. Marseau		
8 Charles	(6) M. Angé Rodrigue		
		Beauport 1754	
Michel			
9 Michel	(8) Louise Dufresne		
		Beauport 1778	
Le même	Euphrosine Simart		
		S. Anne 1817	
Michel			
10 Michel	(9) M. Sophie Martineau		
		S. Frs. 1800	

MAINDEL.

1 François	Fse. Hurteau	S. Malo	
François			
2 François	(1) Marg. Roy	S. M. 1827	
Marguerite	Jos. Dion	S. M. 1847	
Marie Marthe	Magl. Hamel	" 1849	

MALBŒUF.

1 Jean Baptiste	Marg. Picard		
		Cap S. Ign. 1692	
Marguerite	René Bolduc	C. R. 1717	
Joseph			
Augustin			
Noël			
Le même	Marie Renaud	C. R. 1703	
Marie Agnès	Jos. Cochon	" 1729	
Jacques			
2 Augustin	(1) Agnès Mercier		
Marie Marthe	Barth. Gagné S. P. S. 1750		
Angélique	Pierre Chevanel	" 1757	
Jean Baptiste			
3 Joseph	(1) Mad. Gagné	C. R. 1721	
Dorothée	Frs. Morin	" 1749	
Joseph			
4 Noël	(1) Marg. Quessy		
Françoise	Jean Cyr	S. P. S. 1761	
Pierre Noël			
Jacques François			
Jean Baptiste			
5 Jacques	(1) M. Genev. Huret		
		S. P. S. 1750	
6 Pierre	Jeanne Moyen		
Benjamin			
Le même	M. Anne Fontaine		
		S. P. S. 1750	
7 Jean Baptiste (2)	Cloutier	" 1748	
8 Joseph	(3) Reine Morin	" 1750	
9 Jean François (4)	M. Jeanne Mercier		
		S. F. S. 1750	
10 Jean Baptiste (4)	M. Jos. Morin S. P. S. 1752		

MALBŒUF.

Josette	Ambr. Gagné	S. H.	1773
Le même	Genev. Fournier		
		S. P. S.	1758
11 Pierre Noël	(4) Marg. Fontaine	"	1761
12 Benjamin	(6) M. Marthe Fontaine		
		S. P. S.	1787

MANSEAU.

1 Jacques	Marg. Latouche Que.		1673
Marie	Chs. Delage	S. L.	1697
Marguerite	Jos. Godbout	S. L.	1700
Françoise	André Pouliot	S. L.	1703
Angélique	Michel Fortier	S. L.	1706
Charles			
François			
Jacques			
Joseph-Alias			
Jean			
2 Charles	(1) Marianne Ioane S. L.		1701
3 François	(1) Marg. Pouliot	S. L.	1706
Le même	M. Anne Guion S. Frs. 1718		
Jean Baptiste			
4 Joseph-Alias			
Jean	Marie Ouimet	S. J.	1713
5 Jacques	(1) M. Jos. Lajoue S. L.		1716
6 Jean Baptiste (3)	Josette Godbout S. P.		1751

MARANDA

1 Jean	Jeanne Cousin Que.		1677
Jeanne	Julien Brulé Que.		1680
Jeanne	2° Jean Boilard Que.		1673
Elisabeth	Zacharie Lis B.		1718
Elisabeth	2° Pierre Molleur S. P.		1682
Marie	J. B. Hallé		
Michel			
Jean Baptiste			
Jean			
Charles			
2 Michel	(1) Marie Jeannes Que.		1685
Susanne	Jean Valière	S. P.	1707
Madeleine	Joachim Vautour S. P. 1712		
Geneviève	Jos. Dubord	S. P.	1719
Marthe	J. B. Asselin	S. P.	1724
Héléne	Pierre Noël Morin		
		S. P.	1731
Joseph			
3 Jean	(1) Marie Paradis	S. P.	1688
Marie Louise	Frs. Nollet	Qué.	1711
Marie Louise	2° Pierre Monciau		
		Sault au Récolet 1739	
Gabriel			
Jean			
Pierre			
Le même	Genev. Sureau	S. L.	1703
Héléne	Jacq. Baudon	Qué.	1722
Le même	Anne Jousselot Chs.		
		Bourg.	1712
4 Charles	(1) Denise Fiset	A. G.	1695
Charlotte	Pierre Cadoret	S. L.	1720
Madeleine	Jos. Lavigne	S. L.	1743
Joseph			
Charles			
5 Jean Baptiste (1)	Angé Duquet Qué.		1698
6 Joseph	(2) Fse. Crépeau	S. L.	1734
7 Pierre	(3) Fse. Rageot Chs.		
		Bourg.	1717
8 Jean	(3) Marg. Guilbaut Chs-		
		Bourg.	1717
9 Gabriel	(3) M. Ls. Lavoie Qué.		1728
10 Joseph	(4) Eliz. Roberge	S. P.	1726
Geneviève	Michel Morin	S. L.	1750
Françoise	Jean Bouffart	"	1756
Marie Anne	J. B. Griaut-Larivière		
		S. L.	1759
Isabelle	Amable Gosselin	"	1765

MARANDA.

	Charles			
11	Charles	Marg. Fagot Lévis		1739
	Josette	Pierre Drapeau Lévis		1776
	Ignace			
	Charles	(10) Cécile Leclaire	S. L.	1763
	Cécile	Etn. Morin	"	1785
	Françoise	J. B. Girard	"	1796
	Charlotte	Ant. Grenier	"	1796
	Véronique	Ign. Bouffart	"	1798
	Charles			
13	Ignace	(11) Marg. Drapeau Lévis		1776
	Ignace			
	Charles			
14	Charles	(12) Marie Baudoin S Frs.		1799
	Marie	Jos. Delisle	S. L.	1829
	Justine	Olivier Noël	"	1834
	Charles			
	Pierre			
	Joseph			
	François			
	Edouard			
	Félix			
15	Ignace	(13) Angé Bourassa Lévis		1817
	Marie	Pierre Turgeon	B.	1855
16	Joseph	(14) Fse Dupile	S. P.	1822
	Henriette	Frs. Quemeneur	S. P.	1844
	Joseph			
	Le même	M. Anne Plante	S.P.	1829
17	Charles	(14) Marg. Dupile	"	1824
	Hombeline	Ls. Célestin Pichet	S. P.	1864
	Charles Alfred			
18	Pierre	(14) Mad. Plante	S. P.	1830
	Rose de Lima	Magl. Turcot	S. J.	1855
19	Félix	(14) Emelie Delisle	S. L.	1839
20	François	(14) Marg. Delisle	"	1831
	Marie Sara	Ed. Guay	"	1855
	Hombéline	Hubert Guay	"	1855
	Sophie	Ls. Audet	"	1859
	François			
	Joseph			
	Jean Baptiste			
21	Edouard	(14) Marie Lemelin	S. L.	1833
	Edouard			
	Jean			
	François			
	Narcisse			
22	Joseph	(16) M. Agathe Plante	S.P.	1847
	Le même	M. Jos. Langlois	"	1851
23	Charles	(17) M. Delphine Ferlant		
	Alfred		S. P.	1856
24	François	(20) Esther Defoi	S. L.	1860
	Le même	Marcelline Leclaire	S. Isidore	1872
25	Joseph	(20) Agnès Denis	S.L.	1865
	Le même	Clarisse Coté	S.Claire	1867
26	JeanBaptiste	(20) Flavie Gosselin	S. L.	1869
27	Edouard	(21) Joséphine Audet	S.L.	1865
28	François	(21) M.Delphine Ruel	"	1867
	Narcisse			
29	Jean	(21) M. Mathilde Coulombe	S.L.	1875
	Charles	(13) M. Anne Coté	S.H.	1820

MARCOUX.

1	Pierre	Marthe Rainville	Qué.	1662
	Noël			
	Jean Baptiste			
	André			
2	André	MarieParantBeauport		1686
	Le même	M.Mad.Lenormand		1715
	Le même	M.Mad. Amelot		1721
	Marguerite	Etn. Turgeon	B.	1759

18—26

MARCOUX.

	Catherine	Nicolas Parant Beauport		1750
3	Jean Baptiste	(1) Mad. Magnan	Chs. Bourg.	1684
	Jean			
	Joseph			
4	Noël	(1) Marg. Chapleau	Qué.	1698
	Le même	Marg. Coté	Beauport	1701
	Le même	Jeanne Baugy	"	1710
	Pierre			
	Jean			
5	Jean	(3) M. Angé Miville	"	1724
	Jean			
6	Joseph	(3) Eliz. Toupin	"	1730
	Marie Angélique	Pierre Jos. Marseau	S.F.S.	1759
	Geneviève	Frs. Baudoin	S.M.	1765
	Michel Marie	Ordonnée en 1757		
	Antoine			
	Joseph			
7	Noël	Marg. Bélanger Beauport		
	Louise	Guill Lemieux	Bert	1749
	Jean François			
	Alexandre			
8	Denis	Marg. Bélanger		
	François			
A	Germain	Genev. Marchand		
	Pierre			
9	Jean	(4) Angé Maheu Beauport		1740
	Etienne			
10	Pierre	(4) Véronique Trenier	Beauport	1752
	Basile			
11	Jean	(5) M. Apolline Mercier	Bert	1748
	Marie Louise	Cyriac Soucy	"	1786
	Joseph			
	Jean Baptiste			
12	Joseph	(6) Genev. Laurent	Beauport	1750
	Marguerite	Jos. Viger	S.Chs.	1779
13	Antoine	(6) Marg. Bourgot	Bert	1758
	Le même	Marie Vermet	Bert	1765
14	Jean François	(7) M. Jos. Lemieux	"	1749
	Marie Josette	Jos. Savoie	"	1773
	Marguerite	Lazare Buteau	"	1780
	Marie Francoise	Ant. Vuel	"	1780
	Marie Francoise	2e Jérome Paré	"	1793
	Marie Elizabeth	J. B. Bilodeau	"	1783
	Marie Anne	Andre Tangue	"	1791
	Marie Thérèse	Jos. Charbonneau	"	1808
15	Louis Alexandre	M.Thècle Mercier	"	1753
	Marie Thècle	Ant. Rousseau	S.M.	1775
	Marie Madeleine	Ls. Lainé	"	1778
	Marie Angélique	Jos. Gagnon	"	1791
	Jean Baptiste			
	Michel			
	Marc			
	Antoine			
	Alexandre			
16	François	M. Mad. Cochon	S.M.	1768
	Marie	Ant. Coté	S.G.	1802
	Michel			
	François			
17	Etienne	(9) M.Ls.Lortie Beauport		1777
			S.Marie	
	Joseph			
	François			
18	Basile	(10) Agathe Roberge	S.P.	1785
19	Pierre	(8)A Genev. Lepage	Que.	1754
			Quebec	
	Pierre			
20	JeanBaptiste	(11) M. Anne Pepin	S.F.S.	1776
	Madeleine	Pierre Lacroix	"	1817
	Marie	Pierre Martineau	"	1823

MARCOUX.

	Charlotte	Romain Quemeneur	S.F.S.	1826
	Charlotte	2⁰Jean Létourneau	"	1842
	Noël			
	Antoine			
21	Joseph	(11) M. Chs.Couture	S.Chs.	1784
	Marguerite	Ls. Fortier	Bert.	1805
	Marie	Frs. Blais	"	1808
	Marie Charlotte	Jacq. Quirouet	"	1808
	Geneviève	J.B.Blais	"	1813
	Thècle	Laurent Boucher	"	1817
22	JeanBaptiste(15)	Fse. Gagnon	S.M.	1788
	François			
	Jean Baptiste			
	Simon			
	Pierre			
	Le même	M. Jos. Dalaire	S.M.	1814
23	Marc (15)	M.AnneTangué	S.Chs.	1788
	Marie Madeleine	Ls. Pepin	"	1811
	Marie Victoire	Michel Asselin	"	1812
	Marguerite	J. B. Chabot	"	1813
	Angèle	Pierre Bacquet	"	1818
	Marie	Thomas Paré	"	1825
	Anastasie	Flavien Roy	S.Chs.	1831
	Alexandre			
	Charles			
	Pierre			
	Marc			
	Ambroise			
	Bénoni			
24	Alexandre	(15) Fse. Fortier	S.F.S.	1783
	Elisabeth	J. B. Martel	S.Chs.	1816
	Alexandre			
	Laurent			
	Isaac			
25	Michel	(15) Marthe Larrivé	S.Chs.	1788
26	Antoine	(15) Genev.Nadeau	S. Chs.	1795
			S. H.	
	Geneviève	Jean Coté	S.G.	1821
	Angèlique	Frs. Bilodeau	S.G.	1830
	François			
27	François	(16) Fse. Valière	S.G.	1812
			S. Claire	
	Jean			
	Edouard			
28	Michel	(16) Susanne Plante	S.Chs.	1806
	Susanne	Ezechiel Nolin	S.Chs.	1824
	Marie Reine	Michel Genest	S.Chs.	1832
	Françoise	Jos. Pouliot	S.Chs.	1838
	Jean			
	Le même	Barbe Cochon	S.Chs.	1832
	Célina	Benj. Naud	S.Chs.	1851
29	Joseph	(17) Cécile Cantin	S.P.	1815
	Symphorienne	Frs. Boutin	S.P.	1852
	Eléonore	Ant. Boutin	S.P.	1864
30	François	(17) Marg. Drouin	S.F.	1827
31	Pierre	(19) M. Anne Dunière	Bert.	1783
32	Antoine	(20) M. Adé Minville	S.P.S.	1820
33	Noël	(20) M. Adé Danison	S.F.S.	1840
34	Jean Baptiste	(22) Julie Couillard	S.M.	1809
	Julie	Jos. Noël	S.M.	1833
35	Simon	(22) Rosalie Roy	S.G.	1812
	Marie Josette	Pierre Coté	S.M.	1832
	Euphrosine	Ls. Coüet	S.M.	1843
	Eléonore	Mag. Lemelin	S.M.	1844
	Claire	Ls. Marcoux	S.M.	1844
	Simon			
	Alcier			
	Nazaire			

MARCOUX.

36	Pierre	(22) M. Délima Boutillet	S.G.	1819
37	François	(22) M. Anne Métivier	S.M.	1824
38	Pierre	Angé Benoit		
	Marie	Pierre Lecours	S.Chs.	1836
39	Louis	Angèle Couture		
	Angèle	Jean Métayer	S.J.	1841
	Elisabeth	Frs. Noël	S.J.	1841
	Louis			
40	Alexandre	(23) Angèle Couture	S.Chs.	1815
41	Pierre	(23) Thérèse Gosselin	S.Chs.	1815
	Emélie	Chs. Tangué	S.Chs.	1848
	Emélie	2⁰ Jos. Bonneau	S.Chs.	1862
	Marie	Damase Filteau	S.Chs.	1858
	Jean Baptiste			
	Etienne			
42	Marc	(23) Marg. Bernier	S.Chs.	1819
	Marie	Jos. Baudoin	S.Chs.	1847
	Hélène	Laurent Chabot	S.Chs.	1838
43	Bénoni	(23) Cécile Roy	S.M.	1827
	Le même	Justine Chabot	S.Chs.	1831
	Marie Célina	Jos. Naud	S.Chs.	1853
44	Ambroise	(23) Angèle Nadeau	S.G.	1828
	Angèle	Octave Carrier	S.Chs.	1852
	Marguerite	Jos. Chabot	S.Chs.	1855
	Marie	Cyrille Plante	S.Chs.	1859
45	Charles	(23) M. Désanges Fournier	S.Chs.	1843
46	Alexandre	(24) M. Anne Gagnon	S.Chs.	1809
	Louis			
	Isaac			
	Edouard			
	Joseph			
	Le même	Eliz. Gosselin	S.Chs.	1835
47	Laurent	(24) M.Thécle Cochon	S J.	1818
	Le même	Euphrosine Coulombe	S.J.	1825
48	Isaac	(24) Julie Aubin, Lévis		1822
49	François	(26) Charlotte Quéret	S.G.	1826
50	Jean	(27) Rosalie Gourdeau	S.P.	1843
51	Edouard	(27) Emélie Langlois	S.P.	1842
	Emélie Célina	Jean Pichet	S.P.	1866
	Georges			
52	Jean	(28) Hermine Turgeon	B.	1843
	Marie Hérosias	Ls. Dalaire	S.Chs.	1863
53	Simon	(35) Cécile Bacquet	S.M.	1839
	Simon Néré			
54	Alcier	(35) Lo⸗ise Tangué	S.M.	1840
	Le même	M. Ls. Cookson	S.M.	1854
55	Nazaire	(35) Eliz. Coüet	S.M.	1842
56	Louis	(39) Marie Coulombe	S.J.	1850
57	Jean Baptiste	(41) Célanire Gosselin	S.Chs.	1858
58	Etienne	(41) Marie Paquet	S.Chs.	1863
59	Louis	(46) Claire Marcoux	S.M.	1844
60	Isaac	(46) Emélie Dion	S.M.	1846
61	Edouard	(46) Eliz. Blais	S.Chs.	1853
62	Joseph	(46) Marie Fauchon	"	1857
63	Georges	(51) Rose Métayer	S P.	1859
64	Simon Néré	(53) M. Belzémire Lacroix	S.M.	1865

MARSEAU.

1	François	M. Ls. Bolper	S.F.	1671
	Reine	Jos. Roger	S.Frs.	1694
	Susanne	Jean Cojean	S.J.	1699
	Jacques			
	Louis			

MARSEAU.

2	Jacques	(1)	Eliz. Ginchereau		
				S.Frs.	1694
	Marie		Pierre Gautron	S.V.	1720
	Marie Marthe		Pierre Cadrin	"	1727
	Brigitte		Ls. David Roy	"	1739
	François				
	Jacques				
	Augustin				
	Louis				
3	Louis	(1)	Jeanne Dumas		1697
	Dorothée		Pierre Coté	S.Frs.	1720
	Marie Marthe		Ls. Asselin	S.Frs.	1728
	Marie Josette		Ls. Bastien Dalaire		
				S.Frs.	1729
	Marie Josette		2° J. B. Lefebvre	"	1730
	Marie Jeanne		Jean Gagnon	. "	1731
	Jean				
	Antoine				
	Augustin				
4	François	(2)	M. Fse. Baudoin Bert.		1721
	Jean Baptiste				
5	Jacques	(2)	Marg. Baudoin Bert.		1730
	Marie		René Pelchat	S.V.	1763
	Pierre Joseph				
	Paul				
	Le même		Agathe Boulet S.F.S.		1751
	Marie Marthe		Jos. Cochon	"	1783
	Jean Bernard				
6	Augustin	(2)	Marg. Corriveau S.V.		1737
	Marguerite		Jos. Gosselin	"	1762
	Marie Genev.		Athanase Roy	"	1762
	Marie Françoise		Ant. Vallée	"	1767
	Augustin				
	Joseph				
7	Louis	(2)	Marie Labbé	B.	1747
	Marie		Ls. Gontier	S.Chs.	1777
	Marie Anne		Pierre Memaux	"	1780
8	Jean	(3)	Mad. Lepage	S.Frs.	1753
	Madeleine		Frs. Dupont	"	1758
	Elisabeth		Pierre Bourque S.F.S.		1772
	Elisabeth		2° Aug. Gaudin	"	1783
	Jean				
	Augustin				
9	Antoine	(3)	Mad. Gagné	S.Frs.	1731
	Madeleine		Jos. Labbé	"	1762
	Marie Louise		Jos. Dalaire	"	1774
	Marie Thècle		Jean Marie Thivierge		
				S.Frs.	1783
	Marie Thècle		2° J. B. Charlan S.F.		1810
			V. deFélicité Dion		
	Ignace				
	Louis				
	Antoine				
	Augustin				
	Joseph				
10	Augustin	(3)	Fse. Asselin	S.Frs.	1737
	Le même		M. Jos. Gagné	"	1768
	Marie		Dominique Lhortie		
				S.J.	1789
	Le même		M. Mad. Drouin S.F.		1775
11	Louis		Mad. Fontaine		
12	Jean Baptiste	(4)	M. Jos. Boissonneau		
				S.F.S.	1758
	Marie Barbe		Laurent Roy	S.V.	1786
	Marie Josette		Frs. Brochu	"	1788
	Marie Françoise		Laurent Roy	"	1791
	Marie Ursule		J. B. Boutin	"	1796
	Marie Ursule		2° J. B. Thibaut	"	1810
	Marie Rose		Paul Boutin	"	1798
	Marie Agathe		Jos. Dion	"	1808
	Marguerite		Ls. Vermet	Bert.	1787
	François				
	Jean Baptiste				
	Jacques				
13	Pierre Joseph	(5)	M. Angé Marcoux		
				S.F.S.	1759

18—26½

MARSEAU.

	Marie Thérèse		Pierre Bolduc	S.M.	1797
	Marie Thérèse		2° Pierre Lavoie	S.V.	1810
	Joseph				
	François				
	Le même		M. Anne Cadrin S.M.		1802
14	Paul	(5)	Marie Pouliot	S.V.	1767
	Marie		André Fleury	"	1794
	Marie Charlotte		Ls. Tangué	"	1801
	Paul				
	Joseph				
	Jacques				
15	Jean Bernard	(5)	Genev. Quéret	S.V.	1792
	Marie Anne		Ign. Clément	S.G.	1812
	Geneviève		Chs. Turgeon	Lévis	1824
	Ursule		Frs. Dalaire	"	1830
	Louis				
16	Augustin	(6)	Marg. Gautron	S.V.	1765
	Marguerite		Jos. Denis	"	1782
	Le même		M. Céleste Malboeuf		
				S. Tho.	1723
	Marie Rose		Chs. Maillou	S.V.	1792
	Marie Apolline		Ls. Morisset	"	1797
	Marie Victoire		Michel Dessaint	"	1801
	Marie Victoire		2° Jean Frs. Lemieux		
				S.F.S.	1843
	Marie Louise		Frs. Goulet	S.V.	1804
	Catherine		J. B. Ruel	"	1809
	Marie Lucie		Frs. Gautron	"	1818
	Antoine				
	Edouard				
	Etienne				
	Augustin				
	Bernard				
17	Joseph	(6)	Louise Julienne Mercier		
				S.F.S.	1775
	Marguerite		J. B. Boivin	"	1797
	Ursule		Germ. Morin	"	1806
	Françoise		Chs. Dandurand	"	1808
	Joseph				
	Marie				
18	Joseph	(8)	Cath. Canac	S.F.	1758
	Catherine		Aug. Emond	S.J.	1794
	Marie		Jos. Gendreau	"	1796
	Marie		2° Michel Corriveau		
				S.L.	1829
	Joseph				
	Jean				
19	Augustin	(8)	Genev. Blouin		
	Marie Geneviève		Laurent Jahan	S.J.	1780
	Le même		M. Ls. Turcot		1783
20	Antoine	(9)	M. Jos. Blais	S.F.S.	1755
	Marie Anne		Jos. Fortier	"	1776
	Marie An e		Jos. Fradet	"	1790
	Françoise		Noël Dupont	"	1781
	Françoise		2° Chrysostôme Arbour		
				S.F.S.	1808
	Antoine				
	Louis				
	Jacques				
	Michel				
	Le même		M. Mad. Quemeneur		
				S.F.S.	1770
	Marie Madeleine		Jos. Dumas	"	1792
	Marie Margue-rite		Frs. Campagna	"	1795
	Marie Josette		J. B. Harnais	"	1810
	Joseph				
21	Louis	(9)	M. Ls. Goupy	S.M.	1763
	Marie Françoise		Jean Penin	S.F.S.	1797
22	Joseph	(9)	Reine Morin	S.F.S.	1786
23	Joseph	(9)	Vict. Morin	"	1774
	Victoire		Pierre Huot	S.L.	1806
			V. Marg. Couture		
	Marie Madeleine		Frs. Forgue	S. Frs.	1815
	Catherine		Frs. Bigaouette	"	1824
	Antoine				

MARSEAU.

24	Jean	(*)	Félicité Rouleau	S.F. 1766
25	JeanBaptiste(12)		M. Angé Roy	S.V. 1787
	Marguerite		Gab. Duquet	S.M. 1814
	Jean Baptiste			
	Augustin			
26	François	(12)	M. Chs. Bazin	S.V. 1798
	Pierre			
27	Jacques	(12)	M. Jos. Roy	S.G. 1808
	Jacques			
28	Joseph	(13)	Eliz. Paquet	S.M. 1785
	Marguerite		Frs. Mercier	" 1809
	Elizabeth		Philippe Richard	" 1810
	Archange		Jos. Roy	" 1814
	Angélique		Jos. Lemelin	" 1822
	Joseph			
	Paul			
29	Françoise	(13)	M. Mad. Fortin	" 1800
30	Paul	(14)	M. Ls. Bolduc	S.V. 1797
	Marie Louise		J. B. Tangué	" 1821
	Marie Ursule		Ant. McNeil	" 1823
	Flavie		Pierre Parant	" 1825
	Marie Marguerite		Ls. Corriveau	" 1827
	Marie Olive		M. Rémillard	" 1829
31	Joseph	(14)	M. Mad. Blondeau	" 1802
	Madeleine		Frs. Durand	" 1826
32	Jacques	(14)	Marg. Rémillard	" 1805
	Apolline		J. B. Aubé	" 1838
	Antoine			
	Joseph			
33	Louis	(15)	Marie Nadeau	Lévis 1837
34	Augustin	(16)	M. Jos. Bolduc	S.V. 1797
	Bernard			
	Marguerite		Prisque Catellier	" 1824
	Henriette		J. B. Aubé	" 1827
	Marie		F. X. Harpe	" 1830
	Hilaire			
	Augustin			
	Michel			
35	Etienne		Louise Ainse	S.G. 1823
36	Antoine	(16)	Marg. Martineau	S.M. 1802
	Séraphine		Aug. Marseau	S.V. 1837
	Adrien			
37	Edouard	(16)	Marg. Lemieux	" 1818
	Damase			
	Le même		Mad. Couture	B. 1847
38	Joseph	(17)	Marg. Paré	S.V. 1805
	Marguerite		Laurent Gagnon	" 1828
	Geneviève		Pierre Guilmet	" 1836
	Antoine			
	Joseph			
	Le même		Genev. Jolin	" 1822
	Reine Désanges		Aug. Naz. Harpe	" 1866
	François			
39	Pierre	(17)	Marg. Morin	S.F.S. 1806
	Flavie		Abraham Paré	S.V. 1827
40	Michel		Mad. Roy	
	Madeleine		Frs. Gontier	S.G. 1826
41	Joseph	(18)	Cath. Plante	S.J. 1796
	Marie Louise		Frs. Campagna	S. Frs. 1825
	Marie		Jos. Emond	" 1831
	Emélie		Jean Blouin	" 1843
	Flavien			
	Basile			
	Etienne			
	Pierre			
42	Jean	(18)	Ursule Paquet	S.J. 1809
	Joseph			
	Jean			
	Louis			
	Evariste			
43	Antoine	(20)	Mad. Picard	S.F.S. 1778
44	Louis	(20)	Reine Langlois	" 1788
45	Jacques	(20)	Marie Gagné	" 1792
46	Joseph	(20)	Marg. Blais	" 1797
	Augustin			

MARSEAU.

47	Michel	(20)	M. Claire Clément	L. 1792
			V. D. Alexis Gagné	
48	Antoine	(23)	Ursule Paquet	S.J. 1803
49	JeanBaptiste(25)		M. Mar. Dupont	S.M. 1808
	Thomas			
	François			
	Jean Baptiste			
	Le même		Soulange Cadrin	" 1842
50	Augustin	(25)	M. Cath. Fradet	" 1812
	Constance		Pierre Guilmet	S.Chs. 1847
	Abraham			
	Paul			
	Jacques			
51	Pierre	(26)	Séraphine Harpe	S.V. 1822
	Elizabeth		Jean Couture	" 1861
	David			
	François Xavier			
	Ludger			
52	Jacques	(27)	Josette Blais	" 1834
53	Paul	(28)	M. Angéle Denis	S.M. 1813
	Emélie		J. B. Moumeny	" 1846
54	Joseph	(28)	M. Jos. Lémelin	" 1819
	Emélie		Jos. Mercier	" 1847
	Marie Vitaline Alexandre Launière			S.M. 1852
55	Antoine	(32)	Marie Roby	S.V. 1841
56	Joseph	(32)	M. Célina Tangué	" 1851
57	Michel	(34)	M. Angéle Tangué	" 1835
58	Augustin	(34)	Séraphine Marseau	" 1837
	Cyprien			
59	Hilaire	(34)	M. Hermine Cochon	S.V. 1835
60	Adrien	(36)	M. Emélie Audet	" 1840
	Marguerite		Luc Martineau	" 1861
	Honorine		Vital Roy	" 1865
	Delphine		Cyp. Marseau	" 1870
61	Damase	(37)	M. Julie Anna Pepin	S.M. 1848
62	Antoine	(38)	Fse. Langlois	S.V. 1842
66	Joseph	(38)	Luce Guilmet	" 1835
64	François	(38)	Reine Boivin	S.Frs. 1844
65	Etienne	(41)	Julie Lepage	" 1840
66	Pierre	(41)	Constance Gagnon	S.Frs. 1840
67	Basile	(41)	Sophie Roberge	S.F. 1840
	Philomène		F.X. Vaillancour	" 1865
	Sophie		Elzéar Bouffart	" 1867
	Bruno			
68	Flavien	(41)	Marie Picard	S.Frs. 1850
	Marie		Frs. Pouliot	
69	Joseph	(42)	M. Emélie Dion	" 1838
	Le même		Marie Campagna	" 1859
70	Louis	(42)	Hombeline Emond	" 1843
71	Evariste	(42)	Mathilde Lemelin	" 1845
72	Jean	(42)	Emérentienne Emond	S.Frs. 1850
73	Cyprien	(58)	Delphine Marseau	S.V. 1871
74	Bruno	(67)	Marie Drouin	S.F. 1869
75	Augustin	(46)	Rosalie Savard	B. 1835
76	François	(49)	Anastasie Coulombe	S.Chs. 1838
77	Thomas	(49)	Euphrosine Gautron	S.V. 1853
78	JeanBaptiste(49)		M. Clr. Daniau	S.F.S. 1838
79	Jacques	(5)A	A. Julienne Jalbert	" 1838
80	Paul	(5)A	A. Archange Turgeon	S.Chs. 1848
81	Abraham	(50)	Marg. Comeau	" 1849
82	David	(51)	Soulange Mercier	S.V. 1849
83	François Xavier	(51)	Eliz. Chabot	" 1851
84	Ludger	(51)	M. Cédulie Cochon	" 1868

MARTEL.

1	Honore	Marg. Lamireault Q. 1665		
	Joseph Alphonse			
	Paul			
	Jean François			
	Antoine			
2	Paul	(1) Mad. Guillot	S.P.	1698
3	Joseph Alph-	(1) Marg. Grosnier	S.F.	1701
	onse			
4	Antoine	(1) Cath. Guillot	S.P.	1706
	M. Anne	Martin Ratté	„	1731
	Marie Jeanne	André Ratté	„	1736
	Marie Josette	Frs. Fortier	„	1744
	Antoine			
	Ignace			
	Charles			
	Augustin			
	Jean Baptiste			
5	Jean François	(1) Mad. Levannier		
			Chs. Bourg.	1695
	Joseph			
6	Antoine	(4) M. Fse Ratté	S.P.	1732
	Marie	Basile Paquet	„	1761
	Marie Pélagie	Laurent Gosselin	„	1773
	Rose	Jos. Létourneau	„	1800
	Ignace			
7	Ignace	(4) Hélène Ratte	„	1736
	Marie	Chs. Fortier	„	1777
	Françoise	Pierre Crépeau	„	1777
	Louis			
	Ignace			
	Le même	M. Mad. Pichet	S.P.	1762
8	Charles	(4) Mad. Ratté	„	1748
9	Jean Baptiste	(4) Dorothée Fortier	S.J.	1750
10	Augustin	(4) Louise Asselin	„	1752
11	Joseph	(5) Agnés Paquet Chs.		
			Bourg	1730
	Louis			
12	Jean	Rose. Gagnon		
		Eboulements.		
	Louis			
13	Ignace	(6) M. Angé Crépeau	S.P.	1773
	Marie	Jos. Coté	„	1800
	Geneviève	Ignace Goulet	„	1814
	Josette	Jos. Gosselin	„	1826
	Angélique	Jos. Cantin	„	1837
	Antoine			
14	Jean, Jean et	Eliz. Paquet Lorette		1802
	Mad. Hamel			
	Louis	Lorette		
15	Ignace	(7) M. Reine Pichet	S.P.	1763
	Marie Reine	J. B. Thivierge	„	1788
	Charlotte	Ls. Racine	„	1803
	Le même	Marg. Baillargeon	S.L.	1766
16	Louis	(7) M. Ls. Bélanger,		
		Beauport		1774
	Marie Reine	Jean Drouin	S.F.	1813
	M. Louise	J. B. Bonneville	„	1830
	Thérèse			
	Marie	Patrice Dubois	S.P.	1832
	Ignace			
	Louis			
17	Louis	(11) M. Verret Chs. Bourg.		1773
		S. Ambroise.		
	Jean Baptiste			
18	Louis	(12) M. Marg. Nadeau	S.M.	1787
19	Antoine	(13) Angéle Chatigny	S.P.	1816
	Le même	Marg. Noël	„	1822
	Hermelande	Pierre Daniau	„	1841
	Rosalie Artémise	Chs. Honoré Roberge		
			S.P.	1861
	Jacques			
20	Louis	(14) Angéle Ruel	S.L.	1829
21	Louis	(16) Mad. Dorval	S.F.	1804
22	Ignace	(16) Rose Vaillancour	„	1808
	Magloire			
23	Jean Baptiste	(17) Eliz. Marcoux S. Chs.		1816

MARTEL.

24	Jacques	(19) Emélie Leclaire	S.P.	1849
25	Magloire	(22) Emélie Pichet	„	1839

MARTINEAU.

1	Pierre	Marie Leblond	S.F.	1691
	Véronique	Jos Deblois	S.Frs.	1724
	Véronique	2° Alexis Guerard	„	1726
	Germain			
	Jean Baptiste			
	Pierre			
	Philippe			
2	Germain	(1) Jeanne Paradis	S.F.	1718
	Angélique	Pierre Labbé	„	1746
	Jogeph			
	Augustin			
3	Pierre	(1) Genev. Labbé	S.Frs.	1718
	Geneviève	Claude Guion	„	1744
	Félicité	Jos. Guion	„	1745
	Félicité	2° Prisque Turcot	„	1759
	Thécle	Frs. Guion	„	1757
	Marie	Basile Lavoie	„	1759
	Pierre			
4	Jean Baptiste	M. Anne Dupont	„	1727
	Marie Josette	Jos. Asselin	„	1766
	Hyacinthe			
	Joseph			
	Victor			
	Augustin			
	Jean Baptiste			
5	Philippe	(1) Mad. Corriveau	S.V.	1727
6	Joseph	(2) Dorothy Drouin	S.F.	1643 1743
	Marie Dorothy	Pierre Blouin	„	1764
	Marie Louise	Jos. Marie Gagnon	„	1767
	Joseph			
7	Augustin	(2) Fse. Mercier	S.Frs.	1746
	Augustin			
	Jean Baptiste			
	Jacques			
8	Pierre	(3) Marie Bissonet	„	1746
	Madeleine	Simon Nadeau	„	1789
	Madeleine	2° Jos. Caron	„	1804
	Marie Josette	Jos. Gagné	„	1785
	Marie Louise	Frs. Plante		
	Charles			
	Pierre			
	Augustin			
	François			
	Jean Baptiste			
	Joseph			
	Le même	M. Mad. Pepin	„	1784
9	Jean Baptiste	(4) Cath. Rouleau	„	1754
	Pierre			
	Jean Baptiste			
	Pierre			
10	Augustin	(4) Félicité Rouleau	S.F.S.	1760
	Marie Félicité	Jos. Pepin	S.Frs.	1778
	Angélique	Amb. Gaulin	Qué	1785
11	Hyacinthe	(4) M. Ls. Deblois	S.Frs.	1764
12	Joseph	(4) Marie Deblois	„	1766
	Le même	M. Thérèse Racine	S.M.	1768
	Le même	M. Genev. Quemeneur		
			S.F.S.	1771
	Marguerite	Ant. Marseau	S.M.	1802
	Paul			
	Joseph			
13	Victor	(4) M. Ls. Dalaire	S.Frs.	1770
14	Joseph	(6) Thérèse Baudon	„	1778
	Thérèse	Jean Julien	S.P.	1816
	Jean			
	Joseph			
15	Augustin	(7) Monique Canac	S.F.	1770
	Augustin			
16	Jean Baptiste	(7) M. Mad. Drouin	„	1777
	Fébronie	Alexandre Beaucher		
			S.F.	1807

MARTINEAU.

Hélène	Jean Beaucher	,,	1807
Jean Baptiste			
17 Jacques	(7) Genev. Drouin	,,	1782
Geneviève	Jos. Leblond	,,	1807
Marguerite	David Asselin	,,	1811
Marie	Frs. Asselin	,,	1813
Martin			
Jacques			
Le même	M. Anne Asselin	,,	1797
18 Charles	(8) M. Anne Gagné	S.Frs.	1772
Angélique	Jacq. Roberge	S.F.	1806
Madeleine	Frs. Pichet	S.P.	1810
19 Pierre	(8) M. Ls. Gagné	S.Frs.	1775
20 Jean Baptiste	(8) M. Ls. Gagné		1781
Marie Louise	J. B. Blouin	,,	1807
Marguerite	Michel Morin	S.J.	1815
Jean			
21 Joseph	(8) M. Chs. Guion	S.Frs.	1787
22 François	(8) M. Angé Dalaire	S.J.	1789
23 Augustin	(8) M.Jos. Lheureux	S.F.	1796
24 Jean Baptiste	(9) Reine Blais	S.P.S.	1783
Reine	Frs. Girard	S.F.S.	1803
Le même	Françoise Paré	,,	1786
Jean Baptiste			
Le même	Vict. Morin	,,	1793
Marie Rose	Bonaventure Caron		
		S.F.S.	1828
Marguerite	Damase Bélanger	,,	1832
Jérome			
Louis			
Romain			
25 Pierre	(9) M. Thècle Baudoin		
		Bert.	1804
Thècle	J. B. Morin	S.P.S.	1822
26 Pierre	(9) Marie Marcoux	S.F.S.	1823
27 Joseph	(12) M. Fse. Dalaire	,,	1806
Catherine	Paul Lacroix	S.M.	1832
Anastasie	Frs. Cotin	,,	1842
Marguerite	David Cotin	,,	1843
Marie Henriette	Jos. Ed. Morisset	,,	1851
Michel			
Jean Baptiste			
28 Paul	(12) M. Anne Brochu	S.V.	1812
Mathilde	Jos. Bacquet	S.M.	1835
Marie Anne	Firmin Queret	,,	1859
Joseph René			
Joseph			
Jean Gualbert			
Paul			
Marc			
Luc			
Nazaire			
Damase			
29 Joseph	(14) Marg. Deblois	S.F.	1807
30 Jean	(14) M.Ls.Létourneau	,,	1827
Pétronille	Régis Asselin	,,	1855
Marie Zoé	Martin Asselin	,,	1862
François Xavier			
31 Augustin	(15) M. Anne Roy (Audy)		
		S.F.	1794
Marie Anne	Pierre Asselin	,,	1824
Marie Josette	Jean Labranche	,,	1833
Madeleine	Jos. Déry	,,	1839
Henriette	Alexis Létourneau	,,	1841
Jean Baptiste			
Augustin			
32 JeanBaptiste	(16) Mad. Guérard	,,	1806
Le même	Julienne Foucher	,,	1809
Michel			
François			
Pierre			
Jean Baptiste			
33 Edouard	Cath. Verreau		
Catherine	Alexis Crépeau	S.J.	1843
34 Jacques	(17) Angé Paquet	S.F.	1811
Geneviève	Ls. Fournier	,,	1845

MARTINEAU.

Jacques			
35 Martin	(17) Marie Guion	,,	1818
36 Jean	(20) Josette Gagnon	,,	1812
37 JeanBaptiste	(24) Thérèse Denaut	S.Tho.	1817
MarieMarguerite	Frederic Letellier		
		S.F.S.	1840
François	Césarie Fréderic Proulx		
		S.F.S.	1841
Marcelline	Fabien Baudoin	,,	1844
38 Romain	(24) Marg. Peltier	S.P.S.	1821
Marie Elisabeth	Roch Thibaut	S.F.S.	1844
39 Jérome	(24) M. Edwidge Peltier		
		S.F.S	1822
Marie Edwidge	Chs. Tho. Bouchard		
		S.F.S.	1844
40 Louis	(24) Sophie Quemeneur		
		S.F.S.	1828
41 Michel	(27) Genev. Asselin	S.M.	1831
George			
42 JeanBaptiste	(27) M. Eliz. Morisset	,,	1839
43 Pierre	Cécile Furois	,,	1824
Jean			
44 Joseph René	(28) Julienne Bacquet	,,	1848
45 Joseph	(28) Sara Bacquet	,,	1848
46 Jean	(28) Sophie Audet	S.M.	1850
Gualbert			
47 Nazaire	(28) Célina Nadeau	B.	1854
48 Paul	(28) M. Luce Racine	S.M.	1855
49 Marc	(28) M. Adèle Racine	,,	1855
50 Luc	(28) Marg. Marseau	S.M.	1861
51 Damase	(28) HenrietteCélérineMétivier		
52 François	(30) Hombeline Asselin		
Xavier		S.F.	1854
53 Jean	(31) Genev.Létourneau	,,	1827
Baptiste			
Hombeline	Isaïe Dery	,,	1852
Le même	M. Jos. Pepin	S.J.	1832
54 Augustin	(31) Vict. Lheureux	S.F.	1832
55 Pierre	(32) Marie Bureau	,,	1836
56 JeanBaptiste	(32) Olive Deblois	,,	1841
57 François	(32) Mad. Dalaire	S.J.	1841
58 Michel	(32) Sophie Guérard	S.Frs.	1848
59 Jacques	(34) Marg. Gagnon	S.F.	1836
60 Georges	(41) M. Ls. Genev. Hélie		
		S.M.	1854
61 Jean	(43) Philomène Gourgue		
		S.V.	1870

MATAUT.

1 Jean	Gabrielle Gagnon		
Pierre			
Le même	Louise Cloutier	C.R.	1684
2 Pierre	(1) Louise Mailhot	,,	1706
Le même	ScolastiqueToupin Dufault		
		C.R.	1715
Scolastique	Chs. Haulbois	S.M.	1753
Joseph			
3 Pierre	Scolastique Dusaut		1715
Françoise	JeanChamberlan	S.M.	1757
4 Joseph	(2) Angé Valière	S.Chs.	1772
5 Joseph	Angé Gautron		
Jean			
Joseph			
Augustin			
6 Jean	(5) Eliz. Terrien	S.G.	1826
7 Joseph	(5) Angé Terrien	,,	1826
8 Augustin	(5) M. Chs. Turgeon	B.	1840

MATHIEU.

1 Jean	Anne Du Tertre	C.R.	1669
René			
2 René	(1) Genev. Roussin	A.G.	1669
Charles			

MATHIEU:

3	Charles	(2)	Thérèse Dufresne S.L.	1735
	Marie Thérèse		J.B. DuchesneauS.P.S.	1761
	Geneviève		Ls. Picard "	1763
	Monique		Jos. Coté "	1770
	Françoise		Chs. Morin "	1779
	René Isaac			
	Prisque			
	Augustin			
	Charles			
4	Prisque	(3)	Marg. Blanchet S.P.S.	1754
	Marguerite		Jos. Blais "	1774
5	Augustin	(2)	M.UrsuleFournier "	1764
	Marie		Jos. Couillard "	1786
	Marguerite		Jos. Marie Picard "	1792
	Marie		Jos. Martin "	1794
	Euphrosine			
	Michel			
	Charles			
	Augustin			
	Le même		M. Agathe Blondeau Bert.	1798
6	Charles	(3)	M. Chs. Létourneau S.P.S.	1773
	Marie Angélique		Pierre Baudoin "	1797
	Marie Angèle		Jos. Gagné "	1812
	François			
7	René Isaac	(3)	M. Barbe Solieu S.V.	1778
8	René Isaac		Mad. Bélanger	
	Madeleine		J. B. Casault S.V.	1804
	Geneviève		Jos. Roy "	1811
9	Augustin	(5)	M. Genev. Couillard S. Tho.	1789
	Charles			
	Augustin			
	Marcelle			
10	Charles	(5)	Angèle Levasseur S.P.S.	1797
11	Michel	(5)	Marie Lamare "	1801
12	François	(6)	M. Genev. Baudoin S.F.S.	1788
13	Joseph		Angé Gautron	
	Angélique		Jacq. Labrecque S.G.	1819
14	François		M. Ls. Morin	
	Joseph			
	Le même		M. Anne Quéret S.M.	1803
15	Nicolas		M. Ls. Vézina	
	Nicolas			
16	Charles	(9)	Julie Gaumon S.P.S.	1812
	Clarisse		F. X. Laberge "	1838
	Césarie		Jos. Valière "	1838
17	Augustin	(9)	M. Mad. Morel "	1812
18	Marcelle	(9)	Thérèse Létourneau S.P.S.	1824
19	Joseph	(14)	9 M. Anne Patry S.G.	1823
20	Nicolas	(15)	M. Céleste Dion S.Frs.	1839
21	Joseph			
	Pre et Mag.		Anne Mathieu S.G.	1817
	Guérin			
	Eléonore		Jos. Légaré S.L.	1859

MAUPAS—ST. HILAIRE.

1	Nicolas		Agnès Guilmet S.J.	1698
	Marie		René Adam B.	1734
	Nicolas			
	Pierre			
	Joseph			
	Jacques			
	Louis			
2	Nicolas	(1)	Jeanne Monmeny B.	1723
3	Pierre	(1)	Marie Tessier Repantigny	1729
4	Joseph	(1)	M. Jos. Forgue S.M.	1740
5	Jacques	(1)	M. Thérèse Godbout Lévis	1750
			V. de Ls. Pichet	

MAUPAS—ST. HILAIRE.

6	Louis	(1)	M. Jos. Jahan Lévis	1751
	Anne		Jos. Leroux S.M.	1785
7	Pierre (1)		M. Jos. Chamberlin S.M.	1764
	Jean Marie			
	Pierre			
8	Jean Marie	(7)	M. Anne Vallée S.M.	1786
	Josette		Frs. Rousseau S.M.	1813
	Marie		J. B. Rousseau B.	1815
	Euphrosine		J. B. Filteau B.	1826
	Marie Anne		Frs, Coté S.P.	1807
	Jean Marie			
9	Pierre	(7)	Mad. Cotin B.	1788
10	Jean Marie	(8)	Louise Enouf B.	1827
11	Pierre		Françoise Lecours	
	Le même		Louise Lefebvre Lévis	1823
	Jean		M.Anne Mercier S.V.	1851

MAURICE.

1	Jean		Marthe Bussière S.Malo.	
	Le même		Isabelle Couillard B.	1761
2	Joseph		Marg. St. Jean Montréal	
	Michel			
3	Michel	(2)	M. Jos. Corriveau S.V.	1816
	Judith		Isidore Tangué	
	Marie Josette		Jos. Quemneeur S.V.	1841
4	Joseph		Marg. Lefebvre S.G.	
	Stanislas			
5	Stanislas		Charlotte S.L.	1842
	Stanislas			
6	Stanislas	(5)	M.Caroline Ruel S.L.	1867

MAUVIDE.

1	Jean (Chirurgien)		M. Anne Genest	
	Marie Anne		René Amable Durocher S.J.	1773
	Marie Madelanie		Jean Pierre Volant de Champlain S.J.	1788
	Laurent			
2	Laurent (2)		M. Anne Genest S.J.	1781

MÉNARD.

1	René		Judith Veillon	
	Barbe		Ant. Vermet S.F.	1669
2	Pierre		Fse. Pie Ev. de Poitiers.	
	Pierre			
3	Pierre	(2)	M. Jeanne Blais Bert.	1735
	Jean Baptiste			
	Le même		Marie Chartré "	1752
			V. de Michel Chartier	
4	Pierre		Louise Ménard Qué	
	Le même		Marg. Guay B.	1780
	Augustin			
5	Jean	(3)	M. Jos. Hélie S.V.	1773
	Baptiste			
	Jean Baptiste			
	François			
	Pierre			
6	Pierre		M. Ls. Lamothe	
	Marie Anne		Michel Dubord B.	1794
	Marie Anne		2°Aug. Bilodeau Bert.	1806
7	Augustin	(4)	Louise Couture Lévis	1809
	Joseph			
	Augustin			
8	Jean	(5)	M. Vict. Carbonneau Bert.	1798
	Baptiste			

---

(1) Enfant adoptif de Jean Marie Ruellan.
(2) Noyé en 1792 avec M. Hubert curé de Québec.

MÉNARD.

Marguerite	Jos. Garant	S.V.	1829
Françoise	Jos. Gagnon	"	1846
Etienne			
François Xavier			
François Régis			
9 Pierre	(5) M. Mad. Gosselin S.V.		1803
Marguerite	Etn. Guilmet	S.V.	1831
Delphine	Ign. McKinna	"	1845
Marie Louise	Édouard Roy	"	1829
Marie Louise	2° Jacq. Lemieux Bert.		1844
Samuel			
Régis			
Thomas			
10 François	(5) M. Angé Bouchard		
		S.M.	1831
Antoine			
11 Louis	M. Rose Mailhot		
Louis			
12 Augustin	(7) Cécile Turgeon	B.	1839
13 Joseph	(7) Caroline Couillard	B.	1846
14 François	(8) Marie Gosselin		
Xavier		S.M.	1837
15 François	(8) Angé Gagnon		
Régis		S.V.	1837
Flore Eliz.	Hippolyte Gourgeo		
Délima		S.V.	1861
Catherine	Ludger Lefebvre S.V.		1862
Michel			
16 Régis	(9) Marie Nadeau	Bert.	1837
17 Samuel	(9) Angéle Carbonneau		
		Bert.	1841
18 Thomas	(9) Marg. Guilmet Bert.		1843
19 Jean Baptiste	Marg. Bélanger Islet		1791
Adrien	Islet		
Le même	M. Anne Jolin S.F.S.		1837
20 Antoine	(10) Marie Ratté	S.M-	1860
21 Louis	(11) Marie Noël	S.P.	1824
22 Michel	(15) Constance Dion S.V.		1865

McINTYRE—RODRIGUE.

1 Rodrique	Marie McBan		
Joseph			
Jean			
2 Joseph	(1) Ange Gosselin S.Chs.		1795
Angélique	Jean Frédéric Costin		
		S.Chs.	1819
Joseph			
3 Joseph	(2) M. Ls. Lecours S.Chs.		1820
Sophie	André Lemelin	"	1838
4 Jean	(1) Marie Charlan	Qué.	1790
		Qué.	
Luce	Chs. Fortier S.Chs.		1820
5 Pierre	Esther Bédard		
Flore	Ed. Larrivé	B.	1857

McKINNAL.

1 Daniel	Angé Rinfret		
Marie Madeleine	Aug. Brousseau Bert.		1798
Louis			
Joseph			
2 Louis	(1) M. Jos. Baudoin	"	1798
3 Joseph	(3) Rose Gautier	"	1809

McNEIL.

1 Jean	Marie Onell Ecosse		
Ignace			
2 Ignace	(1) Louise Terrien S.F.S.		1764
Marie Reine	Michel Morin	"	1787
Marie	Michel Bétel	S.M.	1787
Le même	Cath. McLean, Que.		
Marie	Nic. Boissonneau S.V.		1789
Marie	Chs. Gourgue	"	1802

McNEIL.

Marie Anne	Jos. Lavergne S.P.S.		1803
Maurice			
Jacques			
Antoine			
Ignace			
3 Antoine	(2) Eliz. Denis	S.V.	1795
Marie	Jacq. Bolduc	"	1820
Isabelle	Germ. Baudoin	"	1840
Osite	F. X. Bilodeau	"	1845
Pierre			
Antoine			
Ignace			
Benoit			
Jacques			
Jean			
Nil			
4 Jacques	(2) M. Marg. Racine S.M.		1809
Louise	J. B. Turgeon	"	1836
Catherine	Ovide Turgeon	B.	1844
Marie	Pierre Télesphore		
	Turgeon	B.	1851
5 Maurice	(2) M. Fse. Gourgue S.V.		1806
6 Ignace	(2) Mad. Levasseur Que.		
Luce	Michel Bilodeau Que.		
Marie Emélie	Pierre Boissonneau		
		S.M.	1847
Nil			
7 Etienne	M. Jos. Carrier Lévis		1817
Remi			
8 Antoine	(3) M. Ursule Marseau		
		S.V.	1823
Ursule	Cyrille Normand	"	1852
Emélie	F. X. Lepage	"	1857
9 Ignace	(3) Ursule Roy	"	1828
Flore	Marg. Mercier S.M.		1851
Hermine	Romuald Asselin	"	1858
10 Benoit	(3) M. Angele Roy S.V.		1837
11 Jacques	(3) Emérentienne Bilodeau		
		S.V.	1838
Emélie	Henri Michel Boutin		
		S.V.	1869
12 Jean	(3) Sophie Tangué S.V.		1839
13 Nil	(3) Dosithé Tangué	"	1843
14 Pierre	(3) Isabelle Gagné	"	1849
15 Nil	(6) M. Jos. Bacquet S.M.		1856
16 Rémi	(7) Léocadie Nadeau	B.	1854

MENEUX—CHATEAUNEUF.

1 Jacques	Marg. Lepeuvrier S.R.		1663
Marie Madeleine	Mathurin Meunier		
		S.F.	1684
Françoise	Michel Peltier	"	1697
Reine	Jos. Ouellet	"	1700
Catherine	Noël Lizotte, Riv. Ouelle		
			1702
Angélique	Jos. Lévesque, Riv. Ouelle		
			1704
René			
2 René	Eliz. Rochon	S.F.	1710
Thérèse	Jacq. Faucher	"	1737
Elizabeth	Jos. Jolin	"	1743
Marie	Ls. Boutin	"	1746
Brigitte	Jos. Roy	S.V.	1749
Marie Marthe	Jérome Hélie	"	1751
Jacques			
Joseph			
Joseph			
René			
3 Jacques	(2) Marg. Leblond	S.F.	1740
Julie	Frs. Guérard	"	1762
Marie	Jos. Guérard	"	1763
Catherine	Jos. Vaillancourt	"	1771
4 Joseph	(2) M. Eliz. Gendron	"	1744
5 Joseph	(2) M. Cath. Blouin S.J.		1747
Marie Catherine	Ls. Gagnon	S.F.	1771
Joseph			

MENEUX—CHATEAUNEUF.

6 René	(2) Louise Bilodeau		
		S. Frs.	1747
7 Joseph	(5) M. Rose Canac	S.F.	1775

MERCIER.

1 Julien	Marie Poulin,	Qué.	1654
Paschal			
Charles			
Louis			
Jean			
Pierre			
A Martin	Mathurine Roux S.F,		1674
	V. de Gab. Rouleau		
2 Paschal	(1) M. Anne Cloutier		
		C.R.	1681
Pierre			
3 Charles	(1) Anne Berthelot		
		S. Anne	1691
Isabelle	Pierre Blais,	Bert	1734
4 Louis	(1) Marg. Rabouon, Que.		1685
Le même	Anne Jaguereau	"	1685
Marguerite	Jean Loiseau,	"	1713
Le même	Louise Simon S. Foye		1703
Joseph François			
Joseph Marie			
5 Jean	(1) Barbe Monmagnier		
		S. Anne	1691
Julien			
A Pierre	(1) Marie Chamberlan		
		S.F.	1717
6 Joseph Paschal	M. Mad. Boucher		
Geneviéve	Jacq. Tangué	Bert	1829
Marie Anne	Ls. Blais	"	1733
Joseph			
Paschal			
François			
Jean			
7 Pierre	(2) Mad. Gagné		
Marie Anne	Ls. Boutin	Bert	1731
Marie Madeleine	Jos. Asselin	Bert	1739
Marie Madeleine	2° Gervais Emond		
		S. Frs.	1764
Marie François	Jacq. Labbé	Bert	1743
Marie François	2° Aug. Martineau		
		S. Frs.	1746
Pierre			
Augustin			
Le même	Mad. Asselin	"	1718
Marie Apolline	Jean Marcoux	Bert	1748
Marie Josette	Pierre Picard	"	1754
Marie	Ls. Dupuis	"	1760
Joseph			
8 Joseph Fran-	(4) M. Ursule Lafontaine		
çois			
9 Joseph Marie	(4) Eliz. Duprat,	Que.	1729
10 Julien	(5) Agnés Meunier		
		S. Anne	1718
Agnés	J. B. Morin	S.F.S.	1738
Marie Geneviéve	Frs. Malbœuf	"	1750
Marie	Jean Valier Roy,		
		Bert	1759
François			
Julien			
11 Jean	Cath. Caron		
Le même	Genev. Asselin		
		S. Frs.	1715
Pierre Joseph			
Louis Joseph			
François			
Jean			
12 Alexandre	M. Jos. Gaudin		
Marie	Jean Harnais	S.P.S.	1749
Ursule	Ign. Gaudreau	"	1758
Simon			

MERCIER.

13 Augustin	(7) M. Anne Joly,	Que.	1747
Angélique	Ang. Blais	Bert	1765
Marie Anne	J. B. Blais	" .	1771
14 Joseph	(6) Eliz. Lebrun	S.V.	1729
Angélique	Ls. Bolduc	Bert	1751
Marie	Alexandre Marcoux		
		Bert	1753
Marie Josette	Jean Valiére Bilodeau		
		Bert	1754
Elisabeth	Ls. Boutin	"	1757
Marie Geneviéve	Gab. Blouin	"	1763
Marie Geneviéve	2° André Beaucher		
		Bert	1807
Marie François	Frs. Mercier	"	1757
Marie François	2° Jacq. Genchon		
		S.F.S.	1761
Paschal			
Jean Baptiste			
Jean			
Joseph			
Augustin			
15 Paschal	(6) M. Ls. Fortier	Bert	1736
Marie Louise	Nic. Pouliot	S.M.	1763
Ursule	Paul Cadrin	"	1765
Marie Anne	Ls. Lebrun	"	1771
Geneviéve	Jos. Labrecque	S.M.	1775
René Paschal			
Pierre			
16 François	(6) M. Mad. Fortier	S.J.	1747
Marie Anne	Jean Jos. Lacroix		
		S.M.	1772
Marie Madeleine	Ls. Nadeau	"	1788
Pierre Noël			
Jean-Baptiste			
François			
Paul			
Augustin			
Le même	M. Cath. Cadrin	S.M.	1776
17 Jean	(6) M. Anne Roy	"	1755
Marie Anne	Jos. Fradet	"	1786
Paschal			
Nicolas			
18 Pierre	(7) M. Ls. Tangué	S.V.	1744
Geneviève	Chs. Lacasse	S. Chs.	1778
Françoise	J. B. Paquet	"	1785
Louise	Ls. Labrecque	"	1788
Joseph			
Augustin			
19 Joseph	(7) Mad. Guilmet	"	1770
Madeleine	Pierre Gagnon	S.H.	1794
Marguerite	Jacq. Hélie	"	1794
20 Julien	(10) Marthe Roy	S.V.	1755
Marie Josette	Henri Audet	"	1785
Marguerite	Ls. Alaire	"	1797
Julien			
Guillaume Pros-			
per			
Louis			
21 François	(10) M. Fse. Mercier	Bert	1757
Marie Françoise	Ls. Quemeneur	S.F.S.	1777
Jean François			
22 Jean	(11) Marg. Moreau	Bert	1748
23 Louis Joseph	(11) M. Jos. Guion	"	1750
Marie Josette	Aug. Blais	"	1788
Le même	M. Reine Gaudreau		
		S.Tho.	1776
Marie Marguer-	J. B. Blais	Bert.	1802
ite			
24 François	(11) M. Agathe Blondeau		
		Bert.	1754
Agathe	Ign. Gagnon	"	1783
Françoise	Ant. Létourneau	"	1796
Germain			
François			
Augustin			

MERCIER.

MERCIER.

25	Pierre Joseph(11)	Cécile Couture	S.Chs.1760
	Cécile	Ls. Vermet	Bert.1787
	*Marie Angèlique	Pierre Morin	„ 1790
	Marie Anne	J. B. Quemeneur	„ 1791
	Marie Anne	2° Jean Boulet	S.H.1812
	Catherine	Aug. Lefebvre	Bert.1797
	Augustin		
	Pierre		
26	Pierre	Marie Coté	
	Le même	M. Anne Fontaine	
			Lévis 1763
	Marguerite	Pierre Jos. Fontaine	
			S.J.1788
27	Simon (12)	M.Mad. Picard	S.P.S.1751
	Marie Josette	Pierre Noël Morin	„ 1773
	Antoine		
	Simon		
28			
29	Joseph (14)	M. Genev. Asselin	
			S.F.S.1751
	Marie Geneviève	Frs. Allaire	S.F.S.1766
	Marie Anne	Aug. Blais	„ 1773
	Louise Julienne	Jos. Marseau	„ 1775
	Marguerite	Michel Blais	„ 1775
	Françoise	Jos. Buteau	„ 1788
	Reine	Ls. Boissonneau	„ 1798
	Augustin		
	Joseph		
30	Jean Baptiste(14)	Eliz. Blais	Bert.1757
	Elizabeth	Laurent Genest	S.Chs.1777
	Madeleine	Alexandre Couture	
			S.Chs.1782
	Angèlique	Gab. Gagnon	„ 1784
	Paschal		
	Joseph		
	Jean Baptiste		
31	Augustin (14)	M.Genev. Paré	S.F.S.1765
	Marie	J. B. Bilodeau	Bert.1783
	Marie Josette	J. B. Lemieux	„ 1801
	Marie Reine	Guill. Lemieux	„ 1805
	Marie Victoire	Jacq. Daniau	„ 1807
	Gabriel		
	Jacques		
	Joseph		
	Augustin		
32	Paschal (14)	M. Thècle Fortier	
			S.F.S.1766
	Marie Louise	Ls. Marie Bilodeau	
			Bert.1791
	Marguerite	J. B. Blais	„ 1812
	Jean Baptiste		
	Louis		
	Joseph		
	Paschal		
33	Jean (14)	M. Genev. Daniau	
			S.F.S.1771
	Marie Louise	Aug. Blais	Bert.1800
	Reine	Félix Dépont	S.V.1821
	Jos. Jean Baptiste		
	Jean Baptiste		
	Etienne		
	Pierre		
34	René Paschal(15)	Thérèse Rouillard	
			S.M.1772
	Marie Thérèse	Jos. Bacquet	„ 1795
	Marie Madeleine	Simon Corriveau	„ 1779
	Marie Madeleine	2° Jos. Denis	„ 1814
	Marie Françoise	Michel Bêtel	„ 1801
	Marguerite	Frs. Genest	„ 1801
	Paschal		
	Joseph René		
35	Pierre (15)	M. Mad Roy	S.M.1777
	Angèle	Michel Vallée	S.G.1803
	Madeleine	Jean Marie Dalaire	
			S.G.1803

	Marie	Barth. Royer	S.G. 1803
	Marguerite	Ant. Boutin	„ 1809
	Marthe	Austache Roy	„ 1819
	Marie Anne	Louis Bêtel	S.G.1830
	Pierre		
	Le même	M. Anne Campagna	
			S.G.1823
	Angèle	Amable Turcot	S.F.1850
36	François (16)	M.Mad. Cadrin	S.M.1777
	Michel		
	Augustin		
	François		
	Pierre		
37	Paul (16)	Marg. Bacquet	S.M.1781
	Marguerite	Etn. Gaumont	„ 1814
	Joseph		
	Paul		
	Le même	M.Marthe Picard	
			Bert.1790
	Marguerite	J. B. Bacquet	S.M.1813
38	Jean Baptiste(16)	M. Mad. Leblond	„ 1784
	Marie Madeleine	Michel Ouimet	„ 1811
	Marie Anne	Paul Roy	„ 1830
	Jean Baptiste		
	Charles		
	Louis		
39	Pierre Noël (16)	M. Jos. Nadeau	B.1785
40	Augustin (16)	M. Chs. Balan	S.M.1787
	Le même	M. Jos· Nadeau	„ 1791
	Marie Josette	Jos. Gautron	„ 1812
	Marie Louise	Jos. Dion	„ 1812
	Marie Angèle	Ant. Chamberlan	„ 1828
	Luce	Jos. Gagné	„ 1833
	Luce	2° Prudent Balan	„ 1843
	Marie Zoé	Frs. Gosselin	„ 1838
	Jacques		
	Joseph		
	Alexis		
	François		
41	Paschal (17)	Cath. Gontier	S.G. 1796
42	Nicolas (17)	Marg. Richard	S.G. 1796
	Euphrosine	Moise Royer	S.G. 1822
	Soulange	Jos. Denis	S M. 1834
	Louis		
	Jean		
43	Augustin	Genev. Ferland	S.Chs.1775
	Joseph		
44	Joseph (18)	Marg. Gagnon	S.M. 1783
	Angèlique	Jos. Gontier	S.G. 1875
	Pierre		
	Joseph		
45	Julien (20)	Mad. Cochon	S.V. 1786
	Marie	Ls. Bernard	S.V. 1820
	Le même	M. Chs. Cotin	S.V. 1791
		V. de Pre. Bernard (?)	
	Le même	M. Chs. Fradet	S.V. 1818
A	Guillaume (20)	Angé Fortier	S.H. 1793
	Prosper		
	Catherine	Pierre Gendron	S.H. 1814
B	Louis (20)	M. Rose Gagnon	S.H.1810
46	Jean (20)	Thérèse Bonneau	S.F.S.
			1782
	Francois	Isidore Coté	S.Tho. 1811
	Véronique		
	Bernard		
	Jacques		
47	Augustin	Cath. Goupy	S.M. 1782
	Marie Josette	J. B. Corneau	S.Chs. 1807
	Etienne		
	Pierre		
48			
49	Joachim	Susanne Bilodeau	
	Angèlique	Jos. Plante	S.H. 1809
	Marie Anne	Jérôme Arguin	S.H. 1815
	Pierre Noël		
	Joachim		
	Joseph		

MERCIER.

	Augustin			
50	François	(24)	Angèle Gravel	S.M. 1786
	M. Josette		Frs. Audet	S.Chs. 1808
	Le même		Marie Bissonnet	S.M. 1821
51	Germain	(2)	Thérèse Veau	S.V. 1786
52	Augustin	(24)	Angé Lavoie	S.V. 1796
	Marie Rose		Simon Arbour	Bert. 1831
	Joseph			
	Augustin			
	Pierre			
53	Augustin	(25)	M. Anne Blais	Bert. 1794 S.H.
	Michel			
	Joseph			
	Pierre			
54	Pierre	(25)	Mad. Baudoin	Bert. 1797
	Rose		Aug. Mercier	Bert. 1828
	Madeleine		Aug. Bolduc	Bert. 1832
	Catherine		J. B. Bilodeau	Bert. 1842
A	Julien		Agathe Giguère	
	Le même		Rose Asselin	S.F. 1803
55	Antoine	(27)	Cecile Morin	S.P.S. 1781
	Marie Cécile		Ant. Leclaire	S.Chs. 1809
	Marie		Aug. Lacroix	S.Chs. 1820
	Madeleine		Michel Blais	S.Chs. 1822
	Marguerite		Aug. Alaire	S.V. 1829
	Antoine			
56	Simon	(27)	Marie Lepage	S.Chs, 1786
	Simon			
	Le même		M. Jos. Gosselin	S.P.S.1816
57	Joseph	(29)	Fse, Fraser	S.F.S. 1792
	Angèle		Ls. Morin	S.F.S. 1817
	Marie Julie		Frs. Marie Fournier	S.F.S. 1821
	Adelaide		Frédéric Letellier	S.F.S. 1829
	Marguerite		F. X. Balan	S.P.S. 1815
58	Augustin	(29)	Louise Boulet	S.F.S. 1799
59	Joseph	(30)	Marg. Genest	S.J. 1786
	Marguerite		J. B. Turgeon	S.Chs. 1804
	Marie Angèle		J. B. Couture	S.Chs. 1812
	Marthe		F. X. Couture	S.Chs. 1823
	Dominique			
	Joseph			
	Jean			
60	Jean Baptiste	(30)	Cécile Turgeon	S.Chs. 1778
	Marguerite		Jos. Lacasse	S.Chs. 1804
	Marie Louise		Clément Réaume	S.Chs. 1809
	Cécile		Jacq. Naud	S.Chs. 1816
	Marie		Jos. Paquet	S.Chs. 1821
	Louis			
	Jean Baptiste			
61	Paschal	(30)	Genev. Roy	S.Chs. 1788
	Geneviève		J. B. Fouquet	S.Chs. 1810
	Elizabeth		J. B. Boulet	S.G. 1814
	Paschal			
	André			
62	Paschal		Angé Roy	
	Marie		Pierre Martin	S.Chs. 1810
63	Jean Baptiste		Josette Corriveau	
	Emélie		Jos. Morin	S.G. 1824
	Pierre			
64	Jean Baptiste		Marie	
	Le même		Cath. Duquet	S.Chs. 1810
	Constance		Michel Coté	S.Chs. 1830
	Catherine		Frs. Trépanier	S.M. 1861
65	François		M. Anne Blais	S.Tho.
	François			
66	Michel		Marg. Morin	
	Marguerite		Ls. Pruneau	S.G. 1828
67	Pierre		M. Chs. Chartier	
	François Xavier			
68	Gabriel	(31)	M. Ursule Bouchard	S.V.
	Marie Ursule		Pierre Bouchard	S.V. 1836

MERCIER.

	Marie Emélie		Marg. Veau	S.V. 1838
	Soulange		David Marseau	S.V. 1849
	Eusèbe			
69	Jacques	(31)	Marg. Beaucher	Bert. 1812
70	Augustin	(31)	M. Anne Carbonneau	Bert. 1812
	Joseph			
71	Joseph	(31)	Archange Roy	Bert. 1817
	Onésime		Frs. Blais	Bert. 1845
72	Jean Bapt.	(31)	M. Marg. Fortier	Bert. 1802
	Thècle		André Carbonneau	Bert. 1830
	Emélie		J. B. Coulombe	Bert. 1831
	Julie		Ls. Bilodeau	Bert. 1840
	Marguerite		Basile Buteau	Bert. 1846
	Paschal			
	Jean Baptiste			
73	Joseph	(32)	Marie Baudoin	Bert. 1807
74	Paschal	(32)	Reine Morin	S.F.S. 1809
	Reine		J. B. Blais	Bert. 1831
	Joseph			
75	Louis	(32)	M. Angéle Balan	Bert. 1812
	Jean Baptiste			
	Louis			
76	Jean Bapt.	(32)	M. Jos. Carbonneau	Bert. 1801
	Simon			
	Jean Baptiste			
77	Pierre	(33)	Marg. Langlois	Bert. 1804
	Marguerite		Ls. Bouffard	S.G. 1824
	Le même		Josette Langlois	S.F.S. 1818
78	Jos. Jean Baptiste	(33)	M. Eliz. Lemieux	Bert. 1816
79	Etienne	(33)	Euphrosine Langlois	Bert. 1816
	Etienne			
	Augustin			
	Edouard			
	Joseph			
80	Joseph René	(34)	Angé. Morisset	S.M. 1802
	Amable			
	Joseph			
	Jean			
81	Paschal	(34)	M. Mad. Roy	S.M. 1805
	Madeleine		Héliodore Girard	B. 1830
	Madeleine		2° Victor Corneau	B. 1849
82	Pierre	(35)	M. Reine Bêtel	S.M. 1805
	Le même		Mad. Curodeau	S.J. 1822
83	François	(36)	Marg. Marseau	S.M. 1809
	Eléonore		Bing. Gagnon	S.M. 1835
	Constance		J. B. Bacquet	S.M. 1843
	Marie Marg.		Fréderic Corriveau	S.M. 1854
	André			
	François			
84	Augustin	(36)	Mad. Pilote	S.M. 1815
	Marcelline		Jacq. Morin	S.M. 1841
	Félicité		Ls. Roy	S.V. 1844
	Olive		Gab. Nadeau	S.V. 1851
	Hubert			
	Edouard			
85	Michel		Marg. Boissonneau	Qué. 1822
	Marie Désanges		André Couture	S.Chs. 1847
86	Pierre	(36)	Marg. Dutile	S.G. 1828
87	Paul	(37)	Fse. Bacquet	S.M. 1804
	Françoise		Jos. Dion	S.G. 1822
	Le même		Marie Roy	S.V. 1810
	Le même		Sophie Delaire	S.M. 1846
88	Joseph	(37)	M. Ls. Boutillet	S.Chs. 1815
	Joseph			
89	Jean Bapt.	(38)	M. Mad. Gagné	S.M. 1811
	Michel			
	Jean Baptiste			

MERCIER.

	Augustin			
	Léon			
90	Charles	(38)	M. Angé. Cland S.V.	1815
	Reine		Frs. Rousseau S.V.	1838
	Hombéline		Abraham Couture	
			S.V.	1846
	Sophie		Chrysostome Arbour	
			S.V.	1846
91	Louis	(38)	Marie Lacroix S.M.	1820
92	Alexis	(40)	M. Genev. Bolduc	
			S.V.	1814
93	Jacques	(40)	Marie Bacquet S.M.	1820
	Mathilde		F. X. Baudoin S.M.	1845
	Suzarine		Jos. Bissonnet S.M.	1854
	Marie Zoé		Frs. Bélanger S.V.	1843
	Marie Anne		Jean Maupas S.V.	1851
	Ursin			
	Le même		Julie Gautron S.M.	1845
94	François	(40)	Julie Demuth	
	Eulalié		Geo. Brisson S.M.	1848
	Marie Zoé		Narcisse Chartier	
			S.M.	1850
	Marie		Théophile Baker S.M.	1858
	M. Jorique			
	François Xavier			
95	Joseph	(40)	Marg. Beaucher B.	1833
96	Jean	(42)	Angé. Roy S.G.	1822
97	Louis	(42)	M. Anne Asselin S.L.	1846
98	Joseph	(43)	Marie Bolduc S.V.	1806
	Thomas			
	Le même		Mad. Dandurand	
			S.H.	1820
	Marcelline		Narcisse Pepin S.M.	1849
99	Joseph	(44)	Rosalie Roy S.M.	1823
100	Pierre	(44)	Victoire Roy S.G.	1827
101	Bernard	(46)	M. Fse. Talbot S.F.S.	1820
102	Jacques	(46)	Genev. Talbot S.F.S.	1820
103	Etienne	(47)	M. Marg. Gautron	
			S.V.	1816
	Marguerite		Laurent Labrecque	
			S.J.	1852
104	Pierre	(47)	M. Anne Dandurand	
			S.H.	1820
	Marie Anne		Chs. Bussière S.Chs.	1841
	Marie Désanges		Athanase Rouleau	
			S.Chs.	1853
	Paul			
105	Joseph	(49)	M. Eliz. Guilmet Bert.	1798
106	Augustin	(49)	Fse. Guilmet Bert.	1798
107	Pierre Noël	(49)	Marie Gagné S.G.	1799
108	Joachim	(49)	Fse. Patry S.M.	1806
109	François		Rose Lefebvre	
	Marie Rose		Alexandre Paquet	
			S.Chs.	1834
	Emelie		Etn. Couture S.Chs.	1839
110	Louis		Marg. Morin	
			S.P.S.	
	Joseph			
111	Pierre-Michel		Genev. Giguère	
	et Genev.		S. Anne	1819
	Lacroix			
	Marie			
113	Joseph		Genev. Coltière	
			S. Tho	
	Magloire			
114	Joseph	(12)	Marg. Boucher Bert.	1826
115	Augustin	(52)	Rose Mercier Bert.	1828
116	Pierre	(52)	Marg. Blais Bert.	1830
117	Pierre	(53)	M. Anastasie Picard	
			S.F.S.	1822
118	Joseph	(53)	Marg. Blais Bert.	1826
119	Michel	(53)	Adé Turgeon B.	1837
120	Antoine	(55)	Genev. Alaire S.F.S.	1807
	Marguerite		Ed. Quéret S.V.	1833
	Sophie		Guill. Bolduc S.V.	1841

MERCIER.

	Michel			
	Louis			
	Antoine			
121	Simon	(56)	Eliz. Fortier S.J.	1821
122	Joseph	(59)	Anastasie Audet	
			S.Chs.	1828
	Le même		M. Chs. Coté S.Chs.	1842
123	Dominique	(59)	Euphrosine Dalaire	
			S.Chs.	1830
	Marie Anne		Pierre Bolduc S.Chs.	1853
124	Jean	59		
125	Jn. Baptiste	(60)	Marie Harlevin S.Chs.	1804
	Jean Baptiste			
126	Louis	(60)	Judith Bisson S.Chs.	1820
	Louis			
127	Paschal	(61)	Marg. Patoine S.G.	1812
A	André	(61)	Thérèse Bilodeau S.H.	1817
128	Pierre	(63)	Thérèse Théberge	
			S.G.	1826
129	François	(65)	M. Luc. Corriveau	
			Bert.	1824
130	François Xa-	(67)	M. Lorette Fraser B.	1830
	vier			
	François Xavier			
131	Eusèbe	(68)	Caroline Vézina S.V.	1853
132	Jn. Baptiste	(72)	M. Mad. Bernier	
			S.P.S.	1828
133	Paschal	(72)	Marg. Buteau S.F.S.	1830
134	Joseph	(74)	Sophie Fortier Bert.	1841
135	Jn. Baptiste	(75)	Caroline Bilodeau	
			Bert.	1845
136	Louis	(75)	Eliz. Blais Bert.	1845
137	Jn. Baptiste	(76)	Judith Blouin	
			S. G.	1823
138	Simon	(76)	Angéle Blais S.G.	1826
139	Joseph	(79)	Marg. Thibaut	
			S. V.	1843
140	Etienne	(79)	Marie Lemieux	
			Bert.	1844
141	Augustin	(79)	Marie Thibaut S.V.	1844
142	Edouard	(79)	Scholastique Dion	
			Bert.	1846
145	Pierre		Caroline Guimet	
	Le même		Delvina Bernard	
			S. J.	1862
146	Augustin		Elénore Coté	
	Le même		Soulange Lebrun	
			S. M.	1863
147	Amable	(80)	Angé Mullen S.M.	1845
148	Joseph	(80)	Emélie Marseau	
			S.M.	1847
149	Jean	(80)	Eléonore Lemieux "	1856
150	François	(83)	Archange Pouliot "	1857
	Marie		Pierre Couture "	1861
	Le même		M. Genev. Asselin "	1857
151	André	(83)	Marie Racine "	1845
152	Hubert	(84)	Soulange Lemieux	
			S.V.	1843
153	Edouard	(84)	Marcelline Roy S.V.	1844
154	Joseph	(88)	Marg. Picard S. Chs.	1840
	Marguerite		Magl. Blanchet	
			S.Chs.	1863
155	Jn. Baptiste	(89)	M. Marcelline Claret	
			S.M.	1844
156	Michel	(89)	Milanie Quemeneur	
			S.M.	1850
157	Augustin	(89)	Sophie Lessart S.M.	1851
158	Léon	(89)	M. Philomène Gagnon	
			S.M.	1856
159	Ursin	(93)	Marcelline Forgue	
			S.M.	1844
160	François Xa-	(94)	M. Hélène Poliquin	
	vier		S.M.	1841
	Le même		Vitaline Fortier "	1855
161	Majorique	(94)	M. Sara Gagnon "	1854
162	Thomas	(98)	Archange Tangué S.V.	1834

MERCIER.

163	Paul	(104)	M. Ls. Pigeon S.Chs.	1855
164	Joseph	(110)	M. Angèle Blais S.F.S.	1842
165	Magloire	(113)	Flore M. Neil S M.	1851
166	Antoine	(120)	Sophie Boivin S.V.	1829
	Marie Délina		Nap. Catellier ,,	1861
	Luce		Jos. Roy ,,	1865
	Virginie		Michel Bernard ,,	1867
	Guillaume			
	Antoine			
167	Michel	(120)	Julie Bernard ,,	1834
168	Louis	(120)	Eliz. Bernard S.V.	1836
169	Louis	(126)	Sophie Gautron ,,	1851
170	François Xa-	(130)	M. Rose Fortier S.M.	1854
	vier			
171	Antoine	(166)	Désanges Richard S.V.	1855
172	Guillaume	(166)	Philomène Cochon ,,	1857
173	Jean Bap-	(125)	Marg. Paquet S.Chs.	1830
	tiste			

MESNY.

1	Etienne	Cath. Lainé S.F.	1671
	Marie Anne	Nic. Vérieul ,,	1692
	Jeanne	Jacq. Bourgouin ,,	1706
	Catherine	Jacq. Baron S.Frs.	1698
	Anne	Jean Gagnon ,,	1699
	Reine	Jean Lefebvre S.Anne	1697
	Catherine	Nic. Croteau ,,	1709
	Marguerite	Prisque Paré ,,	1715

MÉTAYER.

1	Louis		Fse. Beaucher	
	Augustin			
	Jean			
2	Jacques		Levesque	
	Prisque			
3	Augustin	(1)	Josette Richet S.P.	1812
	Jean			
	Augustin			
	Vincent			
4	Jean	(1)	Judith Rouleau S.L.	1816
5	Prisque	(2)	Marie Coulombe ,,	1816
	Le même		M. Anne Coulombe ,,	1823
6	Jean	(3)	Angèle Marcoux S.J.	1841
	Edouard Elzéar			
7	Augustin	(3)	Marg. Bilodeau	
	Rose de Lima		Geo. Marcoux S.P.	1859
8	Vincent	(3)	Julie Thivierge S.J.	1851
9	Edouard El-	(6)	Philomène Dupont	
	zéar		S.F.	1869

MÉTIVIER.

1	Jacques		Fse. Beausier	
	Mathurin			
2	Louis		Louise Perrochon	
	Louis			
3	Mathurin	(1)	Louise Binet	
	Jean			
4	Louis	(2)	Louise Savaria	
			Beauport	1698
	Marie Louise		Michel Derome Qué.	1718
	Marie Angélique		Chs. Amiot ,,	1719
5	Jean	(3)	Genev. Couturier ,,	1701
	Noël			
	Jean			
	Le même		Angé Gab. Duchesne	
			Qué.	1717
A	Jean		M. Simone Béland	
	Françoise		J. B. Huret	
	Marie		F. Jobin	
6	Noël	(5)	Genev. Roy S.V.	1731
7	Jean	(5)	M. Jos. Fradet ,,	1738
8	Louis		Eliz. Peltier S.Tho.	1747
	Louis Abraham			

MÉTIVIER.

9	Jacques François	M. Cath. Miville		
			S. Tho.	1772
	Marie Théotiste	Aug. Goupy S.V.	1806
	Marie Catherine	J. B. Morrisset ,,	1805
	Michel			
10	Louis Abra-	(8)	M. Royer Pruneau	
	ham		Bert.	1789
11	Pierre		Louise Gauthier Montréal	
	Marie Anne		Frs. Marcoux S.M.	1824
	Félicité		Jean Dalaire ,,	1825
	Félicité		2° Pierre Fortin ,,	1839
	Félicité		3° Gab. Goupy ,,	1851
	François			
12	Michel	(9)	Marie Quemeneur	
			S.F.S.	1802
	Pierre			
13	François	(11)	M. Jos. Coulombe	
			S.Chs.	1815
14	Pierre	(12)	M. Rufine Kéroack	
			S.P.S.	1832

MEUNIER.

1	René		Marie Leroux Clermont	
	Mathurin			
2	Jean		Jacquette Gouron	
			Ev. de Larochelle	
	Julien			
3	Mathurin	(1)	Fse. Fafart Montréal	1647
	Françoise		Chs. Pouliot	1667
	Françoise		2° Jean Paul Maheu	
			S.L.	1700
	Elizabeth		Isaac Paquet S.R.	1670
	Marguerite		Pierre Labbé S.Anne	1674
	Marguerite		2° Jean Deblois S.Frs.	1710
	Mathurin			
	François			
4	Julien	(2)	Louise Frost Que.	1670
	Marie Madeleine		Etn. Bouchard Que.	1692
	Marie Charlotte		Philippe Gusillier Que.	1706
	Marie Charlotte		2° Mathieu Cotin	
			S. Aug.	1709
	Françoise		Simon Morin Lorette	1696
	Marie Françoise		Frs. Travers Que.	1712
5	Mathurin	(3)	M. Mad. Meneux S.F.	1684
	Marie		Pierre Bouvier S.Anne	1702
	Le même		Cath Bonhomme	
			Lorette	1705
6	François	(3)	Angé Jacob A.L.	1692
	Agnès		Julien Mercier S.Anne	1718
	Monique		Jos. Boulet ,,	1723
	Marie Margue-		Jacq. Talbot ,,	1726
	rite			
	Geneviève		Etn. Simard ,,	1726
	Jeanne		Zach. Bolduc S.Joa.	1728

MICHON.

1	Abel		Marie Thibodeau S.L.	1699
	Charles			
	Jean Baptiste			
	Laurent			
	Augustin			
2	Laurent	(1)	Anne Blanchet S.P.S.	1728
	Guillaume			
	Joseph			
	Charles			
	Jean Marie			
	Louis Marie			
3	Jean Baptiste	(1)	Marg. Lemieux	
	Marie		Jacq. Campagna	
			S.Tho.	1754
	Marie Marthe		Frs. Picard ,,	1761
	Le même		Marie Morisset S.M.	1744
	Marie Rosalie		J. B. Casault S.Tho.	1767
	Marie Elizabeth		Jos. Blais ,,	1773
4	Augustin	(1)	M. Marthe Blanchet	

MICHON.

Madeleine	Jacq. Adam	S.Chs.	1775
Madeleine	2° Pierre Patry	S.G.	1784
Abel Charles			
5 Charles	(1) M. Anne Dufresne		
		S.G.	1755
Elizabeth	Frs·Paré	S.Anne	1772
6 Guillaume	(2) M.Mad.Morisset	S.M.	1753
Le même	M. Jos. Terrien	S.M.	1773
7 Jean Marie	(2) M. Jos. Picard	S.P.S.	1757
8 Joseph	(2) M. Ls. Terrien	S.M.	1772
9 Louis Marie	(2) M.Eliz. Morin	S.P.S.	1762
Marie Elizabeth	Ls. Lacroix	S.M.	1786
10 Charles	(2) M. Eliz. Paquet	"	1775
Marie Elizabeth	Michel Roy	"	1779
Marie Louise	Ls. Bernier	"	1806
11 Abel Charles	(4) Dorothée Talon	S.P.S.	1777

MIMAUX.

1 Pierre	Mathurine Renaud		
Jean			
2 Jean	(1) Susanne Filteau	S.J.	1698
Josette	Pierre Leclaire	S.V.	1726
Le même	Cath. Rondeau		
Marie Madeleine	Jean Turgeon	S.M.	1737
Catherine	Pierre Garant	"	1746
Pierre			
Joseph			
3 Joseph	(2) M. Cécile Charron		
		S.M.	1746
Le même	M. Anne Forgue	"	1756
4 Pierre	(5) M. Jos. Rome	B.	1752
	Derome		
Marguerite	Jos. Duquet	S.Chs.	1796
Pierre			
Charles			
5 Pierre	(4) M. Anne Marseau		
		S. Chs.	1780
Marie Reine	Chs. Boucher	S.H.	1802
6 Charles	(4) M. Thérèse Fouquet		
		S.H.	1804

MINEAU.

1 Jean	Jeanne Caillet		
Marie	Jean Mourier	S.F.	1678
Marie	2° Jean Rabouin	S.J.	1706
René			
2 René	Jeanne Dufresne	S.L.	1682
Anne	Etn. Fontaine	S.L.	1706
René			
3 René	(2) Anne Moreau	S.L.	1703

MIRAND.

1 Nicolas	Marg. Robidoux		
Marguerite	Pierre Ferland	S.P.	1803
Elizabeth	Ls. Aubin	"	1807
2 Michel	Marie Robitaille		
Le même	Constance Roberge		
		S.P.	1832

MOLLEUR—LALLEMAND.

1 Pierre	Jeanne Queneville	Qué.	1671
Joachim			
Michel			
Le même	Eliz. Maranda	B.	1718
2 Joachim	(1) Jeanne Civadier	S.L.	1793
Geneviève	Nic. Alaire	Que.	1723
Marie	Jacq. Vivier	B.	1729
Marie Josette	Frs. Alaire	B.	1738
Pierre Louise			
Antoine			
3 Michel	(1) M. Fse.Civadier	S.L.	1694
Jeanne	Pierre Garant	B.	1709

MOLLEUR–LALLEMAND.

Jean Baptiste			
Le même	M. Jeanne Lis	B.	1703
4 Pierre Louis	(2) M. Fse. Labadie	B.	1728
5 Antoine	(2) M. Ls. Labrecque	B.	1739
6 Jean Baptiste	(3) M. Fse. Quéret	B.	1721
Jean Baptiste	Fse. Bourbeau		
Josette	Frs. Couillard	B.	1758
Françoise	Jos. Dodier	B.	1758
Jean			
François			
7 Jean	(7) Thérèse Guay	B.	1756
Jean Baptiste			
8 François	(7) M. Marcelline Bacquet		
		S.M.	1773
9 Jean Baptiste	(3) Agathe Rouleau	B.	1820
Agathe	Jean Chamberlan		
		S.L.	1861
Jean			
10 Jean	(10) Eliz. Pomela Montigny		
		S.L.	1862

MONMÉNY.

1 Guillaume	Marg. Gobeil	S.J.	1688
Jeanne	Nicolas Maupas	B.	1723
Joseph			
Jean Baptiste			
2 Joseph	(1) Angé Forgue	S.M.	1715
Marguerite	Pierre Bacquet	S.M.	1741
Marie Josette	Michel Quéret	S.M.	1745
Marie Angélique	André Plante	S.M.	1754
Marie Angélique	J. B. Tangué	S.M.	1749
Michel			
Joseph			
Jean Baptiste			
3 Jean Baptiste	(1) Marie Bissonnet	B.	1723
Marie Anne	Jean Garant	S.M.	1747
Marguerite	J. B. Blais	S.M.	1757
Marie Geneviève	Aug. Lacroix	S.M.	1763
Marie Madeleine	Ant. Bleau	S.M.	1777
Marie Madeleine	2° Ls. Lefebvre	S.M.	1793
Jean Baptiste			
Le même	M. Genev. Lavoie		
		S. V.	1742
Pierre			
Nicholas			
Le même	M. Fse. Hélie	S.V.	1752
Le même	Jeanne Fontaine		
		S.M.	1764
4 Joseph	(2) Genev. Fournier	S.M.	1739
Marie Angélique	Pierre Dalaire	S.V.	1784
Marie Angélique	2° Jos. Marie Boulet		
		S.F.S	1799
Etienne			
Pierre			
5 Michel	(2) M. Jos. Lacroix	S.M.	1750
Michel			
Le même	Marie Letourneau		
		S.L.	1764
Marie Marg.	J. B. Nadeau	S.M.	1789
Marie Marg.	2° Dieudonné Carbonneau		
		S.M.	1797
Marie Angélique	Alexis Fortier	S.M.	1796
Jean Baptiste			
6 Jean	(2) Genev. Gontier		
		S.Chs.	1750
Angélique	Chs. Prevost	S.Chs.	1787
Charles			
Jean Baptiste			
Le même	Genev. Paquet	S.M.	1759
	v. d'Ant. Quéret		
7 Jean Baptiste	(3) M. Cath. Chamberlan		
		S.M.	1749
Jean Baptiste			
8 Pierre	(3) M. Fse. Rémillard		
		S.M.	1771

MONMÉNY.

9	Nicholas	(3)	M. Mad. Forgue S.M. 1771	
10	Pierre	(4)	M. Félicité Laplanche	
			(Bellay) S.V.	1768
	Marie Geneviève	Ls. Lecours	Lévis	1814
	Marguerite	Jos. Turgeon	Lévis	1816
	François			
	Jean Baptiste			
11	Etienne	(4)	M. Jos. Bleau S.M. 1776	
			v. de Ls. Paquet	
	Marie Madeleine	Jos. Balan	S.M.	1795
	Marie Louise	Pierre Bisson	S.M.	1819
12	Michel	(5)	Marie Simart S.M. 1782	
	Cécile	Ant. Gosselin	S.G.	1807
	Augustin			
	Louis			
	Michel			
	Charles			
13	Jean Baptiste (5)	M. Anne Fortier S.M. 1795		
	Jean			
	François Xavier			
	Jacques			
14	Jean Baptiste (6)	Susanne Coulombe		
			S.P.S.	1778
	Angélique	Math Dutile	S.G.	1818
	Michel			
	Joseph			
	Augustin			
15	Charles	(6)	Mad. Polequin S.Chs. 1783	
	Marie Josette	Frs. Letellier	S.Chs.	1809
	Marie Madeleine	Jos. Diers	S.Chs.	1811
	Angélique	Ant. Couture	S.Chs.	1819
	Pierre			
	Etienne			
	Jean			
16	Joseph		M. Mad. Poliquin	
	Jacques			
17	Pierre		Marie Polequin	
	Jean			
18	Abraham		Marie Guilmet Bert. 1796	
	(Inconnu.)			
19	Jean Baptiste (7)	M. Mad. Rousseau		
			S.V.	1783
	Jean Baptiste			
	Le même		M. Ls. Nicole S.V. 1809	
20	François	(10)	Josette Pouliot S.Chs. 1805	
	Marie Josette	Pierre Turcot	S.Chs.	1837
	Marcel			
	Joseph			
21	Jean Bapt.	(10)	Jeanne Gontier S.G. 1809	
22	Michel	(12)	Mad. Rousseau S.G. 1808	
23	Louis	(12)	Marie Labrecque S.G. 1819	
24	Augustin	(12)	Charlotte Gautron ‚‚ 1824	
25	Charles	(12)	Marg. Ainse ‚‚ 1821	
26	Jean	(12)	Fse. Labrecque SChs. 1827	
27	Jacques	(13)	Flavie Bernier S.P.S. 1837	
28	François	(13)	Marie Morin S.V. 1841	
	Xavier			
29	Augustin	(14)	Marie Sampson Lévis 1818	
30	Michel	(14)	Charlotte Octeau ‚‚ 1821	
31	Joseph	(15)	Marg. Lambert ‚‚ 1824	
A	Jean	(15)	Louise Clément S.H. 1820	
32	Pierre	(15)	Marg. Ruel S.G. 1825	
	George			
33	Etienne	(15)	Angé Rouillard S.G. 1825	
34	Jacques	(16)	M. Ls. Vien S.Chs. 1827	
35	Jean	(17)	Anatole Vien ‚‚ 1822	
	Natalie		Jacq. Daniau ‚‚ 1842	
36	Jean Baptiste(19)	Marthe Lemieux Bert 1811		
	Sara		Chs. Roy S.M. 1855	
	Jean Baptiste			
37	Marcel	(20)	Appoline Coté S.Chs. 1831	
	Julie		Ant. Nadeau ‚‚ 1854	
38	Joseph	(20)	Louise Emélie Lefrançois	
			B.	1836
39	Georges	(32)	M. Alvine Couture ‚‚ 1858	
40	JeanBaptiste(36)	Emélie Marseau S.M. 1846		

MONTIGNY.

1				
2				
3	Jean		Mad. Turpa	
	Jean Baptiste			
4	Michel		Thérèse Cantin	
	Michel			
5	Jean Baptiste (3)	Dorothée Gauthier		
			S.V.	1734
	Marie	Jacq. Touron	‚‚	1758
	Ursule	Philippe Fontaine	‚‚	1763
	Zacharie			
	Jean			
6	Michel	(4)	Mad. Ferlant S.P. 1730	
	Madeleine	Jos. Létourneau	‚‚	1752
	Marie Anne	Jean Létourneau	‚‚	1753
	Reine	Chs. Blancard	‚‚	1761
	Thérèse	Amb. Gosselin	‚‚	1765
	Thérèse	2° Alexis Bedard	‚‚	1801
	Le même (?)	M. Anne Leblanc	‚‚	1743
	Thècle	Amb. Roberge	‚‚	1771
	Angélique	Ls. Ferlant	‚‚	1773
	Marie Anne	Ls. Ouellet	‚‚	1781
	Michel			
	François			
7	Jean	(5)	M. Jos. Larrivé SF.S. 1753	
8	Zacharie	(5)	M. Mad. Vérieul S.M 1764	
9	Michel	(6)	Agathe Paradis S.P. 1782	
	Marie Anne	Julien Tessier	S.P.	1812
	Agathe	Ign. Paquet	‚‚	1818
	Marie	Presque Turcot	‚‚	1830
	Laurent			
10	François	(6)	Fse. Nolin S.P. 1787	
	Michel			
	François			
11	Laurent	(9)	Euphrosine Roberge	
			S.P.	1820
	Dorothée	Ed. Gourdeau	‚‚	1841
	Dorothée	2° Ls. Thivierge	‚‚	1852
	Marie Céleste	Alexis Lafrançois	‚‚	1853
	Flavie	F. X. Létourneau	‚‚	1854
	Eliz. Pomélie	Jean Molleur	S.L.	1862
	Celestin			
12	Michel	(10)	M. Angé Paradis S.P. 1821	
13	François	(10)	Julie Leclaire ‚‚ 1816	
14	Célestin	(11)	Olive Deblois ‚‚ 1853	

MOOR.

1	Emond		Cécile Richard Angleterre	
	Thomas			
2	Thomas	(1)	Jeanne Lemelin Que. 1690	
	Marie	Ls. Malet	S.L.	1734
	Pierre			
3	Pierre	(2)	Louise Genev. Gendreau	
			S.L.	1724
	François			
	Thomas			
4	François	(3)	Louise Demeule S.J. 1753	
	Stanislas			
	François			
	Joseph			
5	Thomas	(3)	Isabelle Denis S.L. 1763	
	Marie Anne	J. B. Paquet	‚‚	1784
	Jean			
	Thomas			
6	François	(4)	Susanne Paquet S.F. 1787	
	Marie	Jos. Couture	B.	1822
	Françoise			
7	Stanislas		Genev. Gourdeau S.P 1796	
8	Joseph	(4)	Marie Lacasse S.G. 1799	
9	Laurent		Marg. Poliquin	
	Laurent			
	Pierre			
10	Jean	(5)	M. Jos. Gosselin S.F. 1798	
	Marie Josette	Chs. Binet	S.M.	1818
	Sophie	Jos. Polquin	S.M.	1830

MOOR.

11 Thomas	(5) Thérèse Vaillancour	S.F. 1805
12 François	(6) Angè Audet	S.G. 1810
13 Laurent	(9) M. Hélène Patry	Lévis 1806
Laurent		
14 Pierre	(9) Marg. Quéret	B. 1818
	V. d'Ign. Guay	
15 Louis	Angéle Boissonneau	
Adélaïde	Clément Giguère	
Hubert		
16 Laurent	(13) M. Anne Couture	Lévis 1833
17 Hubert	(15) Philomène Royer S.J. 1860	

MOREAU.

1 Jean		Anne Couture	C.R. 1667
Jeanne		Jos. Dalret	S.L. 1695
Jeanne		René Simoneau	S.L. 1699
Anne		René Mineau	S.L. 1703
Pierre			
2 Louis		Eliz. Gagnon	S.F. 1678
3 Pierre	(1)	Cath. Burlon	S.L. 1703
Le même		Anne Mondain	
Le même		Genev. Fontaine S.J. 1710	
Marie		¹ asile Cloutier	S.L. 1735
Thérèse		Louis Isabel	S.L. 1746
Geneviève		Chs. Cloutier	C.R. 1748
Laurent			
Pierre			
Jean Baptiste			
4 François Noël		M. Marg. Bélanger	
Marguerite		Jean Mercier Bert. 1748	
5 Jacques		Louise Petitclere	Qué.
Le même		Cath. Pruneau S.Chs. 1752	
6 Pierre	(3)	Angé Demeule	S.J. 1742
Angélique		Ant. Brousseau	S.L. 1773
Marie Louise		Michel Létellier S.V. 1774	
Catherine		Ant. Vallée	S.M. 1776
Le même		Thècle Lainé	S.J. 1760
Marguerite		Pierre Blouin	S.G. 1794
Marguerite		2° Amable Lacasse	S G. 1808
Joseph			
7 Laurent	(3)	Hélène Coulombe	S.L. 1748
8 Jean Baptiste	(3)	Cath. Réaume	C.R. 1755
Jean Baptiste			
9 François		M. Ls. Constantin	S. Foye
Michel			
10 Joseph	(6)	M. Anne Corriveau	Bert 1794
Marie Anne		André Labbé	S.G. 1818
Marie		Noël Poirier	S.G. 1822
Archange		Ambr. Chabot	S.G. 1829
11 Jean Baptiste	(8)	Fse. Fournier S.Chs. 1789	
12 Michel	(9)	Mad. Roy	S.V. 1791
Michel			
13 Charles		Marie Routier	
Marie Josette		Germ. Levesque	B. 1828
Marguerite		Victor Poitier	B. 1828
Henriette		Jos. Carrier	B. 1831
14 Louis		Rosalie Puuliot	
Virginie		Pierre Geo. Peltier B. 1849	
Joseph			
15 François	(10)	Fse. Dodier	S.G. 1821
16 Michel	(12)	Charlotte Chatigny	S.G. 1819
17 Joseph Alfred	(14)	Célina Lepage S.Chs. 1860	

MOREL.

1 Oliver		Fse Du¹,uet	Qué 1670
Louis Joseph			
Olivier			
2 Louis Joseph	(1)	Eliz. Ramé, Seigneur de la Durantaye	
Marie Anne		Jean Damour	B. 1719
Marie Catherine		Jos. Gagnon	Kamouraska 1730
Brigitte		Chs. Berthody	Kamouraska 1743
Chs. Alexandre			
André			
3 Olivier	(1)	M. Susanne Guyon	
4 Joseph		Marie Thivierge	
Marie Anne		Jos. Lecours	B. 1723
5 Chs. Alexandre	(2)	Marie Couillard	B. 1724
Marie Madeleine		Thomas Fournier	S. Tho. ¹652
Jean Baptiste			
Joseph			
Le même		Marthe Normand	Kamouraska 1746
Le même		M. Anne Ouimet	
6 André	(2)	Thérèse de la Bourlière	Kamouraska 1736
Jean			
7 Joseph	(5)	Genev. Valière S.P.S. 1761	
Le même		M. Fse. Boulet	S.H. 1807
8 Jean Baptiste (5)		Genév. Picard S.P.S. 1764	
Le même		M. Salomé Blanchet	S.P.S. 1788
Marie Madeleine		Aug. Mathieu S.P.S. 1812	
Jean Baptiste			
9 Jean	(6)	Cath. Boucher S.P.S. 1764	
Marguerite		Jos. Labonté S.P.S. 1787	
10 Nic. René		Mad. Leblond	
Marie Hélène		Frs. Greffart	S.M. 1772
11 Jean Baptiste (8)		Fse. Renaud	S.G. 1816
Marguerite		Marie Ant. Paquet	S.M. 1848
Léocadie		Hilaire Roy	B. 1850

MORIN.

1 Noël		Hélène DesportesQue. 1640	
Agnès		Nic. Gaudry	Que. 1653
Louise		Chs. Cloutier	Que. 1659
Madeleine		Gilles Rageot	Que. 1673
Alphonse			
Jean			
2 Pierre		Marie Martin Port Royal	
Charles			
Jean			
Jacques			
Le même		Fse. Chiasson	
Michel			
Pierre			
Antoine			
3 Jean	(1)	Cath. Belleau	Que. 1667
4 Alphonse		Mad. Normand	Que. 1670
Pierre Noël			
Alphonse			
Joseph			
Le même		AngéPicard	Cap. S. Ign. 1692
Marie		Jacq. Bilodeau S.Tho. 1720	
Louis			
5 André		Marg. Morean	Que. 1670
Jean			
6 Jacques	(2)	M.AnneLavergneQue.1699	
7 Pierre		Marie Boulet	S.Tho. 1707
Marie Françoise		René Picard	
MarieFrançoise		2°André Boucheau	S.P.S. 1765
Reine		Jos. Malboeuf S.P.S. 1750	

MORIN.

Jacques
Jean Baptiste
Augustin
François
François
Joseph
Jean Baptiste
Jean Baptiste
8 Jean (2) Eliz. Hubert Qué. 1715
9 Charles (2) Thérèse Minet Qué. 1719
10 Michel (2) Marie Fregeot Bert. 1727
11 Antoine (2) Marg. Daniau S.F.S. 1734
M. Marguerite Jean Frs. Chouinard
S.F.S. 1754
Marie Louise Jos.PierreJean S.F.S. 1757
Marie Thérèse Jacq. Tangué S.F.S. 1761
M. Geneviève Jos. Dumas S.F.S. 1762
Marie Françoise J. B. Bourque S.F.S. 1770
Pierre Noël
Eustache
Michel
Louis
Martin
12 Pierre Noël (4) Marg.Rousseau S.Tho.1696
Germain
Jean
Isidore
Joseph
Le même Hélène Maranda S.P. 1731
13 François Al- (4) Cath. Chamaillart
phonse S. Tho. 1697
François
14 Joseph (4) Agnès Bouchard
Cap. S. Ign. 1701
Elizabeth Jacq. Campagna
S. Tho, 1731
Elizabeth Agnès Joachim Dion S.P.S. 1727
Pierre
Isidore
15 Louis (4) Eliz. Bilodeau S. Frs. 1721
16 Jean (5) Angé Lerreau
Chs. Bourg. 1712
Thomas
17 Denis Mad. Boulet
Marie François Pierre Pellerin S.P.S. 1749
Marie Josette J.B.Malboeuf S.P.S. 1752
Geneviève Michel Rousseau
S.P.S. 1757
Jean Marie
Denis
18 Jean Jeanne Bonhomme
Lorette
Michel
François
19 Sebastien Marie Fse. Blanchet
Jean Baptiste
Pierre
Le même M. Anne Frégeot
S. F. S. 1743
20 Charles Claire Picard
Marie Claire Jacques Thivierge
S.F.S.1752
Charles
21 Pierre Noël Thérèse Peltier
Marie Josette J. B. Daniau Bert. 1753
Marie Anne Gab. Bilodeau " 1753
Geneviève Frs. Daniau
Geneviève 2" Jos. Chamberlan
S.P.S. 1759
Pierre Noël
Jean Baptiste
22 Joseph Marie Gagné
Marie Josette Jos. Gaudreau S.P.S. 1754
23 François (7) Genev. Langelier
Joseph
Le même Félicité Plante S.F.S. 1764
18—27

MORIN.

Cécile Michel Coté S.H. 1788
François
Pierre Noël
Henri
24 Jacques (7) Thérèse Quemeneur
Jacques S. Frs. 1733
Louis
Augustin
Pierre
François
Jean Baptiste
25 Jean Baptiste (7) Agnès Mercier S.F.S. 1738
M. Geneviève Jos. Gagnon " 1764
Laurent
Jacques
26 Joseph (7) Dorothée Terrien S.J. 1741
Marie Louise Alexis Picard S.P.S. 1773
27 Augustin (7) M. Théotiste Talbot
S.F.S. 1750
Marie Anne Basile Bonneau " 1796
Marie Thérèse Jos. Amand Foret
S.P.S. 1772
Marie Madeleine Aug. Bouchard " 1784
MarieMarguerite Jos. Samson " 1787
René
Jean Baptiste
Joseph
Augustin
28 Jean Baptiste (7) Genev. Blanchet
S.P.S. 1758
François Mad. Ruel
Louis
29 Pierre Noël (11) Anne Bourque S.F. 1767
30 Eustache (11) M. Jos. Boulet S.F.S. 1777
Marie Josette Pierre Gosselin " 1798
MarieMarguerite Ls. Michel Mercier
S.P.S. 1807
Marie Claire Ign. Gaudin S.V. 1812
31 Louis (11) Marg. Paré S.F.S. 1778
32 Michel (11) M. Reine McNeil
S.F.S. 1787
33 Joseph (12) Marg. Isabel S.L. 1725
Geneviève MauriceCoupard S.V.1749
Marie Charlotte Chs. Auray S.F.S. 1761
Reine Aug. Picard " 1762
Marie André Fleury " 1795
Jean François
Basile
34 Joseph (12) Thérèse Dufresne S.L. 1730
35 Germain (12) Ursule Valière S.P. 1731
Marie Frs. Cloutier S.P.S. 1761
Marguerite Michel Chartier " 1753
Elizabeth Ls. Marie Michon " 1761
Marie Anne Paul Bolduc " 1773
Marie Angèlique Jacq. Gendron S.F.S. 1774
Germain
36 Isidore (12) Eliz. Nolin S.P. 1735
37 François (13) Genev. Bossé
Cap. S. Ign. 1726
Marie Madeleine Ign. Dessaint S.Tho. 1753
38 Thomas (16) Marg. Parant
Beauport 1743
Etienne
39 Jean Josette Audet
Augustin
40 Pierre (19) Reine Fortier
Cap. S. Ign. 1742
Marie Reine Guill Pellerin S.P.S. 1770
François
Le même M. Genev. Blais Bert. 1751
Marie Genev. Basile Beaucher S.P.S.1775
Marie Victoire Pierre Blanchet S.P.S.1784
Marie Claire Pierre Dessaint " 1788
Marie Marg. Pierre Basile Fournier
S.P.S. 1792

MORIN.

```
   Augustin
41 Jean              Félicité Lemieux
   Marie Félicité    Jos. Bourque    S.F.S. 1776
   Marie Madeleine Jacq. Gagné     "    1782
   Marie Anne        J. B. Pichet    "    1784
   Marie Josette     Bernard Gagné S.P.S.1778
   Chrysostome
   Jérome Lambert
   Louis
   Antoine
42 François      (7) Dorothée Malboeuf
                           C.R. 1749
   Le même           M. Eliz. Brideau
                           S.P.S.1753
43 Claude            M. Agnès Gagné
   Pierre
44 Pierre       (14) M. Claire Langlois
                           S.Tho. 1748
   Martin
A  Isidore      (14) Louise Fse. Mivette
                           S. Tho. 1738
   Isidore
45 Jean Moïse        M. Jos. Gagné  S.M. 1750
   Marie Josette     Nic. Gosselin S.F.S. 1803
   Jean Moïse
   Louis Marie
   Pierre
   François
   Augustin
46 Denis        (17) Cécile Fontaine S.P.S.1754
   Marie Reine       Martin Morin    "    1777
   Marie Reine       2° Jacq. Dandurand
                           S.P.S. 1777
   Cécile            Ant. Mercier    "    1781
   Marie Josette     Chs. Dandurand
                           S.Tho. 1782
   Antoine
47 Michel       (18) Genev. Maranda S.L. 1751
   Le même           Genev. Cornelier S.F. 1757
   Le même           Thècle Leclaire  S.P. 1763
   Marie Louise      Jos. Leclaire    S.P. 1794
   Marie Louise      2° Tho. Bourassa S.H. 1813
   Le même           Mad. Perrot      S.F. 1777
   Marie Madeleine J. B. Langlois    "   1803
   Michel
48 François      (18) Marie Bouffart S.L. 1753

49 JeanBaptiste(19) Fse. Blais     Bert. 1753
   Marie Françoise  Jean Marie Sénécal
                           S.P.S. 1782
   Sebastien
   François
   Simon
50 Charles       (20) M. Genev. Larrivé
                           S.F.S. 1753
   Marie Victoire    Aug. Marseau    "    1774
   Marie Josette     Jacq. Parant    "    1774
   Madeleine         Jos. Foucher    "    1783
   Reine             Jos. Marseau    "    1786
   Marie Susanne     Jacq. Gagnon    "    1788
   Agathe            Etn. Voyer      "    1788
   Charles

51 JeanBaptiste(21) Angé Blanchet S.P.S. 1751
52 Pierre Basile     Angé Blanchet
   Charles
   Augustin
   Alexis
   Jean Baptiste
   Pierre
53 Pierre Noël  (21) M.Jos. Mercier S.P.S.1723
   Charlotte         Aug. Labrecque S.G. 1806
   Michel
   Simon
54 Pierre       (24) Marg. Daniau  S.P.S 1756
55 Jacques      (24) M. Anne Gendron "  1765
```

```
   Marie Thérèse     Joachim Lainé S.H. 1792
   Marie Anne        Michel Morriset  "   1787
   Marie Brigtite    Jas. Turgeon    "   1803
   Josette           Pierre Hélie    "   1805
   Jacques
   Pierre
   François
   Jean Baptiste
   Joseph
56 François     (24) Rosalie Foret  S.P.S. 1761
57 Augustin     (24) Cath. Lefebvre Lévis 1771
58 Louis        (24) M. Ls. Terrien S.F.S. 1774
   Le même           UrsuleGaudreauS.P.S1795
   Louis
   Augustin
59 Jacques      (25) Josette Gaudin S.F.S.1769
   Marie Josette     Frs.Théberge    "   1793
   Victoire          J.B. Martineau  "   1793
   Marguerite        J.B. Daniau     "   1803
   Reine             Paschal Mercier "   1809
   Jacques
   Louis
   JeanBaptiste
60 Laurent      (25) M. Jos.Harnais S.P.S.1775
   M. Marguerite     René Abraham Daniau
                           S.F. 1802
   Jean Batiste
   Joseph
   Laurent
   Louis
61 Augustin     (27) Fse Bélanger S.P.S. 1779
   Augustin
62 JeanBaptiste(27) M. Pélagie Blanchet
                           S.P.S. 1790
   Rose              Jos. Félix Tétu  "  1831
   Jean Isidore
   Jean Baptiste
63 René         (27) M. Mad. Bouchard
   Toussaint               S.P.S. 1791
   AugustinCharles
   René
   François
   Le même           M. Genev. Proulx "  1829
64 Joseph       (27) M. Fse. Blais   "  1799
   MarieFrançoise    Noël Picard     "  1820
   Eléonore          Jean Frs. Boutin "  1827
   Constance         Vital Boissonneau " 1833
   Euphémie          Bénoni Buteau   "  1836
   Joseph
   Augustin
   Benoit
   Magloire
65 JeanFrançois(33) Ursule Richard S.F.S.1755
66 Joseph       (33) M. Thérèse Vérieul
                           S.F.S 1755
   Marie Charlotte   Frs. Bacquet    "  1786
   Marie Dorothée    Pierre Bilodeau "  1787
   Jean Alexis
67 Basile       (33) Mad. Picard     "  1771
   Marie Madeleine Jean Marie Boulet
                           S.F.S. 1802
   Marguerite        Ign. Bouchard   "  1806
   Germain
68 Germain      (35) Thérèse Coté  S.P.S. 1760
   Le même           Marg. Bolduc  S.M. 1765
   Le même           M. Cath. Méthot
                           V. d'Etn. Lebrun
                           Cap. S. Ign. 1788
   Le même           M. Anne AubéS.P.S. 1813
69 Etienne      (38) Cécile Maranda S.L. 1785
70 Augustin     (39) Eliz. Doiron   B. 1766
71 François     (40) M.Ls.Vaillancour
                           S.P.S. 1773
   Jean François
72 Augustin     (40) M.Jos.BouchardBert. 1781
   Marie Josette     Ant.LetourneauS.P.S.1807
```

MORIN.

MarieMarguerite	Jos. Fournier	P.S.	1821
Marie Claire	Jos. Blais	S.F.S.	1824
Augustin			
Etienne			
Pierre			
Le même	Eliz. Bilodeau	Bert.	1809
73 Charles	Genev. McNeil		
Marguerite	Gab. Thivierge	S.J.	1792
Le même	Cécile Duquet	S.H.	1803
74 Antoine	M. Anne Pellerin		
Marie Anne	PierreNoëlParé	S.P.S.	1787
Marie Rose	Ign. Dessaint	"	1788
Pierre René			
Pierre			
Augustin			
Jean Baptiste			
75 Alexis	Genev. Couture		
Jean Baptiste			
77 Isidore (44)	A Brigitte Fournier		
		S. Tho	1778
Brigitte	Jacq. Létourneau		
		S. G.	1801
Angélique	Pierre Gontier	"	1803
Marie Anne	Jean Gontier	"	1806
Catherine	Michel Létourneau	"	1812
Pierre			
Charles			
78 JeanBaptiste(24)	M.BarbePeltier	S.Tho.	1769
MarieMarguerite	Jos. Coté	S.Tho.	1811
Isaac			
Le même	M. Brigitte Fortier		
		S. M.	1813
79 François	M. Marthe Proulx		
Le même	M. Eliz. Bélanger		
		S. Tho.	1780
Marie Elizabeth	Jacq. Camiere	S.F.S.	1802
MarieMarguerite	Pierre Tangué	S.Frs.	1829
Jean François			
Michel			
Jean Baptiste			
80 Louis	Marg. Mercier		
Marguerite	PierreMarseau	S.P.S.	1806
81 Jean Marie (29)	M. Claire Caron	Islet	1785
		Islet.	
Louis			
82 Jacques	Josette Duchesne		
Pierre			
83 Chrysostome(41)	Fse. Dion	S.F.S.	1765
		S. Hyacinthe.	
Marie	J. B. Boutin	S.F.S.	1790
Françoise	Jos. Boutin	S.V.	1796
84 Louis (41)	Marg. Thibaut	S.F.S.	1777
Marie Catherine	J. B. Alaire	"	1797
Marie	Joseph Baudoin	"	1806
Le même	M. Ls. Lemieux	"	1798
Marie Angélique	André Rémillard	"	1817
Marie Angélique	2° Pierre Bouchard		
		S.F.S.	1832
Marie Archange	David Roy	"	1838
Marie Flavie	Jos. Dion	Bert	1845
Joseph			
85 Antoine (41)	M. Isabelle Beaudoin		
		S.F.S.	1781
		S.Frs. Beauce.	
86 Jérome (41)	Vict Terrien	S.F.S.	1787
Lambert			
Marie Victoire	Ed. Fortin	"	1819
Lambert			
87 Pierre (43)	Thérèse Fournier		
		S.P.S.	1771
88 Martin (44)	Reine Morin	"	1777
89 Martin (11)	Fse. Peltier	S.Tho.	1773
Martin			
90 Jean Moïse (45)	M. Brigitte Buteau		
		S.F.S.	1780

18—27½

MORIN.

Marie Archange	Ambroise Roberge		
		S.H.	1807
Marie Brigitte	J. B. Fortier	"	1808
Marie	Ls. Clément	"	1805
Ambroise			
91 Louis Marie (45)	Genev. Pepin	S.F.S.	1784
Reine	Aug. Guilmet	Bert.	1829
14 Pierre (45)	M. Ange Mercier	"	1790
Marie Josette	Pierre Veau	S.Chs.	1812
Le même	Reine Bonneau	S.F.S.	1794
93 Augustin (45)	M. Reine Jolin	"	1798
94 François (45)	M Angé Boissonneau		
		S.F.S.	1798
Ursule	Ant Bactaelt	"	1824
Sophie	Prudent Langlois	"	1830
Julie	Marcel Dessaint	"	1835
Séraphin			
François			
Hubert			
François Xavier			
95 Antoine (46)	M.Ls.Beaudoin	S.M.	1794
Marie Archange	Jac. Théberge	S.F.S.	1821
Louise	Jos. Bruneau	S.G	1825
Alexandre			
Antoine			
96 Michel (47)	AngéVaillancour	S.F.	1807
Magloire			
Le même	Marg. Martineau	"	1815
97 Sébastien (49)	Mad. Sénécal	S.P.S.	1782
98 François (49)	M.Ls.Sylvestre	"	1790
99 Simon (49)	Marie Gaumont	"	1793
Geneviève	Chs. Talbot	"	1832
100 Charles (50)	M. Ls. Quémeneur		
		S.F.S.	1784
Marguerite	Jean Bilodeau	"	1812
Marie Archange	Guill. Fournier	"	1817
Geneviève	Pierre Fournier	S.P.S.	1820
Charles			
Joseph			
101 Charles (52)	Fse. Mathieu	"	1779
Marie Angélique	Clément Cazeau	"	1806
Marie Angélique	2° Frs. Boutin	"	1822
Pierre Basile			
102 Alexis (52)	M. Anne Bélanger	"	1784
103 JeanBaptiste(52)	M. Ls. Gagné	"	1788
Marie Luce	Guill. Rousseau	"	1812
M. Françoise	Olivier Fournier	"	1822
Geneviève	J. B. Blais	"	1820
Marie Agathe	André Lemieux	"	1820
Bonaventure			
104 Augustin (52)	M. Genev. Gagné	"	1794
Geneviève	Ls. Demers	S.H.	1815
Augustin			
105 Simon (53)	Marg. Bilodeau	Bert.	1811
Marie	F. X. Monmeny	S.V.	1841
Elizabeth	Frs. Boulet	S.F.S.	1842
Le même	Marg. Thivierge	S.V.	1832
106 Michel (53)	Ange Toussaint	S.Chs	1815
107 Jacques (55)	Louise Morisset	"	1790
Louise	Jos. Nadeau	"	1811
Françoise	Michel Lemieux	"	1816
Marie Anne	Frs. Bégin	"	1819
Catherine	Ant. Lemieux	"	1819
107A François (55)	M. Chs. Pilet	S.H.	1791
Catherine	Clément Fradet	"	1813
107B Pierre (55)	Marg. Turgeon	"	1799
Angèle	Ant. Filteau	"	1819
107C Jean Baptiste(55)	M. Mad. Plante	"	1800
107D Joseph (55)	Marie Morin	S.H.	1803
108 Augustin (58)	Josette Denis	S.G.	1819
109 Louis (58)	Genev. Gagnon	S.M.	1820
Marguerite	Eloi Dion	"	1843
110 Jacques (59)	Marg. Bolduc	S.V.	1795
Le même	Marcelline Mercier		
		S.M.	1841

MORIN.

111	Louis	(59)	Angèle Mercier	S.F.S.1817
112	JeanBaptiste(59)		Julie Gagnon	„ 1827
	Charles Fréderic			
113	Joseph	(60)	M. Genev. Vien	B. 1805
	Marie Constance		Vital Gagnon	S.M. 1834
	Marie Geneviève		Basile Bonneau	„ 1837
	Marie Angélique		Jos. Provost	„ 1842
	Marguerite		Florent Baudoin	S.V. 1836
	Magloire			
	Jean			
	Laurent			
	Antoine			
	Ferdinand			
	Joseph			
114	JeanBaptiste(60)		M. Rose Gagnon	S.M.1809
	Olivier			
	Jean Baptiste			
	Eusèbe			
	Laurent			
115	Laurent	(60)	M. Angé Rouillard	S.M. 1814
116	Louis	(60)	Angé Audet	S.Chs. 1814
117	Augustin	(61)	M. Anne Cotin	S.M. 1803
	Olive		J. B. Bissonnet	„ 1833
	Constance		Frs. Dumas	„ 1841
	Marcelline		Michel Bacquet	„ 1844
	Marie Désanges		Pierre Bélanger	„ 1845
	AugustinNorbert			
	Olivier			
	Honoré			
	Georges			
	Louis			
118	JeanBaptiste(62)		Thècle Martineau	S.P.S. 1822
	Mathieu			
	François Xavier			
119	Jacques Isi-dore	(62)	M. Henriette Fraser	S.F.S. 1834
120	AugustinChs.(63)		Genev. Létourneau	S.P.S. 1818
121	Réné	(63)	M.Anne Gendron	„ 1826
122	François	(63)	Fse. Cochon	S.F.S. 1826
123	Joseph	(64)	M. Cécile Picard	„ 1822
124	Benoit	(64)	Restitut Gendron	„ 1834
	Pierre Octave			
125	Augustin	(64)	M.Eléonore Blais	„ 1836
126	Magloire	(64)	Lorette Boissonneau	S.F.S. 1843
127	Jean Alexis	(66)	M.Genev.Thibaut	„ 1794
128	Germain	(67)	Ursule Marseau	„ 1806
	Sophie		Pierre Théberge	S.V. 1836
	Anastasie		Frs. Honoré Théberge	S.V. 1840
	Germain			
	Vital			
	François Xavier			
129	JeanFrançois(71)		M.Angé Bacon	S.P.S.1803
130	Augustin	(72)	Adé Chartier	„ 1812
	Étienne		Islet	
	Adelaïde		Jérome Deroy	„ 1833
131	Pierre	(72)	MarieLétourneau	„ 1820
	Le même		M.Angé Paré	S.V. 1840
132	Pierre	(74)	M. Angé Lamothe	S.P.S. 1774
	Marie Désanges		Chs. Couture	S.Chs. 1799
	Thècle		Jos. Gosselin	„ 1805
	Thècle		2° Frs. Fournier	„ 1809
	Antoine Charles			
	Joseph			
133	JeanBaptiste(74)		M.Mad.Proulx	S.P.S.1778
134	Augustin	(74)	M. Jos. Babineau Nicolet	S.F.S. 1785
135	Pierre René	(74)	M. Angé Chevanel	S.P.S. 1791

MORIN.

	Adelaïde		Michel Morin	S.F.S. 1843
	Martial			
136	JeanBaptiste(75)		M. Eliz. Blais	Bert. 1790
	Elisabeth		Jos. Nadeau	S.Chs. 1809
137	Henri	(23)	M.Ls. Lemelin	S.M. 1799
138	Pierre	(77)	Fse. Fradel	S.G. 1810
139	Charles	(77)	Angé Turgeon	„ 1814
	Le même		Angé Nadeau	„ 1821
140	Isaac	(78)	Reine Arbour	S.F.S.1804
141	JeanFrançois(79)		M. Ls. Chartier	„ 1813
	Henriette		Césaire Fréderic Proulx	S.F.S. 1836
	Marie Restitut		Martial Morin	„ 1842
142	JeanBaptiste(79)		Eliz. Boivin	„ 1837
143	Michel	(79)	Adé Morin	„ 1843
144	Louis	(81)	Marg. Coulombe	Bert.1813
145	Pierre	(82)	Adé Picard	S.F.S. 1815
	Adelaïde		Ls. Prudent Lavergne	S.F.S. 1836
	Catherine		Ant.Létourneau	„ 1839
146	Joseph	(84)	M. Julie Blais	„ 1843
147	Lambert	(86)	M.Fse. Baudoin	„ 1816
	Elisabeth		Henri Emond	„ 1841
	Marie Onésime		Jacq. Labrecque	„ 1843
148	Martin	(89)	M.Angé Blais	S.P.S. 1797
	Marie	(89)	J. B. Labonté	S.P.S. 1824
	Julienne			
	Emérence		J. B. Picard	S.P.S. 1830
	Le même		M. Claire Bornier	S.P.S. 1814
A 149	Ambroise	(90)	M. Anne Samson	S.H.1811
	Pierre	(52)	Fse. Rouleau	„ 1786
	Marie		Jos. Morin	„ 1803
	Marie Francoise		Ant. Nadeau	„ 1806
	Angèle		Frs. Roy	„ 1812
	Gaspard			
	Louis			
150	Joseph	(23)	Marg. Coté	„ 1787
	Madeleine		Jos. Royer	S.G. 1821
	Joseph			
	François			
	Le même		Angé Bedard	„ 1824
A	François	(23)	M. Rose Blais	S. H. 1787
	Pierre			
151	Pierre Noël	(23)	Marie Quemeneur	S.H.1800
	Le même		M. Ls. Pilote	S.M. 1805
152	Michel		Angèle Lafrance	
	David			
153	Louis		Charlotte Savard	
	Madeleine		Zach. Couture	S.G. 1826
154				
155	Augustin	(104)	Agathe Rouleau	S.H. 1819
				S.Marie
	Augustin			
156	Jean Baptiste		Julie Bard	
	Jean Baptiste			
157	Michel		Louise Julien	S.Roch.
	Le même		Christine Nollet	B. 1835
158	Michel	(96)	Marg. Martineau	S.F.1815
	Marie Angé-lique		Olivier Emélien Pepin	S.F. 1850
	Michel			
	Antoine			
159	François	(94)	Reine Paré	S.F.S. 1827
	Le même		Angèle Lessart	S.V. 1851
160	Hubert	(94)	Olive Quemeneur	S.F.S. 1828
161	Séraphin	(94)	M. Sophie Laurandeau	S.F.S. 1839
162	Frs. Xavier	(94)	M. Céleste Cadrin	S.F.S. 1844
163	Alexandre	(95)	Thérèse Brochu	S.G. 1824
164	Antoine	(95)	M. Jos. Gagnon	S.F.S.1829
165	Magloire	(96)	Luce Emond	S.Frs. 1843

MORIN.

166	Maxime		Fse. Coté		
			Lévis		
	Onésine				
167	Joseph		M. Marcelline Macé		
			S. Roch des Aulnets		
	Marie Scolio		Vital Pepin	S.M.	1851
168	Charles	(100)	Marg. Nadeau	S.F.S.	1835
169	Joseph	(100)	M. Marthe Picard	,,	1821
170	PierreBasile	(101)	Modeste Talbot	S.F.S.	1803
171	Bonaventure	(103)	Agathe Bélanger	,,	1826
172	Chs. Frédéric	(112)	M. Adeline Roy	S.V.	1858
173	Jean	(113)	Julie Bolduc	,,	1834
174	Joseph	(113)	Mathilde Thibaut		
				S.F.S.	1835
175	Antoine	(113)	Françoise Blais	S.M.	1836
176	Magloire	(113)	Marie Aubé	S.V.	1837
177	Ferdinand	(113)	Marg.Coulombe	S.Chs.	1840
178	Laurent	(113)	Marcelline Tangué		
				S.V.	1847
179	Augustin	(117)	Adèle Raimond	Qué.	
	Norbert				
180	Louis	(117)	Eliza Blais	S.P.S.	1829
181	Olivier	(117)	Emélie Dubord	S.M.	1830
	Le même		Eliz. Chabot	S.Chs.	1852
182	Honoré	(117)	Marcelline Gagnon		
				S.M.	1842
183	Georges	(117)	Genev. Pigeon	S.V.	1843
184	Jean Bapt.	(114)	M. Flavie Bonneau		
185	Olivier	(114)	Apolline Chamberlan		
				S.M.	1844
186	Eusèbe	(114)	MarcellinePigeon	S.V.	1846
187	Laurent	(114)	Julie Boutin	S.Chs.	1847
188	Frs. Xavier	(118)	M. Esther Balan	S.V.	1845
189	Pierre	(124)	M. Angèle Turgeon		
	Octave			S.Chs.	1860
190	Vital	(128)	Emérentienne Théberge		
				S.V.	1836
191	Germain	(128)	M. Ls. Bilodeau	,,	1843
192	Frs. Xavier	(128)	Marie Rousseau	,,	1846
193	Joseph	(132)	Marie Charrier	S.Chs.	1803
	M. Madeleine		Guill. Pouliot	,,	1831
	Marie		Jos. Clément	,,	1840
	Joseph				
194	Antoine	(132)	M.Vict.Dessaint	,,	1804
	Le même		Marie Vermet	S.G.	1821
195	Charles	(132)	M.Vict.Guénet	S.Chs.	1812
196	Martial	(135)	M. Restitue Morin		
				S.F.S.	1842
197	Gaspard	(149)	M.ReineServais	S.P.S.	1815
A	Louis	(149)	VéroniqueFôrtier	S.H.	1814
198	Joseph	(150)	Emélie Mercier	S.G.	1824
			S. Hénédine		
199	François	(150)	Josette Brisson	S.G.	1826
			S.Hénédine		
200	David	(152)	Eliz. Gendreau	S.P.	1825
	Isaac Guillaume				
201	Augustin	(155)	Anastasie Bazin	S.V.	1846
	Augustin				
202	J. Baptiste	(156)	Cécile Audet	S.J.	1825
203	Michel	,(158)	Josette Drouin	S.F.	1849
204	Antoine	(158)	Archange Drouin	S.F.	1853
205	Onésine	(166)	M. Désanges Hébert		
				S.Chs.	1863
206	Joseph	(193)	M. Jos. Leclaire	S.Chs.	1833
207	Isaac Guillaume	(200)	Flavie Goulet	S.P.	1855
208	Augustin	(201)	Joséphine Gaulin	S.V.	1869
209	Jean Norbert		Monique Pepin		
	Le même		a Eliz. Plante	S.V.	1864
	Pierre	(150)	Théotiste Bouffart		
				S.H.	1818

MORISSET.

| 1 | Jean | | Jeanne Choret | Qué. | 1669 |
| | Marie | | Jacq. Asselin | S.F. | 1687 |

MORISSET.

	Madeleine		Chs. Loignon	S.F.	1695
	Jeanne		Léonard Clément	S.F.	1699
	Anne		Jean Cloutier	C.R.	1714
	Pierre				
	Nicolas				
	Gentien				
2	Pierre	(1)	Cath. Létourneau	S.F.	1698
3	Nicolas	(1)	Anne Cadrin	S.F.	1709
	Marie		Gab. Ouimet	S.M.	1730
	Marie		2° Jos. Patry	S.M.	1746
	Le même		Anne Cloutier	C.R.	1714
	Madeleine		Gab. Plante	S.M.	1734
	Madeleine		2° Guill. Michon	S.M.	1753
	Marie Marthe		Ls. Leblond	S.M.	1742
	Marie Marthe		2° Etn. Roy	S.V.	1747
	Marie		Jean Michon	S.M.	1744
	Agathe		Jean Gautron	S.M.	1747
	M. Geneviève		J. B. Dion	S.M.	1754
	Joseph				
	Nicolas				
4	Gentien	(1)	Genev. Simon	C.R.	1710
	Geneviève		J. B. Prémont	S.F.	1731
	Geneviève		2° Jacq. Pichet	S.F.	1758
	Françoise		Hyacinthe Lehoux		
				S.F.	1741
	Marguerite		Jean Gagnon	S.F.	1745
	Michel				
	Jean Baptiste				
5	Nicolas	(3)	Cath. Blais	S.V.	1747
	M. Françoise		Frs. Coté	S.M.	1774
	Marie Catherine		Jos. Lefebvre	S.M.	1774
	Marie		Claude Lacroix	S.M.	1777
	Apolline		J. B. Ruel	S.M.	1781
	Elizabeth		Ls. Boissonneau	S.M.	1792
	Marie Josette		Chs. Lecours	S.M.	1793
	André				
	Nicolas				
	Jean Baptiste				
	Michel				
	Joseph				
6	Joseph		Marie Guilmet	S.V.	1749
	Marie Anne		André Lacroix	S.M.	1772
	Marie Anne		2° Ls. Voisin	S.M.	1786
	Marie Josette		Ls. Roy	S.M.	1777
	Marie Louise		Frs. Bélanger	S.M.	1786
	Joseph				
	Le même		Louise Genest	S.J.	1757
	Marie Marthe		André Rémillard	S.M.	1792
	Marie		Ant. Tangué	S.M.	1794
	Michel				
	Charles				
	Le même		Cath. Girard	Lévis	1796
7	Michel	(4)	Agathe Deblois	S.F.	1745
8	Jean Baptiste	(4)	Louise Larrivé	S.F.	1747
	Louis				
9	Michel		M. Claire Fortin		
				S.H.	
	Marg. Angélique		J. B. Gosselin	S.Chs.	1796
	Geneviève		Joachim Gosselin	S.Chs.	1802
	Josette		Jos. Bilodeau	S.Chs.	1804
	M. Angèlique		Etn. Denis	S.Chs.	1805
	Louise		Jacq. Morin	S.Chs.	1790
	Marie Claire		J. B. Gosselin	S.Chs.	1795
	Nicolas				
	Louis				
	Michel				
10	Nicolas	(5)	M. Eliz. Brousseau		
				S.M.	1775
11	Jean Baptiste	(5)	M. Mad. Jolin	S.Chs.	1780
	Marie Madeleine		Jos. Paradis	S.H.	1801
	Marie		Ls. Lainé	S.H.	1802
	Angèlique		Frs. Jalbert	S.H.	1803
	Véronique		Pierre Vaillancour		
				S.H.	1810
	François				

MORISSET.

12	André	(5) M. Ls. Pepin	S.M.	1798
			S.H.	
	Louise	Chs. Blouin	S.G.	1823
	Marie Anne	Jos. Fournier	S.G.	1828
	André			
13	Joseph	(6) Cath. Blais	Bert.	1781
	Angélique	Jos. RenéMercier	S.M.	1802
	Françoise	André Roy	S.M.	1808
	Marguerite	Frs. Fradet	S.M.	1825
	Charles			
	Joseph			
14	Michel	(6) M. Ls. Fradet	S.M.	1785
	Archange	Jean Gagnon	S.M.	1819
	Marguerite	Ls. Roy	S.M.	1822
	Marie	Jacq. Richard	S.M.	1824
	Angèle	J. B. Lacroix	S.M.	1832
	Joseph			
	Pierre			
	Louis			
	Georges			
	Ignace			
	Michel			
15	Charles	(6) M. Mad. Aubé	S.Chs.	1789
	Marie	J. B. Bacquet	S. M.	1813
	Louise	Guill. Corriveau	S.M.	1819
	Luce	Michel Clément	S.M.	1822
	Geneviève	Flavien Couillard		
			S. M.	1822
	Marie Marianne	Jean Fortin	S. M.	1828
	Joseph			
	Edouard	Prêtre		
	Jacques			
	André			
	François			
16	Michel	(5) M. Mad. Gagné	S.H.	1786
	Marie Madeleine	Chs. Clément	S. H.	1811
	Rose	Pierre Boutin	S. H.	1820
	Michel			
	Le même	Marie Plante S.	Chs.	1802
17	Louis	(8) M. Ls. Binet	S.Marie	1785
			S. Marie	
	Le même	Marg. Boucher	S.Chs.	1812
A	Michel	(9) M. Anne Morin	S. H.	1787
	Marie	Roch Duquet	S. H.	1810
	Joseph			
18	Nicolas	(9) Marie Lebrun	S. Chs.	1794
	Angélique	Ant. Roy	S. H.	1819
	Apolline	Amb. Roy	S. H.	1820
	Le même	Marg. Patry	S. Chs.	1821
19	Louis	(9) M. Apolline Marseau		
			S. V.	1797
20	François	(11) Angé Couture	Lévis	1810
			S.H.	
	Le même	Rosalie Roy	S. V.	1817
21	Joseph	(5) Marg. Gagné	S. H.	1777
	François			
22	André	(12) Josette Guérard	S.Frs.	1825
23	Joseph	(13) M. Barbe Couture		
			S. V.	1805
	Marie Julie	F. X. Lemieux	S. V.	1835
	Joseph			
	Edouard			
24	Charles	(13) Hélène Chamberlan		
			S. M.	1818
	Marcelline	Frédéric Brochu	S.M.	1841
	Marcelline	2° Ant. Roy	S. M.	1851
	Hélène	Jos. Bélanger	S. M.	1844
	Marguerite	Jean Gosselin	S. M.	1845
	Joseph			
	Le même	M. Théotiste Roy		
			S. M.	1832
25	Jean	Marie Dutile		
	Telesphore			
26	Joseph	(17) A. Cath. Turgeon		
	Restitut	Fréderic Jean Castin		
			S. Chs.	1849

MORISSET.

	Didace			
	Dominique			
27	Germain	Célestine Lepage		
	Auré	Zep. Audet	S. L.	1861
28	Michel	Rose Audet		
	Le même	Justine Turcot	S. J.	1865
29	Michel	(14) Marie Fortier	S.F.S.	1809
30	Louis	(14) Francoise Roy	S. M.	1820
31	Pierre	(14) M. Olive Lacroix	S.M.	1828
32	Joseph	(14) M. Marg. Gagnon		
			S. M.	1813
	Elisabeth	J. B. Martineau	S.M.	1839
	Marguerite	Frs. Genest	"	1850
	Le même	Angé Roy	"	1822
	Séraphine	Chs. Lacroix	"	1844
	Marie Emérence	Etn. Roy	"	1851
	Joseph Edouard			
33	Ignace	(14) Angèle Remillard		
			S. V.	1825
34	Georges	(14) Sara Roy	S. M.	1834
	Marie Célina	Ls. Bissonnit	"	1862
35	Jacques	(15) Euphrosine Rouillard		
			S. V.	1826
36	André	(15) Angélique Veau	S.M.	1833
	Marie Philoméne	Ls. Ed. Eliezer Cochon		
			S. M.	1857
	Marie Mathilde	Jos. Perrot	"	1864
	Prudent			
	Romuald			
A	François	M. Mad. Leclaire		
			S.H.	1814
37	Michel	(16) Louise Belan Levis		1811
38	François	(21) M. Jos. Lainé	S. F.	1826
39	Joseph	(23) Vict. Gougne	S. V.	1837
40	Edouard	(23) Marie Boulet	S. F. S.	1839
41	Joseph	(24) Archange Badeau		
			S.M.	1850
42	Télesphore	(25) Philomène Fournie;		
			S. Chs.	1864
		S. Marguerite		
43	Didace	(26) Constance Gosselin		
			S. M.	1846
44	Dominique	(26) Apolline Briart	S.Chs.	1860
45	Joseph	(32) Henriette Martineau		
	Edouard		S. M.	1851
46	Prudent	(36) Philomène Gosselin		
			S.M.	1861
47	Romuald	(36) Philomène Bacquet		
			S. M.	1864

MOURIER.

1	Pierre	Susanne Levalet	Qué.	1677
	Susanne	Nicolas Filteau	S. J.	1699
	Marie	Chs. Genest	"	1699
2	Jean	Marie Mineau	S. F.	1678
	Marie	Marc Semeur	S. J.	1700
	Marie Jeanne	Pierre Galien	"	1704
	Marguerite	Michel Chiasson	"	1706
	Francoise	Ls. Greffart	"	1710

MUNRO.

1	Jean Philippe	M. Chs. Girard		
	Marie Louise	Louis Coté	B.	1793
	Marie Charlotte	J. B. Coté	B.	1794
	Angélique	Ignace Turcot	S.Chs.	1794
	Jean Philippe			
2	Jean Philippe (1)	M. Marg. Plante	S.H.	1800

NADEAU.

1	Joseph Osanny	Marg. Abraham		
	Catherine	Jean Roy	S.L.	1694
	Denis			
	Jean Baptiste			

NADEAU.

Jean			
2 Jean	(1)	Anne Lacasse	
Marguerite		Chs. Gesseron	B. 1712
Angélique		Denis Gontier	B. 1714
Elisabeth		Pierre Couillard	B. 1727
Louis			
Antoine			
· François			
3 Denis	(1)	Charlotte Lacasse	
Joseph			
Jean			
Alexis			
Guillaume			
Le même		Eliz. Le Roy	B. 1724
Geneviève		Nicholas Hélie	B. 1748
Geneviève		2° Ls. Bélanger	Bert. 1755
Josette		Jean Chs. Frs De la Houssay	S.M. 1765
Cécile		J. B. Fortier	S.M. 1765
Marie Angélique		Jos. Quéret	S.M. 1773
Marie Angélique		2° Jos. Bissonnet	S.M. 1786
Marie Angélique		3° Ls. Godbout	S.Chs. 1792
Marie Louise		Claude Poliquin	S.Chs. 1753
Denis			
François			
4 Jean Baptiste	(1)	M. Anne Dumont	S.J.1696
Marie Anne		Aug. Gignard	Bert. 1712
Isabelle		Jean Hélie	Bert. 1734
Geneviève		Barth. Carbonneau	S.V. 1726
Louis			
Jean Baptiste			
5 François	2	Genev. Martineau	
6 Antoine	2	Marg. Turgeon	B. 1726
Marguerite		Jean Couture	B. 1764
Thérèse		Chs. Grenet	S.M. 1768
Jean Baptiste			
Antoine			
7 Louis	(2)	Anne Genev. Duquet	Lévis 1732
Simon			
Louis			
8 Joseph	(3)	Angé Turgeon	B. 1723
Marie Angélique		Jean Lecours	B. 1742
Louise		Frs. Labrecque	B. 1748
Thérèse		Guill. Gosselin	S.Chs. 1763
Alexandre			
Ambroise			
9 Jean	(3)	Louise Turgeon	B. 1727
Charlotte		Jean Bussière	B. 1758
Charlotte		2° Chs. Roy	S.M. 1771
Zacharie			
Jean Baptiste			
10 Alexis	(3)	M. Claire Albert	Kamouraska 1729
11 Guillaume	(3)	Thérèse Le Roy	B. 1737
Louis		Frs. Coté	S. Chs. 1768
Alexandre			
Jean			
12 Guillaume		Ursule Jahan	
Marie		Aug. Aubert	S.Chs. 1773
Pétronille		Michel Paquet	S.Chs. 1779
Louis			
Charles			
Guillaume			
A Ignace		M. Ls. Bourassa	
Marie Louise		Frs. Roberge	S.H. 1799
Marie Geneviève		Nic. Roberge	S.H. 1823
Thérèse		Ls. Roberge	S.H. 1807
Josette		Jean Rouleau	S.H. 1811
Euphrosine		Joachim Paradis	S.H. 1812
Marie Luce		Ls. Huard	S.H. 1815
Marguerite		Ls. Goulet	S.H. 1819
Etienne			

NADEAU.

13 Denis	(3)	M. Eliz. Gosselin	S.M. 1753
Marie Josette		Pierre Noël Mercier	B.1785
14 François	(3)	M. Ls. Hautbois	S.M.1762
Marie		Marc. Isabel	S.G. 1786
Marie		2° Chs. Carbonneau	S.G. 1830
Félice		Nic. Gosselin	S.G. 1794
André			
Augustin			
François			
15 Jn. Baptiste	(4)	Marg. Carbonneau	Bert. 1721
18 Louis	(4)	Isabelle Hélie	S.V. 1734
		Berthier	
Elizabeth		Jos. Guinard	Bert. 1750
Jean Valier			
Charles Claude			
Jean Baptiste			
Louis			
Joseph			
17 Antoine	(6)	Thérèse Marchand	Lévis 1761
Louise		Frs. Blouin	S.H. 1779
Etienne			
Louis			
Le même		Marie Cochon	S.H. 1782
Marie Archange		Jos. Carrier	S. H. 1808
Le même		M. Jos. Dorval	S. H. 1791
18 Jn. Baptiste	(6)	Marg. Dalaire	S.M. 1767
Marguerite		Jos. Patouel	S.Chs. 1792
Geneviève		Ant. Marcoux	S.Chs. 1795
Marie Anne		Pierre Adam	S.G. 1809
Pierre			
19 Louis	(7)	Genev. Dorval	S.P. 1755
Le même		M. Mad. Giguère	S.F. 1757
Marie		Chs. Guérard	S.Frs. 1782
Geneviève		Ls. Audet	S.Frs. 1800
Pierre			
Louis			
François			
20 Simon	(7)	Mad. Martineau	S.Frs. 1789
21 Ambroise	(8)	Marie Harnais	S.Chs. 1756
Josette		Jean Larrivé	S.Chs. 1789
Ambroise			
Charles			
Joseph			
22 Alexandre	(8)	M. Thérèse Picard	S.P.S. 1757
Thérèse		Jacq. Corriveau	S.Chs. 1881
Marie		Chs. Pouliot	S.Chs. 1785
Josette		Chs. Nadeau	S.Chs. 1792
Joseph			
Le même		Mad. Roy	S.M. 1783
23 Zacharie	(9)	Fse. Gosselin	B. 1763
Charlotte		Ls. Labrecque	S.G. 1791
Charles			
Joseph			
A Antoine		Louise Demers	
Marie Anne		Nicolas Tardif	S.H. 1805
Marie Archange		Germain Baudoin	S.H. 1807
Catherine		J. B. James	S.H. 1809
Ursule		Louis Fortier	S.H. 1810
Antoine			
François			
Jean Baptiste			
Joseph			
24 Jean Baptiste	(9)	M. Anne Boilard	B. 1764
Marie Apolline		Chs. Couillard	B. 1787
Judith		Ant. Fournier	B. 1802
Jean Baptiste			
Joseph			
Charles			

NADEAU.

NADEAU.

```
25 Alexandre   (11) Marie Ls. Hélie      S.V. 1773
   Le même          Genev. Gagné         S.V. 1816
                        V. de J. B. Guay
26 Jean        (11) Genev. Hautbois
                                         S.M. 1766
   Marie            Ls. Baillargeon   S.Chs. 1785
   Josette          Chs. Dumas        S.Chs. 1809
   Angélique        Ls. Hizoir           S.G. 1795
   Joseph
27 Louis       (12) Cath. Gontier        S.G. 1774
28 Guillaume   (12) Judith Bacquet       S.M. 1783
   Judith           Aug. Boucher      S.Chs. 1806
   Geneviève        Laurent Gosselin
                                      S.Chs. 1807
   Louise           André Carbonneau
                                      S.Chs. 1815
   Guillaume
   Le même          Marie Boulière    Bert. 1812
29 Charles     (12) Josette Nadeau
                                      S.Chs. 1792
   Ignace
30 André       (14) Marie Gosselin   S.Chs. 1793
   Angélique        Chs. Morin           S.G. 1821
   Zacharie
   André
   Le même          Fse. Chartier        S.G. 1827
                        V. de Gab. Thibaut
31 François     (14) M. Jos. Nadeau   Bert. 1800
32 Augustin     (14) Josette Coté    S.Chs. 1804
   Le même           Charlotte Briart  S.G. 1807
33 Jean Bapt.   (16) M. Jos. Balan    Bert. 1761
   M. Marguerite     Ls. Martel         S.M. 1787
   Marie Marthe      Jos. Chamberlan    S.M. 1818
   M. Geneviève      Chs. Fisback       S.M. 1795
   M. Geneviève      2º Jos. Leclaire   S.V. 1812
   Louis
   Jean Baptiste
   Gabriel
34 Louis       (16) M. Jos. Bilodeau
                                       Bert. 1765
   Marie Josette    Frs. Nadeau       Bert. 1800
   Geneviève        Ls. Audet         Bert. 1800
   M. Angélique     Ignace Rouel      Bert. 1801
   Marie Anne       Jos. Beaucher      S.V. 1810
   Joseph
35 Joseph      (16) Louise Goupy       S.M. 1768
   Marie Josette    Aug. Mercier       S.M. 1791
   Marie Marthe     Mathieu Labrecque
                                       S.M. 1793
   Marie            Jos. Roy           S.M. 1799
   Marie Brigitte   Pierre Fortier     S.M. 1808
   Joseph
36 Charles     (16) Eliz. Gagnon       S.M 1774
   Claude
   Le même          Apolline Gontier
                                     S.Chs. 1788
37 Jean Valier (16) M. Genev. Daniau
                                       Bert. 1780
   Geneviève        Ignace Noël        S.G. 1806
   Archange         Jos. Audet         S.G. 1808
38 Etienne     (17) Genev. Chabot   S.Chs. 1791
   Geneviève        Jos. Ferland       S.H. 1814
   Josette          Pierre Carrier     S.H. 1817
   Marie Pélagie    David Brown        S.H. 1818
A  Louis       (17) M. Anne Gosselin
                                       S.H. 1789
   Antoine
39 Pierre      (18) Marie Tangué    S.Chs. 1808
40 Louis       (18) Angé. Dalaire   S.Frs. 1775
   Marie Josette    Aug. Ginchereau
                                     S.Frs. 1802
   François
41 François    (19) Mad. Guérard    S.Frs. 1798
   Madeleine        Olivier Labbé      S.F. 1875
   François
```

```
42 Pierre      (19) M. Ls. Guérard   S.Frs. 1802
   Susanne          J. B. Létourneau   S.F 1835
43 Charles     (21) M. Anne Audet
                                     S.Chs. 1776
44 Ambroise    (21) Louise Fournier
                                     S.Chs. 1785
   Marie Louise     Ls. Bouffart       S.G. 1806
45 Ambroise         Genev. Fournier
                                       S.H.
   Le même          Genev. Fortier  S.Chs. 1790
   Geneviève        Pierre Gautron  S.Chs.1812
   Jean
   Le même          Marie Lefebvre     S.G. 1809
   Gabriel
46 Joseph      (21) Charlotte Gosselin
                                     S. Chs. 1787
   Marie Charlotte  Pierre Turgeon    „  1823
   Joseph
   Roch
   Magloire
   Charles
47 Joseph      (22) Genev. Blais    S.Chs. 1799
   Le même          M. Joseph Pénin   „  1801
A  Joseph      (23) Cath. Lasanté     S.H. 1801
B  Antoine     (23) A M. Fse. Morin   „  1806
C  Jean Baptiste(23) A M. Anne Gagné  „  1807
D  Joseph      (23) A M. Ls. Morin    „  1810
   Joseph
   Antoine
E  François    (23) A Angé Turgeon    „  1817
48 Charles     (23) Marie Lacasse     S.L. 1798
   Archange         Jos. Labrecque    „  1841
   Angèle           Amb. Marcoux      „  1828
   Zacharie
49 Jean Baptiste(24) Josette Boucher   B. 1787
   Angèle           J. B. Carrier      B. 1823
   Josette          Louis Demers       B. 1824
   Abraham
   François
   Jean Baptiste
A  Etienne     (12) Genev. Cantin     S.H. 1817
50 Joseph      (24) Fse. Laine     S.Chs. 1802
   Jean Baptiste
   Antoine
   Joseph
   Le même          Julienne Mathieu C.R.1817
   Marcelline       J. B. Chabot       B. 1847
   Marie Louise     Frs. Aubé          B. 1852
51 Charles     (24) Marie Laine        B. 1809
   Archange         Pierre Boucher     B. 1846
   Louise           Cyp. Gosselin      B. 1849
   Marie            Jean Poulin        B. 1859
   Charles
52 Joseph      (26) Eliz. Morin     S.Chs. 1809
   Elizabeth        André Lemelin     „  1841
   Cécile           Germ.Quemeneur    „  1857
   Marie            Ls. Couture       „  1859
   Scolastique      Alexandre Turgeon B.1840
   Scolastique      2º Hyppolite PouliotB.1847
   Angèle           Ant. Gosselin      B. 1845
   Anastasie        Ls. Levasseur      B. 1853
   Anastasie        2 Romain Chabot    B. 1857
   Pierre
   Augustin
   Honoré
53 Guillaume   (28) Marie Roy         S.M. 1812
   Marie            Pierre Boulet   S.Chs. 1837
   Laurent
   Charles
54 Guillaume        Charlotte Bussière
   Flavie           Jean Arthur        B. 1821
   Elizabeth        Michel Couët       S.M. 1831
   Berthélemi
   Charles
55 Ignace      (29) Marie Audet        S.G. 1814
   Ignace
```

NADEAU.

56 André	(30)	Marg. Charron S.G.	1817
57 Zacharie	(39)	Soulange Carbonneau	
		Bert.	1840
58 Louis	(33)	M.Mad.Mercier S.M.	1788
Le même		Mad. Paquet S.Chs.	1790
Judith		Jean Goulet S.G.	1809
Madeleine		Jos. Labrecque S.G.	1811
57 JeanBaptiste	(33)	M.Marg. Monmeny	
		S.M.	1789
Marguerite		Jos. Patry B.	1814
JeanBaptiste			
60 Gabriel	(33)	Genev. Talbot S.G.	1806
Geneviève		Basile Tangué ,,	1825
Le même		Marthe Lainé ,,	1812
61 Joseph	(34)	Marie Gontier ,,	1798
Marie Angèle		Jean Corriveau Bert.	1818
Marie		Pierre Langlois ,,	1820
Victoire		Jos. Bilodeau ,,	1829
Marguerite		Chs. Morin ,,	1835
Marie		Régis Ménard ,,	1837
Joseph			
62 Joseph	(35)	M.Marthe Balan S.V.	1797
Thomas			
François Xavier			
63 Charles		Eliz. Gagné	
Joseph			
64 Jean Baptiste		Marie Roy	
Marie		Jean Leblarie S.G.	1822
Geneviève		Jean Chamberlan ,,	1827
Augustin			
65 Jean Baptiste		Josette Patouel	
Rosalie		Alexandre Duquet	
		S. Chs.	1822
66 Charles		Eliz. Nadeau	
Brigitte		Isidore Guilmet S.G.	1800
67 Charles		Marie Lessart	
Marie		Frs. Blais S.G.	1829
68 Charles		Thérèse Godbout	
Thérèse		Etn. Lebrun S.G.	1830
69 Jean		Eliz. Patry	
		Lévis.	
Jean			
70 Antoine	(38)	A M. ClaireGouletSH	1817
		S. Isidore	
Charles			
71 Joseph		Eliz. Marois	
Catherine		Ls. Marc Turgeon B.	1850
72 Guillaume		Marie Clément	
Philomène		André Brochu S.Chs.	1861
Constance		Denis Rouillard	
		S.Chs.	1856
Narcisse			
73 François	(40)	Ursule Ginchereau	
		S.Frs.	1814
74 François	(41)	Marie Lemelin S.Frs.	1819
75 Jean	(45)	Fse. Lefebvre S.L.	1821
Marie		Ls. Gontier S.J.	1843
Madeleine		Jérémie Gontier S.J.	1849
76 Gabriel	(45	Emérence Lainé B.	1842
Le même		Olive Mercier S.V.	1851
77 Joseph	(46)	Euphrosine Paquet	
		S.Chs.	1814
78 Roch	(46)	M. Anne Chamberlan	
		S.Chs.	1815
Marie Anne		Magl. Brousseau S.L.	1840
Roch			
Joseph			
79 Maglorie	(46)	Fse. Rémillard S.Chs.	1827
Sara		J. B. Carbonneau	
		S.Chs.	1864
Joseph			
80 Charles	(46)	Marg. Terrien S.Chs.	1829
Leocadie		Rémie McNeil B.	1854
81 Zacharie	(48)	Marie Turgeon S.M.	1848
82 JeanBaptiste	(49)	Véronique Tangué	
		S.G.	1812

NADEAU.

83 Françoise	(40)	Emélie Chabot B.	1818
Marie Délina		Ed. Guay B.	1840
Marie Hermine		Simon Gravel B.	1840
Esther		Aug. Boulet B.	1853
Marie Olive		Ls. Gérard B.	1853
François Xavier			
84 Abraham	(49)	M. Ls. Provost B.	1845
85 Joseph	(50)	Fse. Cameron B.	1832
86 Jean Bapt.	(50)	Christine Bergeron B.	1841
87 Antoine	(50)	Dorothée Lacroix B.	1850
88 Charles	(51)	M. Fse. Paquet B.	1848
89			
90 Pierre	(92)	Anastasie Lefebvre	
		S.Chs.	1841
91 Augustin	(52)	Angé Gosselin S.Chs.	1845
92 Honoré	(52)	Célina Gérard B.	1858
93 Charles	(53)	M. Ls. Tangué S.Chs.	1841
94 Laurent	(53)	Génév. Tangué S.M.	1843
Le même		Restitut Charier	
		S.Chs.	1853
95 Barthélemi	(54)	Julie Campeau B.	1831
96 Charles	(54)	Délina Naud S.Chs.	1845
97 Ignace	(54)	Hermine Labrecque	
		S.Chs.	1842
98 Jean Baptiste	(59)	M. Anne Quéret S.M.	1815
99 Joseph	(61)	Emélie Proulx S.F.S.	1827
100 François Xavier	(62)	Luce Roy S.V.	1820
101 Thomas	(62)	Luce Marg. Dalaire	
		S.F.S.	1823
102 Joseph	(63)	Marie Shinck S.G.	1808
Marie		Frs. Rémillard S.G.	1830
103 Augustin	(64)	Marg. Fradet S.G.	1830
104 Jean	(69)	Julie Forgue B.	1834
105 Charles	(70)	M. Phèbè Turgeon	
		S.Chs.	1846
106 Narcisse	(72)	Aurélie Turcot S.Chs.	1857
107 Roch	(78)	Clotilde Rouleau S.L.	1846
108 Joseph	(78)		
109 Joseph	(79)	Sara Paquet S.Chs.	1859
110 François Xavier		M. Flavie Guay	
		S.Chs.	1847
111 Joseph	(47)	A M. Rosalie Pouliot	
		S.Chs.	1850
112 Antoine	(47)	A Julie Monmeny	
		S.Chs.	1854

NAUD—LABRIE.

1 François		Marg. Jobidon A.G.	1676
Jean François			
Le même		M. Thérèse Chaillé	
		Pte. Trembles	1688
2 Pierre		M. Thérèse Garant	
		S.L.	1692
Jean			
Jacques			
Pierre			
Le même		Marie Gaboury S.M.	1716
Jean Baptiste			
3 Jean François	(1)	Génév. Paquin S.F.	1711
4 Pierre	(2)	Marg. Huart, Lévis	1716
Jacques			
Pierre			
Le même		M. Cath. Poliquin,	
		Lévis	1755
Marie Charlotte		André Guay Lévis	1784
5 Jean	(2)	Mad. Desmoliers, Islet	1723
Marie Jeanne		Jos. Roy S.V.	1760
Marie Madeleine		Frs. Perrin S.V.	1723
Marguerite		Ant. Drapeau S.V.	1773
Pierre			
6 Jean Baptiste	(2)	Genev. Gravel, Islet	1741
7 Jacques	(2)	M. Chs. Marchand	
Le même		Genev. Jourdain	
		Lévis	1756

NAUD—LA RIE.

8	Jacques	(4) Genev. Couture	B 1749
	Thérèse	Jos. Labrecque	S.Chs 1776
	Marthe	Jacq. Létourneau	" 1777
	Marie	Pierre Labrecque	" 1786
	Marguerite	Ls. Chabot	" 1790
	Euphrosine	Frs. Guay	" 1791
	Geneviève	J. B. Bertrand	" 1791
	Jacques		
	Joseph		
9	Pierre	(4) Marg. Turgeon	Lévis 1746
10	Louis	Louis Roy	
	Guillaume		
11	Pierre	(5) Anastasie Daigle	S.V 1760
12	Jacques	(8) LouisBrousseau	S.Chs.1783
	Louise	Raimond Patry	" 1809
	Angèle	Alexandre Turgeon	
			S.Chs. 1818
	Ambroise		
	Joseph		
	Jean		
	François		
13	Joseph	(8) Genev. Paquet	S.Chs. 1784
	Marie Anne	Jos. Boutin	" 1812
	Joseph		
	Jacques		
	Ambroise		
	Gabriel		
14	Guillaume	(10) Genev. Samson	S.G. 1787
15	Ambroise	(12) Josette Couture	S.Chs 1811
	Marie Louise	Joachim Provost	" 1841
	Marie Josette	Cyp. Denis	" 1842
	Angèle	Pierre Goupy	" 1847
	Ambroise		
16	Jean	(12) M. Ls. Ruel	S.Chs. 1812
	Marie Ls. Ozine	Frédéric Couture	" 1840
	Angèle	Jos. Gosselin	" 1842
	Didace		
	Jean		
17	Joseph	(12) Scolastique Couture	
			S.Chs. 1814
	Angèle	Magl. Couture	" 1841
	Délina	Chs. Nadeau	" 1845
	Pierre		
	Louis		
	Hubert		
	Le même	Angé Dangueuger	
			S.Chs. 1840
		V. de Jos. Rousseau	
18			
19	François	(12) Marg. Gosselin	S.Chs 1825
	Marie Louise	Jos. Turgeon	" 1847
	Dina	Pierre Pelchat	" 1850
	Marguerite	Ls. Lacasse	" 1863
	Sara	Ls. Bédard	" 1864
	Benjamin		
	Joseph		
	Ferdinand		
20	Joseph	(13) Marg. Bisson	S.Chs. 1812
	Marguerite	Ant. Gonzier	" 1833
	Delphine	Jos. Fournier	" 1841
	Mathilde	Pierre Brochu	" 1850
	Marie	Frs. Chrétien	" 1850
	Christine	Jos. Guilmet	" 1852
	Joseph		
	Prosper		
	Denis		
	Magloire		
	Modeste		
	Bénoni		
21	Jacques	(13) Cécile Mercier	S.Chs. 1816
22	Gabriel	(13) Angé Gosselin	" 1821
	Angélique	Narcisse Boutin	" 1853
	Le même	Angèle Tangué	S.V. 1831
23	Ambroise	(13) M. Ls. Lepage	" 1822
24	François	Thérèse Canac	
		S.Marie	

NAUD— LABRIE.

	Jean		
25	Raimond	Angé Bonneau	
	Le même	M. Lucie Fournier	B. 1844
26	Pierre	Barbe Mousseau	
	Le même	Marie Jos. Dacrot	
			S.Chs. 1835
27	Ambroise	(15) Adé Euphrosine Coniau	
			S.Chs 1839
	Le même	Fse. Couture	" 1862
28	Jean	(16) M. Anne Dalaire	" 1836
29	Didace	(16) Marcelline Boucher	
			S.Chs. 1850
30	Louis	(17) Marie Couture	" 1844
31	Pierre	(17) Angèle Gourgue	S.M. 1846
32	Hubert	(17) Constance Paquet	
			S.Chs. 1855
33	Benjamin	(19) Célina Marcoux	" 1851
34	Joseph	(19) M. Célina Marcoux	
			S.Chs. 1853
35	Ferdinand	(19) M. Eléonore Genest	
			S. Chs. 1856
36	Joseph	(20) M. Chs. Fournier	
			S.Chs. 1836
	Marie	Godfoi Bertel	" 1858
37	Denis	(20) M. Marg. Chabot	" 1840
38	Prosper	(20) Rosalie Fournier	" 1842
	Le même	M. Caroline Lepage	
			S.Chs. 1862
39	Magloire	(20) Emélie Patry	" 1847
40	Bénoni	(20) M. Ls. Fournier	" 1847
41	Modeste	(20) Hermine Audet	" 1849
42	Jean	(24) Angé Pouliot	" 1828
	Le même	M. Archange Bonneau	
			S.V. 1838

NICOLE.

1	Luc	Gilette Bapé	Coutance
	Olivier		
1	Andre	Marie Desroches, Londres	
	Henri		
A	Jacques	Eliz. Thibaut	S.Tho. 1770
		V. de Thérèse Chouinard	
	Jacques		
	Louis		
3	Olivier	(1) M. Ls. Brochu	S.V. 1765
	Marie Louise	J. B. Monmeny	" 1809
	Marie Geneviève	Ls. Louineau	S.F.S. 1787
	Olivier		
	Joseph		
4	Henri	(2) M. Mad. Boutin	S.J. 1789
	Le même	Mad. Turcot	
	Le même	M. Rose Campagna	
			S.Frs. 1798
5	Jacques	(2) A Archange Crépeau	
			S.H. 1802
	Archange	Guill. Roy	S.V. 1816
	Jacques		
	Jacques		
6	Olivier	(3) M. Fse. Fleury	S.V. 1797
7	Jean Baptiste	Céleste Boulet	S.Tho. 1796
		f. de Jos. & Genev.	
		Lefebvre	
	Charles		
8	Joseph	(3) M. Reine Vallée	S.V. 1804
	Magloire		
	Joseph		
	Marcel		
9	Louis	(2) A M. Rose Laberge	
			S.Tho. 1808
	Le même	M. Roger Pélagie Blais	
			S.P.S. 1813
	Le même	M. Rosalie Bacon	
			S.P.S. 1818
10	Jacques	(5) Marie Lebrun	S.M. 1825
		S. Claire	

NICOLE.

11 Jacques	(5) Mad. Bacquet	S.G.	1826
12 Charles	(7) Sophie Létourneau		
		S.P.S.	1829
13 Joseph	Vitaline Têtu		
Thomas			
14 Magloire	(8) Caroline Roy	S.M.	1840
15 Marcel	(8) Angèle Bacquet	,,	1840
16 Joseph	(8) Marie Anne Lacroix		
		S.M.	1845
17 Thomas	(13) M. Constance Azilda		
	Dumas	S.M.	1863

NIEL.

1 Pierre	Anne Noël	S.P.	1724
Marie Josette	Gab. Paradis	,,	1749
Marie Josette	2° René Blouin	,,	1788
Marie Anne	Nic. Paradis	,,	1760
Marie Anne	2° Jacq. Rousseau	,,	1767
Geneviève	Paul Bedard	,,	1757

NOEL.

1 François	Nicole Legrand	S.F.	1669
Marguerite	Frs. Chabot	S.L.	1698
Marguerite	2° Pierre Parent	,,	1706
Madeleine	Ant. Fortier	,,	1706
Madeleine	2° Ant. Pepin	S.J.	1752
Philippe			
Françoise			
Pierre			
Ignace			
Michel			
2 Philippe	(1) Marie Rondeau	S.P.	1692
Angélique	Frs. Gosselin	,,	1720
Ursule	Adrien Leclaire	,,	1722
Marie Anne	Pierre Niel	,,	1724
Philippe			
3 François	(1) Cath. Burlon	S.P.	1699
Catherine	Nic. Duverney	Que.	1728
4 Pierre	(1) Louise Gosselin	S.P.	1703
Dorothée	Ls. Pichet	,,	1838
Geneviève	Chs. Fortier	,,	1843
Elizabeth	Jos. Fortier	,,	1849
Elizabeth	2° Guill. Daniau	S.M.	1762
Louise	Barth. Terrien	S.P.	1749
Marguerite	Pierre Filteau	,,	1749
Hélène	Jos. Baillargeon	,,	1754
Joseph Marie			
Pierre			
François			
5 Ignace	(1) M. Anne Huart	Lévis	1707
Ursule	Jos. Leclaire	S.L.	1734
Cécile	Ant. Rousseau	,,	1746
Ignace			
François			
Jean Baptiste			
Le même	Marie Crépeau		
Madeleine	Bernard Duberger	S.P.	1746
Louise	Jean Frs. Pouliot	,,	1751
Josette	Zach. Bonneau	,,	1757
Marguerite	Aug. Chabot	,,	1764
Ursule	Ls. Leclaire	,,	1765
Benoit			
Ignace			
6 Michel	(1) Agnes Marg. Garant		
		S.P.	1713
Madeleine	Benet Gilaudi	S.P.	1747
Ignace			
7 Philippe	(2) Genev. Leclaire	S.P.	1729
Marie Thècle	Prisque Paquet	,,	1756
Marie Josette	Jean Ferlant	,,	1761
Geneviève	Ls. Aubin	,,	1767
Marie Victoire	Pierre Poulin	,,	1772
Thérèse	Chs. Roberge	,,	1775

NOEL.

Philippe			
Louis			
Jean			
Antoine			
8 Jean François	Louise Millecent	Mans.	
Jean François			
9 Pierre	(4) Marie Anne Pepin	S.J.	1737
Marie Anne	Pierre Leclaire	S.P.	1757
Le même	Marie Bilodeau	S.F.	1748
Marie Thècle	Jos. Gourdeau	S.P.	1783
Marie	Amb. Lecours	,,	1784
Pierre			
Augustin			
Louis			
10 François	(4) M. Marthe Nolin	S.P.	1745
Marie	Jean Simon Turcot	,,	1780
Jean Basile			
11 Joseph Marie	(4) Mad. Bilodeau	S.F.	1749
12 Ignace	(5) Mad. Gosselin	S.L.	1735
Marie Madeleine	J. B. Valière	S.M.	1763
Marie Geneviève	Etn. Roy	,,	1764
Marie Geneviève	2° J. B. Labbé	S. Chs.	1798
Marie	Louis Coté	S.M.	1770
Marie Marthe	Pierre Roy	,,	1771
Cécile	Jos. Lacasse	,,	1778
Laurent			
Joseph			
Ignace			
13 François	(5) Genev. Ruel	S.L.	1750
14 Jean Baptiste	(5) M. Jos. Bourget	Lévis	1754
15 Benoit	(5) Agathe Parant	S.P.	1764
Victoire	Jos. Rousseau	,,	1801
Benoit			
Louis			
Ignace			
A Ignace	(2d m.) M. Ls. Ainse	S. Tho.	1768
Jean Bernard			
Joseph			
16 Ignace	(6) Rose Coulombe	S.L.	1763
17 Jacques	M. Jos. Fontaine		
Hélène	Pierre Goulet	S.P.	1771
Marie Thècle	Ign. Choret	,,	1778
Pierre			
Le même	Mad. Dupile	,,	1757
Madeleine	Chs. Goulet	,,	1774
François			
Le même	Hélène Ratté	,,	1769
Le même	Genev. Plante	,,	1778
18 Jean	(7) Rénée Ferlant	,,	1754
Le même	Genev. Dussaut	Lévis	1756
19 Philippe	(7) Agathe Aubin	S.P.	1755
20 Louis	(7) Marg. Paradis (¹)		
Marguerite	Etn. Réaume	S.L.	1780
Thérèse	Chs. Labrecqne	,,	1790
Geneviève	Chs. Poulet	,,	1792
Marie	Abraham Delisle	,,	1811
Louis			
21 Antoine	(7) Agnès Goulet	S.P.	1775
22 Jean François	(8) Véronique Cochon	S.V.	1733
23 François	Eliz. Fiset		
Marie	Jean Bouffart	S.P.	1799
Madeleine	Pierre Bouffart	,,	1801
Pierre			
François			
24 Laurent	Marie Aubry		
Michel			
Louis			
Laurent			
25 Louis	(9) M. Zacharie Cloutier		
		Lévis	1780
Antoine			
26 Pierre	(9) Thècle Coté	S.P.	1784
Thècle	Jean Langlois	,,	1808

(¹) Voir St. Laurent, Baptème du 30 janvier 1760.

NOEL.

Thècle	2° Aug. Boissonneau		
Marie	Ls. Menard	S.P.	1822
Olivier		„	1824
François			
27 Augustin	(9) Angé L'hortie		
		Beauport	1785
Geneviève	Jos. Delisle	S.P.	1807
Marguerite	Ls. Langlois	„	1811
28 Joseph	(12) Eliz. Guénet	S. Chs.	1778
29 Ignace	(12) M. Mad. Frégeot S.G.		1783
	V. d'Alexandre Blanchet		
Marie Louise	Guill. Roy	„	1803
Ignace			
30 Laurent	(12) Marie Laflèche	S.V.	1785
A Ignace	(15) Marg. Gosselin	S.H.	1808
Le même	Judith Boucher	„	1815
31 Benoit	(15) Agathe Réaume	S.P.	1792
Thérèse	Ls. Paradis	„	1819
Benoit			
32 Louis	(15) M. Anne Godbout	„	1809
33 Pierre	(17) Marg. Poiré	Lévis	1778
Cécile	Adrien Cantin	S.P.	1807
Marie	Pierre Crépeau	„	1810
Félicien			
34 François	(17) M. Fse. Coté	„	1780
Françoise	Aug. Dupile	„	1804
Marguerite	Ant. Martel	„	1822
Pierre			
Louis			
François			
35 Louis	(20) M. Mad. Dupille S.L.		1788
Madeleine	Frs. Godbout	„	1810
Louise	Michel Boucher	„	1832
Marie	Pierre Cinqmars	„	1838
Constance	Marc Dufresne	„	1848
Louis			
François			
Joseph			
Augustin			
Antoine			
Le même	Mad. Loignon	S.F.	1814
Jean			
36 Jean Bernard(15)	A Genev. Coté S.Tho.		1796
		S.G.	
Le même	Marie Garant	S.F.S.	1812
37			
38 Jean Basile	(10) Angé Guay	S.H.	1783
Marie	Ls. Turgeon	B.	1818
Basile			
39 François	(23) Marg. Tessier	S.P.	1801
Joseph			
40 Pierre	(23) Fse. Leroux	S.L.	1816
41 Laurent	(24) Marie Gautron	S.G.	1806
Constance	Frs. Genest	S.M.	1842
Laurent			
42 Louis	(24) Angé. Charron	S.G.	1811
Le même	Marie Quemeneur	„	1822
43 Michel	(24) Marg. Terrien	„	1816
Marguerite	Jean Guay	S.Chs.	1843
Le même	M. Ls. Royer	„	1851
A Antoine	(25) Josette Goulet	S.H.	1818
44 François	(26) Dorothée Boulet S.P.		1818
45 Olivier	(26) Justine Maranda S.L.		1834
Le même	M. Judith Pichet S.P.		1838
46 Ignace	(29) M.Genev.Nadeau S.G.		1806
Angélique	Frs. Bacquet	S.G.	1821
47 Benoit	(31) Mad. Bouliane	S.P.	1848
48 François Fé-	(33) Monique Gourdeau		
licien		S.P.	1813
Brigitte	Ed. Genest	S.P.	1840
Marcelline	Ls. Daniau	„	1841
Henriette	Ign. Goulet	„	1848
Marie Catherine	Chs. Eugène Gourdeau		
		S.P.	1851
Marguerite	J. B. Tailleur	S.P.	1854

Félix			
49 François	(34) M. Jos. Plante	S.P.	1808
Adélaïde	Pierre Gourdeau	„	1840
Luce	David Pichet	„	1841
François			
50 Pierre	(34) Cécile Henry	„	1818
Edouard			
51 Louis	(34) Thérèse Dupile	„	1820
Louis			
52 Ignace	M. Mad. Laberge		
		S.Tho.	
Le même	M. Osile Baudoin		
		S.F.S.	1813
53 Louis	Marie Cloutier		
Marie	Amb. Bédard	S.G.	1823
Marie Anne	Frs. Cloutier	„	1823
54 Louis	(35) Marg. Royer	S.J.	1816
Marcelline	Jacq. Tremblay	„	1839
Emélie	Gab. Dich	„	1842
Marguerite	Frs. Toussaint	„	1845
Rose de Lima	Pierre Gosselin	„	1851
Henri			
55 Augustin	(35) Marie Labrecque S.L.		1822
Marie Philomène	Jos. Valére Coté	„	1856
Marcel			
Joseph			
56 Antoine	(35) M. Genev. Brousseau		
		S.L.	1824
Marcelline	David Cinqmars S.L.		1848
Henriette	F. X. Blouin	„	1854
Marie Eléonore	Jean Ginchereau	„	1855
Philomène	Adeline Pouliot	„	1863
Euphémie	Jovite Vézina	„	1866
Célestin			
Louis			
57 Joseph	(35) Julie Marcoux	S.M.	1833
58 Jean	(35) Louise Coulombe S.L.		1847
59 François	(35) Josette Labbé	„	1812
Josette	Jean Ruel	„	1839
Marie Louise	Pierre Roberge	S.J.	1840
60 Joseph	(15) A Adé. Baudoin	S.V.	1815
		S.Tho.	
Louis David			
A Basile	(38) Charlotte Plante S.J.		1809
61 Joseph	(39) Scolastique Langlois		
		S.P.	1827
62 Laurent	(41) Marie Catellier	S.M.	1839
Le même	Marg. Duquet	„	1852
63 Barthélemi	M. Anne Pedneau		
Julie Hombeline	Honoré Vézina		
Frs. Marcellin			
Evariste			
Félix	(48) Olympiade Tailleur		
		S.P.	1848
64 François	(49) Eliz. Marcoux	S.J.	1841
65 Edouard	(50) Henriette Langlois		
		S.P.	1845
66 Louis	(51) M. Zoé Fréchet		
		S.Nicolas	1847
67 Henri	(54) M. Anne Blouin S.J.		1849
68 Marcel	(55) Apolline Audebert	„	1850
69 Joseph	(55) Genev. Gosselin S.L.		1853
70 Célestin	(56) Marg. Pouliot	„	1862
71 Louis	(56) M. Adéline Labrecque		
		S.L.	1872
72 Louis David	(60) M. Zoé Roy	S.M.	1842
		S.Claire	
73 Frs. Marcel-	(63) M. Adé. Ferlant S.P.		1855
lin			
74 Evariste	(63) Virginie Rousseau	„	1860

NOLIN.

1 Jacques	Fse. Chalifour	Qué.	1671
Louise	Pierre Joncas	S.P.	1696
Louise	2 Jos Langlois S.Tho.		1705

NOLIN.

Louise	3ᵉ Ls. Couillard S.Th.		1719
Françoise	Martin Boulet	S.P.	1693
Jeanne	Pierre Ratté	,,	1702
Jeanne	2ᵉ Ant. Basset	,,	1722
Marie Madeleine	Guill. Ratté	,,	1710
Michelle	Jean Trudel	,,	1715
Marie Anne	Jean Judon	Qué.	1724
Gabriel			
Pierre			
Guillaume			
Jacques			
2 Gabriel	(1) M. Mad. Dorval S.P.		1704
Elisabeth	Isidore Morin	,,	1735
Marie Madeleine	Jos. Talbot	,,	1735
3 Pierre	(1) M.Mad.Presseau	,,	1708
Héléne	Jean Langlois	,,	1739
Marie Thérése	Pierre Choret	,,	1745
Agathe	Aug. Dupile	,,	1768
Joseph			
Jean Baptiste			
Pierre			
4 Jacques	(1) Marie Rinville		
		Beauport	1715
5 Guillaume	(1) Thérése Trudel	S. P.	1715
Marie	Pierre Dalaire	,,	1744
Marie Marthe	Frs. Noël	,,	1745
Marie Marthe	2ᵉ Frs. Leclaire	,,	1763
Marie Benjamin	Pierre Gosselin	,,	1750
Marie Benjamin	2ᵉ Jean Alexandre	,,	1753
Marie Louise	Jos. Nadeau	,,	1750
Marie Josette	Frs. Leclaire	,,	1755
Marie Josette	2 Chs. Couture S.Chs.		1784
Guillaume			
6 Pierre	(3) M. Rose Dorval S. P.		1743
7 Joseph	(3) Thérése Paradis	,,	1746
Thérése	Aug. Dupile	,,	1776
François	Frs. Montigny	,,	1787
Geneviève	Jean Gosselin	,,	1788
Augustin			
Joseph			
8 Jean Baptiste	(3) Mad. Poulet	S. P.	1748
Madeleine	Ign. Paradis	,,	1782
Marie Angélique	Jean Gendreau	S. L.	1790
9 Guillaume	(5) Mad. Leclaire	S. P.	1746
Marie Thérése	Frs. Roberge	,,	1773
Marie	Paul Paradis	,,	1790
Pierre			
François			
10 Joseph	(7) Angé Dupile	S. P.	1776
Marie Angélique	Joseph Marois	,,	1809
Thérèse	Jean Fouquet	,,	1827
Augustin			
Charles			
11 Augustin	(7) Marie Jacques	S. P.	1790
François			
Augustin			
Le même	Marie Coté	S. P.	1817
12 Pierre	(9) M. Vict. Paquet	,,	1777
Le même	M. Jos. Chabot	,,	1780
13 François	(9) Angé Couture S. Chs.		1789
Le même	Ursule Duquet S. G.		1814
14 Augustin	(10) Christine Cantin S. P.		1810
Luce	Jean Gosselin	,,	1835
Apolline	Pierre Goulet	,,	1840
Apolline	2 Narcisse Rousseau		
		S. P.	1857
Marie Sara	Gilbert Roberge	,,	1852
Thécle	Frs. Vézina	,,	1852
Augustin			
Antoine			
15 Charles	(10) Thérése Roberge S.P.		1819
16 François	(11) Fse. Bouffart	S. L.	1826
Marie Olympe	Cyrille Labrecque S.P.		1860
Célimée	Ed. Tremblay	,,	1864
Eugène			
François Agapit			

NOLIN.

17 Augustin	(11) Eliz. Aubin	S. P.		1831
18 Augustin	(14) Ediliré Baudoin	,,		1843
19 Antoine	(14) M. Noflette Goulet			
			S. P.	1847
20 Eugène	(16) Emilienne Plante	,,		1858
21 François	(16) M. Zoé Roberge	,,		1859
Agapit				

NOLLET.

1 Sébastien	Jeanne Auger	Qué	1671
François			
André			
Jean François			
Louis			
Jacques			
2 François	(1) Marie Maranda	Qué	1701
3 André	(1) Marie Brault		
Jean			
4 Louis	(1) Marg. Lis	B.	1710
Louis			
Jean Marie			
5 Jean François	(1) M. Anne Thibaut S.L.		1728
Le même	Angé Fontaine S. V.		1754
6 Jacques	(1) Marie Coulombe	B.	1727
Claude			
7 Jean	(3) Marg. Martin S. L.		
8 Louis	(4) Mad. Peltier	S. P.	1744
Madeleine	Jos. Guilmet S. Chs.		1770
Louis			
9 Claude	(6) Marie Doiron	B.	1759
10 Jean Marie	(4) M. Ls. Parant S. Marie		
			1754
François			
11 Basile	Susanne Carrier		
Claude			
12 Louis	(8) M. Thécle Godbout		
		Que.	1775
13 Louis	Marthe Poiré	S. H.	1799
		S. H.	
Louis			
Le même	Josette Daniau S.F.		1816
14 François	(10) Josette Bégin	Lévis	1794
Elie			
15 Claude	(11) M. Apolline Couillard		
		S.Chs.	1805
Christine	Michel Morin	B.	1835
16 Louis	(12) M. Ls. Lacasse S.Chs.		1813
17 Louis	(13) Angé Picard	,,	1831
18 Elie	(14) Théotiste Roy	B.	1833

OUEL—WELLS—GALIBOIS.

1 François	Geo. Isle	Louisbourg		
Marie	Frs. Quiroüet	Bert.		1767
Françoise	Frs. Vermet	,,		1772
Antoine				
François				
2 François	(1) Eliz. Dodier	Bert.		1761
Marie Elisabeth	Pierre Bissonnet	,,		1789
Marguerite	Ant. Bouffart	,,		1798
François				
3 Antoine	(1) M. Fse. Marcoux	,,		1780
4 Étienne	Marg. Laviolette			
Rose	Michel Blais	Bert.		1825
Sophie	Basile Emond	,,		1830
Angèle	Jos. Emond	Bert.		1833
Luc				
5 André	Marg. Turcot			
Marguerite	Prosper Gaumon Bert.			1828
Catherine	Ls. Dubé	Bert.		1833
Jacques André				
6 François	(2) M. Chs. Roy	S.V.		1800
Le même	Josette Gagnon S.Chs.			1802
7 Luc	(4) Fse. Lessart	Bert.		1824

OUEL—WELLS—GALIBOIS.

8 Jacques André	Marg. Boulet	S.F.S. 1835
9 Georges	Reine Lessart	" 1840

OUELLET.

1 René	Anne Rivet	Qué. 1666
Mathurin		
Joseph		
2 Mathurin	(1) AngéLebel Riv.Ouelle 1691	
Louis		
Augustin		
3 Joseph	(1) Reine Meneux	S.F. 1700
4 Augustin	(2) Anne Antin	
Joseph		
Le même	Cath. Soulard	
Le même	Anne Michaud	
	Kamouraska 1735	
5 Louis	(2) M. Jos. Lacasse	B 1733
6 Joseph	(4) M. Thérèse Jahan	
		S.M. 1749
7 Louis	Cath. Brousseau	
Le même	Anne Montigny	S.P. 1781
8 Jean Baptiste	M. Jos. David	
Le même	Genev. Babineau	
		S.F.S. 1789
9 Henri	Louise Peltier	
	S Roch des Aulnets	
André		
10 Antoine	Ange Duquet	
Antoine		
11 François	Prescille Gagnon	
Clément	S. Paschal	
12 André	(9) M. Mad. Tangué S.M.1829	
13 Antoine	(10) Fse. Asselin	S. G.1829
14 Jean Gabriel	M. Eliz. Fournier	
fils d'André et	Cap. S. Ign. 1807	
Louise Gagnon		
Elisabeth	Frs. Florent Turgeon	
		B. 1845
15 Clément	(11) Seraphie Tangué S.V. 1866	

OUIMET.

1 Jean	Renée Gagnon	
Marguerite	Frs. Turcot	S.F. 1688
Louis		
Jean		
2 Louis	(1) M. Anne Genest S.F. 1693	
Marie	Jean Manseau	S.J. 1713
Thérèse Cath.	Simon Chamberlan	
		S.Foye 1723
M. Josette	Alexis Fleury	
Albert		
Jacques		
3 Jean	(1) Marie Juin	S.Frs. 1702
Le même	Marie Bissonnet	B. 1705
Michel		
Gabriel		
4 Albert	(2) Eliz. Marié	
5 Jacques	(2) Marg. Fontaine	S.J. 1752
6 Gabriel	(3) M. Anne Morisset	
		S.M. 1730
Marie Anne	Jos. Lacroix	S.M. 1757
Marie Agathe	Jean Nic. Delenteigne	
		S.M. 1770
7 Michel	(3) M. Marg.Tangué S.M.1765	
Michel		
Pierre		
8 Michel	(7) M. Mad. Mercier S.M.1811	
Marie	J. B. Tangué	" 1832
Cécile	Ls. Patry	" 1836
Cécile	2° Frs. Vien	B. 1843
9 Pierre	(7) Marie Chamberlan B. 1815	
Sara	David Quéret	B. 1849
10 François	(9) Julie Patry	S.M. 1845

OUELLET.

11 Pierre	(9) Emélie Labbé	B. 1848
12 Elis	(9) Eléonore Colombe	
		S.L. 1850
13 David	(9) Rose Fournier	B. 1850

PAGEOT.

1 Thomas	Cath. Roy	Qué. 1675
Joseph		
Jean Baptiste		
2 Joseph	(1) Mad. Boesmi	
Pierre	Chs.Bourg. 1716	
3 Jean Baptiste	(1) Marie Paradis	
	Chs.Bourg. 1703	
Thomas		
4 Pierre	Mad. Vermet	
Françoise	Chs. Rouleau	S.Frs. 1765
5 Thomas	(3) Mad. Gervais	
	Chs.Bourg. 1729	
Madeleine	Jos. Vermet	
	Chs.Bourg. 1749	
6 Pierre	(2) Marg. Jobin	
	Chs.Bourg. 1761	
Marie	Jos. Gosselin	S.F. 1788
Geneviève	Pierre Giguère	S.F. 1792
Marguerite	Frs. Paradis	S.P. 1790

PAQUET—LAVALLÉE.

1 Mery	Vincent Beaumont Poitiers	
Maurice		
2 Etienne	Jeanne Poussart, Poitiers.	
Etienne		
3 Mathurin	Marie Fremillon Mortaigne.	
Isaac		
4 Maurice	(1) Fse. Forget	1668
François		
5 Etienne	(2) Henriette Rousseau	
		Qué. 1668
Philippe		
6 Etienne Isaac	(3) Eliz. Meunier	C.R. 1670
Elisabeth	Pierre Guénet	S.L. 1690
Marguerite	Jacq. Labrecque	S.L. 1693
Jeanne	Jean Bertrand	
		Chs.Bourg. 1696
Angélique	Denis Desève	C.R. 1703
Françoise	Chs. Lacasse	B. 1703
Madeleine	Jos. Lessart	S.Anne. 1715
Joseph		
Charles		
François		
Antoine		
7 Pierre	Marie Caillet	1672
Pierre		
8 Philippe	Fse. Gobeil	S.F. 1671
Philippe		
Jean		
Pierre		
Françoise		
9 François	Marie Marcoux	
	S. Chs. Beauport 1710	
Noël		
10 Philippe	(5) Jeanne Brosseau	
	Chs.Bourg. 1699	
Jacques		
11 Pierre	(7) Marie Charlan	S.F. 1694
Jean Baptiste		
12 Charles	(6) Jeanne Coulombe S.L.1694	
Marguerite	Jos. Forgue	B. 1717
Marie	Jacq. Bilodeau	B. 1721
Marie	2° Jos. Chrétien S.M. 1740	
Marie Josette	Chs. Ls. Roy	B. 1746
Marie Josette	2° Etn. Fournier S.M. 1766	

PAQUET –LAVALLÉE.

	Charles		
	Jacques		
	Louis		
	Louis		
	Joseph		
	Pierre		
	Etienne		
	Jean Baptiste		
	Jean François		
13	François	(6)	M. Anne Bernard S.L. 1703
14	Antoine	(6)	Genev. Poulet S.P. 1708
	Anne		Jean Thibaut S.L. 1733
	Catherine		Jean Frs. Coté S.L. 1737
	Elizabeth		Ign. Ruel S.L. 1750
	Antoine		
	Jean Baptiste		
15	Joseph	(6)	Fse. Cloutier C.R. 1711
16	Philippe	(8)	Marie Fontaine S.J. 1700
	Guillaume		
	Joseph		
	Pierre		
	Le même		Dorothée Plante
	Marie		Pierre Vincent S.J. 1757
17	Jean	(8)	Marie Charlan S.J. 1708
18	François	(8)	M. Angé.Paradis S.P. 1715
	Angélique		J. B. Marcot S.F. 1738
	Angélique		2° Jean Ferland S.F. 1741
	Marthe		Frs. Canac S.F. 1744
	Madeleine		Jos. Pouliot S.F. 1747
	Basile		
	Joseph		
	Prisque		
19	Pierre	(8)	Elénore Roberge S.L. 1717
	Le même		Agnès Bilodeau S.Frs. 1736
	Marie Agnès		Chs. Fortier S.J. 1760
	Catherine		Jos. Chabot S.P. 1764
	Joseph		
20	Noël	(9)	Genev. Campagna S.Frs. 1728
21	Jacques	(10)	Jean Renaud Chs.Bourg. 1738
	Michel		
	Alexis		
22	Jean Bapt.	(11)	Thérèse Presseau S.P. 1738
23	Etienne	(12)	M. Anne Le Roy B. 1717
	Marie		Pierre Labrecque B. 1734
24	Charles	(12)	M. Chs. Delaire B. 1725
25	Joseph	(12)	Marie Mignot B. 1731
			V. de Frs. Dallaire
26	Jean Baptiste(12)		Anne Bilodeau S.Frs. 1731
	Le même		Genev. Plante S. Frs. 1734
	Le même		M. Ls. Tessier S. J. 1743
	Marie Angélique		Chs. Plante S.J. 1772
	Le même		M.ThècleCharlan S.J.1760
27	Jacques	(12)	Génev. Guay Lévis 1733
	Jacques		
	Le même		Génév. Lacasse B. 1735
	Charles		
28	JeanFrançois(12)		Angé Pepin S.J. 1737
	Angélique		Jos. Chabot S. J. 1782
	Françoise		Ls. Demers S.J. 1761
	M. Madeleine		Jos.MarieDemers S.J.1761
	Jean Baptiste		
	Joseph		
29	Pierre	(12)	M. Ls. Filteau S.M. 1738
	Michel		
	Jean Baptiste		
	Pierre		
30	Louis	(12)	Fse. Filteau S.M. 1742
31	Louis	(12)	M. Genev. Semart S. Anne 1749
	Elizabeth		Jos. Marseau S.M. 1785
	Barthélemi		
	Jean Baptiste		

PAQUET—LAVALLÉE.

32	Phillippe		Louise Gaudreau
	Jean Henri		
33	Antoine	(14)	Ange Rousseau
	Angélique		Etn. Couture
	Angélique		2° Frs. Ruel
	Le même		M. Jos. Coté
			V. de Pierre Goulet
34	JeanBaptiste(14)		Judith Leclaire S.L. 1746
	Marie		Pierre Gontier S.Chs. 1779
	Geneviève		Jos. Naud S. Chs. 1784
	Madeleine		Ls. Nadeau S. Chs. 1790
	Alexandre		
	Jean Baptiste		
	Gabriel		
35	Pierre	(16)	Marthe Labbé S.Frs. 1740
36	Guillaume	(16)	Fse. Labbé S.Frs. 1740
37	Joseph	(16)	Genev. Greffart S.J. 1744
38	Joseph	(18)	Louise Filiau S.F. 1747
	Marie Louise		Ls. Asselin S.F. 1775
	Susanne		Frs. Morr S.F. 1787
	Marie Victoire		Pierre Nolin S.P. 1777
	Michel		
39	Basile	(18)	Thérèse Dorval S.P. 1749
	Le même		Marie Martel S.P. 1747
	Barthélemi		
	Joseph		
	Ignace		
40	Prisque	(18)	M. Thècle Noël S.P. 1756
41	Joseph	(19)	M. Marg. GosselinS.J.1773
	Ursule		Ant. Marceau S.J. 1803
	Ursule		2° Jean Marseau S.J. 1809
	Hyacinthe		
	Joseph		
	Amable		
42	Michel	(21)	Charlotte Martin Chs. Bourg 1767
	Thérèse		J. B. Guénet S.Chs. 1808
			S. Amb.
	Claude		
	Etienne		
43	Alexis	(21)	Charlotte Dubois Lévis 1787
	Charlotte		J. B. Couture B. 1808
	Marie Louise		Chs. Roberge B. 1812
	Anastasie		Frs. Perouard B. 1812
	Esther		Barth. Paquet B. 1822
	Angélique		Chs. Goulet B. 1825
	Joachim		
	Alexis		
	Le même		Charlotte Cantin Lévis 1806
	Louis Octave		
	Charles		
	Maxime		
44	Jacques	(27)	M. Anne Gagne B. 1751
45	Charles	(27)	Fse. Bouffart B. 1763
	Marie Angélique		Frs. Roy B. 1791
	Geneviève		Frs. Carrier B. 1793
	Françoise		J. B. Filteau S.Chs. 1792
46	Joseph	(28)	M. Fse. Fortier S.J. 1782
	Marie Françoise		Jos. Plante S.J. 1808
	Geneviève		Barth. Pepin S.J. 1809
	Marie Angélique		Jos. Blouin S.J. 1812
	Marie Josette		Jos. Hélie S.J. 1810
	Marie Josette		2° Michel Fradet S.J. 1832
	Laurent		
47	Jn. Baptiste (28)		Marie Moor S.L. 1784
	Jean Baptiste		
	Le même		Marie Drapeau S.L. 1788
	Le même		M. Marianne Audet S.J. 1789
48	Michel	(29)	Pétronille Nadeau S.Chs. 1779
	Marguerite		J. B. Boivin S.F.S. 1801
	Le même		Marg. Terrien S.Chs. 1804
49	Jn. Baptiste (29)		Marg. Fournier S.M. 1783
	Marie Louise		Michel Roy S.M. 1821

PAQUET--LAVALLÉE.

Angèle	Jos. Hélie	S.M.	1838
Jean Baptiste			
50 Pierre	(29) Angé Racine	S.Chs.	1785
51 Louis	(30) M. Jos. Bleau	S.M.	1765
Joseph			
52 Joseph	(30) M. Genev. Chabot		
		S.M.	1773
Jean			
Joseph			
Le même	Fse. Picard	S. Chs.	1784
Françoise	Ant. Gosselin	S.M.	1819
Charles			
53 JeanBaptiste(31)	Fse. Mercier	S. Chs.	1785
Marie Anne	André Labbé	S.M.	1822
Angèle	Michel Labbé	"	1822
Marguerite	Ls. Labbé	"	1825
Marie	Pierre Paschal Labbé		
		S.M.	1827
Michel			
Jean			
Louis			
54 Barthélemi	(31) Angéle Labbé	S.G.	1787
Angélique	Michel Chiasson	"	1815
Pierre			
Barthélemi			
55 Jean Henri	(32) Fse. Hélie	C.R.	1785
Le même	Héléne Barillau	"	1792
Pierre			
Le même	Marg. Martel	C.R.	1796
56 Gabriel	(34) M. Angé Gontier		
		S. Chs.	1773
François			
Jean Baptiste			
57 JeanBaptiste(34)	Cath. Gontier	"	1773
Euphrosine	Jos. Nadeau	"	1814
Euphrosine	2° Pierre Duquet	"	1840
Euphrosine	3° Pierre Coten	S.M.	1842
Marie	Ant. Quemeneur	S.G.	1800
Alexandre			
Jean			
58 Alexandre	(34) M. Chs. Gosselin		
		S. Chs.	1782
Marie Charlotte	Jos. Gontier	"	1812
Joseph			
Le même	Thérèse Robertson		
		S. Chs.	1794
Marguerite	J. B. Mercier	"	1830
Angélique	Frs. Gagné	"	1831
59 Michel	(38) Genev. Émond		
Marie Angèlique	Amb. Lacroix		
Marguerite	Pierre Coté		
Angélique	Chs. Bilodeau		
Cécile	Amb. Baillargeon		
Joseph			
Le même	Mad. Roy	S.G.	1806
	V. de Michel Custos		
Elizabeth	Ls. Samson	S.G.	1827
60 Ignace	(39) Thérèse Coté	S.P.	1786
Thérèse	Jean Goulet	"	1812
Josette	Olivier Goulet	"	1851
Laurent			
Oliver			
Ignace			
61 Joseph	(39) Pélagie Racine	S.F.	1787
Angélique	Jacq. Martineau	"	1811
Prisque			
Joseph			
62 Barthélemi	(39) M. Jos. Coté	S.P.	1803
63 Joseph	(41) M. Jos. Lepage	S.Frs.	1805
Adélaide	Marcel Letellier	S.J.	1837
Sophie	Ls. Pouliot	"	1844
Sèraphine	Jean Pouliot	"	1852
64 Amable	(41) Lucie Brochu	S.V.	1818
Luce	Alexandre Vaillancour		
		S.M.	1838

PAQUET—LAVALLEE.

Marie	Simon Forgue	S.M.	1839
Marie	2° Pierre Drouin	"	1843
65 Hyacinthe	(41) M. Vict. Lainé	S.Frs.	1819
66 Etienne	(42) Charlotte Girard	B.	1797
Marie Charlotte	Aug. Blais	"	1825
Etienne			
67 Claude	(42) Marg. Labrecque	"	1799
Marie Charlotte	Etn. Guay	"	1830
Charlotte	Jos. Hélie	"	1831
Louise	Jos. Prudent Girard		
		B.	1838
Marie Françoise	Chs. Nadeau	"	1848
Marguerite	Ls. Baudoin	S. Chs.	1820
Marc Antoine			
Claude			
Bénoni			
François Xavier			
Louis			
68 Joachim	(43) Apolline Fournier	B.	1818
69 Alexis	(43) Euphrosine Turgeon		
		B.	1818
70 Louis Octave	(43) Archange Dion	"	1832
71 Charles	(43) M. Rose Coté	"	1835
Marie	Chs. Cotin	"	1851
72 Maxime	(43) Hermine Fournier	"	1845
73 Laurent	(46) M. Jos. Hélie	S.J.	1810
Josette	Laurent Labrecque		
		S.J.	1845
Laurent			
André			
74 JeanBaptiste(49)	Marie Mercier	S.M.	1813
75 Joseph	(51) Thérèse Emond, Bert	1793
76 Joseph	(52) Marg. Corriveau		
		S.M.	1803
Emélie	J. B. Audet	"	1848
Joseph			
77 Jean	(52) Charlotte Denis	"	1806
78 Charles	(52) Marg. Brochu	"	1822
79 Michel	(53) Julie Fradet	S.V.	1812
Michel			
80 Jean	(53) Angéle Menard	B.	1816
Henriette	Aug. Poulin	B.	1845
Marie Louise			
Zoé	Urbain Lessard	"	1846
81 Louis	(53) Genev. Valière	S.F.S.	1835
82 Pierre	(54) Louise Bolduc	S.G.	1818
83 JeanBaptiste(47)	Josette Pouliot	S.L.	1811
84 Barthélemi	(54) Esther Paquet	B.	1822
Marie Esther	Chs. Ed. Turgeon	"	1851
Barthélemi			
Le même	Marg. Couture	"	1838
85 Pierre	(55) Cécile Hélie	S.J.	1825
Cécile	Frs. Pouliot	"	1862
Paul			
Joseph			
Léon			
Pierre			
86 JeanBaptiste(56)	M. Natalie Bacquet		
		S.Chs.	1797
Marguerite	Thomas Roy	"	1827
Marie	Chs. Chabot	B.	1827
Jean Baptiste			
Antoine			
Le même	M. Angéle Audet		
		S.Chs.	1817
Damase			
François			
87 François	(56) M. Eliz. Balan	Bert.	1798
Marguerite	Jos. Mercier	"	1826
Marie	Paschal Baudoin	"	1830
Henriette			
Euphémie	Jos. Haule Desruisseaux		
		Bert.	1833
Charles			
Jacques			
François			

PAQUET—LAVALLEE.

88	Alexandre	(57)	Mad. Quemeneur	S.F.S. 1802
	Marie		Romain Lémelin S.M.1848	
	Alexandre			
89	Jean	(57)	Susanne Leclaire S.G.1812	
	Susanne		Guill. Lemieux	„ 1830
	Thomas			
	Le même		Reine Paré	S.V. 1842
90	Joseph	(58)	Marie Mercier S.Chs.1821	
	Constance		Jos.Carbonneau	„ 1849
	Marie		Protois Dion	„ 1849
91	Joseph	(59)	M. Jos. Blouin	S.J. 1826
92	Jacques		Mad. Huart	
	Madeleine		Michel Lacroix S.M. 1841	
93	Ignace	(60)	Agathe Montigny S.P.1818	
	Jean Bruno			
	Laurent			
94	Laurent	(60)	Félicité Racine	„ 1836
95	Olivier	(60)	M.Honora Hébert	„ 1840
96	Joseph	(61)	M.Ls.Létourneau S.F.1811	
	Joseph			
97	Prisque	(61)	Marg. Asselin	„ 1813
	Stanislas			
98	Etienne	(66)	Fse. Goupy	B. 1827
	Charles			
99	Claude	(67)	M. Eliz. Goupy	B. 1834
100	Bénoni	(67)	M. Ls. Hélie	B. 1836
101	François Xa-	(67)	Genev. Emélie Girard	
	vier			B. 1846
102	Louis	(67)	Caroline Turgeon B. 1848	
103	MarcAntoine	(67)	Marg. Chevalier S.M.1848	
104	Laurent	(73)	M. Anne Gosselin S.J.1838	
105	André	(73)	Julie Dion	„ 1850
106	Joseph	(76)	Angéle Forgue S.M. 1832	
	Napoléon			
107	Barthélemi	(84)	Natalie Pepin S.L. 1851	
108	Michel	(79)	Marg. Gagnon S.V. 1837	
109	André		Sophie Lepire	
	Le même		M. Hermine Turgeon	
			S.Chs. 1843	
110	Paul	(85)	Léocadie Delisle S.J. 1854	
111	Léon	(85)	M. Virginie Pouliot	
			S.J. 1867	
112	Pierre	(85)	MarcellineGosselin „ 1857	
113	Joseph	(85)	Marie Blouin	„ 1862
114	JeanBaptiste	(86)	Scolastique Couture	
			S.Chs. 1821	
	Constance		Hubert Nand	„ 1855
115	Antoine	(86)	M. Ls. Chabot	„ 1843
116	François	(86)	M.Anne Terrien	„ 1844
	Marie Anne		Laurent Audet	„ 1862
117	Damase	(86)	Emélie Chabot	„ 1862
118	Pierre		Genev. Dion	S.F. 1845
119	François	(87)	SophiePruneau S.Tho.1824	
	Sara		Jos. Nadeau S.Chs. 1859	
	Emélie		Frs. Chabot	„ 1861
	Le même		Archange Douget „ 1850	
120	Jacques	(87)	Fse. Valière S.P.S. 1831	
121	Charles	(87)	Apolline Hudon Bert.1846	
122	Alexandre	(88)	M.RoseMercierS.Chs.1834	
	Marie		Etn. Marcoux	„ 1863
123	Thomas	(89)	Domitille Couture B. 1852	
124	Jean Bruno	(93)	Firmine Cantin S.P. 1848	
125	Laurent	(93)	Cécile Cantin	„ 1851
126	Joseph	(96)	Marcelline Gagnon	
			S.F. 1841	
127	Stanislas	(97)	Marie Pichet	„ 1857
	Le même		Olive Gagnon	„ 1860
128	Charles	(98)	Marie Turgeon B. 1858	
129	Napoléon	(106)	DelphineBacquetS.M.1863	

PAQUIN.

1	Nicolas	M. Fse. Plante C.R. 1676	
	Marie	J. B. Marcot S.F. 1708	
	Geneviève	Jean Frs. Nault „ 1711	

18—28

PAQUIN.

	Marie Madeleine	Jacq. Perrot	S.F. 1711
	Nicolas		
2	Nicolas	(1) M. Anne Perrot	„ 1707

PARADIS.

1	Pierre	Barbe Guion	
	Marie	Guill Beaucher. Qué. 1656	
	Louise	Thomas Mezeroy „ 1678	
	Jacques		
	Pierre		
	Guillaume		
2	Jacques	(1) Jeanne Milois	„ 1668
	Marie	Jean Maranda S.P. 1688	
	Madeleine	Guill. Cantin C.R. 1716	
	Pierre		
	Joseph		
	Guillaume		
	Jean		
3	Guillaume	(1) Genev. Milois Qué. 1670	
	Geneviève	Adrien Leclaire S.P. 1694	
	Anne	Frs. Lemieux „ 1698	
	Elizabeth	J. B. Dorval „ 1705	
	Gabriel		
	Ignace		
	Pierre		
	Guillaume		
4	Pierre	(1) Jeanne Fse. LeRoy	
	Jeanne	Ls. Dupont S.P. 1701	
	Jeanne	2° Germ. Martineau	
		S.F. 1718	
	Marie	Pierre Aubin S.P. 1693	
	Claire	Pierre Hudon „ 1707	
	Anne	Pierre Dorval „ 1709	
	Angélique	Frs. Paquet „ 1715	
	Geneviève	Pierre Poulet „ 1724	
	Charles		
5	Pierre	(2) M. Mad. Drouin „ 1701	
6	Guillaume	(2) Jeanne Hudon	
		Riv. Ouelle 1701	
	Marie	Aug. Dionne S.P. 1726	
	Marie Jeanne	Chs. Amadoe Ratté	
		S.P. 1734	
	Marie Anne	Gab. Bussière „ 1734	
	Marie Josette	Ign. Ratté „ 1741	
7	Joseph	(2) Genev. Cochon C.R. 1712	
	Geneviève	Pierre Goulet S.P. 1741	
	Geneviève	2° Ant. Valière S.Chs.1764	
	Pierre		
	Etienne		
	Paul		
	Joseph		
8	Jean	(2) M. Fse. Hudon	
		Riv. Ouelle 1718	
9	Gabriel	(3) Genev. Lemieux	
		Cap. S. Ign. 169	
10	Guillaume	(3) Marg. Cath. Hudon	
		Riv. Ouelle 1701	
11	Pierre	(3) Marg. Dorval S.P. 1711	
12	Ignace	(3) M. Anne Turcot S.F. 1719	
	Marie Anne	Pierre Choret S.P. 1741	
	Thérèse	Jos. Nolin „ 1746	
	Marie	Jos. Coté „ 1750	
	Marie Josette	Ign. Coté „ 1753	
	Geneviève	Jos. Leclaire „ 1765	
	Marguerite	Ls. Noël „	
	Ignace		
	François		
	Nicolas		
	Jean Baptiste		
13	Charles	(4) Claire Deblois S.F. 1714	
	Marie Thérèse	Jean Goulet S.P. 1750	
	Marie Madeleine	Ant. Goulet „ 1761	
	Gabriel		
	Charles		
	Louis		

5-6 EDWARD VII., A. 1906

PARADIS.

14	Joseph	(7)	Genev. Boivin	S. Anne	1742
15	Pierre	(7)	Ursule Cantin	S.P.	1744
16	Paul	(7)	M. Jos. Rouleau	S.L.	1748
	Geneviève		Pierre Grénier	S.P.	1785
	Madeleine		Frs. Roberge	"	1786
	Louis				
	Joseph				
	Paul				
	Le même		M. Anne Pouliot	S.L.	1770
	Marie Anne		Ls. Vermet	S.P.	1794
	Jean				
17	Etienne	(7)	Marie Tremblay	S.J. Qué.	1755
	Le même		M. Genev. Demers	Lévis	1756
	François				
	Louis				
	Joseph				
18	Ignace	(12)	Thérèse Gaulin	S.P.	1747
	Agathe		Michel Montigny	"	1782
	Thérèse		Jean Goulet	"	1783
	Angélique		Ls. Pichet	"	1793
	Marie Anne		Benoit Gendreau	"	1805
	Jean Baptiste				
	Ignace				
19	François	(12)	Ursule Coté	"	1749
	Pierre				
	François				
	Le même		M. Reine Ratté	"	1761
	Marie Reine		Pierre Chatigny	"	1783
	Josette		Chs. Paradis	"	1794
	Louis				
20	JeanBaptiste	(12)	Véronique Carrier	Lévis	1755
21	Nicolas	(12)	M. Anne Niel	S.P.	1760
22	Gabriel	(13)	M. Jos. Niel	"	1749
	Antoine				
	Charles				
	Gabriel				
23	Charles	(13)	Marg. Goulet	"	1750
	Le même		Marie Langlois	"	1775
24	Louis	(13)	Marg. Demers	Lévis	1764
	Marguerite		J. B. Fortier	S.H.	1786
	Marie Thècle		Frs. Lheureux	"	1801
	Louis				
25	Etienne		Eliz. Beaulieu		
	Le même		M. Jos. Bidet	S.V.	1790
26	Louis	(16)	Thérèse Langlois	S.P.	1782
	Marguerite		Jos. Talbot	S.G.	1812
	Hélène		Michel Vérieul	"	1821
	Judith		Etn. Bussière	"	1822
27	Joseph	(16)	Josette Desruisseaux	Lévis	1784
	Josette		Frs. Gosselin	S.H.	1808
	Louise		Jos. Leclaire	"	1819
	Joachim				
	Joseph				
28	Paul	(16)	Marie Nolan	S.P.	1790
	Constance		Pierre Chatigny	"	1812
	Geneviève		Jos. Cluriau	"	1813
	Félicité		Maurice Leclaire	"	1830
	Marie Angèle		Frs. Manet	"	1833
	François Xavier				
	Le même		Agathe Ferland	"	1806
	Archange		Amb. Létourneau	"	1831
	Agathe		Jos. Roberge	"	1831
	Anastasie		Pierre Pichet	"	1839
	Domitile		Frs. Campagna	"	1856
	Godfroi				
29	Jean	(16)	Thérèse Blais	S.H.	1807
30	François	(17)	M. Anne Taillon	"	1788
	Pierre				
	Etienne				
31	Louis	(17)	Marg. Langlois	"	1791
32	Joseph	(17)	Mad. Morisset	"	1801
33	Charles		M. Ls. Noël		
	Marie Louise		Pierre Larrivé	"	1812

PARADIS.

34	JeanBaptiste	(18)	Agathe Coté	S.P.	1781
	Agathe		Ant. Vaillancour	"	1812
	Laurent				
	Ignace				
	Jean Baptiste				
35	Ignace	(18)	Mad. Nolin	"	1782
	Thérèse		Laurent Ferlant	"	1808
	Madeleine		Jean Choret	"	1816
	Ignace				
36	François	(19)	Thècle Roberge	"	1785
	Le même		Marg. Pageot	"	1790
	Geneviève		Frs. Gourdeau	"	1811
	Marguerite		Pierre Godbout	"	1816
	Marie Angélique		Michel Montigny	"	1821
	Elizabeth		Amb. Godbout	"	1838
	Gabriel				
	François				
37	Pierre	(19)	Thérèse Asselin	"	1784
	Thérèse		Frs. Gagnon	"	1805
38	Louis	(19)	Mad. Rouleau	S.L.	1788
	Reine		Jos. Canac	S.P.	1811
	Madeleine		Nicolas Julien	"	1813
	Louis				
39	Gabriel	(22)	Cécile Chabot	S.L.	1781
40	Antoine	(22)	Thérèse Dupile	S.P.	1782
41	Charles	(22)	Josette Paradis	"	1794
	Le même		Josette Ferlant	"	1810
	François				
42	Pierre		Rosalie Bussière	S.H.	1797
	Joseph				
43	Louis	(24)	Marie Boucher	S.Chs.	1800
44	Joseph	(27)	Josette Gosselin	S.H.	1808
45	Joachim	(27)	Euphrosine Nadeau	S.H.	1812
46	François	(28)	Genev. Thivierge	S.P.	1825
	Xavier				
	Le même		Genev. Grenier	S.I.	1846
47	Godfroi	(28)	Domitile Vézina	S.P.	1852
48	Etienne	(30)	Anastasie Hallé	S.H.	1817
49	Pierre	(30)	M. Reine Bilodeau	S.Chs.	1835
50	JeanBaptiste	(34)	Marg. Genest	S.P.	1811
	Marguerite		Magl. Giguère	S.F.	1836
51	Laurent	(34)	Cath. Vézina	S.P.	1821
	Catherine		Pierre Gagnon	"	1847
	Le même		Josette Rousseau	"	1828
	Marie Aglaé		Alexis Ferlant	"	1856
52	Ignace	(34)	Marg. Beaucher	S.F.	1824
	Martine		Firmin Létourneau	S.F.	1851
	Adelaïde		Jacq. Guay	"	1854
	Philomène		Michel Canac	"	1859
	Pierre				
	Frs. Xavier				
53	Ignace	(35)	M. Ls. Choret	S.P.	1810
	Marie Archange		Jean Rousseau	"	1833
	Marcelline		Ed. Ferlant	"	1840
	Sophie		Stanislas Thivierge	"	1840
	Angèle		Lazare Beaucher	"	1845
	Ignace				
54	François	(36)	Pélagie Roberge	"	1822
55	Gabriel	(36)	Eliz. Rousseau	"	1836
	François Nap				
	Pierre Octave				
56	Louis	(38)	Thérèse Noël	"	1819
57	François	(41)	Angé Julien	C.R.	1821
	François				
58	Joseph	(43)	Cécile Shinck	S.G.	1825
59	Etienne		Olivette Chamberlan		
	Le même		Marg. Coté	S.L.	1842
60	Pierre	(52)	Scolastique Létourneau	S.F.	1856
61	François	(52)	M. Céline Drouin	S.F.	1862
	Xavier				
	Le même		Marie Leblond	S.F.	1865

PARADIS.

62 Ignace (53) Justine Canten S.P. 1838
Marie Justine — Jean Sylv. Leclaire S.P. 1869
Joseph Ignace
63 François (55) M. Virginie Létourneau
Nap. — S.P. 1862
64 PierreOctave(55) M. Anastasie Letourneau — S.F. 1867
65 François (57) Marie Ferland S.P. 1857
Le même — Rosalie Cinqmars S.L. 1869
66 Joseph Ignace (62) Genev. Octavie Leclaire S.P. 1865

PARANT.

1 Pierre — Jeanne Badeau Qué. 1654
Jean François
Charles
Pierre
Etienne
2 Pierre (1) Marg, Baugy, Beauport 1683
Michel
Pierre
3 Jean François (1) Marie Vallée, Beauport 1687
Mathieu
4 Charles (1) M. Anne Duprac, Beauport 1696
Antoine
5 Etienne (1) Thérèse Chevalier, Beauport 1696
Etienne
Le même — Genev. Trudel A.G. 1727
Jean Marie
Nicolas
6 Pierre (2) Marg. Noël S.L. 1706
Pierre
7 Jean Michel (2) Génév. Chrétien Chs. Bourg. 1728
Geneviève — Ls. Gagnon S.P. 1762
Marie — Michel Bélanger S.P. 1762
Agathe — Benoit Noël S.P. 1764
Marie Madeleine — Gab. Langlois S.P. 1779
8 Mathieu (3) M. Marthe Deblois S.F. 1720
9 Antoine (4) M. Angé Delaunay
Joseph Antoine
A Joseph — Louise Blondeau
Joseph
10 Etienne (5) Marie Lefebvre Beauport 1730
Marie Louise — Jean Marie Nollet S. Marie 1754
Etienne
11 Jean Marie (5) Marie Barbeau Beauport 1765
Marie — Pierre Deblois B. 1793
12 Pierre (6) Jeanne Chevalier, Beauport, 1729
Michel
13 Nicolas (5) Cath. Marcoux, Beauport 1750
Etienne
14 Joseph Antoine (9) Charlotte Auclair, Chs. Bourg. 1762
Antoine
15 Etienne (10) M. Chs. Lefebvre S. Marie S.M. 1764
Etienne
16 Michel (12) Cath. Claire Parant Beauport 1761
Le même — Mad. Garneau, Beauport 1768
Le même — Thérèse Bussiere S.P. 1769

18—28½

PARANT.

17 Jacques — Toinette Camiré S. Marie
Jacques
18 Joseph (9) Josette Legris, Que. 1762
Joseph
19 Jacques — Angé Charlau
Jacques
20 Etienne (13) Marg. Grenier, Beauport 1777
Etienne
21 Antoine (14) M. Chs. Poulin S.F. 1795
22 Etienne (15) Marie Leblond S.Chs. 1798
23 Jacques (17) M. Jos. Morin S.F.S. 1774
Charles
24 François — M. Félicité Dessaint — M. Reine
Marie Félicité — J. B. Gontier S.V. 1813
Céleste — Ant. Pigeon S.V. 1825
Marie Antoinette — Michel Bilodeau S.V. 1831
Marie Louise — Nazaire Brousseau S.V. 1846
François
Louis
Pierre
Jean
25 Joseph (18) M. Reine Crépeau S.P. 1802
26 Jacques (19) M. Chs. Valière S.Chs. 1813
27 Michel — Louise Dominy
Le même — Fse. Leclaire S.V. 1822
28 Etienne (20) Adé Drouin S.F. 1845
Le même — Henriette Coté S.F. 1849
29 François (24) M. Vict. Corriveau S.V. 1815
V. de J. B. Corriveau
30 Pierre (24) Flavie Marseau S.V. 1825
31 Louis (24) Marg. Tangué S.V. 1831
Louis
32 Louis (31) Angéle Plante S.V. 1853
Charles (23) M. Claire Jalbert S.H. 1815
Jean (24) Marg. Gendron S.H. 1819

PARÉ.

1 Robert — Fse. Lehoux Qué. 1653
Jean
François
Noël
Joseph
2 Jean (1) Jeanne Racine C.R. 1682
Prisque
Etienne
Timothée
Le même — Cath. Lainé S.F. 1709
3 François (1) Marg. Racine S.Anne 1690
Le même — Claire Lacroix " 1704
4 Noël (1) Marg. Caron " 1685
Louis
5 Joseph (1) Mad. Berthelot " 1685
Marie Josette — Pierre Guignard " 1722
Marie Josette — 2° J.B. Larrivé S.F.S. 1742
6 Prisque (2) Marg. Mesny S.Anne 1715
Jean
Joseph
7 Etienne (2) Anne Lacroix S.Anne 1716
8 Timothée (2) Genev. Barret " 1725
9 Louis (4) M. Jos. Guay B. 1719
Marguerite — Jos. Boulet S.F.S. 1762
Angélique — Pierre Boudoin " 1765
Pierre
Louis

PARÉ.

10 Jean	(6) Thérèse Racine	
		S. Anne 1744
Jérome		
11 Joseph	(6) Judith Amable Simard	
		S. Anne 1751
12 Joseph	Cath. Terrien	
		S.H.
Catherine	Jos. Bilodeau S. Chs. 1775	
Antoine		
13 Louis	(9) M.Ls.Fournier S.Tho.1742	
Marie Geneviéve	Aug. Mercier S.F.S. 1765	
Madeleine	J. B. Dion „ 1770	
Marie Josette	Jos. Blais „ 1773	
Marguerite	Ls. Morin „ 1778	
Marie Reine	Simon Bourque „ 1783	
Française	J.B.Martineau „ 1786	
Thérèse	Jos. Marie Bilodeau	
		S.F.S. 1788
Louise	Aug. Blais S.F.S. 1795	
14 Pierre	(9) Marg. Gagnon	
		S. Joachim 1760
Marie Reine	Etn. Lebrun S.F.S. 1778	
Marie Louise	Jos. Lemieux „ 1783	
Pierre Noël		
Louis		
Jean Baptiste		
Jérome		
Antoine		
Simon		
Amable		
Augustin		
15 Jérome	(10) Marie Canac S.Anne 1771	
Brigitte	Ls. Gérard S.F. 1792	
16 Etienne	(11) M.Agnès ParéS.Anne 1795	
Prisque		
17 Antoine	(12) Marg. Forgue S.M. 1785	
18 Louis	(14) Angé Fortier S.F.S. 1775	
Marie Angélique	Jean Frs Thibaut „ 1804	
19 Jean Baptiste	(14) M. Thérèse Asselin	
		S.M. 1782
20 Jérome	(14) M. Fse. Beaucher	
		S.F.S. 1783
Pierre		
Jérome		
Le même	M. Fse. Marcoux Bert 1793	
21 Antoine	(14) Mary Boulet S.F.S. 1784	
Marguerite	Jos. Marseau S.V. 1805	
Marie Archange	Pierre Morin „ 1840	
Reine	Jean Paquet „ 1842	
Abraham		
Michel		
Augustin		
Pierre		
22 Pierre Noël	(14) M.Anne Morin S.P.S 1787	
23 Simon	(14) M. Agathe Picard	
		S.F.S. 1787
Reine	Frs. Morin „ 1827	
Joseph		
Simon		
24 Amable	(14) M. Reine Dumas „ 1798	
Thomas		
25 Louis	Hélène Bossé	
Adelaïde	Jos. Bernier , 1812	
Joseph Prudent		
26 Etienne	Vict. Jacques C.R. 1817	
Etn.	Thérèse Pepin	
Etienne		
27 François Xavier	Reine Angéle Lapane	
Angéle Eleonore	Jean Oliver Fraser	
		S.F.S. 1839
28 Prisque	(16) Justine Dalaire S.Frs. 1823	
29 Augustin	(14) Marie Brigitte Brie	
		S. Tho. 1788
Marguerite	Ant. Fournier S.Tho. 1815	
Marie Louise	Jos. Fournier „ 1821	
André		

PARÉ.

30 Jérome	(20) M. Marg. Savoie	
		S.F.S. 1808
Archange	Simon Boivier S.V. 1832	
Marie	Etienne Roy „ 1841	
31 Pierre	(20) M. Ls. Bonneau „ 1809	
32 Pierre	(21) Marg. Dumas S.F.S. 1818	
Louis		
33 Michel	(21) Archange Gagnon	
		S. M. 1824
Joseph Michel		
34 Abraham	(21) Flavien Marseau S.V.1827	
35 Augustin	(21) Angéle Bilodeau Bert 1841	
36 Simon	(23) Soulange Gendron	
		S.F.S. 1827
37 Joseph	(23) Eliz. Boissonneau „ 1835	
38 Thomas	(24) Marie Marcoux S.Chs 1825	
39 Jos. Prudent	(25) Cath. Fraser S.F.S. 1821	
40 Etienne	(26) Apolline Guay S.F. 1860	
41 André	(29) M. AngéTurgeonS.Frs.1831	
42 Louis	(32) Dmitille Roy S.Chs. 1853	
43 Jos. Michel	(33) Eliz. Bélanger S.V. 1861	
44 Ambroise	Marie Racine	
Marie	Pierre Gagnon S.F. 1866	

PATENOTRE

1 Nicolas	Marg. Breton Que. 1651	
Marie	Claude Plante S.F. 1678	
Marguerite	Pierre Plante „ 1691	
Marin		
2 Marin	(1) Marg.Mercier S.Anne 1691	
François		
3 François	(2) Eliz. Guion S.F. 1734	

PATOUEL-PATOINE DESROSIERS.

1 Jean Nicolas	M. Anne Louineau Q 1727	
Nicolas		
2 Nicolas	(1) M. Rosalie Saucier	
Le même	M. Cath. Tangué S.V.1761	
Marie	Pierre Adam S.Chs. 1787	
Rosalie	J. B. Campagna S.G. 1799	
Marguerite	Aug. Bilodeau „ 1801	
M. Anne	Amb. Goulet S.V. 1801	
Joseph		
Etienne		
Pierre		
Antoine		
3 Joseph	Genev. Cochon	
François		
4 Joseph	(2) Marg. Nadeau S.Chs. 1792	
Marguerite	Paschal Mercier S.G. 1812	
Angélique	Laurent Genest „ 1820	
Angélique	2 Jean Godbout „ 1824	
Théotiste	Ignace Dion B. 1829	
Françoise	Ls. Gesseron „ 1835	
Pierre		
Joseph		
Le même	Marg. Jacques S.G. 1825	
5 Etienne	(2) Eliz. Ainse „ 1794	
Elizabeth	Frs. Fradet „ 1821	
Marguerite	Frs. Talbot „ 1828	
Angélique	Pierre Guilmet „ 1828	
Louis		
Le même	Angé Delisle „ 1826	
	V.de Chs. Bisson	
6 Pierre	(2) Cécile Trahan S.G. 1805	
7 Antoine	(2) Louise Ainse „ 1795	
Louise	Etn. Labrecque „ 1820	
Antoine		
Etienne		
François Xavier		
8 François	(3) Marie Audet S.G. 1795	
9 Joseph	(4) Archange Goulet „ 1817	
Le même	Genev. Audet S.V. 1821	
10 Pierre	(4) Angéle Forgue S.G. 1830	

PATOÜEL PATOINE—DESROSIERS.

11	Louis	(5) Angé Fournier	S.G.	1829
12	Antoine	(7) Genev. Bedard	„	1821
13	François Xav-	(7) Archange Darveau		
	ier		S.G.	1829
14	Etienne	(7) M. Marg. Dion	B.	1836
15	Jean	Restitut Audet		
	Marie Georgina	Vilbon Blais	S.V.	1862

PATRY.

1	André	Henriette Cartois	Qué.	1675
	André			
	René			
	René			
2	André	(1) Cath. Pruneau	Bert.	1711
	M. Anne	Chs Lacroix	S.M.	1750
	André			
	Joseph			
	Clément			
	Michel			
3	René	(1) M. Chs. Dupuis		
	Michel			
	Jean			
	Pierre			
4	René	M. Cath. Gérard	B.	1721
	Louis			
	Jean Baptiste			
5	Clément	(2) Dorothée Brochu	S.V.	1744
	Marie Dorothée	Frs. Plante	S.M.	1774
	Ignace			
	Gabriel			
	Clément			
	Jacques			
6	André	(2) M. Agathe Roy	S.V.	1744
7	Joseph	(2) Marie Morisset	S.M.	1746
	Catherine	Chs. Fortier	„	1773
	Joseph			
8	Michel	(2) M. Angé Quéret	„	1759
	Geneviève	Pierre Roy	„	1786
	Marie Hélène	Michel Hélie	„	1793
	Le même	M. Ls. Roy	„	1776
	Michel			
9	Michel	(3) Marie Lacroix	S.M.	1743
	Catherine	Frs. Cochon	„	1773
	Marie Anne	Amable Bacquet	„	1786
	Marie Louise	Ls. Terrien	„	1761
	M. Louise	2ⁿ Chs. Turgeon	S.G.	1790
	Michel			
	Joseph			
10	Jean	(3) Marg. Gromelin	S.M.	1748
	Marie	Jos. Roy	S.Chs.	1766
	Le même	Mad Quemeneur	S.H.	1806
	M. Madeleine	J. B. Boucher	„	1820
11	Pierre	(3) M. Mad. Danau	S.M	1748
	Marie Félecité	Etn. Lajoint	„	1778
	M. Madeleine	Mathurin Labrecque		
			S.M.	1774
	M. Geneviève	Ign. Lacasse	„	1779
	Pierre			
	Le même	Mad. Michon	S.G.	1784
12	Jacques	Genev. Guay		
	Le même	Genev. Lacasse	B.	1735
13	Louis	(4) M. Genev. Turgeon		
			Lévis	1754
	Michel			
	François			
	Joseph			
14	Jean Baptiste	(4) Véronique Raimond		
		Beauce.	S.Jos.	1764
	Marie Hélène	Laurent Moor	Lévis	1806
	Jean Baptiste			
15	Clément	(5) Thérèse Quérit	S.M.	1770
	Marie	Etn. Fournier	S.Chs.	1808
	Marie Josette	Hippolyte Poliquin		
			S.Chs.	1815
	Marguerite	Nic. Morisset	„	1821

PATRY.

	Marie Louise	Frs. Dumas	S.L.	1817
	Thérèse	Gab. Lepage	S.H.	1817
	Lazare			
	Féréal			
16	Jacques	(5) M. Fse. Furais	S.M.	1773
	Marie	Ls. Gousse	S.M.	1797
	Marguerite	Ign. Carrier	„	1798
	Françoise	Joachim Mercier	„	1806
	Julie	Ls. Germ. Chouinard		
			S.M.	1813
	Joseph			
	Antoine			
17	Ignace	(5) Genev. Quéret	S.Chs.	1779
	Marguerite	Pierre Gagnon	S.M.	1803
	Marie	Frs. Roy	B.	1811
	Marie Josette	Jacq. Asselin	S.Chs.	1813
	Angélique	Chs. Lacasse	„	1816
	Louis			
	Charles			
	Ignace			
	Jean Baptiste			
18	Gabriel	(5) Marg. Roy	S.V.	1781
	Scolastique	André Langlois	„	1808
	Scolastique	2° Jean Darveau	„	1844
19	Joseph	(7) M. Jos. Leclaire	„	1774
	Marie Josette	Joachim Gosselin	S.M.	1829
	M. Louise	Eustache Bacquet	„	1845
	Jean			
	François			
20	Michel	(8) M. Anne Lémelin	S.M.	1799
	Marie Anne	Jos. Mathieu	S.G.	1823
21	Michel	(9) Charlotte Balan	Bert	1779
	Marie Charlotte	J. B. Asselin	S.M.	1797
22	Joseph	(9) M. Jos. Beaucher	„	1783
	Marie Angélique	Frs. Labrecque	B.	1809
	Catherine	Pierre Roy	B.	1817
	Raimond			
23	Pierre	(11) Marie Girard	S.M.	1782
	Agathe	J. B. Martin-Beaulieu		
			B.	1808
	Susanne	Chs. Desroche	„	1811
	Etienne			
24	Michel	(13) Marie Crépeau	S.P.	1793
25	François	(13) M. Jos. Naud	Lévis	1824
26	Joseph	(13) Angèle Nadeau	„	1830
27	JeanBaptiste	(14) Fse. Baudoin	S.F.S	1806
28	Lazare	(15) Genev. Fournier	S.Chs.	1810
	Marguerite	Chs. Couture	„	1844
	Célanire	Thomas Roy	„	1846
	Jean			
	Léon			
29	Féréol	(15) Angèle Labé	S.G.	1829
30	Joseph	(16) Marg. Nadeau	B.	1814
			S.H.	
A	Antoine	(16) Genev. Coulombe	S.H.	1819
31	Ignace	(17) Marg. Lemieux	S.G.	1810
32	Louis	(17) Josette Couture	B.	1822
	Louis Jos. Nap.			
	Le même	Euphrosine Roy	B.	1844
33	Charles	(17) Josette Baudoin	S.G.	1819
		V. de Jacq. Garant		
34	JeanBaptiste	(17) Luce Carbonneau	S.G	1822
35	Jean	(19) Cath. Lefebvre	S.M.	1805
	Adélaïde	Laurent Lacroix	„	1836
	Rose	Louis Vien	„	1841
	Julie	Frs. Ouimet	„	1845
	François Ed.			
	Louis			
	Joseph			
	Jean			
36	François	(19) Marg. Aubé	S.G.	1818
	Emélie	Magl. Naud	S.Chs.	1847
37	Raimond	(22) Louise Naud	„	1828
	Marie Louis	Guill. Roy	B	1828
	Marie Dina	F· X. Corriveau	„	1835
	Délina	Abraham Fiset	„	1845

PATRY.

Zéphirine	Samuel Fournier	,,	1845
Jos. Raimond			
Didace			
38 Etienne	(23) Marie Guay	Lévis	1829
39 Jean	(28) Angèle Filteau	S.Chs.	1844
40 Léon	(28) Marie Couture	,,	1846
Le même	M. Luce Hébert	,	1855
41 Louis Jos.	(32) Angé Shinck	B.	1853
Nap			
42 Jean	(35) Angé Perrot	Qué.	
Emond			
43 Louis	(35) Cécile Ouimet	S.M.	1836
44 François Ed.	(35) Luce Clément	Lévis	1833
45 Joseph	(35) ÉmélieTurgeon	Lévis	1835
46 Jos.Raimond	(37) Anastasie Fournier	B	1835
47 Didace	(37) Mathilde Beaucher	B	1845
48 Emond	(42) M. Luce Jeanne Audet		
		S.M.	1864

PEDEAK.

1 Jacques	Qué.		
Jacob			
Le même	M. Chs. Asselin Qué.		
Angélique	J.B. Bouffart	S.F.	1840
2 Jacob	(1) VéroniquePouliot	S.J.	1835
Scolastique	Frs. Pouliot	,,	1853
Sara	Ferd. Blouin	,,	1856

PELCHAT.

1 Julien	Olive Foursin Avranches		
François			
2 Jean	Julienne Caruel Avranches		
René			
3 François	(1) M.Jos.Verieul S.F.S.		1760
Françoise			
Joseph			
4 René	(2) Marie Marseau S.V.		1763
Joseph			
Le même	M.Ls. Lacasse S.Chs.		1772
Marie Louise	Ls. Audet	,,	1801
Marguerite	Jos. Picard	,,	1811
Angélique	Gab. Guénet	,,	1814
Charlotte	Ign. Dépont	,,	1839
Louise	André Laurandeau		
		S.F.S.	1816
Louise	2° Jacq.Frs. Minville		
		S.F.S.	1841
René			
Jean Baptiste			
Etienne			
5 François	(3) Marg. Fauchon	,,	1792
Marie Françoise	Jos. Roy	,,	1814
MarieMarguerite	Basile Thibaut	S.V.	1811
Geneviève	Basile Garant	,,	1813
M. Louise	J. B. Audet	S.Chs.	1812
Michel			
François			
6 Joseph	(3) JeanneLangloisS.F.S.		1793
	S. Marie		
Ambroise			
Louis			
Joseph			
7 Joseph	(4) Véronique Lacasse		
		S.Chs.	1788
Veronique	Aug. Dessaint	S.G.	1811
Véronique	2° Ls. Bacquet	S.G.	1816
Marguerite	Pierre Roy	,,	1825
Brigitte	J.B. Fournier	,,	1827
Philippe			
Joseph			
Pierre			
8 René	(4) Louise Jobin S. Chs.		1802
Geneviève	Jos. Julien	B.	1831
René			

PELCHAT.

9 Jean Baptiste	(4) M.Angé Denis S. Chs.		1804
Scolastique	Chs. Bernier	,,	1828
Hermine	Germ. Lebrun	,,	1836
Marie Louise	Jean Blais	,,	1840
Euphrosine	Jos. Proteau	,,	1862
Ignace			
Etienne			
10 Etienne	(4) Cécile Chabot	,,	1812
Marie Agnès	Michel Genest	,,	1856
François			
Georges			
Pierre			
11 Joseph	Jeanne Clément		
François			
12 François	(5) Reine Roy	S.V.	1821
13 Michel	(5) Julie Boulet	S.F.S.	1824
14 Joseph	(6) Fse. Labrecque	S.G.	1821
15 Ambroise	(6) Louise Cochon S.Frs.		1825
16 Louis	(6) Fse. Bacquet	S.G.	1828
17 Joseph	(7) M. Jos.BacquetS.Chs.		1815
18 Pierre	(7) Mad. Fortin	S.G.	1816
19 Philippe	(7) Angéle Coté	,,	1821
20 René	(8) Angé Drouin	B.	1834
21 Etienne	(9) Genev. Bégin	Lévis	1835
22 Ignace	(9) Dina Naud	S.Chs.	1850
23 Françoise	(10) Emérence Gosselin		
		S.Chs.	1845
24 Pierre	(10) Rosalie Bernier	,,	1856
25 Georges	(10) M. Marg. Quéret	,,	1859
26 François	(11) Marie Boucher S.F.S.		1827

PELLERIN.

1 Pierre	M. Genev. Picard		
Le même	M. Fse. Picard S.P.S.		1749
2 Guillaume	Charlotte Hédan		
	Avranches		
Guillaume			
3 Louis	Genev. Huart		
Marie Anne	J. B. Gagné	S.P.S.	1774
Marie Josette	Jos. Daniau	,,	1782
Michel			
Pierre			
4 Guillaume	(2) M. Reine MorinS.P.S.		1770
5 Pierre	Reine Morin		
	Islet		
Louis			
6 Michel	(3) M. Jos. DureposS.P.S.		1779
Marguerite	Jacq. Langlois	,,	1822
Marie Louise	Pierre Roy	S.V.	1820
Simon			
Benoit			
7 Pierre	(3) M. Marg. McDonald		
		S.P.S.	1787
8 Louis	(5) Marg. Picard Bert.		1805
Le même	Eliz. Langevin	,,	1819
9 Simon	(6) M. Anne Pepin S.M.		1817
10 Benoit	(6) M. Thérèse Chamberlan		
		S.P.S.	1819
11 Damase	Mad. Théberge S.P.S.		1822
Salomé	Geo. Raby	S.V.	1849
Marie	Aug. Valière	S.M.	1863

PELTIER.

1 Guillaume	Michel Moville		
Jean			
2 Nicolas	Jeanne Roussy		
François			
Marie	1° Nicolas Goupy		
Marie	2° Denis Jean Dit St.		
	Onge	Qué.	1655
3 Jean	(1) Anne Langlais	Qué.	1649
Noël			
Jean			
Charles			

PELTIER.

	René			
4	François	(2)	Marg. Mad. Morisseau	Qué. 1661
	Louise		J. B. Deblois	S.F. 1703
	Michel			
	Pierre			
5	Noël	(3)	Mad. Mignot	1676
	Noël			
	Charles			
	Guillaume			
	Jean François			
	Joseph			
6	Jean	(3)	M. Anne Huot Riv.	Ouelle 1689
	Jean Baptiste			
	Joseph			
	Charles			
7	Charles	(3)	Thérèse Ouellet Riv.	Ouelle 1697
	Joseph			
	Le même		Barbe Dessaint Riv.	Ouelle 1711
	François			
8	René	(3)	Mad. Leclaire	S.P. 1691
	Marie Madeleine		Jacq. Picard	„ 1710
	Jean			
	Le même		Marie Baillargeon S.L.	1703
	Michel	(4)	Fse. Meneux	S.F. 1697
10	Pierre	(4)	Marg. Rousseau	„ 1703
11	Charles	(5)	M. Anne Soucy Riv.	Ouelle 1701
12	Noël	(5)	M. Anne Thiboulotte	Riv. Ouelle 1708
13	Guillaume	(5)	Louise Pinel Riv. Ouelle	1706
	Angélique		Chs. Rousseau S.F.S.	1766
	François			
	Antoine			
14	Jean François	(5)	Mad. Lavoie Riv.	Ouelle 1710
	Le même		Mad. Morin	S.Anne 1722
15	Joseph	(5)	Marie Lumina	Que. 1714
16	Jean Baptiste	(6)	Marg. Angé Ouellet	Riv. Ouelle 1714
17	Joseph	(6)	M. Anne Boucher	Riv. Ouelle 1726
18	Charles	(6)	M. Anne Boucher	S. Anne 1726
19	Joseph	(7)	Ursule Dessaint	1728
20	François	(7)	Genev. Morneau Islet	1741
21	Jean	(8)	M. Chs. Gosselin S.P.	1714
	Le même		Ursule Ferlant	„ 1715
	Madeleine		Ls. Nollet	„ 1744
	Madeleine		2° Jacq. Guilmet S.Chs.	1762
	Marguerite		Béonet Gilaudi	S.P. 1750
	Marguerite		2° Ant. Gagnon	„ 1767
22	François	(13)	M. Anne Guignard	Bert. 1744
	Marie Anne		Jean Boutin	S.F.S. 1767
	Le même		Héléne Gendron	„ 1750
	Frs. Hyacinthe			
23	Antoine	(13)	Marg. Guignard Bert.	1748
	Marguerite		Ls. Bilodeau	S.F.S. 1775
24	Antoine		M. Jeanne Tessier	
	Marie Angélique		Jos. Daniau	S.M. 1772
A	Pierre		Mad. Lebel	
	Germain			
25	Joseph fils de Jos. & M. Eliz. Thibaut		M. Thérèse Rousseau	S.P.S. 1795
	Marie Thérèse		J. B. Blas	„ 1795
26	Antoine		Marg. Gingras	
	Marie Thérèse		Gab. Goupy	S.M. 1777
27	Frs. Hyacinthe	(22)	Anne Fse. Blais S.P.S.	1778

PELTIER.

	Marie Victoire		Jos. Joncas	S.P.S 1805
	Jean Baptiste			
	François			
	Le même		Marg. Gaumon	
28	Augustin		Angé Morin S.Roch	
	Henri			
29	Jean Baptiste		M. Angé Boucher	
	Archange		J. B. Frs. Talbot	S.P.S. 1814
	Michel Henri			
30	Joseph		Genev. Viger	
	Victor			
31	Germain	(24)	A Scolastique Sauc ier	
	Pierre George		S. Roch. des Aulnets 1814	
32	Joseph Olivier		Sophie Coté St. Lambert	
	Olivier			
33	Jean Baptiste	(27)	Rosalie Blanchet	S.P.S. 1799
	Marie Florence		Chs. Provost	S.Chs. 1833
34	François	(27)	M.Mad. Picard S.P.S.	1804
	M. Marguerite		Romain Martineau	S.P.S. 1821
	Soulange		Ant. Hubert Blais	S.P.S. 1828
	Marie Edridge		Jérome Martineau	S.F.S. 1822
35	Henri	(28)	M. Jos. Dodier	S.V. 1809
36	Michel Honoré	(29)	Genev. Coulombe	
	Eulalie		Jos. Emond	
	Romuald			
	Bruno			
37	Victor	(30)	Marg. Moreau	B. 1828
38	Pierre George	(31)	Virginie Moreau	B. 1849
39	Olivier	(32)	Angèle Beaucher	S.Chs. 1859
40	Henri		M. Genev. Gagnon S.Anne	
	Edouard			
41	Edouard	(40)	Esther Boucher S.F.S.	1841
42	Romuald	(36)	Philomène Roberge	S.L. 1861
43	Bruno	(36)	Luce Vallée Beauport 1870	
	Joseph			
	Bruno			
	Marie Anne			
	Alphonse			

PENIN—LAFONTAINE.

1	Michel		Marie Pothier Montréal	1699
	Le même		Marie Meunier Montréal	1704
	Jean Baptiste			
2	Jean Baptiste	(1)	Angé Guénet	B. 1731
	Marie		Chs. Lacasse	S.Chs. 1765
	Michel			
	Jacques			
	Ambroise			
	François			
3	Jacques	(2)	J. Jourdain	S.Chs. 1758
	Jeanne		Jean Terrien	S.Chs. 1781
	Charlotte		Jos. Poulin	S.Chs. 1792
	Marguerite		Paschal Bisson S.Chs.	1795
	Angélique		Ls. Terrien	S.Chs. 1797
	Marie Josette		Jos. Nadeau	S.Chs. 1801
	Louis			
	Jacques			
4	Michel	(2)	Marg. Plante	S.M. 1765
	Le même		M. Jos. Lefebvre S.V.	1781
	Catherine		Aug. Picard	S.M. 1808
	Michel			
5	Ambroise		Marthe Lacasse	S.M. 1772
	Charles			

258   CANADIAN ARCHIVES

PENIN—LAFONTAINE.

6	François	(2) Mad. Naud	S.V. 1773
	Jean		
	François		
7	Jacques	(3) Cath. Hayot	S.G. 1799
8	Louis	(3) M. A. Comeau	S.Chs. 1809
9	Michel	(4) M. Chs. Turgeon	S.Chs. 1806
	Bibiane	Pierre Savard	B. 1837
	Elizabeth	Michel Aubé	B. 1846
10	Charles	(5) M. Anne Goulet	S.G. 1800
	M. Anne	Amb. Bilodeau	S.G. 1824
	Basilisse	Etn. Couture	S.G. 1830
	Charles		
11	Jean	(6) M. Fse. Marseau	B. 1797
	Angéle	J. B. Coté	Lévis 1823
	Françoise	(6) Eliz. Cadrin	S.M. 1799
	Le même	Genev. Bizin	Lévis 1817
13	Charles	(10) Eulalie Brochu	S.G. 1830
14	Francois Xavier	Marg. Lacasse	
	Marie	NicolasBaudoin	S.Chs.1853

PEPIN—LACHANCE.

1	André	Jeanne de Bourville	
	Antoine		
2	Jean	Jeanne Dumont	
	Robert		
3	Antoine	(1) Marie Testa	Contrat 1659
	Elizabeth	Olivier Gagné	S.F. 1679
	Marie	Jean Guion	S.F. 1688
	Catherine	Amb. Migneron	S.F. 1703
	Igance		
	Jean		
	Jean		
	Gervais		
4	Robert	(2) Marie Creste	Qué. 1670
	Marie Rosalie	Pierre Hélie	Qué. 1700
	Robert		
	Louis		
	Jean		
5	Ignace	(3) M. Mad. Gaulin	S.F. 1687
	Antoine		
	Le même	Marie Lefort	S.P. 1689
	Elizabeth	Pierre Balan	S.Chs. 1715
	Geneviève	J. B. Groinier	S. Frs. 1719
	Louis		
6	Jean	(3) Rénée Guion	S.F. 1688
	Antoine		
7	Gervais	(3) M. Mad. Fortier	S.L. 1698
	Madeleine	Pierre Fontaine	S.J. 1722
	Marie Anne	Pierre Noël	" 1737
	Joseph		
8	Jean	(3) Mad. Fontaine	S.J. 1703
	Madeleine	Etn. Lessart	S.Anne 1732
	Joseph Marie		
	Jacques		
	Gervais		
	Le même (?)	Louise Marchard	
	Brigitte	Pierre Protain	S.J. 1761
	Genev. Euphro-	Amb. Gaulin	" 1780
	sine		
9	Jean	(5) Marg. Moreau	Que. 1699
	Louis Joseph		
10	Robert	(4) Isabelle Royer	S.J. 1700
11	Louis	(4) Eliz. Boutin	Lorette 1710
12	Antoine	(5) Rose Lepage	S.Frs. 1709
	Marie Josette	Jos. Gagnon	" 1732
	Louise	Aug. Desmolier	" 1747
	Hélène	Ign. Bélanger	" 1749
	Madeleine	Michel Balan	" 1752
	Antoine		
	Joseph		
	Louis		
13	Louis	(5) Louise Lepage	S.Frs. 1729
	Hélène	Jean Baudon	" 1754
	Marie Josette	Jos. Dompierre	" 1757

PEPIN—LACHANCE.

	Marie Thècle	Aug. Landry	S.Frs. 1764
	Louis		
14	Joseph	Marg. Fontaine	
	Marie Josette	Jos. Audet	S.J. 1732
	Angélique	Aug. Royer	" 1732
	Pierre Noël		
	Joseph		
	Jean Charles		
15	Gervais	Jeanne Fontaine	
	Madeleine	Joachim Greffart	S.J. 1751
	Madeleine	2' Guil. Guilmet	S.M. 1773
	Madeleine	3 Jean Garant	" 1781
16	Antoine	(6) Mad. Blouin	S.J. 1722
			S.H.
	Jean François		
	Antoine		
	Joseph		
	Le même	Mad. Noël	
		V. d'Ant. Fortier.	
17	Joseph	(7) Genev. Délage	S.L. 1736
	Joseph Marie		
18	Antoine	Eliz. Bidet	S.J. 1739
	Marie	Jos. Bissonnet	S.M. 1763
	Jean Baptiste		
	Charles		
19	Jacques	(8) Thérèse Lessart	
			S.Anne 1739
	Jos. Marie		
20	Gervais	(8) Angé Blouin	S.J. 1743
	Marie Angélique	Jacq. Tremblay	" 1770
	Marie Louise	Pierre Lefebvre	" 1787
	Marie Geneviève	Etn. Papillon	S.Frs. 1778
	Gervais		
	Michel Olivier		
21	Joseph Marie	(8) Genev. Paré	S. Anne 1750
	François		
A	Louis Joseph	(9) Marg. Bergevin	
			Chs. Bourg. 1736
	Louis		
22	Antoine	(12) Genev. Arbour	S.F.S. 1745
	Marie Madeleine	Jos. Dessaint	" 1773
	Marie Anne	J. B. Marcoux	" 1776
	Louise	Ign. Gosselin	" 1779
	Marie Geneviève	Ls. Marie Morin	" 1784
	Clément		
23	Joseph	(12) M. Ls. Boulet	S.F.S. 1750
24	Louis	(12) M. Thérèse Boulet	
			S.F.S. 1752
	Marie Thérèse	Frs. Langlois	S.Frs. 1771
	Marie Josette	J. B. Leclaire	" 1775
	Marie Julie	Frs. Perrot	" 1787
	Marie Josette	Basile Deblois	" 1801
	Marie Madeleine	Chs. Deblois	S.F. 1791
	Pierre		
	Joseph		
	Antoine		
25	Louis	(13) Mad. Emond	S.Frs. 1757
	Marie Madeleine	Jean Bornais	" 1785
	Marie Victoire	Jean Marie Lainé	S.F. 1790
	Marie Josette	Frs. Guérard	" 1792
	Geneviève	Jean Guérard	" 1796
	Marie Thècle	Etn. Dalaire	" 1811
	Joseph		
26	Joseph	(14) Louise Thivierge	S.J. 1732
27	Jean Charles	(14) M. Anne Fortier	" 1744
28	Pierre Noël	(14) Charlotte Rondeau	
	Marie Louise	Jos. Pouliot	S.J. 1770
	Angélique	Frs. Audet	" 1773
	Marie Charlotte	G. B. Thivierge	" 1776
	Françoise	Frs. Chabot	" 1784
	Madeleine	Jos. Demeule	" 1785
	Barthélémi		
	Gabriel		
29	Antoine	(16) M. Fse. Hélie	S.V. 1749
	Charles		
	François Marie		

PEPIN - LACHANCE.

30	JeanFrançois(16)	Mad. Blanchard	S.P.S.	1750
	Augustin			
31	Joseph	(16) Susanne Bélan	Lévis	1762
32	Joseph	Marg. Filteau		
	Marie	Ant. Rosa	S.J.	1777
33	JosephMarie(17)	M. Jos. Dalaire	„	1757
	Marie Josette	Ls. Genest	„	1787
	Barthelemi			
	Antoine			
34	JeanBaptiste(18)	M. Ls. Bissonnet	S.M.	1773
	Marie Louise	André Morisset	„	1798
	Marie Louise	2' Gab. Quéret	„	1821
	Joseph			
35	Charles (18)	M. Ls. Hélie	S.V.	1774
	Isabelle	Clément Royer	S.Chs.	1805
	Marie	Philippe Leclaire	„	1708
	Marie Marthe	Jos. Cameron	„	1823
	Charles			
	Louis			
	Etienne			
36	Jean Baptiste	Charlotte Blouin	S. Joa.	1779
	Jean Marie	Mad. Paré		
	Jean Marie			
37	Jean Marie (19)	Genev. Dupile		
	Jean Marie			
38	JosephMarie(19)	Marie Canac	S.F.	1767
39	Gervais (20)	Anne Hébert	S.J.	1874
	Madeleine	Laurent Fortier	„	1808
	Madeleine	2' Job. Fortier	„	1848
	Jean Marie			
	Gervais			
	François			
40	Mich.Olivier(20)	Agathe Rousseau	S.L.	1785
	Agathe	Barth Pepin	S.J.	1823
	Marie Josette	J. B. Martineau	„	1832
	Michel			
	Gervais			
	François			
41	François (21)	Thérèse Bolduc	S.Joa.	1788
42	Clément (22)	M. Marg. Quemeneur	S.F.S.	1785
	M. Marguerite	Frs. Boulet	„	1821
	Chs. Vincent			
	Pierre Noël			
	Joseph			
	Michel			
43	Jean Baptiste	Marg. Quemeneur		
	Jean Baptiste			
44	Joseph (24)	Félicité Martineau	S.Frs.	1788
	Marie Louise	Ls. Dalaire	„	1803
	Félicité	Frs. Leblond	„	1814
	Christine	David Letourneau	„	1815
	Marguerite	Frs. Plante	„	1829
	Louis			
	Le même	M. Vict. Morin	„	1828
45	Antoine (24)	M. Angé Plante	S.F.	1789
	Marie Josette	J. B. Loignon	S.F.	1815
	Marie Catherine	Ls. Pepin	„	1819
	Marie	Jos. Dompierre	„	1825
	Christine	Chs. Dompierre	S.Frs.	1847
	Antoine			
46	Pierre (24)	M. Mad. Gagné	S.F.	1792
	M. Madeleine	Jean Plante	S.Frs.	1811
47	Joseph (25)	Thècle Drouin	S.F.	1790
	Josette	J. B. Emond	„	1814
	Anastasie	Jos. Dalaire	„	1820
	MarieMadeleine	Jos. Dompierre	„	1822
	Marie	Frs. Dompierre	„	1824
	Catherine	Jos. Giguere	„	1825
	Louis			
	Jean			
	Joseph			

PEPIN—LACHANCE.

48	Louis	Julienne Asselin		
	Julienne	Boniface Aubé	S.Chs.	1799
	Marie	Etn. Lacroix	„	1806
	Marguerite	Guill. Bacquet	„	1807
	Elizabeth	Pierre Cochon	„	1823
	Charlotte	Jos. Labrecque	S.G.	1815
	François			
	Louis			
49	Louis Marie	M. Ls. Avare		
	Marie Louise	Jos. Leclaire	S.Frs.	1835
	Jean			
	Joseph			
	Chrysostôme			
50	Barthélemi (28)	M. Anne Thivierge	S.J.	1782
	Marie Anne	Paul Pouliot	„	1811
	Marie Anne	2'Simon Pellerin	S.M.	1817
	Luce	Ls. Ferland	S.J.	1815
	Gabriel			
	Joseph			
	Barthelemi			
	Guillaume			
	Le même	Julie Cotin	S.M.	1822
51	Gabriel (28)	Marie Chatigny	S.J.	1785
	Marie Angèle	Pierre Boissonneau	„	1807
	Cécile	René Blouin	„	1811
	Archange	Jos. Johan	„	1814
	Joseph			
	Gabriel			
	Louis			
	François			
	Pierre			
52	Augustin (30)	Marg. Thivierge	S.J.	1780
A	Charles (29)	Thérèse Audet	S.H.	1790
C	François (29)	M. Fse. Larose	Que.	1779
	Marie	S. Jos. Beauce		
B	Pierre Noël	Marg. Turgeon		
	Marie	Pierre Lefebvre	S.H.	1816
	Pierre			
	Antoine			
53	Antoine (33)	M. Mad. Blouin	S.J.	1795
	Marie	Jos. Dion	B.	1826
	Joseph			
54	Barthélemi (33)	Charlotte Blouin	S.J.	1801
	Charlotte	Frs. Turcot	„	1830
	Théotiste	Jos. Demeule	„	1836
	Pierre			
	Le même	Genev. Plante	„	1827
55	Charles	Angé Roby		
	Gervais			
56	Louis fils de Ls.	Marg. Bédard		
	Jos. et Marg.	Charles Bourg		1784
	Bergeron			
	Louis			
57	Jean Baptiste	Louise Carrier	S. M.	
	Rose	Ls. Cochon	S.M.	1834
	Emérentienne	Michel Clément	„	1838
	Jean Baptiste			
58	Joseph (34)	Marg. Blais	„	1801
			Que.	
59	Charles (35)	Mad. Bêtel	S. Chs.	1806
60	Etienne (35)	Eliz. Couture	„	1809
		fille de Marie Couture.		
	Etienne			
	Vital			
61	Louis (35)	Marg. Couture	Lévis.	1815
62	Jean Marie (36)	Félicité Amable Giguère	S. Féréol	1803
	Joseph			
63	Jean Marie (37)	M. Ls.Campagna	S.F.	1809
	Emérence	Régis Bisson	S.J.	1836
	Marie	Jos. Blouin	„	1817
	Christine	Vital Simard	„	1863
	Catherine	Jean Jos. Poulin	S. Frs.	1833

PEPIN—LACHANCE.

Hubert
Pierre
64 Jean Marie (39) M. Anne Coulombe
S.J. 1798

Marie Anne	Aug. Audet	"	1819
Cécile	Ant. Gobeil	"	1826
Cécile	2° J. B. Audet	"	1845
Marie	Jos. Audet	"	1827
Josette	Alexis Delisle	"	1831
Angèle	Hyacin. Jolicœur	"	1838

Marie Antoine
François-Xavier
Pierre
65 Gervais (39) Angèle Thivierge " 1804
66 François (39) M. Jos. Drouin S.F. 1806
Baie St. Paul.

Maurice
Joseph
67 Gervais (40) Cath. Drouin S. Frs. 1813
Luce Jos. Jahan S.J. 1840
François
Louis
68 Michel (40) Josette Drouin S.Frs. 1813
Isle aux Grues.
Anatalie J. B. Emond
Magloire
Louis
69 François (40) Julie Desruisseaux S.F. 1824
Julie Jos. Thivierge S.J. 1846
Rose de Lima Jos. Baillargeon " 1850
Philomène Séraphin Arel " 1862
Emélie Hubert Raimond " 1863
François Nap.
Adolphe
70 Joseph (42) M. Frs. Buteau S.P.S 1822
71 Charles (42) Dorothée Boutin " 1835
Vincent
72 Pierrre Noël (42) Marie Thibaut S.F.S. 1838
73 Michel (42) Modeste Minville
S. P. S. 1840
74 Jean Baptiste (43) Angé Hizoir S.G. 1824
75 Louis (44) Josette Lepage S.F. 1819
Marie Natalie Jos. Dalaire S. Frs. 1844
Olivier Emilien
76 Antoine (45) Cath. Savoie S.F. 1820
Flavie Chs. Dompierre S.Frs 1845
Anastasie Basile Dion " 1854
Magloire
Le même Marie Asselin " 1837
77 Joseph (47) Angèle Giguère S.J. 1817
Marie Jean Pouliot S.Frs. 1837
78 Louis (47) M. Cath. Pepin S.F. 1819
79 Jean (47) Justine Giguère " 1825
80 François (48) M. Jos. Voisin S.M. 1810
Josette Jos. Bouchard " 1835
81 Louis (48) M. Vict. Lacroix
S. Chs. 1806
Louis
Le même M. Mad. Marcoux " 1811
Marie Anne Isidore Duquet " 1834
Marie Louise Damasse Mongeon " 1835
Marie Madeleine Prudent Provost " 1840
Angèle Frs. Gosselin " 1842
Marguerite Marc. Lefebvre " 1846
Marguerite 2° Ed. Roy " 1849
Mathilde Jérome Bilodeau " 1854
Emélie Romain Couture " 1859
Marc
Pierre
Marcel
Célestin
Joseph
Charles
Edouard
82 Guillaume (50) M. Anne Pinchaud
Cap S. Ignace 1819

PEPIN—LACHANCE.

Henriette Laurent Gautron S.M.1838
M. Julie Anna Damase Marseau " 1848
Adèle Césarie Alfred Blais " 1852
Célina
Julie Cath. Eliz. Auguste Annibal
Furois " 1857
Charles Numa
83 Jean (49) Cath. Guérard S.F. 1812
Sophie Isaïe Bilodeau " 1841
Jean
84 Joseph (49) Marg. Drouin S.Frs. 1820
Pierre
Joseph
Le même Marie Dompierre
S.Frs. 1833
85 Jean Chry- (49) M. Cath. Lepage
sostôme S.Frs. 1825
Catherine Michel Campagna
S.Frs. 1846
Caroline Jos. Létourneau
S.Frs. 1861
86 Louis Marie (49) M. Jos. Couillard S.F.1823
Marie Flavie Ls. Prosper Gagnon
S.Frs. 1847
Delima Jean Dion S.Frs. 1856
Marie Geneviève Jos. Picard S.Frs. 1858
87 Antoine (49) M. Adé Létourneau
S.Frs. 1829
88 Barthélemi (50) Genev. Paquet S.J. 1809
Marie Pierre Forbes S. J. 1830
Marie 2° Jos. Lainé S.J. 1850
Adélaïde Pierre Gaudreau S.J. 1835
Adélaïde 2° Thomas Dick S.J. 1852
Barthélemi
Le même Agathe Pepin S.J. 1823
Célina Abraham Royer S.J. 1856
Ovide
François-Xavier
89 Joseph (50) Mad. Turcot S.J. 1818
90 Gabriel (50) Marg. McKinnon
Gabriel
91 Joseph (51) M. Ls. Fortin S.J. 1812
Joseph
Louis
Le même M. Archange Cochon
S.J. 1828
Emélie Frs. X. Simart S.J. 1853
Marie Jos. Pouliot J. 1865
Célestin
Nazaire
92 Gabriel (51) M. Marg. Thivierge
S.J. 1818
Henriette Benj. Blou i S.J. 1845
Henriette 2° F. X. Pepin S.J. 1856
Réparate Ls. Thivierge S.J. 1853
Marguerite Frs. Curodeau S.J. 1858
Joseph
Gabriel
Nazaire
93 Louis (51) M. Mad. Blouin S.J. 1819
Marcelline René Blouin S.J. 1852
Louis
Joseph
Jérémie
Célestin
94 François (51) Cécile Pouliot S.J. 1821
Cécile Pierre Gosselin S.L. 1844
Henriette F. X. Gosselin S.L. 1844
Natalie Barth. Paquet S.L. 1851
Judith Pierre Labrecque S.L. 1851
Célestin
François
95 Pierre (51) Marg. Labrecque S.J. 1824
Cécile Mag. Pouliot S.J. 1824
Judith Frs. Gagnon S.J. 1849
Anatolie Frs. Bédard S.J. 1853

PEPIN—LACHANCE.

Marguerite		Jos. Hébert	S.J. 1855
Pierre			
Charles			
Gabriel			
A Pierre	(52 B)	Cath. Lefebvre S.H.	1813
B Antoine	(52 B)	Archange Leclaire	
			S.H. 1814
96 Joseph	(53)	Louise Bilodeau S.G.	1825
97 Pierre	(54)	Charlotte Clavet S.J.	1835
98 Gervais	(55)	Angèle Cloutier S.G.	1820
99 Louis	(56)	M. Ursule Bouchard	
			S.V. 1821
100 Jn. Baptiste	(57)	Thérèse GontierS.Chs.1826	
Narcisse			
Jean Baptiste			
Rémi			
101 Étienne	(60)	Marg. Langlois S.M.	1835
102 Vital	(60)	M. Scolia Morin S.M.	1851
103 Joseph	(62)	Marg. Lepage S.Frs.	1834
104 Hubert	(63)	Eliz. Létourneau S.J.	1846
105 Pierre	(63)	M. Anne Gosselin S.J.1842	
Marie Anne		Hubert Blouin S.J.	1865
106 Antoine	(64)	Emélie Pouliot S.J.	1832
Moïse			
Moïse			
107 Pierre	(64)	Soulange Rouleau S.L.1832	
108 François Xavier	(64)	Séraphine Pouliot S.J.1839	
Virginie		Jos. Premont S.J.	1863
Marie Sara		Elzéar Turcot S.J.	1865
109 Joseph	(66)	Cath. McFarlan S.J.1831	
Rose		Ferd. Lambert S.J.	1862
110 Maurice	(66)	Flavie Crépeau S.J.	1844
111 Louis	(67)	Délina Robertson S.P.1854	
112 François	(67)	Soulange Thivierge	
			S.J. 1857
113 Louis	(68)	Rose Cotin S.J.	1855
114 Magloire	(68)	Cécile Dion S.J.	1861
115 Adolphe	(69)	Soulange Baillargeon	
			S.L. 1851
116 Frs. Napoléon	(69)	Adèle Roberge S.L.	1854
117 Olivier Emilien	(75)	M. Angé Morin S.F.	1856
118 Magloire	(76)	Desanges Laurent	
			S.Frs. 1862
119 Louis	(81)	Susanne Gontier	
			S.Chs.1829
120 Marc	(81)	Hermine Fournier "	1839
121 Pierre	(81)	Olive Audet "	1845
122 Marcel	(81)	Apolline Brochu "	1846
123 Célestin	(81)	M. Rose Labrecque	
			S. Chs. 1847
124 Joseph	(81)	M. Luce Bouchard	
			S. Chs. 1852
125 Charles	(81)	Virginie Couture "	1861
126 Charles	(82)	M. Josephine Olive	
Numa		Grenier S.M.	1858
128 Jean	(83)	Marie Vermet S.Frs.	1841
129 Joseph	(84)	Martin Leblond S.F.	1846
130 Pierre	(84)	Marg. Dompierre	
			S. Frs. 1852
131 Barthélemi	(88)	Anatolie Pouliot S.J.	1842
132 Ovide	(88)	M. Luce Lainé "	1845
133 François Xavier	(88)	Henriette Pepin "	1856
134 Gab. Laughton	(90)	Emélie Pouliot "	1840
135 Joseph	(91)	Venerande Audet "	1836
Cécile		Ls. Guerard S.F.	1856
136 Louis	(91)	Angèle Blouin S.J.	1842
Angèle		Barth. Deblois S.F.	1864
137 Célestin	(91)	Hortence Pouliot S.J.	1857
138 Nazaire	(91)	Eléonore Blouin "	1857
139 Joseph	(92)	Marcelline Thivierge	
			S.J. 1846

PEPIN—LACHANCE.

140 Gabriel	(92)	M. Anne Thivierge	
			S.J. 1852
141 Nazaire	(92)	Seraphine Audet "	1858
142 Louis	(93)	Constance Chatigny	
			S.P. 1843
143 Jérémie	(93)	Marcelline Thivierge	
			S.J. 1851
144 Célestin	(93)	Rose Thivierge "	1854
145 Joseph	(93)	Philomène Blouin "	1862
146 François	(94)	Scolastique Labrecque	
			S.J. 1845
Marie Adéline		Cyp. Langlois S.L.	1866
Séraphine		Jos. Herménégilde Chabot	
Cédulie			S.L. 1872
Angèle		Naz. Audibert "	1877
Marie Célina		Jos. Gobeil "	1878
Frs. Edmond			
147 Célestin	(94)	Emélie Dufresne S. Tho.	
148 Pierre	(95)	Adé Gosselin S.J.	1848
149 Charles	(95)	Genev. Pouliot "	1853
150 Gabriel	(95)	Cécile Hébert "	1856
151 Narcisse	(100)	Marcelline Mercier	
			S.M. 1849
152 Jean Baptiste	(100)	Julie Quemeneur S.V. 1853	
153 Rémi	(100)	Philomène Roy S.M.	1860
154 Moïse	(106)	Marie Langlois S.J.	1861
155 Edouard	(81)	M. Desanges Rousseau	
			S.M. 1857
156 Frs. Edmond	(146)	Genev. Plante S.L.	1878

PERROT.

1 Jean		Jeanne Valta	
Anne		Pierre Blais	S.F. 1669
2 Jean		Mathurin Rigot	
Jacques			
3 Simon		Marg. Cerisier	
Paul			
4 Jacques	(2)	Michelle Leflot Que.	1654
Marie		Frs. Jaret de Verchères	
			S.F. 1667
Anne		Gab. Thivierge "	1676
Catherine		Jean Janhot "	1694
Joseph			
Jacques			
5 Paul	(3)	Marie Chertien	
			Montréal 1670
		Deschambault	
Jacques			
Paul			
6 Joseph	(4)	Marie Gagné Laprairie1688	
Marie		Frs. Mercure S.F.	1707
Geneviève		Nic. Drouin S.F.	1717
Antoine Jacques			
Bertrand			
Louis			
7 Jacques	(4)	Anne Gagné Montréal 1690	
8 Paul	(5)	Marie Montambault	
			S.F. 1702
		Deschambault	
9 Jacques	(5)	Mad. Paquin S.F.	1711
		Deschambault	
10 Bertrand	(6)	Mad. Guion S.F.	1715
Marie Madeleine		Gab. Blouin "	1741
Josette		Jos. Marie Gagné "	1741
Le même		Ange Simon C.R.	1717
Angélique		Jos. Gagnon "	1748
François			
Le même		Marie Gagnon "	1731
11 Louis	(6)	Fse. Simon Montréal 1723	
Geneviève		Chs. Vérieul S.F.	1745
Françoise		Frs. Demeule "	1748
12 Antoine	(6)	M. Fse. Guion "	1729
Jacques			

PERROT.

Le même	Marthe Létourneau		
		S.F.	1739
Marthe	Ant. Simon	"	1761
Marie Madeleine	Michel Morin	"	1777
Geneviève	Frs. Reinfret	"	1777
Pélagie	Pierre Turcot	"	1778
Marguerite	René Picard	"	1799
Augustin			
Jean Baptiste			
Joseph			
13 François	(10) Brigitte Drouin	S.F.	1743
14 Joseph	(12) M. Chs. Blouin	S.J.	1763
Marie	Chs. Amable Drouin		
		S.F.	1771
Cath. Pélagie	Ls. Poulin	"	1771
Judith	J. B. Leblond	"	1780
Marie Marg.	Frs. Couture	S.H.	1791
Jos. Marie			
Joseph			
Jean Baptiste			
Le même	Marie Drouin	S.F.	1767
Geneviève	Jos. Gagnon	"	1787
François			
15 Jean Baptiste	(12) M. Ls. Bussière	S.P.	1769
16 Augustin	(12) Angé Premont	S.F.	1778
17 Joseph	(14) Cath. Deblois	"	1777
18 Joseph Marie	(14) M. Thérèse Fournier		
		S.P.S.	1786
19 François	(14) M. Julie Pepin	S.Frs.	1787
20 Jean dit Poitevin	M. Mad. Genest	S.J.	1775
21 Jean Baptiste	(14) M. Thérèse Bedard		
		S.H.	1801
		S.H.	
Marie Thérèse	Frs. Gagné	S.V.	1820
Marguerite	J. B. Fortier	S.G.	1830
Jean Baptiste			
Joseph			
Le même	M. Marguerite Breton		
		S.V.	1806
Marguerite	Jos. Jolin	"	1832
22 Jean Baptiste	(21) Josette	"	1827
Marie Henriette	Chs. Denis	S.M.	1850
23 Joseph	(21) M. Adé Bernard	S.V.	1843

PETITCLERC.

1 Pierre	Fse. Paris	Qué.	1673
Jean Baptiste			
Charles			
2 Jean Baptiste	(1) M. Fse. Provost	"	1709
3 Charles	(1) Cath. Provost	"	1715
4 Louis	Genev. Belleau		
Geneviève	Frs. Labrecque	S.Chs.	1775
Marie	Gab. Lepage	"	1784
Le même	Marg. Vacherie	"	1775
"	Marg. Queret	S.G.	1788
5 Claude	M. Mad. Elot-Julien		
		S.G.	
Le même	Marthe Labrecque	B.	1781
Charles			
Louis			
Joseph			
6 Charles	(5) Marg. Provost	S. Chs.	1832
7 Louis	(5) Fse. Rousseau	S.G.	1812
8 Joseph	(5) Eliz. Lemieux	"	1822

PICHET.

1 Jean	Mad. Leblanc		
Jean			
Louis			
Pierre			
Jacques			
2 Jacques	(1) Louise Asselin	S.F.	1696
Madeleine	Jean Turgeon	S.P.	1735
Jean			

PICHET.

Louis			
Jacques			
3 Jean	(1) Genev. Crepeau	"	1700
Madeleine	Chs. Denis	S.L.	1719
4 Pierre	(1) Eliz. Côté	S.P.	1703
5 Louis, notaire	(1) M. Anne Côté	"	1710
Josette	Gab. Ferland	"	1740
Geneviève	Claude Vaillancour	"	1747
Marie Anne	Chs. Carrier	"	1752
Marie Madeleine	Ign. Martel	S.F.	1762
Louis			
Le même	Marg. Godbout	S.P.	1730
Marie Reine	Ign. Martel	"	1763
6 Jean	(2) Marie Valière	"	1725
Le même	M. Fse. Létourneau		
		S.F.	1731
Marie	Ls. Turcot	S.P	1763
Thérèse	Jos. Vaillancour	"	1765
Louis			
Jean			
7 Louis	(2) M. Jos. Beaucher	S.F.	1733
Gertrude	Jean Roberge	S.P.	1754
Le même	M. Dorothée Noël	"	1838
Hélène	Gab. Côté	"	1768
Marie Josette	Ls. Blouin	"	1777
Marie Josette	2° Frs. Plante	S.J.	1809
Pierre			
François			
Joseph			
Louis			
8 Jacques	(2) M. Thècle Beaucher		
		S.F.	1733
Thècle	René Picard	"	1755
Marie Gertrude	Gab. Foucher	"	1762
Pierre			
Jacques			
Le même	Genev. Morisset	"	1758
9 Louis	(5) Thérèse Godbout	S.P.	1737
Thérèse	Nic. Couture	Lévis	1760
10 Jean	(6) Rose Vaillancour	S.F.	1766
Rose	Jos. Leclaire	S.P.	1808
Marie	Jean Noël	"	1810
Pierre			
Jean Baptiste			
11 Louis	(6) Gertrude Gendreau		
		S.J.	1794
12 Pierre	(7) Angé Ratté	S.P	1766
Angélique	Julien Gendreau	"	1791
Thècle	Amb. Coté	"	1795
Thècle	2° Jacq. Cantin	S.H.	1816
Marie Josette	Frs. Crepeau	S.H.	1800
Louis			
François			
Pierre			
13 François	(7) Marie Dorval	S.P.	1768
Pierre			
Louis			
Le même	Mad. Dorval	"	1784
Marie Anne	Ls. Dufresne	"	1809
Ignace			
Le même	CharlotteChatigny	"	1811
14 Louis	(7) M. Jos. Côté	"	1774
Josette	Aug. Métayer	"	1812
Reine	Ign. Beaucher	"	1812
Germain			
Pierre			
15 Joseph	(7) Marg. Filteau	S.F.	1775
Marie Josette	Frs. Fortier	S.J.	1799
Joseph			
Gabriel			
Louis			
Laurent			
16 Paul	Charlotte Couture		
Hélène	Pierre Grenier	S.P.	1799
Geneviève	Ant. Grenier	"	1799

PICHET.

```
      Louis
      Paul
17  Jacques        (8)  M. Rosalie Létourneau
                                          S.F. 1767
18  Pierre         (8)  M. Claire Canac      „  1767
      Michel
      Pierre
19  JeanBaptiste(10) Claire Leclaire    S.P. 1797
      Pélagie            Pierre Turcot     „  1824
20  Pierre         (10)  MoniqueGourdeau „  1801
21  Pierre         (12)  M. Thérèse Aubin „  1798
      Jean
      Pierre
22  Louis          (12)  Marg. Leclaire    „  1807
      Marie Judith        Olivier Noël      „  1838
      Françoise           Bénoni Rousseau   „  1840
      Geneviève           Jacq. Plante      „  1841
      David
      Louis
23  François       (12)  M. Mad. Martineau
                                          S.P. 1816
      Emélie              Magl. Martel      „  1839
      Rosalie             Pierre Crepeau    „  1839
      François
24  François            Josette Clairmont
                                          S.F.
      Josette             Jos. Gosselin   S.M. 1832
25  Louis          (13)  Julienne Charlan S.P. 1801
      Elizabeth           Barth. Simart     „  1836
26  Pierre         (13)  Génev. Crépeau  S.J 1809
      Pierre
27  Ignace         (13)  Cath. Chatigny  S.P. 1816
  A Pierre         (14)  Mad. Dumas      S.H. 1810
28  Germain        (14)  Josette Frémont S.L. 1828
29  Joseph         (15)  M. Cath. Bidet  S.J. 1803
      Catherine           Jérémie Blouin    „  1841
      Ursule              J. B. Blouin      „  1841
      Magloire
      Jean Baptiste
      Honoré
      Joseph
30  Gabriel        (15)  Cath. Cochon      „  1810
      Marie               Stanislas Paquet S.F. 1857
      Joseph
      Gabriel
31  Laurent        (15)  Fse. Tremblay     „  1812
32  Louis          (15)  Fse. Bidet      S.J. 1818
      Seraphine           Guill. Blouin     „  1846
      Theotiste           Ls. Audet       S.L. 1843
      Theotiste           2° Jérôme Audet   „  1864
      Reparate            Jos. Gosselin     „  1848
      Le même             Hélène Blouin   S.F. 1830
33  Louis          (16)  Angé Paradis    S.P. 1793
      Elizabeth           F. X. Caron       „  1847
      Louis
34  Paul           (16)  M. Anne Jacques „  1803
35  Pierre         (18)  M. Fse. Demeule S.J. 1792
      Ursule              Amable Boissonneau
                                          S.L. 1821
36  Michel         (18)  Marie Paquet    S.P. 1794
      Marie               Jac. Dion       S.F. 1839
      Michel
      Jean
37  Jean           (21)  Thérèse Coté    S.P. 1833
38  Pierre         (21)  Thérèse Crepeau   „  1831
      Marie Adéline       Jos. Godbout      „  1863
      Louis Fidèle
      Pierre Phydime
      Jean
39  Louis          (22)  Marie Rousseau    „  1834
      Louis Célestin
40  David          (22)  Luce Noël         .  1841
41  François       (23)  Flavie Goulet     „  1840
42  François            Mad. Canac
      Pierre
43  Pierre         (26)  JustineThivierge S.J. 1835
```

PICHET.

```
44  JeanBaptiste(29)  M. Ursule Hélie   „  1831
      George
45  Magloire       (29)  Mad. Boissonneau „  1838
46  Honoré         (29)  Christine Hélie S.J. 1841
      Christine           Ls. Hercule Simart
                                          S.J. 1864
47  Joseph         (29)  Théotiste Terrien S.J. 1844
48  Joseph         (30)  Emélie Thivierge S.J. 1841
      Joseph
49  Gabriel        (30)  Henriette Jahan S.J. 1842
50  Louis          (33)  M. Mad. Chabot S.P. 1823
      Marie Césarine      Jos. Turcot     S.P. 1858
      Marg. Adélaïde      Pierre Turcot   S.P. 1863
      François
51  Michel         (36)  M. Anne Drouin S.F. 1821
      Le même             Domitilde Roberge
                                          S.F. 1852
52  Jean           (36)  M. Genev. Foucher
                                          S.F. 1831
53  Louis Fidèle (38)  Adé Gourdeau    S.P. 1864
54  Jean           (38)  Emélie Célina Marcoux
                                          S.P. 1866
55  Pierre         (38)  Vict. Malvina Tailleur
      Phydime                             S.P. 1869
56  LouisCélestin(39)  Hombéline Maranda
                                          S.P. 1864
57  Pierre         (42)  Anastasie Paradis S.P.1839
58  Georges        (44)  Sophie Cochon   C.R. 1854
59  Joseph         (48)  Lumina Blouin  S.J. 1864
60  François       (50)  M. Apolline Ferland
                                          S.P. 1855
```

PIGEON.

```
 1  Joseph              Fse. Contin    Auranches
      Julien
 2  Julien         (1)  M. Thérèse Garant
                                          S.F.S. 1753
      Marie Louise        Germ. Landry S.F.S. 1787
      Marie Thérèse       Laurent Théberge S.F.S.
                                          1788
      Joseph
      Julien
 3  Julien         (2)  Génev. Thibaut S.P.S.1778
      Louise Reine        Jean Marie Tangué
                                          S.V. 1806
      Géneviève           Frs. Boulet     S.V. 1807
      Henri
      Jacques
      Jean Baptiste
      Antoine
      Pierre
      Julien
 4  Joseph         (2)  M. Gertrude Chamberlan
                                          S.F.S. 1794
      Marguerite          Jos. Lacroix  S.F.S. 1830
 5  Henri          (3)  Marg. Rey       S.V. 1804
 6  Jacques        (3)  M. Angé Richard S.V.
                                          1815
      Angèle              Isaïe Caouet  S.P.S. 1840
      Marie Louise        Jos. Blais    S.Chs. 1843
      Marie Louise        2 Paul Mercier S.Chs. 1855
      Marie Sophie        Hubert Garant S.F.S. 1844
 7  Jean Baptiste (3)  Clotilde Gagnon S.M. 1816
 8  Julien         (3)  Angé Bisson    S.Chs. 1817
 9  Antoine        (3)  M. Génev. Bolduc
                                          S.M. 1820
      Géneviève           Geo. Morin      S.V. 1843
      Le même             Céleste Parant  S.V. 1825
      Marie Marcelline    Eusebe Morin    S.V. 1846
      Delphine            Gilbert Gagnon  S.V. 1855
      Marie Césarie       Nazaire Cochon  S.V. 1856
      Marie Césarie       2° Chs. Dussaut S.V. 1860
10  Pierre         (3)  M. Marth. Carbonneau
                                          S.V. 1821
      Marie               Paul Cadrin     S.M. 1844
```

PIGEON.

Marie Anne	Michel Lebrun	S.M. 1845
Augustin		
11 Augustin	(10) Angèle CoulombeS.M.1847	

PILOTE.

1 Leonard		Denise Gautier	
Pierre			
Jean			
2 Jean	(1)	M. Fse. Gaudry	Que 1678
Jean			
Pierre			
3 Pierre	(1)	Jeanne Brassard	Que 1694
Marguerite		Jos. Racine	Que 1715
4 Jean	(2)	Cath. Brassart	Que 1710
Jean François			
Jean			
5 Pierre	(2)	Louise Chalifour	Que 1716
Joseph			
6 Jean	(4)	Dorothée Bissonnet	
			S.V. 1734
Marie		Jos. Bolduc	S.M. 1761
Marguerite			
Marie		Jean Lacasse	S.V. 1723
Ignace			
Jean Baptiste			
Augustin			
7 Jean François	(4)	M. Anne Chamberlan	
			S.M. 1754
8 Joseph	(5)	Angé. Mignot	S.P.S. 1760
9 Jean Baptiste	(6)	M. Anne Gautron	
			S.M. 1759
Marie Anne		André Goulet	S.M. 1779
Marie Anne		2° Ls. Labrecque	S.G. 1816
Le même		M. AgatheBolduc	S.V.1765
10 Augustin	(6)	Marg. Bolduc	S.V. 1763
Madeleine		Nic. Frs. Boissonneau	
			S.M. 1802
Madeleine		2° Aug. Mercier	S.M. 1815
Marie Louise		Pierre NoëlMorin	S.M.1805
Joseph			
Augustin			
François			
11 Ignace	(6)	M.Cath.Clément	S.M.1765
		S.H.	
Marie		Jean Gosselin	S.Chs. 1796
Marie Marg.		Frs. Baudoin	S.H. 1839
Marie Anne		Michel Gautron	S.H. 1794
Françoise		Ls. Côté	S.H. 1793
Le même		Ursule Roy	S.M. 1794
12 François	(10)	M. Reine Bilodeau	
			S.F.S. 1808
Marie Reine		Frs. Couture	S.M. 1839
Emérentienne		Ls. Audet	S.M. 1842
Sophie		Ls. Lacroix	" 1845
Marguerite		Barnabé Gagnon	" 1848
François			
13 Joseph	(10)	Marg. Lacroix	S.M. 1810
		S. Claire	
Pierre			
Joseph			
François Xavier			
14 Augustin	(10)	M. Génév. Boissel	
			S. Chs. 1817
15 François	(12)	Christine Bolduc	S.M. 1839
16 Joseph	(13)	Marie Fortier	S.V. 1836
17 Pierre	(13)	Henriette Ducrot	
			S. Chs. 1850
18 François	(13)	Olive Cochon	" 1856
Xavier			

PLANTE.

1 Jean	Fse. Boucher	Que. 1650
Marie Françoise	Nic. Pasquin	C.R. 1676
Geneviève	Jacq. Cochon	" 1689
Angélique	Michel Chabot	" 1690

PLANTE.

Louise		Pierre Coignac	C.R. 1702
Claude			
Jacques			
Jean			
Pierre			
Georges			
Thomas			
François			
2 Claude	(1)	Marie Patenotre	S.F. 1678
Angélique		Ls. Turcot	" 1721
Marguerite		Pierre Lainé	S.J. 1720
Charles		Curé de S. Michel	
Jacques			
Le même		Cath. Dufresne	S.L. 1706
3 Georges	(1)	Marg. Crépeau	S.P. 1685
Marguerite		Chs. Delage	S.J. 1706
Geneviève		Jacq. Blouin	" 1715
Angélique		Jean Leroux	" 1715
Susanne		Jos. Fortier	" 1721
Josette		Chs. Delage	" 1725
Josette		2° Jacq. TanguéS. Frs. 1758	
Jos. Marie			
4 Jacques	(1)	Fse. Turcot	S.F. 1686
Le même		Genev. Duchesne	C.R. 1696
Geneviève		Jean Paquet S. Frs. 1734	
Pierre			
Joseph			
5 Jean	(1)	Mathurine Delengré	
			S.F. 1687
Jeanne		Frs. Cochon	S.J. 1711
Marie		Chs. Lefebvre	" 1711
Le même		Susane Lefebvre	" 1699
Susanne		Chs. Quéret	S.M. 1730
Louis			
6 Thomas	(1)	Marthe Pallereau	S.J 1687
Marie		Jos. Racine	" 1725
Marie Marthe		Ls. Fortin	" 1734
Georges			
François			
Thomas			
7 Pierre	(1)	Marg. Patenotre	S.F. 1691
Catherine		Prisque Racine	S.J. 1735
Madeleine		Ls. Clément	" 1733
Madeleine		2° Michel Lefebvre	
			S.M. 1754
Joseph			
Pierre			
Charles			
Paul			
8 François	(1)	Louise Bérard	C.R. 1694
Le même		M. Anne Coignac	" 1700
Louis			
9 Jacques	(2)	M. Chs. Vaillancour	
			S.F. 1711
10 Joseph Marie	(3)	Eliz. Pepin	S.J. 1744
11 Pierre	(4)	Marg. Cochon	" 1726
Marie		Jacq. Bilodeau	S. Frs. 1750
Marie Claire		Jos. L'heureux	" 1767
Marie Josette		Pierre Gagné	" 1773
Marie Josette		2° Zach. Bolduc	" 1789
Marie Geneviève		Jos. Alexis Roy	S.V. 1761
Joseph			
Jacques			
12 Joseph	(4)	M. Chs. Bizeau	S.V. 1733
Marie Félicité		Frs. Roy	" 1765
Marie Madeleine		Jacq. Furois	S.M. 1753
Joseph			
13 Simon		M. Mad. Londeau	
Marie Josette		Jos. Adam	S.M. 1753
Marie Eliz.		Jos. Quéret	" 1764
André			
Pierre			
14 Louis	(5)	M. Jos. Bissonnet	" 1740
Marguerite		Michel Pénin	" 1765
Marie		J. B. Hélie	S. Chs. 1782

PLANTE.

	Eustache		
	Joseph		
	François		
	Louis		
15	François	(6) M. Mad. Caron	
		S. Anne	1732
	Marie Louise	Frs. Fontaine S.J.	1763
16	Georges	(6) M.Mad.MorissetS.M.	1734
	Madeleine	Jos. Hélie S.V.	1775
A	Thomas	(6) Louise Bacquet S.M.	1747
	Le même	M, Jos. Gautron „	1748
17	Pierre	(7) Angé Avare S.J.	1717
	Thècle	J. B. Fortier „	1739
	Marie Madelaine	Jean Frs. Audibert „	1742
	Marie Josette	René Blouin „	1756
	Pierre Noël		
	Basile		
	Prisque		
	Jean		
	Charles		
18	Charles	(7) M. Mad. Avare S.J.	1723
	Madeleine	J. B. Daniau „	1747
	Geneviève	Nic. Boissonneau	
		S.F.S.	1755
	Geneviève	2° Prisque Daniau „	1762
	Félicité	Frs. Morin „	1764
19	Joseph	(7) Jeanne Clément S.M.	1732
	M. Angélique	Chs. Rémillard „	1757
	M. Anne	Gab. Bilodeau „	1770
	Jean		
20	Paul	(7) Perpetue Greffart S.J.	1734
	M. Madeleine	Pierre Gagné „	1770
	M. Marguerite	Ls. Boissel S.M.	1775
	Josette	Noël Gromelin „	1780
	François		
21	Louis	(8) Véronique CochonS.J.	1732
	Le même	Josette Crepeau	1746
22	Nicolas	Marie Brochette	
	M. Josette	Jos. Hélie S.J.	1770
	Jos. Marie		
23	Joseph	(11) Isabelle Emond S.Frs.	1765
	Jean Baptiste		
24	Jacques	(11) M.Jos.Chs.Guion S.F.	1771
	Catherine	Jos. Marseau „	1796
	Charlotte	Frs. Gaulin S.Frs.	1800
	Jacques		
	François		
25	Joseph	(12) M.Jos.Dumont S.P.S.	1753
	Marie	Ls. Vérieul S.V.	1785
	Joseph		
26	André	(13) M. Angé Monmeny	
		S.M.	1754
27	Pierre	(13) M. Cath. Chartier „	1771
28	Louis	(14) M. Jos. Bolduc S.V.	1768
	Marie Anne	Ls. Terrien S.M.	1812
	Antoine		
29	Joseph	(14) Marie Gourgue „	1770
	Marie	Jacq. Manet S.Chs.	1812
		V. de M. Anne Trudel	
	Le même	M. Anne Gosselin	
		S.Chs.	1781
	Susanne	Michel Marcoux „	1806
	M. Marguerite	Ign. Bilodeau S.H.	1800
	M. Madeleine	J. B. Morin „	1800
	M. Angélique	Pierre Bilodeau „	1806
	Charlotte	Basile Noël „	1809
	Antoine		
30	François	(14) M. Dorothée Patry	
		S.M.	1774
	Marie	Michel Morisset „	1802
	François		
	Joseph		
	Le même	Fse. Daniau S.Chs.	1786
	Monique	Laurent Gosselin „	1815
	Geneviève	Barth. Pepin S.J.	1827

PLANTE.

	Joachim		
	Pierre		
	Louis		
	Jean Baptiste		
31	Eustache	(14) M. Marg. Hélie S.M.	1775
	Catherine	Pierre Blouin S.Chs.	1816
	Marie	Jos. Blouin „	1818
	Marie	Ant. Gosselin S. Chs	1818
	Eustache		
	Antoine		
32	Charles	(17) Dorothée Audibert	
		S.J.	1740
	Jean		
33	Charles	Eliz. Boissonneau	
	Elizabeth	Ign. Fortin S.J.	1789
	Joseph		
	Le même	M. Angé Paquet „	1772
	Marie Louise	Ls. Bacquet „	1803
	Charles		
	Louis		
34	Pierre Noël	(17) Eliz. Boissonneau „	1746
	Josette	Ls. Guion „	1785
	M. Elizabeth	Frs. Fortier „	1776
	Joseph		
	Basile		
	Pierre Noël		
	Jean		
	François		
	Jean Marie		
35	Prisque	(17) Jossette Leclaire S.P.	1747
	Josette	Pierre Ferland „	1771
	Thècle	J. B. Langlois „	1772
	Catherine	Jacq. Huot „	1780
	Marie Anne	Frs. Tailleur „	1787
	Marie Anne	2° Pierre Goulet „	1794
	Geneviève	Frs. Côté	
	Prisque		
	Ambroise		
	Joseph		
36	Basile	(17) M. Fse. Fortier S.J.	1753
	Basile		
37	Jean	(17) Marthe Vérieul S.Frs.	1759
	M. Josette	Barth. Gagnon „	1782
	M. Angélique	Ant. Pepin S.F.	1789
	Jean		
38	Jean	(19) M.Genev.FortierS.M.	1765
	Jean Vincent		
39	François	(20) M. Anne Dépont S.V.	1770
	Madeleine	Pierre Quemeneur S.G.	1795
	Charles		
	François		
40	Jos. Marie	(22) M. Fse. Gosselin S.L.	1771
	Marie Frs.	J. B. Emond S.J.	1794
	Elizabeth	Jac. Carbonneau „	1820
	Jos. Marie		
	Jacques		
41	Joseph	M. Jos. Pénin	
	Josette	Chs. Terrien S.G.	1804
	Joseph		
42	Jean Baptiste	(23) M. Anne Charron „	1796
43	François	(24) M. Ls. Martineau S.J.	1794
	Louise	Aug. Emond S. Frs.	1828
	Jacques		
	François		
	Le même	Marg. Pepin S.Frs.	1829
44	Jacques	(24) M. Anne Picard S.Frs.	1801
	Marguerite	Guill. Blouin S. Frs.	1820
45	Marie Josette	(24) M. Fse. Lacroix S.V.	1778
	Jacques		
	Le même	Marie Roby S. V.	1795
	Marie Louise	Jos. Quemeneur „	1816
	Antoine		
	André		
46	Antoine	(28) Thérèse Larrivé S. G.	1819

PLANTE.

47	Antoine	(29)	Marg. Bilodeau S.Chs.1827
	Jean Baptiste		
48	François	(30)	Marg. Gosselin S.Chs.1801
	Etienne		
49	Joseph	(30)	Marg. Nolin S. Chs. 1808
50	Louis	(30)	Marie Ruel " 1812
51	JeanBaptiste	(30)	M. Jos. Gosselin
			S. Chs. 1822
	François		
52	Joachim	(30)	Julienne Canac S. G. 1828
			S. Anselme
	Le même		Félicité Charier S.Chs.1835
53	Pierre	(30)	M. Agnes Blais S.P.S.1828
	Le même		M. Jos. Drolet S.Chs. 1844
54	Eustache	(31)	Mad. Blais " 1799
55	Antoine	(31)	M. Fse. Boulet " 1806
	Marie Thérèse		Frs. Ruel " 1826
	Le même		Barbe Cochon " 1816
	Frs. David		
	Antoine		
56	Jean	(32)	Fse. Boissonneau
			S. Chs. 1773
	M. Marguerite		Jean Philippe Munroe
			S. H. 1800
57	Charles	(33)	Rosalie Dubé S. J. 1805
	Rosalie		J. B. Plante " 1830
	Adélaïde		Jos. Giguère " 1832
A	Joseph	(33)	Angé Mercier S. H. 1809
	Le même		Vict. Genest " 1818
	Le même		M. Anne Rouillard
			S. G. 1820
58	Louis	(33)	Mad. Giguère S. J. 1823
59	Basile	(34)	M. Mad. Hélie " 1772
	Basile		
	Le même		M. Cath. Blouin " 1776
	Marie Mad.		Pierre Turcot " 1808
60	Pierre Noël	(34)	M. Jos. Fortier " 1776
	Le même		Marie Madeleine " 1820
	Marguerite		Chs. Bisson " 1839
	Marguerite		2° Pierre Forgue " 1841
	Pierre		
61	JeanFrançois	(34)	Genev. Thivierge " 1777
	Marie Louise		Basile Plante " 1805
	Jérémie		
	Joseph		
	Le même		M. Jos. Pichet S.J. 1809
62	Joseph	(34)	Genev. Fortier " 1794
63	Jean Marie	(34)	M. Anne Fortier
			S. F. S. 1780
	Marie Anne		Ls. Chamberlan S. V. 1812
64	Prisque	(35)	Marie Dupile S. P. 1782
	Marie Josette		Frs. Noël " 1808
	Marguerite		Ign. Beaucher " 1821
	Prisque		
	Pierre		
65	Joseph	(35)	Agathe Gosselin S.P. 1790
	Agathe		Jean Leclaire " 1820
	Marie Anne		Jos. Maranda " 1829
	Madeleine		Pierre Maranda " 1830
	Brigitte		Stanislas Camiré " 1835
	Prisque		
	Augustin		
	Jacques		
	Clément		
66	Ambroise	(35)	Josette Leclaire S. P. 1797
67	Basile	(36)	M. Ls. Plante S. J. 1805
	Julie		Jos. Gosselin B. 1827
68	Jean	(37)	Josette Doyon C. R. 1788
	Marie		Jos. Drouin S. Frs. 1809
	Angèle		Frs. Drouin " 1809
	Catherine		Prisque TremblayS.F.1823
	Jean		
	François		
69	Charles	(39)	Angèle Thibaut S. G. 1800
70	François	(39)	Brigitte Blais " 1802

71	Jean (Inconnu)		M. Vict. Bétil S. M. 1794
	Josette		Amb. Gontier S. Chs. 1826
	Victoire		Pierre Fortin S. G. 1828
	Pierre		
	François		
72	Jos. Marie	(40)	M. Marg. Bidet S. J. 1798
	Jos. Marie		
	Jean Baptiste		
	Basile		
	George		
	Ignace		
73	Jacques	(40)	Hélène Fortier S. J. 1809
	Emérence		Chs. Blouin " 1836
74	Joseph	(41)	MartheGontier S.Chs.1801
	Marie Marthe		Ls. Balan S. M. 1822
	Marie		Jean Terrien " 1828
	Philippe		
	Pierre		
	Jacques		
	Joseph		
75	François	(43)	Cath. Emond S.F. 1818
	Joseph		
76	Jacques	(43)	Marg. Dalaire S.J. 1825
77	Jacques	(45)	Marg. Buteau S.F.S. 1807
78	Antoine	(45)	Angèle Thivierge S.V.1830
	Angèle		Ls. Parant " 1853
	Esther		Jean Norbert Morin
			S.V. 1864
	Marie Desanges		Ls. Thivierge " 1866
79	André	(45)	Angèle Pepin " 1835
80	JeanBaptiste	(47)	M. Philoméne Gosselin
			S. Chs. 1860
81	Etienne	(48)	Olive Nolin " 1823
	Marie Geneviève		Laurent Hébert " 1845
	Olive		Michel Coulombe " 1854
	Domitille		Ant. Olivier Briant
			S. Chs. 1855
	Philomène		Ant. Gontier " 1862
	Damase		
	François		
	Etienne		
82	François	(51)	M. Salome Audet
			S. Chs. 1859
83	Antoine	(55)	Archange Ratté S.M. 1833
	Aurélie		Chs. Ruel S. Chs. 1863
	Antoine		
	Le même		Anastasie Gosselin
			S. Chs. 1861
			V. d'Anselme Ruel
84	Frs. David	(55)	M. Henriette Trahan
			S. Chs. 1843
			S. Claire.
A	Basile	(59)	M. Euphrosine Bilodeau
			S.H. 1800
	Le même		Genev. Rousseau " 1819
85	Pierre	(60)	Hombéline Picard
			S.J. 1842
86	Joseph	(61)	M. Fse. Paquet " 1808
87	Jérémie	(61)	Genev. Lauglois S.P. 1817
88	Prisque	(64)	Louise Gourdeau " 1812
	Jacques		
	Pierre		
	Prisque		
89	Pierre	(64)	Rosalie GourdeauS.P. 1820
	Marie Caroline		Paul Audet " 1846
	Pierre		
90	Prisque	(65)	Genev. Ruel S.L. 1816
	Geneviève		Amb. Pouliot " 1840
	Apolline		Onésime Couture " 1854
	Marie Desanges		Germ. Lemay " 1856
	Ignace		
	Joseph		
	Isidore		
91	Augustin	(65)	Marg. Cantin S.P. 1828
	Marie Agathe		Jos. Maranda " 1847
	Marie Hermine		Frs. Chartré " 1855

PLANTE.

	Emélienne	Eugène Nolin	S.P. 1858
	Marie Eulalie	Laurent Nicodème	
		Gosselin	S.P. 1865
	Elzéar Augustin		
92	Jacques (65)	Firmine Langlois	S.P. 1839
	Jos. Octave		
	Jos. Eustache		
93	Clément (65)	Marie Asselin	S.P. 1839
94	Jean (68)	M.Mad. Pepin	S.Frs. 1811
	Justine	F. X. Lessart	" 1843
	Frs. Xavier		
95	François (68)	Henriette Drouin	S.F. 1828
	Henriette	Pierre Nap. Pouliot	
			C.R. 1866
	Adéline	Bellarmine Cinqmars	
			C.R. 1869
96	Pierre (71)	Marie Blouin	S.G. 1820
97	François (71)	Rosalie Boutin	" 1821
98	Georges (72)	Esther Thivierge	S.J. 1829
99	Joseph Marie(71)	Cécile Audet	" 1827
100	JeanBaptiste(72)	Rosalie Plante	" 1830
	Rose	Ls. Terrien	" 1860
	Jean		
	François Xavier		
101	Ignace (72)	Ursule Fleury	S.J. 1835
102	Basile (72)	Delphine Poulin	" 1861
103	Pierre (74)	Marthe Hélie	S.M. 1829
	Martine	J. B. Clavet	" 1862
	Marie Célina	Pierre Chrétien	" 1864
	Pierre		
104	Jacques (74)	Angèle Hélie	" 1831
	Proxède		
	Antoine		
105	Philippe (74)	M. Anne Hélie	S.M. 1831
	Florence	Proxède Plante	" 1863
106	Joseph (74)	Fse. Terrien	" 1832
107	François (81)	Constance Fournier	
			S. Chs. 1853
108	Damase (81)	Marg. Gontier	" 1859
109	Etienne (81)	Julie Olive Blanchet	
			S.Chs. 1860
110	Antoine (83)	Eudoxie Chabot	" 1856
111	Prisque (88)	M. Scolastique Létour-	
		neau	S.F. 1835
	Héliodore Ulric		
112	Jacques (88)	Genev. Pichet	S.P. 1841
113	Pierre (88)	M. Emélie Godbout	
			S.P. 1844
114	Pierre (89)	Genev. Drouin	S.F. 1846
115	Ignace (90)	M.Anne Ferland	S.P. 1846
	Marie Anne	Jean Pouliot	S.L. 1874
	Geneviève	Frs. Edm. Pepin	" 1878
	Marie Desneiges	Julien Gendreau	" 1881
	Jos. Onésime		
161	Joseph (90)	M. Anne Célanire	
		Cinqmars	S.L. 1855
117	Isidore (90)	M. Zoé Labrecque	
			S.L. 1855
	Marie	Xavier Hamel	S.L. 1876
118	Eliz. Augus- (91)	Flavie Gagnon	S.P. 1862
	tin		
119	Jos. Octave (92)	M. Emérence Goulet	
			S.P. 1867
120	Jos Eustache (92)	Delphine Célina Fer-	
		land	S.P. 1867
121	Jean Vincent(38)	Brigitte Gendreau	
			S.Tho. 1811
	Judith	Jacq. Légaré	S.V. 1858
	Herménégide		
	Cyrille		
	Valère		
	Joseph		
122	François (75)	Justine Gagnon	
	Le même	Célina Gautier	S.Frs. 1861
124	Frs. Xavier (94)	M. Mad. Lepage	" 1847

18—29

PLANTE.

125	Frs. Xavier (100)	Philomène Terrien	
			S.L. 1863
126	Jean (100)	Eliz. Dupuis	S.J. 1863
127	Pierre (103)	M. Zoé Terrien	S.M. 1851
128	Antoine (104)	Vict. Terrien	S.M. 1856
129	Proxède (104)	Florence Plante	S.M. 1863
130	Héliodore (111)	Marie Chabot	S.P. 1867
	Ulric		
131	Valère (121)	Sophie Garant	S.V. 1847
132	Joseph (121)	Sophie Gagnon	S.V. 1851
133	Cyrille (121)	Marie Marcoux	S.Chs. 1859
134	Herméné- (121)	M. Christine Fournier	
	gilde		S.Chs. 1863

POIRIER.

1	Jean	Marie Gautier	
	Charles		
2	Michel	Marie Brun Beauséjour	
			Acadie
	Grégoire		
3	Bertrand	Mad. Michel	
			Qué.
	Madeleine	Simon Hébert	S.Chs. 1758
	M. Madeleine	Aug. Lefebvre	S.Tho. 1773
4	Charles (1)	M. Anne Lacasse	B. 1730
5	Grégoire (2)	Génév. Guenet	
			S.Chs. 1759
	Marguerite	Ign. Gosselin	S.Chs. 1798
	François		
6	François (5)	Genev. Queret	S.G. 1798
	Marie	Pierre Quemeneur	
			S.G. 1820
	Marguerite	Jacq. Roy	S.M. 1844
	François		
	Noël		
7	François (6)	Mad. Quemeneur	S.G. 1819
8	Noël (6)	Marie Moreau	S.G. 1822

POLIQUIN.

1	Jean	Anne Adam	Que. 1671
	Marie Anne	Chs. Lecours	Lévis 1708
	Claude		
	Jean		
	Le même	Louise Ledran	Lévis 1713
2	Jean (1)	M. Ls. Lecours	Que. 1718
	Marie Louise	Pierre Baudin	S.M. 1751
	Marie Jeanne	Pierre Charier	S.Chs. 1758
	Claude		
	Jean		
	Jacques		
3	Claude (1)	Marie Labbé	S.V. 1718
	Catherine	Pierre Naud,	Lévis 1755
	Jean		
	Jean Baptiste		
	Claude		
	Jos. Dominique		
4	Jean (2)	M. Angé Filteau	S.M. 1745
5	Jacques (2)	Marie Coté	S.Chs. 1751
	Marie Louise	Jos. Duquet	S.Chs. 1781
	Marie Louise	2° Frs. Guay	S.Chs. 1813
	Marie Anne	Jos. Brochu	S.Chs. 1786
	Catherine	Jos. Lefebvre	S Chs. 1800
	Pierre		
	Jean		
	Charles		
	Jacques		
	Le même	M. Genev. Hautbois	
			S.G. 1799
		V. de Jean Nadeau	
6	Claude (2)	M. Ls. Nadeau	S.Chs. 1753
	Bibiane	Ls. Pruneau	S.Chs. 1783
	Madeleine	Chs. Monmeny	
			S.Chs. 1783

POLIQUIN.

	Charles		
7	Jean	(3)	M. Anne Le Roy B. 1744
8	Claude	(3)	Susanne Jourdain
			Lévis 1751
9	Jos. Domin-	(3)	Ange Dangueuge B. 1752
	ique		
	Marie Angé-		Aug. Thibaut S.M. 1793
	lique		
	Laurent		
	François		
10	Jean Baptiste	(3)	Marg. Sustier, Lévis 1753
	Le même		Eliz. Goupy S.M. 1762
	Marie Génév.		J. B. Turgeon, Lévis 1795
	Jean Baptiste		
11	Augustin		Marie Adam S.M. 1778
12	Jean	(5)	Marg. Dumas S.Chs. 1787
	Marie		J. B. Baudoin S.H. 1807
13	Pierre	(5)	Marie Lefebvre
			S.Chs. 1787
14	Charles	(5)	Josette Guay, Lévis 1805
	Landry		
	Le même		M. Jos. Patry S.Chs. 1815
	Eddoce		Michel Daniau S.Chs.1836
	Charles		
15	Charles	(6)	Marie Hébert S.Chs. 1785
	Charles		
16	Laurent	(9)	M.Thérèse Veau S.M.1786
	Marie Adélaide		Ls. Richard S.M. 1811
	Marie Thérèse		Amb. Bacquet S.M. 1839
	Alexis		
	Edouard		
	Michel		
	Joseph		
	Jacques		
	Laurent		
17	François	(9)	M. Agathe TurgeonB.1787
	Marie Agathe		Pierre Bussière S.M. 1804
18	Joseph		Genev. Fafart
			Lévis
	Le même		Marie Anne B. 1790
19	JeanBaptiste	(10)	Angé Guay Lévis 1804
20	Landry	(14)	Françoise Roy S.Chs. 1830
	François		Benj. Couture S.Chs. 1848
	Le même		Ursule Bacquet S.M. 1834
21	Charles	(14)	M. Désanges Guilmet
			S.Chs. 1847
22	Charles	(15)	Agathe Goupy S.G. 1811
23	Jacques	(5)	Brigitte Gautron S.H.1797
	Jacques		
24	Alexis	(16)	Genev. Forgues S.M. 1812
	Marie Genev.		Jean Audet S.M. 1837
	Anastasie		AthanaseGagnonS.M.1838
	Marie Hélène		F. X. Mercier S.M. 1841
	Marie Eléonore		Frs. Bourget S.M. 1848
	Octavie Flavie		Jos. Rousseau S.M. 1854
	Alexis		
	Joseph		
	Honoré		
25	Laurent	(16)	M. Jos. Drapeau S.V. 1814
26	Michel	(16)	Marie Boissel S.Chs. 1825
27	Joseph	(16)	Sophie Moor S.M. 1830
28	Edouard	(16)	M. Genev. Vien B. 1831
29	Augustin	(16)	Marcelline GagnéS.M.1842
30	Jacques	(23)	Angèle Olive Provost
			S.Chs. 1826
31	Alexis	(24)	Genev. Audet B. 1839
32	Honoré	(24)	M. Genev. Bourget
			S.M. 1846
33	Joseph	(24)	M. Jos. Leclaire S.L. 1847

POULET.

1	Antoine	Susanne Minville Qué.1655
	Marguerite	Mathurin BlouardS.F.1671
	Antoine	

POULET.

2	Antoine	(1)	Renée Graton S.P. 1685
	Le même		Anne Loignon S.P. 16·5
	M. Anne		Frs. Ferland S.P. 1708
	Geneviève		Ant. Paquet S.P. 1708
	Geneviève		2° Jos. LabrecqueS.P.1722
	Hélène		Ls. Coulombe S.P. 1710
	Catherine		Frs. Marchand S.P. 1720
	M. Madeleine		Pierre Bergeron S P. 1730
	M. Madeleine		J. B. St. Laurent S.P.1732
	Pierre		
	Jean		
3	Pierre	(2)	Genev. Paradis S.P. 1724
	Le même		Mad. Gosselin S.P. 1729
	Marie Madeleine		J. B. Nolin S.P. 1748
4	Jean	(2)	Marie Roy S.L. 1726
	Geneviève		P. Noël Fortier S.P. 1752
	Madeleine		Paul Langlois S.P. 1754
	Marie Marthe		J. B. Toupin S.P. 1765
	Jean François		
5	Jean Baptiste		M. Anne Lemieux
	Le même		Mad. Coté S.P. 1740
6	Jean François	(4)	M. Ls. Noël S.P. 1751
	Josette		Frs. Pouliot S.P. 1786
	Agathe		Benoit Audet S.P. 1791
	Jean		
	Charles		
7	Jean	(6)	Marie Cantin S.P. 1785
	Le même		M. Jos. Couture B. 1796
8	Charles	(6)	Genev. Noël S.L. 1792
			S. Anselme
	Geneviève		Pierre Godbout S.G. 1815
	Jean		
	Charles		
	François		
	Etienne		
9	Charles	(8)	Marie Pouliot S.G. 1812
10	François	(8)	M. Ls. Choret S.P. 1824
11	Jean	(8)	Louise Vallée S.L. 1833
12	Etienne	(8)	M. Reine FerlandS.P.1835
			S.G.
13	Augustin		Cath. Chiquet
	Léonie		Honoré Chabot S.Chs.1861

POULIN.

1	Jacques	Marie Violette
	Jean	
2	Claude	Jeanne Mercier Qué. 1639
	Martin	
	Ignace	
	Pierre	
3	Jean	(1)	Marie Paré S. Anne 1667
	Paschal	
	Julien	
	Jean	
4	Ignace	(2)	Marg. Paré S. Anne 1783
	Claude	
	Ignace	
	Joseph	
	Guillaume	
5	Martin	(2)	Jeanne Barret
			S. Anne 1788
	Marie		Jean Terriau S.F. 1713
	Françoise		Jean Drouin C.R. 1723
	André	
	Jean	
6	Pierre	(2)	Anne Giguère S.Anne 1639
	Louis	
7	Julien	(3)	JeanneRacine S.Anne 1700
8	Jean	(3)	Louise Paré 1702
	Pierre	
9	Paschal	(3)	Marg. Gagné S.Anne 1709
	Josette		Chs. Guerard S.Frs. 1760
	Josette		2° PierreTerrien S.Frs.1778
	Charles	

POULIN.

10	Claude	(4)	Marg. Nevers	C.R. 1713
	Claude			
	Joseph			
11	Joseph	(4)	Louise Bolduc	S.Joa. 1716
	Pierre			
	Louis			
	Ignace			
12	Ignace	(4)	Marg. Caron	S.Anne 1724
A	Guillaume		Genev. Caron	
	Pierre			
13	André	(5)	Cath. Drouin	C.R. 1718
	Cath. Françoise		Jean Demeule	C R. 1741
	Le même		ThérèseCaron	S.Anne 1725
14	Jean	(5)	Agnès Drouin	C.R. 1724
15	Louis	(6)	Fse. Drapeau	S.Frs. 1734
			Isle Jésus	
16	Pierre	(8)	M. Anne Doyon	C.R. 1743
	Pierre			
17	Charles	(9)	M.Claire Deblois	S.Frs. 1744
	Charlotte		Jos. Hébert	S. Frs. 1762
	Benoni			
18	Joseph	(10)	Charlotte Savoie	S. Joa. 1751
	Augustin			
19	Claude	(10)	Louise Trudel	A. G. 1764
	Jean			
20	Pierre	(11)	Louise Cloutier	C.R. 1750
	Joseph			
21	Joseph	(11)	M. Dorothée Cloutier	C.R. 1751
	Marie Josette		Jos. Faucher	S.F. 1775
	Marguerite		Frs. Deblois	S.Frs. 1776
	Joseph			
	Louis			
22	Ignace	(11)	Louise Filion	S.Joa. 1747
	Le même		M. Marthe Jolivet	S.V. 1761
	Marguerite		Chs. Lepage	S.Chs. 1792
	Joseph			
A	Pierre	(12) A	JosetteLeforet S	Anne 1751
	Jérôme			
23	Ignace		M. Marthe Poulin	
	M. Marthe		Aug. Guilmet	S. V. 1778
24	Pierre	(16)	M. Vict Noël	S.P. 1772
			Beauport	
	Louis			
25	Augustin	(18)	MarieMénard	S.Anne 1811
	Augustin			
26	Jean	(19)	Fse. Rancour	S-Joa. 1799
	Jean Joseph			
27	Joseph	(20)	Josette Filion	S.Joa. 1774
	Louis			
	Joseph			
	Le même		Mad. Gagnon	C.R. 1781
28	Louis	(21)	Cath. Pelagie	S.F. 1771
	Catherine		Jos. Hébert	S.F. 1791
	Josette		Etn. Drouin	S.F. 1792
	Marie Charlotte		Ant. Parant	S.F. 1795
	Marguerite		J. B. Lamothe	S.F. 1800
	Dorothée		Ign. Létourneau	S.F. 1804
	Louis			
	Le même		Angé Loiseau	S.F. 1794
	Le même		Louise Ruel	S.L. 1806
29	Joseph	(21)	Angé Foucher	S.F. 1786
			S. Isidore	
	Angélique		Maurice Giroux	S.L. 1811
	Jacques			
	Jean			
	Louis			
	Joseph			
30	Joseph	(22)	Cath. Penin	S.Chs. 1792
A	Jérôme	(22) A	Marie Filion	S.Joa. 1787
	Jérôme			
31	Louis	(24)	Julienne Blouin	S.J. 1822
			Beauport	

18—29½

POULIN.

32	Augustin	(25)	Henriette Paquet	B. 1845
33	Jean Joseph	(26)	Cath. Pepin	S.F.S. 1833
34	Louis	(27)	Julie Provençal	C.R. 1819
	Louis			
	Le même		M. Thérèse Goulet	S.P. 1854
35	Joseph	(27)	Mad.Lessart	S. Anne 1812
	Célestin			
36	Louis	(28)	M.Anne Létourneau	S.F. 1798
	Henriette		J. B. Turcot	„ 1827
	Henriette		2° André Asselin	„ 1847
	M. Anne		J. B. Ferland	„ 1825
	Sophie		Frs. Canac	„ 1832
	Sophie		2° Ls. Prémont	„ 1840
	Joseph			
	Moïse			
	Edouard			
	Alexandre			
	Frs. Xavier			
37	Joseph	(29)	Angé Crépault	S.P. 1808
38	Jacques	(29)	Marg. Asselin	S.F. 1811
	Geneviève		Greg. Labrecque	S.L. 1835
	Anastasie		Jos. Royer	S.F. 1854
	Jacques			
39	Louis	(29)	Marg. Thivierge	S.I. 1812
	Marguerite		Jean Bte. Hélie	„ 1833
	Henriette		Jos. Blouin	„ 1841
	Delphine		Basile Plante	„ 1861
	Régis			
	Louis			
40	Jean	(29)	Adé. Roberge	S.P. 1825
	Constance		Jean Tessier	S.L. 1847
A	Jérôme	(30)	A. Vict. Chouinard	S.H. 1813
41	Louis	(34)	Angèle Pouliot	S.L. 1838
42	Célestin	(35)	Ls. Beaucher	S.F. 1844
43	Louis (Inconnu)		Chas. Gonthier	S.Chs. 1819
	Marie		Abr, Filion	S.M. 1842
44	Joseph	(36)	M. Colette Guérard	S.F. 1824
	Le même		Genev. Vézina	„ 1831
45	Edouard	(36)	M. Ludwine Canac	S.F. 1836
46	Alexandre	(36)	Elénore Turcot	S.I. 1840
	Virginie		Pierre Imbleau	S.F. 1868
47	Moïse	(36)	M. Fdélise Ferland	S.P. 1843
	M. Démerise		Ign. Léon Aubin	S.P. 1867
	M. Joséphine		Pierre Luc. Pouliot	S.P. 1871
	Joseph			
48	François	(36)	—— Blanchet	
	Xavier			
49	Jacques	(38)	M. Anne Bureau	S.F. 1841
	M. Philomène		Ign. Létourneau	S.F. 1862
50	Régis	(39)	Margt. Gosselin	S.I. 1839
51	Louis	(39)	M. Lse. Audet	S.I. 1842
52	Jean		Angèle Busgue,	S.Evariste.
	Le même		Marie Nadeau	Bert. 1859
53	Louis	(46)	Démerise Raimond	S.I. 1863
54	Joseph	(47)	Belzémire Goulet	S.P. 1877

POULIOT.

1	Michel	(1)	Jacqueline Laurens	
	Charles			
	Pierre			
2	Charles	(1)	Frse. Meunier	1667
	Jeanne		Joseph Audet	S.L. 1703
	Marguerite		Frs. Manseau	S.L. 1706
	Françoise		Jos. Chabot	S.P. 1692
	Charles			
	Antoine			

POULIOT.

	André			
	Jean			
3	Pierre	(1)	Marie Deschamps	Q. 1667
4	Charles	(2)	Marie Chabot	S.L. 1689
	Marie		Joseph Carreau	S.L. 1721
	Jeanne		Pierre Carreau	S.L. 1723
	Madeleine		Jos. Carreau	S.L. 1723
	Le même		Genev. Crépeau	S.P. 1703
	Geneviève		Ls. Lemelin	S.L. 1725
	Marie		Ls. Coulombe	" 1734
	Josette		Ls. Isabel	" 1743
	Pierre Frs.			
	Charles			
	Innocent			
	Nicolas			
5	Antoine	(2)	M. Ls. Chabot	S.L. 1696
6	André	(2)	M. Marg. Chabot	S.L. 1699
	Françoise		Jean Giroux	S.L. 1721
	Le même		Frs. Manseau	S.L. 1703
	M. Marguerite		Ant. Huppé	S.L. 1738
	André			
	Charles			
	Joseph			
7	Jean	(2)	M. Mad. Audet	
	M. Madeleine		Chs. Delâge	S.L. 1723
	Marie		Jean Godbout	S.L. 1735
	Jean			
	Charles			
	François			
8	Pierre	(4)	M. Anne Audet	S.L. 1750
	Marie Anne		Aug. Roberge	S.L. 1762
	Marie Louise		Alex. Couture	S.L. 1763
	Marie Louise		Jos. Lecours	S.Chs. 1779
	François			
	Joseph			
	Nicolas			
	Pierre			
	Jean			
9	Innocent	(4)	Jeanne Isabel	S.L. 1735
	Marg. Angé		Jean Vien	S.L. 1774
	Geneviève		Pierre Clement	S.M. 1764
	Marie		Paul Marseau	S.V. 1767
	M. Thérèse		2° Ant. Lamy	S.V. 1781
	M. Anne		Thos. Fournier	S.V. 1779
	Louis			
10	Nicolas	(4)	Thérèse Lemelin	S.L. 1742
11	Charles	(4)	Thérèse Isabel	S.L. 1743
	Thérèse		Jos. Lefebvre	S.Chs. 1767
	Louis			
	Charles			
12	André	(6)	Thérèse Joanne	S.L. 1730
	Thérèse		Jean Hébert	S.Chs. 1761
	François			
13	Charles	(6)	Lse. Lanoue	S.L. 1744
14	Joseph	(6)	M. Mad. Paquet	S.F. 1747
	M. Françoise		Ign. Bouffart	S.P. 1768
	Charles			
	Le même		M. Lse. Labrecque	S.M. 1781
15	Jean	(7)	Anne Denis	S.L. 1724
	Marie Anne		Ign. Gosselin	" 1750
	Gertrude		J. Bte. Bégin	" 1750
	Angélique		Jos. Marie Fontaine	S.L. 1756
	M. Madeleine		J. B. Hélie	Lévis 1758
	Jean Frs.			
16	Charles	(7)	Genev. Godbout	S.L. 1727
	Marguerite		Jos. Fortier	S.J. 1754
	M. Angélique		Ant. Gobeil	" 1772
	M. Angelique		2° M. Blouin	" 1781
	Joseph			
17	Francois	(7)	Marg. Ruel	S.L. 1733
	Le même		M. Anne Chabot	" 1735
	Cécile		Ant. de la Crouzette	S.L. 1764

POULIOT.

	Cécile		Bernd. Duberger	S.L. 1771
	M. Anne		Paul Paradis	" 1770
	Geneviève		Pierre Gosselin	" 1774
	M. Josette		Pierre Godbout	" 1778
	Jean Frs.			
	Pierre			
18	Charles		M. Frse. Crepeau	
	Charles			
19	Nicolas	(8)	M. Lse. Mercier	S.M. 1763
	M. Anne		Jean Bte. Aubé	S.G. 1786
	Marie		Laurent Couture	" 1786
	Françoise		Michel Dessaint	" 1794
	Nicolas			
	Pierre			
	François			
	Jean			
20	Le même		M. Lse. Vallée	S.V. 1783
	Pierre	(8)	Isabelle Lacroix	S.M. 1764
	Angélique		Pierre Filteau	S.Chs. 1783
	Françoise		Guill. Gosselin	" 1788
	Elizabeth		Etn. Couture	" 1792
	Pierre			
21	Jean	(8)	Marie Dulignon	S.Chs 1773
	Pierre			
	Le même		Monique Hélène Leclair	S.M. 1779
22	François	(8)	Lonise Chabot	S.L. 1775
	M. Louise		Jacques Coulombe	" 1805
	Le même		M. Jos. Paulet	S.P. 1786
	Josette		J. B. Paquet	S.L. 1811
	Geneviève		Laur. Audet	" 1813
	Philippe			
23	Joseph	(8)	Genev. Gosselin	S.L. 1780
	Pierre			
24	Louis	(9)	M. Angé Vien	S.M. 1773
	Marie		Ls. Lemelin	S.L. 1803
	Louis			
	Joseph			
	Le même		Thérése Vaillancourt	S.L. 1810
25	Louis	(11)	Cath Boissel	S.Chs. 1770
	M. Anne		Michel Guilmet	" 1820
	Nicolas			
	Charles			
26	Charles	(11)	Marie Nadeau	S.Chs. 1785
	Josette		Etn. Guillot	" 1807
	Magloire			
	Joseph			
	Alexandre			
	Charles			
27	Francois	(12)	M. Char. Bazin	S.Chs.1769
	Marguerite		Ign. Clément	" 1804
	Josette		Frs. Monmeny	" 1805
	Josette		2° Frs. Turgeon	" 1820
	Thérèse		J. B. Labrecque	S.G. 1803
	Thérèse		2° Jos. Labrecque	S.Chs. 1812
	Marie		Chs. Gesseron	Lévis 1815
	Charles			
	François			
28	Charles	(14)	Frse. Chabot	S.L. 1777
29	Jean Franç	(15)	M. Jos. Fortier	S.J. 1753
	M. Josette		Ant. Gosselin	S.L. 1780
	Jos. Marie			
	Jean			
30	Joseph	(16)	M. Lse. Pepin	S.J. 1770
	Marguerite		Ant. Gobeil	" 1797
	M. Louise		J. B. Turcot	" 1793
	M. Louise		2° Pierre Asselin	S.F. 1816
	Julie		Jean M. Boissonneau	S.J. 1803
	Cécile		Ant. Roussel	" 1806
	François			
	Paul			
	Joseph			
	Pierre			

POULIOT.

	Barthélemi			
31	Jean Frs.	(17)	Eliz. Campeau	S.L. 1763
	Louise		Amb. Roberge	„ 1793
	Cécile		Frs. Gagné	S.G. 1802
32	Pierre	(17)	Genev. Godbout S.L.	1774
	Antoine			
	François			
	Pierre			
33	Charles	(18)	Genev.Corriveau S.V.	1761
	Josette		Jos. Clusiau	S.Chs. 1792
	Josette		2° Michel Dubé	„ 1811
	Ambroise			
	François			
	Alexis			
24	Nicolas	(19)	M. Marg. Blouin Bert	1794
	Marguerite		Guill. Lemieux	S.G. 1813
	Marie		Chs. Paulet	„ 1818
	M. Anne		Frs. Carbonneau	„ 1821
	Rose		Alex. Lefebvre	„ 1826
	Elizabeth		Ed. Bêtil	„ 1830
	Nicolas			
	Le même		Isabelle Carbonneau	
				Bert. 1818
35	Jean	(19)	Mas. Dutile	S.G. 1795
	Marguerite		Jos. Carnac	S.G. 1820
	Archange		Alex. Roberge	Levis 1831
	Jean			
	Le même		Cath. Carbonneau	
				S.G. 1815
	Le même		Marg. Hélie	S.G. 1824
36	François	(19)	Genev. Gosselin	S.G. 1797
	Angéle		Louis Paulin	S.L. 1838
37	Pierre	(19)	Margt. Valiére	S.G. 1800
	Marguerite		Pierre Lemelin	S.G. 1823
	Marguerite		2° Dieudonné Carbonneau	
				S.G. 1827
	Rose		Frs. Lemelin	S.G. 1826
	Angélique		J. B. Naud	S.G. 1828
	Pierre			
	Le même		Margt. Hilrari	S.G. 1814
	Gervais			
38	Pierre	(20)	Margt. Gosselin	
				S.Chs. 1798
	Elizabeth		Ign. Duquet	S.Chs. 1817
39	Pierre	(21)	Genev. Thérien	S.G. 1796
	Geneviève		Frs. Turgeon	S.G. 1816
	Pierre			
	Edouard			
40	Philippe	(22)	Genev. Roberge	S.L. 1812
	Angéle		Jean Savard	S.G. 1832
	Angéle		2° Ign. Bouffart	S.G. 1837
	M. Esther		Jos. Maleux	S.G. 1833
	Luce		Simon Pouliot	S.G. 1844
	Caroline		Ed. Poliquin	S.Chs. 1850
	Jean			
	François			
	Philippe			
41	Pierre	(23)	Marie Roy	S.G. 1801
42	Louis	(24)	Marie Baillargeon	
				S.L. 1803
	Marie		Ls. Godbout	S.G. 1835
	Justine		Pierre Coulombe S.G.	1845
	Louis			
43	Joseph	(24)	Margt. Coulombe S.L.	1821
44	Nicholas	(25)	M.Angé Gaupy S.Chs.	1799
	Angélique		Michel Lebrun S.Chs.	1829
	Nicolas			
	Le même		Marie Tangué S.Chs.	1805
45	Charles	(25)	M. Barbe Tangué S.M.	1802
46	Alexandre	(26)	Archange Cameron	
				S.G. 1725
47	Charles	(26)	Archange Coté	S.G. 1826
	Alexandre			
	Le même		Marie Leroux S.Chs.	1842
48	Magloire	(26)	Rosalie Labrecque	
				S.Chs. 1834

POULIOT.

49	Joseph	(26)	Frs. Marcoux S.Chs.	1838
50	François	(27)	Frse. Roy	S.G. 1795
	Le même		M. Jos. Blanchet	
				Bert. 1823
51	Charles	(27)	Angé Coté	S.Chs. 1809
52	Jean	(29)	M. Mad. Létourneau	
				S.L. 1786
	Euphrosine		Jos. Deblois	S.J. 1815
	Euphrosine		2°PierreTremblay S.J.	1842
	Jean François			
	Joseph			
	Louis			
53	Jos. Marie	(29)	Genev. Godbout	S.L. 1788
	Angélique		Ls. Godbout	S.L. 1823
	Augélique		2° Pierre Fradet	S.G. 1830
	M. Angéle		Jos. Pouliot	S.L. 1828
	Thérése		Mich. Dumais	S.L. 1836
	Nicholas Jos.			
	Françoise			
	Louis			
	Jean			
	Guillaume			
	Nicolas			
54	Joseph		Marie Lacasse	
	Angéle		Pierre Royer	S.Chs. 1821
	Marguerite		Jos. Fortier	S.Chs. 1824
	Marie		Jacq. Gontier S. Chs.	1825
	Joseph			
55	Barthélemi	(30)	Louise Blais	Ste Foy
	M. Rosalie		Ls. Moreau Q.	
	M. Rosalie		2° Mag. Jos. RattéB.	1857
	Barthélemi			
56	Joseph	(30)	Marie Gobeil	S.I. 1800
	M. Cécile		Frs. Pepin	S.I. 1821
	Marie		Julien Gendreau	S.I. 1823
	Lse. Lucie		Pierre Toussaint	S.I. 1829
	Joseph			
	Pierre			
	Hippolyte			
	Jérémie			
57	Pierre	(30)	Marie Brousseau	S.L. 1803
	M. Marguerite		Michel Robitaille	S.J. 1827
	M. Charlotte		Frs. Cinqmars	S.J. 1836
	M. Geneviève		David Brissson	S.J. 1846
	Pierre			
	Charles			
	Paul			
	Jean			
58	François	(30)	M. Jos. Blouin	S.I. 1808
	Cécile		Frs. Royer	S.I. 1828
	Emélie		Ant. Moïs Pepin	
				S.I. 1832
	Emélie		2 Gabriel L. Pepin	
				S.I. 1840
	Véronique		Jack Pedeak	S.I. 1835
	Véronique		2° Chs. Wagner	S.I. 1847
	Seraphine		F. X. Pepin	S.I. 1839
	Anatolie		Barth. Pepin	S.I. 1842
	Eleanore		Ant. Gabriel	S.I. 1850
	Léandre			
	Pierre			
59	Paul	(30)	M. Anne Pepin	S.I. 1811
	M. Anne		Pierre Daniau	S.M. 1833
	Barthélémi			
60	Pierre	(32)	Thérèse Denis	S.L. 1801
	François			
	Ambroise			
	Simon			
61	François	(32)	Julie Damien	Q.
62	Antoine	(32)	M. Angé Gobeil	S.J. 1803
	Archange		Jos. Mercier	S.M. 1837
	M. Constance		Paulin Catellier	„ 1843
	Edouard			
	Antoine			
	Hyppolite			
	Pierre			

POULIOT.

63	Alexis	(33)	Margt. L. Bilodeau	S.Chs.	1790
	Angélique		Jos. Baudoin	S.H.	1814
	Le même		Marg. Bernier	S.Chs.	1808
64	François	(33)	Mad. Goupy	"	1791
	Le même		M. Anne Leclair	S.M.	1808
65	Ambroise	(33)	Genev. Gosselin	S.V.	1794
	M. Angèle		Ls. Dubé	S.Chs.	1819
	Angélique		Noël Cochon	"	1821
	Marie		J. B. Cochon	"	1825
	Ambroise				
66	Nicolas	(34)	Ls. Gaulet	S.G.	1824
	M. Louise		Jos. Vermet	S.Chs.	1848
	Eulalie		Pr.Theop.Provost	"	1850
67	Jean	(35)	Frse. Beaucher	S.G.	1824
	Jean				
68	Pierre	(37)	Margt. Labrecque	S.Chs.	1860
69	Gervais	(37)	Clarisse Goupy	S.M.	1852
70	Pierre	(39)	Brigitte Lebrun	S.G.	1821
71	Edouard	(39)	Angèle Gontier	S.Chs.	1826
	Geneviève		Norbert Labbé	S.M.	1853
72	Philippe		Seraphic Turgeon	B.	1842
73	Jean	(40)	Célina Moreau		
74	François	(40)	Vitaline Baudoin	S.L.	1858
75	Louis	(42)	Martine Racine	S.L.	1836
			Ste-Croix		
76	Nicolas	(47)	Marie Côté	B.	1824
	M. Rosalie		Jean Naud	S.Chs.	1850
	Le même		M. Ang. Couture	"	1836
77	Alexandre	(47)	Constance Gautron	S.V.	1854
78	Jean	(52)	Genev. Turcot	S.I.	1812
	M. Catherine		F. X. Bertrand	"	1847
	Geneviève		Chs. Pepin	"	1853
	Elizabeth		Tho. Dupuis	"	1854
	Jean-Baptiste				
	Joseph				
	Magloire				
	Gilbert				
	Paul				
79	Joseph	(52)	Ursule Curodeau	S.I.	1822
	Joseph				
	François				
80	Louis	(52)	Margt. Thivièrge	S.I.	1829
	Marie		Pierre Gendreau	"	1857
	Le même		Geneviève———	S.L.	1845
81	Jos. Nicolas	(53)	Margt. Lefebvre	S.Chs.	1825
82	Nicolas	(53)	Reine Lacroix	S.G.	1830
	Nicolas				
83	Guillaume	(53)	M. Mad. Morin	S.Chs.	1831
84	Jean	(53)	M. Anne Guénet	"	1833
85	François	(53)	Marie Létourneau	S.F.	1840
	M. Elmire		F. X. Audet	S.L.	1871
86	Louis	(53)	Sophie Paquet	S.I.	1844
87	Joseph	(54)	Salomé Leclaire	S.Chs.	1829
	M. Salomé		Jos. Leclaire	"	1852
	Joseph				
88	Barthélémi	(55)	Marine Fraser	B.	1835
89	Joseph		M. Anne Lemieux	S.H.	
	Nazaire				
90	Pierre	(56)	Eliz. Denis	S.I.	1826
	Elizabeth		M. Audet	"	1845
	Cécile		Chs. Blouin	"	1852
	Hortense		Célestin Pepin	"	1857
	Madeleine		Charles Blouin	"	1860
	Philomène		Jérémie Pouliot	"	1864
	Marie		Jérémie Audet	"	
	Pierre				
	François				
	Paul				
	Célestine				
	Joseph				
	Jérémie				
91	Joseph	(56)	M. Angèle Pouliot	S.L.	1828

POULIOT.

	Marie		Pierre Gaulin	S.I.	1856
92	Jérémie	(56)	M.SophieRoberge	S.F.	1834
	Jérémie				
93	Hyppolite	(56)	M.CécileGodbout	S.L.	1836
	Le même		Flavie Langlois	"	1844
	M. Sophie		Jérémie Pouliot	"	1874
	Pierre Nap.				
	Le même		Marcelline Turcot	S.I.	1857
94	Pierre	(57)	Josette Gobeil	"	1830
	Jean				
95	Paul	(57)	Rose Flavie Roberge	S.L.	1835
	M. Rose		Chs. Bégin	"	1860
	Adèle		Alexis Bouffart	"	1864
	M. Lumina		Ign. Roberge	"	1865
	Henriette		Guill. Bolduc	"	1869
	Paul				
	Thomas				
	Delphin				
96	Charles	(57)	Margt. Turcot	S.I.	1836
	Marguerite		Célestin Noël	S.L.	1862
	Rose de Lima		Frs. Leclaire	"	1862
	Adeline				
97	Jean	(57)	Luce Turcot	S. J.	1836
98	Pierre	(58)	Rosalie Jahan	S.I.	1835
	Philoméne		Paul Gosselin	"	1859
	Marie		F. X. Giguère	"	1894
	Barthélémi				
	François				
	Frs. Xavier				
99	Léandre	(58)	Marie Dion	S.I.	1851
100	Barthélemi	(59)	Eugènie Grenier		
101	François	(60)	Julie Audet	S.I.	1832
	Marie		Pierre Hébert	S. L.	1865
	M. Natalie		Rémi Laroche	"	1867
	M. Délima		Zöel Desroches	"	1873
	Frs. Xavier				
	Damase				
	Pierre				
	Fs. Achilles				
102	Ambroise	(60)	Genev. Plante	S. L.	1840
	M. Mélanie		Pierre Denis	"	1876
	Pierre Luc				
	Thomas				
	Georges				
103	Simon	(60)	Luce Pouliot	S. L.	1844
	Artémise		Jos. Audet	"	1872
104	Antoine	(62)	Soulange Cotin	S. M.	1835
105	Edouard	(62)	Zoé Bacquet	"	1840
	M. Philoméne		Jos. Hélie	"	1864
106	Hyppolite	(62)	Scolastique Nadeau	B	1847
107	Pierre	(62)	Adé. Tangué	S. V.	1848
108	Ambroise	(65)	M. Clothilde Fortier	S. F. S.	1817
109	Jean	(67)	Marie Roy	S. M.	1855
110	Jean Bte.	(78)	Marie Pepin	S. Frs.	1837
	M. Virginie		Léon Paquet	S.I.	1857
111	Joseph	(77)	Marcelline Savoie	S.F.	1841
	Philoméne		F. X. Blouin	S.I.	1864
	M. Demérise		Paul Bussiére	"	1865
	Joseph				
112	Gilbert	(78)	Scolastique Godbout	S. L.	1846
	Joseph				
113	Paul	(78)	M. Fse Picard	S.I.	1849
114	Magloire	(78)	Cecile Pepin	"	1849
115	Joseph	(78)	Désanges Picard	"	1854
116	François	(79)	Cécile Paquet	"	1862
117	Nicolas	(82)	Margt. Provost	S.Chs.	1861
118	Joseph	(87)	Julie Cochon	S. Chs.	1854
119	Nazaire	(89)	Eliz. Bétil	S. M.	1865
120	Pierre	(90)	Théotiste Ruel	S. L.	1849
	M. Théotiste		Jacques Quemeneur	S. L.	1869
	M. Philomène		Saml. Mainguy	"	1872

POULIOT.

121	Paul	(80) M. Virginie Langlais	
			S. L. 1867
	Le même	Adé Labrecque	" 1876
122	François	(90) Scolastique Pedeak	
			S.I. 1855
123	Célestin	(90) Julie Hebert	" 1860
124	Joseph	(90) Marie Pepin	" 1865
125	Jérémie	(90) M. Sophie Pouliot	S.L. 1874
126	Jérémie	(92) Philoméne, Pouliot	S.I. 1864
127	Pierre Napo-	(93) Henriette Plante	C.R.
	léon		
128	Jean	(94) Séraphine Paquet	S.I. 1852
129	Paul	(95) Flore Jobin, Lévis	
130	Thomas	(95) Corinne Peltier Lévis	
131	Delphin	(95) Eléonore Gosselin	S.I. 1864
132	Adelme	96) Philoméne Noël	S.L. 1863
133	François	(98) Philoméne Giguére	
			S. F. 1866
134	Frs. Xavier	(98) Adè Giguére	" 1866
135	Barthélémi	(98) M. Ant. Labrecque	
			S. L. 1872
136	François	(101) Soulange Denis	" 1858
137	Pierre	101) Luce Ferland	S. I. 1859
138	Damase	(101) Amélie Audet	S. L. 1864
139	Ls. Achilles	(101) Caroline Leclaire	" 1864
	Le même	Emélie Leclaire	" 1881
140	Thomas	(102)	
141	Pierre Luc	(102) M. Joséphine Poulin	
			S. P. 1871
142	Georges	(102) Adéle Betourné	
			Montreal 1879
143	Joseph	(111) Sophronie Turcot	S.I. 1865
144	Joseph	(112) Almanda Drolet	S.L. 1875

PRÉMONT

1	Jean	(1) Marie Aubert	C.R. 1663
	Anne	Nic. Thivierge	S. F. 1701
	Elisabeth	Ls. Gautier	" 1706
	Jean		
2	Jean	(1) Marie Gerbert	S. F. 1703
	Jean Bte		
	Le même	Thérése Bélanger,	
			Beauport 1709
	Le même	Anne Bolduc Q.	1716
3	Jean Bte	(2) Genev. Morisset	S.F. 1751
	Geneviève	Jérome Drouin	S.F. 1771
	Marie	Joseph Drouin	" 1777
	Jean Bte.		
4	Jean Bte.	(3) Angé Beaucher	" 1756
	Angélique	Aug. Perrot	" 1778
	Geneviève	Gab. Côté	" 1798
	Charles Amable		
	Pierre		
	Jacques		
	Le même	Josette Lacroix	S.F. 1804
5	Chs. Amable	(4) Fse. Guérard	" 1794
	Geneviève	Jos. Beaucher	" 1826
	Scolastique	Ign. Létourneau	" 1832
	Pierre Magl.		
	Jean Bte.		
6	Jacques	(4) Thérése Foucher	S.F. 1794
	Josette	Germ. Pichet	S.L. 1828
	Françoise	Pierre Bouffart	S.P. 1831
7	Pierre	(4) Brigitte Létourneau	
			S.F. 1809
	Pierre		
	Louis		
8	Jean Bte.	(5) M. Jos. Asselin	S.F. 1830
	Justine	Jos. Létourneau	" 1852
	Bruno		
	Joseph		
9	Pr. Magloire	(5) Marie Gagnon	" 1846
10	Pierre	(7) M. Constance Canac	
			S. F. 1835
	Philomène	Siméon Turcot	" 1859

PRÉMONT.

	Pr. Cyrille		
11	Louis	(7) Sophie Poulin	" 1840
	Le même	M. Hombeline Drouin	
			S.F. 1846
12	Bruno	(8) Marie Blouin	S.F. 1862
13	Joseph	(8) Virginie Pepin	S.I. 1863
14	Pr. Cyrille	(10) Marie Vaillancourt	
			S.D. 1862

PROULX.

1	Jean	(1) Josette Fournier	Q. 1673
	Louise	Pierre Gagné	S.Tho. 1700
	M. Anne	Jacq. Thibaut	" 1705
	M. Barbe	Ls. Isabel	" 1704
	Angélique	Jean Frs. Thibault	" 1705
	Denis		
	Thomas		
	Jean Bte.		
	Louis		
	Pierre		
2	Denis	(1) Anne Gagné	
			Cap S. Ign. 1699
3	Jean Bte.	(1) Louise Rousseau	
			S. Tho. 1701
	Veronique	Ant. Dandurand	" 1738
	Jean Bte.		
	Joseph		
4	Pierre	(1) Agathe Picard	S.Tho. 1711
	M. Madeleine	Marin Métayer	" 1749
	François		
	Pierre		
5	Thomas	(1) Cath. Caron	S.Tho. 1714
	M. Thérèse	Germ. Gaumont	" 1761
	François		
6	Louis	(1) Marie Dufresne	S.L. 1730
	Marie	Clément Aimé	S.Tho. 1756
	Jean Bte.		
7	Jean Bte.	(3) Marie Claire Joly	
			Bert. 1727
	Elizabeth	Chs. Claude Côté	
			S.Tho. 1754
	Nicolas		
	François		
8	Joseph	(3) Marthe Gagné	S.Tho. 1730
	Jean Bte.		
	Augustin		
9	Pierre	(4) Marie Gagné	Cap S.Ig. 1736
	Marie	Ant. Dembonville	
			Bert. 1761
	Madeleine	Ign. Dessaint	S.Tho. 1769
10	François	(4) M. Char. Grondin	
			S.Tho. 1744
	M. Ursule	Pierre Jolin	S.P.S. 1774
	François		
11	Joseph	Theodora Bouchard	
	Le même	Angé Laberge	S.Tho. 1736
	M. Madeleine	J. B. Morin	S.P.S. 1778
	Louis		
12	Augustin	Fse. Fortin	
	M. Josette	Pierre Fournier	S.Tho. 1769
	M. Françoise	Frs. Isaac Gendron	" 1775
	Marguerite	Frs. Lemieux	" 1779
	Louis		
	Augustin		
13	Louis	(5) M. Rose Quemeneur	
			S.F.S. 1761
14	François	(5) Modeste Poirier	
			S.Tho. 1764
	Thomas		
	Joseph		
15	Jean Bte.	(6) M. Ursule Buteau	
			Bert. 1763
	M. Josette	Michel Charron	S.Tho.1791
	M. Genev.	Ls. Fournier	" 1797

PROULX.

Reine		Thos. Fournier S.Tho.	1804
Jean Bte.			
16 François	(7)	M. Cath. Létourneau	
		S.Tho.	1764
M. Catherine		Chs. Duchesneau	
		S.P.S.	1788
17 Nicolas	(7)	Lse. Therrien S.F.S.	1774
18 Jean Bte.	(8)	Marie Oresteille	
		S.Tho.	1760
Marie		Alexis Blais S.Tho.	1786
François			
Joseph			
Augustin			
Le même		Marie Gamache ,,	1775
André			
19 Augustin	(8)	Eliz. Oresteille ,,	1761
M. Modeste		J. B. Gendreau ,,	1802
Etienne			
20 François	(10)	Josette Michaud	
		S. Tho.	1767
M. Josette		Pierre Proulx ,,	1795
Charles			
21 Louis	(11)	M. Lse. Denaut ,,	1771
Augustin			
22 Augustin	(12)	Fse. Denaut ,,	1770
Pierre			
23 Louis	(12)	Thérèse Buteau S.F.S.	1805
24 Thomas	(14)	Marg. Rouleau ,,	1807
25 Joseph	(14)	M. Rose Boulet S.Tho.	1808
Joseph			
26 Jean Bte.	(15)	Scolastique Fournier	
		S. Tho.	1799
Prudent			
27 Joseph	(18)	M. Anne Robin ,,	1787
M. Rosalie		Felix Dandurand	
		S.F.S.	1825
Jean Bte.			
28 Augustin	(18)	Marg. Langlois S.Tho.	1796
M. Henriette		F. X. Dessaint S.F.S.	1841
Marguerite		Laurent Gendron ,,	1844
Olympiade		Ls. Picard S.P.S.	1836
29 François	(18)	Margt. L. Robin ,,	1807
Césaire Frédéric			
30 André	(18)	M. Genev. Picard ,,	1804
Le même		Franç. Blais Bert.	1824
31 Etienne	(19)	M. Genev. Denaut	
		S. Tho.	1794
Etienne			
32 Charles	(20)	Margt. L. Cottière	
		S. Tho.	1799
Henriette		Etn. Dion Bert.	1827
Sophie		Ls. Beaucher ,,	1828
Emélie		Jos. Nadeau S.F.S.	1827
33 Augustin	(21)	Monique Coté S.P.S.	1798
34 Pierre	(22)	M. Jos. Proulx S.Tho.	1795
Marcel			
35 Joseph	(25)	Bibiane Fournier	
		S. Chs.	1846
36 Prudent	(26)	Euphrosine Couture	
		S.V.	1827
7 Jean Bte.	(27)	Soulange Simoneau	
		S.P.S.	1833
38 Césaire Fred-	(29)	Henriette Morin ,,	1841
eric			
39 Etienne	(31)	Thérèse Coté ,,	1823
40 Marcel	(34)	Luce Coté S. Tho.	1825
Jos. Désiré			
41 Joseph Dé-	(40)	Rose de Lina Picard	
siré		S.I.	1861

PROVOST.

1			
2			
3 Charles		(2) M. Char. Ricasse (?)	
Charles			

PROVOST.

4 Charles	(3)	Marie Coté S. Chs.	1764
Josette		Basile Chabot	1787
Charles			
Jean Bte.			
Louis			
Le même		Angé Monneny	
		S. Chs.	1787
5 André		Louise Coté S.P.	1769
Reine		Ign. Howard S.F.	1796
Reine		2° Pr. Foucher ,,	1801
Reine		3° Etn. Duprat ,,	1816
6 Charles	(4)	Lse. Gosselin S. Chs.	1792
Josette		Frs. Poiré ,,	1822
Angèle Olive		Jacq. Poliquin ,,	1826
Euphrosine		Marcel Ruel ,,	1832
Marie		Frs. Turgeon ,,	1812
Marie		2° Abr. Nadeau B.	1845
Stanislas			
Joseph			
Charles			
Marcel			
Delphin			
Prudent			
7 Jean Bte.		Angé Roberge S.H.	1797
Marie		Jos. Tardif ,,	1816
8 Louis	(4)	Margt.L.Beaucher B.	1805
Julie		Hubert Blanchet	
		S. Chs.	1826
Marguerite		Chs. Petitclerc ,,	1832
Olive		Ed. Hospice Ruel	
		S. Chs.	1841
Théophile			
Joachim			
Magloire			
Charles			
Joseph			
Joachim			
Louis			
9 Marcel	(6)	Marie Gosselin S.Chs.	1828
Sophie		Rigobert Guenet ,,	1864
Charles			
10 Charles	(6)	Marg. Guay B.	1827
Philomène		Ls. Lefebvre S. Chs.	1856
Isidore			
11 Stanislas	(6)	Sophie Ruel ,,	1831
12 Prudent	(6)	M. Mad. Pepin ,,	1840
13 Delphin	(6)	Charlotte Labrecque	
		B.	1841
14 Jos. Damase	(6)	Flavie Coté S. Chs.	1847
15 Charles	(7)	Florence Peltier ,,	1833
16 Magloire	(7)	Margt L. Fournier	
		S. Chs.	1837
Marguerite		Mich. Pouliot ,,	1861
17 Joseph	(7)	M. Perpétue Ruel	
		S. Chs.	1837
Le même		M. Angé Morin S.M.	1842
18 Louis	(7)	Josette Latouche	
		S. Roch.	1837
19 Joachim	(7)	M. Lse. Naud S. Chs.	1841
20 Théophile	(7)	Eulalie Pouliot ,,	1850
21 Charles	(8)	Angèle Bisson ,,	1864
22 Isidore	(9)	Marg. L. Gosselin	
		S. Chs.	1852

PRUNEAU.

1 Jean		Susanne Emond S.M.	1691
Catherine		André Patry Bert.	1711
,,		2° Jos. Forgues S.M.	1744
Madeleine		J. B. Lacasse Detroit	1731
,,		Vital Caron ,,	1735
René			
Jean			
2 René		(1) Susanne Dumart S.M.	1716
Le même		Anne Leroux Chs.brg.	1721
René			

PRUNEAU.

3	Jean	(1)	Genev. Boutin (Boulet)
	Geneviève		Ign. Gagnon Bert. 1765
	Pierre		
	Louis		
	Joseph		
4	René	(2)	Thérèse Forgues S.M. 1745
5	Louis	(3)	M. Anne Talbot, Bert. 1748
	M. Geneviève		J. B. Guilmet „ 1768
	M. Reine		Clément Gagnon „ 1783
	Louis		
	Le même		M. Génév. Picard
			S.P.S. 1762
	M. Roger		Ls. Alra Métivier
			Bert. 1789
	Marie		Gabl. Gosselin S.Chs. 1786
6	Joseph	(3)	M. Jos. Bouchard
			Bert. 1752
	Reine		Aug. Guilmet „ 1781
	Marie Josette		Jos. Fradet S.M. 1789
	Joseph		
7	Pierre		M. Claire Bouchard
			S.V. 1754
	M. Claire		Frs. Guilmet S.Tho. 1795
	Jean Bte.		
	Joseph		
8	Louis	(5)	Bibiane Poliquin
			S.Chs. 1783
	Charles		
	Louis		
9	Joseph	(6)	M. Roger Fournier
			S.Tho. 1789
	Marie		J. B. Picard Bert. 1809
	Archange		J. B. Bouffard „ 1826
	Charles		
	Joseph		
10	Jean Bte.	(7)	Marie Leblond S.M. 1775
	Sophie		Frs. Paquet S. I ho. 1824
11	Joseph	(7)	M. Anne Leblond
			S.Tho. 1799
12	Louis	(8)	Margt. Martin S.H. 1810
14	Joseph	(9)	Eliz. Thibault S.P.S. 1820
	Joseph		
13	Charles	(8)	M. Louise Couture
			S.H. 1810
15	Charles	(9)	M. Soulanges Leblond
			S.Tho. 1826
	Marie		Jacq. Brochu S.Chs. 1854
16	Pierre		Marie Duchesne
	Marguerite		
	Louis		
17	Jean Bte.		M. Vict. Bélanger
			S. Roch
	Joseph		
18	Joseph	(14)	Margt. Richard S.V. 1852
19	Louis	(16)	Margt. Mercier S.G. 1828
20	Magloire	(16)	Eulalie Cothière,
			Bert. 1852
21	Joseph	(17)	Léocadie Lefebvre
			S.Chs. 1854

QUEMENEUR—LAFLAMME.

1	François		Marie Chamberland
			S.Frs. 1700
	Marie		Chs. Bissonnette „ 1727
	Thérèse		Jacq. Morin „ 1735
	M. Geneviève		Ls. Giasson S.F.S. 1745
	François		
	Charles		
	Louis		
	Jean Bte.		
	Antoine		
	Joseph		
2	François	(1)	Marg. Brochu S.V. 1739
	Le même		M. Jos. Frégeot
			S.F.S. 1745

QUEMENEUR—LAFLAMME.

3	Joseph		Angé Pepin
	Michel		
	Joseph		
	Jean Bte.		
4	Jean Bte.	(1)	M. Louise Poulin
	M. Louise		Pr. Noël Frégeot
			S.F.S. 1744
	Marguerite		Michel Gagnon „ 1750
	M. Rose		Louis Proulx „ 1761
	M. Françoise		Jos. Gravel „ 1774
	M. Anne		Ls. Ouellet Bert. 1748
	Jean Bte.		
	Jacques		
	Joseph		
	Le même		M. Frs. Métivier
			S.P.S. 1750
	Madeleine		Ant. Marseau S.F.S. 1775
5	Antoine	(1)	M. Angé Clomart
	Pierre		
	Noël		
6	Louis	(1)	M. Cath. Rouleau
			S.F.S. 1746
	M. Geneviève		Jos. Martineau „ 1771
	Louis		
7	Charles	(1)	Brigitte Gagné
	Le même		M. Jos. Vermet, Bert. 1747
	M. Josette		Ls. Pinet S.H. 1777
	Joseph		
	Marie		
	Pierre		
	Noël		
	Jean Bte.		
	Charles		
8	Joseph	(3)	M. Ls. Thibault
			S.P.S. 1760
9	Michel	(3)	M. Claire Blancher
			S.P.S. 1762
	M. Agathe		Ant. Jacq. Fortier
			S.F.S. 1789
	Pierre		
	Noël		
	François		
10	Jean Baptiste	(3)	Angé Bouchard S.V. 1769
	Josette		Jacq. Christophe S.G. 1807
	Prisque		
	Antoine		
	Jean Baptiste		
11	Jean Baptiste	(4)	M.Mad.Gagnon S.F.S.1753
	Rose		Clem. Langlois „ 1781
	Victoire		Ls. Blais „ 1788
	Angélique		Basile Thibaut „ 1797
	Madeleine		Alexr. Paquet „ 1802
	Judith		Mich. Terrien S.G. 1809
	M. Jeanne		Jean Hoopman S.V. 1814
	Pierre		
	Joseph		
	Antoine		
	Jean Baptiste		
12	Joseph	(4)	M. Lse. Huret S.F.S. 1761
	M. Louise		Chs. Morin „ 1784
	M. Marguerite		Clement Pepin „ 1785
	Michel		
	Pierre		
	Joseph		
13	Jacques	(4)	M. Mad. Boulet
			S.F.S. 1764
	Madeleine		Ls. Allaire „ 1805
	Joseph Jacq.		
	Pierre Noël	(5)	M.Marg Tangué S.V. 1762
15	Louis	(6)	M. Frse. Mercier
			S.F.S. 1777
	Marie		Michel Métivier „ 1802
	M. Marguerite		Thos. Talbot „ 1802
	Reine		Jos. Crepeau „ 1809
	Elisabeth		Ls. Théberge „ 1811
	M. Josette		Ang. Rousseau „ 1812

QUEMENEUR—LAFLAMME.

M. Thècle		Jos. Quemeneur	S.F.S	1817
M. Angèle		Ls. Alaire	"	1819
M. Archange		Aug. Tangué	"	1821
Olive		Hubert Morin	"	1828
Romain				
Jean Baptiste				
Thomas				
Louis				
16 Charles	(7)	Marie Hullé	S.H.	1778
Marie		Frs. Lemelin	"	1800
Ursule		Sévère Bussierès	"	1808
Le même		Mad. Lainé	"	1794
M. Madeleine		Basile Boutin	"	1817
17 Joseph Marie	(7)	M. Thérèse Baudoin		
			Bert	1782
Madeleine		Jean Patry	S.H.	1806
Madeleine		2° Pierre Turcot	"	1816
Catherine		Basile Roy	"	1812
Euphrosine		Jos. Roy	"	1812
Marie		Pr. Noël Morin	"	1800
M. Louise		Vital Talbot	"	1819
Louis				
18 Jean Baptiste	(7)	M. Anne Mercier	Bert	1791
M. Anne		Pr. Bélanger	S.H.	1820
Antoine				
Jean				
19 Pierre Noël	(7)	M. Lse. Coté	S.H.	1795
20 Pierre Noël	(9)	Margt. Denaut S.Tho.		1794
Joseph				
François				
Etienne				
Le même		Lse. Corriveau	Bert.	1833
21 Francois	(9)	M. Jos. Thibault	S.F.S.	1800
Sophie		Lse. Martineau	"	1828
François				
22 Jean Baptiste	(10)	Marie Bolduc	S.V.	1797
Marie		Jos. Catellier	"	1824
David				
Louis				
Joseph				
François				
Jean Baptiste				
23 Prisque	(10)	Cath. Fournier	S.Chs.	1805
24 Antoine	(10)	M. Mad. Lainé	S.V.	1821
M. Vitaline		Olivier Bonafé	"	1857
Antoine				
25 Pierre	(11)	Margt Louineau	S.F.S.	1787
25 Joseph	(11)	Genev. Fauchon	"	1792
Geneviève		Michel Fortier	S.M.	1824
Jean Baptiste				
Joseph				
Le même		M. Jos. Jacques	S.F.S.	1798
27 Jean Baptiste		Genev. Racine	S.G.	1797
Marie		Ls. Noël	"	1822
Madeleine		Ign. Ratté	"	1829
28 Antoine	(11)	Marie Paquet	"	1800
Marie		Ant. Couture	"	1829
Honoré				
Jacques				
Joseph				
Paschal				
Louis				
29 Joseph	(12)	Cath. Blais	S.F.S.	1787
Joseph				
Le même		Thérèse Proulx	S.Tho	1793
Flavie		Ls. Simart	S.F.S.	1828
Simon				
30 Michel	(12)	Genev McIntyre		
			S.F.S.	1791
M. Geneviève		Jos. Blais	"	1814
M. Reine		Alexis Fournier	"	1820
Michel				
Ignace				
Jean Baptiste				
31 Pierre	(12)	M. Rose Picard	S.P.S.	1800
Rosalie		J. B. Baudoin	"	1822

QUEMENEUR—LAFLAMME.

M. Louise		Pierre Catellier	S.P.S.	1825
Jacq. Pierre				
32 Jacques	(13)	M. Genev. Lamare		
			S.F.S.	1791
33 Joseph	(13)	M. Jos. Fauchon	"	1792
Jean				
34 Pierre		Margt. Samson		
Le même		Mad. Plante	S G.	1795
Marie		Frs. Poirier	"	1819
Françoise		Lse. Charert	"	1825
Pierre				
Le même		Marie Poirier	"	1820
35 Louis		M. Frse Métivier (?)		
Michel				
36 Louis	(15)	Marie Chartier	S.F.S.	1810
Marguerite		André Baudoin	"	1833
Luce		Narcisse Blais	"	1843
Thomas				
Le même		Marie Lemieux	Bert.	1835
37 Jean Baptiste	(15)	Hélène Leclair	S.G.	1810
Le même		Rose Adam	"	1815
38 Thomas	(15)	Marie Labrecque	S.G.	1822
Emérence		Ls. Turgeon	B.	1857
Le même		M. Margt. Théberge		
			S.F.S	1829
39 Romain	(15)	Charlotte Marcoux	"	1826
40 Louis	(17)	Josette Morin	S.H.	1812
41 Antoine	(18)	Frse. Denis	Bert.	1819
42 Jean	(18)	Vict. Brochu	"	1824
Olive		Marie Godbout	S.L.	1853
43 François	(20)	M. Lse. Fiset	S.Tho.	1824
44 Etienne	(20)	Julienne Proulx	"	1826
45 Joseph	(20)	M. Anne Royer	S.Chs.	1830
46 François	(21)	M. Saly. Blais	S.P.S.	1839
Hilaire				
47 François	(22)	M. Angé Rouillard		
			S.M.	1820
M. Des Anges		Pierre Lessart	"	1844
Mélanie		Michel Mercier	"	1850
Domitelle		Benj. Lessart	"	1854
Damase				
François				
48 Jean Baptiste	(22)	M. Angèle Corriveau		
			S.M.	1839
49 Joseph	(22)	M. Jos. Maurice	S.V.	1841
50 Louis	(22)	Marie Lacroix	S.M.	1842
51 David	(22)	Marcel Guilmet	Bert.	1845
52 Charles		Angé Drouin		
53 François		Luce Denis		
Michel				
54 Antoine		Archange Richard		
55 Joseph	(26)	M. Louise Plante	"	1816
56 Jean Baptiste	(26)	Margt. Bolduc	S.M.	1840
57 Louis	(28)	Rosalie Couture	S.G.	1827
58 Paschal	(28)	Clémentine Boutin	"	1829
59 Joseph	(28)	Marie Campagna	"	1830
60 Joseph	(29)	M. Thècle Quemeneur		
			S.F.S.	1817
61 Simon	(29)	M. Anne Rousseau	S G	1822
62 Jacques	(28)	Marie Bonneau	S.L.	1842
Rose		Nap. Royer	"	1866
Philomène				
Jacques				
Le même		Archange Tessier	"	1858
63 Honoré	(28)	Sophie Tangué	"	1847
64 Michel	(30)	Agathe Roberge	S.G.	1823
65 Ignace	(30)	Louise Baudoin	Bert.	1837
66 Jean Baptiste	(30)	Angèle Fournier		
			S.F.S.	1837
67 Pierre	(31)	Marie Boissel	S.M.	1833
68 Jacques	(31)	Scolastique Carrier		
			Lévis	1836
69 Jean	(33)	Cécile Dupil	S.P.	1818
Marcelline		Ls. Roberge	"	1866

QUEMENEUR—LAFLAMME.

François				
Georges				
70 Pierre	(34)	Angé Labrecque	S.G.	1819
71 Michel	(35)	M. Marg. Arbour	S.V.	1821
Archange		Ls. Lemieux	„	1843
Soulanges		Frs. Fradet	„	1847
Vitaline		Jos. Blanchet	„	1851
72 Thomas	(36)	Anastasie Beaudoin	S.F.S.	1840
73 Hilaire	(46)	M. Egyptienne Bélanger	S.V.	1869
74 Germain		Emérence Morin		
Le même		Cécile Nadeau	S.Chs.	1857
75 Damase	(47)	Julie Hélie	S.M.	1856
76 François	(47)	Marie Voisin	„	1857
77 Jean	(52)	Olive Roy	S.V.	1843
78 Michel	(53)	Phil. Blouin	S.F.	1863
79 Jacques	(62)	M. Théotiste Pouliot	S.L.	1869
80 François	(69)	Henriette Maranda	S.P.	1844
81 Georges	(69)	Emélie Fournier	„	1845

QUÉRET—LATULIPPE.

1 Michel		Frse. Davenne		
M. Françoise		J. B. Molleur	B.	1721
Josette		Jos. Balan	Bert.	1756
Antoine				
Joseph				
Simon				
Pierre				
Michel				
Charles				
2 Joseph	(10)	Angé Gautron	B.	1726
Marie		J. Bte. Bacquet	S.M.	1750
Angélique		Jos. Lefebvre	„	1752
Angélique		2° Etn. Labreque	„	1764
M. Anne		Jacq. Rochon	„	1756
Marguerite		And. Baquet	„	1758
Jean Baptiste				
Joseph				
Le même		M. Anne Lacroix	S.M.	1762
Marie Anne		Ls. Labreque	„	1762
Le même		M. Eliz. Plante	„	1754
Marguerite		Jos. Ratté	„	1791
M. Thérèse		Michel Terrien	„	1794
Le même		M. Angé Nadeau	„	1773
3 Simon	(3)	M. Claire Roy	S.V.	1728
M. Claire		Jean Bissonnette	S.M.	1748
M. Angélique		Frs. Greffart		1757
M. Gertrude		M. Rémillard	S.V.	1760
M. Gertrude		2° René Daniau	„	1800
Le même		M. Bissonnette	S.M.	1750
Simon				
4 Charles	(1)	M. Suzanne Plante	S. M,	1730
M. Angélique		Ls. Bissonnette	„	1756
M. Angélique		2° Michl. Patry	„	1759
M. Madeleine		J. B. Ratté	S.M.	1758
M. Madeleine		2° Ls. Petticlerc	S.G.	1788
M. Josette		Jérome Hélie	S.M.	1767
M. Josette		2° Pr. Labreque	S.G.	1786
Geneviève		Chs. Roy	S.M.	1775
Le même		Hélène Bacquet	„	1750
M. Hélène		Jos. Denis	„	1771
„		2° Mich. Letellier	„	1808
Agathe		Andrè Roy	„	1774
5 Pierre	(1)	M. Anne Lefebvre	„	1776
Charlotte		Amb. Fortier	„	1777
„		2° Ant. Fortier	„	1808
Marie Anne		Ls. Isabel	„	1782
Josette		René Bouchard	S.G.	1795
Michel				
Le même		Genv. Coulombe	Bert.	1769

QUÉRET—LATULIPPE.

M. Geneviève		Jean Bern. Marseau	S.V.	1792
Marthe		Michel Richard	„	1793
6 Antoine	(1)	Marie Paquet	S.M.	1742
		V.de Thom. Plante		
7 Michel	(1)	M.Jos.Monmeny	S.M.	1745
M. Frse		Pierre Giguère	„	1773
M. Louise		Ant. Fortier	„	1775
Marie Louise		2° Jos. Carbonneau	S.V.	1795
M. Josette		Jos. Gagnon	S.M.	1793
Joseph				
François				
Pierre				
8 Joseph	(1)	Margt. Bissonnette	S.M.	1754
Thérèse		Clement Patry	„	1770
Geneviève		J. Bte. Boissel	S.M.	1774
Geneviève		2° Aug.Bazin	S Chs.	1778
Geneviève		3° Ign. Patry	„	1779
Jean Baptiste				
9 Joseph	(2)	M.Anne Gosselin	S.M.	1763
Marie Anne		Chs. Furois	„	1789
Marie Anne		2° Jos. Gourgue	„	1805
Rosalie		J.Bte.Couture	S.Chs.	1803
Joseph				
10 Jean Baptiste	(2)	Cath. Lefebvre	S.M.	1764
Geneviève		Frs. Poirier	S.G.	1798
Joseph				
Nicolas				
Jean Baptiste				
11 Jean		M. Charl. Genesse	Jeune Lorette	
Jacques				
12 Simon	(3)	M.Jos.Remillard	S.V.	1772
13 Michel	(5)	Frse. Cochon	S.V.	1781
M. Françoise		J. Bte. Lemelin	S.M.	1798
Marie Anne		M. Mathieu	„	1803
Michel				
14 Joseph	(7)	Judith Remillard	S.V.	1779
Angélique		Frs. Blouin	„	1806
Joseph				
Michel				
Pierre				
Jean				
Ignace				
15 Pierre	(7)	Marg. Gautron	S.M.	1790
Victoire		Jean Lefebvre	„	1816
Louise		Etn. Langlais	„	1817
Marie		Ang. Denis	„	1821
Joseph				
Pierre				
16 François	(7)	M.Lse.Gagnon	S.F.S.	1792
17 Etienne		M. Jos. Remillard	Kamouraska	
M. Josette		Ant. Richard	S.V.	1788
18 Jean Baptiste	(8)	M. Thécle Roy	S.M.	1791
Marie		Jos. Fradet	S.G.	1814
Marie		2° Claud Audet	„	1826
Charlotte		Ant. Guillot	„	1821
19 Joseph	(9)	M. Ther. Furois	S.M.	1792
20 Jean Baptiste	(10)	Marg. Boucher	Bert.	1793
22 Joseph	(10)	Marg. Dion	S.G.	1803
21 Nicolas	(10)	M. Cath. Bilodeau	„	1799
23 Jacques	(11)	M. Lse. Octeau,	Lévis	1796
Charlotte		M. Marcoux	S.G.	1826
Madeleine		Js. Guilmet	„	1822
Jean Baptiste				
Jacques				
Le même		Marie Goupy	S. H.	1817
24 Pierre		Ange Coté	S.V.	1812
Angélique		F. X. Bolduc	S.M.	1842
Christine		Etn. Lainé	„	1848
Emelie		Chs. Lainé	„	1849
Constance		J. B. Bissonnette	„	1857
André				

QUÉRET-LATULIPPE.

Charles		
25 Gabriel	Marie Bourbeau	
	St. Anselme	
Marie	Chs. Corriveau S.G.	1828
Marguerite	Ant. Gosselin S.Chs.	1838
Pierre		
Le même	M. Lse. Pepin S.M.	1821
26 Joseph	(14) M. Anne Lavoie S.V.	1803
27 Jean	(14) Louise Brochu S.G.	1810
Vital		
Edouard		
28 Michel	(14) Genev. Boutin S.V.	1812
Elizabeth	Ls. Bolduc „	1849
Pierre		
Antoine		
Michel		
29 Pierre	(14) Frse. Bacquet „	1819
Firmin		
Frs. X.		
David		
30 Ignace	(14) Reine Corriveau S.G.	1824
31 Pierre	(15) M. Anne Lefebvre S.M.	1867
Frederic		
32 Joseph	(15) Marg. Gagnon „	1820
M. Margt	Aug. Lacroix, S.M.	1847
Frédéric		
Etienne		
33 Jacques	(23) Marie Coté S.G.	1821
34 Jean Baptiste	(23) M. Lse. Guay Lévis	1833
25 Charles	(24) Rosalie Ratté S.M.	1833
Rosalie	Lau. Gagnon S.Chs.	1852
„	2° Tho. Fournier „	1863
Henriette	F. X. Bilodeau „	1855
M. Marguerite	Geo. Pelchat „	1859
36 André	(24) Eliz. Letellier S.V.	1866
37 Pierre	(25) Emelie Couture S.Chs.	1835
38 Edouard	(27) Marg. Mercier S.V.	1833
39 Vital	(27) Adé Gourgue „	1842
40 Antoine	(28) Marie Bilodeau „	1860
Elisabeth	Ant. Langlais „	1862
Le même	Marie Roy „	1864
41 Michel	(28) Lucie Brousseau „	1847
42 Pierre	(28) Lucie Brochu „	1852
43 Frs. Xavier	(29) Flavie Gagnon S.M.	1854
44 David	(29) Sara Ouimet B.	1849
45 Firmin	(29) M. A. Martineau S.M.	1859
46 Frédéric	(31) Dorothée Gagnon „	1859
47 Frédéric	(32) Eliz. Noreau S.Roch	1845
48 Etienne	(32) M. Natalie Turgeon	
	S.M.	1846
Le même	Luce Goupy „	1851
49 Joseph	Zoé Césarie Bolduc	
Le même	Marie Langlais S.V.	1870

QUIROUET.

1 Pierre	Marie Flauquet (Bordeaux)	
François		
2 François	(1) Thérèse Amiot Q.	1746
Jacques		
Le même	Marie Ouel Bert.	1767
Marguerite	Thos. Goodchild „	1796
Françoise	Ls. Talon „	1807
Veronique	Chs. Fournier „	1807
Jean Baptiste		
3 Jacques	(2) Angé Boucher „	1779
Françoise	Michel Brochu „	1803
Jacques		

RABOUIN.

1 Jean	Marg. Ardiou Q.	1663
Le même	Marg. Leclaire S.F.	1679
Marguerite	Noël Roy „	1700
Jeanne	Etn. Corriveau „	1703
Le même	Marie Mineau S.I.	1706

RACINE.

1 Etienne	M. Marg Martin	Q.	1638
Louise	Simon Guyon	Q.	1655
Madeleine	Noël Simard	C.R.	1661
Pierre			
François			
Etienne			
Noël			
2 Noël	(1) Marg. Gravel	„	1667
Etienne			
Jean			
Pierre			
3 François	(1) Marie Baucher	S.F.	1676
Joseph			
4 Pierre	(1) Louise Guion	„	1683
Etn. Prisque			
Prisque			
Claude			
Jean			
6 Pierre	(2) Cath. Cochon (Con-		
	trete)		1697
Geneviève	Ls. Alaire	S.Joach.	1730
Prisque.			
Le même	Genev. Guimont		
	S.Anne	1711	
7 Etienne	(2) Thérèse Lessard		
	S.Anne	1713	
Louis			
8 Jean	(2) Anne Lessart S.Anne		1701
Jean Bte.			
9 Joseph	(3) Mad. Paré	S.Anne	1710
Joseph			
François			
Le même	Marg. Veau	S.Anne	1721
Le même	Marie Plante	„	1725
10 Claude	(5) Genev. Gagnon	C.R.	1710
Françoise	M. Tremblay S.Anne		1740
Catherine	Jacq. Huot	„	1747
Jean Bte.			
11 Etn. Prisque	(5) M. Anne Gagnon S.A.		1724
Marie	Alex. Vaillancourt S.F.		1747
12 Prisque	(5) Lse. Giguère	S.A.	1729
Prisque			
Etienne			
Le même	M. Vaillancourt	S.F.	1745
13 Jean	(5) Mad. Dorval S.Anne		1722
Charles			
14 Prisque	(6) Cath. Plante	S.I.	1735
15 Jean Bte.	(8) M. Anne Bolduc S.Joal		1737
M. Anne	Joseph Fortier S.M.		1757
Marie Josette	Joseph Solin	„	1763
M. Thérèse	Jos. Martineau	„	1768
16 Louis	(7) Ant. Boivin S.Anne		1748
Charles			
Le même	M. Agnès Paré	„	1776
Louis			
17 François	(9) Marie Gagnon	„	1736
François			
18 Joseph	(9) Marie Gervais	S.F.	1737
19 Jean Bte.	(10) Marg. Leclair	S.V.	1746
M. Marguerite	Louis Dion	S.M.	1772
M. Geneviève	Frs. Leclair	„	1789
Jean Charles			
Paul			
20 Prisque	(12) Lse. Vaillancourt S.F.		1756
21 Etienne	(12) M. Jos. Mon. Dorval		
	S.F.	1767	
Pélagie	Jos. Paquet	„	1787
Joseph			
22 Charles	(13) Pelagie Gagnon S.A.		1761
Marie	Laur Gosselin S.Chs.		1783
Angélique	Pierre Paguet	„	1785
Josette	Etn. Leclair	„	1796
23 Charles	(16) Josette Paré	S.A.	1772
Pierre			
24 Louis	(16) Charlotte Martel S.P.		1803
Marcelline	Ls. Simart	„	1835

RACINE.

Félicité	Laur. Pacquet	S.P. 1836
Apolline	Anselme LefebvreS.P.1843	
Eléonore	Ls. Roberge	" 1846
Martine	Lse. Pouliot	S.L. 1836
Louis		
Jean		
25 François	(17) Genev. Blouin S.Anne1767	
Le même	Charlotte Lessart	1772
Geneviève	J. B. Quemeneur S.G. 1797	
26 Jean Charles(19)	M. Lse. Lessart S.M. 1780	
M. Madeline	Paul McNeil	" 1809
Laurent		
Jean Bte.		
27 Paul	(19) M. Angé. Rouillart	S.M. 1791
Marguerite	J. B. Dion	" 1810
M. Angélique	Pierre Bacquet	" 1812
Rosalie	Aug. Roy	" 1818
Marie Angèle	Pr. Bissonnette	" 1835
Jean		
Paul		
28 Joseph	(21) Mad. Letourneau S.F.1804	
Scolastique	Etn. Giguère	" 1833
Joseph		
29 Pierre	(23) Frse. Pepin S.Anne 1802	
Jean Frs.		
Pierre		
Louis		
30 Louis	(24) M. Thècle AsselinS.F.1831	
31 Jean	(24) Angé Chatigny S.P. 1828	
Sifroi	Romule Chrysostome	
32 Jean Bte.	(26) M. Genev. FleuryS.V.1813	
33 Laurent	(26) Genev. Gaumont S.G. 1826	
34 Paul Norbert(27)	Frse. Fleury S.M. 1818	
Marie	Andre Mercier	" 1845
M. Anne	Frs. Guay	" 1851
Caroline	Odilon Jean	" 1860
Benjamin		
Paul		
35 Jean	(27) Mad. Corriveau S.M. 1821	
M. Luce	Paul Martineau	" 1855
M. Adèle	Marc Martineau	" 1855
Le même	Mad. Lacroix	" 1846
36 Robert	M. Anne Gautron	
M. Anne	David Blanchet	" 1847
37 Joseph	(28) Marg. Asselin	S.F. 1827
38 Pierre	(29) Marie Paré	S.Anne 1827
Pierre		
39 Louis	(29) Marie Dalaire	S.A. 1826
Christine	Frs. Fortier	S.I. 1853
40 Jean Frs.	(29) Cath. Lepage	S.Frs. 1846
41 Romul Chry-(31)	Scolastique Coté S.P. 1858	
tome		
42 Sifroi	(31) Esther Malv. Pouliot	S.P. 1862
43 Benjamin	(34) Eliz. Pellerin	S.M. 1852
44 Paul	(34) M. Oct. Fortier	S.M. 1857
45 Pierre	(38) Marg. Canac	S.F. 1859

RAIMOND.

1 Joseph	Salomé Paradis (Kamour.)	
Joseph		
2 Joseph	(1) Justine Turcot	S.I. 1831
Marie Anne	Jos. Labrecque	S.I. 1851
Demerise	Lse. Poulin	S.I. 1865
Hubert		
3 Hubert	(2) Emélie Pepin	S.I. 1863

RATTÉ.

1 Jacques	Anne Martin	Q. 1658
Marie Anne	Ign. Gosselin	S.P. 1686
Anne	Jacq. Trépanier	S.P. 1691
Geneviève	Jean Sicard	S.P. 1694
Louise	Ls. Martin	S.P. 1700

RATTÉ.

Jean Bte		
Ignace		
Pierre		
Guillaume		
2 Jean Bte	(1) Mad. Blouard	S.P. 1698
Geneviève	Jos. Goulet	" 1722
Marie	Paul Vaillancourt	" 1736
Angélique	J. B. Bazin	" 1744
Madeleine	Chs. Martel	" 1748
Thérèse	Ls. Asselin	" 1734
Thérèse	Jean Turcot	S.J. 1752
Martin		
André		
Ignace		
3 Pierre	(1) Jeanne Nolin	S.P. 1702
M. Françoise	Ant. Martel	" 1732
Cécile	Pierre Dorval	" 1737
Ignace		
Jean Baptiste		
4 Ignace	(1) Helène Dorval	S.P. 1725
Marguerite	Basile Crépeau	" 1725
Josette	Paul Gourgue	" 1744
Véronique	Jos. Marie Charlan	
Chs. Amador		S.P. 1746
Pierre		
Ignace		
Jean Baptiste		
Le même	Genev. Langlais	S.P. 1729
Gertrude	Ls. Bussière	S.P. 1761
Hyacinthe		
5 Guillaume	(1) M. Mad. Nolin	S.P. 1710
M. Madeleine	Claude Vaillancourt	S.P. 1731
Helène	Frs. Goulet	S.P. 1734
Helène	2° Jacq. Noël	S.P. 1769
Agathe	Pierre Dorval	S.P. 1737
Agathe	2° Nic. Fortier	S.P. 1751
Marguerite	Pierre Chatigny	S.P. 1742
M. Anne	Joseph Voyer	S.P. 1747
M. Anne	2° Jos. Ferland	S.F. 1753
Ignace		
6 Martin	(2) M. Anne Martel	S.P. 1731
7 André	(2) M. Jeanne Martel	S.P. 1736
Marie Rose	Pierre Dostie	S P. 1754
Charles		
8 Ignace	(2) Marg. Charlan	S.F. 1747
9 Ignace	(3) M. Anne Dorval	S.P. 1730
Josette	Pierre Roberge	" 1753
M. Reine	Chs. Paradis	" 1757
M. Anne	J. B. Roberge	" 1774
Germain		
10 Jean Baptiste (3)	Josette Duval	S.P. 1744
11 Chs. Amador (4)	M. Jeanne Paradis	S.P. 1731
Marie	Etn. Grenier	S.P. 1760
Marie Thècle	Jean Crépeau	" 1764
Angélique	Pierre Pichet	" 1766
M. Reine	Chs. Crépeau	" 1769
12 Pierre	(4) M. Lse. Crépeau	S.P. 1732
13 Ignace	(4) M. Jos. Paradis	S.P. 1741
14 Jean Baptiste (4)	Agathe Tremblay	S.I. 1750
M. Agathe	J. B. Lessart	S.M. 1774
Marie Louise	Chs. Lacroix	S.M. 1804
Madeleine	J. B. Guénet	S.Chs. 1795
Madeleine	2° Pierre Bacquet	S.Chs. 1798
Madeleine	3° Louis Dion	S.M. 1816
Jacques		
Joseph		
Ambroise		
Alexandre		
15 Hyacinthe	(4) Marie Gobeil	S I. 1768
M. Angélique	Frs. Turcot	S.I. 1812
Joseph		

RATTÉ.

16	Ignace	(5) M. Thérèse Leclair	S.P. 1747
	M. Josette	Jacq. Blais	S.Chs. 1773
	Gertrude	Jean Tangué	S.Chs. 1776
	Thècle	Michel Larivé	S.Chs. 1781
	M. Thérèse	J. B. Bedard	
	François		Chs.Bourg. 1771
	Ignace		
	Jean		
17	Charles	(7) Rose Dorval	S.P. 1761
18	Germain	(9) Marie Coté	S.P. 1779
16	Basile	Josette Coté	
	Laurent		
	Augustin		
	Charles		
	Antoine		
20	Jacques	(14) Genev. Denis	S.M. 1783
	M. Josette	Michel Bolduc	,, 1808
	Geneviève	Pierre Bolduc	,, 1810
	M. Anne	Pierre Richard	,, 1821
	Marguerite	Joseph Roby	,, 1827
	Marie	Benoni Roby	,, 1828
	Rosalie	Chs. Quéret	,, 1833
	Archange	Ant. Plante	,, 1833
	André		
21	Joseph	(14) Margt. Quéret	,, 1791
22	Ambroise	(14) M. Susanne Roy	,, 1804
	Archange	Jos. Gagné	S.F.S. 1834
	Pierre		
23	Alexandre	(14) Marie Voisin	S.V. 1807
	M. Esther	Pierre Bisson	,, 1836
	Alexandre		
24	Joseph	(15) M. Lse-Lainé	S.I. 1809
25	François	(16) Frse. Forgues	SChs. 1773
26	Ignace	(16) M. Marthe Gagnon	
			S.M. 1783
	Marthe	Jean Audet	S.G. 1802
	Ignace		
27	Augustin	(19) Marie Asselin	,, 1813
28	Laurent	(19) Marie Blais	S.V. 1822
29	Antoine	(19) M. Angèle Boulet	
			S.F.S. 1823
	Le même	Théotiste Roy	S.Chs. 1832
30	Charles	(19) Sophie Bruneau	S.G. 1826
31	André	(20) Frse. Lemelin	S.M. 1819
	Le même	Mad. Thivierge	S.I. 1824
	M. Madeleine	Am. Lemieux	S.M. 1847
	Henriette	André Coté	,, 1858
	Flavie	Nap. Leclair	,, 1860
	Marie	Ant. Menard	,, 1860
	Archange	Jean Lemelin	S.Chs. 1855
	André		
32	Thomas	Margt. Guilmet Q.	
	Magloire		
	Georges		
33	Pierre	(22) Adé Talbot	S.G. 1836
34	Alexandre	(23) Céleste Boutin	S.V 1835
	Delphine	Jean Boutin	,, 1863
35	Ignace	(26) Josette Terrien	S.G. 1818
	Le même	Mad. Quemeneur	,, 1829
36	André	(31) Sophie Durand	S.V. 1865
37	Magl. Geor-	(32) M. Rosalie Pouliot	B. 1857
	ges		
38	Jean	(16) Josette Guilmet	S.H. 1805

RÉAUME.

1	René	Marie Chevreau	Q. 1665
	René		
2	René	(1) Marie Guion	C.R. 1694
	Marie	Pierre Dubeau	,, 1716
	Gabriel		
	Simon		
3	Simon	(2) Mad. Julien	Chs.Brg. 1724
	Réné		
	Jacques		

RÉAUME.

4	Gabriel	(2) Cath. Simard	C.R. 1727	
	Etienne			
	Charles			
5	Jacques	(3) Margt. Allard		
			Chs.Brg. 1751	
	François			
6	René	(3) Cath. Dion	C.R. 1762	
	Jean			
	François			
7	Etienne	(4) Lse. Cloutier	,, 1751	
	Etienne			
8	Charles	(4) Marie Gravel	,, 1751	
	Agathe	Benoit Noël	S.P. 1792	
	Marguerite	J. B. Guay	Chs.Berg. 1785	
9	François	(5) J. Eugénie Crepin		
			C.R. 1787	
	Alexis			
10	Jean François	(6) Louise Godbout	,, 1794	
	Isaac			
	François			
11	Etienne	(7) Margt. Noël	S.L. 1780	
	Clement			
	Charles			
12	Alexis	(9) Véronique Trudel	A.G.1816	
	Narcisse			
13	Isaac	(10) Mad. Coulombe	S.L. 1819	
14	François	(10) Thérèse Coulombe	,, 1820	
15	Clement	(11) M.Lse. Mercier	S.Chs.1809	
	Etienne			
16	Charles	(11) Julie Miray	Lévis 1824	
17	Narcisse	(12) M. A. Malv. Turcot		
			S.J. 1858	
18	Etienne	(15) Margt.Baudoin	S.Chs.1832	

RÉMILLARD

1	François	Anne Gaboury	Islet 1681	
	Marie	Guill. Corriveau	S.M. 1709	
	Marie	2° Ign. Quevillon	S.V. 1719	
	Marie	3° Hilaire Martin	,, 1727	
	François			
	Etienne			
	Antoine			
2	Etienne	(1) M. Anne Bolduc	Q. 1726	
	M. Anne	André Aubé	S.V. 1748	
	Agathe	Joseph Loubier	,, 1759	
	Marguerite	Jos. Roy	S.V. 1762	
	Marthe	Jos. Roy	,, 1782	
	M. Josette	Claude Dion	,, 1758	
	,,	2° Bapt. Blais	Bert. 1762	
3	François	(1) Fse. Hélie	S.V. 1720	
	M. Josette	Etn. Beau	,, 1763	
	Angélique	Michel Bernatchez	,, 1765	
	Marie	Guill. Fournier	,, 1766	
	Jacques			
	Joseph			
	Charles			
	Pierre			
	François			
	Ambroise			
	Augusta			
4	Antoine	(1) Margt. Marié	Q. 1728	
	Marie	Chs. Boucher	S.V. 1758	
	Jean-Baptiste			
	Antoine			
5	Etienne	(2) Genev. Blais	Bert. 1757	
	Geneviève	Felix Fleury	S.V. 1794	
	André			
	Etienne			
	Jean Baptiste			
	Hyacinthe			
	Michel			
6	François	(3) M. Jos. Alaire	S.V. 1746	
	M. Josette	Simon Quéret	,, 1772	
	Judith	Jos. Quéret	,, 1779	
	Le même	M. Gert. Quéret	,, 1760	

RÉMILLARD.

7	Augustin	(3)	Mad. Denis	S.V.	1746
8	Pierre	(3)	Charlotte Thibault	„	1755
	Madeleine		Joseph Blouin	„	1784
	M. Charlotte		Ant. Chrétien	„	1793
	Antoine				
	Jacques				
9	Jacques	(3)	Genv. Couture	S.M.	1754
10	Joseph	(3)	Clotilde Denis	„	1755
	M. Françoise		Pierre Monmeny	„	1781
11	Charles	(3)	Angé Plante	„	1757
	M. Angélique		J. B. Roby	„	1790
	„		2° Laurt. Morin	„	1814
	Marie		Ign. Roby	„	1799
	Joseph				
12	Ambroise	(3)	Mad. Evé	S.V.	1764
	M. Louise		Michl. Bolduc	S.M.	1797
	M. Françoise		Jos. Théberge	„	1812
	M. Reine		Pierre Bolduc	S.F.S.	1787
	André				
13	Antoine	(4)	Eliz. Couture	B.	1756
	Marie		Jos. Roy	S.V.	1777
14	Jean Bte	(4)	Eliz. Défourneau	„	1764
	M. Thérèse		Frs. Rey	„	1803
	Louise		Ls. Jérome Arbour		
				S.G.	1796
	Pierre				
	François				
	Le même		Marie Goupy	S.V.	1788
	Augustin				
15	Etienne		M. Jos. Arbour	S.V.	1782
	M. Victoire		Jos. Carbonneau	„	1802
	„		2° Pierre Joncas	„	1823
	Marie		Julien Fleury	„	1804
	Marguerite		Jacq. Marrein	„	1805
	Marianne		Chs. Cloutier	„	1812
	Catherine		Ls. Audet	„	1814
	Angèle		Ign. Morisset	„	1825
	Etienne				
	Joseph				
	Le même		Claire Thibault	S.G.	1810
			Thècle Dion	Bert.	1830
16	André	(5)	M. Marthe Morisset		
				S.M.	1792
	M. Geneviève		Jos. M. Baudoin	S.V.	1812
	M. Archange		Pierre Tanguay	„	1826
	Olive		Ign. Gautron	„	1831
	Marcel				
	André				
17	Jean-Baptiste	(5)	M. Marthe Gosselin		
				S.V.	1792
	Marthe		Jean Forgues	S.G.	1809
18	Pr. Hyacinthe	(5)	M. Fse.Corriveau	S.V.	1796
	Françoise		Margt. Nadeau	S.Chs.	1827
	Angèle		Jos. Fournier	„	1842
	Adrien				
	Hyacinthe				
19	Michel	(5)	Marie Forgues	S.G.	1808
	Luce		Pierre Bolduc	„	1828
20	Antoine	(8)	Marie Roy	S.V.	1789
21	Jacques	(8)	M. Cath. Baudoin		
				Bert.	1789
	Rémi				
22	Joseph	(11)	M. Lse. Lacroix	S.M.	1804
	Restitue		Frs. Leblond	„	1839
	François Xavier				
23	André	(12)	Josette Lacasse	S.Chs.	1812
24	François	(14)	Marie Brochu	L.G.	1806
	François				
25	Pierre	(14)	Reine Chartier	S.G.	1806
	Angélique		Ed. Rouleau	„	1829
	Le même		Angé. Bélanger	„	1826
26	Augustin	(14)	Marg. Roy	„	1817
27	Etienne	(15)	Margt. Audet	S.V.	1814
28	Joseph	(15)	M. Angèle Boucher	„	1829
29	André	(16)	M. Angé Morin	S.F.S.	1727

RÉMILLARD.

30	Marcel	(16)	M. Olive Marceau		
				S.V.	1829
	Théodore				
31	Adrien	(18)	Margt. Boucher	S.G.	1822
32	Hyacinthe	(18)	Angèle Bilodeau	S.G.	1825
33	Rémi	(21)	Margt. Vermet	S.V.	1820
	Le même		Marie Dodier	S.M.	1843
34	Frs. Xavier	(22)	Charlotte Roy	„	1843
35	François	(24)	Marie Nadeau	S.G.	1830
36	Théodore	(30)	M. Désanges Boutin		
				S.V.	1857
	Michel		Genev. Vallée	S.H.	1857

RENAUD.

1	Mathurin		Marie Peltier	Q.	1669
	Michel				
2	Joseph		Marie Lehoux	S.F.	1680
	M. Anne		Gabriel Gosselin	„	1716
3	Michel	(1)	Renée Réaume		
				Chsbourg	1698
	Charlotte		Jos. Alaire	„	1731
4					
5	Pierre		Eliz. Côté	S.Tho.	1761
	Roger				
	Jean Bte.				
6	Jean Bte.	(5)	Josette Godbout	S.H.	1800
	Françoise		Pierre Vermet	S.G.	1819
	Charlotte		Frs. Bilodeau	„	1824
	Jean Bte.				
7	Roger	(5)	M. Frs. Hélie	S.M.	1801
	Françoise		J. B. Morel	S.G.	1816
8	Jean Bte.	(6)	Josette Pénin	„	1819
	Louise		David Bisson	S.P.	1845

RICHARD.

1	Pierre		Fse. Miville	Cap S.Ig.	1680
	Ursule		J. Bte. Morin	S.F.S.	1755
	Ursule		2° Jos. Daniau	„	1762
	Jean Bte.				
	Pierre				
2	Pierre		Eliz. Gamache		
				Cap S.Ig.	1709
			Anne Gamache		
3	Jean Bte.			Cap S.Ig.	1713
	M. Anne		Frs. Thibault	„	1746
	Lazare				
	François				
4	Barthélémi		Marie Martre		
				Ev. de Luçon	
	Jos. Barthélémi				
5	J. Bte. (anglais)		Anne Tangué	S.V.	1726
6	Michel		M. Angé Mercier		
	Françoise		J. B. Harnais	S.V.	1774
	M. Josette		Frs. Tardif	„	1781
	M. Angélique		Jos. Christophe	„	1784
	M. Anne		Jos. Gosselin	„	1789
	Philippe				
	Joseph				
	Antoine				
	Michel				
	Paschal				
7	Jacq. François	(2)	Marie Bore		
				Ev. de Coutances	
	Jacques				
	François				
8	Joseph		Genev. Chaplain		
	Pierre				
9	Lazare	(3)	M. Marthe Guignard		
				Bert.	1757
10	Jos. Barthélémi	(4)	Marie Fortin	S.V.	1752
11	François	(3)	Salomé Gosselin		
				Cap S.Ign.	1752
	Jerome				

RICHARD.

12	Joseph	(6)	M.Jos.Rouillard S.M.	1775
	Marie Reine		Pierre Daniau	„ 1802
	Marguerite		Nic. Mercier	S.G. 1796
	Le même		Marie Thérien	„ 1801
	Joseph			
13	Paschal	(6)	M. Jos. Boulet S.F.S.	1784
	Archange		Ls. Bernard	S.V. 1816
	Marie		F. X. Bernard	„ 1824
14	Philippe	(6)	M. Anne Fortier S.M.	1785
	M. Anne		Pierre Bolduc	„ 1803
	Philippe			
	Louis Jean			
	Le même		Margt. Gaudin	S.V. 1800
	Marguerite		André Shinck	S.G. 1822
	Julien			
	Le même		Marie Roy	S.M. 1811
15	Antoine		M. Jos. Quéret	S.V. 1788
	M. Angélique		Jacq. Pigeon	„ 1815
	Marguerite		Simon Brousseau	„ 1832
	Pierre			
	Antoine			
	Jacques			
	Michel			
16	Michel	(6)	Marthe Quéret	S.V. 1793
	M. Madeleine		Thos. Roy	„ 1841
	Germain			
17	Jacq. François	(7)	M. Margt. Vien S.M.	1777
	Archange		Ls. Campeau	B. 1809
	Archange		2° Jos. Beaucher	„ 1815
	Jacques			
18	Pierre	(8)	Genev. Dupile S.P.	1779
19	Augustin		Genev. Beaulieu	
			C.S.Ign.	
	Charlotte		Jos. Bacquet S.Chs.	1784
20	Louis		M. Rose Thibault	
				Islet 1782
	Charles			
	François			
21	Nicolas		M. Jeanne Bourgot	
			S.J. Portjoli	
	M. Jeanne		Ls. Chabot S.Chs.	1813
22	Ls. Noël		Julie Guimont	
				Cap S.Ign.1805
	Frs. Narcisse			
23	Jérôme	(11)	M. Jos. Larrivé Bert.	1786
24	Joseph	(12)	Genev.Clément S.Chs.	1830
25	Philippe	(14)	Eliz. Marseau S.M.	1810
	Philippe			
26	Louis	(14)	M. Adé. Poliquin	„ 1811
	Louis			
27	Jean	(14)	M. Ls. Lacroix	„ 1815
28	Julien	(14)	Marie Guilmet S.G.	1830
29	Antoine	(15)	M. Ls. Baudoin S.V.	1815
	Sophie		Etn. Ménard	„ 1841
	Marceline		Frs. Goulet	„ 1849
30	Michel	(15)	Marg. Bernard	„ 1815
31	Pierre	(15)	M. Anne Ratté S.M.	1821
	Marcelline		Jacq.BoissonneauS.V.	1845
	Marguerite		Jos. Pruneau	„ 1812
	Esther		Jacq. Boulet	„ 1855
	Desanges		Ant. Mercier	„ 1855
	Archange		Ant. Quemeneur	„ 1860
	Séraphine		Urbain Cyriac	
			Gourgue	„ 1862
	Constance		Ferd Turgeon	„ 1863
	Elizabeth		Eusèbe Dion	„ 1864
	Marie Anne		Chs. Lainé	„ 1866
	Geneviève		Damase Gourgue	„ 1867
	Pierre			
32	Jacques	(15)	Archange Hébert S.M.	1834
33	Paschal		M. Ls. Ainse	
	Marguerite		Jacq. Guilmet S.V.	1841
34	Germain	(16)	Marie Fortier	„ 1837
35	Jacques	(17)	Vict. Blanchet B.	1802
	Marie Victoire		Pierre Huot	„ 1821
	Le même		Marie Morisset S.M.	1824

RICHARD.

63	Charles	(20)	M. Angèle Bartaelt	
			S.F.S.	1815
37	Frs. Xavier	(22)	Genev. Picard S.P.S.	1835
38	Philippe	(25)	GertrudeLemelinS.M.	1832
39	Louis	(26)	MarieClément S.Chs.	1846
40	Pierre	(31)	Marg. Dion S.M.	1858
	Flavien		Marie Blais	
	Le même		Sophie Lacroix	„ 1841
42	François	(20)	Rosalie Chenel	
			Cap S.Ign.	1813
			Cap. S. Ign.	
	Elisabeth		J. B. Dupaleau S.Frs.	1852

ROBERGE.

1	Pierre		Antoinette de Beau-	
			renom S.F.	1672
	Le même		Fse. Loignon	„ 1679
	Marie		J. B. Blouard S.P.	1711
	Elisabeth		Jos. Maranda	„ 1726
	Jean			
	Charles			
	Ambroise			
	Pierre			
	Le même		MarieLeFrançoisC.R.	1684
	LouiseHyacinthe		Joachim Audet S.L.	1716
	Eléonore		Pierre Pichet	„ 1717
	Pierre			
	Joseph			
2	Jean	(1)	Anne Blouard S.P.	1709
3	Charles	(1)	M. Mad. Coté S.P.	1720
	Marie Josette		Frs. Brousseau	„ 1843
	Geneviève		Frs. Bertrand	„ 1747
	Angélique		Ls. Blouin	„ 1755
	Jean			
	Louis			
	Le même		Claire Chantal	„ 1762
4	Pierre (3° M.)	(1)	M. Anne Jeanne S.L.	1710
	Marie Louise		Frs. Mazureau	„ 1748
	Pierre			
5	Joseph	(1)	M. Mad. Lemelin	„ 1715
	Gertrude		Ign. Civadier	„ 1753
	Geneviève		Jean Bilodeau S.Chs.	1764
	Michel			
	Joseph			
	Augustin			
6	Pierre (2d M.)	(1)	Marie Lefrançois C.R.	1726
	Marie Josette		J. B. Drouin S.P.	1773
	Prisque			
	Pierre			
7	Ambroise	(1)	M. Ls. Goulet	„ 1730
	Marie		Frs. Mignot	„ 1779
	Ignace			
	Ambroise			
	François			
	Jean Baptiste			
	Charles			
	Le même		Mad. Leclaire	„ 1777
8	Jean	(3)	Gertrude Pichet	„ 1754
	Thécle		Frs. Paradis	„ 1785
	M. Angélique		Etn. Blouin	„ 1887
	Victoire		Laurent Gosselin	„ 1800
	Ambroise			
	Jean Baptiste			
9	Louis	(3)	M. Reine Vachon	
			Beauport	1764
	Jacques			
10	Pierre	(4)	Marie Civadier S.L.	1747
11	Joseph	(5)	Eliz. Couture B.	1742
	Elizabeth		Michel Turgeon S.Chs.	1766
	Benjamin			
	Joseph			
12	Michel	(5)	Louise Civadier S.L.	1757
13	Augustin	(5)	M. Anne Pouliot	„ 1762
14	Pierre	(6)	Josette Ratté S.P.	1753
	Catherine		Frs. Chatigny	„ 1786

ROBERGE.

	Josette	Pierre Beaucher	S.P.	1793
	Pierre			
15	Joseph	Cécile Lefebvre		
	François			
16	Nicolas	Angé Demerse		
	Félicité	Jean Pierre Vermet		
			S.H.	1801
	Nicolas			
17	Prisque	(6) M. Agathe Goulet	S.P.	1761
	Josette	Pierre Ferland	"	1785
	Agathe	Basile Marcoux	"	1785
	Reine	Ant· Bégin	"	1793
	Thérèse	Jacq. Couture	"	1798
	Ambroise			
	François			
	Pierre			
	Louis			
	Joseph			
18	Ignace	(7) Thérèse Aubin	S.P.	1760
	Thérèse	Pierre Coté	"	1803
	Ambroise			
	Louis			
	Ignace			
19	Ambroise	Thècle Montigny	S.P.	1771
	Marie Thècle	Frs. Fortier	S.H.	1791
	Thérèse	Jos. Gosselin	"	1803
	Louis			
	Ambroise			
	Etienne			
20	Francois	(7) Thérèse Nolin	S.P.	1773
	Angélique	J. B. Provost	S.H.	1797
	Germain			
	Francois			
	Louis			
21	Jean Baptiste	(7) M. Anne Ratté	S.P.	1774
22	Charles	(7) Thérèse Noël	"	1775
	Geneviève	Philippe Pouliot	S.L.	1812
	Thérèse	Michel Tremblay	"	1822
	Charles			
23	Jean Baptiste	(8) Héléne Gagnon	S.F.	1789
	Jean Baptiste			
24	Ambroise	(8) Marie Gosselin	S.P.	1796
	Marie	Pierre Chatigny	"	1816
	Pélagie	Frs. Paradis	"	1822
	Geneviève	Pierre Hébert	"	1825
	Ambroise			
25	Jacques	(9) M. Mad. Couture	S.P	1802
	Le même	Angé Martineau	S.F.	1806
	Sophie	Benoit Giguère	S.P.	1848
	François Régis			
	Jacques			
26	Joseph	(11) M. Angé Corriveau		
			S.V.	1773
27	Benjamin	(11) Thérèse Lambert		
			Lévis	1790
	Joseph			
28	Pierre	(14) Genev. Coté	S.P.	1787
	Josette	Laurent Dumas	"	1816
	Euphrosine	Jos. Begin	"	1826
	Reine	Aug. Couture	"	1827
	Pierre			
	Jacques			
29	François	(15) M. Reine Duperron		
			S.H.	1791
30	Nicolas	(16) M. Genev. Nadeau		
			S.H.	1803
31	François	(17) Mad. Paradis	S.P.	1786
	Madeleine	Etn. Simoneau	S.H.	1808
	Josette	Chs. Bacon	"	1817
	François			
32	Joseph	(17) Cath. Poulin	S.P.	1791
	Thérèse	Frs. Tailleur	S.P.	1817
	Josette	J. B. Langlois	"	1825
	Dorothée	Alexis Langlois	"	1829

18—30

ROBERGE.

	Prisque			
	Joseph			
	Binjamin			
33	Ambroise	(17) Louise Pouliot	S.L.	1793
	Agathe	Jos. Lacroix	S.G.	1813
	Agathe	2° Michel Quemeneur		
			S.G.	1823
	Marguerite	Pierre Jolin	"	1819
	Ambroise			
34	Pierre	(17) Josette Lebrun	S.G.	1793
	Agathe	Jos. Lemieux	"	1817
	Josette	Ign. Dorval	"	1819
	Marguerite	Jos. Lacasse	"	1824
	Marie	Ls. Lacasse	"	1828
	Angélique	Ls. Bissonnet	"	1828
	Monique	Alexandre Paquet	"	1829
	Louis			
	Pierre			
35	Louis	(17) Céleste Lebrun	S.G.	1796
	Marguerite	Samuel Willet	"	1827
	Jean			
	Louis			
36	Ambroise	(18) Barbe Bussière	S.P.	1788
			S.H.	
37	Ignace	(18) M. Angé Aubin	S.P.	1797
	Thérèse	Chs. Nolin	"	1819
	Euphrosine	Laurent Montigny		
			S.P.	1820
	Abraham			
38	Louis	(18) Marg. Cinqmars	S.P.	1807
	Adelaïde	Jean Poulin	"	1825
	Constance	Michel Mirand	"	1832
	Emélie	Bénoni Tremblay	"	1846
	Marie	Jean Blouin	S.J.	1850
	Domitille	Michel Pichet	S.F.	1852
	Ignace			
	Louis			
39	Ambroise	(19) M. Archange Morin		
			S.H.	1806
40	Louis	(19) Thérèse Nadeau	"	1804
41	Etienne	(19) M. Thècle Coté	"	1816
42	François	(20) M. Ls. Nadeau	"	1799
43	Germain	(20) M. Hélène Gosselin		
			S.H.	1808
44	Louis	(20) Archange Delisle	"	1809
45	Charles	(22) M. Ls. Paquet	B.	1812
	Rose Flavie	Paul Pouliot	S.L.	1835
	Adèle	Frs. Nap. Pepin	"	1854
	Pierre			
	Louis			
46	Jean Baptiste	(23) M. Ls. Drouin	S.F.	1813
	Marie Sophie	Jérémie Pouliot	"	1834
	Marie Sophie	2° Basile Marseau	"	1840
47	Ambroise	(24) M. Mad. Coll	S.P.	1822
	Philoméne	Jos. Gagnon	"	1861
	Narcisse Nap.			
	Jean			
	Prudent			
48	Jacques	(25) Scolastique Coté	"	1833
	Chs. Honoré			
49	François Ré-	(25) Euphrosine Coté	"	1836
	gis			
50	Joseph	(27) Adé Lacroix	S.G.	1820
51	Pierre	(28) Judith Shoret	S.P.	1815
	Olive	Moïse Vaillancour	"	1834
	Adélaïde	Ed Giguère	S.F.	1840
52	Jacques	(28) Justine Hebert	S.P.	1832
53	François	(31) M. Jos. Gosselin	S.H.	1811
54	Prisque	(32) M. Angé Ferlant	S.P.	1819
	Marie Zoé	Frs. Agapit Nolin	"	1859
	Gilbert			
55	Binjamin	(32) Archange Langlois	"	1829
56	Joseph	(32) Agathe Paradis	"	1831
57	Ambroise	(32) Angé Turgeon	S.G.	1818
58	Pierre	(34) Marie Turgeon	"	1820

ROBERGE.

59	Louis	(34) Josette Lacasse	S.G. 1821
60	Louis	(35) Marie Gautron	S.V. 1818
61	Jean	(35) Julie Talbot	S.G. 1829
62	Abraham	(37) Archange Pouliot	
			Lévis 1833
63	Ignace	(38) Cecile Denis	S.L. 1831
	Philoméne	Romuald Peltier	„ 1861
	Cécile	Félix Picard	„ 1875
	Célina	F. X. Ainse	Lévis
	Pierre		
	Ignace		
64	Louis	(38) Eleonore Racine	S.P. 1846
	Le même	Marcelline Quemeneur	
			S.P. 1866
65	Pierre	(45) Louise Noël	S.J. 1840
	Louise	Ismael Delisle	S.L. 1870
	Marie	Célestin Dumas	„ 1872
	Délima	F. L. Gosselin	„ 1875
	Pierre Cyrille		
	Elzéar		
66	Louis	(45) Marie Anne (Cookson)	
			S.L. 1847
67	Jean	(47) M. Esther Ferlant	
			S.P. 1852
68	Prudent	(47) M. Rose Leclaire	„ 1858
69	NarcisseNap.	(47) M. Célina Coté	„ 1869
70	Chs. Honoré	(48) Rosalie Artémise Martel	
			S.P. 1861
71	Jean	Esther Marcotte	
	Le même	Julie Celeste Leclaire	
			S.P. 1865
72	Gilbert	(54) Sara Nolin	„ 1852
73	Ignace	(63) Marie Pouliot	S.L. 1865
74	Pierre	(63) M. Philoméne Denis	
			S. Féreol
75	PierreCyrille	(65) M. Sophie Cinqmars	
			S.L. 1870
76	Elzéar	(65) M. Alice Gosselin	„ 1879

ROBERTSON.

1	Robert *	Marie Bazin	S.V. 1764
	Thérèse	Alexandre Paquet	
			S. Chs. 1794
	Angélique	Pierre Roy	„ 1795
	Marguerite	Ant. Gosselin	„ 1812
	Marie Françoise	Amand Asselin	S.F. 1792
	Geneviève	Jacq. George	S.G. 1811
2	Charles	Christine Wilson	
	Le même	Euphremie Ruel Bert	1846

ROBY-SANSCHAGRIN.

1	Jean Limaurin	M. Anne Paquet	B. 1761
	Marie	Jos. Plante	S.V. 1795
	Joseph		
	Guillaume		
	Jean Baptiste		
	Jacques		
	Ignace		
2	Joseph	(1) M. Barbe Roy	S.V. 1789
	Barbe	Frs. Aubé	„ 1820
	Reine	Pierre Emond	S.G. 1824
	Judith	Jos. Vallée	„ 1824
	François		
	Joseph		
	André		
3	Jean Baptiste	(1) M. Angé Remillard	
			S.M. 1790
	Marie Marguer-ite	Ant. Bolduc	„ 1834
	Bénoni		
4	Guillaume	(1) M. Ls. Charron	S.V. 1792
	Louise	Jacq. Lacasse	S.G. 1816
5	Jacques	(1) Marie Fradet	S.M. 1799

* Montagnard Ecossais.

BOBY—SANSCHAGRIN.

6	Ignace	(1) Marie Remillard	S.M. 1799
	Marguerite	Jos. Théberge	S.V. 1824
	Joseph		
7	Joseph	(2) M. Anne Brochu	S.G. 1810
			S.Claire
	Marie	Ant. Marseau	S.V. 1841
	Joseph		
8	François	(2) Marg. Alaire	„ 1823
	Marie Emérie	Michel Boulet	„ 1859
	Georges		
	Le même	Josette Coté	„ 1836
9	André	(2) Marg. Aubé	„ 1823
10	Benoni	(3) Marie Ratté	S.M. 1828
11	Joseph	(6) Marg. Ratté	„ 1827
12	Joseph	(7) Marg. Lemieux	S.V. 1837
13	Georges	(8) Salomé Pellerin	„ 1849

ROCHON—ROCHERON.

1	Julien	Martine Lemaire	
	Simon		
	Gervais		
2	Simon	(1) Martine Bisson	C.R. 1663
	Etienne		
3	Gervais	(1) Mad. Guion	S.F. 1671
	M. Madeleine	Jacq. Gagnon	„ 1695
	Marie	Bernard Létourneau	
			S.F. 1698
	Catherine	Etn. Audibert	„ 1699
	Anne	Nicolas Dumets	„ 1700
	Cécile	J. B. Leblond	„ 1702
	Thérèse	Jean Gagnon	„ 1704
	Elisabeth	René Meneux	„ 1710
	François		
	Gervais		
4	Etienne	(2) Eliz. Bégin	Lévis 1693
5	Gervais	(3) Mad. David	C.R. 1714
	Marguerite	Etn. Drouin	S.F. 1744
	Céleste	Frs. Bilodeau	„ 1756
	„	2° Jacq. Blouin	„ 1761
	Clément		
	Jacques		
6	François	(3) M. Chs. Gingras	
7	Clément	(5) Véronique Gosselin	
			S.F. 1750
8	Jacques	(5) M. Anne Quéret	S.M. 1756

ROLANDEAU—LORANDEAU.

1	Jean	Marie Thibaut	Qué. 1680
	Marie Anne	J. B. Marot	S.Tho. 1716
	Catherine	J. B. Boutin	„ 1717
	Louise	Pierre Gendreau	„ 1724
	Geneviève	Jos. Lefebvre	„ 1726
	Louis Joseph		
2	Louis Joseph	(1) Angé Fournier	
	Marie	Jos. Baudoin	S.P.S. 1754
	Joseph		
	Louis Charles		
3	Joseph	(2) Marg. Gagnon	S.V. 1747
4	Louis Charles	(2) M. Claire Mignot Aubin	
			S.P.S. 1752
	M. Marguerite	André Langlois	„ 1775
	Le même	M.Ls. Chrétien	S.Tho. 1776
	Marie Thècle	Alexandre Fortin	
			S.P.S. 1814
5	Louis	Thérèse Picard	
	Marie Claire	J. B. Boissonneau	
			S.P.S. 1781
	François		
6	François	(5) M. Ls. Moyen	„ 1765

RONDEAU.

1	Thomas	André Remondier	
	Isabelle	Pierre Leclaire	S.P. 1690

RONDEAU.

Madeleine	Philippe Noël	S.P.	1692
Françoise	Chs. Dumas	„	1693
Ursule	Jean Bussière	„	1693
2 Pierre	Cath. Verrier	S.F.	1669
Françoise	Jean Daniau	S.J.	1686
Marie	Ign. Chamberlan	„	1699
Elisabeth	Simon Chamberlan		
		S.F.	1692
Pierre			
Le même	Marie Asselin	S.J.	1683
Jean			
3 Etienne	M. Ls. Moreau		
Catherine	J. B. Audet	„	1732
4 Pierre	(2) M. Anne Jouin	„	1700
5 Jean	(2) Mad. Guignard Con-		
	trecœur		1718

ROSA.

1 Barthélemi	Marie Portuguais		
Barthélemi			
2 Joseph	Marie		
Antoine			
3 Barthélemi	(1) Hélène Guérard S.Frs.1756		
Marie Louise	J. B. L'heureux	„	1786
Hélène	Aug. L'heureux	„	1792
Pierre			
4 Antoine	(2) Marie Pepin	S.J.	1777
Barthélemi			
5 Pierre	(3) Véronique Julien S.P.1800		
6 Barthélemi	(4) M. Mad. Thivierge		
		S.J.	1800
Le même	Marg. Bisson	„	1837
Le même	Susanne Gontier	„	1838

ROUILLARD.

1 Antoine	Marie Girard	Que.	1653
Noël			
Pierre			
2 Noël	(1) M. Mad. Larchevêque		
		Que.	1688
Catherine	Ls. Girard	„	1727
Jean			
Joseph			
Noël			
Michel			
Charles			
3 Pierre	(1) M. Renée Charlan		
		Que.	1719
4 Jean	(2) Cath. Bureau Lorette 1713		
5 Michel	(2) M. Fse. Reinfret Que.1716		
6 Joseph	(2) Jeanne Thérèse		
		Lecompte, Qué.1726	
7 Charles	(2) M. Jos. Gaboury Qué.1731		
8 Noël	(2) M. Jos. Brideau S.M.1741		
Marie Thérèse	René Mercier	S.M.	1772
Marie Josette	Jos. Richard	S.M.	1775
Joseph Charles			
Etienne			
9 JosephCharles(8) M. Angé Gravel S.M.1767			
M. Angélique	Paul Racine	S.M.	1791
Marguerite	Guill. Corriveau S.M.1797		
M. Geneviève	Jean Frs. Veau S.M.1798		
Noël Charles			
René			
Jacques			
10 Etienne	(8) Marie Roy	S M.	1770
Josette	Jos. Shinck	S.G.	1797
Marie Anne	Jos. Plante	S.G.	1820
Adrien			
Etienne			
Noël			
11 Joseph René	Marie Tangué	S.M.	1794
M. Angélique	Frs. Quemeneur S.M.1820		
Euphrosine	Jacq. Morisset	S.M.	1826

18—30½

ROUILLARD.

Charles Claude			
12 Noël Charles (9) M. Jos. Roy		S M.	1798
Josette	Pierre Bolduc	S.M.	1825
13 Jacques	(9) M. Barbe Roy	S.M.	1802
Louis			
Jacques			
14 Etienne	(10) Agathe Godbout S.G.1803		
Agathe	Jean Leclaire	S.G.	1826
Angélique	Etn. Monmeny	S.G.	1825
Etienne			
15 Adrien	(10) Marie Fortier	S.G.	1811
16 Michel	M. Anne Larue		
		Q	
Anastasie	J. B. Solter Blais S.V.1837		
Edridge			
17 Noël	(10) Mad. Fortier	S.H.	1810
Anselme			
18 Charles Claude	Ursule Roy	B.	1824
19 Jacques	(13) Génév. Blais	S.G.	1825
Le même	Adé Gaulin	S.V.	1840
20 Louis	(13) Angèle Baillargeon		
		S.Chs.	1835
21 Charles	Marie Asselin		
		S. Hénédine	
Denis			
22 Etienne	(14) Monique Lebrun S.G.1826		
23 Edridge	(16) Soulange Roy	S.V.	1823
Marie Soulange	Nic Bernard	S.V.	1847
Jean			
24 Ansèlme	(20) Cath. Audet	S.Chs.	1840
25 Denis	(21) Constance Nadeau		
		S.Chs.	1856
26 Jean	(23) Emélie Gagne	S.V.	1855

ROULEAU.

1 Gabriel	Mathurine Leroux		
Anne	Jean Houde	S.F.	1678
Marie	Pierre Dussaut	Que.	1687
Guillaume			
Gabriel			
2 Gabriel	(1) Jeanne Dufresne S.L.1687		
Marguerite	Frs. Dumas	S.L.	1717
Jeanne	Nic Baillargeon S.L.1707		
Jeanne	2° Frs. Dumas	S.L.	1717
Gabriel			
Louis			
Le même	Cath. Roulois	C.R	1713
Catherine	Ls. Tremblay	S.P.	1739
Pierre			
3 Guillaume	(1) Cath. Dufresne S.L.1688		
Geneviève	Ant Godbout	S.L.	1721
Catherine	J. B. Rousseau S.Tho.1712		
4 Guillaume	Cécile Gaudin		
Marie Catherine	Ls. Quemeneur S.F.S.1746		
Geneviève	Ls. Guffart	S.F.S.	1749
Félicité	Aug. Martineau		
		S.F.S.	1760
Marie Rose	Ls. Terrien	S.F.S.	1762
Pierre			
Joseph			
Joseph Marie			
Charles			
5 Jean	M. Mad. Picard		
Marie Reine	Ls. Lasanté	S.P.S.	1766
6 Gabriel	(2) Génév. Petitclerc		
		S. Foye 1717	
Marie Josette	Paul Paradis	S.L.	1748
Louis			
Charles			
7 Louis	(2) Marg. Denis	S.L	1730
Le même	Cath. Coulombe S.L.1738		
Judith	Chs. Baillargeon		
Marie	Simon Brousseau S.L.1773		
Marguerite	Jacq. Gaboury	S.L.	1775

ROULEAU.

```
    Louis
    Gabriel
    Antoine
 8  Pierre        (2) Mad. Daniau      S.M.1741
    Jean Marie
    Pierre
    Pierre        (4) Marg. Gagnon S.F.S. 1757
10  Joseph Marie  (4) M. Ls. Aubé      S.V. 1758
    Abraham
    Joseph
    Le même           M. Marthe Martin
                                       S.F.S. 1775
11  Joseph        (4) Rosalie Chartier S.P.S.1764
    Le même           Reine Durand
                                  Cap.S.Ign. 1768
    Marie Reine       Jos. Tho. Picard S.F.S.1790
    Marie Louise      Jos. Beaucher    ,,   1795
    Marguerite        Tho. Proulx      ,,   1807
    François
    Joseph
12  Charles       (4) Fse. Pageot      S.Frs. 1765
13  Charles       (6) Genev. Gosselin S.L. 1753
    Agathe            Pierre Vien      ,,   1778
    Geneviève         Ant. Rousseau    ,,   1780
    Françoise         Ls. Bouffart     ,,   1798
    Madeleine         Ls. Paradis      ,,   1788
    Madeleine         2° J. B. Côté    S.P. 1794
    Madeleine         3° Pierre Loignon S.P.1809
    Guillaume
    Antoine
    Jean
14  Louis         (6) Genev. Ruel      S.L. 1756
    Geneviève         Ign. Ruel        ,,   1788
    Judith            Alexis Couture   ,,   1800
    Julien            2° Jean Métayer  ,,   1816
    Pierre
    Louis
15  Jean          (7) Genev. Duquet S.Chs.1760
    Marie Françoise   Pierre Morin     S.H. 1786
    Jean
    Charles
16  Louis         (7) M. Véronique Rousseau
                                       S.L. 1774
    Josette           Jos. Leclaire    ,,   1809
    Le même           Genev. Chatigny  ,,   1786
    Agathe            J. B. Molleur    B. 1820
17  Gabriel       (7) M. Thérèse Coté S.P. 1777
    Marguerite        Pierre Boissonneau ,, 1810
    Joseph
    Jean
18  Antoine       (7) M. Anne Létourneau
                                       S.L. 1778
                                       S.H.
19  Pierre        (8) Genev. Couture S.Chs. 1767
                      V. de Sauvage
20  Jean Marie    (8) M. Fse. Girard  ,,   1773
    Marie Françoise   Jos. Balan       S.M. 1800
21  Joseph        (10) M. Eliz. Lefebvre
                                       S.H. 1788
    Joseph
22  Abraham       (10) M. Jos. Blais S.F.S. 1795
    Edouard
23  Joseph        (11) Reine Bilodeau ,,   1799
    Pierre
24  François      (11) M. Fse. Gendron
                                       S.F.S. 1813
25  Guillaume     (13) M. Reine Laverte S.H.1786
    Agathe             Aug. Morin      ,,   1819
26  Antoine       (13) Genev. Godbout S.J. 1793
    Judith             Guill. Cinqmars S.L. 1824
    Soulange           Pierre Pepin    ,,   1832
    Pétronille         Ant. Labrecque  ,,   1833
    Geneviève          Gaspard Dion, Rimouski
    Réparate           Chs. Fortier, S.Claire
    Clément
    Antoine
    François
```

ROULEAU.

```
27  Jean          (13) Genev. Carrier    B. 1795
28  Pierre        (14) Mad. Hamel
    Marguerite         Magl. Cameron S.L. 1831
    Clotilde           Roch. Nadeau  ,,   1846
    Moïse
    Louis
    Pierre
29  Louis         (14) Marie Chabot  S.L. 1798
    Le même            Ls. Boucher  S.Chs. 1822
30  Jean          (15) M. Claire Gerbert S.H.1783
31  Charles       (15) Marg. Gosselin ,,   1792
32  Jean          (17) Josette Nadeau ,,   1311
33  Joseph        (17) M. Jos. Guérard S.F. 1819
34  Joseph        (21) Fse. Boutin   S.H. 1814
    Abraham
    Joseph
35  Pierre             M. Anne Bazin.
                                       S.H.
    Athanase
36  Edouard       (32) Angé Rémillard S.G. 1829
    Le même            M. Anne Emélie Larue
                                       S.V. 1840
    Le même
37  Pierre        (23) M. Angé Tarte Lévis 1824
38  Antoine       (26) Cécile Coté   S.L. 1824
39  Clément       (26) Henriette Gosselin ,, 1842
    Napoléon
40  François      (26)
41  Louis         (28) Genév. Gagné, S.H
    Zoé                Jean Audet     S.L. 1866
    Rose               Désiré Asselin  ,,   1880
    Didace
42  Pierre        (28) Eliz. Couture S.P. 1830
    Théodule
43  Moïse         (28) Clarisse Lebreux S.L. 1846
44  Joseph        (34) Henriette Duquet
                                    S. Chs. 1847
45  Abraham       (34) Dina Labrecque  B. 1850
46  Athanase      (35) M. Desange Mercier
                                    S. Chs. 1853
47  Napoleon      (39) M. Emma Audibert
                                       S.L. 1876
48  Didace        (41) Félicité Labrecque
                                       S.L. 1866
49  Theodule      (42) Eléonore Guérard S.L.1877
```

ROUSSEAU.

```
 1  Mathurin           Frs. Cormeron
    Symphorien
 2  Honoré             Marie Boilerot
    Thomas
 3  Symphorien    (1) Jeanne Sinallon Que. 1658
    Marguerite         Jos. Deblois     S.F. 1686
    Françoise          Jean Deblois     S.F. 1688
    Le même            Marg. Renaudière S.F.1670
    Marguerite         Frs. Dupont      S.F. 1688
    Marguerite         2° Pierre Peltier S.F. 1703
 4  Thomas        (2) Mad. Olivier    Que. 1667
    Catherine          Simon Fournier  S.P. 1691
    Geneviève          Jean Langlois   S.P. 1692
    Marguerite         Pierre Noel Morin
                                     S. Tho. 1696
    Louise             J. B. Proulx  S. Tho. 1701
    Antoine
    Jean Batiste
    Le même            Charlotte Bélanger
 5  Jean               Marie Rigot
    Jean
 6  Antoine       (4) Cath. Bouffart  S.L. 1709
    Geneviève          Frs. Gosselin   S.L. 1734
    Marie              Ign. Gosselin   S.L. 1738
    Angélique          Ant. Paquet     S.L. 1742
    Agnès              Frs. Coté       S.L. 1751
    Jacques
    Antoine
    Jean Baptiste
```

ROUSSEAU.

#	Name	Spouse	Place/Date
7	Jean Baptiste (4)	Cath. Rouleau	S.Tho. 1712
	Antoine		
	Antoine		
	Jean Batiste		
8	Jean (5)	Marie Picard	Cap. S. Ign. 1699
	Marie Génév.	Pierre Daniau	S.P.S. 1770
	Geneviève	J. B. Boutin	Bert. 1773
	Madeleine	J. B. Foucher	S.F.S. 1773
	Michel		
	Joseph		
9	Louis	M. Anne Huret	
	Jean Baptiste		
	François		
10	Charles	M. Cath. Talbot	
	Marie	Jacq. Fournier	S.P.S. 1755
	Marthe	Jacq. Aubin	S.P.S. 1763
	Marie Anne	Jean Langlois	S.P.S. 1765
	Marie Clotilde	J. B. Bélanger	S.P.S. 1777
	MarieMarguerite	Jacq. Joncas	S.P.S. 1784
	Thérèse	Jos. Peltier	S. Tho. 1773
	Charles		
	Le même	Angé. Peltier	S.F.S.1766
11	Louis	M. Angé Dubé	
	Marie Josette	Frs. Boulet	S.P.S. 1766
12	Jacques (6)	Véronique Bussière	S.P. 1744
	Marie Véronique	Ls. Rouleau	S.L. 1774
	Agathe	Michel Olivier Pepin	S.L. 1785
	Antoine		
	Jacques		
13	Antoine (6)	Cécile Noël	S.L. 1746
	Marie Louise	Jacq. Bélanger	S.M. 1768
	Cécile	Pierre Trahan	S.M. 1778
	Marie Catherine	Simon Bacquet	S.M. 1779
	Marie Josette	Jean Gontier	S. Chs. 1787
	Jean		
	Antoine		
14	Jean Baptiste (6)	M. Jos. Coté	S.P. 1751
	Marie Josette	Jos. Couture	S.P. 1772
	Thérèse	Frs. Dumas	S.L. 1773
	Madeleine	Ls. Dumas	S.L. 1783
	Jean Baptiste		
15	Antoine (7)	Anne Jannot	S.P.S. 1749
	Elisabeth	J. B. Boulet	S.P.S. 1780
	Antoine		
16	Jean Baptiste (7)	M. Genev. Valière	S.P.S. 1751
	Marie Madeleine	J. B. Montmeny	S.V. 1783
17	Antoine (7)	Rose Guillet	S.P.S. 1759
18	Michel (8)	Genev. Morin	S.P.S. 1758
	Geneviève	Frs. Landry	S.H. 1786
	Reine	Frs. Gagné	S.H. 1794
	Michel		
	Le même	M. Claire Jalbert	S.H.1807
		V. de Jean Rouleau	
19	Joseph (8)	M. Fse. Fontaine	S.P.S. 1785
	Marie Louise	Ls. Huot	S.H. 1812
	Julien		
20	François (9)	Rose Guillet	S.P.S. 1751
21	Jean Baptiste (9)	M. Fse. Picard	S.F.S. 1754
	Le même	M. Genev. Fournier	S. Tho. 1767
	Marie Génév.	Laurent Roy	S.F.S. 1793
	Marie Roger	Amb. Motté	S.V. 1811
	Marguerite	Ls. Baudoin	S.V. 1812
	Jacques		
	Guillaume		
22	Charles (10)	Marie Baudoin	Bert. 1762
23	Jacques (12)	M. Anne Niel	S.P. 1767
	Marie	Amb. Hamel	S.P. 1803
	Joseph		
	Jacques		
	Louis		

ROUSSEAU.

#	Name	Spouse	Place/Date
24	Antoine (12)	Genev. Rouleau	S.L. 1780
45	Augustin	M. Mad. Isabel	
	M. Madeleine	J. B. Dandurand	S.P.S. 1796
	Michel		
	Augustin		
	François		
	Jean Baptiste		
	Gabriel		
	Pierre		
26	Antoine	M. Angé. Cloutier	
	Antoine		
27	Antoine (13)	M. Thécle Marcoux	S.M. 1775
	M. Angèle	André Labbé	S.Chs. 1815
	Angélique	J. B. Bolduc	S.G. 1819
	Marie	Chs. Lemieux	S.G. 1822
	François		
	Joseph		
28	Jean Baptiste(13)	Angé. Couture	S.Chs. 1789
	Abel		
	Jean Baptiste		
	François		
	Joseph		
	Louis		
29	Jean Baptiste(14)	Thérèse Baillargeon	S.L. 1786
	Thérèse	Laurent Tessier	S.L. 1812
	Cécile	Ls. Boissonnaau	S.P. 1825
	Josette	Laurent Paradis	S.P. 1828
	Pierre		
	Jean Baptiste		
	Charles		
	Le même	M. Anne Civadier	S.L. 1807
30	Antoine (15)	M. Genev. Gaudreau	Cap.S.Ign. 1779
	Geneviève	Etn. Fradet	S.F.S. 1799
	Marguerite	René Bouchard	S.F.S. 1804
	Madeleine	Michel Monmeny	S.G. 1808
	Madeleine	2° Alexandre Filto	S.G. 1817
	Madeleine	3° Simon Quemeneur	S.G. 1822
	Françoise	Ls. Petitclerc	S.G. 1812
	Reine	Jos. Labrecque	S.G. 1813
	Charlotte	Jean Baillargeon	S.G. 1820
	Antoine		
31	René	Josette Perron	
	Christine	Ign. Turgeon	S.Chs. 1822
	Adélaïde	J. B. Lebreux	S.G. 1828
32	Michel (18)	Genev. Carrier	S.H. 1791
	Michel		
	Jean Baptiste		
	Antoine		
	Pierre		
	Louis		
	Hubert Marie		
	Marg.		
33	Julien (19)	Marie Audet	S.L. 1819 S.H.
34	Guillaume (21)	Louise Luce Morin	S.P.S. 1812
	Marie Anne	Etn. Cadrin	S.V. 1834
	Marie Léocadie	Tho. Théberge	S.V. 1843
	Marie	F. X. Morin	S.V. 1846
	François		
35	Jacques (21)	Angèle Langlois	S.V. 1812
	Le même	M. Reine Théberge	S.P.S. 1819
	Angèle	F. X. Roy	S.Chs. 1841
	Marguerite	Joachim Bernier	S.Chs. 1846
	Thomas		
36	Jacques (23)	M. Ls. Binet	Beauport. 1798

ROUSSEAU.

Marie Félicite		Ign. Turcot	S.P. 1828
Jean Baptiste			
37 Joseph	(23)	Vict. Noël	S.P. 1801
38 Louis	(23)	Marie Turcot	S.P. 1804
Marie		Ls. Pichet	S.P. 1834
Elizabeth		Gab. Paradis	S.P. 1836
Narcisse			
Bénoni			
Jean			
Louis			
39 Jean Bapt.	(25)	Mad. Daniau	S.P.S. 1772
Marie Madeleine		Chs. Dandurand	S.P.S. 1802
Thérèse		Fs. Gaudreau	S.P.S. 1814
Marie Angèle		J. B. Normand	S.P.S. 1818
M. Victoire		Jos. Bouchard	S.P.S. 1820
M. Geneviève		Etn. Bouchard	S.P.S. 1827
Louis			
Jean Baptiste			
40 Augustin	(25)	M. Fse. Colin	S.P.S. 1872
41 François	(25)	M. Claire Roy	S.V. 1775 S.Claire.
Jean Baptiste			
François			
Pierre			
Augustin			
42 Pierre	(25)	M. Genev. Bedard	S.H. 1785.
43 Gabriel	(25)	Marg. Angé. Thibault	S.P.S. 1786
44 Michel	(25)	Marie Chabot	S.Chs. 1793
45 Antoine	(26)	M. Anne Hayot	S.F.S. 1802
46 François	(27)	Rose Fournier	S.G. 1804
Thérèse		Pierre Guilmet	S.G. 1829
François			
Le même		Josette Campagna	S.G. 1815
47 Joseph	(27)	Marie Dutile	S.G. 1808
48 François	(28)	Josette Maupas	S.M. 1813
François			
49 Joseph	(28)	M. Anne Blais	S.H. 1814
50 Jean	(28)	Marie Maupas	B. 1815
Marie		Pierre Shinck	S.M. 1836
Olive		Elie Bouffart	S.M. 1839
Marie Louise		F. X. Turgeon	S.M. 1854
Majorique			
Alexis			
Pierre			
Joseph			
François			
51 Louis	(28)	Josette Lacasse	S.H. 1819
52 Abel	(28)	Sophie Adé. Bouchard	S.V. 1827
53 Pierre	(29)	Angéle Savoie	S.L. 1815
54 Joseph	(29)	Mad. Simart	S.P. 1819
Firmin			
55 Charles	(29)	Marg. Bouffart	" 1829 S.H.
56 Antoine	(30)	Genev. Gaumont	S.G. 1821
57 Michel	(32)	M.Anne Brochu	S.Chs. 1812
58 Jean Bte.	(32)	Thérèse Bélanger	S.G.1815
59 Pierre	(32)	Charlotte Brochu	S.Chs. 1822
60 Antoine		Adé Roy	B. 1838
Marie Désanges		Ed. Pepin	S.M. 1857
61 François	(34)	Reine Mercier	S.V. 1838
62 Thomas	(35)	SophieTurgeon	S.Chs 1845
Le même		Eléonore Voisin	" 1858
63 Jean Bte.	(36)	M.Anne Leclaire	S.P. 1828
Léocadie		Norbert Alexis Leclaire	S.P. 1856
64 Jean	(38)	M. Archange Paradis	S.P. 1833
65 Louis	(38)	M. Olive Couture	S.P. 1837

ROUSSEAU.

Marie Josephine		Amable Durand	" 1859
Virginie		Evariste Noël	" 1860
66 Bénoni	(38)	Fse. Pichet	" 1840
67 Narcisse	(38)	Apolline Nolin	" 1857
68 Jean Bte.	(39)	M.Jos.Durepos	S.P.S.1803
69 Louis	(39)	Julie Blais	" 1827
70 François	(41)	Mad. Bolduc	S.V. 1801
Emérence		Jos. Goulet	S.Chs. 1830
Luce		André Clément	" 1830
Anastasie		Aug. Goulet	" 1830
Edouard			
François			
Le même		Fse. Bisson	S.Chs. 1813
Marcelline		Germ. Lacroix	" 1834
Florence		Camile Veau	" 1845
71 Pierre	(41)	Marg. Bedard	S.G. 1808
72 Jean Bte.	(41)	M. Claire Tangué	S.Chs. 1811
73 Augustin	(41)	M. Jos. Quemeneur	S.F.S. 1812
74 François	(46)	Cath. Couture	S.G. 1838
75 François	(48)	Rose de Lima Fortier	S.M. 1841
76 Majorique	(50)	Adé Chamberlain	" 1846
Alexis		Vitaline Gourgue	" 1847
78 Pierre	(50)	M. Eliz. Fiset	" 1853
79 François	(50)	Emelie Bacquet	" 1842
80 Joseph	(50)	Octavie Flavie Poliquin	S.M. 1854
81 Firmin	(54)	M. Emelia Couture	
82 François	(70)	Marie Forgues	B. 1830
Frederic			
83 Edouard	(70)	Archange Lacroix	S.M. 1834
Edouard			
84 Fréderic	(82)	Henriette Boilard	B. 1859
85 Edouard	(83)	Emélie Cochon	S.Chs.1862

ROUSSEL.

1 François		Reine Lemarchand	S.Malo
François			
2 François	(1)	Marie Roy	S.V. 1743
3 Jacques Frs.		Mad. Borel	Ev.d'Aavanches
4 Robt. Leonard	(3)	Marg. Bacquet	S.M. 1771
Michel			
Louis			
Antoine			
Pierre			
5 Michel	(4)	M. Anne Lacroix	" 1805
Marie Anne		Frs. Bacquet	" 1832
Angèle		Jean Brisson	" 1838
Marie		Pierre Royer	" 1840
Marcelline		Laurent Royer	" 1843
Marie		Paul Fradet	" 1846
Marguerite		Flavien Bélanger	S.V. 1845
Michel			
6 Antoine	(4)	Cécile Pouliot	S.J. 1806
Cécile		Basile Turcot	" 1824
Marie Louise		F. X. Cotin	" 1830
Luce		Ls. Thivierge	" 1830
Antoine			
7 Pierre	(4)	Vict. Bilodeau	Eboulement
8 Louis	(4)		
9 Michel	(5)	M. Angéle Fortier	S.M. 1842
10 Antoine	(6)	Emelie Thivierge	S.J. 1836

ROY.

1 Nicolas		Jeanne Lelièvre	1658
Marie		Jean Gautreau	Que. 1679
Elizabeth		Zach. Turgeon	Beauport 1691

ROY.

Louis			
Guillaume			
Jean Baptiste			
Jean			
Noël			
Nicolas			
2 Siméon (Audy)	Claude des Chatelets		
		Que.	1668
Jean			
3 Joseph (Porte-	Susanna Forgue	Lévis	1683
lance)			
Louis Paul			
Joseph			
4 Louis	(1) Marie Ledran		1683
Marie Anne	Jacq. Forgue	B.	1705
Geneviève	J. B. Gontier	B.	1708
Marie	Pierre Guenet	B.	1723
Elisabeth	Denis Nadeau	B.	1724
Jean			
Louis			
5 Nicholas	(1) Mad. Leblond	S.F.	1686
Angélique	Ls. Baudoin	S.M.	1705
Angélique	2° Nic. Delaunay	Bert.	1729
Anne	Jean Navare	S.V.	1720
Alexis			
Etienne			
François Nicho-			
las			
Le même	M. Rénée Desrivières		
		Que.	1723
Marie Ursule	Noël Lebrun	S.V.	1743
Marie Ursule	2° Pierre Bouchard		
		S.V.	1750
6 Guillaume	(1) Angé Bazin		
Marguerite	Gab. Filteau	B.	1711
Marie Anne	Etn. Paquet	B.	1717
Marie Françoise	J. B. Filteau	B.	1721
Marie Françoise	2° Jacq. Copin	B.	1742
Angélique	Jos. Couture	B.	1731
Madeleine	Jean Valière	B.	1734
Thérèse	Guill. Nadeau	B.	1737
Pierre			
Charles			
Guillaume			
Joseph			
7 Noël	(1) Jeanne Lacasse	Levis	1670
Jeanne	Ign. Bouchard	B.	1712
Le même	Marg. Rabouin	S.F.	1700
Marguerite	J. B. Blais	S.V.	1726
Marie Agathe	André Patry	S.V.	1744
François			
Augustin			
Louis			
Pierre			
Etienne			
Jacques			
Joseph			
8 Jean	(1) Cath. Nadeau	S.G.	1694
Geneviève	Ign. Ruel	S.G.	1722
Madeleine	Paul Baillargeon	S.G.	1823
Geneviève	Jean Poulet	S.G.	1826
Pierre			
9 Jean Bap-	(1) Marg. Bazin	S.M.	1798
tiste			
Jean			
Le même	Claire Cadrin	S.M.	1701
Marie Claire	Simon Quéret	S.V.	1728
Geneviève	Noël Métivier	S.V.	1731
Théodore	Guill. Guilmet	S.V.	1738
Marie Claire	J. B. Thibaut	S.V.	1749
Etienne			
Augustin			
Jean Baptiste			
A Olivier	Mad. Rentier		
Pierre			
10 Jean	(2) Thérèse Jobin		
		Chs. Bourg	1691

ROY.

Charles			
11 Joseph	(3) Jeanne Gautron	B.	1714
12 Louis Paul	(3) Angé Dalaire	B.	1723
13 Jean	(4) Jeanne Bizeau (Larose)		
		B.	1716
Marie Anne	Jean Poliquin	B.	1744
Jean			
Le même	Anne Guénet	B.	1725
Marguerite	Etn. Lacasse	B.	1745
Elisabeth	Jacq. Fournier	B.	1746
Marie	Jos. Lacasse	S.Chs.	1749
Cécile	Ls. Labrecque	S.Chs.	1759
Pierre			
Etienne			
François			
14 Louis	(4) M. Fse. Lacasse	B.	1722
15 Etienne	(5) Marie Lacasse	B.	1709
Marguerite	Jos. Fortier	S.V.	1739
Marie	Andre Tangué	S.V.	1743
Elisabeth	Jos. Gautron	S.V.	1744
Geneviève	Pierre Brochu	S.V.	1753
Etienne			
Joseph			
Pierre			
16 Alexis	(5) Marie Leclaire	S.L.	1716
Marie	Pierre Noël Cochon		
		S.V.	1746
Pierre Alexis			
Joseph Alexis			
Alexis			
Jean Baptiste			
17 Frs. Nicholas	(5) M. Thérèse Alard		
		Chs. Bourg	1731
Marie Genev.	Michel Terrien	S.M.	1765
Marie Françoise	J. B. Hélie	S.M.	1769
Pierre			
Louis			
Jean Baptiste			
Jacques			
18 Guillaume	(6) Genev. Couture	B.	1712
Marie	Jos. Labrecque	B.	1734
Marguerite	Chs. Lecours	B.	1742
Marie Louise	Louis Labrecque	B.	1745
Charles			
Jean			
Joseph			
Pierre			
19 Joseph	(6) Jeanne Couture	B.	1716
Marie	Jos. Lalime	B.	1743
Charlotte	Pierre Ruel	B.	1744
Joseph			
Le même	Cath. Prudhomme	B.	1746
20 Césaire	(6) M. Jos Lecours	B.	1728
Marie Josette	Chs. Girard	"	1750
Le même	M. Anne Mignol	"	1733
Charles			
21 Pierre	(6) Marg. Couture	B.	1730
Marie	Jos. Royer	"	1763
Guillaume			
Charles			
Henri			
Pierre			
Le même	Marie Audet	B.	1756
22 Pierre	(9)A Madeleine Roy		
		Chs Bourg	1704
Bernardine	Jean Vézina	"	1741
24 Jean	Angé. Lacasse		
Marie	Frs. Roussel	S.V.	1743
Marguerite	Julien Mercier	"	1755
Agathe	Jean Lebœuf	"	1762
Jean Valier			
Augustin			
Le même	Marg. Fradet	S.V.	1770
25 Joseph	(7) Agathe Fradet	"	1729
Marguerite	Ls. Brochu	"	1759
Marguerite	2° Pierre Goupy	S.M.	1761

5-6 EDWARD VII., A. 1906

ROY.

Christine	Jos. Dodier	S.V.1769
Marie Claire	Frs. Rousseau	" 1775
Athanase		
Joseph		
François		
Le même	Brigitte Meneux	S.V.1749
Marie Rose	Jos. Corriveau	" 1774
Ursule	J. B. Gautron	" 1775
Ursule	2° Ign. Pilote	S.M.1794
Ursule	3° Jos. Chamberlan	S.M.1810
Michel		
André		
Le même	M.Jeanne Nand	S.V.1760
Marie Josette	Pierre Viau	" 1788
Thomas		
26 François (7)	M. Anne Fortier	S.V.1734
Marie Anne	Jean Mercier	S.M.1755
Marie Anne	2° Hilaire Brisson	" 1773
Marie	Etn. Rouillard	" 1770
Marie	2° Jean Thibault	S.G.1891
Alexis		
Louis		
Joseph		
François		
27 Augustin (7)	M.Isabelle Fradet	S.V.1735
MarieMarguerite	André Hélie	" 1702
Françoise	Tho. Cameron	" 1772
Marie Charlotte	Ant. Bazin	" 1779
Louis		
Noël		
Augustin		
François		
Michel		
28 Pierre (7)	M. Fse. Dalaire	S.V.1737
Françoise	Jos. Cauchon	" 1767
Eustache		
Jacques		
Le même	Genev. Dorval	S.P.1750
Marie Geneviève	Pierre Lefebvre	S.V.1771
28 Louis David (7)	Brigitte Marseau	" 1739
Madeleine	Alexandre Nadeau	S.M.1783
Madeleine	2° Chs. Lacasse	S.Chs 1801
Augustin		
Louis		
30 Pierre (8)	Mad. Bussière	S.P.1733
31 Michel	Marg. Emond	
Marguerite	Jean Roy	S.Chs.1752
Guillaume		
Joseph		
Etienne		
32 Jean	M. Angé. Huart	
Joseph		
33 Etienne (7)	M. Reine Fradet	S.V.1742
Marie Louise	Jacq. Lavoie	" 1765
Reine	Pierre Lebrun	" 1772
Marie Angélique	J. B. Leclaire	" 1774
Marie Josette	Frs. Baillargeon	" 1776
Marie	André Brochu	" 1781
Marguerite	Gab. Patry	" 1781
Marguerite	2° Ls. Fortier	" 1825
Catherine	Jean Lefebvre	" 1789
Jean Baptiste		
34 Jacques (7)	Cécile Fradet	S.V.1746
Le même	Eliz. Courteau	" 1751
Le même	M. Jos. Brochu	" 1755
Marie Félicité	Paul Goupy	S.M.1797
Marie Josette	Ls. Gautron	" 1805
Marie	Tho. Fortier	" 1808
Geneviève	Ant. Gosselin	S.G.1817
Jacques		
Jean Baptiste		
Le même	Louise Lanoue	S.F.S.1774
Marie	Jos. Lacroix	S.M.1811

ROY.

Marie	2° Philippe Richard	S.M.1811
Marguerite	Henri Pigeon	S.V.1804
Jacques		
35 Jean (9)	Mad. Bourget	B. 1728
Marie Marthe	Jos. Dion	S.V.1751
Marie Geneviève	Pierre Guilmet	" 1781
Alexandre		
Augustin		
Jean Laurent		
36 Augustin (9)	Agathe Aubé	S.V.1740
Marie Agathe	Ant. Blanchet	" 1768
Marie	Jean Boucher	" 1770
Michel		
Joseph		
Augustin		
Le même	Catherine Dorval	S.P.1750
Catherine	Ls. Chretien	S.V.1782
M. Angélique	J. B. Marseau	" 1787
Pierre		
François		
Etienne		
37 Jean Baptiste (9)	M. Mad. Tangué	S.V.1748
Marie Fse.	André Théberge	S.F.S. 1786
Etienne		
Basile		
Jean Baptiste		
Joseph		
Augustin		
Jacques		
38 Etienne (9)	Fse. Lamelin	S.V. 1752
Geneviève	Pierre Terrien	S.Chs. 1781
39 Charles (10)	Cath. Parant	Beauport 1737
Jean Baptiste		
40 Jean (13)	Marg. Roy	S. Chs. 1752
Marguerite	Frs. Blais	" 1780
Angélique	J. B. Lacasse	" 1806
Pierre		
41 Jean Baptiste		
Etienne (13)	Genev. Joncas	S.Tho. 1757
Marie	J. B. Leclaire	S.Chs. 1780
Le même	M. Genev. Noël	S.M. 1764
Geneviève	Paschal Mercier	S.Chs.1788
Cécile	Jean Couture	" 1790
Jean Baptiste		
42 Pierre (13)	M. Marthe Noël	S.M. 1771
Le même	M. Jos.Gerard	S.Chs. 1773
Etienne		
43 Joseph (15)	Genev. Filteau	S.M. 1739
Joseph		
Le même	M. Marthe Cadrin	S.M. 1749
Marie Marthe	Jos. Lavoie	" 1767
Marie Madeleine	Pierre Mercier	" 1777
Marie Geneviève	Philippe Leclaire	S.V. 1775
Michel		
44 Etienne (15)	Marthe Morisset	S.V. 1747
Marie Cécile	Frs. Gosselin	" 1765
Nicolas		
45 Pierre (15)	Marie Gautron	S.V. 1750
Le même	M. Hélène Bidet	" 1755
Marie Hélène	Michel Forgues	" 1773
Marie Hélène	2° Jacq. Kéroack	S.M.1814
Eustache		
François		
Pierre		
Antoine		
46 Alexis (16)	M. Anne Marie	S.V. 1749
Maguerite	Chs. Gagnon	" 1779
Marguerite	2° Ant. Boissel	S.Chs. 1794
47 JeanBaptiste(16)	Véronique Defourneau	S.V. 1753
Véronique	Chs. Dubord	" 1788

ROY.

Le même	M. Fse.Osite Baudoin		
		S.F.S.	1762
Marie Thérèse	Jean Fse.Boutin	"	1792
Germain			
François Alexis			
48 Pierre Alexis(16)	M. Jos. Bidet	S.V.	1757
Marie Rosalie	Michel Bolduc	"	1783
Marie Josette	Jos. Corriveau	"	1785
Marie Charlotte	Jos. Thibaut	"	1783
Marie Barbe	Jos.Marie Carbonneau		
		S.V.	1790
Marie Hélène	Frs. Roy	"	1792
Pierre Alexis			
49 Jos. Alexis (16)	M.Genev. Plante	S.V.	1761
Marie Françoise	Ls. Gautron	"	1792
Marie Charlotte	Ls. Thivierge	"	1800
Jacques Alexis			
50 Jean Baptiste(17)	M. Marthe Goupy		
		S.M.	1753
51 Pierre (17)	M. Ls. Goupy	"	1759
Marie Louise	Pierre Asselin	"	1782
52 Joseph (17)	M. Genev. Clement		
		S.M.	1768
Véronique	Pierre Valière	"	1808
Joseph			
Le même	Josette Lecours	S.M.	1778
Françoise	Ed. Bussière	"	1826
Angele	J. B. Bissonnet	"	1833
Louis			
Thomas			
53 Jacques (17)	Marg. Terrien	S.M.	1767
Michel			
François			
Ignace			
Charles			
54 Louis (17)	M. Jos. Morisset	S.M.	1777
Marie Marthe	Jos. Aubé	"	1796
Marie	Alexandre Baudoin		
		S.M.	1798
Marie Josette	J. B. Langlois	S.M.	1803
Marguerite	J. B. Gautron	"	1810
Catherine	Ls. Isabel	"	1815
Thomas			
Augustin			
Le même	M. Mad. Coté	S.M.	1794
Marie	Guill. Nadeau	"	1812
Louise	André Couet	"	1819
55 Charles (18)	Louise Gontier	B.	1734
Marie	Jos. Lacroix	S.V.	1771
Marie Louise	Michel Patry	S.M.	1776
Charles			
Le même	M. Jos. Paquet	B.	1746
Pierre			
56 Joseph (18)	M. Mad. Gontier	B.	1741
Marie Louise	Aug. Lacroix	S.V.	1775
François			
Joseph			
57 Jean (18)	Genev. Guay	B.	1759
Jean Baptiste			
Ignace			
58 Pierre (18)	Charlotte Dalaire	B.	1760
Le même	Cath. Drouin	Que.	1768
Marie Angélique	Paschal Turgeon	B.	1791
Charlotte	Jos. Filteau	"	1795
Marguerite	Ign. Hélie	S.M.	1806
Joseph			
Pierre			
Louis			
59 Joseph (19)	M. Gabrielle Sarant		
		S. Chs.	1756
Gabrielle	Ls. Blais	B.	1781
Charlotte Angèle	Jos. Gerard	B.	1785
Etienne Feriol			
60 Charles (20)	Marg. Goutier	S.Chs.	175?
61 Pierre (21)	M.Agathe Turgeon	B.	1759
Marie	Aug. Fournier	B.	178?

ROY.

Marie Elizabeth	Jos. Fournier	B.	1800
M. Charlotte	Ant. Fournier	B.	1802
Marguerite	J. B. Fournier	S.M.	1803
Agathe	LaurentLemelin	S.M.	1792
M. Marthe	Aimé Tremblay	S.F.	1792
Pierre			
François			
62 Henri (21)	Cecile Audet	S.L.	1763
Le même	Marie Couillard	S.M.	1767
63 Guillaume (21)	Mad. Gravel	B.	1764
Madeleine	Ls. Bussière	B.	1792
Charlotte	Jean Turgeon	B.	1797
Jean			
Louis			
Le même	Genev. Chouinard	S.F.S.	
Geneviève	Jacq. Fournier	B.	1802
Euphrosine	J. B. Turgeon	B.	1808
Angèle	Chs. Hebert	B.	1808
Guillaume			
François			
64 Charles (21)	Eliz. Thiviérge	S.J.	1769
Charles			
Le même	CharlotteNadeau	S.M.	1771
65 Augustin (24)	M. Angé Clement		
		S.V.	1757
Madeleine	Pierre Noël Tangué		
		S.V.	1789
66 Jean Valier (24)	Marie Mercier	Bert.	1757
Marie Josette	J. B. Guilmet	S.V.	1779
Basilisse	Jos. Lemieux	S.V.	1780
Marguerite	Frs. Lemieux	S.V.	1785
Marie	Guill. Aubé	S.V.	1786
Francoise			
Joseph			
Chs. Abraham			
Jean Baptiste			
Antoine			
67 Alexis	M. Anne Carrier		
Jean Baptiste			
68 Augustin	Marie Marie ?		
Marie	Michel Lepage	S.Chs.	1782
69 Michel	Justine Fradet		
Justine	Jacq. Buteau	S.V.	1790
Marguerite	Germ. Lemieux		1797
70 Laurent			
70 Joseph (25)	Marg.Rémillard	S.V.	1762
Marguerite	Jos. Tangué	S.V.	1783
Marie Agathe	Jacq. Abraham Durando		
		S.V.	1791
Etienne			
Joseph			
Michel			
71 Athanase (25)	M.Genev.Marseau		
		S.V.	1762
M. Françoise	Amable Durand	"	1793
M. Victoire	J. B. Bernier	"	1794
M. Geneviève	J. B. Bélanger	"	1800
M. Marthe	Ls. Dion	"	1803
Jean Valier			
Jean Baptiste			
Antoine			
Joseph			
Thomas			
François			
Athanase			
72 François (25)	M. Ls. Leblond	S.V.	1763
Le même	Rosalie Tangué	S.M.	1764
Rosalie	J. B. Cameron	S.V.	1788
Marie Louise	Prisque Bélanger	"	1795
Marguerite	Pierre Bélanger	"	1797
M. Josette	Frs. Balan	"	1797
M. Josette	2° Paul Mercier	"	1810
Denis			
Etienne			
Jacques			
François			

ROY.

No.	Name	(Gen.)	Spouse	Place	Year
73	André	(25)	Agathe Quérel	S.M.	1774
	Agathe		Michel Lemelin	„	1803
	Marie Anne		J. B. Bilodeau	„	1803
	Marguerite		Ls. Chrétien	„	1810
	François		Ls. Morrisset	„	1820
	Pierre				
	Joseph				
	André				
	Le même		M. Genev. Dorval	S.V.	1797
	Angélique		Jos. Morrisset	S.M.	1822
	Marie Louise		Pierre Lemelin	„	1827
	Josette		Jean Lemelin	„	1828
74	Michel	(25)	Mad. Pouliot	S.V.	1783
			V. de J. B. Hélie		
75	Thomas	(25)	M. Genev. Tangué	S.V.	1784
76	François	(26)	Genev. Roberge	Lévis,	1764
	Marthe		J. B. Lainé	S.G.	1791
	Marie Anne		Jean Gosselin	„	1798
	Marguerite		J. B. Lemieux	„	1798
	Eustache				
	François				
77	Louis	(26)	Marie Dion	Bert.	1766
	Marie Josette		J. B. Leblond	S.M.	1788
78	Joseph	(26)	Marie Patry	S.Chs.	1766
79	Alexis	(26)	M. Anne Fortin	S.M.	1782
			V. de Pierre Denis		
	Alexis				
80	Augustin	(27)	Louise Couillard	S.Chs.	1765
	Michel				
	Louis				
	Laurent				
	Le même		M. Jos. Bidet	S.V.	1793
81	Noël	(27)	M. Ange Boissonneau	Bert.	1767
82	Louis	(27)	Susanne Derome	S.V.	1771
			V. de Jos. Samson		
83	François	(27)	Marg. Bruneau	S.V.	1780
	Marie Victoire		Ls. Talbot	„	1809
	Marie Victoire		2° Eustache Fortin	S.V.	1817
	Marie Geneviéve		Frs. Roy	„	1807
	Luce		F. X. Nadeau	„	1820
	Pierre				
	Le même		Marie Balan	„	1807
	Cécile		Bénoni Marcoux	S.M.	1827
84	Michel	(27)	M. Fse. Leclaire	S.V.	1784
	Le même		M. Ls. Paquet	S.M.	1821
85	Eustache	(28)	Mad. Chabot	S.L.	1763
	Marie Josette		Frs. Roy	S.V.	1786
	Madeleine		Michel Moreau	„	1791
	Geneviève		J. B. Bacquet	„	1791
	Marie Charlotte		Frs. Ouel	„	1800
	Marguerite		Guill. Audet	„	1801
	Marie Cécile		Ls. Corriveau	„	1803
	Michel				
	Eustache				
	Pierre				
86	Jacques	(28)	M. Susanne Brochu	S.V.	1767
	Susanne		Jacq. Bolduc	„	1791
	Susanne		2° Amb. Ratté	„	1804
	Susanne		3° Ing. Chartier	S.F.S.	1837
	Marie Reine		Jos. Cochon	S.V.	1791
87	Louis	(29)	M. Chs. Boutin	„	1772
	Marie		Paul Lacroix	S.M.	1797
	Marie Angélique		J. B. Gautron	„	1804
	Marie Madeleine		Paschal Mercier		1805
	Marie François		Pierre Noël Lessard	S.M.	1806
	Paul				
	Louis				

ROY.

No.	Name	(Gen.)	Spouse	Place	Year
	Augustin				
	Le même		M. Genev. Vérieul	S.M.	1805
88	Augustin	(29)	Agnés Bolduc	„	1774
	Le même		M. Anne Beaucher,	Que.	1791
89	Etienne	(31)	Anne Doiron	S. Chs.	1761
90	Joseph	(31)	Claire Asselin	S. Frs.	1762
	Marie		Jos. Thivierge	S. Chs.	1783
91	Guillaume	(31)	M. Anne Terrien	„	1768
	Marie Anne		Jos. Catellier	S.V.	1796
	Marie Angélique		Jacq. Bilodeau,	Bert	1816
	Michel				
	Guillaume				
	Le même		Mad. Fregeot	S.G.	1798
			V. d'Ign. Noël		
92	Joseph	(32)	M. Jos. Cochon	S.V.	1771
	Marie Josette		Ls. Bolduc	„	1794
	Marie Josette		2° Jean Asselin	„	1824
	Cècile		Isidore Corriveau	„	1796
	Susanne		Gab. Terrien	„	1798
	Marie		Aug. Roy	„	1804
	Marie		2° Jacq. Terrien	S.G.	1817
	Marie Marg.		Jos. Gagnon	S.V.	1814
	Rosalie		Frs. Morisset	„	1817
	Marie Anne		Louis Bernier	S.H.	1820
	Joseph				
	Michel				
	Jean				
	Charles				
	Pierre				
93	Jean Bte.	(33)	M. Anne Joncas	S.V.	1776
	Marie Anne		Pierre Turgeon	„	1797
	Thérèse		Ign. Royer	S.G.	1806
	Barbe		Barth. Lacasse	„	1806
	Marguerite		Pierre Asselin	„	1809
	Marie		J. B. Filteau	„	1826
	François				
94	Jean Baptiste	(34)	M. Fse. Fortier	S.M.	1799
	Guillaume				
	Jean				
	Jean Baptiste				
	Joseph				
95	Jacques	(34)	M. Céleste Chrétien	S.V.	1808
96	Jacques	(34)	M. Genev. Roussin	S.V.	1793
97	Jean Noël		Marie Boissonneau		
	Marie Anne		Ls. Baudoin	S. Tho.	1793
	Marie Romaine		Amb. Belleau	S.P.S.	1801
	Thérèse		J. B. Gagné	„	1802
	Marie Barbe		Chs. Poiré	S.H.	1807
	Marie Marg.		Jean Blais	„	1807
	Noël				
98	Augustin	(25)	M. Anne Fradet	S.V.	1753
	Madeleine		Laurent Dumas	„	1781
	Marie		Ant. Rémillard	„	1789
	Barbe		Frs. Gosselin	S.G.	1811
	Jean Marie				
	Laurent				
	Augustin				
99	Jean Laurent	(35)	Marg. Boulet	S.F.S.	1754
	Joseph				
100	Alexandre	(35)	Fse. Boulet	„	1764
	Marie Barbe		Jos. Roby	S.V.	1789
	Marie Josette		Jacq. Gosselin	„	1795
	Catherine		André Baudoin	„	1795
	Le même		M. Marg. Dépont	S.F.S.	1783
	Marguerite		Aug. Rémillard	S.G.	1817
	Euphrosine		Frs. Clément	„	1818
	Augustin				
	Jean Baptiste				
101	Eloi		M. Jos. Dion		
	Marie Thècle		J. B. Quéret	S.M.	1791
	Marguerite		J. B. Bolduc	„	1797

PRUNEAU.

3	Jean	(1)	Genev. Boutin (Boulet)	
	Geneviève		Ign. Gagnon Bert. 1765	
	Pierre			
	Louis			
	Joseph			
4	René	(2)	Thérèse Forgues S.M.	1745
5	Louis	(3)	M. Anne Talbot, Bert.	1748
	M. Geneviève		J. B. Guilmet „	1768
	M. Reine		Clément Gagnon „	1783
	Louis			
	Le même		M. Génév. Picard	
			S.P.S.	1762
	M. Roger		Ls. Alra Métivier	
			Bert.	1789
	Marie		Gabl. Gosselin S.Chs.	1786
6	Joseph	(3)	M. Jos. Bouchard	
			Bert.	1752
	Reine		Aug. Guilmet „	1781
	Marie Josette		Jos. Fradet S.M.	1789
	Joseph			
7	Pierre		M. Claire Bouchard	
			S.V.	1754
	M. Claire		Frs. Guilmet S.Tho.	1795
	Jean Bte.			
	Joseph			
8	Louis	(5)	Bibiane Poliquin	
			S.Chs.	1783
	Charles			
	Louis			
9	Joseph	(6)	M. Roger Fournier	
			S.Tho.	1789
	Marie		J. B. Picard Bert.	1809
	Archange		J. B. Bouffard „	1826
	Charles			
	Joseph			
10	Jean Bte.	(7)	Marie Leblond S.M.	1775
	Sophie		Frs. Paquet S. Jho.	1824
11	Joseph	(7)	M. Anne Leblond	
			S.Tho.	1799
12	Louis	(8)	Margt. Martin S.H.	1810
14	Joseph	(9)	Eliz. Thibault S.P.S.	1820
	Joseph			
13	Charles	(8)	M. Louise Couture	
			S.H.	1810
15	Charles	(9)	M. Soulanges Leblond	
			S.Tho.	1826
	Marie		Jacq. Brochu S.Chs.	1854
16	Pierre		Marie Duchesne	
	Marguerite			
	Louis			
17	Jean Bte.		M. Vict. Bélanger	
			S. Roch	
	Joseph			
18	Joseph	(14)	Margt. Richard S.V.	1852
19	Louis	(16)	Margt. Mercier S.G.	1828
20	Magloire	(16)	Eulalie Cothière,	
			Bert.	1852
21	Joseph	(17)	Léocadie Lefebvre	
			S.Chs.	1854

QUEMENEUR—LAFLAMME.

1	François		Marie Chamberland	
			S.Frs.	1700
	Marie		Chs. Bissonnette „	1727
	Thérèse		Jacq. Morin „	1735
	M. Geneviève		Ls. Giasson S.F.S.	1745
	François			
	Charles			
	Louis			
	Jean Bte.			
	Antoine			
	Joseph			
2	François	(1)	Marg. Brochu S.V.	1739
	Le même		M. Jos. Frégeot	
			S.F.S.	1745

QUEMENEUR—LAFLAMME.

3	Joseph		Angé Pepin	
	Michel			
	Joseph			
	Jean Bte.			
4	Jean Bte.	(1)	M. Louise Poulin	
	M. Louise		Pr. Noël Frégeot	
			S.F.S.	1744
	Marguerite		Michel Gagnon „	1750
	M. Rose		Louis Proulx „	1761
	M. Françoise		Jos. Gravel „	1774
	M. Anne		Ls. Ouellet Bert.	1748
	Jean Bte.			
	Jacques			
	Joseph			
	Le même		M. Frs. Métivier	
			S.P.S.	1750
	Madeleine		Ant. Marseau S.F.S.	1775
5	Antoine	(1)	M. Angé Clomart	
	Pierre			
	Noël			
6	Louis	(1)	M. Cath. Rouleau	
			S.F.S.	1746
	M. Geneviève		Jos. Martineau „	1771
	Louis			
7	Charles	(1)	Brigitte Gagné	
	Le même		M. Jos. Vermet, Bert.	1747
	M. Josette		Ls. Pinet S.H.	1777
	Joseph			
	Marie			
	Pierre			
	Noël			
	Jean Bte.			
	Charles			
8	Joseph	(3)	M. Ls. Thibault	
			S.P.S.	1760
9	Michel	(3)	M. Claire Blancher	
			S.P.S.	1762
	M. Agathe		Ant. Jacq. Fortier	
			S.F.S.	1789
	Pierre			
	Noël			
	François			
10	Jean Baptiste	(3)	Angé Bouchard S.V.	1769
	Josette		Jacq.Christophe S.G.	1807
	Prisque			
	Antoine			
	Jean Baptiste			
11	Jean Baptiste	(4)	M.Mad.Gagnon S.F.S.	1753
	Rose		Clem. Langlois „	1781
	Victoire		Ls. Blais „	1788
	Angélique		Basile Thibaut „	1797
	Madeleine		Alexr. Paquet „	1802
	Judith		Mich. Terrien S.G.	1809
	M. Jeanne		Jean Hoopman S.V.	1814
	Pierre			
	Joseph			
	Antoine			
	Jean Baptiste			
12	Joseph	(4)	M. Lse. Huret S.F.S.	1761
	M. Louise		Chs. Morin „	1784
	M. Marguerite		Clement Pepin „	1785
	Michel			
	Pierre			
	Joseph			
13	Jacques	(4)	M. Mad. Boulet	
			S.F.S.	1764
	Madeleine		Ls. Allaire „	1805
	Joseph Jacq.			
	Pierre Noël	(5)	M.Marg Tangué S.V.	1762
15	Louis	(6)	M. Frse. Mercier	
			S.F.S.	1777
	Marie		Michel Métivier „	1802
	M. Marguerite		Thos. Talbot „	1802
	Reine		Jos. Crepeau „	1809
	Elisabeth		Ls. Théberge „	1811
	M. Josette		Ang. Rousseau „	1812

QUEMENEUR—LAFLAMME.

```
   M. Thècle          Jos. Quemeneur S.F.S 1817
   M. Angèle          Ls. Alaire           "  1819
   M. Archange        Aug. Tangué          "  1821
   Olive              Hubert Morin         "  1828
   Romain
   Jean Baptiste
   Thomas
   Louis
16 Charles       (7)  Marie Hullé       S.H. 1778
   Marie              Frs. Lemelin         "  1800
   Ursule             Sévère Bussières     "  1808
   Le même            Mad. Lainé           "  1794
   M. Madeleine       Basile Boutin        "  1817
17 Joseph Marie  (7)  M. Thérèse Baudoin
                                        Bert 1782
   Madeleine          Jean Patry        S.H. 1806
   Madeleine          2° Pierre Turcot     "  1816
   Catherine          Basile Roy           "  1812
   Euphrosine         Jos. Roy             "  1812
   Marie              Pr. Noël Morin       "  1800
   M. Louise          Vital Talbot         "  1819
   Louis
18 Jean Baptiste(7)   M. Anne Mercier Bert 1791
   M. Anne            Pr. Bélanger      S.H. 1820
   Antoine
   Jean
19 Pierre Noël   (7)  M. Lse. Coté      S.H. 1795
20 Pierre Noël   (9)  Margt. Denaut S.Tho. 1794
   Joseph
   François
   Etienne
   Le même            Lse. Corriveau Bert. 1833
21 Francois      (9)  M.Jos.Thibault S.F.S.1800
   Sophie             Lse. Martineau       "  1828
   François
22 JeanBaptiste(10)   Marie Bolduc      S.V. 1797
   Marie              Jos. Catellier       "  1824
   David
   Louis
   Joseph
   François
   Jean Baptiste
23 Prisque      (10)  Cath. Fournier S.Chs. 1805
24 Antoine      (10)  M. Mad. Lainé     S.V. 1821
   M. Vitaline        Olivier Bonafé       "  1857
   Antoine
25 Pierre       (11)  Margt Louineau S.F.S.1787
25 Joseph       (11)  Genev. Fauchon       "  1792
   Geneviève          Michel Fortier S.M. 1824
   Jean Baptiste
   Joseph
   Le même            M.Jos.Jacques S.F.S.1798
27 Jean Baptiste      Genev. Racine     S.G. 1797
   Marie              Ls. Noël             "  1822
   Madeleine          Ign. Ratté           "  1829
28 Antoine      (11)  Marie Paquet         "  1800
   Marie              Ant. Couture         "  1829
   Honoré
   Jacques
   Joseph
   Paschal
   Louis
29 Joseph       (12)  Cath. Blais      S.F.S. 1787
   Joseph
   Le même            Thérèse Proulx S.Tho 1793
   Flavie             Ls. Simart       S.F.S. 1828
   Simon
30 Michel       (12)  Genev McIntyre
                                       S.F.S. 1791
   M. Geneviève       Jos. Blais           "  1814
   M. Reine           Alexis Fournier      "  1820
   Michel
   Ignace
   Jean Baptiste
31 Pierre       (12)  M.Rose Picard S.P.S.1800
   Rosalie            J. B. Baudoin        "  1822
```

```
   M. Louise           Pierre Catellier S.P.S.1825
   Jacq. Pierre
32 Jacques      (13)   M. Genev. Lamare
                                         S.F.S. 1791
33 Joseph       (13)   M. Jos. Fauchon    "  1792
   Jean
34 Pierre              Margt. Samson
   Le même             Mad. Plante      S G. 1795
   Marie               Frs. Poirier       "  1819
   Françoise           Lse. Charert       "  1825
   Pierre
   Le même             Marie Poirier      "  1820
35 Louis               M. Frse Métivier (?)
   Michel
36 Louis        (15)   Marie Chartier S.F.S. 1810
   Marguerite          André Baudoin      "  1833
   Luce                Narcisse Blais     "  1843
   Thomas
   Le même             Marie Lemieux Bert. 1835
37 JeanBaptiste(15)    Hélène Leclair S.G. 1810
   Le même             Rose Adam          "  1815
38 Thomas       (15)   Marie Labrecque S.G. 1822
   Emérence            Ls. Turgeon        B. 1857
   Le même             M. Margt. Théberge
                                         S.F.S 1829
39 Romain       (15)   CharlotteMarcoux "  1826
40 Louis        (17)   Josette Morin  S.H. 1812
41 Antoine      (18)   Frse. Denis   Bert. 1819
42 Jean         (18)   Vict. Brochu       "  1824
   Olive               Marie Godbout  S.L. 1853
43 François      (20)  M.Lse. Fiset  S.Tho. 1824
44 Etienne       (20)  Julienne Proulx    "  1826
45 Joseph        (20)  M. Anne Royer S.Chs. 1830
46 François       (21)  M. Saly. Blais S.P.S. 1839
   Hilaire
47 François      (22)  M. Angé Rouillard
                                         S.M. 1820
   M. Des Anges        Pierre Lessart     "  1844
   Mélanie             Michel Mercier     "  1850
   Domitelle           Benj. Lessart      "  1854
   Damase
   François
48 JeanBaptiste(22)    M. Angèle Corriveau
                                         S.M. 1839
49 Joseph       (22)   M. Jos. Maurice S.V. 1841
50 Louis        (22)   Marie Lacroix S.M. 1842
51 David        (22)   Marcel Guilmet Bert. 1845
52 Charles             Angé Drouin
53 Jean
   François            Luce Denis
   Michel
54 Antoine             Archange Richard
                                         S.V. 1860
55 Joseph       (26)   M. Louise Plante "  1816
56 JeanBaptiste(26)    Margt. Bolduc  S.M. 1840
57 Louis        (28)   Rosalie Couture S.G. 1827
58 Paschal      (28)   Clémentine Boutin " 1829
59 Joseph       (28)   Marie Campagna "  1830
60 Joseph       (29)   M. Thècle Quemeneur
                                         S.F.S. 1817
61 Simon        (29)   M.AnneRousseau SG 1822
62 Jacques      (28)   Marie Bonneau S.L. 1842
   Rose                Nap. Royer         "  1866
   Philomène
   Jacques
   Le même             Archange Tessier "  1858
63 Honoré       (28)   Sophie Tangué      "  1847
64 Michel       (30)   Agathe Roberge S.G. 1823
65 Ignace       (30)   Louise Baudoin Bert. 1837
66 JeanBaptiste(30)    Angèle Fournier
                                         S.F.S. 1837
67 Pierre       (31)   Marie Boissel S.M. 1833
68 Jacques      (31)   Scolastique Carrier
                                         Lévis 1836
69 Jean         (33)   Cécile Dupil  S.P. 1818
   Marcelline          Ls. Roberge        "  1866
```